D1571783

COLLEGE OF MARIN LIBRARY
COLLEGE AVENUE
KENTFIELD, CA 94904

The Cambridge Biography

D. H. LAWRENCE

1885–1930

◆

DAVID ELLIS

MARK KINKEAD-WEEKES

JOHN WORTHEN

From reviews of John Worthen's *D. H. Lawrence: The Early Years 1885–1912*, Volume I of the Cambridge Biography

'it is hard to imagine that this biography will soon be superseded'.

Sir Frank Kermode, *The Guardian*

'[This is] a work of impeccable scholarship, and comes provided with an impressive apparatus of notes, appendices, chronological tables, family trees, an exemplary index, and complete lists of Lawrence's prose and verse writings in the relevant period, making it an invaluable resource for serious students of Lawrence; but it is also written in a lucid, unpretentious style which lay readers will find accessible and enjoyable.'

David Lodge, *The New York Review of Books*

'This is a superb biography. Apart from the compelling narrative there are judicious excursions into the mix of rurality and the mining industry that formed the background to Lawrence's life. There are portraits of the family members and . . . insights into Lawrence's admiring bluestockings and into the less well-known early works that led up to *Sons and Lovers* . . . Cambridge have already given us . . . a decent edition of Lawrence's fiction; now they are embarked on what should be the definitive life.'

Anthony Curtis, *The Financial Times*

'One of this biography's greatest merits is that Worthen understands the dangers of creating a life from a work of fiction. He uses Lawrence's fiction intelligently. He never forgets that even the most apparent autobiographical novels rearrange real events in order to make an artistic point. They cannot be trusted, as too many biographers trust them, to do the biographer's work for him. The other great merit, apart from the wonderfully detailed and engrossing reconstruction of a period and a society, is its attitude to Lawrence himself. Worthen is unfailingly sympathetic, as a biographer should be, yet he never falls into the trap of supposing his hero to be perfect . . . This definitive book will be a hard act . . . to follow.'

Allan Massie, *Weekend Telegraph*

From reviews of Mark Kinkead-Weekes's *D. H. Lawrence: Triumph to Exile 1912–1922*, Volume II of the Cambridge Biography

'It is, quite simply, the best book on Lawrence I have ever read, a really magnificent piece of work. Quite apart from the light it sheds on Lawrence's intellectual, spiritual and artistic development, it should be read by anyone with an interest in the relationship between philosophy and literature . . . Its theme is the interplay between Lawrence's ideas and his fiction. Nowhere has that dialectic been described more plausibly and more sensitively than in this marvellous book.'

Ray Monk, *The Observer*

'The expanse of this particular study . . . testifies to the almost Lawrentian care and richness with which Kinkead-Weekes has explored the novelist's private dramas.'

Peter Ackroyd, *The Times*

'Mark Kinkead-Weekes combines alert and readable prose with a staggering depth of scholarship.'

Boyd Tonkin, *New Statesman and Society*

'As a repository of factual scholarship, Kinkead-Weekes's monumental biography . . . is clearly a well from which readers and scholars will be drawing insight for years to come.'

Washington Post

D. H. LAWRENCE

DYING GAME

1922–1930

♦

DAVID ELLIS

Eh, one wishes things were different. But there's no help for it. One can only
do one's best, and then stay brave. Don't weaken or fret. While we live, we
must be game. And when we come to die, we'll die game too.

D. H. Lawrence to Gertie Cooper
23 January 1927

CAMBRIDGE
UNIVERSITY PRESS

PUBLISHED BY THE PRESS SYNDICATE OF THE UNIVERSITY OF CAMBRIDGE
The Pitt Building, Trumpington Street, Cambridge CB2 1RP, United Kingdom

CAMBRIDGE UNIVERSITY PRESS
The Edinburgh Building, Cambridge CB2 2RU, United Kingdom
40 West 20th Street, New York, NY 10011–4211, USA
10 Stamford Road, Oakleigh, Melbourne 3166, Australia

© Cambridge University Press 1998

This book is in copyright. Subject to statutory exception
and to provisions of relevant collective licensing agreements,
no reproduction of any part may take place without the written permission
of Cambridge University Press.

First published 1998

Printed in the United Kingdom at the University Press, Cambridge

Typeset in Ehrhardt 10/12.5pt

A catalogue record for this book is available from the British Library

Library of Congress cataloging in publication data

Ellis, David, 1939–
D. H. Lawrence: dying game, 1922–1930/David Ellis.
p.   cm. – (The Cambridge biography – D. H. Lawrence, 1885–1930):
Includes bibliographical references and index.
ISBN 0 521 25421 3
1. Lawrence, D. H. (David Herbert), 1885–1930 – Death and burial.
2. Lawrence, D. H. (David Herbert), 1885–1930 – Last years.
3. Lawrence, D. H. (David Herbert), 1885–1930 – Journeys.
4. Authors, English – 20th century – Biography.   I.Title.
II Series: Cambridge biography.
PR6023.A93Z62617   1997
823′.912–dc21   96–52443 CIP
[B]

ISBN 0 521 25421 3 hardback

CONTENTS

CONTENTS

PART TWO: *The Second Visit to America*

CONTENTS

CONTENTS

PART FOUR: *The Marvel of Being Alive*

PREFACE

The preface which appears in the two previous volumes of this biography explains the rationale for a life of Lawrence by three different authors. This third and final volume seemed to me to require an additional note on a question of biographical method. More obviously than in the lives of most authors, Lawrence's writing was associated with his daily living. The people he met, the places he visited and the particular human situations in which he found himself were a constant stimulus to how and why he wrote. Lawrence did not need to keep a diary because he was able to respond to his experience on an almost daily basis in novels, stories, poems, and all the other forms of writing he practised. In his case especially, any biographical account which made a strict partition between life and art would be absurd.

Perhaps the most obvious illustration of the way in which the two are inter-related is Lawrence's tendency to base characters in his fiction on people he knew. There is here a familiar area of danger for biographers which was defined by F. R. Leavis many years ago in a review of Harry T. Moore's edition of Lawrence's *Collected Letters*. For Leavis, Moore's annotations showed 'how lamentably an industrious scholar' (who was also a biographer) 'specializing in a great creative genius, may be unaware of his own limitations and misconceive his place in the scheme of things'. After reviewing various of Moore's attempts to make connections between the people Lawrence knew and the characters in his fiction, for which, Leavis says, the reader who is a 'real admirer of Lawrence's genius will not be grateful', he concludes: 'such a reader, faced with the assertions of "Lawrence scholarship", will be sufficiently justified in asserting that Lawrence *never* put people into his tales and novels: he was a great creative writer'.[1] 'Sufficiently justified' would seem to warn Leavis's own readers that they need to take into account the degree of provocation, and the final reference here to great creative writers carries an implicit appeal to T. S. Eliot's insistence on the incompatibility between writing at the highest level and the transcription of personal experience. But these flanking phrases only partially moderate the force of the central assertion: 'Lawrence *never* put people into his tales and novels'. Of this claim one can say what can be said of very few statements in literary criticism: that it is quite plainly wrong.

There is of course a sense in which no writer can 'put' someone into a book.

Human beings have well-defined biological and social characteristics, but what they 'are' depends on whether one is paying more attention to their impression of themselves or other people's very varied impressions of them. There is no central core upon which all parties could agree (if there were, biography would be a less complicated matter than it is). The proof that Leavis did not have these considerations in mind when he claimed that Lawrence '*never*' – the emphasis is important – put people into books, lies in the way he contrasted Lawrence's habits in these matters with those of Huxley in *Point Counter Point*, very much to the latter's disadvantage. Huxley was the kind of writer who portrayed the people he knew in his fiction (Lawrence among them), whereas Lawrence himself never did.

How can one be so certain that this is not true? Continually during Lawrence's career, and long after he was dead, people recognised themselves in works of his they read. 'Funny you calling me Pan', Middleton Murry wrote to Frieda Lawrence in 1955, 'Lorenzo, you remember, used Pan to kill me off in one of his stories – a queer one which I have never quite understood – all about me and Brett and a policeman in snowy Hampstead. Quite a good picture of me.'[2] The story to which he was referring is entitled 'The Last Laugh'. Like 'The Border-Line' and 'Jimmy and the Desperate Woman', this does certainly contain a 'picture' of Murry so that, in this instance, his identification of himself confirms what can already be established from other evidence. Yet if self-recognition is often a useful guide, it is not infallible. John Worthen has described how Louie Burrows, who had been engaged to Lawrence between December 1910 and February 1912, recognised in H. G. Wells's 1932 novel *The Bulpington of Blup* a portrait of her relationship with her former fiancé, and wrote to congratulate its author on the depth and accuracy of his understanding. She was acutely embarrassed when Wells, who did not know her, wrote back to deny that his novel had anything to do with Lawrence. On the letter of apology she then sent ('I'm sorry that my impulsive assumption embarrassed you – the coincidences in the book are however extraordinary'), Wells wrote: '*File*. This lady is a mythomaniac.'[3] In the moving account of the mental breakdown which led to his attempted suicide, William Cowper describes how he opened a newspaper in a coffee-house and read a letter which appeared to be a satire on himself: 'The author seemed to be acquainted with my purpose of self-murder and to have written that letter to secure and hasten the execution of it.'[4] Louie Burrows's state was not similarly pathological, but there is a condition of inflamed sensitivity where everything we hear or read seems to bear on our own condition.

A more reliable criterion than self-recognition for deciding whether Lawrence ever put people into books, therefore, is authorial confession. In the late 1920s, impatient with the frequent requests for biographical details he received, Lawrence would sometimes refer to *Sons and Lovers*, and even *The Rainbow*, in a way that implied that those anxious to know about his early background could find all they wanted there (vi. 465); and throughout his adult life, he would freely confess that he had portrayed his parents and Jessie Chambers in the first of these novels. Only on the assumption that he did sometimes put people into books does his telling Achsah Brewster, in Ceylon, that 'he had not done justice to his father in *Sons and Lovers* and felt like rewriting it', make proper sense.[5] Even more pertinent to the issue are the occasional letters he wrote to friends hoping that they did not mind the portrait of them in this or that story or novel. But perhaps the simplest and clearest example of Lawrence acknowledging that on occasions his practice was no different from Huxley's is the letter he wrote in 1926 to Koteliansky, in response to an enquiry as to whether or not he knew Gertrude Stein. 'I have never met Gertrude Stein', he told Kot, 'but you remember that deaf fellow in *Aaron's Rod*, that is her brother' (v. 418). The 'deaf fellow' in question is a minor character in *Aaron's Rod* called Walter Rosen. The Lawrence who casually admits Rosen 'is' Leo Stein cannot be the same Lawrence who *never* put people into his tales and novels.

There are certainly then cases where Lawrence set out to provide a 'portrait' of someone he knew, and kept the characteristics of that person clearly in mind throughout the writing process. Yet these are relatively few. More often a particular friend or acquaintance provides a starting-point and, as the character then becomes involved in the autonomous world of the fiction, and responds to the exigencies of the plot, the stricter aims of portraiture are abandoned. In these instances the relation between art and life becomes highly complex as it does in those, also frequent, where Lawrence has taken for one of his characters different features from different people. In the resulting creative amalgams it is doubtful whether the pursuit of which characteristics of the fictional figure belong to which people in real life has much point.

Although roughly similar qualifications as these about Lawrence's depiction of friends and acquaintances could be applied to the use in his writing of the places where he lived, the way he is inclined to integrate into it episodes and situations from his current life calls for a different caveat. There is no doubt that Lawrence worked out in fiction and poetry attitudes to problems which happened to be preoccupying him at the time of composition. Yet it is also true that there are a number of concerns to which he returned time and time again. In certain cases therefore, the immediate context which a biographer will usually seek to establish may be less significant than difficulties rooted in the subject's early life. Of no other twentieth-century author would it have been more difficult to predict how the art would develop: what kind of book Lawrence would write next. Our present judgements are made easy by hindsight, but in the period covered by this volume it would have taken a very shrewd reader of *Kangaroo* to have predicted *The Plumed Serpent*, and an even shrewder one to have seen in that novel the seeds of *Lady Chatterley's Lover.* All three of these works are a response to immediate concerns yet, at the same time, although Lawrence once talked memorably of shedding sicknesses in his books (ii. 90), they also deal with a number of problems and anxieties which never went away. Quite rightly in my view, biographers are inclined to lay a great deal of store by chronology as a key to understanding; but one of Freud's more useful suggestions is that, in the unconscious, there is no such thing as Time.

None of this should be taken as providing justification for any widening of the gap between Lawrence's life and art: so much of the former consisted in writing that the two demand to be treated together even when, evidently enough, the relation is not simple. What these qualifications might more legitimately prompt, however, is one more reason for insisting on the obvious truth that a biographical approach to literature is not the only one possible. Irritated by those who had suggested that *A la recherche du temps perdu* should be treated as a 'closed system', because it contained within itself 'all the elements necessary for its under-standing', George Painter was driven to write in the preface to his pioneering biography of Proust that there was no aspect of the novel which could be studied 'without an accurate and detailed study of [Proust's] life, or has so far escaped distortion for lack of such knowledge'.[6] That was to protest far too much. Just as 'il n'y a pas d'homme nécessaire' neither is there biographical knowledge which is indispensable. The number of possible approaches to literature is very great and what seems appropriate at any one moment depends on the author concerned, and the taste of the reader.

Because this is volume iii of Lawrence's biography, no reader will be surprised to discover that the approach to literary works adopted in it is biographical. That crucially determines its shape. The degree and kind of attention accorded to specific texts here is partly governed by what Lawrence himself valued, and what has come to be valued since. It is a result, also, of an effort to suggest that the extraordinary achievements of Lawrence in the last decade of his life cannot be properly appreciated by anyone inclined to feel that it is as a novelist he must always be finally judged. But it is clear, in addition, that the biographical emphasis in what follows is usually responsible for quite what and how much is said about individual works, and that if the only aim had been to establish among them some elusive hierarchy of literary value, the proportions would have been quite different.

The biography of a literary figure is not solely to be judged by the light it throws on the subject's work but, for many of us, literary value is in the end what matters most, and it is only because Lawrence is generally considered a great writer that the degree of attention his life has received can be justified. Writing someone's life is so labour-intensive that no-one involved can avoid the occasional twinge of nostalgia for the now old 'new critical' stance, or fail to feel on occasions

the attractions of its structuralist and post-structuralist successors. Announce-
ments of the death of the author may have been convincingly shown to be much
exaggerated,[7] but the notion of liberating the text from all its surrounding
impedimenta, of untrammelled communion with (in Arnold's famous phrase)
'the object as in itself it really is',[8] still retains its appeal. The difficulty is that
there are no circumstances in which the mind of the reader is a *tabula rasa*: no-
one comes to a text without information, preconceptions; and much of that
information is likely to be of a biographical nature. In those circumstances, it is
surely better when the biographical information in question is not false or
distorted. The authors of this biography would not have undertaken it had they
been satisfied with the views of Lawrence's character and life currently available.
That does not mean that they feel their view is always the correct one. Describing
a life is full of having to make do, as well as sometimes getting it wrong; and
biographers know they must sometimes be wrong because of information which
arrives at the last minute and allows them to correct the record. The most they
can therefore hope for is that their work should be more or less right or, since the
situation in which they find themselves is often competitive, less wrong than that
of others. If either of those descriptions were to be applied to this biography, if it
could be authoritative in that sense, then its three authors, unkindly if not
perhaps too inaccurately described in a review of volume ii as having grown aged
in their task, could look forward to the twilight of their years with tranquil minds.

David Ellis
November 1996

ILLUSTRATIONS

Between pages 396 and 397

CHRONOLOGY

(February 1922–March 1930)

20–26 February 1922	From Taormina to Naples, via Palermo
26 February 1922	Leaves for Ceylon on the *Osterley*
2 March 1922	Port Said
13 March 1922	Met by Earl Brewster on the dock at Colombo
14 March–*c.* 23 April 1922	At 'Ardnaree', Lake View Estate, Kandy, with the Brewsters
23 March 1922	Attends the special perahera in Kandy in honour of the Prince of Wales
c. 23 April 1922	Stays with Judge and Mrs Ennis in Colombo
24 April–4 May 1922	Sails to Fremantle on the *Orsova*
4–6 May 1922	Savoy Hotel, Perth, Western Australia
6–18 May 1922	At a guest house ('Leithdale') in Darlington near Perth, partly run by Mollie Skinner
18 May 1922	Sails to Sydney on the *Malwa*
22 May 1922	Ship stops in Adelaide
24–25 May 1922	Spends the night in Melbourne
27 May 1922	Arrival in Sydney, New South Wales
c. 29 May–10 August 1922	At 'Wyewurk', Thirroul, New South Wales
30 June 1922	Excursion to Wollongong
4 July 1922	Goes to Sydney
9 August 1922	Leaves Thirroul for Sydney
11 August 1922	Sails for San Francisco on the *Tahiti*
15 August 1922	Wellington, New Zealand
20 August 1922	Raratonga, Cook Islands
22–23 August 1922	Papeete, Tahiti
4–8 September 1922	Palace Hotel, San Francisco
8–10 September 1922	Train to Lamy, New Mexico
10–11 September 1922	Witter Bynner's house, Santa Fe
11 September–1 December 1922	On Mabel Sterne's estate in Taos

12 September 1922	Case against Seltzer for publication of *Women in Love* dismissed
14–18 September 1922	Visit to the Jicarilla Apache Reservation with Tony Luhan and Bessie Freeman
31 October 1922	First visit to what would become Kiowa Ranch with Mabel Sterne
1 December 1922–18 March 1923	In a cabin on the Hawks' Del Monte Ranch with Danish friends, Knud Merrild and Kai Gótzsche, close by
25 December 1922– 2 January 1923	Seltzers at Del Monte
1 January 1923	Robert Mountsier arrives
28 January 1923	Mountsier moves from Del Monte to Taos
2 February 1923	Learns of Katherine Mansfield's death on 9 January at the Gurdjieff Institute in Fontainebleau
3 February 1923	Dismisses Mountsier as his literary agent
19 March 1923	Leaves Taos for Mexico, via Santa Fe
21 March 1923	Crosses the border at El Paso
23–24 March 1923	Hotel Regis, Mexico City
24 March–27 April 1923	Hotel Monte Carlo, Mexico City
1 April 1923	Attends a bullfight in Mexico City
3 April 1923	Visits the pyramids at Teotihuacán
5 April 1923	Excursion to Cuernavaca
13–21 April 1923	Visits to Puebla, Tehuacán and Orizaba
27 April 1923	Leaves for Chapala, Jalisco
28? April–1 May 1923	Hotel Arzopalo, Chapala
2 May 1923	Meets Frieda in Guadalajara, at the Purnells'
2 May–9 July 1923	At Calle Zaragoza #4, Chapala
c. 10 May 1923	Bynner and Johnson arrive in Chapala and stay at the Hotel Arzopalo
4–7 July 1923	Excursion with Frieda on Lake Chapala with Bynner, Johnson, the Purnells
9 July 1923	Leaves Chapala for Guadalajara and visits Bynner in hospital
10 July 1923	Leaves Guadalajara for New York via Laredo, San Antonio, New Orleans and Washington
19 July 1923	Arrives New York City
20 July–21 August 1923	At the Seltzers' cottage in Morris Plains, New Jersey ('Birkindele')

2 August 1923	Lunch with editors of the *Nation*
18 August 1923	Frieda leaves for England on the *Orbita*
22–27 August 1923	Leaves New York and visits Bessie Freeman in Buffalo
25 August 1923	Trip to Niagara Falls with Mabel Luhan's mother
27–30 August 1923	To Los Angeles via Chicago and Salt Lake City
31 August–12 September 1923	Hotel Miramar, Santa Monica
9 September 1923	Trip to Santa Barbara with Merrild and Gótzsche
10 September 1923	On to Lompoc to observe total eclipse of the sun
12–25 September 1923	Back in Los Angeles
25–27 September 1923	To Guaymas, Mexico, with Gótzsche, via Palm Springs
1 October 1923	To Navojoa
c. 3–4 October 1923	Visits Minas Nuevas near Alamos
5 October 1923	To Mazatlán
7 October 1923	Arrives in Mazatlán
14–17 October 1923	To Guadalajara via Ixtlán, La Quemada and Etzatlán
17 October–17 November 1923	Hotel Garcia, Guadalajara
21 October 1923	Visit to Lake Chapala with the Purnells
17 November 1923	To Mexico City
22 November 1923	Sails with Gótzsche for Europe from Veracruz on the *Toledo*, via Havana
11 December 1923	Arrives in Plymouth
12? December 1923–23 January 1924	110 Heath Street, Hampstead, London
31 December 1923–3 January 1924	Visits his family in the Nottingham area
3–5 January 1924	Visit to Frederick Carter in Pontesbury, Shropshire
23 January–6 February 1924	In Paris at the Hotel de Versailles, 60 Blvd Montparnasse
2 February 1924	Visits Gurdjieff Institute in Fontainebleau
4 February 1924	Meets Sylvia Beach at her bookshop in the rue de l'Odéon
6 February 1924	To Baden-Baden via Strasbourg
7–10 February 1924	With Frieda's mother in Baden-Baden
20 February 1924	Back to Paris via Strasbourg
21–25 February 1924	Hotel de Versailles

26 February–5 March 1924	Garland's Hotel, Suffolk Street, Pall Mall, London
5 March 1924	Sails from Southampton on the *Aquitania* with Frieda and Dorothy Brett
11 March 1924	Arrives in New York
15 or 16 March 1924	Calls on Willa Cather and has tea with her the next day
18 March 1924	To Chicago. Sees Harriet Monroe
21 March 1924	Arrives in Santa Fe
22 March 1924	Back in Taos on Mabel Luhan's estate
c. 28 March 1924	Mabel Luhan returns from California with Ida Rauh
c. 30 March 1924	The Lawrences move into the two-story house and Brett into 'the studio'
3 April 1924	Tony Luhan and Jaime de Angulo arrive in Taos
by 4 April 1924	Mabel Luhan has given Frieda Lawrence her ranch at Lobo
22–23 April 1924	To Santo Domingo pueblo for Sprouting Corn dance, with Jaime de Angulo who leaves from there for California
5 May 1924	The Lawrences and Brett go to live on the Lobo Ranch
24–27 May 1924	The Luhans and Clarence Thompson visit Lobo
31 May–1 June 1924	Weekend in Taos
16 June 1924	Geronimo helps Lawrence build an adobe oven
18–23 June 1924	In Taos. Alice Sprague present. Quarrel with Clarence Thompson
c. 28 June–3 July 1924	Builds a kitchen porch with Brett's help
30 July–7? August 1924	Johnson visits Lobo
3? August 1924	Haemorrhage. Confined to bed. Visited by Dr Martin the following day
by 9 August 1924	Lobo Ranch renamed Kiowa
13–23 August 1924	Excursion with the Luhans, taking in the Cañon de Chelly (the 20th)
late August 1924	Trip with Brett and the Hawks to Columbine Lake
10 September 1924	Death of Lawrence's father
11 October 1924	Moves down to Taos

16 October 1924	To Santa Fe
19 October 1924	To El Paso
23 October–8 November 1924	Hotel Monte Carlo, Mexico City
25 October 1924	Lunch with Zelia Nuttall in town
26 October 1924	Lunch with Zelia Nuttall at Coyoacán. Dinner with the British Consul-General, Norman King
31 October 1924	Guest of honour at the PEN dinner
2 November 1924	Introduced by Quintanilla to Edward Weston
4 November 1924	Photographed by Weston
5 November 1924	Lunch with Somerset Maugham
8 November 1924	Hotel Mexico, Tehuacán
9–18 November 1924	Hotel Francia, Oaxaca
ante 14 November 1924	Calls on Governor Ibarra in his palace
18 November 1924–14 February 1925	Avenida Pino Suarez #43, Oaxaca
c. 30 November 1924	Excursion to Mitla
21 December 1924	Walk to San Andrés Huayapan
19 January 1925	Brett takes the train for Mexico City (leaves for Del Monte 8 February)
14 February 1925	Moved to Hotel Francia suffering from what is diagnosed as malaria
25 February 1925	To Mexico City via Tehuacán
26 February–25 March 1925	Hotel Imperial, Mexico City. Diagnosed as tubercular
by 11 March 1925	On doctors' advice has cancelled return to England and decided to go back to New Mexico
18 March 1925	Lunch at the Conways'
25–29 March 1925	To Santa Fe via El Paso. Held up at the border
1 April 1925	From Santa Fe to the Del Monte Ranch
5 April–9 September 1925	At Kiowa Ranch
c. 16–20 May 1925	Ida Rauh comes to Kiowa to hear *David*
19 May–18 July 1925	Friedel Jaffe at Kiowa
1 June 1925	Susan, the cow, arrives at Kiowa
by 18 June 1925	Trinidad and Ruffina Archuleta have left
ante 29 July 1925	Willa Cather visits Kiowa
ante 19 August 1925	Visit of the Crichtons
9 September 1925	At Del Monte
10–13 September 1925	To New York City via Denver

13–21 September 1925	Staying with Nina Witt at 71 Washington Place, New York
18 September 1925	Dinner with Harold Mason and the McDonalds
21–30 September 1925	To Southampton on the *Resolute*
30 September–8 October 1925	Garland's Hotel, Pall Mall, London
4–5 October 1925	Visits the Carswells near High Wycombe (and the Seckers at Iver just before or after)
8–14 October 1925	With Emily King at Sneinton in Nottingham
14–22 October 1925	With Ada Clarke at Ripley, Derbyshire
22–29 October 1925	At 73 Gower Street, London
23 October 1925	Meets William Gerhardie
25 October 1925	Lunch with Lady Cynthia and Herbert Asquith
29 October 1925	Leaves London for Baden-Baden
30 October–12 November 1925	Hotel Eden, Baden-Baden
12–15 November 1925	With Carl and Maria Seelig in Kastanienbaum, near Lucerne
15–23 November 1925	Hotel Miramare, Spotorno, Italy
23 November 1925–20 April 1926	At Villa Bernarda, Spotorno
c. 13 December 1925	Barbara Weekley comes from Alassio to visit
12 December 1925–18 January 1926	Martin Secker visits his wife in Spotorno
25 December 1925	Visit of Barbara Weekley for a 'few days' (comes again 20–26 January)
10–22 February 1926	Visit of Ada Clarke and her friend Lizzie Booth
12 February 1926	Elsa and Barbara Weekley at the Albergo Ligure in Spotorno; Frieda has joined them there by the 16th
22 February 1926	Goes to Monte Carlo with Ada and her friend
25 February 1926	Puts his sister on the train in Nice
26 February 1926	To Capri via Ventimiglia and Rome
27 February–c. 10 March 1926	With the Brewsters at Villa Torre dei Quattro Venti, Capri
11 March 1926	To Ravello with Brett
c. 15 March 1926	Brett leaves Ravello
22 March–3 April 1926	Rome, Assisi, Perugia, Florence, Ravenna

	with Millicent Beveridge and Mabel Harrison
3–20 April 1926	Back at the Villa Bernarda
20 April–6 May 1926	Pensione Lucchesi in Florence
28 April 1926	Elsa and Barbara Weekley leave for England
6 May 1926	Moves into Villa Mirenda, San Polo Mosciano, Scandicci
16 May 1926	Visit to Villa Mirenda of Reggie Turner and Giuseppe ('Pino') Orioli
2 June 1926	Visits Sir George and Lady Ida Sitwell at Castello di Montegufoni, Montagnana, near Florence
12 July 1926	Leaves for Baden-Baden
13–29 July 1926	With Frieda's mother in Baden-Baden
29 July 1926	To London via Strasbourg, Brussels and Ostend
30 July–9 August 1926	At 25 Rossetti Garden Mansions, Chelsea
7?–8 August 1926	Weekend with Richard Aldington and Arabella Yorke at Padworth, near Reading
9–21 August 1926	With Mary and Millicent Beveridge in Newtonmore, Inverness-shire, Scotland
16–18 August 1926	Visit to Fort William, Mallaig and Isle of Skye
21 August 1926	Leaves Newtonmore for Nottingham
22 August 1926	Travels with Eddie Clarke and Peggy King to Mablethorpe, Lincolnshire
27 August 1926	Joined by Frieda and moves to Sutton-on-Sea
13 September 1926	To Emily King's house in Nottingham
14–16 September 1926	With Ada Clarke in Ripley. Visits the Eastwood area for the last time
16–28 September 1926	At 30 Willoughby Road, Hampstead
22 September 1926	Sees the Untermeyers
28 September 1926	Leaves London for Paris
1 October 1926	From Paris to Lausanne
3 October 1926	Lausanne to Florence–Villa Mirenda
6–11 October 1926	Visit from Richard Aldington and Arabella Yorke
22–28 October 1926	Aldous and Maria Huxley in Florence

19 December 1926	Visit to the Stenterello Theatre in Florence with Orioli and the Wilkinsons
24 December 1926	Party for the peasants on the estate
16–18? January 1927	Visit from Earl Brewster
18 January 1927	Visit with Brewster to the studio of Alberto Magnelli
c. 1 March 1927	Huxleys visit, with Mary Hutchinson
17 March 1927	Frieda leaves for Baden-Baden
19 March 1927	Leaves for Rome and stays with Christine Hughes
21–28? March 1927	With the Brewsters in Palazzo Cimbrone, Ravello
28? March–3 April 1927	Walking with Brewster on Sorrento peninsula
4–6 April 1927	Rome. Sees Christine Hughes again
6–11 April 1927	An Etruscan tour: Cerveteri, Tarquinia, Vulci and Volterra
11 April–4 August 1927	Villa Mirenda
12 April 1927	Visit of Barbara Weekley (leaves 3 May), accompanied by Mrs Seaman
23 May 1927	Visit of Edith and Osbert Sitwell
8 June 1927	Takes Christine and Mary Christine Hughes to the Uffizi
12 June 1927	Maria Huxley and the Franchettis at Villa Mirenda
15 June 1927	Driven by Maria Huxley to Forte dei Marmi, returns 16 or 17 June
6 July 1927	Serious haemorrhage. Confined to bed
19 July 1927	Further haemorrhages, after slight recovery
4 August 1927	Takes night train to Villach, Austria
5–30 August 1927	Hotel Fischer, Villach
8 August–3 September 1927	Frieda's sister Johanna and her husband Emil Krug at Grand Hotel, Annenheim
30 August 1927	Leaves for Munich and stays overnight there
31 August–4 October 1927	At Else Jaffe's house in Irschenhausen
5 September 1927	Johanna Krug arrives. Stays until 8th. Else Jaffe leaves 12th for Heidelberg
18–21 September 1927	Barbara Weekley in Irschenhausen

29 September 1927	Visit from Franz Schoenberner and Hans Carossa (Max Mohr also calls about this time)
4 October 1927	Leaves Irschenhausen for Baden-Baden and stays at Hotel Eden
18 October 1927	Leaves Baden-Baden for Florence
19 October 1927	Met at Florence station by the Wilkinsons and taken to Villa Mirenda by car
c. 9 November 1927	Car trip with the Wilkinsons to San Gimignano
ante 14 November 1927	Visit from Scott-Moncrieff, Orioli, Turner and Harold Acton
17 November 1927	Lunch at Turner's house in Florence. Meets Michael Arlen on the Lungarno
19 November 1927	Arlen at Villa Mirenda for tea
18 December 1927	Wilkinsons take tea at Villa Mirenda before leaving to spend Christmas in Rome
21 December 1927	Aldous and Maria Huxley visit
24 December 1927	Party for the peasants on the estate
25 December 1927	Huxleys take the Lawrences to eat at the Petterichs' house in Florence
27 December 1927	Huxleys at Villa Mirenda for lunch
13 January 1928	Has to postpone departure for Switzerland because of illness
20 January 1928	Leaves for Les Diablerets via Milan, the Simplon and Aigle
20 January–6 March 1928	Chalet Beau Site, Les Diablerets
5 February 1928	Picnic on Pillon Pass
9–12 February 1928	Visit of Rolf Gardiner
12?–16 February 1928	Visit of Max Mohr
27 February 1928	Frieda leaves for Baden-Baden
6 March 1928	Leaves Les Diablerets accompanied by Juliette Huxley as far as Aigle. Meets Frieda in Milan
7 March 1928	From Milan to Florence
10–11 March 1928	Else Jaffe and Alfred Weber at Villa Mirenda
16 March 1928	Barbara Weekley arrives from Alassio
28 March 1928	Barbara Weekley returns to Alassio. The Wilkinsons leave for England

2 April 1928	Else Jaffe and Alfred Weber at Villa Mirenda again
11 April 1928	Frieda goes with Else to see Barbara Weekley in Alassio
13 April 1928	Muriel Moller and Nellie Morrison at Villa Mirenda for tea
15? April 1928	Visit of Margaret Gardiner. Mary and Millicent Beveridge come to tea
16 April 1928	Frieda returns from Alassio
4 May 1928	Decides to rent Villa Mirenda for a further six months. Mary Foote for tea
ante 24 May 1928	Enid Hilton and her husband at the inn at Vingone for a 'fortnight or more' (back in London by 31st)
c. 6 June 1928	Brewsters in Florence
10 June 1928	To Turin with the Brewsters
11–13 June 1928	Chambéry, Aix-les-Bains, Grenoble
14–15 June 1928	Hotel des Touristes, Saint-Nizier-de-Pariset. Required to leave because he coughs in the night
17 June–6 July 1928	Grand Hotel, Chexbres-sur-Vevey
19 June 1928	Frieda leaves for Baden-Baden
23–28 June 1928	Maria and Aldous Huxley visit
25 June 1928	Frieda returns
27 June 1928	Excursion in the Huxleys' car to Château de Chillon
6 July 1928	Moves to Hotel National, Gstaad
9 July–18 September 1928	Chalet Kesselmatte, near Gsteig
11 July 1928	Brewsters arrive at Hotel Viktoria in Gsteig
by 28 July 1928	Wm. Jackson Ltd have refused to accept over seventy copies of *Lady Chatterley's Lover* they ordered
31 July 1928	Brewsters bring Dhan Gopal Mukerji to tea
11 August 1928	Frieda's birthday 'feast' at the Hotel Viktoria
c. 24 August 1928	The Brewsters' Indian friend Boshi Sen gives Lawrence a massage
26 August–7 September 1928	Visit of Emily King and her daughter Peggy

29 August 1928	Brewsters leave for Geneva
15–18 September 1928	Else Jaffe stays for the weekend
18 September 1928	Leaves for Baden-Baden
18 September–1 October 1928	Hotel (zum) Löwen in Lichtenthal, with Brewsters and Frieda's mother
1 October 1928	Leaves Lichtenthal with Brewsters for south of France
2–15 October 1928	Grand Hotel, Le Lavandou. Else Jaffe, Alfred Weber and the Huxleys also there till the 4th
3 October 1928	Visits Port Cros with Huxleys, Else Jaffe and Alfred Weber
12 October 1928	Frieda arrives in Le Lavandou
15 October–17 November 1928	At La Vigie on Port Cros with Richard Aldington, Arabella Yorke and Brigit Patmore
17 November 1928	Leaves Port Cros for Bandol
17 November 1928–11 March 1929	Hotel Beau Rivage, Bandol
29 November–2 December 1928	Visit of Rhys Davies
18–22 December 1928	Davies's second visit, with P. R. Stephensen who leaves on the 19th
1–2 January 1929	Julian and Juliette Huxley call, on their way to see H. G. Wells in Grasse
2–12 January 1929	Barbara Weekley at Beau Rivage
4–15 January 1929	Visit of Brewster Ghiselin
c. 7–10 January 1929	Second visit of Stephensen
18 January 1929	Police inform Pollinger that six copies of *Lady Chatterley's Lover* have been seized
21 January–1 February 1929	Visit of Aldous and Maria Huxley
23 January 1929	Police inform Pollinger that typescripts of *Pansies* have been seized
12–22 February 1929	Visit of Ada Clarke
27 February 1929	Sends Ada £50 towards the rent she had paid for Mountain Cottage in 1918–19
28 February 1929	Home Secretary answers questions in the Commons on seizure of *Pansies*
4–7? March 1929	Davies's third visit
11–12 March 1929	Travels to Paris with Davies
12–18 March 1929	Grand Hotel de Versailles, with Davies
15 March 1929	Lunch with the Crosbys

18–25 March 1929	Stays with the Huxleys in Suresnes
23 March 1929	Tea with Daniel Halévy, François Mauriac and other French intellectuals
25 March 1929	Frieda returns from Baden-Baden
29 March–1 April 1929	Spends weekend at Ermenonville with the Crosbys
3 April 1929	Visits the Crosbys in the rue de Lille with Frieda and Aldous Huxley
5 April 1929	Signs agreement with Edward Titus for new edition of *Lady Chatterley's Lover*
7 April 1929	Leaves Paris for Spain via Orléans, Toulouse, Carcassone and Perpignan
9–10 April 1929	Hotel de la Cité in Carcassone
13? April 1929	Arrives Barcelona
16 April 1929	Takes overnight crossing for Majorca
17–22 April 1929	Hotel Royal, Palma de Majorca
18 April 1929	Meets Robert Nichols in the street
22 April–18 June 1929	Hotel Principe Alfonso, Palma de Majorca
8 May 1929	By car to Valldemosa and Soller
10–13? May 1929	Weekend at Cala Ratjada
14 June 1929	Exhibition of Lawrence's paintings opens at Warren Gallery with private view
18 June 1929	Leaves Majorca by boat for Marseilles
22 June 1929	Arrives in Forte dei Marmi
29?–30? June 1929	Orioli spends weekend in Forte dei Marmi
30? June 1929	Maria Cristina Chambers also arrives there
5 July 1929	Police raid on Warren Gallery. Thirteen paintings seized
6 July 1929	Driven to Pisa by Maria Huxley; takes train to Florence
6–11? July 1929	Stays in Orioli's flat in Florence. Very ill
11 July 1929	Frieda responds to Orioli's telegram and arrives in Florence
11?–16 July 1929	Hotel Porta Rossa, Florence
16–18 July 1929	To Baden-Baden via Milan
18–23 July 1929	In Lichtenthal with Frieda and her mother
23 July–3 August 1929	Hotel Plättig, near Bühl
3–25 August 1929	Back at Hotel Löwen, Lichtenthal

11 August 1929	Celebrates Frieda's fiftieth birthday
25 August 1929	Leaves Lichtenthal for Munich
26 August–18 September 1929	At the inn belonging to the Kaffee Angermeier in Rottach-am-Tegernsee, to see Max Mohr
2 September 1929	Visit of Else Jaffe and Alfred Weber
18 September 1929	Leaves Rottach for Bandol via Munich and Marseilles
23 September–1 October 1929	Hotel Beau Rivage, Bandol
1 October 1929–6 February 1930	Villa Beau Soleil, Bandol
18? October 1929	Brewsters arrive from Capri
21 October 1929	Max Mohr goes back to Rottach
ante 20–30 November 1929	Frederick Carter at Beau Rivage
ante 9 December 1929	The Di Chiaras and Ida Rauh arrive at Beau Rivage
10 December 1929	Harry Crosby shoots himself and his mistress in New York
15–20 January 1930	Pollinger at Beau Rivage
17–26 January 1930	Else Jaffe at Villa Beau Soleil
20–21 January 1930	Dr Andrew Morland and his wife at Hotel Beau Rivage
c. 30 January 1930	Barbara Weekley arrives to stay with the Lawrences
6 February 1930	Leaves for the sanatorium in Vence
6 February–1 March 1930	At the Ad Astra sanatorium
13 February 1930	Visit from Earl Brewster
24 February 1930	Visit from H. G. Wells
25 and 28 February 1930	Huxleys visit
26 February 1930	Jo Davidson makes bust of Lawrence
27 February 1930	Visit of the Aga Khan and his wife
1 March 1930	Leaves the Ad Astra for the Villa Robermond in Vence
2 March 1930	Lawrence dies around 10 in the evening

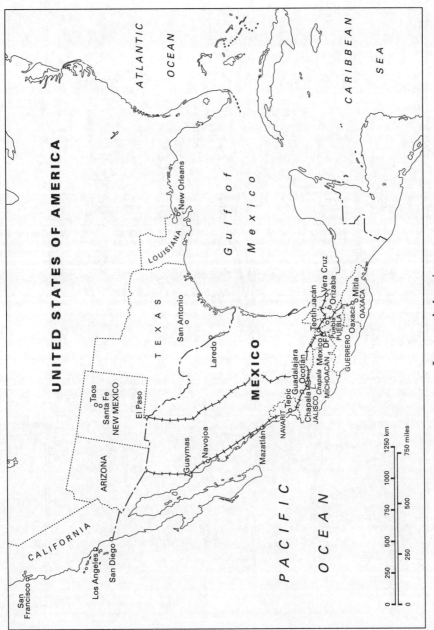

1 Lawrence's America

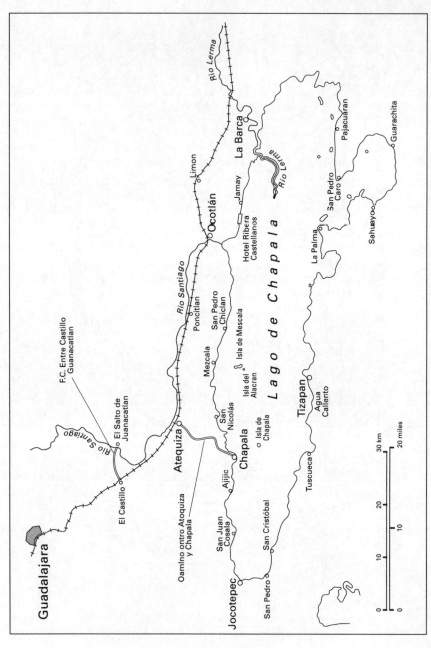

2 Map of Lake Chapala from the 1923 edition of Terry's *Guide*

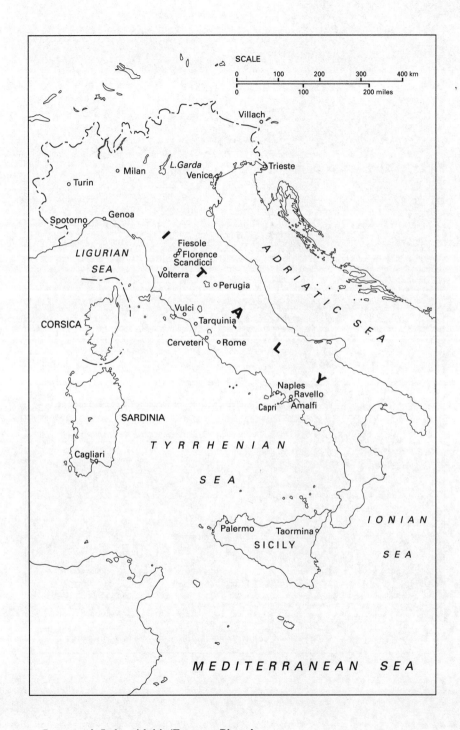

3   Lawrence's Italy, with his 'Etruscan Places'

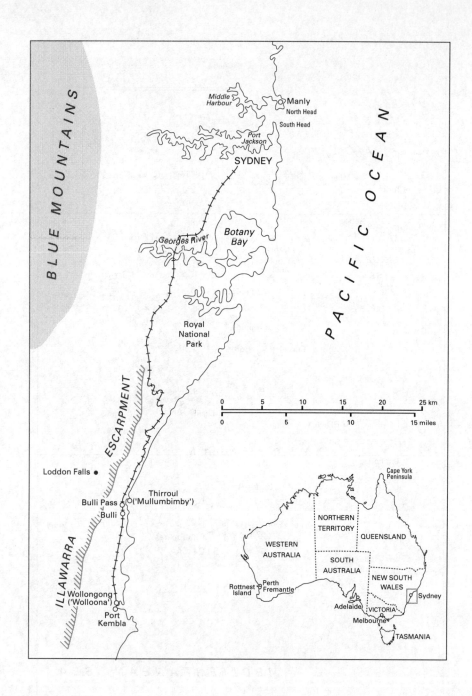

BLUE MOUNTAINS

Middle
Harbour

Manly
North Head

South Head

Port
Jackson

SYDNEY

PACIFIC OCEAN

Georges River

Botany
Bay

Royal
National
Park

ESCARPMENT

0   5   10   15   20   25 km

0   5   10   15 miles

Loddon Falls ●

ILLAWARRA

Thirroul
('Mullumbimby')

Bulli Pass
Bulli

Wollongong
('Wolloona')

Port
Kembla

Cape York
Peninsula

NORTHERN
TERRITORY

QUEENSLAND

WESTERN
AUSTRALIA

SOUTH
AUSTRALIA

NEW SOUTH
WALES

Rottnest
Island
Perth
Fremantle

Sydney

Adelaide

VICTORIA

Melbourne

TASMANIA

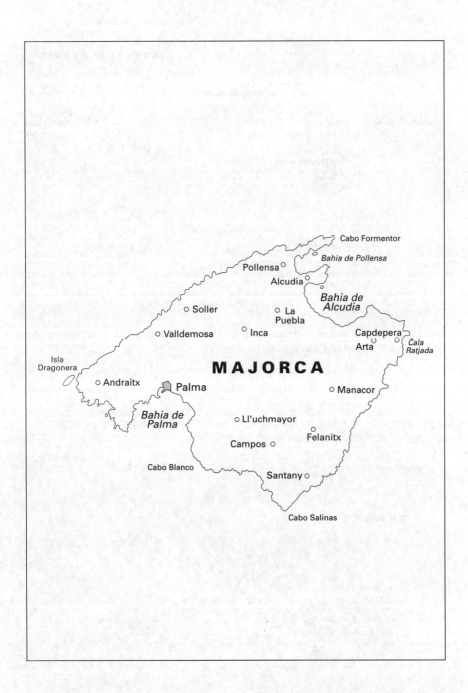

Cabo Formentor

Bahia de Pollensa

Pollensa

Alcudia

Bahia de Alcudia

Soller

La Puebla

Capdepera

Cala Ratjada

Valldemosa

Inca

Arta

Isla Dragonera

MAJORCA

Andraitx

Palma

Manacor

Bahia de Palma

Ll'uchmayor

Campos

Felanitx

Cabo Blanco

Santany

Cabo Salinas

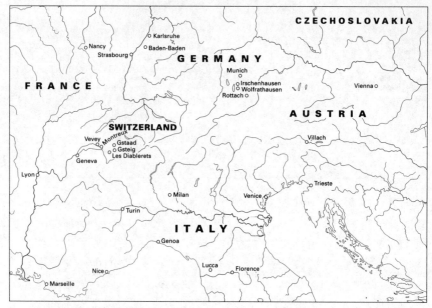

6 France, Switzerland and southern Germany

7 The Riviera

D. H. LAWRENCE

1922–1930

PART ONE

◆

Faring Forth

CHAPTER ONE

◆

February–April 1922

CEYLON

I No More Bad Meals

It is not immediately obvious why any Englishman born and bred in the industrial Midlands should ever want to leave Taormina. Winter could be surprisingly cold, and there were periods in summer when it became too hot to move; but for most of the year there was in that small Sicilian town a light, warmth and colour which any impartial observer might think compared very favourably with the climate in Nottinghamshire. Lawrence and Frieda lived in the top two stories of the Fontana Vecchia, a house on a steep slope ten minutes from the main streets (iii. 517). At its back Mount Etna, which on his bad days Lawrence was inclined to hope would bury the locals in lava (iv. 139), was hidden from sight by other peaks; but from the verandahs in front there were fine views leftwards across the straits of Messina to the Calabrian shore and, to the right, the open Ionian Sea. Lying in bed in the morning Lawrence could watch the water change its colour as the sun came up and think of the Greeks – not Plato or Aristotle but the ancient Homeric adventurers, somewhat 'Asiatic' and 'tinged' (as he once put it) 'with phenoecian' (iv. 97, 100; iii. 488). Powerfully attracted by romantic visions of the past, he often indulged his own nostalgia while simultaneously suspecting it as the sign of a regressive urge towards evasion, forgetfulness and death.[1]

The Lawrences got on well with their Sicilian landlords but relations with the small expatriate community, whose presence the exchange rate made inevitable in such an attractive spot, were more difficult. What Lawrence saw as the aimlessness and snobbery of its non-artistic component often irritated him; and the activities of the artists could either leave him sceptical or disgusted (this last in the case of the Baron Wilhelm von Gloeden who specialised in photographs of naked adolescents, artistically posed in a 'Greek' decor).[2] Yet through the 45-year-old Marie Hubrecht, who painted and had once herself owned the Fontana Vecchia, he met two young artists he came to like a good deal (Jan Juta and Alan Insole); and it was in Taormina that he was first introduced to the Scottish painter Millicent Beveridge who was to become one of his closest friends when the Lawrences returned to Europe in 1925.[3]

As far as his own art was concerned, Lawrence had good reason to be satisfied with what he had achieved since he began to rent Fontana Vecchia in March

5

1920. *The Lost Girl* had been completed, he had prepared second versions of what would become *Studies in Classic American Literature*, and written most of the poems which would appear in *Birds, Beasts and Flowers*. *Mr Noon* may have been abandoned at an intriguing but perhaps also awkwardly personal juncture, but he had finally managed to finish *Aaron's Rod* and had also written both *Sea and Sardinia* and *Fantasia of the Unconscious*. Not all of these texts belong to the time at the Fontana Vecchia itself – he had been away from the villa between August and October 1920, and then again between April and September 1921 – but enough do to suggest that it was highly conducive to productive labour. When he came back to Taormina at the beginning of October 1921, he relied on his recent memories of a holiday at Zell-am-See in writing 'The Captain's Doll', added a substantial new ending to 'The Fox' (so that it was more than twice its original length), and completely transformed a short story called 'The Thimble' into 'The Ladybird'.[4] By general agreement, these three novellas are among the best works he ever published. In his own view, the long introduction he sent off to his agent on 26 January 1922 for a memoir of life in the Foreign Legion by Maurice Magnus was 'the best single piece of writing, *as writing*, that he had ever done'.[5] A homosexual, Magnus had come to Taormina to borrow more money from Lawrence and, when he was refused, slipped over to Malta where several months later he committed suicide in order to escape his creditors. The responsibility Lawrence felt because of his refusal, and because he had himself introduced Magnus to Maltese friends from whom he *did* succeed in borrowing, lends special force to the introduction where two topics central to all Lawrence's writing, homosexuality and the role of money in our lives, are treated in a remarkably complex and lively way.

Looking back at the beginning of 1922, this impressive list of writings can have been no more successful than the climate or the landscape in persuading Lawrence that he ought to take on Fontana Vecchia for a third year. By his standards, two in the same place was already something of a record. Restlessness was, or had become, natural to him. His unhappy experiences during World War I had left him rootless, bitterly alienated from English life, but also from Western European ways in general. On 19 February 1922 Lawrence told his mother-in-law that he and Frieda were sitting ready to travel ('reise-fertig') with four trunks: 'one household trunk, one book trunk, F's and mine – and then two valises, hat box and the two quite small pieces: just like Abraham faring forth to a new land' (iv. 198). They left Taormina for Palermo three days later, staying with a friend named Ruth Wheelock, who worked at the American consulate and had done some typing for Lawrence,[6] before sailing to the Italian mainland on the evening of the 24th. Notes which Lawrence wrote on Friday 24th are on the headed notepaper of the Grande Albergo Santa Lucia in Naples (iv. 200–1). At 8 p.m. on the evening of Sunday 26 February, the Lawrences sailed out of Naples

6

harbour on the P & O liner *Osterley*. Although their immediate destination was Ceylon (Sri Lanka as it is now called), they were embarked on what would prove to be a journey around the world.

With some reluctance ('You don't mean to travel to Ceylon with this object?'), Lawrence had agreed that Frieda should include in her luggage the side of a Sicilian cart with, as she describes it, a joust painted on one panel and St Geneviève on the other.[7] It was a memento of a continent which Lawrence had been declaring himself anxious to leave for several months. In July of the previous year he had told his friend Mary Cannan that he would like to 'break out of Europe', that it had been like a bad meal, every course of which had given him indigestion (iv. 49). At that time, however, the only alternatives seemed to be sailing round the world with a few friends in a small boat[8] or, more practically, finally going to America. Announcing on 17 August 1921 to Scofield Thayer, the wealthy editor of an American 'quality' periodical called the *Dial*, that he intended to be in the United States in the following spring, Lawrence had added, 'Needless to say my knees lose their brassy strength, and feel like chocolate fondants at the thought' (iv. 73).

In ways which were described in volume ii of this biography, Lawrence had always been fascinated by America. During the war, his unsuccessful attempts to escape there had been accompanied by copious evidence of a continuing interest in the first versions of *Studies in Classic American Literature*. He was convinced that in many ways Europe was played out and America would eventually see, as he put it in an introduction to his *Studies*, 'the inception of a new era of living'.[9] His feelings were nevertheless complex. Some of the complexities are apparent in 'The Evening Land', a poem which is signed 'Baden-Baden' where he stayed from May until early July 1921. In its opening lines he addresses America directly and asks, 'Shall I come to you, the open tomb of my race?' The rest of the poem makes it clear that in Lawrence's view white America is ahead of Europe only in the sense that it is further down both the materialistic and the idealist track, and closer therefore to the inevitable catastrophe from which a new era of living would emerge. He describes his soul as only 'half-cajoled'; confesses himself apprehensive of what he expects to find in the States: 'I am so terrified, America, / Of the iron click of your human contact'; and in conclusion asks to be allured until all his reservations disappear.[10]

The letter to Thayer in which Lawrence describes his knees as 'chocolate fondants' was written from Zell-am-See. Towards the end of August 1921 he and Frieda moved from there to Florence but on 21 September broke an agreement to meet Catherine Carswell and her husband in Siena and left for Capri in order 'to see the Brewsters who are leaving for India' – by which Lawrence meant Ceylon (iv. 89). A week later, back in Taormina, he wrote a warm letter to the Brewsters announcing that, instead of going to America in January or February of the coming year, he would be accepting the invitation they had proffered and following them eastwards. Seven years older than Lawrence, Earl and Achsah Brewster were expatriate Americans who painted, but not so successfully that they could abandon their reliance on a small private income.[11] He had known them for only five months but his return to see them in Capri must have confirmed the trust they initially inspired. Their invitation was clearly fairly specific ('They will find me a place', he wrote on 9 October – iv. 96); yet his decision to satisfy his need to break out of Europe as soon as possible by accepting it may also have had something to do with the disagreeable mail which was waiting for him when in October he got back to Taormina from Capri: news that Philip Heseltine was threatening to sue over the portrait of Halliday in *Women in Love*, a copy of the rabid attack on that novel in Horatio Bottomley's populist journal *John Bull*, but also, and perhaps more significantly for his travel plans, hostile comments on his latest novel, *Aaron's Rod*, from his American literary agent Robert Mountsier (iv. 90–2). For a while he stressed the consolations of the view from the front of Fontana Vecchia (the same villa where, by a strange coincidence, the Brewsters had begun their married life roughly ten years before[12]); yet he still felt he had to move even if at this point he is clear both with himself and with others that following the Brewsters would only be a way of postponing the evil hour of the confrontation with America. 'I will go east', he tells them, 'intending ultimately to go west' (iv. 90).

Very soon however Lawrence began to waver, deciding not to persist in his commitment to his new friends until they had written to him from Ceylon and described conditions there. In the meantime all his dreams of escape began to have a Western rather than Eastern context. 'My plan is, ultimately', he explained to Brewster in a letter written on 8 October, ten days after the one in which he said he would go east, 'to get a little farm somewhere by myself, in Mexico, New Mexico, Rocky Mountains, or British Columbia. The desire to be away from the body of mankind – to be a bit of a hermit – is paramount' (iv. 95). Nothing is more typical of Lawrence than that in the next paragraph he should express the hope that, if he did find a farm, the Brewsters would settle 'somewhere near'. His ambition was rarely to be a hermit in the full sense but rather the animating presence of a small group as firmly convinced as he usually was of the irredeemable decadence of Western culture.

It may be that Frieda had more behind-the-scenes influence on her husband's decision-making than emerges from the surviving documents but, as befits the author of 'The Captain's Doll', Lawrence nearly always expresses himself in the letters of this period as if any decision about his next move was essentially dependent on his own inclinations and needs. With one or two very important exceptions described later, all the evidence suggests that Frieda was happy

8

enough to follow where he led. For someone brought up in upper-middle or (more accurately) minor aristocratic comfort, she was remarkably adaptable; but she was also fully committed to the idea of her husband as a genius and probably understood that his extraordinary abilities (and therefore earning power) were more dependent than those of most other great writers on the stimulus of new environments. There seems to have been no objection from her therefore when, in November 1921, Lawrence abruptly changed his mind about going to Ceylon and decided that he would go directly to America after all. The immediate reason was a letter he had received from Mabel Dodge Sterne (as she then was) inviting him to come to Taos in New Mexico. To use the German term Lawrence was fond of applying to Lady Ottoline Morrell, Mabel Sterne had already had a distinguished career as a *Kulturträger*, having established before and during the war highly intellectual and artistic *salons* in first Florence and then New York; but by the early 1920s she was settled in the small New Mexican town of Taos and very active in the growing movement to safeguard what was left of Indian (Native American) culture. What made her invitation so attractive to Lawrence was not so much her evident enthusiasm for his work, particularly for an extract from *Sea and Sardinia* recently serialised in the *Dial*,[13] nor her offer to provide him with a house, but the opportunity she offered of going to America without having too much immediate contact with the dynamic capitalist culture he had come to associate above all with New York. Over the next few weeks he actively explored ways of travelling as directly as possible to Taos – by sailing to Galveston, Texas, for example – or of fulfilling the barely rational wish he had to approach America from the Pacific so as to ensure that his first encounter should not be with that north-eastern seaboard where most of white America's industrial and commercial activity was then concentrated.

Always susceptible to the cold, Lawrence was ill at the end of 1921. For neither the first nor the last time he spent Christmas in bed and found what he describes as the 'flu' difficult to shake off. As he began to feel better he insisted that, if he had been well, he would have booked a passage on a boat due to leave Bordeaux for New Orleans on 15 January; and he faced up also to the fact that there might after all be no alternative to sailing from Palermo to New York on 5 February and quickly moving on to Taos from there (iv. 157–8). Brewster's first letter from Ceylon had failed to change his plans. 'I feel I can't come,' he had written on 2 January 1922, 'that the east is not my destiny' and, because Brewster's chief reason for going to Ceylon was to study Buddhism, he went on to contrast the serenity Buddhists aim to achieve with the pain, frustration and 'struggling through' which he believed to be essential to life. 'Let nobody try to filch from me even my influenza. – I've got influenza at the moment, but it only makes me more unbuddhing' (iv. 154). This mood lasted for sixteen days until on 18 January Lawrence announced to Mountsier, 'Suddenly that I am on the point of

coming to America I feel I *can't* come . . . I would rather go to Ceylon, and come
to America later, from the east' (iv. 168). On the same day he replied to Brewster's
second letter from Ceylon, taking back some of his previous, hostile remarks
about the Buddha and acknowledging that, 'Probably there, east, is the *source*: and
America is the extreme periphery'. 'Shall I come to Ceylon?', he asked, 'Dio mio,
I am so ridiculous, wavering between east and west' (iv. 170–1). He promised to
write to the travel agents at once about ships to Colombo, and from then on
persevered with his eastern plans until he had secured his two berths on the
Osterley.

Quite why Lawrence suddenly changed his mind once again is the kind of
hermeneutic puzzle of which biography is full but which no amount of biographical enquiry is ever likely to solve. Mabel Sterne was convinced that he had
been dissuaded from going to Taos by one of her many enemies,[14] and the letters
do in fact show that Mountsier warned Lawrence off, but not that he took much
notice (iv. 150). Catherine Carswell assumed that Lawrence 'was most reasonably
afraid of disobeying doctor's orders by going to America in midwinter'.[15] That is
possible and the failure to find a convenient boat which would take him directly
to the *southern* states of America may therefore be significant. Yet Lawrence's
respect for the advice of doctors was notoriously minimal. So many motives may
have played a part in his *volte-face* that it becomes impossible to isolate one and
be sure that it was over-riding. The news, which he received in early December,
that he had won the James Tate Black Memorial prize for *The Lost Girl* certainly
made him feel richer (it was worth £100), and perhaps also therefore that he
could be more ambitious in his travel plans; and just before the announcement of
his change of mind on 18 January his efforts to bowdlerise *Aaron's Rod* for his
American publisher Thomas Seltzer had once again put him out of temper with
his New York publishing contacts (iv. 146, 167). If either of these factors has any
importance, its degree cannot be measured exactly, especially in the absence of
that utopian state called 'full documentation' (it would be especially interesting to
know, for example, what it was in Brewster's second letter from Ceylon which
Lawrence found so convincing and whether it was only by the time he wrote it
that Brewster could be more specific about accommodation).

We cannot know for certain how Lawrence's new decision was arrived at, but
eminently recognisable and familiar are the terms in which he explained it,
especially in the difficult letter he was obliged to write to Mabel Sterne on 27
January. He says there that he has become convinced it is after all his destiny to
go east before coming west; yet his more important appeal is to an episode from
the Old Testament: 'But I have a Balaam's Ass in my belly which won't budge,
when I turn my face west' (iv. 181). The story of Balaam, invited by Balak the
King of Moab to come and curse the Israelites but then encouraged by his ass not
to set out on his journey because she can see the angel of the Lord blocking the

way whereas he cannot, was a favourite point of reference for Lawrence (before his letter to Mabel Sterne he had already used it twice in order to explain why he was going to Ceylon rather than America – iv. 177, 180). It is only after Balaam has beaten his ass three times to persuade her to go forward that she is allowed by the Lord to speak and her master's eyes are finally opened to what stands before them both. With its talking animal and its realistic details – 'And when the ass saw the angel of the Lord, she thrust herself unto the wall, and crushed Balaam's foot against the wall; and he smote her again'[16] – the story was one which any child brought up as Lawrence was would be likely to carry forward with him from Sunday school. Its special force lay in the way it suggested that in the decisive moments of our life we are, or should be, directed by powers beyond our overt mental control. In the Bible, those powers come down from above whereas for Lawrence (as his use of 'belly' implies) they are more likely to emerge from below, from the *dark* gods.

Richard Aldington attributed Lawrence's waverings between east and west to his 'chronic indecision and almost pathological self-mistrust',[17] and it is true that on several occasions subsequent to this he exhibited a similar inability to decide quickly what he wanted to do. Partly this was because, with a wife who was often if not always accommodating, no children, and the ability to earn money with his writing wherever he happened to be living, Lawrence had more opportunities to think where he wanted to live than most people do. Partly also it was that his hatred of repression, and his determination to hold himself receptive to all his feelings, made for behaviour which by ordinary standards often seemed wildly inconsistent. In this particular case, however, the process of his decision-making was perhaps not so very far from the norm as to deserve any reference to pathology. Important choices are rarely made easily or on purely rational grounds, especially when the pull in opposite directions is roughly equal. The difficult question for Lawrence was to be able to recognise the right mood in which an important decision could be taken. Much later, in *Sketches of Etruscan Places*, he was to defend the way the Etruscan augur or haruspex scrutinised the hot liver of a recently sacrificed bird on the grounds that this practice 'made him capable of that ultimate inward attention which alone tells us the last thing we need to know'.[18]

II   Kandy and the Brewsters

From Naples, the *Osterley* took the Lawrences back on their tracks through the straits of Messina and gave them the opportunity of once more saying goodbye to Sicily. In *Sea and Sardinia* Lawrence had cast Mount Etna as a wicked white witch depriving men of their souls and he was now once again conscious of having to resist her blandishments: 'She said to me, "Come back here" – I only said no, but wept inside with pain – pain of parting', he wrote in German to his mother-in-law (iv. 205). As they sailed past Crete, through the Suez Canal at five miles an hour ('takes 18 hours – and you see the Arabs and their camels and the rosy-yellow desert with its low palm-trees and its hills of sharp sand' – iv. 208), and then into the Red Sea, there was more occasion for symbolic geography. Mount Sinai seemed to Lawrence 'unnaturally sharp', like a dagger covered in dried blood, and with its surrounding countryside 'Semitic and cruel', represent-ative of the 'murderous will and iron of idea and ideal'. 'Jahveh is father of the ideal', he declared, 'and Zeus and Jupiter and Christ are only sons.' In coming through the Straits of Bab-el-Mandeb to Aden, and then heading for the Indian Ocean, he clearly felt some exhilaration in leaving behind both the hebraic and hellenic components of Western culture. In Lawrence's conception of that culture, Plato and Jesus are the two 'idealists' he most commonly blames for initiating the process which he felt had eventually led to the disastrous triumph of the spiritual over the physical, the mind over the body, and who were therefore also responsible for the ruthlessly exploitative attitudes to the natural world characteristic of his own, science-dominated time. Yet in the more casual mode of letter-writing it is not just these two figures but the whole of Greek thought and the whole of the Judeo-Christian tradition which he is glad to feel he is putting behind him: 'Behind lies at last Jerusalem, Greece, Rome and Europe – fulfilled and past, a great terrible dream' (iv. 211–12).[19]

We know how Lawrence was feeling aboard ship largely because of the two letters he wrote to his mother-in-law, one of which was posted in Port Said and the other when the *Osterley* docked in Colombo on 13 March 1922. Together with other, shorter letters he wrote at the time these suggest that the fortnight's voyage was one of the most contented periods of his troubled life. Half-way through, and on a boat as 'steady as a street', he and Frieda had not had 'a single bad moment' (iv. 208, 212). With some apprehension, he had booked second rather than first-class accommodation but the *Osterley* was less than half full ('except the third class' – iv. 208), and like a luxurious floating hotel. Lawrence's typically detailed description of what was on offer at breakfast – 'stewed pears, porridge, fish, bacon, eggs, fried sausages, beefsteak, kidneys, marmalade – all there' (iv. 205) – was clearly designed to demonstrate to the Baroness von Richthofen how heroic one then had to be in order to grapple with the cup of Bovril at eleven in the morning, the one-o'clock lunch ('soup, fish, chicken or turkey, meat entrées'), four-o'clock tea and seven-o'clock dinner. But he declared himself up to the challenge – 'But one also has an appetite at sea' (iv. 204, 206). Frieda later remembered how unusually well he felt during the trip.[20] His attitude to comfort was in general deeply ambiguous and in *Kangaroo* he makes the principal character criticise the kinds of Englishmen who 'wanted just to hang against the warmest wall they could find, . . . till some last wind of death or disturbance shook them down into earth, mushy and over-ripe'.[21] On this occasion, however, he very reasonably allowed himself to bask in physical well-being and enjoy that illusion of a former, conflict-free world of privilege which great shipping companies and their not always well-paid employees work hard to produce. Frieda had caught a cold in Naples and Lawrence was deeply impressed by the considerate way a steward and stewardess looked after her. 'After Italy it is remarkable. No, civilisation is a beautiful and fine thing, if only it remains alive, and doesn't become ennuyée' (iv. 206).

Rarely idle, he was himself saved from boredom on the *Osterley* by work on a translation of Giovanni Verga's great novel *Mastro-don Gesualdo*. He had first come across Verga in 1916 but only became seriously interested by his writing in late autumn 1921.[22] The cultivator of an Italian offshoot of European realism known as *verismo*, Verga in his most successful works is an even grimmer pessimist than the Conrad whom Lawrence had stigmatised in 1912 as one of the 'Writers among the Ruins' (i. 465), and an apparently unlikely object, therefore, for Lawrence's enthusiasm. Yet after his time in Taormina, he felt he could appreciate Verga's inwardness with Sicilian life, and he was fascinated (his own word) by a style heavily influenced by Sicilian speech – 'it would need somebody who could absolutely handle English in the dialect, to translate him' (iv. 115). Italian specialists are usually dissatisfied with Lawrence's translations of Verga because he makes so many simple mistakes, but for all its occasional incoherences his version of *Mastro-don Gesualdo* is still absorbing to read. He had finished half of it by the time he embarked and must therefore have been involved with all the harsh details of Mastro don Gesualdo's decline and fall while he was enjoying the comforts of the ship. (Incessantly concerned with the accumulation of wealth, the peasant protagonist of the novel ensures a miserable end to his life by marrying into the aristocracy.)

An important addition to the shipboard comforts was evidently the company. The Lawrences were placed at table with Anna Jenkins, a wealthy Australian widow with artistic interests, and the social preliminaries must have been made easier when they learned that one of the novels she had brought to read on the trip was *Sons and Lovers*. Finding Lawrence 'friendly and companionable', Mrs Jenkins got on well with him and it is clear from their subsequent relations that she was one of the reasons he developed on the *Osterley* a very favourable idea of Australia and Australians.[23] 'I believe Australia is a good country, full of life and energy', he told Rosalind Baynes (iv. 213). Before he embarked, Lawrence had spoken of staying in Ceylon 'at least a year' and 'at least six months' (iv. 181, 192), but five days from Colombo and encouraged by Mrs Jenkins, he had begun to think, 'If we don't want to go on living in Ceylon I shall go to Australia if we can manage it' (iv. 213). For the moment, however, that was a vague prospect, subordinate to the excitement of shortly being able to set foot in the east for the first time.

On the morning of 13 March 1922, the Lawrences were met on the wharf in Colombo by Earl Brewster and on the afternoon of the following day they travelled with him to the old inland capital of Kandy. 'Think I shall love these tropics' (iv. 214), Lawrence wrote to Mountsier before they left Colombo, but nine days later he told his agent that he doubted whether he would stay very long in Ceylon. On 28 March he sounded out Mrs Jenkins about coming to call on her in Perth (iv. 218); and on 3 April there is a flurry of letters and postcards announcing a settled dislike of the east and plans for moving on to Australia. The paradise he had told friends he was setting out to rediscover in Ceylon (iv. 207) had failed to materialise, even though in many ways the circumstances could scarcely have been more promising. The Brewsters had rented a roomy bungalow with broad verandahs giving 'each of us a quiet corner of our own' ('I shall never leave it', was Lawrence's *first* response).[24] It stood on a hill about a mile and a half outside Kandy looking down on one side to the famous lake and on another to the Maheveli, Ceylon's longest river. There were four servants, an 'ayah' for the Brewsters' young daughter Harwood, two men (including the cook), and a water-boy. For someone of Lawrence's interests the vegetation and animal life ought to have provided an absorbing experience, and neither was far to seek. The bunga-low stood in what he describes as a 'half-wild estate' of coconut and cocoa (iv. 216). 'We sit on the verandahs', he wrote to his sister Emily, 'and watch the chipmunks and chameleons and lizards and tropical birds among the trees and bamboos – there's only a clear space of about three yards round the house' (iv. 215).

Perfect conditions, one might have thought, for a man whose contentment always depended so much on his relations with the natural world; but that would be to reckon without the heat, not the dry heat of Sicily which Lawrence had found uncomfortable enough, but an enervating combination of high tempera-tures and humidity. He was unlucky enough to have arrived in Ceylon when it was even hotter than usual for the season. 'Ceylon steams heat', he was to conclude as he sailed away (iv. 234). Unwell from the first few days, he never seems to have accommodated himself completely to the tropical luxuriance which the climate fostered. Achsah Brewster describes how appalled he was when he went to put on his topee one morning and discovered that during the night it had become a home for a family of rats. 'The teeming life of the place', she comments, 'horrified him.'[25] Every room in the bungalow had a skylight so that the Lawrences could lie in bed not only listening to the wild-cats fighting on their roof but seeing them too. The loud nocturnal activity of animals and birds so close at hand made such an impression on Lawrence that in 1926 he asked Aldington if he had ever 'heard the night noises of a tropical jungle, and then instantly emitted a frightening series of yells, squawks, trills, howls and animal "help-murder" shrieks'. Only when he had lived in the tropics himself was Aldington able to realise that Lawrence's widely praised talents as a mimic extended beyond the human world and that he had 'accomplished the seemingly impossible task of remembering and being able to imitate all that medley of fantastic noises'.[26] This account comes from *Portrait of a Genius, But* . . . In his earlier book of reminiscences, *Life for Life's Sake*, first published in 1940, Aldington recalled the same episode and also how at this period Lawrence indulged in 'satirical acting of an American friend burning joss-sticks to Buddha'.[27]

Earl Brewster, who in his younger days had been much taken with Theosophy, was studying Buddhism at the famous Temple of the Tooth which stands by the lake in Kandy and is an important contributory factor to the picturesque appeal of the site. On 28 February Lawrence had written to Lady Cynthia Asquith, 'Perhaps I too shall study in that same molar monastery' (iv. 207), but there is no indication he ever set foot there. Once in Kandy his previous expression of interest in Buddhism was proved to be an aberration ('he never again showed as much interest in it as in his last letter from Sicily', Brewster reported ruefully), and he confirmed his former prejudices. They had been that it was a religion which encouraged introspection, passivity, escapism – a lack of active engagement with the world which he was to summarise by saying of the seated Buddha, 'Oh, I wish he would *stand up*!'[28] Now he added to these objections an aesthetic distaste. The art associated with Buddhism in Ceylon failed to catch his interest and his letters of the time are full of references to 'hideous little Buddha temples, like decked up pigsties', or 'rat-hole temples' of a 'rat-hole religion. Better Jesus' (iv. 221, 234). The crucifixes along the road from Germany into Italy had so fascinated him that their description had provided the striking opening chapter of *Twilight in Italy*; but Achsah Brewster remembered that although Lawrence would accompany them to 'old rock temples', he refused to join them in 'removing shoes and hats to pay homage to the silent Buddha figures in the caves', and that 'coming out, there would be Lawrence standing in his shoes, hat tight on his head, declaring that there was no use, he did not belong there and could not join in'.[29] The ill-health that soon afflicted him apart, it is not surprising that Lawrence's visit to Ceylon lasted only six weeks when its religion and culture interested him so little.

III   Perahera

There were nonetheless episodes in this short period which had a significant effect. The most important of these was the visit to Kandy on Thursday 23 March of Edward, Prince of Wales, who had landed in Colombo on Tuesday the 21st and was to leave Ceylon the following Saturday. A description of his activities

15

can be found in the text Sir Percival Phillips wrote to accompany the many photographs in *The Prince of Wales' Eastern Book*, published in aid of blinded servicemen at the end of 1922. After a 'Durbar' in which he met the local Kandyan dignitaries, the Prince was taken in the evening of 23 March to the room in the Temple where the famous tooth, reputed to have come from the Buddha's own mouth, was held. A reliquary, and then six caskets, one inside the other, had to be unlocked before it could be displayed. 'Whatever the origin of the relic, it cannot by any stretch of the imagination be regarded as the tooth of a human being, for one thing it is much too large', is Phillips's dry comment,[30] discounting the possibility that, as in the Christian tradition, 'There were giants in the earth in those days.'

The Buddha's left eye tooth is the most prized possession of Sinhalese Buddhists. Carried under a golden dome on the back of a richly decorated and specially trained elephant, it was and is the centrepiece of the religious festival known as a perahera which lasts two weeks and is held in Kandy every August. A special perahera was organised for the Prince with well over a hundred elephants, in addition to the one bearing the relic.[31] The animals paraded in lines of three or four and in between them came groups of Kandyan chiefs ('like peg-tops swathed round and round with muslin', Lawrence described them – iv. 234), musicians and dancers. The Prince reviewed the procession from the balcony of an octagonal pagoda in the Temple which gave on to the Victoria Esplanade and which was where the former kings of Kandy had traditionally received the homage of their subjects (see Fig. 1). Because it was night-time, the whole spectacle was illuminated by the light of blazing torches of coconut fibre and at its conclusion there were fireworks over the lake.

There are vivid and appreciative descriptions of the perahera in Lawrence's letters: it was 'wonderful', he 'loved it', and the impression it made on him was 'enormous' (iv. 221, 216, 234). Much later he would claim that as he watched near-naked villagers from remote jungle areas performing the so-called 'devil dances' at midnight 'under the torches', with their bodies glittering with sweat 'as if they had been gilded', he had come to understand as he had never done before quite what it meant to *feel* religion.[32] At the time he celebrated the occasion in his poem 'Elephant', which was later to be included in *Birds, Beasts and Flowers*. A description of the elephants in the procession is certainly part of this poem but they receive no more attention than the chiefs, tom-toms, naked devil-dancers or torches; and Lawrence's central interest is not in animals but the inadequate response to all the splendour of 'That pale fragment of a Prince up there, whose motto is *Ich dien*'. The phrases he uses to characterise the future Edward VIII in the poem are in tune with those in the letters where he is called 'thin and nervy: all twitchy', 'worn out', 'sad and forlorn', as well as 'nervous and irritable' (iv. 215, 216, 218, 221). Because Lawrence describes himself as 'just opposite the

Prince' and able to note how 'he nearly jumped out of his skin' when a woman threw a bouquet, or complain that he 'would hardly open his mouth to anybody' (iv. 215, 221), they must all have been the result of reasonably close observation.[33] The discrepancy between the exotic ceremony and the individual in whose honour it was being held is summed up in 'Elephant' when Lawrence writes,

> As if the homage of the kindled blood of the east
> Went up in wavelets to him, from the breasts and eyes
>   of jungle torch-men,
> And he couldn't take it.[34]

He is not reluctant to declare that he himself would have done better, replacing 'Ich dien' with 'Dient Ihr' ('you serve me' rather than 'I serve'), and reasserting the old idea of kingship against a modern conception which makes a 'weary diffident boy . . . / . . . Drudge to the public'. The Prince's failure to be sufficiently regal seems to Lawrence to frustrate the needs and expectations of both the elephants and his Sinhalese subjects so that, as the fireworks light up countless dark faces round the lake, he sees in them 'the faintest twist of mockery . . . the shadow of a jeer, of underneath disappointment'.

Nothing is more likely than that the Prince of Wales was not at his best on 23 March. By then he was five months into a gruelling official programme which had often been undertaken in unusually difficult circumstances.[35] He had come on to Colombo from India where the Congress Party, still incensed by the notorious incident two years before when a British general opened fire on an unarmed crowd in Amritsar and killed nearly 400 people, was continuing to agitate for independence and had called on its supporters to boycott the tour. Ceylon was quiet by comparison but, by the time the Prince arrived there, one elaborate local ceremony might have begun to seem very like another. He was not a man of strong cultural interests – the tone of the comments by Phillips on the Buddha's tooth give a hint of the intellectual character of his entourage – and best enjoyed riding, field sports and night-life. His physical courage and boyish good looks made him popular in England and on tours of Canada and Australia there had been praise for the informality of his manner. But his father George V had rather anxiously warned him that informality would not go down well in India, and an inability always to look appropriately solemn and dignified appears to have been one of the several ways (some of which were to become more evident later) in which the Prince of Wales was miscast for his role in life.[36] There is no reason to suppose therefore that Lawrence's impressions of the Prince were inaccurate and, however surprising some of the political thoughts they gave rise to may appear, they can be considered as part of an important contemporary debate about the responsibilities of modern kingship, and how well the Prince of Wales was likely to fulfil them.

The perahera gave a significant stimulus to Lawrence's political as well as religious thinking. He was oppressed by a sense of 'teeming millions' in the east (iv. 227), and seems never to have shaken off a feeling of potential menace from both the human and animal worlds. As the four servants gathered in the evening on the front verandah of the Brewsters' bungalow to chant prayers to the Buddha he would say, 'Who knows whether they are praying; they may be planning to kill us in cold blood!'[37] He felt that the local people jeered behind his back as they had begun to jeer at the Prince of Wales (iv. 225). What was required was authority, but authority of the right kind. A week after the perahera, he wrote to Robert Pratt Barlow, a rich Englishman who lived in Taormina, and recalled a political discussion they had both had with a man he calls 'Cunard'.[38] In a further illustration of the fluidity of his travel plans, Lawrence says he is thinking of returning to England during the summer and then regrets that Englishmen of the right type do not understand the need to unite in order to carry through 'the vital spark'. 'I know now', he writes, 'it is a shirking of the issue to look to Buddha or the Hindu or to our own working men, for the impulse to carry through. It is in ourselves, or nowhere, and this looking to the outer masses is only a betrayal'; and he goes on, 'the responsibility for England, the living England, rests on men like you and me and Cunard – probably even the Prince of Wales – and to leave it all to Bottomleys etc is a worse sin than any sin of commission' (iv. 219).[39]

An even more explicit statement of his political feelings at this time can be found in the letter he wrote to Mabel Sterne on 10 April. Explaining his dislike of Ceylon, and his plans for seeing Australia before coming to Taos and 'fulfilling my real desire to approach America from the west', Lawrence says that he wishes he could do this without meeting those Americans who believe in the 'detestable negative creed of liberty and democracy. I don't believe either in liberty or democracy. I believe in actual, sacred, inspired authority: divine right of natural kings: I believe in the divine right of natural aristocracy, the right, the sacred duty to wield undisputed authority' (iv. 225–6). Nothing could be clearer – about his feelings at the precise moment he wrote this letter at least. Lawrence had of course both experienced and explored many like them before, but in a novel such as *Aaron's Rod*, where the main interest is in the authority one individual ought to have over another, they take a predominantly personal form. In two novels he wrote after leaving Ceylon – *Kangaroo* and *The Plumed Serpent* – he is concerned to investigate in increasing detail their overtly social and political implications.

It is a mistake to ignore how extreme Lawrence could often be in the declaration of his opinions but dangerous also to place too much emphasis on any one statement in his letters when his attitudes were always so highly volatile and full of contradictions. 'His humanity was outraged', Achsah Brewster reports, 'at driving in rickshaws. When, frail as he was, he needed to be carried uphill through the heat, he simply could not allow a rickshaw boy to pull him, but got out and walked.'[40] It evidently was not included in Lawrence's concept of the divine rights of natural aristocrats that they should be spared uphill walks in a climate where, as he put it, 'even at night you sweat if you walk a few yards' (iv. 216).

IV   Moving On

Towards the end of the Lawrences' stay in Kandy the rains came ('at exactly ten in the morning and four in the afternoon, timed to a minute', Achsah Brewster noted),[41] and the temperature dropped a little. Earlier there had been some discussion about moving to Nuwara Eliya, a hill station thirty miles from Kandy which the British had developed to escape excessive heat. Achsah Brewster remembered that, 'The season was unusually hot, yet we none of us wished to leave for the higher hills.'[42] Lawrence's letters show 'none of us' to be a simplification but it is hard to see how the Brewsters could have left Kandy when their daughter was in school there and Brewster himself – who had after all come to Ceylon in order to study Buddhism – was spending all his mornings at the Temple and all his afternoons on his lessons (he was learning Pali, the language of the Buddhist sacred texts, and four years later would use the knowledge he acquired to publish a *Life of the Buddha*).[43] When on 15 April Lawrence did eventually visit Nuwara Eliya, winding his way with the others through jungle and then tea plantations, he found that he did not in any case like it. By that time he felt that, 'All Ceylon has a lid down over it' and, although there was hoar frost on the ground,[44] there was no getting through the lid even at 6,000 feet – 'no, it presses tighter there' (iv. 227).

He had begun to be ill soon after his arrival and in a letter to Brewster, written from Western Australia on 15 May, said that in Ceylon he had never felt so sick in his life (iv. 239). Precisely what was wrong with him is hard to determine. Catherine Carswell says that he had suffered his first attack of malaria in Ceylon but adds in a footnote, 'So, at least, Lawrence and his doctor took it to be.'[45] She was not a person to throw away any of his letters but in none of those which survive does Lawrence ever mention seeing a doctor in Kandy (or indeed being warned by a doctor in Sicily that he ought to avoid going to America in mid-winter). He may of course have told her about these things when they met again in 1923 but, whether he did or not, what matters in both cases are her hints that Lawrence was already suffering from tuberculosis at this time. In discussions of people who have died of this disease there is always a tendency to push back as far as possible the date at which it could be said to have declared itself and then use it as an explanatory device.[46] Whether it would be technically correct to say that Lawrence already had pulmonary tuberculosis in Ceylon cannot be known. If 'having' it only means harbouring the bacillus then his condition was no different from that of most of his compatriots.[47] In the absence of properly controlled sputum tests, or X-rays, recognising when the disease became active was hard because the symptoms – fever, weight loss, night sweats, coughing, dyspnoea (difficult breathing) and general weakness – were not always present simultaneously, and in any case were the same as in several other conditions. The one reasonably certain external sign was a hemorrhage, blood of a disturbingly bright, 'arterial' colour gushing from the mouth. That in Lawrence's case there is no wholly reliable report of one of these before August 1924 does not prove that areas in his lungs had not previously become infected but then healed of their own accord after a few weeks' illness, without the cause of the trouble ever having been identified correctly.[48] What is reasonably certain however is that the weight loss he complains of at this period had no necessary connection with tuberculosis. The combination of the heat and the local food made them all ill. 'We all were miserable and Lawrence could scarcely drag about', Achsah Brewster puts it, and she has a charming account of Frieda handing round teaspoonfuls of 'liver mixture' while Lawrence mournfully wondered whether the cook could provide bread pudding instead of 'coconut cream with meringue on the top'.[49] Food to which he was unaccustomed, as well as levels of hygiene poorer than those he had known in Europe, seem to have taken their toll. On 5 April he told Mary Cannan that 'my inside has never hurt me so much in all my 36 years as in these three weeks' (iv. 224), and the context makes clear that his reference is to his bowels rather than his chest.

Illness and lack of interest in Sinhalese religion made Lawrence anxious to leave Ceylon, but also the feeling that it was a place where he would never do any proper work. Shortly before leaving Taormina he had told his British publisher Martin Secker, that he hoped to do a 'Ceylon novel' (iv. 193), but on the day of the perahera, ten days after his arrival, his message to Mountsier was that he did not believe he would ever write a line there and two days later he repeated the same thought to Catherine Carswell. On 3 April he wrote to Mountsier, 'I'm not working and feel I never should work in the east' (iv. 214, 217, 220). By Lawrence's own criteria, and with the likely exception of the poem 'Elephant',[50] that proved to be the case. He had sent off the first half of his translation of *Mastro-don Gesualdo* before leaving Sicily and worked with sufficient steadiness on the remainder to be able to post it to Mountsier on 2 April (iv. 219). After that he turned his attention to Verga's *Novelle rusticane*. According to Achsah Brewster he would sit curled up on the verandah transcribing English versions of these grim Sicilian stories in a steady, unhesitating hand while Frieda, who was busy with embroidery, would sometimes consult him as to whether the rabbit's leg should be in yellow or white and he himself would occasionally ask the two women what they understood by a particular Italian word.[51] With Brewster at the monastery and his daughter at school, this passed the time, but it was not felt by

Lawrence to be real work because it was neither fully creative nor likely to bring in much money.

Not being able to work properly excited in Lawrence financial anxieties which were never far below the surface. The James Tait Black prize, and news from Mountsier that he had quite a few dollars to his credit in America (iv. 156), must have given him a temporary feeling of security before he left Europe; but the tickets to Colombo were £70 each and when he booked to travel to Sydney via Perth the cost for them both was about £112. This meant that before he could begin to consider how much it was going to take to get to San Francisco he had already spent over £250 (a large sum for someone who had begun his professional life as a qualified teacher on £95 a year[52]). On 10 April he had told Mabel Sterne that he hoped he would arrive in Taos with 10 cents left in his pocket, 'ten cents left to me in the world, even' (iv. 225). In saying this he must have been aware that she was the kind of person able and willing to give him temporary help if he ran into difficulties. Writing to an old friend like Mary Cannan five days earlier he could afford to be more explicit. 'If I cable you from some corner of the earth to lend me money', he told her, 'don't leave me in the lurch' (iv. 224).

Despite illness, distaste for the local culture and anxiety about money, it was not quite all misery for Lawrence in Ceylon. Towards the end of his stay there were other excursions apart from the one to Nuwara Eliya, and throughout there was the delight of shopping. Frieda always remembered Casa Lebbes at 1 Trincomalee Street in Kandy where Lawrence bought her sapphires and moonstones; and Achsah Brewster describes how, after he had come home from the bazaars 'full of enthusiasm', they would all try to fashion the materials he had bought into Eastern-style garments.[53] In Nuwara Eliya, Lawrence 'with one glance discovered the treasure there among the usual tawdry array . . . some fine red lacquer candlesticks from Cashmere painted with flowers'. These were doubly interesting to him, he explained, because at one time he had 'saved all the tin boxes and glass bottles that came his way and had decorated them with lacquer-painted flowers'.[54] The Cashmere candlesticks joined a blue Persian rug and the other items in the small travelling stock of belongings which Frieda used to create a homely atmosphere wherever she and Lawrence happened to be living.[55]

The bungalow may have seemed to be in the middle of the jungle but that did not preclude either a local school for Harwood Brewster or a 'local carpenter' who built a special carriage for her doll. After the Brewsters had decided that the climate was too much for them also and were doing some preliminary packing, Lawrence staunchly supported Harwood in her demand that this 'white hearse of a chariot' should not be left behind and 'worked hours in the wilting heat, removing the solid wheels and massive handles, packing them around the body of the cart which he filled with her books'.[56] (Achsah Brewster thought this arrangement neat but heavy and discreetly left it behind when they returned to Europe a few weeks later.) A local carpenter implied a local community and it is certain that the Lawrences and Brewsters were visited by young Sinhalese, one of whom delighted Frieda by saying that she had the face of a Buddhist saint.[57] What there are no indications of are sustained contacts with the expatriate community in Ceylon. The exception is Lawrence's announcement to Mountsier on Saturday 22 April that he and Frieda were leaving Kandy for Colombo that afternoon and would 'stay with Judge Ennis till Monday, when we sail for Fremantle' (iv. 232). A reference to Achsah Brewster's 'brass incense-bowl / bought second-hand from Mrs Justice Ennis / for $3\frac{1}{2}$ rupees' in a satirical poem Lawrence wrote about Earl's inclination to become a monk in Burma, suggests that the contact was initially the Brewsters',[58] but how either they or the Lawrences came to know well an English judge who had spent all his career in the colonies, and had been at the Supreme Court of Ceylon since 1912, is at first sight puzzling. The explanation is that in 1904 George Ennis had married Ethel Kirkland, an American but also the daughter of a reasonably well-known Chicago novelist. The cultured Brewsters would certainly have heard about Joseph Kirkland and either known Ethel in America before she married or discovered a community of interest when they came across her in Ceylon. After Brewster had met the Lawrences in Colombo on 13 March it is possible that he took them to stay with the Ennises; but the fellow feeling which enabled Lawrence to rely on their hospitality six weeks later would have had time to develop when Mrs Ennis accompanied the Lawrences and Brewster to the perahera.[59] Writing from their house 'Braemore' in Bullers Road, Colombo, on the morning before Lawrence left Ceylon, he asks Martin Secker to send to Mrs Ennis a copy of *Women in Love*, repeating in a postscript 'name *Mrs Ennis*, wife of Judge Ennis' (iv. 233). It must have given him satisfaction to show Secker, who was unlikely to know how literary a family Mrs Ennis came from, and who had been fearful of legal proceedings against *Women in Love*, that it could be sent with impunity to the wife of a judge (iv. 233).

Lawrence left Ceylon with very few regrets. Much of what he had seen would stay with him all his life, but the letter in which he told Brewster that his visit there had become a precious and invaluable memory is also the one in which he insisted that wild horses would never drag him back (iv. 239). In a flamboyant summary of his response which he offered to Mabel Sterne on 10 April, one can sense how a quite literal nausea became metaphorical and affected all he saw and did. Complaints about 'the scents that make me feel sick, the perpetual nauseous overtone of cocoanut and cocoanut fibre and oil' are immediately followed by disparaging references to 'the nasty faces and yellow robes of the Buddhist monks' and 'the little vulgar dens of the temples'. All this meant, he concluded, that Ceylon was a place he could not bear: 'Je m'en vais, Me ne vo'. I am going away. Moving on' (iv. 225). Move on he did, as quickly as he could find a boat in which to do so. When much later Brewster asked him why he had written so little about Ceylon he replied that 'because of his illness there he did not trust his impressions'.[60] The sweet reasonableness of this reply seems to have been prompted by something 'reasonable' in Brewster himself, with all the strengths and weaknesses that word implies. When Lawrence first arrived in Kandy he told the Brewsters that he considered them his true friends and would therefore tell them all their faults. Brewster notes that Lawrence was as good as his word but adds, disarmingly, 'Occasionally the "elements of my being" were disturbed by his criticisms, but as I cannot recall what they were I fear I did not profit from them.'[61] Whether a high degree of natural equanimity led Brewster to the study of Buddhism or was stimulated by it, the consequences helped him to remain always one of Lawrence's most loyal friends.

CHAPTER TWO

April–August 1922

AUSTRALIA

I   Perth and Mollie Skinner

In the only surviving letter from his ten-day voyage between Colombo and Fremantle, Lawrence writes of 'flying fishes sprinting out of the waves like winged drops, and a catholic Spanish Priest playing Chopin at the piano – very well' (iv. 233). Once again he passed his time translating. On 22 April, two days before sailing, he had sent to Mountsier his translation of the first 88 pages of *Novelle rusticane* and told him that there were 70 more still to do (iv. 231). Since his version of these 70 was posted off from Perth (iv. 245), a good deal of it is likely to have been completed on the *Orsova* and there would therefore have been once again the contrast for Lawrence between daily life on a comfortable ship and his imaginative involvement in Verga's world of suffering, greed, heartlessness and exploitation. As in *Mastro-don Gesualdo*, nearly all the characters in *Novelle rusticane* are obsessed with money but in their case it is because they are permanently threatened with starvation. The stories are a sardonic illustration of how dependent the finer feelings are on a minimum standard of living. The 'History of the St. Joseph's Ass', later published separately in Middleton Murry's *Adelphi*,[1] records the miseries of Sicilian peasant life via the life-cycle of an ass which is eventually worked to death, and shows fondness for animals to be a luxury the very poor cannot afford. In 'Black Bread' the obligation they are under to maintain a wholly utilitarian attitude to sexual relations is illustrated when a young peasant girl is forced to sleep with her aging employer to secure herself a dowry.

There are twelve stories in all, one of which deals with the ravages of malaria on the plain of Catania and could have encouraged Lawrence, as he looked back to his time in Ceylon, to associate his illness there with that disease.[2] The editor of the Penguin edition of Lawrence's translation of *Novelle rusticane* claims that, for any purist who analysed it, there would be more than 1,100 points to comment on (a great number for a small book).[3] His notes do in fact direct attention to numerous howlers, the word for a dwelling translated as an obligation, or 'as soon as she got up' rendered as 'as soon as he got up'; but in the commentary on the story in which these mistakes occur ('Don Licciu Papa') the reader is told that Lawrence's 'had to leave his flock in charge of the boy' should be 'had to leave the boy in charge of the flock'; that a character's desire not to see a certain house again 'while the world stood' should be 'as long as he lived'; and that another who speaks 'straight and flat' to her father ought to be doing so 'clearly and plainly'.[4] Lawrence translated *Novelle rusticane* very rapidly, and with minimal assistance, but he made fewer gross errors than some purists suggest and he was clearly committed to the belief that the spirit of an author could only be conveyed by some deviation from a literal rendering.

There seems to have been no equivalent of Anna Jenkins on the *Orsova* although Bruce Steele has tracked down one couple – John and Dolores Walker – who were travelling from Darjeeling in northern India to Melbourne in order to see a newly born grandson, and with whom Lawrence later corresponded. According to his grandson, Walker was an ardent socialist and he and Lawrence apparently argued at length on the boat about India and Indian politics.[5] Another fellow passenger was Annie Besant, on her way to attend a Theosophical Convention in Sydney, and also to lend support to her old associate Charles Leadbeater whose pederastic activities had recently attracted the attention of the Australian police.[6] The way in which Lawrence mentions her presence is a clear enough indication that he did not speak with her (iv. 235). Although she was well over seventy at the time, that was an opportunity missed. Annie Besant had eventually succeeded Mme Blavatsky as President of the Theosophical Society and, for all his occasional derogatory remarks, Lawrence had a strong if intermittent interest in Theosophy and the occult generally. (Shortly before leaving Italy for Ceylon he had asked Koteliansky to send him the latest number of the *Occult Review* and a catalogue of books on occult science – iv. 171.) Before she was converted to Theosophy by a review copy of Blavatsky's *The Secret Doctrine*, Mrs Besant had been a free-thinking radical and then socialist (she first became well-known in England when with Charles Bradlaugh she was prosecuted for publishing an American book on birth-control), and as Theosophy's leader she maintained some continuity with her former career by energetically championing home rule for India, where of course many of Theosophy's roots were supposed to lie.[7] Had she and Lawrence in fact exchanged views, they would have found themselves more in accord in their opposition to the dominant scientific rationalism of their time than on political matters. Less than a month later he would tell Mountsier that 'corruption and semi-anarchy' would follow all the 'civil jobs' eventually going into the hands of the natives in India: 'And anyhow, the dark races *don't have* any sense of liberty, in our meaning of the word. They live and move and have their being according to the inspiration of *power* – always *power*, whether private or public, just or unjust' (iv. 246).

Fremantle is Perth's port and the *Orsova* arrived there on 4 May. Before leaving Ceylon Lawrence had told his friends that he could be contacted via Mrs Jenkins, who lived in a fashionable area of the city, but whether from his choice or hers his first two nights were spent at the Savoy. This was, Lawrence told Mountsier, the most expensive hotel in which he had ever stayed (iv. 235), but he and Frieda were out of it by 6 May thanks to the combined efforts of Mrs Jenkins and a local author, William Siebenhaar. On the morning of 5 May Mrs Jenkins took the Lawrences to the Booklovers' Library, a bookshop run by an American woman (Mrs Zabel) which served as an intellectual centre for the Perth *literati*. Invited to meet them there was Siebenhaar, who had been born in Holland but emigrated to Western Australia after a short period in England, and who had published in his adopted country both poetry and translations. When the conversation came round to accommodation it was he, he later claimed,[8] who reminded the others of the mixture of guest house and convalescent home in the hills at Darlington, some sixteen miles to the east of the city, one of whose proprietors was another local author named Mary Louisa (Mollie) Skinner. As Mrs Jenkins knew Mollie Skinner she was able to ring her up to make the necessary arrangements. Before they left for Darlington on the following day, the Lawrences called on Siebenhaar at his office (he was a civil servant), and discussed among many other things their common admiration for the poetry of Heine.[9]

Mollie Skinner left at least two accounts of her first impressions of Lawrence when Mrs Jenkins, with some other friends, first brought him and Frieda to 'Leithdale', as the guest house at Darlington was called. In one of them, she remembered wondering which of the two men in the party was Lawrence 'for surely the frail little red-bearded man' Mrs Jenkins was gushing over could not be he. 'But of course it was.'[10] In a second, she says that, 'There were other ladies I did not know, and two or three men, and I hoped the little one with a red beard was not Lawrence. It turned out that it was.'[11] Another friend of Mrs Jenkins's, May Gawler, who around this time was taken for a picnic with the Lawrences in the hills near Darlington, thought when she first met Lawrence that he was a cross between 'a reddish bearded able-bodied seaman and a handy man at the back door' and wondered 'how this rather shabby, slightly coarse, far from spruce and tidy little man could possibly have caused such a flutter, apart from his books'.[12]

First impressions are notoriously unreliable, especially when they are recorded long after the event: Mollie Skinner remembered Lawrence's eyes as green yet for May Gawler they were 'blue, gentle and wistful'.[13] The interest of these, however, is that they coincide in one particular with a radical change which had taken place by this time in Lawrence's way of looking at himself: in his self-image. When he began writing his Australian novel *Kangaroo* a few weeks later, he chose a hero, Richard Lovatt Somers, who in almost every way corresponds to himself and who is described repeatedly as 'small' or 'little'. The tendency to think of himself in this way is already evident in *Aaron's Rod*,[14] but the authorial figures in Lawrence's earlier writings are not 'little' and the surviving photographs show that Lawrence himself could hardly be described as below average for his time and country, in height at least. At 5ft 9in., he is rarely shorter than the other men he is seen with, and usually taller.[15] What is clear from them however is that Lawrence was lightly built with narrow shoulders and (though this is not revealed in the photographs!) thin legs. In his earlier fiction the legs of those protagonists who share many of the characteristics of their creator are frequently one of their assets; but in the chapter of *Kangaroo* which recalls his experiences during the war ('The Nightmare') he remembered how, as he was waiting in his shirt to be examined at Bodmin, a 'fat fellow pointed to his thin, delicate legs with a jeer', and that in Derby he was made to stand before the doctors in just his jacket 'with his ridiculous thin legs'.[16] The self-consciousness about his legs which appears to have originated with these experiences was exacerbated in Lawrence by the sight of hefty young men on Australian beaches. In chapter II of *Kangaroo*, Somers observes a young man with a jacket over his bathing suit who has 'huge massive legs, astonishing' and he wonders at the 'thick legs' of another: 'They seemed to run to leg, these people.'[17] Englishmen have fewer occasions to appear on beaches than Australians and were in any case at this time almost certainly smaller on average than the inhabitants of a country which could and still can offer a healthier, more outdoor life than England. These facts help to explain both why Lawrence was more than ever inclined to see himself as 'a little fellow', 'a little man'[18] in Australia, and why he should have been perceived as such by May Gawler and Mollie Skinner. Yet after his humiliating experiences during the war, and his periodic bouts of illness, it would not be surprising if, by the time he arrived in Perth, Lawrence had begun to hold himself in a way which gave these two women a false first impression of his height, if not of his slight build.

May Gawler and Mollie Skinner were unimpressed when they first saw Lawrence but they quickly came to appreciate and admire him. Mrs Gawler decided he had 'an infinite charm in his make-up, a kind of feminine sympathy', and for Mollie Skinner he was a man of 'great spiritual integrity'.[19] There is in her quite elaborate character sketch a maternal note which may have become natural to her after nursing wounded soldiers in the war, but could also be explained by both the way slightness suggests boyishness and a significant difference in age. Born in 1876 Mollie Skinner was nine years older than Lawrence. Mrs Gawler and Mrs Jenkins were both three years older still. What these three mature women had in common, apart from their admiration for Lawrence, were good connections. An uncle of Mollie Skinner had been the Premier of Western Australia, Mrs Jenkins was a daughter of an Attorney General of that state and Mrs Gawler had been married to the son of a Governor of South Australia.[20] Difficult as it may be to see in Mrs Jenkins the Antipodes' answer to Lady Ottoline Morrell, a chance shipboard encounter had meant that the circle with which Lawrence was chiefly associated during his stay in Perth was a West Australian version of that small fraction of the English aristocracy with an active interest in the arts that he had known so well during the war.

This comparison will be particularly misleading if it suggests that good connections in Australia always went with money. Mrs Jenkins was certainly well-to-do but Mollie Skinner had been a working woman for most of her life. It was through her mother that she was related to what she calls in her excellent autobiography the 'leading families' of Western Australia,[21] but her father was an Irish army captain temporarily stationed in Perth. He was called home in 1878 with the result that his children were educated in the United Kingdom. Born with a hare lip, Mollie Skinner developed a serious eye disease in her childhood which left her with unusually poor sight, but she was clearly a courageous person and as a young woman showed what she calls her pioneer spirit by persuading her parents, against the prejudices of their class, that she ought to train as a nurse. She had just finished her basic training when in 1900 there was a family decision to move back to Perth. Last there when she was only two years old, she returned at twenty-four to find herself among 'the highest in the land, the local aristocracy'.[22] Her father had been obliged to stay in England for two years before he could retire, but soon after rejoining his family he died, leaving too little money for either his unmarried daughters or his somewhat shiftless sons to do anything but fend for themselves. Mollie Skinner worked on a newspaper for a while, as the social correspondent, but then took to nursing in the West Australian outback. Her account of this period provides evidence of both her gift for anecdote and her unusually hardy, enterprising and tolerant character. After a while she went back to England to take a course in midwifery, one consequence of which was her first book (*Midwifery Made Easy*), published in 1913. When the war came, she found herself in India and, transposing her experiences of nursing soldiers there to the Western Front, loosely fashioned them into an epistolary novel entitled *Letters of a VAD*. (The series of letters which weakly sustain the narrative are all addressed to a putative sister.) This work appeared in 1919 under the pseudonym R. E. Leake (her mother's maiden name) by which time Mollie Skinner was back nursing and then running a convalescent home in Australia. She came to 'Leithdale' when it was bought by another nurse who offered her a partnership on equal terms, even though she had no capital to contribute. Lawrence remembered her in Darlington as 'darting about rather vaguely in her white nurse's dress, with the nurse's white band over her head, looking after her convalescents who, mercifully, didn't need much looking after'.[23] Her past experiences in nursing mean that her description of Lawrence as frail, with scarlet lips and a 'hectic flush' on the cheekbones of his otherwise white face, has a special authority.[24]

A recently married couple named the Cohens were among the other guests at 'Leithdale'. Maudie Cohen had been reading *The White Peacock* and with an Australian directness to which Mrs Gawler had first introduced Lawrence, and which it appears he liked,[25] told him that his novel was not up to much and incited him to read *Letters of a VAD*, because it was just as good.[26] If Mollie Skinner was ever technically a member of a Voluntary Aid Detachment in India she would have been an unusually experienced and well-qualified one.[27] VADs were more frequently lady amateurs who, after minimal training, were often to find themselves having to cope with both major medical responsibilities and the hostility of career nurses, still struggling at that time to establish nursing as a profession. The VAD posture in Mollie Skinner's novel and its title could both have been determined by market considerations: in the year before its publication, for example, Vera Brittain had published a volume entitled *Verses of a VAD*. Religious and sentimentally patriotic, *Letters of a VAD* is full of the kind of emotional perversities which Lawrence was so sharp at detecting and which one would have thought he would detest. In the finale, the heroine discovers that both one of the army doctors and her Colonel have fallen in love with her. After luxuriating in their passionate declarations she tells the doctor that he must marry not her but another nurse, with whom he has been flirting, and after he has agreed to do this, she then refuses to marry the Colonel on the grounds that he is divorced. In the final pages she prepares for her conversion to Catholicism to the accompaniment of numerous quotations from Francis Thompson's 'The Hound of Heaven'. It is possible that Lawrence never reached this finale and it was the preceding, often vivid account of the day-to-day horrors of war-time nursing which made him feel that *Letters of a VAD* was 'good, so good'.[28] Possible also, or even very likely, given that Eurocentric condescension must have been even more prevalent in 1922 than now, is that the imperfections of Mollie Skinner as a novelist seemed to him trivial in comparison with the wonder of her being a novelist at all. He must have been surprised to discover that *The White Peacock* was circulating in a guest house 16 miles from the centre of Perth, and one can imagine that his surprise was accompanied with satisfaction when he learned that there were copies of *The Rainbow* in the library of the Perth Literary Institute.[29] He probably felt then like an English farmer travelling abroad who accidentally comes across the sturdy plant he managed to export to far-off parts just before the government pest control official moved in to destroy his crop.

There was a division of responsibilities in the management of 'Leithdale' whereby Mollie Skinner's partner looked after the inside of the house and Mollie herself took care of the household washing and outside jobs.[30] To discuss her work, Lawrence had therefore to track her down in the wash-house, armed with a pair of white socks that he wanted to wash himself because they had been knitted for him by a friend. He quickly secured from her the manuscript of the next novel on which she was working (*Black Swans*) and, with Frieda's help, arranged a series of after-lunch conversations about her writing.[31] Lawrence evidently discovered in talking to Mollie Skinner the shrewdness, spirit and resourcefulness which make her autobiography so much more interesting than the two, distinctly mediocre novels he was able to read. Her past experiences were much more striking than anything she could imagine and, like most people, she wrote best when she knew what she was talking about. His advice to her was to write 'an Australian book about things you *actually* know, which you don't have to invent out of an ink- bottle'.[32]

In urging her to make the most of her local knowledge (the *Letters of a VAD* are unconvincingly attributed to the daughter of an English country doctor), Lawrence suggested that Mollie Skinner should write about the Australia of her youth rather than the present. This was strange advice to a woman who had spent all her youth in England but in offering it Lawrence was influenced both by Mollie Skinner's evident predisposition towards historical fiction in *Black Swans*, and a history of Western Australia which prefaced the *Western Australian Year-Book for 1902–1904*, given to him by Siebenhaar.[33] He felt this history was full of promising subjects, and that Mollie Skinner would be able to handle them if she confined herself to a period she would have heard about from her relations, if not known herself. He told her that if she needed a model for her hero she could not do better than study her brother Jack.[34] Jack Skinner had been wounded in the war and granted a few acres under the Returned Soldiers' Settlement Scheme. He had exchanged these for a small-holding in Darlington chiefly because his mother had moved there, and could thus be seen around 'Leithdale' during Lawrence's stay. Lawrence proposed him as a model because he was aware that Mollie Skinner admired and understood her brother, but he did not do so without making clear – in what sounds like an indirect protest against the uncritical patriotism of *Letters of a VAD* – that he did not 'like that sort of man himself, *giving* himself for his country'.[35] There is no evidence that Jack Skinner ever spoke with Lawrence long enough to defend himself from this charge, or indeed that the two men ever spoke at all, so that his only, unwitting response to Lawrence's dislike was an enquiry his sister remembered him making to her about the identity of the 'creeping Jesus' who was 'mooching around the bush'.[36] Mollie Skinner protests that neither Jesus nor Lawrence ever crept but points out that, with his reddish beard, Lawrence did bear some resemblance to the Jesus of one popular iconographic tradition.

Lawrence's words of advice to Mollie Skinner were similar to those he himself had once received from Jessie Chambers: to write more directly, and with less transposition, about what he knew. They had been instrumental in helping him to make the transition between *The White Peacock* and *Sons and Lovers* but their consequences for the giver had been enormously hurtful. In rewriting *Sons and Lovers* according to Jessie's advice, Lawrence not only made 'Miriam' much more like her but also revealed that they had slept together.[37] According to his friend George Neville, he had developed early a certain ruthlessness about how people would feel when they identified themselves in his books. In discussing the impossibility for himself of telling all he knew, while some of the people involved were still alive, Neville claims that Lawrence would have said 'that it did not matter whose feelings were hurt, or whose happiness was jeopardized, so long as the result added to the sum of human knowledge'.[38] This was certainly one of Lawrence's usual defences; another, not consistent with it, was that in fact most people did not realise they were being used as models anyway and were therefore unaffected. When Lawrence told Mollie Skinner to take inspiration from her brother she protested that to write of those she knew intimately would bring 'hell's fire' on her head, and that she was 'scared' of describing what went on around her. He replied that, having been given 'the Divine Spark', she had no right to bury it in a napkin and added, 'away with anyone's feelings – they won't recognise themselves when they read it, so why worry?'[39] His encouragement was sufficient to prompt Mollie Skinner to write a novel about Western Australia not long after he had left. She called it 'The House of Ellis' and, relying on Lawrence's assurance that he would try to get whatever she wrote published, sent it off to him in 1923. The first person to read the typescript when her novel came back to her as *The Boy in the Bush*, not only much revised by Lawrence but in many parts totally rewritten, was her sister, who said, 'How dare you send those stories about Jack to that odious little redheaded devil who crucifies every soul he meets.'[40] She was saved the anxiety of wondering what her brother would think of the work by the certain knowledge that he would never read it.

Lawrence swept aside Mollie Skinner's worries about working as much as possible from personal observation or experience, and he was equally decisive when she complained that her responsibilities at 'Leithdale' did not leave her time for writing. He told her to forget about a story or construction and, taking an hour every day – 'the same hour – that's very important' – simply to 'write bit by bit of the scenes you have witnessed, the people you know, describing their reactions as you know they do react, not as you imagine they should'. When she asked how, with no story or construction, she would know when to stop he replied, 'When you've done 80,000 words, throw down your pen.'[41] Critics have observed that there are some similarities between this advice and the procedure Lawrence himself was to adopt a few weeks later when he began to write *Kangaroo*. Its spirit is, *mutatis mutandis*, like that of the advice given by thousands of supervisors to research students with a 'writing block'. Although it seems paradoxical to say so, there is a case for believing that Lawrence himself was suffering from something of a writing block at this time. He had of course been remarkably prolific in the months before leaving Europe, but in forms other than the novel. It had taken him several years to complete *Aaron's Rod* and he had left *Mr Noon* unfinished.[42] One of the many reasons for *Kangaroo* being written with such speed and intensity may well have been his fear of being bogged down. As he did so, he made effective use of his recent experience at 'Leithdale'. A striking episode in *Letters of a VAD* describes how the Australian soldiers in the hospital would express their disapproval of anyone they disliked with a slow, collective chant of the 'One, two, three . . .' of boxing referees: they would 'count them out'.[43] Lawrence may have learned more about this habit between reading Mollie Skinner's novel and making such successful use of it in the sixteenth chapter of *Kangaroo*: 'A Row in Town'; but it is to her he owes his first, decisive knowledge. To her also can be attributed the fact that in *Kangaroo* the character called Jack Callcott has had – exactly like Jack Skinner – a bullet lodged in his jaw since the war, which has taken many months to fall out.[44]

Lawrence spent just two weeks in Western Australia but his brief stay would give rise to one of the most important of his literary collaborations. Earlier in his life he had collaborated on one published short story with Louie Burrows, and *The Trespasser* was based on an autobiographical narrative supplied to him by Helen Corke. Once in Taos he and Mabel Sterne would begin writing together a novel based on her life.[45] By May 1922 there had already been, and would in future be, several either proposed or realised collaborations with both men and women friends. Lawrence was unusually quick to see the potential in other people's work or projects, and naturally sympathetic and unselfish in his offers of help. But it is true also that the habit of almost ceaseless literary activity which he developed meant that other people's ideas were often very useful to him, and that his eventual 50 per cent share in the royalties of *The Boy in the Bush* represented a less arduous method of maintaining his income than the composition of *The Plumed Serpent*. An additional reason for collaboration might have been that it lessened that inevitable isolation of an author's life, of which Lawrence complained several times.[46]

   Whatever his exact motives for choosing to collaborate with Mollie Skinner there is no doubt that Lawrence had a genuine admiration and liking for her, just as she had for him. When she posted off 'The House of Ellis' in March or April 1923 she could have had no idea that a rewritten version would appear under their joint names in the following year. Because Lawrence did not have her manuscript in his hands until August 1923, it was only on 2 September that he wrote suggesting he re-cast it because as it stood it would 'never find a publisher' (iv. 495). He began revising the novel before receiving her agreement, confident that she would say yes and knowing how long it might be before he received her reply. Paul Eggert has established that his letter of 2 September only reached Perth on 25 October.[47] When it did arrive Mollie Skinner discussed its offer with William Siebenhaar who accurately predicted that the critics would be inclined to minimise her role in the novel but encouraged her to feel that the opportunity of being Lawrence's co-author was too good to miss.[48] She may have momentarily wished she had missed it when the typescript of *The Boy in the Bush* arrived with an ending, entirely written by Lawrence, which transformed the character of the hero based on her brother and helped to stimulate the angry complaints of her sister about 'that odious little redheaded devil'. Largely on account of her sister, Mollie Skinner wrote to Lawrence asking him to make deletions which would have more or less restored her original ending, but because her letter arrived late in the publishing process, Lawrence's publisher was hostile to her proposal, and Lawrence himself gave it only lukewarm support, the deletions were never made.[49] Her experience of 'collaboration' with Lawrence was therefore very like Helen Corke's and consisted of providing a narrative which without consultation – impractical of course in their case – he then revised and altered as he thought fit. Yet since most of the changes he made increased rather than lessened Mollie Skinner's admiration for Lawrence, and *The Boy in the Bush* was a commercial success (it is virtually certain that without it she would not have been able to arrange for the London publication of her next work, *Black Swans*), Mollie Skinner could hardly have made, and never in fact did make, a serious complaint.

Lawrence celebrated the sky in Western Australia, 'high and blue and new, as if no one had ever taken a breath from it' (iv. 238), but it took him a while to accustom himself to the more characteristic features of the Australian landscape. From the front of 'Leithdale' there was a spectacular view to Perth and its harbour at Fremantle (at night one could see the lighthouse winking on Rottnest Island[50]), but behind the house much of the land was uncultivated and quickly ran into what Australians call 'the bush': 'gum trees, rather thinly scattered, like a thin wood, with a healthy sort of undergrowth: like a moor with trees' is how Lawrence first defined this term (iv. 241). In the particular case of the land behind 'Leithdale' he was struck by how pale and ghostly the trees looked – especially in the company of many which had been charred by fire, and by the 'grey-green iron' of the foliage. This phrase comes from a passage in the first chapter of *Kangaroo* which describes an experience of the protagonist very clearly identifiable as Lawrence's own. Although his solitary excursions made Mollie Skinner nervous, he had gone out alone for a walk in the bush on the evening of a full moon. Jessie Chambers left a vivid account of how powerfully Lawrence could be affected by the moon and on this occasion it helped to induce an 'icy sensation of terror'. He felt there was 'a presence' among 'the weird, white dead trees', a 'spirit of the place . . . watching, and waiting. Following with certainty, just behind his back. It might have reached a long black arm and gripped him.' (Previously in the passage there is a reference to 'tree-trunks like naked pale aborigines among the dark-soaked foliage'.) Attributing this experience to Richard Somers, Lawrence surrounds it with qualifications, noting that 'as a poet', Somers 'felt himself entitled to all kinds of emotions and sensations which an ordinary man would have repudiated'. Yet these in no way lessen the importance of the experience as a safeguard against imagining that Lawrence's dealings with the 'spirit of place' in his writings are metaphorical. Like Wordsworth, he was quite literally inclined to feel that a landscape lived with a special life of its own, and readily sympathetic therefore to the various forms of animism he would shortly encounter in America.[51]

Mollie Skinner began to instruct Lawrence in the secrets of the bush and, with a precision which must have cheered his own botanist's heart, provided him with an account of how it would look in September, once the wild flowers were in bloom.[52] But his initiation cannot have proceeded very far when it was clear that, as far as Perth was concerned, Lawrence was only passing through, on the way to Sydney, probably because, when he consulted the map, it had seemed to him the most appropriate final resting-place before the inevitable voyage to America. He looked at a bungalow in Darlington where he and Frieda could have settled for a while but from the letters it is evident that he was never seriously interested. Exactly a week after they had gone to 'Leithdale' he came into Perth for an hour or so in order to finalise arrangements for taking the boat to Sydney on the following Thursday, 18 May. He was leaving on the earliest possible date the shipping schedules allowed.

The Lawrences' boat was due to leave Fremantle at 4 p.m. on the 18th but they themselves left 'Leithdale' for Perth in the morning. William Siebenhaar and his wife had invited them to lunch. A letter to Mrs Jenkins, whom they had also expected to see, provides a rare example of Lawrentian two-facedness with Lawrence offering to put the Siebenhaars off – 'I can always invent a story' – so that Frieda and he can lunch with Mrs Jenkins in moderate peace (iv. 241). In later letters to her he describes how he dropped overboard the two volumes of verse by Siebenhaar their author had given him – *Dorothea* and *Sentinel Sonnets*[53] – and indulges in some mild linguistic mockery of Mrs Siebenhaar as Madame Sept-cheveux and Signora Settecappelli (iv. 251, 272). Yet he wrote to Siebenhaar himself about his poetry with tactful directness – 'When it comes to writing poetry, we are at opposite ends of the rope. For me you are too classical – and for you I am afraid I should be just outside the pale' (iv. 270); and showed by his actions that he was fundamentally well disposed. Before he left Perth Siebenhaar had given him an essay that he had written for the centenary of the birth in 1820 of the Dutch writer E. D. Dekker but had failed to have published. Dekker's most

34

famous work was the novel *Max Havelaar* (1860) which had appeared under the pseudonym Multatuli ('I have suffered much'), and which denounces corruption in the administration of the Dutch East Indies by telling the story of an idealistic, brilliantly gifted official whose efforts to bring reform lead to his dismissal and ruin. It must have had a particular appeal for Siebenhaar in that, during the war, he had been temporarily suspended from his post in the Registrar General's office at Perth for openly showing his support for an imprisoned member of the IWW (Industrial Workers of the World).[54] Lawrence read Siebenhaar's essay on Dekker when he was settled in New South Wales, and encouraged him to begin a translation of *Max Havelaar* (iv. 270).

A lunch party involving the Lawrences, the Siebenhaars, Mrs Jenkins and Mrs Zabel did in fact take place on 18 May before the Lawrences left Perth. Their short stay had allowed Lawrence to make his first contacts with the Australian landscape and also to begin to come to terms with Australian democracy. Explaining to Brewster why he did not want to stay in Darlington, even though he could have had a 'nice little bungalow' there, he wrote, 'it is *so* democratic, it feels to me infra dig. In *so* free a land, it is humiliating to keep house and cook still another mutton-chop' (iv. 239); yet his own day-to-day contacts had not been especially 'democratic'. 'The funny thing about the Lawrences' stay at Leithdale', Mollie Skinner remembered, 'was that they liked not being known as celebrities';[55] but it is apparent that, because of Mrs Jenkins, they were lionised to some extent. Lawrence himself may have disliked the process but he never bore a grudge against the principal participants. He was sufficiently fond of Mrs Jenkins to invite her to join them in Sydney, and on their voyage to America (iv. 251, 271), and his references to Mollie Skinner in his letters are always appreciative. Siebenhaar clearly had absurd aspects to his personality, evident enough in the occasional pomposities of his writing; but when portions of the translation of *Max Havelaar* which Lawrence had initiated began to reach him in New Mexico, he loyally did what he could to find a publisher. Two weeks in Western Australia had led to three lasting new relationships whereas more than two-and-a-half months in New South Wales appear to have resulted in no Australian friendships at all.

II New South Wales

On its way south, the *Malwa* made a short stop in Adelaide and on 24 May there was an overnight stay in Melbourne (where the Lawrences might well have seen the Walkers). They visited the art galleries in both cities. The only picture to stay in Lawrence's mind was Melbourne's *L'hiver* – a scaled-down version of one of two designs which Puvis de Chavannes had used in the early 1890s for the decoration of a room in the Paris Town Hall (the Hotel de Ville).[56] He was to say

35

a few weeks later that Puvis was the only painter he knew whose landscape came close to conveying an impression of what it was really like to be in Australia. This seems at first an absurd claim, not so much because Puvis de Chavannes might well have had difficulty in locating Australia on a map but because, in *L'hiver*, the ground is appropriately covered with snow and the various figures involved in winter activities seem like refugees from the landscapes of Poussin or Claude. Yet in a letter written on 13 June to Earl Brewster, whose own painting was much influenced by Puvis, Lawrence makes clear that it is not the Frenchman's 'foolish human figures', his 'classic remains' which interest him but the use of colour, and particularly the way horizontal bands are deployed in a 'detaily pattery subtle layering of distances'. It is this which reminds Lawrence of the Australian landscape, 'so apparently monotonous, yet when you look into it, such subtly different distances, in layers, and such exquisite forms' (iv. 265).[57]

Although they must have had a quiver of apprehension when they learnt in Adelaide that their captain's previous command, the *Egypt*, had only a few days before gone down in the Bay of Biscay with the loss of nearly 100 lives (iv. 249), the Lawrences were as contented on the *Malwa* as they had been on the two other P & O ships. He had the knack of absorbing himself in reading or writing wherever he happened to be and Frieda the even more valuable one of being able to allow time to slip by without anxiety. (On this occasion it is likely that she spent some of it on an embroidery of the Buddha begun in Kandy – iv. 280.) They were once again travelling second-class and discovered once again that there was ample room – 'less than thirty passengers' (iv. 244). Travelling with them were two migrant couples from the Nottingham area. The men, Denis Forrester and Bill Marchbanks, were hosiery mechanics who were being brought out to knitting mills in Sydney.[58] Lawrence felt sufficiently at ease in their company to seek them out a few weeks later and ask one of them to lend him money. The other passengers were mostly from India, 'some fleeing to a surer land', as Lawrence puts it, because of the uncertain political situation, and it was their presence which prompted him to predict that 'India will fall into chaos once the British let go. The religions are so antagonistic.' He thought 'this "nationalism" and "self-government" and "liberty" are all tripe . . . The whole thing is, like Bolshevism, anarchistic in its inspiration – only anarchistic: just a downthrow of rule, and a chaos' (iv. 246).

These thoughts were not the best preparation for Lawrence's further encounters with the Australian democratic manner once the *Malwa* had docked on the east side of Sydney's Circular Quay (where the Opera House now stands) at 6.40 on the morning of 27 May, with the rain pouring down.[59] He had already felt uneasy about Australian 'democracy' in Perth but something, or more likely somebody, seriously aggravated that feeling in Sydney. On the 30th he was inveighing against 'the hateful newness, the democratic conceit, every man a little

36

pope of perfection' and complaining that, 'If every American is a King or Queen, I'm sure every Australian is a little Pope all on his own, God's Vicar. "There is nothing better than me on earth", he seems silently to proclaim, not with tongues of angels or tones of silver either: and not always silently' (iv. 247, 250). Sydney's large Irish Catholic population may account for the references to the Pope here. Around the time he was making them, Lawrence was beginning to write *Kangaroo* (he was certainly embarked upon it by 3 June – iv. 251). In the opening pages of that novel, R. L. Somers, a 'foreign-looking little stranger' and his 'mature, handsome, fresh-faced wife' want to take a taxi from outside their hotel but are shocked at being told that they will be charged a shilling for each of their bags. With calm indifference, the taxi-driver tells them they can take it or leave it and they are obliged to call instead a hansom cab. ' "But the taxi-drivers," ' exclaims Mrs Somers, as they are 'clock-clocking' along in the hansom, ' "And the man charged you eight shillings on Saturday for what would be two shillings in London". "He rooked me" ', her husband replies, ' "But there you are, in a free country, it's the man who makes you pay who is free—free to charge you what he likes, and you're forced to pay it. That's what freedom amounts to. They're free to charge, and you are forced to pay." '[60] Luggage is always a trial and a tribulation when travelling as Lawrence often demonstrates in *Sea and Sardinia* where he is inclined to judge the state of the nation by its drivers, porters or waiters. None of these essential aspects of a 'service' industry are always undertaken with good grace in such a fiercely egalitarian country as Australia.[61] When one considers that the Lawrences were carrying with them more or less all they owned, they could accurately be described as travelling light; but four trunks, a few bags and the side of a Sicilian cart are nevertheless difficult to move around and it seems likely that the difficulties and expense of doing so had a lot to do with Lawrence's hostile first impressions of Sydney. (In the letter in which he complains that every Australian is 'a little pope of perfection' he also says, 'living is fairly cheap. But it's *awfully* expensive getting about' – iv, 247.)[62]

Yet if Lawrence did base the Somerses' experience on his and Frieda's, which seems virtually certain, then they would not have been going, as his characters are, from a hotel to a rented house in another part of Sydney. We know that they stayed in their Sydney hotel or boarding house for one or two nights,[63] and that they then rented a house in Thirroul, forty miles south of Sydney on the New South Wales coast. Their problem would have been to move all their belongings from the hotel to the station and then to load them on and off the Thirroul train. Robert Darroch identified the hotel as Mrs Scott's in Macquarie Street (conveniently close to where the *Malwa* had docked) where the cost was 'around £1 a night'.[64] Whether or not this precise identification is correct, a hotel in the Macquarie Street area would certainly compare unfavourably with the rent for the house in Thirroul (30s a week). The pattern was similar to the one the

Lawrences had followed in Western Australia: one or two nights in an expensive central location followed by a rapid retreat to cheaper accommodation out of town. The difference was that this time they went to a rented house of their own and that, as far as we know, there were no intermediaries such as Mrs Jenkins or William Siebenhaar in the picture. In *"Not I, But the Wind . . ."* Frieda said that she and Lawrence took a train with all their trunks and decided that they would get out as soon as the surroundings looked nice. When they came to Thirroul, 'we got out at four and by six o'clock we were settled in a beautiful bungalow right on the sea'.[65] Frieda is not always a reliable witness to her life with Lawrence. She admits in *"Not I, But the Wind . . ."* (published in 1934) that their time in Western Australia had become 'all vague' to her, and she remembered the copies of *The Rainbow* as being in the Thirroul rather than the Perth library.[66] It is unlikely that the Lawrences set off with no idea at all about where they were going and that a practical man such as Lawrence had not picked up some hints through casual conversations and enquiries, or from advertisements in the newspapers. In *D. H. Lawrence at Thirroul*, Joseph Davis reprints a list of advertisements of houses to let which appeared in the *Sydney Morning Herald* for 28 May 1922 and suggests that the Lawrences' investigation of possibilities on Sydney's North shore, before they settled for Thirroul, explains descriptions of that area in the early part of *Kangaroo*.[67]

Lawrence wrote an account in his novel of what could be seen from the railway line between Sydney and Thirroul[68] and there are many details in the novel about Thirroul itself, the accuracy of which has been vouched for by Davis who was brought up there. As Davis engagingly explains, it was chiefly a small and (at this period) declining holiday resort of around 2,500 people which straggled between what Lawrence calls 'a great long hill like a wall' (iv. 263) on one side, and the Pacific Ocean on the other. 'Dark greyish with gum trees', there were small coal mines worked into this wall-like hill (the Illawarra Escarpment) which helped to make Lawrence feel 'quite at home', and many of the wooden houses along the unpaved streets of the township had corrugated iron roofs (iv. 263, 254). By contrast the Lawrences were able to rent a large and well-built house in red brick which was cheap because the holiday season had finished long ago (they arrived of course in the Australian winter), but also because it was in a poor state. Frieda's memoir shows that, just like the Somerses in *Kangaroo*, the Lawrences took the house over from a very large family and had to go to work with dusters, carbolic and elbow grease to make it habitable.[69] Frieda then gave the rooms a personal touch by artful distribution of the stock of rugs and ornaments which had been brought from Europe and added to in Ceylon – in the novel there is a reference to the 'two tall red lacquer candlesticks on the mantlepiece' which they had bought in Nuwara Eliya;[70] and in a letter to the Brewsters, Lawrence tells Achsah that, 'Your little black embroidered *Greek* bag, given in Capri, also hangs on a nail for ornaments' (iv. 266). Once installed, Lawrence must have plunged almost immediately into the Australian adventures of R. L. Somers.[71]

III   *Kangaroo*

The first, manuscript version of *Kangaroo* filled 4 exercise books. Lawrence announced that he had begun it on 3 June and it was finished by 15 July: an average rate of composition, Bruce Steele has calculated, of 3,500 words a day.[72] This is remarkable when one considers how long it takes to *copy out* that number of words in a legible hand, or that 1 day off in 7 would push the daily rate over 4,000 and a free week-end raise it to nearly 5,000. On 21 June Lawrence was about half-way through his novel but in difficulties and wrote to Seltzer, 'I do hope I shall be able to finish it: not like *Aaron*, who stuck for two years, and *Mr Noon* who has been now nearly two years at a full stop' (iv. 267); but the block was only temporary.

There is evidence of the speed with which Lawrence wrote *Kangaroo* in the published work. In chapter x ('Diggers'), the point at which Lawrence had complained to Seltzer he was stuck,[73] a couple called Jack and Victoria Callcott pay a weekend visit to the Somerses'. The Callcotts have previously been their next-door neighbours in Sydney, Victoria is in fact the owner of the house they are now renting in Mullumbimby (Thirroul), and Jack has begun to interest Somers in the right-wing political group of which he is a member. The two men begin discussing politics but their discussion is interrupted by Harriett Somers asking her husband to 'come and rescue the tea-towel from the horns of a cow',[74] whereupon Lawrence forgets completely about politics, Jack and the Callcotts, sliding instead into an account of stray incidents from the Somerses' life in Mullumbimby: the popular fiction on offer at the local library, for example, or Harriett's dismay (which the letters confirm as being also Frieda's – iv. 268) at the town's scandalous neglect of its war monument. The Callcotts' visit has ended in mid-air. This is the major narrative disjunction in the novel, but there are others. When Lawrence came to revise *Kangaroo* in New Mexico he must surely have noticed them. If he took no action, it was probably because rapidity of composition was for him a sign of authenticity and minor carelessnesses of construction did at least indicate that a writer was not self-consciously pre-occupied with making everything neat and tidy but rather swept along by the principal things he had to say.

Carelessly handled transitions are in any case only one of several, more obviously deliberate attacks on the more familiar conventions of novel-writing in *Kangaroo*. Included in chapter VIII ('Volcanic Evidence'), for example, is a long article on earthquakes taken directly from the Sydney *Daily Telegraph*; and chapter XIV ('Bits') would be much shorter – although also less interesting –

without a series of miscellaneous items culled and copied down verbatim from the Sydney *Bulletin*, a newspaper which Lawrence particularly appreciated for its dry Australian humour. Liberties of this kind provoke at the end of chapter XIV a sudden flurry of self-conscious gestures which, by advertising the illusion of Lawrence's fictional world, are meant also to protect it from criticism. With Somers once again struggling to define his attitude towards life in society Lawrence comments 'the record was taken down for this gramophone of a novel'. Two pages later he writes, 'I hope, dear reader, you like plenty of *conversation* in a novel: it makes it so much lighter and brisker', the joke being that all the conversation the reader is hearing at that moment is, as in so many of *Kangaroo*'s other moments, of Somers with himself. This uncomfortably playful and suspicious mood, which those familiar with Lawrence would shortly find in *Fantasia of the Unconscious* (and more recent readers were able to discover in the second half of *Mr Noon*), carries over to the beginning of the next chapter whose first words are, 'Chapter follows chapter, and nothing doing.' There then follows a scornful and parodic attempt to satisfy the conventional expectation that readers should always be kept informed of what the main characters in a novel are up to – the seriousness of which may be gauged from the fact that it includes the injunction, 'If you don't like the novel, don't read it.'[75]

Because chapter XV comes well towards the end of *Kangaroo*, the temporary anxiety which gives rise to these gestures can be associated with the letter written to Koteliansky on 9 July 1922. Kot must have mentioned the controversies which followed the publication of *Ulysses* four months earlier since Lawrence writes, 'I shall be able to read this famous *Ulysses* when I get to America. I doubt he is a trickster'; and adds, 'I have nearly finished my novel here – but such a novel! Even the Ulysseans will spit at it' (iv. 275). He evidently felt that he had given *Kangaroo* features which would put him in very roughly the same avant-garde camp as Joyce. When he had reached America and was eventually able to read *Ulysses*, he quickly discovered his error. On 28 November 1922 he told Seltzer that it had wearied him: 'so like a schoolmaster with dirt and stuff in his head: sometimes good, though: but too mental' (iv. 345).[76] 'Mental' indicates Lawrence's recognition that although he and Joyce were the two serious novelists who had most successfully challenged the Anglo-American reading public, they had achieved that effect by very different routes. Whereas all Joyce's deviations from linguistic and structural norms were carefully calculated, Lawrence's were more often a consequence of his continuing commitment to a Romantic spontaneity. Many of the formal differences between their two novels are related to the fact that whereas *Kangaroo* was completed in six weeks, and the major revisions of the typescript occupied Lawrence for about one week more, the composition of *Ulysses* stretched over several years.[77]

Many features of *Kangaroo* which might at first sight seem 'modernist' are in fact only superficially so. A rapid or even entirely omitted transition is hardly likely to bother a reasonably experienced reader for long, and the newspaper articles Lawrence includes turn out on inspection to be much less disruptive of a conventional narrative than one might expect. The first allows him to establish an image which will prove crucial in the material which follows – human beings as walking volcanoes always in danger of erupting;[78] while the extracts from the Sydney *Bulletin* are offered in illustration of the 'sheer momentaneous' quality of life in Australia, as well as being part of his argument that the bulk of people have no 'central selves . . . They're all bits'.[79] The uncomfortable dialogue with the reader at the end of the 'Bits' chapter and the beginning of chapter xv, although it illustrates how uncertain and pessimistic Lawrence could feel about his audience, is an aberration in the work as a whole. Behind features of this kind is a novel in fact more traditional, in many ways less unusual or original in method, than *Women in Love*. The triad *Portrait of the Artist/ Ulysses/ Finnegans Wake* does not imply that all novelists proceed along a line of increasing technical innovation, or that it is a necessarily good thing that they should. Despite his often casual handling of narrative sequence, Lawrence is, for good or ill, more concerned with 'telling a story' in *Kangaroo* than in many of his previous novels.

Arriving in Sydney, Richard Lovatt Somers quickly discovers that the semi-secret political movement to which his neighbour Jack Callcott belongs is led by a charismatic Jewish lawyer whose name is Ben Cooley but who is known to his devoted followers as 'Kangaroo'. (Lawrence had fixed on this word as the title of his novel by 11 June – iv. 261.) Cooley feels that Somers's literary abilities would make him an important ally and exerts all his considerable intellectual and physical charm in an effort to persuade the new arrival to throw in his lot with his movement. Yet later Somers is also introduced to Willie Struthers, a powerful trade union leader in Sydney, who knows that the Englishman has a working-class background and plays on that fact in order to convince him that he ought to lend his support to the Left rather than the Right. In the climax of the novel, the Labour rally which Struthers is addressing is broken up when a group led by Jack Callcott 'count him out' and during the fighting which follows Cooley is shot in the stomach. Lawrence's self-conscious dialogue with his reader around chapters xiv and xv is part of a break in the action which might be seen as a traditional treading of water before the novel moves with reasonable rapidity to this final, violent crisis. There are many other breaks of course, mostly because of long sections in which Somers reflects on his dilemmas and, in one case (the 'Nightmare' chapter), because he recalls in detail his experiences during the recent war. Expertly though its climax ('A Row in Town') is handled, that is, *Kangaroo* is not primarily a novel of action – not a 'story' in that sense – but rather, to use a term its author insists on several times, a 'thought adventure': a drama of political choice in a world increasingly polarised between those who had felt encouraged by the Russian Revolution of only five years before, and those who regarded with either enthusiasm or at least sympathetic interest the rapid development of movements such as that of Mussolini in Italy.

It is in Somers's reflections on political as well as many other matters that what is most genuinely disconcerting and original about *Kangaroo* can most conveniently be located. Because these are always tending to develop into essays, they could be taken as part of a characteristically modernist confusion of genres, and indeed *Kangaroo* is sometimes a novel in the traditional sense but sometimes also an essay or a travel diary. What is specifically Lawrentian however is that in describing Somers's responses to Cooley, or to various other aspects of Australian life, the author seems deliberately to make no distinction between himself and his protagonist. That is to say that, as in *Sea and Sardinia*, he chooses to describe Somers's experiences without the benefit of hindsight. The impression he creates is that, if we have very little idea of how things will resolve themselves, it is because he does not know either. 'Autobiographical novel' is not a complete misnomer for *Kangaroo* but in the classics of that genre from the nineteenth century the point of view is usually retrospective: however strong an impression of indecision and fluctuating feeling their authors set out to give, we are usually made aware simultaneously that these crises of their *alter egos* are in the past, and that there is thus a degree of distance between the creator and his character. In accordance with the aesthetic principles he had announced in the preface to *New Poems*: 'One realm we have never conquered: the pure present. One great mystery of time is terra incognita to us: the instant',[80] Lawrence often sacrifices this distance for a sense of the here and now. In *Sea and Sardinia* certainly but in *Kangaroo* also, his special gift is to create the illusion that what his protagonists experience is being recorded as it occurs. The advantages in immediacy of this deliberate abandon of perspective, which is of course linked to, although not wholly determined by, the rapidity with which the novel was written, need to be stressed because the disappointment of conventional expectations makes many readers complain that, as a 'character', Somers is irritatingly inconsistent and volatile. The same readers are likely to find the ending, in which Somers leaves Australia, having decided that he has not been profoundly interested in either Cooley or his politics after all, disappointingly inconclusive. What then has all the fuss been about?

The truth is that though the narrative of the novel has a relatively conventional form, very little interest can be attached to how it is concluded. The emphasis falls on the process of decision-making rather than the nature of the decisions themselves. To enjoy the book the reader's satisfaction has to be deflected from wondering how things will turn out to living through Somers's struggle to take account of all the contradictory factors which, in a man of his particular background and sensibility, might determine an appropriate response to Australia and certain real or imagined Australians. In the conclusion as we now have it, the Somerses' ocean liner slowly moves away from the quay in Sydney. The manuscript version ended with a discussion between Somers and William James Trewhella ('Jaz'), a Cornish migrant with an important linking role in the novel. 'Now Jaz, goodbye', Somers and this version of *Kangaroo* conclude, 'Goodbye to you, goodbye to everybody. I've finished on this side.' Modernist in their self-reflective spirit but also indicative of a certain nonchalance in Lawrence about endings, these words refer to the 'side' of the world Somers is about to leave, but they are also a private joke which could not be carried forward to the published work. This is because they fit neatly on the last lines of the last page of the last of the four notebooks Lawrence was using, and spare him the necessity of beginning a fifth.[81]

In the closeness of author and protagonist, and the refusal of hindsight so that one particular mood or opinion might easily find itself contradicted by the next, *Kangaroo* is like *Sea and Sardinia*. But in a travel book we assume that the action relates – in however complicated or distorted a fashion – to episodes which once took place. That we know this is not necessarily true of a novel makes *Kangaroo* an awkward text to handle for a biographer. Letters and other documents show that it is in very many ways a faithful record of Lawrence's day-to-day experiences in Australia. A trip the Somerses are described as taking to 'Wollona' in chapter XIV, for example, is demonstrably based on the Lawrences' excursion on 30 June to Wollongong, a town a few more miles down the New South Wales coast, the main feature of which seems to have been Frieda's hysterical amusement at her husband's frantic efforts to retrieve the hat which had been blown off his head into the sea (iv. 272). There are many episodes, however, for which there is no corroborative evidence and plenty of ways of showing that Lawrence would not only invent when it suited him but also use odd details from his daily life in the development of a wholly fictional situation. As has been indicated already, the Lawrences did not stay in Sydney for weeks as the Somerses do but only for a couple of days. The fictional couple get to know their next-door neighbours when Harriett admires the dahlias in the Callcotts' garden. The estate agents in Thirroul through whom the Lawrences rented their house were called Callcott and their daughter recalled how her mother once picked a bunch of dahlias from her garden for Frieda. At the same time she makes it quite clear that neither of her parents knew the Lawrences at all well.[82] It would be foolish to decide that *Kangaroo* could never be used as evidence for what did happen or had happened to Lawrence simply because it went into the world as a novel. Ever since it was published, the 'Nightmare' chapter has rightly been regarded as Lawrence's record of what happened to him during the war. Minor details which could not be corroborated from elsewhere have been accepted, presumably because people have felt the pertinent question to be why, in a general context which one can show to be historical, Lawrence should have gone to the trouble of inventing what would otherwise be gratuitous and serve no fictional purpose. And yet in Lawrence the transitions between reportage, semi-reportage and 'pure' invention are very hard to spot: it would be an unusually bold reader who claimed they could be detected in the quality of the writing. This means that although it would be perverse for the biographer of such an autobiographical writer as Lawrence to ignore the evidence of this or other novels, they nevertheless need to be handled with wary discrimination.

This is much more the case as far as the secondary rather than the principal characters in *Kangaroo* are concerned. When Ben Cooley first meets Somers he attributes to him a 'series of articles on Democracy' which have appeared in what Somers himself calls 'that absurd international paper published at the Hague'.[83] The paper in question was the *Word* and the articles concerned are indubitably Lawrence's own.[84] Between him and Somers there is the close degree of identification which this attribution suggests and in appearance, gestures and responses, Harriett is similarly very close to Frieda. This gives a special biographical interest to chapter IX ('Harriett and Lovatt at Sea in Marriage') where we learn that in Somers's view the days of 'perfect love' are long over and the choice now lies between companionship on the one hand and Harriett's acceptance of her husband's lord-and-mastership on the other. We can hear Frieda (as we could previously hear her voice in the Ursula of *Women in Love*) as Harriett responds to Somers's preference for the latter alternative:

Him, a lord and master! Why, he was not really lord of his own bread and butter, next year they might both be starving. And he was not even master of himself, with his ungovernable furies and his uncritical intimacies with people . . .

All he could do was to try and come it over her with this revolution rubbish and a stunt of 'male' activity. If it were even real!

He had nothing but her, absolutely. And that was why, presumably, he wanted to establish this ascendancy over her, assume this arrogance.[85]

As in *Mr Noon*, the often bantering tone of chapter IX indicates how far the Lawrences had moved from the remarkable intensities of their early days together; but it hardly suggests their relationship had become 'settled'. The grounds for conflict were still there: in Frieda's temperamental aversion to playing a subsidiary role, and the painful struggle in her husband between desire for freedom and emotional dependency. As chapter IX makes clear, it cannot have been comfortable for Lawrence to have continually at his side a critic as shrewd and acerbic as Frieda but, aware of a tendency towards both solipsism and megalomania in his highly imaginative nature, he often acknowledged the force of what she had to say, and dramatised it as he does here.[86] Other parts of *Kangaroo* however are an eloquent and often moving testimony to occasions when he turned away from conflict and sought relief in a solitary interchange with nature, roaming the sea-shore in front of their house, or exploring the bush in the hills behind.

In almost all respects that matter, Harriett and Richard Somers 'are' Frieda and Lawrence but this does not mean that the other characters in the novel must also be closely based on 'real-life' originals. It is a tribute to the verisimilitude with which these others are often presented that such strenuous efforts have been made recently to prove that they were. In 1981 Robert Darroch claimed that Jack Callcott was a portrait of Jack Scott, the treasurer of the 'King and Empire Alliance' whose president was a former Major General Rosenthal (mistakenly assumed by Darroch at that time to be Jewish and all the more likely therefore to have been the model for Cooley). In deciding that Lawrence must have known Scott well, met Rosenthal more than once and also (probably) had a meeting with 'Jock' Garden, the communist secretary of the Sydney Trades and Labour Council and the possible model therefore for Willie Struthers, Darroch was encouraged by the knowledge that Aldington had been wrong in assuming that *all* the details of right-wing para-military activity in *Kangaroo* must have been transposed from Italy (because Australia was too much of a political backwater for that kind of thing).[87] In the seventeen years since Darroch first published his book more and more evidence has continued to emerge for the existence of para-military groupings associated with right-wing organisations such as the 'King and Empire Alliance'; yet in all that time there has been a singular lack of support for his main thesis. Lawrence may have picked up from casual conversation in Thirroul and elsewhere information about secret movements very roughly along the lines of the 2,000-strong 'Army to Fight Bolshevism' organised quite openly in Queensland in 1919 by the Returned Servicemen's League,[88] but no convincing evidence has been found to suggest that, while he was in New South Wales, he became even remotely intimate with the leaders of a group of that kind.[89]

The controversy which followed Darroch's claim is interesting from a biographical point of view since it obviously matters whether we imagine Lawrence spending most of his time at home in Thirroul or busy meeting the Scotts, Rosenthals and Gardens of Sydney's political world. It is additionally interesting, however, because *Kangaroo* is in fact a remarkable drama of sexual as well as political choice. Most of the alternatives on offer to Somers are present in summary form in 'The Battle of Tongues'. Towards the beginning of this seventh chapter it is made very clear that Cooley's appeal to Somers has a strong sexual as well as ideological component; but although distinctly attracted ('Richard's hand was almost drawn in spite of himself to touch the other man's body'[90]) Somers rejects it for the time being. The encounter makes him uncomfortable and leaving Cooley's office he feels the counter-appeal of separation, 'cold separation', and wonders why close encounters with another human being cannot be like 'a stoop as a gannet stoops into the sea . . . A touch and away. Always back, away into isolation.'[91] He is going to meet Harriett at the Callcotts' house in Sydney where they are staying the night. It has always been evident that Victoria Callcott is attracted to him and, left alone with her, after Jack has left the house for a while and Harriett has decided to go to bed, they are presented with the opportunity of making love. Somers is strongly drawn to Victoria and asks himself, 'Why not know them all, all the great moments of the gods, from the major moment with Hera to the swift short moments of Io or Leda or Ganymede. Should not a man know the whole range? And especially the bright, swift, weapon-like Bacchic occasion, should not any man seize it when it offered?' The occasion is offering itself now in the form of Victoria but because 'his heart of hearts was stubbornly puritanical' Somers turns it down and goes to bed – like the Lawrences when circumstances made it possible, the Somerses have separate bedrooms. The next day he and his wife return to Mullumbimby. It is raining when they arrive but Somers takes off his clothes, runs in the sea and, after standing under the shower in the 'little wash-place . . . to wash off the sticky, strong Pacific', he then makes love to Harriett.

To the end she was more wondering than anything. But when it was the end, and the night was falling outside, she laughed and said to him:
  "That was done in style. That was *chic*. Straight from the sea, like another creature".
  Style and *chic* seemed to him somewhat ill suited to the occasion, but he brought her a bowl of warm water and went and made the tea.[92]

Of these three human encounters in 'The Battle of Tongues', with Cooley, Victoria and Harriett, it is only the last we are able to think of as having in some sense 'happened'. This is because it is only in the last that the setting and both the participants are demonstrably historical ('we bathe by ourselves – and run in and stand under the shower-bath to wash the *very* seaey water off', Lawrence wrote to Catherine Carswell on 22 June – iv. 271). As far as the Lawrences' marriage is concerned, the dialogue in this last encounter reveals an interesting clash of attitudes. Implicit in Lawrence's was the belief that sexual intercourse must always *be* an 'occasion' and the likelihood therefore that, after the early passionate years of marriage – the years described in chapter IX as those of 'perfect love' – it would inevitably tend to become infrequent. Yet the novel suggests other reasons for a lack of frequency. In the cancelled conclusion to the manuscript version, shortly before Somers tells Jaz that he has finished 'on this side', he says,

46

Now I don't like love, and I don't like sex. Yet I'm never going to deny that this is a great and sacred sacrament, sexual love. But there are other sacraments . . . What I finally want is my own male power. Something beyond sex. And sex subservient to this. I don't want to cast out sex, or cut it out. But to set it subordinate to the living male power in my soul.[93]

It is not at all by accident that 'Ganymede' is included in the list of moments Somers recalls when he is wondering whether or not he should sleep with Victoria. More thoroughly than in any other of his fictions, Lawrence explores in *Kangaroo* the homoerotic and also frankly homosexual alternatives to relationships with women. Early in the novel Jack Callcott has offered Somers 'mateship': a distinctively Australian version of Whitman's 'love of comrades'. He has looked at him with an expression 'almost like love', with 'something desirous' in his eyes; and then put his arm round Somers as he reveals the secrets of Cooley's movement in a voice which is 'a kind of caress'.[94] But he is unlucky in arriving on the novelistic scene a couple of years too late and discovering an authorial figure no longer interested in mateship, at least when it is offered rather than sought.[95] As Somers reflects in chapter VI, in a passage which inevitably makes the reader think of Birkin and Gerald in *Women in Love,*

He had all his life had this craving for an absolute friend, a David to his Jonathan, Pylades to his Orestes: a blood-brother. All his life he had secretly grieved over his friendlessness. And now at last, when it really offered—and it had offered twice before, since he had left Europe[96]—he didn't want it, and he realised that in his innermost soul that he had never wanted it.

Yet he wanted *some* living fellowship with other men; as it was he was just isolated. Maybe a living fellowship!—but not affection, not love, not comradeship. Not mates and equality and mingling. Not blood-brotherhood. None of that.[97]

The approaches Jack makes to Somers are warm and tinged with homoeroticism, but the reader is given no sense that his interest is homosexual. Cooley is another matter. Too unusual and dominating to be looking for a 'mate' in the meaning which Jack or indeed Willie Struthers give to that term, he is attracted to Somers partly because he is an intellectual whose scepticism and resistance to his charm represent a challenge to be overcome; but also because he finds him physically appealing. After several preliminary overtures, including the one in 'The Battle of Tongues', the crisis comes in chapter XIII when Somers visits Cooley after having previously called on his political rival Struthers. His confession that he has not found Struthers physically attractive – 'something thin and hairy and spiderish. I didn't want to touch him'[98] – hardly moderates Cooley's jealous fury at what he regards as an act of emotional as well as political betrayal. Much bigger than Somers, Cooley makes one last effort to win him over:

47

Suddenly, with a great massive movement, Kangaroo caught the other man to his breast.

"Don't, Lovatt," he said, in a much moved voice, pressing the slight body of the lesser man against his own big breast and body. "Don't!" he said, with a convulsive tightening of the arm.

Somers, squeezed so that he could hardly breathe, kept his face from Kangaroo's jacket and managed to ejaculate:

"All right. Let me go and I won't".

"Don't thwart me", pleaded Kangaroo. "Don't—or I shall be forced to break all connexion with you, and I love you so. I love you so. Don't be perverse and put yourself against me."[99]

But Somers remains stiff within the embrace, still refusing to yield. He feels that Cooley's 'blind yearning' somehow fails to take account of himself as an individual and the attempt to oblige him to respond – 'Damn his love. He wants to *force* me' – arouses in him feelings of murderous hostility. After he is eventually released Cooley leaves the room for a moment and, on his return, tells Somers that they must have no more to do with each other. He warns him against revealing to others what he now knows about the movement and advises him to leave Australia. It has been a characteristic of the way Cooley is presented that he can seem at some moments very beautiful and at others hideously ugly. Now he is like 'some great ugly idol that might strike'. For what seems like miles Somers makes his way to the outer door as if in a dream with Cooley following 'slowly, awfully behind, like a madman. If he came near enough to touch!'[100]

Although when he had left the building where he met Struthers Somers felt it was like 'escaping from one of the medical-examination rooms in the war',[101] it is above all this experience with Cooley which causes his memories of his humiliations during the war years to 'erupt'. This is because at their epicentre is the fear and anger associated with the final medical inspection when, with nothing on, he (the pronoun can refer here to either Lawrence or Somers) is obliged to bend over in front a group of army medical officials while, to the accompaniment of general sniggers (or so he feels), one of them inspects his anus. Lawrence had always tended to associate the army with homosexuality, especially in its more unpleasant forms; that Cooley's overtures should provoke in Somers memories of his treatment at the army's hands, indicates how decisively they are being rejected.[102]

Another way of regarding this rejection is as Lawrence's own settling of accounts with Whitman. He had once been enormously impressed by Whitman's insistence on the need for men to form close relationships with other men, over and above whatever relationships they might have with women; he had clearly responded warmly to the homoeroticism in the poems; and on one occasion he had endorsed, although rather ambivalently, the implication in them that such close relationship might naturally lead to homosexual practice.[103] Yet now the somewhat incongruous attribution of Whitmanesque ideals to Cooley, who is after all distinctly not a democrat but who on several other occasions before this has been used as the spokesman for ideas his creator had once himself favoured but has now outgrown, allows Lawrence to dramatise his disillusion with the Whitman world-view. In a powerful scene towards the end of *Kangaroo*, with the hospital room smelling strongly of the consequences of Cooley's stomach wound,[104] Cooley speaks to Somers of 'the perfect love that men may have for one another, passing the love of women' and insists, 'Perfect love casteth out fear, Lovatt. Teach a man how to love his mate with a pure and fearless love.'[105] But Lawrence has Somers reject Cooley's dying appeal with the same unease but resolution that Stephen Daedalus exhibits at the deathbed of his mother. Whatever models for relationships with men Lawrence retained after *Kangaroo*, they would not include Whitman's. He had come to diagnose the Whitmanesque love of comrades he attributes to Cooley as both egotistical and Christian-derived: part of that worn-out Western idealism which, by allowing people to hide from themselves their true feelings during the war, had made those feelings so much more pernicious.[106]

IV   Last Days in Thirroul

To have composed *Kangaroo* so rapidly, but also so well, was a great feat of creative labour and an ironic triumph in a house whose owners, manifesting what Lawrence took to be typical Australian humour, had called 'Wyewurk'. The Lawrences were settled there for the whole of June and July and the first nine days of August 1922. They had not been in a house of their own since February. Mrs Jenkins remembered Frieda telling her that she was anxious to settle down for a while[107] and in letters Lawrence wrote from the *Malwa* he reported that she was 'tired of moving on', wanted to stay 'at least three months in or near Sydney', and hankered after 'a little 'ome of 'er own' (iv. 241, 243, 244). For his own part, he declared himself satisfied with their wandering life. Despite the pressure from his wife to pause a little, he rented 'Wyewurk' for only four weeks in the first instance and on his first full day there wrote of leaving Australia as quickly as he could, on either 6 or 12 July (iv. 247). There was thus a conflict of interest between himself and Frieda which disappeared when he suddenly discovered he could write and launched himself into his Australian novel.

'Wyewurk' was a large, three-bedroomed bungalow whose attractive main room was given a distinctive character by liberal use of jarrah wood – a eucalyptus resembling mahogany. It had low, red-tiled roofs projecting out over its verandahs and a back garden leading to a cliff, twenty feet below which was the beach. Despite the season, it was clearly warm enough for the Lawrences (if not the other inhabitants of Thirroul) to go in the water from time to time although to say they swam much in a sea where there was a good deal of typically Australian surf would be to overestimate their expertise. Every morning Lawrence would get up first, light the fire (it was not *that* warm) and clean a little. He then brought in the coal and wood, made the breakfast and did the odd outdoor job. After he had helped to wash up and settled the fire he was free to write.[108] Given the number of words he managed to produce, that is what he must have done most of the time. The Lawrences appear to have made no close friends in Thirroul. The local doctor[109] called, probably to see Frieda who on 21 June was 'just a bit seedy' – as Lawrence remarked, a 'change for her' (iv. 268); and they must have had contacts with the local tradespeople: part of the township's semi-rural charm was that both the postman and newspaper boy made their deliveries on a horse (iv. 256). But in general they not only experienced but positively gloried in a virtual isolation.

Lawrence's daily work-rate tells powerfully against the thesis of Darroch and his followers but so does the distance between Thirroul and Sydney. If the Lawrences had possessed a car it would be easier to imagine how he could have kept dashing into Sydney for another dramatic encounter with an important political figure and still have had his manuscript completed by 15 July (iv. 278). The number of visits for which there is any kind of evidence is small. Lawrence may have had to go back to Sydney to collect his trunks and there must have been at least one trip to check shipping schedules or make arrangements with Cooks about the receipt of money from America (iv. 257). We know, from some very desultory diary notes of his activities between February 1920 and November 1924, that on 3 July 1922 he was planning to go to Sydney on the following day in order 'to see about berths for San Francisco, & visas'.[110] The Fourth of July is not a good time to try and secure visas from an American consulate so that it may be that Lawrence took a hotel room on the night of the 4th and arranged to acquire his visas on the 5th. His experiences during the war had made him feel a marked man and apprehensive therefore that there might be some difficulty in securing even the standard six-month tourist visa, but in the event there were no problems. 'I saw the Consul in Sydney and the visas will be all right', he wrote on the 7th (iv. 274). This expedition would have given him plenty of time for the visit to the Sydney zoo which is described in the penultimate chapter of *Kangaroo* and is the likely origin of the fine poem in *Birds, Beasts and Flowers* with the same title as the novel; but his rhythm of work would have made overnight stays infrequent and a round trip of more than eighty miles did not make Sydney a place which could be popped into. There is no convincing evidence that he was ever drawn there by any people other than the Nottinghamshire couples he had met on the boat. Mrs Jenkins had given the Lawrences a letter of introduction to a journalist friend who worked on the Sydney *Bulletin* but although his novel provides ample evidence that Lawrence read the *Bulletin* (Frieda later claimed that with the

Corriere della Sera it was the only newspaper or magazine he had ever read regularly[111]), the letter was never presented. 'I don't present any letters of introduction', he wrote to his sister-in-law Else Jaffe on 13 June, 'we don't know a soul on this side of the continent' (iv. 262).

If there was only one claim of this kind in the letters Lawrence wrote from Thirroul its implications for Darroch's belief that he got to know such relatively prominent people as Scott and Rosenthal would be serious enough, but there are in fact several more. On the same day that he wrote to Else he told Earl Brewster, 'But within 1000 miles there isn't a soul that knows us . . . I never knew before how wonderful it was to know absolutely nobody' (iv. 265). A week later he wrote to Seltzer that, 'Here in N.S.W. not a soul knows about me' and on 9 July there is a similar refrain in a letter to Koteliansky, 'We don't know a single soul – not a soul comes to the house' (iv. 267, 275). On 17 July he told Mountsier 'we don't know anybody – don't want to – prefer it alone' and on the 24th, after *Kangaroo* had been dispatched to America for typing, he wrote to Achsah Brewster, 'We haven't known a single soul here – which is really a relief' (iv. 278, 280). The relief was perhaps a consequence of having been lionised in Perth and must have encouraged him to tell Seltzer, Mountsier and Mabel Sterne that they should not advertise his imminent arrival in America: 'I want you please *not* to tell anybody we are coming. I want to be really apart from most people – same as here' (iv. 259). Lawrence had many faults but calculated hypocrisy was not one of them. He was unusually open and straightforward, often disconcertingly or even woundingly so. Darroch tried to deal with the evidence in the letters by speculating that the information given to him by Scott and Rosenthal was so sensitive that it required a cover-up. This makes Lawrence not only a liar but someone who would take the trouble of telling lies to Americans or English people far removed from the Australian political scene, and quite indifferent to it.[112]

The letters Lawrence wrote from Thirroul suggest that, after the irritations of the first few days had faded away, he was comparatively happy there. The house pleased him and he liked the continual background noise of the ocean: it was like having 'the Pacific in the garden' with 'the surf seeming to rush in under our feet as we sit at table' (iv. 253, 249). That nobody appeared especially curious about him and Frieda or inclined to ask questions was a relief. 'I suppose', he commented wryly, 'there have been too many questionable people here in the past' (iv. 263). He felt Australians lacked an active inner life: 'just a long lapse and drift. A rather fascinating indifference, a *physical* indifference to what we call soul or spirit', but he was attracted by a complementary easy-going or happy-go-lucky attitude – 'a relief from the moral and mental and nervous tension of Europe' (iv. 271, 264). It was a country into which he felt it would be tempting to disappear and he celebrated, in memorable passages of his novel, its 'fern-dark indifference'.[113]

Yet if in many ways Lawrence was unusually at ease in New South Wales, *Kangaroo* would suggest that his fundamental state of mind was hardly tranquil. The novel is at its best in its depiction of Somers's consciousness which is nearly always troubled and often anguished. He is a man who, just like Lawrence, suffers from bad dreams. On one occasion he is terrified by the appearance in a dream of a woman whose face is bloated with grief and who seems an amalgam of his wife, his mother, his sister and the girls he had known in his youth. He has betrayed this woman and she now repudiates him.[114] Other disturbing dreams are recorded[115] and the whole 'Nightmare' chapter of *Kangaroo* is in one sense a bad dream of the protagonist's difficulties and humiliations in England during the war. Although one can see what in the novel gives rise to this chapter, it is nevertheless felt by readers as an irruption: something that the author has suddenly found himself compelled to write. There is no need here to imagine that there must necessarily have been some obviously relevant and important episode in Lawrence's daily life in Thirroul which unexpectedly obliged him to relive and thereby exorcise what had happened to him during the war. Reading the *Letters of a VAD* may have begun to bring back painful memories and it is perhaps significant that when he first arrived in 'Wyewurk', with its views out to sea, he was reminded of Cornwall where many of his unpleasant war-time experiences had taken place (iv. 249). But the trigger might well have been some event in life which was trivial and apparently inconsequential or some underground logic of the fictional situation he had created. Freud is skilful at demonstrating how the seemingly unimportant becomes significant because of its associative links with material the mind would like to suppress. Lawrence's approach to the 'return of the repressed' is less analytical but more dramatic. Given that the country was at war, it was, he agrees, necessary that Somers should have been treated as he was and that the 'secret parts of a man' should be investigated. After all, 'many men were put through things a thousand times worse'; and yet . . . 'He was full of a lava fire of rage and hate, at the bottom of his soul. And he knew it was the same with most men.'

. . . He cared for nothing now, but to let loose the hell-rage that was in him. Get rid of it by letting it out. For there was no digesting it. He had been trying that for three years, and roaming the face of the earth trying to soothe himself with the sops of travel and new experience and scenery. He knew now the worth of all sops.—Once that disruption had taken place in a man's soul, and in a stress of humiliation, under the pressure of *compulsion*, something has broken in his tissue and the liquid fire has run out loose into his blood, then no sops will be of any avail. The lava fire at the bottom of a man's belly breeds more lava fire, and more, and more—till there is an eruption. As the lava fire accumulates, the man becomes more and more reckless. Till he reaches a pitch of dehumanized recklessness, and then the lid is blown off, as the top is blown off a hill to make a new volcano.—Or else it all sets into rocky deadness.[116]

Even as a non-combatant, Lawrence was a supremely articulate representative of that generation of men trying in the early 1920s to recover from the trauma of World War I. 'Rocky deadness' not being an option, the anger he felt compelled him to try to imagine a world whose social and moral co-ordinates would be quite different from those he believed the war had so comprehensively discredited. For a man in that state, and with that mission, the most favourable environments could provide only the mildest of palliatives.

The manuscript of *Kangaroo* was packed and ready to be sent off to Mountsier by 17 July but the boat on which the Lawrences had retained a cabin (the *Tahiti*) was not due to sail until 10 August. Lawrence was thus at a loose end – 'have done my novel and have nothing further to do here' (iv. 279). The cabin was retained but it was not paid for because the money Lawrence had asked Mountsier to cable through to Cooks had not yet arrived. In telling his agent to send £160 (he needed £120 for the boat tickets) Lawrence stoically assumed that he would be emptying his American account or even borrowing money from Seltzer (iv. 268). Of the money which Mountsier had previously cabled to Ceylon, he had on 9 June only £31 left and at that point the rent for more than half of his stay in 'Wyewurk' (£9) was still to be paid (iv. 256). It was probably in the latter half of July therefore, when the old supplies were gone and the new ones had not yet appeared, that, with or without Frieda, he took a trip to the Sydney suburb of Camperdown, where the two migrant couples he had met on the boat were settled and borrowed a small sum of money from one of them (the Marchbanks). The Marchbanks and the Forresters are the one proven exception to Lawrence's claim that he knew no-one in New South Wales but he may have excluded them because they were neither prominent nor local, or – more probably – because he did not renew his contacts with them until the end of his stay. Denis Forrester's memory was of losing sight of the Lawrences once they all landed and not seeing Lawrence again until he sought them out in Camperdown.[117] What is certain is that the Lawrences invited the Forresters and Marchbanks to 'Wyewurk' for the weekend of 29–30 July, providing an occasion (commemorated in several photo-graphs) both to thank the Marchbanks for the loan and to pay it back. The money from Mountsier must have arrived by then since on the Sunday Lawrence hired a car and driver to take the six of them to the Bulli Pass: a well-known beauty spot behind Thirroul (iv. 281).

The Bulli Pass excursion is not included in *Kangaroo* but it could have been because Lawrence expanded the novel's last chapter when he was in America and included in it episodes from his time in Thirroul after the middle of July. He wrote an account, for example, of the huge storm which broke out shortly before the weekend with the Marchbanks and Forresters – 'nearly blew the sea out of its hollow' (iv. 281); and he described how a little later the Somerses hired a two-wheeled trap, called in Australia a 'sulky', and drove into the bush. 'Sometimes they had gone in a motor-car, but they both much preferred the little, comfortable sulky.'[118] What they see on this occasion makes them both feel reluctant to leave Australia, which was the Lawrences' case also. Lawrence was always inclined to like a place best once the arrangements for leaving it had been finalised, but there is no doubt that the Australian landscape had come to have a special appeal and fascination for him. Somers's precise description of the different kinds of wattle he was able to distinguish on this excursion is an indication of how at home Lawrence had by now come to feel in the bush after his first, intimidating encounter in Western Australia. The Australian critical response to *Kangaroo* has been mixed but almost all its admirers and detractors are united in their praise for the descriptions of the bush, and of the sea-scapes near Thirroul.

Lawrence's fondness for Australia was intensified by an apprehension about going to America which five months away from Europe had not helped him to shake off. 'For some reason', he had written to Mountsier on 21 June, 'the U.S.A. is the only country in the world that I shrink from and feel shy of'; and on 3 July he told Katharine Pritchard, 'As for America, I go to it rather with dread, and fully expect to hold my ears and cover my eyes and bolt, as you did' (iv. 268, 273). Yet the tickets were now paid for and the clothes, the few books, the household effects and the side of the Sicilian cart had to be packed up once again. The Lawrences left Thirroul on 9 August and, in spite of some previous anxiety that the *Tahiti*'s sailing date would be put back by a week (iv. 277), they were on their way to San Francisco by the 11th. Although there had been some delay, and although they had chosen what could fairly be described as the long way round, they were taking up Mabel Sterne's invitation at last.

CHAPTER THREE

◆

August–December 1922
NEW MEXICO

I America at Last

The *Tahiti*'s first stop on its way to San Francisco was Wellington. Delay in obtaining a landing-card for the German-born Frieda irritated Lawrence so much that he denounced the town as a 'cold, snobbish, lower middle-class colony of pretentious nobodies';[1] but his animus did not stop him posting from there a reminder to Katherine Mansfield of her birthplace. She told Middleton Murry that the postcard Lawrence sent her bore no more than the single Italian word 'Ricordi' ('Remembrances'). It was a tentative peace-offering after the bitterness of their recent disagreements yet, without it, the *rapprochement* with Murry which took place shortly after Mansfield's death in January 1923 might not have been so rapid.[2]

From New Zealand, Lawrence was finally on his way to 'the glamorous South Seas'.[3] Stevenson must have played a part in making the South Sea islands seem so alluring to him but at least as influential were Herman Melville's two 'travel' books: *Typee* and *Omoo*. In what is likely to have been the second version of his essay on these books, dating from the summer of 1920, he had written: 'The Pacific Ocean holds the dream of immemorial centuries: in the same way it is nascent with a new world. It is the great blue twilight of the vastest of all evenings, the most wonderful of all dawns. This great ocean, with its peoples, is still latent with the common unknown.'[4] A modern economist who found these remarks prescient would be misunderstanding what Lawrence meant by 'a new world'. When he came to revise them, three or four months after his arrival in America, he could no longer be so confident that the Pacific held a clue to the future as well as the past. It is now 'the great blue twilight . . . perhaps of the most wonderful of all dawns. Who knows?' After noting the paradox that although life for the Melville of *Typee* appears paradisal in the Marquesas Islands, he is nevertheless desperate to leave them, Lawrence now adds, 'But I should not have been happy either. One's soul seems under a vacuum, in the South Seas.' It is however in the description of the inhabitants of the South Sea islands that the effect of personal experience on the final version of this essay is most evident. Previously he had protested against the common notion that the 'savages' Melville finds himself among in *Typee* are somehow child-like; but now he himself calls them children and insists on the impossibility of retreating back to their state: 'But we can't go back. Whatever else the South Sea islander is, he is centuries and centuries behind us in the life-struggle, the consciousness-struggle, the struggle of the soul into fullness.'[5]

Some of Lawrence's alterations to the Melville essay can be attributed to his thoughts about American Indians as well as South Sea islanders; but there is no doubt that although Raratonga (where the ship called first) lived up to his expectations, Papeete was a great disappointment. From Raratonga, on 20 August, he had sent a postcard to Compton Mackenzie who had once so enthusiastically seemed to share his interest in the South Seas. 'Calling here for the day – very lovely – Tahiti next' it said, but once in Papeete, the main town of Tahiti, there was a second postcard: 'If you are thinking of coming here don't. The people are brown and soft' (iv. 284, 286). In a letter to Mary Cannan written from the ship on 31 August he enlarged a little on how two days in Papeete had affected him and concluded, 'These are supposed to be the earthly paradises: these South Sea Isles. You can have 'em.' 'Travel', he wrote in the next paragraph, 'seems to me a splendid lesson in disillusion – chiefly that' (iv. 286).

Lawrence's letter indicates that his disillusion was made more acute by growing dissatisfaction with the life at sea. For the first time a long sea voyage was failing to have its usual, calming effect. This was partly because, even though the Lawrences were travelling first-class, the *Tahiti* struck him as too full: like a large, over-crowded boarding house, 'staggering over the sea' (iv. 284), whereas in the second class of the *Osterley*, *Orsova* and *Malwa* there had always been plenty of room. On the whole they got on well with their fellow-passengers and made friends among them whom they continued to see once they had landed in San Francisco (iv. 289), but in Tahiti a 'Crowd of cinema people' (iv. 287) had embarked whose dissipations offended the puritanism of both Lawrence and – more surprisingly – Frieda. These were the actors and crew of a film directed by Raoul Walsh, eventually to be entitled *Passions of the Sea*. One of its female stars, Frieda complained (as if she herself had always been a model of fidelity), flirted openly with a passenger but then tripped innocently into the arms of the young man who was waiting for her when the ship docked.[6] When Lawrence tried to remonstrate with some of these people over behaviour he felt was inconsiderate and disruptive, they treated him with contempt.[7] Their presence helped to spoil the last days of the voyage for him but it is likely that, despite the resource of more Verga translation,[8] the main trouble was that it had simply gone on too long. His longest previous voyage had lasted fifteen days whereas this one took twenty-five.

The Lawrences arrived in San Francisco on Monday 4 September and went to stay at the expensive Palace Hotel ($7 or almost £2 a night). 'Arrived penniless'

Lawrence telegraphed to Mountsier, asking him to send some money (iv. 287). In a letter to Mabel Sterne almost immediately on his arrival, he explained that he had in fact landed with less than $20 in his pocket but that there was 'money in the bank' (iv. 288). He was no doubt thinking principally of the $1,000 which he had recently heard *Hearst's International* had agreed to pay for 'The Captain's Doll'.[9] With a stroke of good fortune as exceptional as this ($1,000 was almost twice as much as all his writing had recently been earning in England during a whole year – iv. 299), he could well afford a few days at the Palace Hotel.

When he was in Australia, worrying about how he would manage in America once his money had run out, Lawrence had unrealistically hoped that he might be met in San Francisco by either Seltzer or Mabel Sterne. The absence of the former he could now justifiably attribute to Seltzer's concern over an event which was to have significantly favourable consequences for Lawrence's financial future: an attempt by the New York Society for the Suppression of Vice to have *Women in Love* banned, along with two other Seltzer publications.[10] Lawrence learned of the prosecution in a newspaper cutting sent to him by Mabel Sterne who compensated for her own absence by also sending two railway tickets for New Mexico with the message that once the Lawrences left San Francisco she would regard them as her guests (iv. 289, 292). It was a gesture which touched Lawrence at the time ('So American!' – iv. 289) although later, when relations with his hostess had deteriorated, he was to make clear that he had insisted on reimbursing her for the tickets.[11]

The Lawrences felt impressed but also a little confused by San Francisco. Frieda remembered how, when they went into a self-service cafeteria, they did not know what to do – 'how to take our plates and food'.[12] Unimpressed by the trams, her husband wrote of 'black, glossy streets with steel rails in ribbons like the path of death itself' and, allowing his grammar to mimic his disarray, described the city at night as 'bewildering, beautiful too, a sort of never-stop Hades. I went to a cinema and with jazz orchestra and a huge and voluminous organ. Either it is all crazy or I am going' (iv. 290). They did a little sight-seeing in the area with the friends they had made on the boat but dropped the vague plans they had for taking in the Yosemite valley, or even the Grand Canyon, on their way to Taos. Lawrence felt, he said in the same letter in which he wonders about going crazy, that he would drop dead if any more stupendousness assailed him (iv. 290). By Friday 8 September the money from Mountsier had arrived and the Lawrences were ready for their two-day rail journey to New Mexico.

Because there was no train to take them directly to Taos they were heading for Lamy, the closest stopping-place on the main line, twenty or so miles to the south of Santa Fe. Waiting for them there on the afternoon of 10 September were Mabel Sterne and her Indian companion, Tony Luhan. For her, the effort to attract Lawrence to New Mexico, which had begun almost twelve months before,

57

had finally proved successful. She later explained how it was extracts from *Sea and Sardinia* which had convinced her Lawrence was ideally equipped to describe life in Taos and thus promote the Indian cause; but she had read other works of his before sending off her invitation, including *Sons and Lovers*.[13] It would be surprising if she had not also seen 'America, Listen to Your Own' when it appeared in the *New Republic* in December 1920. This short piece, dated 'Florence 1920', urged Americans to stop being so respectful of European and in particular Italian culture, and to turn again to catch the spirit of their own 'dark, aboriginal continent', to 'take up life where the Red Indian, the Aztec, the Maya, the Incas left it off'.[14] There was a suggested life-choice here which had been precisely Mabel Sterne's own.

Born into a wealthy Buffalo family in 1879 (and the same age therefore as Frieda), Mabel Ganson's first marriage was to Karl Evans, a young man from her own milieu – his father owned a steamship company.[15] After the birth of what would prove to be her only child she appeared set for the life of a provincial socialite with artistic leanings, but the death of her husband in a hunting accident changed all that. To break up an affair she was having with her doctor, Mabel's mother sent her to Europe and on the voyage out she met and later married a young Boston architect named Edwin Dodge. With his help, she renovated a beautiful old house on the outskirts of Florence – the Villa Curonia – and from the winter of 1905–6 established there an increasingly well-known *salon* for avant-garde writers, painters, musicians and actors. One of her frequent guests was Gertrude Stein who on one of her visits wrote 'A Portrait of Mabel Dodge at the Villa Curonia', the text through which both women first became well known in the United States.

Chiefly so that her son could be educated at home, Mabel returned to New York in 1912 and soon began another *salon* in her apartment on Fifth Avenue, near Washington Square. Almost immediately she became heavily involved in the organisation of a controversial exhibition of modern and chiefly French art at the old Armory building in New York: an event with a role in American cultural history as influential as that of Roger Fry's 1912 Post-impressionist exhibition in England. She then turned her attention to left-wing politics and it was partly through her initiative that a great pageant was held in Madison Square Garden on 7 June 1913 in support of a group of silk workers from Patterson, New Jersey. They were involved in a strike organised by the IWW whose leader, Bill Haywood, frequented Mabel's *salon* along with other 'movers and shakers' of the radical Left such as the anarchist leader, Emma Goldman, once sent to jail for recommending that women kept 'their minds open and their wombs closed', and Max Eastman, the highly influential editor of the *Masses*.[16] Mabel worked on the pageant for the silk workers with John Reed, best remembered now as the author of *Ten Days Which Shook the World*, with whom she proceeded to have a well-publicised affair. When she divorced Dodge in 1916, however, it was to marry not Reed but the painter Maurice Sterne – 'Are you a relative of the Maurice Sterne, artist, who was at Anticoli this summer?' Lawrence had asked, with inadvertent ineptitude, in response to Mabel's initial invitation to Taos (iv. 111).

By the time of her third marriage Mabel Sterne had more or less abandoned her life in New York. She spent most of her time in the country, helping to found and then support a 'progressive' school run by Isadora Duncan's sister, Elizabeth, at Croton on the Hudson; or encouraging her new husband in his artistic career at Provincetown on Cape Cod. When Maurice Sterne decided to visit New Mexico in order to paint Indian subjects, and wrote back enthusiastically to his wife about the area, Mabel decided to follow him there. She arrived in Santa Fe in December 1917, found she felt uncomfortable with the 'Anglos' already established in the town and bullied Sterne into taking a house for six months in the more remote and as yet less colonised Taos. When the six months were up and Sterne left, Mabel stayed on to begin or continue her affair with Tony Luhan, a handsome Indian carpenter from the Taos pueblo who would soon be involved in building her a fine house. Turning her back on New York and Europe, Mabel Sterne made Taos her base for the rest of her life, much of which she would devote to the safe-guarding and promotion of Indian culture.[17]

Waiting for Lawrence on Lamy station, 'Mabel' was at least as well known in her way as he was in his.[18] The dubious privilege of being commemorated by Stein, in the title at least of a characteristically enigmatic piece, was well in the past, but before the 1920s were over there would be at least four more published portraits of her in fiction or drama.[19] She had written a good deal herself but was known best as a woman able to encourage men to realise their full potential in either art or political action. Mabel saw herself as a contemporary, that is to say active and entrepreneurial, version of the Muse although, unlike Frieda (whose self-image was similar), she usually had quite specific notions as to what her men should be inspired to do. She described in *Lorenzo in Taos* how she seemed to want to use all her power 'upon delegates to carry out the work' and in the same context explained, 'I wanted Lawrence to understand things for me, to take *my* experience, *my* material, *my* Taos, and to formulate it all into a magnificent creation. That was what I wanted him for.'[20] Her powerful personality was no more fitted than Frieda's for a minor role amongst the hand-maidens. Warm and generous, no-one would ever have accused her of the emotional perversions which often accompany the self-sacrificing temperament. 'Mabel's desire to control others', writes her chief biographer, 'was at least as strong as her need to submit to direction.'[21]

Lawrence was to become acquainted with the strength of Mabel's will very quickly and in his own unfinished portrait, written after a few weeks in Taos, described her as having eyes which were as 'dangerous as the headlights of a great machine coming full at you in the night'.[22] Her will to attract him had been frustrated when he had first accepted her invitation but then taken a boat east – despite the magic power which she believed lay in the Indian necklace she had sent to Frieda.[23] Nothing daunted, Mabel had then persuaded a reluctant Tony Luhan to help her in making telepathic appeals to the Lawrences across the seas, resisting the suggestion at one moment that instead of their coming to her she should join them: 'Certainly I wouldn't budge to go and see them in Ceylon! I'd had the idea of having *him* come to *Taos*, and I'd sit there and draw him until he came.'[24] The late afternoon of Sunday 10 September 1922 was when all her efforts finally bore fruit.

Mabel seems to have been too excited to have had any very distinct first impressions of Lawrence. She was aware only of his 'slim fragility besides Frieda's solidity, of a red beard that was somehow too old for him, and of a nervous incompetence. He was agitated, fussy, distraught, and giggling with nervous grimaces.' The nervousness was partly a consequence, she implied, of Tony Luhan's presence and indications given previously, or conveyed now by her behaviour, that he was something much more to her than an Indian chauffeur.[25] Lawrence's subsequent writings make this likely enough. It became an important problem for him whether there ever could, or should, be a successful sexual relationship between two people of different races. A preliminary and unpleasant conclusion was to appear shortly in the part of his revision of the essay on *Typee* and *Omoo* in which he describes the South Sea island woman 'with her knotted hair and her dark, inchoate, slightly sardonic eyes. I like her, she is nice. But I would never want to touch her. I could not go back on myself so far. Back to their uncreate condition. She has soft warm flesh, like warm mud. Nearer the reptile, the Saurian age. *Noli me tangere*.' The same hostility to miscegenation would emerge in 'Quetzalcoatl', the first version of *The Plumed Serpent*, but in the final version of that novel the heroine's marriage to the Indian Cipriano takes place with quite evident authorial approval.[26]

After an early evening meal in the restaurant room at Lamy station, Luhan set out to drive Mabel and the Lawrences to Santa Fe. Their car broke down on the way and as Luhan spent some time trying to repair it, Frieda unrealistically urged her husband to get out and help. Lawrence protested that he did not know anything about cars and then, according to Mabel, leaned forward to its owner confessing himself 'a failure as a man in the world of men'.[27] She did not indicate the tone in which Lawrence pronounced these words and, so soon after having met him, was probably in no position to tell. Eventually Luhan persuaded the car to start again but when they arrived in Santa Fe the accommodation Mabel had envisaged for all four was no longer available. She decided therefore to entrust the Lawrences to her friend Witter Bynner while she and Luhan went to stay the night with other people she knew. Outside Bynner's house, about half a mile from town just off the old Santa Fe trail, Lawrence began to unload the piles of luggage. Since the Lawrences' departure from Taormina in February, the various suitcases and trunks had now come more than half-way round the world. As he was stepping out of the car with the large Sicilian cart panel under his arm, Luhan backed slightly with the result that the edge of the panel, already resting on the ground, split. An enraged Lawrence at once declared that he had carried the panel far enough at Frieda's bidding and was not now prepared to carry it any further. It was left with Bynner the next day and could still be seen in his Santa Fe house when he was interviewed there by a French writer in 1960.[28]

Witter Bynner was a poet of some distinction who after twenty years of literary and academic life in New York, Europe and California had retreated to Santa Fe only seven months previously.[29] Mabel recorded that when she delivered the Lawrences to his house she was too tired to notice 'how it seemed'.[30] The reference is probably less to the possible rudeness of leaving newly arrived guests with people they did not know than to the fact that Bynner was a homosexual who was then living with another writer almost twenty years his junior: Willard Johnson (familiarly known as 'Spud'). Apart from Tony Luhan and Mabel, other guests at the dinner Bynner and Johnson hastily improvised for the Lawrences were the Hendersons. Alice Corbin Henderson had been the co-founder with Harriet Monroe of *Poetry* (the Chicago-based journal in which Lawrence had already published a good many of his poems), and was one of the women to have 'discovered' Santa Fe before Mabel. Her husband William was a painter and architect and her daughter, also named Alice ('la Corbinetta' as Lawrence would call her – iv. 339), was to be married before the end of the year to Mabel's son, John Evans, even though by then she would be only sixteen.[31]

Bynner's recollections of Lawrence did not appear until the early 1950s by which time he had grown increasingly hostile and malicious. He was nevertheless an intelligent man whose observations are always worth attending to. His first impressions of Lawrence's physique were unfavourable – 'The beard and hair . . . seemed like eaves he was cuddling under – a weasel face hiding under the warm fur of its mother and peeking out' – but he remembered being drawn by the magnetism of his guest's conversation and he was one of the very many to record how entertainingly Lawrence could mimic members of the London literary scene – Middleton Murry as well as Norman Douglas (whom Bynner had met) were evidently included on this occasion.[32] In those days his adobe house, which is on a rise that gives a fine view of Santa Fe and the surrounding semi-desert landscape (it is now the Buena Vista Art Center), was still in a primitive state and consisted of only three rooms. He had therefore given up his bedroom to the Lawrences while he and Johnson slept in the living room on couches. In the morning he got up early intending to clear away the dishes from the night before

61

and make sure the Lawrences had some breakfast before they left for Taos. But when he went in the kitchen he found that his guests had already washed the dishes, laid the table and cooked the breakfast, all before his maid could arrive from across the street.[33] There was therefore time for more conversation before Mabel and Luhan arrived to pick up the Lawrences. With a late start and the likelihood of a stop for lunch, it took all day to drive the seventy or so miles to Taos, all the day-light hours (that is) of 11 September 1922, Lawrence's thirty-seventh birthday.[34]

II Finding his Feet

The trip from Santa Fe to Taos in those early days was described by Mabel in the *Edge of Taos Desert*, the fourth volume of her *Intimate Memories*.[35] Although the roads have improved and there is far more building on the outskirts of both towns, the effect is hardly less spectacular today than it must have been over seventy years ago. Shortly after the climb out of Santa Fe, there is an expanse of gentle foothills whose yellow, desert-like soil is dotted with pines and sage-brush. The route is undulating until it dips down into the valley of the Rio Grande. After Velarde, the old road follows that valley closely until, near to Taos, it has become a precipitous gorge. Leading back to the Taos plateau is a narrow zigzag up the right side of the gorge, with the rushing river down below on the left and, beyond it, seemingly perpendicular walls of rock which have the look of reddish clay scarred into huge, irregular building blocks. Conglomerations of these blocks overhang the gorge dangerously or have settled in untidy heaps below. Although for a European, there are somewhat similar sights in the Alps, the light, the colours and the vegetation make the effect entirely different.

Years later Lawrence was to call New Mexico the 'greatest experience from the outside world' he had ever had. His time in Sicily, he wrote, 'right among the old Greek paganism that still lives there', had not shattered the essential Christianity on which his character was established. His stay in Kandy had not touched 'the great psyche of materialism and idealism' which dominated him, and Australia had been 'a sort of dream or trance'. The glimpse of Tahiti had repelled him, as had California. 'But the moment I saw the brilliant, proud morning shine high up over the deserts of Santa Fe, something stood still in my soul, and I started to attend . . . In the magnificent fierce morning of New Mexico one sprang awake, a new part of the soul woke up suddenly, and the old world gave way to a new.'[36] The transition from old to new was in reality far more gradual than these last phrases suggest, but the New Mexican landscape is an experience for the dullest observer and Lawrence's sensitivity to his surroundings was praeternaturally acute. Mabel claimed he caught his breath, as well he might, when the car had climbed to the point where its occupants could look down across the flat sage-brush desert to a Taos made green by water from the mountains that curve round behind it.[37]

They arrived at her estate a mile beyond the village when it was dark and too late therefore for the Lawrences to appreciate fully her extraordinary house – a model in many ways of the Villa Curonia but entirely transformed by the substitution of elegant, Renaissance lines with the thick, lumpy irregularities of adobe.[38] The new adobe house which Mabel had ready for the Lawrences was only about 200 yards from the back of her own. With its 4 rooms and kitchen it stood just beyond the boundary of her estate on ground only Indians had the right to build on and as a result was often referred to as 'Tony's house'.[39] Aware that Mabel was 'a sort of queen with various houses scattered round; and dependants', and that she had prepared the house for him 'because she wants me to *write* this country up', Lawrence nevertheless found it 'charming' and its owner 'very nice' (iv. 295–6). Before he had time to enjoy it however, or to get to know the Taos pueblo – 3-miles away and a staggering visual testimony to 1,000 years of remarkable cultural resilience in what were often very hostile circumstances – he was taken off to the Jicarillo Reservation, about 100 miles to the north-west of Taos. Tony Luhan and another Indian were driving there to attend the celebrations which the Apaches still hold every year on 14 and 15 September at either the Horse or Stone Lake. While she stayed behind with Frieda, Mabel persuaded Luhan to take with him not only Lawrence but also Bessie Freeman, an old friend from Buffalo days who was staying with her.

The impressions of the Apaches which Lawrence wrote after his return were published in the *Dial* five months later under the title 'Indians and an Englishman'. He describes very well in this article the confusion, for an outsider, of the Apache gathering and records the beginning of what was to be a continuing fascination with one of the more common forms of Indian dancing: the curiously hypnotic rhythmic shuffle. He also makes it clear, however, how destructive *real* Indians were to the expectations of someone 'born in England and kindled with Fenimore Cooper' and that, although he believed he and they shared the same origins ('Our darkest tissues are twisted in this old tribal experience'), there was now a gap between him and them which seemed unbridgeable.[40] Looking round at the Apaches, and coming to terms with the 'unbearable sulphur-human smell' that was a consequence of their 'cult of water hatred',[41] it is evident that he saw no-one whom he felt could have played Chief Chingachgook to his own Natty Bumppo or any young Indian at all reminiscent of the noble Uncas, last of the Mohicans.

Lawrence was often accused of coming to very rapid conclusions about the places he visited and the people he met.[42] The accusations were frequently justified but on this question of what to think of the Indians he took his time and seemed reconciled if not content to remain in indecision, for a while at least.

Since it was chiefly because of the Indians that he had been drawn to America in the first place, responding to what Witter Bynner called 'the Red Indian lure',[43] the matter was a vital one with profound implications for Lawrence's previous views on religion, history and modern civilisation. His opportunities for considering it could not now be any better. The two Indians who had taken him to the Jicarillo Reservation had themselves participated in the Apache celebrations, and ten days after he was back Lawrence was able to watch the dances and ceremonies which take place in the Taos pueblo at the end of September. But his account of these is even more straightforwardly descriptive than his article on the Apaches,[44] and in his first letters from Taos snap judgements are less in evidence than a certain bewilderment at all the new sights and sounds he was experiencing. 'I am still strange here, not orienté' he told Seltzer on 19 September (iv. 298). The next day he described himself to E. M. Forster as 'a great stranger' in New Mexico and said the Apaches were 'so different – yet a bit chinesey. I haven't got the hang of them yet' (iv. 301). On 29 September, after Mabel had invited some young Indians from the pueblo to play and dance in a house on her property, which she called 'the Studio', and after Lawrence and the other 'Anglos' who were present had been persuaded to join in, he wrote to Catherine Carswell that, 'The Indians are much more remote than negroes' (iv. 313). The definition of what he could feel would be a correct attitude towards Indians was to preoccupy him for the next three years and have an important bearing on his writing. Yet he had understood enough at the end of his first fortnight in Taos to ask Mountsier to send him the complete copy of *Studies in Classic American Literature* which he had been holding for him, and to feel that he would 'like to go through them again' (iv. 306).[45] If he was not yet quite sure what to think of New Mexico he must have rapidly become aware that many of the confident generalisations he had made in the *Studies* about America in general, and Indians in particular, were no longer valid.

Lawrence was under some pressure to decide what he felt about the Indians because of the controversy surrounding the Bursum Bill. One of the other people Mabel had attracted to Taos was John Collier, the Lawrences' next-door neighbour on her estate, and a prominent social reformer and propagandist for Indian rights. (In the 1930s, under Roosevelt, he was to become the US Commissioner for Indian Affairs.) It was Collier who, in the month of the Lawrences' arrival, alerted Mabel to the danger for the Indians of a bill which had been introduced into Congress by Senator H. O. Bursum of New Mexico on 20 July, and which purported to bring some clarity to the complicated issue of land tenure in and around the pueblos. When Mexico had been obliged to cede large tracks of the Southwest to its more powerful neighbour in 1848, the United States had agreed that the Southwestern Indian tribes could retain title to about

700,000 acres of land granted to them by their previous colonisers. But a decision of the Supreme Court in 1876 that the Pueblo Indians were not wards of the government had the effect of leaving their lands open for both purchase and squatting. The reversal of this decision in 1913, after New Mexico had become a state, created a confusion about who owned what that the Bursum Bill was intended to clear up. According to Collier its provisions were spoliatory and representative of yet one more stage in the federal government's attempt to destroy the pueblos and force the Indians into the mainstream of American economic life. The establishment view of the Indians at this time can be suggested by the way they were referred to in the Supreme Court's 1913 reversal of its 1876 decision: 'Though they are sedentary and disposed to peace, they adhere to primitive modes of life, influenced by superstition and fetishism and governed by crude customs. They are essentially a simple, uninformed, and inferior people.'[46] Collier believed, as did Lawrence in his very different way, that on the contrary the Indian way of life, communal and unmechanised, held a clue to the salvation of 'Anglo' civilisation. His warnings stimulated Mabel into taking a leading role in the organisation of a nation-wide and eventually successful campaign against the Bursum Bill, in the course of which she mobilised many of her former New York associates and encouraged everyone within her orbit (including Lawrence) to play a part. In the company of novelists such as Zane Grey and Edgar Lee Masters, as well as Harriet Monroe and another poet from Chicago, Carl Sandburg, Lawrence signed a 'Protest of Artists and Writers Against the Bursum Bill'; and he wrote the article which appeared in the *New York Times Magazine* on Christmas Eve under the title, 'Certain Americans and an Englishman'.

Admitting at the outset that he was having difficulty in finding his feet, Lawrence was neither as firm nor as committed in this article as Mabel must have hoped. He pointed out that, as far as he understood the situation, Taos Plaza itself was on Indian land and that to recognise this fact fully was no less impractical than the general dispossession of all long-term squatters. He referred disparagingly to the 'highbrow palefaces' who had stimulated the Indian into resistance and said he felt that, whatever happened, the pueblos were doomed. Yet he did denounce the Bursum provisions as bare-faced and began his conclusion by suggesting that 'in some curious way, the pueblos still lie here at the core of American life'. He then resorted to a favourite image he had used in 'America, Listen to Your Own'. Americans, he had said there, 'must pick up the life-thread where the mysterious Red race let it fall'.[47] 'Let us try to adjust ourselves again to the Indian outlook', he now wrote, 'to take up the old dark thread from their vision, and see again as they see, without forgetting we are ourselves.' The final phrases represent a new emphasis and there is something slightly plaintive about the way Lawrence next alludes to what had been part of his ideal vision of the future of America before he went there, 'Before the pueblos disappear, let there be just one moment of reconciliation between the white spirit and the dark.' 'And then, again', he concludes, 'what business is it of mine, foreigner and newcomer?'[48]

III   Cooper, Indians and Wilful Women

As Lawrence acknowledges in his article on the Apaches, most of his ideas about Indians were derived from James Fenimore Cooper. The degree of his admiration for this writer had been remarkable. Turgenev, Tolstoy, Dostoyevsky, Maupassant and Flaubert were all 'so very *obvious* and coarse, besides the lovely, mature and sensitive art of Fenimore Cooper or Hardy' he had told Catherine Carswell in November 1916 (iii. 41). In the first version of his essay on 'Fenimore Cooper's Leatherstocking novels', published in the *English Review* in March 1919, he had called *Deerslayer* 'one of the most beautiful and the most perfect books in the world: flawless as a jewel and of gem-like concentration'. 'Leatherstocking' is one of the names given to the white frontiersman Natty Bumppo and the five novels in the series trace his history from his old age in *The Pioneers* back to his youth in *Deerslayer*; but for Lawrence, 'This is biography in futurity, record of the race-individual as he moves from the present old age of the race into re-birth and the new youth which lies ahead.'[49] He saw this re-birth as largely dependent on the relationship between Natty and the Indian Chingachgook: an ideal as powerfully operative in his mind as the bond between David and Jonathan. The Leather-stocking novels represented, he felt, a 'myth of atonement' for white expropria-tion of the Indians' land and a remedy for the situation whereby the souls of dead Indians lived 'unappeased and inwardly destructive in the American'.[50] At the end of *The Last of the Mohicans* Natty and Chingachgook are:

isolated, final instances of their race: two strangers, from opposite ends of the earth, meeting now, beholding each other, and balanced in unspeakable conjunction – a love so profound, or so abstract, that it is unexpressed; it has no word or gesture of intercommu-nication. It is communicated by pure presence alone, without contact of word or touch. This perfect relationship, this last abstract love, exists between the two isolated instances of opposite race.

And, this is the inception of a new race.[51]

The Leatherstocking essay was the second of two pieces on Cooper which Lawrence contributed to the *English Review* (the first dealt with what he called the 'Anglo-American' novels).[52] Both are full of acute observations about the psychological sub-structure of Cooper's work but are perhaps inevitably inclined to take the authenticity of his depictions of American life, and of frontier life especially, too much on trust. After Lawrence had been living in Taos for a couple of months, he was ready to blame Cooper for having given him ideas about

America which were false. 'This popular wish-fulfillment stuff', he wrote, 'makes it so hard for the real thing to come through, later.'[53] The manner Lawrence decided to adopt for all of the revised essays was short, sharp and slangy, more adapted, he felt, to the American public and more suited to the fast pace of American life. That alteration made it easy to substitute for the lyrical enthusiasm of the original Cooper essays a more sceptical and occasionally mocking approach. Conveniently typical of the changes he made is his treatment of a declaration by Cooper's wife that it was only natural her husband 'should dwell on the better traits of the picture rather than on the coarser and more revolting, though more common points' of Indians. In the first version of the Leatherstocking essay Lawrence took these remarks as indicative of Mrs Cooper's impatience with her husband's 'Indian passion'.[54] In the Taos revisions they became a sign that Cooper's wife 'had to look things in the face for him . . . He himself did so love seeing pretty-pretty, with the thrill of a red scalp now and then.' 'But men see what they want to see', Lawrence went on, 'especially if they look from a long distance, across the ocean, for example'.[55] He is referring here to the seven years Cooper spent in Europe after the publication of *The Last of the Mohicans* in 1826, but the phrases might just as easily have applied to himself. Being in America required difficult adjustments to previous notions and the often regretful admission that former enthusiasms were not entirely justified. Thus from being 'flawless as a jewel', *Deerslayer* becomes 'a gem of a book. Or a bit of perfect paste. And myself, I like a bit of perfect paste in a perfect setting, so long as I am not fooled by pretence of reality.'[56]

Not very reasonably, Lawrence feels that even his former admiration for Cooper's descriptions of natural scenery has to be modified now that he is actually living in America. In the first version of the Leatherstocking essay he had said that, 'No man could sufficiently praise the beauty and glamorous magnificence of Cooper's presentation of the aboriginal American landscape, the New World', and described Lake Glimmerglass, the setting for *Deerslayer*, as 'perhaps, lovelier than any place created in language: lovelier than Hardy or Turgenev, lovelier than the lands in ancient poetry or in Irish verse'.[57] But proof that he was not able to adapt to the variety and splendour of New Mexican scenery as quickly as he implied when, towards the end of his life, he wrote the article on New Mexico, can be found in the revised version of the Leatherstocking essay. Cooper too often, he reiterates there, looked back to his homeland across the Atlantic but, 'When you are actually *in* America, America hurts, because it has a powerful disintegrative influence upon the white psyche. It is full of grinning, unappeased aboriginal demons, too, ghosts, and it persecutes the white men, like some Eumenides, until the white men give up their absolute whiteness'. The opening scenes of *The Pioneers* still contain 'some of the loveliest, most glamorous pictures in all literature' but, 'Alas, without the cruel iron of reality.'[58]

Now that he could observe them at first hand, relations with the Indians seemed to Lawrence a far more complicated affair than his reading of Cooper had led him to believe. He had always assumed that the friendship between Natty and Chingachgook was based on a recognition of difference, otherness; but the need for that recognition acquires new emphasis in his revisions as he complains about whites who 'intellectualize the Red Man and laud him to the skies', or protests, 'In the white man – rather high-brow – who "loves" the Indian, one feels the white man betraying his own race. There is something, unproud, underhand in it. Renegade.' He had also always recognised that the structure of the Leather-stocking novels was mythic but now it is a question of 'a wish-fulfilment vision, a kind of yearning myth': Natty and Chingachgook's blood-brotherhood is at present 'sheer myth . . . wish-fulfilment, an evasion of actuality'. Yet this still leaves open the prospect of regarding 'a stark, stripped human relationship of two men, deeper than the deeps of sex' as a possibility for the future which would provide the 'nucleus of a new society, the clue to the new world-epoch'.[59] Lawrence, that is, retains his idealism but in a much more attenuated, less confident form. In the original Leatherstocking essay he had explained why he felt two *men* could be said to be at the inception of a new race,[60] but Mabel might and did in fact sometimes claim that her association with Tony Luhan provided a more practical example to follow. In his revisions, Lawrence repeats his previous suggestion that, by having both General Munro's daughter Cora and her Indian admirer Uncas die in the finale of *The Last of the Mohicans*, Cooper was indicating his disapproval of mixed marriages; but in his new version of the essay on the Anglo-American novels he now gives his own view, 'I doubt if there is possible any real reconciliation, in the flesh, between the white and the red', and a few paragraphs later adds, in illustration:

Supposing an Indian loves a white woman, and lives with her. He will probably be very proud of it, for he will be a big man among his own people, especially if the white mistress has money. He will never get over the feeling of pride at dining in a white dining-room and smoking in a white drawing-room. But at the same time he will subtly jeer at his white mistress, try to destroy her white pride. He will submit to her, if he is forced to, with a kind of false, unwilling childishness, and even love her with the same childlike gentleness, sometimes beautiful. But at the bottom of his heart he is gibing, gibing, gibing at her. Not only is it the sex resistance, but the race resistance as well.

There seems to be no reconciliation in the flesh.[61]

These observations were not of course in the previous essay. They reflect in part Lawrence's own tendency to feel he was being jeered at whenever he began to settle in a new place,[62] but it is hard not to regard them as above all a direct commentary on the relationship between Mabel and Tony Luhan.

These revisions to the Cooper essays were made in November when relations between Mabel and the Lawrences had reached a low ebb. For a few weeks after the Apache trip things went well enough. There was an exciting new environment to come to terms with, the challenge for Lawrence of continuing to learn Spanish (he had begun in Australia and continued on the boat),[63] and above all what was probably his first experience of riding. As the conclusion of *The Rainbow* indicates, horses had already played a prominent part in Lawrence's imaginative life, but it is doubtful whether he had ever before *been* on one. Thanks to Mabel, and often in her company, he and Frieda would soon be exploring the surrounding countryside on horseback every afternoon. Together they would make periodic visits to the Manby bath-house (so called after the Taos resident who had built it over one of the hot springs in the gorge of the Rio Grande), ride over to the pueblo, or pick their way through the foothills of the nearby Sangre de Cristo mountains.

The day after his arrival in Taos Lawrence heard from Seltzer that the case against *Women in Love* had been dismissed by a New York judge. Even if he did not realise them immediately, it would not take long for the financial implications to become apparent. (The 3,000 copies of an ordinary trade edition published in October had, Lawrence was able to report on the 19th of that same month, sold out – iv. 326.[64]) Now he was actually in America and able to examine his financial state with more confidence and accuracy he felt that, even without the likely future proceeds from *Women in Love*, he was reasonably well off, and on 18 September he wrote to Koteliansky urging him to say if he was hard up: 'I have taken money from you and not felt in any way constrained, so surely you can do the same with me.' He had decided, he went on, to pay back at last 'the little bit that Eddie Marsh and Ottoline once gave me: so long ago' (iv. 297). A generous patron of many other promising young artists and writers, Marsh was someone with whom Lawrence had never seriously quarrelled (as he had with Ottoline Morrell), and when, on the same day that he wrote to Kot, he sent him a friendly note enclosing 'that £20 which you so nobly lent me long ago', he also acknowl-edged having received from Marsh two comparatively recent letters (iv. 297).[65] On 22 September he wrote to Lady Ottoline, from whom he is unlikely to have received any correspondence, the single sentence, 'Will you please let me pay back the £15 which you so kindly lent me during the hard days?' (iv. 305). It was the final settling of accounts with one great *Kulturträger* at the very moment when he had been drawn into the ambit of another; and when – it has to be said – he was also benefiting from her largesse. Lawrence was conscious of the dangers from the beginning, telling Brewster – on the same day that he returned the £15 to Lady Ottoline – that Mabel was 'generous and nice – but still, I don't feel free. I can't breathe my own air and go my own little way'; and writing to Mountsier, 'It is very nice here: we learn to ride horseback, Frieda and I. But I don't altogether like living under anybody's wing. Too smothering. And I don't want anybody to be *kind* to me' (iv. 305, 306). On 27 September he told Else Jaffe that 'Mabel Sterne is very nice to us – though I hate living on somebody else's property and accepting their kindnesses', and two days later he made clear in a letter to Mountsier that he had begun to take steps to ensure that his independence would not be too compromised: 'I am settling down a bit better here, and Mabel Sterne is learning to leave us alone, and *not* to be a padrona. I pay for everything I have, so don't feel indebted – though I must say she is naturally generous' (iv. 310, 315).

If one were able to calculate a realistic rent for the attractive house which Mabel claimed, and Lawrence certainly believed, had been built and furnished especially to receive him, and appropriate payments for the hire of horses, frequent motorised transport and all the other incidental advantages of living in what Lawrence came to regard as 'Mabeltown', it is unlikely that he could ever have had enough money in the bank to pay for 'everything' he would have received over an extended period. He was in a situation of inevitable financial dependence which was bound to become galling without great tact on the benefactor's side, as well as a good deal on his; but an enterprising vitality rather than tact was Mabel's forte. Once she had an aim in view she directed all her energies to achieving it and, as her previous history showed, was not above using her wealth to bring emotional pressure to bear on any individual who might benefit or had already benefited from it. After Maurice Sterne had left Taos he raised the possibility of a divorce but Mabel postponed that move until *she* was ready by reminding him of the $100 a month he received from her as an allowance.[66] Her background, temperament and past successes had accustomed her to having her own way and she was therefore ideally suited to personify for Lawrence what he felt was a distinctively American version of the 'will' he had found similarly alarming in Ottoline Morrell. (The episode in *Women in Love* where Hermione Roddice obliges Rupert Birkin to accept from her a Persian carpet is almost certainly relevant here.[67]) 'What you dislike in America', he told Brewster, 'seems to me really dislikeable: everybody seems to be trying to enforce his, or her, *will*, and trying to see how much the other person or persons will let themselves be overcome. Of course the *will* is benevolent, kind, and all that, but none the less it is other people's will being put on me like a pressure' (iv. 305). Less than a year after Lawrence's arrival in Taos, Mabel had humbly accepted his characterisation of her as the archetypal wilful woman of white America.[68]

Initially directed towards bringing Lawrence to America so that he could write about the Indians, Mabel's 'will' further complicated the situation when, almost immediately after his arrival, she set herself the additional aim of luring him away from Frieda. In *Lorenzo in Taos* she very frankly admits that this was her intention, justifying it on the grounds that she felt Frieda had become a clog to Lawrence and could no longer provide him with the stimulus he needed.[69] Mabel characterised her brief struggle with Frieda for possession of Lawrence as a battle between body and spirit. That she should cast herself in the *latter* role may seem bizarre given how notorious she had become for the number of her ex-husbands and lovers; yet she shared with Lawrence an interest in matters such as Theosophy, sympathetic magic or telepathic exchange that Frieda was altogether too *terre-à-terre* to take much notice of. Delighting in ideas, she found it difficult to rest easy without some ideal to pursue or some cause to which she could devote herself. By the time she met Lawrence, her life had suggested that she was more interested in the power and influence to be gained from sexual relationships – the way they allowed her to direct the energies of men – than in the sex itself. (In *Lorenzo in Taos* she lets slip that Lawrence was not physically attractive to her.[70]) She claimed that in a few rare moments of intimacy Lawrence had told her that Frieda had the soul of a German soldier, 'strong because it does *not* understand – indelicate and robust'; that he had complained bitterly of having to feel the hand of Frieda on him when he was sick, 'the heavy German hand of the flesh'; and that he had denounced her as 'inimical to the spirit'. 'You *need* something new and different', she had told him. 'You have done her. She has mothered your books long enough. You need a new mother.'[71] More mothering was precisely what Lawrence usually felt he did not need, but Frieda was in any case by no means prepared to move over. 'I had always regarded Lawrence's genius as given to me', she wrote in her very short account of how she beat off Mabel's predatory incursions.[72]

According to both Mabel and Frieda, their short conflict was brought to a head by the novel which Lawrence began writing in collaboration with Mabel. This was to be an account of her life from the time she arrived in New Mexico and to explain, in its first part at least, how she came to abandon Maurice Sterne for Tony Luhan. Mabel describes the first extended discussion of this project with Lawrence as taking place on the flat sun-roof outside her bedroom. After his passing glance at her unmade bed had seemed to turn her whole room into a brothel, and when she herself was still dressed in 'a voluminous, soft, white cashmere thing like a burnous' ('I never dressed early in the morning but took a sun bath'), she reports Lawrence as saying nervously, 'I don't know how Frieda's going to feel about this'. Realising how different a proposition from Mollie Skinner Mabel Sterne was, Frieda in fact insisted that all future meetings between the collaborators should take place in the Lawrences' house. On the one occasion Mabel remembered going there, any vital communication between her and Lawrence was prevented by Frieda stamping round, 'sweeping noisily, and singing with a loud defiance'.[73] As Frieda wrote of the collaboration between Lawrence and Mabel in *"Not I, But the Wind . . . "*, 'I did not want this',[74] and whatever Frieda did not want had seriously reduced chances of taking place.

It is not clear precisely when the collaboration was abandoned. Mabel places

Frieda's opposition in September but a letter Lawrence wrote to Mountsier on 6 October suggests it must have declared itself later. 'Am doing a M. Sterne novel of *here*', he says, 'with her Indian: she makes me notes. Wonder how we shall get on with it. I don't let her see my stuff'. That Lawrence was thinking of pressing on with the novel in spite of his wife, but with 'notes' as a substitute for meetings, is made improbable by Frieda's own pencilled addition to this letter: 'you ought to come here – I *love* the land and like Mabel D . . . Lawr has actually begun a novel about here and Mabel D – It's *very* clever the beginning, it will be rather sardonic!' (iv. 319). It must therefore have been later in October, when other reasons for animosity were beginning to emerge, that Frieda decided that this new collaborative venture was not a good idea.

In an undated letter to Mabel in which Lawrence asks her for some 'notes', he says he wants to know how she felt when she met Maurice Sterne on Lamy Station or when she drove to Taos, what her first words with Luhan were and the details of the 'fight with Tony's wife'.[75] He warns that she needs to remember things she does not want to remember and suggests that he might incorporate into his text one of her own short stories and some of her poems so that her 'indubitable voice' could be heard sometimes. At the end of the letter he tells her, 'I have done your "train" episode and brought you to Lamy at 3 in the morning' (iv. 317–18). The seven surviving pages of the Mabel novel seem in fact to end with the heroine in the small town of Wagon Mound at 8 in the evening waiting for the 11 p.m. slow train to Lamy but, as the Cambridge edition made clear, a deleted final sentence does in fact bring Mabel to Lamy and makes it very doubtful whether any more of the novel was ever written. The opening describes her agony of impatience on the train from New York, the way she impulsively leaves it at a country station in order to hire a car which she hopes will get her to Lamy ahead of time, and how the failure of this expedient obliges her to fall back on the railway system. Sybil Mond is the name Lawrence gives to Mabel[76] and he describes her as 'a sturdy woman with a round face, like an obstinate girl of fourteen'. She seemed, 'so naive-looking, softly full and feminine. And curiously heart-broken at being alone, travelling alone . . . '; but, 'Mr Hercules had better think twice before he rushed to pick up this seductive serpent of loneliness that lay on the western trail. He had picked a snake up long ago, without hurting himself. But that was before Columbus discovered America.' It would seem that, well before the crisis in his relations with Mabel, Lawrence had understood how formidable she would be. What appears to have impressed him most was her power. Sybil, he writes, was at forty, 'heavy with energy like a small bison', someone in whom the 'old colonial vigour' had culminated. Yet the portrait is by no means unsympathetic and the description of her journey is lively enough to make his abandon of the narrative a matter for considerable regret.[77] As both Lawrence's agent and someone not fond of Mabel, Mountsier must have expressed interest in its progress. On 28 November, only a few days before he escaped from Mabel's influence, Lawrence told him, 'I think if I wrote the M[abel] S[terne] novel, and the Indian, it would be just *too* impossible. Might make me also *too* sick' (iv. 344). It would be a long time before he again attempted a 'portrait' of Mabel in the way Mrs Morel could be said to be a portrait of his mother or Harriett Somers of Frieda. Critics have frequently discovered connections between her and the protagonist in 'The Woman Who Rode Away', Mrs Witt in 'St. Mawr' or even Kate Leslie (who also has an Indian lover) in *The Plumed Serpent*; but the differences between these three figures and Sybil Mond are very great.[78]

In addition to this fragment of the Mabel novel, the three articles on or about Indians, and the major revision of *Studies* which was to preoccupy him from about the beginning of November, Lawrence revised *Kangaroo* during his first stay in Taos. This involved adding a last chapter but deciding to keep the long account of Somers's experience during the war ('The Nightmare') despite the feeling of Mountsier, and to some extent Frieda, that it didn't belong (iv. 318–19). He also wrote five poems. Four of these are responses to his new environment,[79] but the fifth – 'Spirits Summoned West' – was written after he had received news from England that Sallie Hopkin, one of his old friends from Eastwood, had died. Although she was almost twenty years his senior, there are passages in *Mr Noon* which might suggest that Lawrence had once felt something more than friendship for Sallie.[80] His reaction to the news of her death came first in a letter of condolence to her husband Willie Hopkin on 25 October which ends 'England seems full of graves to me' (iv. 327). 'Spirits Summoned West' begins with this same phrase and goes on in a way which shows that, even after so much varied experience and now that he was in such a stimulating fresh environment, the old problems were still not far below the surface (a truth also apparent in his record of Somers's dreams in *Kangaroo*). Sallie Hopkin, Lawrence implies, was one of those women who, just like his mother, loved him in the old way but whom he had to tell to die (he may be recalling here how he and his sister Ada had given Mrs Lawrence an overdose of her sleeping draught on the night before her death[81]). Now 'the divided yearning is over', and now that death has made these women 'husbandless indeed', he invites them all to travel westwards and lodge at last with him. But his invitation is especially addressed to his mother.

> Come back, then, mother, my love, whom I told to die.
> It was only I who saw the virgin you
> That had no home.
>
> The overlooked virgin
> My love . . .

73

Come, delicate, overlooked virgin, come back to me
And be still
Be glad.

I didn't tell you to die, for nothing.
I wanted the virgin you to be home at last
In my heart.[82]

There are unsettling signs in this poem of guilt, a jealousy some psychoanalysts would call 'oedipal', and a feeling that it is only in death certain kinds of mature, married women can be entirely his own. Although anyone who knew Lawrence's work well would not find 'Spirits Summoned West' especially unusual, that he should have been happy to publish such an uncomfortably intimate piece, not only in *Birds, Beasts and Flowers* but also in Murry's *Adelphi*,[83] can still seem surprising. When he was busy with *The Trespasser* in 1912, Lawrence had written to Edward Garnett,

I give myself away so much, and write what is my most palpitant, sensitive self, that I loathe the book, because it will betray me to a parcel of fools. Which is what any deeply personal or lyrical writer feels, I guess. I often think Stendhal must have writhed in torture every time he remembered *Le Rouge et le noir* was public property: and Jefferies at *The Story of my Heart*. (i. 353)

These feelings pre-date his encounter with Frieda and her insistence (more Otto Grossian than authentically Freudian) on the evils of repression;[84] but it is nevertheless remarkable how far he had come since he expressed them, and how willing he was to publish the most private material. His willingness may on occasions have been because he felt that what he said was unlikely to be properly understood. It is hard to make too much sense of 'Spirits Summoned West' without *some* biographical material (although the relevance of that material to elucidation does not mean that it has any necessary significance for the question of literary value).

The complications of Lawrence's attitudes to frankness, if not self-exposure, are apparent in another of his writings from this period, the review of a boldly avant-garde composition entitled *Fantazius Mallare* by a Chicago-based author Ben Hecht (destined later to achieve world-wide fame as a playwright and screen writer).[85] This had been sent to him by Spud Johnson who, while he was in Berkeley, had founded with fellow students an irreverent magazine entitled *Laughing Horse*.[86] The editors must have felt that one author with a reputation for being 'sex-obsessed' (a phrase used about Lawrence in the title to an American review of *Psychoanalysis and the Unconscious*[87]) would be an appropriate commentator on another. But the different tone Hecht chose to adopt in dealing with sexual matters in *Fantazius Mallare* is evident in its eponymous hero's characteristic reflections on love.

74

The egotist beautifying himself with love, finds himself removing his shoes, tearing off his underwear, fondling a warm thigh and steering his phallus toward its absurd destiny. The transvaluations – the ineffable and inarticulate mysteries he fancied himself embracing – turn out to be a woman with her legs wrapped around him. His desires for the infinite sate themselves in the feeble tickle of orgasm. Cerberus seduced from his Godhead by a dog biscuit![88]

With echoes of Hoffmann, Huysmans and Dada, the novel recounts the bizarre relations of a former painter with a gipsy girl and a paralytic Negro dwarf and is illustrated with Beardsley-inspired drawings in which the erect penis is much in evidence. Lawrence did not like it and clearly set out to show that there was more than one way of being outspoken.

Really, Fantazius Mallare might mutilate himself, like a devotee of one of the early Christian sects, and hang his penis on his nose-end and a testicle under each ear, and definitely testify that way that he'd got such appendages, it wouldn't affect me. The word penis or testicle or vagina doesn't shock me. Why should it? Surely I am enough a man to be able to think of my own organs with calm, even with indifference. It isn't the *names* of things that bother me; nor even ideas about them. I don't keep my passions, or reactions, or even sensations *in my head*. They stay down where they belong.[89]

His review takes the form of a letter to 'Chère Jeunesse' and goes on to denounce the masturbatory impetus of Hecht's book, urging young people to 'let all the pus of festering sex out of your heads, and try to act from the original centres'.[90] After it was written, he learned that Hecht and his illustrator had been arrested on obscenity charges (with the assistance of one of Chicago's best-known lawyers, Clarence Darrow, their troubles were to be short-lived).[91] Lack of familiarity with how such matters might resolve themselves in a country like America must have contributed to Lawrence's alarm and he sent a telegram to Roy Chanslor, one of Johnson's fellow editors still at Berkeley, asking him not to print the review. As he wrote to Johnson on 30 October, 'But heaven, they might put me in prison as they have done him. Martyred in such a cause' (iv. 331).

According to Bynner, Chanslor had not liked Lawrence's review and had no intention of publishing it until he received the telegram. When it did appear he replaced all the references to the sexual organs, to sexual acts and even such expressions as 'wetleg' with dashes enclosed in brackets. (The underlinings in the quotation above indicate the words which he omitted.) The effect was probably to make Lawrence's review seem even more outspoken than it was but, given that it denounced Hecht's book, Chanslor's claim that its publication led directly to his expulsion from Berkeley appears dubious.[92] More instrumental probably were his decision to use one of the illustrations from *Fantazius Mallare* as the frontispiece to that number of *Laughing Horse*, and the fact that it mainly consisted of attacks on his university's teaching staff and officials. Despite his fears, there were no obvious unfortunate consequences for Lawrence himself from this first, modified experiment in calling the sexual organs by their 'real' if – at this early stage in seeing what could, or ought to be, said in public – anatomical or learned names. Later he would come to feel that one needed to use a more popular language but, in defence of that use, he would insist on the importance of not being frightened by mere words, just as he does in his review of Hecht.

IV New Style *Studies*

It was on 22 September that Lawrence had asked Mountsier to send him a copy of *Studies* but not until 11 November that he told him to tell Seltzer he was 'doing *Studies in Classic American Literature* again' (iv. 307, 338). On the 18th of that month he reported that he had 're-written the first five' and on the 28th said he was sending Mountsier 'the first eight – out of twelve' (iv. 341, 343). If the twelve essays which make up the 1923 edition of *Studies* are compared with Lawrence's first attempts to write about 'Classic American Literature' in the final years of the war then 're-writing' is a far more appropriate term for the changes they underwent in New Mexico than 'revision'. The wholly altered manner he now adopted, the racy, colloquial aggression, is at least one consequence of arriving in America for the first time, but other results of his being there are not hard to detect. To a quite different, more jaundiced view of Cooper's Indians (for example), can be added changes in Lawrence's essay on Hawthorne's *Scarlet Letter* which give every indication of reflecting his difficulties with Mabel.

In so far as it illustrates best Lawrence's main contention about the great American writers – that they said one thing when meaning another – the *Scarlet Letter* essay is central to *Studies*. In support of his now, most well-known literary-critical principle – 'Never trust the artist. Trust the tale'[93] – he had rightly observed in his first version that, prone as Hawthorne is to explicit condemnation of his two sinners – Hester Prynne and Arthur Dimmesdale – in apparent endorsement of puritan public opinion, his novel is written in a way which evokes in the reader very considerable support as well as sympathy for Hester's pride and passionate nature. One of the features of its action is of course that it takes place after Arthur and Hester have slept together. In his original essay Lawrence had taken it for granted that Hester must have 'seduced' the saintly clergyman (an inference perhaps justified by her dominance over Arthur on the one occasion in chapter XVII when they are shown alone together), and gone on to point out the evils which result from women being obliged to take the lead in relationships: 'Woman cannot take the creative lead; she can only give the creative radiation.'[94] This familiar prejudice may easily obscure, in our time, the remarkable acuity of many of Lawrence's observations in this first essay on *The Scarlet Letter*. He notes, for example, how Hester's seduction of Arthur is a well-merited punishment for the way spiritual clergymen of his variety feed off their 'female devotees'. Arthur

is a pure lambent flame sucking up and consuming the very life-stuff of mankind. But particularly he sucks up the life-stuff of the woman who loves him . . . Unless the woman will be holy prostitute to him in sacred spiritual love, given to him as wax is given to the candle-flame, to be consumed into light, he is done, for his own substance is spent.

He draws out the paradox that although, in bringing down Arthur, 'Hester Prynne has struck the blow that will kill for ever the triumphant spiritual being in man', she can thereafter 'only exaggerate the old life of self-abnegation and spiritual purity. She becomes a sister of mercy'; and he then skilfully selects from the novel passages which show the hostility with which several beneficiaries of that mercy respond to its unconscious hypocrisy.[95]

Eight of the twelve, original versions of the *Studies* appeared in the *English Review* between November 1918 and June 1919. It would have been an exceptional reader of that journal who was not disconcerted by them, and there is no evidence that their extraordinary originality was properly recognised. The situation was complicated by the inclusion in them of views on the functioning of the body's nerve-centres even more disconcerting than their criticism of American writers. After Lawrence had detached these views from *Studies* and developed them into *Psychoanalysis and the Unconscious*, the response of American reviewers was distinctly unsympathetic. The aggressively flippant, take-it-or-leave-it tone of the 'preface' to *Fantasia of the Unconscious* – successor to *Psychoanalysis and the Unconscious* – is partly a consequence of a score of reviews of the first psychology book which had been sent to Lawrence by Seltzer in September 1921 (iv. 86). The similarities between the tone of this preface and indeed many other parts of *Fantasia* on the one hand, and the manner Lawrence adopted for the final version of *Studies* on the other, suggest that, in re-writing the latter, adaptation to what he thought of as American taste could not have been his *only* concern. A certain lurking despair over whether his audience would ever understand the kind of thing he wanted to say also helps to account for why the final versions of the *Studies* are so different from their predecessors, even though they are organised around the same quotations. It means, for example, that they are more allusive and therefore more difficult (why bother to spell things out to people who are not going to understand anyway?); and it probably helps to explain why in them Lawrence allows himself to be more self-indulgently autobiographical, or abandons himself so easily to whatever happens to be on his mind, even when the resulting revision makes a poor fit with the original material.

An example of this last process is his treatment of Hester as the seducing female in the version of the *Scarlet Letter* essay written in New Mexico. 'Oh, Hester', he now writes, 'you are a demon. A man *must* be pure, just that you can seduce him to a fall. Because the greatest thrill in life is to bring down the Sacred Saint with a flop into the mud', adding a little later, 'Look out, Mister, for the Female Devotee. Whatever you do, don't let her start tickling you.' This can still be seen as Lawrence's imaginative recreation of the undescribed episodes which precipitate the action in *The Scarlet Letter* (Hester Prynne is after all Arthur Dimmesdale's admiring parishioner); but moving on to repeat that in both Hawthorne and his characters, belief in spiritual ideals is accompanied by subtle hostility to them and that this is also true of 'modern Believers . . . modern Saviours', Lawrence writes: 'If you meet a Saviour, today, be sure he is trying to make an innermost fool of you. Especially if the saviour be an UNDER-STANDING WOMAN, offering her love.'[96] The theme of the understanding woman reappears two pages later after Lawrence has noted that Hester, with what Hawthorne describes as her 'voluptuous, oriental characteristic' (and he himself had called in his first version of the essay, 'the aboriginal American principle working in her, the Aztec principle'[97]), 'would not betray the ithyphallic gods to this white, leprous white society of "lovers"'. 'Neither will I, if I can help it', Lawrence goes on, 'These leprous-white seducing, spiritual women, who "understand" so much. One has been too often seduced, and "understood."' The look in the eyes of a gipsy woman he once saw is 'so different from the hateful white light of understanding which floats like scum in the eyes of white, oh, so white English and American women, with their understanding voices and their deep, sad words and their profound, *good* spirits. Pfui!'[98] Hester is linked to the female salvationists through her after-life in the novel as a Sister of Mercy, but it is not in *that* role she figures as a seductress. The introduction of 'seducing, *spiritual* women', therefore, is a distraction from the main issue and seems a direct consequence of Mabel's ambitions (Lawrence had felt threatened by 'understanding' women before but Mabel was a peculiarly formidable example).[99]

In re-writing his *Studies* Lawrence loses very little of their startling originality (in either of its versions the essay on Poe is a marvel of penetrating psychological as well as stylistic insight), and the new manner has advantages as well as drawbacks, leaving readers altogether freer and forcing them to be more active in interpreting thoughts that are now often merely suggested rather than earnestly expounded. Yet the extent to which new interests and concerns infiltrate the essays can sometimes threaten their coherence. The *Scarlet Letter* essay becomes somewhat confused in revision because Lawrence's preoccupation with Mabel makes some parts of his description of the kind of women to whom men can fall victim seem quite foreign to Hester. But more serious confusion derives from Lawrence having changed his opinion of some of his American writers by the time of his final versions. The most obvious example here is the essay on

Whitman which begins with a humorously effective attack on that poet's predilection for 'aching with amorous love', or 'merging', his offer to embrace the world which Lawrence has now decided is not only impractical but fundamentally false and egotistical. For example,

As soon as Walt *knew* a thing, he assumed a One Identity with it. If he knew that an Eskimo sat in a kyak, immediately there was Walt being little and yellow and greasy, sitting in a kyak.

Now will you tell me exactly what a kyak is?

Who is he that demands petty definition? Let him behold me *sitting in a kyak*.

I behold no such thing. I behold a rather fat old man full of a rather senile, self-conscious sensuosity.

DEMOCRACY. EN MASSE. ONE IDENTITY.

The universe is short, adds up to ONE.

ONE.

I.

Which is Walt.

His poems, *Democracy, En Masse, One Identity*, they are long sums in addition and multiplication, of which the answer is invariably MYSELF.[100]

The shrewdness here derives from disillusion with qualities once thought overwhelmingly attractive and the comic ease from having so recently exorcised the attraction in *Kangaroo*. Passages such as this work so convincingly, however, that they co-exist uneasily with the material Lawrence retains in the essay in support of his assertion that 'Whitman, the great poet, has meant so much to me.'[101]

The *Scarlet Letter* is the seventh of the twelve essays which make up *Studies* and Lawrence would therefore have been working on it between 18 and 28 November. By that time his relations with Mabel were very poor. They had had their ups and downs (during one of the former, Mabel had been persuaded by him to dress like Frieda and scrub her own floors[102]), but November was full of crises. On 20 September Lawrence had told E. M. Forster he would probably stay in Taos all winter and on 18 October that was still his intention (iv. 301, 324), but there are increasing signs of dissatisfaction throughout the month. Near the end of it, on 28 October, he told Mountsier, 'I don't think I can bear to be here very long: too much on Mabel Sterne's ground, she arranges one too much as if one were a retainer or protégé of hers: and thank you, I don't choose to be anybody's protégé . . . I won't be bullied, even by kindness. I won't have people exerting their wills over me.' 'In the end', he continued, 'it costs one more, also, paying them back for the things they have arranged for one, and which one didn't really want than it would if one had been left to make one's way all alone' (iv. 330).

A temporary easing of the strain was brought about by plans for making use of

Mabel's 'ranch'. This was a small house, about seventeen miles away, in a beautiful position among the mountains northeast of Taos. Lawrence was taken up to inspect it on 31 October and immediately wrote an enthusiastic letter to Bessie Freeman telling her to sell her house in California and come down to Taos to 'plan a new life'. His idea was that, while he and Frieda occupied the ranch, she could 'take up the next "homestead" lot to us, and have your house: and Mabel would take up another lot adjoining. And the rule would be, no *servants*: we'd all work our own work, no highbrows and weariness of stunts' (iv. 333–4). On the same day, he invited Mountsier to join his already imagined community: 'If we go, come there with us, and we'll make a life. It's a wonderful place, but difficult to get at. If we like it in the long run, MS. says she will let us have it' (iv. 334). For the next few days he and Frieda camped on the ranch and once back in Taos, in letters dated 6 November, Lawrence again declared to Seltzer and Mountsier his intention of living there (iv. 335–6).

It is not hard to imagine how Mabel must have felt about these developments. Here was Lawrence escaping her influence, proposing to establish a community rival to her own, and all by making use of her own property. It would have taken a different generosity from the kind she usually displayed for her to have been entirely happy at the prospect. 'I shall pay M[abel] S[terne] a rent for the ranch, not much' Lawrence wrote rather airily in his 6 November letter to Mountsier, but rent would have been poor compensation to Mabel for having provided the Lawrences with the means of evading her influence.[103] She was no more inclined than Lawrence himself to endure with patience any feeling that she was being used.

Frieda's bar on private interviews had driven Mabel into writing long and intimate letters to Lawrence (after he had admitted showing one of these to Frieda – 'Just to make everything square and open' – they became less intimate[104]). Very shortly after his return from camping near the ranch, and an even shorter time after his letters to Seltzer and Mountsier confirming his intention of going to live there, Lawrence must have received a letter from Mabel whose contents can be partly inferred from his stinging and obviously immediate reply. Quoting it in full will help to convey what must have been the flavour of their exchanges as the relationship deteriorated.

Dear Mabel,
    I too will put it in black and white.
1. I don't believe in the 'Knowing' woman you are.
2. I don't believe in the 'good' woman you are: that 'good' woman is bullying and Sadish. i.e. I utterly disbelieve in your 'heart'.
3. I don't believe in the lie of your 'submission' to Tony. As well say you 'submit' to Lorraine.

4. I believe that, at its best, the central relation between Frieda and me is the best thing in my life, and, as far as I go, the best thing in life.

5. You are *antagonistic* to the *living* relation of a man and his wife: because you only understand a sort of bullying: viz Tony, John Evans and the rest. – So, I count you antagonistic to the living relation between Frieda and me.

6. I have to pay for 'stamps and cigarettes' because you would find some way of insulting me on their score if I didn't.

7. It strikes me I have paid you pretty fully for all the 'emotion' you have expended, and more than paid for all the 'goodness'. I have still to pay for some of the bullying and mischief.

8. It disgusts me when you say it is chic for Lorraine to have one red eye.

9. I don't care a straw for your money and the things you 'give' – because after all it is on these you finally take your stand. It is on these you base your generosity. Bah, generosity!

10. I will *never* help you to think, and 'flow' as you want: neither do I want to prevent you from so doing. Bubble as the hell you like.

Which is my Bursum Bill, and Basta.

Basta!

D. H. Lawrence

Nina Witt having arrived a propos – you believe in 'conjunctions' – has read your letter and this.

DHL
(iv. 337)

The first three of Lawrence's points seem to quote back at Mabel terms she had used about herself, and in the next two he reaffirms his loyalty to Frieda against the threat which Mabel represented. His main concern, apart from the reference to Mabel's dog Lorraine in points 3 and 8, is then to throw off the feelings of dependence which had plagued him since his arrival in Taos (the cigarettes he mentions in point 6 would have been for Frieda rather than himself). In a final blast, he rules out the idea of any future collaboration and hints at the reluctance he had felt in being enrolled in Mabel's campaign against the Bursum Bill. It is an indication of the kind of open and volatile relation Lawrence had with Mabel that communications did not immediately and irrevocably terminate with this letter. The comparison between Luhan and Lorraine in point 3 must have been registered by her as peculiarly and designedly offensive.

Life went on in Mabeltown much as before but with an increased determination on Lawrence's part to get away. Not surprisingly, the ranch proposal was dropped. Writing to Mountsier on 11 November Lawrence explained that this was because the 'House can't be mended: and too much snow. We could have it in spring' (iv. 338). The dilapidated condition of the house is not to be doubted, but it is likely that it could have been mended and that the effort to do so was more than Mabel was willing to make or Lawrence ask for. His difficulty in looking for instant alternatives was that in Taos he was largely confined to Mabel's circle.

81

Two weeks after his arrival there, hedging his bets, he had written to Alice Corbin Henderson, 'Will you tell me, supposing we should ever want to move a little way off from Taos, if you think we could find a little furnished house in the Santa Fe neighbourhood, and what, approximately the rent would be' (iv. 308). But there were not many people in Taos itself, outside Mabel's sphere of influence, of whom he could make the same enquiry. This was not entirely her fault. When he had first responded to her invitation he had expressed anxiety that Taos might harbour 'a colony of rather dreadful sub-arty people' (iv. 111), and Mabel had reasonably taken this as an indication that he wanted to be kept away from the artists who had settled there. (There had been a 'Society of Artists' in Taos since 1915.[105]) It was not as if she herself could not provide a variety of company. Apart from Bessie Freeman with whom – as her inclusion in the ranch proposal shows – Lawrence had got on very well, there was Nina Witt, another friend of Mabel's from the early Buffalo days but one who, having followed her down to Taos, stayed there and married the local sheriff.[106] Lawrence's reference to Nina in the postscript of his angry letter is the sign of a friendship that was to strengthen over the next few months. Andrew Dasburg, a well-known painter and friend of Mabel from the New York days had also been attracted by her to the Taos area, bringing with him the actress Ida Rauh, once the wife of Max Eastman.[107] They were often to be met at or after dinner in the 'Big House' along with Collier and a stream of others, not all of whom were Bursum Bill activists. There can have been no shortage of varied and informed conversation as Mabel's guests were served excellent food in her dining room and could glance out to the magnificent sage-brush plain which still allows a breath-taking and totally unimpeded view of the mountains, or as they gathered in one of the sitting rooms to play charades.[108] To have the convenience of his own house, 'very smartly furnished with Indian village-made furniture and mexican and Navajo rugs, and old European pottery' (iv. 310); to dine at Mabel's whenever he felt like it; to meet interesting and often talented people who were either settled there because of her or merely passing through; to be able to ride round the area in the afternoons and take hot baths next to where the Rio Grande wound its way through its spectacular gorge – all this, and more, could have made Taos a happy valley for Lawrence, even at 7,000 feet above sea-level, had he not been of too restless, dominating and fiercely independent a spirit to endure the discomforts of patronage for long.

Mabel did not encourage contacts with the colony of artists in Taos but the Lawrences made enough of them to be invited to dinner one evening by Walter Ufer and his wife, both of whom were painters. It was there they first met two young and impecunious Danish artists, Knud Merrild and Kai Götzsche. 'The Danes', as they were often conveniently called, were also newcomers in Taos having left New York for New Mexico in their old Ford on 1 September.[109] They became friendly with the Lawrences, through whom they were invited to the dancing in the Studio, and were privy to several of Lawrence's outbursts against Mabel including, 'She wants to bully me into writing a book on her. Never, never, in my life shall I write that book.'[110] The four of them ate and went riding together and, according to Merrild, the Danes were with the Lawrences when they camped near Mabel's ranch and were therefore witness to Lawrence's fury after Mabel informed him that a cabin close by, which he had earmarked for them, had to be kept free in case her son should ever want to use it on a hunting trip. Merrild claimed that it was there and then Lawrence established that the Hawk family, who ran a genuine farm or ranch called Del Monte a short ride away, had a five-roomed log cabin they were willing to rent to the Lawrences, and that there was also a smaller cabin very near which the Danes could use. Gótzsche and Merrild had vague plans to move on from New Mexico to California but for the moment they were both broke and entirely free. Since they liked Lawrence they were willing to accept his suggestion that he should pay the rent for all four.[111] From being the recipient of favours Lawrence was now about to dispense one although, as he soon discovered or as he almost certainly anticipated, conditions were so harsh in the mountains that he and Frieda could not have lived there in winter without the help of the Danes.

It is not possible to say when precisely in November final decisions were made but around the 20th Lawrence wrote a note to Mabel which ends, 'We'd better not come tonight to supper – give ourselves time to cool down' and then included the postscript, 'Mrs Hawke offered us their cabin for the winter. Perhaps we'd better accept that and simplify everything' (iv. 343). Since he had arrived in America, Lawrence had been encouraging both Mountsier and Seltzer to visit him. When he wrote to the latter on 28 November, two days before leaving Taos, he assured him, 'Of course there is no breach with Mabel Sterne – no doubt she will want us all to come and stay here a bit, when you come'; and the note he sent to Mabel on 1 December, thanking her for lending him the house, is very friendly (iv. 345–6). Yet the efforts to be magnanimous in victory cut no ice with his hostess who, as she explains in her memoir, was so upset at losing him that she deliberately disappeared for a while to Santa Fe to avoid having to look on helplessly as the Lawrences packed their bags.[112]

CHAPTER FOUR

◆

December 1922–March 1923

CHRISTMAS AT DEL MONTE

I Publishers and Agents

The Lawrences left Taos for their log cabin on the Hawks' ranch on 1 December 1922. They were driven north towards the mountains and then up an increasingly narrow and dangerously rutted track by Götzsche in the Danes' Ford, Merrild having temporarily to stay behind while he recovered from the effects of an abscess in his mouth.[1] Towards the end of the journey the car stalled and they had to be towed the remaining distance by horses (iv. 347). The first few days were spent in making essential repairs: the Danes' cabin – one main room with a kitchen and store room – had to be fumigated before it became habitable, and there was much 'roofing, carpentering, plastering, glazing, paperhanging, white-washing etc.'[2] Shortly after his arrival Lawrence told Mabel that 'Life has just been a business of chopping wood, fixing doors, putting up shelves, eating and sleeping, since we are here' (iv. 358).

He described their own cabin as being in 'The last foothills of the Rocky Mts. – forests and snow mountains behind – and below, the desert, with other mountains very far off, west' (iv. 349). The site was beautiful but living conditions were rough and primitive. It began snowing the day after his arrival (iv. 348), and there cannot have been many times after that when snow was not on the ground. Although the days were often warm and sunny, the temperature could drop to '25° below freezing point at night' (iv. 384). Water had to be carried into the cabins from outside and there would be occasions when the four newcomers were reduced to melting snow for cooking and drinking, or rubbing themselves down with it in order to keep clean. The visits to the Manby hot springs which from Taos had been a pleasant diversion, now became a minor necessity. They would go not in the Danes' car, soon a synonym in Lawrence's vocabulary for unreliability, but on the four horses they almost immediately secured on semi-permanent hire from 'the Hawks', an expression which at this period chiefly meant William Hawk, the son of the family (his parents having temporarily migrated to warmer climes), his young wife, Rachel, and the elder of William's two sisters, Elizabeth (iv. 343).

An immediate priority, apart from the repair of the cabins, was an adequate store of firewood. Lawrence's early letters from Del Monte seem unduly preoccupied with satisfying this need until one learns (from Merrild) that the balsam pine he and the Danes felled and then cut up into logs was eight to ten feet in circumference and 'perhaps seventy-five to eighty feet high'.[3] It is obvious that he could not have accomplished this feat on his own, and that in general, for the heavier labour that 'living rough' entailed, the presence of two fit companions – Merrild had qualified for the Danish Olympic swimming team in 1920 – was a practical necessity.[4] Obvious too is that Lawrence very much enjoyed all the bustle and hard physical exertion of settling in. When he was proposing to Bessie Freeman a community based around Mabel's ranch, he spoke of making everything 'real' and complained that life under Mabel's wing was too 'unreal' for him (iv. 334). Having to protect himself more actively against the elements gave him a stronger impression of 'reality'.[5] Wordsworth, in his notes to the 'Immortality Ode', talks of how, when he was a boy, he needed to grasp a gate in order to save himself from the 'abyss of idealism'. Lawrence was a similarly imaginative individual, similarly fearful of his own solipsism, and in need of frequent confirmation that the external world was really there. With pack rats to contend with and coyotes that howled around the cabins at night (iv. 360, 362), conditions at Del Monte during the winter of 1922–3 certainly gave him that.[6]

Battling against these conditions – establishing a minimum degree of comfort in a hostile environment – was made more satisfying for Lawrence by the company of his own sex. Ever since his days of hay-making with the male members of the Chambers family, he had entertained a special fondness for working together with other men in some collective physical labour. He had especially rediscovered its satisfactions in Cornwall when he had worked on the farm with the Hockings.[7] In both these earlier experiences there was a powerful erotic component, but there are no signs of this in his relations with the Danes: no indication, for example, that he strongly preferred one to the other. They were simply fellow labourers in a common task with whom he could share the camaraderie members of a successful football team enjoy (in his schooldays he had been incompetent at all the traditional sports), alleviate the necessary solitude of a writer's life, and perhaps lessen the feeling that, in the phrase Mabel claims Lawrence had used to her, he was a failure in the world of men.

Lawrence's move to Del Monte made the arrangements for the impending visits of his publisher and literary agent, already complicated by their strong dislike of each other, more difficult. It was not now so easy to call on Mabel for help with transport and accommodation. When Seltzer announced that he would be leaving New York on 22 December, accompanied by his wife, Lawrence suggested that they should all meet in Taos, attend the dance always held in the pueblo on Christmas Day and then perhaps stay a couple of days with Mabel. She (he had again assured Seltzer on 3 December) remained 'quite friendly. She was always nice – only somewhat *blind* to anything except her own way' (iv. 348).

Around 10 December, therefore, he wrote to Mabel suggesting this arrangement (iv. 358). She replied that because her houses would be full at Christmas, partly because of the marriage between her son and the daughter of Alice Corbin Henderson on the 20th, it would not be possible for her to put up the Lawrences and Seltzers, but that she had arranged for her friend Elizabeth Harwood to do so instead. The exchange was courteous but behind it a good deal of anger was simmering. Mabel admits in her memoir that she refused his request out of pique and because she felt she was being used.[8] Lawrence himself, after initially agreeing to stay with Elizabeth Harwood, decided to remain on his mountain and on 19 December wrote to Mabel:

I have decided not to come to Taos at all for Christmas. Mountsier remains indefinite, and the Seltzers are no more definite than they were. So I'll have them brought straight out here when they do come: and I must be here to receive them.

No, I don't feel convivial.

Hope you'll have a good time with your festivities. (iv. 363)

Between this note and a previous, mild reply to Mabel's explanations of why she could not accommodate him (iv. 359), there is a distinct change of tone. One way or another it had been brought home to him that she had not remained friendly after all and he was not someone who could easily ignore the hostility of others. At times during his stay in Del Monte his rage against Mabel would reach dizzy heights. Merrild remembered him saying with great earnestness how he felt he could enjoy killing someone and that some killings were necessary for the world at large. When asked who would be his first victim Lawrence had replied that he would kill Mabel – cut her throat.[9] Feelings of this intensity are unlikely to have been provoked merely by her refusal to put him up, and were more probably the consequence of rumours about the Lawrences which, Mabel admits, she and her son began spreading in Taos once they had left.[10] The gist which seemed to have reached Lawrence's own ears was that they were spongers whom she had been forced to turn out.

Refusing to go to Taos to pick up the Seltzers meant that Lawrence would miss seeing the Christmas dance in the pueblo. The Danes thought that a pity but after failing to persuade him to accompany them, decided to ride off alone. When they had finished seeing some of their artist friends in Taos however and then went on to watch the dance, they discovered that both the Lawrences were there in the pueblo before them. They had been brought down from Del Monte by Nina Witt. It was with the Witts that the Lawrences and Seltzers stayed one of the nights they had imagined they would spend at Mabel's, and on at least two further occasions their house would become a useful Taos base for Lawrence and Frieda.[11] It was to the Witts and not to her, Mabel noted with bitterness, that Lawrence sent his postcards after he left Taos for Mexico in March 1923 (iv. 370,

410).[12] Mabel had grown up with Nina Wilcox, as she was known in her Buffalo days, and describes in the first volume of her *Intimate Memories* how their two destinies had been 'linked together from the earliest days'. To find someone she had known so long siding with the Lawrences against her must have been galling but she herself might have provided part of the explanation when, describing her childhood in Buffalo, she wrote, 'I liked playing with Nina because I could make her do just as I liked.'[13]

The Seltzers arrived on Christmas Day and, to judge by Adele Seltzer's account immediately on her return to New York, their short visit was a great success. In two letters to a woman friend she gives an excited description of fetching water from the water-hole at 'a distance equal to three city-blocks', chopping wood for the three fires that were kept burning in the Lawrences' cabin and riding over the countryside with Lawrence in the afternoons. 'As for the bath question', she wrote, 'one *can* keep clean with an all-over wash, can't one?'[14] There were animated discussions in the evenings with the Danes, the only other company. Much later, Seltzer was to write to Merrild recalling their New Year's Eve in the Lawrences' cabin and the 'haunting beauty' with which Lawrence sang 'Good King Quentin' in his 'small but sweet voice'.[15] Late on New Year's Day Mountsier arrived and on 2 January Adele Seltzer left for home while her husband went off to California in an attempt to sell the film rights for *Women in Love*.[16]

The visit of Mountsier was much less successful, although, given that on his last appearance he had provoked a 'strong distaste for Yankees' (iv. 67),[17] it began promisingly enough ('Personally he is being very nice,' Lawrence wrote to Seltzer on 4 January – iv. 367). It had been arranged that he should stay in the Hawks' ranch house, take breakfast with the Danes and his other meals with the Lawrences. Quite early on he seems to have blotted his copybook by complaining about the quality of the breakfast the Danes served,[18] and there is a general sense of his failing to fit in with the rhythm of life they and the Lawrences were establishing. He went riding with Rachel Hawk but at some point had a bad fall which left the Hawks with one horse less, himself with a broken wrist and Lawrence with confirmation for his suspicion that Mountsier was accident-prone.[19] ('We were so sorry about the tonsils', he had written on 28 November, 'But you are a terror. What do you imagine you will have next?' – iv. 344.) Yet Mountsier's most serious failing was probably to overstay his welcome. With no pressing obligations back east and a vague intention of radically altering his way of life,[20] it was not until 28 January that, on Lawrence's suggestion, he moved down to Taos, staying then with the painter Victor Higgins.[21] A week later, with very strong prompting from Seltzer, Lawrence wrote to Mountsier and told him that he no longer wanted him to act as his literary agent (iv. 376).

The degree of hostility between Seltzer and Mountsier was such that it had become inevitable Lawrence should have to dispense with one or the other. In the last months of 1922 it was Mountsier who was the aggressor, having on several occasions to be calmed down by Lawrence. He was prejudiced against Jews, even by Lawrence's own far from rigorous standards on that matter; but there was more to his dislike than anti-semitism.[22] He had been annoyed at what he felt had been Seltzer's failure to promote adequately his own book on Europe's post-war debt to America,[23] and had come to consider him an incompetent, small-time businessman who served Lawrence's interests poorly. In the months before Christmas, in letters whose tone is aggressive and threatening, he concentrated on two main complaints: that Lawrence's royalty should always begin at 15% rather than 10%, and that the copyright for each work should be in Lawrence's name from the date of publication, and not transferred from Seltzer to him later. He was particularly irritated by Seltzer's delay in transferring the copyright of previous publications to Lawrence, conscious – as no doubt Seltzer himself was – that in the meantime they could not be offered to another publisher.[24] In the long letter he wrote to Seltzer from Del Monte as late as 19 January, he reiterated these complaints, enclosed proposed contracts for Lawrence's imminent publications which would obviate them in the future, and pointed out that now Lawrence was becoming well known there were plenty of other people around who would publish him on more favourable terms. It must have been after he had received this missive that Seltzer told Lawrence – not for the first time – how Mountsier was a man with whom it was impossible to do business, and Lawrence made the decision, now that he was actually in America, to look after his literary affairs himself (iv. 376).

And yet the letter which Mountsier sent to Seltzer from Del Monte on the 19th must certainly have been written with Lawrence's knowledge and tacit approval,[25] and its author could reasonably have protested that all it aimed at was conscientious protection of his client's interests. The reasons why Lawrence allowed him to write it and then, pressed by Seltzer, withdrew his support are varied. The longer Mountsier stayed at Del Monte the more irksome his company became, and he had not Seltzer's advantage of a lively wife – 'A-day-la' rather than Adèle – who had been brought up in a German-speaking household and got on very well with Frieda.[26] If it was true that Lawrence was now sufficiently well known to be courted by bigger and more efficient publishers that was largely because, he must have reasoned, Seltzer had triumphantly defended *Women in Love* against prosecution; and he would by now have known that it was after all Seltzer, not Mountsier, who had secured the $1,000 from *Hearst's*. On a quite different level of explanation, there was also the minor matter of $300. Four days after Mountsier had left Del Monte, Lawrence explained in a letter to Seltzer that, although he had reassumed sole control of his bank account, 'I haven't yet broken with [Mountsier] as my agent, because I feel he tried. But I think the break has got to come. Voyons!' (iv. 374). The letter to Mountsier which announces the break was written only two days later and begins, 'Thank you for your letter, and statement. Does the railway fare from New York cost as much as $300? You remember you said you would let me pay the railway fare only' (iv. 375–6). When Lawrence had urged Mountsier to visit him in New Mexico he had said he would pay the travel costs ('You had better come and see me here, and pay the railway expenses from my account' – iv. 300), but he was obviously surprised to find them so high.

Over-riding reasons of this and other kinds however was the question which Lawrence himself defined as one of 'belief'. The short stay of the Seltzers allowed him to discover just how enthusiastic they were about his work and learn that Seltzer had said to his wife, only *half*-jokingly, that each letter from Lawrence was so precious she needed to wash her hands before reading it (iv. 396).[27] Adele's letters about the visit give some indication of what the attitude of herself and her husband must have been. 'Lawrence is a Titan, a wizard, one of those human marvels like Shakespeare or Goethe. He loses nothing by being seen at close range', she wrote in one; and in another,

Lawrence is a Titan, and I go about with an ever-present sense of wonder that we, Thomas and I, little, little Jews, should be the publishers of the great English giant of this age, publishers of him, not because with Jewish shrewdness we outwitted some other publisher and got Lawrence first, but because Lawrence's 'Women in Love' went begging for a publisher, and we were the only people who understood its greatness and had faith in him as a writer.[28]

These letters explain why, in one of his many references to Seltzer's height (he was only 5 feet tall) – as well as to his notion that there was a destructive analytic power characteristic of the Jewish mind – Lawrence should have referred to his publisher on 24 January 1923 as 'such a tiny little Jew: but nice, one of the *believing* sort' (iv. 372). By contrast, Mountsier must have figured as someone who had lost his faith. When Lawrence had sent him both *Aaron's Rod* and *Kangaroo* he had been apprehensive that they would not be well received; and in fact he had become accustomed in the previous two years to hearing far more criticism than praise from this journalist who had been a graduate student at Columbia.[29] 'Mountsier didn't believe in me', he told Seltzer on 7 February, 'he was against me inwardly' (iv. 378). Forced to choose, any author would prefer the party warmly enthusiastic about his work to the one who was not, but in doing so Lawrence was aware that, as a person who – however tactlessly – had battled hard on his behalf, Mountsier might be entitled to feel hard done by, and he was anxious to make as fair a final financial settlement as possible.[30] He was almost certainly conscious also – because he had felt them himself – that by no means all Mountsier's objections to Seltzer's business efficiency were ill founded and that there might well come a day when his former agent would enjoy the satisfaction of an 'I told you so.' (The year which Seltzer began in California trying – unsuccessfully as it turned out – to sell *Women in Love* to Warner Bros. ended for him with a net overall loss of $7,000.)[31]

After abandoning the novel about Mabel, Lawrence began no new major work during his first stay in New Mexico. In the first days at Del Monte, he had finished working on the last of the *Studies* and sent them to Mountsier to be typed. When he got them back he must have gone through the complete typescript, making minor alterations, before having it posted off to Seltzer at the end of the third week in January 1923 (iv. 369). Part of the evidence for this assumption is the inclusion in the *Scarlet Letter* essay of a few minor details from *Americans*, by Stuart P. Sherman, a book on American literature which on 8 December he had told Mountsier he would be willing to review – he was going through proofs of his review at the end of February (iv. 398).[32] Although Sherman dealt with only three of the American writers discussed in the *Studies* – Franklin, Hawthorne and Whitman – his general comments on the past and future of American literature and his sub-Arnoldian manner meant that in Lawrence, the very recent author of a book which was on the same general subject but written in a manner not at all Arnoldian, he had the misfortune to meet the ideally qualified reviewer. One of Sherman's chapters is on Emerson who is a surprise absentee from *Studies* – given that they were once called 'The Transcendental Element in American Literature' (iii. 155) – and whom Lawrence admits in the review he once liked very much. Now he regards Emerson as being of 'museum-interest' only, especially as 'The great virtue of one age has the trick of smelling far worse than weeds in the next.' Sherman's intention, Lawrence explains, is to urge some middle way between the jeering, iconoclastic up-to-the-minute H. L. Mencken on the one hand, and on the other the snobbish worship of past values (especially when they happen to be eighteenth-century and *risqués*) of the Princeton luminary, Paul Elmer More. It is possible in Sherman's view to be both a worshipper at the shrine of American Democracy and an admirer of 'Great Men of the Great Past'. This taste for compromise, associated as it is in Sherman with the academic habit of looking conscientiously at both sides of every question and an inclination to mask his own views in irony, allows Lawrence to indulge in mildly sarcastic remarks about professors of literature.[33] (When he reviewed *Studies* for the *New York Evening Post Literary Review* on 20 October, Sherman was able to retaliate by referring to Lawrence's 'coal-heaver style . . . now regarded as rather out of date'.) Lawrence's review is sarcastic rather than ironic and makes no attempt to mediate between opposed positions, but it is a compellingly original and lucid piece which benefits greatly from his own recent immersion in Sherman's subject.

In January Lawrence went through what was probably the manuscript (rather than typescript) of his translation of the Verga stories before sending it to Seltzer (iv. 367),[34] and wrote an article on the novel, the origins of which were similarly in his pre-American days. In July 1922 he would have seen in his favourite Sydney *Bulletin* a lengthy account of a book by Meredith Starr entitled *The Future of the Novel*, and in the same month he had heard from Koteliansky about the interest Joyce's *Ulysses* was arousing in England.[35] After he had read and responded to *Ulysses*, Seltzer suggested that his brief, off-the-cuff remarks should appear in print but Lawrence demurred, 'Do you really want to publish my James Joyce remarks? No, I don't think it's quite fair to him' (iv. 355). As an alternative he incorporated some of the objections they represented in an essay which he also called 'The Future of the Novel' but which, after it had been sent off to Seltzer on 1 February, was finally published under the title 'Surgery for the Novel – Or a Bomb'.[36]

Lawrence criticises in this piece Joyce, Proust and Dorothy Richardson for being too 'mental', too concerned with the minutiae of their own psychology. The 'serious' novel, he suggests, is 'dying in a very long-drawn-out fourteen volume death-agony, and absorbedly, childishly interested in the phenomenon'.

"Did I feel a twinge in my little toe, or didn't I?" asks every character in Mr Joyce or Miss Richardson or Monsieur Proust. "Is the odour of my perspiration a blend of frankincense and orange pekoe and boot-blacking, or is it myrrh and bacon-fat and Shetland tweed?"[37]

The popular novelists of the day (with whom Lawrence associates Sinclair Lewis) do not please him any better and his survey of the contemporary novelistic scene leads him to define his own conception of the novel's role in society. If a bomb were put under the whole present scheme of things, he asks, what feelings would carry us through. 'What is the underlying impulse in us that will provide the motive-power for a new state of things, when this democratic-industrial-lovey-dovey-darling-take-me-to-mammy state of things is bust? *What next?* That's what interests me. *What now?* is no fun any more.' As examples of 'What next?' novels from the past which he admires, Lawrence cites the Gospels and Plato's *Dialogues*, and he goes on to complain that it was 'the greatest pity in the world, when philosophy and fiction got split'. He admits that in the past he also cared about whether or not he loved a particular girl, or what his mother felt about him, but now 'the purely emotional and self-analytical stunts are played out', he is 'blind to the whole blooming circus'.[38] Self-analysis, and the analysis of others to which it leads, had been a major strength of the great novels Lawrence had written just before and then during the war. It had still been very important in *Aaron's Rod* and *Kangaroo* but there the need to provide a new gospel for the one so comprehensively discredited during that war is increasingly evident. In the 'Future of the Novel' Lawrence made clear where he stood in relation to his modernist competitors while at the same time preparing the ground – without as yet fully realising it – for *The Plumed Serpent*.

It was also while he was at Del Monte that Lawrence wrote the four, final contributions to *Birds, Beasts and Flowers*. When he looked over this collection (most of which had of course been composed in Europe), he felt it would be the best volume of poetry he had published and spoke of it being 'remarkable', of having it very much 'at heart' (iv. 378, 379, 383). As *The Plumed Serpent* might be taken to show, Lawrence's judgement of his own work was not infallible but in this case it has been endorsed by almost everyone who has ever taken an interest in his poems. One of the final four ('The American Eagle') is political, but the other three deal with aspects of daily life in the Del Monte area. 'Bibbles' describes the antics of a pup from one of the litters of Mabel's dog Lorraine, given to Lawrence by Mabel and then brought up with him from Taos. This same dog features in 'The Blue Jay' where it seems disconcerted by the mocking sounds the jay appears to make as master, dog and bird are pictured moving round in the snow near the Lawrences' cabin. 'Mountain Lion' is the account of an unexpected meeting with two armed Mexicans who are returning home with the dead body of a beautiful mountain lion. Like so many others in *Birds, Beasts and Flowers*, these three poems demonstrate Lawrence's flair for describing episodes which reveal unostentatiously but to full advantage, his exceptional sensitivity to nature and the animal world. The common view that he succeeds so well with birds, beasts and flowers because he finds them a relief from human society gains some support in the last lines of 'Mountain Lion' when, after having discovered the lair from which the lion's 'bright striped frost-face will never watch any more', Lawrence reflects,

> And I think in this empty world there was room for me
> and a mountain lion.
> And I think in the world beyond, how easily we might
> spare a million or two of humans
> And never miss them.
> Yet what a gap in the world, the missing white frost-face
> of that slim yellow mountain lion![39]

There were times in Del Monte when the difficulties Lawrence had experienced, or continued to experience, with Mabel and Mountsier strengthened the misanthropy which he had begun to feel most acutely during the war.

II Bibbles

Merrild recalled being with Lawrence when he met the Mexicans with the dead mountain lion; but then nothing much can have happened in and around Del

Monte which he did not recall. 'Although we maintained separate households', he wrote, 'we spent much time together, seldom less than three to five hours daily and frequently all day from breakfast to bedtime.'[40] The isolation of the foursome was interrupted by only very occasional visits. When her annoyance with Lawrence had moderated, Mabel made a surprise visit to Del Monte but Lawrence and the Danes, hearing a car coming, went for a walk leaving Frieda to do the honours on her own. Bynner brought a party including both his mother and Johnson to lunch and alienated the self-consciously masculine Merrild by appearing in 'a lot of Indian silver jewelry – bracelets, rings, necklaces and what-not'. ('If he must wear all that silver,' Merrild complained, 'why doesn't he put a ring in his nose, too, to make it complete?')[41] An artist friend of the Danes from Taos, Meta Lehmann, who was busy arranging an exhibition of their work in Santa Fe, came up and scandalised Lawrence by spending the night with Merrild and Gótzsche in their small cabin.[42] For the most part however the Lawrences and the Danes saw no-one but each other. To lessen their sense of dependence Lawrence persuaded Seltzer to commission three book covers from Merrild and he asked Gótzsche to paint his portrait – gestures which must have brought them all closer together.[43]

At the start, they all took their evening meal in the Lawrences' cabin but later the Danes ate there only once or twice during the week, although they always came on Sundays. Merrild is one of the many to have sung the praises of Lawrence's cooking and he also makes clear that he baked all the bread. Frieda cooked when her husband's constant interfering allowed her to, but spent more of her time sewing, making curtains, bedsheets and pillows for the Danes and knitting both of them woollen caps.[44] She seems to have 'mothered' them, to the satisfaction of all three parties. The well-being of this community of four depended heavily on regular trips – sometimes by car – to the nearest villages, Valdez and San Cristobal, or more infrequently to Taos, as well as on the kindness and co-operation of the Hawks; but its relative self-sufficiency must nevertheless have been pleasing to Lawrence. This was a time when, according to Merrild, his denunciations of the 'modern world' were particularly ferocious and he refused to read any newspapers. But his misanthropy could not now extend, as it had done in Australia, to celebrations of knowing no-one and being alone with Frieda, and there is a convincing ring to Merrild's claim that Lawrence's social, as well as practical, need of the Danes was at least as strong as their need of him. 'I don't think the Lawrences passed the winter evenings with the same ease we did, or they shouldn't have asked us to "come up" as frequently as they did.'[45] If a cynic is a disappointed sentimentalist, a misanthropist might well be someone whose unusually strong social instincts have been frustrated. With the Danes, Lawrence could begin to feel that he had the beginnings of one of those ideal communities he dreamed about so often. When Seltzer went off to sell the film rights of *Women in Love* for what turned out to be the literally fabulous sum of $10,000 there were long discussions about how all four of them would spend the windfall;[46] and even after those hopes were disappointed, they made plans for travelling together once the winter was over. Mexico was easily the most-favoured destination although the influence of the Danes sometimes made Greenland another (iv. 361–2, 373).

Frieda was to tell Merrild that the closeness of their life together in Del Monte meant that he and Gótzsche knew the Lawrences 'more intimately than any human beings' before or after.[47] It is a great pity therefore that his record is partly ruined by the adoption of a disastrously mistaken method. Fearful that he would inadvertently put into Lawrence's mouth different words from the ones he had used in Del Monte, Merrild chose to represent him as continually spouting long passages from his published works. Thus his dubious claim that, during their first weeks in New Mexico, Frieda resented Lawrence getting to know one or two people from the artist colony in Taos is immediately followed – with no kind of introduction or explanation – by a long extract from *Kangaroo* in which Somers (whom Merrild calls Lawrence) explains to his wife why he feels the need of other company apart from her own.[48] This device becomes particularly absurd when the words Merrild decides to attribute to Lawrence are taken from a work which post-dates the episodes being described. There is in his memoir, for example, an interesting account of what he and Gótzsche felt was wrong with the copy of Piero di Cosimo's *Death of Procris* which Lawrence had made in earlier days, carried with him in his luggage, and had now hung on the cabin wall.[49] But it is interrupted by four paragraphs on copying paintings which are prefaced by 'And [he] further went on to say', but which are in fact taken from the essay 'Making Pictures' written by Lawrence in 1929.[50]

What remains of Merrild's account when a line is drawn through all the quoted extracts is nevertheless of great interest. He provides details of day-by-day living in Del Monte too gratuitously specific to be inauthentic and a predominantly favourable description of Lawrence clearly derived from close observation. Like others before him, Merrild testifies to Lawrence's vitality, charm and kindness but above all to his capacity to inspire interest. 'One was never bored in his society. On the contrary, no matter how often one saw him, it was always a revelation.' The disadvantages of Lawrence's enterprising, energetic nature he regarded as foibles. Gótzsche could play the violin and Merrild himself the flute but when they gave a classical recital Lawrence was bored ('he hated to be left out') and only happy when all four of them were singing and playing folk tunes together. (On 28 January Lawrence asked Adele Seltzer to send him his old favourite, the *Oxford English Song Book*, as well as a collection of German songs – iv. 373.) He was bossy and interfering in everything, not only incapable of allowing Frieda to cook on her own, but trying on one occasion to grab the paint brush from Merrild's hand in order to demonstrate how things should really be done. 'I had to engage in a bodily struggle to get my brush back', Merrild records and he says that he told Lawrence, 'If you *have* to paint pictures, paint your own.' It was good for the Danes that they were both convinced that this was one area where Lawrence was ignorant and his self-confidence unjustified.[51] Of the various summaries of Lawrence which Merrild attempted, the following is probably the one which accords best with all the incidental information he provides.

When I think of him now, he appears as a kind, serious man – a man who took life, or being, very seriously. Sometimes he would brood, but more often he was gay, even to playfulness. He could be bitter and sometimes exploded in a fury of hatred toward the humbug and rottenness of present-day civilization, its society and people. He hated bullying, people trying to alter one into an approximation of themselves. He had no social, moral or intellectual affectations and was free from any kind of snobbery. He had his fits once in a while, but on the whole, in everyday life he was easy going. A man of strong personality and character, almost overpowering and absolutely fearless.[52]

It says a great deal for both the Danes' tolerance and the attractiveness of Lawrence's personality whenever he was feeling reasonably contented with the world, that the occasional 'fits', casually referred to in Merrild's character sketch, did not make life in the small Del Monte cabins impossible. One of them concerned Frieda's smoking, or rather her fondness for allowing a lighted cigarette to dangle from the corner of her mouth. (As Mabel noted, and as several photographs confirm, Frieda had in any case the habit of putting her lower jaw 'a little sideways . . . rather like a gunman'.) Already in Taos there had been an episode when Frieda, with head cocked and one eye closed against the smoke from her cigarette, had begun criticising her husband: 'Take that dirty cigarette out of your mouth! And stop sticking out that fat belly of yours', Mabel remembered him shouting, whereupon Frieda retorted, in not quite the manner of Browning's 'Any Wife to Any Husband', 'You'd better stop that talk or I'll tell about *your* things.' Appalled at first, the company was later amazed to observe Lawrence and Frieda walking home from the 'Big House' arm in arm.[53] When he was with the Lawrences in Mexico, Bynner would be witness to a similar Lawrentian outburst against Frieda's smoking.[54] In Merrild's account, Lawrence's annoyance at Frieda's 'very nonchalant way with a cigarette' made him attempt to knock it out of her mouth. When he failed, 'he grabbed the almost full package of cigarettes lying on the table and in a hysterical rage crushed and ground the cigarettes in the palm of his hand and then threw the remains on the fire, scolding Frieda all the while and calling her all sorts of names.' When Frieda defiantly continued smoking, Lawrence hit out again but she evaded him and retreated to the kitchen.[55]

In the second of the 'fits' which Merrild witnessed the connection with Frieda is not so direct. The prelude to it can be found in 'Bibbles' where Lawrence complains that his dog bestows affection on all and sundry ('You love 'em all. / Believe in the One Identity, don't you / You little Walt-Whitmanesque bitch'), and describes how she deserts him after he has had occasion to punish her: 'Then when I dust you a bit with a juniper twig / You run straight away to live with somebody else.'[56] The *Letters* show that this refers to an occasion when William Hawk, whose family kept over a hundred head of cattle (iv. 362), killed a steer and 'Pips' (one of the Lawrences' alternative names for Bibbles) 'would not be kept away – became shamefully sick – got well spanked – and so has gone to live with the Danes'. 'There let her stay', Lawrence goes on to Seltzer on 4 January, 'She's got no loyalty. To me, loyalty is far before love. Love seems usually to be just a dirty excuse for disloyalties' (iv. 367–8), a sentiment which Frieda's first husband, Ernest Weekley, might well have echoed. After considerable effort on the part of the Danes, Lawrence and Bibbles were reconciled and the dog returned home. Shortly afterwards she went on heat. By that time the Danes were temporarily in charge of the Airedale of their friend Ufer, who had left Taos for a while, and there was another Airedale at the ranch. Bibbles was a small French bull terrier and, according to Merrild, Lawrence was disgusted at the possibility of a 'bull-dale' ('All afternoon he talked about ill-breeding, in Pips and in humans, intermixture of races'). He did his best to make her obedient and around the time he told Seltzer that his poem about Bibbles was finished (1 February) he must have felt that he had succeeded. Yet when he took the dog for a walk shortly after, ignoring the advice of the Danes to keep her on a leash, Bibbles ran off with the Airedale from the ranch in spite of all his efforts to restrain her. When she came home in the evening she was (as Merrild puts it) 'promptly spanked'.[57] The next morning therefore she ran off again and around noon the following day sought refuge with the Danes for the second time.

What happened next is vividly described by Merrild.

In the afternoon, Gótzsche and I were sitting in the big room, Gótzsche on a chair, I on the edge of the hearth of the fireplace. Gótzsche had Pips in his lap and was playing with her. Suddenly we heard rapid footsteps outside. The door was thrown open without a knock or warning and in burst Lawrence, his high rubber boots on, soiling our clean floor. He hesitated for a moment to get his direction and rushed over to Gótzsche's chair. He stopped abruptly, his face pale, eyes on stalks, shivering in rage. He pulled himself erect and burst out in a violent stream of curses, starting: 'So there you are you dirty, false little bitch.' Like lightning out of a clear sky, he struck the little dog with all his enraged force, so that it hurtled from Gótzsche's lap down on the floor where she landed hard and rolled under the table.[58]

Gótzsche jumped to his feet and for a moment appeared about to hit Lawrence. Lawrence himself, Merrild says, 'was completely out of his mind, wholly ruled by the dark mysterious forces, giving way to a concentrated fury towards Pips'. Ignoring Götzsche, he suddenly threw himself on the floor and tried to grab hold of Bibbles while the dog cowered under the furniture. Seeing an opening, it shot through the open door with an almost equally rapid Lawrence in pursuit. When Götzsche and Merrild moved to the door,

There was Lawrence running after the leaping, jumping dog, working the snow up in a haze. In its eagerness to get away the dog had not followed the hard-trodden path of the trail, but trying to make a short cut, jumped into the high soft snow. She was jumping desperately – like a wounded rabbit – to escape, but Lawrence's long legs were better fitted to wade through the snow and he soon overtook the shivering dog. Desperately he kicked her. Out of breath and near collapse with frenzy, he shrieked: 'Go home, you dirty ——.' In utter fear she yelled but did not move; she lay shivering with her paws in the air. Not obeying orders the devil kicked her again. No result, only a heartrending shriek and she rolled only as far as the power of the kick moved her in the snow. 'Don't you hear me, you ——,' shouted Lawrence. He bent down and grabbed the terrified dog, lifted her in both hands up over his head and hurled her with all his might as far as he could through the air, shouting: 'I will teach you.'

Struggling fiercely with legs in the air, Pips tried hard to land in a favourable position. When she fell she disappeared in a cloud of snow-dust, drowned. Motionless she stayed where she had fallen. Lawrence came up to her again. In a wild fury he yelled and kicked, grabbed and again threw her into the air, landing her some feet ahead, perhaps on a rock, perhaps in the soft snow.[59]

Recovering from their surprise, the Danes ran out and placed themselves between Lawrence and the dog. Merrild remembered Lawrence's eyes as 'the deepest, whitest boiling Inferno – a pair of burning piercing eyes of such strength that I saw nothing else, only sensed the bloodless, pale blue-pink lips in a wilderness of beard'. They seemed to belong to someone who was craving for a fight and daring Merrild to hit him: 'I admired his courage. He was panting for air. The break in his pursuit after the dog had brought him to exhaustion and the edge of a hectic collapse, and still his eyes dared me to strike.' Conscious, Merrild complacently although accurately notes, of his own 'trained superior athletic strength against [Lawrence's] inferior underdeveloped body' he refused the challenge and the two parties 'broke away silently and walked off in opposite directions'.[60]

Lawrence's extreme fondness for his dog is evident in several delicately descriptive passages of 'Bibbles'. At Christmas, Adele Seltzer had thought it 'wonderful to see how attached the two are – dog to man, man to dog. Lawrence sitting on a low stool to the side of the hearth fire with Pips on his knees.'[61] When he was about to leave Del Monte for Mexico in the middle of March he asked Bynner, 'I would like awfully to take the little black dog with us. Could we do it, do you think?'; and on the same day he told Seltzer that he could not bear to leave 'the Bimsey' (iv. 408–9). His rage at what he felt was Bibbles's betrayal must have been proportionate to his feeling for her; yet any complete explanation of the wild and violent irrationality of his behaviour must surely also take into account the way his failure to command her complete loyalty was a refraction of past difficulties in his relations with Frieda. It was true in addition, of course, that for Lawrence emotional repression was an unmitigated evil, and likely to make one ill.[62] When he shocked Merrild with his description of how he would like to murder Mabel he was following his belief that any *genuine* impulse (and the homicidal urge is sufficiently widespread for the problem of authenticity not to be relevant here) needed to find expression. Actually killing Mabel rather than merely talking about it would have created difficulties, but if Lawrence could come closer than most to an ideal of uninhibited living it was because he and Frieda had for years now lived in a way which allowed him to 'be himself'. It was a long time since he had been obliged to accept the social restraints of a schoolmaster's life, and he was not therefore likely to be inhibited in his fury against Bibbles by the presence of two friendly and financially dependent Danes. When Frieda reflected back on Lawrence's 'fits' she said little more than that he could be very hot tempered.[63] Certainly the Bibbles episode demonstrates that he was the possessor of what Dryden called a 'fiery soul'.

In Dryden's lines, Achitophel's fiery soul 'working out its way / Fretted the pigmy body to decay'. Lawrence's rages must have taken their physical toll but he was convinced that anger did more harm in than out, and he was in any case no pigmy. Merrild describes in considerable detail an occasion when he and Gótzsche went to the hot springs in Lawrence's company, but without Frieda. He takes the opportunity of indignantly denying that their friend ever gave either of them 'the slightest reason even for suspicion' that he was a homosexual, and describes how, as he sat in the hot spring water in the roughly constructed bathhouse with the Rio Grande rushing by outside, Lawrence looked without his clothes on: 'with his outstretched arms he reminded me instantly of a medieval woodcarving of Christ on the Cross'. This was because he was white-skinned and thin; and yet, Merrild goes on, 'I would not call him skinny, but rather say he was slim with thin legs like the Archbishop of Canterbury, or like most Englishmen, but otherwise a well-proportioned body, harmonious in its slimness. He did not seem frail, but gave you a feeling of sinewy strength rather than muscle strength, a tenacious strength of his own.'[64] (All this of course despite the fact that Lawrence's body was 'underdeveloped, athletically speaking'.) To Merrild at least, Lawrence was in no way a sick man at this time so that the common idea that his rages could be attributed to tuberculosis is not at all helpful as far as the Bibbles episode is concerned. The pain and discomfort of his illness as it developed, or broke out again, after the Del Monte period ought perhaps to have made Lawrence even more inclined than he had been before to lose his temper, but the evidence seems to be that his explosions of rage were in fact less frequent the sicker he became.[65] As Merrild's description of the attack on Bibbles illustrates, they demanded a degree of energy which in his final years he no longer had available.

The day after the Bibbles episode Lawrence brought round to the Danes some freshly baked bread and cake. He had done the same after his battle with Frieda over her smoking.[66] Although he never apologised, he knew how to re-establish a harmony which (the 'fits' excepted) remained remarkably constant between four people who for three and a half months lived so closely together. As a trip to Mexico became increasingly likely it was not lack of enthusiasm on either side which determined that the Danes would not be able to go. They had no money and their Santa Fe exhibition (from which they vainly hoped to make some) was due to finish well after the Lawrences had planned to leave Taos. Their unsold pictures were not in fact taken down until 28 April whereupon they headed west in the hope of finding some design work in Hollywood. The idea was that once they had saved a little they would rejoin the Lawrences in Mexico. This was always supposing that Lawrence liked it there. Having entered the country on a six-month tourist visa, he knew that if he did not soon leave, he would have to apply for an extension; but in March his plans were as usual fairly vague. He felt that, now he could no longer appeal to Mountsier, he would have finally to go to New York himself to sort out his literary affairs some time in the summer; and he had some thoughts (Frieda, who was becoming anxious to see her children, had more) about going on from there to England. After having had sent on to him by Seltzer Murry's favourable review of *Aaron's Rod*, in which he said that Lawrence's sun was now shining forth 'after the darkness of eclipse' (the darkness being *Women in Love*), and declared this new novel 'much more important than *Ulysses*',[67] he heard from Murry at the beginning of February that Katherine Mansfield had died and re-established a correspondence with him which would make going back to England more of a possibility in the coming months. For the moment, however, the priority was to decide on travelling companions for the trip to Mexico (he and Frieda never seemed to have contemplated going on their own). Mabel had made approaches (iv. 372) but the quarrel with her was too recent for Lawrence to accept them. When Bynner brought his party to lunch in early February, he and Johnson had expressed keen interest but Lawrence was at first mistrustful, not because they were a homosexual couple, but because, like Mabel and Mountsier, they were American. 'No Americans if possible. I feel sore with all Americans for the moment' (iv. 386). Yet, as it became clearer that the Danes would not be able to come, he changed his mind and wrote a friendly note to Johnson suggesting that he and Bynner should come along (iv. 388). The last letter Lawrence wrote from Del Monte is dated 14 March. He and Frieda stayed in Taos at the Witts' for three days and then set off for Mexico on the 19th via Santa Fe and Witter Bynner's house.

CHAPTER FIVE

◆

March–July 1923
OLD MEXICO

I The Monte Carlo

The 'Bynners', Lawrence explained to Adele Seltzer, in an uncharacteristically demeaning reference to Johnson's status (iv. 412), were not quite ready to leave on 20 March so he and Frieda pressed on, crossing the border at El Paso on the 21st and then spending two nights 'in an unkempt Pullman trailing through endless deserts'[1] before arriving in Mexico City. The Spartan conditions at Del Monte had made Frieda nostalgic for a little luxury and they therefore registered at the Hotel Regis, described in Philip Terry's standard *Guide*, which Lawrence had acquired from Seltzer (iv. 374), as 'the largest and most modern hotel in Mexico', and a place where guests would find all their 'discriminating friends'.[2] They did not like it there – after months of living wild and with clothes that would have seen better days they must have felt (or imagined) that polite disdain which the staff in grand hotels reserve for those instantly recognisable as not quite the thing. After only one night at the Regis they moved to a cheaper and altogether more modest establishment, a few streets off the Zócalo (the main cathedral square), which was run by Italians. The Monte Carlo, still flourishing, and still cheap, was the hotel Lawrence used on two subsequent visits to Mexico City. He found it 'second-class but kindly' and, after his recent experience of Prohibition in the States, enjoyed being able to speak Italian again with a flask of Chianti at his elbow (iv. 414).[3] In his *Journey with Genius*, Bynner provides a lively account of the informality of its atmosphere, with Italian women coming to table 'their long damp black hair drying loose on towels across their shoulders', and a visiting vaudeville troupe airing 'its trained apes and dogs and cockatoos under the washlines on the roof'. In the kitchen, Signora Forte 'superintended perfectionism of minestrone, ravioli, and spaghetti' which the guests then ate 'under blessings from a colored print of Garibaldi on the dining-room wall'.[4]

Bynner and Johnson had left Santa Fe three days after the Lawrences but their train to Mexico City was fourteen hours late, frustrating Lawrence's attempts to have them met at the station so that he could then explain that he and Frieda were no longer at the Regis. The consequence was that the two parties lost each other until, three days after their arrival, Bynner and Johnson had the good fortune to bump into Lawrence on the street. The two Americans immediately moved into a room next to the Lawrences' at the Monte Carlo. The four of them were to spend the following three months in close proximity. There were the inevitable frictions during this period but there is no sense that these ever had much to do with the nature of Bynner and Johnson's relationship. Whatever Lawrence may have felt about Cambridge homosexuals in 1915,[5] he accepted the bond between these new friends with relative calm, never complaining of it in his surviving letters to third parties. Even Frieda limited herself to saying that Johnson was 'nice but such a "jeune fille" ',[6] or protesting that 'Bynner is an old lady and Johnson a young one' (iv. 434). (What Bynner and Johnson had to say about the Lawrences behind *their* backs was less good-natured.) It became clear later that Lawrence did not fully approve of the decisions Bynner had made about his sexuality but he was tolerant of them, perhaps because he was now more a man of the world, or more understanding of the complexities of his own sexual nature. He was conscious that in any case he and Frieda were in a phase of their relationship when they urgently needed some company other than their own. The Danes had provided relief from the social isolation Frieda especially had begun to fear, and Bynner and Johnson would do the same. The advantage to Lawrence of both arrangements was that neither couple constituted a sexual threat. The relationship Frieda formed with the Danes seems to have been largely maternal, and there was no danger of her embarking on a casual affair with either Bynner or Johnson. This is important when one thinks how many communities of the kind Lawrence had often contemplated have been destroyed by sexual rivalries. But if Bynner was 'safe' he was also no misogynist and developed a warm admiration for Frieda, openly supporting her against what he often felt was her husband's scandalous ill-treatment. Over six feet tall and four years older than Lawrence, he had been educated at Harvard where one of his fellow undergraduates had been Wallace Stevens, and one of his teachers, George Santayana. With wholly reasonable pretensions to regard himself as a successful poet in 1923, Bynner did not lack the self-confidence to stand up to Lawrence on this matter of his treatment of Frieda, as on many others. Far more friction would come from the strength of his personality than from the fact that he was travelling with a 'secretary' more than twenty years his junior.[7]

The Lawrences had arrived in Mexico City on Friday 23 March 1923. Bynner and Johnson got there the following Monday night so that it was probably Thursday the 29th or Friday the 30th before they were all together in the Monte Carlo.[8] On the evening of 27 April Lawrence was to set off for Chapala, a small lakeside village thirty-five miles from Guadalajara, the 'Pearl of the west' (iv. 442). The intervening month was almost wholly taken up with sight-seeing. (The only writing Lawrence appears to have done was the short 'Au Revoir, U.S.A.' published in Johnson's *Laughing Horse* that December.) On Easter Sunday (1 April) the quartet went to their first bullfight. Lawrence was disgusted, and hurried away with Frieda early in the proceedings after having had to watch a bull disembowel a couple of horses. The experience provided him with a graphic opening for *The Plumed Serpent*, the first version of which ('Quetzalcoatl') he was to write in Chapala. In that version, as in the published novel, responses to the bullfight are attributed to the Irish heroine, Kate Burns (in *The Plumed Serpent* she becomes Kate Leslie), but were clearly also Lawrence's own. The cruelty of the event, especially with, as Lawrence records it, its strong sexual component, caused him to follow Frieda out of the stadium 'white with rage'. The disinclination of Bynner and Johnson to leave at this point he attributes in the novel to a characteristic American lust for new experience, more marked in the younger, colder man than in the elder.[9]

Two days later there was the trip to the famous pyramids at Teotihuacán, some twenty-eight miles outside Mexico City. This ancient site of what is likely to have been in its time the world's greatest theocracy would have impressed a visitor such as Lawrence in any circumstances; but only four years previously the Mexican archaeologist, Manuel Gamio, had made it more remarkable by uncovering a series of sculptured heads along the side of the Temple of Quetzalcoatl. One of these represented Tlálac, a rain god, but the other, the 'feathered serpent' himself (this is one of the two meanings of 'Quetzalcoatl' in Nahuatl, the Aztec language), with eyes of obsidian and fangs that had been enamelled.[10] A reference in Lawrence's first essay on Crèvecoeur's *Letters of an American Farmer* shows that he had long been familiar with some Aztec sculpture;[11] and almost immediately on his arrival in Mexico City he had complained to Murry about the 'gruesome Aztec carvings' in the National Museum (iv. 416). After his experience of the bullfight, the distinctly *pre*-Aztec artifacts at Teotihuacán gave Lawrence a similar feeling of violence and cruelty. 'Huge gnashing heads', he wrote, in his description of his visit in 'Au Revoir, U.S.A.', 'jut out jagged from the wall-face of the low pyramid . . . The great stone heads snarl at you from the wall, trying to bite you.' Yet for all this recoil, there is a general sense of an already acute interest strengthened and confirmed. 'Au Revoir, U.S.A.' contrasts the strain North America puts on the nerves with the way Mexico makes one lose one's temper: 'Mexico exasperates, whereas the U.S.A. puts an unbearable tension on one. Because here in Mexico the fangs are still obvious.' Lawrence prefers a country where the violence and unpleasantness of nature (human or otherwise) is apparent to one where he feels there is a pretence of loving kindness. His sense of the greater authenticity of Mexico is conveyed by his reference to it as 'the sort of solar plexus of North America'.[12] He had left Mabeltown for the Del Monte Ranch because he was in search of a life that was more 'real'; now in Mexico he must have felt himself slowly becoming aware of a bedrock upon which he would construct a whole new political and social system in his coming novel. Lawrence is in the line from

Rousseau insofar as he believed passionately that nothing a healthy human being felt could be wrong; but his realisation that the primordial impulses are far less pleasant than many liberals had preferred to believe means that his politics have much less the flavour of Rousseau than of Hobbes.

After Teotihuacán there was Xochimilco, an old part of Mexico City full of canals, and then a few days in the nearby town of Cuernavaca. It was in the cloisters of the cathedral at Cuernavaca that Bynner took a picture of Lawrence which its subject very much liked (Fig. 9):[13] he sent it as a postcard to four correspondents, remarking to one, 'Isn't this a nice photograph' (iv. 435). Photographic portraits of great writers have usually far more sociological than psychological interest. The solipsism of our attempts to see in them the author of this or that great work, with his 'penetrating look', 'imposing brow', etc., could easily be exposed if we did not know what he looked like, and a malicious friend were to pass off, as the author concerned, his milkman or most insensitive critic. If the aim is to understand what Lawrence was really like, in the usual meaning of that expression, most studio portraits of him are relatively worthless, especially as few professional photographers ever seem to have succeeded in persuading their subject to relax. Bynner was interested in photography and had the means to afford decent equipment, but it is above all a tribute to the relationship which, despite their frequent antagonisms, he must on occasions have enjoyed with Lawrence that in this photograph, as in several others taken later in Chapala, the subject seems so willing to present himself to the camera rather than hide from it. Good as it is however, its chief interest is that it was a photograph Lawrence himself liked. Whatever else we may think we learn, what it teaches above all is how Lawrence preferred to see himself: jovial, lively (the eyes sparkle) and patently good-natured. The contrast with a physical description later provided by Carleton Beals – teacher, writer and well-known expert on Mexican affairs – who met Lawrence in Mexico City at this time and was *not* one of his admirers, is striking. 'He was a thin man', Beals wrote, 'with a body that seemed about to fall to pieces; his face was pasty, expressionless, but his greenish eyes glared from out his pale red beard with curious satyr-like luster . . . everything sent him into convulsive loss of self-control, quite un-English, but he was already suffering from incurable consumption.'[14]

In the middle of April, with Terry's *Guide* in support, there were trips to towns within a 130-mile radius of Mexico City, during which Bynner did not always find Lawrence jovial. We know this because Johnson, who had hurt his back in Cuernavaca, was in Mexico City's American hospital at the time and the letters which Bynner wrote to him there have survived. The party of three set off on 13 April in a train which had armed guards riding on its roof, and after fear of rebels or bandits (in a country so politically volatile it was difficult to tell the difference) had marooned it in the countryside for a considerable period, they arrived in Puebla nine and a half hours after having left the capital. An average speed of under ten miles an hour did nothing for Lawrence's temper, especially as he was developing a cold. 'Don't grow a moustache', Bynner wrote to Johnson on the 15th, 'A cold can make it so untidy.' With Puebla as their base they took short trips to Cholula and Atlixco although both the Lawrences were now unwell and had to spend some time in their hotel beds. On 19 April, Bynner could report,

D. H. revived somewhat but cursed the land and despaired of its people. One instant he does that and the next instant wishes a hacienda hereabouts for six months – then curses again. If ever there was a sick soul it is his . . . Poor Frieda! . . . This man whom a generation is thinking intellectual is as set about with superstitions as a parlor of palmistry.[15]

A day or two later they abandoned Puebla and made the seven-hour train journey to Orizaba. It was on Orizaba station, according to *Journey with Genius*, that Lawrence hysterically declared the town too evil to set foot in and had to be bullied into accompanying the others to a hotel. The explanation, Bynner conjectured, was that Lawrence had recently read how in the days before the revolution a government commission had called a meeting of strikers in Orizaba in order to hear their grievances. Once the meeting-place was full, they had locked the building and set fire to it.[16] Certainly an occasional aspect of Lawrence's famous sensitivity to the spirit of place was revulsion from localities where anything especially unpleasant had happened, and it was by a feature of the same processes of association that he so disliked staying in, or revisiting, anywhere he had been seriously ill.

Although there can be no absolute confirmation for this aspect of Bynner's speculations, it is certain that his impression of Lawrence's indecisiveness at this time is accurate. From Orizaba Lawrence wrote eight postcards, in all of which he says that he has had enough of Mexico and announces a definite decision to return to Europe via New York. In one of them he even asks Murry, 'Have you thought of a house for me in the country? I want to come back' (iv. 425). Yet on his return to Mexico City on 22 April Lawrence immediately began to change his mind, writing to Eddie Marsh, 'We are still in Mexico, I tip-toe for a leap to Europe, and then hold back – don't quite know why'; and to the Danes, 'I'm *still* going to look for a place here' (iv. 430).[17]

Lawrence's hesitation about where he should next settle down and write was compounded by not knowing quite what he was going to produce. Frieda felt that he was only completely content when he was writing, and in Mexico City the words, or ideas for the words, would not come. From Orizaba he told Adele Seltzer, 'I should never be able to write on this continent – something in the spirit opposes one's going forth' (iv. 426). The restlessness this feeling produced appears to have been aggravated rather than appeased by all there was to do in the social as well as sight-seeing line. From yet another of Mabel's influential New York contacts, the well-known journalist Lincoln Steffens, who on his return from Russia in 1919 had popularised the phrase, 'I have seen the future and it works', Lawrence had secured one letter of introduction to the University Club of Mexico and another to Roberto Haberman, who worked at the Department of Education, at that time the focus for an unusual degree of reforming zeal.[18] It could have been through Haberman that the visitors met Frederic Leighton, an American who had been brought in to help with the reforms. Through a Dr Lyster, to whom Bessie Freeman had given Lawrence a letter of introduction (iv. 392, 421), they also came to know at this time Zelia Nuttall, a highly distinguished anthropologist in her sixties. Born in San Francisco, Zelia Nuttall had been educated in Europe and must have spoken in a way which deceived Lawrence into thinking she was English (iv. 422). She offered him accommodation in part of her historic, fortress-like house, which was in the suburb of Cayoacán, dated from the Conquest, and was reputed to have once belonged to one of Hernán Cortés's most prominent lieutenants, Pedro de Alvarado. In the second chapter of 'Quetzalcoatl', Lawrence would describe going to tea at the Casa Alvarado and meeting a bad-tempered American judge who, when he heard of the letters of introduction from Lincoln Steffens, exploded, 'Why he's nothing but a rank bolshevist', and who complained of the Mexican government's welcome for 'bolshevistic aliens'.[19] The portrait of this judge shows how much Lawrence must have disliked him, but the views he is portrayed as expressing are not in fact far removed from his own complaints about the imposition of alien ideas on the indigenous culture of Mexico.

More perhaps because of these social contacts than in spite of them (finding enough but not too much company is a balance Lawrence was not the first to find hard to strike), there are rather more records of his irritability for this short period than for most others after the war. Bynner has the most memorable:

I had noticed that his flare-ups were more likely to occur when we had had wine. One day, with the Monte Carlo meal ended but with a little Chianti left, he was still sipping while Frieda smoked. Her cigarette began to slant downward in the left corner of her mouth. I saw his attention light on it, saw him watch grimly fascinated till she gave a pull on the dangling stub and then tilted her head up to ease her eye from watering. Though the dining room was full, he stiffened suddenly, jerked himself to his feet and blared, 'Take that thing out of your mouth!' She gazed at him, wide eyed, without answering. 'Take it out, I say, you sniffing bitch!' And then, though she was seated behind a corner table, half hidden from everyone by the cloth, 'There you sit with that thing in your mouth and your legs open to every man in the room! And you wonder why no decent woman in England would have anything to do with you!' Flinging the remaining drops of his Chianti at her, he darted past the other tables into the lobby and then out into the street.[20]

By the early 1950s Bynner was an unreliable and hostile witness, unreliable because of the time which had elapsed and hostile partly because he had been forced to watch his own literary standing dwindle into insignificance while Lawrence's remained relatively high. As a professional writer he was in any case much more likely than Merrild (for example) to alter what he remembered for the sake of literary effect. Yet both Merrild and Mabel make it clear how much Lawrence could dislike Frieda smoking. According to Bynner, her own explanation was that it angered Lawrence because he had been told by doctors that he must not smoke himself,[21] but it is hard not to believe that there was also an element of outraged propriety. (In *A Passage to India* – to be published in the following year – Ronnie Heaslop's indignation at discovering that his fiancée has been left alone with two Indians is intensified by the fact that he sees her smoking with them[22]). Moral indignation is certainly implied by the insults Lawrence hurls at Frieda along with his remaining Chianti. The words are unlikely to be the actual ones used, but there is plenty of evidence that Lawrence was capable of coarse abuse, and of the cruelty of reminding Frieda how difficult she had found it to be accepted by well-bred Englishwomen such as Lady Ottoline Morrell. It must have been some comfort to her that in America there was a majority of friends, which included Bynner and Johnson, equally if not more at home in her company than her husband's.

Another outburst of a quite different kind which Bynner records is corroborated by others. Frederic Leighton, who had got to know the Lawrences well and would visit them in Chapala,[23] had arranged for their party to lunch on 26 April with, José Vasconcelos, the Minister of Education himself. At the last minute 'urgent matters of State' obliged Vasconcelos to postpone the luncheon until the following day. Lawrence, already apprehensive perhaps about the formality of the occasion, felt insulted and flew into a rage, striding 'back and forth on the third floor inner balcony of the Education building for fully ten minutes before he could be quieted sufficiently to leave'. 'How anyone's body', Leighton's account continues, 'to say nothing of a sick, fragile one, could withstand such berserk bursts of passion I did not know.'[24] Lawrence refused to attend the re-arranged lunch on the 27th and that evening set off alone for Lake Chapala in a last, reconnoitring effort to discover somewhere in Mexico where he and Frieda might settle for a while. He had read about the beauties of Chapala in his *Guide*, but after his experiences in Orizaba and elsewhere was beginning to lose faith in its author. A stronger reason for pinning his last hopes on that small town, rather than any other place, was that Bynner and Johnson had a contact in the area whom they had always intended to visit. Like Johnson, Idella Purnell had been an admiring student of Bynner's when he taught a course on poetry at Berkeley in 1919. Her American father was a dentist who had married a Mexican and settled in Guadalajara where Idella now worked at the American Consulate, wrote poetry and was no doubt nostalgic for her recent university days. Just before leaving Santa Fe, Bynner had written to her, 'I do not know what the Lawrences are planning beyond Easter in the capitol [sic]; but I know that Spud and I, if we go, shall arrive presently in Guadalajara'; and when he was laid up in the American hospital, Johnson reminded Idella that they had met in Berkeley, adding, 'The Lawrences still influence us, strangely enough, in our decision. First they declare flatly that they will *not* go to Guadalajara at all; and then announce calmly that they think they will take a house there. They really are frightfully difficult – beware of 'em.'[25] The house Lawrence was thinking of taking was only in the Guadalajara district, and there was no certainty he would be favourably impressed. But on 1 May he sent a telegram declaring Chapala 'paradise' (iv. 435) and urging them all to come, and by 2 May he and Frieda were installed in their Chapala home. 'He will be writing again there', Bynner reports Frieda as saying when they were waiting for the Guadalajara train to leave Mexico City, 'He will be happier.'[26]

II 'Quetzalcoatl'

The house Lawrence had rented was in Calle Zaragoza, a few hundred yards from both the Plaza and the lakeside. It was sitting by the lake, with his back against a tree, that on 10 May, after two false starts (iv. 442), he began his new novel, racing along at his usual fast pace – by the end of the month he had completed 250 manuscript pages or 10 chapters (iv. 451–2). As in *Kangaroo*, Lawrence incorporated into this new novel details from his immediate environment. He had been obliged to take with the house a family of servants, a situation which in normal circumstances he disliked, but which now gave him the opportunity to improve his Spanish and see at close quarters how ordinary Mexicans lived. Many of the best parts of both 'Quetzalcoatl' and *The Plumed Serpent* derive from observation of his 'criada' or maid-of-all-work, Isabel de Medina. She lived at one end of the long, rambling building with a host of dependants, and Lawrence's complex, and on the whole sympathetic, account of her attitudes and behaviour anchors his novel in a day-to-day reality which provides a useful contrast to the occasional extravagance of its more obviously invented parts.

The handsome church at Chapala, with its two spires, strangely large and imposing for such a relatively small community, figures prominently in 'Quetzalcoatl' as does an ornate stone band-stand in the Plaza around which the dances were held which inspired one of Lawrence's episodes. Then as now Chapala was a place to which the inhabitants of Guadalajara could retreat at the weekend. During the long years of relative stability that the Porfirio Díaz regime had given Mexico (1876–1911),[27] there had been efforts to develop it into a fashionable resort, one sign of which was the nearby villa where Díaz himself used to come to stay with his brother. The chief male character in 'Quetzalcoatl' is Ramón Carrasco and it is this building (El Manglar) that L. D. Clark has established as the model for Ramón's hacienda, where so much of the more distinctly political action of the novel takes place.[28] Yet the most important stimulus for its setting came from the lake itself. The Italian lakes that Lawrence knew well had been encircled by high mountains and well-developed communities. In Chapala he was already in the most populous lakeside community: efforts at civilisation elsewhere along the shores were far more hesitant and primitive, and as he looked across the lake the impression was not at all alpine but of low eroded hills. At its edges the water ran continually into reeds with no apparent sense of where its proper boundaries ought to be. Its peculiar filmy quality, and the effect on the lake as a whole of the heat mists or sudden violent storms (the Lawrences had arrived in Chapala during the rainy season), became features of the new novel which, in its final version especially, many readers encounter with relief after yet another Quetzalcoatl hymn, or one more detailed description of the ceremonies Ramón introduces in his attempt to establish a new religion and a new form of political control.

Lawrence met Frieda, Bynner and Johnson in Guadalajara on 2 May where all four of them were entertained by Idella Purnell and her father.[29] He brought Frieda back to Chapala immediately, Bynner and Johnson (who had minor ailments) following on a few days later. According to Bynner, Lawrence was anxious for the two Americans to share the house in Calle Zaragoza,[30] but they plumped instead for the Hotel Arzopalo which overlooked the lake and had an American manager, Winfield Scott (iv. 436). A pattern of life was then established similar to the one the Lawrences had enjoyed with Götzsche and Merrild in Del Monte, except that Bynner and Johnson were writers not painters – some of the poems Bynner wrote in Chapala were later to appear in *Caravan* (1925), and a few from the far less productive and successful Johnson in his *Horizontal Yellow* (1935). Mornings were dedicated to work but, at the beginning of their stay at least, they would all meet in the afternoons on the beach. Sometimes Bynner would then serve martinis in his hotel room and all four must have eaten together fairly regularly. Separately or in concert the two couples took occasional trips to Guadalajara, or made excursions to villages on the lake. Popular with them was Jacotepec where we know that both Lawrence and Bynner had *serapes* woven to their own designs. At the weekend they would frequently see the Purnells who used to catch the bus from Guadalajara (the journey took two hours), and stay over on Saturday at the Arzopalo.[31]

Lawrence's feelings about Chapala fluctuated, as they did about any place in which he stayed, but they were on the whole positive and he would certainly have investigated even more actively than he did the possibility of renting a hacienda nearby – a place to which he could call the Danes and where they could 'make a life together' (iv. 463) – had he not believed that the countryside was dangerous. Already in his excursions from Mexico City, he had observed some of the effects of the recent turmoil ('Nearly all the big haciendas and big houses are ruins'), and he reported to Merrild from Chapala, 'this little village has twenty soldiers to guard it' (iv. 419, 453). Precisely how risky it was to wander unaccompanied around the area would be impossible to say. Lawrence had first arrived via the railway station at Ocotlán, being then rowed down the river to the lake; and he had stayed at a hotel near Jamay before taking a boat the next morning for Chapala (see the map on p. xxxii).[32] The manager of the hotel where he spent the night may well have regaled him with horror stories which would not have improved his confidence;[33] and this was certainly eroded by the moment on the night of 8–9 May when Lawrence believed his bedroom was being broken into. (From then on the young son of Isabel de Medina was to sleep on the Lawrences' verandah with a loaded gun by his side.) The details of this episode are not included in 'Quetzalcoatl' but eighteen months later Lawrence dramatised them in chapter VIII of *The Plumed Serpent* where all the evidence suggests that Kate Leslie's responses have their origin in her creator's memory of his own.[34]

Bynner believed that Lawrence exaggerated the dangers of life in Chapala but, of all the foreign countries one might have chosen to visit in 1923, Mexico was certainly far from being the safest for foreigners. Both he and Lawrence had met the writer Stephen Graham who, just before they both left New Mexico, had described in a Santa Fe newspaper how the friend he was travelling with had been killed by a stray bullet in Mexico City on the last day of 1922 (iv. 368–9).[35] Since the downfall of Díaz in 1911, there had been continual violence in the country with powerful individuals slaughtering their way to the Presidency only then to find themselves in conflict with former associates. The chief victims of the chaos were the ordinary people of Mexico (between $1\frac{1}{2}$ and 2 million of whom are thought to have been killed in the second decade of the century), but there were also periodic attacks on foreigners. The election in 1920 of Alvaro Obregón to a four-year term as President had at least signalled the beginnings of a return to normal life but, although Emiliano Zapata had been murdered in 1919 and the same fate would overtake Pancho Villa during the period of Lawrence's stay in Chapala, the fairly immediate future would show that revolutionary fervour had still not blown itself out, even with these two legendary figures removed from the picture.

Whatever the degree of actual physical risk to Lawrence himself, the uncertainties of daily life in Mexico were peculiarly suited to stimulate his political thought. In *Aaron's Rod* the clashes between Right and Left he had observed in Italy play only a minor role; and in *Kangaroo*, although there are detailed descriptions of the ideology and organisation of a right-wing movement, it is one to which the protagonist is attracted but which he cannot finally endorse. Now, as he wrote 'Quetzalcoatl' – with some misgiving because of the unfamiliarity of the word, Lawrence was beginning to settle for this title around 15 June (iv. 457) – he began to imagine a political system of which he could wholly approve. Ramón Carrasco and his close friend and ally General Cipriano Viedma are shown striving in this new work to establish a feudal theocracy in which all aspects of life are governed by respect for spiritual authority rather than the power of money or social rank. None of the revolutionary blueprints for a new society which had been drawn up in Mexico during the previous decade had regarded religion as central. If it nevertheless seemed to Lawrence the right country for Ramón and Cipriano's experiment, it was because he felt that, despite centuries of exploitation, the Indian population had retained the potential to live religiously, whereas the busy lives of Americans such as Owen Rhys and Bud Villiers (the Bynner and Johnson figures) concealed a fundamental sterility and an inner emptiness. In a key and very successful scene of the new novel, the Chapala church is reverently cleared of its Christian icons and converted into a centre for a new religious cult inspired by indigenous rather than imported beliefs. As its leader, Ramón takes it upon himself both to represent and physically to embody Quetzalcoatl, the most humane of the gods the Aztecs had incorporated into their pantheon, while Cipriano becomes the old Aztec god of war, Huitzilopochtli.[36]

Lawrence was to be helped in writing a novel concerning a culture so initially alien to him by his reading. He would research the more specifically anthropological aspects of his subject later but, already conversant with Prescott and several other of the more popular works on Mexican history, he now asked Idella Purnell to send or bring him from Guadalajara Bernal Díaz's *True History of the Conquest of Mexico*. Frances Calderón de la Barca's *Life in Mexico*, conveniently available in an Everyman edition, helped him to interpret the daily life he saw around him, even though it dated from the last century; and he now had enough Spanish to be able to read novels in that language (iv. 452). As J.-P. Pichardie has pointed out however, a good deal of Lawrence's former reading – in Theosophy, utopian fiction or English nineteenth-century social commentary – also became important at this time for the kind of novel he was writing.[37] Perhaps as immediately relevant was the irritant of Bynner's presence. A devotee of Whitman (his two other literary idols were Meredith and Housman), Bynner was an egalitarian and socialist – a champagne socialist according to Lawrence who in 'Quetzalcoatl' describes him as 'a bolshevist by conviction but a capitalist by practice. He lived on his income but sympathised fiercely with communism.'[38] When he and Johnson were alone with Frieda in Mexico City, waiting for Lawrence's report from Chapala, the two Americans had joined a rowdy group of people who invaded the cathedral on May Day, raised red flags on its central towers, and then were nearly trapped inside the building by soldiers.[39] Bynner was wholly in sympathy with the young intellectuals in Mexico City who were inspired by the Russian example and dreamed of reforming their country along socialist lines; but for Lawrence, socialism was – like Spanish Catholicism – only another element in the 'white superimposition', 'the great paleface overlay' which, he had claimed in 'Au Revoir, U.S.A.', 'hasn't gone into the soil half an inch'.[40]

In 'Quetzalcoatl' both Ramón and Cipriano are of Indian extraction and base their political thinking largely on the characteristics of Mexican *Indian* culture. Although Lawrence instinctively associates these with a deeper level of the psyche and is therefore obliged to regard them as more authentic, 'real' and true, he had been made well aware by his encounter with Aztec and pre-Aztec remains that not all those aspects of Mexican life he chose to regard as indigenous were pleasant. In both versions of the novel he is able to express through Kate his own dismay at a violence and cruelty in Mexico that he felt obliged to acknowledge as part of the reality of human nature, not least because he could often identify both in himself. To repress these impulses entirely would go against Lawrence's belief in the evil of repression (and he was never much interested in the convenient Freudian escape-route of 'sublimation'). His struggle to confront them, and to work out how they can be made compatible with social life, is apparent in his novel. A vivid sketch which bears all the hallmarks of personal experience shows Kate vainly attempting to rescue a water-fowl from a tiny Mexican boy who has tied it by the leg to a stone in the shallow borders of the lake so that he can then pelt it with stones;[41] but that native (or rather, innate) aggressivity is not always to be reprobated becomes clear in Lawrence's treatment of another key episode: the attack by enemies of the Quetzalcoatl movement on Ramón's hacienda. This occurs when Ramón is being visited by Kate who saves his life when she fires a pistol at one of his assailants. Once the fighting is over, Ramón urges her to dip her finger in the blood of the man she has helped him to kill and then hold it up to the sun as an offering to the god of anger. Despite her horror at the violence she has witnessed, Kate is persuaded to do this, 'Because the dark soul in her, deeper and sterner than pity, knew that it should be so.'[42] This final touch to the description of the attack was omitted from *The Plumed Serpent*, but more for aesthetic than ethical reasons: not, that is, because Lawrence's attitude to the taking of life had become in the meantime more conventionally liberal. In both versions of the novel the survivors from the gang responsible for the attack on the hacienda are executed in public with a minimum of legal formalities; but in *The Plumed Serpent* they include a woman, and the necessity of capital punishment is emphasised when three of them are disposed of, not by subordinates, but by Cipriano himself ('swift as lightning he stabbed the blindfolded men to the heart, with three swift, heavy stabs'[43]). In both versions the prisoners are made to choose from a handful of dried grasses or twigs, one of which is still green at its hidden end. The person lucky enough to pick the piece which is still green is pardoned. Lawrence seems to want to incorporate this kind of lottery into his new society as a reminder to people like Bynner that the arbitrary will always play an important role in human life and that the search for absolute 'fairness', carried on – in judicial as in so many other matters – under the banner of 'Reason', is fruitless as well as irreligious.

The novel Lawrence began writing in Chapala was a stern attempt to face up to human realities he felt liberals such as Bynner preferred to smooth over yet, paradoxically enough, aspects of it would give him at least as many opportunities for wish fulfilment as he had ever had before. On several occasions in the past he had dreamed of founding a community. Now, in his descriptions of how Ramón and Cipriano establish their new society, he could begin to enter into details of its religious and social organisation. More importantly at this stage in his novel's composition, the bond he imagines between the two leaders would allow him to dramatise for the first time in his fiction the *ideal* male relationship. The *Blutbrüdershaft* Rupert Birkin offers Gerald Crich in *Women in Love* is, like the relation of Natty Bumppo and Chief Chingachgook, based on notions of equality; but when in *Aaron's Rod* Rawdon Lilly suggests that he and Aaron Sisson might move closer to each other, it is understood that the pre-condition would be Aaron's acknowledgement of his friend's priority. In *Kangaroo*, although Ben Cooley often talks the language of Whitmanesque comradeship, it is clear that he wants Somers to be his follower rather than his friend. In the years after *Women in Love*, Lawrence had come to feel that a male bond could only be true and lasting if one partner recognised the superiority of the other but, perhaps because of the closeness of his own identification with some of the characters concerned, he had never shown how this might happen in practice. Now, in chapter VII of 'Quetzalcoatl', he has Cipriano swearing to obey his associate and bending down in one moment of their ceremony of bonding to kiss Ramón's bare feet. For his part, Ramón has asked Cipriano to swear that he will kill him should he ever fail to lead.[44]

This scene in which the two leaders of the Quetzalcoatl movement are bound to each other in a union of perfect trust and loyalty is a successor to the wrestling match in *Women in Love*, or the episode in *Aaron's Rod* where Lilly rubs oil into every part of Aaron Sisson's body. That is to say that it is an ideal, entirely satisfactory version of these kinds of encounters. Like them, it has overtones which are homoerotic while never implying that the men involved mean to turn their backs on women for good.[45] In 'Quetzalcoatl', Ramón is unhappily married to a devout Roman Catholic, Carlota, through whom Lawrence is able to investigate what he felt were the weaknesses of Christianity in a Mexican setting: its sentimental idealism and refusal to recognise the true nature of mankind. Once Carlota is dead, he marries Theresa, every unreconstructed male's dream of the perfectly submissive, supportive but yet not colourless female partner. Kate, who owes a lot to Frieda as well as to Lawrence himself, is both puzzled and challenged by Theresa (the puzzlement being easier to associate with Lawrence's own wife than the challenge). She herself is sought after by Cipriano but, although attracted, has not by the end of 'Quetzalcoatl' made any commitment. At one moment she is watching Cipriano swim and ponders: 'Would it be true for her to marry that red man out there in the water? She could not feel it . . . There was a gulf between him and her, the gulf of race, of colour, of different aeons of time'; and a little later, she tells him directly, 'Even if I married you, I shouldn't really change. It would only be betraying my race, and my blood, and my own nature.'[46] Just before the Lawrences left Mexico City, news had come that Mabel had married Tony Luhan (iv. 434). It evoked a not very creditable sense of shock in both of them (iv. 439, 442, 450). Yet however firm Lawrence's belief in the necessity for capital punishment was to remain between the writing of 'Quetzalcoatl' and *The Plumed Serpent*, his views on miscegenation became more easy-going with time and although in the first half of the published novel Kate is still declaring her belief in the inferiority of the non-white races and her disapproval of mixed marriages,[47] towards its end she has become Cipriano's lover and then his wife.

A rhythm of work and relaxation was established in Chapala which allowed Lawrence to come very close to finishing a first draft of *The Plumed Serpent* in two months: 'The novel is *nearly* finished – near enough to leave', he told Bessie Freeman on 27 June (iv. 462). If he did not finish it completely it was in part because the heroine's indecisiveness as to what finally to think of Ramón, Cipriano and the Quetzalcoatl movement was a reflection of his own. When he was writing *Kangaroo*, it was with the intention that it should be published as soon as possible. His implicit assumption that he would need to come back to 'Quetzalcoatl', and his frequently expressed understanding that he was dealing with a rough first draft, can be taken as a sign of the greater importance he accorded it. This was after all his response to those who might have been inclined to say that he only knew how to complain. Disillusioned with the left-wing, 'progressive' programmes of most of those with whom he associated but, as *Kangaroo* had shown, not finally much happier with their right-wing equivalents (in 'Quetzalcoatl' there is an explicit rejection by Cipriano of Italian Fascism), this was his own vision of the way forward even if, as it happened, and as T. S. Eliot might have said, it was also the way back.[48] To elaborate that vision needed time and effort. Not since *Women in Love* had a novel meant so much to him.

III   Chapala Days

In the first weeks of his stay in Chapala, Lawrence would walk Frieda to the main beach in the afternoons and watch while she, Bynner and Johnson swam. Self-conscious about his physique and poor swimming, he himself preferred to bathe alone in a more secluded area. (After catching sight of Lawrence in his bathing costume, Johnson described him to Idella Purnell as 'like an ivory crucifix in trunks: one expected to see the water stained with the blood of wounds in his feet'.)[49] Surrounding the other members of the main party in the area of the lake where they swam would be a crowd of young boys – bootblacks, street sellers and the like – whom Johnson and Bynner had got to know and with whom they enjoyed romping. On one occasion after Lawrence had accompanied Frieda and remained to observe, Bynner remembered him protesting vehemently that the two Americans were making idiots of themselves. Their behaviour was not only undignified but also dangerous because they did not know what diseases the boys who were climbing on their shoulders and clinging round their necks might have. 'Don't you realize how dirty these little chits are?', Bynner reports Lawrence as saying, 'They begin early down here doing everything'.[50] His account portrays Lawrence as a puritan killjoy as well as an author who, however controversial his own books may have been, was afraid of public opinion: it was 'what people will think' that worried him. Later Bynner describes how, when on one occasion he and Johnson were away from their hotel and some of these boys arrived selling knick-knacks or offering to shine shoes (against the manager's express prohibition), Lawrence was instrumental in having them arrested.[51]

It is clear from a passage in chapter VIII of 'Quetzalcoatl' that Lawrence was indeed preoccupied with the bathing question and the status of the young boys. His account corroborates a good many of the details available in *Journey with Genius*, but it offers on them a rather different point of view.

[Owen] lay for hours on the sand cooking like a beefsteak and surrounded by a swarm of little boys, the boot-black boys and the regular urchins of the place, spanking their little posteriors and being spanked back by them, letting them climb over him and dive from his shoulder when he was in the water, letting one of them sit on his naked chest as he lay in the sand . . . Owen and Villiers, like real democrats, pawed and were pawed by the swarming crew, and giggled and crowed as if they were having the time of their lives . . . Some of the boys were really nice little fellows. But some of the louts were vermin.

Owen was really in a wild state of excitement about his boys and youths. He photographed them in all imaginable poses, took nude photographs of them that would let him.[52]

It is perhaps as well that remarks like these did not survive into the final version. Bynner in fact soon came to share Lawrence's suspicion of the beach boys, although he maintained a life-long friendship with one of them, employing Yisidor Pulido and his wife to look after the house he was eventually to buy in Chapala and visit regularly until he was immobilised by a stroke in 1965.[53] Years later, looking back over three letters he wrote to his mother from Chapala in 1923, Bynner discovered that, even then, he must have come to find Lawrence's

view of the boys 'more reasonable than at first'. He quotes himself as discovering
' "as Lawrence warned me I should, that their light fearlessness becomes almost
impertinence, an easygoing ingratitude" '.[54] In a letter written to Idella Purnell in
1949, just after finishing his memoir of Lawrence, he admitted to her for the first
time his own 'tendency towards men. (It used to worry me; but life and Dr
Kinsey have shown me that such a tendency is very common)'; and went on to
reflect on Lawrence's own sexual make-up. 'I do not for a moment think the term
homosexual, with its loose applications, should be applied to him', he told Idella.
He and Lawrence had never mentioned the subject, except once when Lawrence
'spoke with distaste of some "pederast" who constantly took photographs of
naked boys at or near Taormina'. He wondered whether Lawrence's objection to
his and Johnson's romping with the bootblacks was not prompted by a fear that
people would misconstrue their friendliness.[55] The 'pederast' was Wilhelm von
Gloeden and it seems obvious, from the reference to 'nude photographs' in the
'Quetzalcoatl' passage, that Bynner had correctly identified – somewhat late in
the day – the reasons for Lawrence's unease.

As the disagreement over the bootblacks demonstrates, 'Quetzalcoatl' and
Journey with Genius offer rival accounts of the Lawrences' first Mexican stay from
two powerful personalities. In Chapala, the 25-year-old Johnson soon found
himself caught in the crossfire between them. As Bynner's secretary – the title
was not *merely* honorific – he typed letters and poems by Bynner which reflected
unfavourably on Lawrence (the reproduction of some of these in various sections
of *Journey with Genius* suggest Lawrence was right when he complained, 'But you
don't understand me, Bynner'[56]). Yet while he was doing this, Lawrence had
employed him to type also the opening parts of 'Quetzalcoatl', with their not
especially flattering references to himself and Bynner; and Johnson would also
have typed a passage in which the character based on himself is characterised as
hollow, without 'even the rags of liberalism and idealism to flutter'.[57] The analysis
does not seem to have worried Johnson unduly, although it may be that, with so
much lightning flashing round his young head, he cultivated the calm indifference
to everything which all the others decided at the time was part of his character.
They found him both cool and enigmatic, so much the latter in fact that
Lawrence would join the others in teasing him with being a 'fifi' (one of the
young men about town who came from Guadalajara at the weekends in pursuit of
women); or later suggest that the good-looking Idella was in love with him (iv.
515).[58] In the middle of June Lawrence wrote to Seltzer, 'By the way, if ever you
want a man clerk, do you think you might have Spud Johnson? He's very reliable
and does good work. I think he ought to have a proper job, not be just Bynner's
amanuensis' (iv. 457). In a passage from 'Quetzalcoatl' which occurs too far on for
Johnson to have typed it, the Bynner character is described as a 'barren bachelor
. . . with all the sterility of an old maid's egotism . . . He was both sensitive and

shrewd, and not easily beaten. But it was as if his adolescent mould had never been broken, smelted down, and recast into full manhood, through marriage.'[59] If the intention in finding Johnson another job was to rescue him from Bynner, so that he too would not remain cast in an 'adolescent mould', the attempt was almost certainly a consequence of a mistaken view of Johnson as wavering in his sexual orientation. That Bynner was once engaged to be married to Edna St Vincent Millay, and did not openly acknowledge his homosexuality until he was well into his thirties, leads James Kraft to refer to him occasionally as bisexual; but the Johnson of Chapala gives the strong impression of being already perfectly sure that he preferred men to women. Perhaps by analogy with himself, Lawrence seems to have made with regard to Johnson the same mistake he had made about Forster in 1915 and assumed that his sexual preferences were still a matter for conscious choice.[60]

The impression that they were not comes from Johnson's letters and diaries, but also from a third major source of information on the Chapala period: the unpublished novel about the Lawrences' visit there which Idella Purnell began soon after they had left, broke off and then completed in 1932.[61] 'Friction' is a *roman à clef* sufficiently inexpert (in 1923 its author was still only twenty-two) to need only minimal deciphering. Her talents were for verse rather than fiction and from spring 1923 she edited a poetry magazine (*Palms*) to which she was able to persuade many distinguished writers, including of course Lawrence himself, to contribute. The best parts of her novel are its descriptions of the Chapala environment but its plot – which eventually involved the Johnson character (Lionel) in political assassination – is unconvincing; and although many of the tensions she describes appear to be identified correctly, her dealings with them lack authority and a sufficient degree of psychological penetration. The conflict between Lawrence and Bynner over the boys on the beach is treated by her as if it were wholly political (which it only *partly* is), although elsewhere in her novel several of the sexual complications of the Chapala situation are acknowledged freely enough. In chapter VI, for example, Dean – who is obviously Bynner – has received a letter warning him of evil gossip concerning his relationship with Lionel and feels he must send Lionel away in order to protect him. 'People back home', he tells Lionel, 'are saying that I'm a sort of latter day Oscar Wilde, and you can see where that leaves you.' But Lionel makes it quite clear that he prefers to stay. With the help of some earlier poetry in which Bynner seemed to be mourning the death of a woman he had loved (his delicate lyrical manner runs towards suggestiveness and abstraction rather than specificity and there are often signs in his work of Proustian transposition), Idella Purnell portrays Dean as unaware of the exclusiveness of Lionel's love for him, someone essentially heterosexual whose Whitmanesque warm-heartedness to all and sundry is easily misinterpreted. She had been devoted to Bynner at Berkeley and her view of

Dean in chapter VI is likely to be an accurate reflection of how she felt about him in 1923. It may well be, therefore, that it was growing understanding of his nature which led her to abandon *Friction* not many pages later, although the portrait which emerged from the completed novel remains highly flattering.[62]

The view she presents of Edmund (Lawrence), on the other hand, is largely hostile. Childishly dependent on his wife Gertrude and unpredictably irritable, he is shown as resenting the affection Lionel and Gertrude develop for each other and jealous of the devotion Dean commands from both Lionel and Judith (the name Idella Purnell gives herself). It is as if the warnings about Lawrence which Johnson had sent to Idealla from Mexico City had been more effective than their sender probably intended. In chapter XV Judith's father, the Colonel,

saw how Lionel's eyes worshipped Dean, and how Edmund bristled in a petty jealousy whenever he caught the boy's shining look fixed on his idol. The addition of Judith to the party increased Edmund's wrath, for Judith too was an open worshipper of Dean. To Edmund she gave a guarded deference, having been warned before she met him of his tantrums and rage, and fearing always that she might provoke him to an outburst against herself. Yet mixed with her alarm was the greatest respect for his literary powers and gratitude for his occasional words of advice.[63]

Idella Purnell appears to have been too nervous of Lawrence to understand him well but her novel is full of details of everyday life in Chapala which provide a very useful addition to the biographical record.

Lawrence was to see Idella again later in the year (some of the impressions of him in the novel clearly derive from this second contact), and it was he who suggested the title for whatever she was to write about Chapala. Yet although there was 'friction', there were also many signs that the situation there suited him. Bynner and Johnson provided an intellectual society he might otherwise have found it hard to discover in such an out-of-the-way spot, and his disagreements with Bynner in particular were a stimulus to define more closely his own quite different political views. There was a reciprocal profit for the two friends from knowing Lawrence whom they both agreed could be fascinating and, in his good moods, very amusing. 'The Lawrences are still quite gay', Johnson wrote to Idella from Chapala.

The other night Hal [i.e. Bynner] fed Lorenzo on several drinks in the Plaza, whereat the gay dog invited Hal and me to dinner and after dinner was a perfect scream, burlesquing the Bohemian set of London. He is a born mimic when he lets himself go. And I was fairly rolling on the floor with mirth.

Looking back later in the year to the time he had spent with Lawrence, Bynner wrote to him, 'I find that, after all, I like to have you infuriate me: it forces me to attention. For the rest, I had a memorably happy time with you and Frieda and the Spoodle; and am hoping that somehow it will be renewed.'[64] ('Spoodle' was another of Johnson's nicknames.) The more the rhythm of Chapala life established itself the more Lawrence himself began to wonder why it should stop, especially as the novel he was composing so freely began to seem to him the best thing he had ever written. Frieda led the way to that view by declaring to Adele Seltzer on 10 June that 'Quetzalcoatl' was 'the most splendid thing [Lawrence] ever did'; but Lawrence himself added in a postscript, 'I like my new novel best of all – much' (iv. 455) – an opinion he was to retain for several years.

IV The Call of Home

Beneath all the surface irregularities which Lawrence's volatility imposed on his and Frieda's movements, there was usually a master plan. In this case it was to go up to New York in the late summer in order to deal with his publishing affairs, and then sail to England. As the time approached for implementation (the house in Calle Zaragoza had been rented by the month and with the intention of leaving it at the end of June – iv. 439–40, 453), Lawrence began to get cold feet. Going back to the England he had left with such relief in 1919 was a major decision for him, and his reluctance to move was immeasurably strengthened by the arrival in mid-June of the first number of Murry's new periodical the *Adelphi*. After having first signaled his reconversion to the idea of Lawrence's greatness with his review of *Aaron's Rod*, and then having been able to re-open his lines of communication with its author in the wake of Katherine Mansfield's death, Murry more explicitly announced his change of mind when praising *Fantasia of the Unconscious* in a Dutch periodical in the spring of 1923: 'Lawrence was right and I was wrong', he wrote then.[65] The *Adelphi*, he would claim, was launched primarily to provide 'the only writer of modern England who has something profoundly new to say'[66] with a platform, and he was also alluding to Lawrence when he described himself in his first editorial as 'only a *locum tenens* for a better man'.[67]

This flattery did not prevent the better man from feeling bitterly disappointed with what he found in the first number. He was annoyed that the extract from *Fantasia* which he had allowed Murry to print had appeared without an indication of the book it came from, and he thought Katherine Mansfield's 'bits' – a sketch called 'The Samuel Josephs' – 'ugly' (iv. 458). What he regarded as a puff of Wells's new novel (*Men Like Gods*) irritated him, and he was rightly disgusted by some sentimental rubbish about a humble clerk discovering the beauties of the Bible and Shakespeare, attributed to 'The Journeyman'. It was, however, Murry's opening address, full of cajoling intimacies and a vague spirituality, which must have disturbed him most (Catherine Carswell was to say that he had 'no printable words in which to describe it'[68]). There was in this an art of implying strong commitment while at the same time never saying anything sufficiently concrete to alienate the general reader which helped to ensure the *Adelphi*'s remarkable initial success.[69] 'No', Murry wrote,

when it comes to the point, the secret deep-down point that sometimes takes years to discover, we know we are not isolated. That is enough. But we can say more. We believe in life. Just that. And to reach that belief, to hold it firm and unshakable, has been no easy matter for some of us . . . Belief in life is not, strictly speaking, an idea at all. It is a faith. A moment comes in a man's life when suddenly all the hard things are made plain, when he knows quite simply that there is good and bad, that he must fight for the one and make war on the other. And the good things are the things that make for life, and the bad things are the things which make for decay.[70]

Here was a celebration of 'life' only parodically Lawrentian. If this was 'the best possible in England' (iv. 462), Lawrence felt, then they could keep it and he became all the more disinclined to respond to the urgings of Murry and Kot that he should join them in the enterprise, and move in their direction. But the often compliant Frieda was not so easily discouraged; she had her mother to see and, above all perhaps, her children.

Frieda's children had often been a cause of conflict in the Lawrences' marriage. Bynner records just one outburst of violent temper in Chapala but that was when Frieda was becoming maudlin over some photographs of her children and, with 'you sniffling bitch!', Lawrence snatched them from her, tore them in two and stamped on the pieces.[71] The details of this episode may be exaggerated but both Merrild and Mabel describe how they had to help Frieda communicate with her children without Lawrence's knowledge, posting her letters to them or sending cables secretly.[72] Frieda's anxiety to see her children again is an evident influence on certain passages in 'Quetzalcoatl' which were either eliminated from *The Plumed Serpent* (the literary outcome of a period when they were less of an issue between her and Lawrence), or received much less prominence there. In chapter v, for example, Kate Burns is made to ponder, 'But since she was in America the real yearning she had always felt for her children had snapped . . . They were the children of her idea, they had nothing to do with her deepest blood or her soul . . . They inherited none of her outward-striving spirit. They had slipped back into the conventional, meaningless mass'; and in chapter xvi Theresa, Ramón's second wife, asks, ' "Do they want you very much in Europe?" "Yes", said Kate, "My mother, and my children". – Then she considered a while, and a sense of truth made her add, "But not *very* much, really. They don't want me very badly. I don't fit in with their lives." '[73] By the time of *"Not I, But the Wind . . ."* Frieda had decided that Lawrence had been right in his feelings about her children at this period: 'they didn't want me any more, they were living their own lives'.[74] In Chapala, however, she was far from sharing the feelings of 'Quetzalcoatl' 's heroine (there is more than one way in which the novel is full of wish-fulfilment), and held Lawrence firmly to their original intention of leaving at the end of June.

Before the Lawrences left there was to be one final excursion involving the Purnells as well as Bynner and Johnson. All kinds of craft traded on the lake but the most attractive of them were large, flat-bottomed, fifty-foot sailing boats called canoas. These furled their sails when they drifted into Chapala at the end of the day but were so attractive with the evening sun shining on their canvas that Bynner went to the trouble of hiring a boat so that he could meet them before they prepared to enter port and take photographs while they were still in full sail.[75] It was decided to hire one of these canoas for a few days and, with a 'crew' of locals, sail round the lake. From Idella Purnell's various accounts, and Johnson's 'Log of the Esmeralda' in the library at Austin, it would seem the expedition was not a great success. According to Johnson, the 'Esmeralda' set sail at 1.07 p.m. on 4 July but was almost immediately becalmed. Even Idella, who was a very poor swimmer, slipped over the side to cool off but as she let go of the boat's ladder she panicked at the thought of the depths below and – with the others looking on from above – went down a couple of times before she could grab it again. Lawrence assured her later that someone would have jumped in to help had they thought her to be in real difficulty, but she resented the 'ghoulish' way he pressed her to explain what it felt like to believe you were on the point of drowning.[76]

In the later afternoon the wind got up and they were able to sail to within a mile of Tuscueca (the village opposite Chapala) when they were again becalmed. Packed like sardines and with very primitive toilet arrangements, the night was made more uncomfortable by rain. But Idella was in any case kept awake by sea-sickness. 'Everyone had to admit', comments Johnson sourly, 'that the motion of the boat was not enjoyable there in the middle of the lake at anchor – but everyone would also have admitted that Idella's way of impressing everyone with her misery was not enjoyable either.' The stormy weather meant that the next day they had the rare opportunity of seeing a water-spout – a tubular column of water stretching down from the storm clouds – towards the eastern end of the lake; but the wind they now had was blowing in the wrong direction and prevented them from sailing into Tuscueca. Idella meanwhile was feeling sicker but much more serious was Bynner's condition. What he began by thinking of as a boil was in fact an infected anal fistula and giving him a great deal of pain. After earnest examination of the inflamed area by Lawrence and Dr Purnell, it was decided that there were two invalids on board and both were put on the steamer back to Chapala when they were eventually able to reach Tuscueca. 'I was glad Idella was to go but wished her father was in Hal's place', wrote Johnson in his log. The rest of the trip passed less eventfully and in more comfort. The remaining sailors spent a second night near Tizapan and a third near La Palma (both on the southern shore of the lake). There was probably a fourth night on the north shore and a return to Chapala on 8 July. It had often been one of Lawrence's dreams to sail the seas with a few chosen companions. The Lake Chapala expedition would be the closest he ever came to its realisation, but there is hardly any direct transcription of the experience in either his letters or his other writings even though, in what L. D. Clark describes as the only recorded instance of its kind, Bynner remembered Lawrence using a notebook to jot down his impressions of the water-spout.[77]

Bynner's case was serious and he had to be operated on immediately in a Guadalajara hospital. He writes very warmly of Lawrence's 'constant, thoughtful tenderness' as a visitor of the sick giving the impression, typical of his dealings with chronology in *Journey with Genius*, that he came to the hospital regularly over a period of two weeks.[78] But back in Chapala by 8 July, Lawrence wrote from the Arzopalo on the 9th that he and Frieda were leaving that day (iv. 467–8). Idella Purnell describes how she and the daughter of Winfield Scott accompanied the Lawrences by boat to the railway station at what must have been Ocotlán ('a trip too short for seasickness').[79] She was temporarily occupying Bynner's room at the Arzopalo and Johnson wrote to her there describing how he had met the Lawrences on the 9th in Guadalajara, dined with them and then accompanied them to the hospital to see Bynner. On 10 July he had taken both breakfast and lunch with the Lawrences (the first 'at the Casa Purnell'), and then seen them off 'on the afternoon train for Laredo and points north'. (It is probable of course that Lawrence had found time to go and see Bynner again on that day.)[80] Their original intention had been to sail to New York from Veracruz but the threat of dock strikes had made them change their plans. With new visas and vaccination certificates,[81] they crossed the frontier at Laredo on 13 July without difficulty, and pushing on to San Antonio, Lawrence sent a postcard to Koteliansky that same day, whose message ends, 'This already feels much nearer England' (iv. 468). It is not clear from the wording, as indeed it was probably not entirely clear to Lawrence himself at this juncture, whether or not he felt being nearer to England was a good thing. Since telling at least eight people he was going home, when he was visiting Orizaba, and then changing his mind a day or two later, his feelings had never entirely settled. 'When I get letters from Europe then I never want to go back. When I forget the letters, I do' (iv. 444) was one of his own versions of his state of mind.

CHAPTER SIX

◆

July–November 1923

NEW YORK, LOS ANGELES, GUADALAJARA

I Separation

From San Antonio the Lawrences moved on to New Orleans – 'this steaming, heavy, rather dead town' he complained on 15 July (iv. 469). Their intention was to sail from there to New York but the ships were full of holiday-makers (iv. 473) and they took instead the train via Washington, arriving at their destination on the 19th. After only one night in New York they moved to a cottage near Morris Plains in New Jersey which the Seltzers had rented for the four of them. 'Birkindele' it had been christened in a strange, amalgamated tribute to Mrs Seltzer and the work which had brought them all most money.[1]

Lawrence was kept very busy in New Jersey correcting the proofs of *Kangaroo*, *Mastro-don Gesualdo*, and *Birds, Beasts and Flowers* (for which he had designed his own cover – iv. 521), and revising Maxim Gorky's *Reminiscences of Leonid Andreyev* which Koteliansky and Katherine Mansfield had translated and which Kot, with Lawrence's friendly help, hoped to have published in the *Dial* (iv. 478, 487). He may have been prompted to spend more time than usual on his proofs by a letter from an American librarian which he had received in Chapala and which pointed out 'rather scaring lists of errors' in *The Captain's Doll* and *Fantasia of the Unconscious*. 'I am afraid a great deal is my own fault,' he had replied, '– hyphen or no hyphen is one to me. However, I will try to mend my ways, especially as far as orthographic inconsistency goes, remembering your eye is on every dot' (iv. 443). The labour of mending his ways, or merely persisting in his old ones, may help to explain why, although he planned to spend quite some time with Bessie Freeman, who was on a flying visit to New York, he and Frieda probably saw her only once; and why, although he talked of taking the train to Boston to see Amy Lowell (iv. 478), who had provided invaluable financial support in the old days,[2] he never in fact did so. More indicative either of his mood or of the amount of work he found on his desk, was that he decided against going to New Haven to see the Brewsters, who were back from Europe on a visit to Achsah's birth-place.[3]

If there was an element of the anti-social in these missed opportunities, then New York, which he had always previously regarded with such apprehension, would not have moderated it. Most of his time he was able to spend alone with

Frieda in the countryside – the Seltzers were commuting to their New York office and only reappeared in the evenings (iv. 477). A four-mile horse and buggy ride from Morris Plains station, 'Birkindele' was 'pretty, rural, remote, nice' (iv. 473); but Seltzer had arranged a number of literary luncheons or dinners which he must have felt were important for maintaining his author's already considerable reputation in America.[4] At one of these Lawrence met Henry Seidel Canby, who dealt with literary matters for the *New York Evening Post*, and at another John Macy, the literary editor of the *Nation*, as well as the owner of that journal, Garrison Villard. To this latter occasion were also invited two members of the British Labour Party with consequences which Joseph Wood Krutch, who reviewed for the *Nation* at this time, later described in a memoir. Lawrence apparently sat in complete silence while the two Labour Party members discussed the living conditions of their supporters and how they expected to ameliorate them once they came to power. Realising that this discussion left his other guest out in the cold, Villard turned to Lawrence and asked him what he thought should be done to save the world. 'Those of us who had read some of Lawrence held our breaths and he rose to the occasion. White beneath his scraggly beard, Lawrence replied with measured ferocity: "I thought, Mr Villard, you understood that I hoped it would go to pieces as rapidly and as completely as possible." '[5]

Lawrence did not like literary dinners very much and he does not seem to have been much happier having his photograph taken by one of New York's leading photographers. In May, Martin Secker had asked Curtis Brown, Lawrence's literary agent in England (Mountsier had only dealt with American matters), to send him copies of any photographs which Lawrence might have taken of himself in New York, and on 15 August Lawrence posted directly to Secker 'a couple of good photographs that Seltzer had taken of me' (iv. 448, 486). These would be two of twelve by the Hungarian-born Nickolas Muray, who had a studio in Greenwich Village, photographed most of the leading literary and theatrical personalities of the 1920s, and worked in close co-operation with the editor of *Vanity Fair*, Frank Crowninshield (to whom Lawrence may also have been introduced at this time). These are 'good photographs' in the sense that they are clearly the work of a competent professional but in all the ones now available Lawrence looks defensive and tense. Muray remembered him as the shyest person he had ever seen, regretted there was not 'a single smiling picture' but explained that Lawrence 'wasn't the smiling type'.[6] Bynner might have disagreed and proposed that the first duty of any portrait photographer, amateur or professional, is to secure his subject's confidence. It is however untrue that Lawrence is not smiling in any of the Muray photographs. In at least two of them a faint smile hovers round his lips but it is the expression which highly self-conscious people assume when threatened by the camera and which appears to be saying to putative observers, 'If you think this allows you to know what I'm like, you are quite mistaken.'

The labour of correcting proofs, and the unease Lawrence felt at being in New York, were not the only reasons why he might have felt tense in Nickolas Muray's studio. In his letters from the end of July and beginning of August he usually takes for granted that he will be going to Europe, but he is clearly reluctant and comes to regret Mexico more and more. By 7 August, having already bought tickets for both himself and Frieda, he has definitely changed his mind, and with the by now familiar allusion to Balaam's ass, decided that if Frieda wanted to stick to their original plans – as she very evidently did – then she would have to return to England on her own. 'I ought to come,' he told Middleton Murry, 'but I can't . . . F. wants to see her children. And you know, wrong or not, I can't stomach the chasing of those Weekley children' (iv. 480). In a letter to Murry a week later, he explains that Frieda would probably arrive in Southampton on 26 or 27 August and adds, 'I wish you would look after F. a bit' (iv. 483). Similar requests to Koteliansky and Catherine Carswell (iv. 482, 485) do not have the same ironic flavour which this one assumes in the light of subsequent events.

Lawrence and Frieda had been away from each other frequently, as they visited their respective families for example, and they had sometimes parted without a clear understanding as to when they would meet again,[7] but they had never before contemplated being on different continents. In *his* correspondence he assumes that either he will rejoin Frieda shortly or – much more probably – she will meet him in California (where he thought he would go and see the Danes), or in some other, warm place by the end of October. It was Catherine Carswell who claimed that when Lawrence went to see Frieda off on the *Orbita* on 18 August they had 'on the quay . . . one of the worst quarrels – perhaps the very worst – of their life together. And when they parted it was in such anger that both of them felt it might be for always.'[8] If there was such a quarrel, it could hardly have been about Lawrence's refusal to return to Europe – a decision taken ten days earlier; and the feeling of having parted for good is not apparent in anything Lawrence wrote at the time. But a week after sailing Frieda complained to Adele Seltzer from the *Orbita*,

I feel so cross with Lawrence, when I hear him talk about loyalty – Pah, he only thinks of himself – I am glad to be alone and will not go back to him and his eternal hounding me, it's too ignominious! I will not stand his bad temper any more if I never see him again – I wrote him so – He can go to blazes, I have had enough.[9]

Her mood softened subsequently but this letter supports at least *one* aspect of Middleton Murry's account, thirty years later, of how he had travelled through France to Freiburg with Frieda in September 1923 and discovered that he loved her as much as she loved him. But even though 'the idea of our sleeping together, waking in each other's arms, seemed like heaven on earth', he refused her offer of a physical relationship out of consideration for Lawrence. 'She had had enough of Lawrence,' he says of Frieda then, 'in his Mexican "moods", and in fact she had left him. She felt – rightly enough – no more loyalty to him.'[10]

It is important that, by the time Murry wrote these words in his journal, he would have been able to read in *Journey with Genius* Bynner's vivid account of Lawrence's 'Mexican "moods"'. Yet if Lawrence's 'bad temper' was more in evidence in Mexico City than usual, he was much calmer in Chapala and, as a letter she wrote to Bynner from the *Orbita* testifies, Frieda had been 'very happy' there.[11] Her husband's outbursts were in any case not merely 'Mexican' and she had been used to dealing with them for years. The far from reliable Mabel Luhan reports her surprise at discovering 'great black and blue bruises' on Frieda's 'blonde flesh' when they went to the hot springs together.[12] There is a fair amount of evidence that when Lawrence was in a temper and lost control he had sometimes physically attacked Frieda, both in New Mexico and the places they had lived together before, although to say he 'beat his wife' would give a false impression of systematic abuse and underestimate the extent to which she was capable of responding in kind. To be even the occasional target of her husband's wild rage must nevertheless have been very unpleasant. What is unlikely is that it was either Lawrence's bad temper in Mexico, or that factor alone which caused her to tell Adele Seltzer she would not go back to him. Weariness with being 'hounded' was almost certainly aggravated on this occasion by frustration at his volatility: for months he had given the impression that, however reluctant he might often appear, he would eventually go with her to Europe; yet now he had changed his mind and seems to have expected her once again to follow suit. What made his decision so important, and may help to explain the unusual severity of the quarrel, was the issue of the children. Frieda's elder daughter Elsa was about to turn twenty-one in September and thereafter Weekley would have no more legal power to prevent her from seeing her mother.[13] For Lawrence, however, attention to the children was often to be interpreted as a betrayal of himself.

When she wrote to Bynner from the ship, Frieda did not tell him she had left Lawrence, and even in the letter to Adele Seltzer she said she did not care *if* she never saw him again. Merely to threaten separation was nonetheless a bold gesture. A remarkably good-looking woman in her youth, at least one of the photos Bynner took in Mexico shows how beautiful she could still on occasions appear (see Fig. 10). But Frieda was forty-four on 11 August 1923 and for a woman who had been in every way conditioned to make her life with and through men this was important. Financially speaking, she was entirely dependent on Lawrence who, as his fortunes began to improve after the war, regularly sent money to her mother, and other of her relatives, in inflation-crippled Germany.

In England he had arranged for her to use Mary Cannan's flat in Queen's Gardens, and afterwards she would move to an apartment in a big house in Hampstead where the Carswells were living. With these friends Frieda was reasonably comfortable but not very popular with other, male members of the Lawrence circle. Koteliansky and Murry had particularly disapproved of her and felt she had been a bad influence on Lawrence. In London she would be able to see her children, but she could hardly have expected much support from the other people she knew there if her intention was really to leave her husband for good. How she would keep herself without Lawrence cannot have been at all clear. What was bold in her refusal to cancel her own trip therefore was that she had entered into a battle of wills with Lawrence when most of the social and economic advantages were on his side. She may have guessed from past experience that the psychological ones were on hers but, after his repeated assertions of the vital importance of male independence, she cannot have been entirely sure.

On the same day on which he saw Frieda off, Lawrence gave an interview to the *New York Evening Post*. He was reported as believing that the present phase of industrial civilisation, whose pre-eminent symbol was now New York, would not last much longer, and as wondering what the modern equivalent could be of the Christianity which had regenerated Europe after the fall of the Roman Empire. He said he had detected in New Mexico the stirrings of an impulse which could carry mankind through to the next phase after the catastrophe, and that the only people who interested him were those few who 'make the destinies of the world'. It was an interview to please Mabel Luhan and, if she saw it, its conclusion would also have intrigued her. 'How long should he be here? His wife, he said, was going back to England, and he drew out his watch. "I guess she's going back to England in half an hour", he went on, "But I think I will go back to the Middle West".'[14] For the moment he went back to 'Birkindele' in order to pack and say goodbye to the Seltzers. Returning to New York on Monday 20 August for a visit to the dentist (iv. 490), Lawrence finally set off westwards on the morning of the 22nd. If he had tried to persuade Frieda that her place was with him, it would have been on the grounds that he was also one of the people who made the destiny of the world. For the moment at least, that belief in his mission would have to be sustained alone.

II West Coast

Having now firmly decided to meet up with the Danes, Lawrence's first stop on his way to California was in Buffalo where he was entertained for five days by Bessie Freeman and her relations. This was not only Bessie's home town but also of course that of Nina Witt and Mabel Luhan (he had lunch with Mabel's mother on a trip to the Niagara Falls on 25 August – iv. 492).[15] To mix with the 'blue blood' of an American provincial city was a new experience which fascinated him – 'It's almost like *Cranford*: more old-fashioned than anything still surviving in Europe' (iv. 492). He left on the 27th, making his way to Chicago where it 'rained and fogged . . . and floods of muddy-flowing people oozed thick in the canyon-beds of the streets' (iv. 493–4); and then pressed on via Salt Lake City to Los Angeles where the Danes met him at the station in their old Ford 'Lizzie'. He was able to spend that night (30–31 August) in Merrild's room on W. 27th Street because both the Danes were temporarily living in the fashionable suburb of Brentwood. After mixed fortunes which included some design work at the film studios and elsewhere (but also some house-painting), they had been commissioned by a geologist named Johnson to decorate his library in exchange for food and board. On the 31st Lawrence moved out to the Hotel Miramar in Santa Monica to be nearer to them. The Danes took him to a beach where Lawrence refused to swim and where they noticed the same physical self-consciousness Bynner and Johnson had observed in Chapala; and they introduced him to their Brentwood patron (it helped that Mrs Johnson was an admirer of Lawrence's writing). As they continued to work on their murals, they had to fight off his insistence that he should lend a hand. On 9 September the three of them drove with the Johnsons to Santa Barbara and after a night there went further up the coast to Lompoc where, with a group of artists and writers from Carmel, they were well placed to observe a total eclipse of the sun. Back in Los Angeles by 12 September, Lawrence rented for the final fortnight of his stay a room on Grand Avenue about a block and a half from where the Danes were living.[16] On one occasion during this last period Lawrence took the Danes, a Danish couple they knew, and the Johnsons to a performance of *Aida*; and on another he was invited to a reception by a Hollywood actor who, dressed in white jodhpurs and carrying a riding whip, thrust 'an appalling pint of whisky and soda' into Lawrence's hand.[17] He was fascinated and not unattracted by a life that seemed to him to be lived entirely selfishly and 'from the outside', but he also found it boring: 'Drunk with trivial externalities: that is California' (iv. 501).

This period of Lawrence's life, on the move from New York and then in California, is apparently aimless and one, moreover, when according to Merrild he was 'restless and lonesome'.[18] But work was second nature and an essential ballast. He had received from Henry Canby *A Second Contemporary Verse Anthology* whose contents did not impress him but which he used in his review – it appeared in the *New York Evening Post Literary Review* on 29 September – to insist that all significant literary activity ought to be dangerous. It was no good 'playing word-games around the camp fire. Somebody has to jump like a desperate clown through the vast blue hoop of the upper air.'[19] The same insistence can be found in an essay entitled 'The Proper Study' which he intended for both Murry's *Adelphi* (it was published in the December number) and the *Nation*. Rejected for the *Nation* by John Macy, to Lawrence's considerable annoyance (iv. 518), it appeared in Crowninshield's *Vanity Fair* in January 1924 complete with one of Nickolas Muray's studio portraits. 'Man is nothing, less than a tick stuck in a sheep's back, unless he adventures', Lawrence claims in this essay and argues that the proper study of mankind inevitably leads to contemplation of man in his relation to the deity. Nothing new can now be wrung from the literary treatment of man in his social relations: 'any new book must needs be a new stride. And the next stride lands you over the sandbar in the open ocean, where the first and greatest relation of every man and woman is to the Ocean itself, the great God of the End.'[20] There was that recoil from human involvement here which he had dramatised so well in *Kangaroo*, and also an implicit denial of his relationship with Frieda as the centre of his life.

So naturally prolific a writer could not be detained by one review and one short philosophical essay for long. The new work he now began was the complete recasting of the novel inspired by her brother which he had urged Mollie Skinner to write and which he had finally received a few days before he left New York (iv. 489). While he was still in Chapala he had heard from her that it was on its way, promised to read it carefully so as to see which publisher it could be submitted to and added, 'If there are a few suggestions to make, you won't mind, will you' (iv. 467). When he had read her typescript he wrote from the Miramar in Santa Monica that it was full of 'good stuff' but 'without unity or harmony', offering to re-write it and have it published as a collaboration. 'If you give me a free hand, I'll see if I can't make a complete book out of it. If you'd rather your work remained untouched, I will show it to another publisher: but I'm afraid there isn't much chance' (iv. 495–6). It would have been hard for an obscure and diffident writer like Mollie Skinner to refuse an offer expressed in these terms. The proof that Lawrence must have more or less immediately begun writing without waiting for her acceptance is that, three weeks later, the day before leaving Los Angeles, he was able to report to Adele Seltzer that he had posted off 'the first part of the *Boy in the Bush*' (iv. 503) – just under a third of the novel as we now have it.

Lawrence may have seized on Mollie Skinner's novel because he was at a loose end, just as he had turned to translation when he had finished one of his own works and was not ready to begin another. But although the text she sent him has disappeared, it is not difficult to deduce why he should have found 'The House of Ellis' attractive. The hero – Jack Grant – must always have been an athletic non-intellectual, sent out to a farm in Australia because he has disgraced himself at his English school in various manly ways. His early fortunes allow Lawrence to evoke, with a pleasure which was evident in the prose and which was reinforced, perhaps, by memories of his time with the Chambers family at Haggs Farm, the relief an apparently 'normal' but in fact deeply unconventional young man derives from the hard, mind-numbing physical labour of farm life, the daily involvement with horses, and the close participation with other young men in common physical activities. Jack Grant who is sensitive but enjoys rude health, and who has the manners of a gentleman but is also a boxer, is the kind of youth Lawrence would have liked to have been but wasn't. The 'first part' of his story referred to in Lawrence's letter to Adele Seltzer is told with a liveliness which suggests that, however lonely and restless he may have been in California, there were long hours of contentment with his notebooks. How much of this first part ought to be attributed to Mollie Skinner is impossible to say because Lawrence re-wrote her novel in longhand without using any of the 'badly typed' text she had sent.[21] Much of the plot and local detail, as well as initial ideas for the characters, must be predominantly hers; but there is a pace in the narrative and a sharpness to the prose foreign to anything she ever wrote on her own. Fairly frequently also, there are passages which can only have been written by Lawrence. The last of the three notebooks he sent to the Seltzers leaves the story in the middle of New Year celebrations at the Ellis farm, just after a cricket match which has been made unintelligible by both writers' ignorance of the rules.[22] There is then a dance. It would be remarkable if this, and the whole description of how Australians living in remote parts of the country celebrated Christmas and New Year in the 1880s, did not have its prototype in the 'House of Ellis'; but the description of Jack's intense dislike of dancing probably owes something to Götzsche and Merrild having persuaded Lawrence to visit a Los Angeles dance hall with them. (They got him inside but could not then induce him to take the floor.)[23] Much as Jack dislikes it, the dancing stimulates further his interest in Monica, the Ellis daughter to whom he has already felt most attracted. Not long afterwards they find themselves alone.

"Kiss me!" she whispered, in the most secret whisper he had ever heard. "Kiss me!"

He turned, in the same battle of unwillingness. But as if magnetised he put forward his face and kissed her on the mouth: the first kiss of his life. And she seemed to hold him. And the fierce, fiery pain of pleasure which came with that kiss sent his soul rebelling in torment to hell. He had never wanted to be given up, to be broken by the black hands of this doom. But broken he was, and his soul seemed to be leaving him, in the pain and obsession of this desire, against which he struggled so fiercely.

. . . Only when he was alone again in the cubby did he resume the fight to recover himself from her again. To be free as he had been before. Not to be under the torment of the spell of this desire. To preserve himself intact. To preserve himself from her.

He lay awake in his bed in the cubby and thanked God . . . he was immune from her, that he could sleep in the sanctity of his own isolation. He didn't want even to think about her.[24]

It would be as reasonable to suppose this is Mollie Skinner as it would to suggest that she collaborated on the remarkable series of poems about tortoises which

Seltzer had published in chap-book form in 1921,[25] or that she had been a secret contributor to *Aaron's Rod*.

While Lawrence was in Los Angeles Bessie Freeman sent on to him a telegram from Mabel Luhan which may have been a tentative move towards making-up; but he was not at this stage interested ('I'm through with her now' – iv. 498). What he wanted was news of his wife but he seems to have received only one letter, although probably not the one telling him she had had enough which Frieda had warned Adele Seltzer she had written. (She may have written it but the assumption in Lawrence's letters that they will be meeting again shortly suggests either that it was never sent or that Frieda had exaggerated its fierceness.) His expectation that she would come to join him did not prevent Lawrence from pursuing a plan he had entertained in New York to sign himself up as a cook, and the two Danes as ordinary seamen, on some ship bound for the South Seas;[26] but when this not surprisingly came to nothing he more and more concentrated on getting back to Mexico: 'It seems realer to me than the US', he told Seltzer (iv. 495). In the few days before he left Chapala, Lawrence had increased his efforts to rent a farm to which he, Frieda and the Danes could return in the winter (iv. 419). The notion of property somewhere in Mexico still preoccupied him and must have helped to nourish the enthusiasm with which he sat down every morning to evoke farm life in the outback of Australia. To make it more than a notion, however, he needed company and when it came to the point he found it hard to persuade Merrild to leave his job (he was back to house-painting) and accompany him and Götzsche on a trip south. Merrild had been keener on the trip to the South Seas and felt – he says in retrospect – both that he was becoming too dominated by Lawrence and that Lawrence would in any case soon find himself missing Frieda so much that he would follow her back to England.[27] Older than Merrild and perhaps therefore less suggestible, but giving the impression also of being more inclined to take life as it came, Götzsche was free of these worries and on 25 September left with Lawrence for the Mexican border. They made a slight detour first of all, in a failed attempt to see Bessie Freeman in Palm Springs (where she was having a house built – iv. 504), but by the 27th they were in the Mexican west coast town of Guaymas, on their way to Guadalajara. The day before leaving Los Angeles, Lawrence had told Frieda that he did not think he would come back to Europe whatever happened: 'I've turned in my return ticket to New York, to get the money back', he wrote; and he ended his letter, 'I wish I heard from you again before I left – Don't stay any longer in Europe if you don't want to.'[28]

Lawrence was long enough in Guaymas to be offered a 6–8 acre plot nearby if he would have a house built on it (iv. 507), but on 1 October he and Götzsche moved 100 miles southwards to Navojoa. From there, armed with letters of introduction from the Forsythes, a Scottish banker and his wife who were friends of Bessie Freeman and whom he had met in Los Angeles,[29] they visited a Swiss couple who owned a silver mine in the appropriately named Minas Nuevas, near Alamos. It was in this latter town that Lawrence saw stretched out in the market place a dead dog which none of the traders would take the responsibility of removing. The sight stayed with him and was used in 'The Woman Who Rode Away' to typify a certain fatalistic hopelessness in Mexican provincial life (although Lawrence's description of the Swiss wife in a letter makes clear that she was in no way a model for that story's protagonist – iv. 506, 510). After Navojoa the two travellers caught the train down to Mazatlán where they thought of taking the boat to Manzanillo and moving on by train from there to Guadalajara. They had introductions to two Germans in Mazatlán, Walther Melcher and Frederico Unger, and were able to view a farm in the area (iv. 510, 518–19). But this west coast landscape, and communities with a 'sentence of extinction' written over them, seemed too wild and desolate even for Lawrence. 'This west is much wilder, emptier, more hopeless than Chapala', he told Bynner, 'It makes one feel the door is shut on one. There is a blazing sun, a vast hot sky, big lonely inhuman green hills and mountains, a flat blazing littoral with a few palms, sometimes a dark blue sea which is not quite of this earth.' A cattle ranch he had visited near Navojoa, in the expectation of finding for himself a similar kind of property, struck him as 'wild, weird, brutal with a devastating brutality' (iv. 505–6).

Lawrence had many more intentions of putting to sea than he was ever able to realise and on 10 October he and Gótzsche abandoned the coast and took the inland route from Mazatlán to Guadalajara which went via Tepic. At Tepic they had to take the 'stage' (a Ford car) to Ixtlán – this was on the 14th, stopping on their way to watch Lawrence's second and last bullfight: no less nauseating, in Gótzsche's account, than the first although, 'There were no horses, I am glad to say.'[30] The next day they went by mule to Quemada only to discover that the railway from there to Etzatlán was washed out and that they were condemned to another day of mule-back riding over unusually rough terrain (iv. 515).[31] They reached Guadalajara by the train from Etzatlán on 17 October, twenty-two days after they had left Los Angeles. Gótzsche's vivid account, in letters back to Merrild, of the rigours of the second part of their journey makes it unlikely that it could have been completed, with such apparent lack of ill-effects, by someone as chronically sick as Carleton Beals (for example) thought Lawrence looked in Mexico City. It also suggests that the writing of that part of *The Boy in the Bush* which describes how Jack Grant and his friend Tom Ellis leave the family farm for a couple of years, in order to try their luck in the north Australian outback, must have come easier to Lawrence after the trek from Mazatlán than it would have done before.

III   *The Boy in the Bush*

Soon after the Lawrences had left Chapala, Winfield Scott – the American manager of the Arzopalo – had also left to run the Hotel Garcia in Guadalajara. It was to this hotel therefore that Lawrence took Gótzsche. He had asked his correspondents to write care of Dr Purnell and now collected from him a large pile of letters, the most important of which was one from Frieda announcing that she liked England, had no intention of coming to America, and wanted Lawrence to rejoin her in Europe (iv. 512). Now he was back in that part of Mexico he knew and liked Lawrence's first thought had been to spend the winter there. Immediately on his arrival in Guadalajara, he had evoked in a letter to Earl Brewster his old idea of a community of like-minded souls: 'I should be happy if I could have a little ranch, and you and Achsah and the child a house two fields away, and perhaps other friends that one could ride over to, on horse-back, not far. I wish that would come true' (iv. 513). A letter of the same date makes clear that the 'other friends' he had in mind included the Carswells. After a few days however, he began to acknowledge that if Frieda was determined not to come over to him then there would be nothing for it but for him to go and see her.

Coincidentally or, in Merrild's view, perhaps not so coincidentally,[32] there was also waiting for him at the Purnells' a letter from Mabel. She explained how angry she had been when she discovered Lawrence had been saying unpleasant things about her but that she now realised his friendship was too valuable to be without.[33] Her telegram had produced no effect, but this more obvious and circumstantial olive branch was one Lawrence was ready to accept. He wrote back making peace and ended his letter by hoping that the rumours he had heard of 'another young man' and divorce from Luhan were not true: 'Tony always has my respect and affection. And when I say in my book: "One cannot go back" – it is true, one cannot. But your marriage with Tony may even yet be the rounding of a great curve; since certainly he doesn't merely draw you back, but himself advances perhaps more than you advance, in the essential "onwards"' (iv. 514).[34] Lawrence's critics (Murry included) had made him sharply aware that his interest in the so-called more 'primitive' forms of social life – as an alternative to the inadequacies and horrors of modern civilisation – was open to the charge of regression;[35] and in Italy, Sardinia, Ceylon and then Tahiti he himself had recognised that there could be no simple lapsing back to a previous form of life. In his remarks to Mabel about her marriage he is quoting an assertion to that effect from the chapter on Melville's travel writing in *Studies*.[36] Yet in that same chapter he writes, 'Our road may have to take a great swerve, that seems a retrogression' and, referring to the South Sea islanders, 'We can take a great curve in their direction, onwards. But we cannot turn the current of our life backwards.' Later he adds, 'we must make a great swerve in our onward-going life-course now, to gather up again the savage mysteries. But this does not mean going back on ourselves'.[37] Lawrence's use of these same metaphors in his letter to Mabel marks a change in his attitude to her marriage which prefigures the alterations he would later make to 'Quetzalcoatl'.

Now he was once again in Mexico, 'Quetzalcoatl' was the work he was anxious to revise, but he had given those parts of the manuscript not typed by Johnson to Seltzer and had not yet received anything back. While he was waiting for a complete typescript, he could get on with *The Boy in the Bush* which he had continued to write as he was travelling with Gótzsche. By 1 November he was able to report that he had come to 'Book IV' of 'The House of Ellis', that is, to what was probably its last section. 'The end', he warned Mollie Skinner on that date, 'will have to be different, a good deal different'. She had left Jack Grant 'psychologically at a standstill all the way' whereas Lawrence confessed to having made 'a rather daring development' which he suspected she might not like (iv. 523–4). The allusion must chiefly be to Jack's relations with women. With the help of an account Lawrence himself later gave of how Mollie Skinner's novel had originally ended, and various statements of her own, Paul Eggert has deduced that in 'The House of Ellis' Jack had gone in search of Monica after she had fled in disgrace – perhaps because (as in *The Boy*) she had given birth to an illegitimate child; that he had then got lost in the bush; and that after being rescued by members of the Ellis family, he had been nursed back to health by a dowdy but dependable cousin named Mary. In a typically Victorian conclusion, Jack would then have realised it was Mary not Monica he really loved and retired with her to a farm he happened to have inherited.[38]

The end of that part of *The Boy* Lawrence wrote in Mexico is quite different. Jack has experienced from the start some mild attraction towards Mary but, after his two years away in the outback, decides there is no reason why he should not be married to both her and Monica. This decision comes near the end of the novel when he is already Monica's husband and when he has been developed psychologically in ways which make him increasingly like Lawrence himself.[39] There is more and more of Lawrence in the later Jack and it becomes a puzzle therefore why, with the evident approval of his author, he should entertain bigamous intentions when, as Frieda complained, Lawrence himself had previously been such a strong advocate of monogamous 'loyalty'. Mollie Skinner was certainly innocent of any credit or blame (she was as dismayed by the changes to the ending of her story as Lawrence in his 1 November letter expected her to be); but whether there was anything in Lawrence's recent experiences which prompted him to experiment with the idea that certain men were entitled to two women without (*The Boy* makes clear) the women in question being entitled in their turn to two men, has to be a matter of speculation only. The idea was startling but not quite so new and sudden as it seems at first. Already in his revisions to his essay on *The Scarlet Letter* he had said, 'It is probable that the Mormons are the forerunners of the coming real America. It is probable that men will have more than one wife, in the coming America';[40] and that thought may have been revived as he passed through Salt Lake City on his way to Los Angeles. But the 'coming America' was rather different from the more immediate future of a protagonist whose development had brought him increasingly close to his creator. The authorial endorsement Jack Grant's bigamous proposal receives may have had something to do with Idella Purnell's physical attractiveness but, if there were in fact features of the way Lawrence was then living which help to explain it, they are more likely to be associated with the renewal of his contact with Mabel. That may well have caused him to reconsider the situation which had arisen in Taos and wonder why he had needed to be so exclusively Frieda's. If it did, it is important that the painful awareness of Frieda not at that moment being exclusively his – or at least, on the question of who should join whom, not being someone over whom he was able to exert that authority which he imagines Jack Grant eventually establishing over Monica – should lead him to imagine for his hero additional rather than alternative female company. There is nothing in *The Boy* from which one could deduce that Lawrence had allowed himself to contemplate with equanimity either abandoning or being abandoned by Frieda permanently.

Dr Purnell offered Lawrence and Götzsche the use of a small house he owned in the lakeside village of Ajijic, not far from Chapala, and on 21 October the three of them went with Idella to look it over. Lawrence thought the lake 'lovelier than before – very lovely: but somehow gone alien to me' (iv. 519). In a letter Götzsche wrote to Merrild the next day Lawrence's disenchantment is attributed to the absence of Frieda ('he is longing for her') and he is described as being very much at a loose end: 'As he lives now, he only writes a little in the morning and the rest of the day he just hangs around on a bench or drifts over to the market place.'[41] His relation with Götzsche was described by Idella as 'entirely casual' and she thought he and Lawrence were 'like people who are friends, without being all-out friends. They did not have the community of interests or of hates which would be necessary for any kind of deep affection.'[42] Apart from Götzsche, Lawrence's only other social resource in Guadalajara was the Purnells themselves and he dined there very regularly – every night according to Idella, with Götzsche in the first instance ('his gargoyle friend'), but then on his own.[43] She remembered him breaking into a brilliant imitation of the young Ezra Pound, complete with earring, being discomfited by the visit to London of his solid mid-western parents; and she was grateful for all the help and advice he gave her over *Palms*. Because 'The House of Ellis' has disappeared we can never be certain how it was transformed, but Lawrence's re-writing of one of Idella's advertisements for

Palms is a surviving example in miniature of his power to make the dead walk by the substitution of a vigorous direct manner for conventional rhythm and phrasing.[44]

It is clear from 'Friction' that she and Lawrence also talked about Murry's editorial in the October number of the *Adelphi* – an unusually vapid one, even for Murry – in which he discusses his alternating moods of hopelessness and optimism along with the plate of mushrooms he is cooking for his dinner. Since its launch in June, Lawrence had received all five numbers of the *Adelphi* and must have been made aware by them that Murry's claim to have launched the magazine largely for his benefit was proving to be not entirely without foundation. Work of his appeared regularly (although not quite as regularly as Katherine Mansfield's), and when in the second number a reference in the extract from *Fantasia* to Jesus as a failure in his dealings with women brought letters of protest (as well – according to Murry's biographer – as a drop in the *Adelphi*'s circulation from 15,000 to 7,000[45]), Murry defended Lawrence stoutly in the next number. This was a courageous gesture, however much it may have made Lawrence wince to read that 'incomparably the most important English writer of his generation' is what he had become 'since Katherine Mansfield's death'.[46] There was nothing by Lawrence in the third number but in the fourth a third and final extract from *Fantasia* appeared (with an explanation of the source of all three), and also Lawrence's translation of Verga's 'The St. Joseph's Ass'. In the fifth, October number which Lawrence discussed with Idella, there were three poems from *Birds, Beasts and Flowers* (including 'Spirits Summoned West') and a reference in the editorial to a possible new direction for the journal being dependent on the return of a 'friend'.[47] Murry had written to Lawrence in support of Frieda's insistence that he should return, and urged him to reassume his natural role as leader in an England which was once more assuming the intellectual leadership of the world (iv. 520, 522). Lawrence's experiences of both England and Murry were too bitter for him to be entirely convinced, however; and when he read the editorials, their sentimentality and above all their vague, late-Romantic and semi-spiritual idealism must have convinced him that he and Murry were very different people. What would have also left him puzzled and uneasy was the realisation from the communications he was receiving that Frieda and Murry who, in the more recent past, had disliked each other intensely, were now in such apparent harmony. To the letter from Frieda he had received in Los Angeles, Lawrence had replied on 22 September, 'I had your letter from London. *Don't trust 'em* – that's my perpetual warning.'[48] By insisting that he should join her in London, and endorsing Murry's faith in the *Adelphi*, Frieda demonstrated that the warning had been without effect.

Idella Purnell's portrayal of Lawrence in 'Friction' as pathetically dependent almost certainly owed more to her contacts with him in October and November

1923 than those she had enjoyed in the summer. Gertrude 'knew', she writes in chapter XVI, 'that her beloved man had become her beloved child, and that he could never leave her . . . She felt however, that she should leave him, for such a shock might make him finally draw himself together and become self-dependent.'[49] Manly authority and self-reliance were such powerful Lawrentian ideals that it must have been shattering for him to realise that he was disoriented without Frieda and would have to submit to her will. Certainly the impression which Gótzsche conveyed of his state of mind was not cheerful. 'I am avoiding L. as much as possible at present', he wrote to Merrild on 25 October,

because, considering all things, he is really insane when he is as now. It is too bad, and I miss someone with whom to talk and have a little fun. You know his ways, and how he bends his head far down, till his beard is resting on his chest and he says (not laughing) 'Hee, hee, hee' every time one talks to him. A cold stream always runs down my spine when he does that. I feel it is something insane about him. I am, considering everything, really glad that we have not been able to find a ranch here, because I realize it would be too difficult to live with a man like L. in the long run. Frieda is at least an absolute necessity as a quencher. I have sometimes the feeling that he is afraid she will run away from him now, and he cannot bear to be alone.[50]

From time to time Lawrence's spirit rebelled and he began to think again about staying put (memories of how he had been affected by the English winter in the past may always have been at the back of his mind), but in general he was resigned. 'Gótzsche will have told you', he wrote to Merrild on 3 November, 'that Frieda won't come back: not west any more. I had a cable yesterday asking me to go to England. So there's nothing for it but to go' (iv. 526). He began to make enquiries about ships to Europe from Veracruz and persuaded Gótzsche he ought to accompany him by offering to pay his fare. By that time they were getting on better and Lawrence apparently excused his behaviour in the last half of October by saying that he had been adversely affected by the Guadalajara air.[51] Yet although on 10 November Gótzsche reported to Merrild that over the previous two weeks Lawrence had been 'himself again', he was still wary: 'Lawrence is a queer snail, and impossible to understand. He seems to be absolutely nuts at times, and to have a hard time with himself.' He reported Lawrence as saying that he was willing to provide a London house for Frieda and her children while he continued to travel alone. ' "She will hate it before long", he says, biting his lower lip and nodding small, quick nods. Do you know him? The fact is that he is afraid she will like that arrangement only too well.'[52] Before the two of them left for Mexico City on 16 November there was one final hesitation. Lawrence came to Gótzsche to say that he felt he would die if he saw England again so they immediately began once again the search for a farm on which to spend the winter. According to Gótzsche, however, Lawrence was already looking 'really sick and so pale' with 'his head hung way down on his chest', and the next day he had decided, 'It is just as well to go to Europe, don't you think?'[53]

Gótzsche was not the only person to have thought Lawrence insane: the charge, explicit or not, was a fairly common if irresponsible one during the war; yet here was a witness it is impossible to dismiss out of hand. He had been an admirer, telling Merrild that he felt he was fortunate to be able to go to Mexico with Lawrence 'no matter how it turns out';[54] and some of his admiration survived the trip. His observations in his letters back to Merrild have a dispassionate ring which appears to derive from his self-sufficiency and lack of involvement in Lawrence's literary affairs. Wherever they were in Mexico he was able to keep himself happy by a sketch or painting of stimulating new sights. Gótzsche clearly cannot have believed that his travelling companion was insane in the technical sense – an idea which Lawrence's letters or the testimony of Idella Purnell immediately dispel; but he must have found in his behaviour features which struck him as abnormal, and well beyond his own range of experience. He deduced a highly troubled state of mind from external signs to which we no longer have direct access (although his impression of Lawrence saying 'Hee, hee, hee' is peculiarly life-like); but he is unlikely to have read the last chapter of *The Boy in the Bush*, finished, according to a letter Lawrence wrote to Mollie Skinner, on 14 November (iv. 532). This became the penultimate chapter in the novel's final version and the least that can be said is that the thoughts attributed in it to Jack Grant are highly troubled also. Jack is riding back to Perth with a Mr George and Mary after the latter, in a late concession to verisimilitude and traditional psychological consistency, has refused his proposal to become his second, additional wife. The feeling of rejection excites in Jack a belief that nearly everyone he knows would like to destroy him.

They would like to destroy me, because I am not cold and like an ant, as they are. Mary would like me to be killed. Look at her face . . . Even Monica, though she is my wife. Even she feels a judgment ought to descend on me. Because I'm not what she wants me to be. Because I'm not as she thinks I should be. And because she can't get beyond me. Because something inside her knows she can't get past me. Therefore, in one corner of her, she hates me, like a scorpion lurking . . . Because I'm not one of them, and just like they are, they would like me destroyed. It has always been so, ever since I was born.[55]

It is, Jack believes, his difference from others which makes them so hostile to him: 'Because inside my soul I don't conform: can't conform. They would all like to kill the non-conforming me. Which is me myself. And at the same time, they all love me extremely the moment they think I am in line with them.' But it is precisely his difference ('I thought they would know the Lord was with me, and a certain new thing with me on the face of the earth') which makes Jack feel that

Mary and Monica are honoured by his wanting them both: 'But since . . . both of them *know* that it is an honour for them to be taken by me, an honour for them to be put into my house and acknowledged there, they would like to kill me. It is *I* who must grovel, I who must submit to judgment.' Their attitude means that he must abandon the idea of taking 'a big wild stretch of land' in the north and living there like Abraham with his wives and dependants, 'With my Lord . . . for the God of my little world. The spontaneous royalty of the other Overlord, giving me earth-royalty.' 'A little world of my own!', the chapter and indeed the version of *The Boy in the Bush* which Lawrence wrote in the United States and Mexico ends, 'As if I could make it with the people that are on earth today! No, no, I can do nothing but stand alone. And, then, when I die, I shall not drop as carrion on the earth's earth. I shall be a lord in death, and sway the destinies of the life to come.'[56]

The mechanisms of Jack's thought-processes in this last chapter are fairly familiar. Rejected by a woman he likes and whom he had assumed was in love with him, he develops a paranoid conviction that everybody else dislikes him and compensates for the consequent sense of isolation by insisting on his value and importance in ways which, to the extent that they would not be endorsed by other people, might well be regarded by them as megalomaniac. It is a credible reaction in a young man whose daring hopes for a new social arrangement have been dashed; but whereas at the beginning of *The Boy* there is a perceptible distance between the narrator and his ingenuous hero, in this last chapter there is no hint of any outside vantage point from which the reader might be allowed to view it as temporarily pathological – the reaction of a character who has failed to come to terms with living in a world of *competing* individual needs. No-one can automatically assume that Jack's thoughts here were also Lawrence's; but one of his strengths as a novelist is certainly the fairly direct attribution to his protagonists of feelings of his own which in most of us go unavowed. When he is writing at his best however, such feelings are given a critical context: other characters contest their validity, or their unreasonableness is demonstrated in the unfolding of events. 'One sheds ones sicknesses in books', Lawrence famously said of *Sons and Lovers* (ii. 90), but in traditional literary criticism at least, there is an important difference between writers working out their problems and merely displaying them.

On 10 November, Lawrence had received two letters from Frieda, posted in Baden-Baden. He wrote immediately to his mother-in-law complaining that her daughter 'must always think and write and say and ponder *how* she loves me. It's stupidity. I am after all no Christ lying on his mother's lap'; and he insisted that what a man needed from his wife was strength ('Kraft, Kraft, Kraft'). To Frieda herself he wrote a letter quite free of what at one point in *The Boy* Jack Grant calls the 'flummery of love': it has no opening form of address and concludes with the non-committal 'tanti saluti' (iv. 532, 529).[57] He told her he still wished he was 'staying the winter on a ranch somewhere not far from this city. I still don't believe in Europe, England, efforts, restfulness, *Adelphis* or any of that. The egg is addled. But I'll come back to say how do you do! to it all.' With what was probably the same openness he had shown in Taos, he sent with his letter one of those he had received in Guadalajara from Mabel Luhan, and he also told Frieda not to bother about money: 'When I come we'll make a regular arrangement for you to have an income, if you wish. I told you the bank was to transfer another £100 to you' (iv. 529). Towards the end of *Kangaroo*, Jack Callcott suggests that Harriett Somers might want to stay on in Australia even though her husband intends to leave: 'Oh, he wouldn't give me any money, and I haven't a *sou* of my own', Harriet replies, 'lightly, laughing it off'.[58] Like the remarks reported by Götzsche about finding a house in London where Frieda could live with her children, Lawrence's 10 November letter shows that he was ready to make the arrangements for Frieda to live independently, if that was what she really wanted. It was not simply because he had never had much money of his own that Lawrence had none of Mabel's inclination to use it as a method of control.

When he and Götzsche arrived in Mexico City on the 17th they checked in at the Monte Carlo. That same evening they were invited to dine with Norman King, the British Consul General, 'all in evening dress. How's that for committing suicide on the spot?', Lawrence lamented. 'My dinner jacket is so green with overripeness' (iv. 534). King was himself a painter and invited Götzsche to make use of the studio in his 'large rich home'.[59] That must have suited Götzsche and it is likely to have been in further deference to his companion's interests that Lawrence next made a point of looking up Miguel Covarrubias (iv. 534), a young painter he had met, not through a letter of introduction but quite accidentally, on his previous visit to Mexico City. The Lawrences had been dining in a bohemian restaurant with Bynner and Johnson where Covarrubias also happened to be eating and where several of his unframed water-colours were hanging on the wall. Both a pupil and a disciple of the famous muralist Diego Rivera, it was almost certainly in response to Lawrence's expressions of distaste at the aggressive, caricatural elements in Rivera's work that Covarrubias had declared, either on that occasion or later, 'Only the ugly is aesthetic now.'[60]

Lawrence found the capital cold, dark and gloomy and he was unnerved by its atmosphere, 'like a criminal plotting his next rather mean crime' (iv. 535). In a warmly affectionate letter to Johnson he reported 'they expect more revolution – Calles and De la Huerta – probably a bad one' (iv. 536). A familiar point in Mexican affairs had in fact been reached when those who had helped an individual to seize supreme power began to feel, like the rebels in *Henry IV*, that they were not properly appreciated. One of Obregón's two principal allies in the overthrow of President Carranza (assassinated by a loyal 'Obregonista' in 1920), was Adolpho de la Huerta. Once the end of his four-year term as President was in sight, Obregón had made it clear that his successor ought not to be De la Huerta but the second of his former allies, Plutarcho Calles, and the consequence had been an ever-increasing rise in tension.[61] In reply to a letter from Mabel which had been sent on to him from Guadalajara, Lawrence said that, because he was sailing in three days' time, they would have to go their separate ways for the moment – 'Mine, I always think, holds the chance of my getting shot' (iv. 539). This was on 19 November. The next day he replied to another letter from her, insisting, just like Jack Grant in the (as yet) final chapter of *The Boy*, that one must be very wary of the world,[62] and confessing, 'Yes, I am glad if you will stand behind me, and I know it. I need someone to stand behind me, badly. – I don't want much to go to England – but suppose it is the next move in the battle which never ends and in which I never win . . . Send me some strength then on my way . . . Don't you see I find it very hard' (iv. 540–1). On 22 November 1923 he and Gótzsche sailed to Europe from Veracruz (two weeks later this port, which had played such an important role in the recent past,[63] was seized by supporters of the De la Huerta faction and the long-running Mexican revolution entered one more violent phase). In marriage, Lawrence had often insisted, it was the husband's duty to lead and the wife's to follow. Boarding the *Toledo* was a crushing defeat for his principles and yet one more consequence of that overly dependent temperament for which, with increasing bitterness after 1919, he was always inclined to hold his mother responsible.

1 The octagonal pavilion, attached to the Temple of the Tooth in Kandy, at the time of the perahera (1922)

2 Mabel Dodge, *c.* 1922 (in the middle of the back row between Alice Corbin Henderson and her husband. Witter Bynner is at the front with the dog)

3 The 'Big House' at Taos

4 Taos pueblo

5 Frieda Lawrence, Witter Bynner and Willard Johnson
outside Bynner's house in Santa Fe

6 Knud Merrild at Del Monte, in the hat knitted for him by Frieda

7 Thomas and Adele Seltzer, *c.* 1920

8 The Temple
of Quetzalcoatl
at Teotihuacán

9 Lawrence in Cuernavaca

10 Frieda Lawrence in Guadalajara

11 Lake Chapala now . . .

12 . . . and then (Frieda paddling)

13 The Lawrences at the window of their house in Chapala

14 Idella Purnell

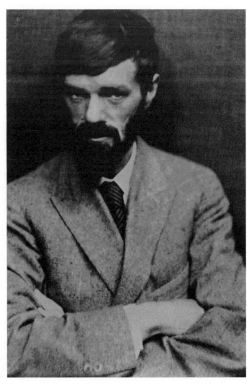

15 Portrait of Lawrence
by Nickolas Muray

16 Dorothy Brett in her Western costume

17 Portrait of Lawrence
by Edward Weston

18 Lawrence at the PEN dinner in
Mexico City (31 October 1924)

19 The Lawrences on the verandah of their house in Oaxaca

20 Frieda, Lawrence, their landlord, Corasmin and the parrot,
in the garden of their house in Oaxaca

21 José Clemente Orozco – sketch for *Reactionary Forces*

22 *Reactionary Forces*, 1924 (showing defacement)

23 Ida Rauh

24 Lawrence with Walton Hawk

25 The Lawrences at Kiowa

26 Painting of Kiowa Ranch by Dorothy Brett, with additions by Lawrence

27 The Lawrences on the SS *Resolute*, about to leave the USA in 1925

PART TWO

◆

The Second Visit
to America

◆

CHAPTER SEVEN

November 1923–March 1924
EUROPEAN INTERLUDE

I On Coming Home

The ship Lawrence and Gótzsche took from Veracruz belonged to a German company. After two or three days it docked in Havana from where, on 25 November, Lawrence sent a postcard in which he described himself to Merrild as 'already sick' of life at sea (iv. 541). We would have no more detailed clue to his feelings if, fifteen months later, when he was lying seriously ill in Mexico City, Lawrence had not begun a novel entitled 'The Flying-Fish'. The hero of this fragment (Gethin Day) takes a German ship from Veracruz towards the end of the year and with one young Danish companion, and an older one who has worked in the Mexican oil fields, spends an unsatisfactory day in Havana. He is travelling second-class with only sixteen other people – this boat is 'nearly empty' Lawrence had told Merrild – and does not appreciate their table manners. A description in 'The Flying-Fish' of a meal in which all seventeen second-class passengers are sat 'at one long table in the dining-saloon' is clearly a memory of Lawrence's own trip fifteen months earlier and has all the sharpness of similar scenes in *Sea and Sardinia*, without any of that book's comic exuberance. To escape the irritation of his travelling companions Gethin Day spends hours 'at the very tip of the ship, on the bow-sprit' watching the dolphins and the porpoises. The movements of these fish are described with a felicity reminiscent of the best poems in *Birds, Beasts and Flowers* and they provide an answer, or rather the model for an answer, to one of the problems which we know most tormented Lawrence. How can a man both associate with others and remain himself? As Gethin Day gazes at the water he thinks, 'This is the purest achievement of joy I have seen in all life: these strong, careless fish. Men have not got in them that secret to be alive together and make one like a single laugh, yet each fish going his own gait.' But the opportunity to observe the porpoises and dolphins does not last long. After Havana the ship heads north, to about the latitude of New York, in order to pick up (one of the officers explains) 'the current running east'. Whereupon no more dolphins and no more blue sky. 'It was December, grey, dark December on a waste of ugly, dead-grey water, under a dead-grey sky.'[1]

The change of light and weather was to have an important effect on Lawrence.

He was returning to Europe unwillingly, at Frieda's behest (the archaism modulates usefully between 'command' and 'request'), and he was in no mood to be easily pleased. Shortly after he had landed in England, in an essay entitled 'On Coming Home', intended as the first in a whole collection of reflections all beginning with the preposition 'On', Lawrence gave a detailed account of his feelings as his ship approached Land's End and then made its way at night into Plymouth Sound. The darkness and the quiet efficiency of the English sailors and officials on the wharf gave him the impression of a 'curious muteness' which stayed with him during the succeeding days. 'I have not had one single sharp impression in England. Everything seems sand-bagged, like when a ship hangs bags of sand over her side to deaden the bump with the wharf.'[2] After the brightness and the animation of a country where the scale was always large and the sky rarely grey or overcast, England struck him as gloomy, shut-in, half-alive: a tight little island peopled with the walking dead. We learn from 'On Coming Home' that Lawrence spent whatever was left of the night of 11 December 1923 in a Plymouth hotel and took an early train to London the next morning. In the breakfast car he is struck by the complacent self-sufficiency of his compatriots and an air of superiority which he feels is unjustified now England is no longer the leading world power. He repeats two stories he is likely to have heard at Norman King's table in Mexico City, both of which illustrate, in his view, that however hard Britain's representatives abroad struggle to maintain her prestige, it will always be undermined by the spinelessness of the authorities at home.[3] As he had in Ceylon (but on this occasion just six weeks before Britain's first Labour government), Lawrence regrets the passing of the old proud reckless England and of Englishmen who were brave and manly even when, like Palmerston, they dyed their whiskers. 'Look at us now. Not a man left inside all the millions of pairs of trousers. Not a man left. A host of would-be amiable cowards shut up each one in his own bubble of conceit, and the whole lot within box after box of safeguards.'[4]

Murry published three of the 'On' series in the *Adelphi*: 'On Being Religious' in February 1924, 'On Human Destiny' in the following month, and 'On Being a Man' in September of the same year; but he refused to accept 'On Coming Home'. 'Murry said to me last year', Lawrence would complain on 9 August 1924, ' "Come, only come, and do what you like with the *Adelphi*." I came in December. He went green at my first article, and – wouldn't print it. *No Lorenzo, you'll only make enemies.* – As if that weren't what I want. I hate this slime of all the world's my friend, my half friend, anyway I'm not going to make an enemy of him' (v. 94). He was not being entirely fair. The *Adelphi*, as both Murry and Frieda had explained in their letters to Mexico, was to be the means by which England recovered her intellectual prestige, and Lawrence was being called home to lead the others towards the achievement of that goal. 'England seems to me', he now wrote in 'On Coming Home', 'the one really soft spot, the rotten spot in the empire.'[5] To declare in the *Adelphi* that the cause to which Murry had pledged himself was hopeless from the start, would have been to destroy the journal's rationale.

When Lawrence's train arrived in London on 12 December he was met by Frieda, Murry and Koteliansky (now acting as the *Adelphi*'s business manager, its 'busy bee' – iv. 556). Describing this reunion at the station in reminiscences which began to appear in the *Adelphi* in June 1930, Murry wrote of Lawrence's 'greenish pallor' on his arrival.[6] It was a phrase he must have lived to regret. Commenting on it in the first edition of *The Savage Pilgrimage*, Catherine Carswell wrote that Lawrence's complexion could be attributed both to his conviction that he had made a mistake in coming back to England and to his immediate realisation that Frieda and Murry were too 'chummy': 'In Lawrence's marriage there was no place for any kind of lieutenancy.' After Murry had forced Carswell to withdraw her first edition with threats of legal action, this last sentence became, 'In Lawrence's marriage there was no place for any kind of lieutenancy, however platonic.'[7] The letters Frieda and Murry exchanged much later indicate that their relationship had in fact remained 'platonic' (in the strictly technical sense at least);[8] but, from what he was to write in the next few weeks, it is clear that either Lawrence himself was not entirely convinced or the extent to which he realised (or was told) things had gone deeply disturbed him. He had no overwhelmingly rational grounds for complaint. The angry mood in which Frieda had left New York ought to have led him to anticipate she might choose to go her own way, and there was a half-recognition of that possibility in his talk to Götzsche of making financial arrangements which would allow her to live alone (or at least without him) in Europe. Meanwhile in Mexico he had written letters to Mabel which could fairly be described as intimate and, via the intermediary of Jack Grant, permitted himself to wonder in *The Boy in the Bush* why a man could not have two women rather than just one. A strict view of infidelities might not distinguish too sharply between what Lawrence allowed himself to imagine and what Frieda allowed herself, or would have allowed herself, to do.

For all that, it is not difficult to see why Lawrence found it hard to take the chumminess of Murry and Frieda in his stride. To have recovered Frieda after their brief separation, with no questions asked, would have been one thing; to discover a possible sexual rival in a man who had once been his closest friend but whom he periodically hated with a peculiar intensity was quite another. The resentment Lawrence felt is evident in three remarkably transparent short stories which he began in Europe and posted back to England from America on 4 April 1924 (v. 26). The strength of feeling against Murry in these stories makes it surprising that there was no positive breach with him while Lawrence was still in England. There was a sexual libertarianism prevalent among many of his friends before the war to which, for all his puritanism, Lawrence always partly subscribed, in theory if not in his heart of hearts. This had several unsavoury aspects, yet it is perhaps one of its strengths that instead of quarrelling with Murry or refusing to see him, Lawrence began instead to explain that, because the situation in England was so hopeless, Murry ought to accompany him and Frieda back to the New World. In a dinner he gave a fortnight later, he was to extend the invitation to seven more of his friends; but it is evident from Murry's reminiscences, and those of Catherine Carswell, that a familiar scheme for a community of chosen souls, with the energy and will to save themselves from what Lawrence saw as the catastrophe of modern life in Europe, was in his mind as soon as he arrived in London. That Murry may have been, or might become, Frieda's lover was no bar to his being urged to return with the Lawrences to New Mexico.

More immediately Murry left the Lawrences to settle in at 110 Heath Street in Hampstead while he and Kot went their separate, although not especially lengthy, ways (at this period Murry had lodgings next to Dorothy Brett in Pond Street and Koteliansky lived in St John's Wood). Heath Street was where Frieda had been living prior to Lawrence's arrival, in a flat just above the Carswells – a circumstance which allows Catherine to note in *The Savage Pilgrimage* that Murry had been Frieda's 'constant visitor'. She recalls in that book how she was 'asked upstairs' on the afternoon of the 12th and could then observe an animated Lawrence vigorously rejecting Frieda's suggestion that after his long journey he ought to rest a little. He was keen to show Catherine some of the things he had brought back from abroad – an Indian belt of plaited horse hair, for example, or a painted Mexican vase – and in doing so gave her an impression of unusual vitality.[9] The impression conveyed by the first two letters he wrote to foreign correspondents from England is different. Both of them state how much he loathes London – 'Frieda is nice, but England is hateful', he told his mother-in-law (iv. 542) – and both are somewhat despairingly brief (iv. 544). They were written on 14 December and by the 17th he was confined to bed with a bad cold (iv. 544). Mabel Luhan felt that it was irresponsible and uncaring of Frieda to oblige Lawrence to return to England when she knew how dangerous an English winter might be for his health.[10] Lawrence himself, however, as the exchange Carswell witnessed indicates, did everything he could to prevent his wife from treating him as an invalid. He would never have consciously admitted that his fear of the cold and damp should be a major factor in the struggle which had gone on between them about who should rejoin whom. In the figure of Mr Morel in *Sons and Lovers* Lawrence had shown how little he believed that illness entitled one to self-pity. Since writing that novel he had come more and more to regard his father as a role model; but towards the 'bad invalid' which the depiction of

Mr Morel suggests his father may have been, his attitude remained as sternly disapproving as that he attributes to Mrs Morel. When in her autobiography Frieda wrote, 'I should have gone to meet him in Mexico, he should not have come to Europe', she may nevertheless have been thinking, at least in part, of the effect of the English climate on Lawrence's health.[11]

While Lawrence was confined to his bed, he sent Frieda to ask Catherine Carswell to come to see him and, without asking for a direct yes or no, broached his idea for a small community in America. He had first known her as Catherine Jackson, a struggling writer more than five years older than himself and still scarred by a disastrous first marriage to a schizophrenic and a tormented love affair with Maurice Greiffenhagen, who was head of the Life department in the Glasgow art school where she studied and whose painting, *An Idyll*, the young Lawrence had found so fascinating. Since 1915 she had been married to Donald Carswell, a journalist who had found no financial advantage in qualifying as a barrister and been obliged to return to earning a meagre living with his pen.[12] Catherine explained that however much she would like to come to New Mexico, with the expectation of then moving down to Mexico proper once that country had stopped 'revolving' (iv. 546), her husband probably would not; and that there was also her five-year-old son John Patrick to consider. Admitting these difficulties, Lawrence went on to ask her about her writing and listened with obvious interest when Catherine explained that she had recently found a promising theme for a novel in an account of how a group of savages kidnapped a baby girl and reared her as a goddess. A short while after she had returned to her flat, Lawrence called her upstairs again and showed her a detailed sketch of the beginning of her proposed novel, suggesting that they should write it in collaboration: 'You do the beginning and get the woman character going and let me have it, and I'll go on and fill in the man.' There are echoes of this sketch in 'The Princess', but Lawrence wrote that story alone, Catherine Carswell having quickly decided that she was 'not up to' collaborating with him.[13]

The offer Lawrence made her was characteristic and has many different determinants, but it can be associated with the same sense of isolation that prompted the invitations to America. By the 19th two of these had been more or less accepted. 'We seriously think of New Mexico in early spring', he wrote to Mabel Luhan on that date, 'and Middleton Murry wants to come along – also, probably Dorothy Brett, who paints, is deaf, forty, very nice, and daughter of Viscount Esher' (iv. 546). With Mark Gertler and Dora Carrington – two other former Slade students – Brett (as she was usually called) had been a member of the Garsington set during the war years and Lawrence had met her then; but it was only now that he got to know her well. His brief description, repeated to other correspondents, covers the salient points but inevitably ignores, in its brevity, how Brett's prominent and politically influential family had proved almost as great a disability to someone of her temperament as the severe deafness which had begun to afflict her in her early thirties. She was now brought into Lawrence's more immediate circle by Murry, with whom she had begun to sleep soon after Katherine Mansfield's death. In a diary she kept through most of 1923 and the beginning of 1924, Brett poignantly recorded the progress of this affair: the shock of her first sexual relationship at the age of thirty-nine and the sentimental conviction that in making love with Murry she was obeying Katherine's dying injunction to look after the 'little lad'. She described her anxieties about pregnancy but also her hopes of a possible marriage, much tempered by the knowledge that while Murry was sleeping with her, he was simultaneously interested in a number of younger, more physically attractive women (she does not seem to have been aware of his attraction to Frieda).[14] Once the Lawrences had returned, Brett soon became, Carswell records, 'as constant a visitor as Murry' to their rooms;[15] and when he was fit enough Lawrence frequently called at her studio in Hampstead where she appears to have endured far more patiently than Merrild his advice about how she ought to paint.[16]

II Dinner at the Café Royal

Lawrence's bad cold helps to fix the approximate date of the famous dinner he gave for his friends at the Café Royal. Carswell reports that he was only obliged to stay in bed for a day or two and by 31 December he had left London to visit his sisters in the Midlands. Brett describes a meal she prepared for the Lawrences on Christmas Day, dating it after the Café Royal occasion.[17] It seems probable therefore that Lawrence's dinner took place between 21 December, when he was on his feet again (iv. 548), and the 24th (after which some at least of his guests would have had family commitments).

There are three usable accounts of the dinner at the Café Royal: those by Catherine Carswell, Murry and Dorothy Brett. The one offered by Mabel Luhan, not of course an eye-witness, begins by assuming that it was given for Lawrence by his friends whereas it is clear that Lawrence himself chose this way of marking his return to Europe. Perhaps also, now that he had dollars in the bank or (not having heard from Seltzer recently) hoped he had, he wanted to thank some of those who had helped him, in financial and other ways, during the war. When Catherine Carswell first heard of the dinner from Frieda her assumption was that she and her husband would not be invited because they could see the Lawrences every day. 'But you and Don are coming!' Frieda shouted, going on to explain, 'This is for Lawrence's real friends. Are you not his real friends?' It was then that Carswell realised that she was not enthusiastic about sitting down at the same table with some of Lawrence's other 'real friends'.[18] Apart from herself and Donald, Koteliansky, Murry and Brett, the party was to include Mark Gertler and Mary Cannan. Of these only Mary Cannan might not have been aware of the intimacy which had developed between Frieda and Murry in the preceding weeks, or not have known that they had travelled together through France in September. From this last fact, and with their knowledge of the two parties, all but Brett would have drawn what would seem to them the obvious conclusion; and she was only diverted from it by being herself Murry's lover. According to her biographer, Murry had suspended the sexual aspect of their relationship when Frieda came to England but then resumed it on learning that Lawrence was due home. Murry and I, Brett was to write to Kot on Boxing Day 1923, 'are lovers still . . . I never refuse him'.[19] There were complications here which help to explain why Catherine Carswell did not expect the dinner at the Café Royal to be especially carefree or relaxed.

The chapter in *Women in Love* entitled 'Gudrun at the Pompadour' would suggest that Lawrence's choice of the Café Royal was not in any case a particularly good omen. He had never himself been an habitué nor did he approve of its bohemian atmosphere; but it was an institution with which most of his guests would be familiar and also perhaps the only decent restaurant in London he knew well. (For Catherine Carswell, the Café Royal dinner was 'the one and only formal gathering' she had 'ever known Lawrence to initiate'.)[20] The three chief witnesses are in broad agreement about what went on there although there was an acrimonious dispute between Carswell and Murry as to what, at one particular moment, might have been said. At some point, Kot made an impassioned speech in which he declared that Lawrence was a great man and no woman could ever understand him. Not everybody agrees that Frieda was excluded from this generalisation. If she was, it represented a major concession on Koteliansky's part given that, less than three weeks before he must have made the same point directly to Frieda who replied, in a letter, 'If the day came, which God forbid, that I should see Lawrence as the "great man", he would be a dead thing to me and it would bore me.'[21] To give emphasis to his remarks Kot smashed a number of the Café Royal's glasses, with their distinctive 'N' monogram,[22] on the floor or table. This may have been in tribute to his Russian background or simply a sign that, like everyone else present, he had drunk too much of the claret which was liberally available. Alcohol makes good linguists and at one other moment Lawrence and Donald Carswell could be heard rattling away in Spanish together.[23]

It is not clear whether it was before or after these episodes that Lawrence, with what Carswell describes as 'quiet urgency', made a public appeal to all his guests to follow him to the New World and start a fresh life there. 'Did the search, the adventure, the pilgrimage for which he stood, mean enough to us for us to give up our own way of life and our own separate struggle with the world?' Drink, and the perception some of those appealed to felt they had of Lawrence's desperate loneliness, must explain why all but one of those present responded in the affirmative. The honourable exception was Mary Cannan who, in an echo of Lawrence's own straightforwardness, is reported by Carswell as saying, 'I like you, Lawrence, but not so much as all that, and I think you are asking what no human being has a right to ask of another.'[24] This is how most if not all the others ought to have responded, especially as Lawrence does not seem to have resented the reply. Mary Cannan had offered him financial support more than once in the past, but if he returned her liking it was also because, like two of his other, younger favourites, Cynthia Asquith and Frieda's sister Johanna ('Nusch'), she was, or at least once had been, unusually attractive and well-groomed. What he may have admired in addition was the way that, via first the stage and then marriage to two writers (J. M. Barrie before Gilbert Cannan), she had progressed from modest social origins to her present position of relative independence. Yet in retrospect the idea of Mary Cannan traipsing around a ranch in the mountains above Taos, with or without her usual elegant attire, must surely have seemed incongruous even to him. On the evening of the Café Royal dinner she is described as leaving early along with Mark Gertler, whom Lawrence had known well during the war and whose painting *The Merry-Go-Round* had been the inspiration for Loerke's frieze in *Women in Love*. But Gertler was more a friend of Brett (the Slade connection) and Kot (another member of the Jewish immigrant community) than of Lawrence, and never one of his intimates.[25]

Of those who indicated that they were willing to follow Lawrence to the New World, only Brett and Murry made it clear after the dinner (as they almost certainly had before) that they were to be taken seriously. In the opinion of Brett's biographer, she at this stage was willing to leave England less on account of her growing attachment to Lawrence (who had after all been back home only a couple of weeks) than because she hoped to continue her relationship with Murry.[26] Much later in his life, Murry himself explained that although he had disagreed from the start with Lawrence's analysis of the hopelessness of the situation in England, and with his belief that there was no point in trying to appeal through the *Adelphi* to what was still capable of regeneration, he nevertheless responded positively to the invitation because of his love for Lawrence as an individual human being.[27] It is doubtful whether he could have given a similarly coherent account of his motives in December 1923, but his affection was demonstrated at the Café Royal dinner when he took the unusual step, for an Englishman, of kissing Lawrence. What he then said was the subject of the dispute between him and Catherine Carswell already mentioned. According to her, Murry became conscious of her distaste and addressed her as follows:

'Women can't understand this', he said. 'This is an affair between men. Women can have no part or place in it.'

'Maybe', said I. 'But anyhow it wasn't a woman who betrayed Jesus with a kiss.'

At this Murry again embraced Lawrence, who sat perfectly still and unresponsive, with a dead-white face in which the eyes alone were alive.

'I *have* betrayed you, old chap, I confess it.' continued Murry. 'In the past I *have* betrayed you. But never again. I call you all to witness, never again.'[28]

By the time Catherine Carswell wrote this description, Murry had already given a preliminary account of the exchange in his biography of Lawrence, *Son of Woman*. 'Suddenly', one reads there, 'you put your arm about my neck, for the first and last time, and said: "Do not betray me!"' Murry adds that although he did not understand these words, he never forgot them. Commenting later on the Carswell version he concedes that he did kiss Lawrence, 'for the first and last time in my life', but is able to cite a letter which Lawrence sent him in January 1925 for confirmation of his own lines. Referring in an ironic vein to 'that charming dinner' at the Café Royal, Lawrence writes, 'You remember saying: "I love you Lorenzo, but I won't promise not to betray you.?"' (v. 205).[29]

The accounts of Murry and Carswell are difficult to reconcile although, if they are taken to refer to different moments of the same episode, they could both be broadly accurate. Where they crucially coincide is in showing that the question of betrayal was in the air. Carswell's reference to Judas is consistent with her whole approach to the dinner which, by implication at least, she continually compares to the Last Supper. Given the group in which she moved this is not at all outlandish or surprising. Many of Lawrence's friends were inclined to compare him with Jesus and he himself occasionally considered his own sufferings, persecution and sense of mission in the same light. One self-critical consequence of these considerations was his conclusion that figures like Jesus, necessarily and, what is more, deservedly, attract disciples such as Judas. This was a topic on which he could have talked and perhaps did talk for hours with Murry whose interest in the subject was shortly to lead to a *Life* of Jesus, and who would have agreed that Judas was a necessary figure. In this context, the betrayal Murry either regretted or could not guarantee might not happen in the future, would be of the *cause* Lawrence represented: his commitment to establishing a new life on earth. Yet with characteristic if unconvincing ingenuity, Murry himself later wrote that the secret he alone had discovered and could not promise that he would not betray, was that Lawrence had reached a stage when he was no longer committed to 'life' but to death and despair.[30] For most people at the dinner table who overheard the exchange between him and Lawrence, however, the significance would almost certainly have been more local and particular. They would have taken the appeal which Murry claims preceded his own words ('Do not betray me') and those words themselves – whatever they were – as allusions to Frieda. Catherine Carswell shows that she understood the exchange in this way by immediately following her version of events with, 'Throughout all this Frieda remained aloof and scornful – excluded . . . One could not but admire her.'[31] True enough: one of Frieda's strengths appears to have been to sit by and do nothing, resignedly but not too uncomfortably, when there was really nothing much she could do.

Catherine Carswell records that Lawrence was excited at the prospect of his dinner and displayed a certain boyish enthusiasm in arranging it. Yet there must also have been tension in his mind as he contemplated the likely responses to his invitation, or wondered what thoughts the other people around the table might have about Murry and Frieda. These factors, together with his very recent illness, help to explain the adverse effects the wine had on him. After the claret, Donald Carswell and Murry called for port, one or other of them insisting that port was a man's drink. 'Not in Eastwood it isn't', Lawrence could reasonably have replied; but either out of anxiety to play the gracious host or determination to meet a challenge to his manliness, he allowed his mild remonstrance that port did not agree with him to be over-ruled. Not long after drinking some, Lawrence slumped forward and, paler even than usual, was sick over the table. It may or may not be Catherine Carswell's undoubted animus which places this moment 'immediately after the strange episode with Murry'.[32] She and Brett then ministered to the unconscious Lawrence with Frieda still looking on – 'stonily detached'[33] – after which Kot and Murry carried him downstairs to a taxi and took him back to Hampstead. Donald Carswell was left to pay on the host's behalf and deal with the waiters who, his wife later reported, remained remarkably unperturbed. Given the Café Royal's clientèle, they were probably more used to vomit and broken glass than their colleagues at other establishments.

Harry T. Moore has written of the 'repulsiveness' of the Café Royal dinner.[34] Others might well regard it as high farce or recall Matthew Arnold's well-known words in his essay on Shelley, 'What a set!'[35] Lawrence himself hardly looked back on it with any pleasure. As Catherine Carswell was passing his sitting-room the next morning, he called her in to say that he had made a fool of himself the night before, but insisted that there was no harm in this as long as the fact was first admitted and then forgotten.[36] Five months later, however, he was to write to her, 'I never forget that fatal evening at the Café Royal. That is what coming home means to me. Never again, pray the Lord' (v. 46–7). What was foolish in his behaviour, a shade King Learish, was the public appeal; but to understand in full how he could have come to make it, one needs to realise how completely and passionately Lawrence believed he was living in the modern equivalent of the Dark Ages. This conviction is evident enough in two articles he wrote a few weeks after the dinner: the essay 'On Human Destiny' which would appear in the *Adelphi*, and a piece entitled 'Books', never published in his life-time and probably the combined result of two projects he mentions on 24 December 1923 as 'On Writing a Book' and 'On Reading a Book' (iv. 549). Both the completed articles begin with reflections on the nature of thought and man as a thought-adventurer; but both then go on to ponder how the human spirit is kept alive in periods of general dissolution and decay. One of Lawrence's favourite symbols for this endeavour had always been the Ark. 'But for the living germ of Noah in his ark, chaos would have redescended on the world in the waters of the flood', he writes in 'Books'.[37] After having worked on *Movements in European History*, however, the plight of Christianity in the Dark Ages had also seized hold of his imagination, and in 'On Human Destiny' he describes how,

In the howling wilderness of slaughter and débâcle, tiny monasteries of monks too obscure and poor to plunder, kept the eternal light of man's undying effort at consciousness alive . . . A scattered, tiny minority of men who had found a new way to God, to the life-source, glad to get again into touch with the Great God, glad to know the way and to keep the knowledge burningly alive.[38]

In 'Books', Noah and the monks are brought together: 'There were the lonely fortified monasteries, the little arks floating and keeping the adventure afloat.'[39] It was this vision of how 'the adventure' could be sustained, together with a strong personal sense of isolation, which caused Lawrence to presume too much on friends who did not share his own apocalyptic horror at what the recent war had implied about the future of Western civilisation. The man who vomited on the table at the Café Royal could on occasions be a monstrous egotist, and a victim of the Carlylean delusion that his pre-eminence in one field made him infallible in others; but he was also an irrepressible as well as warm-hearted idealist who, now that he felt Christianity was discredited, perpetually looked for ways of keeping the flame alive in the 'howling wilderness' of modern life. As he would explain in a more matter-of-fact idiom to Mabel Luhan on 9 January 1924, 'One's got to put a new ripple in the ether' (iv. 555).

III   Carter, Horses and Pan

Lawrence had promised to visit his family immediately after Christmas but he delayed his trip, mentioning to his sisters the snow and a recurrence of his cold but telling Mabel Luhan, on 27 December, that he simply did not want to go north: 'It's all the dead hand of the past' (iv. 552). On New Year's Eve he was nevertheless in Nottingham where he saw Emily (although almost certainly not his surviving brother, George, with whom his relations were not good[40]), and on New Year's Day he went to spend some time with Ada in Ripley. At some point during this time with his two sisters, he would also have gone to see his father in Eastwood. Frieda stayed behind in London, perhaps with her children and away from these Lawrence family reunions which were in any case brief since on 3 January Lawrence took the train to Shrewsbury in order to visit a painter and book illustrator by the name of Frederick Carter. While in Chapala, he had received from Carter a manuscript and some accompanying drawings which offered to interpret the symbolism in the Book of Revelation. Since reading *The Apocalypse Unsealed* by the Irish Theosophist James Pryse during the war, Lawrence himself had been wedded to the idea that the central clue to Revelation was to be found in the human body.[41] The seven seals, for example, were in his view 'ganglia of nerve-consciousness' and what the Bible's last book in fact revealed was 'a conquest, one by one, of the lower affective centres by the mind' so that the New Jerusalem then became that dubious triumph: 'the mind enthroned' (iv. 460). The direction of Carter's interest was quite different; his approach was astrological rather than physiological, and he had a special concern with the signs of the zodiac. Lawrence nonetheless found his work fascinating, even if '*absolutely* unintelligible to the general reader' (iv. 461). When he was in Los Angeles, he had hinted at the possibility of collaboration and, having recently received a second version of Carter's manuscript, suggested that he might be able to help it into print by providing an introduction (iv. 497). In several other of his letters, he had promised that once he was back in England he would meet with Carter to discuss his work, and one of the first things he did on his arrival in London was to propose a time and place (iv. 542).

The meeting in Shropshire went well, with Lawrence especially interested, according to Carter,[42] in the ubiquity of the dragon symbol – a matter very much on his mind at this time in its Mexican form of the plumed serpent (several times during his stay in England he wrote of needing to get back to Mexico shortly in order to re-write 'Quetzalcoatl' – iv. 549, 559, 591). Together they drew up a synopsis for the first of what was meant to be a whole series of articles on 'astronomical symbolism'.[43] But there were literary consequences of their meeting which were more significant. Carter and his wife lived a few miles outside Shrewsbury in a village that is now rather characterless, in part because the old rectory they rented, which overlooked the graveyard, and which figures so effectively in *St. Mawr*, was pulled down many years ago. Lawrence's stay was short – startling his host with the completely new set of clothes which he had bought shortly after disembarkation,[44] he arrived at Shrewsbury station on 3 January and was back in London on the 6th. He saw enough, however, to be able to use Pontesbury in *St. Mawr* for one of his most memorable analyses of the decadence of post-war English society. It was the topography of the place rather than any prominent individuals he encountered there which caught his imagination (the curate Carter describes him as meeting and immediately loathing, 'bovine, red-faced and naive',[45] hardly seems a model for *St. Mawr*'s egregiously urbane Dean Vyner). On the day after his arrival, Lawrence was taken for a long walk which ended with a stiff climb to a high point in the area dotted with outcrops of strangely formed rocks. The most bizarrely shaped group of these –

the one that includes 'the devil's chair' – runs along the crest of a hill from which those who have laboured to it have the satisfaction of looking out across the border country far into Wales.

These rocks are known as the Stiperstones. An excursion to them provides a dramatic centrepiece to *St. Mawr*, but in the story they are visited not on foot but on horseback. This is appropriate given the crucial importance of horses in the novella, but appropriate also for Lawrence in general. Three days after he got back to London, he wrote to Spud Johnson (iv. 554–5) acknowledging receipt of the latest number of *Laughing Horse* which opened with Natalie Curtis Burlin's translation of the Navajo 'Song of the Horse' – 'How joyous his neigh! / Lo, the Turquoise Horse of Johano-ai!' etc. It was not so much the banal words of this song which would have stimulated him but an introduction which referred to one legend from California 'to the effect that the fabulous animal, the laughing horse, is a brute which expends all of its energy emitting ribald horse-laughs at any and everything which it sees or hears about', and which goes on to mention another legend 'among the Navajo tribes of Arizona and New Mexico about a turquoise horse on which the Sun-God travels across the sky on clear, happy days'.[46] The effect of this information is clear in the 'London Letter' Lawrence immediately wrote for Johnson (it appeared in *Laughing Horse* in May 1924). Beginning 'Dear old Azure Horse, Turquoise Horse', Lawrence complains of the awfulness of London – 'I've been here exactly a month' – and he protests:

Oh Horse, Horse, Horse, when you kick your heels you shatter an enclosure every time. And over here the horse is dead, he'll kick his heels no more . . . Two-legged man is no good. If he's going to stand steady, he must stand on four feet. Like the Centaur.[47]

In the second and third weeks of January, before he and Frieda set off for Paris on the 23rd, Lawrence added a final chapter to *The Boy in the Bush* and made revisions to the rest. He had left Jack Grant riding back to Perth in an angry and paranoid mood after Mary's rejection of his bigamous proposal. In the new conclusion he is found leaving town in order to join his wife Monica in the northwest of Australia. His anti-social mood has continued and he feels he can be intimate with no other human being: 'his horse was the only creature with which he had the right relation . . . between them, they made a sort of centaur'.[48] He goes into a roadside inn and, as he sits there eating, hears his horse Adam neighing fiercely. A previously minor character in the novel, named Hilda Blessington, has been following him on a mare to which his stallion is wildly attracted. Jack shuts his horse in the stables but when it threatens to kick its way out he decides to let it into the paddock with Hilda's mare. ' "But you won't mind if your grey mare gets a foal to my horse?" ', he asks. ' "Oh no, she said, "I shall like it." '[49] The Hilda Blessington of this final chapter is very clearly based on Dorothy Brett. She tells Jack that she wants to escape her environment, would like to join him and Monica in the northwest, and that she dislikes men.

"You want to be a virgin in the virgin bush?" he asked.

She glanced at him quickly.

"Something like that," she said, with her little chuckle. "I think later on, not now, not now—" she shook her head—"I might like to be a man's second or third wife: if the other two were living. I would never be the first. Never.—You remember you talked about it."[50]

They agree that she should come to the northwest at Christmas and the possibility of Jack having two wives is thereby salvaged after his disappointment with Mary.

In a number of small ways Paul Eggert has described,[51] the completion of *The Boy in the Bush* in this fashion is clearly related to the *Laughing Horse* articles; but it also forces one to wonder what exactly Lawrence's feelings were at this time for Dorothy Brett. The resemblances between her and Hilda Blessington are unmistakable, and Hilda's willingness to go to the northwest with Jack is quite plainly analagous to Brett's decision to accompany the Lawrences to New Mexico. Some further indications of quite what this might mean can be found in 'The Last Laugh', the 'Murry story' which Lawrence may have begun to compose now, before he and Frieda left for Paris. In his 'London Letter' for *Laughing Horse*, he had written, 'It's a turquoise centaur who laughs, who laughs longest and laughs last'; and in a letter he wrote to Mabel Luhan on 9 January he urges her to call into action her 'common horse-sense . . . the centaur's way of knowledge', and to dare to laugh at things: 'My Gods, like the great God Pan, have a bit of a natural grin on their face' (iv. 555).

Lawrence's story deals with the return to London of both himself and a mysterious pagan figure the reader is encouraged to associate with Pan (when it was completed he referred to it directly as a 'Pan story' – v. 50). It opens naturalistically with a 'thin man with a red beard' called Lorenzo 'grinning like a satyr' as he says goodnight to two friends outside his house in Hampstead. One of these friends (Marchbanks[52]) is clearly based on Murry: a good-looking man with 'dark, thin, rather curly hair' and a bald spot; the other has similar facial characteristics to Hilda Blessington and (like Brett) is both deaf and the 'daughter of a peer'.[53] As these two are making their way home, Marchbanks becomes excited because he feels he can hear a mysterious laughing sound in the atmosphere, and he encourages his companion to attach the 'listening machine' she carries with her so that she might hear it also.[54] Their behaviour attracts the attention of a young policeman and the trio move over to some trees where the woman – referred to by Marchbanks as 'James' (her surname) – is the only one privileged to catch sight in the gloom of the source of the laughter.

These events have a strange effect on all three. As Marchbanks is passing a garden path, a front door opens and he accepts an alluring invitation from a Jewish woman to come inside. James and the policeman continue on to her home together but, as they do so, she hears voices crying 'He's come back!', and when they pass a church a strong wind runs over the organ 'like pan pipes', a window is blown out and the altar cloth sails upwards to lodge in a tree. The laughter continues – 'Such laughter! He laughs longest who laughs last' – making the woman feel full of fresh life, but frightening the policeman.[55] It is snowing and fear has made the policeman so cold that James agrees to let him spend the night in a room of her house while she retires upstairs to her painter's studio. In the morning James becomes aware that she is no longer deaf and, pondering her two-year relationship with Marchbanks during which they have never become lovers – 'Never that at all' – she realises that her love for him has been spurious. Her glimpse of the figure among the trees has also made her realise that she has 'never really wanted a man, *any* man . . . But I believe, if that man kept on laughing something would happen to me . . . Wouldn't it be wonderful if he just touched her. Even touched her.'[56]

Before Marchbanks arrives as usual for his breakfast, after his escapade with the Jewish woman, she wonders whether the fact that he has heard but not seen the laughing figure in the bushes will make any difference. When the two of them move downstairs from her studio to see the policeman, they discover that one of his feet has become 'curiously clubbed, like the weird paw of some animal'. While they are contemplating this transformation, the strange laughter is heard again. This time James sees nothing, but Marchbanks has a vision of its origin which strikes him dead – 'A man who should see Pan by daylight fell dead, as if blasted by lightning', Lawrence was to write in an article on 'Pan in America' a few months later.[57] As Marchbanks dies there is 'in the rolling agony of his eyes . . . the horrible grin of a man who realises he has made a final, and this time fatal, fool of himself'.[58]

Although it exhibits a characteristic skill in merging realism with the super-natural, 'The Last Laugh' is one of Lawrence's more bizarre stories. There is a hint of the messianic in the way Lawrence's own return to Europe is conflated with the emergence of a new liberating atmosphere associated with Pan – ' "He's come back! Aha! He's come back!". There was a wild, whistling, jubilant sound of voices in the storm of snow';[59] and the story is manifestly hostile to Murry who, in one of the two other 'Murry stories', is also disposed of by a returning spirit from another world. Yet the chief interest in this context is what 'The Last Laugh' suggests about Lawrence's attitude to Brett. He was right to imply in the story that in her physical dealings with men Brett had been either fearful, disgusted or uninterested; and he may already have heard, even at this stage, about an unpleasant experience in her early adolescence with one of her father's friends which she felt had had a profoundly inhibiting effect on her.[60] What he clearly did not know was that Brett's hostility to sexual relations with men had very recently been conquered by Murry. In 'The Last Laugh', the figure James sees in the bushes is credited with the possible future power of doing what Marchbanks can not: reconciling her to heterosexual love-making.

When this story was begun both Brett and Murry were committed to accompanying the Lawrences to New Mexico. In *Lawrence and Brett: A Friendship*, Brett gives the impression that she attached herself to him as soon as he arrived in London whereas her main interest must for at least some time have remained Murry. The effusiveness of the declarations of immediate devotion one finds in her memoir obscure how interested in *her* Lawrence must at this point have been.[61] As so often one is left wondering how Frieda responded to the situation. It was complicated enough to explain a mistake Koteliansky made at this time which permanently destroyed his friendship with Brett (given to hero-worship as they both were, they had previously been closely united in their devotion to Katherine Mansfield). In the Lawrence circle Kot was often looked up to as a moral arbiter. His Spartan life-style, impressive physique and genuine disinterestedness gave considerable weight to the severe condemnations he was inclined to pronounce. At some point while Brett was still in Europe, he must have criticised her for thinking she might be able to lure Lawrence away from his wife and palm Murry off on Frieda. We know this from Brett's angry response on 25 February and Frieda's reference to the episode in a letter to Brett written in 1932: 'How Lawrence would have hated [Kot] for practically putting it into your head that Lawrence might marry you and I Murry.'[62] It is impossible to know precisely what was in the heads of any of the participants in this imbroglio, but Kot's inference from what he had observed may have been unreasonable only insofar as he seems to have assumed that any interest Lawrence showed in Brett meant that he might be inclined to abandon Frieda.

IV Paris and Baden-Baden

As soon as he returned to England, Lawrence had begun planning a trip to Spain via Paris (iv. 546). By 22 January Paris was still the intermediary point but Spain had been replaced by what, for Frieda, would be a second visit to her mother in Baden-Baden (iv. 559–60). No doubt she felt this was necessary now that she was sure she would be going back to America soon. Immediately on her husband's return, she had accepted that her future lay with him; or at least, with an increasingly clear view of Murry's emotional volatility, had fallen in with her husband's assumptions on that score. 'F is well – and says she's prepared to come west. I swear at her for having brought me here', Lawrence had written to Idella Purnell on 17 December (iv. 545). Although Frieda's son Monty (now at Oxford) remained under the influence of her first husband and his family, she had at least been able to see a good deal of her two daughters – the younger one, Barbara, was only nineteen and technically therefore still in Weekley's control, but she was a rebellious, unconventional girl, now a student at the Slade.[63] With that natural inclination temporarily satisfied, and with what was probably a shrewd assessment of the letters Mabel had been writing to Lawrence (it is Mabel herself who confirms he must have shown all of them to Frieda[64]), she was ready for America again.

In Paris the Lawrences stayed in the Grand Hotel de Versailles on the Boulevard Montparnasse. The middle-aged painter they had known well in Taormina, Millicent Beveridge, had a close friend named Mabel Harrison who also painted and for a while these two had lived together in Paris. Now Milly Beveridge had moved elsewhere – it was perhaps to her that Lawrence was referring when he wrote on 18 January of having to 'go to Chelsea to tea' (iv. 558)[65] – but her friend still had a studio opposite the Hotel de Versailles and this is what is likely to have recommended it to the Lawrences. Mabel Harrison showed them round and was able to tell Frieda where to shop for clothes. Although Seltzer's continuing failure to communicate with him was beginning to make Lawrence anxious, the Café Royal dinner had been one sign of what he must have experienced as a new affluence, and the complete set of new clothes with which he surprised Carter was another. A third was now the decision to refurbish Frieda's wardrobe, and where else to do that but in Paris? In *"Not I, But the Wind . . ."* Frieda recalls her husband's amazement, when he accompanied her to the tailor, that any man could 'throw all his enthusiasm into clothes for women'.[66] Lawrence had some taste for the more luxurious refinements of modern civilisation, but it did not extend very far.

Widely travelled, he had never before visited the French capital. In the 'Paris Letter' which he now wrote for *Laughing Horse*, he ponders the futility of Parisian grandeur in a democratic age and insists on the uselessness of attempting to revive the old notions of aristocracy. What was required was an elite based on natural rather than adventitious attributes. Modern Parisians, he felt, were worn out with devotion to Aphrodite (all those nudes in the art galleries and museums), and the pleasures of the table.[67] His letters and postcards to friends from Paris are more appreciative, and he certainly preferred being there to staying in London (iv. 569). He paid a visit to Sylvia Beach's famous bookshop, 'Shakespeare and Company', where he was pleased to find his own books on sale (iv. 569), and with Frieda made a few excursions, one of which was to 'that Ouspensky place at Fontainebleau' (iv. 568): the centre for spiritual and physical regeneration, presided over by the Armenian mystic George Ivanovitch Gurdjieff. Since they had buried the hatchet, Lawrence and Mabel Luhan had continued to correspond regularly and in one of her letters she had asked him what he thought of the Gurdjieff Institute. On 9 January he had replied peremptorily, 'I have heard enough about that place at Fontainebleau where Katharine Mansfield died to know it is a rotten, false, self-conscious place of people playing a sickly stunt. One doesn't wonder about it *at all*. [This in evident rebuke to Mabel's own wondering.] One knows' (iv. 555). Now he paid a brief visit to confirm his prejudice ('seems a rotten place to me', he told Brett on 4 February – iv. 568).[68] Lawrence referred to his excursions in a postcard to Murry sent on 2 February which begins, 'Keep myself amused here dodging round a bit and trying to write a story' (iv. 568). If Murry had known the story which is likely to have been concerned, he would not have found the postcard friendly.

Having possibly begun 'The Last Laugh' before leaving for Paris, Lawrence appears to have finished its first version there. He turned next to the second of his 'Murry stories', 'The Border-Line', which begins with its heroine travelling to see her relations in Baden-Baden. The route she takes from Paris, via Nancy and then Strasbourg, exactly parallels that of the Lawrences when they left the French capital on 6 February 1924. Evidence that Lawrence did at least begin 'The Border-Line' about this time rests on a number of minor similarities in wording between a preliminary draft of this story and an article whose date of composition can be established from internal evidence. Once he was settled in Baden-Baden, Lawrence pursued his interest in the topics he had raised with Carter by writing a review of Dr John Oman's study of the Book of Revelation which was to appear in the April number of the *Adelphi* under the pseudonym he had used for *Movements in European History*: L. H. Davidson;[69] but he also wrote a 'Letter from Germany' to match his previous two letters from Paris and London. This latest and last letter begins, 'We are going back to Paris tomorrow' (the Lawrences left Baden-Baden on 20 February), and in it Lawrence claims that, although two years ago Germany was still looking 'to western Europe for a reunion, for a sort of reconciliation', now it was turning towards 'the destructive East, that produced Attila'. After describing the effects of economic collapse in Baden-Baden ('Money become insane, and people with it'), he says that Germany is now turning, 'Back, back to the savage polarity of Tartary, and away from the polarity of civilized Christian Europe.'[70]

Echoes of this letter can be found in the first draft of 'The Border-Line' which, in its opening description of the heroine's trip from Paris to the Rhine, employs the same similes as Lawrence's account of that 'miserable journey' in the 'Letter from Germany'. (In the Marne country the trees are like pieces of thin wire and the smashed houses in the villages like rotten teeth in an otherwise healthy mouth.)[71] These survive into the second, much fuller version where the 'Cynthia' of its predecessor has become 'Katherine Farquar'. From the beginning, however, the figure was based on Frieda with Murry immediately recognisable this time as Philip Farquar, a journalist who has married Katherine after the disappearance of Alan Anstruther, her first, soldier husband in the war. Alan was a 'red haired fighting Celt' with 'a weird instinctive conviction that he was beyond ordinary judgment . . . [a] silent, indomitable assumption that he was actually first-born, a born lord'. This did not make him easy to live with, especially as Katherine also has a high opinion of herself: 'when it came to innate conviction of lordliness, it was a question which of them was worse. For she, in her amiable queen-bee self thought that ultimately hers was the right to the last homage.' (As readers of *Sea and Sardinia* know, the 'queen bee' or the 'q-b' was one of Lawrence's favourite nicknames for Frieda.) Philip is Alan's friend and, after 'rather despising him for years', Katherine falls under his spell. Six years after Alan has been reported missing in action, she marries Philip but gradually experiences 'a curious sense of degradation . . . She realised . . . the difference between being married to a soldier, a ceaseless, born fighter, a sword not to be sheathed, and this other man, this cunning civilian, this subtle equivocator, this adjuster of the scales of truth.' Even immediately after Alan had left for the war, she had begun to realise that, in spite of all her 'queen-bee love, and queen-bee will', it is men and not women who change 'the flow of history'. Philip flatters her female ego, but with 'the subtle, fawning power that could keep her always blindfolded'.[72]

On her way to Germany Katherine is obliged to spend some time in Strasbourg – as indeed the Lawrences would in going both to and from Baden-Baden – and decides to walk to the cathedral square. There in the twilight of this border town she has a strange meeting with the ghost of her supposedly dead husband. 'He was a stranger: and yet it was he, no other', Lawrence writes in one of several phrases which seem to anticipate the narrator's description of his encounter with the ghost in T. S. Eliot's 'Little Gidding'. She and Alan do not talk but as they walk together Katherine realises that she has again 'the one enduring thing a woman can have, the intangible soft flood of contentment that carries her along at the side of the man she is married to', and wonders why in the past she has fought against it. At the bridge head, Alan draws his hand from her arm and waves her goodbye 'as if in the farewell he promised never to leave her'.[73]

The next morning Katherine takes a train to Oos where there is a connection for Baden-Baden. Philip is waiting for her there as – in a major addition Lawrence made to the first draft – is her sister. After her meeting with Alan she feels for the first time how humiliating it is to be married to Philip 'even in name' and exchanges disparaging remarks in German with her sister, referring to him as 'the little one' (one obvious physical advantage Lawrence had over the good-looking Murry was in height, another – also referred to in all three stories – was that Murry was balding).[74]

The second version of 'The Border-Line', which was published in September 1924 in both the American magazine the *Smart Set* and in the English periodical *Hutchinson's*, mostly fills out the preliminary draft Lawrence almost certainly completed in Europe; but from this point in the action it differs markedly from a third version which is much more generally known because it appeared in the collection *The Woman Who Rode Away* (and, until the recent appearance of the Cambridge edition, had been reprinted ever since). This is because when the proofs of the *Woman Who Rode Away* collection were sent to Lawrence in January 1928 the unaccountable absence of the last four pages of 'The Border-Line' led him to re-write the ending (vi. 269–70, 272, 275). In both published endings of the story the return of Alan from the dead leads to the death of Philip, just as in 'The Last Laugh' the return of Lorenzo's mysterious *alter ego* is fatal to Marchbanks. But there are details in the magazine version which make it far more graphic and enigmatically disturbing. The conclusion of the story which appeared in 1924 is much longer and includes an episode where Katherine and Philip go into town to try the water from the hot spring. Katherine catches sight of Alan among the people there and drinks a secret toast to him 'in the hot, queer, hellish-tasting water'. When Philip takes his turn, the water induces a violent fit of coughing. She walks him home with the ghostly Alan – unseen of course by Philip – holding her hand on the other side. When they get to the hotel, Katherine notices that there is blood on Philip's chin and overcoat. Refusing his request to sleep with him, she sits by his bed with Alan opposite her. Once Philip is asleep, she returns to her own room but towards morning there is a 'hoarse, horrible cry' that brings her rushing back. Philip is sitting up in bed with blood running down his chin. Previously he had complained to Katherine that he had dreamt an inert, cold Alan was lying outside the bedclothes, trapping him in the bed as though he were in 'a lead coffin-shell'. Now he explains, 'He lay on top on me, and turned my heart cold, and burst my blood vessel in my chest.' There is blood all over the sheets.[75]

The following evening Katherine has a sofa bed moved into Philip's room. As in the re-written ending, he calls to her for comfort in the middle of the night and she is prevented from providing it by Alan's intervention. Yet whereas in the later version it is no more than a question of Alan disengaging Philip's hands from around Katherine's neck, in this one she has already slipped into bed with her second husband and has to be pushed out of it onto the bedroom floor. As she lies there in her nightdress, she momentarily feels she wants to protect Philip, 'But a greater power, the knowledge of the uselessness and fatal dishonorableness of her womanly interference made her desist.' After a while Alan comes to lift her up. When in the re-written version she makes love to him, it would seem to be in a familiar way; but in 1924 Lawrence made clear that something quite different and unusual was involved: 'He was hard and cold like a tree, and alive. And the prickling of his moustache was the cold prickling of fir-needles. He held her fast and hard, and seemed to possess her through every pore of her body. Not now the old, procreative way of possession.' Whatever way replaces the old one, it leads her to fall asleep and when she wakes up Philip is lying dead in a pool of blood. This does not disturb her.

After all, she belonged to the man who could keep her. To the only man who knew at all how to keep her, and could possess her through all the pores of her body, so that there was no recoil from him. Not just through one act, one function holding her. But as a cloud holds a shower.

The men that were just functional men: let them pass and perish.

In a strange coda to the magazine version of the story, Katherine walks that afternoon to the old castle. Alan mysteriously joins her there and then leads her down into the woods. The text from the *Woman Who Rode Away* collection ends with a reference to 'the silent passion of a husband come back from a very long journey', but the concluding note in the periodical version is both more explicit and more bizarre.

And again, as he pressed her fast, and pressed his cold face against her, it was as if the wood of the tree itself were growing round her, the hard live wood compressing and almost devouring her, the sharp needles brushing her face, the limbs of the living tree enveloping her, crushing her in the last, final ecstasy of submission, squeezing from her the last drop of her passion, like the cold white berries of the mistletoe on the tree of life.[76]

Like 'The Last Laugh', 'The Border-Line' is a ghost-*cum*-horror story in a genre whose perhaps most immediately relevant practitioner, as far as Lawrence is concerned, was Edgar Allan Poe. As in the Poe stories Lawrence had analysed so acutely in *Studies in Classic American Literature*, eerie and supernatural happenings are continually suggestive in 'The Border-Line' of powerful but subterranean psychological conflicts. This is far truer of the conclusion to the original published version and makes it more compelling. There are at least three significant differences from the ending Lawrence re-wrote in 1928. One is that in 1924 he had transferred to the Murry figure his own fear and, *possibly*, his own personal knowledge of the tubercular haemorrhage. Although Murry himself had once been threatened with consumption, it must have galled his rival to have to recognise his own inferiority in terms of health; and perhaps Lawrence was tormented by the idea that, if once he were conveniently out of the way, there would be no bar to the development of Frieda and Murry's relationship. (In fact, although they may not have slept together in 1923, they certainly hurried to do so in 1930 only a few weeks after Lawrence's death.)[77] In 'The Border-Line', it is Philip who shows the pre-disposition to tubercular infection and then has it confirmed in him through a strange physical contact with Alan.

The second, and possibly associated, difference is that the love-making which Alan enjoys with his reclaimed wife does not seem to involve penetration. Drawing biographical inferences from fiction is always dangerous but in this case, where the story is so patently peopled with figures very close to Lawrence, it seems reasonable to conjecture that at the beginning of 1924 Lawrence and Frieda were no longer having sexual relations in the usual sense of that term. If that was in fact so, then Lawrence's response in the story was to claim superiority for alternative methods of gratification; but its finale indicates in a painful manner his awareness that these might not have seemed superior to Frieda ('crushing her in the last, final ecstasy of submission, squeezing from her the last drop of her passion . . .'). His re-writing of this ending post-dates the composition of *Lady Chatterley's Lover* where the descriptions of love-making are to some degree coloured by nostalgia for earlier and happier days. When he wrote 'The Border-Line' he may have been struggling hard to come to terms with a situation which was new to him, although not one it is legitimate to assume was necessarily permanent or inclusive (his possible inability to make love in the usual way with Frieda could not be taken, at this stage at least, as a proof of total impotence).

The third difference is the hardest of all to interpret. The chilling handshake of the Commendatore in *Don Giovanni* is an instance everyone remembers of contact with the resurrected dead proving fatal; but however associated with literary convention Alan's dealings with Philip may be – and certainly in a story of this kind literary convention is important (ghosts, stories in this mode insist, cannot make love) – to kill a man by lying on top of him seems very peculiar. As in Poe, the detail arrests the attention precisely because it has no obviously explicit significance. Of the several things it might indicate, one is that Lawrence, who had of course once been strongly attracted to Murry, felt in some obscure part of his being that he had been physically betrayed by him, as well as by Frieda.

The main impulse behind 'The Border-Line' is nevertheless quite clearly hetero- rather than homosexual jealousy. Lawrence must have resented bitterly the idea that a supposed friend could have slept with Frieda. This, and the other two 'Murry stories', obviously helped him resolve a series of inner conflicts which – untypically enough – the special orthodoxy of his milieu could have prevented him from discussing openly. If Frieda had slept with Murry, was that so significant? Was she not a free agent? And what more odious and ridiculous figure than the jealous husband? How could he complain openly of treachery in a group where the feelings of the moment had such a privileged status? Another man in his situation might nevertheless have decided on a complete breach with Murry. It is difficult to establish how much of the second version of 'The Border-Line' had been completed before Lawrence took the boat back to America, and how much was written or revised either on the sea-trip or in the period between his arrival there on 11 March and his despatch of the three stories to England on 4 April. What seems reasonably certain, however, is that all of them were begun in Europe, and it is in any case a simple truth that, during the *whole* of the period when 'The Border-Line' was being written, Lawrence's expectation was that he and Murry would soon be living together in New Mexico. That sometimes made him uncomfortable but more often it was a situation which, on a conscious level, he accepted and even on occasions welcomed.[78]

V   Gathering the Troops

After dining in Strasbourg, the Lawrences travelled to Paris through the night of 20 February on their way back from Baden-Baden. They went once again to the Hotel de Versailles from where Lawrence informed his mother-in-law, with whom his relations had as usual been warm and cordial, 'It was very nice with you in Baden: we have pleasant memories' (iv. 588). At the beginning of their first Parisian stay, Lawrence had discouraged Catherine Carswell from coming to join them for a holiday on the grounds that the differences between Paris and London were insufficiently marked – 'I'll help you to a *real* holiday in place of this' (iv. 563). Now, as he continued to sight-see with Frieda (Versailles and Chartres on this second occasion) and Frieda bought herself two new hats (iv. 590), he made it clear that he did not want to go back to Heath Street when they returned to London. There are no signs that this was the consequence of any suddenly developed dislike for Catherine: more probably he simply felt a need for independence and wanted to be in the centre of town so that he could more easily make the arrangements for sailing to America. The Lawrences travelled back to London on 26 February and registered at Garland's Hotel in Pall Mall.

According to a passage which formed part of Brett's first attempt at her memoir of Lawrence, but which she discreetly omitted from the published version, it was during the following week in London that, with herself, Kot and Gertler also present, Murry described to the Lawrences the situation which gave rise to the third of the stories that concern him, 'Jimmy and the Desperate Woman'.[79] Too much paraphrase of Lawrence's more famous works would be otiose, but the 'Murry stories' are relatively unknown, and they deal so directly with Lawrence's feelings that an account of their action seems biographically essential. This third one concerns the editor of a London magazine with the same physical characteristics as Marchbanks or the Murry figure in 'The Border-Line'. Jimmy Frith is thirty-five, small but good-looking, with dark thin curly hair and a bald patch at the crown. He has an idea of himself as 'a Martyred Saint Sebastian with the mind of a Plato' and writes 'rather personal, very candid editorials' in his magazine which bring him 'shoals, swarms, hosts of admiring acquaintances. Realise that he was handsome and could be extraordinarily "nice", when he liked, and was really very clever, in his own critical way, and you see how many chances he had of being adored and protected.' But Jimmy has recently been divorced by a wife who had pronounced him a man who would always need looking after and he is determined now to find a woman whom he can protect: someone who will restore his pride by nestling on *his* bosom.[80]

In *Point Counter Point* Aldous Huxley was to satirise far more savagely than Lawrence Murry's well-known weakness for cultivating amorous relations with his female contributors. Here Jimmy has received some poems from a miner's wife – in the story they read like clever parodies of Lawrence's own early verse – and discovered from their author that she is 'married to a man who lives in the same house with me, but goes to another woman'. Since he has to give a lecture in Sheffield he decides to visit her home in Yorkshire, especially as having himself 'scarcely set foot north of Oxford', he has the feeling that it is in 'these dark and rather dreadful mining villages' reality lies. When he meets Emily Pinnegar he discovers the opposite of the frail and wilting female he had imagined rescuing but after a brief conversation he nevertheless ('little gambler he was') invites her and her young daughter to come and live with him in London. Although in Brett's account this is what Murry actually did, the decision feels unconvincingly rapid in an otherwise 'realistic' story but it paves the way for an excellent scene in which Jimmy and Mr Pinnegar, who returns from his shift down the mine at nine o'clock, confront one another. In the first instance Jimmy has to sit uncomfortably by as Pinnegar squats in front of the fire and has his bare back washed by Emily; but when the two men then discuss their situation the miner insists that he is not at all reconciled to losing his wife, even if he does have another woman. He has gone to her only because Emily has not been what he regards as a proper wife, someone who will submit to him: '*I* don't want my wife writing poetry! And sending it to a parcel of men she's never seen. *I* don't want my wife sitting like Queen Boadicea, when I come home, with a face like a stone wall with holes in it.' Pinnegar nevertheless acknowledges that he will not try to stop his wife doing whatever she decides she really wants to do, and it is agreed both that Emily will follow Jimmy to London in a day or two and that her husband will divorce her.[81]

The interest of the confrontation lies in the way that Pinnegar, thin yet energetic and the kind of figure Lawrence is obviously imagining he might have been had he followed his father's line of work, dominates Jimmy whose decision-making processes are shrewdly satirised: 'even as he seemed to look straight at her, the curious cast was in his eye, and he was only looking at himself, inside himself, at the shadows inside his own consciousness.' The exchanges between the two men are understandably tense and in the course of them there is a reference to the major political event of Lawrence's brief period back home: the inauguration on 22 January 1924 of Britain's first Labour government under Ramsay MacDonald. '"After all, best be logical," says Jimmy, "If you *are* democratic, the only logical thing is a Labour Government."' Pinnegar responds with a toned-down version of Lawrence's own response to Garrison Villard at the

New York dinner the two Labour Party members had attended: ' "Maybe so", said the collier, "But *something*'s got to come to an end, sooner or later".'[82]

When Jimmy returns to London and tells a friend what has happened, he is berated for getting himself into yet another mess. As he had left the Pinnegar home after making his proposal and thought what the atmosphere would now be like, he had been described as someone who could never bear 'extreme tension. He always had to compromise, to become apologetic and pathetic.' Now the friend – in Brett's account it was Lawrence – tells him he is a fool but will no doubt outlive all the female storms he prepares for himself by playing the 'weeping willow' as usual. The next morning he feels much less sure about what he has done and writes to Emily in order to say that she must only come to London if she is sure she wants to. According to Brett it was Lawrence who took it upon himself to meet the real-life contributor in London and send her back home, but in the story the friend does not interfere. Emily decides she does want to take up Jimmy's offer but when he goes to meet her the next day at the station he feels immediately about her the presence of her husband (to whom Emily is 'helplessly married'). This awareness goes to his head 'like neat spirits' and represents a revenge for the way in which, in spite of his 'resonant Oxford voice', Jimmy has been made to feel inferior by Pinnegar. 'Which of the two', he asks himself as the story ends, 'would fall before him with a greater fall? – the woman or that man, her husband?'[83]

Emily Pinnegar bears no resemblance to Frieda but Lawrence is able to use his descriptions of her for indirect allusions to what he must have felt had made Murry attractive to his wife, as to so many other women.

He looked up at her as he spoke, with the wide, shining, childlike, almost coy eyes that were his peculiar asset. She looked down at him in a sort of interested wonder. She seemed almost fascinated by his childlike, shining, inviting dark-grey eyes, with their long lashes: such an absolute change from that resentful unyielding that looked out always from the back of her husband's blue eyes. Her husband always seemed like a menace to her, in his thinness, his concentration, his eternal unyielding. And this man looked at one with the wide, shining, fascinating eyes of a young Persian kitten, something at once bold and shy and coy and strangely inviting. She fell at once under their spell.[84]

Jimmy's question to himself as to which of the Pinnegars would suffer the greater fall ends the story with a suggestion of what Lawrence must have felt was at least part of Frieda's attraction for Murry. It indicates his understanding of the resentment people will usually feel when forced by either real or imaginary differences to acknowledge their inferiority. In Lawrence's political thinking at this time there is the ideal of a society whose members freely and gladly recognise the superior attributes of certain individuals and become their followers. Yet as *Aaron's Rod* and *Kangaroo* show, there were times when he understood very well the pitfalls of the leader/follower relationship and how, when it is badly managed by the dominant party, leaders will get the followers they deserve. The extreme illustration of this was a Jesus who, offering love in the way he did, becomes responsible for the treachery of Judas. There are signs – never very marked admittedly – that when Lawrence contemplated the largely distressing and unsatisfactory course of his long association with Murry, he was not unwilling to blame himself.

Almost totally obscured though they are by an angry and aggressive tone, some of these signs can be detected in the letter Lawrence had written to Murry on 7 February when he and Frieda were still in Baden-Baden – 'Dear Jack, / We've just got here – all snow on the Black Forest, but down in here only wet.' He had told Murry that because he seemed unsure about New Mexico he ought to come only if it really suited him to do so: 'decide for yourself, and purely for yourself. Don't think you are doing something for me. I don't want that . . . I don't really want any allegiance or anything of that sort. I don't want any pact.' The pact which Birkin had sought from Gerald Crich in *Women in Love* had been closely associated with Lawrence's early fondness for Murry, but in *Kangaroo* he had made clear his disillusionment with Whitman's love of comrades and notions of *Blutbrüderschaft*. Murry would have indicated that although he did not believe in Lawrence's reasons for fleeing Europe, he was willing to go with him because of his admiration and affection for Lawrence as an individual. But that would not do: 'a man like you', Lawrence had written, 'if he does anything in the name of, or for the sake of, or because of somebody else, is bound to turn like a crazy snake and bite himself and everybody on account of it'. Some people might be able to devote themselves to others without complication but in Lawrence's view Murry was not one of them. Forgetting whatever he might have said in his appeal at the Café Royal (or more likely the tone in which he made it), he insisted that it was not loneliness which led him to ask others to follow him abroad: 'Let us clear away all nonsense. I don't *need* you. That is not true. I need nobody. Neither do you need me. If you pretend to need me, you will hate me for it' (iv. 572).

The anger of this letter could partly be explained by the view Lawrence expresses through one of the characters in his fiction, 'If Jesus had been a kind master he would have hit Judas across the mouth and said, "Get back you swine". It was a very subtle cruelty on Jesus's part to take that kiss . . . It is a master's duty to *prevent* his man from treachery.'[85] A more immediate explanation – Frieda can reasonably be assumed to have been the chief underlying one – was a meeting Lawrence had had in Paris two days before with Vivian Locke-Ellis, who had been the *Adelphi*'s chief financial backer. He had met Locke-Ellis to discuss a scheme devised by himself, Kot and Murry for the establishment of a small publishing house (one of its first books would have been Frederick Carter's *Dragon of the Apocalypse*).[86] Perhaps because Locke-Ellis was so obviously not interested, Lawrence took an intense dislike to him and allowed his feeling to lap over on to Murry ('I very much dislike any attempt at an intimacy like the one you had with Lock Ellis and the others' – iv. 572). Yet more important than this was that, before he wrote his letter, Lawrence had received the latest number of the *Adelphi* with a strange editorial by Murry entitled, 'Heads or Tails?' 'Your articles in the *Adelphi*', he complained, 'always annoy me' (iv. 572).

If the Murry stories could be said to benefit from a biographical context, this is even more true of 'Heads or Tails?' because its terms of reference are so vague. Murry's concern in his editorial is to describe his own divided personality. His first formulation for the division is the world within and the world without but, obviously mindful of Lawrence's criticisms of his solemnity, he quickly abandons these terms as too pretentious: 'O Lord, deliver me from my besetting virtue, which is solemnity!' ('I'm sure seriousness is a disease today', Lawrence had written to Mabel Luhan on 9 January, 'It's an awful disease in Murry!' – iv. 555.) Murry next refers to the way he feels divided into the night before and the morning after (a distinction Jimmy Frith would have appreciated), and then describes himself as half fish and half land-animal. He is hoping for the day when he will be 'a fish indeed, as Mr Lawrence says I ought to be'. The reference is to 'The Proper Study', published in the *Adelphi* three months earlier, in which Lawrence had urged his readers to plunge courageously into a sea of new, alien experience and commit themselves, like fishes in the deep, to a new form of life. More particularly, Murry seems to be alluding, throughout his piece, to the tendency one side of his nature has for making impulsive decisions – such as Jimmy Frith's in asking Emily Pinnegar to come and live with him in London, or his own in agreeing at the Café Royal dinner to follow Lawrence to New Mexico – when another, more worldly, calculating side is likely to lead him to renege on them soon after. This kind of dilemma is so familiar that Murry's pondering of it in his own behaviour ought to make his reader feel sympathetic, and there are in fact moments in the editorial which have a certain appeal. He points out, for example, that other people's ideas of when we are at our best do not always coincide with our own.

For instance, when the waters seem to have covered me indubitably and I begin to swim about with a sensation of speed and ease that is positively alarming, the chances are that somebody whom I have been accustomed to regard as a perfect fish, instead of admiring my beautiful evolutions, as I expect him to or at least acquiescing in them, suddenly changes into an unmitigated land-animal, and begins to beat me about the head with his walking-stick. He is angry, and he shouts at me: 'Don't make such a damned fool of yourself! Can't you *see* what a spectacle you are? If you don't leave off this instant, I'll have done with you for ever.' And at the very moment when I think I am doing something superlative, some dolphin-roll that took an unusual amount of courage, he smites me with a quite special vehemence and cries, 'Really, you make me sick!'[87]

As a description of how problematic relations with Lawrence could often be – which is precisely what it is – this is quite attractive; but in general Murry forfeits sympathy because of his exhibitionism. His 'besetting virtue' is not in fact solemnity but a self-indulgent inclination to wring his hands in public and display the rather sticky underside of his feelings with an ease and frequency which cast doubt on their authenticity. 'Why care so much about your own fishiness or fleshiness? Why make it so important?', Lawrence had asked in his letter; and he had added, in an implied judgement which is at the heart of his satirical analysis of Murry in 'Jimmy and the Desperate Woman', 'Can't you focus outside yourself? Not forever focussed on yourself ad nauseum?' (iv. 572). Lawrence was hardly a happily integrated personality and he had been known to change his mind, but there was a directness in his dealings with his feelings which helps to explain why his essay-writing is so much more satisfyingly specific than Murry's, and why he did not have that power of easy rationalisation which allowed Murry to negotiate a succession of messy situations with his self-regard intact, frequent public gestures of self-abasement notwithstanding.

After the angry letter partly provoked by the *Adelphi* editorial, Lawrence had written to Kot, 'If Murry talks to you about America at all, dissuade him from going, at least with me' (iv. 574). Yet a week later, on 13 February, responding to letters from both Brett and Murry, he was reconciled to their all being in America together. The difficulty was that Murry had decided he could not get away until the first week of April whereas Lawrence had now come to feel that he had to be back in the United States as early as possible. The chief reason he gave was the need to pay his American taxes for 1923 before the 15th (all the necessary documents were in one of the trunks he had left with the Seltzers – iv. 559); but behind this lay acute anxiety as to the state of his publisher's business affairs, and a fear that the considerable amount of money he was owed might never materialise. He had begun to hear unsettling rumours of Seltzer's difficulties as soon as he arrived in London (iv. 543), and these appeared to be confirmed by a complete lack of response to his own frequent requests for information – 'That hateful Seltzer never writes a word' (iv. 580). When his publisher did finally respond on 23 February it was to report that Lawrence's balance in the Chase National Bank was 'about $600. I cannot tell you the exact figure because it is a holiday and my bookkeeper is away. I will put some more in soon, so that you will have enough for expenses.'[88] Here was a sum far below what Lawrence knew was due to him from his royalties, and Seltzer's accompanying gloss was hardly encouraging.[89] The sooner he got to New York the better and he and Frieda now made arrangements to leave England in the first week of March. The question then became whether Brett would accompany them then or follow on with Murry later. Her choice of the first option suggests that she was already detaching herself from Murry having finally accepted that any possibility of marriage to him was illusory. If her dating of his episode with the Yorkshire miner's wife is reliable that truth must have come home to her with a special force in the first week of March.[90]

One of the several reasons Murry himself later gave for not following the Lawrences to America was that, 'Lawrence, without consulting me, asked a fourth person to go. The presence of that fourth person made my participation impossible.'[91] The general nature of Lawrence's invitation at the Café Royal (which Murry accepted) makes his complaint about an absence of consultation absurd, if not patently disingenuous; but if by February he was trying to escape from his involvement with Brett, who in late December had told Kot that she 'never refused him', then one can understand why he might not want to be condemned to her company in the wilds of New Mexico, especially in view of whatever complications the presence of Frieda might give rise to. Even easier to understand is that he should be reluctant to abandon the powerful position he had built up in London 'quality' journalism and in the academic world (*The Problem of Style*, which he published in 1922, had been the result of lectures he had been invited to give at Oxford and *Keats and Shakespeare*, which appeared in 1925, derived from a similar invitation to lecture at Cambridge). There was some talk of editing the *Adelphi* from America (iv. 550), but he must have known how unrealistic that was, and wondered quite how he would pass his time in Taos. A new environment would be a stimulus for Brett's painting and she had a small private income, but Murry must have doubted that he had the creative talent to earn his living away from his London contacts, and realised that even the handsome income he was soon to derive from Katherine Mansfield's royalties was partly dependent on his promotional efforts at home.[92] The most cursory glance at Murry's private and professional situation at the beginning of 1924 would tend to support Catherine Carswell's assertion that he never had the slightest intention of leaving Europe;[93] and yet in some part of his nature – the one which in the *Adelphi* editorial he refers to incongruously as the world within, the night before or the fish – he almost certainly did.

By the time the Lawrences were back in London the situation nevertheless seemed clear. 'Dorothy Brett is coming with us: but Murry not yet', he warned Mabel Luhan on 29 February. On Saturday 1 March there was a tea party at Brett's house which Dora Carrington described to Gerald Brenan three days later, in vintage Bloomsbury style. She had gone to Hampstead merely to say goodbye to Brett and was dismayed to find herself in a 'dreadful assembly of Adelphites'. Lawrence (she complained) had come back in the winter expecting to be greeted as a new messiah and he now held forth to the faithful like a lecturer to 'minor university students'. Carrington noted accurately that the four principals were inclined to talk of going to Mexico when their more immediate destination was the United States; and she told Brenan that although Murry – 'that great decaying mushroom' – said nothing, merely swaying backwards and forwards on the sofa 'with hollow eyes, toothless gums and a vacant smile', it was generally understood that he was about to give up the *Adelphi*. The idea of a fresh start for any of these people clearly left her unconvinced, but then she was predisposed to scepticism by dislike.[94]

On 3 March, two days before he sailed, Lawrence wrote to Mollie Skinner hoping that she would be pleased with *The Boy in the Bush*, now 'in the printer's hands, both here and in New York'. 'You may quarrel a bit with the last two chapters', he told her. 'But after all, if a man really has cared, and cares, for two women, why should he suddenly shelve either of them? It seems to me more immoral suddenly to drop all connection with one of them, than to wish to have the two' (iv. 596). On 5 March, off he sailed for America with his two women on a ship called the *Aquitania*, which he had chosen for its speed. 'The Brett is going along: Murry is coming afterwards' (iv. 598), he had confidently informed his mother-in-law two days before. A new experiment in communal living was about to begin.

◆

CHAPTER EIGHT

March–October 1924

BACK TO NEW MEXICO

I   Mabeltown Once More

It would have been unlike Lawrence had he not continued to work on at least one of the Murry stories during the six-day voyage to America. His ship arrived on 11 March 1924 in a blizzard and almost immediately he wrote to their chief inspiration, 'When you come, don't declare anything on your customs declaration paper – put "Personal Effects and Clothing" – no more' (iv. 601). He may have sought some psychological relief in disposing of Murry in his imagination, but in everyday life he was reconciled to seeing him soon.

On *her* customs paper, Brett had made the mistake of declaring her painting materials and provoked a discussion as to whether or not they were liable for duty. Yet although the doctors who accompanied the immigration officials quizzed her about her deafness, and there was some bemusement as to how a woman with her family name could be the daughter of a man who appeared to call himself Esher, the formalities for both Brett and the Lawrences were relatively simple (v. 18). Instead of having to wait in queues on Ellis Island, the officials came to their ship and dealt with them and the other passengers on board. Cleared for landing, the members of the Lawrence party were following a porter towards the taxis when they were intercepted by the Seltzers, who had been waiting patiently to greet them. Lawrence had not written to announce the time of his arrival but they had discovered it from Curtis Brown in what was no doubt an effort to make the best impression possible (iv. 600).

The news from Seltzer was much as Lawrence expected and in more ways than one he was already prepared for it. Before he left London, recovered from his experiences with Mountsier, or at least made uncomfortably aware of the disadvantages of having no-one in New York who could establish why Seltzer remained so silent, he had agreed that his British agent should also act for him in America (iv. 559). The result was that he was now able to appeal for help to Curtis Brown's American representative: A. W. Barmby, a Yorkshireman whom he immediately liked and trusted (v. 16). Together with Barmby, and after some intervention from a lawyer, it was agreed that Seltzer should pay what he owed 'bit by bit' (v. 18). In September Lawrence could report to his sister Ada that, during the current year, he had been able to 'wring' a total of $3,000 out of his publisher (v. 126); but by the time he left the United States in September 1925 he was still owed a sum in the region of $5,000, most of which he would never be able to recover.[1]

Even before, but especially after, the dismissal of Mountsier, Seltzer had been more than a publisher for Lawrence, often acting as his unpaid agent.[2] For this and other, more utilitarian reasons – to force Seltzer into bankruptcy would have been counter-productive – he had no wish to be too hard; and he was pleased that arrangements for the future could be made with 'friendly relations preserved' (v. 18). Yet although the letters suggest that Lawrence responded to his financial anxieties with admirable calm, he was inclined to blame Adele for her husband's misfortunes and to let off some steam against her, in private at least. He blamed Adele for goading her husband into trying to become a more commercially successful publisher than his nature allowed. 'No Thomas', he would lecture Seltzer on 23 July from Taos,

You wanted to be a big publisher, and to beat Knopf etc. But men must serve at the altar they're dedicated to. You're not born for success in the Knopf sense, any more than I am. I don't 'sacrifice' myself: but I do devote myself: and to something more than the arts. You began by so doing. You began to serve – and to serve, let us say, the arts. Then you wanted the arts to serve you, to make you a rich and prosperous publisher. So you sat down between two stools. And it is distasteful. (v. 78–9)

It was not until his sixth letter to Seltzer from Taos – on 18 May – that Lawrence alluded to his wife ('Greet Adele – I hope she is well and sporting' – v. 46), whereas during his previous stay in America his letters had been full of affectionate messages and he had written to her directly on a dozen occasions.[3]

When he first arrived in New York it would have been hard for Lawrence not to remain friendly towards the Seltzers because they let Frieda and Brett have their flat while he went to a hotel and they themselves camped in the firm's office (v. 17). For the week they were there, the new arrivals saw a good deal of Willa Cather whom Earl Brewster had urged Lawrence to contact. (Achsah had been a room-mate of Cather's life-long companion, Edith Lewis, when she and Edith were both sophomores at Smith.[4]) In her late fifties, Cather was the only American writer of major importance he ever met. She had a reputation for being brusque and difficult, but apparently found both the Lawrences 'very unusual, charming, and thrilling people' and planned so many things for them and Brett to see that her biographer claims, 'when they left after a week she had to go to a resort in the Pocono Mountains in Pennsylvania to rest up'.[5] With all this hospitality, Lawrence found it difficult to carry on writing and on the day he left New York told Curtis Brown, 'I want to get quiet, and do some stories' (v. 19). These were unlikely to have been new stories but rather the same ones he had been busy with in England, and no doubt also on the boat.

On 18 March the Lawrence party left New York for Chicago where they were shown the sights by the editor of *Poetry*, Harriet Monroe, whom Lawrence had often corresponded with but had never previously met.[6] Impressed with the view on Lake Michigan, with its 'stripe of snow like a skunk's nose' (v. 28), Lawrence had an enjoyable afternoon; but on the 19th he took the night train to Santa Fe, arriving on the 21st. For at least one other member of his party, card games helped to pass the time during the long journey and Brett remembered fondly how, with Frieda in a doze and (she remarks with quiet malice) 'fitted none too comfortably in the small seats', Lawrence wrote the words 'Lui et Elle' at the top of their scoring pad.[7] In Santa Fe they were met by the always hospitable Bynner, who was accompanied by Johnson, but Lawrence was anxious to get settled and the next day they took the 'stage' (a large car rather than a bus) for Taos. Brett describes how, while they negotiated the narrow and precipitous second half of the journey, she annoyed Lawrence by continually clutching his knee as the car corkscrewed up towards Taos from the bottom of the Rio Grande canyon and she peered fearfully out of the window at the drop below.[8] She was too dazed to make much of the scenery whereas normally one of the strengths of her writing is its recall of physical appearance. Her memoir has the misfortune of being addressed directly to the dead Lawrence (just as Mabel's *Lorenzo in Taos* is addressed to the Californian poet who replaced him as her idol, Robinson Jeffers). This is a difficult mode to handle and often makes both books sound preposterous. Brett's account nevertheless conveys very well an impression of someone cut off from a good deal of social life by her deafness but able to notice much of what others did not because of the compensatory sharpness of her 'painterly' eye.

The Lawrences and Brett arrived in Taos a few days before Mabel Luhan returned from a stay in California. She had gone there with her husband and a new protégé who had been recommended to her by Alice Sprague, another friend from Buffalo days who had kept in touch, although one much older than Bessie Freeman or Nina Witt.[9] The protégé in question was Clarence Thompson, a recent Harvard student with literary and artistic interests whom Mabel herself describes as 'effeminate'.[10] At the house she took in Mill Valley, near San Francisco, she had been visited by the anthropologist and linguist Jaime de Angulo. Born in Paris of Spanish parents in 1887, De Angulo had come to the United States in 1905. After more than a year as a cowhand in Colorado, and then a period as the foreman of a ditch-digging team in Honduras, he had trained as a doctor. It was only when he had given up physical medicine and settled near Carmel in 1916 that he seriously turned his attention to anthropology and the recording of Indian languages. In 1922 he had been paid by the Mexican government to make part of a team studying these languages in the area round Oaxaca. The following year, pursuing yet another of his interests, he went to

Zurich to work with Jung, but was called back from there in the autumn of 1923 after a fire in Berkeley had destroyed the house where his wife was living.[11] This background, and these interests, explain why he should have intrigued Mabel, although his own fascination was more with Tony Luhan than her. On his visits to her house, De Angulo quizzed Luhan on linguistic matters but also took the opportunity of practising a little amateur psychoanalysis on Clarence Thompson whom he diagnosed as almost totally identified with his feminine side, his 'anima'. According to Mabel, he succeeded in inducing 'the border states of what we have learned to call madness' in both Clarence and herself.[12] De Angulo's influence explains why at the beginning of 1924, when Lawrence was still in Europe, Mabel had pestered him for his opinion of Jung. She was enthusiastic about what her new acquaintance could tell her but still anxious at this stage that Lawrence should be her mentor in all things, and prepared therefore to have her ardour dampened with responses such as, 'Now don't you keep on going on to me about introverts and extroverts and insides and outsides. It's all in the head, and no good will come out of the head' (iv. 576).[13]

In letters she had written to Lawrence in the winter of the previous year, Mabel had promised him her 'submission' and, returning home in the company of Ida Rauh (Tony was driving back from California with de Angulo and would only arrive on 3 April – v. 22–3), she was determined to turn over a new leaf. As she later explained to Jeffers,

Truly I had tried to seduce his spirit so that I could make it work for me instead of doing the work myself. Now I only longed to pour myself out to him and let his will be done as he would have it done. I submitted my will to him and told him so. I luxuriated in submission for a change and hoped I pleased him by it.[14]

The results, for reasons Mabel herself came to understand ('He simply loathed *conscious* endeavour, do you see?'), were very like those Murry had described in the *Adelphi* editorial he had entitled 'Heads or Tails?'

Lawrence did however detect some change – 'Mabel is very mild', he told Seltzer on 4 April, adding in a reference to her recent Jungian enthusiasms, 'no longer mythological' (v. 22); and from time to time during this second stay he was to observe that she was not quite the 'wilful woman' she had been when they first met. But radical transformation was not to be hoped for, whether or not an impartial observer would have thought it desirable. A woman of Mabel's egotism, forcefulness or strength of character could no more become self-effacing than Lawrence could have become six inches taller by taking thought. This is evident enough in her book about Lawrence even when every allowance is made for its largely retrospective character. It emerges, for example, in the bluntness with which she confesses why she immediately disliked Brett and was irritated by her deafness: 'Do you think', she wrote referring to the ear-trumpet which Brett found more convenient for everyday use than her Marconi 'listening machine', that 'I liked it when I saw that brass dipper swallowing up Lorenzo's talk to me? Good heavens! It was worse than Frieda's restraining presence!'[15] Brett's deafness – always looking but seldom speaking – made her seem like a spy to Mabel who resented the way she seemed to hang on Lawrence's every word, the brass dipper always pointed towards *him*. Her own hero-worship was impeded by this new variety. In most things she might sense that she was superior to Brett but there were situations where, given the priorities she was obliged to accord to Frieda, she could feel her nose doubly out of joint.

After Mabel's return, the Lawrences went to a two-story house across the alfalfa field at the back of hers (where they had been sleeping), while Brett was put into what was known as 'the studio'. Next to where the Lawrences stayed was the small 'pink house' which Clarence Thompson had started to build the previous summer. (Tiring of his presence in California, Mabel had packed him off to see Jung in Zurich; but he would only get as far as Paris and be back in Taos in May.) In a passage naively revealing of how casually she could exploit her economic advantage, Mabel explains, 'when I found that [Clarence] was having most of my men do the work, I got impatient and wrenched [the pink house] away from him and said he couldn't have it and that I'd finish it for myself'.[16] It was Lawrence who suggested that they should all take a hand in painting this house. He began with the decoration of the outside toilet which he succeeded in making such a scandalously visible landmark that Tony Luhan would never use it.[17] While Frieda painted a chest of drawers, Lawrence and Brett next began carving Adam and Eve on a bedroom door. In London they had modelled figures from the Garden of Eden in plasticine and clearly enjoyed this kind of activity together.[18] But it was work for which Mabel had no gift. 'They both liked *doing* things with their hands and I hated to – so that was that.'[19] Provoked by Lawrence's and Brett's derogatory asides on the character of Eve, Mabel abandoned her own half-hearted attempts at painting window-frames and flounced back to the big house. At dinner that night she sulked ('I was cold and *digne*') so that after only two games of mah-jong – the new craze she had brought back from California – Lawrence decided to leave:

In a flash I was after him, opening the door and closing it behind me so swiftly that I found him still on the threshold out in the warm darkness. I put my hands up on his shoulders and leaned up to him in a flood of yearning.

'Oh, *don't* be mad', I breathed. He bowed his head over me until I felt his beard brushing my cheek, and he put his arms about me in an instant's silence. Then:

'Nay, nay, lass', he said, in a voice ever so gentle and low. 'I am never really mad any more.'[20]

Mabel's determination to make Lawrence pay attention to her, and her refusal to play a humiliating third fiddle, are not the signs of a temperament naturally 'submissive'. With a frankness which makes her engaging, she goes on to describe how 'jubilant' her mood was the next morning. When she told Tony how wonderful she felt, his response was no more than a curt, 'Maybe too wonderful.' Unabashed, she went down to take her breakfast in her hammock at the back of her house from where she could look across the field at Frieda vigorously shaking a blanket over an adobe wall, or Lawrence going to the well for water, 'his shoulders always bent, his eyes on the ground. "There goes Lorenzo, looking at his feet", the Indians used to say.' There also would be Brett hovering near her door, 'forever watching Lorenzo, *forever*!' On this particular morning Mabel could not stop herself rushing over to see the Lawrences. They greeted her sourly, Lawrence no doubt regretting his contribution to her triumph of the night before and Frieda having rebuked him for it. When Mabel told them how good she felt, Lawrence attributed her jubilation to 'sheer unrestrained ego'. Not to be deflated, she then went over to the studio to try her message on Brett. The resulting exchange shows that if Mabel Luhan had neither the caustic, intelligent humour of Mrs Witt in *St. Mawr* (a figure with whom she is often associated), nor much charity, she at least possessed a rough, knock-about sense of comedy.

'Isn't it a wonderful day', I screamed into her ear-trumpet.

'What?' she screamed back, always unable to hear a word I said. 'Hay? Is José cutting the hay?'

'No!' I bellowed. 'You *idiot*', I added in a lower tone, 'I said, isn't it a wonderful *day*!'

'Oh! *Day*.' She frowned, looking bored and supercilious. 'Well, what of it? What about the day?'

'Oh, *shut up*!' I snapped – and turned homewards.

The sight of her face as she made her way back caused Tony to remark, 'Guess you better ride horseback this morning.'[21]

In April Mabel took the Lawrence party to two Indian dances. One was in the Taos pueblo on the 9th but the other involved a trip to Santa Fe, where they saw Bynner and Johnson and then went on to the pueblo in Santo Domingo. Having spent three weeks studying the Taos pueblo language with Tony's uncle Antonio Mirabel, Jaime de Angulo came with them on this latter occasion; but after the dance was over he set off in his rope-soled sandals, blue beret and Indian serape declaring that he meant to walk back to California. With their shared interests, he and Lawrence ought to have got on well but, in Mabel's view, Jaime tried too hard to impress and shocked Lawrence by his exhibitionism, tearing off his shirt in the dining room on one occasion and strutting up and down to display the muscles in his back: ' "He's not quite all right", [Lawrence] told me presently. "You must keep an eye on him. Next time he'll rip his trousers off, I wouldn't wonder!" '[22] Regarding De Angulo as an exhibitionist in all things, Lawrence assumed that his talk of walking to California must be mere bravado, and remonstrated with Mabel for letting her visitor go off in this way: 'How could you, Mabel! He never meant to do it!' Yet the letter De Angulo wrote to his wife on 18 April, five days before, suggests that he knew what he was doing: 'I plan to walk back. The railroad fare is too much. I think I will get rides nearly all the way. I ought to make it in a couple of weeks or ten days.' He must have enjoyed waving goodbye to the others and striding off alone down the road outside Santo Domingo, but he was not quite all show.[23]

Lawrence may not have found De Angulo sufficiently congenial to profit from his expertise, but two essays he wrote in April demonstrate that his interest in the Indians had continued and developed. The second of them – 'The Dance of the Sprouting Corn' – is a lively description of what he had seen on 23 April in Santo Domingo, and further confirmation of his admiration for practices which bound man and nature closer together; but in the earlier piece – 'Indians and Entertainment' – he offers to tackle the characteristically anthropological task of explaining ritual: in this case the Indians' ceremonial dances. Relying partly on his memories of Jane Harrison's *Ancient Art and Ritual*, which he had read as long ago as 1913 (ii. 90), he draws a contrast between the Greeks' religious festivals and those of the Indians. The earliest Greek religious dances, he claims, those from which Western drama supposedly derived, were always performed *for* someone: at the very beginning, a god. This was the origin, he says (the causal chain is highly elliptical), of the situation in modern entertainment whereby 'the individual watching the shadow-spectacle sits a very god' and looks down on a representation of his own doings. There was always in the Western tradition, that is, the potential for self-consciousness and a split between ideal Mind (observing itself) and body. For the Indian on the other hand 'God is immersed, as it were, in creation, not to be separated or distinguished. There can be no Ideal God.' One consequence, he feels, is that Indian ceremonies are in no way moral in the Greek sense; they celebrate the life of man in nature without attempting to make Western distinctions between good and evil. 'There is, in our sense of the word, no God. But all is godly . . . The Apache warrior in his war-paint, shrieking the war-cry and cutting the throats of old women, still he is part of the mystery of creation. He is godly as the growing corn.'[24] Whenever Lawrence thought about the superiority of so-called primitive life over modern civilisation, he tried hard not to overlook its violence and cruelty; but precisely in its harsher aspects, the old animistic religion seemed to him to have the advantage over Christianity, or Greek culture, in not being tarred with an idealist brush.

'Indians and Entertainment' was a manifestation of an interest in the Indians very different from Mabel's. On the same day on which Lawrence sent the essay to Curtis Brown (20 April), suggesting that it would be more suitable for 'a heavier sort of periodical' (v. 36), the Commissioner of Indian Affairs visited the Taos pueblo and rebuked its Council for keeping two young boys out of school so that they could receive religious training (state education for Indian children had become compulsory in 1920). At the same time, he warned its members against paying too much attention to long-haired writers, artists and anthropologists whose livelihoods depended on maintaining Indian culture in a primitive state.[25] Mabel and her friends mounted a counter-attack to which, as he had done at the time of the Bursum Bill, Lawrence made an equivocal contribution. This time it was in the form of a poem, never published in his life-time, entitled 'O! Americans'. His difficulty was that he sympathised neither with the government nor the white liberals. 'It is almost impossible', he wrote in 'Indians and Entertainment', 'for the white people to approach the Indian without either sentimentality or dislike. The common healthy vulgar white usually feels a certain native dislike of these drumming aboriginals. The highbrow invariably lapses into sentimentalism like the smell of bad eggs.'[26] When these were the only alternatives, Lawrence had been inclined to prefer common healthy vulgar dislike, but on this occasion he protests in his poem against the obtuseness of the government, suggesting that Americans ought to act with all the responsibility of those who have the germ of the future in their hands: 'It is much more difficult and delicate to be true to an unborn future, than to an accomplished past.' His rallying call is *noblesse oblige*. The Indian, he goes on, 'is a savage with his own peculiar consciousness, his own peculiar customs and observances. / Don't sentimentalize his savage consciousness, customs and observances.' But nor should these customs be utterly quashed.

> Turn the Poles, the Germans, the English, the Italians, the Russians,
> Turn them into hundred-per-cent Americans.
> What else have they come to this country for?

> But the Indian never came.
> It was you who came, Americans.
> And before you put out the old savage light for ever, hesitate.[27]

Mabel and her allies must have felt that the situation required something rather stronger than this. Towards the end of her memoir, Mabel tells Robinson Jeffers that she called Lawrence to Taos 'but he did not do what I called him to do. He did another thing. Perhaps you are the one who will, after all, do what I wanted him to do: give a voice to this speechless land.'[28] Speaking on behalf of the Indians, however, was a task the complexities of which Lawrence may have understood better than she did.

Life at this time, Mabel mused, was made up of 'funny little everyday ups and downs'.[29] Helping to provide them was her usual collection of unusual individuals with one or two new faces always filling the gaps left by the bored, exasperated or disillusioned. When Clarence Thompson returned from Europe in May Lawrence initially got on with him well, and an acquaintance from his previous visit whom he now came to know better was Ida Rauh. Born in 1877, Ida Rauh had a law degree from New York University but she had never practised, involving herself instead in many of the same causes with which Mabel had been associated. A strong advocate of women's rights, she had been arrested in 1916 for distributing birth-control pamphlets; and before that, had been instrumental in founding a theatre company in Provincetown on Cape Cod (where many Greenwich Villagers of her type would retreat during the summer). When the 'Provincetowners' played in New York, she was known as the 'Duse of MacDougal Street', after both the famous Italian *tragédienne*, Eleonora Duse, and the location of their theatre, just south of Washington Square; and she demonstrated her versatility by directing the first production of at least one of Eugene O'Neill's plays.[30] After her divorce from Max Eastman and her move to Santa Fe with Andrew Dasburg, she had given up the theatre for painting and sculpture but still retained enough of the associated skills to be the co-star, with Lawrence, of the charades Mabel's guests would play when they were not busy with mahjong. Brett remembered Lawrence and Ida lying under a blanket on the floor and convulsing the company, which appears to have recognised the allusion to the episode in Chapala, with an imitation of a wife and husband trying to persuade each other to get up and check whether there was a burglar in the house.[31] A likely onlooker who would have been particularly appreciative of this performance was Spud Johnson who (like Ida) also seems to have been in Taos often during this time. When Johnson did come, however, it was without Bynner. This was because Mabel was in the process of trying to lure Spud away from Bynner and make him *her* secretary (in which case the word would no longer need its inverted commas). Lawrence told Bynner that he did not want to interfere in this quarrel (v. 48) although, given the efforts he himself had made in Chapala to 'save' Johnson from his homosexuality by finding him a job with Seltzer, it is unlikely that the division of his sympathy was entirely equal. One consequence of Mabel's endeavours was that Bynner kept away from Taos but another, more indirect, was a satirical play partly inspired by her which he wrote a year or so later and called *Cake*.[32]

It is possible that the idea for *Cake* owed something to the comedy Lawrence probably began in late June, when he was only an occasional visitor to Mabel's house, but abandoned after two scenes.[33] His play – much more light-hearted than Bynner's – was to be called 'Altitude' in reference to the strange effects that being 7,000 feet above sea-level was supposed to have on people in Taos. The part he wrote is not very funny but it provides an interesting glimpse of a day in the life of Mabeltown, or rather of a morning since the opening has several of Mabel's guests – there is no attempt to disguise their identities by changing names – coming down to breakfast and discovering that the cook has not turned up (her absence is attributed by Johnson to Mabel having been 'temperamental'). The first to appear is Mary Austin, a prolific writer and fellow campaigner with Mabel in the Indian cause who settled in Santa Fe in 1924. She is shown celebrating Nature, Woman, and the Indian in a fatuous mixture of mysticism and a particularly milk-and-water version of the fashionable liberalism of the day.[34] When Clarence Thompson enters it is in 'rose-coloured trousers and much jewellery', and he is later followed by Alice Sprague, his sponsor from Buffalo: 'If we take care of him, and protect him, and *love* him, he may be a Great Teacher', she says of Thompson at one point in 'Altitude'. When Mabel herself appears, she is comically domineering in her response to the problem of who will prepare the breakfast in the absence of the servant, and sings the praises of the Indians while persistently ordering one of them about. Ida Rauh is cast as the intelligent sceptic in this company and Mabel's opponent in the chief topic discussed in the scene: whether Thompson ought to walk down to the plaza in his rose-coloured trousers (Mabel objects that the locals will see them as, 'Another sign of vice from over here'). Apart from Luhan and the milkman, the other character in this fragment of a play is a young girl named Elizabeth whom Mabel had discovered as an eight-year-old in an orphanage in 1914 and looked after ever since.[35] In the second scene Elizabeth is shown trying to persuade Johnson to come for a ride and eliciting strong disavowals of his interest in either falling in love with girls or getting married. The exchange suggests that it was not only Lawrence who was puzzled by Johnson and who wondered whether he might not be reclaimed for heterosexuality. 'Spud *is* queer', Mabel says at one point in 'Altitude', 'I wonder what it is. Whether we can't fix it.'[36] Offering to employ Johnson was a characteristic example of Mabel's 'fixing' which Bynner found hard to forgive.

The opportunity to be once again part of Mabel's entourage was hardly what had brought Lawrence back to New Mexico. Almost immediately he wanted to return to the mountains and probably asked Mabel about the Del Monte cabin he had rented the year before. This enquiry, or others like it, prompted in her a striking act of generosity. 'Mabel', Lawrence was able to report to Seltzer as early as 4 April, 'has given Frieda the ranch above Lobo – legally made over' (v. 23). This was of course where the Lawrences had wanted to go when they were first in Taos. Handing it to Frieda rather than Lawrence was a tactful recognition of how much Lawrence disliked being indebted to anyone. It may also have been a consequence of an awareness of Frieda's complete financial dependence on her husband which must have become particularly acute in both the Lawrences during their recent separation. Now she had something of her own. Pleasure in the gift was therefore considerably enhanced by the manner of the giving yet it was not long before the Lawrences, or more likely one of them, decided that it nevertheless implied too much obligation and decided to send to Germany for the manuscript of *Sons and Lovers* as a gift in exchange. Mabel was distressed at having to recognise either that the Lawrences lacked the graciousness to accept freely what was freely given, or that they understood too well one of her principal means of wielding power. Matters were hardly improved when in July, with the second honeymoon period with Mabel by then definitely over, Frieda wrote to her that she had recently been told the *Sons and Lovers* manuscript was worth over $50,000, far more than the value of the ranch, for which Mabel had originally paid $1,200 (v. 74, 111). Frieda's informants in this matter were the Ufers, but they were merely relaying the opinion of Swinburne Hale, a Harvard-educated poet who had come to Taos to be near his sister and brother-in-law (Joseph Foster), following a nervous breakdown. Hale later went mad and the price he assigned the manuscript was hardly an indication that his mind was sound in 1924. It might well have been the case that, even in these early days, the manuscript was worth more than the ranch but if on occasions the Lawrences were eager to suggest to Mabel that the slate was more than clean, they never seriously felt they had had a raw deal. Later in this year, Mabel also had what could be described as a breakdown and went back to New York to be treated by her psychoanalyst A. A. Brill, the translator of *The Interpretation of Dreams* and other of Freud's major texts. Some time later she gave the *Sons and Lovers* manuscript to Brill in payment for his help in treating a friend, so little did she appreciate having her urge to give transformed into a *quid pro quo*.[37]

II Lobo

Mabel's ranch, 2 miles further up from Del Monte and described by Lawrence as comprising 150 or 160 acres (v. 29, 49), very few of them usable because of an inadequate water supply, was on a slope of the mountain known as Lobo, which is the Spanish word for wolf and also the name that, for a while, he gave to the property. (When it was briefly in the possession of Mabel's son, he had called it 'The Flying Heart'.[38]) Chiefly consisting of two reasonably sized cabins, a barn and a tiny, one-roomed shed which Brett deliberately chose for herself, all its buildings were in an advanced state of disrepair.[39] The gaps in the log walls had to be filled in, and there was an urgent need for plastering, re-roofing, painting and the replacement of windows. Later Lawrence would decide he had to rebuild the chimney of his cabin with home-made adobe bricks, and he and Brett would work hard on equipping it with a porch (v. 46, 62). In all this he was helped by an occasionally drunken Mexican carpenter and several Indians who camped near the ranch when they were working there.[40] (On 6 June Lawrence recorded in his diary that he had spent $217.65 in wages as well as $245 on building supplies.)[41] Periodic trips to the ranch during April meant that the Lawrences and Brett were able to live there permanently from 5 May – although the Lawrences did not move into their cabin until the 24th (v. 48); but for at least six weeks afterwards there was still a lot left to do as Lawrence's frequent requests for materials from 'Gerson's' testify (Gerson Gusdorf was the owner of a general store in Taos). It was all very hard work with Lawrence always wanting to take the lead. Brett remembered how he insisted on climbing into the space between the tin ceiling and the wooden roof of his own cabin with a handkerchief tied round his mouth, and how white and tired he looked when he emerged sweating from that 'oven' carrying a dust pan of rat-dirt and birds' nests (although sunshine had alternated with snow when the Lawrences first arrived in Taos (v. 15), this was now late spring or early summer).[42] But he relished these occasional bouts of hard physical labour. In a letter to Mabel on 12 May, he asked if she could have sent up to the ranch the 'adobe tools', whitewash, brushes, white and turquoise paint, a packet of tin tacks, 'another pound of putty', hinges for cupboards, and screws; and he also enquired about the loan of 'the little grindstone'. On the evening of that same day, he followed his letter with a note asking if he could have a sack of fine straw for his plastering and concluded, 'Been a very busy day – very satisfactory' (v. 40–1). In the first of these communications, he also told Mabel that he hoped to finish the first half of his article, 'Pan in America', that evening.

'Pan in America' is mostly what its title suggests it might be, but in the course of the essay Lawrence deplores once again the way machinery has alienated people from the realities of their physical environment. While striving to establish a life for himself and Frieda on Mabel's former ranch, and while enduring in the process a good deal of physical discomfort and hardship, there is no doubt that Lawrence felt closer to those realities. The Indian, he writes in 'Pan in America', respects the tree even when he has cut it down to provide him with heat.

Is it better, I ask you, to cross the room and turn on the heat at the radiator, glancing at the thermometer and saying: "We're just a bit below the level, in here?" . . . what does life consist in, save a vivid relatedness between the man and the living universe that surrounds him? Yet man insulates himself more and more into mechanism, and repudiates everything but the machine and the contrivance of which he himself is master, god in the machine.[43]

'Naturally,' Lawrence told Seltzer on 18 May, 'I don't write when I slave building the house' (v. 45). Once having sent off the three Murry stories, he does not seem to have felt like embarking on any more fiction until he was satisfied that the ranch was relatively habitable. Short essays such as 'Pan in America' were another matter. The piece is in some respects a gloss on 'The Last Laugh' although Lawrence's interest in defining accurately what the Pan figure meant to him stretched back a long way. In 1915, for example, he had rebuked E. M. Forster for tending to confuse Pan with 'universal love' and for giving him 'attributes of Christ' in his 'The Story of a Panic' (ii. 275). This first item in Forster's *Celestial Omnibus* is nevertheless a likely source of the story with which

'Pan In America' opens: 'At the beginning of the Christian era, voices were heard off the coasts of Greece, out to sea, on the Mediterranean, wailing: "Pan is dead! Great Pan is dead!" '[44] After this reference to the displacement of Pan by Christ, Lawrence goes on to describe the unsatisfactoriness of various subsequent reincarnations of Pan, as Satan for example, or in the pantheism of Wordsworth or Whitman, only to find the true Pan still alive and kicking in the landscape of New Mexico.

Brett appears to have settled down to life in New Mexico very quickly. Her English upper-class background meant that she did not have to be taught how to ride, she went fishing regularly and she would tramp round the ranch with a rifle, hunting for rabbits. When she was not doing these things, or helping Lawrence with building and repairs, or painting, she assumed the laborious task of typing whatever Lawrence wrote (it was laborious because she had very little previous practice).[45] But Lawrence paid Johnson to type 'The Last Laugh' (v. 27), presumably because it involved her. Warning Curtis Brown not to send any of the three 'Murry stories' to the *Adelphi*, he characterised them as a consequence of 'the depression of that Europe' which he was busy trying to forget (v. 26). This would have been hard with Murry about to appear but there was now some uncertainty in that direction – 'Another letter from Murry – still putting up little catty defences – leaves me cold' (v. 42), Lawrence told Mabel on 14 May; and a day or two later Brett received from Murry the only one of his letters she appears not to have wanted to preserve. In it Murry explained that he was going to marry a 23-year-old woman named Violet le Maistre whom he had come to know after she had sent some stories to the *Adelphi*.

When Lawrence wrote his letter of congratulation on 16 May he assumed that the wedding was to take place four days later whereas, with something of the impulsiveness of a Jimmy Frith, Murry had been married on 24 April, less than two months after he had said goodbye to the Lawrences and Brett at Waterloo. 'If you can settle down with [Violet] and be happy I am sure it is the best for you', wrote Lawrence, 'Better, as you say, than wild-goose-chasing in other continents'; and he went on: 'I hope you'll have a nice place in Dorset and make friends with your own destiny. I'm sure you can, if you will, take the rest of your life peacefully, with a wife, a home, and probably children. Anyhow that's what I wish you – an acquiescent, peaceful happiness' (v. 43). Lawrence had no doubt come to expect Murry's defection and he may well have been relieved by it, but his response was nonetheless surprisingly mild, as it was to the confirmation of Seltzer's financial difficulties and to other crises which blew up during this period. There was some truth in his claim to Mabel, 'I don't get mad any more' – although only some. Brett records an episode before they left London when, enraged by Frieda, Lawrence picked up the poker and began breaking the cups and saucers saying, 'If ever you talk to me like that again, it will not be the tea things I smash, but your head'; and she describes how at the ranch he once felt so angry with Mabel that he broke in pieces a heavy chair which, in accordance with his belief in the moral value of practical activities, she had struggled to make for him.[46] Mabel herself describes how, when Frieda was once 'joking with Jaime, a cigarette dangling from the corner of her mouth', Lawrence 'began to shout invectives at her, calling her a bitch and so on'.[47] Confirmation of this kind of behaviour can be found in the letters De Angulo wrote to his wife from Taos describing the Lawrences. Frieda struck him as much older than her 'neurotic' husband – 'more like his mother than his wife . . . She mothers him and adores him and cuffs him. He is absolutely dependent on her, and rages and quarrels with her, and utterly loses his temper. "Pull in your belly, you big bitch", – this in public – her eyes flash, "Oh! you are such an ass!" '[48] The evidence that even at this stage in their marriage Lawrence still called Frieda unpleasant names in public, and that Frieda could on occasions give as good as she got, is too copious and comes from too many varied sources to be suspect.

Because Brett had chosen the smallest of the three cabins on the ranch Lawrence was able to reserve one of the other two for Mabel. The idea was that she and Tony Luhan could spend the night there whenever they felt like it, just as when the Lawrences were in Taos they could sleep in the two-story house where they had left some of their belongings. The road between the ranch and Mabel's house was difficult but only seventeen miles long. Her first extended stay with the Lawrences around 24 May was not however a success. She was accompanied by Clarence Thompson, and by Tony Luhan, who was angry to realise that, now the ranch was no longer his wife's, he had no legal right to pasture horses in the surrounding fields, or invite his Indian friends to camp there. The first thing he did on his arrival was to go out and shoot a porcupine. Tolerant though he was of Brett's rabbit hunting, Lawrence protested that he did not want porcupines shot on his property, however much damage they did to the trees (whose trees were they anyway?), and Mabel became offended on Luhan's behalf. It was an awkward situation with Lawrence clearly anxious to demonstrate that the ranch was now his (or at least Frieda's), and Mabel always reluctant to lose the power of patronage.[49]

Tony spent the night with the Indians who were still helping Lawrence with repairs and camping on the ranch, while Mabel and Thompson slept in the second cabin. The next morning Mabel sent Thompson to tell Lawrence that she wanted to confer with him and, when he refused to come, rushed over to his cabin and brought him back to hers, insisting that she had to speak to him alone. Once they were together Mabel began to cry with a distressed Lawrence sitting beside her on the bed 'bent over, his hands clasped between his parted knees'. She cried for a long time, long enough for Frieda, Brett and Thompson to pass by and observe her through the open door, fascinated by the uniqueness of the event. 'It was a great gift I made Lorenzo that day. I knew it at the time, as I know it now. I kept my sobs jerking up long after they had naturally subsided.'[50] She and Lawrence settled whatever differences there were between them but, after this visit, Mabel never stayed overnight in the spare cabin again.

One of the excursions Lawrence made with Mabel in May was to an Indian ceremonial cave in the hills behind Taos. When he saw it a stream of water would have been falling perpendicularly across its face but, as Mabel explained, this turned to 'an icy column' in winter, and at the winter solstice 'as the sun turns to go south, it shines through the erect, transparent pillar of ice and falls precisely upon the altar'.[51] In 'The Woman Who Rode Away' which he wrote in June (once he had settled in at the ranch), this altar is where the female protagonist is taken to be sacrificed by a tribe of Indians. In 'Indians and Entertainment' Lawrence had challenged the anthropologists in their own, discursive terms, perhaps because he had been given the opportunity by Mabel of looking again at Frazer's *Golden Bough*, an experience which led him to complain to Brett about 'people who write books from their armchairs; men who never go out and experience anything for themselves'.[52] Now, in this new story, he took up the challenge on what might properly be considered his own ground. 'The Woman Who Rode Away' is not principally concerned to analyse *why* there could develop a practice so instinctively repellent to the modern Western mind as human sacrifice; but to make the reader feel the reasonableness of this ritual within a 'primitive' context.

The eventual sacrificial victim is an American woman in her thirties, tired of the life she lives with her much older husband and two children near an exhausted silver mine in the northwest of Mexico. (For details of her environment Lawrence relied on memories of his trip from California to Guadalajara with Götzsche the previous autumn.) She rides off into the mountains vaguely in search of a remote tribe of Indians with a sinister reputation, and on a symbolic journey which signals her death as a modern woman of the West (she is described as coming from California). There is some implied criticism of the protagonist's arrogance in failing to recognise the complete otherness of the Indians she encounters: inclined to assume that her physical attraction will either expose her to assault or give her some power over them, she takes some time to understand how completely indifferent they are to her sexuality; but she is not named and little stress is laid on her individual shortcomings. Lawrence's interest centres instead on the religious earnestness with which the Indians prepare their victim for sacrifice, washing her, providing her with new clothes and in some ways honouring her as a benefactress; as well as on the woman's half-acquiescence in the process. The story is complicated by the fact that her passivity is shown to be partly a consequence of the drugs the Indians administer,[53] and there is a sophisticated irony in the woman's failure to realise – it takes the reader some time – that for the Indians she fulfils a prophecy of a white woman who will willingly sacrifice herself to their gods and allow them to recover the powers of the sun and moon wrested from them by the white races. The story does not set out to justify human sacrifice. Its aim, or at least its effect, is rather to oppose to the Scottish rationalism of a Frazer a remarkable effort of imaginative understanding of practices it is hard to contemplate steadily in any *other* than a coolly rationalist fashion.

'The Woman Who Rode Away' is associated with an incident at Mabel's in late June which marked an end of easy relations between the ranch and the 'Big House' in Taos. The Lawrence party had been persuaded to come down from their mountain for the week-end, and in the studio which Brett had previously occupied Mabel had arranged for dancing. In April and perhaps May some of Luhan's friends would be invited to the studio and there would be Indian dancing in which Lawrence was happy to participate.[54] But this was the western variety, with a gramophone playing popular dance tunes, and Mabel had always previously been unsuccessful in persuading Lawrence to join in. Before this particular occasion, however, he and Clarence Thompson had been down to the Plaza and returned with some moonshine which everyone sampled, Brett so liberally that she confesses in her memoir to having fallen down at one point in a drunken stupor.[55] The alcohol – a more accurate generic term with moonshine than other concoctions – seems to have had its effect on everyone and allowed Mabel to overcome temporarily Lawrence's disapproval of modern dancing. While she danced with him Frieda danced with Thompson until, with much bumping and jostling, a tense situation developed that ended with Frieda and Thompson suddenly disappearing into the night. This behaviour – 'I couldn't believe my eyes' (records Mabel) 'That was simply not done among us' – had a sobering effect and put an end to the party. After accompanying Alice Sprague to her cabin, Lawrence decided to go to bed. Mabel meanwhile sat peering out of her bedroom window waiting for the return of Frieda and Thompson. When they finally appeared, and she saw that Frieda had gone back to the two-story house, Mabel found it impossible to restrain her curiosity and, slipping on her dressing gown ('my thin kimono'), went out to speak to Thompson. Half-way to his cabin she heard Tony Luhan, who had been wakened by her exit and might have suspected an assignation with Lawrence, commanding her sternly to come back, but she crept on regardless. When she spoke to Thompson, he excitedly told her how Frieda had explained that it was Lawrence's intention to kill Mabel: '[Frieda] says he has *told* her he will destroy you, and every time he comes down here he goes a little farther with it, and every time you are a little weaker and more sick after he has left'. As they talked Mabel heard a car start and realised that an angry Luhan had decided to retreat to the pueblo (where he would sometimes visit his ex-wife). Alarmed, she begged Thompson to go and fetch him back but he promised to do so only on condition that she swore never to see or write to Lawrence again. Mabel agreed and while he was gone went over to see Frieda who, after explaining that she and Thompson had simply walked round the Taos Plaza, invited Mabel to listen to Lawrence mumbling angrily in his sleep in the room below.[56]

It is hard to fix the degree of Frieda's irresponsibility in confiding in Clarence Thompson as she did because he was an obviously unbalanced personality who may have wildly exaggerated what she said. It is hard also because Frieda herself never took very seriously her husband's occasional claims to have special psychic powers. In this area Mabel perhaps understood him better than she did. 'He really thought he was able to deal death – to destroy and to create; and he was here on earth for that purpose; that if he could overcome evil and destroy it, he would have fulfilled his destiny', Mabel writes at one point. She notes that although he would talk about this aspect of his mission, he was too 'canny' to commit it to paper: 'Something held him back. Perhaps Frieda? When he talked about these things and she was there – "Bosh!" she frequently exclaimed!'[57] Mabel may have understood better that there were times when Lawrence did seriously succumb to a belief in the omnipotence of thoughts, but Frieda's scepticism was surely better for him.

In spite of her understanding, Mabel does not seem to have been unduly worried by Clarence Thompson's mediated accounts of Lawrence's violent outbursts against her. It was rather Luhan who, fired up by Thompson, became seriously hostile, motivated by either protectiveness or jealousy. The two men formed a pact against Lawrence and on the morning after the dance Thompson came close to hitting him. According to Mabel it was on this morning also that Lawrence presented her with 'The Woman Who Rode Away' to read. Given the context it was perhaps inevitable that this should then become what it has remained for many critics, 'that story where Lorenzo thought he finished me up'.[58] Yet whereas Marchbanks, Farquar and Jimmy Frith are obviously Murry, the protagonist of 'The Woman Who Rode Away' bears not the slightest physical resemblance to Mabel, who was not in her thirties and had not been to Berkeley. It is true that she has some of the qualities of that modern American womanhood which Lawrence tended to find conveniently personified in Mabel, and that the story contains declarations such as, 'The sharpness and the quivering nervous consciousness of the highly-bred white woman was to be destroyed again, womanhood was to be cast once more into the great stream of impersonal sex and impersonal passion.'[59] The first phrase, however, hardly sounds like Mabel, and what misogyny there is in the story as a whole is clearly general rather than specific, and in any case far less prominent and important than an inwardness with 'primitive' thinking which contrasts so sharply with the bafflement Lawrence had displayed when he first arrived in Taos almost two years before.

Inured by this time to crises in his relationship with Mabel, Lawrence's first response to the events following the dance in the studio seems to have been weary stoicism. When Clarence Thompson, whom Mabel calls the 'hero of the moment',[60] asked for and was granted the two-story house Lawrence made arrangements for clearing it of his and Frieda's belongings with calm efficiency. But his anger built up and he was less composed when Luhan, now seriously alienated, sent his nephew for two horses which grazed on the ranch and were used by the Lawrence party. It was as if, Lawrence complained, they were being accused of having stolen them (v. 72). On 10 July, in a note which indicates that Mabel's promise to Thompson never to write to Lawrence again had not been kept very long, he nevertheless told her, 'you know quite well there is no need for either Clarence or Tony to be "mad" . . . I refuse myself to get "mad." – We'll remain friendly at a distance – or at least, I will.' It was to this same letter, however, that Frieda added a postscript letting Mabel know that the manuscript of *Sons and Lovers*, which had arrived from Germany on 5 July, was worth 'at least, $50,000' (v. 73–4). It is easier to strike the right note in the aftermath of a quarrel if there is no previous history of obligation.

III   Kiowa

In July Lawrence must have spent a lot of his time writing, but it was also in this month that he read and admired *A Passage to India*. He and Forster had lost contact with each other after their occasional meetings in the middle war years, but they had begun to correspond again in 1922 and in February 1924 Lawrence had written from Baden-Baden thanking him for *Pharos and Pharillon* and adding, 'To me you are the last Englishman. And I am the one after that' (iv. 584). In New Mexico he saw in the *Adelphi* some comments by Murry on *A Passage to India*,[61] and sent a reminder to Forster that he had promised to provide him with a copy of the novel. This was on 14 July. A week later it arrived and on the 23rd Lawrence, not usually lavish in his praise of his better-known contemporaries, wrote to say he thought it 'very good'. 'The day of our white dominance is over, and no new day can come till this of ours has passed into night' was his opening comment (a rather different view on British imperialism from any he had expressed in Ceylon); and he ended his letter, 'there's not a soul in England says a word to me – save your whisper through the willow boughs' (v. 77).[62]

A Passage to India must have interested Lawrence particularly because he too was busy on a satire of English civilisation. Forster's attack – if that is not too strong a word – was of course on the English in India where various aspects of English social life are shown as having ossified to the point of self-parody, whereas Lawrence's target in *St. Mawr* was on the one hand a well-heeled, cosmopolitan group of devotees to the 1920s cult of enjoyment, and on the other the snobberies of English village life. Yet there is no difficulty in imagining the two characters who most obviously illustrate these snobberies – Dean Vyner and his wife – as members of the Anglo-Indians' Club in Chandrapore. The difference between Lawrence and Forster is less in what they chose as objects of satire than in the quality of the satire itself, one gentle and Austenite, the other exuberantly and uncompromisingly savage. The quite different tone of Lawrence's novella is partly a result of his use of the formidable Mrs Witt as a critic of English society. She is by no means exempt from authorial satire herself – as an American aristocrat from New Orleans she expects young men to be as 'democratic as Abraham Lincoln and as aristocratic as a Russian Czar' – but she functions on Lawrence's behalf as a withering *spectator ab extra*, thinking of Texas as she sarcastically endorses Dean Vyner's characterisation of his village as 'isolated' ten miles from Shrewsbury, and commenting, as she decides to provide the local pub with a weekly barrel of beer which the landlord can sell to his working-class clientele at only a penny a glass, 'My own country has gone dry. But not because we can't *afford* it.'[63] Mrs Witt allows for a scorn in the hostility to most things English which at this stage was obviously Lawrence's own. He would write, Brett recalls, sitting against a tree 'somewhere in the woods' and become so absorbed that he would not hear the whistle she blew to signal lunch. When he finally appeared one day he was 'full of [his] new story' and read to her and Frieda the scene in which Mrs Witt scandalises the Dean and his wife by refusing to blame the horse, St Mawr, for her son-in-law's riding accident: 'You laugh so much over it, that you have to stop – and we are laughing too.'[64]

Brett assumes in her account that it is this son-in-law (Rico) who is kicked in the face by St Mawr whereas, in the story as we have it (forty-one manuscript pages of an earlier version were destroyed by fire in 1961[65]), he crushes his ankle and breaks two ribs as the horse falls back on him, and it is in fact a representative young Englishman named Fred Edwards, also a member of the group riding to the Stiperstones, who has two teeth kicked out as he moves to control the horse. Frieda was apparently horrified by this episode telling Lawrence he was cruel and that he frightened her.

But you are too immersed in the people and the story to care what anyone says. With great relish and giggling, you describe Rico's plight. You hate Rico so, that for the moment you are the horse; in fact, you are each person yourself, so vivid are they to you. With each character your voice and manner change: you act the story rather than read it, and we sit entranced, horrified, amused – all by turns, while your lunch gets colder and colder on your plate.[66]

Lawrence's indifference to Frieda's complaint is evident enough in the story when the narrator remarks with obvious irony, 'Poor Rico, he would limp for life', or its usually mild-mannered heroine, Mrs Witt's daughter Lou, writes in a letter of the family with which Fred Edwards is associated, 'I hate their ways and their bunk, and I feel like kicking them in the face, as St. Mawr did that young man.'[67] There is a lack of quarter here which helps to explain why Lawrence's satirical manner seems so different from Forster's.

It is characteristic also of a difference between the two writers that the positive alternative to a decadent English society is much more boldly asserted in the novella than in *A Passage to India*. In his letter, Lawrence criticised Forster for making too much depend on the understanding between Aziz and Fielding: 'You saying human relationships don't matter, then after all hingeing your book on a very unsatisfactory friendship between two men! *Carito!*' (v. 77). In the first part of *St. Mawr*, it is a horse which convinces the heroine of the sterility of her social relations and in the second it is an American landscape. The prominence of St Mawr in the first part allows Lawrence to display at length both the depth of his interest in horses and the knowledge he had acquired of them in Taos by riding almost every day. St Mawr is a handsome stallion bought by Lou, ostensibly so that her husband Rico can ride him in Rotten Row, but really because she so admires his appearance and what it seems to represent. Hard to domesticate, the horse will only behave with people he trusts, such as his Welsh groom Lewis, and almost immediately begins a battle of wills with Rico that ends with the episode on the excursion to the Stiperstones. It is after this that Rico's friends conspire to geld St Mawr, prompting Lou and her mother to take him with them to America along with Lewis and a servant of Mrs Witt who is half-Indian and called Phoenix. This move across the Atlantic makes for an uneasy narrative transition. St Mawr, discovering an interest in mares which he did not have in England, disappears from the picture along with his groom; Mrs Witt, rebuffed in the attempt to repopulate the space which her sarcastic wilfulness has cleared around her by persuading Lewis that he and she should marry, collapses into lethargy; and Lou, after recognising how little she would like the hopeful Phoenix as a sexual partner, is left buying a dilapidated ranch in the mountains near Santa Fe which is obviously modelled on Lawrence and Frieda's own (it costs her $1,200).

This final action in the story is somewhat arbitrary but it does allow for extended descriptions of the history of Kiowa Ranch, as Lawrence had by 9 August now chosen to call Frieda's property after the Indian tribe which had once camped in that area (v. 94, 228). With his remarkable gift for evocation, he also describes the immediate surroundings of the ranch and the staggering beauty of the view from its front fence down to a desert plain below, circled round with mountains. It is this view which comforts Lou while at the same time she recognises (as she had also done in thinking about St Mawr) the menace always present in 'nature'. In Lawrentian terms, this American landscape is where Pan can still be found yet it is entirely different from how he imagines its prelapsarian, European equivalent in 'Pan in America'.[68] The nature which surrounds Lou on the ranch demands to be battled against and has defeated the previous owners' heroic attempts to establish themselves there. Pack rats are integral to it, as well as blue-jays and squirrels. But this element of 'reality', which appeared to announce so clearly *'There was no merciful God in the heavens'*, is inseparable from Lou's sense of the landscape's overwhelming beauty and her conviction that, at this stage of her life, there is more for her in communion with this version of nature than in relations with men. 'Either my taking a man', she tells her mother, 'shall have a meaning and a mystery that penetrates my very soul, or I will keep to myself'; and when her mother comments that in that case she will probably spend all her life keeping to herself, Lou replies,

Do you think I mind! There's something else for me, mother. There's something else even that loves me and wants me. I can't tell you what it is. It's a spirit. And it's here, on this ranch. It's here, in this landscape. It's something more real to me than men are, and it soothes me, and holds me up . . . It needs me. It craves for me. And to it, my sex is deep and sacred, deeper than I am, with a deep nature aware deep down of my sex.[69]

From finding an alternative to human society in a relation with a horse, Lou has moved by the end of *St. Mawr* to seeking a non-sentimental salvation in the landscape of the country above Taos. In humanist and perhaps Forsterian terms, this gives to the ending of Lawrence's story a resonance which is deeply misanthropic.

The ranch portrayed in such detail at the end of *St. Mawr* is so patently Lawrence's that it would be unreasonable to assume that many of the feelings which it is described as prompting in both Lou and its previous owner were not also his. The pine tree which stood near the buildings ('the guardian of the place'), and which he had written about in greater detail in 'Pan in America', is celebrated here as 'A passionless, non-phallic column, rising in the shadows of the pre-sexual world, before the hot-blooded ithyphallic column ever erected itself.'[70] This is consonant with Lou's new determination to abjure sexual relations for the time being but the conclusion to 'The Border-Line' (in its magazine version) might suggest that the phrases also have biographical implications. At the end of that story, the Alan Anstruther who returns from the dead to embrace Katherine Farquar is like a tree whose potency is non-sexual, or at least not sexual in the usual way. The inference one might draw from this collocation is that a major difference between Lawrence at Kiowa in early summer 1924, and Lou settling down in her ranch at the end of *St. Mawr*, is that he was making a virtue of necessity. But if Lawrence was indeed no longer having sexual relations with Frieda at this time, the reasons may not necessarily have been the health problems which were very shortly to declare themselves. Equally relevant may well be the kinds of feelings expressed in *St. Mawr* by the Welsh groom Lewis when Mrs Witt asks him to marry her. Of several similar declarations, one is, 'No woman who I touched with my body should ever speak to me as you speak to me, or think of me as you think of me'; and another, 'Nothing in the world . . . would make me feel such shame as to have a woman shouting at me, or mocking at me, as I see women mocking and despising the men they marry. No woman shall touch my body, and mock me or despise me. No woman.'[71] In these matters the line between 'can't' and 'don't want to' is notoriously difficult to draw.

In at least one important respect Lou is in any case a character very remote from Lawrence himself, and we can be sure that the impression he conveys at the end of *St. Mawr* of her likely future life on the ranch is biographically misleading. She, we are led to believe, will be isolated and solitary whereas his own retreat from social life was partial only. Apart from the two women he lived with, and the relations he still maintained with Mabel, Lawrence must have seen almost every day during this period members of the Hawk family, from whom he and Frieda had rented the Del Monte cabin the year before. As he would explain in an appealingly descriptive letter he took the trouble to write to his young niece Peggy at the end of August, Frieda, Brett and he would gather the horses every evening 'after tea' and ride down to the Del Monte Ranch for 'milk, butter, eggs and letters' – the postman did not come as far as Kiowa (v. 111). They resumed their friendship with the owner's son Bill and his wife Rachel, as well as now developing one with Bill's younger sister Bobby who had married a man named Gillete and was building a house close by.[72] They clearly ate with one or other of these Hawks occasionally and also invited them up for a meal to the ranch. There was, that is, a reasonable amount of congenial society on the mountain as well as seventeen miles below, should he choose to go down (or Taos residents choose to come up).

One person from Taos who did visit the Lawrence party was Joseph Foster. If there were a prize for the memoir of Lawrence whose manner least inspires confidence in the accuracy of its details, Foster's *D. H. Lawrence in Taos* – written fifty years after the events it describes – would be an easy winner. Yet the substance of his account of a visit to the ranch in late July appears to be confirmed by a reference in Lawrence's letters. Foster and his wife Margaret were driven there by his brother-in-law Swinburne Hale, whose dubious authority Frieda had relied on in the matter of the *Sons and Lovers* manuscript.[73] Foster claims that Frieda and the good-looking Hale were strongly attracted to each other when they first met in Taos, but there would be other reasons why she would be likely to welcome a visit from him and his two companions. At this period Lawrence wrote all morning and then worked in the afternoons on the ranch, building or baking bread in the adobe oven which two Indians had helped him to construct at the side of the cabins (v. 57, 62). When she was not hunting or painting, Brett typed what he wrote, and it is nearly always she who is described as helping Lawrence with the building and repairs. Frieda meanwhile 'kept house', what little there was of it to keep, washed clothes and sheets, which she very much enjoyed doing, baked and even cooked when Lawrence allowed her to. She enjoyed riding as much as the others did – it is to this period that Brett assigns the anecdote of Frieda exclaiming how wonderful it was to feel her horse's 'great thighs moving, to feel his powerful legs' only to be rebuked with her husband's, 'Rubbish, Frieda! don't talk like that. You have been reading my books';[74] and she could spend hours with a book and cigarettes in bed, or relaxing in the hammock Mabel had given her. There must nevertheless have been times when she was glad the Hawks were close by and glad also to see visitors, whether they came up only for the day, like the Fosters and Hale, or stayed for a while as Spud Johnson did in early August.

Johnson had meant to come with Bynner who at the last minute was prevented from making the trip by an illness, real or diplomatic (v. 84). Mabel was by this time sufficiently reconciled to the Lawrences to drive Johnson to the ranch and even think of staying there herself: that she did not meant that he could sleep in the second cabin and not the barn (v. 83). He had been there only a day or two when, on 3 August or thereabouts, Lawrence began to spit 'bright red blood'. The description of the colour is from Brett who had become painfully aware of its significance during her friendship with Katherine Mansfield. She and Johnson were both in Lawrence's bedroom when, in a 'wild fury', he threw at Frieda a piece of iron he was using as an egg-cup because she had been worried enough to call the doctor. Johnson she describes as 'aghast and astonished' that a man so obviously weak and ill could have the strength to be so furious. Lawrence threatened to refuse to see the doctor but relented when Clarence Thompson (his previous anger forgotten) drove Dr Martin up to the ranch. After the visit both Lawrence and Frieda became relaxed and smiling. 'It's all right', Frieda explained to Brett, 'Nothing wrong; the lungs are strong. It is just a touch of bronchial trouble – the tubes are sore.' This was a diagnosis her husband was to adopt for the rest of his life. Two months later, when he had still not completely recovered, he was to write from the ranch to Murry, 'The high thin air gets my chest, bronchially. It's *very* good for the lungs, but fierce for tender bronchi' (v. 143).

Brett's account of Lawrence's haemorrhage is supported by references in his letters and makes it as certain as these things can be that from August 1924 it is legitimate to regard him as tubercular. That an old frontier doctor like Dr Martin, who had served the Taos community for many years, was not prepared to make this diagnosis is not surprising. He certainly did not bother with anything as scientific as a sputum test and, according to Foster, simply told Lawrence and Frieda what they rather insistently made clear they wanted to hear.[75] Lawrence's own refusal to entertain the idea of tuberculosis, with his talismanic distinction between sound lungs and tender bronchi, is a complicated psychological posture and became more so the more the evidence of the true state of affairs accumulated. What helped him to sustain it was an important difference between his case and that of someone like Katherine Mansfield. From the time she is first recorded as spitting blood her decline was rapid. Lawrence, on the other hand, was to live another $5\frac{1}{2}$ years after the visit of Dr Martin and for almost half that period he was often physically active. Whether this was because of a sounder constitution, or of one with some previous practice in fighting and overcoming tuberculosis is impossible to establish, just as it is impossible to know how much his refusal to recognise that he was suffering from a disease for which in his time there was no cure helped him to resist it.

IV Southward Bound

Lawrence was not in bed for long but for the rest of his stay at the ranch he complains in his letters of a sore throat and chest. His illness made him dissatisfied with his surroundings and all the more anxious to stick to the plan he had conceived in England of moving down to Mexico for the winter and finishing 'Quetzalcoatl'. He was still far from well when on 13 August he and Frieda were taken on a fortnight's trip into Arizona by Mabel and Tony Luhan. Along with 3,000 others, they went to see the annual ceremony at the Hopi Reservation, which was famous because it involved the priests dancing with live snakes held between their teeth.[76] It was a long way to drive and the accommodation was not always comfortable, so it is perhaps not surprising that in the short account of the snake dance he wrote on the 22nd, once the four of them were back in Santa Fe, Lawrence should have allowed his irritation with the way the Indians of the Southwest were being turned into a tourist attraction to spill over onto the Indians themselves. He gave this first account the appropriate title of 'Just Back from the Snake-Dance – Tired Out' and could only acquiesce in Mabel's disapproval of it.[77] Back at Kiowa he wrote a second, much longer piece which pleased them both far more.

The radical difference between two descriptions of the same event written within a few days of each other dramatises the obvious truth – inherent but not so apparent in the various versions of *Twilight in Italy* – that what can be said to have happened to a person alters with an altered perspective; and that even for someone as committed to Romantic spontaneity as Lawrence, second thoughts can often seem on reflection truer than the first. The details of the snake dance are recognisably the same in both with, for example, the priests carrying the snakes in their mouths towards the circling crowd and then allowing them to drop and slither away until other participants come forward at the last minute with forked sticks to pick them up and carry them back to the centre. In the first account this is made to seem like a circus turn whereas in the second it is a moment in a genuine religious ceremony which illustrates the Indians' distinctive view of the world. As in 'Indians and Entertainment' or 'Pan in America', Lawrence contrasts their relationship to the environment with that of the Western world which he sees as always concerned to dominate and exploit natural forces by the use of scientific knowledge. The Indians understand the cruelty of nature too well to sentimentalise it, and they are also concerned with appropriating its powers; but their rituals for doing so mean that they never lose a certain awe and respect for a world of which they always feel themselves an integral part. For the Hopi the snakes which they wash and oil for several days before the dance, are emissaries sent on their behalf to the dark sun at the centre of the earth.[78]

Lawrence's second account of the dance is eloquent and appreciative and he showed his fondness for it when he told Murry on 30 August that it 'defines somewhat my position' (v. 109). Sending it to the Curtis Brown office in London on the same day he warned, 'If you offer this to Murry for the *Adelphi*, tell him not to cut it, even though it's long' and concluded, 'I value my "Hopi Snake Dance" article rather highly, so if nobody wants it as it is, let them go without it' (v. 110). On 10 September he asked Forster to read it – 'let me know what impression you get' (v. 116). He must have been conscious that the article was his own equivalent of the final 'Temple' section in *A Passage to India*: the attempt, that is, to explore a challenging different alternative to the post-Christian culture of the West. For Forster, as the letters home on which the 'Temple' section is based reveal, the Hindu ceremonies to celebrate the birth of Krishna are a partly attractive but essentially baffling muddle which it is consequently difficult for him to treat without at least some hint of condescension.[79] More completely alienated from Western culture than Forster (and more savage therefore in his satire), Lawrence felt that he could understand and identify with a quite different form of worship more easily than the man whom he had described on 8 August as 'about the best of my contemporaries in England' (v. 91). The topic seems to have come up when Murry wrote to say that he approved of the snake-dance piece since on 2 October Lawrence replied,

I'm glad you like the Hopi Dance article. All races have one root, once one gets there. Many stems from one root: the stems never to commingle or 'understand' one another. I agree Forster doesn't 'understand' his Hindu. And India to him is just negative: because he doesn't go down to the root to meet it. But the *Passage to India* interested me very much. At least the repudiation of our white bunk is genuine, sincere, and pretty thorough, it seems to me. Negative, yes. But King Charles *must* have his head off. Homage to the headsman.

(v. 142–3)

The trip to see the Hopi snake dance, which included a diversion to the impressive Indian ruins in the Cañon de Chelly,[80] meant over 1,000 miles of driving (v. 110). Lawrence was anxious that while he and Frieda were away Brett should not be alone on the ranch and arranged for two Indian women to stay with her. During her first months in Taos Brett had been fearful of sexual assault. As part of the outlandish 'Western' dress she quickly adopted, she wore calf-high leather boots in one of which she carried a stiletto to protect herself from attack. Mabel claimed that this made the locals afraid of *her* and that one old Mexican once refused to drive her up to the ranch with: 'Senorita with dagger very dangerous!'[81] However unreal the threat was, Lawrence felt responsible for Brett, and there were other ways in which her presence could complicate his life. She records how on one occasion he suddenly accused her of having no respect for Frieda and of wanting to talk only to him, never to her. As he voiced these complaints Frieda popped out of the bedroom to goad him on.[82] Yet at this stage the inevitable tensions which arose from such an unusual *ménage à trois* remained manageable, and in moments when Lawrence did find Brett a nuisance he must have reminded himself that it was after all he who had invited her. Writing to Catherine Carswell on 8 October, a week before leaving for Mexico, his tone is resigned: 'Brett will go down with us. But if we take a house, she must take a little place of her own. Not be too close' (v. 147).

While the Lawrences were away, Brett had in fact a good time riding with the 'dudes' who were staying at the Del Monte Ranch. Like other ranchers in the area the Hawks, profiting from the fashion amongst city-dwellers for the wild (South)west, supplemented their farming income by taking paying guests. One of her excursions was to a small, isolated lake a long way into the mountains behind where she and the Lawrences were living. It so impressed her that she insisted Lawrence should also make the trip when he came back from Arizona. The long day's ride, which there is no suggestion Lawrence was not by now fit enough to make, was organised by Rachel Hawk. As Brett points out, its details were shortly to be recalled by Lawrence in the climax of 'The Princess'.[83]

The beginning of this story goes back to the sketch which Lawrence had written for Catherine Carswell the previous December after she had told him about her idea for a novel.[84] Colin Urquhart is an eccentric Scottish widower who brings up his only daughter in the conviction that she is a being apart, quite different from the people she is obliged to mix with in the normal course of her life. This conception of her as an unacknowledged 'Princess' is partly a consequence of his being the chief of his clan but also the result of a belief – more explicitly attributed to him in the sketch than in the story but present in both – that his daughter is a changeling, a gift of the Tuatha De Danaan. Colin Urquhart is more circumspect than Lewis in *St. Mawr* about declaring his belief in the fairies of Celtic mythology, but his author draws freely on that world to convey the impression of Dollie Urquhart's perfectly formed but diminutive physique and her puzzled, fastidious distaste for the gross physicality of ordinary people. Ghosts may have *lost* their sexuality but in one tradition fairies have never had any. Dollie is fairy-like in that the sexual behaviour of humans belongs for her to another world.

While her father lives, Dollie is content enough but after his death she finds herself at a loose end and thinks vaguely of marriage as a means of having someone to look after her as he did. She is living in America at this time (her mother's country) and with a female companion decides to go to a dude ranch in the Southwest which is obviously based on Del Monte. There, the only man who interests her is a handsome Mexican called Romero who used to own all the surrounding property but is now – a dispossessed Prince – working on the ranch as a guide. Dollie contrives to go with Romero alone on a long trip into the mountains which is, in a literal sense, the same trip Lawrence took with Brett and Rachel Hawk in late August but also (in the context of the story) a symbolic expedition on Dollie's part into territory whose wildness intrigues but also frightens her.

Because Dollie wants to see wild animals, she has agreed with Romero that they will need to stay overnight in a hut near the lake to which they have ridden. Woken by the cold she calls out to Romero and then says 'yes' when he asks whether she would like him to make her warm. What follows satisfies her curiosity but only by convincing her of how alien sexual activity is to her nature. The bluntness with which she makes clear to Romero on the following morning that she has not liked what took place during the night so wounds his masculine pride that he throws all her clothes into the frozen pond and forces her to have sex with him on the assumption that he can somehow make her appreciative. In a stalemate whose bleakness is a reflection of the cold and bleak environment, Romero keeps Dollie a prisoner, determined that he would rather die than have to accept his sexual failure while she does all she can to make it evident that a couple of (for her) insignificant sexual encounters do not make her any less independent, intact and self-sufficient than she was before. When two forest rangers eventually appear on the scene, Romero shoots at them and is then shot and killed himself. The power and effectiveness of this conclusion derives largely from an even distribution of sympathy. The reader is made to understand Romero's fierce resentment, which is economic as well as sexual, without in any way finding it attractive – but is also led to recognise in Dollie a genuinely special being. There is a reminder in her treatment that there is no reason why we should all be the same, which is similar to what one finds in Lawrence's discussion of Sue Bridehead in the *Study of Thomas Hardy*: 'Why must it be assumed that Sue is an "ordinary" woman – as if such a thing existed? Why must she feel ashamed if she is special? And why must Jude, owing to the conception he is brought up in, force her to act as if she were his "ordinary" abstraction, a woman?'[85] Yet since it is

Dollie who initiates the tragedy with her curiosity, and who has insufficient self-knowledge to follow the rules of her own nature, the irony of the final sentence works powerfully against her. The episode which leads to the death of Romero leaves her permanently unbalanced and with the conviction that she had met a man in the mountains who had gone mad and shot her horse from under her. 'Later', 'The Princess' ends, 'she married an elderly man, and seemed pleased.'[86]

Of the three longer short stories or novellas Lawrence wrote during his second stay in New Mexico, 'The Princess' is the best constructed. 'The Woman Who Rode Away' has an ending which is unhelpfully equivocal and the move to America in *St. Mawr* breaks that story in two. After an opening in the witty summarising manner which became increasingly typical of Lawrence in his later work and which he also employs successfully at the beginning of *St. Mawr*, an opening which demonstrates how effectively he could combine omniscient narration with free indirect speech, 'The Princess' moves steadily to its grim conclusion with impeccable emotional logic. This does not necessarily mean that it is the best of the stories, all three of which are remarkable for the originality of their concerns. Different though that makes them from each other, they have a number of features in common – female protagonists, 'symbolic' journeys, the landscape of New Mexico – which made Lawrence feel that it would be appropriate for them to appear together (v. 136, 141, 147). It is a pity that his idea for a volume containing all three, equivalent to the one which had included 'The Fox', 'The Captain's Doll' and 'The Ladybird', came to nothing and has never been realised since. Even today its appearance would draw attention to the extraordinary achievement they represent and throw useful light on the complicated issue of Lawrence's supposed 'decline'. There are of course unevennesses in the three stories as there always are in his work, in particular perhaps a long splenetic outburst in *St. Mawr* about the pervasiveness of evil in the world, which is insufficiently contextualised;[87] but in general there is a vividness in the rapid characterisation, a sharp edge to the dialogue and an utter convincingness in the evocation of setting which one can only imagine possible for the greatest of writers.

Lawrence realised that his three novellas were not exactly cheerful ('They are all sad. After all they are true to what is' – v. 148) but also that they were good – *St. Mawr* he described as a 'corker' (v. 91). If he was nevertheless inclined to take them more for granted than we can or should, it was because they had been written or, as in the case of *St. Mawr*, re-written (v. 58 n.2), with his usual speed. Rapidity of composition is an important aspect of Lawrence's creativity when the quality of what is composed is as high as in these three works. His ability to write so quickly had meant that, although when his birthday came round on 11 September he was still only thirty-nine, he already had a large mass of important work to his name. At the end of June he had been approached by Professor Edward McDonald of the Drexel Institute of Technology in Philadelphia who was preparing a bibliography of his writings. After receiving drafts from McDonald on the 31st of that month, he wrote back, 'The list of books horrifies me by its length' (v. 87).

Lawrence had responded to the first news of the bibliography rather as he had to the librarian who had written to him in Chapala pointing out all the printing errors in his recent works. 'I don't really care a snap about first editions', he told McDonald, 'or whether e's are upside-down or not' (v. 64). He was glad to have a record of his writings all the same, answered McDonald's enquiries conscientiously, and went to considerable trouble to get Secker to clear up difficult points. He also agreed to supply an introduction which, when he wrote it on 1 September, became 'The Bad Side of Books'. He chose to discuss the bad side mainly so that he could describe how William Heinemann had been shocked by *Sons and Lovers* ('I should not have thought the deceased gentleman's reading had been so circumspectly narrow'[88]); the way Mitchell Kennerley had cheated him out of royalties for that, his 'most popular' novel;[89] and the banning of *The Rainbow*. Lawrence made it clear in his introduction that he continued to find the process of exposing himself to the public painful: 'One writes, even at this moment, to some mysterious presence in the air. If that presence were not there, and one thought of even a single solitary reader, the paper would remain for ever white'; and he recalled the discouraging aspect of his early days rather than their excitement. He remembered for example how his mother had been too ill to read *The White Peacock* and the consequences of his father's efforts to do so once she was dead:

After the funeral, my father struggled through half a page, and it might as well have been Hottentot.

'And what dun they gi'e thee for that, lad?'

'Fifty pounds, father'.

'Fifty pounds!' He was dumbfounded, and looked at me with shrewd eyes, as if I were a swindler. 'Fifty pounds! An' tha's niver done a hard day's work in thy life.'

I think to this day, he looks upon me as a sort of cleverish swindler, who gets money for nothing: a sort of Ernest Hooley. And my sister says, to my utter amazement: 'You always were lucky!'[90]

It is hard to believe entirely in Lawrence's amazement. A man with his background must have understood the difference between working as hard as he did at his vocation and being compelled to perform repetitive tasks for at best only moderate reward. An awareness of the difference is apparent in his writing. The guilt at having escaped the common working-class fate must have played at least some part in Lawrence's unusual industriousness, and also contributed to the note of defiance in his celebrations of leisure. On these latter occasions he is a little like the Carlyle who, as Lawrence himself reports it, wrote 50 vols. on the value of silence (i. 504).

Two weeks after recalling his father's response to *The White Peacock*, and ten days after having sent him £10, Lawrence received a cable from his sister Emily to say that Arthur Lawrence had died (v. 114, 124).[91] The *idea* of his father was to become increasingly important to Lawrence in the subsequent years but he accepted the fact of his death calmly and continued his preparations for moving down to Mexico. In addition to 'The Princess' he wrote in his last weeks in the Taos area an essay entitled 'Climbing Down Pisgah' and an 'Epilogue' for a new and this time illustrated edition of his *Movements in European History*. Neither of these pieces appeared in his lifetime. In the essay Lawrence attacked once again pre-war idealism: the urge men have to identify themselves with some vast Spirit of the Universe; and in the 'Epilogue' he repeated his belief that World War I had destroyed Western civilisation's capacity for leading the world forward. Faced with a choice between the bullying of either Soviet Communism or Italian Fascism the only salvation, he argued, lay not in parliamentary democracy but in the new generation's willingness to recognise and accept the natural aristocrats in the world around them. The power with which Lawrence chose to denounce the futility of the war in this 'Epilogue' – coupling together at one point Lloyd George and Horatio Bottomley as 'voices of the people' and claiming that everyone now knew it would have been better to have lost it – suggests that the refusal of Oxford University Press to print this resumé of his political thinking cannot have come as too much of a shock.[92]

While the Lawrences were preparing to move at the ranch there was also movement in the big house in Taos. Clarence Thompson, having previously driven up to the ranch to make his apologies to Lawrence,[93] had gone back to New York and Mabel was also preparing to go there in order to be analysed by Brill. Her problems had become acute during the Hopi trip when she had begun to feel detached from her companions and indifferent to any kind of stimulus. In her memoir she is inclined to blame her breakdown on Lawrence – 'He would not let me live my life in the only way I knew, and actually the man had overcome me' – and recalls his reported threats to destroy her.[94] If there is any truth at all in this diagnosis the relevant literary evidence is not the sacrificial death of 'The Woman Who Rode Away' but Lewis's rejection of Mrs Witt in *St. Mawr*. Mabel never disguised the fact that her aim was to have Lawrence fall in love with her and she had felt that his return to Taos with two women in tow, rather than just one, made her prospects only very marginally slimmer. 'What is it about Brett you like?' she once asked him. Lawrence replied that Brett had something of a touchstone about her – an ability to show things up which he could not properly explain.

'Something like a Holy Russian idiot?' I asked with seeming innocence, but with inner rage.

'Perhaps', he answered, but with an inattentive voice that forgot what we were speaking of; and with an intense blue look in his eyes, he rode his horse alongside me until his thin leg and thigh brushed against me. I was satisfied for the moment about Brett. I knew he would never do that with her, that he would never, with sudden forgetfulness, unconscious of himself, need, like Icarus, to reach out, and replenish himself from her life.[95]

Both 'The Last Laugh' and the conclusion to *The Boy in the Bush* cast doubt on this diagnosis, but even if it was not Brett who in Mabel's view prevented her from having her own sexual way but Frieda, there were also perhaps constitutional changes in Lawrence more difficult to overcome than his wife. Whether or not being baulked was the chief factor which led Mabel to put herself under Brill's care, as her account would suggest, Lawrence was sympathetic and helpful once she had decided to do so, and despite his contempt for psychoanalysis wrote her two letters of stern encouragement and counsel (v. 125–6, 129–30). But after Tony Luhan had driven her to Santa Fe to put her on the train for New York in late October and she learned from 'friends' that Lawrence, who was in Santa Fe from the 16th to the 19th of that month on his way to Mexico, had been calling her destructive and dangerous, she wrote a letter which put a temporary end to their relationship: 'I gave up Lawrence then. That is, I gave up expectation, so far as he was concerned.'[96] Although she was in Taos when he returned to the ranch in 1925 they did not meet; and although Mabel was to begin corresponding with him again once he was back in Europe, she never saw him again.

◆

CHAPTER NINE

October 1924–February 1925
OAXACA AND *THE PLUMED SERPENT*

I Back at the Monte Carlo

After five days in Taos, the Lawrences and Brett were driven down to Santa Fe by Tony Luhan on 16 October 1924 (v. 150–1). With Bynner out of town, they stayed at the Hotel Vargas (now the St Francis), but saw Johnson, Ida Rauh and her partner Andrew Dasburg. For what was probably the first but would certainly not be the last time, they also met Christine Hughes, a friend of these three who lived with her daughter in Santa Fe (v. 158, 199). Johnson was too preoccupied with whether or not he was going to work for Mabel to think of accompanying the Lawrence party to Mexico (v. 150); but there was still a chance that Bynner might join it later. He was interested in attending the inauguration of the new Mexican President, Plutarcho Calles, which was due to take place at the beginning of December. Calles was supported by the labour movement in his own country but also had strong links with the American Federation of Labor. Fiercely anti-clerical, he was widely regarded in American left-wing circles as a good Socialist: an impression which Bynner's journalist friend, Carleton Beals, had done much to encourage.[1]

'Bynner, are you coming to see us?', Lawrence asked in a note he left for him at his house on 19 October as he was leaving Santa Fe (v. 151). At El Paso on the following day there was an incident which Brett recounts with evident relish. 'Your wife?' asked the passport official pointing at Brett and when Lawrence said 'no' tried again with 'Your sister?' Told that Brett was only a friend, the official then pointed at Frieda, enquiring of Lawrence with an engaging smile, 'Your mother?'[2] Age differences are notoriously more difficult to detect in people of a different nationality, but what may have led the official into error was the contrast – striking in photographs of the time – between the slight build of Lawrence, who remained throughout his life young in figure if not face, and Frieda's maternal amplitude. With the error rectified and the passports stamped, the Lawrence party took the train again and arrived in Mexico City in the early morning of the 23rd. They checked in at the Hotel Regis, perhaps because of the hour,[3] but moved that same day to the Monte Carlo from where Lawrence could tell Bynner that Brett was in his old room, 'we in the one inside'. He went on: 'With a bowl of candied fruit, a flask of chianti, those coloured majolica cups and tea, we only need you two to push back the clock' (v. 153).

Lawrence expected his time in the Mexican capital to be enlivened by meetings with two potentially interesting new acquaintances. In May, Manuel Gamio had sent him one of his books and encouraged Lawrence to look him up if ever he happened to come to Mexico again (v. 45).[4] As that country's Director of Archeology and the leading expert on Teotihuacán, Gamio would have been a very useful person for Lawrence to meet as he prepared to re-write 'Quetzalcoatl', but unfortunately he was busy at a site in Yucatán – 'digging up the dead instead of looking after the living', Lawrence complained (v. 155).

The other new acquaintance was to be Somerset Maugham who had come to Mexico from New York in order to find material for a new book; but Lawrence's initial efforts to get in touch were met around the 25th by a telegram which explained that Maugham had gone to Cuernavaca – sixty miles away – ' "to work" ' (v. 155). There were times when Lawrence arranged his own life so that he could concentrate on his writing but there was for him an uncomfortable kind of self-importance, related to his ambivalent feelings about being a 'writer', in offering literary work as an excuse for evading a social demand. He was contemptuous of the terror he imagined Maugham feeling at not being able to 'do his next great book, with a vivid Mexican background, before Christmas'; and he consoled himself for not seeing Maugham with the thought that, from all he had heard, this particular colleague was in any case no great loss: 'A narrow-gutted "artist" with a stutter' (v. 157).

Maugham did in fact return to Mexico City before Lawrence left and they were finally able to lunch together at Zelia Nuttall's house on 5 November (v. 161).[5] According to Frieda, there was a further unpromising preliminary to their meeting when, to Lawrence's disgust, the suggestion that they should share a taxi to the Casa Alvarado came not from Maugham himself but Gerald Haxton, who was Maugham's secretary in the way Johnson had been Bynner's.[6] Even if the circumstances preceding this lunch had been ideal, it is hard to see how two people so different from each other could have got on. 'Sehr unsympatisch' was Lawrence's verdict on Maugham when he wrote to Murry two days afterwards (v. 162). Many years later, in his *Introduction to English and American Literature*, Maugham wrote that Lawrence's view in his short stories was that of 'a sick man of abnormal irritability, whose nature was warped by poverty and cankered with a rankling envy'.[7] It certainly irked Lawrence that writers like Maugham were so commercially successful, but there are no indications that he ever envied them.

Not being able to see either Gamio or Maugham on his arrival in Mexico City annoyed Lawrence and his bad temper was aggravated when both he and Frieda caught the flu (v. 159–60). A principal reason for leaving the ranch had been anxiety about the likely effects of the winter temperatures on his chest; but for the moment it now seemed as if he were worse rather than better off. Yet there were old friends to take him out of himself: on 24 October the Lawrences and Brett invited Zelia Nuttall to lunch in town (v. 155), and the lunch with Maugham was only the last in a series of invitations to her house which followed (Frieda reports that they ate there three times).[8] One possible new contact, moreover, did not disappoint. By no means consistently anti-social, Lawrence had responded positively in August to an invitation from the founder of the PEN club to become a member. Enclosing his guinea, he asked if he could have a 'card to the Mexico City branch' because he would be 'down there shortly' (v. 88). Now he dropped a line to the president of the club in Mexico City, Genaro Estrada, who called on him promptly and then proceeded to organise a dinner in his honour.[9]

Both Frieda and Brett describe Lawrence as apprehensive of the likely formality of this event, which took place on 31 October (v. 157), and as regretfully assuming that it would require a rare appearance of his black tie and dress suit. A photograph taken at the dinner confirms Brett's memory of Lawrence's complaint afterwards that, 'There was nothing but beer to drink',[10] yet shows it to have been a relaxed, intimate affair in the distinctly modest surroundings of a Chinese restaurant, with the sixteen Mexican writers who had been gathered to meet Lawrence wearing ordinary suits (Fig. 18). Its chief benefit for him was a first meeting with Luis Quintanilla, the blond young man seated on his right. Born in Paris in 1900, Quintanilla had been to school in the United States and spoke both English and French fluently, in addition to his parents' Spanish. Like many of his fellow writers he combined an interest in literature with a career in government (although only a lowly official in the protocol division of the Foreign Ministry when Lawrence knew him, he was later to have a distinguished diplomatic career).[11] After the meal, Genaro Estrada gave an address in Spanish, which was later published by the Mexican branch of the PEN club in a pamphlet, along with a review of *Aaron's Road* (sic) by Genaro Fernández MacGregor and a short tribute to Lawrence by Xavier Villaurrutia.[12] Estrada admitted that Lawrence's visit was something of a surprise and he had not therefore had the time to study their guest's work, but he compensated for his ignorance by describing Lawrence as a David who, weak and simple like his predecessor, had thrown his stone at the stars and found a blaze of glory raining down in reply. In terms which the guest was, on this occasion, clearly too tolerant and good-natured to find embarrassing or offensive, Estrada compared Lawrence's head to that of Antonin Proust in the painting by Manet, and he said that his beard would look well 'poised meditatively on the shoulders of a character from *Richard III*'. Picking up the prevailing rhetorical manner – but no doubt relieved now that he had hedged his bets in telling Amy Scott Dawson, when accepting her invitation to join the PEN club, that writers were '*perhaps* the only people who *may* be capable of imaginative international understanding' (v. 88 – my italics) – Lawrence replied to this address by urging his hosts to remember that, in spite of all their differences of nationality, and in spite of their common interest in literature, they were first and foremost men together. But one of the party then replied that in Mexico one had to be first and foremost a Mexican, implying (presumably) that there were things then happening in the country from which it was not only impossible but also wrong for intellectuals to remain apart.[13]

Quintanilla was a member of a prominent avant-garde group of poets and artists known as 'Los Estridentistas' ('the strident ones') and almost certainly the only one present who knew enough of Lawrence's work to be intelligently enthusiastic about it. During the days following the dinner he was often with Lawrence and on 2 November introduced him to Edward Weston, the American photographer who, after leaving his wife and four sons in California, was then living in Mexico City with an Italian-born former actress of striking looks, Tina Modotti. Lawrence made a 'most agreeable' first impression on Weston and agreed to sit for him two days later, on the 4th; but in Weston's view the sitting was a failure because 'the contact was too brief for either of us to penetrate more than superficially the other'. He was also disappointed by the technical quality of the negatives of his portraits whose preparation he had been obliged to hurry in order to attend a dinner for the American ambassador (the opposite of worldly, he had gone to the dinner as part of a general effort to drum up new business and avoid the embarrassment of having to be supported in his new life by occasional cheques from his wife).[14] Lawrence himself, on the other hand, liked the two portraits which Weston sent on to him in Oaxaca a few weeks later (v. 185). One shows him looking down with a kindly half-smile on his face. In the other photograph, for which he expressed a surprising preference, he is standing or sitting with his back to a wall, his head slightly turned to the right and his chin slightly up (Fig. 17). The effect here is of melancholy and strain. In comparison with Weston's portraits of the people he got to know well in Mexico City, or his famous nude studies of Tina Modotti, neither of these photographs is remarkable. As 'close-ups', however, they do convey the impression that this is how Lawrence really looked, with his nose unattractively rounded at the end, his too-prominent chin covered by the beard, the thick, abundant hair growing forward and a skin unusually leathery and lined for someone still under forty. No-one who saw them could have mistaken *this* man for his wife's son.[15]

In his letter of thanks to Weston, Lawrence did not explain why he liked the photographs. He was too concerned with suggestions of how they and other work by Weston might be published and lead to his becoming better known. '*Vanity Fair* might like some of your less startling nude studies, if you could stand seeing them reproduced and ruined', he wrote, and he added, 'Let me know if I can help you in any way' (v. 186). Some similarity of interests may have helped prompt this degree of concern – Lawrence and Weston were both interested in the occult, for example, inclining to a belief in the Atlantis myth, and both strongly distrusted 'scientific' medicine – but the more likely stimulus was Lawrence's perception of a similarity of situation. Only six months older than Lawrence, Weston had broken away from his old way of life much later; and it was he rather than Tina Modotti who had abandoned a family. Yet the financial problems of starting out again in defiance of conventional society were ones which Lawrence was in a position to understand very well. He liked Weston, admired his work and felt generously inclined to give him the kind of encouragement he would have appreciated when he first began his life with Frieda.

As happened quite often in his relationships, Lawrence offered more warmth than he received in return. Weston's initial liking was soon accompanied by serious reservations and on Lawrence's death he wrote an appreciation that was comparatively cool. 'Of one thing I feel sure:' his summing-up included, 'Lawrence had no plastic sense.'[16] This judgement he describes as having been formed during their time together and then verified by the remarks on the Rivera murals in *The Plumed Serpent*. Weston was a passionate admirer of Diego Rivera and had become a close friend of his before he met Lawrence. It is this advantage which helps to make his portraits of the painter and, more especially, his wife – Guadelupe Marin de Rivera – peculiarly impressive. Looking at these makes one regret Lawrence was not able to spend more time with the one great portrait photographer for whom he ever sat.

Weston remembered that he and Tina walked in Chapultepec Park with Lawrence,[17] and Quintanilla introduced the Lawrence party to his lively American wife. There was (that is) no shortage of company for all three of them. On 26 October they had dined with Norman King, in the suburb of Tlalpam where Lawrence had taken Gótzsche almost a year before, and where he could now have first met an expatriate couple, George and Anne Conway, who were to prove a tower of strength a few months later.[18] Sympathetic to King's complaints about his superiors back home, Lawrence's relations with the British Consul-General were clearly good and he also liked King's assistant, Constantine Rickards, whom he describes as 'very attentive' (v. 156). Rickards had been born in Oaxaca, where his Scottish father had mining interests, and his brother still lived there, a priest in the cathedral chapter.[19] In spring 1923 Lawrence had already seriously considered a visit to Oaxaca ('you pronounce it Wa-há-ka', he would explain in a letter to Murry on 15 November – v. 167); and since then he had habitually mentioned it as the place where he would go to finish his 'Mexican novel' (iv. 545, 582, 596). Jaime de Angulo would have told him more about the area but meeting Rickards, who could provide him with all he immediately needed to know and smooth his way once he got there, confirmed Lawrence in his choice and he, Frieda and Brett set out for Oaxaca on 8 November. His idea was to see what the town was like and perhaps afterwards take up Idella Purnell's invitation to go back to the Guadalajara area ('If we stay [in Oaxaca]', he had written to Bynner, 'whatever will Idella say!' – v. 153). It is an interesting side-light on Lawrence's dependence on setting in his writing that he did not feel any pressing need to return to Chapala in order to re-write 'Quetzalcoatl'. Another novelist might have wanted to verify this or that detail of topography or architecture, but Lawrence was not concerned that his 'Mexico' should be too local or specific, and was in any case confident of his memory. Great writers are born just as much as they are made. Like the 'ear' which allowed Lawrence to mimic others so effectively, his phenomenal powers of visual recall never let him down.

II   First Impressions

Via the junction at Esperanza, the Lawrence party travelled on the 8th to Tehuacán where they spent the night. The next morning they took the narrow-gauge railway to Oaxaca through the Tomelin Canyon (v. 162). The line to Oaxaca had only recently been re-opened and nearly every station they passed was pock-marked with bullets.[20] Soldiers crowded the platforms and, as always during this period in Mexico, travelled either on or in the trains as guards. 'Only about forty passengers – two little coaches – and twenty soldiers to guard us', Lawrence wrote (v. 166). The Huerta revolt which had begun only a week or two after Lawrence last left Mexico was by now over, but the country was still unsettled and there was apprehension over the coming transfer of power. Obregón and Calles were political allies, and it had been amicably agreed between them that – the electorate willing! – one should succeed the other; but the actual moment of succession was yet another possible occasion for their enemies to make a move (v. 161). Noting the innumerable wooden bridges on the Oaxaca line made Lawrence realise how easily the town could once more be isolated from the capital, as it was – temporarily – on at least one occasion during his stay (v. 182). They arrived on the evening of 9 November and went to a hotel called the Francia which is a few hundred yards from the Zócalo. There they discovered that Brett's ear-trumpet (the instrument Mabel referred to as her 'brass dipper' but Brett herself called her 'Toby') had been either lost or stolen. This was particularly unfortunate because her cumbersome 'listening machine' was not working very well (eventually it had to be sent to Veracruz for repair).[21] In the next few days she and Lawrence busied themselves with having a substitute for Toby made by a local tinsmith, but for a while at least she must have felt as cut off from the outside world as her new, provisional home had recently been.

Oaxaca in 1924 was a small, provincial centre of around 27,000 inhabitants: in 1909, under Díaz, the population, which was predominantly Indian (Zapotec), had been over 36,000. Its previous governor, García Vigil, had declared for

Huerta, been chased from the town with 600 of his men, and was finally captured and shot in April.[22] José Vasconcelos, the Minister of Education with whom Lawrence had only narrowly failed to lunch eighteen months before, had unsuccessfully contested the ensuing election for the governorship. Like Díaz and Mexico's most famous revolutionary hero, Benito Juárez, Vasconcelos was from the Oaxaca area. He had resigned his post and chosen to challenge the government in an election because he had been disillusioned by the methods Obregón employed to crush the Huerta revolt.[23] The government candidate was the victor (only, Vasconcelos was always to insist, because the election was rigged), and was shortly to be installed; but in the interim the town was being governed by Isaac Ibarra to whom Estrada, an under-secretary at the Ministry of Foreign Relations as well as the PEN club president, had written about Lawrence's visit. The consequence was that a few days after his arrival Lawrence was invited to call on the Governor in his palace. He was unreasonably dismayed to discover that Ibarra was 'an Indian from the hills'. That seemed to him an illustration of the 'absurd sort of socialism' which now infected every area of Mexican life (v. 164, 167). Around Christmas he was to write the four marvellously vivid and entertaining sketches of life in Oaxaca which later provided the opening chapters for *Mornings in Mexico*. In what now appears as the second of these, 'The Walk to Huayapa', he describes with some scorn how candidates for election in the Oaxaca area had to be distinguished by symbols because most electors could not read (at 70 per cent, illiteracy rates were in fact higher there than in most other regions of Mexico).[24] Not only socialism ('socialism is a dud. It makes just a muck of people: and especially of savages' – v. 168) but also Western democracy itself seemed to him as much an imposition on Indian culture as Christianity. Lawrence was now even more out of sympathy with the left-wing proclivities of his friends in Mexico City than on his first visit there with Bynner, and he was shortly to tackle once again his own description of a society which would allow the Indians to reach their natural fulfilment rather than subject them to the distorting effects of Western models. 'Believe me,' Ramón Carrasco tells his first wife in *The Plumed Serpent*, 'if the real Christ has not been able to save Mexico,—and He hasn't; then I am sure, the white Anti-Christ of charity, and socialism, and politics, and reform, will only succeed in finally destroying her.'[25]

Before he began re-writing, Lawrence spent some time with Frieda and Brett getting to know what was and still is an unusually pleasant town. There were the inevitable churches to visit and a local icon to pay homage to: the Virgin of Soledad. Like the better-known Virgin of Guadelupe in Mexico City (which Lawrence had taken Brett to see), this statue was associated with miracles dating back to the seventeenth century.[26] Pottery and blankets in the attractive local manner could be bought in Oaxaca – 'This is where they make the serapes like the one with the eagle hung on the wall', he told William Hawk, in what was obviously a reference to the decoration at Kiowa; and there was an unusually busy and colourful market, 'humming like a bee-hive', where one could get anything from 'roses to horse-shoes' (v. 164). He made an amalgam of his many visits to this market the subject for the fourth of his Mexican 'Mornings', insisting that what brought so many local Indians to this magnetic centre on a Saturday morning was not primarily the economic need to sell their wares but an irresistible desire for human contact.[27] On one occasion he was able to provoke an uncontrollable hilarity in the sandal sellers by indicating with pantomimic gestures that what they had to offer stank to high heaven. Since a passage in Bernal Díaz had led him to assume (quite wrongly according to Ross Parmenter) that it was still traditional in Mexico to tan leather with human excrement, the joke might have been partly on him; but the suggestion to Brett that this was why the sandals smelled as they did produced a comic consternation in her which made him also shake with laughter.[28] A further stimulus to good humour was the weather in Oaxaca. 'The climate here is perfect, just like midsummer, with a bright sun in a perfect blue sky every day, and roses and hibiscus flowers in full bloom', he wrote to one of his sisters on the 15th; and on the same day he told the other, 'The climate is lovely: just like midsummer, cloudless sun all day, and roses and tropical flowers in full bloom. My chest had got very raw, up at the ranch: that very high altitude' (v. 166, 168). It comforted him to feel that Oaxaca was at 5,000 rather than 8,000 feet.

There was a small expatriate community in Oaxaca which quickly made itself acquainted with the new arrivals – very soon Lawrence would claim to know them all (v. 179). A Swiss dentist and his wife (the Kulls) entertained them several times and remembered how Brett would exclaim 'O, bother!' when she missed the ball at tennis.[29] Around the end of the month, Donald Miller, an American mining engineer, would take them in his car to Mitla where there are the impressive ruins of a palace (v. 182).[30] Danger and hardship had made this community close-knit and friendly. Before the revolution, when the Díaz regime was providing a secure environment for foreign investment, there were 300 British and American families in the town.[31] Now these were reduced to a beleaguered handful. The cutting of the railway line had made things difficult and in August expatriates all over Mexico had been shocked when a Mrs Rosalie Evans, who had defied the Obregón legislation which would have obliged her to surrender her hacienda, was assassinated: as she fell from her carriage, her hair caught in one of its wheels and she was scalped before the horses could be stopped.[32] The countryside around Oaxaca, like that around Chapala eighteen months before, was not considered entirely safe. This gave Lawrence the same feeling of constriction he had experienced in Chapala, although even before the 'Walk to Huayapa' (a village a few miles northeast of Oaxaca whose real name was and is San Andres Huayapan), he seems to have rebelled and decided to take his chances (v. 165). In his first weeks, however, not being able to walk or ride at will was one of the factors which, along with worries about his health and Frieda's growing irritation with Brett, quickly took the shine off his highly favourable first impressions.

Soon after he arrived, Lawrence followed the advice of the British Vice-Consul in Mexico City and made contact with Father Edward Rickards. On 18 November he and Frieda moved from the Hotel Francia into a part of Rickards's house on the north edge of town, near the military hospital (v. 169). A few days before, they had taken the mule-drawn tram and gone to inspect this accommodation with Brett. There were five large rooms: plenty of space for all three. By their manner if not in words, however, the Lawrences made it clear that they would like Brett to stay on at the hotel.[33] 'One gets tired of being always with other people', Lawrence told Emily on the 15th, the 'one' in this case referring much more to his wife than himself (v. 166). The part of Father Rickards's house the Lawrences occupied formed two sides of a square. Each room had a large window on the street and was bordered on the other, inner side by a red-tiled verandah. The house was turned inwards in the Mexican fashion so that one entered the rooms via this verandah which formed an intermediate living-space between the inside of the house and the large inner garden or patio. A photograph shows Lawrence and Frieda on this broad verandah, sitting on chairs and at a table all borrowed from the expatriate community (See Fig. 19).[34] When it was not too hot, they could stroll in the large garden where there were 'orange trees and lemon, and hibiscus and roses' (v. 179) – but also parrots who, according to the first and very lively sketch in *Mornings in Mexico*, spent a good deal of time imitating the bark of Father Rickards's little white dog, Corasmín, so that he would have to creep away and hide, crippled with embarrassment (v. 178). Lawrence's descriptions of this and other aspects of 43 Avenida Pino Suarez, with its discreet and agreeable landlord, make it sound an ideal place for him to settle down and work.

As in Chapala, taking a house, or even part of one, meant taking a servant; but whereas Isobel de Medina had brought a whole family with her, the obligation this time was limited to a single young 'Mozo' (the Spanish word for a boy) named Rosalino. A cook – Natividad – and 'two youngsters', Maria de Jesus and Maria del Carmen, also formed part of the household (v. 177); but they appeared to have been the landlord's responsibility rather than Lawrence's. The portrait of Rosalino in the third essay in *Mornings in Mexico* is touching and affectionate, and one of the most immediately appealing sketches Lawrence ever wrote. He had been impressed by reading in Lewis Spence's *Gods of Mexico* that one of the Aztec goddesses had begun the process which led to the creation of humankind by giving birth to an obsidian knife.[35] This seemed to him an apt symbol for the hardness and incipient cruelty he found in many aspects of Mexican life. But

Rosalino struck him as gentler and more vulnerable than most of the young Indians he had seen or met, 'as if he were a mother's boy'.[36] A further fellow feeling must have developed when Lawrence learned how Rosalino had been beaten unconscious for refusing to be conscripted by various revolutionary factions: 'He is one of those, like myself, who have a horror of serving in a mass of men, of even being mixed up with a mass of men.'[37] He admired his *mozo*'s efforts to improve himself by learning Spanish (inevitably taking a hand as he had done with Isobel's daughters),[38] and tracked closely a bout of nostalgia which nearly took Rosalino away from the Lawrences and the town, back to his native hills. As in writing 'Quetzalcoatl', having a servant was for Lawrence the best way of gaining insight into Indian life. 'Her servants were the clue to all the native life, for her', Kate reflects in *The Plumed Serpent*.[39]

III   Re-writing 'Quetzalcoatl'

On the day after Lawrence had moved into Father Rickards's house, he began re-writing what he had often previously referred to as his 'Mexican novel' (iv. 559, 591): it was his agent's fright at the idea of an unpronounceable title which would lead to its going out into the world as *The Plumed Serpent* (v. 250). Working very hard, and under increasing pressure from sickness and domestic difficulties as he neared completion, he produced in around two and a half months a manuscript nearly twice as long as the version he had written in Chapala.[40] When he was finishing the former version he had regarded it as temporary and he now 'filled out' his draft with more detailed, evocative writing, expanding old material but at the same time incorporating into it experiences which belonged to the period after he had left Chapala. A typical example of the latter process occurs in the part of *The Plumed Serpent* which deals with Kate's stay in Mexico City, before she goes to 'Sayula'. When he had been in the capital a month before, Lawrence had taken Brett to the National Museum. As he was examining various Aztec deities there, an attendant touched him on the arm and asked him to take his hat off. He complied momentarily but then quickly put his hat back on again. When the attendant returned with the same request Lawrence stormed out of the building complaining (according to Brett), 'They want to show their power over strangers, that's all it is. They want to show they have authority to make a white man take off his hat!'[41] This experience, and something like this reaction, is attributed to an American military attaché in Lawrence's revision of chapter II – the account of the tea-party at the home of Mrs Norris (Zelia Nuttall).[42]

Coming to Oaxaca led Lawrence to change completely his account of Cipriano's background. In 'Quetzalcoatl' he is a peon's son who had been sent to Oxford by an Englishwoman with a coffee plantation 'somewhere near Jalapa';[43] but in *The Plumed Serpent* his benefactor becomes Bishop Severn of Oaxaca, a figure clearly based on a real cleric with English origins: Eulogio Gillow who had been Archbishop of Oaxaca until his death in 1922. Lawrence's landlord had been Gillow's secretary and could therefore tell him all that he needed to know about him.[44]

One or two entirely new figures in the novel were based on people Lawrence had recently met. An addition to the Mexico City scenes, for example, is a 'pale young man called Mirabal' who speaks Spanish with a French accent (as Luis Quintanilla did), and who later appears briefly at one of Ramón's prayer-meetings in Sayula.[45] There is now some talk in the Mexico City scenes of the coming inauguration of a new President ('Montes'), as there was no reason to be in 'Quetzalcoatl'; and later in his revised novel Lawrence makes creative use of Plutarcho Calles's well-known anti-clericalism. Montes is shown as sympathetic to the Quetzalcoatl cult because it is indigenous and because he is hostile to Christianity. By the end of the novel he has endorsed it as the national religion, further stimulating a violent Catholic reaction: 'it looked like the beginnings of a religious war'.[46] On this topic *The Plumed Serpent* has a genuine right to be regarded as prescient in that Calles's moves against the Church early in his Presidency did very quickly provoke a civil war in Mexico between the government and those who called themselves 'cristeros'.[47]

Both versions of Lawrence's Mexican novel are full of 'pure' invention: passages not directly based on something that had happened to him or on people he had met; but there is also a fair proportion of direct transcription. In *The Plumed Serpent* this is either elaborated (attracting in the process new memories of his first visit to Mexico) or, as in the passages I have cited, amalgamated with more recent experience. But sometimes there are signs that a recent experience recalled episodes from the first Mexican visit which had not found their way into 'Quetzalcoatl' at all. This is the case, for instance, in the scene from chapter III of *The Plumed Serpent* in which Kate is shown the murals of 'Ribera' and those of another painter (not named) whose work she likes even less.

The virtues of Diego Rivera had been extolled to Lawrence by a young and enthusiastic Covarrubias in 1923. It was almost certainly with Covarrubias, as well as with Frieda, Bynner, Johnson and Frederick Leighton, that Lawrence went to the National Preparatory School (where university students spent their first year) to see Rivera and his young team of muralists at work. One of the team – Jean Charlot – claims that he acted as a guide on this occasion and that Lawrence dismissed the murals as imitations of Gauguin.[48] Bynner has many more details of Lawrence's response at that time but some of these may be derived from his later reading of *The Plumed Serpent*.[49] In that novel it is important that, just before Kate goes to see the murals, she is powerfully struck by the Indian couples selling their wares in the cathedral square, the men, large-limbed, silent and handsome 'looking up with their black, centreless eyes, speaking so softly, and lifting, with small, sensitive brown hands the little toys they had so carefully made and painted'. At the same time as she admires them however, Kate takes account in the couples of 'the dirty clothes, the unwashed skin, the lice, and the peculiar hollow glint of the black eyes, at once so fearsome and so appealing'.[50] This finely written portrait in words, reflecting as it does the complexity of Lawrence's attitude to Indian life, serves as the positive pole to Kate's negative response to the murals, which might otherwise appear wholly philistine. She grants that Ribera is interesting, and a man who knows his craft; but she finds his Indians too stylised, mere 'symbols in the weary script of socialism and anarchy'. The sympathy he has for them, she feels, thinking back to the Indians she has just seen, is 'always from the ideal, social point of view. Never the spontaneous answer of the blood.'[51] A defender of what Charlot calls the 'Mexican Mural Renaissance' might well agree that, of course, the Indians are not represented naturalistically, and that they do have a certain static, monumental quality which one might associate with Gauguin (or perhaps, more relevantly, Rivera's friend Picasso).[52] He would also have pointed out, however, a little like Loerke in *Women in Love*, that art is not necessarily an exact copy of life and in mural art especially symbolism is traditional. But Kate's objection, like Ursula's in her discussion with Loerke, is to what she perceives to be the spirit behind the art. She feels that for Ribera the Indian is merely a pretext, and that the impulse directing his art is hatred of the oppressor rather than any genuine interest in the oppressed.[53]

From what Lawrence calls 'the University' Kate and her party pass on to a building L. D. Clark has identified as an annexe of the Preparatory School.[54] There she sees the work of another man which is so caricatural, ugly and crude that it repels her. In an argument she has with a young Mexican called García who is accompanying her and Owen (Bynner), there is a reference to 'a hideous picture of a fat female in a tight short dress, with hips and breasts as protuberances, walking over the faces of the poor'.[55] This identifies the other artist as José Clemente Orozco, the one other experienced painter among the muralists. It also proves that Lawrence must have looked at the murals again during his recent stay in Mexico City, because Orozco did not join Rivera's group until July 1923, when Lawrence was already in Chapala, and the mural in question (*The Reactionary Forces*) is attributed by all the experts to 1924. Like many of the others it was partly defaced in student riots, but a preliminary sketch which survives shows vividly a grotesquely ugly woman in furs, with a contemptuous expression on her face and a large breast half-exposed, kicking the point of one of her high heels into the head of a female beggar who is lying with a skeletal baby on the floor.[56] The design and drawing are very effective – Orozco had spent many years as a political cartoonist – reminiscent for a European of the kind of work George Grosz was doing in Germany at this time. For Kate, however, to have these things in an educational establishment is a 'misdemeanour' to 'anyone with a spark of human balance'. She protests to García that they are too ugly. Bynner is no doubt right that García, who does not appear in 'Quetzalcoatl', is partly based on Covarrubias since the arguments he had with Lawrence were – in Bynner's memory of them at least – very like those Kate has with García. Yet García is 'a rather short, soft young fellow of twenty-seven or eight, who wrote the inevitable poetry of sentiment, had been in the government, even as a member of the House of Deputies'.[57] This suggests that Lawrence's chief or additional model for García had been encountered more recently, an impression strengthened by the fact that his exchanges with Kate are a version of the disagreement Frieda reported Lawrence having had with one of his fellow diners at the PEN dinner.

Kate protests that no-one is like the figures in Orozco's mural and that, 'One must keep a certain balance.' García replies that this is not true for Mexico: 'In Mexico you can't keep a balance, because things are so bad. In other countries, yes, perhaps you can remain balanced, because things are not so bad as they are here. But here they are so very bad, you can't be human. You have to be Mexican. You have to be *more* Mexican than human—no?' Kate replies, in a repetition of the charge she had made against Ribera, that the 'twelve million poor—mostly Indians—whom Montes talks about' only matter for the left-wing artists as a *casus belli*, 'Humanly, they never exist for you.'[58] Her opinions are not *necessarily* Lawrence's own, but every reader takes them as authorially endorsed. There is no specifically determining dramatic context to be considered and they make no particular dramatic point about her character. One of the weaknesses of *The Plumed Serpent* in fact is that, while Lawrence tries to dramatise a developing response to Mexico which is specifically female (and partly influenced by his knowledge of Frieda), he at the same time uses Kate for the convenient working-out of many of his own views on Mexico. The effect can be confusing and detract from the psychological drama which is, or perhaps more accurately, should be, at the centre of *The Plumed Serpent*: Kate's struggle to decide what she feels about the Quetzalcoatl cult and its organisers.

The major plot difference between 'Quetzalcoatl' and *The Plumed Serpent* has already been described and is related to precisely this struggle of Kate's. In the published novel, the invincible repugnance she had previously felt for physical union with someone of another race is easily overcome, partly (one has to suspect) because of the way Lawrence had come to feel about Mabel and Tony Luhan. The earlier version had contained a scene in which Kate and Cipriano visit a weaver's shed in a village across the lake. In this later one, their boat trip to Jamiltepic is accompanied by heavily insistent phallic imagery;[59] when they arrive they sleep together; and, in a change to the previous version's plot movements, they afterwards return to Ramón's hacienda where he marries them in a distinctive 'Quetzalcoatl' ceremony. That they have indeed slept together in Jameltepic is never made explicit. Here, as later in the novel, the future author of *Lady Chatterley's Lover* resorts to versions of the familiar 'And afterwards . . . ' formula; yet at one point, just before the death of Ramón's first wife Carlota, when Kate and Cipriano are in a boat together, he feels 'the mysterious flower of her woman's femaleness slowly opening to him, as a sea-anemone opens deep under the sea, with infinite soft fleshiness'. This image will be important to Lawrence in *Lady Chatterley* and so too will be a distinction between clitoral and vaginal orgasm first introduced by Lawrence in a final, although still not especially explicit account of Kate and Cipriano's love-making which celebrates the abandon of her search for 'the white ecstasy of frictional satisfaction'.[60]

Kate's 'Marriage by Quetzalcoatl' (the title of chapter xx in *The Plumed Serpent*) is followed by two more marriage ceremonies. The first of these comes after she has agreed to join Cipriano and Ramón in the pantheon of the Quetzalcoatl cult and represent or embody the goddess Malintzi (something the Kate of the earlier version was far too sceptical to do). In this ceremony she is united to Cipriano in his guise as the war god Huitzilopochtli. The second is a conventional civil ceremony which she goes through at a time when she is contemplating returning to Europe for a while. In 'Quetzalcoatl' Kate definitely decides to return; the implication at the end of *The Plumed Serpent* is that she will stay in Mexico, although there is still some indecision (the more positive ending is a result of alterations DHL made in the proofs).[61] In the later version, that is, Lawrence still uses Kate, Ursula-like, as a critic of the ideas of the male characters: a spokeswoman, as it were, for the doubts and worries of his more commonsensical readers; but he weakens his novel by using her much less or, because now she commits herself so much more completely to Cipriano and the new religion, much less effectively. A great deal of the interest of *Kangaroo* had centred on Somers's irresolution and allowed Lawrence to deploy his impressive powers of psychological analysis. In *The Plumed Serpent*, his energy tends to go out rather than in, away from the inner life of Kate, who partly in consequence has, as a character, neither the sharp particularity of Ursula Brangwen nor the same degree of autobiographical investment found in Somers. It is not her hesitations which now chiefly preoccupy Lawrence but rather the effort of imagining, in what is often obsessive detail, the clothing and liturgy of Ramón and Cipriano's new religion.

The much greater length of *The Plumed Serpent* is chiefly accounted for by Lawrence's absorption as he re-wrote, in the costume, ritualistic gesture, dance[62] and, above all, the hymns of his imagined Quetzalcoatl cult. The ceremonies of the new religion receive far more attention than its social organisation, although it now emerges more clearly that Ramón runs his estate very much on the lines of

William Morris; and there is now even less engagement with the likely political realities of transforming a whole society than there had been in 'Quetzalcoatl'.[63] Lawrence disclaims any great interest in these by having Ramón say: 'Politics, and all this *social* religion that Montes has got is like washing the outside of the egg, to make it look clean. But I, myself, I want to get inside the egg, right to the middle, to start it growing into a new bird.'[64] What fascinates Lawrence is the idea of creating *ab ovo* a whole new series of religious practices and beliefs of which Ramón is both the initiator and – as the representative of Quetzalcoatl on earth – the object. The last time he was in Mexico he had made jottings in a notebook for an essay which would eventually become 'On Being Religious' (published in the *Adelphi* in February 1924). Lawrence claims in these that there was no real battle between himself and Christianity, perhaps only one with non-conformity 'because, at the depths, my nature is catholic'.[65] He was attracted to Catholicism because its structure was hierarchical; but *The Plumed Serpent* shows that it must also have appealed to him because of its rituals – even if he was still enough of a non-conformist to reject those already available and invent his own.

The charge that Lawrence's description of how the Quetzalcoatl cult becomes established is insufficiently detailed, or that Lawrence writes (for example) as if industrialisation had never been heard of in Mexico or could be reversed, has been met by the suggestion that, like *News from Nowhere* and other works in the same tradition as Morris's novel, *The Plumed Serpent* is 'utopian'.[66] It is a moot point how self-consciously impractical Lawrence ever intended to be in any of his writing, and certainly several of the leading ideas in his novel were not only current in his day but associated with political activity of a highly practical kind. This is apparent to anyone who reads George L. Mosse's account of German 'Volkish' ideology, which he sees as closely linked with the rise of the Nazi Party.[67] Yet to assume from the similarities between many of Ramón's beliefs and various aspects of the Volkish movement that the politics of *The Plumed Serpent* (what little of them there are) should be called Fascist, and that the hotel keeper at Orilla is therefore right when, early in the novel, he describes the 'Men of Quetzalcoatl' as just 'another dodge for national-socialism',[68] would be inaccurate and unfair. Cipriano's explicit condemnation of Italian Fascism does not survive into *The Plumed Serpent*, but for Lawrence himself Fascism was always associated with bullying, and he took considerable care to show Ramón as someone who never attempts to impose his views and whose power is never very actively sought but comes as a consequence of the people's freely granted allegiance.

Ramón is not a Mexican version of Mussolini. Yet the views he expresses, and the society he seeks to establish, are of course highly authoritarian. This may well make a whole class of readers dislike the book but is hardly a reason for thinking it a failure in literary terms. (Lawrence is by no means the only writer of the 1920s with opinions which could be thought of as reactionary.) What makes *The*

Plumed Serpent hard to read for many is less the ideas its characters express than having to pay attention to yet another description of the costumes Ramón and Cipriano wore, and the gestures they made, during yet another Quetzalcoatl ceremony; or having to struggle through yet another of Ramón's hymns. Very impressive passages can be found in most of these, but they are too few in comparison with the large number of the hymns and their often inordinate length; too few also to compensate for the slackening of dramatic tension they inevitably induce. Since the novel was published there have almost certainly been a majority of readers who feel that the degree of Lawrence's absorption in these matters is greater than theirs could ever be and who therefore regard *The Plumed Serpent*, not as the culminating triumph of Lawrence's American years, but as the consequence of seriously misguided effort: a work whose development took him too far away from the areas of his greatest strength.

It should go without saying that this is not everyone's view, and that Lawrence's Mexican novel has always had its admirers. Catherine Carswell thought it the 'most ambitious and most impressive novel of [her] generation' and, perhaps more significantly, in an obituary talk he gave two months after Lawrence had died, E. M. Forster called it his 'finest novel', full of his 'essential qualities – the poetry that broods and flashes, the power to convey to the reader the colour and the weight of objects'.[69] Forster's admiration suggests that he might have been affected by Lawrence's criticism of the 'Temple' section in *A Passage to India* and been persuaded, first by the essay on the Hopi snake dance and then by *The Plumed Serpent*, that Lawrence had more insight into what it meant to be religious but not Christian than he had. More recently, both L. D. Clark and J.-P. Pichardie have written impressive accounts of why *The Plumed Serpent* should be regarded as a great novel; and there are increasing signs of it beginning to benefit from the burgeoning interest in 'part-colonial studies'. Firmly anti-colonial in its hostile attitude to the effects on the Indian population of the Spanish Conquest, *The Plumed Serpent* is nevertheless a tricky text for workers in this field to handle because the post-colonial future it imagines for Mexico is so far from being conventionally liberal.

No work Lawrence ever wrote divides his admirers as sharply as *The Plumed Serpent*. Those who think highly of it can appeal for support to its author's own judgement. In Chapala Lawrence had regarded the novel as his most important creative endeavour since *Women in Love*, and there is no evidence that in Oaxaca he was any less excited than he had been then about its merits and value. He committed himself to it with a tenacity and depth of engagement which he had not shown since the war. Yet in the last years of his life he rarely mentioned *The Plumed Serpent*, and in an interview he gave in the late 1920s he said that he thought *Sons and Lovers* was the best novel of the first phase of his career, *Women in Love* the best of the second, and then went on to insist that *Lady Chatterley's*

Lover was his favourite from the third.[70] He may have forgotten *The Plumed Serpent* because he had come to feel he had over-rated its quality; uncharacteristically, he may have been affected by some of the harsh reviews it received; but it is also likely that he shied away from the novel because it was irredeemably associated in his mind with the misfortune which overtook him as, at the beginning of February 1925, he completed the revisions of its previous version.[71]

IV Literary Distractions

Re-writing 'Quetzalcoatl' meant a major and exhausting effort for Lawrence and, by his own standards at least, he allowed himself few distractions. One of these was reading Tolstoy's *Resurrection* for the first time. We know he did this, not through the letters, but because he says he has just finished it in an essay which he wrote shortly after Christmas. Detailed comment on Tolstoy's story of the Prince, spiritually re-born after he has found himself on a jury which unjustly condemns to hard labour in Siberia a woman whom he has previously seduced, would come later, in Lawrence's essay on 'The Novel'. At this point, despite or because of his absorption in *The Plumed Serpent*, he largely ignores the challenge Tolstoy's remarkably radical and subversive Christian Socialism presents to his own idea of the 'political novel', and concentrates rather on defining what spiritual re-birth ought really to be after the years in the tomb which have followed World War I. He accuses Tolstoy of wanting to crucify Jesus anew and insists that 'Christ and the Father are at one again. There is a new law.' In the biblical idiom of Ramón's hymns, he urges those who are capable of acceding to the new, integrated life to seize their chance: 'For the multitudes shall be shaken off as a dog shakes off his fleas. And only the risen lords among men shall stand on the wheel and not fall.'[72]

An essay such as this would have meant no more than an hour or two with his notebook, but Lawrence did take more time off in an attempt to help two friends: one old, one new. The old friend was Mollie Skinner. In summer 1924 he had heard that she had gone to London to try to place the novel (*Black Swans*) which he had seen in draft and which had prompted his advice that she should stick, in her writing, to what she knew best. That advice had eventually resulted in *The Boy in the Bush*, which came out while Mollie Skinner was still in England. It distressed Lawrence that so many reviewers gave her little or no credit for her part in its composition, and his discomfort was increased when he learned that the novel she had brought to London with her had been rejected by his own publisher (v. 113). But with the help of Edward Garnett, Mollie Skinner persuaded Jonathan Cape to take it, and then asked Lawrence if he would provide a preface (v. 190). The request was hard to refuse but to write about a novel of which his memory was vague, and which he had felt was no more than a promising mess, was not easy either. On Christmas Eve 1924 he solved the problem by writing mostly about *The Boy in the Bush*, taking the opportunity to explain its relation to 'The House of Ellis'; accepting responsibility for 'the last chapters and anything in the slightest bit "shocking"'; but also complaining about the way Mollie Skinner's role in the whole enterprise had been ignored.[73] He was not however a man to leave it quite like that. To the account of *The Boy*'s origins he added a defence of the morality of his own ending, and to the complaints about the reviewers an attack on the established 'literairy' world in general:

the first business of anybody who picks up a pen, even so unassuming a pen as Miss Skinner's now, is to put no trust in the literary rabble, nor in the rabble of the critics, nor in the vast rabble of the people. A writer should steer his aristocratic course through all the shoals and sewerage outlets of popular criticism, on to the high and empty seas where he finds his own way into the distance.[74]

Both these additions are lively and interesting but they do not have much to do with *Black Swans* which Lawrence remembered as 'always hovering over the borderline where probability merges into magic: then tumbling, like a bird gone too far out to sea, flopping and splashing into the wrong element, to drown soggily.'[75] Although he goes on to say that he believes the novel has been improved, these phrases are hardly encouraging to a prospective reader; and either Mollie Skinner or her publisher must have decided that *Black Swans* would do better without a preface by Lawrence. 'I'm sure', he wrote four months later, without rancour and confirming the wisdom of the decision, 'it's best for it to appear absolutely without any connection with me' (v. 245).

His second attempt to help a friend was no more successful. When he had almost finished *The Plumed Serpent*, he took the trouble to refashion completely an essay which had been sent to him by Luis Quintanilla. On 19 December he had written to Quintanilla to say he had received Weston's portraits and thought them very good. He wondered whether they might not serve for a little article Quintanilla could write 'on Mexico D.F. – and me thrown in – and Weston thrown in – for *Vanity Fair*'. On his most recent passage through New York he had lunched with Crowinshield, *Vanity Fair*'s editor (v. 185), and he was anxious to use his influence both to make Weston better known and at the same time to launch Quintanilla on a career in the lucrative American market. His disclaimer that he made this proposal because he wanted publicity for himself is patently true. 'You, with your Paris-Post-bellum amusing style', he told Quintanilla, 'you could very successfully do little articles – two or three thousand words – for a paper like *Vanity Fair*, which everybody reads' (v. 186–7). But when the young writer responded with a piece about the irritations and indignities of being obliged, as part of his official duties at the Foreign Ministry, to show American visitors round the capital, Lawrence was bewildered by its rancour: 'There must be a terrible bitterness somewhere deep down between the U.S.A. and Mexico, covered up. When one touches it, it scares one, and startles one' (v. 196).

Quintanilla's article is quite sharp in its observation, although not at all 'amusing'. He denounces all the various types of Americans who have decided to come south now that the Mexicans have, as he puts it, 'stopped revolutionaring for a while' (he can afford the strange verbal form because his English is otherwise faultless). Apart from industrialists, businessmen, labour-leaders and salvationists, he complains, the influx includes women in search of Latin lovers such as Rudolph Valentino or Ramón Navarro, and betrayed husbands looking for a town where they can carry a gun, get drunk, swear and live with a prostitute. After ironically delineating these and other visitors, Quintanilla writes that 'at last comes the American artist' and pays a tribute to Edward Weston for 'catching the very heart of Mexico . . . The Indian pyramids pierce the sky more majestically, since you have seen them.' Signing his piece 'Louis' rather than 'Luis', he ends by referring to the PEN dinner in honour of Lawrence and wonders whether 'in spite of the "strained" anglo-mexican relations, the subtle and deep talent of the great English writer will catch the strange beauty of this Mexican atmosphere; with her crimes and poetry, with her ruins and her social utopias, with her bandits and her dreams'.[76]

There is a bitterness in Quintanilla's article, a settled anti-Americanism, which would have made it difficult or perhaps impossible to publish in an American periodical; but in trying to alter the tone Lawrence only succeeded in producing a version awkwardly and uncomfortably facetious. The material is entirely re-worked, and in an addition of supposedly comic business, he has 'Luis Q.' meeting Americans in his office in Mexico City, fielding their mindless questions, but rushing upstairs after each one to the window from where he can see the nearby Popocatépetl whom he then consults as to the correct answer. (Popocaté-petl is one of the two volcanoes just outside Mexico City which in Lawrence's day were not yet permanently obscured by a blanket of smog.) The revised version of Quintanilla's article is exceptional in that although Lawrence did not perhaps make it any worse, neither did he make it any better. Returning it to its author he displayed an uncharacteristic but justified lack of confidence in his work and he cannot have been surprised when his friend did not try to place the piece. The grounds Quintanilla gave later were that, as re-written by Lawrence, his article contained remarks with which he could not agree; but to have had it published in the form he received it, under his own, unknown name, would in any case have been very difficult.[77]

Lawrence returned the transformed article to Quintanilla on 12 January 1925. It was roughly three weeks before then that, in by far the most important of his literary distractions, he had also taken time off to write the first four essays in *Mornings in Mexico*. The lightness and charm of these suggest the relief he must have felt at a temporary respite from the hard labour of *The Plumed Serpent*; but they had also allowed him to express responses to his immediate environment which could not be incorporated into a novel he had begun and set in Chapala. There was, for example, already a market scene in 'Quetzalcoatl'. Lawrence re-wrote this in a characteristic way, expanding the original material to more than double its length so that the 'little gangs of donkeys' which come 'trotting to be laden' become, in *The Plumed Serpent*, 'little gangs of donkeys' which 'come trotting down the rough beach, to be laden, pressing their little feet in the gravelly sand, and flopping their ears'.[78] Expanded also is Kate's central feeling about the market, her surprise that there is 'never a shout, hardly a voice to be heard', or that the vendors 'never asked you to buy. They never showed you their wares.' These phrases are virtually identical in both versions but in 'Quetzalcoatl' she feels, 'It was as if they didn't want to sell the things: didn't care' whereas by the time of *The Plumed Serpent* this has become, 'It was as if their static resentment and indifference would hardly let them sell at all.'[79]

Because Lawrence's impressions of the market at Oaxaca were quite different from these, it would have been difficult for him to incorporate them into his re-written novel. Instead they form what was originally the second of his 'Mornings' ('Market Day'), where his extraordinary gift for an apparently casual *reportage* is on full display. The contrast they provide to the heavier parts of *The Plumed Serpent* has led some critics to prefer them to the novel. This, an admirer has responded, is like preferring one of Rubens's tiny preliminary sketches for 'The Flaying of Marysas' to the picture itself.[80] It is hard not to feel in disputes of this kind the influence of that hierarchy of literary forms we inherit from the nineteenth century. Matthew Arnold found it difficult to be fair to Flaubert and Tolstoy because they were not poets, and poetry was after all the 'crown of literature'.[81] We now have no problem in acknowledging that poetry has no inherent superiority over fiction, but are not always so open-minded about travel books, short sketches or any form of writing that can be ruled out of the higher court by its association with the world of journalism. Less avant-garde than its author imagined, *Kangaroo* is at least thoroughly 'modernist' in its radical assault on its readers' preconceptions concerning genre. Without taking the point of that assault, and without therefore learning to think of the novel in its traditional aspects as just one more literary form among many, there is little hope of a just assessment of Lawrence's literary output in the years which followed the publication of *Women in Love*. The relative positioning in that estimate of *The Plumed Serpent* and the first four sketches in *Mornings in Mexico* will always remain debatable; and it is quite true that works of such different scope are difficult to compare. But what one could assert the sketches certainly do offer, with their sharpness and humour, is a reminder of a psychological principle the Romantic poets were fond of illustrating: that when the mind has been concentrating fiercely in one direction, its sudden relaxation towards another can often result in unexpected felicities. *The Plumed Serpent* was Lawrence's attempt to imagine a radically new way of living for a world which, as he puts it in the 'Epilogue' he had recently written for *Movements in European History*, had been left 'directionless' in 1919: 'We none of us believe in our ideals any more. Our ideal, our leading ideas, our growing tip were shot away in the Great War.'[82] Although revulsion from an always incipient savagery in Mexican life is more apparent in the re-written version of the novel than in 'Quetzalcoatl', it dealt with a country where he felt there was most reason for hope, or least reason for absolute despair. From an author who was too much of a perversely defiant optimist to regard politics as necessarily and inevitably a choice between available evils, it attempted to steer a course between all the political alternatives then on offer ('I must Creat a System', Lawrence would have said with William Blake, 'or be enslav'd by another Man's');[83] and was composed with an earnestness which reveals an indebtedness to that nineteenth-century tradition which had declared poets the unacknowledged legislators of their world. Yet it is a sign of the complexity of his nature that, when he took time off to write his sketches, he should begin the first ('Corasmin and the Parrots'), in a spirit which, if it does not contradict his chief labour, at least qualifies it,

One says Mexico: one means, after all, one little town away South in the Republic: and in this little town, one rather crumbly adobe house built round two sides of a garden patio: and of this house, one spot on the deep shady verandah facing inwards to the trees, where there are an onyx table and three rocking chairs and one little wooden chair, a pot of carnations, and a person with a pen. We talk so grandly, in capital letters, about Morning in Mexico. All it amounts to is one little individual looking at a bit of sky and trees, then looking down at the page of his exercise book.

It is a pity we don't always remember this.[84]

CHAPTER TEN

◆

November 1924–March 1925
BRETT IS BANISHED

I Ultimatum

Although the Lawrences and Brett were now living at some distance from each other, tension continued to grow. Frieda patently found Brett's devotion to her husband galling. Its nature emerges from numerous passages in Brett's memoir which have a touching quality for third parties, but which one can easily imagine having a quite different effect on anyone who happened to be married to their principal subject.

> I have been waiting for you in the hotel for so long that I begin to wonder if you are coming after all. I stroll slowly to a corner of the Zócalo and stand for a few minutes watching the people. Suddenly I see you, walking along the street. Your head is up, your feet move over the ground lightly, so lightly that you might be floating. You drift along dreamily, looking as if you were seeing nothing, hearing nothing; your head is slightly tilted back, your pointed beard sticking out. Slight, narrow-shouldered, in pale grey, your big Stetson shadowing your face, your face pale, luminous in the shadow of the hat – you are almost a dream figure. I watch, wonderingly, so little do you seem to belong to this earth.
>
> What is it that flows from you? It is hard to describe. It is that something from the heart, that has nothing to do with upbringing or training. Compassion . . . can it be that? I wonder, watching you. Compassion . . . understanding . . . or both . . . or what? I can find no word. How describe the real aristocracy of the heart and mind? I have tried to so often, from the first days I knew you, but I never have been able to find the words. I watch you now and know that it surrounds you, gives you that strange 'quality' that others see and feel as well as I, and which clothes you even from that distance as I watch you drifting lightly across the street and round the corner. I know the way you must come, so I hurry to meet you.[1]

Brett would usually go to see or meet the Lawrences in the afternoons around four o'clock. In the mornings she typed *The Plumed Serpent* ('our spelling does not match any better in Mexico than it did in America!'[2]). On those afternoons or parts of afternoons when she was alone, she painted. Her memoir suggests that the occasions on which she was able to have Lawrence to herself were fairly frequent. On one of these they were walking together in the town when they saw a giggling crowd gathered round a shop window. On investigation they discovered the object of the mirth to be a caricature of Lawrence which amused them also. They went off to have drinks with the Kulls in the Zócalo and then back to that couple's flat for brandy. Suddenly Lawrence realised it was nine o'clock and ran home to an enraged Frieda. The next day Brett was witness to Frieda's complaints: ' "He kept me waiting", she cries, "Kept *me* waiting!" The emphasis on the "me" astonishes me. "Why not?" I ask, rather tactlessly and fruitlessly.'[3] There was certainly a lack of tact in Brett's assumption that her own sense of insignificance in comparison with Lawrence should necessarily be shared by his wife.

On another occasion Lawrence and Brett decided they had had enough of feeling trapped within Oaxaca because of the supposed risk of wandering outside the town. They set off into the countryside along the Mitla road and found two bushes within hailing distance of each other. Under one, Brett began a painting of the plain bordered by the mountains to the north of Oaxaca, which has survived and to the foreground of which Lawrence added some figures of people and animals.[4] Under his own bush he began the first sketch in *Mornings in Mexico* – it was intended for *Vanity Fair*, a periodical very much on his mind when during these same couple of days in late December he wrote to Weston and Quintanilla. The plan was for Frieda to join them for lunch but she failed to turn up. After they had followed the same routine on another day and Brett asked, on leaving Lawrence at his door, whether it was going to continue, he replied, 'I don't know . . . You had better come up and see. I don't think Frieda likes it.'[5]

On one of their meetings to which Brett does not give a date she remembered being so much in harmony with Lawrence that she was able to tell him about the 'strange, wonderful, mystical experience' she had a month or so before Katherine Mansfield died. This is likely to have been visions of the absent (and later dead) Katherine which Brett felt she had often been granted. Lawrence was not at all sceptical but rather 'excited, happy, exhilarated'. 'You talk to me of —, too', Brett writes, 'of her difficulties, her likes and dislikes, your mutual difficulties.' (The last phrase suggests the dash must stand for Frieda.) When they arrived back at the Lawrences' house they were both in a joyous mood. Frieda was again not pleased but, 'I am still immersed in the talk I have had and notice nothing: for the moment I am obtuse.'[6] Only after tea does it dawn on Brett that it is time to go. Her deafness had both cut her off from the world and made her unusually self-sufficient. It seems in addition to have helped her to become a person who was unusually slow to take offence, but also not quick to recognise when her company was no longer wanted.

Frieda gave her view of the situation involving Brett in a lightly fictionalised autobiography she began in the 1930s but never finished. This has the disadvantage, like much of Frieda's writing, of sounding uncomfortably 'sub-Lawrentian' in many of its analyses, and it is of course retrospective. Yet the gist of her account corresponds with what she said, or was reported as saying, at the time. Brett is easily recognisable in the fragment as 'S-': 'S- did not hear very well, so whatever Paula [Frieda's name for herself] said was one thing and what S-'s ears heard was another'; and she is presented as one of two women in America 'who were determined to take Andrew [i.e. Lawrence] under their wing'. But whereas 'R-' (equally easy to recognise as Mabel) was possessed of a 'terrific will', S- was a different type: 'the serving self-effacing, adding herself to another's being, but feeling very superior in her self-abnegation'. Paula admires the way S- adapts herself to the rigours of life on the ranch where the three of them are living, given the comforts of her previous background, and she does all she can to make her happy; but she knows that S- is not grateful and that, because of her adolescent crush on Andrew, she has a '*parti pris* against Paula from the beginning'.

It exasperated Paula, chiefly that her own good will towards this incomplete being was so ignored. She put up with her because she helped Andrew in many things, she was a faithful servant but the kind of servant that bosses you in the end with its service . . . She encroached more and more on the privacy of Andrew and Paula's daily life, till Paula would stand it no more. 'She goes or I', she had declared one morning.[7]

It is possible to attach a reasonably precise date to Frieda's ultimatum. In a letter Lawrence wrote to William Hawk on Tuesday 6 January 1925, explaining that Frieda was once again anxious to see her family in Europe, there are signs that a friendly accommodation may have been attempted before the ultimatum was delivered. He himself, he said then, needed to go to London, 'So probably we shall sail for England from Vera Cruz in February' (v. 191). (Lawrence had described Frieda as 'sniffing Europe-wards once more: her mother and children' as early as 10 December and, with his father having so recently died, was himself under some pressure from his sisters to visit Nottingham – v. 185, 197.) Brett, he told William Hawk, did not want to go to Europe with them because she was worried that she would not then have enough money to get back to America: 'Her heart is set on the ranch . . . Therefore probably you'll hear from her soon, saying she's wending her way north, to Del Monte. She could stay in one of your houses till we get back, couldn't she?' (v. 191). What appears to have been envisaged at this stage was not any dramatic break from Brett but an amiable, temporary separation. The drama comes with a note which is dated 'Friday evening' and which the Cambridge editors suggest was delivered to Brett by Rosalino three days later than Lawrence's letter to William Hawk:

Dear Brett,
   The simplest thing perhaps is to write, as one can't shout everything.
   You, Frieda and I don't make a happy combination now. The best is that we should prepare to separate: that you should go your own way. I am not angry: except that I hate 'situations', and feel humiliated by them. We can all remain decent and friendly, and go the

simplest, quietest way about the parting, without stirring up a lot of emotions that only do harm. Stirred up emotions lead to hate.

The thing to do is to think out quietly and simply, the best steps. But believe me, there will be no more ease between the three of us. Better you take your own way in life. Not this closeness which causes a strain.

I am grateful for the things you have done for me. But we must stand apart.

Yrs D. H. Lawrence

(v. 192)

In his letter to Hawk, Lawrence had spoken of sailing to England in February. This would have meant that in only a few weeks he and Frieda could have travelled up to Mexico City with Brett and parted amicably from her there. But now he felt impelled to make a more immediate and obvious break. The likelihood therefore is that, between 6 and 9 January, Frieda had discovered that she could not contain her exasperation any longer – possibly because Brett was not very good at taking hints – and forced her husband into this apparently decisive and in some ways cruel gesture. (The cruelty is in the first sentence where the reference to Brett's deafness might also be seen as providing Lawrence with a convenient excuse for writing what it would be very difficult for him to say.)[8]

In Brett's account of how she responded to this note the efficacy of her defence mechanisms is evident when she recalls (as always, in the present tense), 'I sense behind it all, something that has no bearing on me and my doings.'[9] She chose to go and see the Lawrences at four o'clock as usual. Nothing was then said about a separation but the atmosphere was tense enough for her not to stay too long. After she had returned to her room at the Francia and begun typing more of *The Plumed Serpent*, Lawrence suddenly appeared to explain that Frieda had made a scene immediately Brett had left, that he was in despair, and that the only thing he could do was to ask her not to come to the house again.

I tell you to sit down, and down you sit. You rumple your hair, despairingly. 'Look here, Lawrence', I say, 'Let us be calm and sensible. This is too much of a strain for you; it makes you ill, doesn't it?'

'Yes', you reply, wearily, 'It is unbearable. I shall be ill if it goes on.'

'Well', I say, 'The simple, easy way out is for me to go. I will go back to Del Monte for awhile. This will relieve you of the strain.'[10]

One might doubt whether, in 1925, Brett was quite so calm and in control of the situation as is suggested here where she seems to take a retrospective revenge on Lawrence by patronising him. Yet she clearly did decide to go to Del Monte. This was less of a generous concession than the dialogue above implies, when it was only because of the Lawrences that Brett had somewhere to stay in the Taos area and Frieda (as Lawrence's note indicates) would have liked to see her out of their lives altogether. They were now at a point, however, where a compromise was acceptable to all three. At some time during the next nine days, as Brett made her arrangements to leave, Lawrence explained that Frieda hated her: ' "But", I say, astonished, "Do you mean to say that all this time while I have been thinking Frieda likes me, that she has been hating me?" "Of course", you reply, impatiently. "Of course she hates you. What do you suppose all our quarrels are about?" ' At some time also Frieda paid Brett a surprise visit. If it is true that on this occasion Frieda said she resented the fact that Lawrence and Brett did not make love together, and accused them of being like a curate and a spinster, then she was being disingenuous because she would have no more tolerated Brett as her husband's mistress than Mabel in that role. Brett claims that in the course of their conversation Frieda remarked, 'Lawrence says he could not possibly be in love with a woman like you – an asparagus stick!' and that her reply was, 'He is none too fat himself . . . If you goad a man long enough, he will say anything'; but that their exchanges eventually ended in laughter.[11] The more appropriate response to the 'asparagus stick' jibe might have been that Brett could only seem thin to anyone who compared her with Frieda; but then there would have been much less likelihood of a reconciling good humour. A semblance of friendliness does in fact seem to have been maintained until on 19 January the Lawrences rushed to the Oaxaca station just in time to see Brett take the train for Mexico City (v. 199).[12]

Lawrence had always been anxious about Brett and felt responsible for her safety. It was after all only because of his invitation that she found herself in America. When on one occasion he was confined to bed, and she and Rosalino were at the market, there was a minor incident which involved a drunken Indian throwing a punch at her. This alarmed Lawrence considerably once he heard about it. It was fear of attack in Taos that had led Brett to carry a knife there. Now she took great interest in procuring another knife in Oaxaca, where they are a local speciality, making Lawrence laugh by suggesting that the upshot of her fascination with knives would be that she might become like the Aztec goddess and give birth to one.[13] She would have had this knife with her on the 19th, for psychological comfort at least. In the Mexico of that time there cannot have been many European women travelling to the capital from Oaxaca unaccompanied. Although that must have made Lawrence very uncomfortable, for him it was a case of *force majeure* in the ample form of Frieda. All he could do was write letters which might make the later stages of Brett's journey easier. On 12 January, for example, he had asked Quintanilla and his wife to look after Brett when she arrived in Mexico City and added, 'If you hear of anybody nice with whom Miss Brett might travel up to El Paso, tell me, will you. I don't like to think of her going alone' (v. 196). The Lawrences had met in Oaxaca an American secretary named Rosalind Hughes who had been on an extended holiday there but was now in Mexico City and could be asked – at least twice according to her own account – to keep an eye on Brett.[14] Lawrence also wrote to Ida Rauh in Santa Fe saying that he would tell her when Brett was due to arrive there, 'Just look after her a little bit, will you? I don't like her travelling all that way alone' (v. 199).

II Guilt

Lawrence was as susceptible to guilt feelings as the next person, probably much more so, but he was also highly intolerant of them. In *Sons and Lovers* the young Paul Morel accidently breaks his sister's doll, Arabella. After a day or two of feeling miserably guilty, he persuades his sister that they should build a funeral pyre in the garden and sacrifice what is left of the doll. Lawrence describes the evident relish, the 'wicked satisfaction', with which Paul then watches Arabella – his victim but at the same time the cause of his unease – melt into the fire.[15] Adult life rarely permits such frank expression of the irrational but familiar urge to take revenge on people or objects we have already harmed, but there are faint traces of this process in Lawrence's dealings with the Seltzers while he was in Oaxaca. His New York agent Barmby had obviously recommended that for Lawrence to let Seltzer publish any more of his books, when he owed him so much for those which had already appeared, would be a mistake and suggested the more soundly based firm owned and run by Alfred and Blanche Knopf. The issue came up with the long and brilliant introduction he had written for the *Memoirs of the Foreign Legion* by Maurice Magnus (now at last about to be published along with Magnus's text); and then again, more significantly given its greater commercial potential, with *St. Mawr*. Lawrence's first response was to try to avoid the problem: 'But I leave it to you and Barmby to decide whether to go to Knopf with a book of mine, or not', he told Curtis Brown on 6 November 1924 (v. 161). Eventually however he was obliged to take responsibility, explaining to the same correspondent on 10 January, 'I wired Barmby to proceed with Knopf for the next book' (v. 193). He did not however tell Seltzer that he was moving to Knopf until 15 February and only after receiving a cable from him asking what was going on. Even then, although his reply begins 'Dear Seltzer' instead of his usual 'Dear Thomas', Lawrence is anxious to make clear that the move is not necessarily definitive: 'Let us see how things work out: and if Knopf does one book, why should you not do another, if you wish to?' (v. 213). His decision was a reasonable one: Seltzer had let him down badly and, although he could ask Lawrence how he was expected to get his business back on its feet when his best-known author was deserting him – 'You endanger all if you leave me', he had said in his cable[16] – he had become a bad risk. For Frieda's sake as well as his own, Lawrence could not afford to be negligent of his own financial interests. Leaving the Seltzers nevertheless made him uneasy and he must have felt guilty as he remembered their visit to the ranch in 1922–3, and how enthusiastically they had championed his cause in America. Revenge for this guilt is apparent in short spurts of aggression which accompany his discussion of them with third parties. Telling Curtis Brown that Barmby had arranged to give the Magnus book to Knopf he writes, 'Adele Seltzer – spouse of Thomas – will say as I heard her say before: the English are all treacherous. But Jews are all Judases, and that's how Judas always talks, of other people's treachery. Basta!'; and two months later, after having told Curtis Brown that Knopf was also to have *St. Mawr*, Lawrence explains, 'As for Seltzer, if only he'd have been open and simple with me, I'd have borne with him through anything. But a furtive little flea who hides his hand from me as if I was going to fleece him – whether fleas have hands and fleece or not – why – Basta!' (v. 165, 194). It was quite true that Seltzer had been less than forthcoming in his dealings with Lawrence, but the reasons for his failure to write to him in Europe were much more likely to have been associated with shame than any fear his favourite author might fleece him, and it should hardly have been counted a failing of Adele's that she was Jewish. Lawrence could have offered sound, rational explanations for having to leave the Seltzers but these evidently would have provided less immediate relief for his unease than complaints of this variety, and the dismissive impatience of 'Basta!'

Because he must have felt far more uneasy about Brett than about the Seltzers, one might have anticipated that his anger, when it did break out, would be proportionately greater. Yet it seems likely that he was too decent a human being to unleash it on Brett herself, as he did in the letter he wrote to her on 26 January 1925, without some immediate, precipitating cause. One can be reasonably sure that this was associated, in a way not now possible to define precisely, with Middleton Murry. On Friday 23 January Frieda wrote a friendly note to Brett, who was staying for some time in Mexico City, to which Lawrence added a reasonably friendly postscript (v. 202–3). On the following Monday morning, Lawrence received both a letter from Brett and at least two from Murry in the same envelope. These latter are likely to have been letters from Murry to Lawrence which Brett had collected for him from the British Consulate (whose address he often gave to his friends). The account they must have given of the struggle between Murry and Kot for control of the *Adelphi* which had been going on the previous year ('an absolutely prize sewer-mess' – v. 205) enraged him.[17] After suggesting in writing back to Murry that he would discover the truth about himself in 'Jimmy and the Desperate Woman', which had appeared in the *Criterion* three months previously, he recalled the 'charming dinner' at the Café Royal and Murry's declaration that he loved him but could not promise never to betray him. 'Let's wipe off all that Judas–Jesus slime', he said and went on to tell Murry that, 'in Kot you met a more ancient Judas than yourself'. He insisted that since he (Lawrence) was not lovable he was 'hence not betrayable', and in his final remarks made it clear that although he and Frieda might be in England soon, he would have no desire to see Murry there – 'I shall not want to see anybody except just my sisters and my agent. – Last time was once too many' (v. 205–6).

This furious response to Murry was written on Wednesday 28 January. Two days previously, on the same day he had received all three letters, Lawrence had written his angry reply to Brett in which he begins by saying that the enclosures from Murry made him 'sick in the pit of [his] stomach'. It is hard to know how far the tone in which he then addressed her was provoked by these, and how far it was a consequence of her own letter. She must have alluded to her ideal of friendship, the character of which can be inferred from Lawrence's reply:

Friendship between a man and a woman, as a thing of first importance to either, is impossible: and I know it. We are creatures of two halves, spiritual and sensual – and each half is as important as the other. Any relation based on the one half – say the delicate spiritual half alone – *inevitably* brings revulsion and betrayal. It is halfness, or partness, which causes Judas. Your friendship for Murry was spiritual – you dragged sex in – and he hated you. He'd have hated you anyway. The halfness of your friendship I also hate. And between you and me there is no sensual correspondence. (v. 203)

Lawrence continues with a familiar attack on the 'inevitable bunk of love', saying that a marriage based on kindliness and liking, such as the one Maruca, the daughter of the Hotel Francia's owner, appeared to have contracted, was preferable to a love-match. Brett must have written to him about a sea captain at the hotel where she was staying who had shown some interest in her and left his bedroom door open at night, presumably as a form of invitation. Lawrence tells her not to jeer at this or think that she was superior to sex: 'Only too often you are inferior to it.' 'Know from your Captain', he goes on,

that a bit of warm flame of life is worth all the spiritualness and delicacy and Christlikeness on this miserable globe. – No Brett, I do *not* want your friendship, till you have a full relation somewhere, a *kindly* relation of both halves, not *in part* as all your friendships have been. That which is in part is itself a betrayal. Your 'friendship' for me betrays the essential man and male that I am, and makes me ill. – Yes, you make me ill, by dragging at one half at the expense of the other half. I am so much better now you have gone. – I refuse any more of this 'delicate friendship' business, because it damages one's wholeness.

Lawrence protests that in spite of all he says he does not feel unkindly towards Brett – 'In your one half you are loyal enough' – but he concludes by urging her to become whole, 'not that unreal half thing your brothers hated you for, and that all men hate you for, even I' (v. 203–4).

When during the war Bertrand Russell had received a similarly diagnostic if considerably more hostile letter from Lawrence, he claimed that it led him to contemplate suicide for twenty-four hours.[18] It is hard at first to understand how an account of her sexual nature so much more ungenerous and unfair than anything that had been said about Dollie Urquhart in 'The Princess' (for example) did not either devastate Brett or lead her to break off relations with Lawrence completely. In fact, as far as one can tell, it made no essential difference to her feelings for him. Perhaps she concluded, as she had done with regard to the note Rosalino had brought, that it had no real bearing on her. She might have found some support for that view in the inconsistencies of a letter which gives the appearance of control but is no more coherent than Lawrence's minor outbursts against the Seltzers. It might well be these inconsistencies which led Brett's biographer to wonder whether Lawrence might not at some point during his time with her in Oaxaca have 'made some kind of pass which she, in her timidity and not knowing how to behave in a triangle, had refused'.[19] There is no evidence for any kind of approach normally suggested by the word 'pass', but it is obvious enough that Lawrence's letter is full of an uncertainly directed and still more uncertainly justified sexual resentment. When he wrote 'The Last Laugh' he had been attracted to Brett and felt that he could be the person to reconcile her to sexuality; but he did not know then that she had slept with Murry. Fragments of a diary which Brett kept when she first came to New Mexico indicate that she had eventually explained how things had stood with Murry:

what a torment it has been to know I am not what he thinks I am . . . I can't bear hurting him, and yet I can't at the same time bear feeling I have deceived him: no, that's not true, I haven't done that, I have been forced by others to withhold what I should have left to myself told him immediately.[20]

Yet Lawrence cannot have been in possession of many of the facts to accuse *Brett* of having dragged sex into her relationship with Murry. The first 'you' in 'Your friendship for Murry was spiritual – you dragged sex in – and he hated you' reads more naturally as a singular than as a plural; but even if the charge is reduced to a half share in the dragging, it remains grotesque and a complete contradiction of the portrait of Brett which Lawrence is otherwise offering. (If we are all creatures of two equally important halves, bringing in sex should not deserve the pejorative implications of 'drag'.) In the paragraph in which Lawrence refers to the nature of Brett's relationship with Murry there is the reference to betrayal and Judas. Brett had never and would never betray Lawrence. It was Murry who was fixed in his mind as Judas, perhaps because like her he also did not understand that all close relationships, whether between men or women, needed to be physical as well as spiritual. As in 'The Border-Line' what one might be glimpsing here is anger towards Murry as someone who had both let Lawrence himself down and been his successful sexual rival.

In the second half of his letter Lawrence says that he can only be friendly with Brett when she has a 'full relation somewhere'. The ending of *The Boy in the Bush*, as well as 'The Last Laugh', would seem to indicate that he had at least fantasised that this full relation could be with him. This notion finds support in some 'Suggestions for Stories' Lawrence jotted down in a notebook during his second stay in Mexico. The first of these is for the fragment now known as 'The Flying-Fish', which he did at least begin; but it is the last, which never became more than a suggestion, that is relevant here (not long before leaving England for Taos, Brett had bought a motor-bike):

The Woman out of the Water – A woman on a motor bike loses her head & steers into the sea – they fish her out nearly drowned – take her to house – bring her round – she stays on with man & wife – is the insidious separator – wife fires her – she has a vision of Christ. Husband follows her – loves her – finds she is really half a *fish*[21]

Lawrence scholars often write as if he had never found Brett physically appealing but this is not the case. In Oaxaca she appears to have revived in him some of the acute discomforts he had felt in his relationship with Helen Corke, before he had met Frieda and while he was still in Croydon.[22] Here is one explanation for his letter; another is the over-spill of his anger against Murry; and the third and perhaps most important one: the need he felt to assuage his guilt by presenting Brett as someone who had deserved his ill-treatment.

III Collapse

After having been as considerate towards Brett as his difficult position allowed, Lawrence exploded into violent anger just a week after her departure. The reasons already offered here for this sudden change are partly circumstantial (the arrival of Murry's letters), and partly psychological. Yet there is another tradition of biographical explanation, hard to reconcile with all the others, which may be relevant and which is summed up very crudely in the title of a book Mabel Luhan had sent Lawrence while he was still in Australia – Louis Berman's *The Glands Regulating Personality*.[23] The issue here is not of course Lawrence's glands but his general physical state. During the period of the crisis with Brett, which is also the period when he was working hard to finish *The Plumed Serpent*, it is certain that he was not at all well. The accusation that it was she who had made him ill, by stimulating one side of his nature while simultaneously frustrating the other, is as ungenerous as the rest of his letter; but he needed some explanation of why he had been in and out of bed since December, and it is likely enough that the situation involving Brett was a contributory factor. When Frieda wrote her friendly note to Brett on 23 January she had said, 'Lawrence is seedy but getting better, well you must be exhausted after such a work like the novel – I said to my mother, it had grown out of the soil of this country like a cactus' (v. 202); but her optimism was ill-founded, as was Lawrence's own belief two days later in his attack on Brett, 'I am so much better now you have gone' (v. 204).

At the time he wrote that phrase Lawrence still had a few pages of *The Plumed Serpent* to write[24] but he intended to travel to Mexico City in the first week of February (only a fortnight after Brett). According to his own account, corroborated by the local doctor, what then happened was that on the very day he finished his novel he collapsed as the 'tail end of [his] influenza got tangled up with a bit of malaria in [his] inside' (v. 210). 'As if shot in the intestines' was how he was to describe his collapse, a few months later (v. 230). Oaxaca is too high for the malaria-bearing mosquito but the disease is still endemic in the countryside around Mitla (which the Lawrences had visited), De Angulo had come down with it when he was working in Oaxaca almost three years previously, and in the 1920s there were plenty of cases in the nearby military hospital whose director was Lawrence's own doctor.[25] If he himself had no doubts about the immediate cause of the trouble and was prepared therefore to have quinine injections 'shoved' into him (v. 210), it was because his symptoms were the same as those he had suffered in Ceylon: principally acute pain in the lower belly, 'Inflammation of the bowels' as Frieda puts it (v. 210). This is not what one usually or principally associates with malaria and neither in Ceylon nor at this point does one hear of Lawrence having suffered from shivering bouts. Later he developed a standard account of what had happened to him. As he expressed it to Amy Lowell on 6 April 1925, 'I got malaria in Oaxaca: then grippe: then a typhoid inside' (v. 229). Typhoid was certainly also common in Mexico at this time but, although it is invoked here to explain the intestinal pain, that is no more one of its principal symptoms than it is of malaria.

Whatever Lawrence's real complaint at this stage, it laid him very low although he felt a little better on 7 February and ready to leave Oaxaca the following week. So much illness was beginning to put him seriously out of humour with the town. 'Well, I'll never come down here again', he told William Hawk (v. 212). Instead of being able to leave Oaxaca in the second week of February however, Lawrence had a relapse. This was so serious that on the 14th he had to be moved on a stretcher to the Hotel Francia where Frieda felt he would be easier to look after. The expatriate community rallied round and, with a kindness she never forgot, helped her with the nursing: 'I was amazed at the "Selbstverständlichkeit" with which they helped us. It was so much more than Christian, just natural.' For the first time since she had known him, Lawrence seemed to give up hope. 'If I die', Frieda remembered him telling her, 'nothing has mattered but you, nothing at all.' What seemed to give him comfort, she said, was the application of hot sandbags to his 'tortured inside'.[26]

A few weeks later, in 'The Flying-Fish' fragment, Lawrence described how he had felt as he lay sick in the hotel room. His hero, Gethin Day, who is 'nearing forty', has been called back to his ancestral home in the Midlands but is trapped for the moment by a bout of malaria in a 'hotel in [a] lost town of South Mexico'.

Although he knows that England is 'tight and little and overcrowded' he is very anxious to return. Immobile in his bed, he watches 'dark-blue shadows' flitting across the indoor patio and Indians with large straw hats rustling past the large window which gives onto the street and is heavily barred.[27] Passing children occasionally clutch the window bars and stare in 'to see the Americano lying in the majesty of a white bed'; and sometimes a beggar sticks his 'skinny hand through the iron grille' and whimpers 'por amor de Dios'. Eventually Gethin Day is able to crawl out into the plaza where, 'half lying on one of the broken benches', he projects the despair of his condition on to the buildings: 'The low, baroque Spanish buildings stood back with a heavy, sick look, as if they too felt the endless malaria in their bowels, the greater day of the stony Indian crushing the more jaunty, lean European day which they represented.'[28]

In the fragment, Gethin Day gradually recovers sufficiently to take the train to Mexico City. The same was true of Lawrence, who was finally able to leave Oaxaca with Frieda on 25 February, three weeks after he had intended. Given his enfeebled state, the journey back to the capital must have been very difficult. Frieda was later to describe it as a 'crucifixion',[29] and she told her mother at the time that it was '*dreadful*' (v. 216). The distance was only 250 miles but it required an over-night stay in Tehuacán, as it had on the way down. Writing from there to his sister Emily, Lawrence said that Frieda had 'got a bit of flue also', and was 'very depressed' (v. 214). Her own memory is of how, after the strain of recent weeks and tormented by the thought that her husband was doomed – that all her love and strength would never make him well again, 'something broke' and she cried 'like a maniac the whole night'. Lawrence, she reports, 'disliked me for it'.[30]

IV Retreat

In Mexico City, the Lawrences went to a hotel called the Imperial rather than the Monte Carlo because Lawrence was, as he put it in a letter to Brett, 'too feeble to rough it' (v. 214). This move to a better class of establishment, with electric heating and room service, was in any case essential now that Frieda had temporarily to stay in bed. At this point, Lawrence began to have anxieties which were to last the rest of his life about his weight: 'I get thinner and thinner' (v. 215). He was told that to recover properly from malaria he needed to get back to sea-level and thought of settling for a while on the Devonshire coast, once they had landed in Plymouth. Separate cabins were reserved for him and Frieda on a ship which was due to leave Veracruz on 17 March and would be in England on 3 or 4 April (v. 217, 219).

Back in the capital, Frieda could turn for help to the first-rate doctors at the American Hospital. They performed various tests on Lawrence: a blood test certainly and also probably an analysis of his sputum. We know from a letter Frieda wrote in 1930 that in addition they took an X-ray of the lungs.[31] Whatever the immediate cause of his troubles, the underlying truth could no longer be disguised. Quintanilla recalled visiting Lawrence at the Imperial with his brother and being taken on one side by the doctor present who told them that 'it was not a case of grippe but definitely an advanced case of tuberculosis'. He claims that: 'we broke the news as gently as we could to Frieda, and decided not to say anything to Lawrence, for the time being'.[32] On what was clearly another occasion Frieda returned to their apartment at the hotel to find the 'analyst doctor' there. When she went into Lawrence's room he said, 'rather brutally . . . "Mr Lawrence has tuberculosis." And Lawrence looked at me with such unforgettable eyes.'[33] It would be perverse to imagine that Frieda could have invented this moment, but even if Lawrence had never been told the truth directly he must have known what it was. The changed instructions of the doctors were significant enough. They now said that on no account must he go back to England but that he needed to seek out dry, mountain air. 'Take him to the ranch', Frieda remembered one of them urging, 'it's his only chance. He has TB in the third degree.'[34] To Brett she wrote with a more optimistic prognosis, 'The doctor says in a year Lawr's lungs should be quite cured, but he must *not* write', adding that he needed to 'become a vegetable.' Circumstances beyond her control appeared to be rescinding the separation with Brett she had succeeded in bringing about, but Frieda went on in her letter to insist that, when she and Lawrence returned to Kiowa, she would expect Brett to remain further down the mountain in Del Monte and not occupy, as she had before, the tiny cabin next to theirs. In spite of the idiosyncratic punctuation and spelling, her words have a dignity not typical of her usual dealings with Brett, and are evocative of the mood which must have been induced by her understanding of how serious her situation had now become.

you see, Brett, both to Lawr and me you *are* a guest and a friend, any thing else was just your idea – but never a *fact*, it is *bad* – and you are all so good in your *consciousness* but you see a lot of things you also are that you dont know of, there is a strangled self in you that does all sorts of things you never know – And I know that your living with us took the unconscious ease and glamour out of my life – I always later on felt you waiting and watching and I hated it – *That* is'nt what I want – Let us be simple friends and relase [*sic*] all that other soul stuff – And it is'nt that I want myself the adoration you give to Lawrence, it would stifle me – It makes everything tight round me and Lawr feels the same – and surely that silly, poky little house cant in itself mean much to you – anyhow I could'nt have you there again – You will hate me for this, but I also have my life to live and the responsibility.

(v. 222–3)

Frieda's letter shows that Lawrence had been warned by his doctors not to tire himself by writing; but even though he had told her that she was the only thing that mattered in his life, writing was also what he lived for. In an autobiographical essay he would write much later, he said that without his writing he would probably 'have died soon. Being able to express one's soul keeps one alive.'[35] Sick as he was he began 'The Flying-Fish' at the Imperial, dictating the first part to Frieda until he was able to take over the writing himself and carry his hero half-way across the Atlantic.[36] His breaking-off at that point is likely to have been a consequence of his enforced change of plans around 11 March. They meant that he would shortly be seeing Ida Rauh for whom, before leaving New Mexico, he had promised to write a play (v. 160). Ida had declared a fondness for stories from the Bible and on 3 March Lawrence had described to her the 'attractive scheme' he had worked out for a play about Noah and his family (v. 217). Once he knew he was going back to New Mexico instead of England, he could have felt that he now needed to fill the scheme out, and put aside 'The Flying-Fish'.

With encouragement from Genesis, Lawrence imagines in 'Noah's Flood' three sons of Noah who are demi-gods, representative of the old order. In the play's first scene they are being conspired against by three men from what, in a sketch he had sent to Ida, he called the 'democracy of decadence' (v. 217). The conspirators complain that 'the Old One and his demi-god sons' do not do anything to deserve their pre-eminence and that it survives largely because they have the secret of fire. They plan to steal 'the red flutterer' and kill Noah and his sons. In an image which would become very important to Lawrence in the final two years of his life, the creative principle at the heart of the Universe is figured here as a Great White Bird; but it emerges from the discussions of the men that they have ceased to honour it. In good times,

the hearts of men beat the warmth and wildness of an answer to the Great White Bird, who sips it in and is rejoiced, lifting his wings. But now the hearts of men are answerless, like slack drums gone toneless. They say: We ourselves are the Great White Birds of the Universe. It is we who keep the wheel going![37]

The three men are seeking liberation from religious dependence and believe that the secret of fire will make them 'free from the need to answer, masters of the question'.[38] In the term he had employed in 'The Flying-Fish', Lawrence is going back to the moment in culture when the 'greater day', which he had always felt ready to re-emerge in Mexico, was first obscured by the lesser. He did not persevere with 'Noah's Flood' but the play he did shortly afterwards write for Ida Rauh (*David*) is very much concerned with the same transition.

At the beginning of his time in Mexico City Lawrence was confined to his room at the Imperial, but later he was able to go out and see one or two people. We know, for example, that on 18 March he had lunch with George Conway and his wife because he signed a 'Record of Guests' which was in use in the Conway household. Conway had a well-informed interest in Spanish colonial documents – in time his collection would become important enough to be cited as a manuscript source in works on the conquest of Mexico;[39] but he was also the managing director of both the Mexican Light and Power and the Mexican Tramways Company. Writing from Taos on 2 April to Mrs Conway, whose daughter remembers her mother saying that she used to take Lawrence to see his doctor in the family car,[40] he thanked both her and her husband for being so kind: 'Tell Conway I hope his troubles are smoothing out. – Really, Mexico City is not so bad, you know: when one finds one's own countrymen still sterling' (v. 229).

One of Conway's troubles was a Tramways strike in March directed (among other things) at having him expelled from Mexico.[41] As he had before, Lawrence felt strong sympathy for an expatriate fellow-countryman exercising power in foreign lands and is likely to have expressed his disdain for the strike, and other manifestations of socialist activity, when he went out to lunch around this time with Quintanilla. With Quintanilla on this occasion was the poet Maples Arce, one of the leaders of 'Estridentismo' and the editor of an influential avant-garde magazine called *Irradiador* (in which Weston's photographs often appeared).[42] According to Quintanilla, Lawrence not only expressed dismay at the political situation in Mexico but was also scornful at the suggestion that Arce was a genius: 'What genius has Mexico ever produced?' His colleague was sheltered from Lawrence's scorn by his inability to understand English but this tone – and the criticisms of his country – so upset Quintanilla that, to his later regret, he walked out of the restaurant and never saw Lawrence again.[43]

With the basket of food the Conways had given them (v. 229), the Lawrences were at last able to leave Mexico City on 25 March. On the 27th, at Jaurez, on the Mexican side of the El Paso border, they secured entry visas from a friendly American Consulate, having stated that their intention was to remain in the USA no more than six months. But the immigration officials at El Paso were suspicious – under the rules of their Department, issued on 1 February 1924, persons with tuberculosis 'in any form' were excluded from entry – and they subjected Lawrence to something more than the routine medical inspection. Recalling the experience nearly four years later he wrote,

at El Paso we were held up by the U.S. authorities and detained till next day – I was called a liar to my face, when I was speaking plain truth – and kept stripped, being examined by a down-at-heel fellow who was supposed to be a doctor but was much more likely to be a liquor-runner – all of which I have not forgotten and shall never forget. Sheer degrading insult! (vii. 144) [44]

Frieda remembered that the Consulate in Juarez was helpful, although the situation was 'tough' with the 'El Paso people hating to give in';[45] but on 28

March medical certificates were issued testifying to 'No Physical or Mental Defects' and the Lawrences were let through.[46] It cannot have helped Lawrence's nerves during the waiting period that he was conscious of looking very ill even if, in his own view, he had improved the situation with a little artifice. As he told Brett,

I looked so awful when I reached Mexico City from Oaxaca: just pale green. The people stared at me so in the streets that I could not bear it, so Frieda bought me some rouge. I rouged my cheeks and gave myself such a lovely, healthy complexion that no one ever turned to stare at me again. You should have just seen me! I used the rouge all the time until I reached New Mexico – until I got past that terrible doctor at El Paso.[47]

It is doubtful whether even a terrible doctor would be deceived by rouge and more likely that Lawrence was finally allowed entry because he was not after all likely to be in the country very long. The medical inspection was clearly an ordeal, however, bringing back painful memories of those he had been obliged to undergo during the war. From our present point of view, it demonstrates the strong, practical interest individuals might have at this time in not admitting they were suffering from tuberculosis, even to themselves.

Lawrence was relieved to be out of Mexico, which he now associated with his illness and was shortly to refer to in disparaging terms. It was a country which had nevertheless meant a lot to him and he had often been happy there, feeling himself in contact with a deeper reality. Gethin Day's responses in what is obviously the Zócalo in Oaxaca are coloured by illness; but they are essentially the same as those which Lawrence had experienced when he first arrived in Mexico and which he had expressed in 'Au Revoir, U.S.A.' Here was a place where one could see more clearly the sub-structure over which Western, Christian culture lay like a thin film. He tried not to ignore the advantages of this culture: in *The Plumed Serpent* Kate often regrets the amenities and refinements of the life she has previously known, and he tried also not to idealise what he felt lay below. The life he sensed in the Mexican landscape and in Indian culture might be more authentic but he was quick to recognise that it could also be harsh and cruel. There were times when he felt over-powered by its harshness but more often he derived a profound satisfaction from a conviction that what surrounded him was 'real'. He needed to feel that he was in contact with what was genuine and substantial. Mexico (but also the landscape surrounding the ranch in *New* Mexico, to which he was now returning) gave him that reassurance more than anywhere else had, or would.

CHAPTER ELEVEN

◆

March–September 1925

THE RETURN TO THE RANCH

I Road to Recovery

The Lawrences had expected to arrive in Santa Fe on the morning of 28 March 1925 but the unpleasant delays at the border meant that they did not get there until the afternoon of the following day. This time Bynner *was* at home, but without Johnson, now Mabel's secretary and away with her at Croton on the Hudson, where she had often rented the same large property. 'Spud wrote from Finney Farm', Lawrence was later to report, 'Sort of HellO!' (v. 237).

His condition meant that he and Frieda could hardly think of staying with friends so that they went once more to the Hotel Vargas. Apart from Bynner, Ida Rauh was now Lawrence's closest contact in Santa Fe and the discussions he must have had with her about 'Noah's Flood' were probably influential in his decision to abandon it. On 1 April she and Andrew Dasburg drove the Lawrences directly to the Del Monte Ranch (v. 228). Even if Mabel Luhan had been in Taos at this time, it is doubtful whether Lawrence would have been in the mood to make the customary stop and attempt a reconciliation. She was a reminder that not every aspect of life in New Mexico could be anticipated with pleasure, but he was nonetheless relieved to be back. 'I really like this country better than any landscape I know', he told Emily on 31 March (v. 228).

The Lawrences stayed at Del Monte for a few days before moving up to their own ranch on 5 April (v. 230). The Hawk family had always been important to them but became more so now that Lawrence was unwell and estranged from Mabel. He and Frieda got on well with the Hawk parents, but had a particularly close relationship with their son Bill and his wife Rachel (a charming photograph of the time shows Lawrence on horseback with Walton, the young son of this couple[1]). Brett also seems to have been easily accepted by all the family, especially by the two Hawk daughters – Bobbie Gillete and also Elizabeth ('Betty'), now married to a man named Cottam in the Forest Service (v. 57 n.2).[2] They might both have found life in the mountains a bit dull and welcomed such an exotic diversion as the daughter of Viscount Esher.

Immediately the Lawrences arrived, it was confirmed that Brett should stay at Del Monte rather than be within twenty yards of them at Kiowa. But this only meant a recreation of the situation which had existed in Oaxaca and it was not long before the familiar tensions surfaced. These have left their traces in angry notes which Frieda fired down to Del Monte in the succeeding weeks, notes in which she accuses Brett of adopting a condescending attitude towards her and asks to be left alone. 'That I owe *you* something is cool', she says in one, in obvious response to Brett's claim that she had been a great help to the Lawrences. 'I looked after your physical well-being for about a year[;] you thought *nothing* of that, but only the high falute with L.'[3] During only one of the several crises does Lawrence seem to have intervened on Frieda's behalf, writing a letter in which he accuses Brett of being a 'born separator . . . It is instinctive with you' (v. 234). 'Separator' is the word Lawrence had used in his suggestion for the story about a girl with a motor-bike, and there is an echo of it in a charge Frieda made in the note from which I have just quoted:

You did things for Lawrence but *never* for me – You just thought me an inferior fool – I *do* know enough of Katherine and of you to judge – If you were so fond of Murry and yet always let Katherine think you adored her, no I can't swallow it – I believe that Carrington & Gertler *might* perhaps have brought it off, but for you.[4]

There are notes which show that Frieda was not always hostile to Brett, but by this stage she was never going to be reconciled to what she felt was an unwarrantable intrusion in her life ('It's all very simple we *want* to be *alone*'[5]). Apart from his one intervention, Lawrence himself seems to have accepted the situation (which after all quite suited him) and, as he became stronger, clearly spent a good deal of time with Brett, painting, riding or working about the ranch as well as once again relying on her for his typing. If her own account is to be believed, Brett herself did not take much notice of Frieda who at one moment insisted that Brett could only come up to Kiowa three days a week (Mondays, Wednesdays and Saturdays), and at another devised a scheme whereby Brett had to blow a whistle whenever she approached the ranch and Lawrence would then emerge to say whether she could visit.[6] She seems to have enjoyed defying these rules and to have given Lawrence's wife as good as she got when challenged. This cannot have diminished Frieda's feeling that she was being regarded as of no account, an inconvenient appendage to a brilliant man. It was the knowledge that this was how she was seen by most people which had caused her so much distress during the war, and which had given, and still now gave, rise to loud assertions of her own worth, as well as to reminders of how much she had done for Lawrence in the past and how much he still depended on her.

If Brett's defiance re-activated these feelings how or why did Frieda put up with it? Part of the reason must have been that, in between her bursts of anger and resentment, her nature was too essentially easy-going to make much headway against Brett's impercipience and quiet, dogged resistance: she was pitted against someone who not only could not, but very often would not, hear. There was always a side of Frieda which simply could not be bothered. On nearly every occasion when Brett mentions Frieda in her account of these final months together in New Mexico, she is lying in the bedroom to the left of the Kiowa cabin's single main living room (Lawrence occupied the bedroom on the right), with a cigarette in her mouth. This may be as distorted an impression as the one Frieda tries to give of herself working hard to look after Brett, in one of her angry notes ('I cooked for you and you flourished!'[7]). Yet with Lawrence helping a great deal with housework and cooking once he grew better, and all the outdoor work his responsibility, there must in fact have been many hours during which she exercised that talent for doing nothing which her husband both lacked and envied, and forgot entirely her struggle with Brett. This was useful because in the immediate term there was in any case not much to be done. In the most hostile of her notes she had simply told Brett to pack up and go, signing off by calling her a 'beastly nuisance':[8] all to no effect. The only way she could have got rid of her was by applying heavy pressure on her husband. This was what she had done in Oaxaca and it was only through the unhappy irony of Lawrence's illness that they had all been thrown together again. It is reasonable to give Frieda the credit for realising that now was not the time for making Lawrence acutely miserable once again. Her consolation in her discomfort was that she knew it was only temporary. Like the protagonist of 'The Flying-Fish', Lawrence had turned towards Europe when he felt ill; and in Kiowa he was still far from well. From Santa Fe he had told his elder sister, 'I feel rather a hankering after England – perhaps because I was ill, then one wants to come home' (v. 228). The toughness he felt as characteristic of the New World, of its landscape chiefly but also of the primitive living conditions he had often experienced there, had invigorated him; but now he felt that his condition required some kind of relief or reprieve. 'We are due to go to Europe for the winter', he wrote to Edward McDonald on 29 June,

and I want to go. America is so eternally and everlastingly tough: very good for one, for a bit; but after too long, it makes one feel leathery in one's soul. Continual leathery resistance all the time. Mexico more so. I think it's time I was softened down a bit, with a little oil of Europe. (v. 272)

Kiowa was therefore no more than a temporary stopping-place: a forced interruption meant to last only until Lawrence was properly fit to travel. However angry Frieda became with Brett she knew that the crucial decision to break up what had become for her an increasingly uncomfortable situation had been taken in Oaxaca, and that she therefore had only a few more months to endure.

When Bynner saw Lawrence in Santa Fe for what would be the last time, he was so dismayed by the physical change that he could not remember afterwards what they had discussed.[9] Recovering his strength was for Lawrence a hesitant process. The dominant mood of his recuperation in its early stages is suggested by a letter he wrote to Zelia Nuttall on 12 April:

Lying on the porch this warm afternoon, with the pine-trees round, and the desert away below, and the Sangre de Cristo mountains with their snow pale and bluish blocking the way beyond, it seems already far to Coyoacán. Here the grass is only just moving green out of the sere earth, and the hairy, pale mauve anemones that the Indians call Owl flowers stand strange and alone among the dead pine needles, under the wintry trees. Extra-ordinary how the place seems *seared* with winter: almost cauterised. And so winter-cleaned from under three feet of snow. (v. 235–6)

Lawrence grew steadily stronger as the warm weather advanced but there were minor relapses, never attributed to tuberculosis (in his letters at least). 'I am better, but the cold winds do get my bronchi, and then I just stay in bed', he told Dasburg on 1 May; and at some moments he may have fallen back on his belief that there was a 'mountain fever' which came from the rarity of the air (v. 248, 519). Writing to Catherine Carswell on 24 August, when he was as well as he would ever be again, he appealed to his old stand-by malaria: 'I am as well as ever I was – but malaria comes back in very hot sun, or any malaria conditions' (v. 289). Lawrence does not appear to have consulted any doctors during this period, but he did show faith in a French patent medicine called 'Solution Pantenberge' which was a mixture of 'creosote and chalk, unsweetened' and was supposed to 'harden the tissue' (vi. 200). 'Bring me another bottle of Pantenberge from the drug-store, please,' he told Ida Rauh, 'or better bring two bottles' (v. 250).

Having to stay in bed rarely prevented Lawrence from composition and he pressed ahead with a new attempt to write a play for Ida, this time based on the story of David. David had been one of his original ideas for the work (v. 174), and he may have returned to it because Frieda had been reading the Books of Samuel in a German translation of the Old Testament and came to him with questions.[10] The figure had always fascinated him, but this time he approached the story from a quite new angle. Previously he had been especially interested in David's relation to Jonathan but now, although he wrote two scenes in which these two declare their love for each other, his main concern was with David and Saul. At the beginning of the play Saul has the power of the Lord taken away from him because he disobeys Samuel's instructions to kill Agag, the captured king of the Amalekites, and destroy all his cattle. Samuel goes to Judaea to anoint David as the future king, and for the rest of the action Saul struggles to come to terms with the knowledge that he will be supplanted. He does not do this very well, succumbing often to fits of wild irritability, breaking his promise to David – after he has killed Goliath – that he should marry his eldest daughter Merab, and

throwing his javelin at him on several occasions. These are episodes from the
Bible which Lawrence dramatises faithfully enough, and in following his source
he presents David as doing all he can not to antagonise a king who also becomes
his father-in-law – having deprived him of Merab, Saul is eventually obliged to
give David his second daughter, Michal. As the action unfolds, however, it
becomes increasingly clear that it is with Saul Lawrence's sympathy really lies.
That is because he sees him as a last representative of the old, animist world-
order and David as the inaugurator of the modern era of the personal God.
Whereas Saul is careless and lacking in self-control, David (to preserve himself)
is shrewd and calculating. Although David can hardly be blamed for his
shrewdness, he begins a process which will end in man living selfishly for his own
purposes, cut off from the greater life of the natural world, the greater 'Day' as
Lawrence had recently expressed it. The theme of *David* is thus the same as that
which had been adumbrated in 'Noah's Flood'. One of the reasons why Lawrence
may have found it easier to treat in this new form was because it allowed him to
identify with Saul in his anguish over the physical effects of the loss of God's
power.

Ah the blithe boy! Ah God! God! was I not blithe? Where is it gone? Yea, where?
Blitheness in a man is the Lord in his body. Nay, boy, boy! I would not envy thee the head
of the Philistine. Nay, I would not envy thee the Kingdom itself. But the blitheness of thy
body, that is thy Lord in thee, I envy it thee with a sore envy. For once my body too was
blithe. But it hath left me. Not because I am old. And were I ancient as Samuel is, I could
still have the alertness of God in me, and the blithe bearing of the living God upon me. I
have lost the best. I had it and I have let it go.[11]

   By 14 April Lawrence had written six scenes of a play which would eventually
run to sixteen.[12] He had finished *David* a month later (v. 236, 252) – relatively
slow-going for him, but he was taking it easy, gradually recuperating and seeing
very few people. One of his first purchases on his return to the ranch was a
buggy, and with two of their four horses the Lawrences would use it to drive
down to San Cristobal, where there was a blacksmith, or to Arroyo Hondo for
supplies (v. 277, 282–3). By 14 July, however, Lawrence could report that he had
not yet been to Taos, and there is no evidence that he ever did go (v. 277). As he
got better he and Frieda would eat at Del Monte with Bill and Rachel Hawk, or
have them up to dinner at the ranch. In the third week of May Else Jaffe's son,
Friedel, who had been an exchange student at a college in Annapolis, and then at
Johns Hopkins University in Baltimore, arrived and stayed for two months in
Brett's old cabin (v. 63 n.1, 244, 252). The sparse and anodyne references to
Frieda's nephew in the letters suggest he must have fitted in well enough, and to
have a strong young man on the ranch would have been very convenient.
Although Mabel was back in Taos by July (v. 281), she refused to drive up, but

one person who did was Willa Cather, now staying at the Big House while she prepared to write one of the most famous novels of the Southwest, *Death Comes for the Archbishop*.[13] The general Taos view was that she was heavy-going but Lawrence did not mind her and the call she made at Kiowa confirmed Frieda in her strong liking (v. 277, 280, 283). Joseph Foster records that, with his wife Margaret Hale, he visited the Lawrences at least twice and that on one of these occasions Johnson was staying with them.[14] Unreliable as Foster is, it would have been surprising if Johnson had not made sure he saw Lawrence and Frieda, once he was back from Finney Farm. In mid-July he was in Santa Fe and expecting to be driven to see the Lawrences by their new friend Christine Hughes; but both Mrs Hughes and he fell ill so that this particular visit, scheduled for the 25th, had to be cancelled (v. 280, 281, 285).

Well before July, on what was probably the weekend of 16 May (v. 252), Ida Rauh had come to Kiowa and listened quietly while Lawrence read aloud the play he had written for her. According to Brett, she showed no enthusiasm when the reading was over ('yet I know she feels the beauty of the play'), and then said in a flat voice that she was too old to play such a radiant creature as Michal[15] – 'It's only when one *lets go* that one feels old: or is old', Lawrence would rebuke her (v. 282). In 1925 Ida Rauh was forty-eight so that age might have been the chief consideration for her; but she could also have been disappointed to find that, in a play principally concerned with relationships between men, Michal is very much a minor role. She appears in the lively opening, taunting, along with her sister Merab, the captured King Agag who is tied to a post – 'It is a dog', she says, 'that cannot scratch his own fleas';[16] and in the first part of *David* she has other moments of high spirits which, as far as the context of Lawrence's own work is concerned, go back at least as far as the impertinences of Beatrice in *Sons and Lovers*. But in Provincetown and New York Ida had earned a reputation for brooding dramatic power, and she may have felt that, with her species of good looks, flightiness would not become her. With her experience of the theatre, she might also have recognised that Lawrence's one attempt to add some weight to Michal's character was a failure. In the soliloquies he gives to the principal male characters, the occasional direct quotation from the the Bible's Authorized Version is skilfully combined with pastiche of biblical language; but when Michal is alone on the stage at the beginning of scene vi ('As for me, I am sad, I am sad, I am sad, and why should I not be sad?'), his touch completely deserts him. Michal's soliloquy is driven laboriously along with a series of exclamations and rhetorical questions. It is patently being used to inform the audience that Saul and David have gone off to fight Goliath and the Philistines, and its idiom seems out of kilter with the rest of the play. Michal is worried, for example, that Saul will marry her off to 'some old sheik', and she is depressed that the spells she has cast in order to secure David have been 'no good'.[17] The speech would be a nightmare for any actress, and one which Ida was clearly not prepared to endure. More generally, she may have realised that, although *David* has some genuinely dramatic moments, it loses momentum half-way through; or perceived – without our benefit of hindsight – that its chief point concerning the inauguration with David of a new relation to the world was hardly comprehensible without some familiarity with Lawrence's private myths of the history of human culture. Whatever her reasons, Ida made it clear that she did not want to act in *David*, but in such a way that Lawrence bore no resentment, merely complaining mildly that she had been wrong to expect 'a more personal play, about a woman' (v. 276). He retained his belief in *David* and, when his agent suggested that it should be published rather than performed, responded with sentiments which must have been heard all too frequently over the last hundred years whenever there has been some hope of restoring the theatre to its former Shakespearean glory:

Curtis Brown says it is not a 'popular' play. But damn it, how does he know even that? Playgoing isn't the same as reading. Reading in itself is highbrow. But give the 'populace' in the theatre something with a bit of sincere good-feeling in it, and they'll respond. If you do it properly.   (v. 274)

II   Fighting his Corner

The doctors in Mexico City had advised Frieda to take Lawrence back to the ranch because of the belief, widespread at the time, in the therapeutic powers of pure, thin air. This is not now felt to have had much, if any, foundation. When patients rich enough to be able to recuperate in the Swiss sanatoriums (for example) did well, their recovery had less to do with mountains than with a healthy diet and withdrawal from much of the stress of their ordinary lives. The difficult road up to Kiowa ensured that Lawrence was protected from the stress of having to see *too* many people, a position which he did not have to be ill to appreciate. His response to the outside world at this juncture can be deduced from the essay which he called 'Accumulated Mail' and which he wrote for his publishers' House Almanac, the *Borzoi 1925* (sending if off via his agent to the editor, Blanche Knopf, around 18 April – v. 243). This dealt humorously with an experience which someone who travelled as much as Lawrence was bound to have (and which he had already described in *Kangaroo*[18]): being met in a new place by a huge pile of correspondence that had either followed him there or was lying in wait. On this occasion the pile included a letter from a group of high-school students, 'somewhere in Massachusetts or in Maryland', who were in the habit of choosing some famous man as a guide and had lighted on Lawrence ('what on earth am I to say to them?'); and another from a 'soi-disant' friend (clearly Murry) who, after telling him that he would understand people better if he did not think he was always right, goes on to ask if he can have some of Lawrence's articles at a cheap rate for the London magazine he edits. The prize exhibit however was a letter from Nottingham, signed simply 'A Mother', which described how its writer had seen a young woman reading *Sons and Lovers* and successfully persuaded her not to finish it. What a pity, this correspondent wrote, that a book which was so well written could not have been kept clean. 'Let us hope', Lawrence responds, 'the young woman who was saved from finishing *Sons and Lovers* may also be saved from becoming, in her turn, *A Mother!*'[19]

'A gentleman in New York', he reports, had written to ask about the 'controversy' between Lawrence and Norman Douglas. The gentleman in question was referring to *A Plea for Better Manners*, the pamphlet which Douglas had recently published as a counterblast to Lawrence's not especially flattering view of him in the introduction to Magnus's *Memoirs of the Foreign Legion*. In the course of arguing that the introduction contained distorted, 'novelist's' portraits of himself and Magnus, Douglas had implied that its author had made money out of a text to which he had no legal right, since he himself had been designated Magnus's literary executor.[20] In February 1925, Murry's associate H. M. Tomlinson had reviewed *A Plea for Better Manners* favourably and suggested Lawrence had a case to answer.[21] His response in 'Accumulated Mail' was first of all to deny that there was any controversy between himself and Douglas and then to set out clearly and rather wearily the facts: that he had worked hard to find a publisher for the *Memoirs* so that the two Maltese who had been led into lending Magnus money in the last weeks of his life could be paid back. Because they were due to receive 50% of the royalty on the book, they would recover their money, and that he should take the other 50% was reasonable given this correspondent's own view that the *Memoirs* would be unpublishable without his long introduction. What he did not at this stage decide to reveal in public was that he had in his possession a letter from Douglas which told him to do whatever he liked with the *Memoirs* manuscript. On 18 April he was inclined to think that he ought to justify his conduct by having this letter printed in the *Borzoi*, but by 5 June he had decided not to bother: 'No, don't use the Norman Douglas letter at all, please', he told Blanche Knopf. 'I felt sore at him for a while, but now prefer to forget him and all that stuff' (v. 260).

The bulk of 'Accumulated Mail' consists of a sprightly riposte to an essay on Lawrence which Edwin Muir had published in the New York *Nation* in February. The charges must have seemed all too familiar: that his characters were not recognisable as ordinary people and had no will-power; that he himself was unwilling to submit to discipline and had not fulfilled his early promise; and that his gifts were 'splendid in their imperfection'.[22] Lawrence responded to them with wit and restraint, acknowledging that Muir was after all a 'phoenix' in comparison with most of his critics, but regretting nevertheless that he did not have 'A Mother' to take books from him 'before he can do himself any more harm'.[23] The article would have been sent on to him by his agent or publisher. It is likely to have met the same fate as the letters which accompanied it and into which Lawrence would either spit or blow his nose before putting them on the fire. As Sean Hignett has observed, this was a sensible practice in the days before Kleenex; and to burn whatever came from Lawrence's diseased chest was after all more hygienic than washing handkerchiefs in the primitive facilities Kiowa could provide.[24]

During the 1920s there was an increasing frequency of general articles on Lawrence like Muir's, and not only in the English-speaking world. In August of the previous year he had been approached by the Italian critic, Carlo Linati, who was preparing an account of Lawrence's work for the *Corriere della Sera*. He responded encouragingly and made sure that Linati was sent most of his publications – along with the Sydney *Bulletin*, the *Corriere* was after all his favourite newspaper ('about the best paper in Europe' is how he described it in his reply to Linati – v. 90). Yet when the article reached him five months later in Oaxaca it pleased him no more than Muir's would. He must have been dismayed that after he had taken the trouble of having his two psychology books sent to Italy, Linati was incapable of reading them with sufficient care to avoid the conclusion that Lawrence was a disciple of Freud's: 'His thirst for liberty and a shame-free inner sincerity led him to embrace Freud's theories.'[25] In writing to Linati, Lawrence is too polite to point out this misunderstanding, contenting himself at first with expressing surprise that he should seem to another quite so '*frenetico*'[26] – 'You leave me quite out of breath about myself' (v. 200); yet, stung by the charge that he had not yet succeeded in subjecting the 'miraculous intensity of his poetic vision to the rhythm of a vast and powerful composition', he had then proceeded to a strong and lively defence of his own methods against those of the Flaubertian school. He began by saying that he could not bear art 'you can walk round and admire . . . the actor and audience business' and ended, 'whoever reads me will be in the thick of the scrimmage. and if he doesn't like it – if he wants a safe seat in the audience – let him read somebody else' (v. 201).

Muir, and Linati before him, must have made Lawrence feel that his critics judged him by the wrong criteria and had failed to understand that he was in no sense a savage genius, warbling his native wood-notes wild, but someone who had thought hard about novel-writing and developed his own aesthetic. He was more pleased by the article by Stuart Sherman which appeared in the *New York Herald Tribune Books* on 14 June ('Lawrence Cultivates His Beard'). He and Sherman had reviewed each other quite sharply in the past,[27] but Lawrence liked what was said in this piece because, as he told its author on 11 July, 'you do care about the deeper implication in a novel. Damn "holiday reading"!' (v. 275). Sherman dealt summarily with one of his subject's more unqualified admirers, the Herbert J.

Seligmann whose monograph on Lawrence had been published by Seltzer in 1924;[28] but it must have been gratifying to find Dr Joseph Collins disposed of with similar expedition and effect. The highly unpleasant chapter on Lawrence in Collins's *The Doctor Looks at Literature* showed close knowledge of his work but was chiefly concerned to warn the public that he was an advocate of homosexuality.[29] It may be, Sherman observes, that the men and women in Lawrence's novels 'can be referred to definite abnormal types, easily recognized and named by the psychopathologist. But that supplies no principle for annihilating Mr Lawrence's novels. Doubtless Dr Collins has often seen in hospitals or insane asylums men easily recognizable as the type of Orestes or King Lear or Othello.'[30] Sherman was no critical genius but Lawrence appreciated his intelligence, and in his 11 July letter explained that he had written a couple of essays on art and morality which, as the editor of the *Tribune*'s book section, Sherman might like to use. Because he had already found a home for it, he did not add that, two weeks before, he had completed a third essay, later to be called simply 'The Novel'.[31] Taken together, these three pieces, written in May and June 1925, constitute one of the most impressive of all Lawrence's many replies to his detractors and have provided crucial concepts, as well as striking phrases, for which many literary critics have been heavily in his debt ever since.

Although it usually assumed a form less direct than that adopted by Collins, or the 'Mother' from Nottingham, the most common charge against Lawrence was that his work was a threat to public morality. As he told Sherman when referring in his letter to his first two articles, 'Art and Morality' and 'Morality and the Novel', the point was 'easier to see in painting, to start with' (v. 276). Why, he begins by asking in 'Art and Morality', are people so shocked by Cézanne's paintings, not of nudes, but of such apparently unexceptionable objects as apples? The reason he gives is that Cézanne is struggling to define a new relationship to the forever shifting outside world. Most of us are frozen in outmoded notions of what that relationship should be and, in modern life especially, what Lawrence calls kodak vision – the allurements of a putative photographic 'realism' – continually provides us with false ideas of both the outside world and ourselves.[32] The artist shocks us by challenging those ideas and yet the search for a proper relationship with external reality is in fact the key to morality. As Lawrence puts it at the beginning of 'Morality and the Novel', 'The business of art is to reveal the relation between man and his circumambient universe, at the living moment. As mankind is always struggling in the toils of old relationships, art is always ahead of the "times," which themselves are always far in the rear of the living moment.'[33] Van Gogh's *Sunflowers* are the 'revelation of the perfected relation', not the painter's idea of sunflowers nor those flowers 'themselves' but a third thing which exists in what Lawrence calls the 'fourth dimension'.[34] In a world which is never the same and has continually to be re-discovered, the novelist has the same duty as the painter to seek the 'perfected relation' of the moment.

And morality is that delicate, forever trembling and changing *balance* between me and my circumambient universe, which precedes and accompanies a true relatedness.

Now here we see the beauty and the great value of the novel. Philosophy, religion, science, they are all of them busy nailing things down, to get a stable equilibrium. Religion, with its nailed down One God, who says *Thou shalt, Thou shan't*, and hammers home every time; philosophy, with its fixed ideas; science, with its "laws": they all of them, all the time, want to nail us on to some tree or other.

But the novel, no. The novel is the highest complex of subtle inter-relatedness that man has discovered. Everything is true in its own time, place, circumstance, and untrue outside of its own place, time, circumstance. If you try to nail anything down, in the novel, either it kills the novel, or the novel gets up and walks away with the nail.

Morality in the novel is the trembling instability of the balance. When the novelist puts his thumb in the scale, to pull down the balance to his own predilection, that is immorality.[35]

What tempts novelists to put their thumb in the scale according to Lawrence is a mistaken belief in absolutes. This is one of his criticisms of Tolstoy in the third of his three short essays; but here his argument is complicated by a return to the idea he had deployed so effectively in *Studies in Classic American Literature*: that in many great novelists there is a conflict between a 'didactic "purpose"' and their 'passional inspiration'.[36] Tolstoy's instinct, Lawrence writes, urged him to endorse the relationship Vronsky and Anna Karenina achieve, but his conventional social being prompted him to condemn it. This was a view that Lawrence had propounded with particular fierceness, and patent vested interest, in the early years of his relationship with Frieda.[37] He returned to it now fresh from his reading of *Resurrection* which he felt was made dishonest by Tolstoy's obsession with the 'absolute' of Christian Socialism. For Lawrence here was another manifestation of a hated idealism which worked to make people forget that 'Everything is relative' and 'the relatedness and interrelatedness of all things flows and changes and trembles like a stream.'[38]

The first two of these three essays were not taken by Sherman for the New York *Herald Tribune* but published in November and December of 1925 in a new English periodical, the *Calendar of Modern Letters*. The third ('The Novel') had a different fate. In April Lawrence received a letter from Harold Mason, the owner of the press which was about to publish Edward McDonald's bibliography of his work (v. 240). The items in this bibliography had prompted the thought that there was room for a collection of essays which had previously only appeared in journals. Lawrence was receptive to it and by 23 May had decided that such a collection would provide an opportunity to publish the whole of 'The Crown', only three of whose six sections had appeared before the collapse of the *Signature*, the journal he and Murry had tried to run by subscription in 1915.[39] On 29 June he sent 'The Novel' to David Jester (Mason's assistant) in response to the request that the collection being planned should include at least one essay which had not previously appeared in magazine form (v. 271). As the project went forward, however, he became uneasy that it would turn out a mere rag-bag, like those collections of Katherine Mansfield's odds and ends which he had criticised Murry for imposing on the public. 'I don't very much want to re-publish half-baked sort of stuff,' he wrote to Jester on 15 July. 'I'd like to make a complete little book, with more or less a central idea, an organic thing . . . I don't like those volumes of oddments men bring out' (v. 279–80). He therefore wrote five more essays, in addition to 'The Novel', sending them off with a much modified 'Crown' in the third week of August (v. 290). It was one of these essays – 'Reflections on the Death of a Porcupine' – which provided the title for what was now a collection of material of which most was either completely new or had never been published before. For a man who had been at death's door at the beginning of the year, 1925 was becoming remarkably productive, hardly less so in fact than all of Lawrence's other writing years.

III Farm Life

When he first got back to the ranch, Lawrence was too weak to do more than direct the labour of others, but within a month he had recovered enough strength to participate. Water had always been one of his chief preoccupations and, before leaving for Mexico, he and Brett had worked hard cleaning out the spring in the Gallina Canyon which was the source of the ranch's water, all of two miles away.[40] Now he hired a local builder to help build a dam and install pipes up to the ranch, and soon Lawrence was able to celebrate a bright stream running gaily past the front of his cabin in Kiowa's irrigation ditch (v. 257). To help in this, and other more mundane labour, he employed a nephew of Tony Luhan, named Trinidad Archuleta (well-known in the pueblo for his dancing), and also Trinidad's wife Ruffina; but she and Frieda quarrelled violently and, despite the efforts of all the other parties to reconcile them, there had to be a parting of the ways.[41] 'We had an Indian and wife to do for us, till last week', Lawrence wrote impatiently to Catherine Carswell on 20 June, 'then we sent them away. "Savages" are a burden. So a Mexican boy comes up to help: and even him one has to pay two dollars a day: supposed to be very cheap labour' (v. 269).

Both the Lawrences had periodically been attracted by the vision of a self-sufficient rural life, and in Australia Frieda had quite specifically thought of buying a farm and then told Lawrence she was 'determined to have a little farm in America' (iv. 273, 277). Trying to ensure a reliable water supply was part of Lawrence's plan for transforming Kiowa into a modestly 'working' ranch again:

in European terms, making it more farm-like. Although the water in the irrigation ditch ran gaily enough at first, by the middle of a dry summer it did not run at all after two o'clock (v. 268); but there was enough to turn green the fifteen-acre alfalfa field near the cabins, and it allowed the Lawrences to establish a small garden (v. 258). Having recovered their cat Timsy from the Hawks, they also acquired some hens and by the end of May were the anxious owners of Susan, a black and unruly cow. Lawrence milked Susan morning and evening (Friedel Jaffe took an often-reproduced photograph of his uncle at the milking stool); when they were not stolen by skunks, there were sometimes as many as eight eggs a day; and Frieda turned the larger of the spare cabins – the one that had been meant for Mabel and Tony Luhan – into a dairy where she was able to produce two pounds of butter a week (v. 266, 268).

As the summer advanced, Brett worked on an attractive painting of the life that was now developing at the ranch to which Lawrence, as usual, added details. In the background, the splendid view from Kiowa is effectively represented and in the front part of the picture Brett tells a story of life there without too much regard for the usual conventions but rather in the manner of an Italian primitive. Lawrence and Frieda, for example, are shown twice, once round the adobe oven baking bread and again on horseback in the company of Brett. To the right is a tepee of the kind Trinidad and Ruffina might have stayed in before the quarrel, and further back a new corral for the horses, which Lawrence and Brett had worked on (he also made sure that the barn was re-roofed – v. 268). In front of the horses which the Lawrences and Brett are riding cluster the hens, and to the left is Timsy, arching his back. Lawrence was responsible for this last detail as he was for a Susan gambolling in the field beyond the irrigation ditch, which looks wider, more like a real stream, than it can ever have been in reality. In the left front corner, Brett has found room for some of the wild life around the ranch. A rabbit, delightfully if unrealistically airborne in Lawrence's characteristic pictorial manner, shares the confined space with what might be a mountain lion; but more prominent is a large porcupine.[42] Porcupines were a pest in the area because, as Lawrence explains in his reflections on the death of one, they climbed up pine trees and ate the bark, often to such an extent that the trees died. Being a real farmer meant owning a gun and shooting troublesome animals of this kind. On his first visit to Kiowa Luhan had of course done just that, but with the consequence that he and Lawrence had quarrelled. In his 'Reflections' essay, which like many of the others in the volume is full of echoes of life on the ranch, Lawrence explains how, never having owned a gun before, he came to follow Luhan's example.

On 14 July Lawrence described to Emily how he had heard Aaron, one of the horses, 'squealing and running to [the] corral': he had a 'little bunch of porcupine quills in his nose' that had to be pulled out with pliers, one by one (v. 278). The essay on the death of the porcupine in *Reflections* begins with a vivid account of Frieda discovering a dog whimpering with the pain of the thirty or so porcupine quills embedded in its muzzle and chin. Lawrence spends hours pulling out about twenty of these with the dog cowering at each approach of his hand and howling with pain at each extraction. Nervously exhausted with the effort, he tries to chase the dog off home so that its master can assume the responsibility for removing the remaining quills. When it is reluctant to go, Lawrence takes a stick to beat it away but, as he aims a blow at its back, the dog turns round rapidly with the result that Lawrence hits it by accident on its bleeding, swollen muzzle. Then it does rush off, 'with a fierce yelp'.[43] The shooting of the porcupine the next day is therefore in some ways a revenge killing, especially as Lawrence – firing a gun at an animal for the first time in his life – only succeeds in wounding it and is obliged to finish off the unpleasant business with a pole. He does so by hitting the porcupine across its nose. This is a disturbing episode, graphically evoked with all Lawrence's power of telling detail; and it leads him to expatiate on one of the principal themes of his six new essays: that in the realm of what he calls 'existence', where there is an unavoidable struggle for food and survival, members of one species have the right and indeed duty to kill members of a species which is inferior, should it become necessary. Yet one of the interests of the essay lies in the conflict between that hard-line position and the complicated circumstances which led to the death of the porcupine.

More habitually troublesome than the occasional porcupine was Susan the cow. Equal in frequency to Brett's references to Frieda lying on her bed smoking are her descriptions of Lawrence having to go in search of Susan in order to milk her. In the essay which came fourth in *Reflections* after 'The Crown' – '. . . . . . Love Was Once a Little Boy' – Lawrence describes how he often has to hunt for her in the trees where 'Possibly she is lying peacefully in cowy inertia, like a black Hindu statue.' Sometimes,

she is away down in the bottom corner, lowing *sotto voce* and blindly to some far-off, inaccessible bull. Then when I call at her, and approach, she screws round her tail and flings her sharp, elastic haunches in the air with a kick and a flick, and plunges off like a buck rabbit, or like a black demon among the pine trees, her udder swinging like a chime of bells.[44]

But if Susan has been frightened in the night by coyotes or dogs and wandered further than usual, then Lawrence has to look for her on horseback and will be startled by suddenly discovering her 'terribly silent, among the tree-trunks . . . standing like some spider suspended motionless by a thread, from the web of the eternal silence'.[45]

The evocative power of these descriptions is important in conveying how much it matters to Lawrence that he should establish a satisfactory relationship with

Susan, as with all the other manifestations of 'nature' on the ranch. In 'Lawrence Cultivates His Beard' Stuart Sherman had praised Lawrence's descriptions of the natural world and contrasted him with Wordsworth who 'saturated nature with purely human emotion'.[46] Lawrence takes over from Sherman this misunderstanding, accusing Wordsworth at one point, in a fine but misapplied phrase, of 'anthropomorphic lust';[47] and he insists that in any relationship with another living creature, or indeed any inanimate feature of the natural world, there has to be reciprocity and some surrender, on the human side, of characteristic human assumptions and claims. This is in the search for that true relatedness with the external world which Lawrence also proposes in 'The Novel' as the chief aim of art. Such a relationship can only be achieved in the realm of 'being' where each member of each species has the opportunity to become fully itself and thus incomparable with any other form of creation. It is in the realm of 'existence' that everything is necessarily part of a natural hierarchy, according to its degree of 'livingness'. The investigation of these two realms, and of the way they interact, gives to the six new essays that 'organic' quality Lawrence had said he was looking for in his letter to Jester.

In that letter of 15 July, when he was still thinking in terms of revision rather than entirely new material, Lawrence had asked Jester to send him a few of his old essays 'like the one on "Love"' (v. 279). This had appeared in the *English Review* in January 1918, and treats its subject very much in the manner of Birkin in *Women in Love*. In a fine paragraph typical of his philosophical writing at that time, Lawrence had described how,

in the fire of [a man and woman's] extreme sensual love, in the friction of intense, destructive flames, I am destroyed and reduced to essentiality; she is destroyed, and reduced to her essential otherness. It is a destructive fire, this profane love. But it is the only fire that will purify us into singleness, fuse us from the chaos into our own unique gem-like separateness of being.[48]

This is the vision, familiar to readers of the novel, of the mysterious dialectical process whereby individuality, far from having to be surrendered in a relationship, can be defined and intensified by it. ' . . . . . . Love Was Once a Little Boy' bears almost no overt relation to 'Love' but parts of it are a disillusioned commentary on Lawrence's previous beliefs. In 1925, for example, he feels that the trouble between men and women is 'the inevitable result of trying to snatch an intensified individuality out of the mutual flame'. In a relationship between a man and a woman 'each hopes [that their ego] will flourish like a salamander in the flame of love and passion. Which it well may: but for the fact that there are two salamanders in the same flame, and they fight till the flame goes out. Then they become grey cold lizards of the vulgar ego.'[49] How one can surrender oneself to another human being, 'merge' with another – to invoke the word he had deployed so disparagingly in his later remarks on Whitman – and yet simultaneously retain one's identity is a problem which agonised Lawrence (as of course it did Wordsworth) all his life. In his later essay on love, in what often reads like a reflection on his current feelings about Frieda, he largely abandons the search for a solution in the human world and, like Lou Carrington, concentrates instead on the problem of relations with nature in all its manifestations. Having reviewed many of these, he declares in the last of the six new essays to appear in *Reflections* ('Aristocracy') that, 'The true aristocrat is the man who has passed all the relationships, and has met the sun, and the sun is with him as a diadem.' The human world he sees in this essay as 'stuck squalid inside an achieved form, and bristling with a myriad spines, to protect its hulking body as it feeds, feeds: gnawing the bark of the young tree of life, and killing it from the top downwards. Leaving its spines to fester and fester in the nose of the gay dog.' It cannot be attended to when 'man's supreme moment of active life is when he looks up and is with the sun, and is with the sun as a woman is with child.'[50]

Like many people, Lawrence had periods when his strongest urge was to withdraw from human society. This was a tendency powerfully reinforced in 1925 by his recent illness. In the essay provocatively entitled 'Blessed Are the Powerful' he writes, 'Courage, discipline, *inward isolation*, these are the conditions upon which power will abide in us' (my italics).[51] But as in the case of Lou Carrington, who senses on the ranch a 'wild spirit' which craves for her and for which (or whom) her sex is 'deep and sacred',[52] isolation from the human world does not dispense with the need to relate. What Frieda felt about all this would be difficult to say. She could hardly feel threatened by the sun but had she thought about it – which is unlikely – she might well have been disturbed to find her husband expending less energy of thought on their own relationship, which he seems to have regarded as established and therefore to a large extent moribund (when Frieda makes an appearance in the six essays she is referred to as 'Madame'), than on his dealings with hens. 'That brown hen', he writes in 'Him With His Tail in His Mouth',

is extraordinarily callous to my god-like presence. She doesn't even choose to know me to nod to. If I've got to strike a balance between us, I've got to work at it.

But that is what I want: that she shall nod to me, with a *Howdy!*—and I shall nod to her, more politely: *How-do-you-do, Flatfoot?* And between us there shall exist the third thing, the *connaissance*. That is the goal.[53]

Lawrence was however a man whose moods were unusually volatile and upon whose life it would be foolish to impose any crudely developmental pattern of feeling. Besides which, what he wrote and what he did were not always in harmony. This last point is illustrated by an anecdote Brett placed in the period before the second visit to Mexico but which, since it involves the hens, must belong to 1925.[54] The Lawrences' meat-safe was a wooden box hung from a tree, because the meat kept better in the air and no other location was secure from rats and other scavengers. Next to it was another box in which Lawrence shut hens which became broody (as he says one of them is inclined to be in a letter to Ada on 14 July[55]). Brett describes Lawrence taking a hen from this box and putting it back with the others in the belief that it might once again begin to lay.

Later, after tea, you go to the chicken-house to look at the hen. Frieda and I hear a considerable scuffling coming from the chicken-house: you emerge dangling the hen by her legs upside down – she is squawking to wake the dead. You march angrily to the wood-pile, pick up the axe, lay the agitated hen's head on a piece of wood and adroitly chop it off. Frieda and I watch, amazed. You leave the hen twitching headless on the ground and come in.

'Damn her,' you say, 'she was brooding again; after all the trouble I took hanging her for days up in that box to cool her underneath, she still brooded. So I've chopped off her head. Serves her right, too!'[56]

In the realm of 'existence', or that of sensible farming, the only thing to do with a broody hen may well be to eat it. Yet it seems clear from Brett's account that the death of the hen (not, one hopes, 'Flatfoot') is no more a consequence of strictly practical considerations than was the death of the porcupine. It is important that the impression of irrationality here is conveyed by one of the most warmly sympathetic of all Lawrence's commentators. When that same irrationality was evident in a far more startling form in the incident with Bibbles, it was impossible to avoid feeling that there was a connection with the relationship between Lawrence and Frieda. Here too, although far less clearly, Lawrence's complicated attitude to Frieda's sexuality and her maternal feelings seems to underlie the manner in which he disposes of the hen. If that is so, then his relationship with his wife was not quite as quiescent at this time as the six essays might suggest.[57]

Although the death of the hen is not mentioned in them, life on the ranch provided Lawrence with much of the stimulus for his new essays; but they are also the result of a close re-reading of 'The Crown'. Many phrases or themes from the earlier text are picked up for expansion in a new mode: the concern with what the Greeks called equilibrium, for example, or the belief that power comes into us 'from behind'. Yet despite his claim in a 'Note' that 'The Crown' says what he still believes, some ideas are also picked up for implicit rectification. In 1915 Lawrence had been much taken with the ancient symbol of the universe as a snake with its tail in its mouth. Given the style of dualistic and hopefully dialectical thinking to which he was wedded at that period, this had helped him to make a good deal of play with the identification between ends and beginnings, sources and goals: with the idea that, as Eliot puts it in 'The Dry-Salvages', the way up is also the way down.[58] In the essay which takes its title from the snake symbol ('Him With His Tail in His Mouth'), Lawrence is concerned to break away from conceptions which now strike him as too constricting. In 1925 it is still second-nature in him to think in opposites, but doing so on too grand and abstract a scale has come to seem a narrowing of vision. 'Bunk of beginnings and of ends, and heads and tails', he writes, 'Why does man always want to know so damned much? Or rather, so damned little. If he can't draw a ring round creation, and fasten the serpent's tail into its mouth with the padlock of one final clinching idea, then creation can go to hell as far as man is concerned.' And later, 'Equilibrium argues either a dualistic or pluralistic universe. The Greeks, being sane, were pantheists and pluralists, and so am I.'[59]

There are new views in the 1925 essays but also, as the quotation above suggests, a new manner. One important aspect of that manner might be exemplified by comparing two different kinds of attack on sentimental humanitarianism in *Reflections*. In 'The Crown' Lawrence had written, 'Let no one suffer, they have said. No mouse shall be caught by a cat, no mouse. It is a transgression. Every mouse shall become a pet, and every cat shall lap milk in peace, from the saucer of utter benevolence.'[60] In the essay which gave its title to his new collection, he emphasises the need for our acceptance of all nature as a battle for survival between higher and lower cycles of 'existence' by describing in detail how his cat captures and then torments a chipmunk. What he feels compelled to admire in Timsy is her combination of 'soft, snowflakey lightness' and 'lean, heavy ferocity':

I had never realised the latter, till I was lying in bed one morning moving my toe, unconsciously, under the bedclothes. Suddenly a terrific blow struck my foot. The Timsy had sprung out of nowhere, with a hurling, steely force, thud upon the bedclothes where the toe was moving. It was as if someone had aimed a sudden blow, vindictive and unerring.

"Timsy!"

She looked at me with the vacant, feline glare of her hunting eyes. It is not even ferocity. It is the dilation of the strange, vacant arrogance of power. The power is in her.[61]

Whenever Lawrence wants to make a point in the new essays he is inclined to do so with the help of an episode from his immediate experience. His new manner (that is) is more personal, anecdotal as well as more abrupt and colloquial in the 'American' mode he had employed in *Studies in Classic American Literature*. The first sentence of 'Him With His Tail in His Mouth' reads: 'Answer a fool according to his folly, philosophy ditto.' The second – on a new line – is 'Solemnity is a sign of fraud.' After two more sentences in which Lawrence accuses both religion and philosophy of conflating ends and beginnings, he writes, 'It seems to me time somebody gave that serpent of eternity another dummy to suck.'[62] The writing in 'The Crown' is not solemn but it is often confusingly abstract. This is particularly true of the three published parts which convey ideas more effectively expressed in the *Study of Thomas Hardy* or *Twilight in Italy*. The final three sections develop in interesting ways the topic of the last section to have been published in 1915: 'The Flux of Corruption', or what Birkin calls in *Women in Love* the 'dark river of dissolution'.[63] That almost the whole of Western civilisation is involved in a process of inevitable corruption which can be 'divine' when freely submitted to – 'In the soft and shiny voluptuousness of decay, in the marshy chill heat of reptiles, there is the sign of the Godhead'[64] – but becomes 'vile' when 'experienced as a controlled activity within an intact whole' was a concept with which Lawrence was intensely preoccupied in 1915. Ten years later he allows the bulk of his elaborations of it to stand but ignores the theme in the six new essays.

Lawrence's claim in his 'Note' to have altered 'The Crown' 'only very little' depends on what one understands by 'little'. There are small but significant changes in wording throughout, but also several passages entirely omitted or re-written. The conclusion to the fourth section had included a long passage on homosexuality as an inevitable stage of dissolution, in its vile rather than divine aspect, which Lawrence probably felt it would be pointless to court controversy by including – especially as, ten years on, it was a topic which was no longer of burning interest to him. Its omission meant that he could also drop a relatively overt reference to David and Jonathan as homosexuals.[65] In his recent play they had not been shown in that light. With its action fresh in his mind, he re-wrote a passage at the end of section ii in which he had previously presented David as heroically but mistakenly committed to only one of the binary oppositions which constitute the world: to Darkness rather than Light, to the Flesh rather than the Spirit, or to the Lion rather than the Unicorn (if either of these two heraldic beasts manage to appropriate 'The Crown', which is the dialectical aim of their necessary struggle, they are described by Lawrence as losing their integrity). Now it is Saul whom Lawrence casts in the lion-like role while he describes David, not as the unicorn, but as a Judas – 'the individual who knows something of both flames, but commits himself to neither' – and introduces a new opposition which will figure prominently in the new essays: '[David] holds himself, in his own ego, superior either to the creative dark power-flame, or the conscious love-flame. And so, he is the small man slaying the great.'[66] The animus against David is clearer here than it is in the play where closeness to the biblical source means that readers are often aware of him as a young man of good-will doing his level best to avoid having Saul's javelin stuck through him. Lawrence concludes his revision of the end of section ii by applying his 1915 terms to more recent political events. Thus the Russian revolution is an example of 'democracy triumphant, the unicorn and the dove seizing the crown, and on the instant turning into beasts of prey.'[67]

The six new essays pick up this concern with post-war politics, especially as two of their key terms, 'existence' and 'being', are also conceived as 'power' and 'love'. True power is described as the birthright of the 'natural aristocrat' who is able to offer life to others by putting them into a new relation with the universe: 'Whoever can establish, or initiate a new connection between mankind and the circumambient universe is, in his own degree, a saviour.'[68] Lawrence has nothing but contempt for the new breed of Fascist dictators in Europe, referring in 'Blessed Are the Powerful' to 'Papa Mussolini' as 'a little harmless Glory in baggy trousers';[69] but, as always, he is equally hostile to democratic egalitarianism. It is only at a more or less abstract level, he insists, that one thing is the equal of another; closer to the ground there is an inevitable quality of difference between species, males of the same species, and between males and females, which makes any talk of equality inappropriate. If the hen, he says in '. . . . . . Love Was Once a Little Boy', 'likes to crow at sunrise, she may. There is no law against it. And [the cock] can lay an egg, if the fit takes him.'[70] He and Frieda are equal in their capacities as British citizens but not as man and woman. Things are not equal just because they weigh the same on the scales but in any case, 'Alas! my wife is about twenty pounds heavier than I am.' In the Cambridge edition of *Reflections* it is made clear that Lawrence originally wrote 'fifty pounds' and that the correction is in Frieda's 'vigorous hand'.[71] His exaggeration can be taken more as a rueful comment on his own thinness than her bulk.

How is the 'power' Lawrence is concerned with in these essays to be reconciled with 'love'? Very much, it turns out, as 'existence' is reconciled with 'being': through recognition of the inevitably prior claims of the former. 'The clue to all existence is being', he writes in the porcupine essay, 'But you can't have being without existence.'[72] In 'Blessed Are the Powerful' he insists that, 'The communion of love is only a part of the greater communion of power' which will always be a 'communion of inequality'. In the realms of love or being, 'perfect relatedness' is a consequence of balance or equipoise; but as soon as power enters in, there can no longer be anything resembling equilibrium. When it is a question of the love relations between men and women, it enters in very quickly because, in Lawrence's 1925 view, 'The act of love itself is an act of power.' All his key terms have several different meanings. 'Power' can be predominantly spiritual, physical or political according to the context, but it can also be, and often simultaneously is, sexual. 'Even the Phallic erection', he says in 'Blessed Are the Powerful', 'is a first blind movement of power. Love is said to call the power into motion: but it is probably the reverse: that the slumbering *power* calls love into being.'[73] Given that, in spite of his concern with power in these essays, Lawrence persists in believing that it is relationships based on love (or desire as he often calls it) which make life worth living, loss of power is not a misfortune but a catastrophe. If in *David* the most moving moments come when Saul is deploring his loss of power, the reason may partly be because Lawrence is also considering there the loss of sexual potency. He could reasonably regard his own loss as a temporary consequence of illness, but this would not mean he could therefore feel it was an accident. All power comes from God and Saul loses his because he disobeys God's will. The equivalent in Lawrence's own case might be suggested by the first sentence of '. . . . . . Love Was Once a Little Boy': 'Collapse, as often as not, is the result of persisting in an old attitude towards some important relationship, which, in the course of time, has changed its nature.'[74] Illness, with all its consequences, sexual or otherwise, was always regarded by Lawrence as in some sense the sufferer's own fault: the result of a failure in his dealings with himself and the outside world. The advantage of this attitude was that, if a man was ultimately responsible for the illness, then recovery might also lie in his own hands.

IV   Interviews and Farewells

In the 1920s Lawrence was sufficiently well known to be sought out for interview. One of the seekers was an aspiring writer named Kyle Crichton who had suffered from tuberculosis and was then living in Albuquerque.[75] In 1924 he had written a long letter to Lawrence which was ignored; and in January 1925, when they were in Oaxaca, both the Lawrences had been amused by an indignant note from Crichton's wife complaining of this treatment (v. 200, 202). The young man was persistent and, once the Lawrences were back at the ranch, managed to enlist the help of both the Hawks and Brett in his effort to see them. In the middle of June Crichton drove his Model T Ford to within fifty yards of Kiowa and, while he and his wife stayed in the car, Brett went forward to see if Lawrence was willing to receive them. The moment happened to be opportune and soon the visitors were installed on the porch listening to tales of Lawrence's early life. The relative abundance of these indicates that he found Crichton more attractive in person than in his wife's epistolary style. When he later sent a short story about his background to Lawrence – born in Pennsylvania he, also, was the son of a miner – the reply was typically kind and detailed, as well as impressively acute; and it was accompanied by offers to do what he could to help Crichton in his career (v. 293–4).[76]

In his blue shirt buttoned at the neck, Lawrence (Crichton says) was thin and about five feet eight inches tall. Frieda he describes as not only large but also 'handsome'. In a strong German accent she prompted Lawrence as he did his imitations of Ford Maddox Ford (remembered kindly by him but with resentment by her because of an argument they had about Germany in 1915); and pictured Edward Garnett slaving away all afternoon at a single phrase, in regulation Flaubertian fashion, while in the garden his wife Constance piled up page after page of her 'marvellous translations'.[77] They both evoked the memory of Compton Mackenzie in silk pyjamas dictating to his secretary at two in the morning while his wife played the piano in a soft, romantic fashion two rooms away; and Lawrence spoke of his former friend Dikran Kouyoumdjian who, as 'Michael Arlen', had recently published *The Green Hat*.[78] Lawrence shocked Crichton by insisting that, after Katherine Mansfield's death, Murry had promoted her beyond her just deserts; and Frieda described how they both – but she especially perhaps – had liked Willa Cather: 'Everybody said she was blunt and abrupt, but we got along famously.'[79] One way in which Lawrence and Frieda could work as a team in certain social situations became clear when Crichton, remembering that he was supposed to be conducting an interview that he expected to sell to the New York *World*, asked Lawrence what it was that made a writer write.

'Egotism', said Frieda flatly.

'No, no', protested Lawrence. 'It isn't that. You don't write for anybody; you rather write from a deep moral sense – for the race, as it were.'

'And to let everybody know how clever you are', persisted Frieda.

Brett had left her spot behind the little table and now edged her way forward with her horn cocked for battle and a happy smile on her face.

'Of course you want to see it published', admitted Lawrence, 'but you don't really mind what people say about it. It doesn't *matter* what they say. A writer writes because he can't help writing, and because he has something in him that he feels he can say better than it has been said before, and because it would be wrong, entirely wrong, to possess a talent and have thoughts without sharing them with the world.'[80]

Everything we know about Lawrence indicates that these were beliefs he held all his life. Frieda saw it as one of her roles to discourage him from being too solemn about them.

This elevated conception of the writer's role did not mean that Lawrence expected all writers to be as dedicated to saying something important as he was. When Crichton asked what he read, he explained that he relied on books which were sent him or that were lying around, but then shocked his interviewer for the second time by revealing what Brett's memoir confirms:[81] that his favourite reading at that time was the pulp magazine, *Adventure*. Regarded as the aristocrat of the cheap serials, *Adventure* had once numbered Sinclair Lewis among its associate editors and specialised in escapist fiction of reasonably high quality: tales of Cossacks in sixteenth-century Russia, of pirates, French legionnaires, detectives and explorers in the African or the South American jungles.[82] Lawrence told Crichton that he thought the magazine's writers were lively as well as honest and accurate about their facts: 'If they say something happened in a certain way in Africa or Malaya, you can depend on it';[83] but it was the romantic aspect which must also have appealed to an important element in his own nature. Love of adventure is partly what drove Lawrence to visit so many different places, or to try to persuade the Danes to hire a boat and sail off into the Pacific with him when they were together in California. It manifests itself in his own writing in his account of the attack on the hacienda in *The Plumed Serpent* or, more obviously, in the enthusiasm with which he describes Jack Grant's adventures in *The Boy in the Bush*.[84]

Before the Crichtons went, they were offered tea inside the cabin. The spotlessness of the interior they attributed to Frieda's German background only to have two of their stereotypes disposed of with one remark when they were told it was all Lawrence's doing. That morning, before milking Susan, he had baked the bread they ate; and he was also responsible for a jam made from some raspberries Brett had picked. 'I cook when he'll let me', Frieda said, 'but he does it much better himself.' When Lawrence warned her that these kinds of remark would make the Crichtons think that she did nothing on the ranch, Frieda replied, 'If they've ever lived on a farm, they won't.'[85] The 'farming' aspect of the Lawrences' life had already brought half-jocular complaints from him about Susan. When she had them alone, Frieda had asked the Crichtons to compliment Lawrence on the cowshed he and Brett had built behind the corral (a photograph of the time confirms Brett's account of the way they used one of the horses to haul the wood[86]). Because Susan had once again disappeared by the time the Crichtons were leaving, Lawrence asked them to sound their horn if they caught sight of her on their way out.

The visitors did not spot Susan, who continued both to irritate and intrigue Lawrence with her vagaries. Getting to understand her was a process by no means completed by the time the Lawrences were preparing to leave Kiowa. Having spent so much time and money improving the ranch, and having created in the process an excellent therapeutic environment for an invalid, it was perhaps surprising that they should have thought of leaving it at all. But both had been clear from the moment of their return to New Mexico that they would be in Europe in the autumn; the ranch would be a far less comfortable place in winter; and their visas were in any case only valid until the end of September. On the 8th of that month, the Lawrences suspended their furniture from hooks in the cabin ceiling (to prevent it being eaten by the pack rats);[87] took Susan, the hens and the cat back to the Hawk family; and left Kiowa for what, for one of them, would be the last time. Then they made their way to New York via Denver and Chicago, after saying goodbye to Brett. She had gloomily assumed that she would stay on during the winter at Del Monte because she felt she was too deaf to travel much alone. Lawrence, however, urged her to follow him and Frieda to Europe[88] (although not to travel with them!), and he suggested she might try Capri – his own intention was after all to spend the winter in Italy. The Brewsters were now living in Capri again and he promised to write to them on her behalf (v. 305). Once in New York, Lawrence showered her with details designed to make both her coming visit there, and the arrangements for getting to Italy, much easier (v. 298–9). The care he took over these was characteristic – had he not been a writer Lawrence would have made a first-rate travel agent; but some of the energy he expended was no doubt a derivative of an uneasy conscience. 'Born separator' or not, Brett's devotion to him generated a sense of responsibility which he could never entirely shake off.

Transforming the ranch would have been a relatively costly affair and tickets to Europe were not cheap either.[89] One can understand therefore why, on 14 September, Lawrence hoped that his New York lawyer, Benjamin Stern, 'would get a bit of money out of Seltzer' (v. 298). Simultaneously hating to look at *The Plumed Serpent*, because of its association with his illness in Oaxaca, yet still feeling that it was his 'chief novel so far' (v. 272), he had begun revising the typescript at the ranch and could expect it to bring in some money; but for the moment his financial affairs in the United States were precarious and he was to leave the country with only $30 in his account ('but Seltzer telephoned he was *going* to deposit some more' – v. 307). In these circumstances, and given his recent change of publisher, it would hardly have been appropriate for the Lawrences to stay with the Seltzers in New York, although they did see them – 'dangling by a single thread, over the verge of bankruptcy' (v. 305–6) was Lawrence's later description; nor could they invoke Mabel's help. Rather than stay in a hotel, they went to Mabel's arch-rival, Nina Witt, who had a three-story house off Washington Square and let them have the bottom floor. They had seen a lot of Nina Witt during their first stay in the Taos area but, on the two subsequent occasions they were there, she had been in the process of securing a divorce from her Taos-based husband, and an infrequent presence.[90] The city was still 'steamy hot' (v. 305) in September as they were entertained by some of Nina's rich friends and Lawrence waited for the organisers of the New York Guild Theatre – with whom Ida Rauh had put him in touch – to decide whether or not they would produce *David*. (They must have decided against the play soon after he had left – v. 300, 303.) He called on his new publishers for the first time at their office in Fifth Avenue – 'deep carpets, and sylphs in a shred of black satin and a shred of brilliant undergarment darting by' (v. 306) – and, after his troubles with the Seltzers, was reassured by the impression they conveyed of financial reliability. There was an awkward moment when he had to explain to Knopf why he had given *Reflections on the Death of a Porcupine* to another publisher, but relations remained cordial.

On 18 September he and Frieda dined with this other publisher, Harold Mason, and his wife. Also present were Lawrence's bibliographer, Edward McDonald, and Mrs Mcdonald who later recalled that the Lawrences were very natural with each other – 'If Lawrence started to tell an amusing story, Frieda was likely to say, "Shut up Lorenzo, that is my story."' She describes how they all went back to Nina Witt's house from the restaurant only to find that Lawrence had forgotten his key. 'Ach, Lorenzo,' Frieda said as she began tossing pebbles at a lighted window on the second floor of the house, 'for a genius you are a poor ting.'[91]

On 22 September the Lawrences set sail for England on the *Resolute* (v. 305). A reporter's picture shows them boarding on the 21st and standing against one of the ship's iron stairways looking somewhat travel-worn: Lawrence in a crumpled three-piece suit and Frieda in a loose cloak of vaguely Indian style (Fig. 27). Yet they both have nice expressions. The wistful smile on Frieda's face makes her seem young, and Lawrence has the look of a man who might be persuaded at any moment into one of his comic imitations. Although neither of them could then have known it, they were at the end of an extraordinary adventure. Apart from three months around Christmas 1923–4, Lawrence had not been back to Europe for three and half years. In that time he had sailed round the world and fulfilled his war-time ambition of seeing 'America'. For him of course that word had come to have a different meaning from its usual, English ones, then and now. When Frieda's nephew had to leave the ranch in the middle of July because he was not, as a student, allowed to spend more than a year in the United States, Lawrence wrote: 'One would think the place was Paradise, the way it's hedged in. But Friedel will be glad to get back to Germany – he hated the time he spent in the east – New York – Maryland. I would hate to have to stay long in the U.S.A. too – anywhere but here, which is so different, and Mexican really' (v. 278). Lawrence had seen a good deal of what the English now often think of as America – New York, Buffalo, Chicago, Salt Lake City, San Francisco, Los Angeles – but for him that term was synonymous with non-urban, non-white regions in the Southwest, and further down. The life and landscape in these areas he had found a remarkably stimulating challenge, but also hard in a way which called for temporary retreat now that he was often ill and tired. 'I am quite glad to be out of that America for a time', he wrote to his mother-in-law from the boat, 'it's so tough and wearing, with the iron springs poking out through the padding.' A few days later he reported to Brett that he had endured his 'worst headache ever', having attributed it the day before, in a letter to Bill and Rachel Hawk, to 'the old malaria popping up' (v. 304, 305, 307).

In his three and half years out of Europe Lawrence had written an immense amount (as was usual with him), and succeeded in establishing himself fairly firmly in the American market. This had been one of his ambitions during the war. Another had been to found a new way of communal living in America. Although they had been much attenuated versions of 'Rananim', the first of several ideal communities Lawrence would attempt to found, his periods with the Danes, with Bynner and Johnson, and with Brett, had at least gestured towards a more satisfying way of life than any he had known since 1915. This was partly because they occurred in physical rather than merely human contexts which could not fail to make, on a man like Lawrence, a lasting impression. The landscape of the various parts of New and Old Mexico in which he had lived had profoundly affected his sense of the world; but to have been close to a scene of political turbulence in Mexico was also significant because it allowed him to develop further the keen interest in politics he had brought with him to America.

In a favourable review of H. M. Tomlinson's *Gifts of Fortune* Lawrence would write: 'We travel, perhaps, with a secret and absurd hope of setting foot on the Hesperides, of running our boat up a little creek and landing in the Garden of Eden.'[92] For the most part Frieda had been with him on his search for Eden and in September 1925 she was still standing by to be cast in the role of Eve, although on rather different terms from those of three and a half years before. One constant, however, was her resistance to her husband's notions of how their relationship might be strengthened by diversification – on his side at least. Towards the end of the war she had been hostile to Lawrence's belief in his need for a close male friendship in addition to his marriage and, more recently, she had taken exception to his having acquired (not altogether by design) a close woman friend in Brett. Where weaker characters might have been worn down by Lawrence's insistence on his beliefs, or his relentless claim to predominance in their relationship, she had continued to do more than hold her own. But if Lawrence had not had Frieda's opposition to contend with, he would have needed to invent it. Before leaving Italy in 1922 he had explained to Brewster that he disliked Buddhism because of its emphasis on passivity (iv. 154). He had a strong personal need to fight with the world in order to convince himself that it existed; and to protect himself from a regressive solipsism which he identified with death. 'Il faut secouer la vie,' say the French, 'Autrement elle vous ronge.' Lawrence was committed by his nature to grasping life and shaking it hard; but as the photograph of him on the *Resolute* shows, and the portraits by Edward Weston still more, it gnawed away at him all the same.

PART THREE

◆

Europe
Once More

◆

CHAPTER TWELVE

September 1925–April 1926

SPOTORNO

I Old Friends

Arriving on 30 September 1925 in Southampton, the Lawrences went straight to Garland's Hotel. In his most recent letter to Murry, written from Oaxaca eight months earlier, Lawrence had indicated that he would not want to see him again. Yet now he wrote to Murry, who was living on the Dorset coast, announcing his arrival and wondering if he would be coming up to Town (v. 306, 310). That gesture made it difficult to get in touch with Koteliansky because Kot and Murry had quarrelled so bitterly over the running of the *Adelphi*; but Lawrence did go to see Kot's friends David and Edith Eder, practising psychoanalysts whom he had known well just before and then during the war, and with whom he had never quarrelled.[1] When Brett later told him that she was thinking of trying hypnosis as a cure for her deafness, he advised her to get in touch with Eder: 'He knows all about those things, and is a friend of mine, a *nice* man, not a liar' (v. 333).

Two other old friends he saw on his return to London were the Mackenzies, briefly reunited before Faith Mackenzie went off again to live her independent life on Capri. Because he expected Brett to be arriving in Capri shortly, Lawrence was able to urge Faith to look out for her. By this date, the Carswells, who were as usual very short of money, had retreated from London to the country, three miles from High Wycombe. Leaving Frieda behind, Lawrence went to visit them on Sunday 4 October and stayed the night.[2] He did not find the visit cheering and, although he was always glad to see Catherine, described her on the 8th as 'buried alive in a hole of a horrid little cottage in damp and dismal Bucks' (v. 313). High Wycombe is not far from the village of Iver where Martin Secker lived with his Italian wife Caterina Maria ('Rina'), and either just before or just after his stay with the Carswells Lawrence called on his publisher there. It depressed him to learn that, with a million and a quarter out of work, Secker could not find anyone to cut '16 acres of good thick hay still standing' because the eight unemployed men in the village were too frightened of losing their government money: 'If . . . they go off the list of the dole . . . they find it hard to get on again' (v. 312).

As on his last return home, Lawrence was also depressed by the English weather. This seemed to get worse as the Lawrences travelled north to stay with

Emily in Nottingham on 8 October. 'I coughed like the devil with the filthy air' Lawrence was to say later (v. 332); and on 9 October he reported to Secker: 'Of course I'm in bed with a cold, the moment I come here' (v. 315). During their last period in Mexico City the Lawrences had thought of renting a house on the English sea coast. The idea had stayed with them during their journey home but it was now definitively abandoned (v. 315). It must have been very strange for Lawrence, after he had settled whatever there was left for him to settle of his late father's affairs, to look out into the murk of the industrial Midlands from Emily's windows while he was correcting the proofs of *The Plumed Serpent*, still regarded as 'the most important of [his] books' (v. 318), although now with a degree of insistence that might have suggested uncertainty.

He had brought with him from New York two novels in a series the Knopfs published, known as the 'Blue Jade Library', and had arranged to review them for the book supplement of the *New York Herald Tribune* (v. 301).[3] These were reprints of successful works from earlier in the century: Frederick Rolfe's *Hadrian the Seventh* and M. W. Pickhall's *Saïd the Fisherman*. Lawrence wrote shrewdly and entertainingly of how, for all his conversion to Catholicism, Rolfe – or Baron Corvo as he preferred to be known – was essentially Protestant in temperament, one of nature's back-benchers, so that when the protagonist of his novel is miraculously elected Pope and invested with supreme power, his creator cannot find him anything sensible to do; and in discussing *Saïd the Fisherman* he raised again the difficulty of striking the right note in dealing with an alien culture. For Lawrence, Pickhall was too inclined to make his Arab immoral rather than merely amoral, and too anxious to ensure that he received his just deserts. These involved Saïd being taken to London, falling into the 'nightmare of that city' and losing his reason. 'One is appalled, thinking of Saïd in London', Lawrence writes in the final paragraph of a review which (like the one of Rolfe) he posted to his London agent from the Midlands (v. 317, 319). 'When one does come out of the open sun into the dark dank autumn of London, one almost loses one's reason, as Saïd does.'[4]

Frieda had much more reason to feel content with her return to Europe than her husband. For her, there was always the satisfaction of once again being able to see her children. Her eldest, Montague, who was now twenty-five, continued to take his father's side and refused to establish cordial relations with the Lawrences as a couple (because he worked at the Victoria and Albert Museum, Lawrence felt free to predict that he would end up in 'one of the glass cases, as a specimen of the perfect young Englishman' – v. 333). But the two girls were much more friendly. Elsa had a secretarial job in London while Frieda's youngest child, Barby, had just finished at the Slade and was at something of a loose end. She happened (or had arranged) to be staying in Nottingham with friends of her father during the second week of the Lawrences' stay in the Midlands, after they had moved on from Emily's house to the newer, smarter house his more prosperous younger sister Ada had quite recently bought in nearby Ripley (v. 278). Barby paid them a visit there and later recorded, 'When I saw my mother in this house, I thought she seemed a little out of place. I do not think Ada ever liked her, or forgave her for going off with her favourite brother.'[5] Lawrence was once again confined to his bed but had sufficient energy to lecture Barby on the inadequacies of her fiancé of the time, whom she had previously brought to lunch with the Lawrences at Garland's Hotel. Later there was a pleasant meal, for which Lawrence came downstairs, and it was suggested that Barby might stay the night. She telephoned her Nottingham hosts but was then rung back by the wife who had discussed the matter with her husband (a colleague of Weekley's at the University) and been infected with his alarm at what Barby's father would say if he heard that his daughter had spent the night under the same roof as Lawrence. 'Feeling something like a criminal', Barbara Weekley records, 'I crept dejectedly back to my Nottingham friends in the dark.' According to her, when she explained what these Nottingham friends had said, 'Lawrence sprang to his feet, white with rage. "These mean, dirty little insults your mother has had to put up with all these years!" he spat out, gasping for breath.'[6] Yet this painful if indirect reminder of Weekley's hostility, as well as an increasing understanding of Barby, would serve him well when he came to write *The Virgin and the Gipsy* a few months later. So too would trips to the local beauty spots which the car-owning Ada and her husband organised for the Lawrences. 'We've motored all over my native Derbyshire since we are here', Lawrence wrote to Nancy Pearn, his chief contact in the Curtis Brown office, on 20 October. 'It's a very interesting county' (v. 320).

On 22 October the Lawrences travelled back to London. For their last week in England they stayed in a flat in Gower Street owned by the younger of Catherine Carswell's two brothers, to whom they paid a rent.[7] Before they left for Baden-Baden on the 29th, they had been introduced to several new literary people (one of whom was William Gerhardie[8]), and met again two old friends who, since they last saw them, had decided to *become* literary. When in 1910 the aristocratic Cynthia Charteris, daughter of Lord Elcho (later to become the eleventh Earl of Wemyss[9]), married Herbert Asquith, the second son of the Prime Minister, their income was £900 a year.[10] For people of their tastes this sum became woefully inadequate in the inflationary period after the war, especially as Herbert Asquith had by then exchanged his career as a barrister for that of a minor poet, and even more minor novelist. There were two ways in which his wife could be said to have also turned to literature at this period. The first and most effective (given her family's need of money) involved becoming the secretary of J. M. Barrie, one of the most prominent and commercially successful literary figures of his day. That post, soon to bring Cynthia Asquith £1,500 a year, did involve ordinary secretarial work, but it was more importantly the means by which Barrie could satisfy his complicated need for intimate, non-physical relationships with beautiful women and their young sons. (Lawrence would have known about Barrie's peculiarities through his friendship with his first wife, Mary Cannan.) The second way was by becoming a writer herself. By 1925 Cynthia Asquith had already published a book on child care and a children's novel, as well as both an anthology and a book of stories for children; but on 25 October, when the Lawrences came to lunch (v. 324), she was busy trying to compile a collection of ghost stories by various hands. Either then or on the 28th, when she saw Lawrence again, she must have asked him for a contribution.[11] Lady Cynthia was to be very successful as an editor because her charm made her hard to refuse and because she knew so many people in that characteristically English realm (satirised by Lawrence in both *St. Mawr* and *Lady Chatterley's Lover*) where art and letters mingle with high society.

The 28th was the day before the Lawrences were due to leave. Murry came to see Lawrence then for what would be the last time, travelling up from Dorset and staying the night. He was praised by Lawrence for his recent book on *Keats and Shakespeare* but then criticised for having moved on from there to a fascination with the life of Jesus. The older he got, Murry reported Lawrence as saying, the more unsympathetic Jesus became to him: 'Now Judas – that was a different matter. If only one knew a little more about him!'[12] The meeting nevertheless went well and it was agreed that Murry should bring his wife Violet, and their seven-month-old baby girl, to see the Lawrences on the continent early in the new year. On the morning of the 29th Lawrence made an impulsive, last-minute dash to a local shop for a bag of fruit which Murry could eat on the train. The arrangement was that, if he was not back soon, Murry was to ask his taxi driver to pass by the shop on the way to the station so that they could say goodbye. Unfortunately, the driver took a different route to the shop from Lawrence's on his return to the Gower Street flat and goodbyes were never said.[13]

A similar mishap, but on a larger scale, took place at this same time with Brett. To Lawrence's surprise and disapproval, she had written to say that, instead of going directly to Italy as he had advised, she would be calling on her English friends and relations first. ('I don't think it's much good your seeing [Murry]', he warned her – v. 326.) Because her ship had left New York on 24 October, she would be arriving in England just a few days after the Lawrences had left. Writing to her on the 28th Lawrence explained that he would not be able to see her because his arrangements were 'all fixed up when I got your cable'. 'Shall you go on to Capri?', he continued. 'The Brewsters, and Faith Mackenzie, Compton Mackenzie's wife, are both expecting you there. We may stay on the Italian Riviera for a while: Frieda wants to have her children there, not too far. Better, I think, for you to go to Capri' (v. 326). The idea of going to the Italian Riviera, after the statutory visit to Frieda's mother in Baden-Baden, had come from Rina Secker who, as dismayed as Lawrence with how damp and dismal it could be in Bucks., was just about to visit her parents in Spotorno, a small resort not far west of Genoa. Lawrence indicated that there would be no question of Brett being invited to join them there and he was still not clear at this stage whether, if she did go to Capri, she could be quite certain of receiving his visit.

II   Villa Bernarda

In Baden-Baden the Lawrences stayed a couple of weeks at the Hotel Eden, 'once really grand' but now, with the favourable exchange rate, only 9s 6d a day each, 'food and all' (v. 328). When he was not staring out over the Rhine from the top of the town's old castle, or 'running away into the hills and the Black Forest' (v. 330, 329), Lawrence would accompany Frieda on her visits to her mother in the Ludwig Wilhelm Stift, her pink-stoned retirement home not far from the Baths, and play cards with impoverished pensioners, all of whom seemed to have titles: 'I can hardly believe my own ears when I hear myself saying (in German of course) – But, Excellence, those are trumps!' (v. 329). While he was there, Rina Secker arrived in Spotorno and wrote to say that she had seen a suitable house for rent. The Italian Riviera was no doubt more convenient than other parts of Italy for Frieda's daughters to visit, but Lawrence's own willingness to go there would have derived from expectations of a mild climate, and some relief from the illness which was now always threatening. On their way from Baden-Baden to Spotorno at the end of the second week in November, he and Frieda passed through Lucerne in order to meet a Swiss admirer of Lawrence's named Carl Seelig, a literary critic who may have been considering some translation work.[14] Lawrence enjoyed Seelig's company but, with 'slow rain and snow', found Switzerland 'horrid'. 'We went motoring in Switzerland', he wrote to Emily from Spotorno, 'icy cold – I hated it, and got a cold' (v. 336–7).

Rina Secker's father, Luigi Capellero, was the manager of the Miramare, still a fine hotel on the sea-front at Spotorno, where the Lawrences first stayed.[15] The house she had spotted, or heard about from her parents, was the Villa Bernarda – 'a three-decker – or a four decker, with the contadino in the deeps' (v. 338). It stood on a hill at the back of the small town, and had splendid views over Spotorno's attractive broad bay out to the open sea. At the very top of the hill on which the house was situated were the ruins of an old castle but these were close enough to be contained within the Villa's 'big vineyard garden' (v. 338). Apprehensively regretting the absence of fireplaces, Lawrence nevertheless liked the house and its situation, and was in any case pleased to have been greeted during his first days in Spotorno by fine weather. 'The sun shines,' he wrote to Blanche Knopf on 23 November, the eternal Mediterranean is blue and young, the last leaves are falling from the vines in the garden. The peasant people are nice, I've got my little stock of red and white wine – from the garden of this house – we eat fried chicken and pasta and smell rosemary and basalica in the cooking once more – and somebody's always roasting coffee – and the oranges are already on the orange trees. It's Italy, the same forever, whether it's Mussolini or Octavian Augustus. (v. 341–2)

The Villa Bernarda belonged to the wife of Angelo Ravagli who was a lieutenant in the 'Bersaglieri', an infantry regiment of high standing stationed in Savona only eight miles away. When Ravagli came to Spotorno to meet the Lawrences for the first time, it was the Queen of Italy's birthday and he was in dress uniform. Frieda was particularly impressed. As she wrote in early December to Brett: 'We have a nice little Bersaglieri officer to whom the villa belongs I am thrilled by his cockfeathers he is almost as nice as the feathers!' (v. 350). The Lawrences moved into the Villa from the Hotel Miramare on 23 November having agreed to take it – along with Giovanni, the 'contadino' Lawrence mentions who kept the garden and provided general help – for four months at a total cost of £25. Lawrence felt this was reasonable and, as living was cheap in Spotorno, looked forward to saving some money. 'We ought to manage on five shillings a day', he told Brett on 25 November. 'I want to economise, as Seltzer is hardly held together by a safety pin: and he has my five thousand dollars' (v. 343). In sterling, $5,000 amounted to around £1,250 and the prospect of only ever receiving such a large sum in very small instalments over a long period, or never receiving it at all, deprived Lawrence of the security which at this stage in a highly productive career he might reasonably have expected to feel.

Two days before moving, Lawrence had posted off to Nancy Pearn his review of a third book published by Knopf which he had brought with him from New York: J. A. Krout's *The Origins of Prohibition*.[16] Readers of the *New York Herald Tribune* must have found this a strange work for him to be considering after *Saïd the Fisherman*, and he confesses himself that it had proved rather more academic (and therefore dull) than he expected. Yet it did allow him to express his old view that it was the curse of 'distilled liquor' which had driven a healthy and natural fondness for wine and beer into disrepute; and to note wryly that imposing social control over alcohol in a democracy meant legislating for your neighbour while privately reserving the right to take the occasional drink yourself.[17] In the note to Nancy Pearn which accompanied the review – he was asking her to have it typed and sent on – Lawrence said that he was going to try to write a ghost story for Cynthia Asquith's collection (v. 341). The result was lengthy and complex, took him an uncharacteristically long time and was rejected by Lady Cynthia. Yet 'Glad Ghosts', as Lawrence eventually decided to call his story, is no less skilfully written than others of this period and full of biographical as well as critical interest. What also makes it worth describing is that it is now so little known.

The work is unusual for Lawrence in having a first-person narrator, one Mark Morier (M. M.) who has first met the heroine, Carlotta Fell, at 'our famous but uninspired school of art, the Thwaite, where I myself was diligently murdering my talent'.[18] (Discussions with Brett had given Lawrence an unflattering opinion of the Slade but increasing contact with Barby had made him actively hostile – in December he was to call it a 'criminal institution' – v. 364.) Carlotta is an aristocrat, which might suggest that the model is Brett; but even as an art student she had 'appeared in the fashionable papers, affecting to be wistful, with pearls, slanting her eyes'.[19] This sounds like Lady Cynthia whom Lawrence had already portrayed in 'The Thimble' and 'The Ladybird', and there is proof that Lawrence is in fact thinking chiefly of the woman for whom 'Glad Ghosts' was intended in the physical descriptions of his heroine. Carlotta marries Luke Lathkill just before the war and, while he is away at the front, invites the narrator to her box at the opera so that she can discuss her marriage. (Cynthia Asquith had invited the Lawrences to just such a box in 1918[20]). He learns then that the Lathkill family is dogged by bad luck and later hears that although Luke Lathkill has survived the war, with only a wound in his throat, Carlotta's twins have been killed in a car accident and her baby girl has died of a sudden illness. Cynthia Asquith's misfortunes were not as serious as these but there were good reasons why she might also regard herself as unlucky. Many of her young male friends and relations were killed in the war and her first child, the 'fat and smiling John' as Lawrence had called him when he and Frieda first met the Asquiths in 1913 (ii. 63), had proved to be autistic. In August 1926 he was moved from a special school for backward children to the mental institution where he was to spend the remainder of his short life.[21]

The main action of 'Glad Ghosts' concerns the narrator's visit, after the war, to the Lathkills' country house in Derbyshire – prompted by his recent drives round that county, Lawrence situates the house 'at the end of the village of Middleton' where in 1918–19 he himself had once lived; and he takes the family name from a Derbyshire river mentioned in one of the poems by Herbert Asquith which he had read.[22] Morier discovers at 'Riddings' a sepulchral atmosphere, presided over by Luke Lathkill's domineering mother who is a spiritualist and has in her power a certain Colonel Hale, tortured with guilt after the death of his first wife. Lady Lathkill is able to transmit and interpret messages from this dead wife but these have first of all instructed Colonel Hale to marry a young woman, and then forbidden him to make love to her. The narrator learns of this unhappy situation after a dinner at which the Colonel and his young wife, as well as Luke and Carlotta, are present. In its preliminary stages, before the ladies retire, this dinner is made even gloomier than it might have been by Lady

Lathkill's evident disapproval of alcohol. Yet it is partly by encouraging her son to drink more of his own 'good burgundy' that the narrator begins to excite in him some resistance to the old woman's tyranny, and when he, Morier and Colonel Hale do join the ladies, Luke insists that they all dance to records instead of once again listening to Lady Lathkill reading extracts from her books on spiritualism. In the middle of their dancing however, the room suddenly goes cold and the spirit of Colonel Hale's first wife makes an appearance, or at least is publicly addressed by Lady Lathkill in her capacity as a spiritualist medium. This rather puts a damper on things but Luke is too fired up to be discouraged and suggests to Colonel Hale that, if the ghost of his first wife is unappeased, it is because he never in her lifetime worshipped her with his body: 'Ah, if the Church taught us *that* sacrament: *with my body I thee worship*! That would easily make up for any honouring and obeying the woman might do.' He adds that there is nevertheless still time for him to take her to his warm heart. This Colonel Hale does there and then. Quite how he manages this is, in the nature of the case not very clear, but the effect is to break the power of Lady Lathkill who has next to endure hearing her son thanking her for the gift of his own body: 'Goodnight, Mother, mother of my face and thighs.'[23] (When the narrator is leaving next morning he learns that the old lady has been struck down with a sudden illness.)

While talking to Colonel Hale, Luke has had the young Mrs Hale's hand pressed against his breast or thigh. It is evident to every one that he has appropriated her and that Morier is therefore free to approach Carlotta. Yet, Lawrence writes, 'Desire is a sacred thing, and should not be violated.' The narrator has been put in a bedroom with which a female ghost is traditionally associated. Her visits are very rare, but because they are reputed to restore the family fortunes, Luke has hoped that Morier might attract one. During the night he is in fact visited, whether by the ghost or Carlotta he cannot tell: 'I shall never know if it was a ghost, some sweet spirit from the innermost of the ever-deepening cosmos. Or a woman, a very woman, as the silkiness of my limbs seems to attest.'[24] Whatever the true identity of his night visitor, the consequence is that the fortunes of the Lathkills (and of the Hares) *are* restored with all four now rid of the influence of Lady Lathkill and able to live satisfying lives.

'Glad Ghosts' is a sufficiently involved and developed story to deal with several typically Lawrentian themes: the power of the old to blight the lives of the young; the need to appease the spirits of the dead; and the possibility of a renewal or re-birth of the body – of its 'resurrection' – through sexual contact. Perhaps because these topics were to become increasingly important to Lawrence in his last years, the writing did not come easily (he seems to have written it at least twice).[25] Once Brett was in Capri, he resumed his old habit of giving her manuscripts to type but although he seems to imply he sent some part of 'Glad Ghosts' to her on 8 December, on the 12th he complained that he was still struggling with the story and that it was 'growing long' (v. 348, 352). On the 24th he had done three-quarters and got stuck, so that only on the 29th was it 'finished at last', although with the 'usual woe' it was 'much too long' (362, 365). Brett was not a professional typist, and she had several other things of Lawrence's to get through in addition to this story, so that it was not before 29 January that he was able to send 'Glad Ghosts' to the Curtis Brown office with the explanation that he had written it for Cynthia Asquith but wondered if it was suitable (v. 385). She clearly did not think it was and on 9 February wrote to Walter de la Mare: 'I am worried because Lawrence has sent me a ghost story that I really don't think it possible for me to publish. I doubt whether the publisher would. It's very long and I'm afraid he'll be furious. Another portrait of me too, which makes it more difficult.'[26] It was not principally the length which made the story impossible, nor that she felt she was portrayed in it (after 'The Thimble' and 'The Ladybird' she was used if not reconciled to that). What must have made Cynthia Asquith feel that even if she approved 'Glad Ghosts' her publisher would not, was its impropriety. Although the transactions are carried out with the consent of all parties, and in the best possible country-house taste, it is after all a tale of asymmetrical wife-swapping: a temporary switching of partners in order to revive relationships which are moribund. It would not have helped that in telling it Lawrence was on occasions more erotic than any of her other contributors were ever likely to be. When the narrator first meets the second Mrs Hale, for example, he notes the 'hint of a black moustache' and later cannot help thinking of 'the sparse black hairs there would be on her strong-skinned, dusky thighs'.[27] Because, however, Lady Cynthia felt sure that she was being represented in Carlotta Fell, it may not have helped either that the story ended (as indeed 'The Ladybird' had) with suggestions of a fantasised sexual relationship between herself and the figure closest to the story's author.

Having had Lawrence's typewriter shipped over from America as part of her own luggage, it was Brett who had written to ask him to send her manuscripts to type (he insisted on paying her at the going rate – v. 343–4). Almost as soon as she arrived in Capri, she would have received two short prose pieces which were to appear along with two poems by Lawrence in a special number of *Laughing Horse*, entirely devoted to work by or about him and published in April 1926. These are interesting because they show Lawrence attempting to clarify for himself a feeling that he did not want to go back to the ranch in the near future. In 'A Little Moonshine with Lemon' he contrasts the view he has from the balcony of his bedroom at the top of the Villa Bernarda with the landscape around the ranch, recalling nostalgically the horses he and Frieda owned and the fir-tree in front of their cabin; but also remembering the intense cold in winter and the likelihood that at Kiowa there would be snow on the ground. In Spotorno he is drinking vermouth to celebrate St Catherine's day (25 November), whereas at Kiowa he would be demonstrating how little Prohibition affected his own life by sipping moonshine: 'not very good moonshine, but still warming: with hot water and lemon, and sugar, and a bit of cinnamon from one of those little red Schilling's tins'.[28] In this sketch Lawrence does not declare how he feels on the question of 'Europe v. America' but in the second short prose piece, which has precisely that title, he admits that now he is back in Europe he feels a 'real relief'.[29] One of the two poems Lawrence must have sent Johnson is called 'Mediterranean in January' and is unusual for him at this stage in his career because it is rhymed. He draws a comparison in it between 'The Blue anemone with a dark core' and the way 'bank-tellers tell the one tale that is told; / And bank-notes are poetry purer than gold.' He will only go back to New York, he says, 'When I see this sea looking shoddy and dead, / And this sun cease shining overhead.' Meanwhile the Mediterranean before him 'Persuades me to stay, since stay I may'.[30] In his letters Lawrence often refers to the tension of life in America and indicates that he has come to Italy to relax. He speaks also of the effort it would take to travel to New Mexico and, with some apprehension, of the weather one would be likely to find there in winter. Yet he must also have known, after his experiences in El Paso, that he would have had great difficulty in getting back into the United States, even if he had wanted to go. Moreover, once he had been refused entry on the grounds that he was suffering from tuberculosis, it would have been hard for him to continue to deny to others (and perhaps to himself) that this was the true state of affairs. Of this period Frieda writes, 'the ranch too called him. However the idea of having to struggle with immigration officials, thinking of his tuberculosis, scared him.'[31]

Lawrence never publicly admitted to 'thinking of his tuberculosis', but whether or not he secretly knew, or at least suspected, that crossing the Atlantic again was no longer an option, he was still as characteristically full of travel plans as ever. A vague idea of going to Russia, for example, had been encouraged by conversations with Carl Seelig in Lucerne; and in a fence-mending note, written on 6 December, he asked the Russian-born Koteliansky what he thought of it (v. 347). We know from Mark Gertler how Kot replied, not to the specific enquiry but to Lawrence's evident wish to be once again in contact. Gertler was a consumptive who had responded in an entirely different way from Lawrence to his misfortune, openly acknowledging that he was suffering from tuberculosis and spending in consequence a good deal of time in sanatoriums. On 22 December 1925 he wrote to Kot from the Mundesley Sanatorium in Norfolk:

I am surprised Lawrence wrote to you just now, because if he wanted to resume friendship I should have thought it would have been a good opportunity for him to have done so, when he was in London recently. I think you were right to write to him as you did. I have now decided that if Brett writes to me again – I shall also be frank with her.[32]

Whatever Kot's degree of frankness Lawrence was not disconcerted by it, suggesting to him on 18 December that they should neither of them 'bother any more about people and lies'; that they neither of them had changed very much and that, 'We are both much simpler than a man like Murry, whom I don't really understand' (v. 356). Affectionately recalling old times, he re-established the friendship on its former footing so that Kot was soon sending him the recent *After Lenin: The New Phase in Russia* by Michael Farbman, a co-resident at 5 Acacia Road whom Lawrence knew, as well as several books for learning Russian to which he applied himself with his usual diligence. By the beginning of February 1926, in a letter to Harold Mason, he was trying out a few very simple phrases in the Russian alphabet and saying, 'Did I tell you, I half think of going to Russia, instead of coming to America this year. One has to be so tough in America' (v. 387); but an unusually severe bout of illness a few days later signalled the end of his interest. As he told Kot on 17 March, 'Since I had influenza I abandoned my Russian Grammar in despair' (v. 404).

At this period, a more persistently expressed travel plan than a trip to Russia was the old dream of buying a boat and wandering with a few friends around, not in this present case the South Seas, but the Mediterranean. The last time Lawrence was in daily visual contact with the Mediterranean, at Taormina, he had imagined it dotted with peripatetic Greeks: Odysseus, Jason or the Dionysos whose boat, in the frontispiece to an edition of Hesiod which had especially impressed him, has bunches of grapes growing from its masts.[33] Lawrence's favourite idea now was that he and his friends should be in a sailing boat heading for the Greek islands. This would satisfy his desire for freedom as well as his curiosity about new places, because they could call at various ports on the way. Something of the strength of his ingrained romanticism is evident in what he apparently said to Brett when he finally went to visit her in Capri: 'In the old days Brett, the sailing ships had sails of crimson silk. Think of that in the sunlight: crimson silk on a blue sea, with the sunlight and the white waves.'[34]

The trouble with boats, as Lawrence had discovered five years before when he was last seriously looking for one to buy or hire, was that they cost a lot of money, especially as a small crew would be required. The most he could contribute, he explained to the Brewsters when he broached his plans to them on 9 January, was £100 (v. 373). It irked him that, although on the day after the Lawrences had left Taos in September he had turned forty (a moment his letters and other writings show he clearly regarded as an important watershed), he was still prevented from doing what he wanted by shortage of funds. With increasing age and sickness he was now less philosophical about the inequalities of income distribution than he had been in his youth: 'I wish we weren't always poor', he had written to Brett on 25 November, 'I wanted to go to Dalmatia and the Isles of Greece. Why doesn't anybody ever have a yacht, and sail the coasts of the Mediterranean – Greece, and

Constantinople, and Damascus, and Jaffa, and Egypt, and Tunis and Morocco – or at least Algiers. How nice it would be! Why do beastly people like Nina Witt have the millions' (v. 343).

There is a shift in Lawrence's attitude to money but no fundamental alteration. That can be deduced from the second ghost story which he quickly wrote for Cynthia Asquith, once he had realised that 'Glad Ghosts' would not do. In one of many fine moments in 'The Rocking-Horse Winner', the young boy whose ability to predict winners has won him £5,000, and who wants to give this money to his mother in order to secure her love and attention, arranges with his uncle that the mother should receive on her birthday a letter from the family solicitor pretending that a distant relative is to provide her with £1,000 per annum for the next five years. Paul (as the young boy is called) makes sure that he is at breakfast when the letter arrives so that he can be a witness to her pleasure. But the mother's face remains cold and expressionless, and she immediately goes to the solicitor's in order to arrange for all the money to be paid to her at once. There is a rise in the family's standard of living, with new furnishings and a tutor for Paul, and it is decided that he will go to Eton; but as a consequence the mysterious voices which have seemed to him to haunt the house and which whisper, 'There *must* be more money!' become even more loud and tormenting. To satisfy his mother's craving for the kind of life to which she feels entitled, and provide for her the 'luck' which her husband has failed to deliver, Paul is obliged to put more and more pressure on his psychic powers. He can only predict his winners by rocking backwards and forwards on a rocking-horse from his early childhood which he has contrived to keep in his bedroom. In the well-known climax, full of disturbing sexual overtones, Paul feverishly rocks back and forth on this horse until he is able to predict that 'Malabar' will win the Derby whereupon he falls into a coma from which he never recovers. Because Paul's uncle has arranged for the money his nephew had already accumulated to be placed on 'Malabar', he is the one who ends the story by saying to the mother: 'My God, Hester, you're eighty-odd thousand to the good, and a poor devil of a son to the bad.'[35]

As the person who was now dealing with this story at Curtis Brown, Nancy Pearn had been anxious that Lady Cynthia should not use her social prestige to get something for nothing. But Lawrence was doing a favour for a friend and on 6 April 1926 he would tell Miss Pearn, 'Of course it's all right, the £15 for the "Rocking-Horse" story, to Lady Cynthia: if she is suited' (v. 415). £15 is not much for a strong candidate for inclusion in any anthology of the best short stories of the century, but Lady Cynthia might have felt it dear at the price. Although she was less recognisable to an outsider as Paul's mother than as the Carlotta Fell of 'Glad Ghosts' (both of whom feel they have no 'luck'), there were good reasons why she should later have described 'The Rocking-Horse Winner' as 'excruciating' as well as 'unforgettable'.[36] Like most children of aristocrats before the war, her autistic son had been brought up by nannies and nursemaids and she later worried that his difficulties might have been related to a lack of maternal affection, or at least attention. In Lawrence's story Paul kills himself by trying to attract attention in a world whose mercenary values he does not understand. That children need love more than material benefits is the most obvious moral of 'The Rocking-Horse Winner', but another is that our sense of how well or poorly off we are will always depend on our expectations. Lawrence sounded off about being short of money rather more often in 1925 than he had done since first leaving Europe three or so years before, but he could still spend his time writing short pieces for Spud Johnson which he knew would bring him nothing, and be relatively indifferent to what Cynthia Asquith would pay him for a story (even if he later came to feel it had not been very much).[37] As her biographer points out, she was in fact skilful in adjusting fees to expectations, once paying De la Mare £20 for a poem but W. H. Davies only 2 guineas. This was for her first anthology – of children's stories and verse – whose American sales alone brought her £750 'minus about £200 due to the contributors'.[38] If Lawrence had seen these figures he might well have felt that this was an exceptionally good return for an editor but, with his recent story in mind, added wryly but perhaps not too bitterly – he was very fond of Cynthia Asquith – that she, after all, had lots of expenses.

Lawrence had dealt brilliantly with the problem of money four years earlier in his long introduction to the Magnus *Memoirs*. A puzzle for any reader of these concerns the source of the sums of money which are so crucially important to Magnus, allowing him (for example) to pay 5 *sous* to another soldier to clean his kit or to retreat to a local hotel for a bath and a good meal when life in the barracks becomes even more intolerably sordid than usual. Lawrence's introduction makes clear that Magnus himself was sometimes not sure what the source would be either but that he shared with his friend Norman Douglas the belief that the time to spend money was when you had none: ' "Precisely," said Douglas, "Spend when you've nothing to spend, my boy. Spend *hard* then." '[39] Lawrence would have made a distinction between not caring too much about money – not allowing it to rule one's life – and being irresponsible in financial matters. He was appalled when he learned that Brett, just before she left Taos, had given a cheque to the local storekeeper which she now knew would bounce. 'I do think you ought to keep track of your spending and incoming,' he told her. 'I would loathe to draw a cheque if I thought it wouldn't be covered: it's sort of false' (v. 426).

In attempting to have Magnus's memoirs published, and arranging that half the proceeds should go to paying off the author's debts while the other half should come directly to him for the long introduction, Lawrence felt that he was steering an appropriate middle course between a proper regard for his own financial interests, so that he did not stumble into debt and dishonour, and the right degree of disinterestedness in a good cause. Norman Douglas's suggestions in *A Plea for Better Manners* that Lawrence's criticism of Magnus was prompted by resentment at having lent him small sums which were never returned, and that he had succeeded in making money out of effects to which Douglas himself was legally entitled, had upset him; but it was relatively easy to ignore them while the text in which they appeared was only a pamphlet, privately printed in Florence. When however Douglas chose to reprint *A Plea* in a collection he called *Experiments*, published in London in October 1925, Lawrence was urged by Secker to respond (v. 340).[40] Eventually he wrote a letter to the *New Statesman* (where *Experiments* had been reviewed) in which he gave his version of the whole Magnus affair and pointed out that, if he had made some money from the publication of the memoirs, Magnus's unfortunate Maltese creditors were now also re-paid. What made Lawrence's protest so effective, when it finally appeared on 20 February 1926, was that it included extracts from the letter which Douglas had written to him in December 1921. 'By all means do what you like with the MS', was one of the letter's injunctions along with, *'Pocket all the cash yourself.* B-[one of the Maltese] is such a fool he doesn't deserve any.' Douglas had also told Lawrence, 'Put me into your introduction, if you like' and must have been left feeling relieved that at least Lawrence stopped short of quoting in his letter to the *New Statesman* the continuation of that phrase ('drunk and stark naked if you like'); and that he omitted the characteristically vivid manner in which Douglas had expressed how fed up he was with trying to get the Magnus *Memoirs* into print: 'Whoever wants it, may ram it up his exhaust-pipe.'[41]

III Visitors

Celebrations of the warmth on the Italian Riviera are gradually outnumbered in Lawrence's letters by complaints about the biting wind and the periods when it was very cold (this was after all winter). The Villa Bernarda had no fireplaces but behind the sitting room on its top story was a kitchen which contained a stove. In the evenings, or during the daylight hours of the colder days, the Lawrences would sit round this stove (v. 353) but, at the beginning of their stay, it smoked. One Sunday the 35-year-old Ravagli, who would visit his tenants at weekends to see how they were managing, climbed on the roof and energetically cleaned out the relevant tube where it emerged from the chimney. Frieda later recalled that Lawrence then told her Ravagli was the kind of man it would be useful to have with one in Kiowa.[42] She was too free of guilt to have invented this remark so that Lawrence could give posthumous approval to her having taken Ravagli to live with her in New Mexico in 1933.[43]

Lawrence could hardly ever have found himself at a loose end in Spotorno because he wrote so much, but had he and Frieda wanted it, there was an *entrée* into local society available to them through Rina Secker. (On Christmas Day 1925 the Lawrences dined with both the Seckers and Rina's parents at a restaurant in Spotorno – v. 364.) Rina Capellero had married Martin Secker in 1921 and given birth to a little boy in March 1924. Lawrence's references to her in his letters suggest there were tensions in the marriage and that, like the heroine of his story 'Sun' (who also has a little boy at the toddling stage), she had come to Italy to recover her spirits as much as her physical health. 'Sun' was probably the second of two short stories which he asked Brett to type after the work for Spud Johnson: he sent the manuscript off to her around 12 December (v. 352).[44] It describes how a young woman who is nervously exhausted finds a new life by learning to lie naked in the warmth of the Italian winter sun. Obviously expressive of Lawrence's own feelings about light and warmth after his few weeks in England, the story is the fictional counterpart of his remarks in *Reflections on the Death of a Porcupine* about the man who has met the sun and has it with him as a diadem.[45] The female protagonist and her husband are both American, and for the setting Lawrence relied on his memories of the garden of the Fontana Vecchia, rather than Spotorno. For all that, it would have been surprising if the Seckers had not perceived in this story a suspicious similarity to their own situation. Towards the end of its main action, the heroine's husband arrives from his office in New York 'utterly out of the picture, in his dark grey suit and pale grey hat, and his grey, monastic face of a shy business man'.[46] Martin Secker came to Spotorno in the second week of December and did not leave until 18 January. 'Martin Secker is here', Lawrence wrote soon after his arrival, ' – with the Capellero family down the road. He's a nice gentle soul, without a thrill: his wife a living block of discontent' (v. 352).

Lawrence's first impression of Secker on his arrival seems to have been transcribed into the conclusion of 'Sun' but, as time went on, Lawrence spent a good deal of time with him – on 16 December they went to Savona together – and learned to appreciate his quiet decency ('he's a nice mild soul' – v. 366). How appreciative Secker was of Lawrence when he read 'Sun' is not recorded. Given the many transpositions in the story, both he and his wife could have told themselves with some justification that Lawrence had merely used them as a starting-point: that in the way of authors, especially authors like Lawrence, he had allowed his imagination to play around the fundamentals of their situation with consequences which, in the end, had no real bearing on it. Yet that would hardly take away *all* the discomfort Secker himself was likely to experience when he read in the conclusion to 'Sun' that the husband had 'the gold-grey eyes of an animal that has been caught young, and reared completely in captivity', or that he 'smelled of the world, and all its fetters and mongrel cowering'.[47] As Cynthia Asquith understood, knowing Lawrence was not always a comfortable business, especially as his analyses and judgements could never be dismissed as simply a consequence of envy, resentment or malice.

Barby Weekley also arrived on the Riviera at the beginning of December 1925. She stayed in the first instance in a *pensione* at Alassio, about twenty miles down the coast. This was chiefly because, Lawrence explained to Brett on 5 December, 'Pa prefers she shouldn't house here' (v. 347). It was inevitable that at least some of the bitter resentment Lawrence felt at Weekley's attitude should transfer itself to his children who were also on occasions the innocent victims of his anger at what he felt was their mother's unreasonable attachment to them. 'Privately', he had told Brett on 4 November, 'I can't stand Frieda's children. They have a sort of suburban bounce and *suffisance* which puts me off. When they appear, I shall disappear' (v. 332–3). Gradually however he began to warm to Barby. On her visits to Spotorno, they went for walks together and Lawrence advised her on her painting, denouncing her academic training, passing unequivocal judgement on what she did, and making his own contributions to particular canvases. Barby no more resented this treatment than Brett had. After her mother had left home, she had been brought up with her brother and sister in the restrictive or at least conventional atmosphere of her grandparents' house in London. The rebel of the family, she had often clashed with Weekley's unmarried sister Maud who also lived in the London house, had assumed Frieda's maternal duties and who must have felt, when Barby was expelled from St Paul's for drawing male nudes in a textbook, that nurture was going to prove powerless against nature (in its Von Richthofen form).[48] Disconcerted by the look of Lawrence when she had met him with her sister in the winter of 1923–4, Barby now found his company stimulating. Remembering that she 'painted away assiduously at Spotorno', she later wrote: 'The creative atmosphere of the Lawrence household was like a draught of life to me.'[49]

Elsa was due to follow Barby to Italy after Christmas, when the two sisters would stay in Spotorno (although in a hotel rather than at the Villa Bernarda); and so too was Lawrence's sister Ada. Because Murry was also expected with his wife and small child, the Lawrences must have felt that it was a good thing they had rented a large house. At first Lawrence thought it would be convenient for Ada to travel with the Murrys but, after hearing from Murry that they would not after all be coming because of the difficulties his wife was having with a second pregnancy, he suggested to Ada that she might travel with Elsa (v. 365–6).[50] Murry would afterwards claim that it was his failure to keep his promise and visit Lawrence in Spotorno which precipitated a definitive breach between them,[51] but the letters suggest that the trouble centred on matters less private. Lawrence had arranged to have Murry sent a copy of *Reflections* which of course included, in 'The Crown', a striking reminder of those days during the war when they had collaborated to produce the *Signature* (as well as wounding remarks which made that collaboration seem of little importance).[52] Murry had hoped that now, with the withdrawal of Kot, the burden of sustaining the *Adelphi* was falling even more on himself, he and Lawrence might once again collaborate. To Lawrence's somewhat contemptuous dismissal of this notion ('My dear chap, people don't want the one-man show of you alone, nor the punch and Judy show of you and me' – v. 368), as well as to the essays which he found in *Reflections*, Murry responded with what Lawrence thought was 'more spite and impudence than I have yet had from him' (v. 374). He felt, in addition, that Murry had added insult to injury when, shortly afterwards, he asked if he could print one of the essays from *Reflections* in the *Adelphi*, for nothing (v. 380). These difficulties made him aware of just how far apart he and Murry now were. This had been especially brought home to him by Murry's preoccupation with the figure of Jesus. Discussions of Jesus by Murry had been appearing regularly in the *Adelphi* well before he began serialising his recently completed *Life of Jesus* in the issue for June 1926 (the instalments continued until July 1927, which was also the last issue to appear under his editorship). He offered a secularised Christ, a 'man of genius', completely without any supernatural dimension. Lawrence himself was later to write his own version of at least part of the gospel story in *The Escaped Cock*, but how differently he must already have conceived things can be judged from this representative extract from Murry's *Life*:

To those to whom Jesus is God, it must inevitably be almost blasphemous to emphasize so signal a trait in Jesus as his humour. Yet to those for whom Jesus is wholly man, and the more divine for that, this humour of his is infinitely precious. The man of sorrows is the man who called Peter 'the Rock', and James and John 'the sons of Thunder'; he was, before all else, like Shakespeare, a smiling man.[53]

Opinions will differ on the value and quality of this manner, but no-one could dispute how entirely different it is from Lawrence's. 'Surely', Lawrence wrote to Murry on 19 January in a note in which he said he would prefer to have no more of his own pieces in the *Adelphi*, 'you realise the complete incompatibility of my say with your say. Say your say, Caro! – and let *me* say mine. But for heavens sake, don't let us pretend to mix them' (v. 380).[54]

Lawrence's hostility to the more conventional forms of Christian feeling is apparent in the longest and most successful of the stories he wrote in Spotorno: *The Virgin and the Gipsy* (these few months in the Villa Bernarda represent one of his more remarkably creative periods). This classic tale, which occupied him perhaps over Christmas 1925 and certainly in the first weeks of 1926, is heavily reliant on details of the Weekley family with which Barby had supplied him, and has Weekley himself cast as a literary vicar whose wife – 'She-who-was-Cynthia', his 'pure white snowflower'[55] – has deserted him when his children were young.

Elsa is featured as well as Barby, but the story concentrates on the latter who is the obvious model for Yvette, a young woman whose relations with a gipsy allow her to discover alternatives to the narrow and restrictive life which she sees all around her. The gipsy provides her with a standard of manhood by which to judge the conventional young men who court her, and he is at the same time an implicit challenge to her father's system of morality.

Yvette first meets the gipsy when she is motoring in Derbyshire with friends, and the girls in the party decide to have their fortune told by his wife. She is struck by the penetrating stare of this 'pagan pariah woman' and feels that her handsome husband looks at her with a frankness of desire she has never encountered before. On a later occasion she is just about to enter his caravan for what it appears is going to be her first, full sexual experience when a couple who are passing in a car enter the camp site to warm their hands by the open fire. These are the Eastwoods who are living together while waiting for the woman's divorce to be finalised and who represent a somewhat unsatisfactory, intermediate stage on the road to the gipsy's complete alienation from conventional society. (It is when Yvette's father rebukes her for having developed a friendship with the Eastwoods that she feels how fully he has revealed the meanness and timidity of his moral standards.) The gipsy and Yvette are finally brought together when the rectory in which she lives is half destroyed by a flood, and he first of all helps her to struggle upstairs to the room protected from the rushing water by the chimney ('Where is the chimney? the back chimney? – which room? The chimney will stand');[56] and then, having taken off his sodden clothes, holds her naked body against his in order to protect her from hypothermia and the effects of shock. (It is not made clear whether he does more than this.) *The Virgin and the Gipsy* is a story of awakening – with Yvette as the sleeping princess – and very skilfully modulates between realism and the fairy tale. Although the action is always credible, there is a certain non-realistic element apparent in Lawrence's decision to call Yvette's father the Reverend Mr Saywell; in the references to the Lady of Shallot motif, as Yvette looks out of the window hoping that the gipsy will come by; and in the obviously symbolic import of the cleansing flood. This means that the gipsy can also remain partly symbolic without Lawrence having to bother with the question of how a relationship between an educated middle-class girl like Yvette and a gipsy could be sustained. But the function of the gipsy is in any case to initiate Yvette into a new life, to mark a new beginning. This means that, as in 'Glad Ghosts', only one contact is necessary, sufficient to make Yvette aware of 'some hidden part of herself which she denied; that part which mysteriously and unconfessedly responded to him'.[57]

Much of the power of *The Virgin and the Gipsy* comes from the comic verve of Lawrence's satirical representation of the Saywell household: his remarkably potent evocation of domestic staleness. The spinster aunt modelled on Weekley's sister Maud is so effective and memorable a portrait of that rancorous envy of the young which can develop in people who regret the sacrifice of their own lives that it is amazing Barby could have later told Lawrence his account of the household was 'not bad enough'.[58] The dominating figure is the Rector's mother – 'the Mater' – who has such a shrewd understanding of her son's foibles that she is always in control. Blind, obese, greedy, she is shown feeding off the life of those younger than herself, and associated unforgettably with the image of an old toad sitting outside a bee-hive and snapping up the bees as they launch out 'as if it could consume the whole hive-full, into its aged, bulging, purse-like wrinkled-ness'.[59] Readers are made to feel so strongly the oppressiveness of the Mater that it is hard for them not to experience at least some exhilaration when, having managed to get up the stairs of the flooded house, Yvette looks down and sees 'Granny bob up, like a strange float, her face purple, her blind blue eyes bolting, spume hissing from her mouth'; or when the gipsy, watching one of the Mater's 'old purple' hands clawing 'at a bannister rail', looks down on the 'awful float-like face below' and says, ' "Not good enough! Not good enough!" '[60]

Any suggestion that Lawrence was unaware that he often did portray his friends and acquaintances can be discounted when we find him writing to Bynner in January 1926, 'I hope you won't mind the little sketch of you in *The Plumed Serpent*'; and it was only three months later that he made the remark about a character in *Aaron's Rod* being Leo Stein which I quote in my preface (v. 384, 419). He continually incorporated the people he knew or had met into his fiction, sometimes in the form of what it would be legitimate to describe as direct transcription ('portraits'); but more often using them as starting-points or in creative amalgams. This is how Cynthia Asquith and the Seckers had been used in 'Glad Ghosts', 'The Rocking-Horse Winner' or 'Sun', so that to define the precise relation of the characters in these stories to biographical fact would be a very delicate matter. Each of these cases is different, and so is *The Virgin and the Gipsy*. There are details of the Weekley family in that novella which are extraordinarily accurate but they mostly come, not from direct knowledge, but from what Frieda and above all Barby told Lawrence. He had never met 'Granny Weekley' so that, for the immensely powerful, physical portrayal of 'the Mater', he relied on the drawings with which Barby supplied him (those which were to result later in the impressive painting reproduced as Fig. 30). *The Virgin and the Gipsy* is a great work, and not merely, or indeed at all, because it is anticipatory in many ways of *Lady Chatterley's Lover* (the gipsy, who has been through the war and nearly died of pneumonia – Major Eastwood describes him as a 'resurrected man' – clearly looks forward to that novel's gamekeeper). It was a piece that ought to have made money and for a while Lawrence wondered whether, with the inconveniently long 'Glad Ghosts', there might not be the basis for a successor to the *Captain's Doll* volume, which had sold well. Yet he fairly quickly decided that he would not publish it in spite of its commercial potential. The only clue we have to his motives is from Barbara Weekley: 'Frieda showed me the manuscript and said that Lawrence thought he should not publish it "Because, after all, he is their father." '[61]

One could interpret this act of self-denial as a critical recognition on Lawrence's part that the novella's only serious flaw is an occasional authorial denunciation of the Reverend Mr Saywell which, in contrast to the treatment of the Mater, is not shown to be justified. But the real reason was more probably Lawrence's feeling that there should after all be limits to the portrayal of friends, enemies and acquaintances in books. Although he must have felt that people like the Seckers or the Asquiths were fair game, too sophisticated or too fundamentally well disposed to take serious offence, he may have decided on reflection that to pillory the Weekley family as gleefully and successfully as he had done in *The Virgin and the Gipsy* was not fair, especially as Barby (whom he grew to like more and more) was still after all one of its members. He may also of course have realised, remembering his difficulties with Philip Heseltine over *Women in Love*,[62] that making people too easily identifiable could be troublesome, even dangerous. In February Mabel, having decided that her refusal to communicate with Lawrence had gone on long enough, had sent him the first volume of her memoirs. When he got round to reading them after his return from Capri, he was alarmed: 'In the first place,' he told her on 12 April, 'why oh why didn't you change the names! My dear Mabel, call in all the copies, keep them under lock and key, and then carefully, scrupulously change the names: at least do that: before you let one page go out of your hands again. Remember, *other people* can be utterly remorseless, if they think you've given them away' *(v. 423).* It is a peculiarity of Lawrence that the literary indiscretions of others were sometimes far more vivid to him than his own; but in the case of *The Virgin and the Gipsy* at least, he could have shown Mabel that he knew how to exercise restraint.[63]

Lawrence had finished *The Virgin and the Gipsy* by 21 January, three weeks before more visitors were due to arrive. In that period it was 'cold and rainy' and soon he was obliged to take once more to his bed. He had been ill intermittently ever since his return to Europe, but this time his condition was serious. How serious is apparent from his confession to Brett around 11 February: 'I'm in bed these last six days with flu. It gave me bronchial hemorrhage like at the ranch, only worse' *(v. 390).* He told her that Ada had arrived the day before – she travelled with a friend from the Ripley area named Lizzie Booth; and that Elsa Weekley was due that evening. He also indicated that all Frieda's old hostility to Brett had been revived, probably because his own relations with his wife were once again poor. When the Lawrences had first settled in Spotorno, Frieda had sent Brett a couple of notes so warm and affectionate that there seemed no reason why she would not fall in with her husband's vague plan of perhaps visiting Brett in Capri or travelling down to Sicily with her (v. 344–5, 349–50).[64] Now, however, Lawrence reported his doubt that the three of them would 'ever see comfortable days together. Frieda declares an implacable intention of never seeing you again, and never speaking to you if she does see you – and I say nothing' (v. 390).

Whatever reservations Barby had about not sleeping in the same house as Lawrence had quickly disappeared once she was in Italy, a long way from family pressure; and with the opportunity to observe them closely, she was able to record an occasion when the Lawrences had one of their fierce arguments to the accompaniment of minor violence on Lawrence's part against his wife (after loud noises she rushed upstairs to find her mother with 'her face scratched'[65]). But if their relations were not especially good before the arrival of their extra guests, they deteriorated rapidly with Ada and Lizzie Booth in the villa and Elsa (who had also travelled with a friend) staying with Barby at a local hotel. On 16 February Lawrence reported to Brett, 'I'm up and creeping about, but hope to be more or less solid by the weekend. My sister's coming was occasion for another rumpus: F abandoned the ship, and stays down in the little hotel with her two daughters, pro tem' (v. 392). As Barby had observed, Ada and Frieda did not get on, but it is likely that, with Lawrence in bed and so evidently ill, Ada was shocked – as other observers would later be – by Frieda's nonchalant view of her nursing responsibilities. How it seemed from Frieda's point of view is suggested by her recalling in her memoir, 'Ada arrived and above me in Lawrence's room with the balcony, I could hear him complaining to her about me. I could not hear the words but by the tone of their voices I knew.' She was especially hurt when, after a reconciliation with Lawrence, which was followed by a bitter quarrel with Ada, she went up to his room and found it was 'locked and Ada had the key'.[66] Too weakened to be much more than an object of dispute, Lawrence could only complain to William Hawk on 19 February, 'somehow everything feels in a great muddle, with daughters that are by no means mine, and sister who doesn't see eye to eye with F. What a trial families are!' (v. 394).

IV Capri and After

To escape the conflict at home, and even though he was 'still a bit shaky with [his] flu' (v. 397), Lawrence decided to take Ada and her friend to Monte Carlo for a couple of days before he was due to put them on the train in Nice on 25 February. He found Monte Carlo 'very stupid and boring' (v. 398), but at least had the satisfaction of being able to give William Siebenhaar and his wife, who were on holiday in Europe and met Lawrence there, oral confirmation of his success in persuading Knopf to consider including Siebenhaar's translation of

Max Havelaar in his 'Blue Jade Library'.[67] Once his female compatriots were on their way home he had to decide what to do next. He had felt 'absolutely swamped out' by Frieda and her daughters (v. 394) and talked of needing some time on his own. His latest idea had been to visit Spain by himself (v. 394) and in all his letters to Brett he had been studiously vague about the possibility of coming to Capri. Yet from the railway junction town of Ventimiglia on the day after Ada had left, Lawrence sent a telegram to Brett announcing his imminent visit (v. 400). Arriving on the 27th, he let Frieda know where he was two days later (v. 411) and as a result soon began to receive angry letters from her. If, as seems likely, Frieda began her affair with Angelo Ravagli in March or April 1926, one could fairly say that she did not act without provocation.

In Capri Lawrence stayed with the Brewsters in their Villa Torre dei Quattro Venti. They had occupied this house more or less continuously since their return from Ceylon, but were now just about to give it up in order to go to India. Due to leave Italy on 16 March they nevertheless warmly welcomed Lawrence to stay with them. Their daughter Harwood was now just entering her teens and went down with Brett to meet Lawrence at the little port in Capri. Brett hardly recognised him at first in a 'new brown overcoat, a new grey suit, a brown Homburg hat, brown shoes', but then noted how 'frail, how delicate and collapsed' he seemed.[68] Occasionally making her pause while he recovered his breath, Lawrence nevertheless accompanied Brett to many of the island's beauty spots in the next few days; and they visited together several of its semi-permanent expatriate residents. She had become particularly friendly with a poet named Frederick Branford (whose work Lawrence knew), and Lawrence himself made sure that he looked up the Brett Youngs, with whom he had once been house-hunting in Sicily, and John Ellingham Brooks, Somerset Maugham's first lover and a resident in Capri since the Oscar Wilde trial.[69] In addition to Ferdinando di Chiara and his American wife Anna, there was also of course Faith Mackenzie. Brett remembered how, when they visited Faith, they listened to her 'beautiful gramophone'[70] (if the wife of the founding-editor of the *Gramophone* magazine was not to have a good machine, who was?); but Lawrence later dined with Faith alone and through his 'sensitive understanding and the glow of kindness in his deep eyes' led her to talk more frankly than she usually did about her private affairs.[71] On 2 March he had told his sister Ada how sorry he was that 'there was that bust-up to spoil your holiday – I had so wanted you to have a nice time'; and about a week later he reported that he had seen 'most of the old people in Capri . . . Mrs Compton Mackenzie was there as usual, an unhappy soul, trying to pretend to be gay. She's another who loves her husband but can't live with him. Much good it does her!' (v. 401, 403).

The question of buying a boat was still on Lawrence's mind. He raised it with Brooks, who promised to make enquiries about cost,[72] and he must have discussed it with his hosts. Before the Brewsters left the island there were charades in the library, the empty shelves (all the books were packed away) serving as props in Lawrence's brilliant impersonation of an over-zealous assistant in a shoe shop.[73] The general level of performance would have been high given that, in addition to Brett, Mary Cannan, who happened to be on one of her periodic visits to Capri, also took part. Her loquaciousness was highly irritating to Brett who was anxious to have Lawrence as much to herself as possible, partly so that she could seize the right moment to show him her new painting (a Christ on the cross who looked like Lawrence and was gazing down on a Pan figure with similar facial characteristics[74]); but chiefly so that she could provide him with the comfort which she felt he badly needed. In her account, Lawrence confessed himself completely worn out by the conflict with Frieda; 'you have no idea Brett, how humiliating it is to beat a woman', he apparently told her, 'afterwards one feels simply humiliated'.[75] Barby recalled that her sister Elsa was shocked when she saw that, after one of his disputes with their mother, Lawrence had tears in his eyes;[76] and it certainly seems the case that marriage as a series of pitched battles was less a stimulus to Lawrence than it once had been, especially now that he was so often ill. Brett was there with not only comfort but an alternative. She had decided before Lawrence came to Capri that she wanted to go back to America and that, in order to avoid the bother of having continually to re-apply for visas, it would be as well to have herself put on the immigration list: made part of the quota which had been recently introduced. (This was not a difficult thing for her because the quota for Britain was rarely full in the 1920s and all she needed was a medical certificate, proof of financial means and evidence that in the past she had been neither a criminal nor a Bolshevik.) But after Lawrence had received an upsetting letter from Frieda, Brett offered to delay her return to the United States and asked him whether it would not be better if she were 'nearer at hand, in case of trouble . . . "Yes", you reply, with so much weariness mixed with boredom, that I feel nothing on earth matters very much to you. "It would be best. I don't know what to do. We must wait and see." '[77]

When the Brewster family left Capri around 10 March, Earl remembered Lawrence enthusiastically carrying away all the left-over artist's materials from the studio he and his wife had shared.[78] They would have had a visual reminder of their time with Lawrence if they had seen, or been sent, a photograph which appeared at the end of the month in the magazine *Eve: the ladies' pictorial*. Under the rubric 'More Pictures of Capri: And some of its devotees', and above another photograph showing a beach party which includes Harwood, Mrs Brett Young and Mrs Branford, the Brewster family is seen with Lawrence and Brett posed against one of Capri's many rocky slopes. Achsah Brewster has an arm round Brett, emphasising the youthful, almost schoolgirl, impression Brett here makes, while Lawrence looks fit in his three-piece suit even if, for the man who wrote

'Sun', rather over-dressed. The author of the short text is well informed, hoping that Lawrence 'will dramatise Capri as excitingly as he interpreted Australia in his novel *Kangaroo* or as interestingly as he wrote about *Sea and Sardinia*'. This is in contrast to whoever wrote the words to accompany the photographs which appeared in the *Tatler* a week earlier with the title, 'From Capri, The Land of Cypress and Myrtle'. One of these shows a stiff and awkward Faith Mackenzie and another has Lawrence sitting on a low wall looking thin and harassed. 'Mrs Compton Mackenzie', the caption reads, 'is the wife of the famous author, who has used Capri as a background for many of his plots. He bought one of the Western Isles, Herm, from the late Lord Leverhulme. Mr D. H. Lawrence is the well known author–photographer.'[79]

With the Brewsters having to leave to take their boat to India, Lawrence and Brett decided that they would go to near-by Amalfi in the Gulf of Salerno. He had been there before in 1920 and liked it,[80] but another incentive was probably learning in Capri that, just above Amalfi, at Ravello, Millicent Beveridge and Mabel Harrison were staying at the Hotel Palumbo. When he and Brett arrived at that hotel on 11 March, however, they found it full and had to be given the key to some converted stone cottages which were close by and served as its annexe. For the next few days they explored the beautiful town with Lawrence's two painter friends: 'I have asked Miss Beveridge and Miss Harrison to walk down to Amalfi with us. My throat feels a little sore, and I want to buy some mustard plasters. Just in case, that's all; I'm all right, really', Brett reported Lawrence as saying.[81] Through the Brewsters, she is likely to have met Lucy Beckett whose father, the second Baron Grimthorpe, belonged to the Buddhist Society in London, was a student of oriental philosophy, but also happened to own the Palazzo Cimbrone in Ravello.[82] It was while they were in the Cimbrone gardens that Lawrence and Brett saw a statue of Venus which had turned bluey green, because of the effect of the sunlight on copper, and decided to paint it. Brett characteristically agreed that her version was less satisfactory than Lawrence's – too ladylike; although she thought her colour better than his. ' "Colour is not everything", you reply tartly.'[83] On or about 15 March, this pleasant period of sight-seeing and painting came to an abrupt end and Brett left Ravello in such haste that Lawrence had to send her laundry on after her.

Brett gave two different explanations of why she decided to leave so suddenly. The first more or less concludes the memoir of Lawrence which she published in 1933, and describes how she was summoned to the American Consulate in Naples to deal with her immigration papers. Reluctant to leave Lawrence, she was encouraged by him not to miss the chance of securing her quota number and told that perhaps they could meet again in Florence. The second account does not seem to have been written before the late 1960s. In it Brett explains that the two bedrooms she and Lawrence occupied in the hotel annexe were next to each other.

One evening Lawrence walked into her room in his dressing gown. Saying that he did not believe in a close relationship unless there was a physical dimension as well, he got into bed with her. Brett writes that she felt an 'overwhelming desire to be adequate', was 'passionately eager to be successful', but 'had no idea what to do'. Nothing happened and with 'It's no good', Lawrence suddenly got up and left the room. The next night they tried again with Brett doing her best to be 'loving and warm and female' but the result was a 'hopeless horrible failure'. When Lawrence got up to leave this time Brett's account has him saying, 'Your pubes are wrong.'[84] The remark left her feeling 'ashamed, bewildered, miserable'. The next day she found Lawrence in a rage and packing his bags to leave Ravello. She said that because his two painter friends were expecting to do some travelling with him, it would be better if *she* left and if she gave as an excuse that she had to go to Naples to collect her citizenship papers. Lawrence then accompanied Brett in the carriage down to Amalfi and put her on the boat to Capri. There was some not very precise talk of meeting again shortly, but they never did.

There are of course problems with Brett's second account of what happened in Ravello. If it is true, then the first contained a deliberate falsehood which could make some people wonder what the rest of her testimony is worth. She was moreover devoted to Lawrence and may in her last years have been indulging in an old woman's fantasy, or profiting to the end from the attention which her friendship with him had brought.[85] Even if we could be certain that what she did remember him saying was 'pubes' and not, as in several subsequent accounts, 'boobs' (a slang expression for breasts which only became current after World War II) that word is almost equally bizarre and one which one never finds Lawrence using elsewhere. In addition to these particular objections, there is a general rule that a memoir will be more trustworthy the nearer its composition is to the events described. Brett began writing her first account shortly after Lawrence's death in 1930. Her second belongs to a period almost half a century after she had seen Lawrence for the last time.

A fair review of the evidence nevertheless seems to indicate that, if all the details of Brett's second account are unlikely to be reliable, it must be true in substance. Some such episode as the one it describes was always likely to have been the culmination of Lawrence's long relationship with her. In his hostile letter to Brett from Oaxaca he had made clear how uncomfortable it made him that their closeness should not be physical as well as mental or spiritual; and his temporary alienation from Frieda in 1926, together with the accident of being together with Brett in a building apart from the hotel, provided a natural context for discovering whether they could establish their relationship on a new, more satisfactory footing. Because sex is a subject on which the most truthful of people tell lies, Brett's first account of the episode is no necessary indictment of her general credibility; but in any case how *could* she have told the truth in a book published in 1933, with Frieda still very much alive and given the discretion of publishers in those days? The second account has a narrative coherence which the first lacks: Naples is not far from Ravello so why could Lawrence not have accompanied her there, or why could Brett not have gone and come back? It may be that Lawrence did not refer to Brett's 'pubes'; or even that she was wrong in remembering that he transferred to her all of the blame for the fiasco in Ravello in such a cruel way. Yet that there was some such misfortune seems reasonably certain. In his first surviving communication to Brett after she had left (a postcard written on 17 March), Lawrence says 'Am sending your washing. Letter from Frieda – much milder. She wants to leave on Apr 10th and go to Germany', and he reports that he has moved up to the main part of the hotel (v. 405). A day later he wrote a letter the second paragraph of which reads:

One has just to forget, and to accept what is good. We can't help being more or less damaged. What we have to do is to stick to the good part of ourselves, and of each other, and continue an understanding on that. I don't see why we shouldn't be *better* friends, instead of worse. But one must not try to force anything. (v. 406)

These are not the remarks of a man whose closeness to Brett had been interrupted by a call from the American Consulate in Naples.

'Fiasco' was the word Stendhal adopted for the inability to have or maintain an erection: a sexual misfortune which from time to time overtook him, often when he was at last on the point of making love with a woman to whom he had long been paying court. In him, these episodes were certainly not an indication of any *general* failing of sexual powers. The events in Ravello, on the other hand, have frequently been taken as conclusive proof of Lawrence's physical impotence. Given his state of health that interpretation may well be accurate, but it is impossible to be certain. All the signs are that by March 1926 he had not made love with Frieda for a long time, perhaps because he was no longer physically capable of doing so or because he now found her, from a sexual point of view, increasingly intimidating and overpowering. Brett may have offered him the opportunity of reaffirming his potency with someone much less expert and experienced; but, as her account makes painfully clear, that could well have been part of the trouble. The impression one draws from *Aaron's Rod* is that Lawrence was deeply monogamous, not necessarily out of moral principle but because he was hard to suit. If he was going to sleep with anyone other than his wife, he needed the right encouragement (of the kind which Rosalind Baynes seems to have been able to provide in September 1920[86]). Brett had not had sexual relations with a man before she was thirty-nine and it is possible that Murry had been her only sexual partner until her last meeting with Lawrence. Yet it is possible also that she could have been everything that was required in the difficult circumstances and the result would still have been the same.

Whether the origins of what seems to have happened in Ravello were physical or psychological, it was a sad business for both parties, and a miserable culmination to the kind of fascination with Brett which Lawrence had revealed in 'The Last Laugh' or the ending of *The Boy in the Bush*. In November of the previous year Mark Gertler had written sourly from the Mundesley Sanatorium to Kot:

I do not believe that Lawrence is trying to get away from [Brett]. It is somehow not his way. I do not even credit him with that kind of decency. He seems to me to prefer always hurling himself back and back into relationships with people – even when they have long since become rotten – take for instance his relationship with Murry. Of course he cannot do that with you because you are different. But with Brett, I should not be surprised if he were *still* intrigued – though knowing – in a way – what she is. If he wanted to get rid of a person I think he could be pretty direct – and if he couldn't Frieda could. No, I think he and Brett will drag on for ages yet – probably some conspiracy a little against us.[87]

The last phrase, with its quite groundless suspicion, suggests how unreliable Gertler's impressions might be; yet it is true that when Lawrence liked, or had once liked, somebody a great deal, his feelings for them could be surprisingly persistent. His long association with Murry had now petered out and that with Brett had come to a point which meant either a new, more fulfilling phase or a minor psychic disaster (for one of the two parties at least). Brett describes in her second version of events how devastated she felt by 'the whole misery, the torment of the failure in Ravello', a misery which would have been all the more intense if what she told John Manchester was true: that Lawrence had said he would leave Frieda if he and Brett could develop a relationship which was as successful on the physical as it was on the spiritual plane.[88] She must have written of her distress to Lawrence, who on 21 March wrote back in terms one can hope were as much for his own benefit as hers:

The greatest virtue in life is real courage, that knows how to face facts and live beyond them. Don't be Murryish, pitying yourself and caving in. It's despicable. I should have thought, after a dose of that fellow, you'd have had too much desire to be different from him, to follow his sloppy self-indulgent melancholics, absolutely despicable. Rouse up and make a decent thing of your days, no matter what's happened. I do loathe cowardice and sloppy emotion. My God, did you learn *nothing* from Murry, of how *not* to behave? Even you write the sort of letters he writes![89]   (v. 408)

Brett now did in fact go to Naples to collect her citizenship papers and then (according to the second account) agreed to take charge of a disturbed girl on a visit to Florence where she hoped to bump into Lawrence. 'Had no idea you were in or near Florence' he told her on a postcard when he got back to Spotorno at the beginning of April (v. 410), and on the 4th he wrote: 'I had no idea you had come to Florence – do hope you were not really ill. I went to Perugia and

Ravenna with Mabel Harrison and Milly Beveridge.' In the same letter he said that he felt the best thing for her to do was to go to America, and suggested that she might live at Kiowa, rather than Del Monte, if she could find someone congenial to share such an isolated house (v. 412). By the 8th, Brett had written to say she would like to take up Lawrence's offer and must have suggested a final meeting before she sailed. 'I don't think it would be any use our meeting again just now', he replied, 'we should only be upset. Better get a fresh start on all round: we need it badly' (v. 417). On the 11th, he encouraged Brett in a plan she had to go to Perugia and recommended the Etruscan collection there: 'I might come down there later to see if I can do a book: but at present don't feel like making any effort of any sort' (v. 420). On the same day he told the Brewsters that Brett had determined on America: 'She says she will sail, and I think it's best. She can't stand Capri any more: and I can't stand it when she clings too tight' (v. 421).

On 17 March, after receiving the 'much milder' letter from Frieda he had mentioned to Brett, Lawrence had told Kot that he expected to be in Spotorno the following week (v. 404). Going with his women friends first to Rome, where he arrived on the 22nd, he moved up to Florence via Assisi and Perugia, and then cut across country to Ravenna before arriving back in Spotorno on Easter Saturday, 3 April, about six weeks after he had first left. It may be that he felt he needed the extra time away from both Frieda and Brett, in pleasant but unchallenging company, to calm his nerves. In Perugia he was so taken with the Etruscan artifacts in the museum that, once back in Spotorno, he mentions to several different correspondents the plan he now has for writing a book on Etruscan civilisation (v. 413–15).

On his arrival home, Lawrence was greeted warmly at the station by Frieda and her daughters. They appeared, and perhaps genuinely were, glad to have him back. Elsa and Barby had lectured their mother on the need to keep her temper in order – 'Now Mrs L. (so they called me) be reasonable, you have married him, now you must stick to him';[90] and however much consolation for Lawrence's absence she had already found, or as yet merely perceived, in Angelo Ravagli, she must have felt that at thirty-five, married and with three children, her landlord was unlikely to represent at this stage a viable, permanent alternative. Writing to Kot while Lawrence was in Ravello she had described herself as like a 'proud old hen' as she watched Italian youths hanging around her daughters, told him that she was translating David into German, and said that she was worried about Lawrence's health ('I don't think Lawrence is fit to go to Russia').[91] Once he was back with her, Lawrence told Brett and others that he was in fact feeling well. 'I'm also much better,' he told his mother-in-law on 4 April, 'almost as in the past, only always a touch of bronchitis. But they say, an Englishman of 40 is almost always bronchial' (v. 411). Since he had fallen so ill at the beginning of February, he had not done any writing and on 5 April felt he needed to apologise to Curtis Brown, whose own income of course depended upon his authors' continuing productivity. 'Don't mind if I have blank times when I don't write – I am like that' (v. 415). In retrospect one could feel that a man who, just before he fell ill, had finished 'The Rocking-Horse Winner' and *The Virgin and the Gipsy*, as well as 'Sun' and 'Glad Ghosts', was entitled to a rest.

Family life came to seem more agreeable to Lawrence in April as he observed how Frieda's daughters treated their mother. Whatever had happened in Ravello did not make Lawrence feel that he should no longer keep in regular contact with Brett and on the 11th he told her:

We get on quite well here. Frieda's children are quite fierce with her, and fall on her tooth and nail. They simply won't stand her egotism for a minute: she is furious, then becomes almost humble with us all. I think *they've* taught her a lesson. Being her own family, they can go for her exactly in her own way, and pretty well silence her. It makes me die with laughing. She's caught more than she bargained for, in her own offspring. Makes her really appreciative of me: and she quite sees that you too are not the most terrible person on earth. (v. 420)

He was characteristically indeterminate about what he should do when the lease on the Villa Bernarda expired towards the end of the month. Frieda intended to take her daughters to see her mother in Baden-Baden before they had to return to England, but Lawrence did not want to go to Germany and toyed with various ideas, including settling in Perugia for a while to work on the Etruscans (v. 416, 421). The only thing he was sure of was that, although Frieda would have liked to go back to the ranch in the summer, he would not. Brett was now due to sail for Boston from Naples on 2 May and, in a letter to the Hawks, Lawrence tried to smooth her way, at the same time insisting that if she did go to live on the ranch it should not be alone, and urging Rachel Hawk to do what she could to make Brett more responsible about money (v. 429). Writing to Mabel Luhan, he had also announced Brett's imminent arrival but then gone on to re-iterate his suspicion of Gourdjieff whose influence on Mabel's thinking his previous remarks had clearly not eliminated. 'I do believe in self-discipline', he told her, 'And I don't believe in self-control'; and then, memorably, 'But the fact that your I is not your own makes necessary a discipline more patient and flexible and long-lasting than any [of] Gourdjieff's' (v. 423). This letter was written on 12 April. A week later it had been decided that he would accompany Frieda and her daughters to Florence and then stay on there while they made a short visit to Baden-Baden.

CHAPTER THIRTEEN

◆

April–October 1926

FLORENCE AND ENGLAND

I Villa Mirenda

The Lawrence party arrived in Florence on 20 April and went to the Pensione Lucchesi, on the Lungarno della Zecca Vecchia, where Lawrence had stayed before, and which had been recommended to him by Brett within the last fortnight (v. 418). The following day was 'Natale Romana', a new national holiday that had replaced May Day in the Fascist calendar. Bands played in the streets and there was much singing of 'Giovinezza' ('Youth'), the surprisingly cheerful and inoffensive-sounding hymn of the Fascist movement. Since Lawrence was last in Florence in 1921, Mussolini had gained complete control of Italy, in the first instance largely by means of squads of an unofficial militia organised very much as Lawrence imagines Ben Cooley's Diggers are organised in *Kangaroo*.[1] Through a combination of intimidation and demagoguery, he had emasculated Parliament, compromised the King, crushed or sometimes murdered the opposition and established a dictatorship. Yet his regime was not especially efficient and at this stage its effect on foreign residents was minimal. Lawrence was at first not openly hostile but neither was he enthusiastic. He had written disparagingly of Mussolini in *Reflections on the Death of a Porcupine*, and when the news had reached him in Spotorno that a demented Irishwoman's attempt to assassinate Il Duce on 7 April had only succeeded in leaving him with a damaged nose, Lawrence's response had been, 'Put a ring through it.'[2]

It must have been once they were in Florence that Frieda and her daughters decided against going to Baden-Baden: Elsa and Barby were in any case due to return to England by the end of the month (they said goodbye to the Lawrences on 28 April – v. 442). Lawrence wanted to prepare for his book on the Etruscans but, beyond that, had no very definite plans. Frieda on the other hand was once again anxious to rent a place of their own until July (the Baden-Baden visit having been postponed until then). Through friends in the expatriate community they must have met the Wilkinson brothers, one of whom (Arthur Gair) was settled with his family in a villa to the southeast of Florence. The Wilkinsons knew that the owner of the villa closest to Arthur's – Raul Mirenda – lived in town, visited his country property only intermittently and had a whole top floor which he no longer used. The Lawrences inspected the Villa Mirenda on 29 April and, although they were not able on that occasion to see the top-floor rooms, liked it very much (v. 444). They met the owner who was sufficiently taken with Lawrence to rent his top floor to them – something he later said he had never done before and did not do again.[3] The first price Lawrence mentioned in his letters was 4,000 lire (for a whole year); but in the event he paid only 3,000 (v. 443, 453). This was the equivalent of £25 and the same sum he had paid for four months at the Villa Bernarda. At the Pensione Lucchesi the daily tariff was 45 lire for each of them (v. 446). Although neither of the Lawrences envisaged remaining in Florence for a year, this annual rent was cheap enough for them to regard the Villa Mirenda as a useful *pied à terre* and one which, moreover, could serve as a base for Lawrence's Etruscan excursions. Happy with their choice, they moved in on 6 May (v. 449).

Raul Mirenda (his family was of Spanish origin although its more immediate provenance was Sicilian) called his house the Villa di San Polo because it was in the tiny hamlet of San Polo Mosciano, but everyone else seems to have referred to it by his family name. Lawrence described how to get there many times. You took the tram from the centre of Florence in the direction of Scandicci, as unattractive a place then as it is now, if Walter Wilkinson's reference to 'that long sordid village on the plain' is to be believed.[4] After about half an hour the tram reached its terminus just beyond Scandicci at the Ponte Vingone, from where there was a half-hour walk into the hills. Setting directly off into the country from the terminus, you walked about half a mile uphill past a 'pagoda house' and then turned left for San Polo (a dialect version of Paolo) at a junction marked in Lawrence's time by 'two cypresses' (vi. 451). The road then went down, but as you emerged from the dip, there on the brow of the hill opposite was the Villa Mirenda, squat yet imposing and from that angle the most striking building in all the surrounding Tuscan countryside of vineyards, olive trees and woods. Behind the house, which was said to date from the time of the Medicis, stood a church with half a dozen small houses clustered round. From the villa's windows and terraces there were beautiful views: on one side the foothills of the Apennines and on another a view over Florence to the Duomo, with the hills of the far more fashionable Fiesole rising up beyond. An advantage of not being in the fashionable area for country retreat, which Lawrence immediately noticed, was that the Wilkinsons were the only other foreigners in the area (vi. 453).

The top story of the Villa Mirenda consisted of six bare rooms. Conditions were primitive with oil lamps, charcoal fires for cooking and no running water; but with his increasing fear of the cold Lawrence must have been pleased to discover that there was a large stove in the sitting room (the *salotto*) because the Mirenda family had once bred silk worms. According to Raul Mirenda, the rent included 'service': help in and around the house from two young people from one of the estate's three peasant families – Giulia Pini, who was fifteen, and the twenty-year-old Pietro Degli Innocenti, who was not a blood relation of Guilia's but had been unofficially adopted from an early age into the Pini family.[5] It emerges clearly from the letters however that the Lawrences did in fact pay extra for the assistance of these two. With what one must presume was his landlord's permission, he quickly began painting the woodwork and one or two extra pieces of furniture were acquired. After their return to the house in autumn, these would include a hired piano (v. 599): not to have had one to play in Kiowa, for example, deprived Frieda of what was perhaps her chief form of relaxation.[6] Their surroundings could never be luxurious but both were used to the simple life and, when weather permitted, Lawrence would in any case spend a good deal of his time outside, sitting in the open against an olive tree in order to write, or retreating into the neighbouring woods which were full of nightingales (v. 479).

One of the short essays Lawrence wrote after his arrival at the Villa Mirenda celebrates the nightingales in the area which he says 'sing all the time, save in the middle of the night and the middle of the day'.[7] He wonders why such an 'obstreperous and jaunty bird' made Keats sad, and concludes that, in spite of assertions to the contrary in the 'Ode to the Nightingale', 'it is a sadness which is half envy': that Keats felt sad by contrast. His commentary on the Ode is an indirect reply to Murry's. Lawrence had recognised that *Keats and Shakespeare* was a good book, but also complained that it was 'so die away' and maudlin (v. 337). 'The nightingale never made any man in love with easeful death—except by contrast', he insists; and he goes on to imagine what the response of the female nightingale might be to her mate's singing.

Probably she likes it, for she goes on breeding him as jaunty as ever. Probably she prefers his high cockalorum to the poet's humble moan

"Now more than ever seems it rich to die

To cease upon the midnight with no pain—"

That wouldn't be much use to the hen nightingale. And one sympathises with Keats's Fanny, and understands why she wasn't having any. Much good such a midnight would have been to *her*![8]

Even more indirectly than a reply to Murry, this short piece is also a meditation by Lawrence on how to deal with his 'bronchials', and a characteristic protest against self-pity.

'The Nightingale' was probably written in June[9] but on 13 May, a week after his arrival in the Villa Mirenda, Lawrence had sent off to Nancy Pearn 'Two Blue Birds', a short story only incidentally concerned with ornithology. Its opening sentence – 'There was a woman who loved her husband, but she could not live with him'[10] – echoes precisely a phrase he had used about Faith Mackenzie when writing to Ada from Capri in March (v. 403); and it shows that he had continued to ponder the Mackenzies' unusual marital arrangements. Lawrence hoped that the results of his pondering would not be a 'tribulation' to Nancy Pearn (v. 451). His story is in fact an intelligent and subtle analysis in which the wife has all the good lines; but that did not prevent Faith Mackenzie from bitterly resenting what she regarded as a betrayal of trust. Her husband claimed to have been unaffected but his behaviour later, over another story for which his characteristics were borrowed ('The Man Who Loved Islands'), suggests that he may have secretly shared his wife's resentment.[11]

In 'Two Blue Birds' a woman who lives abroad and has 'gallant affairs' goes back home to visit her husband for a spell. He is a writer who is being made very comfortable by a housekeeper, one of whose daughters acts as a 'sort of upper maid' while the other is his devoted secretary. Because of his large expenses (which include having to pay for the cocktails his wife drinks in fashionable locations on the continent), he is obliged to work very hard, ten or eleven hours a day; but at least he has everything to smooth his path with 'absolutely nobody and nothing, to contradict him'. The wife feels that this situation is unhealthy and in the finale, after her husband has been disturbed in his constant dictation by two blue birds fighting, decides to make her protest. She invites the devoted secretary to stay and have tea with herself and her husband (both the women are wearing blue dresses); and she then proceeds to dominate the potentially awkward situation. When in response to the usual request the secretary timidly says that she will have her tea 'as it comes', the wife retorts: 'It's coming pretty black, if you want to ruin your digestion' and adds some water. She feels that it is not so much her husband's huge output which is affecting the quality of his writing as the too-comfortable circumstances in which it is produced, and offends him mortally by maliciously suggesting his work reads as if his secretary had written it herself: ' "Do you mean to say my books read as if–" he began, rearing up and speaking in a narrowed voice. / "I do!" said his wife. *"Just* as if Miss Wrexall had written them from your hints. I *honestly* thought she did—when you were too busy—" / "How very clever of you!" he said.'[12] In the acid drawing-room comedy manner Lawrence had deployed so successfully in 'The Captain's Doll' and *St. Mawr*, the wife then protests that her husband is taking everything from his secretary and giving her nothing in return:

"But he gives me everything, everything!" cried Miss Wrexall. "He gives me everything!"

"What do you mean by everything," said the wife, turning on her sternly.

Miss Wrexall pulled up short. There was a snap in the air, and a change of currents.

"I mean nothing that *you* need begrudge me," said the little secretary rather haughtily. "I've never made myself cheap".

There was a blank pause.

"My God!" said the wife. "You don't call that being cheap! Why, I should say you got nothing out of him at all, you only give! And if you don't call that making yourself cheap— my God!—"[13]

Faith Mackenzie felt wounded that Lawrence had used in 'Two Blue Birds' intimate details about her marriage which she had given him in confidence. (She cannot have been pleased also that he was so frank about her love affairs.) Compton Mackenzie had much more to complain about in that the story supported a general perception of the time that his work was deteriorating in quality. After claiming to be unaffected, he developed over the years a standard response to having been used as a model in this story and (far less directly) 'The Man Who Loved Islands'. This was that Lawrence had the unfortunate habit of creating figures who, in appearance and surroundings, had a photographic resemblance to others when in fact all of them were versions of himself.[14] Although at the primary level 'Two Blue Birds' will always remain a portrait of the Mackenzies, there is some truth in his claim, and not merely because there is an obvious sense in which *all* Lawrence's characters are emanations of himself. The wife's chief complaint about her husband and his secretary is after all very like the complaint Frieda had made about Brett and Lawrence: she too had felt (or at least claimed to feel) that there was something indecent about a platonic or non-physical intimacy. Moreover the notion that too much comfort, in the form in this case of too much coddling, is inimical to creativity was a rule Lawrence had certainly adopted for his own use. A few months later, on what would be a last visit to Eastwood, his old friend Willie Hopkin had the temerity to ask, as the two of them were looking down on Haggs Farm, why he had not married Jessie Chambers. Angered, Lawrence refused to respond for a while but he is then reported to have said: 'It would have been a fatal step. I should have had too easy a life, nearly everything my own way, and my genius would have been destroyed.'[15]

During the first three weeks of the Lawrences' stay at the Villa Mirenda the weather was very bad, with lots of rain. This, Lawrence complained, was 'bad for one's bronchials' (v. 455). At the end of May, in a letter to Rachel Hawk, he compared himself to her two-year-old son Walton, of whom he had been very fond: 'As for poor old Walton, he's cursed, like me, with bronchials, and a curse they are, though you don't easily die of them' (v. 467). Rachel and her husband had fallen on hard times and were having to move from the house at Del Monte while William took a job in the Forest Service which would involve a good deal of travel. Lawrence's suggestion was that, for the time being, she and her two children should go to live at Kiowa with Brett (v. 466). It was a weight off his mind when this happened. He had been anxious about Brett living at the ranch alone, partly because he was genuinely concerned about the potential for psychological damage in that degree of isolation; but also because he feared that Brett, who he knew had no sense of financial responsibility, would run up debts for general maintenance for which he would then become responsible.

The arrangement with Rachel meant one worry less, but there were other anxieties involving those close to him. At the beginning of May a national coal stoppage began in England, to be accompanied on the 5th by the country's first-ever General Strike. This lasted a little over a week, but the miners held out after it was over, persisting in their resistance to the employers' attempt to make the industry more competitive on the international market by lowering wages. Lawrence was worried about the effects of the continuing coal strike on his sisters, both of whose husbands were shopkeepers in mining areas; but he was also fearful that the conflict would lead to class war. On 17 May he told Koteliansky, 'Myself, I'm scared of a class war in England. It would be the beginning of the end of all things'; and on 1 June he asked his sister Ada how her business was going 'with the beastly strike. Really, it's too bad they let it come to a strike: very dangerous too, because it may start a real class war, and England is the one country where that is most dangerous' (v. 455, 467–8).

Less insouciant than he had been in the past, Lawrence was also concerned about his own writing future. He was being pressed by his publishers for another novel (preferably one like *Sons and Lovers!*), but felt no urge to write one. On the whole the reception of *The Plumed Serpent* had not been enthusiastic.[16] The effort to finish that novel was closely associated in his mind with his collapse in Oaxaca, and he felt resentful that the critical and financial rewards of an endeavour which had almost killed him should be so paltry: 'Why write books for the swine, unless one absolutely must!' (v. 483). At the end of July he would tell Brett: 'I am not doing any work at all: feel sufficiently disgusted with myself for having done so much and undermined my health, with so little return. Pity one has to write at all' (v. 504). On 27 June he told Nancy Pearn that he had another story which was 'nearly done' (he was referring to 'The Man Who Loved Islands'); and he went on, 'But little articles, if people like 'em, are much the easiest' (v. 482). Three days before, he and Frieda had been in Florence for the San Giovanni festival (the Feast of the Nativity of John the Baptist). Lawrence wrote a short, evocative but not especially significant account of the celebrations which he was able to sell. He knew that with slight pieces like this, which cost him only a fraction of the effort required for a story and yet might often bring in at least half as much, he could keep himself going until he once again felt the urge to tackle something substantial.[17]

The increasing concern about money which Lawrence exhibited at this time is a complicated phenomenon with many different determinants, but one of them was certainly a fear of having to commit himself to a major enterprise without really wanting to. A contemporary such as Compton Mackenzie was like Cynthia Asquith in having established a very high standard of living that required for its maintenance large sums of money. In 1922 Eric Pinker (son and successor of the famous literary agent J. B.) had guaranteed Mackenzie an annual £6,000 against his future literary earnings, but this on the assumption that after three years his client would make good any deficit. Wealth of this kind was something Lawrence had never remotely known, even in his best days with Seltzer. A more relevant comparison would therefore be with Aldous Huxley who in 1923 signed a contract with Chatto and Windus which guaranteed him an annual £500 for the next three years on the condition that he provided 'two new works of fiction per annum (one of which two works shall be a full length novel)'. When this agreement was renewed for a further three years in 1926, the annual income went up to £650 and the conditions became two books per annum 'one of which at least a full-length novel' and 'possibly three other books during the said three years'.[18] Welcome though a guaranteed income would have been, Lawrence must have known that his health would no longer allow that kind of rhythm; but he felt in any case a strong repugnance against *forcing* his talent in any way. Once Mabel Luhan had broken the ice, Lawrence corresponded regularly with her about her memoirs, which he thought good but too indiscreet to be published, or at least published in a normal form. He felt that, a little like Mollie Skinner, Mabel only wrote well when she was concerned with what she knew or remembered well, and in November 1926 would give her three of his own general rules: 'Don't write if you're out of mood. Don't force yourself. And wait for grace' (v. 579).

To continue with his plans for a book on the Etruscans was not to force his talent, and Lawrence was in any event reconciled to taking his time. He had read the standard English work on the subject, George Dennis's *Cities and Cemeteries of Etruria* (first published in 1848 but available in Everyman since 1907) and, perhaps because of the research he had been obliged to do for *Movements in European History*, he knew what Theodor Mommsen had to say in his *History of Rome* (v. 413, 465). Now he made arrangements to get hold of a German book on Etruscan art (*Etruskishe Malerei* by Fritz Weege), read a scholarly Italian tome, Pericle Ducati's *Etruria antica*, and received from Milly Beveridge, who was back in England, R. A. L. Fell's *Etruria and Rome* (v. 465, 473). He was disappointed to realise that all the authorities tended to repeat each other and 'There really is next to nothing to be said, *scientifically*, about the Etruscans'; but that at least meant he was free to take 'the imaginative line' (v. 473). One can see him beginning to do this in a letter he wrote to Else Jaffe on 26 May. There he says that the real strength of Italy seems to him to lie in Etruscan physicality 'which is not at all Roman' (v. 465). He must have become aware how important the supposed values of imperial Rome were in Fascist ideology, and begun to perceive Etruscan culture as a necessary counterweight. For the moment however he delayed the visits he was intending to make to the chief Etruscan centres, spending much of his time instead typing the translation of *David* which Frieda had now completed. This was a task he had taken over from her daughter Elsa and he found it laborious, in part because, even on the now very familiar machine

304

he had recovered from Brett, he did not type well, especially in German; but also because he could not help continually altering Frieda's version. She may have known German better than he did but who was it after all who had written the text? Lawrence spent so much of the early summer typing that it must have been a relief to him that Frieda never fulfilled her firmly declared intention of translating *The Plumed Serpent* next (v. 470).

As in June the Italian summer finally arrived and the weather improved, so did Lawrence's mood. He and Frieda began to profit fully from the richness and beauty of their new surroundings and the neighbouring Wilkinsons proved very good occasional company. In a letter to his niece Peggy, Lawrence had described Arthur Wilkinson as having 'the wildest red beard, sticking out all round' and said that wife, son and daughter were all kitted out with 'sandals and knapsacks'. 'But', he had added, 'they're jolly and very clever: paint, and play guitar and things' (v. 447). The Wilkinson family were middle-class bohemians, pacifist, left-wing and vegetarian but shared with the Lawrences a taste for the simple life and a delight in home entertainment: charades, games, singing. In England Arthur had taken a puppet theatre round the sea-side resorts, using puppets he had made himself. This form of cultural revivalism was always attractive to Lawrence and he told Peggy that if the Wilkinsons were to bring their puppet caravan to Italy he would travel around with them, banging the drum. He and Frieda saw the family quite often – as many as eighty times in their two-year tenancy of the Villa Mirenda – and clearly found them an important social resource.[19]

The Lawrences enjoyed the relative isolation of the country (the nearest shop was in Scandicci), but not so much that they did not appreciate visits to the Wilkinsons or go into Florence once or twice a week to see friends. Among the expatriates their chief initial contact was Reggie Turner, a rich minor novelist from the 1890s who had lived for years in the Viale Milton and was well known for his wit and kindness. The kindness had been evident in his continuing loyalty to Oscar Wilde during the difficult last years after Wilde's release from prison. The wit, celebrated most notably by his friend from Oxford days, Max Beerbohm, did not transfer itself to paper and is harder to illustrate, but something of its flavour is perhaps apparent in a remark about a friend who was writing a life of Botticelli: 'Dear Herbert Horne! Poring over Botticelli's washing bills – and always a shirt missing!'[20] Lawrence had been introduced to Turner by Norman Douglas in 1919 but when he first arrived in Florence with Frieda and her daughters, he found that Douglas was in Greece ('Apparently he's deep deep in a book on "The Flowers of the Greek Anthology"' – v. 444); and when in June Douglas reappeared Lawrence was still too irritated by the Magnus affair to renew the contact: 'I saw Douglas in a cafe and didn't speak to him: felt I couldn't stand him' (v. 472).

It would have been through Turner therefore, rather than Douglas, that Lawrence now first got to know well the antiquarian bookseller, Guiseppe ('Pino') Orioli. They had met briefly during the war when Orioli was visiting the Crocker family, who had a bungalow between Penzance and Zennor and were friends of his business partner, Irving Davis, and again when Lawrence came to Florence without Frieda in the summer of 1920;[21] but it was only now that they became close. A year older than Lawrence, Orioli had at the age of twelve been obliged to leave school and go to work in a barber's shop because of the bankruptcy of his shopkeeper-father. At fourteen he had moved from his home town of Alfonsine, near Ravenna, to Florence where one of his brothers was settled and where he once again worked as a barber. In 1907, after three years of military service, he made his way to London and endured some difficult moments before picking up sufficient English to set himself up as a teacher of Italian. He later claimed that one of his pupils was Dr Crippen, executed in 1910 for poisoning his wife, but another was certainly Davis who at that time was still at Cambridge and through whom he met several of the university's personalities, including Lytton Strachey. In spite of his lack of formal education, Orioli had managed by this period to acquire enough culture to be an acceptable companion to highly educated young men (especially when they happened to be homosexual), and he had also developed a keen interest in the antiquarian book trade. When Davis completed his degree in 1910, he and Orioli set up shop in Florence, helped by Davis's father, a wealthy dentist. When they then both fell in love with 'the same creature',[22] they decided in 1913 to move to London in order to preserve their friendship and opened a shop at 24 Museum Street. During the war Orioli was in England quite often, once he had managed to have himself attached to the Italian Military Mission in London; but when it was over he left Davis there and went back to Florence in order to open premises of his own. At the time Turner brought Orioli and Lawrence together again, his shop was on the Lungarno Corsini, near the Ponte Santa Trinità, although he kept a flat in one of the streets which runs off the cathedral square.[23]

Two people still alive in the 1990s who remember Orioli, do so with great fondness. Barbara Barr insists that in company he was even funnier than Douglas; and Ianthe Carswell, wife of John Patrick but also a daughter of Irving Davis, was struck by his kindness and good nature.[24] Richard Aldington, paying tribute to his inexhaustible cheerfulness, felt that he had a 'keener sense of life' than anyone he had ever met, apart from Lawrence.[25] After 1930, Orioli published material highly critical of Lawrence, but while he was still alive the letters suggest how remarkably considerate and accommodating Pino could be. In the months and years to come, Lawrence would have good reason to feel grateful to Turner for bringing them together again.

A less successful but by no means entirely futile meeting for which Turner is also likely to have been responsible was with Sir George and Lady Ida Sitwell. The consequence of this was a visit on 2 June to the Sitwells' immense and sprawling Castello di Montegufoni, fourteen miles out of Florence, where the eccentric Sir George subjected the Lawrences to a guided tour of his collection of beds, principally (Lawrence remarked) 'those four-poster golden venetian monsters that look like Mexican high altars' (v. 474), but where they at least received an invitation to visit the Sitwells' country house in Derbyshire in August, presumably on the understanding that they would then have the opportunity of meeting Sir George and Lady Ida's artistic children.[26] The Montegufoni trip was not an especially enjoyable diversion but others were more so and all in all the Lawrences seem, in these first weeks at the Villa Mirenda, to have discovered the right mix between privacy and social contact: to have temporarily solved (that is) the problem of how much one needs others which Lawrence was pondering very seriously at this period as he wrote 'The Man Who Loved Islands'.

While the sun continued to shine Frieda became so contented with their new rhythm of life that she no longer wanted to move (v. 479), but there was her mother's seventy-fifth birthday on 14 July, and arrangements had already been made to visit Baden-Baden for that. Lawrence himself was quite keen to go to London where two theatrical societies which had recently amalgamated appeared to be on the point of giving *David* its first staging: 'Seems to me I'd better have a finger in that pie' (v. 474). Ada had taken a bungalow in Mablethorpe for August and hoped to be visited there by her brother, although not his wife, who would stay in the Chelsea flat for which Lawrence had been negotiating through Milly Beveridge (v. 476, 490), and enjoy the company of her children. In addition, Lawrence had been invited to Inverness-shire where Milly Beveridge and her sister had a house, and also asked by Compton Mackenzie – 'Two Blue Birds' had not yet appeared – to come and see the third island he had recently acquired (v. 474) – actually a cluster of islands called the Shiants between Lewis and Skye.[27] All these visits, firmly promised or in prospect, meant that there was too much to cancel at short notice and by 12 July the Lawrences had packed their bags and were on the move again.

II Baden-Baden Again

Arriving in Baden-Baden on the 13th, Lawrence drank the hot spring waters. Their taste is no more pleasant than in most spas, but no-one relies on them to slake a thirst and he felt they were good for his 'miserable bronchi' (v. 502). One of the doctors attached to the Baths suggested that he should come back in September and take the 'inhalation cure' and for a time during his coming stay in England he was tempted to do so. Certainly he felt that he ought to try and do something about 'those bronchials of mine' before the winter came on (v. 502, 503).

He was contented enough in Germany, despite the presence of most of Frieda's family for the matriarch's birthday, and found Baden-Baden relaxing after Florence where there was a continual state of nervous excitement as Mussolini promulgated measure after measure in order to tighten his control. On 16 July Lawrence explained to Edward McDonald that he felt he now had a right to take it easy: 'One does get dead sick of struggling ahead among the brick-bats and tin cans of our most modern world. The second half of one's life – I am forty – should surely be one's own, after one has more or less given away the first half, for a pound of imitation tea.' Yet in the same letter he was scathing about the old people in his mother-in-law's Home, whose only concern was to cling on to life. He reports her as proclaiming triumphantly, 'Wir alten, wir sind noch hier!' ('We old ones, we are still here!') and goes on:

And here they mean to stay, having, through long and uninterrupted experience, become adepts at hanging on to their own lives, and letting anybody else who is fool enough cast bread upon the waters. BadenBaden is a sort of Holbein *Totentanz*: old, old people tottering their cautious dance of triumph: 'wir sind noch hier: hupf! hupf! hupf!'

(v. 495–6)

That he had himself still not completely discounted some form of active future involvement in the communal affairs of life is evident from two letters he wrote at this time to Rolf Gardiner. Still in his early twenties, Gardiner was perhaps Lawrence's first genuine disciple. After he had read *Sons and Lovers* in a Cambridge which he felt was dominated by the 'metallist thinkers of Bloomsbury and Kings', Lawrence had become for him 'the torchbearer, the torch leader of [Gardiner's] youth'.[28] While still at university, and then after leaving it, Gardiner had become actively involved in editing journals, forming associations and planning communes, all of which had or would bear the stamp of what he felt were Lawrentian ideals: harmony with nature, acceptance of the principle of leadership and rejection of the post-war modern world of commercialism, suburbia and parliamentary democracy. On the one hand he wanted to revive traditional forms of communal singing and dancing, and foster self-reliance through outdoor activities and the kind of training-schemes for young people associated with the Scout movement; on the other, he had grandiose plans for uniting all the youth organisations of northern Europe in an international organisation which could radically transform the social, political and economic character of the post-war Western world. He had a special interest in the German youth leagues, or 'Bunde', where leaders 'to whom unbreakable allegiance was given' were 'acclaimed rather than voted into office'; and he had founded in Frankfurt a 'Musikheim' or 'centre for social therapy through music, art and husbandry'.[29] In 1924 Gardiner had already written to Lawrence about John Gordon Hargrave, founder of an organisation improbably known as 'Kibbo Kift, the Woodcraft Kindred',[30] and received long replies (v. 66–8, 67 n.1, 93–4). In Baden-Baden Lawrence received a circular from him and, following that, a letter which on 22 July he described as being like 'a bluster in the weather' which made him hold onto his hat. Yet this gentle irony was followed with words of encouragement:

But I should like to come to Yorkshire, I should like even to try to dance a sword-dance with iron-stone miners above Whitby. I should love to be connected with something, some few people, in something. As far as anything *matters*, I have always been very much alone, and regretted it. But I can't belong to clubs, or societies, or freemasons, or any other damn thing. So if there is, with you, an activity I *can* belong to, I shall thank my stars. But, of course, I shall be wary beyond words, of committing myself.   (v. 501–2)

These are not the attitudes of a man exclusively concerned to hang on to what was left of his life. They show a Lawrence whose social instincts had been frustrated, but who also had to recognise how unsuccessful he had been in the past at combining and co-operating with others.

One of the tourist attractions in Baden-Baden was a steep funicular railway which took one up to the top of a hill (the *Merkur*), only two or three miles from the town, where there was a restaurant and a dilapidated altar to Mercury dating from Roman times. In an article published in February of the following year,[31] Lawrence describes an excursion to the Merkur with the 'Sunday crowd' indifferent to the 'very much battered Mercury, in relief' near the altar, and no-one now to throw 'grains of offering in the hollow of the votive stone'.[32] But a sudden and very violent summer storm illustrates the folly of ignoring the old gods and, when it is over and the crowd emerges from its shelter (along with the implied narrator), they find two employees of the railway are lying dead, struck by lightning:

On the south side of the outlook tower two bodies lay in the cold but thawing hail. The dark-blue of the uniforms showed blackish. Both men were dead. But the lightning had completely removed the clothing from the legs of one man, so that he was naked from the hips down. There he lay, his face sideways on the snow, and two drops of blood running from his nose into his big, blond, military moustache. He lay there near the votive stone of the Mercury. His companion, a young man, lay face downwards, a few yards behind him.[33]

Describing a visit to 'Mercury Hill' when she was with the Lawrences in Baden-Baden two years later, Achsah Brewster referred to this article as a profound and beautiful 'allegory'.[34] It is highly likely that Lawrence and Frieda did take the funicular in July 1926, but although the local newspaper reported violent summer storms in the area, with hailstones as large as pigeon eggs and two men in nearby Karlsruhe gravely injured by a falling crane, it specifically noted how fortunate it was that no-one in Baden-Baden had been hurt.[35] Because a chief characteristic of Lawrence's writing is dramatic immediacy, one is tempted to assume that, in his travel sketches especially, he is always describing exactly what had happened. But he was adept at mingling what he had seen with episodes he had imagined, and on occasions a written description could be more important to him than personal experience. 'Mercury' begins realistically enough but, as the crowd is sheltering from the storm, a 'fiery man whose upper half is invisible', and at whose 'naked heels white little flames seem to flutter', passes by.[36] This vision signals a change of gear in the article which appears to have demanded a conclusion more dramatic than any Lawrence and Frieda are likely to have witnessed on their own excursion.

'Mercury' was probably the only writing Lawrence did in Germany given that he had posted 'The Man Who Loved Islands' to Nancy Pearn just before leaving Italy (v. 498). When in 1927 this story was to be included in the *Woman Who Rode Away* collection, Compton Mackenzie put so much pressure on Martin Secker, his publisher as well as Lawrence's, that Secker felt obliged to omit it.[37] Mackenzie is the obvious model for the chief character since not many other men in Britain could have moved from one island to another (from Herm to Jethou in the Channel Islands), and then acquired a third (the Shiants); and at the start of the story the treatment is mildly satirical. But as in 'Mercury' the tone also changes half-way, and by the end of the story it so absolutely justifies Lawrence's own angry claim 'the man is no more he than I am' (vi. 205) that one has to believe that in protesting as he did Mackenzie was objecting to 'Two Blue Birds' by proxy. Lawrence's further claim in his comments on Mackenzie's threats was that 'The Man who loved islands has a philosophy behind him, and a real significance' (vi. 218), and insofar as this story deals rigorously and in a relatively abstract way with a quite specific issue, it is probably the most philosophical fiction he ever wrote.

The man who loves islands is called Cathcart. On the first of them he has a whole retinue and lives in semi-feudal state. But partly because his retainers cheat him, he moves to a second, smaller island accompanied only by one old couple, a widow and her daughter to keep his house, and an orphan boy. Still he loses money. On the second island Cathcart slides automatically and not very willingly into an affair with the widow's daughter.[38] When the daughter becomes pregnant, he marries her but, after the birth of the child, makes a generous financial provision and escapes any further involvement by moving alone to a third island which, like the Shiants, is little more than a rock in the sea. There he becomes irritated by the company of some sheep and has them removed; and when his cat leaves him he is relieved. Cathcart has been writing a reference book to all the flowers mentioned in Greek and Latin literature (this is more or less what Lawrence had believed Douglas was doing but when his book appeared in Florence in 1927 it was in fact entitled *Birds and Beasts of the Greek Anthology*).

On his third island he abandons the book and loses interest in his own powers of visual and linguistic discrimination:

Many gulls were on the island now: many sea-birds of all sorts. It was another world of life. Many of the birds he had never seen before. His old impulse came over him, to send for a book, to know their names. In a flicker of the old passion, to know the name of everything he saw, he even decided to row out to the steamer. The names of these birds! he must know their names, otherwise he had not got them, they were not quite alive to him.

But the desire left him, and he merely watched the birds as they wheeled or walked around him, watched them vaguely, without discrimination.[39]

It is impossible to read this without recalling Lawrence's own extraordinary expertise, in botany especially, and how shocked he was by others who did not seem to know the names of things. One critic has worked out that in his first novel, *The White Peacock*, 145 different trees, shrubs or plants are identified and 40 different kinds of birds;[40] and certainly the success of Lawrence's famous 'nature descriptions' is inseparable from a high degree of technical and linguistic knowledge. For the man on the island words no longer mean anything; he finds it repulsive to read his name on an envelope and, in a master stroke of narrative, he is described as tearing 'the brass label from his paraffin stove'.[41] What Lawrence is showing here is a profound understanding of the relationship between language and society. Without words Cathcart has completely cut himself off from the human world and his human existence has then no meaning. At the end of the story the snow which falls has entirely obliterated the island's distinctive features: all discrimination is lost. With some initial help from Mackenzie, and then with a good deal more from Lawrence's critical understanding of tendencies in himself, 'The Man Who Loved Islands' is a remarkable, general reflection on the impossibility of separating ourselves off from others entirely. In the second of his postcards to Brett after she had left Ravello, Lawrence had written:

Frieda wrote much more quietly and humanly – she says, we must live more with other people: which I think is true. It's no use trying to be exclusive. There's a good *bit* in quite a lot of people. If we are to live, we must make the most of that, and not cut ourselves off.

(v. 406)

III Last Visit to England

The Lawrences left Baden-Baden on 29 July and were in London by the 30th. If Lawrence had negotiated through Milly Beveridge the rent of a flat in her own Chelsea block (Rossetti Garden Mansions, where Philip Heseltine had once lived),[42] rather than in their usual Hampstead stamping grounds, it was partly so that Frieda could be closer to her son Monty at the Victoria and Albert Museum. Perhaps because of the influence of his sisters, Monty was now prepared for

reconciliations and later gave a convincing account of what would have been his
first real meeting with Lawrence since childhood. As he arrived to visit his
mother and step-father, Lawrence appeared first 'so that to save any sort of
awkwardness I went straight up to him, shook him by the hand and said: "how do
you do? how are you?" ' Then Frieda joined them, beaming with pleasure to see
that two men so important to her were getting on. A gifted mimic himself, Monty
remembered being surprised that Lawrence had retained his Midlands accent:
'Sargent', he reports him as saying, 'sooch a bad peynter'; but from an evening
he spent with him in September, when the Lawrences were back in London, he
concluded that his step-father was one of only two men of 'unquestioned genius'
he had ever met. (The other was also a miner's son: the artist Henry Moore, to
whom he would have been introduced by Barby.)[43]

Frieda no doubt made sure she saw her daughters as well as Monty. Kot came
to visit but there was now no question of arranging to see Murry. When Rolf
Gardiner called to see Lawrence for the first time, he was surprised to find him
in a 'starched collar and knitted rope of a tie – little bits of provincial
conventionality which persisted oddly in [his] make-up'; but soon became
involved in a discussion of various kinds of traditional dancing. To match his
young visitor's account of sword dances in Yorkshire, Lawrence began to imitate
not only the New Mexican Indian shuffle but also the movements of the devil-
dancers he had seen at the perahera in Ceylon, 'his piercing blue eyes popping
right and left out of his pale face as he twisted like a cobra, shuffling in his carpet
slippers like one possessed by demons'.[44] Another caller was Aldous Huxley who
dropped round from the Athenaeum where he usually stayed when he was in
London, and who says that this was only the second occasion on which he and
Lawrence had met (the first being in 1915 when Huxley was so fascinated that he
immediately signed on as a candidate for Rananim). Lawrence had read Huxley's
recent travel essays *Along the Road* in Spotorno and written an appreciative note
suggesting they might meet. The note reached the Huxleys when they were still
in India but now he was back in Europe Aldous made sure to look Lawrence
up.[45] It was a renewal of contact which was to prove vitally important for
Lawrence's few remaining years.

Also important for those years was a renewed contact with Richard Aldington,
whom Lawrence had known during the war. Although it was then that Aldington
had formed his relationship with Dorothy Yorke (Arabella as she was always
known), the woman with whom he was now still living, he had remained married
to another old friend of the Lawrences: the American poet Hilda Doolittle
('H. D.'). 'Hilda Aldington is a cat, and won't give them a divorce, though she
herself went off with Gray' had been Lawrence's comment on the situation in
June (v. 475). Richard and Arabella lived in the country near Reading, close
enough to the Seckers for Lawrence to have told Rina she ought to ride over and

introduce herself sometime (v. 443); and both he and Frieda went down to spend the weekend there on 7 August. According to Aldington, Lawrence was initially offended by a 'modest and wineless meal' but improved in spirits once he was assured that the habit he had developed in America of taking a hot toddy before going to bed could be satisfied. During this visit also, he apparently talked of the ranch constantly and with a 'nostalgic regret'. Both these details *may* be accurate but when Aldington says that he had arranged to have sent down to his cottage a 'dozen standard works' on the Etruscans from the London Library he must be exaggerating, firstly because there were not that many 'standard works' in existence, and secondly because Lawrence had read all but one of those he mentions in *Sketches of Etruscan Places* before he came to England. Yet no doubt he and Aldington did discuss Etruscan matters and what is certain is that the visit went well, ending with the Aldingtons (Lawrence refers in a letter to Arabella as Richard's 'wife' – v. 507) promising to come to the Villa Mirenda for the grape harvest a little later in the year.[46]

Back in London, with still no news of the theatrical society which had talked of staging *David* beginning its rehearsals, Lawrence decided to take up Milly Beveridge's invitation to visit Scotland and on 9 August caught the 9.50 for Edinburgh, leaving Frieda to her own devices (v. 507). The Beveridge house was in Newtonmore, Inverness-shire.[47] This was Lawrence's first trip to the High-lands (or indeed Scotland) and although he found the places he visited dampish and too full of tourists, and was unmoved by the opening of the grouse season ('an event for those that shoot, and a still bigger one for those that get shot' – v. 509), he was in general impressed. He particularly enjoyed being taken on a long trip to the west and on the 20th, after his return, effortlessly offered Else Jaffe a travel sketch in his finest manner:

We made an excursion to the west, to Fort William and Mallaig, and sailed up from Mallaig to the Isle of Skye. I liked it very much. It rains and rains, and the white wet clouds blot over the mountains. But we had one perfect day, blue and iridescent, with the bare northern hills sloping green and sad and velvety to the silky blue sea. There is still something of an Odyssey up there, in among the islands and the silent lochs: like the twilight morning of the world, the herons fishing undisturbed by the water, and the sea running far in, for miles, between the wet, trickling hills, where the cottages are low and almost invisible, built into the earth. It is still out of the world, and like the very beginning of Europe: though of course, in August there are many tourists and motor cars.   (v. 512)

On Skye Lawrence would not have been too distant from Mackenzie's Shiant Isles, but perhaps because Mackenzie was no longer in the region (he had visited his new property in June[48]), or because Lawrence felt he was short of time, there seems to have been no plan to go that far.

Very definitely on holiday, not all of Lawrence's time was given over to relaxation. On the same day on which he wrote to Else, he sent to Nancy Pearn an effective demolition of the first volume of *The World of William Clissold* by H. G. Wells. Scornful of Wells's claim for the novel as experimental (mixing as it did autobiography, fiction and discursive prose), he complained that it seemed like the effusion of a 'peeved elderly gentleman', a 'sexagenarian bore'. Lawrence was of course in direct opposition to the characteristically Wellsian positions reiterated in the book: that mental activities are the supremely important ones, for example, or that human history shows a 'gradual and systematic uplift from the ape'.[49] Yet he had once been a great admirer of Wells's fiction ('If *Tono-Bungay* is a novel, then this is not one', he wrote), and his attack was written more in sorrow at someone of great talent not having done himself justice than in anger. 'For, after all', he concluded, 'Mr. Wells is not Clissold, thank God! And Mr. Wells has given us such brilliant and very genuine novels that we can only hope the Clissold "angle" will straighten out in Vol. II.'[50]

Travelling down to Nottingham on the 21st, Lawrence was met at the station by his niece Peggy and taken by her to spend the night at Emily's house. The next morning they were picked up by Ada's husband, Eddie Clarke, and went to Mablethorpe to join the rest of the family, stopping on the way for a last look at Southwell (the scene of Birkin and Ursula's famous tea at the Saracen's Head in *Women in Love*), and talking French some of the time so that Lawrence could make his contribution to Peggy's education.[51] Emily and Sam King's several different forays into the retail trade had never been very successful, but the Clarkes' drapery shop had made them prosperous – in a phrase Lawrence always associated with his mother, they had 'got on'; and it was probably Ada therefore who had rented the Mablethorpe bungalow. A generous woman – the rent for the cottage the Lawrences had occupied between May 1918 and May 1919 had been paid by her – Ada had welcomed into their new house in Ripley an old friend named Gertie Cooper. When the Lawrence family had moved to Lynn Croft in 1905 the Coopers became their neighbours and the five girls had always been close to the Lawrence children. Tuberculosis had been or became the chief factor in the death of all five, and at the end of 1918 he had sat by the bedside of his particular favourite among them (Frances or 'Frankie'), as she was dying.[52] It may be that Ada had invited Gertie to be with them at Mablethorpe; but whether Lawrence saw her there or whether he was simply very struck by his sister's account, he became extremely concerned about her health and actively involved in trying to do something to improve it. Just after his relatives had left Mablethorpe, he told Koteliansky: 'I want to get Gertie away as soon as possible to some cure, *she's delayed too long*. I suppose I shall have to go over next week to see to the business – and probably take her to London – or direct to Mundesley' (v. 521, my italics); and through Kot and Gertler he continued to pursue his enquiries about the Mundesley Sanatorium. A week later he decided that because

Gertie needed a thorough examination, she might as well have it in Nottingham rather than London and instructed Ada to find the best man.

Tell him her case – ask for an examination as soon as possible, and tell him you would like an X-ray photograph. Be sure to tell him that. When we see how the thing is, if it has started, and how far it's gone, we shall know much better where we are. Ask him too if he would suggest an analysis of sputum. But get an x ray photograph, and *don't tell Gertie* – let her imagine she is only being x-ray looked at. Then if the photograph is bad, you need never show it her. And if it isn't at all bad, which I don't believe it will be – then it will reassure her more than anything. (v. 525–6)

Over the next few weeks Lawrence succeeded in getting Gertie Cooper into the Mundesley and, once she was there, wrote to her letters which combined affectionate encouragement with a stern insistence that she should take the business of getting better very responsibly and seriously ('don't fail in small matters like swallowing a drop of Pantanberge, and a raw egg' – v. 541). He was very fond of her (they were more or less exact contemporaries), and rightly alarmed by the way tuberculosis had destroyed nearly all her family; yet his adoption of such an actively interventionist strategy for someone else will seem strange unless one assumes he really had persuaded himself that, whereas Gertie's lungs were affected, his own difficulties were limited to the bronchi.

Lawrence's moods were now very dependent on what it would soon be accurate to call his periods of remission. He felt well in Mablethorpe which brought back memories of his first visit to the sea in his youth. A photograph taken at the time shows him bedraggled but cheerful, clowning on the beach with his favourite sister (Fig. 36). But meanwhile Frieda was feeling bored in London and came to join her husband at the end of August – on the same day that Ada and the rest of Lawrence's family went back home. (Writing from Florence in May, Lawrence had told Ada: 'And sometimes, when F. is away, you can come and stay with me' – v. 448.) He hired a bungalow two miles down the coast at Sutton-on-Sea, taking it for either two or four weeks because he did not know when, or if, the rehearsals for *David* were going to begin. On the whole he continued to enjoy himself, watching Frieda swim but not risking a dip himself because, as he explained to Secker, 'I'm still scared of my brochials' (v. 524). When he had visited the Aldingtons in August he had acknowledged the beauty of the English country-side: 'the same small, green fields with big hedges, and slow canals with white water lilies and yellow, and a kingfisher darting' (v. 506); but felt that he could never live in his native land again. Now, in an area which was more properly native to him, he was less sure, although he continued to be very disturbed by the consequences of the coal strike.

The Lawrences left Sutton on 13 September, two days after his forty-first birthday. Frieda headed back to London while he went to see Emily in

Nottingham and then Ada in Ripley. This last visit to the region of his birth and what he also called, in a famous phrase, 'the country of [his] heart' (v. 592), has been exhaustively researched by Derek Britton who shows how important a part it played in the genesis of *Lady Chatterley's Lover*. On the 14th Lawrence walked round all the old Eastwood landmarks with Willie Hopkin, who had provided such an important centre of intellectual life in the Eastwood of his adolescence and youth; and Hopkin's second wife has described the dinner at Ada's which she and her husband then attended in the evening.[53] In the course of this dinner it is very likely that Hopkin provided Lawrence with information about familiar Eastwood characters which would later feature as part of Mrs Bolton's Tevershall gossip in his last novel. The next day Lawrence toured Derbyshire in the Clarkes' car. He had wanted to go to Hardwicke Hall but found it closed so they may then have pressed on to Renishaw, the country seat of the Sitwells (although he had been invited there, he would have known that it was now too late to find any of the family in residence – v. 532). If he did visit the house, then Renishaw and Lamb Close, the family home of the Barbers near Eastwood (already used as the model for the home of the Crich family in *Women in Love*), would both have contributed to the descriptions of Wragby Hall in *Lady Chatterley's Lover*.[54] Yet more important than ideas for people and places which Lawrence may have picked up on this short visit was the effect of observing at close quarters the crumbling coal strike. This was now in its twentieth week with many miners drifting back to work on humiliating terms while the remainder strove to intimidate their fellow-workers into holding firm. Lawrence was struck by both the genuine hardship he saw and the radicalisation of the local people. As he wrote to Koteliansky on the 15th, from the house in Ripley (which in an unconsciously ambiguous tribute to the brother who had written *Kangaroo* Ada had called 'Torestin'): 'This strike has done a lot of damage – and there is a lot of misery – families living on bread and margarine and potatoes – nothing more. The women have turned into fierce communists – you would hardly believe your eyes. It feels a different place: not pleasant at all' (v. 536).

Lawrence explained how he felt on revisiting his home region in an article which he may have begun while he was at Ada's and which was never published in his lifetime.[55] At the beginning of 'Return to Bestwood', standing in the main street of Eastwood, he is overcome by what is at once 'a devouring nostalgia and an infinite repulsion'; and towards its end he admits that although the local people are the only ones who move him strongly, and with whom he feels himself connected in a 'deeper destiny', they make him both shrink away and feel an 'acute nostalgia'.[56] He describes a group of women, shouting defiance and waving red flags, as they give a raucous send-off in the town market-place to two other miners' wives on their way to court to face charges of abusing and obstructing the police.[57] With the same ambivalence which characterises the rest of the article, he contrasts their behaviour with that of his mother, who belonged to the Co-operative movement and was a member of the Women's Guild, but who would have died of shame before being involved in such a disturbance. Progressive as she was for her time, his mother still believed in the ultimate benevolence of all employers and the necessity of 'getting on'. He reflects on how he and Ada have in fact 'got on' – although 'my sister's "getting on" is much more concrete than mine'; but that reflection brings back an anecdote where the fierce anger and resentment against his mother which Lawrence was more and more beginning to experience is scarcely concealed. When *The White Peacock* was being published, the editor of the *English Review*, Austin Harrison, apparently told Mrs Lawrence that her son would be riding in his carriage by the time he was forty.

To which my mother is supposed to have said, sighing, 'Ay, if he lives to be forty!'
  Well, I am forty-one, so there's one in the eye for that sighing remark. I was always weak in health, but my life was strong. Why had they all made up their minds that I was to die? Perhaps they thought I was too good to live. Well, in that case they were had![58]

From these more private reflections, Lawrence goes on to make a comparison between the miners he had known before the war, 'noisy, lively, with strong underworld voices', and their dispirited post-war successors. He ends 'Return to Bestwood' with a long list of his own beliefs which is both a personal credo and a political programme for creating a better world. Accepting as a premise that 'we are on the brink of a class war', he reaffirms his own commitment to a more intense feeling of being alive rather than material prosperity. Acknowledging that everyone nevertheless needs a decent standard of living, he suggests (as he had done occasionally before) that the solution to economic problems lay in the nationalisation of 'land and industries and means of transport'.[59] This borrowing from the Left is then matched by one from the Right. With Mussolini perhaps in mind as a contrast, Lawrence insists that if there has to be power in a society it ought to be 'sensitive power'; but in an echo of a sinister off-shoot of the eugenics movement which the Fascists favoured, and which had also figured occasionally in Lawrence's previous thinking (i. 81), he immediately goes on: 'I know that we must look after the quality of life, not the quantity. Hopeless life should be put to sleep, the idiots and the hopeless sick and the true criminal. And the birth-rate should be controlled.'[60] Yet all these proposals are useless, he concludes, when the whole of the country's education is based on monetary values. In Mexico Lawrence had been able to imagine very freely how a whole society could be transformed. In England he found that more difficult, perhaps because its economic organisation was so much more modern and his knowledge of the society concerned so much more profound and intimate.

Lawrence rejoined Frieda in London on 16 September. With Kot as the middle man, it was Gertler who was making arrangements for Gertie Cooper to go into the Mundesley; and it was also Gertler who found the Lawrences rooms in a house in Willoughby Road, close to Hampstead High Street, much more to their taste than Chelsea. There was still no firm news of the production of *David* which was being organised by Phyllis Whitworth who had founded the Three Hundred Club in 1923 and then arranged its amalgamation with the much-better-known Stage Society three years later. It might be that the complications of this recent amalgamation added to the difficulties of staging Lawrence's play. Not until 27 September, on the day before Lawrence left England for the last time, did he lunch with the prospective director, Robert Atkins (v. 543). It seemed then as though *David* would go on in December and Lawrence therefore held out to Emily, and Gertie Cooper, the prospect of being home again at Christmas (v. 543, 545).

During their final days in London the Lawrences saw 'such a lot of people' (v. 539); if they had been so socially active in normal times even Lawrence would have failed to do much work. There was Montague Weekley and Kot again, as well as Brigit Patmore, an old acquaintance from the war years now living apart from her husband, the grandson of the Patmore (Coventry) best remembered for 'The Angel in the House'. She had known most of the major writers in the period just before the war but, first introduced to Lawrence by Ford Maddox Ford, it was when he and Frieda were living in Mecklenburgh Square with H. D., Arabella Yorke and (the war permitting) Richard Aldington, that she got to know him well. On the occasion of their reunion, she was invited to tea in the Lawrences' Hampstead lodgings with the novelist Dorothy Richardson and her husband Alan Odle.[61]

Someone from a quite different phase of Lawrence's past whom he now met again, and who would play an important role in his future life, was Willie Hopkin's thirty-year-old daughter, Enid Hilton; and it was at this time also that he first made friends, through Gertler, with a young man named Bonamy Dobrée who taught English at the University of London. With some difficulty, given his crowded schedule and some further work on the Etruscans he had decided he needed to do at the British Museum, Lawrence managed a further, but this time very brief, meeting with Siebenhaar for whose translation of *Max Havelaar* he had dashed off an introduction in May.[62] Dorothy Richardson took both the Lawrences to a party given in a Mayfair flat by an American literary couple, the Lewis Untermeyers, who in admiration of Lawrence's talents, and knowledge of his poverty, had combined with a friend to send him an unsolicited gift of $100 shortly after the war.[63] Jean Untermeyer noted afterwards two features of Lawrence which reoccur in many accounts: a habit of sitting with 'his knees pressed close together, his hands tucked under them', and a resemblance to pictures of Jesus (although in her version this made him seem like 'a sly Christ').[64]

The Carswells were now back in Hampstead, as chronically short of money as they had always been, ever since their marriage. On the two occasions they met with the Lawrences there was much talk of how to make a decent living (at this point in his life the modest sum Lawrence had fixed on as 'decent' was £300 a year – v. 492). During the second meeting, which took place in Willoughby Road on the night before the Lawrences were due to leave, Koteliansky characteristically insisted that *any* unearned income, even including Catherine's own modest £50 a year, hopelessly alienated the beneficiary from the vast majority in the community who had to earn every penny they spent. Their host thought this too harsh but when Catherine's novelist brother, who happened to be present, began to extol the advantages of wealth and speculate on what it would be like to be really well off, Lawrence remarked:

A lot of money has an influence on the nature of a man that is not to be resisted. I *feel* of myself that I, at least, should be able to resist it. But that's just how everybody feels, and I suppose I'd be not so different from the rest of mankind. Money, much money, has a really magical touch to make a man insensitive and so to make him wicked.[65]

During his stay in England Lawrence had toyed with the idea of returning to Baden-Baden for the inhalation cure, and at one point thought that he and Frieda might next go to Bavaria to see Else Jaffe (v. 509, 512). But they had been delayed by the difficulties over *David* and, if they stayed away from the Villa Mirenda much longer, they would both miss the *vendemmia* and not be home to greet the Aldingtons when they made their promised visit. They left London on 28 September 1926 and, after a short but happy reunion with Mabel Harrison in Paris, were back in Florence at the beginning of October. The 'real' importance of events which only assume their significance in retrospect is always difficult to gauge. Lawrence had left England as soon as he reasonably could after the war, and this had been his third short visit home since then. Had he known it was also his last, the complexity of his attitudes towards the country of his birth means that it is doubtful he would have thought potentially sentimental farewells appropriate, or that anyone else would later be entitled to regret their absence. There had been a time, towards the beginning of his career, when a growing success suggested he might one day be able to secure a comfortable niche within the English literary fraternity; but if he had ever entertained serious ambitions of emulating Wells (whose background was also 'disadvantaged') the war had dashed them, and immeasurably sharpened those feelings of alienation to which, in his time, a writer whose parents were working-class was always likely to be subject. Desperately ill in Oaxaca his thoughts had turned homewards, but now even the country of his heart had proved to be more accurately the country of his memories (loyal though he was to those). Travel had certainly made him feel how 'English' he was in many of his attitudes, but it had not noticeably and consistently increased his fondness for England itself. When his ship moved out of Folkestone harbour on this occasion Lawrence must already have known that there was no longer any place which he could legitimately call home. Responding to what he took to be a characteristically American preoccupation with 'freedom' on his first arrival in Taos, he had said: 'Thank God I am not free any more than a rooted tree is free' (iv. 307). To become an integral part of his environment, both human and physical, was however something which neither his feelings nor his circumstances after the war would ever allow.

CHAPTER FOURTEEN

◆

October 1926–March 1927

TWO LADY CHATTERLEYS

I *The First Lady Chatterley*

When the Lawrences arrived back at the Villa Mirenda, the *vendemmia* was nearly over. Bunches of grapes for casual eating were festooned everywhere and already there was in the house a not unpleasant, sourish smell from those left to soften in the cellar's vats. The three peasant families who farmed the land around the villa, as well as that part of it belonging to the local priest, used large white oxen and, as Lawrence was later to note, their traditional farming methods left sufficient margin along the terraces and elsewhere for an astonishing variety of wild flowers to flourish: here was a place where man 'moulded the earth to his necessity without violating it.'[1] In many ways this pastoral setting was idyllic for someone of his temperament and tastes, and during the first weeks of his return it was marred only by his being woken very early in the morning with the sound of gunfire. 'Vivi pericolosamente! must have been intended for the uccellini', Lawrence remarked in sardonic mockery of one of Mussolini's better-known slogans (v. 558);[2] and in a short piece he wrote about this time entitled 'Man is a Hunter', he made fun of the discrepancy between the appearance of the hunters he met as he walked beneath the umbrella pines in the adjoining wood and their intended prey. Whereas the noise they made, and the equipment they carried, might make one feel they were stalking elephants, they were in fact busy shooting little birds. He describes how dismayed he and Frieda were when Giulia Pini, having asked if they would like some game, triumphantly unfolded on the table a handkerchief containing 'three robins, two finches, four hedge sparrows, and two starlings, in a fluffy, coloured, feathery little heap, all the small heads rolling limp.' In New Mexico he had been forced to recognise that hunting porcupines was sometimes very necessary, and in 'Man is a Hunter' he makes clear that he has no objection to eating partridges, hares or rabbits. But the 'small mouthful of little bones each of these tiny carcases must make' was too much for his English sensibilities.[3]

The major labour of the grape harvest was completed by 6 October, the same day on which Richard Aldington and Arabella Yorke arrived. During the five days he stayed at the Villa Mirenda, Aldington found Lawrence unusually cheerful and relaxed. He describes how, when the two women had gone into Florence and he and Lawrence were sitting under the chestnut trees outdoors, barefoot peasant children would creep up to offer grapes. Each time Lawrence would go into the house for a piece of chocolate, or some sugar when the chocolate was gone, apologising 'for the seeming generosity (for at Vendemmia grapes are worth nothing, and chocolate and sugar are always luxuries) by telling me how poor the peasants were, and how the children ought to have sugar for the sake of their health.'[4] At the Villa Mirenda the pastoral setting was idyllic because the modern world had hardly yet intruded; but Lawrence knew the consequences of three families, with a total of twenty-seven mouths to feed, having to give half their produce to their landlords (v. 609).[5]

It was still hot in San Polo, especially within the villa whose thick walls had stored up the heat of the summer. Lawrence felt relieved that he did not yet have to light the wood stove, and continued to prepare the large sitting room on the south side of the house for winter. Many of the doors and window frames of their part of the building were probably painted before he and Frieda left for Germany; but it may have been at this time that he painted both the shutters and the chairs green. The red-tiled floor of the *salotto* was provided with rush matting (of the same Italian variety Connie Chatterley uses in the decoration of her private sitting room[6]); and it was certainly at this period that some of the peasants helped to spray its walls white – employing the same instrument that had been used to spray the vines (v. 564). With the hired piano, a few pieces of furniture and (above all) a stove designed more with the comfort of silk worms than humans in mind, Lawrence felt they could face the cold far more confidently than they had in the Villa Bernarda.

Much of the more essential shopping must have been done when the Lawrences first moved into their new premises but, as Aldington's account suggests, Frieda would still have had things to buy in Florence. She describes how she would take both Giulia and Pietro shopping with her, so that they could help carry parcels on the way back. When they did not accompany her, the Lawrences would pay Pietro to take Frieda down to Ponte Vingone in a tiny dog-cart belonging to the estate, or to have it waiting for her at the terminus when she came back laden with purchases. A specialist as well as enthusiastic shopper, who could compare facilities in Kandy or Oaxaca with those in Sydney or New York, Frieda very much appreciated the Florence shops and the absence there of 'dreary large store drudgery'. She especially remembered an establishment which sold nothing but ribbons where she enjoyed choosing a present for Mabel Luhan – in return for an Indian bracelet she had asked Mabel to send for Arabella Yorke (v. 603).[7]

It was a while before Lawrence himself went into Florence. The Aldingtons provided company almost as soon as he returned from England and there was a happy reunion with his neighbours the Wilkinsons. Lilian Wilkinson describes how on 21 October Frieda took the two-minute walk over to their house (the Villa Poggi) just as they were finishing tea so that they offered her a cup – 'and had a cigarette for her of course'. Because she found Frieda talkative and happy, Mrs Wilkinson sent her husband over to fetch Lawrence, but he was whistling so loudly as he peeled hardboiled chestnuts for supper that he did not at first hear the knocking at the door.[8] His first trip into town is likely to have been on the day after these events. On 22 October he and Frieda had lunch with Aldous and Maria Huxley who were staying in Cortina d'Ampezzo in the Dolomites, for the sake of their young son's health, but who had previously lived in Florence where Aldous was now returning temporarily in order to be 'dentisted' (v. 560, 563). Maria was a Belgian who had been unofficially adopted during the war by Ottoline Morrell, so that with her would have come for Lawrence not entirely happy memories of Garsington (although Frieda had seen Ottoline during the recent visit to London, he had not – v. 559); and at first both the Lawrences found Aldous dry and lacking in vitality. The two couples soon found, however, that they got on very well and the Lawrences invited the Huxleys to lunch at the Villa Mirenda at least once (v. 563). Their guests were travelling in a new car which Lawrence noted cost 61,000 lire (v. 563), and which was the result of Aldous having recently sold two articles in America for the astonishing sum of $1,000 each.[9] Before returning to Cortina soon after the 28th, Maria Huxley had been able to use the car to transport to the Villa Mirenda, and leave behind with Lawrence, four or five canvases on only one of which her brother (to whom they had once belonged) had begun to paint. It was a friendly gesture which inadvertently began a whole new phase of Lawrence's life and career.

With eye-sight so poor that it prevented him from driving, Aldous Huxley was nevertheless very interested in cars. He had bought a six-cylinder, two-litre Itala, and this together with his suggestion that the Lawrences might now like to buy the Citroën he no longer needed (v. 565), explains some bizarre imagery in a short story Lawrence must have been finishing when the Huxleys were in Florence. (He typed it himself, making several changes in the process, and on 1 November told Nancy Pearn that he had sent it off to her a couple of weeks ago – v. 571.) 'In Love' was prompted by Elsa Weekley's recent engagement to Teddy Seaman, a man she had known for most of her adult life.[10] It concerns a young woman called Hester who has also known her fiancé for a long time and is therefore disconcerted when, a month before the wedding, he decides it is incumbent on him to begin 'spooning' with her. Lawrence is interested in making a distinction between loving someone in a straightforward, direct way and the social posture of being 'in love'.[11] In a light comic vein, he describes how his heroine escapes her fiancé's unwelcome attentions by persuading him to play Tchaikovsky on the piano and then slipping out of the house to hide up a tree. When her sister (in whom it is easy to see traces of Barby) unexpectedly arrives on the scene, Hester threatens to go off with her unless the fiancé returns to behaving in the way he did before he decided he needed to demonstrate that he was 'in love'. In the corrected version of the story, the husband-to-be is portrayed as harbouring a genuine desire for the heroine, realises that he has been behaving artificially and everything ends happily. The effect of the Huxleys' new car can be felt in several places but especially at the beginning when Hester is described as being as 'complicated as a motor car! Surely she had as many subtle little valves and magnetos and accelerators and all the rest of it, to her make-up! . . . She needed starting, as badly as ever any automobile did. Even if a car had a self-starter, the man had to give it the right twist.'[12]

'In Love' is a trifle. Roughly around the time he sent it off, and with his recent English experiences still very much in mind, Lawrence began what would prove to be his last novel. Frieda later described how he wrote most of the first version of *Lady Chatterley's Lover* sitting against a pine tree in the neighbouring wood, close to a spring and the little cave dedicated to San Eusebio, where he could shelter if it happened to rain.

He had to walk a little way by the olive trees to get to his umbrella pine. Thyme and mint tufts grew along the path and purple anemones and wild gladioli and carpets of violets and myrtle shrubs. White, calm oxen were ploughing.

There he would sit, almost motionless except for his swift writing. He would be so still that the lizards would run over him and the birds hop close around him. An occasional hunter would start at this silent figure.[13]

One of the dogs from the area had adopted Lawrence and would go out with him every morning. It is to this animal, either already called John or given this name by his new protector, that we owe our knowledge that on 26 October Lawrence had reached page 41 of *The First Lady Chatterley*. On that day, after John had put a wet paw on the notebook Lawrence was using, he celebrated the occasion by writing at the top of the relevant page: 'Smudges made by John, the dog, near the stream behind San Polo Mosciano! 26 Oct 1926.'[14]

He would write all morning and read the results to Frieda after lunch. At the start he was thinking of a 'shortish' story because, as he explained to Secker on 27 October, he did not feel 'like a long effort' (v. 563). Four days later the Lawrences wrote a joint letter to Montague Weekley, urging him to join them for Christmas. 'Lawrence', Frieda reported, 'goes into the woods to write, he is writing a short long story, always breaking new ground, the curious class feeling this time or rather the soul against the body, no I dont explain it well, the *animal* part' (v. 569).

Frieda was unsure whether the first version of *Lady Chatterley's Lover* was going to be about class antagonism or the mind's conflict with the body, but in the event it dealt with both topics. It began as a novella like *The Virgin and the Gipsy*, except that this time Lawrence wanted to ask whether two people such as Yvette and the gipsy could ever have a *permanent* relationship. Connie Chatterley is not a virgin in the technical sense, but she is obliged to re-become one when her husband Clifford returns from the war with the lower half of his body paralysed. (As Lawrence was to write in his second version of the novel, she is a 'married nun, become virgin again by disuse'.)[15] Her situation means that once more there are vestigial traces in the story of the Sleeping Beauty motif, with the awakening agent being in this case not a gipsy but a gamekeeper. Parkin (as the gamekeeper is called in the first two versions) is a kind of 'black man of the woods' for the local children, and he lives in a cottage which has a 'certain fairy-tale atmosphere'.[16] The evocation of this wood clearly owes something to the surroundings in which *The First Lady Chatterley* was written; but it is also dependent on that area of Lawrence's childhood and adolescence he had recently explored again with Willie Hopkin. If (that is) the wood sometimes seems magical, that is partly because features in it such as 'Robin Hood's Well' take Lawrence back to the lost golden age of his youth.[17] At the beginning of her relationship with Parkin, Connie fantasises that she will be able to avoid the considerable social difficulties it raises by limiting herself to being no more than his 'wife in the wood', rather as in 'The Ladybird' Lady Daphne is Count Dionys's 'wife in the darkness'.[18] But fairy-tale or fable elements of this kind, characteristic of Lawrence in his novellas, are not especially prominent in *The First Lady Chatterley*. Remembering his recent impressions of intense class hatred in England, he soon became concerned to treat the efforts of Lady Chatterley and her husband's gamekeeper to build a solid understanding on mutual sexual attraction in a mode which was as sternly realistic as possible.

These efforts were not made any easier by Lawrence's decision in *The First Lady Chatterley* to keep Parkin defiantly working-class throughout. At one moment in the story Connie reflects,

When they were merely two people together, quite pleasant, he spoke more or less good English. When he really loved her, and cooed over her in the strange, throaty cooing voice of a man to his tender young wife, he said 'thee' and 'thou'. And when he was suspicious or angry, he used the dialect defiantly, but said 'you' – or rather 'yer' – and not 'thou.'[19]

This is the general *principle* of the bi-lingualism which Mellors will deploy with such virtuosity in *Lady Chatterley's Lover*; but in this first version of the novel, it is no more than enunciated; and although Parkin may sometimes speak standard English there is no attempt to endow him with any items of what is usually thought of as middle-class culture. His lack of interest in painting, music and literature, or the so-called art of conversation, constitutes a serious drawback for Connie who, in the first part of the book, regards Clifford and Parkin as complementary: 'Her two men were two halves. And she did not want to forfeit either half, to forego either man.'[20] Yet after she has become pregnant by the gamekeeper and goes abroad for a while, she begins to feel that it is with him she must live after all. On her return to 'Tevershall', however, it is then Parkin who reminds her of the social difficulties of their relationship. He has too strong a class feeling, too much sense of solidarity with those without the opportunities being offered him (as well as too much suspicion of Connie's motives), to live with her on a farm purchased from her healthy private income; and yet he knows that she could not survive as an ordinary, working-class wife. Their problems are dramatised in highly effective scenes which did not survive into the novel's final version. After Parkin has been forced to give up being a gamekeeper because of the scandals caused in Tevershall by Bertha Coutts, the wife from whom he had been separated, he takes a job at a Sheffield steel works and lodges with a working-class family there (the Tewsons). Connie's visit to see Parkin at the Tewsons, with whom she takes tea, painfully exposes any illusion she or the reader may still harbour that love can easily conquer all, and that social differences do not matter.

The success of the Sheffield episode leaves its author in a quandary: how is he going to solve the problems which he has now made more acute by dramatising so well? To help in this task, Lawrence introduces a new character called Duncan Forbes: the type of supposedly witty, cultivated young cynic rarely successful in his work, especially when, as on this occasion, the pleasantries we are presumably meant to admire as much as Connie does are so feeble and cheap.[21] Forbes good-naturedly tries to mediate between the two lovers when further discussion of their possible future together leads to a serious quarrel; but his task is complicated by his (and the reader's) sudden discovery that Parkin is a committed Communist, and has become secretary of the Communist League in his Sheffield steel works. This surprising development accurately conveys the impression of a radicalisation of working people which Lawrence had gained on his trip to England, but it makes life difficult for Forbes because he knows that Connie has little faith in the solutions Communism offers. *The First Lady Chatterley* nevertheless ends optimistically with Connie renouncing Wragby and determined that her coming child should not be handed over to Clifford (whom she now begins to wish dead). How Connie and Parkin could make a life together has not however been made clear to the reader. It was perhaps because it was not clear to Lawrence either that he began re-writing the novel almost as soon as he had completed its first version. *The First Lady Chatterley* was finished around the beginning of December 1926 and Lawrence began its successor – the version now known as *John Thomas and Lady Jane* – almost immediately.

Socially and culturally ill-matched as they are, one has less strong a sense of what could keep Parkin and Connie together than one might because there are no detailed descriptions of their love-making. On the whole Lawrence relies in *The First Lady Chatterley* on conventional elisions of the 'afterwards' variety. It is true that the word 'cunt' and variants of 'fuck' are used on a handful of occasions, but at this stage they are not integral and could easily have been omitted for publication. Yet the situation Lawrence had chosen to deal with was such that he must have suspected from the beginning that it would be very difficult to get his novel into print, or that at the very least its publication would cause controversy and attract abuse. (Already in this first version he is exploring the discomforts of being regarded as a moral monster when he describes Parkin's feelings as his separated wife spreads rumours about the peculiarity of his sexual practices.) The problem was not so much that Lawrence's subject was adultery with a social inferior – that theme was familiar, even if it rarely appeared in a form which was authorially endorsed. The difficulty lay in giving Connie a husband who had been deprived of his virility during the war. This was a sensitive topic in 1926 and already in *The First Lady Chatterley* Lawrence shows himself aware of the awkwardness by saying that Clifford's wound was 'really symbolical in him. He was always paralysed, in some part of him'; by suggesting that in many ways it was easier for Clifford to be 'only half a man', that his crippled condition was 'a relief, an escape'; or by having Connie reflect that her husband had 'always hated sex'.[22] But to insist that Clifford would have been like that *anyway* means that he has been deprived by a cruel misfortune of the opportunity which any character – and especially perhaps a Lawrentian one – ought to have of defeating expectation.

Was it then a fundamental error on Lawrence's part to have conceived Clifford as he did? Much later, in 'A Propos of *Lady Chatterley's Lover*', he conceded that it might have been. Agreeing that to have paralysed Clifford 'technically' made it so much more vulgar of Connie to leave him, he explained that, 'the story came as it did, by itself, so I left it alone.'[23] If one juxtaposes this remark with Frieda's suggestion that in *Lady Chatterley's Lover* Lawrence was identifying with both the gamekeeper *and* Clifford,[24] then one might deduce that the story came as it did because he needed to find some way of talking about his own impotence. If, however, Frieda was right in what she implies, then all one can say is that Clifford is treated with remarkably little sympathy. One of the weaknesses of *The First Lady Chatterley* is the way an increasing shift of point of view towards Connie allows Lawrence to load Clifford with a degree of opprobrium for which we are shown very little dramatic justification. If Lawrence did believe that he shared Clifford's plight, he was determined not to make that a reason for the slightest indulgence in his fictional treatment.

In her letter to her son, Frieda had talked of the conflict in the novel between body and soul. By the end of *The First Lady Chatterley* it has become clear that, when no compromise is possible, then Lawrence feels one must plump for the body. Because the struggle between the classes which Frieda had identified as the other theme of *Lady Chatterley*'s first version cannot be resolved in this bold way, Lawrence seems to have abandoned trying to think too hard about practical solutions. By the time he was completing *The First Lady Chatterley* in November, it had turned out to be no more coherent an answer to all the new problems he had faced during his last visit to England than 'Return to Bestwood'. In its final few pages Lawrence uses Duncan Forbes to signal what is not only a discreet confession that one of the dilemmas he had proposed to himself when beginning the work had proved too difficult to resolve, but also a major change of direction for many of his own future creative endeavours. 'I've hated democracy since the war', Forbes confesses, 'But now I see I'm wrong calling for an aristocracy. What we want is a flow of life from one to another.'[25] In the so-called 'leadership novels' of the 1920s: *Aaron's Rod*, *Kangaroo* and *The Plumed Serpent*, Lawrence himself had called for an aristocracy. He would by no means now lose interest in political issues, but over the next year or two he would go back to believing that the mission of the artist was to encourage more satisfactory relations between individuals, even if the only people in a position to profit from the encouragement were those who, from either choice or necessity, were isolated from the body of society as a whole.

II Making Pictures

Lawrence wrote *The First Lady Chatterley* in about six weeks, at an average of over 2,000 words a day; but he took two and a half months over its almost immediate, longer and more elaborate successor. He was diverted from these literary labours by his growing enthusiasm for painting. As a young man he had often painted but, since becoming a professional writer, he had usually settled for occasional copying as a means of relaxation, or for adding details to Brett's pictures. The stretched canvases which Maria Huxley had left behind, and the picture-less walls of the newly decorated *salotto*, inspired him to tackle his own subjects. In 'Making Pictures' he would later describe the joy with which he sat on the floor with one of the canvases propped against a chair, and brushes from the house painting beside him. His material was 'a little stock of oil, turps and colour in powder, such as one buys from an Italian drogheria.' Beginning the first picture was like 'diving into a pond . . . The knowing eye watches sharp as a needle; but the picture comes clean out of instinct, intuition and sheer physical action. Once the instinct and intuition gets into the brush-tip, the picture *happens*, if it is to be a picture at all.'[26] This is a post-Romantic aesthetic of composition, equally relevant to the way Lawrence wrote books.

The first picture he painted shows a well-built blond woman with round, bare breasts. The dark-haired young man with a moustache next to her has his right arm across her body in order to cup her left breast (the position in which Parkin is described as sleeping with Connie except that in their case it is the left hand and the right breast[27]). A child with a continental breakfast bowl in front of him looks on contentedly, and through a kind of porthole at the back of the room there is a gleaming phallic tower. The two adult figures have the golden nimbuses of Renaissance saints, and the back of the chair on which the child is sitting forms a nimbus for him also.

Lawrence began by calling his first, pleasant and essentially unexceptionable picture the 'Unholy Family' (v. 574) and, after a smaller composition of *Men Bathing* (v. 581), a similarly good-natured polemical impulse lay behind his next large canvas (47 × 28 in.). This illustrates an episode from a story in *The Decameron* which describes how a good-looking young peasant secures the gardening job at a convent by pretending to be deaf and dumb. His supposed disability is a guarantee of discretion and leads eventually to his sleeping with all the institution's eight nuns, as well as its Abbess. At the point Lawrence chose to depict, the young man, more worn out by his sexual than agricultural labours, is taking a rest when the wind blows back his clothing and displays to a passing group of nuns who have not yet enjoyed his favours some indication of what they have missed.[28] The 'Unholy Family' had been a very simple painting, cartoon-like in its composition, but *Boccaccio Story*, as Lawrence called his third picture, is much more ambitious. In what may be a tribute to late Cézanne but is more probably a frank confession of the absence of an appropriate technique, the young man has no hands to speak of; but there is quite skilful foreshortening in the treatment of the rest of his body and a well-rendered expression of repletion on his sleeping face. In their charming hats, the nuns are comically intrigued by what they see. The pleats in their dresses echo the furrows on the ground around them; their absorption in the gardener's anatomy is balanced by that of two white dogs who are looking attentively at them; and the composition is framed at the back by attractively fluffy trees. *Boccaccio Story* may not be a great painting but it is an agreeable one and, like 'Unholy Family', essentially humorous. There is a lot of fun in both. Frieda described how boldly and joyfully Lawrence attacked his canvases: 'I watched him for hours, absorbed, especially when he began a new one, when he would mix his paints on a piece of glass, paint with a rag and his fingers, and his palm and his brushes. "Try your toes next", I would say.'[29]

Boccaccio Story was finished in December and in the same month Lawrence began *Fight with an Amazon*. In this picture a Rubensesque nude is being clutched from the side by a naked man while what seem like wolves bay around. The blond pubic hair of the nude occupies a prominent central position; but the main significance of this clumsy painting is that it indicates one important future direction of Lawrence's painterly interests. Indifferent to what he could manage fairly easily, he will often want to depict naked bodies in close contact with each other and, at the same time, to fill his canvases with movement. Characteristic of this tendency is likely to have been 'a little picture of a negro wedding' (v. 623), finished by 12 January and almost certainly inspired by the photograph of African women keeping a gigantic ball in the air with outstretched hands, which he had seen in one of the copies of the *Illustrated London News* Secker was now conscientiously sending him (v. 620).[30] His next surviving large composition after *Fight with an Amazon* – three naked men seen from behind as they linger near a stream which winds its way through a landscape dominated by red willow trees – is static, and perhaps partly for that reason largely successful. (The peacefulness of the scene makes fewer technical demands than most of Lawrence's other large paintings and the colouring has always been regarded as especially appealing.) But after *Red Willow Trees* would come *Flight Back into Paradise* with, at its centre, a crouching Eve retreating from a modern world full of transformers or power generators while Adam struggles with the angel at the gates. If Lawrence had not explained in a letter that this *is* what is happening (v. 639), however, it would be hard to interpret, and the compositional ambition of this painting, together with the attempt to render dynamic interaction, make it very weird indeed. Whether or not Lawrence was inspired in his depiction of Eve by the famous crouching Venus in the Uffizi,[31] he does not make a very good job of her; and the angel's body is equally distorted. The difficulty in saying this is that, as a painter, Lawrence falls between two stools. He is self-evidently not a trained artist so that to use formalist criteria in criticising his work might seem inappropriate. On the other hand, he painted competently in his early days, was a distinguished critic of art and, through his association with painter friends, had a good knowledge of most of their technical terms and procedures. To treat him therefore as one would someone like Grandma Moses would be condescending. The situation is complicated by the fact that, in the 1920s, several major avant-garde artists made it a point of honour not to be seen deploying conventional skills. Many of the things Lawrence would have known he could not do might well have fallen into the category of those which, in his sophisticated familiarity with the way certain artists talked about their work, he could well have decided were not worth doing anyway. For all that it seems reasonable to say that, whereas a case could be made for *Boccaccio Story* and *Red Willow Trees* as pictures in their own right, *Flight Back into Paradise* is only interesting because it was painted by a great writer.[32]

In the first instance Lawrence himself was not especially preoccupied with doubts about the quality of his art. By December he was already thinking of a London exhibition, and that his paintings might provide his future livelihood (v. 600, 601). Producing daily so many words he began to develop a resentment of them, and to feel that painting was not as stressful as writing. Yet there were already signs that it could become so. Both Arthur and Lilian Wilkinson were serious painters and (like Milly Beveridge) Arthur had exhibited his delicate water-colours from time to time.[33] When the Wilkinsons went to spend a couple of months in Florence over the Christmas period, Lawrence borrowed an easel of theirs for his Boccaccio painting, and then used it as a model to have one of his own made by a local carpenter (v. 587, 606). Besides being painters, the Wilkinsons were also of course 'progressive' in their thinking. Yet they were offended by Lawrence's first picture when he showed it to them on 14 November, remarking afterwards that the 'imbecile fat woman with most of her clothes missing' formed, along with her male companion and the 'pert child', a 'most unpleasant group'.[34] As Lawrence painted more, he more and more resented responses of this kind, which he was alert enough to sense even when the onlookers were hiding what they felt. On 27 February 1927 he would tell Brewster that he painted no picture 'that wont shock people's castrated social spirituality' and that he always included somewhere a phallus – 'a lingam you call it' – because for him the phallus was 'a great sacred image' (v. 648). (In *The First Lady Chatterley* he had already written a hymn of praise to 'phallic wonder', the 'mystery of the penis' which is 'the river of the only God we can be sure about, the blood' and what 'connects us sensually with the planets'.)[35] Nine days after this letter he told Brett that although his paintings seemed to him 'absolutely innocent', 'I find people *can't even look* at them. They glance, and look quickly away. I wish I could print a picture that would just *kill* every cowardly and ill-minded person that looked at it' (v. 651). This last remark shows that painting was no necessary haven from stress after all; but it also indicates the polemical direction in which the *Lady Chatterley* enterprise would increasingly evolve.

The Wilkinsons may have been upset by *A Holy Family* (as it was later to be called) but they left a social gap when they temporarily decamped for the town around 18 November. Lawrence wondered whether either the Dobrées or the Seckers would like to rent the Villa Poggia over the Christmas period; and he tried to secure either Gertler or Montague Weekley as a house guest at the Villa Mirenda (v. 581, 597). He had no success in either attempt. Christmas was not however entirely solitary. Some of the local peasant children had spoken of other foreigners who in the past had provided a Christmas tree (v. 609). The result was that Frieda, retaining from her German childhood a special fondness for Christmas celebrations, instructed Pietro to buy one the next time he went into Florence. Instead, he stole a small pine from the part of the wood belonging to the priest and, together with him and Giulia, the Lawrences then wrapped gold and silver paper round its cones and decorated it with ornaments and candles bought in town.[36] On Christmas Eve the Pini and the two other peasant families were invited into the Villa Mirenda. There was wine, biscuits and (where appropriate) cigars for the adults, as well as presents for all the children. Lawrence described the occasion to Ada on 30 December:

The peasants all came up on Christmas Eve, with the children washed beyond recognition, the rascal Filiberto, who as a rule doesn't have much but dirt and his shirt to cover him, looking like a diminutive chauffeur, most amazing. We gave them wooden toys like those I sent, and sacks of sweets, and they were fascinated. The elder ones drank Marsala and sat still, and Tosca and Lilla and Teresina – damsels of 17 and 18 sang and danced. But we were worn out when they departed. (v. 616)

Lawrence goes on to describe how the Wilkinsons and their two children came in from Florence to visit on the 26th – an occasion recorded in the Wilkinson diary as a 'famous reception . . . singing and feasting and all six of us as sympathetic and merry as could be'[37] – but he added, 'for the rest we were alone, which I prefer'.

Lawrence had periods when he did not want to see others, but he was clearly pleased when the Wilkinsons returned to their villa after Christmas and by then he could begin to look forward to the arrival of the two Beveridge sisters and Mabel Harrison, who had decided to take another house in the neighbourhood from the end of February (v. 643). Yet what gave him most pleasure was the return of the Brewsters from India. Their first port of call on their way back to Europe was the Greek island of Syra where they hoped one or both of the Lawrences might join them; but that proved so immediately unsatisfactory that they very quickly retreated to Capri, where they could be temporarily accommodated in the villa belonging to their friends the Di Chiaras (v. 629), and began to look round for a house they might buy in Italy. Lawrence tried to interest them in Tuscany and on 16 January Earl Brewster, prospecting a little but mainly concerned to re-establish contact with the Lawrences and tell them about his Indian trip, made a very welcome visit to the Villa Mirenda. After he had gone Lawrence confessed how apprehensive he had been about showing his paintings to a professional like Brewster, and in a letter to Brett on 20 January he conjectured that Earl had not found them sufficiently modern, 'not mâte [sic] enough – not enough "values" and colour-for-tone substitution' (v. 629). Yet he came to feel his friend had been helpful nevertheless, and had given him good advice. 'Thanks for telling about the hand and elbow', he wrote to him on 6 February, 'you're right' (v. 637).

He was less appreciative about a visit Brewster had arranged to the studio of the Florentine painter Alberto Magnelli. A former associate of the Italian Futurists and a friend of De Chirico, Magnelli had by the 1920s settled for a largely representational method of painting. Lawrence thought him conceited, 'very self-important and arch-priesty', and he complained that, although the work was 'very clever' with 'quite new colour and design', it was essentially hollow: 'all that labour and immense self-conscious effort, and real technical achievement, over the cremated ashes of an inspiration' (v. 629). The paintings he is likely to have seen portray human figures in compositions of a highly geometrical nature and anticipate Magnelli's later move into non-figurative areas as he attempted to rediscover what one French critic calls 'the pure and archetypal forms which lie behind superficial sense impressions',[38] or what in a more specifically English idiom would be one aspect of Clive Bell's 'Significant Form'. Part of their effect comes from a certain monumentalism but also a high degree of finish. 'As for mâte surface', Lawrence wrote to Brewster on 6 February,

I find, for myself, I hate it. I like to paint rather wet, with oil, so the colour slips about and doesn't look like dried bone, as Magnelli's pictures do. And I'm not so conceited as to think that my marvellous ego and unparalleled technique will make a picture. I like a picture to be a picture to the whole sensual self, and as such it must have a meaning of its own, and concerted action.   (v. 637)

It is after making clear his own position in this way that Lawrence thanked Brewster for the advice about the hand and elbow.

Lawrence confessed to Brett that the visit to Magnelli's studio had put him in a 'vile temper' and made him long for a 'bolshevist revolution' (v. 630). He had experienced a similarly, disproportionate reaction years before when he had gone with E. M. Forster and David Garnett to the studio of another avant-garde painter, Duncan Grant (although on that occasion the reasons were more personal and complicated).[39] It is usually assumed that Duncan Forbes, who is an important figure in *The First Lady Chatterley* and becomes reasonably important again in *Lady Chatterley's Lover*, must be loosely based on Duncan Grant. That may be true even if, in *The First Lady Chatterley*, Forbes is a largely sympathetic character. The angry attack on his art only appears in the novel's final version where it is described as full of 'tubes and corrugated vibrations'.[40] During the war years both Grant and Magnelli experimented with abstract art and the kind of figure painting they then developed was clearly influenced by Cubism. But 'tubes and corrugated vibrations' is not at all an apt description of either's work and suggests that, when he denounces Forbes's painting, Lawrence has in mind a representative figure rather than any particular painter. It is nevertheless possible that the animus against that figure was strengthened because Magnelli's work reminded him of some of the paintings he had seen in Duncan Grant's studio in 1915.

This is a highly speculative connection but it is made more probable by the way memories of Garsington, and of many of the figures who now constituted 'Bloomsbury', would have been revived for Lawrence by the renewed contact with Aldous and Maria Huxley. When the Huxleys again visited the Florence area in March 1927, they brought with them Mary Hutchinson who, as a cousin of Lytton Strachey and mistress of Clive Bell, was at the centre of the Bloomsbury group. 'Mary Hutchinson seems nice and gentle', Lawrence reported to

Brett, 'very faded, poor dear – almost a little old woman. Clive Bell and Co. must be very wearing. I feel myself in another world altogether' (v. 651). Because he was already familiar with the ideas which Bell's writings had popularised, it was not only socially but also aesthetically that Lawrence felt himself in another world. Yet this was not because he felt more old-fashioned than they were. In the view he expressed to Achsah Brewster on 19 January, his own painting was more 'modern' than that of 'artistic anarchists' such as Magnelli (v. 627). Reflecting as it did Lawrence's suspicion of a modernity which made 'art out of antipathy to life', and used all its effort and skill to 'dress up a skeleton' (v. 627), that would have been a difficult claim to sustain in terms of subject matter, design or technique; but if a major element in being 'modern' is the capacity to startle common opinion, then it would certainly prove to be justified.

III   The Novelist as Critic

Throughout the period in which Lawrence wrote the first two versions of *Lady Chatterley's Lover* he kept reasonably well, falling worryingly ill only in March 1927, after he had finished the second. On 10 January (with, one can imagine, his fingers crossed), he told his mother-in-law that he had not yet had a bad cold that winter (v. 622). Bad it may not have been, but Lawrence had certainly been in bed with what he began by calling a cold around 23 November of the previous year (v. 582). Three days later he concluded that, instead of a cold or perhaps merely in addition to it, he had been suffering from a bout of malaria (v. 588). In his own mind at least, this would explain the high temperature from which he no doubt suffered. But raised temperature could also be a symptom of tuberculosis. Writing to Gertie Cooper on 28 October he had commiserated with her on having been confined to bed at the Mundesley until a drop in her temperature indicated that the bacillus was no longer active: 'You know, they keep you in bed until the temperature *never* rises above one degree *below* normal. I myself, at that rate, should be in bed for ever, for mine is always up and down' (v. 566). This self-identification can be construed as no more than one, additional item in Lawrence's attempt to cheer Gertie up; but that Frieda was willing to acknowledge openly he was in the same boat as his old friend is made plain in the postscript she added to this letter. One of the symptoms that worried Lawrence most after his illness in Oaxaca was that he continued to remain painfully thin. 'How splendid gaining 5 lbs!', Frieda wrote to Gertie, 'I feel quite envious (not for myself, Lord preserve me) but for Lawr' (v. 567).

Gertie Cooper was continually on Lawrence's mind and he not only wrote regularly to her in the Mundesley but corresponded with her doctors. He was shocked when he learnt from Ada that they had decided she needed to have part of her left lung removed. 'I doubt if *I* should have the operation, if it was me', he told his sister (v. 630); but in writing to Gertie herself he showed an under-standable and yet quite uncharacteristic inability to offer clear advice: 'For myself, I daren't say, either have the operation, or don't have it. It worries me too much' (v. 632). He did however define for her an attitude of mind which he must have felt would be helpful and which is significant because it was so obviously his own.

Eh, one wishes things were different. But there's no help for it. One can only do one's best, and then stay brave. Don't weaken or fret. While we live, we must be game. And when we come to die, we'll die game too.

Listen to the doctors carefully, when they advise you. But when it comes to deciding finally, decide out of your own real self.   (v. 632)

One reason for thinking that Lawrence could not have been seriously ill very often during the six months he spent back at the Villa Mirenda is that he produced so much. Although he and Frieda saw the Wilkinson family regularly, going with them to the theatre in Florence on at least one occasion,[41] and must also have visited their friends in town from time to time, the record of his life in this period is even more than usually a record of his creative work. In addition to the two, preliminary versions of *Lady Chatterley's Lover*, his paintings, articles and short stories, Lawrence found time for several reviews, with all the reading they entailed. His favourable account of H. M. Tomlinson's *Gifts of Fortune: With Some Hints to Those About to Travel*, sent off on 9 November, appeared in the old and well-established periodical, *T. P.'s Weekly*, which had once had the distinction of serialising *Nostromo*; but a week before he had very grudgingly told Nancy Pearn that he would be willing to continue reviewing for a youthful and aggressive newcomer on the periodical scene, the *Calendar of Modern Letters* (v. 570–1). Before his review of Wells's *World of William Clissold* was printed in the *Calendar* in October 1926, Lawrence had published 'The Princess' in its first three monthly numbers, and by the end of 1925 both 'Art and Morality' and 'Morality and the Novel' had appeared there. One of its editors, the young and gifted Edgell Rickword, had wanted to meet Lawrence when he came back to England from America in 1925, but the arrangements fell through (v. 311). Any regrets Lawrence might have entertained must have swiftly disappeared when he read in the *Calendar* for April 1926 a slashing review of *The Plumed Serpent* by C. H. Rickword, Edgell's cousin. With a directness for which the periodical was noted, Rickword called the writing in parts of Lawrence's novel 'nauseating in the extreme', accused him of 'charlatanism' and made the Eliotic complaint of an 'absence of detachment': *The Plumed Serpent* was a work in which 'the fervour of the missionary overcame the integrity of the artist'.[42]

Denunciation from the lively young must have contributed to Lawrence's disillusionment after the publication of *The Plumed Serpent*, and it would certainly explain the marked lack of enthusiasm with which he agreed to continue reviewing for the *Calendar*. It was nevertheless exactly the right context for a demolition of *Pedro di Valdivia*, a work by a writer who had established his reputation before the war and belonged to the Conrad generation, R. B. Cunninghame Graham. This account of the *conquistador* who had helped to colonise Chile seriously annoyed Lawrence for many reasons. As someone who had said, when Secker suggested in November the collection which eventually became *Mornings in Mexico*, that he hated 'the thought of half baked essays in vol. form' (v. 575),[43] Lawrence objected to *Pedro di Valdivia* in the first instance as an example of book-making. Cunninghame Graham's 123-page introduction quoted all the best parts of the Valdivia letters whose translation then constituted the remaining 94 pages of the book: 'He deliberately – or else with the absent-mindedness of mere egoism – picks all the plums out of Valdivia's cake, puts them in his own badly-kneaded dough, and then has the face to serve us up Valdivia whole, with the plums which we have already eaten sitting as large as life in their original position.' Lawrence criticised a failure to give the reader any impression of Chile ('We never see the country, we never meet the man, we get no feeling of the Indians'), and he suggested that Graham's translation of the letters was poor. Above all, however, in a word which was becoming very important for the first two versions of *Lady Chatterley's Lover*, he excoriated him for his 'insentience'. Cunninghame Graham seemed to Lawrence to share the insensitivity of the *conquistadores* without having their excuse. He had made no attempt to conceive what it really meant when Valdivia ordered 200 'rebel' Indians to have their hands and noses cut off:

imagine deliberately chopping off one slender brown Indian hand after another! Imagine taking a dark-eyed Indian by the hair, cutting off his nose! Imagine seeing man after man, in the prime of life, with his mutilated face streaming blood, and his wrist stump a fountain of blood, and tell me if the men of action don't need absolutely to be held in leash by the intelligent being who *can* see these things as monstrous, root cause of endless monstrosity![44]

Challenged, Lawrence might well have said that although Cipriano kills people in *The Plumed Serpent*, he does not mutilate or torture them.

Lawrence sent his thoughts on *Pedro di Valdivia* to Nancy Pearn in December (v. 601). His next review for the *Calendar* would consider four recent works of fiction. To Mabel Luhan's friend from the old New York days, Carl Van Vechten, he was no kinder than he had been to Cunninghame Graham, finding his attempt to evoke Harlem life in *Nigger Heaven* meretricious. *Flight*, which dealt with 'the removal of Creoles . . . from the Creole quarter in New Orleans to the Negro quarter in Atlanta' he thought more respectable, and at least its author, Walter White, had the advantage of himself being black. But Lawrence's real interest was in the other two works, whose distinction he was quick to recognise. What he liked about *Manhattan Transfer* by Dos Passos ('the best modern book about New York that I have read'), and Hemingway's *In Our Time*, was the honesty with which both authors acknowledged the meaninglessness of so much of life, especially in the modern, post-war world: their evocation of it as a place where, in the words of his apt summary of the Hemingway stories, 'Nothing matters. Everything happens.'[45]

By contrast with these young writers, he thought the last author whose work he considered for the editor of the *Calendar* lacking in honesty. This was John Galsworthy whom Rickword had asked him to re-appraise as part of a series of essays which appeared in the journal under the title 'Scrutinies'. By the time Lawrence sent off his contribution at the end of February, the *Calendar* was about to fold (it ceased publication in July 1927, after only two and a half years); but Rickword had arranged to include it in a collection of previous 'scrutinies' from his periodical which he was preparing to publish in book form. Lawrence began by offering a classic definition of a certain tradition in literary criticism. Always impatient with formalist criteria, his premise was that a work of art could only be judged by its effect on 'our sincere vital emotion'. That meant a critic had to be emotionally rather than merely scholastically educated: 'A man with a paltry, impudent nature will never write anything but paltry, impudent criticism.' As if that were not enough, the critic had also to be honest, not someone who like Lord Macauley was 'emotionally very alive' but who 'juggles his feelings'. If the critic passes these tests then what he or she needs to make clear are the standards which have been adopted for each particular critical enterprise. For his reading of Galsworthy ('or most of him, for all is too much'[46]), Lawrence offers a distinction between an individual, and a social, being. With the help of two offprints which had recently been sent him by the American psychoanalyst, Trigant Burrow (whom Lawrence had mentioned favourably in *Psychoanalysis and the Unconscious*[47]), he was able to re-state several old preoccupations in new terms. The individual (he claimed) who is neither too absorbing of his immediate environment nor too absorbed by it, retains an innocent, naïve core while still remaining a part of the living continuum of the natural world. The social being, on the other hand, has lost this core, feels in consequence his own isolation and can only attempt to quieten the resulting fear by insuring himself through the accumulation of money. The trouble with the characters in the Forsyte saga, Lawrence feels, is that they are all social beings: there is not one single individual left in sight. Even those who rebel against a world in which money is the controlling principle are only confirming that principle through contradiction: 'the thing a man has a vast grudge against is the man's determinant'. They are not indifferent to wealth, only resentful that they themselves do not possess it. As a consequence, their retreat into 'passion' has the same effect on the reader as dogs copulating on the pavement. Lawrence's implicit praise for the power of this satiric vision is qualified by the suspicion that it is perhaps unintentional: that Galsworthy could not see 'what you were when you *weren't* a Forsyte';[48] and he is sure that in his later, post-war works the novelist had himself surrendered entirely to the Forsyte ethic and allowed the acuity of a potentially satiric intention to be blunted by sentimentality. But then that, of course, was why he had remained such a popular writer.

Sending his Galsworthy piece to Nancy Pearn, Lawrence described it as 'for a book of *Scrutinies* by the younger writers on the elder, which is being published by that *Calendar* young man Edgell Rickword' (v. 649). In relation to Galsworthy, Lawrence was a younger writer but Rickword and his associates were younger still, one more generation further down. This is why the review of *The Plumed Serpent* in the *Calendar* must have been especially hurtful. There was some consolation in two long letters he received in November and December 1926 from another, but very different, 'young man', Rolf Gardiner. The first described a visit Gardiner had made to the Nottingham area and prompted in response Lawrence's detailed, guided tour to the 'country of [his] heart'. In this same reply, Lawrence spoke of the need for some geographical centre for all Gardiner's revivalist efforts, 'some spot on earth, that will be the fissure into the under world, like the oracle at Delphos, where one can always come to . . . If I did come to England to try such a thing,' he added, 'I should depend on you as the organiser of the activities' (v. 591). Responding enthusiastically, Gardiner wrote:

I take it you meant *The Plumed Serpent* absolutely seriously. For me, it was a most wonderfully courageous essay to think out the course of action that must be taken somewhere. Won't you write us a *Plumed Serpent* for northern Europe, someday? You know, more individuals among my generation are coming to understand, or shall I say accept, your work? Or rather it is for them the most potent agency for breaking down the clogging crust which is imposed by 'modern' knowledge on men, that exists in that form. You have taught me how to feel, I think. And one goes to your books again and again to be warmed and healed by that 'faceless flame' and surging godly rhythm which make all other books seem as dead and dreary as cold mutton in a restaurant window.[49]

Gratified as Lawrence must have been to have proof that not all articulate young men of the post-war period were like C. H. Rickword, the tribute could have seemed paradoxical in that it came at a time when, after the coal strike had indeed forced him to begin thinking of a *Plumed Serpent*, if not for 'northern Europe' then at least for England, he was about to abandon the attempt. By the end of *The First Lady Chatterley*, and with the strike finally over, he was suggesting that the only solutions to the problems of the post-war world would be individual and non-political; and in *John Thomas and Lady Jane*, that was the position he would dramatise.

IV   *John Thomas and Lady Jane*

Lawrence expected to see Gardiner when he went back to England. He had thought this might be as early as December but, after having taken the trouble to write out his own music to accompany *David* and send it to Robert Atkins (v. 557),[50] he learned that the production had once again been postponed and assumed that Atkins had 'funked' it (v. 576). In compensation for the delay, the enterprising Phyllis Whitworth engaged Esmé Percy, an actor much admired for his performances in Shaw, to produce *The Widowing of Mrs. Holroyd*. (Percy had wanted to direct this early play of Lawrence's at the beginning of the war but had to give up all his theatrical plans when he enlisted in December 1915.)[51] Pleased though he was, Lawrence did not feel it was an occasion for which he need risk a journey to London in December. Gardiner and others sent him reports of the production, Mrs Whitworth forwarded photographs and reviews, and on 19 December Lawrence wrote a warmly appreciative letter to Percy, thanking him for his efforts (v. 604). He took on himself the blame for the almost uniform criticism of the play's ending, but on the whole cannot have been too dismayed by its reception, and he must have been especially pleased with the praise of Shaw who, according to Gardiner, 'said the dialogue was the most magnificent he had ever heard, and his own stuff was "The Barber of Fleet Street" in comparison!'[52]

With the London trip postponed and (after Christmas) the Greek island of Syra ruled out of contention by the Brewsters' unfavourable report, Lawrence was even less clear than usual where he would go in the spring when Frieda was likely to visit her mother. A return to the ranch was becoming more and more unlikely in his view and both the Lawrences were thinking more often of selling. Frieda knew very well the chief reason why a trip to America was out of the question, for her husband at least; but raising the somewhat delicate matter of a sale with Mabel Luhan (who had after all given her the ranch in the first place) she said: 'Of course it grieves me too much to think the ranch might go, but then we have so little money and Lawrence is so English' (v. 598).

Her renewed impression of Englishness must have come from having *The First Lady Chatterley*, and then probably its successor, read to her daily. They would make her aware of how deeply Lawrence was now plunged in the environment of his childhood and youth. The letter to Gardiner about the 'country of [his] heart' confirms this impression of looking back, as does a long letter to Gertie Cooper on 23 January 1927 where he reminisces with her about their common past.

I suppose they're warbling away in Eastwood Congregational Chapel at this minute! Do you remember, how we all used to feel so sugary about the vesper verse: Lord keep us safe this night, secure from all our fears–? Then off out into the dark, with Dicky Pogmore and the Chambers and all the rest. And how Alan used to love the lumps of mince-pie from the pantry? And Frances did her hair in brussel-sprouts, and made herself a cup of ovaltine or something of that sort! Sometimes it seems so far off. And sometimes it is like yesterday.[53]

(v. 634)

More and more Lawrence's thoughts took an autobiographical turn as he tried to adjust his memories to a perspective quite different from the one he had adopted in *Sons and Lovers*. That he now saw things differently is apparent in 'Return to Bestwood', and several of his now quite different attitudes to his mother are repeated or developed in 'Getting On', an essay which is likely to have been prompted by news from Ada in January that Henry Saxton was dead (v. 631). As Lawrence explains in 'Getting On', Saxton was a coarse local grocer whom his mother admired because 'she had really just one idol, success'. Looking back he now resents the way she imposed her values on him and taught him to despise his easy-going, working-class father: 'For years I prayed that he might either be converted into a chapel man, or die. They were not my own prayers. They were a child's prayers for his mother, who has captured him and in whom he believes implicitly.' When he had described in *Sons and Lovers* how the young Paul prayed for the death of his father, there had been no blame of the mother.[54] What he resents particularly now is that, for all her apparent love, his mother partly despised him for being to some inevitable degree the son of his father ('She looked on us all as her lower class inferiors'); but also because she had decided that he was too weak to survive – even though 'I always had more vitality than the rest put together.' The story of Austin Harrison and the carriage which Lawrence tells in 'Return to Bestwood' occurs again, and he concludes by wondering, as he also wonders in that piece, what his mother would make of him now. In some ways she might have been pleased,

But she would have been chagrined at my lack of 'real' success: that I don't make money; that I am not *really* popular, like *Michael Arlen*, or *really* genteel like Mr Galsworthy: that I have a bad reputation as an improper writer, so that she couldn't discuss me complacently with my aunts: that I don't make any 'real' friends among the upper classes: that I don't *really* rise in the world, only drift without any *real status*.[55]

As 'Getting On' shows, the circumstances and physical surroundings of his own background, as well as the class conflict within his own family, must have been very much in Lawrence's mind as he wrote what is now usually known as *John Thomas and Lady Jane*. Dividing his novel into chapters (the absence of these in the first version testifies to its 'short long story' origin), he now immensely improved its 'texture', filling out episodes with local detail much as he had done when re-writing 'Quetzalcoatl' in Oaxaca. Moments such as Connie's illness, which alarms her sister Hilda and leads to the engagement of the nurse Mrs Bolton, are brought alive with fresh imaginative investment.[56] Duncan Forbes, so important in *The First Lady Chatterley*, is now virtually eliminated but Lawrence compensates for his loss by introducing several new characters,[57] and several of the previous ones are developed very considerably. This is true of Lady Eva, the figure based on Lady Ida Sitwell, and of Hilda; and in chapter II there is a new and excellent scene of conflict between Clifford and a subtly delineated Sir Malcolm Reid (Connie's father).[58] But the supporting character who is developed most between the first version of *Lady Chatterley's Lover* and the second is Mrs Bolton. Now 'good-looking' rather than 'elderly', she is given much more of her own background and it is especially in this second version that she becomes the channel for the kind of Eastwood gossip Lawrence had heard in the summer from Willie Hopkin. Hopkin himself makes an appearance as Lewie Rollings, 'married again', still talking socialism and still writing for the local newspaper: 'But he hadn't much influence any more. His kind of socialism was all words and being funny about people like Henry Paxton.' Paxton himself, 'the burly self-made grocer', is described by Mrs Bolton as 'over eighty now, and paralysed, but still a tyrant',[59] phrases which might suggest that chapter VII of *John Thomas and Lady Jane* was completed before Lawrence heard from Ada of the death of Saxton in January.

Clifford is not much changed (although his relation with Mrs Bolton is). There are some early indications that he is going to be transformed into a Bloomsbury intellectual,[60] but nothing comes of them. In fact, he is now less obviously interested in intellectual matters and, as a result, his initial intellectual companionship with Connie, which was an important feature of *The First Lady Chatterley*, disappears almost entirely. There is now no question of Connie regarding Clifford as Parkin's complementary other half and her relation with her husband is almost uniformly hostile. So much is this the case that the reader finds it difficult to understand why the couple should stay together, apart from compassion on her part, and Connie shows even less of that in this second version than she had in the first.

The biggest change in *John Thomas and Lady Jane* concerns Parkin. We now learn from Mrs Bolton that Parkin is his stepfather's name and that his real father (Dicky Seivers) was a professional cricketer – the only person Lawrence had met with that distinction in real life was H. G. Wells.[61] Quite new is the attribution to Parkin of a disturbing sexual history. Frightened as an eleven-year-old when Bertha Coutts, five years older than himself, deliberately exposed herself and revealed to his startled young eyes that women have pubic hair, he found that during the first weeks of his marriage to Bertha he could not make love until this hair had been shaved off.[62] In the narrative as a whole, he remains uneducated and working-class; and there are now more practical illustrations of how the dialect can be used to express class resentment. But in this second version of the novel, Parkin's feelings are predominantly personal and he is no longer interested in politics. The difference is crucial and leads to a transformation of the scene in Sheffield and, in consequence, of the novel's ending. When Connie goes to take tea with the Tewsons all the political running is made by Bill Tewson who, like his wife, is now treated by Lawrence much less sympathetically. When called upon to speak, Parkin articulates a version of the view which Connie has arrived at while she has been abroad. This is that there is no such thing as class in the ordinary sense, and that both the haves and the have-nots constitute a vast proletariat of the cold-blooded, from the clutches of which those few remaining individuals whose blood is warm need to escape.[63] There is little question now of Parkin's pride and class solidarity prompting a bitter refusal of Connie's suggestion that she should buy a farm for them both ('It's better to be beholden to a woman, than live a life o' misery'); and indeed he does not much object to her suggestion that a foreman at the Sheffield works should be bribed in order that he might be given a less physically punishing job.[64] In his letters after the Sheffield episode, Parkin apologises for his friend Bill and makes clear that he is leaving the works because he is aware of Connie's anxiety as to the brutalising effect his job might have on him. 'I shouldn't care if the bolshevists blew up one half of the world, and the capitalists blew up the other half, to spite them, so long as they left me and you a rabbit-hole apiece to creep in, and meet underground like the rabbits do', he says; and she replies: 'I am so glad you are leaving Sheffield. I was so afraid you were just going to deteriorate into a socialist or a fascist, or something dreary and political.'[65] In their last encounter, which begins in the church at Hucknall where Lawrence had explained to Gardiner that Byron's heart is buried (v. 592), their future is indeterminate; but he is looking forward to working on the farm Connie will buy once his divorce from Bertha has been finalised.

In *John Thomas and Lady Jane* there is no hope in public action, and love between two individuals has become the only solution to the problems of the modern world. Partly in consequence, Lawrence's descriptions of the love-making between Connie and Parkin are more explicit and he begins to distinguish the particular character of each sexual encounter. His response to having written a potentially unpublishable novel in *The First Lady Chatterley* was to make it more certainly unpublishable. When the second version was finished he referred specifically to its *verbal* impropriety (v. 638, 655). Yet unprintable words are used no more liberally than they were before; the difference lies in greater realistic detail. This can be observed in his re-writing of the first night Connie and Parkin spend together in the cottage, in which there is a new element in her observation of his erect penis: 'the strange gallant phallus looking round in its odd bright godhead'. As in *The First Lady Chatterley* the phallus is presented as the key to any connection with the living continuum of the universe, with much of modern inanity now being attributed to fear of its primordial authority. It was not so much, however, talk at this quasi-philosphical level which would have been so alarming to a publisher (though no doubt alarming enough!). After *Birds, Beasts and Flowers*, Lawrence had written surprisingly little poetry, but on the last day of 1926 he sent to Nancy Pearn two poems for the *Calendar*. Both of these insisted on the centrality of the man/woman relationship, and in 'The Old Orchard' the Eve figure is urged to achieve full knowledge by eating the whole of the apple this time.

> Eat, and lie down!
> Between your thighs
> disclose
> the soft gulf. Be wise!

> Lift up your heads
> O ye gates! Even lift them up
> ye everlasting doors!
> That the king of glory may come in.[66]

An attentive censor might have objected to the first stanza but the second is likely to have been too metaphorical to attract his attention. The description in chapter XI of *John Thomas and Lady Jane* of how Connie 'put her arms round [Parkin's] waist, and her swinging breasts touched the summit of the erect phallus in a sort of homage' would have been another matter; so too would have been Lawrence's account of how Connie, noticing that Parkin's phallus has become 'little and sticky', 'leaned out of bed and touched it delicately'.[67] This is not merely more explicit than the poem but quite different from anything Lawrence had ever written before.

V   Yet More Words

Lawrence finished *John Thomas and Lady Jane* around the second or third week of February 1927. Although he was aware that it was unpublishable as it stood, he told Brett on 8 March: 'I will *not* cut it' (v. 651). But he clearly felt also that the novel was in any case not yet as he wanted it to be. *John Thomas and Lady Jane* is 150,000 words long, but it can only be very shortly after he had completed it that Lawrence finished the Van Vechten review and wrote the 'Scrutiny' of Galsworthy for the *Calendar*. In addition, he now responded with almost 14,000 words to a request which Cynthia Asquith, looking to capitalise on the success of her *Ghost Book*, had made in the November of the previous year for a murder story.[68] 'The Lovely Lady' is hardly a murder story in the ordinary sense. Pauline Attenborough, its central figure, is seventy-two but, in the half-light and with an appropriate exertion of her iron will, manages to look only thirty. She has made a fortune in antiques and lives in a tastefully furnished Queen Anne house just outside London, along with her son Robert and a niece, Cecilia. A relationship might well develop between these two if both were not so completely under Pauline's domination. One day when Cecilia is sun-bathing on the roof of the converted stables, she hears a mysterious voice. Appearing at first to come from nowhere, it turns out to be Pauline talking to herself down below: as she also takes the sun, she has her head towards the opening of a drain-pipe which acts like a speaking-tube and carries her voice up to Cecilia. From Pauline's self-communings, Cecilia learns that the old but still lovely lady feels guilt, not so much because Robert is the son of an Italian priest who was her former lover, rather than of her dead husband, but because her elder son, Henry, had died shortly after she had made clear her disapproval of the young woman he wanted to marry. Exasperated by her failure to get anywhere with Robert while he is still so attached to his mother, Cecilia impulsively decides on another occasion when Pauline is again talking to herself to use the drain-pipe to her own advantage. Speaking to Pauline in the guise of Henry's vengeful spirit, she tells her that she is quite right to feel guilty and that she ought to set Robert free: allow him to live his own life. This message from the apparent beyond devastates Pauline whose will now disintegrates along with her good looks. In a brilliantly written section where Lawrence calls on his memories of *The Picture of Dorian Gray* (although the story as a whole owes rather more to Poe's 'Ligeia'), he describes Pauline's complete physical collapse, how she begins to look as crumpled as 'an old witch' and lose all her previous elegance and refinement.[69] When she dies shortly afterwards, the two young people are left free to marry. Cecilia had realised that unless Robert's mother could be disposed of she herself would have no life, and with a stratagem which is a milder version of Henry's means of getting rid of Bamford in 'The Fox', she has effectively 'murdered' her.

Dealing as it does with the leisured classes, 'The Lovely Lady' looks at first as if it had been written as a relief from those thoughts of his own background which had been preoccupying Lawrence as he wrote the two versions of *Lady Chatterley's Lover*, and autobiographical pieces such as 'Return to Bestwood' or 'Getting On'. This is only partly true. Pauline Attenborough is 'A mother fascinating her sons, and then forcing them into death, rather than let them go.' The parallel with Mrs Morel in *Sons and Lovers*, and therefore with Lawrence's sense of his own mother, is plain. Cecilia suggests to Robert that his dead brother Henry was 'torn in two between the girl he wanted to marry, and your mother, and he died to get out of it'. This is how, after having completed *Sons and Lovers*, Lawrence specifically interpreted the death of William Morel (i. 477), and, by extension, of his own brother Ernest. Yet the most significant parallel with the early novel comes in the description of Pauline's dead body.

When Robert came home he went up to see her. She was pretty again, but shrunken, like a little old child. Something very childish about the poor dead face, that smote his heart suddenly. And at the same time, that look of wilfulness and imperviousness had now fixed and gone cold and chilled the heart. Fixed in her own will, and impervious, even in death. And at the same time, the pathos of a maid who has died virgin and unlived. It is the contradiction of a woman hardened to her own will: she never lives, she only knows what it is to force life.[70]

We know from *Sons and Lovers*, as well as from poems such as 'The Bride' or 'Spirits Summoned West', how struck Lawrence had been by the virginal expression on his mother's face when she was dead.[71] In the past he had interpreted that look in a wholly positive way. 'The Lovely Lady' confirms that hardening of Lawrence's heart against his mother apparent in 'Return to Bestwood' or 'Getting On'. It suggests that he was now blaming Lydia Lawrence more bitterly for the man he had become; resenting that she had loved Ernest more than himself (in the story Pauline regards Robert as very poor compensation for the loss of the handsome, athletic Henry); and doubting that she had cared for him with anything like the fervour with which he had been devoted to her.

The description of the dead Pauline Attenborough is in none of the versions of 'The Lovely Lady' published before the Cambridge edition of *The Woman Who Rode Away*. This is because Cynthia Asquith found the story too long for her collection, and Lawrence obligingly reduced the story to about half its original length of 13,700 words.[72] In order to draw up the list of all he wrote between October 1926 and March 1927, one has to add to all the other thousands of words already mentioned, the two versions of an introduction intended for F. S. Flint's translation of the memoirs of the Duc de Lauzun, the first of which Lawrence probably abandoned at the beginning of this period; and the first two parts of 'Flowery Tuscany'.[73] Small though these additions are, they strengthen the sense that he had been remarkably productive and make one understand better his complaint to his mother-in-law that his pen had become *eine Schwierigkeit* ('a weariness') to him (v. 622). The trouble was that productivity was not the same as profitability; he would have needed a session or two with Mackenzie or Maugham to drive home the point. Much of his time had been spent on two versions of a novel whose financial future was very uncertain, and a lot of it on reviewing for a minority periodical which could not pay well. But Lawrence was reconciled to being neither popular nor rich and prepared to regulate his expenses accordingly. In November the Seltzers had written asking if he would consider publishing with them again. In his reply Lawrence said that he could promise nothing and added, 'Adele says I am to come back with a best seller under my arm. When I have written "Sheik II" or "Blondes Prefer Gentlemen"', I'll come. Why does anybody look to me for a best seller? I'm the wrong bird' (v. 574).[74] It was not that he was inattentive to the relation between writing and money – reading a biography of Voltaire which Mabel had sent him, he told Brett he thought the author cunning and underhand for not explaining how, at Lawrence's own age,

Voltaire came to have 'an *income* of £3000' (v. 585). Yet as he wrote in his essay on Galsworthy, 'Money, of course, with every man living, goes a long way. With the alive human being it may go as far as his penultimate feeling. But in the last, naked him it does not enter.'[75] That being his case he was not prepared at this stage to worry too much about the future. He was fortunate in having a wife who did not feel there was much point in worrying either.

With Frieda having fixed on 17 March as the day on which she would leave for Baden-Baden to see her mother, it was Brewster's availability that determined Lawrence's own plans. He decided that it was not worth bothering with *David* – rightly as it happened since it was only produced in May – and that the time had at last come for the Etruscan trip which he had been thinking of the year before.[76] Thanks to their close friendship with Lord Grimthorpe's daughter, Lucy, the Brewsters had recently been able to move from Capri to his temporarily available Palazzo Cimbrone in Ravello, and Lawrence wrote both inviting himself there and suggesting to Earl an Etruscan walking tour. Given Lawrence's disinclination to go back to places where anything unpleasant had happened to him, there is support for those who are sceptical of Brett's account of the Ravello episodes in his telling Brewster, 'I'm among the people who like Ravello – though Cimbrone is a bit too much of a good thing' (v. 648). But there is support on the other side also, in the suggestion to Brewster in this same letter that both of them were now 'at the *âge dangereuse* [sic] for men'. 'One resents bitterly', Lawrence went on, 'a certain swindle about modern life, and especially a sex swindle. One is swindled out of one's proper sex life, a great deal. But it is nobody's individual fault: fault of the age: our own fault as well. The only thing is to wait; and to take the next wave as it rises. Pazienza!' (v. 648). If Lawrence did in fact identify with Clifford Chatterley, then a crucial difference would be that, whereas for Clifford the sex swindle was permanent, he himself continued to believe in the rise of the next wave.

Writing to Brett on 8 March Lawrence raised the matter of his future movements gingerly: 'The Brewsters, did you know, have moved to Ravello, and are in Cimbrone, Lord Grimthorpe's place, you remember. They invite me for a little while. I might go – but I don't know – It depends if I shake off this flu' (v. 651). In a letter to Secker a week later he said that the flu had been bothering him for three weeks; and four days before he had told his sister Emily that if he was not himself fit enough to travel by the time Frieda left, 'Giulia will look after me, and the Beveridge sisters' – who must therefore have been installed by this time in a small house close to the Villa Mirenda (v. 655, 653). But the precaution was not necessary and on 19 March Lawrence was fit enough to leave. He took the train to Rome, responding to an invitation which had been extended three months before (v. 616), and spent two nights in the flat of Christine Hughes, the friend of Bynner and Ida Rauh, whom he had met several times in New Mexico and who was now visiting Europe, ostensibly so that her daughter Mary Christine could continue her music studies. After an unhappy car trip down to the sea at Ostia with mother and daughter, he moved on and was with the Brewsters in Ravello on the evening of the 21st.[77]

CHAPTER FIFTEEN

◆

March–August 1927
CHANGE OF LIFE

I Etruscan Tour

Frieda had left for Baden-Baden on 17 March. It is likely that on her way to Germany she called on Angelo Ravagli who, newly promoted to Captain, was now stationed in the north of Italy, at Gradisca near Trieste. Since the Lawrences' return to the Villa Mirenda in October 1926, their former landlord had kept in touch. On 15 November Lawrence reported to Secker that Ravagli had recently spent the day with them; and on 20 February he thanked Ravagli for having sent (or left) some sheet music and was clearly expecting another visit (v. 576, 645). In his own account for Nehls, Ravagli explained how he had been sent to Florence as a witness in a court martial during this period and enjoyed a 'very gay lunch' with the Lawrences. A couple of weeks later he had to go to Florence again for the same purpose and decided to make a surprise visit to the Villa Mirenda. He claims that on this occasion Lawrence suspected that Ravagli was finding another excuse to see Frieda and became cordial only after he had insisted on seeing his military travel documents. The visit was in fact 'no trick', Ravagli writes, although, 'it could have been'.[1]

Lawrence might reasonably have wondered why Ravagli was so anxious to see *him* since the two men had precious little in common. Like Parkin, the Captain had no literary or artistic interests. The memory of how, after Lawrence's death, her mother used to urge her to marry 'a common man' has prompted Barbara Barr to comment ironically on the occasional inconvenience for Frieda of living with someone of Ravagli's limited intellectual powers; and that they were indeed limited is confirmed by several letters of his which have recently been published.[2] Interviewed by a journalist from the *Observer*, at the very end of his life, Ravagli admitted that he never read books, 'only magazines. I tried *Sons and Lovers* but it was too heavy – *much* too heavy. We don't need literature to know what to do.'[3]

The difficulty of deciding when, precisely, Frieda first slept with Ravagli is not lessened by the popular reputation she has acquired for being ready to jump into bed with almost any man she met. Yet, however sexually active she may have been before the war, there is little evidence of extra-marital activity in the 1920s, and especially since the time when she first left Europe with Lawrence in February 1922. Ceylon with the Brewsters, Perth, Sydney – in none of these places is there the slightest extant trace of a lover. Both the Lawrences developed close links with Merrild and Götzsche when they left Taos to live on the Del Monte Ranch, but Frieda's relationship with the Danes seems always to have remained maternal. She was close to Witter Bynner on her and Lawrence's first visit to Mexico, but by then his heterosexual days were long since past, and Spud Johnson never appears to have had any. There is little doubt that when she returned to England in the winter of 1923–4 she would have liked to have slept with Murry; but the letters he exchanged with her in the 1950s indicate that, technically speaking, Lawrence's suspicions on this score were unjustified.[4] Back in Taos there may possibly have been some brief dalliance with the sexually confused Clarence Thompson, but there is a singular lack of candidates for an affair in the time then spent in Oaxaca and Mexico City, or during the final period of virtual isolation at Kiowa. Between February 1922 and October 1925 and perhaps beyond, it is possible, indeed rather likely, that Frieda was a faithful wife.

This needs stating as a simple fact rather than as a defence or excuse because, sexual libertarian as she was, Frieda would have felt that she needed neither. For her, marriage was always potentially 'open'; but there is sometimes a gap between theory and practice. In a different way, this holds good for Lawrence also who, bitterly resentful of the idea that he might have been cuckolded by Murry and determined to see Ravagli's travel papers, could nevertheless write in his unfinished introduction to the Lauzun memoirs that their author 'never seems to have made love to a woman unless he really liked her, and truly wanted to touch her; and unless she liked him and wanted him to touch her. Which is the essence of morality, as far as love goes.'[5]

Lawrence spent a week with the Brewsters in Ravello. Although the cold in the cavernous Palazzo had them shivering as they ran from the end of the huge refectory table where they dined to their 'own special hearth corner', his company brought an added warmth as well as jollity to the family group. Something of this is evident in the composite letter which all four sent to Brett on 24 March (vi. 22–4); it was a warmth to which Brett and Mabel Luhan responded by urging them all to come and live in Taos where Mabel had recently been building more cottages on her estate.[6] In Achsah Brewster's account of Lawrence's visit, there is a description of the enthusiasm with which he painted his *Fauns and Nymphs*, she meanwhile using him as a model for one of her own compositions. According to her, *Fauns and Nymphs* began as a treatment of Brett's subject: Pan observing the crucifixion, but Lawrence worked over this painting at the Villa Mirenda and there is no remaining trace of the crucifixion in what we have now.[7] At the centre of the picture a grinning faun, who might once have been more obviously Pan, stands side-ways on, with his right hand across the chest of a large-breasted nymph gazing coyly up ('coy' was Lawrence's own word – vi. 196). Another faun leans his head against that of the central figure, there is a nymph looking on from the left-hand side and, at the bottom of the frame, incongruously staring straight at the viewer, the head of a third faun. All these fauns and nymphs have dark purplish hair which, along with some background of the same colour in the top corners, forms a unifying circle. In this exceptional case, the compositional arrangement through colour appears to have interested Lawrence more than the subject itself.

Harwood Brewster was privileged in always being allowed to refer to Lawrence as 'Uncle David', and he delighted her with tales of his more picturesque relatives, including the one who administered to the miners an ointment known as 'Lawrence's Salve'.[8] As was common when the Lawrences and Brewsters got together, there were corporate renditions of popular arias from opera as well as the usual folk songs.[9] In the letter to Brett, the fourteen-year-old Harwood, whose spelling was still uncertain, had been more sarcastic than she intended about the 'walking tripe' which her father and Lawrence were planning: 'I think it will be mostly trains and motor cars!'; but just before the party broke up the two men did spend the weekend in Sorrento and walked from there to Termini at the end of the peninsula (vi. 26). On that occasion Lawrence apparently discussed his difficulties over Lady Chatterley's Lover, speaking of its tenderness and insisting that it was not an improper book.[10]

Lawrence and Brewster left Sorrento for Rome on Monday 4 April and spent a couple of days there. It is likely that during this time Lawrence again saw Christine Hughes and was able to confirm his impression, already expressed in letters (v. 600), that her daughter was much more interested in boys than in her music studies. That is what he suggests in the portrait of Mary Christine he later wrote. Entitled 'Laura Philippine', this slight sketch records how disconcerted he was by a languid twenty-year-old who smoked, showed 'several yards of good leg',[11] danced the Charleston into the early hours and appeared bored by everything. He must have enjoyed some literary company while he was in Rome because in the introduction he wrote in May for a new edition of his translation of Mastro-don Gesualdo, he refers to a conversation about Verga he has had there recently with 'one of the most brilliant young Italian literary men'.[12] Lawrence and Brewster prepared for their coming trip by inspecting the Etruscan holdings in the Rome museum (the Villa Giulia) until on 6 April, with the former's flu now seemingly 'quite shaken off' (v. 26), they set out on the Etruscan tour at last.

They went first to Cerveteri, about 25 miles from Rome, towards the coast. They then moved on to Tarquinia to see the famous painted tombs and from there made a largely unsuccessful attempt to examine Etruscan remains in the area around Vulci. Finally they moved 100 miles north and visited the Etruscan museum in Volterra. Most of their travelling was by train, bus or horse-drawn cart but on the first day Lawrence demonstrated that he was in fact largely recovered by walking at least ten miles.[13] He was clearly delighted with his trip. He says so in the letters he wrote immediately on his return, and his pleasure is evident in the six *Sketches of Etruscan Places* completed by the end of June. They have a diary form similar to that of *Sea and Sardinia* and are equally impressive in both evoking a sense of the 'here and now', and in exhibiting Lawrence's remarkable capacity for reliving a recent experience as he wrote. But in *Sketches of Etruscan Places* the mundane concrete details of travelling, which his restless curiosity and eye for significant detail always allow him to make interesting, are mingled with a large proportion of art criticism: of Etruscan architectural design, funerary sculpture and, above all, the wall-paintings in the tombs of Tarquinia (to which he devoted two of the six sketches). His intention was to write a book double the length of the one we now have, and to furnish it with about a hundred illustrations (vi. 77, 84). Yet even as it stands *Sketches of Etruscan Places* is still one of Lawrence's best and indeed most coherent texts.[14]

After all his travels, Lawrence felt that he had finally discovered in the Etruscans the traces of a people with the right attitude to life. It was only superficially a paradox that this attitude was manifested, could now in fact only be glimpsed, in their attitude to death. The tombs illustrated the Etruscan refusal to succumb to gloom, in either the Christian or tragic Greek sense, and were (in Lawrence's view) the relics of a people who had sought to live in harmony with their natural environment rather than exploiting or dominating it. This was strikingly apparent to him in the first Tarquinian tomb he and Brewster were shown: the one decorated with scenes of hunting and fishing. With great felicity, Lawrence describes the naked figure who grins as he plunges vertically into the sea, the boat with the beautifully painted eye on its prow so that 'the vessel shall see where it is going', and the flocks of birds that have the 'draught of life' in their wings;[15] and he is equally adept at making his reader see all those, by now well-known, figures in the other tombs who are dancing or playing instruments as they spring along in the open air. The 'real etruscan carelessness and fulness of life' of these figures seems to him to be also a feature of relations between the sexes in the many banqueting scenes where, contrary to Roman habit, women were always present. Having noted with Brewster's help that the tombs at Cerveteri have, or once had, stones at their entrance or on top which are phallic symbols, and which none of the specialists he had read had been anxious to discuss, he attributes the 'natural beauty of proportion' in the now denuded and undecorated burial chambers on that site to the Etruscans' 'phallic consciousness';[16] and describing a banqueting scene in the Tomb of the Painted Vases in Tarquinia, he succeeds at least as well in explaining what he means by 'touch' as he had yet managed to do in his two, preliminary versions of *Lady Chatterley's Lover*.

351

On the end wall is a gentle little banquet scene, the bearded man softly touching the woman with him under the chin, a slave boy standing childishly behind, and an alert dog under the couch. The *cylix* or wine-bowl that the man holds, is surely the biggest on record; exaggerated, no doubt, to show the very special importance of the feast. Rather gentle and lovely is the way he touches the woman under the chin, with a delicate caress. That again is one of the charms of the etruscan paintings: they really have the sense of touch . . . It is one of the rarest qualities, in life as well as in art. There is plenty of pawing and laying hold, but no real touch . . . Here, in this faded etruscan painting, there is the quiet flow of touch that unites the man and the woman on the couch, the timid boy behind, the dog that lifts his nose, even the very garlands that hang from the wall.[17]

It is a help to Lawrence's lyrical evocation of Etruscan life that so relatively little was, and still is, known about their origins, their language, the details of their system of government, or the precise role women did play in their social life. His general impression is so overwhelmingly favourable that he is keen to defend what might be weak points. He emphasises, for example, the evidence for believing that the Etruscans treated their slaves more humanely than the Romans ('Apparently the "vicious Etruscans" had nothing comparable to the vast dead-pits which lay outside Rome beside the great highway, in which the bodies of slaves were promiscuously flung'); and he refuses to accept that a painting in one of the tombs, which shows a man with a sack over his head being attacked by a dog held on a leash, is clear evidence of cruelty.[18] That the Etruscans were not a cruel people is important for the contrast he develops with the Romans who, having once conquered them, had proceeded (in the usual manner of conquerors) to blacken their defeated enemy's name. Lawrence sees the Fascist regime in the Italy of his day as attempting to imitate the Romans, and he is irritated by the Fascist salutes by which he is occasionally greeted in Tarquinia and Volterra. He sets against Roman/Fascist ideals an Etruscan 'art of living . . . science of behaviour': an ability to preserve the 'natural humour of life' which is incompatible with conquest for, as he points out, 'You cannot dance gaily to the double flute, and at the same time conquer nations or rake in large sums of money.' In an emphasis which accounts for a good deal of the pervasive charm of *Sketches of Etruscan Places*, he insists on the eventual power of what is gentle and sensitive. 'Brute force and overbearing may make a terrific effect', he writes, 'But in the end, that which lives lives by delicate sensitiveness'; and he offers a familiar Romantic *topos*: 'The Pyramids will not last a moment, compared with the daisy.'[19]

Gentleness and sensitivity are also the keynotes of Lawrence's response to the people he meets on his Etruscan tour. *Sea and Sardinia* was enlivened by frequent bursts of rage but in *Sketches of Etruscan Places* he loses his temper only once. This is in Città Vecchia, Stendhal's old stamping ground, a town which he and Brewster have to pass through on their way by train from Cerveteri to Tarquinia.

It was there that, glancing out of the carriage window of a train bound for Rome as it stopped at the station, Virginia Woolf described the Lawrence she then happened to catch sight of on the platform as 'pierced and penetrated'.[20] This must have been just before he left the station and was approached by a loutish, furtive individual who asked to see his passport. Although he does not say so, the request made him furious because it brought back painful memories of being spied on during the war. But even this one unfortunate encounter ends happily:

But what do they mean, I said, behaving like this to a simple traveller, in a country where foreigners are invited to travel! – Ah! said the porter softly and soothingly. It is the Roman Province. You will have no more of it when you leave the Provincia di Roma. – And when the Italians give the soft answer to turn away wrath, the wrath somehow turns away.[21]

Stendhal, French consul in Città Vecchia during the 1830s, is an appropriate name to mention because *Sketches of Etruscan Places* often have the attractive, casual almost inconsequential air of his travel writing. The essay on Vulci, for example, succeeds in being fascinating even though it is an account of how on 9 April Lawrence and Brewster failed to see anything of obvious cultural signifi-cance (apart from the famous Etruscan bridge known as the Ponte della Badia). What holds the interest are matters as apparently trivial as the difficulties of hiring a carriage in Montalto di Castro, or the problem, when they finally get to Vulci, of buying candles from reluctant locals and then persuading one of them to act as a guide to the tombs (which turn out to be ruined and bat-infested). The liveliness of Lawrence's description of these encounters makes the reader appreciate better why so many of his friends and acquaintances later insisted that no excursion with him could ever be a waste of time. The boy who drives them out to Vulci is a baker's assistant named Luigi who had formerly been a shepherd in the flat, marshy country behind Montalto di Castro known as the Maremma. In the course of the chapter Lawrence shows himself developing a special feeling for this boy, especially as he suspects Luigi of being, like so many others in that region, a sufferer from malaria. (Because he believed he suffered from malaria himself, Lawrence had stressed in previous references to his Etruscan trip how important it was that he should visit the Maremma before the 'malarial' months of the summer – v. 653, 655.) The gentleness of his presentation of Luigi is reminiscent of the tone in which he had referred, in the previous chapters, to Albertino, the 'little lad in long trousers' who runs a hotel in Tarquinia for his parents. The energy and child-like authority with which Albertino manages everything, when he should really be in school, makes Lawrence think, 'How Dickens would have loved him!' (although he adds that Dickens 'would not have seen the queer wistfulness, and trustfulness, and courage in the boy').

[Albertino] shows us two small rooms, opening off a big, desert sort of general assembly room common in this kind of inn. "And you won't be lonely," he says briskly, "because you can talk to one another through the wall. *Teh! Lina!*" He lifts his finger and listens. "Eh!" comes through the wall, like an echo, with startling nearness and clarity. "Fai presto!" says Albertino.—"E pronto!" comes the voice of Lina.—"Ecco!" says Albertino to us. "You hear!"—We certainly did. The partition wall must have been butter-muslin. And Albertino was delighted, having reassured us that we should not feel lonely nor frightened in the night.[22]

Walls made of butter muslin are not what travellers usually look for in a hotel. The sensitivity of the depiction lies in Lawrence's affectionate appreciation of the discrepancy between the part Albertino is doing his heroic best to play and the real preoccupations and anxieties of a boy his age, which include feeling lonely and frightened in the night.

When Lawrence contrasts Etruscan sensitivity with Roman/Fascist harshness and bullying, he does not of course speak from a democratic or egalitarian point of view. The Etruscan society he admires was in his opinion a religious oligarchy run by the 'Lucumones', aristocratic priests who, like Ramón in *The Plumed Serpent*, would not have thought it wise to reveal all the secrets of their religion to the common people. But he imagines their rule as having been based on popular consent. Mussolini would no doubt have made the same claim. The arrival of Lawrence and Brewster in Volterra on Sunday 10 April 1927 happened to coincide with a dinner to celebrate the installation of a new *podestà*, appointed to govern the city on behalf of Mussolini's regime. With a mildness characteristic of the book as a whole, Lawrence makes fun of the resulting political ferment.

It is amusing to see on the walls . . . chalked fiercely up: *Morte a Lenin: Death to Lenin*: though that poor gentleman has been long enough dead, surely, even for a Volterran to have heard of it. And more amusing still is the legend permanently painted: *Mussolini ha sempre ragione! Mussolini is always right!* Some are born infallible, some achieve it, and some have infallibility thrust upon them.

But he then goes on to add that it is not for him to put even his 'little finger in any political pie . . . Let those rule who can rule.'[23] The scenes sculpted on the funerary urns which he sees later in the Volterra museum nevertheless remind him again of the distinctions *Sketches of Etruscan Places* has been working to develop. The museum keeper is a 'gentle old man' who makes Lawrence reflect 'how much more etruscan than Roman the Italian of today is: sensitive, diffident, craving really for symbols and mysteries, able to be delighted with true delight over small things, violent in spasms, and altogether without sternness or natural will-to-power'; and he concludes, 'The will-to-power is a secondary thing in the Italian, reflected on him from the Germanic races that have almost engulfed him.'[24]

From the museum, the two travellers go out of one of the town's gates and then shelter in the wall of the huge medieval castle that had become a state prison. The chapter ends with Lawrence reflecting on the two former inmates who carved 'marvellous likenesses of themselves out of the huge loaves of hard bread the prisoners get':

Hair and all, they made their own effigies life-like. Then they laid them in the bed, so that when the warder's light flashed on them he should say to himself: There they lie sleeping, the dogs!

And so they worked, and they got away. It cost the governor, who loved his houseful of malefactors, his job. He was kicked out. It is curious. He should have been rewarded, for having such clever children, sculptors in bread.[25]

After finishing the Volterra chapter, it is probable that Lawrence went on to write the beginning of a chapter entitled 'The Florence Museum' in which he summarises many of his general thoughts on the Etruscans.[26] Yet the anecdote about the prisoners provides a better conclusion for *Sketches of Etruscan Places*, and not merely because it rounds off the account, the diary (as it were), of the excursion with Brewster. Its anti-authoritarian content chimes in well with Lawrence's presentation of the Etruscans as a highly creative people crushed by a rival nation addicted to system, order and greed; and in artistic terms, the casualness of this ending, its Stendhalian nonchalance, is consonant with his pleasure in the idea that the Etruscans built wooden temples all of which have now disappeared. 'Why has mankind had such a craving to be imposed upon!', he asks in this context.

Why this lust after imposing creeds, imposing deeds, imposing buildings, imposing language, imposing works of art? The thing becomes an imposition and a weariness at last. Give us things that are alive and flexible, which won't last too long and become an obstruction and a weariness. Even Michelangelo becomes at last a lump and a burden and a bore. It is so hard to see past him.[27]

II Summer in Florence

When Lawrence rejoined Frieda at the Villa Mirenda on 11 April he felt out of sorts. Whether his excursion had exhausted him, or the evidence he felt he had seen of a better life made him more dissatisfied with his own, he was thoroughly unsettled. Developing now a notion which had attracted him before, he decided that he was undergoing the 'change of life'. In a letter to Mabel Luhan he recalled that she was going through the menopause when they first met, and he reminded her of a long poem he had written on the subject, rather forgetting the extent to which it was an adaptation of one of hers. It is clear from this poem, which he had left behind at the ranch, that in 1923 he already believed men could be menopausal too.[28] Writing to Brewster on 3 May he claimed that William Archer, the translator of Ibsen, had told a friend how he had suffered from the change of life: 'But you patiently put up with it, and you come through to something else, another, freer self' (vi. 49).

The letter to Mabel was written a fortnight before this remark, on 15 April, which happened to be Good Friday; and in it Lawrence associated the effort to struggle through the change of life with the Resurrection. 'This is the day they put Jesus in the tomb', he told her, '– and really, those three days in the tomb begin to have a terrible significance and reality to me' (vi. 37). When Lawrence and Brewster had been in Volterra they had passed a little shop, in the window of which was a model of a white rooster escaping from an egg. Brewster remembered saying that this toy, an Easter gift for children perhaps, suggested a title: 'The Escaped Cock – a story of the Resurrection'.[29] It was this enigmatic remark which gave Lawrence the idea for the short story later developed into the first part of the novella *The Escaped Cock*. A daring revision of the account of the Resurrection in the Gospels, this first part was summarised by him in his letter to Brewster of 3 May:

I wrote a story of the Resurrection, where Jesus gets up and feels very sick about everything, and can't stand the old crowd any more – so cuts out – and as he heals up, he begins to find what an astonishing place the phenomenal world is, far more marvellous than any salvation or heaven – and thanks his stars he needn't have a "mission" any more (vi. 50).

This is an accurate précis of the action of the story, but its tone hardly suggests how triumphantly Lawrence avoids bad taste in the handling of such delicate material, the power with which he is able to evoke a 'biblical' atmosphere, and how movingly Lawrence describes the pain and disillusionment of the Jesus figure.

The Escaped Cock begins with a proud rooster tied by the leg in a peasant's yard. His efforts to escape are paralleled with Jesus' struggle back to life as he lies in a cave, imprisoned in his swathing bands after the crucifixion ('They took me down too soon'[30]). Illness increasingly made Lawrence feel that he had destroyed his health in a hopeless cause and his identification with the Jesus figure is evident in the latter's general sense that all his efforts to reform the world have been a mistake which only brought him suffering, and that what he must now do is simply appreciate the world in its 'phenomenal' aspects. It is especially evident, however, in the beginning of the story where perhaps only a man who had battled with illness as hard and as often as Lawrence could have written so effective a description of what it feels like to come back from the dead.

Slowly, slowly he crept down from the cell of rock, with the caution of the bitterly wounded. Bandages and linen and perfume fell away, and he crouched on the ground against the wall of rock, to recover oblivion. But he saw his hurt feet touching the earth again, with unspeakable pain, the earth they had meant to touch no more, and he saw his

356

thin legs that had died, and pain unknowable, pain like utter bodily disillusion, filled him so full that he stood up, with one torn hand on the ledge of the tomb.[31]

For Lawrence, recovery from one of his recurrent bouts of illness could be classified as a minor miracle, yet it was not resurrection in the full sense.[32] That required the complete casting-off of the old way of life (so that there were no more bouts at all), and the entry into a new. 'I hope you're feeling really better from the flu', he wrote in the letter to Mabel, 'In my opinion, flu is one of the diseases of a changing constitution. It changes the very chemical composition of the blood – hence the bad effect on the heart – and the long time one takes to get round'; and he went on, 'when one does get round, one has lost for good one's old self – some of it – though where the new self comes in, I don't quite see' (vi. 37). In *The Escaped Cock*, the Jesus figure says goodbye to Mary Magdalene, tucks the peasant's rooster under his arm and walks out into the world to be a physician. After a Lawrentian version of the encounters on the road to Emmaus, he arrives at an inn where his cock defeats the local rooster in a fight and settles down to lord it over the inn yard. The cock is now provided for but, at this stage in Lawrence's pondering of the events surrounding the Resurrection, Jesus' own future is left much less certain. Where his own change of life would lead was for Lawrence similarly problematic. What he must have fervently hoped was that, after all the pain and discomfort it had already involved, there would at least *be* a change.

The day after Lawrence's return to the Villa Mirenda Barbara Weekley arrived, chaperoned by Eileen Seaman (the mother of her sister's fiancé). Irritated by the sense that Weekley still felt his daughter needed protection, Lawrence reported with some glee that, while Barby stayed at the villa, her disconsolate 'dueña' was packed off down the hill to a 'little Osteria at Vingone' (vi. 34, 31). During the three weeks his step-daughter was with him, Lawrence and Barby seem to have got on less well than usual, partly because of his unsettled state; but partly because she also was out of sorts, with no inclination at that time to paint. His own first composition after his return was a painting he had already begun before leaving (v. 652): Jesus emerging from the tomb with the Virgin Mary supporting him from behind as he leans towards Mary Magdalene in front. In the letter to Brewster on 28 May which allows us to be certain about the identity of the two supporting figures, Lawrence described the Magdalene in his now-finished picture as 'easing [Jesus] up towards her bosom' (vi. 72); and on inspection it becomes evident that the dress she is wearing is unbiblical enough to leave her breast bare. But that feature is hardly noticeable in a painting entirely different in spirit from *Fauns and Nymphs* (where bare breasts are important), and also different in style because here Lawrence is going back to the Italian primitives he so much admired. The imitation of their manner makes acceptable the disproportion in Jesus' hand and arm (realistically speaking, far too small for the rest of his body), especially as to render them in that way intensifies an impression of vulnerability chiefly conveyed by a face full of uncertainty and suffering. In writing of this moving painting to Brewster, Lawrence adopted the same facetious tone which characterises his summary of *The Escaped Cock*, referring to the second female figure as Jesus' 'old ma'. For a man so continually on his guard against appearing to solicit sympathy, there was a certain embarrassment in describing to a friend works which so directly conveyed his feelings about his own plight.

Although Barby was not herself painting, she was on hand for three weeks in the somewhat unlikely event of Lawrence wanting to discuss technical problems. Until the middle of May, so too were Milly Beveridge and Mabel Harrison who on Lawrence's return from his Etruscan trip were still in 'La Massa', the neighbouring 'villino' which he described as 'a little 7-roomed cottage' with 'poky little rooms' (vi. 78).[33] It was with Milly that Lawrence took some of the walks that led to the three descriptions of the surrounding countryside in 'Flowery Tuscany', the last of which was written after his return from his Etruscan tour. She remembered him discoursing on at least thirty varieties of wild flowers; but also that he had to pause for breath every fifty yards or so.[34] In addition to this familiar company, there were also of course the Wilkinsons. Barbara Weekley describes how, before she left Florence on 3 May, she accompanied her mother and step-father to a party at the Villa Poggi where everyone was required to do a 'turn'. Frieda imitated a street-singer she had heard as a child while Barby herself painted her nose red, put on a white veil and sang a music-hall song about an unfortunate Mary Ellen left waiting at the church.[35] Lawrence fell back on an old favourite: his imitation of Florence Farr lugubriously intoning the 'Lake Isle of Innisfree' to the accompaniment of an imaginary psaltery or Irish harp; but for the first time on record, and with an audience which was not especially literary, it flopped badly. According to Barby, 'On the way home Lawrence raved at Frieda for having allowed him to do it.'[36]

By the beginning of May 1927, Lawrence and Frieda would have been in the Villa Mirenda a year and he had therefore to decide whether to extend the lease. He did so despite being irritated by his landlord's suggestion of an increase (whether this materialised, and what it was if it did, is not clear). In his view, they had improved the property so much that to ask them to pay more was 'impudence' (vi. 38). Given how cheap the rent was, this was strong and (he seems to have decided on reflection) unreasonable language; but at this period Lawrence was again becoming anxious about money. In the previous few months the exchange rate had altered very much in the lira's favour: when he first came to Florence in 1926 he had been able to get 120 lire to the pound but now the rate was only 88 or 90 (vi. 60). The effect, as he several times explains to friends by quoting the prices of basic foodstuffs, was to make Italy one of the dearest places in Europe for someone whose income came largely from England. Another worry would come when he learned that from July the British government would levy a 20 per cent tax on the royalties of all British authors living abroad. This was a considerable blow for anyone who rubbed along as precariously as Lawrence; but as he said to Brewster in June, 'The only solution is to need little'; and explaining the new tax situation to his sister Ada in September he would conclude, 'But we're lucky to have got off taxes so long' (vi. 90, 143).

Financial worries did not make Lawrence any more enthusiastic about the compromises which he would have to make if *Lady Chatterley's Lover* were to appear in print; or about agreements to secure his immediate financial future of the kind Huxley had entered into. 'But I don't want to make contracts for *Lady Chatterley*', he would tell Secker, 'that young woman may still go in the fire – and I don't want to make contracts for anything – I don't like it – I feel I've got a string round my wrist and it puts me off. – And don't you bother me about it, I'm much nicer when I'm *not* contracted' (vi. 77). On 12 April he had written to Nancy Pearn that he 'could probably live by little things. I mean in magazines'; and a fortnight later he sent her one of these 'little things' which he called 'Making Love to Music'. This seems to have been inspired by either his recent encounter with Mary Christine Hughes in Rome, or Barby's arrival, because it enquires into the nature of the dream which is 'simmering at the bottom of the soul of . . . this slender, tender young lady just out of her teens, who is varying the two-step with the Black Bottom'. Starting from the premise that present-day behaviour is always a consequence of the dreams which were harboured in secret by our grandparents, Lawrence rather surprisingly concludes that the young women of his day are fulfilling the dream of those of their grandmothers who regretted that their own dancing was spoilt by the coarse sexual importunity of their partners. It follows that in his view the 'popular modern dances' are 'distinctly anti-sexual' even if (or rather partly because) 'Nothing is denied [the tender young lady], so there is nothing to want.' As a model of genuine dancing he offers two Etruscan figures from the 'Tomb of the Triclinium', praising them, as he would do later in the second of his essays on Tarquinia, for showing passion without licence or, as he puts it here, 'a splendour and an abandon which is not at all abandoned'. This is the present-day dream that he somewhat optimistically believes will form the substance of life for young women in three or four generations. The Etruscan dancers are 'wild with a dance that is heavy and light at the same time, and not a bit anti-copulative' – like modern dancers – 'yet not bouncingly copulative either' – like those in the days of the tender young lady's grandmother.[37]

Lawrence sent 'Making Love to Music' to Nancy Pearn accompanied by two photographs of the tomb paintings. These were necessary to make his article fully comprehensible, but they also made it more difficult to place. The frequent use of words like 'copulative' cannot have made that task easier either. Nancy Pearn did not in fact find a home for it, which was ominous given Lawrence's newly stated hope of living off 'little things' in the magazines. Especially ominous perhaps because the stories he was now writing were *also* not especially marketable. Despite its title, which would only become unfortunate when Lawrence later developed the story in order to show how the resurrected Jesus discovered physical love, *The Escaped Cock* hardly involved sex at all; yet it dealt with a topic bound to discourage many magazine editors. After the New York office of Curtis Brown had managed to place it in the *Forum*, whose subtitle was 'A Magazine of Controversy', the editor admitted that no previous publication had aroused 'so violent an outburst of contrary opinions'.[38] By 27 May Lawrence had written another story which he described to Nancy Pearn as 'founded on fact' but also 'more impossible than the last, to print' (vi. 70).[39]

'None of That!' describes how an American woman in Mexico City becomes fascinated by a bullfighter whom she then, on his frequent visits to her house, tries to bring under the domination of her powerful will. Possessing in private the same degree of nerve he displays in the bull ring, he eventually persuades her to visit his own house late at night and then, disdainful of the woman himself, hands her over to his cronies by whom (the implication is) she is raped. During all the time Lawrence was in direct contact with Mabel Luhan he published nothing which contained what could be described as a 'portrait' of her. But with her straight hair cut short 'like a Florentine page boy', her 'rather round cheeks and clear eyes' and her 'American energy' that made her like a 'locomotive engine stoked up', Ethel Cane in 'None of That!' is unmistakably Mabel.[40] Reading her memoirs and continuing to receive her letters had of course kept Mabel firmly in Lawrence's mind and, before his Etruscan trip, he had been involved with Orioli in recovering a number of her books and paintings which had been left in the charge of her second husband, Edwin Dodge, at the beautiful mansion on the outskirts of Florence where she had held court before the war (v. 625, 642). Why Lawrence should have decided to cast Mabel in the sordid Mexican tale whose details he may have heard, or been reminded of, when he stayed with Christine Hughes in Rome, is nevertheless not clear. Nothing in his correspondence, or the story itself, suggests that it was a delayed act of revenge. It seems more that, when he wanted to investigate a power-struggle between a woman who did not really care for men, and a man with no real interest in women, Mabel came naturally to mind.

Ethel Cane believes in the power of the imagination to triumph over all bodily concerns and feels that her life will be over once she loses that belief. She recognises the bullfighter as the biggest challenge she has ever faced and hopes to subdue him as she has subdued so many men before. But he has an elemental power (not at all idealised by Lawrence) which is impervious to hers. The important point about the conclusion is not the rape itself but that after it, and before she commits suicide, Ethel Cane confirms that she still wants to leave half her large fortune to the bullfighter. Both her suicide and the legacy are in not *entirely* ungrateful acknowledgement that (unlike Mrs Witt in *St. Mawr*) she did at least succeed in meeting her match. 'None of That!' is an absorbingly written story which foreshadows Lawrence's preoccupation with power struggles within sexual relations in his final version of *Lady Chatterley's Lover*. In its general tenor, however, it was likely to give Nancy Pearn a headache, as were specific moments such as the bullfighter's reflection that Ethel 'hates a man as she hates a red-hot iron. She is as easy to embrace as an octopus, her gate is a beak. What man would put his finger into that beak? She is all soft with cruelty towards a man's member.'[41] When Nancy Pearn had heard that Lawrence's latest novel was improper she had advised against its publication because his standing in the magazine market might be damaged (v. 29). When she received 'None of That!' she might have felt that this fear was groundless given that, with his 'little things', Lawrence was already doing his best to damage it anyway. But he had always been someone who, more than most professional authors, would usually only write what he felt like writing. 'One can never make success *in* the world', he would shortly say to Mabel, 'only against it' (vi. 74).

When he was sketching in Ethel Cane's background in 'None of That!', Lawrence described a phase in her life when she bought 'old furniture and brocades . . . She coveted such things, with lust, and would go into a strange sensual trance, looking at some old worm-eaten chair.' Relying partly perhaps on his recent visits to the Villa Curonia, he says that Ethel was furious when she failed to secure this or that valuable antique: 'Things! She was mad about "things"!'[42] 'Things' is both the title and a theme of a story which was probably written either shortly before or just after 'None of That!'[43] It deals with an American couple called the Melvilles who have lived in Europe most of their adult life and accumulated in the process a number of beautiful pieces, even though their income is modest ($3,000 a year). When they return to America with middle age approaching, they discover that their 'things' have to be kept in store because they cannot afford a house big enough for their display. The wife finds this especially frustrating and begins to feel it might be time for her husband to find a job. They make one final attempt to live their old life of cultured leisure in Europe, but now the charm has completely gone and the husband decides to accept a post teaching European literature in a university in Cleveland. There they have the money to establish the right setting for their 'Bologna cupboards, Venice book-shelves, Ravenna bishop's chair, Louis-Quinze side-tables, "Chartres" curtains, Siena bronze lamps' which all look 'perfectly out of keeping, and therefore very impressive'. Having started out on their married life as typical

New England idealists, they are shown at the end of 'Things' as wholly succumbing to materialist values. ' "Europe's the mayonnaise all right" ', says the husband,

"but America supplies the good old lobster–what?"

"Every time!" she said, with satisfaction.

And he peered at her. He was in the cage: but it was safe inside. And she, evidently, was her real self at last. She had got the goods. Yet round his nose was a queer, evil, scholastic look of pure scepticism. But he liked lobster.[44]

When he was looking for someone on whom to base the protagonist of 'None of That!', Lawrence clearly thought of Mabel. For Valerie and Erasmus, the couple in 'Things', there is no doubt that he turned in part to the Brewsters, with whom he had only very recently spent happy times. His New England idealists are also (for example) Buddhists; they also had worked for the Red Cross in Europe during the war; and they paint.[45] In September 1928, after he and Frieda had spent several weeks with the Brewster family in Switzerland, Lawrence told Earl, 'Have a most amusing story of mine in Amer. *Bookman* – called "Things" – you'll think it's you, but it isn't. I shall bring it along' (vi. 562). He had a long history of putting friends and acquaintances into books and then denying that he had done so; but there is a wide variety of different cases and in this particular one his denial can be justified. For the Melvilles he certainly borrowed a number of characteristics from the Brewsters but 'Things' is not fundamentally a portrait of them. Whereas the pyschology of Ethel Cane is very recognisably Mabel's there is no evidence of Lawrence thinking that, in their pursuit of culture and spirituality, the Brewsters were frauds and covert materialists. They were not collectors of antiques – that trait was carried over from Mabel if it did not also come from the dozens of people in Florence who must have shown him their valuable 'things'; and they showed no obvious signs of abandoning their life outside America. Very roughly speaking, one could say that the difference between 'None of That!' and 'Things' was like that difference between 'Two Blue Birds' and 'The Man Who Loved Islands' which Lawrence defined in a letter to Martin Secker on 27 May. 'Did Faith Mackenzie object to her portrait-sketch in "Two Blue Birds?" ' he asked. 'Surely not. Nor he! – I hope he won't mind either "The Man Who Loved Islands" when it comes in the *London Mercury*. He only *suggests* the idea – it's no portrait' (vi. 68–9). Although the context is not her own, there is certainly in 'None of That!' a 'portrait-sketch' of Mabel Luhan whereas, however many details Lawrence may have borrowed from the Brewsters for the American couple in 'Things', the exigencies of his theme led him to develop the Melvilles in ways which made it reasonable for his friends, good-natured as they were, to accept his denial that he had meant to portray them. Because the commitment of Erasmus and Valerie to art and culture is false or amateur (they paint but not 'desperately': 'Art had not taken them by the throat, and they did not take Art by the throat'), they become vulnerable to the feeling that it is money which really matters after all. This is a topic which had become very important to Lawrence because of the financial pressures he had recently felt. On 13 June he sympathised with Kot over the refusal of a periodical to print his own review of a book Kot had translated. Like him, Lawrence was beginning to feel that nothing nice ever happened or would happen. 'I dreamed I was made head of a school somewhere', he wrote, 'I think, in Canada. I felt so queer about it: such a vivid dream – that I half wonder if it is *my* destiny! A job! – But I manage to make a living still' (vi. 82). Erasmus may have been the type to cash in his chips but his creator was determined to soldier on. Writing his sour little comedy of the Melvilles was a method of bolstering that determination.

III   Relapse

The Koteliansky translation which Lawrence had reviewed back in April was V. V. Rozanov's *Solitaria*. In spending time on it he was doing a favour for a friend, trying to procure the book some attention; but that did not prevent him from finding Rozanov another of those 'morbidly introspective Russians' with the usual 'tick-tack of lust and asceticisim, pietism and pornography', another 'pup out of the Dostoievsky kennel'. Only in the twenty pages extracted from *The Apocalypse of Our Times*, where Rozanov attacks Christianity and shows himself 'a new man, a risen man, the living and resurrected pagan', did Lawrence feel that he had the importance attributed to him in the book's introduction.[46]

These were hardly phrases to make *Solitaria* a best-seller; but, a plain speaker himself, Koteliansky was accustomed and no doubt resigned to Lawrence's frankness. Walter Wilkinson, the young brother of his neighbour, had not known him anything like as long or as intimately so that, pleased as he must have been when, a couple of weeks after his acount of *Solitaria*, Lawrence did him the favour of noticing a modest book he had written entitled *The Peep Show*, he may also have felt that with friends like that in the literary world he would not have to look far for enemies. Lawrence insisted that Wilkinson's book was enjoyable: that his account of a six weeks' tour with a largely one-man puppet show 'from the Cotswolds down through Ilfracombe to Bideford, then back inland, by Taunton and Wells' succeeded precisely because its author, a vegetarian simple-lifer who 'had enjoyed William Morris's *News from Nowhere* immensely, as a boy', was so naïve, trusting, ordinary and nice. But his choice and analysis of certain passages were devastating. He quoted Wilkinson as saying, 'It is an exquisite pleasure to find oneself so suddenly in the sweet morning air, to tumble out of bed, to clamber over a stone wall and scramble across some rushy dunes down to the untrodden seashore, there to take one's bath in the lively breakers'; and he comments that, because the author of these phrases is so self-evidently sincere and well-meaning, 'the very banalities at last have the effect of the *mot juste*'. So they may and, never a stickler for formal matters if he felt there was some genuine human interest in a book or painting, Lawrence does persuade his reader that there is something worthwhile in *The Peep Show*. That the value must be strictly limited, however, becomes evident when he goes on to say of Wilkinson's style:

It is what the 'ordinary' young man, who is 'really nice', does write. You have to have something vicious in you to be a creative writer. It is the something vicious, old-adamish, incompatible to the 'ordinary' world, inside a man, which gives an edge to his awareness, and makes it impossible for him to talk of a 'bath' in 'lively breakers'.[47]

Doing favours for friends rarely made Lawrence less inclined to speak his mind. But he would back up what he felt he could do in the literary sphere, without any sacrifice of integrity, with help of a more directly practical nature. Since the war he had regularly offered money to the always impecunious Koteliansky; and in September he would write to Secker, 'If you ever want an odd sort of clerk, do try Walter Wilkinson' (vi. 168).

On 29 April Lawrence received a letter from Phyllis Whitworth telling him that there would be two subscription performances of *David* on 22 and 23 May, and asking for his help in their preparation. Reluctant though he was, he told Kot on the following day that he intended to be in London 'by the end of next week'; but on 4 May, in a postcard to his sister Emily, he explained that he had not been able to risk travelling because of a cold on his chest. On 13 May, he was again thinking of setting off for London on the following day (vi. 55). Once more however illness spoiled his plans. Writing on the 16th to Milly Beveridge, only very recently back in Rossetti Garden Mansions, he explained, 'I very nearly started on Saturday – then at the last minute my courage failed me – I thought, what if I get stuck in bed in London, what a frightful bore and bother for other people'.[48] Summing up the whole sorry situation in a letter to Emily on the 19th, he wrote,

I was disappointed not to get to the play. But on top of my cold came malaria, owing to the steaming hot damp weather that suddenly appeared – and I felt a wash-out. I wish to heaven I could really get to feel myself again. Since that whack in Mexico two years ago, I've never been right, and never felt nearly myself. Between malaria and continual bronchial trouble, I'm a misery to myself. I wish I could sort of get over it, and feel a bit solid again. (vi. 59)

On the same day he told Gertie Cooper that on the morning he was supposed to set out for London he had felt 'as miserable as a wet hen' (vi. 64).

From Kot, who had been to see *David* with Gertler, he received a long and essentially cheering account of the production. Although he had several serious criticisms (he thought the acting of Saul 'bad and cheap'), Kot nevertheless insisted that the play had been received enthusiastically, and he felt sure that it could be made a great success, even (he optimistically suggested) a 'great financial success' (vi. 66). This favourable report, with its prospect of the switch some 'Society' productions had succeeded in making to the commercial theatres, may have made Lawrence unusually sensitive to the bad reviews – no more fond of these than most people, he could usually be relied on to take them in his stride. What may also have helped to determine his response on this occasion was that Frieda, who had taken a particular interest in *David*, was, in her husband's own words, especially 'disappointed and downcast' by its critical reception (vi. 75). The reviewer in the *Times* called it 'neither drama nor poetry', and 'Omicron' in the *Nation and Athenaeum* said that what made the play hard to produce was its lack of 'all dramatic movement'.[49] Lawrence's riposte was strange but one which would become common in the more embittered moments of his last years. To Brewster he said that the reviewers were 'eunuchs' who had 'no balls' (vi. 72); and writing to Mabel on 28 May he complained that they hadn't 'enough spunk to hear a cow bellow. The worst of the youngish Englishman is, he's such a *baby*: one can't imagine his backside isn't swaddled in a napkin: and such a prig, one imagines he must either be a lady in disguise, or a hermaphrodite' (vi. 73). These terms might make some sense if *David* had been objected to because of its daring treatment of sexual matters. But as the criticism had nothing to do with sex, they seem excessive and suggest how deeply Lawrence had been disappointed.

He slowly recovered from what was surely a tubercular attack but which he had now got used to describing as bronchial trouble aggravated by malaria. It was while he was recovering that he put the final touches to his grimly moving pictorial version of the Resurrection, turning then to a picture of five black women in complicated poses gathered round a cradle in which lies (the title informs us) the baby Moses. This amused him because he did not 'quite know how to do it' (vi. 74, 81). His progress on the writing-up of his Etruscan tour was meanwhile uncharacteristically slow: because of illness; because he had been writing so many other, disparate things; but also because he felt he needed to collect more photographs and look at certain books again (on 29 April he had announced to Secker that he had begun the essays but also asked if he could send him Dennis's *Cities and Cemeteries of Etruria* because he had left his own copy in America – vi. 45). Lawrence had nonetheless finished the essays on Cerveteri and Tarquinia by 9 June; the one on Vulci was completed by the 14th and all six by the 25th. Although he had previously confessed the public was an ass he did not understand, and suspected that his Etruscan essays would prove a 'piece of hopeless unpopularity', he told Secker on 2 July that he was open to any suggestions as to how to make them sell (vi. 77, 82, 93). He badly needed something that would bring in money.

By May it had already become very hot. There had been a pause after Lawrence first returned from his Etruscan tour when 'at the very ends of the bare boughs of fig trees, spurts of pure green' burnt like 'little cloven tongues of green fire vivid on the tips of the candelabrum';[50] but soon everything was in full bloom. The garden fairly blazed with roses and the fireflies went 'winking round under the olives and among the flowers, at night, like lost souls' (v. 64). Peas, beans and asparagus were in full swing, and the strawberries ripe. It became too hot to sit in the sun for breakfast after seven o'clock so the Lawrences would get up at six and take a siesta later in the day. On the afternoon of 1 June, Lawrence told Else Jaffe that while Frieda was still 'peacefully slumbering' he was going to sit in a deckchair under the medlar tree. The medlars were just ripe, as were the 'big cherries'. 'It seems to me always very pleasant', he not unnaturally reflected, 'when it is full summer, and one ceases to bother about anything, goes drowsy like an insect' (vi. 81, 75).

With the departures of Barby, Mabel Harrison and Milly Beveridge in May, there were fewer people to talk to in San Polo; but on the 23rd of that month Osbert and Edith Sitwell, who were staying with their parents, paid a call which Lawrence found agreeable (vi. 67);[51] and in the second week of June the Lawrences showed Christine Hughes and her daughter round Florence for a few days. (Having had his appetite for retreating to America whetted by the reviews of *David*, Lawrence now found it dulled by the philistinism of this pair: 'They're stone blind, culturally', he complained to Brewster – vi. 79.) This company was in addition to the Wilkinsons and the usual friends in Florence: Orioli and Turner of course, but also several female long-term residents. One of these was Nellie Morrison whom the Lawrences had first met in Capri in 1921, when she had introduced them to the Brewsters (in the same year she had lent them her flat in the via dei Bardi for a few weeks).[52] Another was Violet Paget who wrote under the name of Vernon Lee and was now in her seventies. When Huxley had first visited the Lawrences in Florence the year before, he had also renewed his contact with Vernon Lee and found her 'the most astonishing and brilliant of talkers when she is at her best'.[53] By the summer of 1927, the Huxleys had moved from Cortina to the fashionable Italian coastal resort of Forte dei Marmi, not far from Lucca. Settling in there, Aldous had put aside the ambitious novel on which he was working (*Point Counter Point*) in order to satisfy his publishers with a book of essays on general psychological and political themes entitled *Proper Studies* – Aldous 'wants to *work*', Lawrence wrote, in a friendly version of his criticism of Somerset Maugham, 'He works so much' (vi. 81.)[54] On 15 June, Maria Huxley drove the Lawrences to Forte dei Marmi where they spent a cheerful couple of days, and where Lawrence felt well enough to swim. By 2 July he had sent his six Etruscan essays to Milly Beveridge so that she could find additional accompanying photographs from the British Musuem and then pass the whole package on to Secker (v. 93). This was only half of Lawrence's proposed book and he had decided therefore that, accompanied by Frieda, he would fulfil his original intention of visiting the other cities of the Etruscan League, places such as Arezzo, Chiusi and Orvieto. Writing to Brewster on 27 June he said, 'I want to go etruscanising at the end of this week' (vi. 92). It was hot for sight-seeing but being on the move might well prove no less uncomfortable than staying put in Florence as August approached.

Frieda's account of what happened next has been quoted many times but its troubling directness, the sense it conveys of absolute authenticity, makes it indispensable.

One hot afternoon Lawrence had gathered peaches in the garden and came in with a basketful of wonderful fruit – he showed them to me – a very little while after he called from his room in a strange, gurgling voice. I ran and found him lying on his bed; he looked at me with shocked eyes while a slow stream of blood came from his mouth. 'Be quiet, be still', I said. I held his head, but slowly and terribly the blood flowed from his mouth.[55]

A week later, when he was well enough to correspond, Lawrence continued to insist that his troubles were bronchial, referring on 11 July to 'chronic bronchial congestion' and on the 12th to 'bronchial hemorrhage' (vi. 98). With Orioli's help, Frieda secured a prominent Florentine doctor who seems to have driven up to the Villa Mirenda almost every day. (At the end of July, Lawrence would describe Dr Giglioli as the 'head of the Medical Profession for Tuscany' – vi. 109.) He suggested that the haemorrhage had been brought about by going in the sea at Forte dei Marmi but, although Lawrence may have accepted that as the immediate cause, his own diagnosis was characteristically psychosomatic. Writing to Else Jaffe on 18 July he said, 'My illnesses I know come from chagrin – chagrin that goes deep in and comes out afterwards *in hemorrhage* or what not.' Slowly he got better and by the time he wrote his letter to Else he had been sufficiently recovered to leave his bed and walk in the woods a little; but early on the morning of the following day, 'the hemorrhage came again. Frieda wept, and I felt like all the martyrs in one' (vi. 103, 104).

Lawrence's relapse cancelled all immediate thoughts of 'etruscanising'. Writing to Frieda's mother on the 11th in order to explain what had happened ('Your son-in-law is a poor wretch, and is in bed once more'), he had assured her that he had already succeeded in finding a copy of Fritz Weege's book on Etruscan painting but 'the Etruscans and all work can sleep with the devil – once I'm well, I shall only want to enjoy myself and forget everything' (vi. 95). After the Etruscan trip, the Lawrences had planned to go to a lake resort in Austria where they could avoid the Florence heat and see Frieda's younger sister Johanna, now divorced from her unsatisfactory first husband and married to a solid banker from Berlin, Emil von Krug. Everyone felt that it would be good if Lawrence could be moved to a fresher climate for a while, but ensuring that he would be fit to travel to Austria was clearly not easy. The Wilkinsons and Orioli appear to have been especially helpful, and Lawrence reported that friends came up from Florence almost every day to ask what they could do (vi. 97). In addition to these local visitors, the Huxleys drove all the way from Forte dei Marmi to see him, bringing with them J. W. N. Sullivan, Kot's close friend and one of the regular contributors to the *Adelphi*. After their visit, Aldous reported to his father on his admiration for Lawrence: 'He is a very extraordinary man, for whom I have a great admiration and liking – but difficult to get on with, passionate, queer, violent. However, age is improving him and now his illness has cured him of his violence and left him touchingly gentle.' But he also expressed anxiety about the effect on his friend of 'long standing tuberculosis': 'This is decidedly not a temperature to be ill in, and the poor wretch is not strong enough, nor secure enough from fresh bleedings, to move away from Florence into the cool of the mountains.'[56]

However kind and supportive friends may have been, the main burden of getting Lawrence back on his feet must have fallen on Frieda. In her account of this period she says, 'I nursed him alone night and day for six weeks, till he was strong enough to take the night train to the Tyrol.'[57] No doubt the nursing would have been of a superior or at least more conventional quality if Lawrence had been married to Jessie Chambers or Louie Burrows rather than to her. But in a subtle encounter in *The Escaped Cock*, he had analysed why, at this point in his life, their notions of care might have been less acceptable to him than Frieda's. Returning to the tomb from which he has recently escaped, the Jesus figure meets his former follower 'Madeleine'. Although he recognises in her the greed of 'selfish devotion' (the complementary opposite of her former lust for men), he is troubled enough about the immediate future to ask whether he might lodge in her house for a while. Yet he realises almost immediately that he could never in fact stay with her because of the 'flicker of triumph' in her eyes at his request, their betrayal of the 'greed of giving'.[58] There was nothing in Frieda's temperament which would allow her to transform Lawrence's illness into the kind of opportunity which, according to his criticism of Charlotte Brontë, Jane Eyre is allowed to enjoy after Mr Rochester has been blinded.[59]

While Lawrence was ill, and as he very slowly improved, a correspondence which had previously been brief and desultory developed in important and significant ways. In spite of a period in Zurich with Jung, the American analyst Trigant Burrow was essentially a Freudian; but after several years of practising Freudian analysis, he had become convinced that the root of his patients' troubles lay in the failure of their relations with the social group. Because the one-to-one principle on which pyschoanalysis was based seemed to him to reinforce rather than diminish the separation of individuals from each other, he began to develop in 1923 revolutionary techniques of group analysis. Burrow had already sent Lawrence articles in which the theoretical ground for this change was prepared, and it was probably after receiving an offprint in which he explained further some of his principles that Lawrence sat up in bed on 13 July in order to confess, 'What ails me is the absolute frustration of my primeval societal instinct . . . I think societal instinct much deeper than sex instinct – and societal repression much more devastating' (vi. 99). On 3 August he responded warmly to Burrow's recently published book *The Social Basis of Consciousness*, repeating his earlier, poignant complaint: 'Myself, I suffer badly from being so cut-off. But what is one to do? . . . At times, one is *forced* to be essentially a hermit. I don't want to be . . . One has no real human relations – that is so devastating.'[60] Lawrence pointed out that of course mankind had never been 'fully societal' (the ugly term is Burrow's not his), but agreed that the situation in their day was worse than usual: 'Now is the time between Good Friday and Easter. We're absolutely in the tomb' (vi. 113) – a description he must have had other reasons for feeling apt after his recent collapse. He said he would try to write a review of *The Social Basis of Consciousness* and, weak though he was, must in fact have completed the quite long and detailed account, which appeared in the New York *Bookman* in November, before he left for Austria on the evening of the following day (vi. 120).

Describing in this review how, in Burrow's opinion, almost the whole of life consists in interaction between the false images which people have of themselves, he quoted a sentence from the book's explanation of why these images come into being which has a curiously modern ring for anyone interested in psychoanalysis: 'Captivated by the phylogenetically new and unwonted spectacle of his own image, it would seem [man] has been irresistibly arrested before the mirror of his own likeness and that in the present self-conscious phase of his mental evolution he is still standing spellbound before it.'[61] Nearly all human behaviour is determined by the effort of human beings to adapt themselves to the images of themselves which their upbringing has persuaded them to accept. As a result, there is everywhere in life what Lawrence paraphrases as a 'death of spontaneity', and all so-called normal activity is in fact neurotic. In his version of Burrow, 'the "normal" activity is to push your own interest with every atom of energy you can command. It is "normal" to get on, to get ahead, at whatever cost. The man who does disinterested work is abnormal.' The effects of 'image-substitution' obviously make themselves felt in the sexual sphere as much as in every other. Lawrence claims that in his day 'Sex does not exist; there is only sexuality. And sexuality is merely a greedy, blind self-seeking.' In his letter of 3 August to Burrow, the thoughts about sex which the book had provoked are different and more personal. 'I'm not sure if a mental relation with a woman doesn't make it impossible to love her', he says. 'To know the *mind* of a woman is to end in hating her . . . There is a fundamental antagonism between the mental cognitive mode and the naïve or physical or sexual mode of consciousness' (vi. 114).

This last view does not follow obviously from Burrow's positions but is rather an idiosyncratic addition to them. Yet on the whole Lawrence is very attentive to what Burrow has to say in *The Social Basis of Consciousness*, perceives the originalities of the approach – in spite of its abstractions and obfuscating jargon – and is genuinely grateful for the framework it offered for thinking about his own social failures. Some might argue that these were a consequence of his never having been completely and successfully socialised. Although he learned some caution in later life, there was never far below the surface in Lawrence the impetuous urge to go out to others in search of a genuinely warm human contact. As much as any awareness of his exceptional talents, this quality, which rightly or wrongly Lawrence himself associated with his working-class background, explains why so many people who met him for a short time recalled being in his company with such pleasure. He never learned that art of manoeuvring among others with an eye constantly alert to one's own pyschological advantage which in his view all the Forsytes had mastered so completely. To a large extent he remained child-like, although not childish, in his search for love. Yet those who agree with him in thinking real human contact ('touch' as he sometimes liked to term it) one of the few substantial happinesses of life will not be inclined to call him immature, or dispute his claim that it was the general state of life in society which deserved to be considered 'abnormal' rather than his own. One could say that on many occasions he egotistically expected too much of others, and too much of life (a man who had one friend as faithful as Brewster and another who would prove as loyal as Aldous Huxley did not perhaps have much right to complain); but one would have to be curiously eupeptic not to be affected by his analysis of the unfortunate way we live now, to which he was prompted by Burrow's book. The problem was, how to imagine a state of affairs which could be radically different: 'How to regain the naïve or innocent soul – how to make it the man within man – your "societal": and at the same time keep the cognitive mode for defences and adjustments and "work" – voilà! As for myself', he added to these puzzles in his letter to Burrow,

I'm in despair. I've been in bed this last month with bronchial hemorrhages – due, radically to chagrin – though I was born bronchial – born in chagrin too. But I'm better – shaky – shaky – and we're going to Austria tomorrow D.V. – whoever D. may be – to the mountains. (vi. 114–15)

◆

CHAPTER SIXTEEN

August 1927–January 1928
LADY CHATTERLEY'S LOVER

I Convalescence

On 4 August the Lawrences were due to take the night train into Austria. Orioli had by then left Florence for Vallombrosa (vi. 109), but he had arranged for them to rest in his flat between their coming down from San Polo and going to the station. The Wilkinsons were very helpful in at least the first of these operations. Writing to Arthur Wilkinson from Austria on 7 August, Lawrence said that he was 'eternally grateful to you all for getting me out' (vi. 119). He survived the night in a sleeping-car well and continued to improve, telling all his friends of the relief he felt at escaping from the heat, and Ada that he liked the relaxation of the poverty-stricken Austrians after the 'bossiness of Fascist Italy' (vi. 121). He and Frieda had gone to Villach, a resort surrounded by mountains just over the north Italian border. The plan was to join his sister-in-law Johanna and her husband at a hotel on the nearby lake, the Ossiachersee, six miles away. He liked 'Nusch', the only woman Barbara Weekley ever heard him describe as 'desirable';[1] but because he found himself comfortably installed at the Hotel Fischer in Villach (not an easy thing to manage for a man in his condition), he and Frieda decided it would be best to make their base there. There would be more to see in a town than by a lake for someone who still could not walk very far.

To occupy himself during the three weeks he spent in Villach, Lawrence returned to the translation of more Verga short stories. Back in April, Jonathan Cape's request for a new introduction for the reissue of Verga's *Mastro-don Gesualdo* had reminded him that he had already translated more of Verga's short fiction than had appeared in *Little Novels of Sicily*. The work already done included 'The She Wolf' and 'Cavalleria rusticana', the famous story which would provide the title for a further collection he had by July agreed to prepare for Cape (vi. 110). As part of his convalescence, he now devoted all his time to Verga, sending Orioli on 20 August a short list of linguistic puzzles (vi. 131). This work could be only modestly remunerative but while he was still ill – on the 25th he informed Mabel Luhan that he was 'about a third' recovered (vi. 136) – he could hardly earn much. On 27 August he nevertheless told Ada that, if Gertie Cooper proved to have spent all her money on her treatment, we can manage her between us. I could tell the bank to pay her £50 a year – and I'd never know. . . So don't let her bother about money, but let me know if she still has enough, or I should begin to help her now. I could pay it to you, so she needn't worry. And don't tell anybody. I hate these money things talked about. (vi. 137)

At the end of the month, the imminent return of Johanna's husband to his bank in Berlin was a signal for them all to move. Since coming back from America, Lawrence had talked often of wanting to accept Else's suggestion that he and Frieda should go to the area south of Munich for a while, and this is what he now did. At Irschenhausen, deep in the Bavarian countryside, there was the small wooden summer home which Edgar Jaffe had built and which the Lawrences had occupied for two short periods in 1913.[2] To return there was to recall the vitality, turbulence and joy of the first years of their relationship. It pleased Lawrence to discover that Else was still employing the same servant ('Edgar's Anna of 14 years ago') and, responding favourably to a suggestion Secker made at this time that he ought to think about publishing his collected poems – 'or a selection, for I'd like to leave some out, and put some in' – he reported with pleasure that he had found his own 'first copy of *Love Poems*' still lying in a cupboard of the house (vi. 142, 168).[3] With a forest at the back and a wide open valley leading up to 'blue mountains' in front, the house at Irschenhausen again delighted him. Among the trees the ground was 'uncanny with mushrooms' and small red deer occasionally flitted past. The dark blue gentians of autumn were in bloom and the chicory flowers by the path which led up to the front porch were of an especially striking light blue. 'I love above all', he wrote to Brewster on 17 September,

the stillness of innumerable trees that are none the less silently growing, and pressing themselves on the air so softly yet so indomitably. I am glad not to be in Italy for a while. I don't [mind] if it rains some days, and is dark. I like it . . . I find Italy has almost withered me. Here something softens out again. (vi. 151)

Just over a week later, describing the beauty of his surroundings for the benefit of the Wilkinsons, he wrote, 'The jays are so cheeky they almost steal the tears out of your eyes' (vi. 158).

A friend of Else's named Elizabeth Mayer, whose husband was a psychiatrist in Munich, a 'short train ride away', and who later became closely associated with W. H. Auden, has left a record of visiting Lawrence at Irschenhausen in September 1927. As she walked up the path to the house, 'past the familiar pond with the white ducks' (having borrowed the house from Else in the past, she knew it well), she also was struck by the beauty of the chicory flowers. Lawrence was on the porch playing a variety of Patience called 'The Demon' which he had learned from his mother-in-law (vi. 207). 'He looked frail and not well, a cough frequently interrupting his talk'; but he was surrounded by the three Von

Richthofen sisters and 'one could see how fond he was of them and how well they took care of him'.[4] Else would be there because she had a larger house at Wolfratshausen nearby, and Johanna was following the conventions of her class in letting her husband go back to work on his own while summer was still not quite over. Their occasional presence, together with that of Barby (who was then in Cologne but later paid a short visit[5]) meant that Frieda could share the burden of care and made Irschenhausen an excellent place for Lawrence to recuperate. In a letter to Brett, he described swallowing 'malt and beer and milk and chalk for my fatal tubes' and said that he was determined to 'get them hardened'. They had nagged him all his life and he was going to see what could be done. 'Next week I'll have a talk with a Munich specialist. But it is a thing Englishmen are liable to, and especially at my age, and it usually lasts a year or two' (vi. 154–5).

With her Ph.D. and close association with men who either had been or still were professors at the university, Frieda's sister Else must have been unusually well connected in the intellectual community of the Munich area. It was almost certainly through her that two prominent literary figures, Franz Schoenberner and Hans Carossa, came to see Lawrence at Irschenhausen. It can hardly have been an accident that the second of these two was a doctor as well as a writer, and a doctor who, in addition to writing novels and poems, specialised in the treatment of tuberculosis.[6] Late in September Carossa examined Lawrence who reported his verdict to Else on 7 October, after he had left Irschenhausen. 'He listened to me – I mean to my breathing-passages – could hear nothing in the lungs, says they must be healed – only the bronchials – and doctors aren't a bit interested in bronchials. But he says I shouldn't do any hot-air inhalations: that will start the bleeding again' (vi. 172). This diagnosis differs markedly from the one Carossa apparently gave Schoenberner who was with him on the visit. As the two of them walked to the station, Schoenberner asked what the real situation was: 'He hesitated a moment before he said, "An average man with those lungs would have died long ago. But with a real artist no normal prognosis is really sure. There are other forces involved. Maybe Lawrence can live two or three years more. But no medical treatment can really save him." '[7]

When Lawrence met him, Schoenberner was the editor of a lively and irreverent satirical magazine called *Jugend*; later, and until 1933, he took over the editorship of the much better-known but equally disrespectful *Simplicissimus*. Nazi Germany was never going to be a comfortable place for such a man and his memories of Lawrence were published in 1946 when he was an exile in New York. Normally a biographer will always prefer an account written at the time to one which appeared nearly twenty years later. In this case, however, there is every reason for believing, not that Lawrence's memory was faulty, but that Schoenberner recorded Carossa's true opinion. It seems at first deplorable that a man who was as frank and open as Lawrence should have been lied to, specifically on this (to him) crucial question of 'lungs'. But doctors knew that for someone in a state of advanced tuberculosis there was no medical cure, and that the only faint hope was therefore spontaneous remission. They must have known also that the chances of that wholly exceptional event were likely to disappear once a patient came to believe he or she was lost. In those circumstances, it would not be surprising if some of them learned to say comforting things, or even what they were quickly able to deduce their patients wanted to hear.

Throughout his period at Irschenhausen, Lawrence continued to translate the remaining stories in the *Cavalleria rusticana* collection. When she made her visit, Elizabeth Mayer was already the translator of several contemporary Italian writers into German, so that she and Lawrence had a 'lively conversation' about the difficulties of rendering dialect, even though the sisters had said he was not to talk much because of his condition.[8] By 28 September he was ready to send the final manuscript of the Verga translations, 'together with my Introduction', to Rowena Killick: his contact at the Curtis Brown office while Nancy Pearn took a summer holiday which included two days with a woman friend at the Villa Mirenda, being looked after by Giulia Pini and the Wilkinsons (vi. 165, 167).

The introduction to *Cavalleria rusticana* is substantial and deserves to be better known, including as it does some of Lawrence's most significant critical thinking as well as several of his most memorable formulations. It begins with an account of Verga's flirtation with the *beau monde*, his retreat to his native Sicily and his discovery there of his real subject – peasant life, and the manner in which it should be treated: 'verismo'. Lawrence goes on to note the 'pure human candour' of many of the stories' doomed protagonists, deceived husbands for the most part who kill their rivals and then spend the rest of their lives in jail. Were their women worth it? Of course they weren't: 'Nowadays we have learnt more sense, and we let [a woman] go her way.' And yet, 'hurt [a human being] mortally at its sexual root, and it will recoil ultimately into some form of killing.'[9] It seems to him that these figures have retained their 'naive innocent core' (unlike, anyone who had been reading his latest work might have wanted to add, the characters in Galsworthy); and that as a result they are always being destroyed by the 'sophisticated greedy ones'. Verga, Lawrence wrote, 'found the vulgar and the greedy always destroying the sensitive and the passionate'.[10]

From these remarks on the action of the stories, Lawrence passes to more important reflections on Verga's literary aesthetic. To appreciate these fully it is useful to look back to a number of important paragraphs on Flaubert's realism in the introduction to Cape's reissue of *Mastro-don Gesualdo*, written at the beginning of May. Adopting the Jamesian position that Emma and Charles Bovary are 'too insignificant to carry the full weight of Gustave Flaubert's profound sense of tragedy', Lawrence makes two further criticisms of a novel which he nevertheless feels is self-evidently a great book. Given that 'the human soul has supreme joy in true, vivid, consciousness', and that Flaubert himself clearly has 'a pure satisfaction and joy in his own consciousness, even if the consciousness be only of ultimate tragedy or misery', he regrets that Emma Bovary is conceived as too small a figure to share in that joy. He regrets, too, that she is allowed none of Flaubert's own 'heroic impulse', her own version of her creator's 'heroic effort to be truthful, to show things as they are'. Emma cannot of course have either of these qualities because she has been conceived in a realist mode. Yet in Lawrence's view the discrediting of heroic effort by the realists has almost extinguished in the young 'that instinctive fighting for more life to come into being'. The trouble is that 'life without the heroic effort, and without *belief* in the subtle, life-long validity of the heroic impulse, is just stale, flat and unprofitable. As the great realistic novels will show you.' The impression these convey – that the life they portray is life as it must inevitably be – is an illusion. Flaubertian realism, 'as every one knows, has no more to do with reality than romanticism has. Realism is just one of the arbitrary views man takes of man.'[11]

Verga's 'verismo' was an Italian adaptation of Flaubertian realism and its Naturalist successors, and in his introduction to the stories in *Cavalleria rusticana* Lawrence regrets that their author should have been so dazzled by the French and adopted so many of their literary views. One of these is the need for the writer to practise self-effacement, which Lawrence sees as a reaction to the Romantic, egotistical effusiveness of a writer such as Hugo. He points out, as he had done at the beginning of his literary career in reviewing Thomas Mann's *Death in Venice*,[12] that 'self-effacement is quite as self-conscious, and perhaps even more conceited than letting oneself go'. With the Flaubertian fashion for eliminating all traces of the author goes a cult of form which, for Lawrence, makes Verga's most highly praised stories like 'La lupa', or 'Cavalleria rusticana' itself, just a little too controlled (whereas 'Rosso Malpelo' is one of the 'finest stories ever written'). 'As a matter of fact', he writes, 'we need more looseness. We need an apparent formlessness, definite form is mechanical. We need more easy transitions from mood to mood and from deed to deed. A great deal of the meaning of life and of art lies in the apparently dull spaces, the pauses, the unimportant passages.'[13]

The habit Verga has of missing out transitions so that the effect becomes confused is partly then (Lawrence explains) a question of literary fashion but, more profoundly, it also represents an attempt to mirror the workings of the emotional rather than merely logical mind. 'Instinctively', Lawrence claims, '[Verga] had come to hate the tyranny of a persistently logical sequence, or even a persistently chronological sequence'; and he then defines the alternative in words whose appositeness reveals the importance of the topic for his own practice and beliefs.

Now the emotional mind . . . is not logical. It is a psychological fact, that when we are thinking emotionally or passionately, thinking and feeling at the same time, we do not think rationally: and therefore, and therefore, and therefore. Instead, the mind makes curious swoops and circles. It touches the point of pain or interest, then sweeps away again in a cycle, coils round and approaches again the point of pain or interest. There is a curious spiral rhythm, and the mind approaches again and again the point of concern, repeats itself, goes back, destroys the time-sequence entirely, so that time ceases to exist, as the mind stoops to the quarry, then leaves it without striking, soars, hovers, turns, swoops, stoops again, still does not strike, yet is nearer, nearer, reels away again, wheels off into the air, even forgets, quite forgets, yet again turns, bends, circles slowly, swoops and stoops again, until at last there is the closing-in, and the clutch of a decision or a resolve.[14]

As a riposte to the frequent complaints about Lawrence's own lack of 'form', nothing could be more apt or better expressed. Despite his infatuation with the French, Verga is able (in Lawrence's view) to render unaffectedly these fluctuations of the emotional mind: 'He is doing, as a great artist, what men like James Joyce do only out of contrariness and desire for a sensation.'[15]

On 4 October the Lawrences moved to Baden-Baden for a final fortnight with Frieda's mother. They stayed once again at the hotel whose full title was the 'Kurhaus Eden' (vi. 186), and Lawrence decided to make as much use as he could of the town's medical facilities. He had been examined by one of the doctors in charge at the Baths the last time he was in Baden-Baden. On this occasion, the examination produced a significant, if only temporary, alteration in the way he referred to his condition. He reported the doctor as saying that he was 'really rather better than . . . last year', but that there was catarrh which, though clearer on the 'lower lungs', was 'still not clear at the top'. Writing to Ada about her young son Bertie's measles on 9 October, he warned, 'I do hope you've taken care to see there were no after-effects. I believe all three of us, Emily and you and I, got a lot of catarrh trouble as the effects of measles'; and he went on to say that, although he had no intention of going into a sanatorium now he was on the mend, he wanted to get 'that catarrh of the lungs down' (vi. 177, 179).

'Lungs' had been (and would soon become again) a taboo word for Lawrence; and the sanatorium was close to being a taboo subject. The question had already been raised in Florence, but replying on 31 July to a letter from Gertler, who was an unusually interested party, Lawrence had said that his doctor supported him in not thinking a sanatorium necessary (vi. 109). In Baden-Baden it is clearer that he himself was the one who decided against that option. Gertler's example might have been encouraging (despite Lawrence having meanly described him on 22 September as 'swallowing milk upon milk, and feeling he's triumphed in merely being alive' – vi. 155); but Gertie Cooper's was far less so. He had been appalled by what had happened to her, telling Koteliansky soon after his return from the

Etruscan trip that Gertie's had been 'a horrible business – in a hospital in London these last two months – left lung removed, six ribs removed, glands in the neck – too horrible – better die . . . Why aren't we better at dying, straight dying! What is left, after all those operations?' (vi. 42). Reporting to Emily that the Baden-Baden doctor wanted him to go into a sanatorium for two months so that he could increase his weight he said, 'Look at poor G and sanatoriums. I'm sure the thought of her simply breaks my heart: a year now' (vi. 177). Had he known the statistics he might have taken a gloomy satisfaction in the degree of support they gave to his position. A recent historian of the treatment of tuberculosis in Britain reports that, of all the patients who were treated in sanatoriums in 1914, 80 per cent were dead by 1920; and that, of the 3,000 discharged after sanatorium treatment under the London County Council in 1927, only 24 per cent were still alive by 1932.[16] She does not however give survival rates for those who rejected advice to enter a sanatorium; and there were the examples of Somerset Maugham and Middleton Murry, as well as of Gertler and Gertie Cooper, to suggest that taking this step could on occasions increase life expectancy.

Instead of that solution, Lawrence opted for the inhalation cure, although of the cold air variety because Hans Carossa had told him the hot might produce more bleeding. The benefit was supposed to come from the air being impregnated with radium. He described the setting for the cure to Max Mohr, another German writer who had trained as a doctor, and who had driven from his house in the mountains south of Munich to visit Lawrence in Irschenhausen (vi. 173). This contact came not through Else but from correspondents in England where Mohr had been a prisoner of war, and where he is most likely to have developed his view that Lawrence was 'the greatest living novelist' (vi. 157). After explaining his reactions to several of Mohr's plays he had been reading, Lawrence told him on 10 October that, in addition to listening patiently to concerts in the Kurgarten and taking tea with 'the beloved woman' in the Waldkaffee, he had to sit every morning 'in a white coat and hood, in a vaporous room with other figures vaguely seen through the mists in more white mantles and hoods . . . doing an Inhalationkur' (vi. 183). He thought it did him some good but, four days later, the effects seemed 'not at all miraculous' (vi. 189).[17]

As he looked forward to the future, Lawrence wondered what he would do in the winter. The Baden-Baden doctor recommended the mountains, and the Lawrences had already been thinking of Cortina d'Ampezzo 'because the Huxleys said it did wonders for them last winter – so they're going again' (vi. 179, 155). But Bonamy Dobrée, recently appointed to a university post in Egypt, had written to invite the Lawrences to stay with him and his wife in a house near Cairo. That seemed interesting, and Lawrence sent a letter to Valentine Dobrée, who was still in London, urging her to spend a few days at the Villa Mirenda on her way out to join her husband, partly, no doubt, so that he could glean more details (vi. 170–1). He was worried that the Egyptian climate might not be suitable for his 'beastly bronchials' (vi. 171); but also that travelling to Egypt would prove too expensive. The difficulty was that it was hard to make a living once you were sick. On 26 September, a week before he left Irschenhausen, he had told the Wilkinsons that he and Frieda were spending more than he earned and, 'as Richard Aldington says – you can't even have poor relief if you've been two years out of England!!' (vi. 158). Yet still, after describing his idea for the Etruscan book to Knopf three weeks later, he was able to say that he did not much care whether or not he finished it – 'I can eke out a living on stories and little articles' (vi. 182). To do even that he needed to recover, but it may be that he was able to write to Knopf as he did because, by 10 October, after more than two months in Austria and Germany, he was feeling so much better. For that result Frieda's family, as well as Frieda herself, must take some credit. At Irschenhausen in September he had learned that old Mrs Weekley, the model for the Mater in *The Virgin and the Gipsy*, had died. Any suspicion that his savage treatment of the Mater could relate in a direct way to Frieda's mother is dispelled by the letter which he sent to Ada from Baden-Baden on 9 October. 'My mother-in-law', he tells her, 'is wonderful – seems to get younger . . . She is really very nice – and whatever she can do for me, she does it – thinks of everything possible. Frieda's sisters the same – they really cudgel their brains to think of any way to help. I must say people are kind – so were our neighbours the Wilkinsons, at the Mirenda' (vi. 179–80).

II Home Comforts

On 19 October 1927, Lawrence and Frieda were met by the Wilkinsons at Florence station and taken in a hired car back to the Villa Mirenda. Over the months, Giulia Pini, to whom Lawrence had sent at least two postcards from abroad, and who was entrusted with the surveillance of their flat, had become an important person in their lives, and he noticed on his return how pretty she was becoming (vi. 194). In normal times the Lawrences gave Giulia 20 lire a week, for which she came in at 7 a.m. to make the coffee and stayed on for around 3 hours to clean and wash the dishes. She did no cooking or laundry but returned to the villa at 1.30 p.m. to wash up again; and was often available in the evening for sewing and conversation with Frieda (vi. 392, 398). Helpful and unobtrusive, her presence was one of the many assets of living how and where they did.

Throughout the 1920s Frieda missed the comforts of a settled home. Not at all a socialite, and easily contented with the simple (but not too arduous) routines of domestic life, she was happy in the Villa Mirenda, especially now that the rooms they occupied were furnished to their taste. Yet in spite of his appreciation of

Giulia, Lawrence himself could not wait to leave. He acknowledges very frankly that this was because he now associated Florence, as he had done Oaxaca, with the miseries of illness. Two days after his return he told Brewster, 'Frieda loves it here: but since I was ill, I look round at it all, and it means nothing to me, though it's quite nice'; and ten days later he wrote to Emily, 'It's nice to be quiet and peaceful again but since I was ill here, I've sort of lost my attachment to the place – to Italy altogether' (vi. 195, 200). Understanding the irrationality of his motives did not always make them any less potent.

Lawrence's two-and-a-half months' convalescence in Austria and Germany had improved his condition but he still found it impossible to walk uphill without gasping (vi. 196). He began to think of this as a consequence of his 'asthma' (vi. 211). It was harder for him to find relatively anodyne explanations for the cough which now hardly ever left him. He tried a number of patent medicines. From Germany he had brought back a 'Brust-thee' (a herbal tea for chest conditions) which he religiously allowed to boil slowly for hours; and he was as faithful as he had been in New Mexico to 'Solution Patanberge' (v. 236, vi. 198, 200). Arthur Lawrence had been a strong advocate of these 'natural' remedies; but by 1927 his son was past their help. In the following year Lawrence would take, on Ada's recommendation, capsules supposedly made from a South African plant called 'Umckaloaba' (vi. 336, 350). This was one of several clinically worthless remedies for tuberculosis 'invented' by Major C. H. Stevens of Wimbledon, the medically unqualified proprietor of a 'Consumption Cure Co.' and a likely inspiration for Teddy Ponderevo of Wimblehurst in Wells's *Tono Bungay*. Fond as he had been of that novel, Lawrence was in no state to make the connection.[18]

Very soon after settling back in, he did his best to help Koteliansky who at this period was full of modest money-making schemes which came either to nothing, or to so little that other, supplementary schemes were soon required. On this occasion, and perhaps inspired by his friend Leonard Woolf, Kot was thinking of becoming a publisher. He had in mind a series of short texts, of no more than 10,000 words, in which well-known writers could sound off in a way not possible to them through the normal channels. These would form the 'Intimate Series' and sell at 15 shillings or a pound for each slim volume. Lawrence was not very enthusiastic: 'personally I don't like expensive limited editions', he wrote to Kot from Baden-Baden (vi. 190); and nor was he sanguine about the scheme's commercial possibilities. He was nevertheless keen to help an old friend who was feeling particularly gloomy (vi. 159), and had promised Kot from Germany that he would sound out Aldous Huxley and Norman Douglas once he was back in Florence.

He had been back on speaking terms with Douglas from as long ago as May. 'I've promised to be reconciled to Douglas, since I've been here a year and never spoken nor even nodded to him', he had written to Secker on 29 April (vi. 45);

and we know from unpublished letters that the meeting in Orioli's shop which Aldington later described must have taken place very shortly afterwards.[19] According to Aldington, the tension of their first coming together was only dissipated after Douglas had said, 'Have a pinch of snuff, dearie', and Lawrence then remarked that the only other person ever to have offered him snuff was his father.[20] Born in 1868, Douglas was in fact almost old enough to be Lawrence's father, and tended to assume an elder-statesman air with the younger writers he frequented. In *A Plea For Better Manners* he had referred to Lawrence on several occasions as his 'young friend'.[21]

On 26 October Lawrence wrote to Douglas about the 'Intimate Series', sending his letter to Prato where Douglas was temporarily staying, chiefly to avoid being hounded by the Florentine mother of the young boy he had recently taken to live with him.[22] The reply was friendly enough and Douglas responded positively to the idea that he should come and see the Lawrences at the Villa Mirenda; but he declined to have anything to do with Kot's scheme on the grounds that he was far too embroiled in his own private publishing ventures. As he explained, he was busy distributing to the few enthusiasts who had subscribed, his own recent *Birds and Beasts of the Greek Anthology*; and at the same time he had to oversee the printing of his new novel *In the Beginning*. At that stage, it seemed as if the first of these books, an esoteric labour of gentleman-scholar love, would not sell enough to cover its production costs; and he was pessimistic about the prospects of the second.[23] 'The mania for privately printed books seems to be declining' he told Lawrence, and he regretted that he could not do anything for his 'little Jew' (vi. 203). When Lawrence forwarded this reply to Kot he said, 'Don't mind that he calls you a little Jew, it's merely Douglas' (vi. 203); yet he himself had participated in the casual anti-semitism of the day, with its degrading stereotypes, when in his original letter he had referred to Kot as 'A friend of mine, Jew, but a poor one' (vi. 198).[24]

In addition to writing to Douglas, Lawrence tried to help Kot with what we can assume was his own intended contribution for the 'Intimate Series'. This opens very much in the manner of the autobiographical essays about his home town which he had written during or just after his visit to Eastwood in the summer of 1926: 'Nothing depresses me more than to come home to the place where I was born, and where I lived my first twenty years, here, at Newthorpe, this coal-mining village on the Nottingham–Derby border.'[25] The present-tense mode would suggest that 1926 is when the opening of 'A Dream of Life' was in fact first composed, if it were not for the fact that instead of referring to the strike, Lawrence mentions rather the short-time working which had followed the defeat of the miners and which he would have heard about from his sisters (vi. 178, 245). But after continuing in a naturalistic manner for some time, and elaborating on the idea which had been central to 'Making Love to Music' – that the people of his day were a consequence of the way their grandmothers had dreamed about the future – 'A Dream of Life' is transformed into a fable when the narrator visits the quarry which figures so prominently in *The White Peacock*[26] and finds a womb-like cave in which he can curl up and fall asleep. Having specified the date as October 1927 (helpfully confirming speculation about when 'A Dream of Life' was written), he wakes up exactly 1,000 years later. What greets him is 'intimate' only in the sense that it represents Lawrence's private dream of how his home town of Eastwood should really have been.

We climbed up towards the top of the town, and I felt I must be passing the very place where I was born, near where the Wesleyan Chapel stood. But now it was all softly lighted, golden-coloured porticoes, with people passing in green or blue or grey-and-scarlet cloaks.

We came out on top into a circular space, it must have been where our Congregational Chapel stood, and in the centre of the circle rose a tower shaped tapering rather like a lighthouse, and rosy-coloured in the lamplight. Away in the sky, at the club-shaped tip of the tower, glowed one big ball of light.[27]

When the inhabitants of the transformed Eastwood do not wear cloaks or tunics, they wear nothing at all (which suggests a radical change in the Midlands climate). The men have the look of ancient Egytians, and there is communal dancing and singing amid a general seemliness, calm and beauty. 'A Dream of Life' would have been Lawrence's version of *News from Nowhere*, but the writing was interrupted by morning fogs around San Polo which made him 'bark'. This was the word he used to describe his cough in his response to Huxley's news that he was too committed to Chatto and Windus to be able to participate in Kot's 'Intimate Series': 'Poor Kot, he'll be depressed about his "scheme" . . . I do what I can for him – but why should anybody want to be a publisher?' (vi. 202). He promised Kot that he could have a manuscript for him by Christmas (vi. 203); but his lack of success with both Huxley and Douglas may be sufficient explanation why 'A Dream of Life' was never finished.[28]

During his last days in Baden-Baden, Lawrence had conceived the idea for a picture of Adam and Eve reversing the course of human history by driving God out of Paradise – 'Get out of here, you righteous old bird!' (vi. 190). 'Barking' or not, he completed this water-colour within a month of his return, as well as a brightly coloured oil painting of a jaguar leaping out of the jungle at the throat of a native (vi. 212), which may have been a reminiscence of his time in Ceylon.[29] In the Adam and Eve composition, the crouching female nude, who is handing Adam another apple to replace the one he has just hurled at a fat-thighed Ancient of Days taking evasive action in the background, has a face which is suggestive of Frieda's.

It is likely to have been after he had finished these two paintings, and 'A Dream of Life', that Lawrence wrote 'Rawdon's Roof', an undistinguished and yet, for the biographer, irritatingly intriguing short story which he posted off to Nancy Pearn on 17 November. The Rawdon in question is a man who is separated from his wife and has sworn that no woman will ever sleep under his roof again. He has a liaison with a neighbour named Janet Drummond whose unsatisfactory husband returns from one of his long absences 'in a bigger mess than ever', and wants to make love to her in order to get the mess 'off his mind'.[30] When Janet retreats to Rawdon's house and asks to be allowed to stay there, the story contrasts his ungallant refusal with the fact that his manservant is entertaining a lady friend that night (some women do sleep under Rawdon's roof after all). What makes the story mysterious is that, like 'The Last Laugh' or 'The Border-Line', 'Rawdon's Roof' seems to require some explanation of its biographical origin in order to become fully meaningful (without this, it lacks point as well as literary quality), but that none is obviously available. Derek Britton has made an effort to link the story with Gordon and Beatrice Campbell whom Lawrence had known well during the war and who were now living in Ireland. On 21 October, and again on 16 November, he wrote to the Campbells enquiring about the possibility of going to live in Ireland: one of the several alternatives to the Villa Mirenda he was then considering (the notion of joining the Dobrées in Egypt was ruled out when he heard from Valentine Dobrée at the end of October that her father was ill – vi. 205). Yet as Britton himself admits, there are no 'strong identifying features' to link the Campbells with the Drummonds; and his idea that Rawdon himself could be based on Campbell's former close friend Middleton Murry is in conflict with all the other portraits of Murry in Lawrence's work.[31]

'Rawdon's Roof' *feels* as if it began with the resounding, somewhat Douglasian statement of a friend or acquaintance that 'No woman shall sleep again under my roof!' It may only be a biographer's vice to worry that we have no certain way of knowing who that friend or acquaintance was. As Lawrence has failed in this story to transform personal thoughts and feelings into material of sufficient general interest, what difference would it make if we did know? Of the suspicion that it might make *some* difference, and the lingering curiosity concerning the origin of 'Rawdon's Roof', it can at least be suggested that a biographer of Lawrence who was inclined to experience both would have his subject's support. In the first weeks after his return from Germany, Lawrence worked hard on the preparation for Secker of his *Collected Poems*, dividing them roughly into a first volume he called 'rhyming verse' (*Love Poems and Others*, *Amores*, *New Poems*, *Bay*) and a second of 'unrhyming' pieces (*Look! We Have Come Through!* and *Birds, Beasts and Flowers*). In the process of doing this, he came to regret the absence of a biographical framework for material, much of which, he must have recognised as he arranged or revised it, was deeply and sometimes painfully personal. In the longer of two alternative introductions to *Collected Poems* with which he would provide Secker in May 1928, he tried to supply a minimum of biographical background, referring as he did so to Jessie Chambers and Helen Corke as 'Miriam' and 'Helen', but to his former fiancée Louie Burrows merely as 'the other woman, the woman of "Kisses in the Train" and "The Hands of the Betrothed" '. In the shorter version (which he wrote second and which is the one Secker chose to use), what he can say about himself is necessarily curtailed but in insisting again on the need for a biographical framework, he introduces a fresh comparison:

It seems to me that no poetry, not even the best, should be judged as if it existed in the absolute, in the vacuum of the absolute. Even the best poetry, when it is at all personal, needs the penumbra of its own time and place and circumstance to make it full and whole. If we knew a little more of Shakespeare's self and circumstance how much more complete the Sonnets would be to us, how their strange, torn edges would be softened and merged into a whole body![32]

What Lawrence says here is not only applicable to poetry. It is clear from the way he wrote about fiction and painting that for him all art was fundamentally an act of self-expression and that biographical information had always therefore the potential to be relevant. Certainly he had no compunction about calling it into play himself and would no doubt have extended his impatience with the Flaubertian doctrine of impersonality to its updated version in T. S. Eliot's famous distinction between the man who suffers and the mind which creates.[33]

Preparing an edition of his collected verse was hard work because in typing out individual poems Lawrence also made what were often very substantial alterations (so much so that several need to be considered as quite new). This was a potentially awkward procedure for someone so committed to spontaneity, and so hostile to the stylistic polishing Lawrence most often associated with Flaubert. In order to sanction it, he would describe in both of his introductions how, in his early days, the self inhabited by his creative demon was often stifled by the commonplace youth he also then was: 'A young man is afraid of his demon and puts his hand over the demon's mouth sometimes and speaks for him.'[34] This meant that in altering his early poems he was merely giving them the form they should really have always had, and removing from them the effects of youthful inhibition. As he puts it, 'It is not for technique these poems are altered: it is to say the real say.'[35] The terms in which Lawrence describes the struggle in gifted young writers between creativity and convention were striking and soon picked up. In his biography of W. H. Auden, Humphrey Carpenter quotes a letter of advice written in 1932 to a very young John Cornford in which Auden says, 'Real poetry originates in the guts and only flowers in the head. But one is always trying to reverse the process and work one's guts from one's head. Just when the

Daemon is going to speak, the Prig claps his hand over his mouth and edits it.'[36] Yet whether all the many changes Lawrence made to his early poetry can be justified in terms of this image of the Prig or the Demon is very doubtful. In *Love Poems and Others* (for example), where hardly a single poem is unaltered, there are numerous minor changes whose rationale appears suspiciously stylistic, or which seem to have been introduced for clarification. The change in 'Kisses in the Train' from 'And still my wet mouth / Sought her afresh' to 'And still my blind face / Sought her afresh' could hardly be cited as an example of the young man who wrote the original version having his 'real say'; while the move from 'As I stand on this hill, with the whitening cave of the city beyond, / Helen,' to 'As I stand on this hill, with the whitening cave of the city in front, / And this Helen beside me', in the *Collected Poems*' version of 'Repulsed', is typical of how Lawrence tries in his revisions to make things clearer.[37]

There are, however, many more radical kinds of alteration. 'Repulsed' had ended with the narrator and 'Helen' hating each other so that its last line read, 'As a man hates the dreaming woman he loves, but who will not reply.' In the last line of 'Repulsed' in *Collected Poems*, Helen is referred to as, 'The female whose venom can more than kill, can numb and then nullify.'[38] It is hard to think of this view of her as one the young Lawrence had been too inhibited to express. Two of the poems in *Love Poems and Others* ('Corot' and 'Michael-Angelo') contain frequent references to 'God'. In *Collected Poems* these have all been eliminated or replaced by 'Life' or 'Time', which is not to restore the record to what it should have been but rather to re-write it. The longest piece in Lawrence's first collection is an excellent dialect poem entitled 'Whether or Not'. Concerned with a situation similar to the one he had dealt with in 'Fanny and Annie', or in his play *The Daughter-in-Law*, a reader gathers from the various voices in this poem that a young woman's fiancé has had an affair with a middle-aged widow with whom he has been lodging and made her pregnant. (The limited familiarities the young woman has allowed him, the fiancé says in his defence, have proved so arousing that he has had to find an outlet for his sexual feelings somewhere.) Disgusted though she is with his behaviour, the young woman decides she must make the best of things, use her own money to pay off the widow and ensure that her own marriage can go ahead. Lawrence made minor changes to the first ten sections of this narrative poem but then added an eleventh in which the fiancé declares that he has no more intention of marrying the young woman than he has of doing his duty by the older one. 'Talk about love o' women!', he says, 'Ter me it's no fun'; and he adds, in reference to the widow,

> What bit o' cunt I had wi' 'er
>   's all I got out of it.
> An' 's not good enough, it isn't
> For a permanent fit.[39]

This may be what Lawrence felt he *should* have written as a young man but it is not what he ever *could* have written, demon or not.[40]

III Turning Point

It was a long time after his return before Lawrence felt fit enough to go into town. The Wilkinsons took both the Lawrences on a car trip to San Gimignano around 9 November, and by the 14th he had been visited by Orioli and Reggie Turner who brought with them Charles Scott-Moncrieff and the young Harold Acton (vi. 209, 214).[41] But Lawrence did not himself go into Florence before 17 November when he posted 'Rawdon's Roof' to Nancy Pearn. The consequence of this excursion was having to stay in bed the next morning. He explained how angry this made him in a reply to a letter from Aldington and Arabella Yorke in which they had obviously asked whether he needed to borrow any money. 'You shouldn't offer your hard-earned savings', Lawrence wrote, '– my goodness, I damn well ought to have enough to live on – so I have, by living like a road-sweeper. But basta! But I saw the end of my days, and my only, or chief grief was, I couldn't spit in the face of the narrow gutted world and put its eye out.' Going on to explain that he was not feeling well, even though he had arranged the day before for Pietro to bring the *barrocino* to Ponte Vingone so that he and Frieda would not have to walk back up to the villa, he said that nothing enraged him like not getting well (vi. 220).

Anger was one of Lawrence's characteristic responses to falling ill. Huxley, who knew him as well as anyone during his last years, offered a highly influential analysis of the role it played in the introduction to his collection of Lawrence's letters.

The secret consciousness of his dissolution filled the last years of his life with an overpowering sadness . . . It was, however, in terms of anger that he chose to express this sadness. Emotional indecency always shocked him profoundly, and, since anger seemed to him less indecent as an emotion than a resigned or complaining melancholy, he preferred to be angry.[42]

There is a good deal of truth in this and it is certainly the case that Lawrence was always much more inclined to explode with anger against the unfairness of the world than hope to attract sympathy with a 'complaining melancholy'. Yet this was true long before he fell ill; and the debilitating effects of his disease tended to make his outbursts of rage less frequent and less violent. Huxley suggests that a secret consciousness of his imminent death made Lawrence permanently angry. We have no evidence that *at this period* he was conscious of not having long to live, secretly or otherwise, and, as *Sketches of Etruscan Places* shows, anger was only one, if very important, method he had of responding to ill health.

The trip to Florence on 17 November tired Lawrence out but it was a momentous occasion for him: as near to anything else in these years to that biographer's salvation, a 'turning-point'. The meeting with Turner on that day, as well as with in all probability Orioli and Douglas, largely determined how he would spend his final years. This was because it was suggested to him that he should publish *Lady Chatterley's Lover* privately. The last word Lawrence had received from Douglas about private publication was that the bottom had fallen out of the market; but since then orders for *In the Beginning* had flowed in and, well before the publication date in December, he had already covered his costs.[43] If Douglas could do that, why should Lawrence not do the same, or better, given that he was much better known and given also (Lawrence's memories of the boost which prosecution had given to the sales of *Women in Love* may well have suggested) that the novel he had to offer was regarded in official circles as improper? Orioli would have explained how, with a relatively small outlay, Lawrence might make several hundred pounds, as much as 7 or 8, and without then being liable to either the new 20 per cent tax on royalties or the 10 per cent agent's fee. This would solve his current financial problems and take away the anxiety of the fact that, as he put it to Curtis Brown when on 18 November he broke the news about his plans for private publication, 'It is not cheap, being ill and doing cures' (vi. 222).

As well as being the day when he saw a way of resolving both his increasing financial difficulties and the problem of having written an unpublishable novel, 17 November mattered to Lawrence because, as he was walking by the Arno, he happened to bump into Dikran Kouyoumdjian, who had taken a flat in Florence for a while. He had known Kouyoumdjian during the war when he had introduced both him and Philip Heseltine to Garsington, and had later seen him fall in love with Dorothy Warren, Ottoline Morrell's niece.[44] Since that time Kouyoumdjian had wisely changed his name to Michael Arlen and become immensely rich and famous as the author of one of the most spectacular best-sellers of the 1920s, *The Green Hat* (1924). (When he came to tea at the Villa Mirenda on 19 November, he told the Lawrences that the American stage adaptation of his novel had earned him $5,650 in one week,[45] and the successful film with Greto Garbo which came out in the following year – *A Woman of Affairs* – cannot have done his bank-balance any harm either.) Lawrence had read *The Green Hat* and although he nowhere says so explicitly, it must have been just the kind of would-be avant-garde production he most despised. It suggested that in the 1920s the only way to be massively popular was to let the public have its cake and eat it.

Iris Storm, the heroine of *The Green Hat*, bears a superficial resemblance to Aldous Huxley's amoral, cocaine-sniffing vamps – Myra Viveash in *Antic Hay*, for example, or Lucy Tantamount in the *Point Counter Point* he was then busy writing. Her upper-class friends and relations regard her as having gone sadly off the rails after one of their finest products ('Boy' Fenwick) threw himself out of the window on the evening following his marriage to her. Chiefly because her now-alcoholic brother so admired 'Boy', Iris encourages them to assume that he did this because he discovered his wife was not a virgin whereas the truth, gradually revealed – the novel tips its hat to the avant-garde tendencies of the day by being a highly skilful exercise in delayed information – is that he has had to confess to Iris he is syphilitic. She, in any case, has only married him after the despair of being separated from her only true love, Napier Harpenden, by Napier's cruel, worldly father. In the course of the novel, Napier and Iris rediscover each other and eventually determine to sacrifice the conventions of their class to their abiding love. Yet just before they are about to leave England together, in a demonstration that she is a good sort really, Iris contrives to send her lover back to his wife and then commits suicide by driving her Hispano Suiza into the tree under which she, her brother and Napier used to play as children. This lurid and sentimental tale is unfolded to the accompaniment of both highly coloured descriptions of life in the fast lane in the 1920s (expensive sports cars, drugs, night-clubs, jazz), and a glamourised, nostalgic view of a country-house aristocracy that was fast disappearing in the post-war economic climate. It contains several erotic scenes which reverse the proportions in *Lady Chatterley's Lover* in that they are very high on suggestiveness (unlike Lawrence, Arlen could never have been accused of neglecting the importance of foreplay), and very low on explicit sexual detail.

Lawrence's previous references to *The Green Hat* show that he did not admire it,[46] but he rather warmed to its author, noting with some sympathy that the 'Florence snobs cut him dead' (v. 225). All his life Arlen had been the victim of prejudice. In the Garsington days, the normally tolerant Lady Ottoline had described him as 'a fat dark-blooded tight-skinned Armenian Jew' who was 'very coarse-grained and conceited' (ii. 473); and Rebecca West memorably characterised his standing among the English upper classes about whom he wrote, and with whom he now had more than enough money to mingle, when she called him 'every other inch a gentleman'.[47] Lawrence sympathised with Arlen as the permanent outsider who understood that he would never be properly accepted, and who perhaps never quite genuinely wanted to be. He clearly felt that if Arlen was often despised by people it was because they were envious, and would have been only too happy to make the same huge sums of money out of literature, had they possessed the knack.

What made Arlen endearing to Lawrence also was that he was or had been suffering from tuberculosis. Lawrence talks vaguely about this in his letters to friends but in a rare, almost unique diary entry, dated 19 November, records that Arlen had been obliged to have a tubercular testicle removed. This sufficiently explained why Arlen should be a 'sad lost dog' in spite of all his wealth. Lawrence saw him several times, before he went to San Moritz for (to use Lawrence's own word) his 'lungs'; and he almost certainly lunched with him, Douglas and others on 29 November.[48] About three days before, stimulated both by his scheme for private publication and by suggestions for a new dimension to his novel which meeting Arlen had provoked, he had begun to re-write *Lady Chatterley's Lover*. By 8 January he had completed a third version, very different from the other two.[49] Looking at Lawrence's complete works on the library shelf, most people rightly regard him as remarkably prolific. In terms of an average number of words per day, however, he was not in fact prolific in the manner of Mackenzie or Maugham; and indeed he rather prided himself on only writing when he felt like it. Yet when he did feel like it, he was capable of unusually sustained creative efforts, of the kind (for example) which had allowed him to write *Kangaroo* in six weeks. These periods of intense writing activity punctuate his career; but none is more remarkable than the six weeks in which he completed the almost 120,000 words of *Lady Chatterley's Lover* because during none of the others was he so debilitated by illness, and forced so often (as the letters and other documents attest) to retreat to his bed.

In the final version of *Lady Chatterley's Lover* Michael Arlen becomes the wholly new character Michaelis, an Irish playwright who is commercially very successful but both despised and envied by the 'society' people he depicts. In the diary entry which records having tea with Arlen on 19 November, Lawrence had written of him: 'Wants to marry . . . wants a Greek or Georgian wife, something Oriental, being himself an Armenian.' In the novel's account of Michaelis's first meeting with the Chatterleys, he announces that he is going to get married but not to an English, Irish or American woman: 'No, I've asked my man if he'll find me a Turk or something—something nearer to the Oriental.'[50] The introduction of Michaelis brings a new emphasis on commercial success in art, prostitution to what is repeatedly called the 'bitch goddess' of success. In the first half of the novel, Clifford is now a literary intellectual and the author of essentially insignificant short stories which bring him £1,200 a year. It might be thought ironic that Lawrence's often fiercely satirical concern with the way art is corrupted by the values of commerce should be most evident in a novel which would eventually make him so much money. But no criticism of a society can ever be effective, or even heard, unless the critic has been able to retain some modest standing-ground within it. The invaluable diary entry about Arlen ends:

We talked my poverty – it has got on my nerves lately. But next day had a horrible reaction, & felt sort of pariah. People must feel like that who make their lives out of money. Definitely I hate the whole money-making world, Tom & Dick as well as en gros. But I won't be done by them either.

One would have to be a saint – and Lawrence was very sceptical of sainthood – to feel that only the destitute have the moral right to criticise our present economic arrangements: that the only place from which to speak out against the corruption of most human relations by a concern for financial gain is a cardboard box. If Lawrence had no special responsibility to think about his own future, he certainly needed to be concerned with Frieda's; and had an obligation therefore not to allow himself to be 'done'. He lived modestly and precariously enough for the wholesale assault on the evils of commercialism in the final version of *Lady Chatterley's Lover* to be free of the charge of hypocrisy, whatever else one might think about it.

When he was writing 'The Sisters', Lawrence felt that Ursula needed more previous emotional and sexual experience before her relationship with Birkin and, partly as a result, *The Rainbow* slowly came into being. In *Lady Chatterley's Lover* Connie now has an affair with Michaelis before she becomes involved with her husband's gamekeeper. The descriptions of their sexual encounters introduce two themes which, if not entirely new, now assume much greater importance. The first and less important is infantilism. In his physical relations with Connie, Michaelis is like a little boy seeking maternal comfort; his appeal is that of a child. The same theme is developed in relation to Clifford who in his dependence on Mrs Bolton now regresses more and more. Part of the even more unsympathetic presentation of Clifford in the final version is a new scene where, after Connie has written to say that she wants a divorce, he becomes hysterical and has to be comforted by Mrs Bolton.

After this, Clifford became like a child with Mrs. Bolton. He would hold her hand, and rest his head on her breast, and when she once lightly kissed him, he said: "Yes! Do kiss me! Do kiss me!" And when she sponged his great blond body, he would say the same: "Do kiss me!" And she would lightly kiss his body, anywhere, half in mockery. And he lay with a queer, blank face like a child, with a bit of the wonderment of a child. And he would gaze on her with wide, childish eyes, in a relaxation of Madonna-worship. It was sheer relaxation on his part, letting go all his manhood, and sinking back to a childish position that was really perverse. And then he would put his hand in her bosom and feel her breasts, and kiss them in exaltation, the exaltation of perversity, of being a child when he was a man.[51]

The altered tone of *Lady Chatterley's Lover*'s final version is largely attributable to periodic denunciations of modern industrial society; but passages such as this also help to account for its greater harshness. By the time Lawrence wrote it, the fact that at one early point in the evolution of the novel Connie could have regarded Clifford as complementary to the gamekeeper seems incredible. Some of the hysteria he ascribes to Clifford goes back to his memories of how Weekley had responded when Frieda had told him that she was leaving; but only someone very much aware and fearful of his *own* temptation to seek refuge from the difficulties of the world in the maternal bosom could have infused it with such venom.

The second theme which Lawrence uses Michaelis to highlight is the struggle for power within sexual relations. All his work does of course show a preoccupation with the battle of the sexes; but in this last novel he takes his exploration of this battle much more obviously into the sexual act itself. Comparison of what Lawrence says about Arlen in his letters and diary entry with similar phrases from *Lady Chatterley's Lover* make it certain that he provided the model for Michaelis; and one of Arlen's friends later claimed on his behalf that he had not only recognised himself in the figure but, as a great admirer of Lawrence, felt flattered to have been used.[52] One would have liked confirmation of this from Arlen himself because, although the portrait as a whole is by no means unsympathetic, it has one important feature with which anyone who recognised himself as the model could hardly have felt very comfortable. In addition to his infantilism, Michaelis suffers from chronic sexual inadequacy: Connie refers at one moment to his 'pathetic, two-second spasms'.[53] It may be this was associated in Lawrence's mind with Arlen having to have a testicle removed but if so the association was surely unconscious – he had often shown himself unfeeling in the depiction of people he knew, but never quite that ruthless. More likely is that Michaelis's sexual difficulties illustrate the chances you took when Lawrence based a character on you. Michaelis *is* Arlen in many respects but he is also a figure who, in a process of both broadening and coarsening which goes on in the final version, becomes necessary as a representative of the unsatisfactory youth of the day. 'Like so many modern men', Connie reflects, '[Michaelis] was finished almost before he had begun.'[54] The consequence is that she has to hang on to achieve her own satisfaction. This is what Connie has been described as doing in new material which gives an account of her early sexual experiences as a student in Germany:

But a woman could yield to a man without yielding her inner, free self . . . she had only to hold herself back, in the sexual intercourse, and let him finish and expend himself without herself coming to the crisis; and then she could prolong the connection and achieve her orgasm and her crisis while he was merely a tool.[55]

This practice is what the gamekeeper will later denounce with such startling force in Bertha Coutts; but it could be said that, with Michaelis, Connie has no other choice; and insofar as holding back is an inclination in her, a new direction of the novel is to show how she is educated into better habits by the potent gamekeeper.

The introduction of Michaelis brings important changes to *Lady Chatterley's Lover*, but even more important are the changes to the gamekeeper himself. He now acquires a new name ('Mellors'), and a quite new pedigree. No longer a homogeneous working-class figure, Mellors has risen from the ranks during the war and gained a commission. He not only looks like a gentleman to several of the other characters but is perfectly capable of speaking like one when it suits him. Now a reader of books, Mellors is full of ideas about the state of the world and what might be done to change it. His education makes him much more skilfully and self-consciously bi-lingual: someone who easily switches registers, to the increased discomfort, in this version, of a now less sympathetic and more disapproving Hilda (in the scene preceding the night of 'sensual passion', before Connie goes off to the Continent).

Making Lady Chatterley's lover more articulate and informed brings him closer to Lawrence himself. This process is also evident in the physical descriptions of the gamekeeper who is more frail than his predecessor and suffers from a persistent cough. Mellors's sexual history is also now very recognisably Lawrence's own. In the second version of the novel, Parkin had been disgusted with women after the sixteen-year-old Bertha Coutts exposed herself to him when he was a boy. We have no way of knowing whether this unsettling incident corresponds to anything in Lawrence's own early life. But as Mellors describes his first girlfriend, who so much encouraged him in his reading, and a second who 'loved everything about love except the sex', the references to Jessie Chambers and Helen Corke become unmistakable. (Lawrence had been led to think of them both when he was revising his early poems, an activity which he confessed had brought back painful memories – vi. 223, 318.) Yet if these two women are undoubtedly 'from life' where does that leave their successor, Bertha Coutts, against whose sexual rapaciousness Mellors now fulminates with such vehemence?

By God, you think a woman's soft down there, like a fig. But I tell you the old rampers have beaks between their legs, and they tear at you with it till you're sick. Self! self! self! all self! tearing and shouting! . . . I told her about it, I told her how I hated it. And she'd even try . . . But it was no good. She got no feeling off it, from my working. She had to work the thing herself, grind her own coffee. And it came back on her like a raving necessity, she had to let herself go, and tear, tear, tear, as if she had no sensation in her except in the top of her beak, the very outside top tip, that rubbed and tore.[56]

In initial physical description, Connie Chatterley may owe most to Rosalind Thornycroft, but as the character develops she acquires many of Frieda's attributes and, in later life, Frieda certainly showed no tendency to contradict those who identified Connie Chatterley with her. But if many aspects of Connie are reminiscent of Frieda at her uninhibited best (running naked in the rain, for example), Bertha Coutts must surely often represent what for Lawrence was his wife's dark side. Where else but from his relations with Frieda could he have accumulated such a reserve of intense sexual distaste?

The transformation of the gamekeeper has profound effects for the novel as a whole. The endings of both its first and second versions are unsatisfactory attempts to solve the problem with which Lawrence had begun: how can a woman of Connie Chatterley's background form a lasting relationship with a man from the working classes? With the change from Parkin to Mellors, the problem no longer exists. In *John Thomas and Lady Jane* Connie had visited Parkin at his mother's house in Tevershall where he was recovering after being provoked into a fight by the man with whom Bertha Coutts had previously been living.[57] This well-written scene, as well as all those involving Sheffield and the Tewsons, now disappear and once Mellors has been sacked by Clifford he goes directly to London to meet Connie as she returns from her holiday abroad. There, in what is perhaps Lawrence's least successful attempt to imagine male camaraderie of the locker-room variety – 'the old free-masonry of male sensuality'[58] – Mellors discusses Connie's sexual potential with her father at the latter's club. After playing a prominent part in *The First Lady Chatterley*, Duncan Forbes had been more or less rested in *John Thomas and Lady Jane*. In this final version he returns in a far less sympathetic light, agreeing to be named as the father of Connie's coming child only on condition that she pose for one of his pictures. After Connie has returned to Wragby and revealed that her lover is not in fact Duncan, the novel ends with a long letter from Mellors who is working on a farm while he waits for his divorce from Bertha, and while he learns the skills which will later allow him to begin a life with Connie.

If one thinks of the germ of the *Lady Chatterley* enterprise as already contained in *The Virgin and the Gipsy*, then it is possible to measure the distance travelled from the short, ungrammatical note from 'Joe Boswell', with which that novella ends, through Parkin's stiffly written communications with Connie, to this final fluent letter from Mellors. The evolution of the project is in many ways epitomised in the evolution of epistolary style. Mellors eloquently stresses once again the dismay he feels over a world totally dominated by money-making and he offers alternatives which are far closer to those Lawrence had begun to sketch out for Kot in 'A Dream of Life' than to the Communism of Parkin in *The First Lady Chatterley*. He makes it clear that all that matters to him is his relationship with Connie: 'I believe in the little flame between us. For me now, it's the only thing in the world. I've got no friends, not inward friends. Only you. And now the little flame is all I care about in my life.' They have fucked this flame into being, he says, just as the flowers are fucked into being, 'between sun and earth'; but now is the time for chastity in the 'peace that comes from fucking'. A new feature of the third version is that Mellors has at one moment adopted popular euphemisms for his and Connie's genitalia. This means that he can end his long letter, and the novel, on a cautiously optimistic note: 'John Thomas says good-night to lady Jane, a little droopingly, but with a hopeful heart—.'[59] In all Lawrence's major novels there is this pattern of offering powerful reasons for despair but not then allowing his characters to abandon hope.

A far more articulate, intellectually commanding gamekeeper completely alters the dynamic of his relationship with Connie. He now becomes a much more dominant figure, instructing her in the ways of sex and of the world. Mellors's tendency to lecture Connie, together with the introduction into the discussions of sex at Wragby of new figures (two of whom are based on Huxley and his friend Sullivan[60]), make the final version of *Lady Chatterley's Lover* much more a 'novel of ideas' than it had been before. Many readers have regretted this and complained that the increased discursive element, together with a much stronger strain of denunciatory rage in the reflections of the gamekeeper, obscure the lyrical celebrations of sexual intercourse which make the second version so impressive. Explicit accounts of sexual acts, in a language as direct as Lawrence could make it and with several daring attempts to describe the physical feelings associated with female orgasm, will always be the most arresting as well as the most controversial feature of both the second and third versions of Lawrence's novel. In *Lady Chatterley's Lover*, with now no anxiety about censorship, sexual intercourse continues to be celebrated in an increasingly specific and particularised way; but it is perhaps true that, with Mellors at this stage much more obviously his creator's spokesman, there is sometimes a wilfulness or insistence which makes the reader uncomfortable. The facts are nevertheless complicated, as a quick glance at the evolution of the famous flower scene shows. In *The First Lady Chatterley* there is a brief allusion to Parkin and Connie decorating each other's naked body with flowers; but it is in *John Thomas and Lady Jane* that the episode is properly developed. When re-writing it for the final version, Lawrence often improves the local detail, but he also makes two additions which are problematic. As he caresses Connie, Mellors says, 'An' if I only lived ten minutes, an' stroked thy arse an' got to know it, I should reckon I'd lived *one* life, seestyer!'; but he then adds immediately, with an incongruity which would have been difficult for Parkin (given the way *his* character was initially conceived), 'Industrial system or not!' Just before, Mellors's finger-tips have touched the 'two secret openings' of her body, 'time after time, with a soft little brush of fire'.

"An' if tha shits an' if tha pisses, I'm glad. I don't want a woman as couldna shit nor piss." Connie could not help a sudden snirt of astonished laughter, but he went on unmoved. "Tha'rt real, tha art! Tha'rt real, even a bit of a bitch. Here tha shits an' here tha pisses: an' I lay my hand on 'em both, an' I like thee for it. I like thee for it. Tha's got a proper, woman's arse, proud of itself. It's none ashamed of itself, this isna."[61]

In none of its versions is *Lady Chatterley's Lover only* lyrical in its celebrations of sex, and no charge is more false than that it consists of a number of sexual encounters which are boring because they are repetitive.[62] Increasingly as the novel developed, it became an exploration of a wide variety of sexual contacts, some more satisfactory than others. Tenderness always remained its keynote, but as the inclusion of the 'night of sensual passion' in version two shows, by no means all the encounters between Connie and the gamekeeper are either tender or romantic. That night is described as exorcism, a burning-out of shame; and this addition to the final version about shitting and pissing is clearly complementary to that endeavour. The difficulty is that, from a dramatic point of view, it can sound programmatic, too obviously and unrealistically polemical. Of course, one might be tempted to say that this is because (even today) Mellors's words have the power to shock: an inevitability Lawrence tries to neutralise by having Connie respond to them with a 'sudden snirt of astonished laughter'. But if one makes the perhaps dubious assumption that we now have no more trouble with 'shit' and 'piss' than with 'cunt' and 'fuck', then the criticism that Lawrence is too concerned to force his readers to see the truth must hold. It is not so easy to imagine, however, what his alternatives were. Frieda later made clear that she preferred the first version of the novel and shrewdly remarked, '*The First Lady Chatterley* he wrote as she came out of him, out of his own immediate self. In the third version he was also aware of his contemporaries' minds.'[63] That is clearly true. Yet how could an alert and naturally combative man like Lawrence not be aware of how most of his contemporaries would respond to the degree of explicitness he had become convinced was necessary; and how then could his fictive manner remain entirely free of an implicit, retaliatory aggression?

IV Surviving Christmas

Lawrence's absorption in the re-writing of *Lady Chatterley's Lover* helps to explain why he stayed put in the Villa Mirenda over the Christmas period. He had thought of retreating to Florence, as the Wilkinsons had done the year before (this year, they spent two weeks in Rome – vi. 241). He and Frieda would be more comfortable in a Florence hotel and there he would avoid what he was beginning to apprend as the obligation of another Christmas tree for the peasants. Lawrence was mildly irritated at this time by Frieda's motherly concern for one of the peasant children, the ten-year-old Dino Bandelli whom she had discovered needed an operation for a hernia. In letters to his mother-in-law he suggests that Frieda's preoccupation with Dino was a little forced ('she is already Saint Frieda, butter couldn't melt in her mouth'); and he was maliciously amused when, after Frieda had arranged with Dr Giglioli to pay for an operation in Florence, Dino fled the hospital and was coaxed back, not principally by her, but by the promise of a bicycle from Raul Mirenda. 'This time [Frieda] is no longer the one-and-only saint', he ungenerously crowed, '– the padrone has promised Dino a bicycle. And Dante, the elder brother, says: If someone promises me a bicycle, I'll go too and be operated on' (vi. 243, 251). With both his usual volatility and his old hostility to Christmas celebrations, Lawrence was no longer comfortable with the notion of himself as lord of the manor (or lord to Frieda's lady), and he wanted to withdraw from what had become over the months a relatively complex social situation. Yet after Pietro had again stolen a suitable tree, Lawrence enjoyed the Christmas Eve ceremonies well enough; and to have moved out of the villa in late December would have disrupted his routine. He was someone who could usually write anywhere, but all his major projects in the 1920s – *Kangaroo*, 'Quetzalcoatl', *The Plumed Serpent* – were begun and finished in the same place.

For a man in his condition San Polo nevertheless had its disadvantages when the weather became really cold: if he had gone into town he could at least have found a hotel with central heating. In a letter to Gertie Cooper, written on 19 December, he spoke of the recent 'damp foggy weather' which had made him cough 'a fair bit', and then went on,

On Saturday started a fierce wind, cold enough to blow the skin off your face: but it was sunny. But I stayed indoors by the warm stove, my bronchials won't stand ferocious changes. Today, when I was out just now, the vapour froze in my beard: never been so cold here. At the same time, there is no wind, and a hot sun, so that we don't need any fire. I sit in the sitting-room in the sun writing this, and my head is almost too hot. Yet the other side the house the water freezes if you spill it on the floor. What a world! (vi. 244)

One can easily imagine that in another mood Lawrence would have delighted in these contrasts, but he was very low, confessing to Kot on the 23rd, 'I do think this is the low-water mark of existence. I never felt so near the brink of the abyss' (vi. 247). Kot was often gloomy and many of Lawrence's letters to him are attempts to shake him out of his depressive torpor. For Lawrence himself to admit to such a degree of low spirits is unusual. Remembering that in *Sons and Lovers* the young Paul suffers from unaccountable fits of depression so that his exasperated mother plumps him down in the garden with 'Now, cry there, Misery',[64] or that throughout Lawrence's adult life there are signs of recurring black moods of unusual severity, one could argue that he was constitutionally melancholic. Well before the characteristic response to illness which Huxley mentions in the introduction to his collection of the letters, however, it was always Lawrence's determined policy to take a 'great kick at misery'.[65] What the remark to Kot shows was that he was not always capable of carrying out that policy especially when, in his money worries and above all his illness, he had sound, objective reasons for feeling depressed. Yet after enjoying more than he expected the celebrations with the peasants on the 24th, and after he and Frieda had been invited to share a Christmas Day dinner with a couple named the Petterichs,[66] at whose villa in Florence Aldous and Maria Huxley were staying, he felt better (vi. 250). And during all this time he would have been sustained by the excitement of finishing the final version of his novel. In 1921 Lawrence had told Mountsier: 'If I hadn't my own stories to amuse myself with I should die, chiefly of spleen' (iv. 109). In December 1927, he would have substituted chagrin for spleen and then repeated the claim with more than usual conviction.

With a large family party which would include Aldous's brother Julian and his Swiss wife Juliette, the Huxleys had now arranged to go skiing in Switzerland, rather than returning to Cortina. Thinking no doubt of Lawrence's health, they urged him to come along also and, after much reluctance and hesitation, he agreed to follow them there. Both the Huxleys and Frieda appear to have agreed with the doctor in Baden-Baden that the mountains in winter would do him good. Once *Lady Chatterley's Lover* was finished there was no reason why he should not get away from Florence, except that he needed to have his re-written novel typed. Its content made that task a far from simple matter. He had turned first to Nellie Morrison in whose Florence flat the Lawrences seemed occasionally to have stopped over, when it was too late to get back to San Polo (v. 610), and whose broadmindedness could be inferred from the fact that she had a young Italian lover. Recently he had been helping her with a story she had written and on 20 December, after promising to put her in touch with Nancy Pearn, he had asked whether she was willing to begin typing the parts of his novel which were by that date already re-written (vi. 245).[67] He made this request tentatively, warning her that she might be shocked, and his misgivings proved justified when, in a gentle anticipation of the strong feelings *Lady Chatterley's Lover* would arouse, Nellie Morrison found that her distaste for the material would not allow her to continue beyond chapter v (vi. 259). In desperation – if an old friend like Nellie could not face the typing, who would? – Lawrence sent off the second of his manuscript notebooks to Catherine Carswell in London, and extracted an assurance from Maria Huxley that she would deal with the third.[68]

It might have been as he came to the end of *Lady Chatterley's Lover* that Lawrence finished his most erotic painting: a naked woman perched uncomfortably on the knee of a naked man who, in a manner far more enthusiastic as well as far more naturalistic than that of the male figure in *A Holy Family*, fondles her breast while the eyes of both figures gleam lasciviously.[69] Once the novel was finished he had one more literary task to complete before he was ready to leave Florence: an introduction for an English translation of *La madre* by the Sardinian novelist, Grazia Deledda. Jonathan Cape had asked for this because he was publishing *The Mother* in the same 'Travellers' Library' series in which *Mastro-don Gesualdo* had appeared; but he must also have realised that Lawrence was well placed to write an introduction to a work which dealt with Sardinian peasant life (of which he had at least seen something), and whose theme was the contest between the 'old wild instinct of a mother's ambition for her son' and 'the other wild instinct of sexual mating'.[70] The mother of the title has sacrificed everything

28 View from the terrace of the
Villa Bernarda

29 'Pino' Orioli and Norman
Douglas on a walking holiday
in the early 1930s

30 'The Mater': Barbara Weekley's painting of Granny Weekley

31 Lawrence with the Brewsters and Brett on Capri, February/March 1926

32 Portrait of Barbara
Weekley in her early twenties

33 Giulia Pini as a young woman

34 The Villa Mirenda

35 Lawrence and Frieda round
the well at the Villa Mirenda

36 Lawrence on the beach at Mablethorpe with his sister Ada, August 1926

37 *Dandelions*

38 Scene from
the Tomb of
Hunting and
Fishing

39 Etruscan subulo player:
from the Tomb of the Leopards

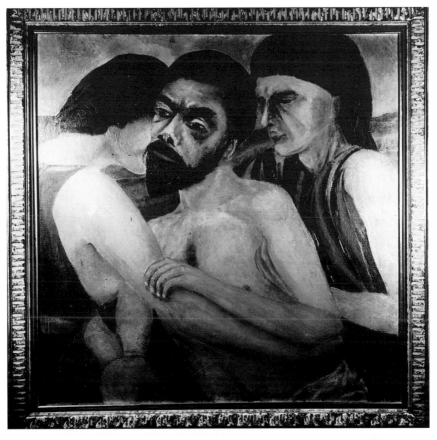

40 *Resurrection*

41 The Crosbys at Le Bourget,
with their dog Clytoris

42 Lawrence, Frieda and Orioli on Ponte Santa Trinità in Florence

43 Lawrence with Frieda at
Kesselmatte in 1928

44 Lawrence with his sister Emily
at Kesselmatte in 1928

45 Portrait of Lawrence by Ernesto Guardia, 1929

46 Lawrence's self-portrait in red crayon for the first, unexpurgated edition of *Pansies*

47 The Trotters in the Warren Gallery at the time of Lawrence's exhibition

48 Villa Beau Soleil

49 Max Mohr, *c.* 1929

50 Maria Huxley, *c.* 1928

51 Clay head of Lawrence by Ida Rauh for the frontispiece of the special 'Lawrence' number of *Laughing Horse* (1926)

52 Mabel Luhan, Frieda Lawrence and Dorothy Brett in the 1930s

so that her son can become a priest and then sees the result of all her efforts threatened by his passion for one of his parishioners. Lawrence admired the novel, especially for its depiction of an isolated, savage community of twenty years before, when the human instinct was 'still uncontaminated' and the 'money-sway' not yet dominant (it reminded him of *Wuthering Heights*); and he thought that Deledda, though not a 'first-class genius', did more than merely reproduce the 'temporary psychological condition of her period'. But perhaps because she had won the Nobel Prize for Literature in 1926, he is keen to insist that 'she does not penetrate, as a great genius does, the very sources of human passion and motive'. To what must have been Cape's wry disappointment, Lawrence ended his introduction by noting that of course the novel 'loses a good deal in translation'. This is because, whereas in Italian there are many 'instinct-words with meanings never clearly mentally defined', in the 'more cut-and-dried northern languages . . . every word has its fixed value and meaning'.[71] For a writer who had been trying to describe female orgasm in *Lady Chatterley's Lover* that was perhaps an appropriate complaint.

Lawrence sent Nancy Pearn the manuscript of his introduction to *The Mother* on 5 January. By the 8th he had heard from Nellie Morrison that she could not go on with her typing stint, and on the 10th he wrote to Catherine Carswell with his request that she should lend a hand (vi. 259–60). The Lawrences had intended to set off for Switzerland on Monday 16 January but by then he was 'in bed with flu – misery' (vi. 265); so that it was not until the 20th that they left for Les Diablerets, near the town of Aigle a few miles from the eastern end of Lake Geneva.

◆

January–June 1928

LAST DAYS AT THE VILLA MIRENDA

I Les Diablerets

As the scenes which conclude both *Women in Love* and 'The Captain's Doll'
suggest, Lawrence had rarely been very comfortable where there was 'snow
grinning on the tops of mountains' (iv. 97). On this occasion its obliteration of the
usual landmarks disconcerted him and he felt oppressed in a world where it was
too cold for almost anything to grow. 'I am no snow-bird', he wrote on 31
January, eleven days after he and Frieda had installed themselves in the Chalet
Beau Site two or three hundred yards from the little station in Les Diablerets: 'I
hate the stark and shroudy whiteness, white and black. It offends the painter in
one – it is so uniform – only sometimes lovely contours, and pale blue gleams.
But against life.' That would not matter so much if he could feel the thin air was
doing him good but, if in the first week or so his responses were mixed, he often
had the opposite impression: 'I think this place is a good tonic, but snow isn't
good for bronchials: it just isn't, it scrapes inside' (vi. 277).

Like Lawrence, the two Huxley brothers worked every morning. Aldous was
busy with *Point Counter Point* and Julian with his contributions to three very
large volumes of a popular handbook of biological science to be entitled, *The
Science of Life. A Summary of Contemporary Knowledge about Life and its Possibilities.* He was writing this in collaboration with H. G. Wells and Wells's son
(G. P.), who was a zoologist. Julian had very recently given up his Chair at King's
College, London, in order to devote himself to this labour, which would
eventually bring him £10,000.[1] After lunch, he and Aldous went skiing with their
wives and children until the light began to fail at about four o'clock. Although
Lawrence had hopes that he might soon be able to join them, telling Secker on 27
January that he was not up to winter sports 'yet', and Emily four days later that
he thought he would 'try ski-ing next week' (vi. 275, 286), his health never
allowed him to do so. But with his own chalet only a 'step away' from theirs, he
and Frieda had tea with the Huxleys almost every day. From the occasions when
the Huxleys came to Beau Site, Juliette Huxley remembered his 'delicious lemon-
curd on crisp little pasties' which he baked himself, as well as the 'radiating
creativeness' of his presence.[2] He seems to have been stimulated by their
company, even if Julian made him more polemically hostile than usual in his

remarks about science. The hostility is not surprising given that the work Julian Huxley was then engaged on turned out to be pervaded with the positivism of its 'senior partner' (as H. G. Wells calls himself in its introduction). The third of its sections is entitled 'The Incontrovertible Fact of Evolution' and in the brief dismissal of Shaw's 'Life Force' and Bergson's 'Elan Vital', the tone is exactly that of Ursula's Dr Frankstone in *The Rainbow*. Julian Huxley remembered infuriating Lawrence by discussing with his brother 'the possibility of mankind's genetic improvement'. 'Lawrence often exploded with a snort of impotent rage when we talked about scientific matters . . . I learnt to disregard his outbursts of fury, but we had many a stormy passage.'[3]

Stormy passages or not, Lawrence seems to have enjoyed having people to talk to, so that, despite his persistent cough and his lack of breath, he began to feel more cheerful, as well as stronger as the short February days went by. He also began to accommodate himself better to the environment. Not being able to ski seemed less important as he watched Frieda spend 'a good deal of the afternoon on her bottom in the snow, unable to rise because of those thundering long sticks on her feet'; or the 6' 4" Aldous – 'thin and half blind' – dragging himself uphill for forty minutes so that he could 'slither down again in four – it's a lot of hard work for a bit of fun' (vi. 287). Short walks and the occasional toboggan ride were, he decided, enough for him; and on 5 February he very much enjoyed being driven to the nearby Pillon Pass, which divides the cleft in which Les Diablerets lies from the neighbouring valley where everyone speaks Swiss German. At the top of the pass, they were met by the Huxley party on skis and were able to picnic in a spot with fine views all round: 'very high, very sparkling and bright and sort of marvellous . . . it sort of puts life into one' (vi. 290).

As usual, Lawrence had plenty to do. The edition of his collected poems which he had been working on was finally ready to be sent off on 3 February and, before that, he had been obliged to write a new ending for 'The Border-Line' because, in the proofs of the *Woman Who Rode Away* collection, that story had arrived with its conclusion missing.[4] But his main task, as he received typescript from Catherine Carswell in London and Maria Huxley nearer at hand (in the mornings she typed Lawrence's novel while her sister-in-law typed *The Science of Life*), was to prepare an expurgated edition of *Lady Chatterley's Lover* for both Secker and Knopf. Norman Douglas was following his usual practice when, shortly after the Florence publication of *Birds and Beasts of the Greek Anthology* and *In the Beginning*, he arranged for both books to appear in ordinary commercial editions in London. He did this to maximise his return. With the Florence editions he appealed to the world of the specialist collector, and then made what he could in the more usual market-place. Lawrence's additional and perhaps principal motive for now wanting to ensure that *Lady Chatterley's Lover* could appear in London and New York, even though previously he had been so determined not to cut his novel, was different. He had been advised by Curtis Brown that it would be impossible to secure copyright for any book published abroad which was generally regarded as obscene; and that it would therefore be difficult to protect a Florence edition of *Lady Chatterley's Lover* from the literary pirates. Thoughts of pirated editions of *Birds and Beasts of the Greek Anthology* were hardly likely to have kept Norman Douglas awake at night; but Lawrence must have realised that *Lady Chatterley's Lover* might be a prime target, and he was therefore anxious that editions of the novel should be copyrighted in London and New York, if not before he published in Florence then at least at more or less the same time (vi. 295). For that to be possible he knew he would have to expurgate. Not surprisingly, he did not find expurgation easy. 'I find I simply don't know how much and how little to expurgate so I'm not doing much', he told Secker. 'You must ponder it carefully, and if you want to take any bits out, then do so: but don't leave raw gaps, and don't make the thing lose its point' (vi. 305). This was to shelve the problem by passing it on to someone else.

Expurgation was also difficult because the typescript was slow in arriving from London. The delay betrayed an impatient Lawrence into some uncomplimentary remarks about Catherine Carswell which got back to her, via her cousin Yvonne Franchetti (a close friend of the Huxleys), and which would require a mollifying letter in April: 'Nay, when things are repeated, always judge the *repeaters*' (vi. 385).[5] Though her typing was a 'simple chicken-pox of mistakes' (vi. 293), Maria herself was more satisfactorily prompt and, with the novel finally together, Lawrence allowed her sister-in-law to read it. Juliette Huxley's initial reaction was one of angry moral shock and she told Lawrence that he ought to call his novel 'John Thomas and Lady Jane' 'because that was really all it was about'. He exploded with laughter ('he had a very special way of laughing, tilting his head and pointing his small red beard at one, his bright blue eyes twinkling') and afterwards decided that those words would do very well for a title – 'Many a true word spoken in spite' (vi. 315).[6] Lawrence had experienced his usual difficulty with titles, experimenting with 'My Lady's Keeper' and then 'Tenderness' before coming back unenthusiastically to *Lady Chatterley's Lover* (vi. 275). He had to come back to it again after Aldous Huxley persuaded him that 'John Thomas and Lady Jane' would be likely to make the novel too easy a prey for Customs officials, on the look-out for pornography.[7]

In spite of the disagreement over his novel, Lawrence developed an excellent relationship with Juliette Huxley who as Juliette Baillot, a young Swiss girl engaged by Ottoline Morrell to look after her child, was only seventeen when he first met her at Garsington, and whom he had previously known only slightly.[8] She remembers him expressing unease that he had quarrelled so badly with Lady Ottoline and promising that he would write to her. Like Brett, she did not object when he insisted on improving the genital organs of the male figure in her conception of Adam and Eve (in an embroidery); and she enrolled her sons in a search for coltsfoot, which was beginning to appear in some rocky crannies, after she learned that Lawrence thought the herb tea that could be made from it might do him some good.[9] Both the Lawrences felt they got to know Juliette well enough to speak intimately with her about difficulties in her marriage; and she later remembered Lawrence calling Julian Huxley an 'expurgated version of a man' – a very likely phrase given Lawrence's preoccupations at the time.[10] Her response in retrospect was not resentment but rather regret that she was at that period too 'repressed' to accept the invitation to unburden herself. Towards the end of the stay at Les Diablerets, Lawrence and Juliette were thrown more together because Julian went back to London and, on 27 February, Frieda left to visit her mother in Baden-Baden. (Juliette Huxley refers to Frieda as going off on one of her 'periodic prowls', so that it may be it was generally accepted at the time that she would also be seeing Ravagli.) When the moment came for the remaining members of the party to leave on 6 March, Juliette thoughtfully accompanied Lawrence down to Aigle because 'the sudden change of altitude might have over-tired him'.[11] Announcing on 2 March to Secker that he would be leaving in three days' time, and that Aldous Huxley had left the day before, Lawrence wrote, 'So Diablerets is nearly over. But it has done me good, and I've been happy here' (vi. 305).

Before Lawrence left, and while Frieda was still with him, Rolf Gardiner paid a visit. He had come on to Switzerland from Bavaria where he had been pursuing his interest and involvement in the German youth leagues, and remembered being met at the station in Les Diablerets by a Lawrence who was 'very pale and shrivelled-looking'. When he was taken to the lodging which had been found for him, so that he could wash after his journey, Lawrence apparently told him that 'one should never use soap on the face', making Gardiner very reasonably wonder how the miners back in Eastwood must have managed. At Chalet Beau Site, with its wood-panelling that made Lawrence feel he was living in the cabins of a ship (vi. 273), he was given tea, and then talked with the Lawrences in German about the youth Bunde. Frieda was impressed but Lawrence himself had doubts about the 'political passions infecting' those groups. Gardiner had recently inherited a farm in Dorset which Lawrence felt could well provide the necessary geographical centre for a new life in tune with the rhythm of the seasons, one where there would be a reliance on handicrafts rather than machine-made goods and communal rituals of dancing and singing: a life, in fact, much like the one Mellors advocates in the final version of *Lady Chatterley's Lover*. As they discussed this prospect at supper and after, Gardiner was struck by the highly practical nature of Lawrence's interest in how the farm might be run. The next day he was taken to tea with the Huxleys and remembered how cheerful Lawrence was in their company. According to him, although Lawrence had a special, affectionate way of referring to Aldous as 'Aldoose', he tried to frighten Huxley off his 'four-square rationalist perch' by describing 'outlandish events in Mexico'. (In the process of doing that, he must also have been providing copy for Huxley's sympathetic portrait of Lawrence as 'Rampion' in *Point Counter Point*.)

The Lawrences occupied four rooms in the large, four-story chalet which stood on one, chalet-dotted side of the narrow valley, looking across at the opposite mountain slope where the winter sports took place. Gathered round the stove in one of these rooms, with its glow patterning the ceiling, the three of them spent the evening talking about their past lives in a way which left Gardiner with a 'great tenderness' for both his hosts.[12] As he left the next day (12 February) he was immediately succeeded by Max Mohr, the doctor/writer who had visited Lawrence in September of the previous year, and had been sufficiently impressed to want to renew the experience. Partly because of Mohr's ability to write English, the two men had corresponded regularly since they last met (Lawrence usually wrote in German to his mother-in-law and sometimes to other German-speaking relatives or friends, but he confesses on occasions to finding it a strain). Mohr stayed until the 16th and, in a spurt of irritation which his future behaviour showed to be without significance, Lawrence described him to Else Jaffe as a gossip or gasbag (vi. 294). Writing to Brett on the same day Gardiner left, he had been kinder to his previous guest, calling him 'very nice, but not much in my line' (vi. 293); and on the 20th he replied warmly to a letter Gardiner had sent and made encouraging noises about the farm project. But on 4 March, two days before he himself left Les Diablerets, something Gardiner must have told him about a struggle for leadership in the Youth League organisations, which looked like leading to his being 'shoved out', led Lawrence to make clear an important point on which he and Gardiner were no longer at one. 'I'm afraid the whole business of leaders and followers is somehow wrong, now', he wrote; 'I'm afraid part of what ails you is that you are struggling to enforce an obsolete form of leadership' (vi. 307–8). Gardiner could have replied that if he was struggling to enforce a form of leadership (obsolete or not), it was in part because he had been such an enthusiastic reader of *The Plumed Serpent*. How Lawrence had now moved on from that novel would have been clearer to him had he been offered the opportunity, when he went to Les Diablerets, of reading *Lady Chatterley's Lover*, whose concerns were only peripherally his own. In the course of writing that work, Lawrence had implicitly abandoned his interest in the need for strong leadership: the necessity for individuals or groups to accept the inherent superiority and therefore natural authority of others, which had increasingly preoccupied him from the middle of the war years, and which had culminated in his account in *The Plumed Serpent* of how Ramón and Cipriano assume the sacred responsibility of commanding others. His explicit admission that, if he had not in the past simply been wrong, then at least he now felt it was time to move on, would come nine days after his letter to Gardiner, once he was back in the Villa Mirenda. At the end of 1927 Witter Bynner, still smarting a little over the way he had been depicted in *The Plumed Serpent*, sent Lawrence a criticism of the novel, in which he accused him of having been influenced by Mabel Luhan and questioned its stress on the importance of the leader.[13] In a letter in which Lawrence told Bynner to expect a batch of order forms for *Lady Chatterley's Lover*, he replied,

On the whole, I think you're right. The hero is obsolete, and the leader of men is a back number. After all, at the back of the hero is the militant ideal: and the militant ideal, or the ideal militant, seems to me also a cold egg. We're sort of sick of all forms of militarism and militantism, and *Miles* is a name no more, for a man. On the whole, I agree with you, the leader-cum-follower relationship is a bore. And the new relationship will be some sort of tenderness, sensitive, between men and men and men and women, and not the one up one down, lead on I follow, ich dien sort of business.   (vi. 321)

Bynner must have been gratified to receive these remarks; but had Gardiner read them, he would have keenly felt the difference between the Lawrence he so admired and the man whose company he had enjoyed in Les Diablerets.

II Business Matters

On 6 March Lawrence was due to meet Frieda in Milan. Their trains arrived at more or less the same time so that they were reunited on the station platform and able to travel on to Florence together shortly afterwards. The Wilkinsons were once again kind enough to meet them at the station and have them driven up to San Polo where they were greeted by several of the local peasants with bunches of primoses, violets and anemones (vi. 313). In mean-spirited remarks on Lawrence which Orioli published in his *Adventures of a Bookseller* in 1938, he claimed that the peasants on the Mirenda estate were never very happy with Lawrence because they 'expected to make a little money out of him with washing and so forth, and never did'.[14] This could only refer to Giulia Pini, who would have been the only person to profit from a decision by the Lawrences not to do their own laundry, but whose relation with them – from all the evidence available – appears to have been warm and trusting. There may well have been occasions when some of those on the estate felt that they could have done better out of different foreign tenants in the villa; but there had been none of these before the Lawrences, and there would be none after, so that there were no immediate comparisons to sharpen a sense of missing out. With their Christmas celebrations, and more especially

Frieda's involvement in the case of the Bandelli boy's hernia, the Lawrences had done enough for the reception they received to be regarded as a genuine sign of welcome and affection. Aldington remembered Orioli, who would certainly have needed someone to correct whatever he wrote in English, always talking very warmly about Lawrence in 1932; and he attributed the malicious remarks in both his books of memoirs to his close friend and collaborator, Norman Douglas. This seems very probable. Douglas never entirely forgave Lawrence for the introduction to the Magnus memoirs and the eminently recognisable portrait of himself as James Argyle in *Aaron's Rod*.[15] At the same time, it is unlikely that Douglas was entirely responsible. Like many others, Orioli fell on hard times in the 1930s and almost certainly felt, as he looked back, that the 10 per cent he had received from Lawrence for over-seeing the printing of *Lady Chatterley's Lover*, and for then playing such a major part in its distribution, was a poor return for all the effort involved.

For a while after Lawrence got back to Florence the weather was very bad – on 15 March he claimed it had rained every day (vi. 323). The cold winds made him feel 'like being in a knife box' and, after frost had ruined the first pea crop, most of the haricot beans 'rotted in the ground, with the rain' (vi. 332, 351). It must have depressed him also that the Wilkinsons, who had been so important to him during their stay in San Polo, packed up and went back to England at the end of March (vi. 343). Despite the welcome from the peasants, he was glad that his lease would expire at the end of April and was now only kept in Florence by work on *Lady Chatterley's Lover*. On 9 March he took his typescript to the same, non-English-speaking printer Douglas had used;[16] and, with Orioli as the essential liaison officer, waited eagerly for the first proofs. Unhappy at the Villa Mirenda, and fearful that the spell of wet weather would undermine all the physical progress he felt he had made during his stay at Les Diablerets (which he now looked back on with increasing favour), he threw himself wholeheartedly into the labour of private publication. His original idea had been to follow Douglas in having 700 copies printed which he would sell at 2 guineas each (vi. 225); but rightly calculating that he had a bigger name than Douglas, especially in the United States, he decided to risk 1,000 copies, 500 for the United Kingdom and the other 500 for America at £2 and $10 respectively. Douglas had sent out about 100 subscription leaflets for *Birds and Beasts of the Greek Anthology*; Lawrence had 1,500 printed and wrote dozens of letters to friends and acquaintances, asking them to distribute the leaflets as well as soliciting their direct support. (On 13 March alone he wrote 20 letters enclosing subscription forms.)[17] Those letters which survive illustrate the trouble he took to adapt his tone to particular correspondents, although it was inevitable that a standard defence of *Lady Chatterley's Lover* should emerge as he sought to justify such a relatively unusual method of publication. If he had to publish it privately it was not, he said, because it was concerned with sex in the familiar way. As he put it to George Conway, the businessman who had been so kind to him in Mexico City:

It is – in the latter half at least – a phallic novel, but tender and delicate. You know I believe in the phallic reality, and the phallic consciousness: as distinct from our irritable cerebral consciousness of today. That's why I do the book – and it's not just *sex*. Sex alas is one of the worst phenomena of today: all cerebral reaction, the whole thing worked from the mental processes and itch, and not a bit of the real phallic insouciance and spontaneity. But in my novel there is.   (vi. 324)

Lawrence was aware that publishing *Lady Chatterley's Lover* would set him apart 'even more definitely than I am already set apart' (vi. 332). As the whole history of his relations with others during the war had shown, and as his more recent correspondence with Trigant Burrow had poignantly underlined, his instincts were not naturally those of an outsider. In taking the steps which he felt would isolate him further, it may have been important that nearly all his male friends in Florence were homosexual, and that their support was therefore buttressed by an experience of social disapproval even more extensive than his own. He was especially nervous of what Secker, Curtis Brown and Nancy Pearn would think, and not only because he was involved in an enterprise from which they could expect no financial gain. 'You hear I am burning my boats by publishing my "shocking" novel here all by myself', he wrote to Nancy Pearn on 1 April. 'I expect everybody will disapprove – you certainly will. So I shan't ask you to buy a copy' (vi. 347). By that date he had already heard from Secker that he did not feel he could publish *Lady Chatterley's Lover* in its expurgated form (vi. 330); but although this decision upset him, and he would later be made very angry by what he felt was his agent's humiliating failure to find an alternative publisher in England, the implications for the copyright issue were less important to him at this stage than the question of whether he was going to cover his costs.[18] As he explained to more than one friend in March and early April, should too few subscribers be forthcoming, the expense of having published the novel would leave him 'broke' (vi. 330). That would be particularly serious if, as Nancy Pearn had predicted, its publication compromised his position in the magazine market and prevented him from making good his losses there. His anxieties were, however, relatively short-lived. Cheques from England quickly began to appear (the mail meant that the American subscribers were slower to show their hand). By 16 April he had already collected over £126, and by the 25th he knew that he had enough in the bank to cover even a pessimistic estimate of his likely publishing expenses (vi. 383).[19]

Some of Lawrence's immediate financial anxiety was in any case relieved by the arrival on or just before 1 April of five gold $20 pieces. These had been sent by Harry Crosby, an American in Paris who, along with his wife 'Caresse' (real name

Mary), made up one of the more astonishing representative couples of the Roaring Twenties. Born into the plutocratic purple of east coast America (they were both quite closely related to the banker J. P. Morgan), the Crosbys had cut loose from their puritanical past to profit from a very favourable exchange rate and live an opulent, bohemian life in Paris. Totally hedonistic as well as mildly literary, they knew and gave financial assistance to many of the leading painters or writers of the day. At the beginning of 1927, they had taken a trip to Egypt where Harry Crosby, already an admirer of 'The Ladybird', had read with growing enthusiasm *The Plumed Serpent*. Two years before, he had become a convert to sun-worship and on the Egyptian trip demonstrated his interest by having his own special design of the sun tattooed between his shoulder blades. The 'Aztec' element in Lawrence's novel especially excited him and he wrote to its author via Secker, expressing his admiration, enclosing some of his own poems about the sun, and asking if Lawrence would consider exchanging a manuscript for gold pieces, talismanic not only because of the gold itself but also because the American $20 coin featured on its reverse side an eagle flying above the sun.[20] In the reply which Lawrence wrote from Les Diablerets, he expressed a liking for Crosby's poems and promised to look for some manuscripts once he got back to Florence (vi. 300–1); but before he had given the matter much thought, the gold pieces had arrived. In her memoirs, Caresse Crosby gives an exciting although in some respects demonstrably inaccurate account of how the coins were sent. Because the export of gold was illegal in America, one of their friends back home had to arrange for it to be smuggled out of the country. The courier was a young painter named James ('Bill') Sykes who had secreted the gold coins in his shoes and brought them to the Crosbys in the rue de Lille just after they had been 'running the dogs at "Le Polo", a smart French club near Longchamp that had recently gone in for whippet racing'. He arrived as they were settling down with some friends to enjoy cinnamon toast accompanied with a glass or two of Cutty Sark. Crosby immediately wrapped up the gold and took his package to the Gare de l'Est where he entrusted its delivery to a passenger on the Florence train whom he chose at random, but who turned out to be (Caresse Crosby claims) the Duke of Argyll.[21]

In acknowledging receipt of the coins, Lawrence (whose own home life was rather different from the Crosbys') makes no reference to the Duke of Argyll; but he was of course pleased to receive the money and mentioned several manuscripts he had been thinking of sending (vi. 348). One which would have been especially appropriate, which Crosby may have specifically requested, but which Lawrence could not find, was 'Sun'. Nancy Pearn soon told him that this was not, as he had rather forlornly hoped, still hanging round the Curtis Brown office but then added, 'Are you sure you burnt them all [i.e. a number of recent manuscripts which had been returned to him]; and tell me, would it be cheating to write out the story again in your own fair handwriting to sell to the eager Yank? If not, why not?'[22] While he had been waiting to hear from her, Lawrence had asked Orioli to have binding put round several other manuscripts he had decided to send to Crosby, and to have printed on the cover the design of a phoenix rising from a nest of flames which he had sent to Middleton Murry in December 1923 as a Christmas greeting (iv. 551), and which he had now decided to use as an emblem on each copy of *Lady Chatterley's Lover*. When the package was finally sent off, it included the manuscript of 'The Man Who Loved Islands' and several poems;[23] but the prize item was a newly written-out version of 'Sun' with an altered ending. '*Sun* is the final manuscript', Lawrence told Crosby, 'and I wish the story had been printed, as it stands there, really complete. One day, when the public is more educated, I shall have the story printed whole, as it is in this MS' (vi. 388).

Lawrence never treated Crosby as an 'eager Yank', but there is just a hint of sharp practice in these phrases. In further correspondence after the arrival of the gold, Crosby had asked Lawrence if he would be willing to write an introduction to the collection of his own poems which he intended to have published by the press he and Caresse had very recently founded. Writing on 17 April to say that he would be willing ('I really like the poems'), Lawrence had added that because the manuscript of 'Eagle' – a poem written in New Mexico which Crosby had specifically requested – had been burnt, he might 'write it out' for him (vi. 372). He could have said that this is what he had done in the case of 'Sun'. Yet he did make important changes to the ending of the original story, amplifying the role of the peasant to whom the heroine is attracted, insisting even more on the difference the sun has made to her, and being far more sexually explicit. Where his words to Crosby are misleading, therefore, are in their suggestion that he had been obliged in the original 'Sun' to tone down what, at the time of writing, he had really wanted to say. There is no evidence for that and thus no justification for his reference four months later to the original 'Sun' as 'expurgated' (vi. 505).[24] The description in the later text of Juliet's womb as 'wide open, spread almost gaping in the violet rays of the sun', or the comparison in its last paragraph between the big roused penis of the peasant and the 'little, frantic penis' of her husband, are very much from the author who, since he wrote the original text, had completed the three versions of *Lady Chatterley's Lover*.[25] Yet in the form in which it was sent, that manuscript was just as valuable to Crosby as the lost one would have been; and since it was accompanied by several others, he certainly got his money's worth. It was nice to have gold – 'One should love it for its yellow life, answering the sun', Lawrence had written, 'I shan't spend it if I can help it' (vi. 348); yet if he *had* decided to spend it, the equivalent in sterling could only have been in the region of £25.

The introduction which Lawrence wrote for Crosby's collection (*Chariot of the Sun*), and which he sent off at the beginning of May (vi. 389), could not be said to have been written for the gold because he had liked the poems from the start. It is in any case one of those gestures of Lawrentian support likely to have made a less self-confident man than Crosby feel much as Walter Wilkinson must have when he read the review of *The Peep Show*. Explaining as eloquently as he had ever done before how genuine art's 'new effort of attention' provides a fresh vision of the world which then soon becomes stale through imitation, Lawrence insists that the glimpse of the chaos surrounding our imagined order which poets like Crosby offer is valuable even when their work has no 'outstanding melody or rhythm or image or epithet or even sense'. At a time when the important thing is to escape conventions and get back to chaos, the fact that Crosby's poetry is often technically incompetent and sometimes silly is less important than its originality: 'What does it matter if half the time a poet fails in his effort at expression! The failures make it real . . . Failure is part of the living chaos. And the groping reveals the act of attention, which suddenly passes into pure expression.'[26] This *was* praise but praise of a highly qualified kind and after Crosby had sent some further poems which he thought of adding to his collection, he was warned against doing so on the grounds that they would not correspond to what Lawrence had said about the others: 'it won't fit if you introduce these new, long, unwieldly, not very sensitive poems' (vi. 390).

In his pleasure at receiving the manuscripts, Crosby suggested that his press (originally called 'Narcisse', after one of the Crosbys' dogs, but now more appropriately 'The Black Sun') should publish 'Sun' in a de luxe edition. If this was what Lawrence had been hoping all along, no-one would know from his cordial but distinctly cool response (vi. 404); and he was positively embarrassed when, to show his appreciation of Lawrence's generosity, Crosby sent three more gold coins and an ornate snuff box which had been presented to the Master of a British warship in 1815 by Caroline Buonaparte, the former Queen of Naples.[27]

My wife went to Florence yesterday and brought the Queen of Naples' snuff-box and three pieces of gold, from Orioli, to my utter amazement. But, cari miei, it won't do. I'm sure you're not Croesuses to that extent: and anyhow, what right have I to receive these things? For heaven's sake, you embarass me! I hope to heaven you're quite quite rich, for if you're not, I shall feel really bad about it . . . I considered myself paid to excess before, so now where am I? . . . Perhaps one day we can square it somehow. (vi. 410–11)

Lawrence signed off by thanking Crosby but telling him that, 'in the future I shall tell you the price of my pen to a centime, and not a button more'. He always hated to be under an obligation and milking the rich was not one of his stronger suits. Throughout the 1920s James Joyce was kept afloat by subsidies from his rich American patron, Harriet Shaw Weaver. Although Lawrence might sometimes have envied that kind of situation, he could never have endured it.

III 'Le Pisseur'

In between sending out subscription forms and correcting the proofs of *Lady Chatterley's Lover* as they slowly came (from a printer without English, they needed a lot of correction), Lawrence continued to paint. He was painting in Les Diablerets when Rolf Gardiner saw him, and he carried on sufficiently in San Polo to be able to report to Maria Huxley as early as 16 March that he had done 'three more water-colours' – though his preference was for oils ('one can use one's elbow, and in water it's all dib-dab' – vi. 329). The five water-colours of this period all show the increasing naturalism with which he wanted to depict naked bodies. In *Fire Dance* the muscular male figure facing the viewer has his head thrown back, his right hand extended and one bent leg raised as it is thrown forward in the next step of the dance. Apart from the leg, this is very similar to the pose in *Yawning*, although in that picture the accompanying figure is a naked woman in the process of stretching both arms above her head. *The Lizard* and *Under the Haystack* are both more melancholy and more static. In the first, a naked couple sit on the ground in complicated postures, their depression somehow exposed by the alertness of the lizard facing them; and in the second, the woman tenderly cradles the man's head against her breast. In these two paintings, the women's faces are different; but in all four the face of the man is the same, and it is the same also in the fifth of the paintings (*Dandelions*) which shows a naked man in profile, urinating. When Lawrence wrote about this composition to Brewster on 27 March he said it seemed to him 'very touching and nice' (vi. 339). In *Lady Chatterley's Lover* he had been concerned to exorcise fear of the so-called natural functions, and certainly in this painting there is a calm naturalness in the quiet self-absorption of the naked figure. His face would reappear in the naked peasant who dominates a picture which Lawrence painted after he left the Villa Mirenda. This is called *Contadini* and is usually assumed to be a portrait of the 'Pietro' habitually and wrongly assumed to be related to the Pinis. The origin of this assumption is Raul Mirenda who told Nehls that Lawrence made 'Piero' pose for a 'nude male figure' he was painting in oils (Pietro degli Innocenti was also often called 'Piero' to distinguish him from Giulia Pini's real brother).[28] Although Mirenda may be right, it seems unlikely that the young man the Lawrences always called Pietro was often asked to take his clothes off; and we know from the letters that, for both *Fire Dance* and the picture of the man urinating, Lawrence was using photographic studies of nudes that he had asked Brewster to send him (vi. 318, 339). If Pietro was often conveniently on hand as a nude model, why should he have bothered to secure these? That the *face* of the principal male figure in all these six paintings (the five I have been discussing and *Contadini*) might be Pietro's, is another matter.[29]

'Le Pisseur', as Lawrence originally entitled *Dandelions*, figures prominently in an account of the short visit Rolf Gardiner's sister Margaret made to Lawrence in the middle of April. She describes how frequently he had to pause for breath when he was accompanying her up to the villa from the tram terminus; and his outburst of misanthropic rage as he compared the beauty of the Tuscan landscape below them with the people living in it. She remembered the *salotto* as having 'striped Mexican rugs' on the floor as well as Lawrence's paintings on the wall; and appreciated the delicious stew he had cooked for them both. With lunch over, he gave her *The Escaped Cock* to read while he reluctantly took the afternoon rest which he explained was now part of his regime. When after an hour or two he rejoined her, he fulminated against those who had written letters of protest to the editor of the American magazine in which the story had appeared. A day or two before, the Beveridge sisters had arrived in Florence (vi. 367), and Lawrence was expecting them to tea.[30] When they appeared, he showed both them and Margaret Gardiner his latest paintings and in particular 'Le Pisseur'. Millicent Beveridge would later confess that, much as she liked Lawrence himself, she 'loathed' his paintings, and according to Margaret Gardiner both sisters were shocked on this occasion and told Lawrence he had gone too far. She herself admits that, although at the time she was careful to disassociate herself from their criticism, she did not like his paintings either. When the Beveridge sisters had gone, Lawrence was very angry that they should have reacted as they did.[31]

Dandelions has obvious technical deficiencies. The left arm, which is too long, seems to be reaching across towards the right-hand wall in a way which would have twisted the body; the body itself is uneasily tilted forwards; and the shadowing is peculiar. In *Sketches of Etruscan Places* Lawrence had suggested that the subtlety of Etruscan painting lay in 'the wonderfully suggestive *edge* of the figures. It is not outlined. It is not what we call "drawing". It is a flowing contour where the body suddenly leaves off, upon the atmosphere. The etruscan artist seems to have seen living things surging from their own centre to their own surface.'[32] In his own work, he was without the resources to achieve this effect. Yet beyond the depiction of an action which is not usually depicted, there is no sense in the painting itself of a desire to shock, and no reason to doubt Lawrence's sincerity when he wrote to Juliette Huxley on 27 March, 'I just did a water-colour of a naked man pissing against a wall, as the Bible says. It's most tender and touching' (vi. 344). Evacuation can be pleasurable and by having his figure unclothed Lawrence emphasises that here is a quotidian action which should be utterly shame-free. His figure is unselfconscious and, surprising though it may seem, Lawrence appears to have been equally unselfconscious when he painted him. Yet there is a typical naïvety in his surprise – anger then deriving from surprise – when friends reacted with distaste; and since all art is social, the response of others could soon involve him in aspects of the same process which had characterised the composition of *Lady Chatterley's Lover*. Recognition of how far he was from playing the same tune as the majority only drove him to play it louder.

There are faint, comic hints of this process in the letter he wrote to Aldous and Maria Huxley on 2 April about *Dandelions*. 'Well, I painted a charming picture of a man pissing . . . Now I'm doing a small thing in oil, called *The Rape of the Sabine Women* or a Study in Arses' (vi. 353). Partly because of an over-reliance on outline, arses are often to the fore in Lawrence's paintings and especially in this one as a large man bends forward with one arm under the knees of a large woman whose efforts to escape twist her buttocks round towards the viewer. Given the way Lawrence refers to this composition, and its title, it could be that it contains some element of parody. A second small oil painting he did at this period is certainly parodic, or at least satiric in intent. In *Close-Up*, two unattractive faces are being brought together in a kiss. The unpleasant way in which the coming encounter is depicted may reflect Lawrence's own general dislike of kissing; but its title indicates how disconcerted he had been on his infrequent visits to the cinema at having to observe kissing magnified. The third oil painting from this busy time is more straightforward. Entitled *Family on a Verandah*, it shows a mother stretched out on a hammock, the husband crouching near her feet and two children approaching her from the side. All the figures are naked and, as in *Fight with an Amazon*, the pubic hair of the woman provides a central point of focus.[33]

On 16 March Barbara Weekley had suddenly appeared: she had come to Florence from Alassio where she had once again been staying. Barby had previously shown photographs of Lawrence's paintings to her friend Dorothy Warren, who had recently opened an art gallery in London, and she now brought a renewed invitation to exhibit from Warren that would have helped to stimulate Lawrence into painting so much during the coming weeks. As he expected to leave the Villa Mirenda at the end of April and would have to pack up his paintings anyway, he was inclined to think an exhibition in London might be a good thing. An opportunity to transport several of the smaller ones to England came in May when Willie Hopkin's daughter Enid turned up in Scandicci with her husband Laurence Hilton. At the time of her marriage, early in 1922, Lawrence had written to Enid, explaining that he was about to leave Europe but giving her advice in his best travel-agent manner on the Italian holiday she and her husband were then planning (iv. 195). According to her, he subsequently sent other, similar letters of travel advice and it was through him that she was able to meet several people in his literary circle. She describes how, when Lawrence heard she was going to Paris, he gave her a letter of introduction to Raymond Duncan (Isadora's brother) because of her interest in ballet. This might well have been when Lawrence met the Hiltons in London in September 1926. On that occasion he had not been too impressed and, although he invited them to come to the Villa Mirenda after learning in April that they were in Italy (vi. 380), he was not keen to put them up. The compromise was the little 'osteria' in Vingone where Barby's 'dueña', Eileen Seaman, had stayed. That must have seemed an eminently reasonable solution to the Hiltons when on their first visit to the villa they found Lawrence in bed and Frieda explained that they could not stay in the house because his nights were so disturbed. From Enid Hilton comes one of what would be many descriptions of Lawrence writing in bed (his 'knees bent up with a writing pad on the uplifted legs'); and she says that at intervals he would call Frieda in order to read to her what he had just written: 'Sometimes they laughed together and at other times she would sound a little shocked and in her deep, throaty voice, said: "Lorenzo, you cannot say that."' The Hiltons stayed over a fortnight and when they left Lawrence entrusted to them seven water-colours and three of the smaller oils (the larger ones from the year before remained for the moment on the walls of the rooms they occupied in the villa).[34] Lawrence had not finally determined whether Dorothy Warren should exhibit his work, but he could at least now show her what it was really like. When he first began painting again, he had immediately thought in terms of exhibitions and of selling enough of his work to live, but now the prospect of showing them was real and fairly immediate, he became nervous and insisted he did not really want to sell any of them (vi. 371). He also felt the need for some professional advice. Suggesting to Mark Gertler that he might go and look at examples of his work from 1 June, when Enid Hilton would be back in London, he insisted that they had a 'certain phallic beauty' comparable to the novel he was just about to publish. But he also added, in the germ for the formulations which most admirers of the paintings have relied on since, 'I know they're rolling with faults, Sladeily considered. But there's something *there*' (vi. 406).

IV   The Lighter Side

When Lawrence had welcomed Margaret Gardiner at the Villa Mirenda on or around 15 April, he had been on his own. Barbara Weekley had gone back to Alassio on 28 March and a fortnight later Frieda went with Else Jaffe (who was on the second of two short stays at the Villa Mirenda) to visit her there. Barby describes Frieda as 'going off alone' once she arrived in Alassio,[35] and Lawrence himself later reported to Secker that on her visit she had seen not only Rina Secker's parents, the Capelleros, but also the 'tenente', who must have been home on leave (vi. 377). Lawrence was no fool, in fact quite exceptionally intuitive about others, and especially about Frieda. By at least this date, he must have known about his wife's relationship with Ravagli. There is no absolute proof of his attitude but several suggestions that he had decided to make the best of it. This is the period with which Barby associates his remark to Frieda, 'Every heart has a right to its own secrets';[36] and there are faint signs of a philosophical or enforced tolerance in some of his letters. Else Jaffe had brought Alfred Weber with her on her first visit to the Villa Mirenda in March, when Lawrence described his visitors to Brewster as having been 'as good as married, and as bad, for many years' (vi. 317).[37] On 13 April, two days after Frieda had left for Alassio, he wrote to Witter Bynner with comments on his satire *Cake*. Bynner's letter had apparently reminded him that one of Mabel Luhan's chief faults was an impulse to interfere in other people's affairs: 'breaking other people's eggs and making a mess instead of an omelette'. The effect of this was apparent in what was then happening betweeen Ida Rauh and Andrew Dasburg. 'I think it's *very silly* for Ida and Andrew to be at outs and made mischief by. People who have lived together had best stick together. You can only change for the worse' (vi. 365–6).

When Frieda returned from Alassio on 16 April, the lease on the Villa Mirenda had only another two or three weeks to run. Lawrence had announced publication of *Lady Chatterley's Lover* for 15 May and presumably expected to be able to leave Florence before then, entrusting to Orioli the final arrangements and the dispatch of copies to subscribers. But there were predictable delays in the printing. The chief trouble was that the Tipographia Giuntina had only enough type to set half the novel, and that the paper which had been ordered failed to arrive. Without the paper, there was a long delay before the first half could be printed off, the type broken up and the second half of the novel set. Because the proofs Lawrence received were full of errors, they required a considerable amount of time also. Meanwhile, as Lawrence's own records show, the money kept coming in: from his many friends round the world; from people who knew him only vaguely but felt a link (such as H. G. Wells, J. M. Keynes or Leonard Woolf); from complete strangers; but also from specialist booksellers. It was these last especially who began to show impatience when the novel failed to appear on time. It may have been in part because he was still busy with *Lady Chatterley's Lover* well into May (it was not in fact until 7 June that he finished the last of the proofs and added his signature to the appropriate sheets – vi. 422) that he decided to secure the Villa Mirenda for a further six months. But the chief reason was Frieda. On 4 May he told Else Jaffe what had happened.

You have heard by now that we are keeping on the Mirenda. I took down the pictures and we began to pack: but Frieda became so gloomy, that I hung the pictures up again and paid six months' rent. Not worth while getting into a state about. So here we are, just the same. And probably we shall stay till the end of the month, as the proofs of the novel are *still* only half done. I wish the printer would hurry up. (vi. 391)

Frieda was anxious to hang on to Villa Mirenda as a *pied à terre*, not because she wanted to continue living there in the summer. With last year's collapse in the

mind of both, she had suggested Switzerland for June and July, and because he
felt more and more that Les Diablerets had done him good, Lawrence had at first
agreed to go and 'do some of [his] coughing there' (vi. 376). But if Les Diablerets
had a disadvantage, it was that it was so steeply sloped, and he now began asking
his friends about villages in the mountains where it would be flat enough for him
to take walks (vi. 384). For the period after July, and on the confident assumption
that he would by then have recovered his old strength, he had very ambitious
plans. He wanted at some point to call in on England, but because it seemed
increasingly likely that *Lady Chatterley's Lover* would make money, he thought
mostly of going back to America, ideally on a ticket which could be bought from
the Messageries Maritimes for £120 and which would allow him to travel all
round the world, stopping off wherever he and Frieda wished (vi. 379). In several
letters he reports that both the Brewsters and the Huxleys had agreed to
accompany them to America but, although their assent seems to have been quite
genuine, it might also have been made easy by the strong suspicion that Lawrence
would never again be in a state to make that kind of journey.[38]

In his last weeks at the Villa Mirenda, between painting and correcting
proofs, Lawrence wrote a number of pieces that demonstrated the lighter side of
his talent as well as, Enid Hilton's testimony confirms, his growing tendency to
work in bed. Nancy Pearn had forwarded a request from the editor of the
Evening News for a newspaper article and he responded with 'When She Asks
Why', which was published on 8 May. This was perhaps the easiest way he had
yet found for making 'ten quid' (vi. 403). When the piece was republished in
1930, 'When She Asks Why' became 'The "Jeune Fille" Wants To Know' and
what she wants to know is quite why certain things cannot be said or done.
Lawrence points out that the prohibitions are not really for her benefit and
protection (smart young women of the 1920s can look after themselves), but for
that of her timid father whose values still belong to the pre-war period. The
'jeune fille' on whose behalf books are censored is thus really a pretext for
calming the anxieties of her elders. The glimpse Lawrence gives of a father and
his daughter in this short piece is reminiscent of the Rector and Yvette in *The
Virgin and the Gipsy* and suggests that, when she came to stay in March, Barby
must have complained again about Weekley's continuing concern for her moral
welfare.

On 13 May Lawrence sent Nancy Pearn 'Laura Phillipine', which was based
on his encounter with the daughter of Christine Hughes in Rome the year before,
and may not therefore have been written recently. The possibility is that it was a
piece for which he only now began to see a market.[39] In fact, Nancy Pearn placed
'Laura Phillipine' with *T. P.'s Weekly*, a relatively familiar outlet; but on 17 May
she was able to report that the editor of the *Daily Chronicle* wanted 'about a
thousand words' for a series with the general title 'What Women Have Taught

Me', to which Compton Mackenzie and André Maurois were also contributing (vi. 403). Lawrence responded with a memory from his childhood of his father swearing that he would make Mrs Lawrence 'tremble at the sound of [his] footsteps', and his mother deflating him completely with, 'Which boots will you wear?' He knew then, he says, who really wielded the power in their house. His mother was dominant because his father had ceded complete moral authority to her: the right to decide what was right and what was wrong: 'Which led me to wonder, as a small child, why God was a man and not a woman.' 'That Women Know Best' appeared in the *Daily Chronicle* on 29 November 1928 and is likely to have earned Lawrence fifteen guineas (vi. 403 n.3).[40] Over the coming months he would continue to write short newspaper articles and thereby consolidate the new financial security he was about to achieve with *Lady Chatterley's Lover*.

It was in these same few weeks, Lawrence also wrote one of the best of his short stories – he sent it off to Nancy Pearn on 7 June, three days before he left Florence. In 'Mother and Daughter' he sides with the younger generation against the old, as he had in 'When She Asks Why', and also satirises once again the power of the mature woman. But the treatment is urbane and witty, light years away from the intensities of the novel whose proofs he was, or had been, correcting. He may have been prompted to write this story by a visit at the beginning of May from Mary Foote, a professional painter in her mid-fifties who was a friend of Mabel Luhan. 'I am asking people if they know of a nice Gasthaus in Switzerland, for me,' he wrote to Else Jaffe on 4 May. 'I hate hotels-pensions, after a few days. I always want to kill the old women – usually English – that come into meals like cats. We just had a very handsome Louis XV sort of a one to tea – but American this time – and of course I'm bristling in every hair' (vi. 391). Rachel Bodoin of 'Mother and Daughter' is a 'well-born Irishwoman' rather than an American, but with her well-preserved good looks, her 'terrible inward energy' and above all her 'merciless, hammer-like humour' she goes back, via Pauline Attenborough in 'The Lovely Lady', to that other handsome American, Mrs Witt in *St. Mawr*. The link with Mary Foote is suggested when Lawrence also describes Rachel Bodoin as being 'perfectly eighteenth century, the early half'.[41]

This powerful mother dominates her daughter Virginia, eventually frightening off an impecunious lover called Henry because of a contempt and sarcasm with which Virginia cannot prevent herself from being complicit. (Sending her daughter a gift of £20, Mrs Bodoin advises her to buy her lover a new suit before 'the sunlight may be tempted to show him for what he is worth'.) After Henry has backed out, mother and daughter 'set up married life together' in Bloomsbury; but the elegance of the home Mrs Bodoin creates does not prevent Virginia from becoming increasingly nerve-worn by her highly paid job in a government department, and increasingly exasperated by her failure to break away from her mother. Her rescuer appears in the unlikely form of a sixty-year-old Armenian widower (who had been obliged to emigrate to Bulgaria, as Arlen's family had, and who also has a 'lot of bouyoums' in his name). He is anxious to marry Virginia for reasons which are by no means exclusively sentimental, and has the power, as well as the dogged imperviousness to insult, which allows him to disrupt the 'flow' that has always bound mother and daughter together. (Wholly underestimating the danger he represents, Mrs Bodoin refers to him as the 'Turkish Delight'.) The implication is that only someone of his age and different cultural background could be strong enough to defeat the power which Rachel Bodoin represents.[42] 'Mother and Daughter' is witty throughout, as well as very tightly and economically written: it is sophisticated comedy from a writer whose last novel would give him a reputation with which it would become impossible to associate pleasing urbanity of this variety. Yet the defeat of the older woman, like the defeat of Pauline Attenborough or Mrs Witt, is not described without respect and hints of a moving personal tragedy. Lawrence feared the power of mature women with strong characters but, Mary Foote aside, it was in their company that he was often most comfortable.

With his lease renewed, Lawrence had written to the Brewsters inviting them to make use of the Villa Mirenda while he and Frieda went to the mountains. They arrived around 6 June but, once they saw how things stood, decided to go to the mountains also. This was because, Achsah Brewster says, they felt they would not be able to enjoy Lawrence's company for very much longer.[43] After an exceptionally cold and wet May, the weather had finally changed. 'There are millions of poppies everywhere in the corn', Lawrence told Emily; 'the peasants are busy cutting the hay – they cut it all with sickles, and carry it in their arms to the wagon – the nightgales sing, and I saw the first firefly' (vi. 413). These attractions did not convince Lawrence he wanted to stay. If the Villa Mirenda was the house he had lived in longer than any other since leaving Europe in 1922, that was not entirely his choice. Despite a location and environment which seems in retrospect ideal for someone of his tastes and occupations, Lawrence had wanted to be off for many months. Whatever the conveniences and beauty of the spot, and even without the associations with illness which it now had for him, his restlessness would always have driven him elsewhere. On previous occasions, a chief motive for moving seems to have been that new places provided him with stimulus for his writing. Now he was primarily engaged in a fruitless search for better health; but it may also have been that the distraction of travel prevented him from pondering too often his real situation.

Before he left Italy, Lawrence confirmed a *rapprochement* with Ottoline Morrell begun when he admitted to Juliette Huxley in Les Diablerets that he still felt uneasy about the quarrel which had divided them. Insofar as she felt betrayed when she recognised features of her own appearance and environment in the figure of Hermione Roddice in *Women in Love*, the quarrel could be said to have been of his own making. On 8 May he had written to say how sorry he had been to hear she was not well and hoped that they might one day meet again, 'because I'm sure we're quite fond of one another really' (vi. 394). After Lady Ottoline had replied with a circumstantial account of her illness, he wrote again on the 24th, warmly expressing his sympathy and responding in the affirmative to her enquiry as to whether he was given to 'feel things very much'.

I do. And that's why I too am ill. The hurts, and the bitternesses sink in, however much one may reject them with one's spirit. They sink in, and there they lie, inside one, wasting one. What is the matter with us is primarily chagrin. Then the microbes pounce. – One ought to be tough and selfish: and one is never tough enough, and never selfish in the proper, self-preserving way. Then one is laid low.

Explaining that he had been in bed again with 'a touch of flu', he went on to say how sad he was that Lady Ottoline had given up Garsington. He wished they could all have two lives: one in which to make mistakes and another in which to profit from them; and he continued with sentences which clearly addressed themselves to the self-doubt and gloom she must have expressed.

But don't say you feel you're not important in life. You've been an important influence in lots of lives, as you have in mine; through being fundamentally generous, and through being Ottoline. After all, there's only one Ottoline. And she has moved one's imagination. It doesn't matter what sort of vision comes out of a man's imagination, his vision of Ottoline. Anymore than a photograph of me is me, or even 'like' me. The so-called portraits of Ottoline can't possibly *be* Ottoline – no one knows that better than an artist. But Ottoline has moved men's imagination, deeply, and that's perhaps the most a woman can do. And in the world today, full of women, how rare to find one that can move the imagination! No, I wish, and wish deeply, there could be Ottoline again and Garsington again, and we could start afresh.   (vi. 409)

In spite of an outrageously masculine vision of woman's role (which both Frieda and Lady Ottoline would have shared), this is both a gracious, moving tribute and, from someone who so rarely excused himself, the nearest Lawrence was ever likely to come to an apology. Self-confidence and self-assertion were nearly always a feature of his behaviour, but he was too committed to honesty in his dealings with his feelings, and too contemptuous of emotional hypocrisy, to be self-justifying in his judgements on his past.

417

◆

PART FOUR

The Marvel
of
Being Alive

◆

CHAPTER EIGHTEEN

June–November 1928

THE SEARCH FOR HEALTH

I Chexbres-sur-Vevey

Achsah Brewster recalled that when she and her husband left the Villa Mirenda with the Lawrences, no-one had any very clear idea of where they ought to go; but in May Lawrence had made enquiries about resorts in Savoy, on the French side of the Alps (vi. 402), and it was in that direction that they all set out. On the train to Turin their compartment emptied, and they began to sing hymns. With his knowledge of not only the revivalist tunes but also 'every word of every verse' in each hymn, Lawrence led the singing.[1] A particular favourite with him was 'Throw out the Life-Line!' with its rousing if somewhat repetitive chorus:

> Throw out the Life-Line!
> Throw out the Life-Line!
> Someone is drifting away:
> Throw out the Life-Line!
> Throw out the Life-Line!
> Someone is sinking today.

This was a Temperance hymn, often 'performed' outside public houses in late Victorian and Edwardian England, with Temperance campaigners dressed as life-boat men and carrying model boats.[2] At its various climaxes, Achsah remembered Lawrence standing up and throwing 'an imaginary lasso to the drowning souls, hauling them in strenuously'.[3]

From Turin they moved on to Chambéry, Aix-les-Bains and Grenoble. On the 14th, among the mountains to the southeast of Grenoble, Lawrence found what he was looking for in a village then called Saint-Nizier-de-Pariset.[4] By this stage, after consultation with his various doctors, he had firm ideas about the degree of altitude therapeutic for people in his condition. At 3,500 feet, the Hotel des Touristes at Saint-Nizier was high enough, and it also had the advantage of being 'on the edge of a plateau' (vi. 424). The slope towards the higher mountains at the back of the village was not steep, and it was surrounded by gently undulating fields, so that it would not be impossible for him to walk a little. Every one in the party agreed they liked the hotel, but after only one night the proprietor came to the Brewsters and told them they would have to leave because Lawrence had coughed so much in the night. Apologetically, he invoked a local by-law which prohibited him taking guests with 'affected lungs'. When she wrote about this episode later, Achsah Brewster was still not certain that Lawrence understood why, after previously declaring their enthusiasm, they all then told him that, on second thoughts, they did not like the look of the place and felt they had to leave.[5] To his sister Emily, to Secker and to Enid Hilton, Lawrence himself gave reasons as specious as theirs for the move, calling Saint-Nizier 'too high and cold and raw' and the hotel 'comfortless' (vi. 426–7); but a letter he wrote to Orioli on 21 June shows that he knew exactly what had happened. 'That St. Nizier place was very rough', he told him, ' – and the insolent French people actually asked us to go away because I coughed. They said they didn't have anybody who coughed. I felt very mad' (vi. 428). Because Lawrence had fully intended to settle for the summer in Saint-Nizier, he now had to write to several of his regular correspondents cancelling it as a forwarding address (vi. 425). But this inconvenience was nothing in comparison with the psychological damage the episode must have caused.

The party moved on, away from the 'insolent French' and across the Swiss border, to a hotel where the Brewsters had stayed immediately after their return from Ceylon (iv. 279). This was at Chexbres, eastwards along the shores of Lake Geneva a few miles from Vevey. Although Chexbres-sur-Vevey was in Lawrence's opinion not high enough, he felt that the altitude would 'do for the moment' (vi. 431), and he appreciated both the hotel's comfort and the fine views from his balcony. He must have had a room at the front of the building where the land slopes steeply down to the water while, across the lake, the French Alps impressively complete the picture. It is an exceptionally attractive site, aspects of which he described in another of the series of articles he was now writing for the *Evening News*. When this particular one appeared in his posthumous collection *Assorted Articles*, it would be called 'Insouciance'; but in its newspaper version its title ('Over-Earnest Ladies') refers to the English women on the balcony next to his, one of whom insists on talking about Mussolini when he is busy watching two mowers on the slopes down to the lake, and listening to the 'slush! slush!' of their scythes softly carrying up to him. 'Why', he complains, 'do modern people almost invariably ignore the things that are actually present to them?'; why are they haunted by 'that mysterious bugbear of "caring"?' As an inveterate carer himself, Lawrence was in a good position to ask these questions; but his authority for doing so also derives from an ability to combine caring with what he calls here 'intuition' – the quality that has allowed him to become totally absorbed in:

the uncanny glassiness of the lake this afternoon, the sulkiness of the mountains, the vividness of near green in thunder-sun, the young man in bright blue trousers lightly tossing the grass from the scythe, the elderly man in a boater stiffly shoving his scythe-strokes, both of them sweating in the silence of the intense light.[6]

At the Grand Hotel in Chexbres, where the 'x' is silent, Lawrence completed two more articles for the *Evening News* ('Master in His Own House' and 'Dull London'),[7] but also worked on a continuation of his version of the Resurrection story. Frieda must have felt him sufficiently settled there, and sufficiently looked after by the Brewsters, to go for a week to see her mother in Baden-Baden. On 21 June he wrote to her, 'I worked over my Isis story a bit' (vi. 429). The composition of the second part of *The Escaped Cock* must therefore have begun before Frieda left Switzerland on the 19th. Two episodes in it where solitary onlookers observe a bustle of mundane activity close to water may well have been written or revised while Lawrence was alone on his hotel balcony, although the water is the sea and not a lake. Yet the action of the continued story clearly does not take place in any precisely identifiable location but in a mythical Bible land of Lawrence's Congregationalist youth. In 'Hymns in a Man's Life' he would explain how magical for him had been words such as Galilee, Canaan, Moab, Kedron; and how uninterested he always was in what such places were really like.[8]

The continuation of his story begins with a beautiful evocation of a wooden temple of Isis, occupying 'a little tree-covered tongue of land between two bays', by 'the shores of Sidon'. On the steep slopes coming down to the sea, the olive trees silver under the wind, 'like water splashing'.[9] The young priestess who presides there has not been able to feel keen interest in any of the men she has met in her former life, even though one of these was Mark Antony; and she has now dedicated herself to the Isis who is in search of the torn and scattered body of Osiris. (In this Egyptian fertility myth, the parts of his body which are always the last to be recovered, and without which regeneration cannot take place, are the genitals.)[10] When the protagonist of the first part of Lawrence's story arrives seeking shelter, she is struck by the 'beauty of much suffering' in the 'delicate ugliness' of his face[11] and roused for the first time. The Indians in 'The Woman Who Rode Away' mistake their American intruder for the white visitor whose sacrifice will restore the fortunes of their race. With much happier results, the priestess of 'Isis in Search' assumes that the resurrected Christ-figure of the first part of *The Escaped Cock*, with his scars and scarcely healed wounds, is the lost Osiris. Her tender desire has a healing effect and touches even the man who is so recently returned from the dead that he has wanted to avoid any close human contact ('Noli me tangere'). With oil, the priestess massages the wound in the man's side and all his lower body so that (in the old phrase) his loins stir and, in what is now a *complete* resurrection of the body, sexual desire springs up again.

'Again' is the word a biographer is tempted to use, thinking of the poignant element of wish-fulfilment in this delicately written story; but insofar as it concerns someone recognising the importance of sex for the first time – 'Father!', the man says, 'why did you hide this from me?'[12] – it is inappropriate. Having read the letters of complaint to the editor of *Forum* after the first part of *The Escaped Cock* appeared there, Lawrence knew that his protest against the Pauline element in Christianity, and the insistence on Christ as virgin, was bound to create controversy. Either because of this, or because of the degree of his own personal investment in it, he was very protective of his story. On 30 June he described it as 'almost finished' but, although three weeks later he certainly had a complete manuscript, he was not inclined to do anything with it (vi. 442, 469). Even by the end of August he was still reluctant to let it go – 'why expose my sensitive things gratuitously? And this story is one of my thin-skinned ones' (vi. 526); and it was not until 2 September that he posted both parts of the story to Enid Hilton (who by then had become important to him for other reasons) so that she could arrange to have them typed (vi. 539). This reluctance to expose his own views, thoughts and feelings was accompanied by outbursts of a fierce disdain for his likely critics in the 'ordinary' world which finds expression in his completion of *The Escaped Cock*. The priestess and the Christ-figure are presented as quite apart from the slaves on the estate where the temple stands, one of whom casually rapes his girl companion towards the beginning of the action. Nor can they hope for any kind of genuine contact with the mother of the priestess and her Roman steward, who direct the labour of the slaves, and who precipitate the conclusion when they force the Christ-figure to flee by plotting his arrest. In the vocabulary of 'The Flying-Fish', which Lawrence would read aloud to the Brewsters in July, these others are people of the 'little day' whose activities are without point unless they can be set in 'the circle of the greater life'. But this does not mean that the lesser day can therefore be ignored. In her preoccupation with 'Isis in Search', the young priestess has handed over all effective, material power to her mother. 'Why did the woman of Isis', the Christ-figure reflects, 'relinquish her portion in the daily world? She should have kept her goods fiercely!'[13]

On 23 June Aldous and Maria Huxley came to visit. They were driving to Forte dei Marmi where they intended to spend another summer, and Aldous found Lawrence 'surprisingly well, all things considered'.[14] They left on the 28th having taken both of the Lawrences – Frieda had returned from Baden-Baden on the 25th – to the Château de Chillon for the day. This excursion to the castle which juts out into the lake on the shore eastwards beyond Montreux does not seem to have interested Lawrence overmuch, in spite of the Byronic connection;[15] yet he must have envied the mobility which their car and good health gave the Huxleys. He himself would feel increasingly trapped and more and more reduced to running the more practical affairs of his life by correspondence. Like many people in his situation, necessity made him increasingly adept at using others. Principal among his agents was Orioli to whom he had written on the 23rd asking him to supervise the packing of the seven large oils which still remained in the Villa Mirenda (after Giulia Pini had wrapped them in blankets and Pietro had brought them into town in the dog-cart, they were to be professionally packed by the same firm Orioli had used to send some of Mabel Luhan's things from the Villa Curonia back to her – vi. 101, 432–3).

Lawrence wanted his paintings to be ready to send off but he did not yet know quite where they should go. Having heard nothing from Dorothy Warren, he was tempted to accept the offer of a show which he had only recently received from the owners of the Claridge Gallery in London. He was interested now in an early London exhibition (the show which the Claridge Gallery had originally planned for July had fallen through and they needed a replacement in a hurry), and he became more interested when the well-known American photographer Alfred Stieglitz, who had admired *Studies in Classic American Literature* and was in touch with both Brett and Mabel Luhan, wrote to confirm that he wanted to exhibit Lawrence's paintings in his own New York gallery some time during November (vi. 432–3, 467).[16] On the same day that he wrote to Orioli, Lawrence sent a curt note to Dorothy Warren explaining that he might well abandon her for the Claridge Gallery, and implicitly justifying himself with a reference to the 'long lapses between her answers' (vi. 434). She wrote back immediately, apologising for the delay and warmly pressing him not to give her up. She had, she explained, been in Berlin with an exhibition of young English painters ('Barbara [Weekley] amongst them'), and her assistant in London had let her down. In her view, a short exhibition in July, such as the Claridge was suggesting, would be no good: to be effective any show needed to last at least three weeks and be held in November, although October would be possible if the pictures had to go to America later that month. She promised to explore Lawrence's suggestion that there might be a joint exhibition of his own work and that of the Brewsters, though it was important in her view that the walls of her gallery should not be too crowded; and she reminded Lawrence of how much she had liked his copy of the *Flight into Egypt* by Fra Angelico which 'used to hang over the mantelpiece in Byron Villas', the house in Hampstead the Lawrences had occupied in 1915 (vi. 435). Responding to this private appeal ('After all, I know you, and the thing is more personal'), Lawrence instructed Orioli to have the remaining pictures sent to Dorothy Warren and told her on 4 July, just before he left Chexbres:

When you have the pictures, let me know how you like them. Probably you will like them better as you get used to them. They are quite simple, with no tricks: but I consider they are, what very few pictures are, organically alive and whole. All the modern smartness only succeeds in putting pictures together, it practically never makes a picture live as a whole thing. (vi. 446)

On the day the Huxleys left, Lawrence received from Orioli his first copy of

Lady Chatterley's Lover. He was delighted, feeling that it had a 'fine shape and proportion' and that his own phoenix design was 'just the right bird for the cover' (vi. 440). But he was also understandably apprehensive about possible difficulties of distribution. There was the question, for example, of whether it ran the risk of being seized by American Customs officials, especially when several copies in a package large enough to attract attention were being mailed to a bookseller. In urging Orioli to keep the packages small, Lawrence also told him not to send too many at once; and he took the precaution of asking several American friends to telegraph Orioli as soon as they received their copies so that he would know they were getting through. It was not long before he heard that many of them were not (vi. 449–50).

At first, there was no trouble of this kind in England and the novel reached its subscribers easily enough. The difficulties began in July when a London firm with a bulk order (William Jackson Ltd) looked at one of the more than seventy copies they had received and decided, on both legal and moral grounds, that on no account did they want to be involved (vi. 477). Because they had asked Lawrence where they should now send the books, he needed someone in London who could collect and store them for him (to tell the firm to send them back to Florence risked attracting more attention than he thought wise). The person he turned to was Enid Hilton who, having already transported a batch of paintings to London for him, now happened to be living at the same address in Mecklenburgh Square where he and Frieda had once stayed with Hilda Doolittle, Richard Aldington and Arabella Yorke.[17] Lawrence was nervous about involving an essentially non-literary person in his literary affairs, someone from the more 'ordinary' world of his early friends and family, particularly as there was some risk of her being compromised if the authorities did decide to act against his novel. But the enthusiastic efficiency with which Enid collected the books, and then distributed them to individual subscribers as further orders came in, fully justified his choice. When two other booksellers reacted in the same way as Jackson's, however, he turned to Koteliansky rather than imposing on her again (vi. 481). If he had not appealed to him in the first place, it was because he felt Kot did not believe Lawrence should ever have written, much less published, *Lady Chatterley's Lover* (vi. 476); but whatever Kot's feelings about the book, he was the last person to let down an old friend.

Very grateful at first (vi. 492), Lawrence became impatient when rumours of the novel's imminent suppression, which Kot passed on to him, proved groundless. They had prompted him to tell Enid Hilton that she should send 32 of her copies to the Aldingtons' cottage in Berkshire for safe-keeping (vi. 494), a move which seemed to him in retrospect unnecessary ('Kot is such a fusser' – vi. 528), and which made the business of supplying late, incoming orders from the recovered copies more complicated. Yet supplied they all were. A total of 108 were returned by the booksellers (vi. 552) but were then all quickly redistributed as Orioli forwarded orders to Lawrence and he told Enid, Kot and the Aldingtons where the books they held were to be posted. He kept a careful check on numbers, advised Enid to conceal her name when she delivered or posted a package, and forwarded money for expenses (which Kot obstinately refused). Another helper was Laurence Pollinger, the young man who had recently taken charge of Lawrence's books at the Curtis Brown office (Nancy Pearn only dealt with his journal contributions), and who on his own initiative found a number of new buyers. Energetically directing these assistants with precise and detailed letters, Lawrence was quickly able to bring his sales to nearly 600 copies and to make a lot of money (by the end of August he was already showing a net profit of over £700, most of which came from the English market). In his letters to England, or in his periodic financial reports to Florence (which conscientiously calculated Orioli's 10 per cent as well as a small token for Carlo Zanotti, Orioli's assistant and lover), Lawrence showed a keen, hard-headed interest in business – now that it was his own – and a sharp grasp of commercial detail. It was on one afternoon in Chexbres that Achsah Brewster remembered 'he veered upon money', growing more and more vehement as they talked:

One must fight for his just share, never mind if peace of heart were dearer than the just share! He was furious.
'It's your duty to be rich. It's a sin for you to sneak off with your peace of heart while other people sneak off with what belongs to you. Fight!'[18]

Of course, the Brewsters were Buddhists and for years Lawrence had been involved in a running argument with them about the virtues of unworldliness and passivity, which may have often prompted him to exaggerate his own positions. But not to be 'done', or perhaps 'done' any longer, was certainly a stronger feeling with him now than it had been in the past. He was so enraged by Jackson's refusal to handle the books they had ordered that he tried to make them compensate him for the cost of postage, only to be answered with a letter from their solicitors (vi. 496, 515).

II   Chalet Kesselmatte

Chexbres was not high enough for the therapeutic effect altitude was supposed to have. Although he increasingly made it clear that he was not in the Swiss mountains by choice (vi. 469), Lawrence was determined to give thin air an extended trial. On 6 July he and Frieda moved to the Hotel National at Gstaad, without the Brewsters, but in order to chalet-hunt for all four. They found something suitable for themselves near the village of Gsteig, in a spot that happened to be only about eight miles from Les Diablerets, but in German-rather than French-speaking Switzerland, across that Pillon Pass where he had picnicked with the Huxleys six months before. At 300 Swiss francs for the season, and with two rooms and a kitchen downstairs, as well as one room up, it was both comparatively roomy and comparatively cheap (vi. 452). They moved in on 9 July and efforts were made to find an equivalent nearby for the Brewsters, both before and after they arrived at the Hotel Viktoria in Gsteig. But Gsteig was in fact where the Brewsters continued to stay during the rest of their time in Switzerland.

The Lawrences' new home was known as the Chalet Kesselmatte and only a mile from the village, but it was steeply uphill all the way. Not until 31 July – after a period when he had felt so 'perfectly wretched' that he thought his tombstone in Gsteig churchyard ought to read, 'Departed this life, etc. etc. – *He was fed up*' – could Lawrence report he had made the trip down and, 'what is much worse', up again (vi. 483). He had now the requisite altitude ('about 4000 feet' – vi. 453), but not the flattish walking ground which had made Saint-Nizier so attractive. From outside the chalet there were once again spectacular views, this time across the beginnings of the Pillon Pass to the Diablerets glacier; but the land behind and in front banked sharply so that, without a car, he was virtually immobilised, isolated. It may have been some apprehension about isolation that led him to invite his sister, almost as soon as he was settled. This was not Ada, Frieda's enemy, but the less prosperous Emily who had never been out of England and to whom he offered money for the trip. Even if she did not come, he was (Lawrence told her) likely to be in England at the end of September for the exhibition of his pictures: 'If only my health were better, I'd be there now. I don't particularly *want* to be in Switzerland. But the doctors say this is where I ought to be – so we'll try it. – I really want to try to get rid of this beastly cough – it's no worse – and no danger in it – but it is such a nuisance' (vi. 456–7).

Lawrence and Frieda were not quite alone on their mountain. Their landlords were supposed to be living in another chalet they owned, 'across on the north side, with the cows'; but the wife and her adopted daughter of fourteen would turn up about tea-time to wash up and cook for their tenants, and they would then stay the night. As there was room, he liked them, and they were off at four in the morning to their farm work, Lawrence did not mind (vi. 459). Outside they arranged a table and chair for him under some pine trees, and there he composed a number of short pieces which required only a limited stretch of concentration. Continuing with his series of articles which he hoped would please the *Evening News*, and earn him a minimum of £15 each, he wrote 'Matriarchy' which expresses vividly the sense of being overwhelmed by women that many men of his generation seem to have had after the war. This was a consequence less of women's numerical advantage, which the war had substantially increased, than of their growing presence in the workplace: the understandable refusal of many women to retreat back into the home after 1919. The suffragist movement had clearly also mattered in creating this sense but so too (Lawrence's descriptions make clear) did 1920s' fashions. 'Women, women everywhere,' he wrote, 'silk-legged hosts that are up and doing, and no gainsaying them. They settle like silky locusts on all the jobs, they occupy the offices and the playing fields like immensely active ants, they buzz round the coloured lights of pleasure in amazing bare-armed swarms, and the rather dazed young male is, naturally, a bit scared.' The solution, he suggested, was for men to give up to women their role as head of the family. After all, among the 'Pueblo Indians of the Arizona desert' (he is almost certainly thinking of the Hopi) there was a matriarchal system which worked well; and what did it matter if when Tommy Smith married Elsie Jones he became Mr Jones? As the Indian example showed, the primary duty of a man was in any case not to his family but to the religious life of the tribe. Matriarchal domestic arrangements would leave him free to spend more time in the *khiva*, the religious meeting place in Indian villages where only men were allowed, or whatever Western equivalent one could conceive where he could satisfy those 'ultimate social cravings which can only be satisfied apart from women'. (His mother would have objected that in Eastwood the *khiva* was the pub) In an article which was sent off for the *Evening News* on the same day (12 July) as 'Matriarchy' (vi. 460), but which pleased its editor no better, Lawrence does not deny that money is important: 'No getting away from it, there is something rather mean about saving money. But still more fatal is the disaster of having no money at all, when you need it.' At the same time, he suggests that because most men find making a living a bore and are no longer interested in property, it might as well be handed over to women, for after all 'the modern excessive need of money is a female need'.[19]

The manager of the foreign department at Curtis Brown had asked him to write a short autobiographical account for a French publishing house intending to publish some of his work in translation.[20] Lawrence was reluctant to do this, saying that all they needed to know could be found in *Sons and Lovers* or *The Rainbow* (vi. 465). On 18 July he nevertheless obliged, sketching in his background and claiming that, although he had always been delicate in health, he had a 'strong constitution'. Firmly committed now to his father's rather than his mother's side of the Lawrence family's social equation, he rather exaggerated the recoil he had felt as a boy from middle-class values, and he went on to suggest that it was the suppression of *The Rainbow* which had marked his definitive breach with 'the British bourgeois public'.[21]

On the day before he posted this sketch off, he had sent to Nancy Pearn a review of four books for *Vogue*. This journal had been in both his and her sights for some time, but he was still doubtful whether he could provide what they required.[22] They had given him that reviewer's nightmare: four books with no connection with each other; yet his brief comments on each disguise the incongruity of the package and demonstrate that, if he was usually disinclined to work to order, it was not because he lacked the requisite skill or flexibility. Praise for *The Station: Athos, Treasure of Man*, by Robert Byron, a rising young star of travel writing, allowed him to compliment the Sitwells whose 'charming butterfly manner', with its 'underneath tenacity of purpose', he took to be one of Byron's models. He strongly approved of the attack on suburban sprawl in *England and the Octopus* by Clough Williams-Ellis – 'As a nation we are dying of ugliness . . . People who live in mean, despicable surroundings become mean and despicable'; but when he came to the fiction he had received, he could only feel dismay. A novel entitled *Comfortless Memory*, by Maurice Baring, struck him as full of 'faked seriousness' and 'utterly boring'. As for Somerset Maugham's latest short stories, involving as they did Ashendon, the eponymous elderly author turned World War I spy, these struck him as 'even more depressing'. In Lawrence's view, Maugham's almost passionate concern was to prove that 'all men and all women are either dirty dogs or imbeciles' and, for him, it was better 'to be a live dirty dog than a dead lion'. 'The author's pet prejudice being "humour"', Lawrence concluded, 'it would be hard to find a bunch of more ill-humoured stories, in which the humour has gone more rancid.'[23] Maugham had been in Florence on at least one occasion while Lawrence was living there (vi. 239), but they had seen enough of each other in Mexico City to prefer not to meet again.

As far as the record of Lawrence's newspaper articles is concerned, the autobiographical sketch and the review for *Vogue*, together with a short story Lawrence wrote at this time entitled 'The Blue Moccasins' (often ill but hardly ever idle is his usual state in these last years), fill the gap between 'Ownership' and the next piece he wrote for the *Evening News* and sent off towards the end of August. Arthur Olley, its literary editor, had specifically asked for something on 'Women are Cocksure but Never Quite Sure', so that why he rejected 'Cocksure Women and Hensure Men' is not clear. From Lawrence's previous pieces Olley would know that, for all the apparent concessions to contemporary female aspirations, he was (or had become) fundamentally conservative on women's issues. To express his conservatism on this occasion, Lawrence returned to the farmyard, pointing out that when the cock crows 'he listens for an answer, alert'. The crowing of a cocksure woman, on the other hand, is 'out of scheme . . . not in relation to the rest of things'; for all her cocksureness, she is always a hen. At some point all she has done will turn into 'pure nothingness' and she will realise that she has lost the 'hensureness which is the real bliss of every female.'[24]

Unimpressed by these views, Olley took a week or so later a piece ('Hymns in a Man's Life') which had not been intended for him; and then 'Red Trousers', which Lawrence sent to Nancy Pearn on 13 September when he was about to leave Gsteig and which provides a neat termination for all those *Evening News* pieces written in Switzerland by returning to the question of insouciance. From 'Red Trousers' itself we learn that one of the newspaper's readers had responded to an earlier piece by Lawrence ('Dull London'), and written directly to its author in order to suggest that at the origin of the capital's transformation into a gloomy city was the cigarette, that 'tubular white ant which is sapping our civilisation'. Lawrence suspected an anti-tobacco 'crusader' and noted that, although crusades make life interesting, they have a tendency to become dull, especially when they achieve their ends. (The original title of the piece was 'Oh! For a New Crusade'.) He remembered how he used to thrill to the Salvation Army and the singing of hymns such as 'Throw Out the Life-Line' but then, if everybody set out to make their lives more exciting by joining that organisation, there would be nobody left to save. Women were all right in that they were still 'thrilling in the last stages of their emancipation crusade. Votes, short skirts, unlimited leg, Eton crop, the cigarette, and see you damned first'; but what could men do. What it needed, Lawrence lightheartedly suggests, was for a dozen men to have the sheer insouciance to walk down the Strand in tight red trousers, little orange-brown jackets and bright green hats. In his view, that would take more courage than an Arctic exploration.[25]

The Lawrences may have been isolated in Chalet Kesselmatte but they were visited regularly. The Brewsters conscientiously puffed up the slope every day for tea and, because they themselves had visitors, the Lawrences would also meet these, either at Kesselmatte itself or on the odd occasions when they either walked or were driven down to Gsteig. (Not only was it possible to drive in the mountains during the summer but there was even a bus which went from Gsteig over the Pillon Pass to Les Diablerets – vi. 468.) Lawrence complains mildly of four American spinsters who came to see the Brewsters (vi. 498) and he had mixed feelings about two Indian visitors. The first was Dhan Gopal Mukerji who was married to an American and wrote books about India. Prompted perhaps by Brewster whose interest in Indian thought had been stimulated by Mukerji's articles in the *Atlantic Monthly* before he and Achsah left for Europe, Lawrence had read Mukerji's autobiography, *Caste and Outcaste*, in 1924 (v. 77). That work does not however seem to have made much impression and although Lawrence found this visitor 'quite amusing', he also thought him a 'bit false' (vi. 510).[26] He warmed more to a scientist named Boshi Sen whom the Brewsters had met in Calcutta and who went on to work at London University. He massaged Lawrence's back and shoulders and persuaded him that a hot poultice of mud might be good for his chest (vi. 519, 538).

The Brewsters visited every day but sometimes Earl would come on his own in the morning in order to paint, patiently accepting (as Brett had done before him) Lawrence's criticism and advice. Trapped as he virtually was under the pine trees, Lawrence was painting a good deal himself. There was a picture eventually called *Sun-Men Catching Horses* which he sent to Harry Crosby but which has disappeared. In mid-August, he painted *Contadini*, the portrait in oils of a seated naked man with the back of another male nude behind, his powerful buttocks showing just above the first figure's left shoulder. One reason why commentators have been inclined to associate this painting with Raul Mirenda's reference to 'Piero Pini' posing nude for Lawrence is that, anatomically speaking, it is unusually closely observed. If one of its 'contadini' is indeed meant to be Pietro, then the portrait is obviously from memory; but the likelihood of its having in fact been painted, like *Dandelions*, with the aid of photographs is strengthened by a letter written on 15 August to Brewster, who had decamped to Paris for a few days with Mukerji. Saying that he had just finished *Contadini* on a panel Brewster had given him, Lawrence asks him if he could buy in Paris some more nude photographs 'that I could use in my sort of painting – natural ones' (vi. 506).

Giving the chief nude figure Pietro's *face* would not however have been unusual for Lawrence. Harry T. Moore has suggested that in another of his paintings from this time, the central female nude who is half-sitting, half-kneeling on the sand stretching back her torso voluptuously while a naked man embraces her from behind, has the facial characteristics of Cynthia Asquith. The photographic evidence, the fact that Lawrence called his painting *North Sea* when it was at Margate that he and Lady Cynthia first met, and the stories in which a figure based on Lady Cynthia succumbs to the attractions of a character rather like himself, make Moore's suggestion not at all improbable. Yet even the absolute certainty that the woman's face was intended to be Lady Cynthia's would not of course mean that Lawrence had ever persuaded her to pose nude for him, or that he had ever seen her in that state. Two other paintings from this period are *Accident in a Mine* (as Lawrence explained to Brewster, miners sometimes worked naked in areas which were especially deep and hot) and *The Milk White Lady*. In spite of the absence of a piano, the Lawrences and Brewsters spent a good deal of their time together singing. This second, little-known picture was inspired by the verses in a song Achsah identifies as 'The Two Magicians' which describe how a woman looks out of a window 'as white as any milk' while a man looks in 'as black as any silk'.[27]

As Lawrence wrote his short pieces for the newspapers, he read them to the Brewsters, Frieda and whoever else happened to be present. (Boshi Sen was particularly taken with 'Cocksure Women and Hensure Men', saying that it was an article every woman in India ought to read.) Achsah Brewster remembered how moved she was when Lawrence read his 1923 fragment 'The Flying-Fish' and reports that he later explained it was a story written 'so near the borderline of death' that he now felt he would never finish it.[28] She also describes how he consulted them about his short story 'The Blue Moccasins'. This was unusual for

Lawrence in having been (like his newspaper articles) commissioned – in June Nancy Pearn had told him that *Eve: the lady's pictorial* would like something from him for their Christmas number (vi. 438). As much as the unpredictability of the creative imagination, this may explain why 'The Blue Moccasins' appears to have little to do with his current concerns but took him back to English provincial life and a woman called Lina McCleod, who is a less extreme version of 'The Princess' in his novella of that name. Well-off, independent, fastidious and not very keen on men, Lina paints flowers and has travelled widely (it is in New Mexico that she has acquired the attractive Indian moccasins of the title). Back at the top of the social hierarchy in her own English village, she becomes interested in a good-looking bank clerk who regards her with awed respect. Although Percy Barlow is not merely her social inferior but also more than twenty years her junior, she decides to marry him just before he is conscripted into the army during World War I.

When Percy gets back to England, Lina's hair has gone white, she finds that she rather resents the way he disturbs her enjoyment of her own company and whatever sexual life they have enjoyed quickly comes to an end. Still naïve and unawakened, he involves himself in church activities and agrees to take part in the Christmas show along with the local vicar's war-widowed daughter, Alice Howells, who is the same age as himself. The show is a Turkish extravaganza in which Alice plays an old Caliph's wife in the habit of kicking off her striking-looking slippers in order to indicate to her young admirer Ali (played of course by Percy) that he can approach her without danger. Because the blue moccasins are ideal for Alice's costume, Percy removes them from his bedroom wall where they have been hanging since the day he once compared their colour to his wife's eyes. Soon after, temporarily tired with flowers, Lina decides she wants to paint them and asks Percy where they are; but he denies any knowledge. On the night of the show, Lina unexpectedly decides that she will demean herself sufficiently to attend; and is shocked both by the sight of Alice in the missing moccasins and by the evidence of the way the innocently unaware Percy is drawn to the younger woman. At the interval, she confronts them both and demands her moccasins back. It was at this point in his reading that Lawrence looked up and asked his listeners how they thought the story ought to finish. The Brewsters replied that Lina should give up her demand, allow the play to continue and thereby retain her husband's allegiance. This is a surprising suggestion for people who had read as much Lawrence as they presumably had. What is more surprising is that this was his conclusion also, and only in the second ending, which one can still see written between the crossed-out lines of the first, does Lina go off with the shoes and Percy become aware that he has had enough of being treated like a 'good doggie' and needs the physical comforts of Alice. The last short story Lawrence ever completed, it would have been strange if 'The Blue Moccasins' had ended in

433

a limp concession to habit and convention, even if it was to appear in *Eve: the lady's pictorial*.[29]

At 4,000 feet Lawrence's health still did not improve and he failed to experience the benefits which he had associated with Les Diablerets six months before. At first he attributed his difficulties to a necessary process of acclimatisation to the altitude; but by the end of July he was becoming sceptical and told Orioli that he felt 'weaker and more upset' than he had at the Villa Mirenda (vi. 476). His 'infernal cough' was not, he explained to an American correspondent on 25 August, 'a death cough at all', but it was an 'unspeakable nuisance' all the same (vi. 522). On the day the Brewsters arrived in Gsteig they had found him in bed with what Achsah describes as a 'slight hemorrhage';[30] and he was periodically laid up thereafter. Never a complainer, he found it harder now to pretend that all was well and recovery just around the corner. At the end of August when he was once more in bed, he told Kot that he wished the Lord would make a new man of him, 'for I'm not much to boast of now'; and he warned Dorothy Warren, 'Don't for heaven's sake get into the way of being ill! That's what I've done – and heaven, I'd give anything to be well' (vi. 530, 535–6).

In this situation, having to supervise the sale of *Lady Chatterley's Lover* was both a burden and a godsend. The difficulties it ran into made him furious and caused intense aggravation at the very time when what he above all needed – any doctor would have said – was calm. With his usual persisting residue of naïvety (it was not for nothing that he could depict with authority bewildered young men like Percy Barlow), he was surprised as well as hurt when various friends or acquaintances indicated that they did not like the novel.[31] He decided that those who were hostile could not by definition be real friends: 'Amusing', he told Bonamy Dobrée on 12 August, 'how many people dislike *Lady C*! I'm afraid I've lost $\frac{9}{10}$ of my few remaining friends. But such friends are well lost; like dead limbs from a tree' (vi. 502). In keeping with this exaggeration was an uncharacteristic inclination to regard appreciation of the novel as a qualifying test (vi. 537), although at the same time he tried to make sure it was a test some of those closest to him did not take and could not therefore fail. He told Earl Brewster, for example, that *Lady Chatterley's Lover* was not his 'type of book' and that he would only give him a copy when they were all about to go their separate ways;[32] and on several occasions he says that he is anxious to keep news of its publication from his sisters (vi. 486, 489).

The difficulties over *Lady Chatterley's Lover* excited him more than was perhaps healthy for a man in his condition; yet at the same time they had a galvanising effect. 'Now the fun begins', he wrote in one of his letters to Kot (vi. 481), and the word was not entirely inappropriate. He must have enjoyed asking Orioli to have false dust-jackets printed so that copies would have a better chance of passing through American Customs unnoticed – *The Way of All Flesh* by Samuel Butler was a nicely ironic choice of disguise, but *Joy Go With You*, by Norman Kranzler, a better (vi. 561, 525); and his enrolment of Enid Hilton and others in the effort to offset the damage done by puritanical English booksellers had all the excitement of conspiracy. In 'Red Trousers' he had said that what men needed in his day was a worthwhile crusade; he had found one for himself in his determination to present *Lady Chatterley's Lover* to the world. Added zest in that endeavour came from his direct financial involvement. As well as being keen that he should not be out of pocket because of English booksellers who had ordered copies and would not then handle them, he was on the look-out for any American dealers who might be tempted to avoid payment by pretending that their shipment had not arrived. When he heard that the copies he had priced at $10 were selling in New York for over $50, he was furious and suspected there might be a trade in those which had been confiscated (vi. 564). Around 600 had been quite quickly disposed of in England and of the 140 sent to America, roughly half appeared to have got through (vi. 552). Although many of those that had been confiscated represented a loss, some would have been pre-paid. As far as they were concerned, Lawrence would write to Orioli at the end of September, 'Tell Mary Foote and others that I refuse to be responsible for the action of the U.S.A. govt. Their books were sent *registered* – they must now apply to the post-office for delivery' (vi. 579).

In addition to 1,000 copies of the signed edition, Lawrence had asked the Tipographia Giutina to print an extra 200 which were unsigned and more cheaply produced. Originally intending to give these away to friends (vi. 364), he was now holding them in reserve. From the beginning he had thought it would be a good idea if he also held back some of the expensive copies in the hope that scarcity would then allow him to raise the price (vi. 393). In September, with the moment fast approaching when there would only be 200 copies of the signed edition left, he felt it could be doubled. Given that his novel was now a product in demand the supply of which was rapidly diminishing, this was a reasonable commercial decision; and to those who complained about the increased price the reply could be that they ought to have had the faith and wit to subscribe at the beginning. Yet writing to people such as Kot and Stieglitz, Lawrence was sufficiently uncomfortable to pretend that it was all Orioli's doing. The fiction he himself had proposed was that the remaining copies had been bought up as a speculation by Orioli and his former partner in London, Irving Davis; and that anyone who bought one at the dearer price was dealing with them. But Davis had virtually no involvement in the *Lady Chatterley* scheme (in January 1929 Lawrence would complain that he had not even paid for the six subscription copies he had ordered – vii. 124), and the letters show very clearly that the price rise had been decided by Lawrence in concert with Orioli (vii. 124; vi. 533, 564, 566).

The lack of improvement in Lawrence's health made him restless and by the middle of August he had begun to feel that he had given altitude a sufficiently long trial. What was the point in being in the mountains if he was not getting any better? The difficulty was that Emily had accepted his invitation to visit and was due to arrive on the 26th with her daughter Peggy. The Brewsters meanwhile had decided to spend some time in Geneva, and on the 28th the Lawrences gave a farewell dinner for all three (their daughter Harwood being with them), and for Boshi Sen. Achsah Brewster and Peggy Needham describe this occasion in some detail, both insisting that, ill though he was, Lawrence took the lead in the after-dinner singing. He knew an Indian war chant, the concluding whoops of which he rendered with such fervour that Achsah wondered whether he was going to burst a blood-vessel; and, switching from one sense of Indian to another, he parodied a sentimental ballad from Amy Woodforde-Finden's four immensely popular 'Indian Love Lyrics': the one entitled, 'Less than the dust beneath thy chariot wheels'. Peggy Needham remembered that he was able to give all eleven verses of the folk song, 'Richard of Taunton Dean', in Somerset dialect, with the rest of the party singing the chorus. (It was not only of the revivalist hymns that he knew 'every word of all the verses'.)[33] The next day he had to stay in bed but that did not stop him writing 'Hymns in a Man's Life'. He dwelt in this attractive essay on the paradox that the often undistinguished words of the hymns he had learned in his childhood were more deeply embedded in his imagination than the greatest poetry. A more important consequence of his religious training was that it nurtured his sense of wonder, the 'most precious element in life': 'You cannot help feeling it in a bean as it starts to grow and pulls itself out of its jacket. You cannot help feeling it in the glisten of the nucleus of the amoeba. You recognise it, willy-nilly, in an ant busily tugging at a straw; in a rook, as it walks the frosty grass.'[34]

From his chair outside the chalet, Lawrence would sit staring across the valley to the Diableret glacier for long periods so that Emily used to ask herself what was going through his mind. She would almost certainly have been right in suspecting that it was not merely wonder at the natural beauty of the world. Though she herself does not seem to have been aware of it, her visit was not a success. Lawrence was ill and depressed and he felt more than usually the gulf between his own interests and those of his relatives: 'I am not really "our Bert". Come to think of it, I never was' (vi. 535). Jessie Chambers had once praised him for his power to transmute the common experiences of life into significance,[35] but that demands a super-abundant vitality and is perhaps in any case associated with a certain time of life, when the world we see about us is still fresh. As he became increasingly ill, there were moments when Lawrence was exasperated by what was common and everyday. 'How I *hate* the attitude of ordinary people to life', he told Huxley on 2 September, complaining of Emily and her daughter. 'How I loathe ordinariness! How from my soul I abhor nice simple people, with their eternal price list. It makes my blood boil' (vi. 542). Ada was the sister to whom he felt close and all the signs are that he found Emily (whose nickname in the family was 'Pamela or Virtue Rewarded') a little dull and unimaginative. Yet his letters show him to have been a caring brother and, whatever the degree of hostility he felt towards her at this time, he seems to have succeeded in hiding it.[36]

Any nastiness which was exceptional would in any case have been attributed by both Emily and Peggy to the state in which they found him. This was recorded in several terrifying photographs Peggy Needham took during her visit. The one most commonly reproduced shows Emily sitting beside Lawrence on a bench outside the Chalet Kesselmatte; but there is another, clearly taken at the same time, where he is sitting next to Frieda (Figs. 43 and 44). Both women were sufficiently stout to emphasise his painful thinness, which can be seen clearly on this occasion as his upper leg, pressing against the bench, shows the outline of his thigh. The sight of that explains why his suit should seem too big for him; but it is his posture and expression which count at least as much as these details. In the photograph with Emily he is staring grimly ahead. With Frieda beside him he has turned to face the camera, but the frown is equally irritable and unhappy, and his tense posture, with the hands clasped awkwardly on his lap, has not changed in the least. Photographs are deceptive because they capture only one specific moment which is not necessarily representative. The difference between these snapshots and the picture of Lawrence and Frieda at the window of their house in Chapala during the summer of 1923 (Fig. 13) nevertheless seems full of significance.

Well before Emily left on 7 September – posting to Harry Crosby on her way through Paris the now lost painting of *Sun-Men Catching Horses* (vi. 549) – Lawrence had been thinking about his next move. He and Frieda were due to go to Baden-Baden in the second half of September and after that he expected to have to be in England for his exhibition. He had sounded out the Huxleys about the possibility of an Etruscan tour in October (using their car), and he thought he might then go to the United States for the exhibition Stieglitz was planning. From New York, it would be a relatively simple matter to return to the ranch. To this rich and optimistic mixture had been added in late August an offer from the Aldingtons to join them for a part of the autumn and winter in Port Cros, a small island off the French Mediterranean coast where the editor of the *Nouvelle Revue Française*, Jean Paulhan, had offered Aldington the use of a house. The attraction of this was that Port Cros was relatively near, and that the Mediterranean was likely to be warmer than England, Florence or New York in the autumn. Besides, if anyone had passed the *Lady Chatterley* test with flying colours it was the Aldingtons. 'I was awfully pleased that you liked the book, both of you', he had written to Arabella Yorke on 4 August:

I'm afraid it's cost me the beaux restes of my friends. – a rugged[?] remnant, anyhow. And I'm really very glad you like to read me, Arabella. Believe me, I get far more insults and impudence about my work, than appreciation: so when anyone comes out a bit whole-heartedly, I really feel comforted a great deal. I must say, I don't find much generous appreciation. It's usually superior disapproval, or slightly-mingy, narrow-gutted condescension. (vi. 491)

An American who had also passed the Chatterley test was Alfred Stieglitz. In telegraphing to say that his copy of the novel had arrived safely, Stieglitz also made clear how much he had liked it. Lawrence was nonetheless wary about seeming to press his paintings on him – 'I'm not really keen on exhibiting, so don't go to any trouble.' At the same time he told him not to be alarmed because the pictures were 'quite good', which was more than one could say for most moderns, 'all excellent rind of the fruit, but no fruit' (vi. 505–6). That a painting had subject matter did not seem to him to make it any the less of a painting; besides, he went on, referring to the Braque composition which he would have seen in a book on modern French artists Harry Crosby had just sent him, 'what's a deformed guitar and a shred of newspaper but subject-matter?' (vi. 505).[37]

This hostility to aspects of Modernism in the pictorial arts is matched at this same time (mid-August) by Lawrence's hostile response to a copy of *transition* which he had also just received from Harry Crosby. The thirteenth number of the journal made famous through its association with writers and artists such as Hart Crane, Man Ray, Gertrude Stein and Max Ernst contained six reproductions of Picasso's paintings, one of which (although not of a 'deformed guitar and shred of newspaper') was in his Cubist mode. But it also included 'Continuation of a Work in Progress' by its most celebrated contributor, James Joyce, extracts from what would later be published as *Finnegans Wake* having already appeared in all but two of *transition*'s previous numbers.[38] Lawrence found this a pain to read and confirmation of his previous opinion of Joyce. 'Nothing but old fags and cabbage-stumps of quotations from the Bible and the rest, stewed in the juice of deliberate, journalistic dirty-mindedness', he complained to the Huxleys (vi. 508); and to Crosby, who was friendly with Eugene Jolas, *transition*'s editor, he explained more moderately that Joyce bored him stiff – 'too terribly would-be and done-on-purpose, utterly without spontaneity or real life' (vi. 548).

Although they liked each other's work so little, Joyce and Lawrence could have commiserated with each other on the difficulty of getting it into America. As August moved into September, Lawrence began to have many of the problems Joyce had already experienced with *Ulysses*. It became evident that if he sent his paintings to New York, they too ran a risk of being confiscated at the Customs, and that he would therefore have to give up the idea of exhibiting in Stieglitz's gallery. This meant that there was now no hurry about the Warren Gallery exhibition, which might just as well take place in November as in October; and that he did not need to worry too much that Dorothy Warren, who had been so anxious that he should not show his pictures elsewhere in London, had once again not been in touch. It meant also that New York, and by extension the ranch, could be crossed off his future travel plans.

It was the season of birthdays. When Earl Brewster was away in Paris with Mukerji, there had been a party at the Viktoria on 11 August in order to celebrate Frieda's – she was 49; and exactly a month later Lawrence was 43. All the Brewsters were now in Geneva for a while and on 13 September Lawrence wrote to Earl there to thank him for the birthday letters and gifts: 'It was nice to be remembered, after all. You and my two sisters and Frieda's mother – that was all. But then I'm not a celebrator' (vi. 562). With the altitude experiment a failure, he had not much to be celebratory about. The 13th was Thursday and the Lawrences would have left Gsteig for Baden-Baden at the weekend if Else Jaffe had not been going to call then on her way for a holiday in the south of France with Alfred Weber. She stayed until the following Tuesday and all three then left Switzerland together. Lawrence had not especially disliked Gsteig or the chalet, but they had not brought the benefits he expected; and he had found them no more comforting places in which to be ill than the Villa Mirenda.

Baden-Baden meant a reunion with the Brewster after the brief separation. Lawrence had tried to find room for them all at the Eden, where he and Frieda usually stayed, but it was full and instead they went to a quiet old inn in Lichtenthal on the outskirts of the town (vi. 562), which is now called Der Goldener Löwe ('The Golden Lion'): that Lawrence always refers to it as the Hotel Löwen suggests that in his day it must have been the Hotel zum Löwen, where 'zum' is the equivalent of 'at the sign of'. They were six rather than five because the Baroness was with them, enjoying a change from her retirement Home. (As before, she and Lawrence spent many hours playing Patience.) Although it was only a seven-minute tram ride from the centre of Baden-Baden, Lichtenthal had only very recently been incorporated into the main town and still retained the characteristics of a village. Lawrence enjoyed sitting in the spacious garden and drinking wine in the evenings as he listened to the local choral society practising in an adjoining hall.[39] Crossing the village square outside the hotel, it was only 200 yards to a convent on the opposite side of the street and then left past its front gates to the famous Lichtenthal Allee. With the Oos flowing clearly on one side and extensive parkland on the other, this broad, tree-lined avenue which led straight to the Kurhaus a mile and a half away was like a time-capsule, 'incurably 1850', as Lawrence was to put it, 'with the romance and the pathos and the bathos of Turgenev rather than Dostoevsky'

(vii. 382). According to Achsah Brewster, they would all stroll gently along the Allee with drinking glasses for the hot spring already in their hand, and then go on to the Kursaal for a concert of arias and overtures Lawrence made clear he had heard many times before. As a treat for the Baroness, and because 21 September was Earl's fiftieth birthday, they hired two horse-drawn landaus and made a long, leisurely excursion to the old ruined castle just outside the town and then on into the fringes of the Black Forest (vi. 568). But as autumn set in, Lawrence was beginning to suffer from the cold. Frieda tried to persuade him to see a 'famous physician' she had met in town, and even spoke of a nun in the nearby convent who had 'the power of healing with the touch of her hands'. Ignoring both these suggestions, Lawrence told her that all he needed was the south and the sun.[40]

Giving up his idea of England, he decided he would take up the Aldingtons' offer and go to Port Cros while Frieda made the long trip to London for the exhibition (vi. 568–9). But then from Dorothy Warren, who was in Vienna and about to get married, came news of more likely delay. With the idea of sending his pictures to New York now abandoned, that did not much concern him. Hearing from Florence that the Pinis were leaving the Villa Mirenda, he was concerned about the few possessions which had been left there, once Giulia was no longer around to keep an eye on them. Although their lease still had a couple of months to run, the Lawrences decided that Frieda should go to Florence and remove all their remaining property from the villa while Lawrence travelled with the Brewsters in the direction of the French Riviera (vi. 577). Assuming that the Pinis were being forced to give up the land they had been farming, he felt sorry for them but without the strength to face the 'great emotional stew' going back to the villa might entail (vi. 574).[41] He and the Brewsters left on 1 October and, caught between trains in Strasbourg, sought warmth in a cinema where *Ben Hur* was showing. Lawrence did not much like films (especially when they involved close-ups of kissing), but he was usually tolerant of them. On this occasion, he was so nauseated by what Achsah Brewster describes as the 'falsity' of the action ('doves fluttering around baby-faced dolls, brutal Romans accursed with hearts of stone, galleys of inhuman slaves'[42]), and the way the open-mouthed public in the cinema accepted it all as true, that he had to leave after half an hour. A mistake with their luggage by the young porter at the Hotel Löwen had meant that they missed the early train from Baden-Baden and were therefore condemned to travelling by night from Strasbourg (vi. 584). At Le Lavandou, where he had arranged to meet Else Jaffe and Alfred Weber, Lawrence left the Brewsters who were continuing on their way to Nice and, eventually, Italy. As they parted, Achsah was struck by how 'white and weary' he looked after his night in the train.[43]

III   Port Cros

Le Lavandou is one of the once-charming resorts on the once-charming French Riviera: 'They are just beginning to mess this coast up', Lawrence told the Brewsters, '- but the messing seems to proceed very rapidly, once it starts' (vi. 588). Responding to a hope he had expressed that he might see them (vi. 574), the Huxleys were also in Le Lavandou, on their way from Forte dei Marmi to the house at Suresnes near Paris where they intended to spend the winter.[44] It was with them therefore, as well as Else and Alfred, that Lawrence hired a motorised fishing boat to investigate the island of Port Cros in advance of the Aldingtons' arrival there.[45] He liked its vegetation but thought the one hotel too 'chic' for his taste; and he was dismayed to discover that there was an 'hour's stony walk uphill' to the fortified wall on the top of a hill, somewhere behind which he and Frieda were due to pass the next couple of months (vi. 584).

His companions all left on 5 October and for a while he enjoyed his solitude as he waited for Frieda to arrive from Florence; but when she was late turning up, he became agitated and anxious. Achsah Brewster describes how nervous Lawrence had become in Chexbres when Frieda was several hours late coming back from Baden-Baden ('He always looked forward so eagerly to her return');[46] but on this occasion the delay stretched to several days. Richard Aldington later explained it by saying that closing down the Villa Mirenda became complicated for Frieda because it involved 'a journey to Trieste'.[47] No doubt she did seize the opportunity of being away from Lawrence to see Ravagli, either at his posting in Gradisca or elsewhere; but what we know for certain is that her journey to the south of France was disrupted by a strike on the branch line coming into Le Lavandou from the Nice direction, so that in the end she was reduced to taking a taxi from Saint-Raphael (vi. 589). This was on the 12th, by which time the Aldingtons, installed in the 'Vigie' in Port Cros for over a week, had sent several telegrams to Lawrence wondering what had happened to him.[48] He and Frieda gave themselves the weekend to prepare and on Monday 15 October took a boat to the island, perhaps from Le Lavandou but more probably from Hyères, a larger resort further west up the coast where (weather permitting) there was a regular, thrice-weekly service to Port Cros which took two hours (vi. 600).

When the Lawrences arrived at the Vigie they discovered that the Aldingtons were not alone. They had with them – in retrospect it would be more accurate to say that Richard Aldington had with him – Brigit Patmore, who had been detached from her husband for several years and was in the process of finishing her second novel.[49] There was also Giuseppe, a 28-year-old Sicilian who went with the Paulhans' house and who regularly made the hour-long trip with his donkey down to the tiny harbour for provisions. Given that virtually everything they needed had to come from Hyères via this harbour, Jasper the donkey was an important asset (vi. 592).

'Vigie' is French for an observation post and Lawrence discovered there was no fortress inside the wall he had seen but a couple of acres of abandoned land, 'all wild lavender and stinking nanny and arbutus and tiny pine-trees really very nice'. The rooms they were to occupy were built against the wall, 'windows facing the inner space, loop-holes looking out to sea', and there were enough for him and Frieda to have a bedroom each. The sitting room was large but, with his fear of the cold and winter coming on, Lawrence may have noted with apprehension that the only forms of heating were open wood fires. More immediately, his problem was that there was nowhere for someone in his condition to go. The nearest beach was forty-five minutes downhill and then at least another forty-five back-up (Frieda went with the others once or twice, but Lawrence not at all). As he explained to the Brewsters, although he found everyone very considerate and nice, he was once again 'perched, as at Kessel-matte' (vi. 592, 593). The situation was not ideal in any circumstances but they were made worse by Frieda having returned from Italy with a bad cold which he promptly caught. Equally promptly, his cold turned into 'influenza'. 'I get scared when this influenza begins biting again', he confessed on 20 October, and a week later he told Orioli: 'I have been in bed all week with that flu cold – and two days hemorrhage and feel rather rotten. I don't think we shall stay here very long, I don't believe it suits me' (vi. 593, 598).

With Lawrence out of action, cooking responsibilities fell chiefly to Frieda and Arabella Yorke, with Brigit Patmore in charge of breakfasts. She describes how exhausted she would find Lawrence when she took breakfast into him each morning at 6.45. While she arranged a coat round his shoulders, she could feel 'his pyjamas soaked with perspiration' but it was apparently 'against the rule to suggest that anything was wrong'. Things were nevertheless wrong enough for Aldington to worry, listening to Lawrence's 'dreadful hollow cough' at night, what would happen if they had to get him to the mainland quickly; and there was a general agreement in the party that he should never be left completely alone. On the one clearly recorded occasion that Frieda went swimming, for example, Brigit Patmore took care to keep him company.[50]

When he had been convalescing in Austria and Bavaria the year before, Lawrence had turned to translation in order to occupy his time, and he did the same now. Encouraged by the commercial success of *Lady Chatterley's Lover*, Orioli was thinking of going into publishing on his own account. But Lawrence was worried that the British Home Office, after having prompted the French into an unsuccessful prosecution of Frank Harris's *Life and Loves*, was about to launch a campaign against the publication abroad of 'indecent' literature in English; and he warned him not to bother for the moment with a book of limericks Norman

Douglas had compiled or Harold Acton's translation of a somewhat scabrous Renaissance text concerning Gian Gastone, *The Last of the Medici*.[51] He suggested instead that Orioli should launch a series of translations of 'Italian Renaissance Novelists', and told him on 21 October that he had himself begun with a story from the 'Terza Cena' ('the third supper') of Antonfranceso Grazzini, who was also known as 'il Lasca' ('the Roach').[52] (On the model of the *Decameron*, Lasca's stories are supposedly told by different members of a group of people from the leisured classes who are waiting by the fire for dinner to be served.) 'It is important', Lawrence said, 'to start the series with an interesting and *not* indecent story. We can come on with the indecent ones later' (vi. 595). Sitting up in bed with his Homburg hat on to protect him from the draughts, he had 'half done' the Lasca story by 27 October, even though he felt rotten ('this is worse than the Mirenda'); and by 1 November he could describe it as 'nearly done' (vi. 598, 605).

Lasca's *Story of Doctor Manente* is of novella length and the most technically adept of all Lawrence's translations from Italian. He simulates well the toppling-over effect of the original Renaissance prose and, with the experienced Aldington on hand to give advice, makes fewer errors than he had done before.[53] When on 1 November he told Orioli that it was 'nearly done', he also said that he ought to make it his enterprise 'and give me 10%' (vi. 605). 10% was what Orioli was receiving for his involvement in the *Lady Chatterley* venture but there were several reasons why the offer was far from being in the nature of a *quid pro quo*. The most obvious of these was that the Lasca translation was certain not to make a similar amount of money. Lawrence told Brigit Patmore at this time that *Lady Chatterley's Lover* had brought him £800;[54] and he continued to maintain the fiction that the price rise on the remaining stock was none of his doing. In reply to a bookseller who had asked for a copy, he repeated on 14 November that Orioli had 'bought up [his] last lot', adding 'I believe his price is now £4. – if you can run to it. – worth it though' (vi. 617).

Rumours continued to filter through to Port Cros about possible government action against Lawrence's novel, and at the end of October he received cuttings of vehement attacks on it in *John Bull* and the *Sunday Chronicle*. His initial response was to tell Nancy Pearn that these could not hurt him because 'I've sold the edition' (vi. 602). Evidence that they did in fact hurt comes from Richard Aldington and Brigit Patmore's accounts of how everyone sat around the wood fire in the large sitting room at the Vigie as extracts from the cuttings were read out. The writer in *John Bull*, never (as Lawrence pointed out) a newspaper with friendly feelings towards him (vi. 598),[55] thought *Lady Chatterley's Lover* 'the foulest book in English literature' and, incongruously as well as unfairly, laid part of the blame for it on 'one L. Franceschini, master of the printing shop called the "Tipographia Giuntina"'. He reported that in Paris copies were changing hands 'among British decadents' for five to twenty guineas each but claimed not to mind: 'If Lawrence-lovers choose to steep their evil minds in the fetid master-piece of this sex-sodden genius we are indifferent.' On the other hand, he called for the circulation of the book in England to be stopped immediately and regretted there was no legislation which would allow its author to be sent to prison 'for a good stiff spell'. Although he thought *Lady Chatterley's Lover* reeking 'with obscenity and lewdness', the writer in the *Sunday Chronicle* was more moderate; yet by reporting (inaccurately) that the British Customs had seized the novel 'with the object of preventing its circulation in this country', he also was inciting the authorities to act.[56]

The company at the Vigie seems to have followed Lawrence's lead in his letter to Nancy Pearn and taken a casually dismissive attitude to these tabloid rantings; but at one point in the evening Lawrence muttered to himself, 'Nobody *likes* being called a cesspool.' Despite Frieda's protests that he would burn the house down, he then began dipping manically into the pile of rosemary, thorn and myrtle on the hearth, piling branch after branch on the fire until the room was full of smoke and perfume. Efforts to stop him merely increased his 'rhythmical rage' and only when the fuel was exhausted and he had (Brigit Patmore suggests) 'served up his enemies symbolically as a burnt sacrifice' was his anger appeased.[57]

An opportunity to express that anger in a more measured way came when he was sent an American book, *To the Pure: A Study of Obscenity and the Censor* by Morris Ernst and William Seagle.[58] Writing to Ernst on 10 November, Lawrence said that the impression of muddle conveyed by its description of legal intricacies made him feel that he was watching 'a great unchained ape fumbling through his hairs for something . . . I see that weird and horrible animal, Social Man, devoid of real individuality or personality, fumbling gropingly and menacingly for something he is afraid of, but he doesn't know what it is.' The book's account of attempts to suppress a wide variety of literary texts had confirmed his feeling that censorship was 'one of the lower and debasing activities of social man'.

Myself, I believe censorship helps nobody; and hurts many. But the book has brought it home to me much more grimly than before. Our civilisation cannot afford to let the censor-moron loose. The censor-moron does not really hate anything but the living and growing human consciousness. It is our developing and extending consciousness that he threatens – and our consciousness in its newest, most sensitive activity, its vital growth. To arrest or circumscribe the vital consciousness is to produce morons, and nothing but a moron would wish to do it.   (vi. 613)

Lawrence would write more extensively about censorship later, but the author of the article in *John Bull* was already answered here, had he but known it.

After he had finished his Lasca translation, Lawrence quickly wrote three more newspaper articles. In 'Is England Still a Man's Country?', he at last admitted that although women were now much more prominent in social or even public life, as well as a 'drain on a man's cigarettes', effective power was still in the hands of men. That being the case, the problem men needed to tackle in order to prove their manliness was the economic slavery to which most people were condemned. He began the second article, 'Sex Locked Out', with his old insistence that neither the peacock's feathers nor the nightingale's song were simply there to ensure propagation, as some biologists claimed; and he went on to emphasise the inseparability of sex and beauty ('Nothing is more ugly than a human being in whom the fire of sex has gone out'). The third piece ('Women Don't Change') is chiefly interesting for the way it confirms Lawrence's belief in the cyclical nature of history. The new woman of the 1920s was not in his opinion really new: 'Modernity or modernism isn't something we've just invented. It's something that comes at the end of civilisations.'[59] An accomplished journalist by this stage, these short pieces represented an ideal way for Lawrence to maintain his income, and have his say, with a minimum of sustained effort.

He was not the only person busy writing at the Vigie. Brigit Patmore was finishing her novel and Aldington, with already over a dozen translations behind him, was preparing a version of the *Decameron*. At some point he put this aside and began what would be by far his most successful work: *Death of a Hero*. He had tried three times before to write about his war experiences but only now, ten years after leaving the army, did the words come easily. In *Kangaroo*, Lawrence had spoken of the accumulation in people during the war as 'a lava fire of rage and hate'.[60] It may be that this took longer to rise to the surface for participants than for non-combatants like Lawrence, and that it was no coincidence therefore that two more remarkable World War I narratives – *Goodbye to All That* by Robert Graves (1929), and R. C. Sherriff's play, *Journey's End* (1930) – both come, like *Death of a Hero*, at the end of the 1920s.

On Port Cros, Lawrence did not discover how powerfully Aldington could write about being under fire because only 30,000 words of *Death of a Hero* were completed there.[61] In a prologue which functions as a grim variation on the music-hall song 'Ain't it Grand to be Bloomin' Well Dead', Aldington imagines how the nearest and dearest of his hero ('George Winterbourne', but identical in most respects to himself) respond to the news of his death in combat. We are introduced to a father feebly converted to Roman Catholicism; a mother on her twenty-second lover; a wife who, when she comes home 'a bit sozzled' to find the telegram from the War Office, is accompanied by an amorous Swedish painter also rather the worse for drink; and a mistress whose response is distinctly cool. The tone is remarkably harsh and bitter, full of a soldier's resentment against civilian ignorance and insensitivity, and with a special animus directed towards women for the way they purportedly derived sexual stimulus from the involvement of their menfolk in bloodshed. Although there is also in this prologue patent anger that conditions during the war allowed women to be more sexually active than before, Aldington moves on in 'Part One' to a violent denunciation of Victorian hypocrisy, especially as it regarded sex. The rationale for this would be stated later when the narrator says, 'It was the regime of Cant *before* the war which made the Cant *during* the War so damnably possible and easy.'[62] In this section, which includes a vicious attack on George's appalling public school, Aldington is unusually outspoken, not mincing words in his description of the catastrophic wedding night of the hero's parents, or in his protests against the damage caused by the taboo of virginity. Many of his targets were also Lawrence's, and it might have been expected that he would respond positively to Aldington's misogyny even though, in *Death of a Hero*, it came in a form that was far more extreme than his own. In fact, Lawrence was disconcerted by what he was given to read, told Aldington that if he published a novel of that kind he would lose his reputation, and apparently expressed anxiety about its author's mental health.[63] In a dedication of *Death of a Hero* to Halcott Glover, written in Paris in 1929, Aldington referred to it as a 'jazz novel'.[64] With its distinctive post-war 'realism', it was certainly a text which revealed Lawrence as essentially a member of the old school. Compared with Forster he was a savage satirist, but compared with Aldington, who was only seven years younger but who, in addition to having a far coarser mind, had separated himself much more completely from the values of the pre-war world, he was full of delicacy and restraint.

After his visit to Les Diablerets in February, Max Mohr had sent Lawrence a novel of his entitled *Venus in den Fischen*, published the year before. On 22 March Lawrence told him frankly, 'No, I didn't really like *Venus and the Fishes*: it is too modern for me: you know I'm a bit "altmodisch" really' (vi. 338). All the weeks he was in Les Diablerets Huxley had been busy with *Point Counter Point* and by the time Lawrence was in Port Cros he had received the published text. Much more than *Venus in den Fischen* or *Death of a Hero*, this novel made him feel how out of sympathy he was with even the more accessible and intelligent avant-garde of his day. Sending his reaction to Huxley on 28 October, he took a line similar to the one he had taken when he first saw a photograph of Mark Gertler's painting *The Merry-Go-Round* years before.[65]

I have read *Point Counter Point* with a heart sinking through my boot-soles and a rising admiration. I do think you've shown the truth, perhaps the last truth, about you and your generation, with really fine courage. It seems to me it would take ten times the courage to write *P. Counter P.* than it took to write *Lady C.*: and if the public knew *what* it was reading, it would throw a hundred stones at you, to one at me. I do think that art has to reveal the palpitating moment or the state of man as it is. And I think you do that, terribly. But what a moment! and what a state! if you can only palpitate to murder, suicide, and rape, in their various degrees – and you state plainly that it is so – *caro*, however are we going to live through the days?   (vi. 600)

The murder victim in *Point Counter Point* is Everard Webley, the charismatic leader of an English Fascist movement who is so remarkably anticipatory of Oswald Mosley that it is hard to remember, when reading the novel, that it was published well before Mosley left the Labour Party.[66] His downfall is plotted by Spandrell, a Satanist whose family background is modelled on Baudelaire's but who has clearly read *Women in Love* since he echoes Birkin's striking notion of the 'murderee'.[67] After the death of Webley, Spandrell organises his own execution and could therefore be said to commit suicide. Actual rape in the novel would be more difficult to identify if Lawrence had not gone on to complain in his letter to Huxley, 'I can't stand murder, suicide, rape: and especially being raped. Why do men only thrill to a woman who'll rape them? All I want to do to your Lucy is smack her across the mouth.' His reference is to Lucy Tantamount, the most successfully conceived of Huxley's many disillusioned female sexual athletes, who torments in the novel a weak, romantically inclined young man called Walter Bidlake. In *Lady Chatterley's Lover*, Mellors had talked about the sexually predatory woman but in *Point Counter Point* Huxley dramatised her with a power which clearly disturbed Lawrence deeply.

Attempting to encapsulate in a fugue-like structure all the different and often contradictory ways in which human behaviour can be conceived, *Point Counter Point* is an impressive achievement. Although Lawrence's letter opens with praise, its general effect is of dislike and disapproval. His comparative lack of appreciation could be attributed to the state of his health: sandwiched between an implied claim that Aldington is just like Huxley in being the kind of sensationalist who *also* thrills to murder, suicide and rape, and the reference to Lucy Tantamount just quoted, there is: 'It makes me feel ill, I've had more hemorrhages here and been in bed this week. *Sporca miseria.*' But another, more obvious explanation of Lawrence's dislike is that *Point Counter Point* contained a very obvious portrait of himself. Mark Rampion is a painter/writer of working-class origins married to an aristocratic German wife inclined to stay in bed in the mornings while he does not at all mind helping with housework. He champions the body rather than the mind, admires 'those naked sunburnt Etruscans in the sepulchral wall paintings', has a particular hostility to Shelley, dislikes Cubism . . . the parallels with Lawrence are everywhere and many of the things Rampion says are clearly taken down verbatim. 'Oh, for God's sake shut up', he tells his wife at one point; and when she protests, 'But isn't that what you say?', he replies, 'What I say is what *I* say. It becomes different when you say it.'[68] Several of the insights into his character could only have come from someone who knew Lawrence well: 'There were moments', the reader is told, 'when his love for his

447

mother turned almost to hatred' and in the same passage Rampion is reported as saying, 'She had no right to bring me up like that.'[69] In his letter to Huxley it was not this degree of intimate revelation to which Lawrence explicitly objected but that, in his view, Rampion was 'the most boring character in the book – a gas-bag. Your attempt at intellectual sympathy!' On the other hand, the way he then went on did suggest that, like many of the people he had portrayed in his own work, Lawrence felt betrayed: 'It's all rather disgusting, and I feel like a badger that has its hole on Wimbledon Common and trying not to be caught' (vi. 601). A fortnight later, writing to William Gerhardie who had twitted him about Huxley's portrait, he said, 'No, I refuse to be Rampioned. I am not responsible. Aldous's admiration is only skin-deep, and out of the Mary Mary quite contrary impulses' (vi. 617).

It is true that what Huxley admired in Lawrence, and what he personifies in Rampion, are qualities he felt were contrary to his own coolly rational nature. Yet his admiration was nevertheless heart-felt rather than skin-deep, and Rampion, even if he does talk too much, is by far the most sympathetic figure in *Point Counter Point*. Through an authorial persona called Philip Quarles, whom Huxley characterises as too analytical and tepid in his emotional involvements, he continually expresses how privileged he feels to know Lawrence well and how much he felt he had learnt from him.[70] Although almost anyone who is 'put' into a book is likely to feel mis-represented, Lawrence might have pondered how well things had turned out for him in comparison with Middleton Murry. *Point Counter Point*'s 'Burlap' is a portrait of Murry incomparably more vicious than anything in his own 'Murry stories', although several of its details almost certainly derived from Lawrence's conversations with Huxley in Florence or Switzerland. Where he may have hinted in 'Smile' that there was something factitious in Murry's grief over the death of Katherine Mansfield, Huxley was happy to refer to it directly as 'incessant spiritual masturbation', and claim that his love for her had been 'as much self-induced and self-intensified as his grief at her death'.[71] He exposed ruthlessly in Burlap an ability to combine seduction with spirituality and to find righteously moral justification for any variety of self-interested behaviour. The influence of *Lady Chatterley's Lover* is felt when Huxley describes in odious detail the infantilism of the foreplay in which Burlap engages with a character called Beatrice Gilray (who has several features reminiscent of Brett).[72] Lawrence had been able to disturb many of his readers with an account of the relationship between Clifford Chatterley and Mrs Bolton in its latter stages; but neither of those characters was easy to associate with a real-life original. If on the other hand, to everyone in the know, Rampion was obviously Lawrence, Burlap was equally obviously Murry and, judging from his own discomfort, he may have asked himself how his one-time friend and associate felt. So alienated was Lawrence from Murry at this period however, that he is unlikely to have felt any sympathy; and yet he must surely have recognised in the treatment of Burlap the same elements of the new tone, the new world of manners, which so dismayed him in both Huxley and Aldington.[73]

Lawrence had said they would stay on Port Cros until at least the middle of December (vi. 599); but illness quickly made him alter his plans. In November, there were storms which must have made it harder to keep warm and which certainly meant that the boat from Hyères could not always deliver its provisions. Although this difficulty could surely have been anticipated, it was adduced by Lawrence as the reason why *everybody* in the Vigie decided they had already endured enough (vi. 612). Aldington, on the other hand, is frank about the way he felt Lawrence's illness had spoilt things for the rest of them and claims that, without the anxiety of being so far from the mainland and a doctor, he would never have left Port Cros.[74] But this supposes that Arabella, Brigit and himself were obliged to leave with the Lawrences who were for some reason incapable of managing on their own. Whatever Aldington said to the Lawrences at the time or to the general public after, the truth was that there were tensions developing between the three members of his own group which made their remaining together too uncomfortable to contemplate. It was after the period on Port Cros that Aldington left Arabella Yorke to begin his ten-year liaison with Brigit Patmore, and his letters make clear that there were very often fierce arguments and rows at the Vigie.[75] Brigit Patmore alludes to these and gives the impression that Lawrence sided with her; but the suggestion she reports him as making that she should leave Port Cros with him and Frieda is equally supportive of Aldington's complaint (in a letter) that he took Arabella's side.[76] There is no sign in his own letters that he took either, and also no indication that Aldington was justified in fearing that, while the Lawrences were at the Vigie, they had discovered that he and Brigit Patmore were already sleeping together. '*Of course*, Lorenzo will try to find out', he wrote to her on 6 December. 'All I fear is that he and/or Frieda came to my bedroom & found me not there.'[77] There were clearly more reasons for Aldington, Brigit Patmore and Arabella Yorke to leave Port Cros than Lawrence's health and the bad weather.

The problem for the Lawrences was where to go next. Had he been fit enough, they would have tried Spain (vi. 608), but instead they opted for Bandol, a resort only a few miles west of Hyères where Katherine Mansfield had stayed twice during the war and where they were sure to find a hotel with central heating. Because they did not intend to be there long, and had still not entirely abandoned the expectation of Frieda being suddenly called to London by Dorothy Warren, it seemed useful that Bandol was on a main rather than branch railway line (vi. 615).

On 15 November 1928, two days before he left Port Cros, Lawrence replied to a letter he had unexpectedly received from Jessie Chambers's younger brother, David. Without mentioning Jessie, he explained how much visits to Haggs Farm, when David was only a small boy, had meant to him: the water-pippin near the door, the maiden-blush roses which the Chambers's old mare would lean over and eat, the stewed figs for tea when it was winter. The memory of that time made him wish that he were nineteen again and coming 'up through the Warren' to catch sight of the farm buildings. When Emily and her daughter had been staying in the Chalet Kesselmatte he had protested that he was not only not 'our Bert' any longer, but that he never had been. This was in the context of a feverishly angry outburst against the ordinary and commonplace. Now, with quite different associations in his mind, he told David Chambers, 'If there is anything I can ever do for you, do tell me. – Because whatever else I am, I am somewhere still the same Bert who rushed with such joy to the Haggs', and he signed off with a rare and untypical 'Ever' (vi. 618).

◆

CHAPTER NINETEEN

November 1928–March 1929

BANDOL

I Pansies

Bandol was meant to be a temporary resting-place where the Lawrences would stay for only two or three weeks (vii. 17), but in fact they were there almost four months. The Hotel Beau Rivage was pleasant but also cheap at forty francs a day (vii. 22), and although Aldous Huxley was later to complain that the revolting dishes cooked in monkey-nut oil had made him ill,[1] Lawrence thought the food good. Towards the end of his stay, he would record that he had eaten all his meals – always a promising sign (vii. 205). At its beginning, he was cheered by the remarkably fine weather. He found it incredible that it could be so hot and sunny in November and, as the sun went down, he spoke of Bandol 'swimming with milky gold light', of 'white boats half melted on the white twilight sea' and of 'palm trees frizzing their tops in the rosy west' (vii. 21).

It was only a few days after he had settled in that Lawrence made his first known reference to the poetry he had begun to write. Since the publication of *Birds, Beasts and Flowers* in 1923, he had written very little verse; but the preparation of his *Collected Poems* had revived his interest and from about this time until November of the following year he wrote almost half of what is now considered as his total poetic output.[2] Yet the manner of this new writing was different from the poetry he had written before. Frieda joyfully said that it was doggerel (vii. 64), and in the first draft of an introduction to what he quickly decided were to be called 'pansies' (a word which, as he points out, is derived from the French *pensées*), he himself explained that each short piece was 'just a thought put down', even if a few of these thoughts did sometimes get 'a poetic way with them'.[3]

By 20 December Lawrence had composed over 160 pansies.[4] The first few are relatively long, as well as sourly satirical, and seem to reflect the discontent of Lawrence's last days in Port Cros which may have carried over to his first days in Bandol; but many of those that follow are very short. Sometimes, like 'The Mosquito Knows', they are also satirical but in a brief, effectively generalised way:

> The mosquito knows full well, small as he is
> he's a beast of prey.
> But after all

> he only takes his bellyful,
> he doesn't put my blood in the bank.

A quite different illustration of Lawrence in a laconic mood is 'Sea-weed':

> Sea-weed sways and sways and swirls
> As if swaying were its form of stillness;
> And if it flushes against fierce rock
> it slips over it as shadows do, without hurting itself.[5]

Whether or not this is a 'thought', it certainly has a 'poetic way' with it. 'Pansies are for thoughts', Lawrence writes in his first introduction,[6] but they are also flowers with an unobtrusive beauty.

The topics which preoccupy Lawrence in his first batch of pansies include the obsession of modern society with money, the prospects facing the young, the fatal triumph of the machine, relations with women and the need for a revolutionary change in social life. But some of the poems are very private, like 'Numbness' which when it was published became 'Man Reaches a Point' and poignantly records its author's sense of a growing deadness in himself:

> I cannot help but be alone
> for desire has died in me, silence has grown,
> And nothing now reaches out to draw
> other flesh to my own.[7]

On other occasions the poems indirectly record various day-to-day happenings in Bandol: a visit to a circus or the purchase in the town bookshop of African bowls from the Bakuba tribe which particularly pleased Lawrence.[8] To add to the variety are songs in a popular ballad style like the well-known 'Red Herring' whose jaunty first verse gives the flavour of the whole:

> My father was a working man
>   and a collier was he,
> at six in the morning they turned him down
>   and they turned him up for tea.[9]

By no means all of these pansies have something distinctive about them, but in general one could say of them what Lawrence had said of the black *bucchero* vases of the Etruscans: that they have a 'naturalness verging on the commonplace, but usually missing it';[10] and many are memorable poems in the conventional sense. Like the newspaper articles, their advantage for a man in his condition was that they could be composed quickly. He would write them in the mornings, sitting up in bed and periodically looking out to sea from his room on the second floor of the Beau Rivage. Around eleven or twelve he would go with Frieda for an aperitif at a favourite café on the sea-front and usually spend the rest of the day relaxing.[11] A diary of Lawrence's thoughts and feelings in a form appropriate to his enfeebled state, pansies were the resolution of the conflict between a need to conserve his diminishing energy and at the same time satisfy, not only a naturally self-reflective nature, but also a life-long creative urge towards passionate involvement in the world's affairs.

Once installed in a hotel as comfortable as Beau Rivage, and with his tuberculosis again in remission, Lawrence felt happy enough; but not unnaturally, especially after the pleasures of the Villa Mirenda, Frieda fretted for a house of her own (vii. 33). There was always therefore some pressure on Lawrence to move, but he was a tangle of conflicting impulses. Once he had heard from Dorothy Warren that his exhibition was now definitely postponed until the new year (vii. 27), his interest in Spain became stronger, partly because he had never been there ('I think new things, new scenes are good for me', he told the Brewsters on 10 December – vii. 54), but partly also because he had increasingly become a seeker-out of the sun. This was as much for fear of the effect on his vulnerable 'bronchials' of cold and damp as for the kind of reasons Harry Crosby might have given. Yet although he must have talked of going south to Spain fairly often, he had not entirely given up America. He was increasingly prepared to admit openly that the trouble here was the difficulty he was likely to have with the immigration authorities. If Brett felt that her coming over to Europe would mean 'a lot of fuss with papers and permits', his going over there (he reminded her) would entail 'a lot more fuss. Then if they *wanted* to be spiteful, they'd hold me up about my health. Altogether it seems too much of a coil and fuss. – But if it were simple and friendly-feeling, I guess we'd slip over soon' (vii. 25). In mid-December a request he received through Mabel Luhan to write a short article on New Mexico for an American journal kept his interest in returning to Taos alive. He had finished the piece a week later and confessed that writing it had given him 'a real longing to be back' (vii. 71, 94).[12]

If the Lawrences were staying in Europe, as deep down they must both have known they had to, then Frieda would have preferred to go back to Italy rather than to Spain. Their trunks were after all still in Florence and it might not be unfair to say that on Lake Garda or even in Taormina, two places where in December Frieda was suggesting she might want to go, she would be closer to Ravagli than in Barcelona, Majorca or Malaga (three of her husband's rival suggestions at this time – vii. 54, 86). He had made it clear that he was no longer much drawn by Italy but there were nevertheless moments when he thought he might have to return there, to finish the Etruscan book, about which his publishers were beginning to nag him (vii. 25), but also to sort out his affairs in Florence. Throughout his stay on Port Cros, and then again while he was in Bandol, Lawrence bombarded Orioli with instructions concerning the *Lady Chatterley* edition. The remaining hard-backed copies continued to sell well, even at double the original price, and before the end of the year Lawrence's net profit had risen to £1,000 (vii. 61). For someone who had been able to rent the Villa Mirenda for £25 a year, and who had felt three and a half years before that he could live decently on £300 per annum (v. 492), this was a considerable sum. But Lawrence may well have calculated that the windfall was no more than the rough sterling equivalent of the royalties Seltzer owed, and he did not feel sufficiently well off to ignore those people who had received *Lady Chatterley's Lover* but then not paid for it. 'After all, why lose about £50', he asked Orioli in December. He suggested that non-payers should be chased up and their names published in a journal, on the assumption that shame would then drive them to settle their bills (vii. 68). Orioli himself, who had been ill for a while in the late autumn of 1928, was understandably less zealous in carrying out all the instructions he so regularly received than he had been in the past. 'He's very unsatisfactory lately' (vii. 59), Lawrence wrote and began to feel that he might have to go to Florence himself. The major, outstanding issue was how best to dispose of the extra 200, more cheaply produced, copies of *Lady Chatterley's Lover*. As more information reached Lawrence about pirated editions of the novel now increasingly prominent on both the European and American markets, he began to wish he had 2,000 of these extra copies rather than only 200 so that he could undersell the pirates and put them out of business (vii. 57).

It was this issue of piracy which led Lawrence to add Paris to the long list of places where he thought he might either want or have to go. On 10 December he wrote to the Huxleys asking them to look out for a copy of his novel the next time they went from Suresnes into town, and to find out whether or not it was genuine. They wrote back with the news that Maria had been offered a pirated copy at the astonishing price of 5,000 francs (or about £77). Aldous thought Orioli ought to come to Paris immediately and dispose of the paper-backed copies ('He would undersell the devils and at the same time turn an honest penny'); but he also wondered whether Lawrence should not think of having a new, photographically reproduced edition published there which he could then sell at a reasonable price (vii. 57–8). To find a printer willing to publish such an edition, however, and then an adequate method of distribution, would certainly require his own presence in the French capital, or at least that of someone as dependable and devoted as Kot (whom Lawrence was later to sound out – (vii. 142) – but without success). If the job did have to be done, he gradually came to realise, he would have to do it himself.

With all these places in mind where he might need or want to go (at one point they included South Africa – vii. 28), Lawrence meanwhile went nowhere. He found life too agreeable at Beau Rivage and felt much better than he had done on Port Cros. In the mornings he wrote his pansies or other short pieces such as the newspaper article sent to Nancy Pearn on 24 November ('Enslaved by Civilisation').[13] After the aperitif and lunch, he would wander along the front where the locals played 'boules', sit by the tiny port to observe 'life' ('chiefly dogs', he would conclude after he had been in Bandol for six weeks – vii. 110), or go out to the jetty to watch the arrival of the fishing boats with, as Frieda put it, 'silvery loads of sardines glittering on the sand of the shores'.[14] The weather was so fine that 9 December was the first day on which it rained in Bandol after his arrival there (vii. 50). He would be happy sitting by himself on a stone in the sun (vii. 110) and just before Christmas he told Rolf Gardiner, 'Myself, I'm afraid I take more and more pleasure in being alone, with just an occasional friend. I think perhaps the nicest thing in the world is to be most of the time alone, then to see a few people with whom one feels a bit of natural sympathy' (vii. 87). Yet Lawrence's implied portrait of himself as largely solitary at this time was, or at least would very quickly prove, false. He had a reasonable amount of company before he wrote these phrases to Gardiner, and after them it was the constant stream of visitors which helps to explain why he and Frieda lingered in Bandol so long.

The first of these was a young Welsh writer named Rhys Davies whom Lawrence came to know through his epistolary contacts with Charles Lahr, the German-born proprietor of the 'Progressive Bookshop' in Holborn. With his wife Elizabeth Archer, Lahr had been largely responsible for launching in the mid-twenties an avant-garde magazine called the *New Coterie*. He had published the first version of 'Sun' in this journal and at the same time printed 100 copies of the story in a limited, signed edition.[15] Not the only political radical who admired Lawrence's work, Lahr was in contact with him at this period over an expurgated edition of *Lady Chatterley's Lover* which he thought Victor Gollancz might be willing to publish (vii. 44), and he had expressed an interest in ensuring the English distribution of the 200 paper-backed copies of the novel still in Florence.[16] He knew Rhys Davies and explained to Lawrence how the young Welshman was then living in Nice on an advance from America for his second novel. The first (*The Withered Root*) Lawrence had quite liked when he had read it fifteen months before, although he objected to the way the protagonist had been killed off in the end: 'Death is so *easy*, in novels. It never kills the novelist: though it is pretty risky for the artist' (vi. 533). Yet if he now wrote to Davies, inviting him to come to the Beau Rivage and making it clear that the visit would cost him nothing, it was not merely out of admiration for his literary talents but because he must have been hopeful of learning through Davies whether Lahr was the kind of person he could trust. The few days the young Welshman spent in Bandol between 29 November and 2 December 1928 were a success, and this was the first of three trips he made to see the Lawrences while they were staying there. Lawrence discovered that his visitor not only knew Lahr well but had 'a great respect for him' (vii. 49), and this quietened his anxieties about dealing with a man he had never met.

Davies remembered Lawrence denouncing the young for their failure to resist sufficiently both the materialism and the antiquated taboos of their rotting world. Although he admitted to his guest that he himself felt he had been successfully constrained by modern society, so that he was like 'a monkey in a cage', at least he was prepared to bite those who put their fingers through the bars.[17] A coarsely funny story Davies told was received in 'blank silence' yet, in his conversations with his wife, Lawrence used freely the sexual vocabulary of Mellors, apparently indifferent to being overheard by other, English-speaking guests at the hotel. He raged against Frieda from time to time, and Davies is therefore one of many to have reflected on the Lawrences' famous quarrels. Mabel Luhan had felt that by provoking her husband Frieda ensured that he never lost interest in her; Davies, who thought his hosts well-matched, took the opposite but equally valid line that, in provoking his wife, Lawrence 'kept her simmering subtly; for a natural inclination to a stout German placidity threatened to swamp her fine lioness quality'.[18]

Like so many other people, Davies was impressed by Lawrence's abilities as a mimic, what he calls 'his magical talent for burlesque'. Most accounts are of imitations of people, but Davies especially remembered Lawrence's descriptions of John, the terrier which had attached itself to him during his days at the Villa Mirenda, and how miraculously he had acted its 'writhing agony after it had been run over, its will to live, its pleased sniffing at life as it recovered, and its sudden bouncing forward into a fresh world of smells'. When they took a horse-drawn carriage to drive out to some spot in the hilly countryside behind Bandol, he and Frieda would get out in order to take a stroll while Lawrence, still not up to walking, would 'squat on his heels collier-fashion and remain thus for an hour, unmoving, hunched up like a very old and meditating bird, his shut eyelids lifted to the sun'. Although he found Lawrence's powerful personality intimidating and felt it would be impossible to be in his presence long without feeling swamped – an explanation in his view of why the various Rananims which had been projected could never have worked – Davies was struck by the lack of pomposity in a writer who was by now so well known. When one day after a heavy lunch during his second visit, Lawrence read out loud a selection of his pansies, Davies fell asleep 'to the sound of verses about the harsh flight of swans clonking their way over a ruined world'. Their author was not angry but amused, even if his wife's face at tea-time did contain 'a surprised rebuke'.[19]

All these recollections were first published in Cyril Connelly's journal *Horizon* in 1940. An additional memory only appears in the slightly amended version of the article which is included in Davies's autobiography, *Print of a Hare's Foot*, published in 1969, nine years before his death. This is perhaps because by that time Middleton Murry was dead. Lawrence had not known of Katherine Mansfield's association with Bandol and as late as 28 December was able to write to Ottoline Morrell, 'I didn't know Katherine had been here – wonder where she stayed' (vii. 105). She had of course spent a good deal of her time at the Hotel Beau Rivage itself, according to Davies in the very large corner room which he was given on his first visit, down the corridor from the two smaller but communicating rooms the Lawrences occupied.[20] Back in England Davies had read 'a moving and emotional recital' by Murry of his last, peaceful reunion with Katherine, 'all past differences forgiven and resolved'. Lawrence listened to his account of this with growing agitation,

He squirmed, he yelped. 'Wrong! *Wrong*! This is what really happened. When Murry turned up at that crank's institute a friend staying there went to Katherine's room to tell her of his arrival. She said, "Keep that bugger away from me", then had her last haemorrhage.' He did not reveal his source of this.[21]

Just before he left Bandol Lawrence would receive a letter from Murry asking whether he still had a copy of *The Rainbow*. His reply, on 1 March 1929, was pleasant and conciliatory but showed no signs of wanting to renew the old friendship. To Brett on the day following he merely said, 'Murry wrote the other day – a bit feeble' (vii. 200, 206).

II   More Painting

Lawrence could write in his hotel room, but during his first weeks in Bandol he complained that it did not provide him with enough space to paint (vii. 25–6, 55). He had nevertheless completed six small paintings by the time he left, prompted into activity by an exciting new development. When Frieda had been in Florence, finally clearing their belongings from the Villa Mirenda, she and Orioli had met Jack Lindsay, a writer who had moved to London from Australia in 1926 and helped to found the Fanfrolico Press. The expensive limited editions of the more licentious classical writers in which this press specialised were illustrated with erotic drawings by Lindsay's well-known painter father, Norman. When his son was shown a couple of Lawrence's paintings, it must have struck him that there was no reason why the Fanfrolico should not publish a whole book of reproductions, and he casually mentioned the idea to Orioli. (Although at this stage he was too much under the influence of his father's aesthetic ideas to approve of Lawrence's, he and his Australian associates at the Fanfrolico were committed to supporting almost any tendency in contemporary English culture which opposed the ruling cultural elites.)[22] Very interested by the idea of a 'portfolio of reproductions', Lawrence followed up the suggestion enthusiastically, writing to Lindsay and immediately offering to accompany whichever of his pictures were reproduced with a 'little introductory essay' on modern painting (vii. 60). The disapproval of his own work by several of his painter friends, the visit to

Magnelli's studio, the book on modern French painting which Crosby had sent him, and the insight into prevailing views which he must have gained from reading the copies of *The Times Literary Supplement* he regularly received from Secker – all these factors had brought him to a point where he was anxious to make a public declaration of his own position.[23]

In the event, it was not because of Lindsay that the idea for a book of reproductions of Lawrence's paintings, with an introduction, was realised. The moving spirit quickly became P. R. Stephensen, business manager at the Fanfrolico, and a man whose activities with Communist groups in Australia and then among the more challenging and provocative bohemian circles in London, justify his biographer's description of him as a 'Wild Man of Letters'.[24] In partial manifestation of his wildness, Stephensen was at this time co-editing with Lindsay a journal entitled the *London Aphrodite* which was hostile to both the modernist tendencies in Eliot's *Criterion* and the much more old-fashioned ones in what it contemptuously referred to as the 'Squirearchy', after the influential editor of the *London Mercury*, J. C. Squire. Rhys Davies was one of the *London Aphrodite*'s contributors but when Stephensen came to Nice in December 1928 it was less to see him than to unload a few of the Fanfrolico's de luxe editions on wealthy English expatriates, and visit the Irish writer, Liam O'Flaherty, another friend and collaborator who was living nearby.[25] He did however accompany Davies on his second visit to the Lawrences, which began on 18 December, and was so impressed that he took the trouble of returning for two days in the new year. It was at the first meeting, however, that arrangements for the book were made. At this time Stephensen was beginning to detach himself from Lindsay so that Lawrence's paintings would be published not by the Fanfrolico but by a new press run by Stephensen and financed by Edward Goldston, a rich antiquarian bookseller from the same Museum Street where 'Orioli and Davis' were to be found (it was from Goldston that Lawrence had finally been able to secure a copy of Fritz Weege's *Etruskische Malerei* – vi. 102). They called it the Mandrake Press and the book of paintings, which was its first offering, sold in its ordinary edition at 10 guineas and made a profit of £2,000.[26] Lawrence would be embarrassed to be associated with a book which was so dear and several times in this period stressed how anxious he was for his work to be seen by poor people – at one point he even began exploring schemes for publishing his pansies in cheap broadsheet form.[27] Yet he was also clearly gratified by the plan to have the reproductions available when Dorothy Warren opened her exhibition in the spring. It can hardly have been a coincidence that he began to paint again soon after Stephensen's first visit.

Of the paintings Lawrence had completed before he left Bandol, two are in oil and four in water-colour.[28] The strangest is entitled *Renascence of Men* and shows one naked man with his head between the feet of another (a reminiscence, perhaps, of Lawrence's former leadership ideas). We know that *Spring* began as a painting of a group of workmen in blue cotton trousers playing *boules* but that Lawrence then took the trousers off (vii. 150, 169). The effect of the removal is startling given that the two male couples in the foreground are embracing, their naked bodies pressed close together. This image no doubt derives from an Englishman's observation of the greater degree of physical familiarity permitted to men in Mediterranean culture; and his painting of two naked men drying themselves after bathing in the sea, which he called *Summer Dawn*, also reflects aspects of his life in Bandol (Brewster Ghiselin, a young and clearly very fit American who visited the Lawrences in January did not find it too cold to swim). But these three paintings also illustrate something else. A biographer of Lawrence is inevitably led to think of his life in terms of 'phases', with a major shift in attention between the so-called 'leadership' novels of the early and middle twenties, and *Lady Chatterley's Lover*. This does not, however, mean that previous interests and preoccupations were entirely extinguished. Local life in Bandol certainly, but also the visits of young men who admired him, seem to have temporarily revived in Lawrence that yearning for male comradeship which in the past had made him feel Whitman was such a crucially important figure. Although he himself was a believer in the kind of radical transformation he often associated with ideas of re-birth and resurrection, and preferred to the gradualism of Darwinian evolution the Aztec mythology in which the transition to a new evolutionary period is effected by a huge, world-wide explosion, many if not most lives are more convincingly described in terms of shifting emphases.[29] We grow and develop, casting aside old interests to embrace the new. But as Lawrence had indicated in his letter to David Chambers, there is also a sense in which we are always the same.

In a fourth painting entitled *Dance Sketch* the naked man and woman are deliberately thin and elongated (the man's left leg tapering into infinity), in order to suggest vivacious movement, and this oil painting is enlivened by a sprightly billy goat prancing on its hind legs in half-comic accompaniment of the human dancers.[30] The other two paintings, both water-colours, reveal Lawrence's growing preoccupation at this period with swans. In *Singing of Swans* the two birds in the sky have thrown the naked figures down below into disarray and recall Davies's aural memory, just before he dropped off, of a 'harsh flight of swans clonking their way over a ruined world'. This was the last of the paintings Lawrence completed in Bandol. The first was probably the graphic yet very fine representation of Leda being raped by Zeus.[31] Brewster Ghiselin remembered Lawrence telling him that although the ultimate symbol was of course the sun, sometimes he preferred 'the great white bird beating the water with its wings and sending out waves'.[32] As Davies's memory indicates, this preference is reflected in the poetry he was writing as well as in his painting. In *Swan*, for example, Lawrence describes how:

> . . . we men are put out
> as the vast white bird
> furrows our featherless women
> with unknown shocks
> and stamps his black marsh-feet on their white and marshy flesh.[33]

Another pansy of this period is, however, a better illustration of the often disconcerting strangeness and power of Lawrence's imagination, and the extraordinary success with which he was often able to deploy the new poetic form he had developed. It is called, 'Won't It Be Strange–?' and sounds very much like the poem Davies half-heard:

> Won't it be strange, when the nurse brings the new-born infant
> to the proud father, and shows its little, webbed greenish feet
> made to smite the waters behind it?
> or the round, wild vivid eye of a wild-goose staring
> out of fathomless skies and seas?
> or when it utters that undaunted little bird-cry
> of one who will settle on icebergs, and honk across the Nile? –
>
> And when the father says: This is none of mine!
> Woman, where got you this little beast? –
> will there be a whistle of wings in the air, and an icy draught?
> will the singing of swans, high up, high up, invisible
> break the drums of his ears
> and leave him forever listening for the answer?[34]

Many of Lawrence's pansies are banal but examples such as this recall Dr Johnson's exasperated demand when, with Romanticism looming, people were beginning to question Pope's credentials: 'If Pope is not a poet, where is poetry to be found?'

III   The Artist as Hero

As Christmas approached, Frieda was hoping to see her two daughters, and Lawrence at one point thought that the four of them might take the boat from Marseilles to Naples. The idea was to spend the holiday with the Brewsters who had retreated from Nice to Capri where they had once again been able to borrow (or share) the villa belonging to the Di Chiaras. This plan fell through when Elsa discovered she could have only one week's break from her work (vii. 56, 68), and it was perhaps because of this that she did not make it to Bandol at all. Barby only managed to come early in the new year so that the Lawrences were obliged to spend Christmas on their own, even though the hotel 'filled with strangers' for the festivities (vii. 107).

For Lawrence on Christmas Day came the gift of a silk dressing gown from Davies, who must have felt indebted for recent hospitality and who received for his thoughtfulness a note which did include thanks but was chiefly a lecture on the importance of saving money: 'There do I try to keep you within decent bounds of economy, *knowing* your finances and having lived for years with similar ones, and then you break out into silk dressing-gowns Christmas gifts! It's worse than an expensive tart' (vii. 93). Lawrence had a special feeling for Davies because he came from a mining village in the Rhondda and had never had much money. According to Barby, that her mother had no presents on Christmas Day reduced her to tears and Lawrence to angry outbursts about her thoughtless children.[35] The youngest of those children turned up on 2 January in a troubled state because of her involvement with what Lawrence would describe as a 'messy second-rate Studio crowd' (vii. 125). Three weeks before, in a newspaper article originally entitled 'Oh These Women!', which he may now well have felt was relevant to Barby's difficulties, he had complained that men refused to accept women as real human beings, and that when women did succeed in living up to some pattern men had provided, they only found themselves disliked for it: 'There is intense secret dislike for the Eton-young-man girl, among the boys, now that she is actually produced.'[36]

It was two days after Barby's arrival in Bandol that Brewster Ghiselin introduced himself. Recently registered at Oxford for graduate studies, Ghiselin had secured Lawrence's address from Sylvia Beach in Paris, written to ask if he could visit him and then travelled down to Bandol on the assumption that the answer would be in the affirmative.[37] At first Lawrence was wary. 'A young man appeared from California – to admire me', he told Huxley, 'and you know what a depressing effect admirers have on me' (vii. 118). But he quickly decided he liked Ghiselin, whose intention was to stay in Bandol only a few days, and suggested that he should move from his hotel on the outskirts of town to the Beau Rivage and spend the rest of his vacation with them. The invitation to become (Ghiselin soon discovered) 'virtually a member of the Lawrence household' was one he accepted willingly, and it was 15 January before he left Bandol, three days after Barby. This was the second occasion on which the man who wrote to Rolf Gardiner on 23 December about the pleasures of solitude had been active in providing company for himself and Frieda, and Ghiselin was incorporated into the Lawrences' daily routine just as Davies had been. His descriptions of it confirm the other accounts although, for him, Lawrence sang the Hebridean Seal Woman's song of which he had always been so fond and the 'words' of which the police had seized from his cottage in Cornwall during the war because they suspected they were part of a code.[38] It is from Ghiselin we learn that the 'life' which Lawrence was happy to observe in Bandol did not merely consist of dogs, important though they clearly were.

The townspeople and the free animals of the town crowded the public areas. Dogs foraged along the shore or haunted the market place, standing or lying in the luxury of human presence, among the booths, the racks of clothing, the live catch heaped in wet baskets or dropped on bare concrete. Women passed back and forth on their errands or in idleness, many of them wearing their fashionable bright red, purple, green, or black bedslippers. Fishermen in blue jeans sat against the railing around the war monument, talking and laughing while they mended their nets or baited their lines with small prawns and wound them into a basket like a nest, the hooks plunged in along the rims. Drying nets like a gross brown lace striped the quay. Lawrence liked the warm scene, the contentment of the men and their pleasure at their work.[39]

According to Ghiselin's meticulously dated account, it was on the afternoon of 9 January 1929, when Stephensen was on the second of his brief visits (Barby remembered Lawrence's introduction of the Australian to her as his one attempt at match-making), that he felt the sea was warm enough for a swim. Having left his swimming costume back at the hotel, he was encouraged by Lawrence to improvise with three coloured handkerchiefs. 'You're perfectly decent; you're perfectly decent', Lawrence reassured him from the rocks where he and Stephensen were sitting.[40]

Unlike Davies, Ghiselin managed to stay awake during a pansies' reading and he had a clear memory of a second introduction Lawrence had written for them which is far more polemical than the first, and which accompanied a typescript of the poems sent off to the Curtis Brown office on 7 January 1929 (vii. 122). The more provocative element in this second attempt to define and defend his new form is associated with a letter Lawrence had written to Ottoline Morrell on 28 December in which he described *Lady Chatterley's Lover* as an attempt to make 'an *adjustment in consciousness* to the basic physical realities', and suggested that if a man had been able to say to *her* when she was young that (in the words of Mellors) one 'wouldna want a woman who couldna shit nor piss', it would have been a liberation and helped to have kept her heart warm.[41] As an example of the psychic damage which the taboo about natural functions and the words that describe them could cause, he referred to poems by Swift that include the line, 'Oh! Celia, Celia, Celia shits' (vii. 105–6).[42] The identical reference occurs in the second *Pansies* introduction where he now defines the thought which each poem is as coming 'as much from the heart and the genitals as from the head'. Although there are few so-called obscene words in the collection he was about to send to his agent, and neither sex nor the natural functions are especially prominent topics in it, with his mind more on *Lady Chatterley's Lover* than *Pansies*, Lawrence goes on to refer to such words as 'poor simple scapegoats . . . that the cowardly and unclean mind has driven out into the limbo of the unconscious, whence they return upon us looming and magnified out of all proportion, frightening us beyond all reason'. Citing Swift as someone whom these words had literally frightened out of his wits, he said how much worse it would be if Celia did not shit, and he suggested that it was not the fact itself which so deranged a great mind but the thought. According to Ghiselin, when Lawrence had finished reading out the passage in his introduction about Swift he looked up in concern 'for whatever embarrassment his stepdaughter might be suffering. "Poor Barby! *Poor* Barby!" he said, in caressing tones of sympathy tinged with amusement.'[43]

Barby's presence, as well as Stephensen's brief visit and the new project with what would be the Mandrake Press, must have helped stimulate Lawrence into more painting; but so too may the fact that Ghiselin also painted. Of a picture he was doing of some 'brilliant fingerlings' he had bought in the market, he remembered that Lawrence thought the feeling for the fishes themselves was true but that 'they were isolated in the midst of bare space in a way that deprived them of their actual relation to other things'; and he recalled Lawrence praising Cézanne for trying to catch 'all the aspects of the apple he was painting, as it continually changed in the flux of death'. (According to Lawrence a similar need to follow the developments in the object being rendered 'accounted for the flowing and changing form of free verse'.)[44] These comments were clearly an offshoot of the essay on painting which had been promised to Stephensen and which Lawrence had finished by 11 January 1929 (vii. 125). To prepare for it, he had asked Kot on 21 December to have him sent a copy of 'Roger Fry's *Cézanne* book. It would make a good starting point for me to write a good peppery foreword *against* all that significant form piffle' (vii. 82). Taking the hint, Kot had arranged that he should receive not only Fry's recent monograph on Cézanne but also a copy of Clive Bell's *Art*, in which the doctrine of Significant Form had first been enunciated (vii. 125).

Lawrence's 'peppery foreword' is the most explicit and extended of his confrontations with Bloomsbury, and justifies his own estimation of it as one of the best things he ever did (vii. 117). Its length demonstrates that, however impaired by illness his unusual capacity for prolonged effort may have been, it was by no means destroyed. He begins by asking why England and America have produced so relatively few great painters. The reason, he believes, is that painting depends above all on physical awareness – 'the instinctive-intuitive consciousness'[45] – and it is the Anglo-Saxons who are the worst victims of that shift from the physical to the mental (the ideal), initiated by Plato and then reinforced by Christianity. This view of Western culture would be familiar to anyone who had read Lawrence's previous writings, but it now includes a new component. Why is it, he asks, that things became so much worse after the Renaissance so that sex could be treated much more freely in Chaucer than in Shakespeare, and why were the Italian primitives far less seduced by purely 'optical vision' than their successors? The answer, he decides, had a lot to do with the appearance of syphilis in Europe and the fear of both sex and the body which it so quickly engendered.[46]

It was above all since the Renaissance that English painting especially had sought an escape from 'the *reality* of substantial bodies'. Although there were honourable exceptions such as Blake, when the English painted human figures in the eighteenth or nineteenth centuries clothes became increasingly more important than the bodies inside them. It was to avoid having to deal with the body that the English became so proficient in landscape, especially in the more diaphanous medium of water-colour. Lawrence confesses that for himself, although he admires English water-colours and especially those of Turner, a landscape always gives the impression of a background waiting to be occupied. Turner led on to the French Impressionists yet, great painters though they were, it was always evident that there would one day have to be an attempted return 'to form and substance and *thereness*'.[47] It was as the initiator of this attempt that Cézanne was so important.

The notion of painting as a downward spiral since the Renaissance was one which Lawrence shared with Clive Bell who at one moment in *Art* suggests that 'more first rate art was produced in Europe between the years 500 and 900 than was produced in the same countries between 1450 and 1850'.[48] But on the question of *Art*'s main thesis they were of course at odds. In two high-spirited pages Lawrence mocks the doctrine of Significant Form, imagining critics like Bell and Fry as 'Primitive Methodists' who have 'renounced the mammon of "subject" in pictures', no longer go 'whoring . . . after the Babylon of painted "interest"', and hanker no more for 'the flesh-pots of artistic "representation"'. Now, he says, they are like evangelical preachers urging others to know 'the one supreme way, the way of Significant Form' because that is 'the revelation of Spiritual Life, moving behind the veil'.[49] To call them 'Primitive Methodists' is partly an allusion to their enthusiasm for early Italian painting (which he himself fully shared), but chiefly a joke at the expense of Bell's cultural elitism. In *Art*, the insistence on how few people are fitted for the more refined experiences of 'aesthetic ecstasy' can easily shade off, at its Bloomsbury edges, into social snobbery. A knowledgeable ex-Congregationalist, Lawrence makes fun of this tendency by associating the proponents of Significant Form with a denomination which tended to take its clientèle from the lower strata of the working classes.

From Fry's book on Cézanne, published in 1927, Lawrence gleaned a good deal of useful information and he shared several of its views, believing with Fry (for example) that the still-lifes were of central importance, and that what was so impressive about Cézanne was his heroic sincerity.[50] But the tone clearly irritated him, and he must have found many of its commentaries too technical for his taste.[51] Bell's doctrine of Significant Form had been frankly Platonic and Lawrence was quick to detect in Fry also a lurking Platonism. In retiring from

Paris to Provence, Fry says, Cézanne gave himself up entirely to a 'desperate search for the reality hidden beneath the veil'; and he stresses Cézanne's interest in the geometry or architecture of composition: that aspect of his work which helped give rise to Cubism and then led on to the abstract canvases of painters such as Mondrian.[52] Lawrence has a low opinion of Cézanne's successors, comparing them to a Chinese dressmaker who reproduces in exact replica the darned rent in a Western dress he is copying. Cézanne did indeed make an 'assault on representation' but because he was battling with the 'hydra-headed cliché' not searching for something beyond or behind what was there: 'I am convinced that what Cézanne himself wanted *was* representation. He *wanted* true-to-life representation. Only he wanted it *more* true to life. And once you have got photography, it is a very, very difficult thing to get representation *more* true-to-life: which it has to be.'[53]

In Lawrence's opinion, Cézanne was a realist, determined to let an apple (for instance) 'exist in its own separate entity . . . to shove [it] away from him, and let it live of itself'. That might seem a small thing to do, 'yet it is the first real sign that man has made for several thousands of years that he is willing to admit that matter *actually* exists.'[54] For Fry, on the other hand, the return to substantiality after the Impressionist excursus was in no sense 'materialistic'. Although Lawrence feels that Cézanne only fully succeeds in still-lifes, he admires the well-known portrait of Mme Cézanne for its 'appleyness', 'which carries with it also the feeling of knowing the other side as well . . . intuition needs all-roundedness, and instinct needs insideness. The true imagination is for ever curving round to the other side, to the back of the presented appearance.'[55] These terms are crucially different from those in which Fry celebrates the portrait of Mme Cézanne:

The transposition of all the data of nature into values of plastic colour is here complete. The result is as far from the scene it describes as music. There is no inducement to the mind to retrace the steps the artist has taken and to reconstruct from his image the actual woman posing in her salon. We remain too completely held in the enchantment of this deep harmony. Though all comes by the interpretation of actual visual sensations, though the desire to remain absolutely loyal to them was an obsession with Cézanne, the word realism seems as impertinent as idealism would be in reference to such a creation. It belongs to a world of spiritual values incommensurate but parallel with the actual world.[56]

Like Fry, Lawrence stresses the heroism of Cézanne's struggles as a painter: his life-long battle to achieve what in the terms of this essay is a form of resurrection: 'All we know is shadows, even of apples. Shadows of everything, of the whole world, shadows even of ourselves. We are inside the tomb . . . Spectres we are to one another.'[57] The Frenchman may only have succeeded by the end of his life in knowing and therefore representing with *complete* success a few apples, and perhaps ('not quite so fully') a jug or two, but that was a major step, 'a great deal more than Plato's Idea', and it 'rolled the stone from the mouth of the tomb'.[58] As Lawrence describes the isolation of Cézanne in his later years, his refusal to compromise ('He didn't betray himself in order to get success, because he couldn't: to his nature it was impossible'[59]), and his utter commitment to his art, a strong element of self-identification emerges. Here was an artist whose bitter struggles to put himself back in touch with the material world were beneficial to the race as a whole. Lawrence responds with scorn to Fry's suggestion that he could not draw. The apparent ineptitudes in Cézanne's draughtsmanship, he suggests, come from his horror of the cliché, an initial ignorance of what it was really in his nature to paint, and his inability to 'prostitute one part of himself to the other. He *could* not masturbate, in paint or words. And that is saying a very great deal, today.'[60]

Lawrence's portrait of Cézanne is eloquent and moving; his attacks on Fry and Bell often shrewd and witty; and although the historical framework he establishes is dubious (someone, he suggests, implicitly admitting that his own treatment is no more than suggestive, ought to make a 'thorough study' of the impact of syphilis on the European consciousness[61]), it is at least lively and thought-provoking. Not clear, however, is precisely what relevance his remarks are meant to have to the reproductions they would eventually precede in the Mandrake Press edition. When the essay appeared it was called 'Introduction to These Paintings', as if the paintings in question supplied the lack which had been defined and Lawrence had succeeded with the human form when Cézanne, whose frustrated ambition it always was (Lawrence suggests) to paint female nudes with which he could be satisfied, had only ever got as far as the apple. That title was, however, something of an accident. Once he had received the proofs of his essay in February 1929, Lawrence discovered it had been given a title he had never intended – 'Introduction to Painting' – and he added the 'These' and an 's' as a simple, economical way of making it seem less fatuous (vii. 198). His remarks are certainly a defence of his painting but more a justification of the direction in which he had tried to move than a celebration of what he had miraculously achieved.[62]

IV Bad News

After Brewster Ghiselin left on 15 January to go back to Oxford, the Huxleys were expected. Julian and Juliette Huxley had spent a night in Bandol at the beginning of the month, on their way to visit H. G. Wells in Grasse (vii. 114, 116); and now Aldous and Maria, who were driving from Paris to Florence in order to sell their car, were due on the 21st.[63] Just before, or on the same day they arrived, Lawrence had some bad news. He learned from Pollinger that on the

18th two officers from Scotland Yard had called at the Curtis Brown office to say that six copies of *Lady Chatterley's Lover* mailed from Florence had been confiscated, and that any further copies entering the country would be seized and destroyed (vii. 146 n.4). Lawrence had been anxious for some time about the fate of these copies, as well as of six more he had asked Orioli to send to Brigit Patmore (he learned later that the police had also called at her house – vii. 153). News of the seizure a week or two before of a copy of Norman Douglas's *Limericks*, also posted from Florence (vii. 143–4), had made him feel the net was closing in, but now his fears were realised.[64] As he wrote to Orioli, 'the blow has fallen' (vii. 146); but worse was to follow. Less than a week after his first letter, Pollinger sent two more. In the first he described how the same two Scotland Yard officers who had visited him previously had reappeared to say that Lawrence's typescript of *Pansies*, with its provocative introduction, had also been seized. In the second letter he reported that the *manuscript* of the painting essay (the only copy) had clearly been opened and inspected before it was delivered (vii. 149 n.1). Stimulated by journals such as *John Bull*, which printed another attack on *Lady Chatterley's Lover* on 19 January (vii. 141), the authorities were now thoroughly alerted. Lawrence could comfort himself with the thought that they were closing the stable door after the horse had bolted, with only a few strands from the tail likely to be trapped; but he must have immediately wondered how he would get his pansies published, and whether his paintings could now be reproduced or shown without interference from the police.

The intervention of Scotland Yard could be discussed with the Huxleys who were understandably indignant on Lawrence's behalf. They suggested that Mary Hutchinson's lawyer husband might be approached and it was through him, as well as other of their influential contacts, that questions about the seizure of private mail in a supposedly democratic country came to be asked of the notoriously puritanical as well as aggressively interventionist Home Secretary, William Joynson-Hicks ('Jix' as he was known), in the House of Commons at the end of February. He claimed that the package containing Lawrence's pansies had only been opened as part of a routine, random check of the 'open book post' to see whether its contents were travelling at the right rate, a reply that assumed it had been sent unregistered (which was not true). He further explained that once those contents were in his office he had been advised they were indecent and instructed they should be forwarded to the Director of Public Prosecutions; but that he had nevertheless ruled that the poems should be detained for two months in order to 'enable the author to establish the contrary if he desires to do so'.[65] Lawrence did so desire but although he instructed the Curtis Brown solicitors to apply for their release, and St John Hutchinson also made an effort to retrieve them (vii. 167, 190), the typescripts were never returned.

Almost immediately after the seizure Lawrence must have begun typing another version of the poems in which he made numerous alterations to the pansies already written, often improving them considerably, and added a good many more. When he sent this new typescript to Secker at the end of February, with a new introduction in which the fiery paragraphs about obscene words no longer appeared, he said that the poems contained in it had been 'expurgated', and that he had kept back all those 'that might – falsely – be considered improper' (vii. 195). There is some mild degree of bowdlerisation in the second version but these words were clearly written on the expectation they would be read by the police, and Lawrence made arrrangements for the number of poems that might be falsely considered improper to reach Secker by indirect means. His eventual solution was to instruct Davies to post the missing pages to England from Nice. This explains his telling Secker on 10 March: 'After all I sent you the missing pp. of the Poems, or had them sent by post, as it seems all right now' (vii. 215).[66] Confiscating his work, even before it was published, was too radical a challenge to his sense of justice not to be taken up, especially when the reason the Home Secretary publicly gave for inspecting it in the first place was false. 'But I *do* wish it could be shown in the House', Lawrence would tell Hutchinson in March, 'that [Joynson-Hicks] is a *liar*, and he did open my sealed and registered *letter*' (vii. 227).

Towards the end of January it had turned very cold and this, together with what he regarded as nauseating food, made Aldous ill. Frieda also caught a chill so that on 27 January Lawrence could report that he and Maria had been obliged to go down to dinner alone: 'Of course the old waiter wouldn't believe that Frieda was ill, while I survived' (vii. 157). No-one seems to have been in a state for excursions, and the four of them must therefore have spent most of their time together in conversation. This was the first time Lawrence had seen Aldous since he wrote the angry letter about *Point Counter Point* from Port Cros; but he was now less angry, having reminded himself that any one person is an amalgam of different selves and decided that if *Point Counter Point* was unpleasant, Huxley himself was nice.[67] He was to make a public reference to *Point Counter Point* about a month later when he sent Nancy Pearn a foreword to the first novel of a young American writer, Edward Dahlberg (vii. 191). Part of the manuscript of *Bottom Dogs* had been sent to him in December from London (vii. 65), where an impoverished Dahlberg was being encouraged and introduced to the English literary fraternity by Arabella Yorke. Born in a Boston charity hospital to a Polish immigrant, who had been deserted by her husband (or companion) shortly before the birth, Dahlberg's novel derived its power from its relation to the hardships and miseries of his own childhood and youth, especially his five years as an inmate of a Jewish Orphan Asylum in Cleveland.[68] Once he had been sent the whole of *Bottom Dogs*, Lawrence did not much like it, but he felt it gave a vivid impression of the 'mass of failure that nourishes the root of the gigantic tree of dollars' in America, and showed how the struggle to survive, against the landscape as much as in competition with other people, broke the 'sympathetic heart', making people lose faith in a universe which was *ultimately* kind'. Once blood-sympathy has been destroyed, human beings became 'intensely repulsive to one another'. This was illustrated in modern writers such as Joyce, Gide and Huxley and could be linked to the reaction against the previous century's transcendentalism. 'An English novel like *Point Counter Point*', Lawrence wrote in his foreword, 'has gone beyond tragedy into *exacerbation*, and continuous nervous repulsion'; yet *Bottom Dogs* was 'in psychic disintegration, a good many stages ahead of *Point Counter Point*.'[69]

The Huxleys' visit was the eighth the Lawrences had received since arriving in Bandol but when Aldous and Maria left on 1 February 1929 there were still two more to come. Before Christmas he had finally sent a copy of *Lady Chatterley's Lover* to the Brewsters, telling them it was not in their line and they need not read it if they didn't want to (vii. 54); but after all the fuss in the English papers he had also felt obliged to send copies to his sisters. He firmly advised Emily not to read the novel ('you'll find it mostly rather heavy'), and told her not to let her daughter read it either: 'just keep it uncut, its value is then higher' (vii. 69). He would have had more confidence in Ada and must therefore have been disappointed when she indicated her disapproval and accused him of having hidden aspects of himself from her. In reply, Lawrence said there had been no concealment but that Ada had refused to see and accept what had always been elements in his nature. He advised her to look out for an article by him which was about to appear in the *Sunday Dispatch* entitled 'Myself Revealed', although he felt 'much more strongly, really' (vii. 127). 'Myself Revealed', which when it appeared on 17 February was described as being 'By D. H. Lawrence: The Most-Discussed Novelist of the Day' and was accompanied by a 'portrait study . . . Specially drawn by Joseph Simpson', had been adapted by Nancy Pearn from a longer piece clearly written while Lawrence was still living in the Villa Mirenda (vii. 64–5, 123). It describes briefly Lawrence's background and career and then how stranded he felt between a working class which had retained a warmth of human contact but was intellectually and culturally constricting, and a middle class 'broad and shallow and passionless'.[70]

With time, the animosity between Frieda and Ada had temporarily subsided and on 12 February, a month after Lawrence's correspondence with his sister over *Lady Chatterley's Lover*, she arrived in Bandol for a ten-day holiday. Although Lawrence was very fond of Ada, her presence filled him with 'tortures of angry depression. I feel all those Midlands behind her, with their sort of despair' (vii. 183). Trade was very poor in the deepening economic depression; yet it was also that his sister, having now turned forty, had begun to feel that all she had previously lived for – 'business, house, family, garden even' (vii. 213) – was worthless. On the day she left, Lawrence, too depressed to go to the circus that was then in town (vii. 190), wrote to say how unhappy her misery had made him and urged her to regard her present state as transitional; 'it's a different kind of happiness we've got to come through to – but while the old sort is dying, and nothing new has appeared, it's really torture . . . it's taken me three years to get even so far' (vii. 186). When he learned that she had arrived home just in time to have her father-in-law die in her arms, he wrote again, enclosing £50 'towards the money' she had paid in rent for Mountain Cottage in Derbyshire where the destitute Lawrences had once lived (vii. 193). To the Brewsters he attributed the transformation of the previously lively and energetic Ada to 'something organic in women, and not to be argued with'; but he also said it was largely 'the result of having been too "pure" and unphysical, unsensual. The organism itself reacts at last, and makes havoc' (vii. 214). Just after she had left, he sent to Nancy Pearn an article entitled 'The State of Funk' in which he discussed the damage done to the English by their disastrous fear of sex, confessing how long it was before he had been able to tell himself that he was no longer going to be ashamed of his sexual feelings. Although there was no birth without birth-pangs, the great changes which were inevitably in the offing could prove advantageous if men remained adaptable and courageous. Fear of the body was destroying silent sex-sympathy, 'a form of warm-heartedness and compassionateness' which had no necessary connection with sexual intercourse. It was this, Lawrence said, that he wanted to restore into life, 'just the natural warm flow of common sympathy between man and man, man and woman'. Yet as he had told Ottoline Morrell, and as he had hinted to Ada, that meant accepting sex 'fully in the conscious-ness'.[71] 'The State of Funk' was one of Lawrence's several replies to his critics but because they were in full cry when Nancy Pearn received it, she held the article back a while and it was never published in his life-time.

While Ada was in Bandol the weather became even colder than it had been during the Huxleys' visit. Centrally heated though it was, there were times when the hotel was without water, and others when the trains stopped running (vii. 176, 181). Adding to Lawrence's sadness over his sister were frosts so exceptional that many of the palms and eucalyptus trees in the town never recovered (vii. 183). Difficulties related to the threats to his work in England were a constant worry, with even the Mandrake Press's printers now complaining about *Mango Tree* and *Dandelions* so that in his irritation Lawrence told Stephensen, 'Leave 'em all out if you like, and print blank pages with the titles at the bottom' (vii. 199). At the beginning of his stay in Bandol, while the weather was still fine, he reported to several friends his feeling that he was growing stronger; but now, with winter finally arrived, and the English authorities having finally made the kind of move which, from the moment he began to send out

Lady Chatterley's Lover, he had apprehended, there are increasing complaints in the letters about his health. A visit to Toulon at the end of February left him feeling 'so shoddy' and with such a 'beastly cough' that he told Brett and Mabel there was no chance of his coming to America that year. It was too far to travel and anyway 'they might again begin fussing about letting me in' (vii. 203, 205). Spain was temporarily out of the picture because of political trouble there (vii. 169), but the latest 'southern' possibility was Corsica. On 24 February the Lawrences were intending to visit Davies in Nice on the following Saturday (2 March), and sail from there to Ajaccio; but having met some people who had just arrived back from Corsica and were still looking frozen (vii. 213), they abandoned the plan. They then decided to go to Spain after all and invited Davies over for a last visit (vii. 194). On the day he was due to arrive Lawrence explained to the Huxleys that he would still have to go to Toulon again to pick up the new suit he had ordered: 'I believe it will look nice – shall buy some nutty shirts and new shoes and see if I can't come out a butterfly for once – I want a metamorphosis or metempsychosis or both – a reincarnation into a dashing body that doesn't cough' (vii. 207).

At the end of January Lawrence had described his future movements as being on 'the knees of the gods, always an uncomfortable place' (vii. 155). What next finally determined them was a letter he received from a Paris bookseller, saying that he would be willing to help with the distribution of a new edition of *Lady Chatterley's Lover*. Spain would have to be postponed while he went to Paris to supervise his counter-attack on the pirates. This decision was made easier when Davies declared a willingness to travel up to the French capital with Lawrence, and it suited Frieda, who had never been keen on Spain, and now decided it was time for her to revisit Baden-Baden. On 11 March all three of them took the train north rather than south, Frieda to see her mother (and perhaps Ravagli), Lawrence to make arrangements that he hoped would prevent others from scooping up any more of the profits which he was fully entitled to feel should really have been his.

◆

CHAPTER TWENTY

March–July 1929

OLD HAUNTS AND NEW

I   More Business

At the station in Marseilles, Frieda took a fast train while Davies and her husband settled for one which would mean spending a night in a provincial town before their arrival in Paris. The reason for this, Davies explained, was that Lawrence, who described himself as of course having 'a sore throat to travel with' (vii. 215), did not want to have to 'sustain the long journey at one go'. In their gloomy hotel on the night of the 11th the two men shared not only a room but also a bed, and as he watched Lawrence drying himself after a bath Davies remembered feeling that he had never seen 'such a frail, wasted body, so vulnerable-looking'. It gave him 'an elusive sense of foreboding'.[1]

Once in Paris they went to the Grand Hotel de Versailles, later remembered by a jaundiced Edward Dahlberg, who paid a visit there after Frieda had rejoined her husband, as a 'plushy name for a hostel'.[2] The Lawrences had stayed in this hotel on two previous visits to the French capital because it was close to Mabel Harrison's studio: 49 on the Boulevard Montparnasse whereas the Grand Hotel de Versailles was at number 60; but on this occasion she appears to have been out of town.[3] Almost immediately on his arrival Lawrence made contact with the Crosbys (vii. 216). Like *Lady Chatterley's Lover*, their de luxe limited edition of *Sun*, published the previous October, had both attracted the attention of American Customs officials and been pirated, but they were not a couple easily deterred.[4] It was on them therefore that Lawrence was relying to publish both parts of *The Escaped Cock* which he had good reason to feel no ordinary publisher would touch.[5] When he was invited to lunch at the Crosbys' luxurious apartment in the rue de Lille on 15 March, they must have confirmed their interest in the book even though, on a personal level, fundamental differences now emerged. As Harry Crosby put it in his diary, displaying the fashionable, 'Modernist' disdain for punctuation, he and Lawrence 'disagreed on everything. I am a visionary I like to soar he is all engrossed in the body and in the mushroom quality of earth and the body and in the complexities of psychology.' This is a recognisable and familiar distinction – making one think of the hostility Lawrence had developed early in his career to the 'soaring' quality in 'Ode to a Skylark';[6] but Crosby was no Shelley and respect for his right to sustain the 'visionary' side of the argument is undermined when he goes on to say of Lawrence: 'He admits of defeat. I do not. He is commonplace. I am not. He is unthoroughbred. I am thoroughbred' (what he meant was rich). Although Crosby felt that those who had pirated *Lady Chatterley's Lover* were 'skunks', he could see no excuse for having written it but 'I guess he is a sick man' and 'I forgive him a great deal because of *The Plumed Serpent*.' Like Rolf Gardiner, he had been attracted to Lawrence by that novel and found it difficult to accept the change in emphasis. The conversation with Lawrence became so animated that Crosby missed the opening of the races at Maisons Laffite where (he takes the trouble to record) a horse on which he had bet 1,000 francs came in at 7 to 1.[7]

The purpose of the Paris visit was to see Frank Groves of 'Groves et Michaux', a bookshop in the Palais Royal area. Lawrence's understanding, and the main reason for his having postponed a trip to Spain, had been that Groves was interested in helping him publish a new, cheap edition of *Lady Chatterley's Lover*; but when the two met the situation turned out to be quite different. Groves had acquired pirated copies of the novel which he felt would be difficult to dispose of, because of the competition from other pirates but also because the more respectable Paris booksellers, Sylvia Beach included, refused to handle them. His suggestion was that, in exchange for 20 per cent of the net profits, Lawrence should allow a slip to appear in each copy that would describe him as 'authorising' the edition. The wholesale price was fixed at 100 francs, so that if all the 1,500 copies sold Lawrence stood to receive 30,000 francs (about £460). Compared with the effort and risk of publishing his own edition, this would be easy money and as he told Orioli on 18 March, when he was 'almost inclined' to accept the deal, an agreement with Groves would not necessarily preclude his own edition later (vii. 219). Had Lawrence settled with him he would have had no reason to linger in a Paris which he would soon begin to feel was very bad for his health, after Frieda had returned from Baden-Baden. But although he hesitated for a while, his pride eventually rebelled and he broke off negotiations with Groves. As he said when he described the episode a week or two later, 'It is understood that Judas is always ready with a kiss. But that I should have to kiss him back—!'[8]

Monday 18 March was the day on which he went to spend a week with the Huxleys at Suresnes, but before he arrived there he was already seriously ill. Brigit Patmore described how exhausted Lawrence could look after a night struggling with the effects of his tuberculosis in Port Cros; but Davies left an eye-witness account of the struggles themselves. Woken by Lawrence's coughing in the hotel room next to his, he hurried through the communicating door to find him 'as though in mortal combat with some terrible invisible opponent who had arrived in those mysterious dead hours that follow midnight'.

The dark tormented face and haggard body was like some stormy El Greco figure writhing on the bed. Was this the perky bird or lizard figure of Bandol! He seemed to be violently repudiating some evil force, a wretched man nearly overcome by a sinister power of superhuman advantages. Alarmed, I suggested a doctor and went towards the telephone. But at once he flew into anger. No, he would *not* have a doctor. But if I would sit by the bed for a while . . . I think he needed the aid of some human presence. Soon he was calmer, lay back exhausted, unspeaking but triumphant. The opponent had gone.[9]

Seriously alarmed by his state, the Huxleys succeeded in interesting Lawrence in a Dutch specialist's regime which Maria knew or had heard about ('perhaps we'll go to Holland to sit in a village and drink milk and be looked after by a doctor Maria believes in', he told Juliette Huxley – vii. 227). They made him pay one visit to a French doctor and agree to a second when he would be X-rayed. Lawrence had not had an X-ray since the dark days in Mexico City but when he returned from Suresnes to the hotel on the 25th he appeared reconciled, telling Orioli on the following day, 'Have got a bit of grippe – don't feel very well – must be x-rayed again' (vii. 229). Yet as the time for the appointment approached he backed out – according to Davies, half an hour before he was due to keep it and was all dressed to go.[10] On 25 March Frieda had reappeared (accompanied by her nephew Friedel), and the Huxleys laid the responsibility for his change of mind on the encouragement Lawrence derived from her return.[11] Davies makes it clear that he was indeed encouraged. Out of the hotel when Frieda arrived, he casually knocked on Lawrence's door once he was back and was told to come in. Tired perhaps from her recent journey, Frieda had joined her husband in his afternoon's rest: 'The couple lay in bed under a tumbled counterpane of crimson velvet, Lawrence's bearded head nestling contentedly on a hearty bosom refreshed by a fortnight's breathing of its native air.' Frieda laughed at Davies's embarrassment and immediately asked to share the bar of Montélimar nougat he was carrying with him.[12]

Lawrence was not so ill at the Huxleys that he could not participate in their social life, nor accept an invitation from the historian Daniel Halévy to go to a literary tea with Aldous on the 23rd, where the other guests included François Mauriac as well as Denyse Clairoun, the future translator of *The Plumed Serpent* (vii. 223). Contacts like this may have been useful in his search for someone who could help with an edition of *Lady Chatterley's Lover*, but the crucial tip is more likely to have come from Sylvia Beach after Lawrence had made an unsuccessful negotiating trip to Shakespeare and Company, her famous bookshop in the rue de l'Odéon. Beach was anxious not to become further associated in the public mind with what was regarded as erotica; her contacts with Joyce had satisfied all her publishing ambitions ('what could anybody offer after *Ulysses*?'); and she did not in any case admire *Lady Chatterley's Lover*. Yet she found Lawrence full of personal charm and felt sympathetic towards him because he seemed so ill.[13] It was Beach who was in the best position to tell him all he needed to know about Edward Titus, an American bookseller who was married to Helena Rubinstein, of cosmetics fame, and operated from premises in the rue Delambre, just around the corner from the famous Dôme Café in Montparnasse and very close therefore to the Grand Hotel de Versailles.[14] Shortly after his return there, Lawrence had worked out the details of an arrangement with Titus: 3,000 copies of a new edition of *Lady Chatterley's Lover* were to be photographically reproduced at a cost not exceeding 12 francs a copy. In his desire both to undersell the pirates and also to make his novel as widely available as possible (Davies said that he badly wanted it to 'reach the masses – of England particularly'[15]), Lawrence had decided it should retail at 60 francs and that the price to the trade must therefore be 40. He and Titus were to launch the edition with a deposit of 1,500 francs each (vii. 229, 244), but the profits were to be shared on a ratio of 8 to 7 in his favour. Compared with what he had been offered by Groves, this agreement with Titus was a risk because there would always be the danger of the edition not selling. Yet a second printing was required by August and in February 1930 Lawrence was able to authorise a third. Production costs were much lower than expected: only 6.50 francs a copy (vii. 451), and within a few months Lawrence would receive from Titus £1,200, about as much as he had made out of the first Florence edition.[16]

Part of the agreement with Titus was that the new edition should include a 'little peppery foreword' (vii. 229). Lawrence had finished this by 3 April (vii. 234) and called it 'My Skirmish with Jolly Roger'. It gave him the opportunity to describe the various pirated editions of his novel which he had seen or heard about, and reveal that, while he had been in Bandol, a New York bookseller with a conscience (Terence B. Holliday) had sent him a cheque for $180 which represented a 10 per cent royalty on the pirated copies he had been selling in his shop.[17] In an accompanying letter, Holliday explained that he had been obliged to resort to the pirates because the genuine copies he had ordered for his clients had been seized at the American Customs, and he must also have apologetically described the money he was sending as no more than a drop in the bucket. 'He meant, of course', Lawrence commented in 'My Skirmish with Jolly Roger', 'a drop out of the bucket. And since, for a drop, it was quite a nice little sum, what a beautiful bucketful there must have been for the pirates!'[18]

Having referred in the foreword to his recent refusal to deal with Frank Groves, Lawrence then offered the defence of the language in *Lady Chatterley's Lover* which he had sketched out in letters such as those to Ottoline Morrell, or in the most controversial of his three introductions to *Pansies*. Developed in more detail, this begins to seem curiously 'un-Lawrentian' in many of its emphases, perilously close to a previously anathematized 'sex in the head', or working the body from the mind. There are, Lawrence now claims, two mutually exclusive realms of thought and action which have nonetheless to be related in harmony. As far as the former is concerned, we are now surely civilised enough to be able to separate word from deed and not be overwhelmed by certain terms in the way our recent ancestors were. 'In the past,' he says, 'man was too weak-minded, or crude-minded to contemplate his own physical body and physical functions, without getting all messed up with physical reactions that overpowered him.'[19] But this does not of course mean that twentieth-century man has all the advantages. For Lawrence, whose generalisation of his own situation does not necessarily and automatically invalidate his point, satisfactory sexual contact in the modern world has become a virtual impossibility:

Ours is the day of realisation rather than action. There has been so much action in the past, especially sexual action, a wearying repetition over and over, without a corresponding thought, a corresponding realisation. Now our business is to realise sex. Today, the full conscious realisation of sex is even more important than the act itself. After centuries of obfuscation, the mind demands to know and know fully. The body is a good deal in abeyance, really.[20]

Knowing fully, with a 'fresh mental realisation' which will 'freshen up' the experience of sex, means (in Lawrence's view) 'being able to use the so-called obscene words, because they are a natural part of the mind's consciousness of the body. Obscenity comes in when the mind despises and fears the body, and the body hates and resists the mind.'[21] As an example of the ravages of fear, he once again cites Swift's anxieties over Celia; but also the recent case of a venerable clergyman who had lived blamelessly until the age of sixty-five but then found himself in the police courts for molesting little girls. Still smarting over the confiscation of his pansies, Lawrence pointed out that this case had come to light 'at the moment when the Home Secretary, himself growing elderly, is most loudly demanding and enforcing a mealy-mouthed silence about sexual matters'.[22] Ought that not, he asks (showing how, even more rigorously than Freud, Lawrence was committed to the belief that any repressed feeling would inevitably emerge at some point in a perverted form), make the Home Secretary pause? The difficulty for *Lady Chatterley's Lover* was that it was not only disliked by puritans such as Joynson-Hicks but also the 'modern young jazzy and high-brow person' who found it too simple and ordinary. Between the perversions of puritanism and the perversions of 'smart licentiousness' (as well as those of the 'low uncultured person with a dirty mind'), there was hardly space to turn; but, Lawrence concluded, 'I stick to my book and my position: Life is only bearable when the mind and the body are in harmony, and there is a natural balance between the two, and each has a natural respect for the other.'[23]

For smart, jazzy young people who did not like *Lady Chatterley's Lover*, Lawrence would have had to look no farther than the Crosbys. There is strong evidence that this is precisely where he did look, and that the person he describes in 'My Skirmish with Jolly Roger' as telling him the novel revealed the mentality of a boy of fourteen was therefore Harry Crosby.[24] On 29 March, four days before he reports having finished his short foreword, the Lawrences had gone to spend the weekend with the Crosbys in their converted mill at Ermenonville, thirty miles to the north of Paris.[25] The photographs which survive from the visit show Lawrence enjoying the sun on the paving stones of the courtyard, inspecting the Crosbys' horses in the new overcoat and hat he had bought, along with a new suit, in Toulon,[26] and taking drives in a donkey cart with Caresse (who seems to have retained her admiration for her guest longer than her husband). Their aim in these drives, she explained, was to seek out the first daffodils and they would return to find 'Harry still writing and Frieda still playing the gramophone'.[27] Through the figure of Clifford in *Lady Chatterley's Lover*, Lawrence had expressed vehement disapproval of the new, essentially passive instruments of entertainment: the radio in particular but by extension the gramophone. It may not have calmed his irritation on this occasion that a song to which Frieda particularly enjoyed listening again and again was Bessie Smith's 'Empty Bed Blues' and either at Ermenonville, or later in the rue de Lille, he demonstrated that he was still susceptible to fits of rage by breaking that recording, and perhaps several others, over Frieda's head. It was in response to these events that Harry Crosby promised, and indeed did eventually send, Frieda a gramophone of her own.[28]

In addition to Bessie Smith (blues, jazz and black musicians were all the rage in the fashionable Paris nightclubs of 1929), the Crosbys possessed a record of Joyce reading from the Aeolus episode in *Ulysses*.[29] When they played this to Lawrence it only confirmed him in his dislike: 'Yes, I thought so, a preacher, a Jesuit preacher who believes in the cross upside down.'[30] There was more talk of Joyce when the Lawrences visited the Crosbys in the rue de Lille on 3 April, taking with them a part of the typescript of *The Escaped Cock*, and also Aldous Huxley who joined Lawrence on the anti-Joycean side during the discussions which took place. After tea and glasses of sherry, the Crosbys rushed off to sign a contract with Joyce for publication by their press of more 'Work in Progress'. Although they invited him to meet Lawrence he declined on the grounds that his eye hurt.[31] In the past Joyce had paid very little attention to Lawrence but the success of *Lady Chatterley's Lover* in the same avant-garde Parisian circles in which *Ulysses* had long been pre-eminent must have irritated him. After he had asked Stuart Gilbert to read aloud some pages of the novel, he pronounced it 'lush!', and when at some point in 1929 Joyce had agreed to be on the editorial committee of a new journal, he met the suggestion that Lawrence should be asked to contribute with, 'That man really writes very badly. You might ask for

something from his friend Aldous Huxley, who at least dresses decently.'
Whether this means that he had at some point seen Lawrence, as he had
certainly seen Huxley (with whom he shared the prospect of going blind), is
difficult to say.[32]

Lawrence blamed his continuing ill health on life in a big city ('Bandol did me
good, Paris does me harm'), and he increasingly longed to return to the south
(vii. 230, 241). Davies had been visited in Paris by his mother and sister and on 2
April he returned with them to England (vii. 233). By then, or shortly after,
Friedel Jaffe must have gone back to his job in the town hall in Baden-Baden. On
5 April Lawrence confirmed his agreement with Titus for the new edition of
Lady Chatterley's Lover and on the 7th he and Frieda set off for Spain,
determined not to aggravate his condition with the usual rush of travelling and to
make the journey in leisurely stages.

II Palma

With nights in Orléans and perhaps Toulouse (vii. 246), it was 9 April before the
Lawrences reached Carcassonne. He was relieved to be once again close to the
Mediterranean but shocked that his bill for bed and dinner at the Hotel de la
Cité, a converted medieval priory on the ramparts, came to 400 francs (vii. 251).
In possible revenge, he took enough of the hotel's notepaper to accommodate an
article entitled 'Making Pictures', which he wrote once he and Frieda had
reached Barcelona. This had been requested by a well-established art magazine
(the *Studio*), and because it appeared together with a reproduction of his painting
The Finding of Moses, provided a useful advertisement for both the Mandrake
Press edition of his paintings and what he was still hoping was his coming
exhibition at the Warren Gallery.[33] Having described Maria Huxley's role in
bringing him back to painting late in life, Lawrence insisted on how much more
important than training or technique was 'visionary awareness': 'One may see the
divine in material objects; I saw it today, in the frail, lovely little camellia flowers
on long stems, here on the bushy and splendid flower-stalls of the Ramblas in
Barcelona.' His own training in awareness, he explained, had mostly come from
copying other painters' work. When one thinks of Lawrence's aesthetic, with its
emphasis on spontaneity and its dislike of any form of self-conscious artistry, one
could easily be led to predict that copying would have been abhorrent to him. But
it is a paradoxical truth that he had copied pictures all his life. His copy of Fra
Angelico's *Flight into Egypt*, which Dorothy Warren remembered (vi. 435), and
his version of Piero di Cosimo's *Death of Procris*, to which Merrild had taken
exception in New Mexico,[34] are only two of more than a dozen copies Lawrence
refers to directly in 'Making Pictures'. As he is keen to stress, it was not in order
to improve his technique that he copied but to learn 'what life, what powerful life

478

has been put into every curve, every motion of a great picture'.[35] When Birkin is copying a Chinese drawing of geese in *Women in Love* Lawrence has him say to Hermione Roddice, 'One gets more of China, copying this picture, than reading all the books.'[36]

Having moved on to Barcelona via Perpignan, Lawrence found it rougher, more ' "proletariat" in feeling' than he expected (vii. 250), and quickly made arrangements which would allow him and Frieda to sail to Majorca after only three days. His judgement on the town and news of his plans come in one of what would be several irritated exchanges with Secker about his pansies. Writing from Paris he had already insisted to Secker that, in the typescript he had sent, 'my "expurgation" was merely for the post' (vii. 249), and he now wanted his publisher to sail as close to the wind as possible. 'Do you imagine', Lawrence wrote, referring to the Home Secretary by his universally adopted nickname, 'I would haul down my flag to such an extent in front of the public, for all the Jixes in Christendom?'; and he told Pollinger, 'this is a black sheep that refuses to be whitewashed all over – must at least be piebald' (vii. 249, 257). When he saw that Rebecca West had published an article in *Time and Tide* in which she attacked Joynson-Hicks and said that 'a gentleman who opens another gentleman's letters ceases at that exact hour, moment, minute, second, to be a gentleman', he wrote to encourage and congratulate her.[37] 'We are going over to Majorca', he concluded, 'to see if my cough will calm down a bit there. Jix would say it's my sins – I say it's his' (vii. 252). It was always a moot point to what extent (if any) the aggravation Lawrence suffered from the authorities, and the persecution he began to feel, worsened his condition. When he first heard his poems had been seized, Rhys Davies felt 'the charge of indecency had an effect on [Lawrence] like vomiting. It was almost painful to look at him. It was in such moments as these that I felt that, more than his consumption, an evil destructive force was attacking him successfully.'[38]

Since posting the second typescript of *Pansies* to Secker in January, Lawrence had continued to write his short poems. The initial, although sometimes also final, versions of most of those he sent off had been written down in a notebook brought with him to Europe from Oaxaca; but in Bandol he had purchased a new one, written on the inside cover '23rd. Nov. 1928', and begun writing more poems in that.[39] The first nineteen poems in this French notebook were crossed out to indicate that most of them had been, or were going to be, published. From the first poem after these nineteen ('Image-Making Love') until the one which indicates it must have been written in Majorca because it refers in its title to one of the villages on the island (Andraitx) and begins, 'It is June, it is June / the pomegranates are in flower', there are only eleven poems. The eleventh ('Intimates'), which could have been written at any time between February and June, is one of a small group that dramatises the fatal effects on love, and by

extension on sexual relations, of what Lawrence had referred to in his review of
Trigant Burrow as 'image-substitution'. It does so with an urbanity characteristic
of several of the late short stories:

> Don't you care for my love? she said bitterly.
>
> I handed her the mirror, and said:
> Please address these questions to the proper person!
> Please make all requests to head-quarters!
> In all matters of emotional importance
> please approach the supreme authority direct! –
> So I handed her the mirror.
>
> And she would have broken it over my head,
> but she caught sight of her own reflection
> and that held her spell-bound for two seconds
> while I fled.[40]

After 'Intimates' there are fifty-eight more poems before 'Forte dei Marmi',
which would seem to announce Lawrence's arrival in Italy on 22 June. A number
reflect a phase in the perennial conflict between wanting to be associated with
other people and what Lawrence describes in one of the more traditionally
'poetic' and beautiful of these new poems as the 'Delight in being alone'. Others
contrast the danger of becoming 'finally self-centred', which one form of being
alone might seem to entail, with a human life which has still retained its
'connection with the living cosmos'. As the poem ('Fatality') from which these
two phrases are taken explains: 'No one, not even God, can put back a leaf on to a
tree / once it has fallen off.'[41] Many are very short like 'All-Knowing' – 'All that
we know is nothing, we are merely crammed waste-paper baskets / unless we are
in touch with that which laughs at all our knowing'[42] – and only four of these
poems deal specifically with the experience of living in a part of Spain.[43] But
although Lawrence often responded fairly immediately to his experiences, he also
reflected on them, and wrote about them later. An example would seem to be
'The Scientific Doctor' which comes twelve poems before 'Forte dei Marmi' and
describes how the speaker abandoned the doctor of the title because he did not
want to have 'so-called science' wreaked on him, or be reduced to the 'level of a
thing'.[44] This poem almost certainly provides a useful side-light on Lawrence's
refusal to be X-rayed in Paris but it is less interesting biographically than the one
which follows – 'Healing':

> I am not a mechanism, an assembly of various sections.
> And it is not because the mechanism is working wrongly, that I am ill.
> I am ill because of wounds to the soul, to the deep emotional self
> and the wounds to the soul take a long, long time, only time can help
> and patience, and a certain difficult repentance

long, difficult repentance, realisation of life's mistake, and the freeing oneself
from the endless repetition of the mistake
which mankind at large has chosen to sanctify.[45]

Lawrence's attribution of his illness to non-physical causes is familiar, but less so is quite this degree of self-blame and the emphasis at the end of the poem on our inevitably social nature, the difficulty of treading our own path.

The Lawrences visited Majorca only a few months before Robert Graves came to settle there. At that time it was not yet the popular haven it later became for painters and writers, although on the day following his arrival Lawrence met in one of Palma's streets the poet Robert Nichols, an acquaintance of Graves in the immediate post-war days (vii. 260).[46] From Barcelona, they had booked in at Palma's Hotel Royal but after a week they moved to the Principe Alfonso which has been described by Paul Hogarth as 'a marvellously flamboyant example of Catalan *modernismo*' and which still survives, without its 'park-like gardens', as a Chinese restaurant.[47] Lawrence's first impressions of Majorca and its capital changed only in emphases during his two months' stay there. He found the landscape attractive but less beautiful than Sicily, and the people either irritatingly or therapeutically dull, depending on his mood. Writing to the Crosbys on 18 April the accent fell on the therapeutic aspect and he spoke of a population which had not reached the stage of having nerves. That could be exasperating, but also helped to create an atmosphere which had the 'charm of the sleep trance' (vii. 255). He predicted it would do him good and in fact felt, for the most part, much better there than he had in Paris or Port Cros.

Frieda, on the other hand, was discontented. After her fortnight away from Lawrence, she had abandoned her plans to attend her daughter Elsa's London wedding on 5 April (vii. 211, 241) and, with her husband so obviously unwell, seems to have dropped her opposition to Spain. That did not, however, mean she was happy to be condemned to yet more hotel life. Too disgruntled at first even to try to speak Spanish (vii. 253) she began, as Lawrence would put it, 'moaning for a house' (vii. 293), and prompted him to begin looking around. On the assumption that he was not going to die in the very near future, or that, after his death, Frieda would need money to live on, this was a sound financial move. The bill at the Royal for a week had been £11 and the Principe Alfonso would turn out to be only £1 cheaper (vii. 260, 309). Given that there would be other expenses in addition to these hotel bills, what they implied was an annual income of something in the region of £750. Lawrence was now making a lot of money but he would have to keep on making it to live in hotels for the rest of his life. A rented house would therefore be a useful economy but his search for one was halted suddenly by a fit of shivering ('my teeth chattered like castanets' – vii.

260), which he took to be the return of his malaria. This convinced him that Majorca might not be good for his health after all, and that he ought to give up any idea of staying there for long.

Lawrence's impressions at this stage in his life were unusually dependent on his physical condition but, because it was so brief, his attack of shivering in Palma illustrates that fact in a dramatic way. Its immediate consequence, apart from the abandon of the house-search, was a letter to Davies on 25 April which contrasts sharply in tone with all his letters from Majorca before or after. He admitted he liked the hotel but complained of a cold little wind in the previous few days: four days later it was still whistling round the hotel 'like ten errand boys' (vii. 268). The food was good but the people at the hotel gave him too much of it and as for Spanish wine, 'my God, it is foul, cat-piss is champagne compared, this is the sulphureous urination of some aged horse.' The people were 'dead and staring . . . I can't bear their Spanishy faces, dead unpleasant masks, a bit like city English.' Everything was dearer than it ought to be, Robert Nichols and his wife – whom Lawrence and Frieda had both liked very much – had now left, and they themselves thought of staying on only another twelve days, or at most a month. 'I don't want to take a house here, to stay. I think, all in all, Italy is best when it comes to living, and France next. *Triumphat Frieda!*' (vii. 260).

Lawrence's recovery from his disillusionment was rapid. The cold wind he complained of turned out to be an aberration, and it was warm and dry for the rest of his stay. The hotel was by the sea and Frieda could therefore swim regularly; at one point Lawrence was feeling so much better that he thought it would not be long before he himself took a dip (vii. 326). There were very few other people at the hotel (four at one period and then six – vii. 286, 313), so that the Lawrences were treated very well. They enjoyed the company of these other guests and also that of a number of the island's residents to whom Nichols, who had been in Majorca three months before the Lawrences came (vii. 260), is likely to have introduced them. Because one of these included the British Vice-Consul they had an *entrée* to the whole expatriate community.[48] Even in his letter to Davies, where anger over his illness had already subsided sufficiently for the display of bad temper to sound a touch theatrical, he had admitted that 'we know some rather nice people, residents, who invite us to lunch and dinner, quite social'. With contacts like these, he and Frieda would be able to explore the island by car in the coming weeks.

By 29 April Lawrence had recovered sufficiently from his brief attack either to have completed or, more likely, given his habits of composition, entirely written the article entitled 'Pornography and Obscenity' which he sent off to Nancy Pearn on that day (vii. 268). This was a favour for Titus who was attempting to relaunch *This Quarter*, a Paris journal largely for American expatriates, with which Hemingway had once been associated;[49] but it gave Lawrence the chance to speak his mind once again on the censorship issue. In his view, the fact that 'obscenity' is redefined in every phase of culture meant that the present triumph of democracy had necessarily transformed the concept into a 'mob' phenomenon. Every word including, he implies, those which some readers had found so shocking in *Lady Chatterley's Lover*, has a mob as well as individual meaning; but nowadays 'hardly one person in a million escapes mob-reaction'. As for pornography, the taste for that arises from a confusion between the sexual and excremental flows in our nature. It is this which leads people to insult sex, 'to do dirt on it', and to a vast, hole-in-the-corner production of dirty books, jokes and pictures which Lawrence here says he would be perfectly prepared to censor 'rigorously'. In an implicit advertisement for the translation series he had urged Orioli to launch, he suggests that, because an open, frank attitude to sex is the only solution to pornography, its best literary antidote was to be found in 'the Renaissance story-tellers, Boccaccio, Lasca, and the rest'.[50]

Lawrence would have liked to paint but he complained, as he had done before, that this was difficult when you were living in a hotel (vii. 263). In Bandol the difficulty had been overcome but, according to his report to the Wilkinsons at the end of May, whatever picture he was painting when their letter arrived – 'sitting in my pyjamas on bedroom floor' – was the only one he had tackled in Majorca (vii. 313). His interest in his previous work remained nevertheless very acute. As the proofs of the Mandrake Press edition of his paintings came through in stages, he criticised each reproduction minutely, and with an impressive display of technical expertise, complaining that this or that colour was wrong, or the modelling of a particular torso had been lost (vii. 270–1, 279–80). His first reactions were of disappointment but he gradually came to feel that the printers had done a reasonable job and grew excited at the prospect of the book. He was both pleased and embarrassed to learn that advance orders indicated it would do well, and that the ten copies on vellum which Stephensen and Goldston had decided to offer at the huge sum of fifty guineas could have been sold six times over (vii. 319). The plan was still for the publication of the book to coincide with the opening of his exhibition yet, as 'that wretch, Dorothy Warren' (vii. 329) consistently failed to write to him, he could not be sure it would be realised.

The Lawrences had now settled into an agreeable rhythm of life which made them feel they might as well stay on in Majorca until it became too hot. Frieda's 'triumph' in persuading her husband they ought to go back to Italy still held good; but they now thought that, before sailing to Marseilles, they might well take a trip round several of Spain's more famous towns (vii. 282–3). Like his prediction that he would soon be able to swim, this plan illustrates how much better Lawrence was feeling. He talked now of wanting a proper house in Italy, rather than the top story (or stories) of someone else's; and his preference was for something in the Florence, Lake Garda or Forte dei Marmi areas (vii. 281, 276). When a Taos painter offered to pay $5,000 for the ranch,[51] it struck Lawrence that the money might come in useful to help set up a home rather more permanent than anything they had known before (vii. 289). He had addressed himself to the topic of house decoration in an article sent to Nancy Pearn at the beginning of May (vii. 269), arguing that the interiors of our homes should change as we do, and that as a result there should be a periodic clearing out of all paintings and photographs. His suggestion in 'Pictures on the Wall' is that when pictures have gone dead on us they should be burnt, just as dead flowers are. The reason we keep them is the same reason which makes decorating houses with pictures so problematic: any single one is usually a relatively expensive item of the householder's property. One solution which he suggests and which has since been adopted by a number of enlightened galleries or local authorities, is a 'pictuary' where paintings could be borrowed in the same way as books are. 'We all have to stare at the dead rags our fathers and mothers hung on the walls, just because they are *property*', he complains; with access to a pictuary, we might be able to keep a painting no longer than it is still alive to us. In those circumstances he calculates that he would want to keep 'some Picassos' about six months, 'some Braques' (violins and bits of newspaper notwithstanding) about a year; but Titian's *Adam and Eve*, from the Prado, all his life. In general, 'the cheapening of books freed them from the gross property valuation and released their true spiritual value. Something of the same must happen for pictures.'[52]

The financial success of Lawrence's private publication of *Lady Chatterley's Lover*, and a burgeoning market in the late 1920s for expensive limited editions, made him even more impatient than usual with his publishers. It had not helped that his total English royalties for the previous year from Secker had amounted to only £165 (vii. 18). Increasingly he felt that he had done a great deal of work in the past for an inadequate return and was determined to fight his corner more effectively in the future. When Secker proposed that there should be 250 numbered and signed copies of the coming edition of *Pansies*, which could be sold at 4 times the price of the the ordinary ones, Lawrence refused to agree until he had persuaded him that the extra revenue these would generate should be split equally between publisher, booksellers and author. He clearly had an instinctive dislike of having to sign his name many times over, but he also reasoned that, when it was above all his signature which gave the special copies their value, there was no reason why he should be limited to the author's usual 10 or 15 per cent (vii. 352, 358).[53]

Arranging this matter through Pollinger made him irritable and not at all receptive therefore when Secker began to suggest which lines needed to be altered in the typescript of *Pansies* he had received, and which poems omitted.

His irritation would have been greater if, while he was discussing this issue, Lawrence had not simultaneously begun negotiating with Charles Lahr over a limited, 'privately published' edition of *Pansies* which would include all those poems Secker finally decided to leave out, and the inflammatory introduction which had accompanied the first, confiscated typescript.[54] 'I shall be my own pirate, this time', he told Kot (vii. 302). A general election was due in England on 30 May and there was a possibility therefore of a new Home Secretary. But this hardly eliminated all the risk of publishing material which had been described in the House of Commons as obscene. In a defiant gesture of solidarity and friendship, Stephensen insisted that his name, rather than Lahr's, should appear on the proposed volume's inside cover: if there was going to be trouble he was eager and willing to be first in the firing line.[55] Lawrence realised that Lahr's edition would have to appear after Secker's had been offered to the general public and at first thought in terms of 250 copies (although later he secured an agreement from Secker for 500 – vii. 301, 324). As he had insisted, his description of the second typescript of *Pansies* sent to London after confiscation of the first as 'expurgated' (vii. 195) had been for the benefit of whoever he thought might be reading his mail. Yet once readers were offered the opportunity of comparing Lawrence's collection as he had conceived it, with his 'official' publisher's notions as to how he felt it must appear, it became a wholly apt description of Secker's *Pansies*.

Lawrence was angry with Secker for rejecting certain poems as impossible and insisting on changes in others; yet, as a group, the fourteen additional poems in Lahr's limited edition make one feel that this was a dispute in which there was more than one valid point of view. In the first pansy he ever wrote, Lawrence appears to have relied on Arabella Yorke's analysis of Aldington as someone driven to womanising by repressed homosexuality, and in what would now be the final version of 'The Noble Englishman', 'Ronald' (the Aldington figure) is described openly as a 'sodomist', too frightened to acknowledge his real nature and sadistic therefore in his dealings with women.[56] 'Ego-Bound Women' begins, 'Ego-Bound women are often lesbian, / perhaps always', and in 'There is No Way Out', Lawrence claims that 'If you copulate with the finest woman on earth / there's no relief, only a moment's sullen respite.' 'My Naughty Book' is a comically ironic apology for having used words 'like sh— and f—!' in *Lady Chatterley's Lover*, and 'The Little Wowser' a complaint in a similar vein about the trouble his own wowser, or John Thomas, has caused him. With some rueful poignancy in view of the circumstances, this pansy ends, 'I've chucked him, I've repented.' Two poems in the group are directed against predatory females. In 'What Does She Want?' the 'she' of the title is a 'volcanic Venus' who thinks lovers will assuage her dissatisfaction but 'the penis won't do it. / She bites him in the neck and passes on.' 'Don't Look at Me' (a 1920s forerunner of Bob Dylan's 'It's not me, babe') warns that type of woman to keep away: 'No, my poor little penis would be of no use to you / dear ladies, none whatsoever.' Several of the poems are in comic ballad form and in 'Demon Justice' Lawrence fashions a proleptic reply to those critics who would later claim that the prevalence of buttocks in his paintings is an indication of his own latent or repressed homosexuality. One of the sins of omission for which demon justice is in order, he says, is giving 'not even a hint / that a pretty bottom / has a gay little glint / quite apart from Sodom.' He prescribes 'sixty slashes' for the guilty parties across the 'rusties' (a dialect term for buttocks) and concludes, 'Then with a sore / arse perhaps you'll remember / not quite to ignore / the jolly little member.'[57] None of these poems is at all exceptionable in a modern context, but in 1929, with a certain amount of newspaper hysteria over *Lady Chatterley's Lover*, Secker might well have found himself in court had he published them.

To make the private, unexpurgated edition more attractive, Lahr asked for a signed portrait. Having photographs taken of himself had become increasingly disagreeable to Lawrence, but shortly before he left Majorca he promised Lahr several which had been taken there by a local photographer, Eduardo Guardia. He also said that he would send drawings made of him by an artist named Tom Jones who was living on the island, as well as his own attempt at a self-portrait in red crayon (vii. 333). Although he told Lahr that drawing his own face was unpleasant to him (vii. 325), he nevertheless felt that his efforts were preferable to those of either Guardia or Jones. The photographs help explain the surprise young men like Davies and Stephensen experienced when they first met Lawrence: although he was someone whose writings could suggest a tough combative nature, the first impression was often of unusual delicacy and sensitiveness. His expression in the Guardia portraits is humorous but with the limp hair, a right cheekbone that has come to seem high because of a sunken cheek, and a neck too thin for its collar, they also suggest the frailty of ill health.[58] The drawing in red crayon, which demonstrates considerable competence, must clearly have represented how Lawrence preferred to think of himself at this time. The staring eyes give it the anguished look of some of Van Gogh's self-portraits, but also a hint of demonic energy. That impression is reinforced by the tense posture and the way the right ear, in contradistinction to the more commonplace shape shown in the photographs, comes to a point, like the ear of some faun, or even of Pan himself (see Figs. 45 and 46).

In Paris, the Huxleys had been so concerned by Lawrence's condition that when they visited London they told their English friends he had not long to live. The consequence was a number of anxious enquiries he found irritating: 'Take it for granted everything Maria says is a gross exaggeration', he told Catherine Carswell on 20 May (vii. 293).[59] One of the letters of enquiry was from Murry who had heard the Huxleys' news via Sullivan and, anxious to see an old friend before he died, offered to come out to Majorca, even though his wife was at that time also very ill with tuberculosis.[60] Lawrence politely discouraged him, agreed that as far as friendship went they had 'missed it',[61] but insisted that they belonged to 'different worlds, different ways of consciousness' so that the best thing they could do was let each other alone 'for ever and ever'. In any case although his health was a 'great nuisance', it was by no means as bad as all that and he had 'no idea of passing out' (vii. 294–5). Five days later, on 25 May, he told Max Mohr that he had been 'pretty well' in Majorca: 'My cough is still a great nuisance, I wish it would get better. Yet I am a bit fatter and stronger' (vii. 304).

On the 8th he had certainly been well enough to take a car trip to the monastery at Valldemosa, once the home of another famous consumptive, Frédéric Chopin, who spent three months there with George Sand.[62] On the way from Valldemosa to Soller, Lawrence defined the colour of the sea which lay below their picnic place as the bluest he had ever seen, 'not hard like peacocks and jewels, but soft like the blue feathers of the tit' (vii. 275). The subsequent weekend he and Frieda went with two other people staying at the hotel to Cala Ratjada, across from Palma on the eastern side of the island, and there was at least one further excursion after this (vii. 286, 326). Yet though he grew to like Majorca more and more, and any place where he began to feel better pleased him, Frieda had no intention of allowing Lawrence to go back on his agreement that the house they would now look for should be in Italy. Her determination was strengthened when towards the end of May she had her bottom pinched in a tram. That, Lawrence said, made her despise every letter in the word 'Majorca' and 'rampant' to sail to Italy – 'to Marseilles anyhow – on June 4th. – where her squeamish rear has never been nipped' (vii. 309). There seem, however, to have been difficulties over booking – the boat to Marseilles sailed only once a week – and in the end, the notion of a trip round Spain abandoned, they settled for the 18th as the date of their departure (vii. 321).

By 8 June Lawrence had still not heard from Dorothy Warren about the exhibition but on the 12th he learned that it would open on the following day (vii. 330) – the private view did not in fact take place until the 14th. The Lawrences had always intended that one of them should be present when the paintings went on show, and Dorothy Warren's unreliability had made them both concerned about arrangements for storing or shipping the pictures once the exhibition was over. Even before its date was confirmed, they had agreed that Frieda would have to go to London while Lawrence made his way alone to Forte dei Marmi where the Huxleys were now installed for the summer (vii. 335). He felt that a journey to England might be too much for him; but in addition he had heard that the detectives who called on Pollinger in January had said he would be arrested if he ever did come home (vii. 222), and was in no mood to take the risk. When on 18 June therefore the Lawrences left Majorca, it was once again with different destinations in view. They travelled together to Marseilles but from there went their separate ways, Frieda northwards towards Paris and Lawrence on the line that ran eastwards through Cannes.

III   The Exhibition

Before leaving Palma, Frieda had badly sprained or, according to her account, actually fractured her ankle. Bathing at midday, she had been disturbed in her solitariness by the sight of a 'Spanish officer on a splendid horse'. Hurrying to fetch her bath robe, she trod on a pile of sea-weed covering a hole in the rocky beach. Too incapacitated to accept the officer's suggestion that she should ride home on his horse, a sad waste (in her view) of a 'romantic situation', she had to be driven back to the hotel in a car Lawrence ordered.[63] By the time she left Marseilles she was still limping badly, but mobile enough to take time off in Paris to see Titus on her husband's behalf. Lawrence was understandably anxious to be kept abreast of a publishing venture, of which he was financing half, and Frieda found she enjoyed discussing publication schedules and distribution plans. By the time she was back from her trip to England Lawrence would say that she fancied herself 'quite a business-woman', although he would also tell Titus: 'You mustn't expect my wife ever to remember any of the really business matters in business – she remembers only the romantic incidents, no more. So if you were thinking that she will have given me a solid report of what you told her, disillusion yourself' (vii. 392, 432).

Frieda arrived in London from Paris on 22 June. One of her first visits was to a Park Lane specialist who charged twelve guineas to treat her ankle; but she was also able to see her children. Although Barby had been with her and Lawrence just after Christmas, she had not seen Monty since the summer of 1926 and must have been especially anxious for news from the recently married Elsa. In addition to these private matters, and reunions with Koteliansky as well as others of the old circle, she had more Lawrence business to transact. Frieda would have arrived with messages for Secker whose expurgated edition of *Pansies* was just about to appear (a pre-publication copy was reviewed in *The Times Literary Supplement* on 4 July);[64] and she had brought for Lahr the photographs and drawings from which he was invited to choose a frontispiece for the unexpurgated one (vii. 333). Then there would be discussions with Stephensen about the Mandrake Press edition of Lawrence's paintings: how the copies were selling, whether there were going to be difficulties about getting them into the United States, and who should have received complimentary copies. Frieda got on so well with Stephensen that at some time during her stay she left her London hotel (the Kingsley in Hart Street) and spent a few days with him and his partner, Winifred Lockyer, in their cottage at Knockholt in Kent.[65] Like Davies and Ghiselin, Stephensen was one of

Lawrence's new young admirers especially inclined to make a fuss of Frieda, although there were several other people in London who were glad both to see Lawrence's wife for her own sake and to renew their contact with him through her. A consequence was that she had a 'coruscating fortnight' and was everywhere 'fêted and champagned' (vii. 367, 373). These words of Lawrence are in the ironic mode he often adopts in talking about his wife; but in a letter Frieda herself wrote in late July or early August she tells one of the friends she had made in Majorca that she had enjoyed a 'terrific time' in London, and had been made to feel 'no end of an important person' (vii. 373 n.3).

The main item of Lawrence 'business' Frieda had to deal with, and the one that brought her most excitement, was of course the exhibition of her husband's paintings. There was a gay flag bearing his name flying above the Warren Gallery in Maddox Street when she first went there; and she noted how different the paintings seemed ('a little wild and overwhelming') in those elegant surroundings after the big, bare rooms of the Villa Mirenda.[66] This difference is confirmed by contemporary photographs, one of which features Dorothy Warren and Phillip Trotter themselves, and suggests how relatively unlikely this recently married couple were as champions of Lawrence's art (Fig. 47). Fashionable aesthetes of the 1920s, they were also well connected;[67] more at home in Bloomsbury, one would have thought, than in Lawrentian circles. Some equivocation in Dorothy's support is apparent in her having kept Lawrence's paintings so long without showing them (Stephensen, who had to deal with her over the Mandrake Press edition, came both to distrust and to dislike her as a snob and a neurotic[68]), while the tone in her husband's long and invaluably detailed account of the exhibition is not always free of social condescension. As St John Hutchinson explained when he later appeared in court on the Trotters' behalf, the Warren Gallery had made a speciality of showing work by artists who came from the working classes – 'like Mr Lawrence, who began as a miner in England' (*sic*) – and the previous show had been of work by Henry Moore.[69] Yet both the Trotters give the impression that the last thing they would ever have wanted to acquire was the common touch. That they were keen to support such work was nevertheless admirable and one great quality they both seemed to possess (partly, perhaps, because of precisely those connections with Bloomsbury which Dorothy had through her aunt, Lady Ottoline Morrell) was a contempt for conventional notions of propriety in art. If they were hardly the types to rub shoulders with the parents of some of their artists in a working men's pub, neither would they ever have wanted to sit down to tea with Mrs Grundy.

In one sense, the Trotters' exhibition of Lawrence's paintings was a great success. Offers to buy were rare but in the first week their gallery was visited by 3,500 people (vii. 348). With entry at a shilling a head, that was good business. Phillip

Trotter saw an obvious relation between the crowded rooms and what he calls the 'first phase' of hostile press coverage, which included an attack on the show in the *Observer* for 16 June in which the pictures were described as pornographic. This first phase brought visitors whose motives were not simply aesthetic. As he puts it: 'The daily litter of cast-away catalogues on the stairs and landings was interpreted as a manifestation of outraged modesty; but disappointed prurience was at least an equal contributor.'[70] Whatever people's reasons for coming to the Gallery, hordes of them did in fact come (around 13,000 by the time the show closed[71]).

After discussions with Lawrence by letter, Frieda decided she would go to Baden-Baden on 6 July (vii. 356) and wait for her husband there until at least the 19th, her mother's seventy-eighth birthday. To celebrate the success of the exhibition, and repay some of the hospitality she had received, there was a party at the Gallery on the evening of 4 July which Frieda insisted should be 'her show'.[72] By then the exhibition had been running just a day short of the normal period of three weeks and might be expected to close soon. Catherine Carswell, who reports that Frieda wore a 'gay shawl, red shoes and a sheaf of lilies',[73] was one of the old friends present; new ones like Stephensen, Davies and Lahr had no doubt also been invited; and Ada made the trip down from Nottingham. Lawrence would be gratified later to learn how enthusiastic his favourite sister was about the paintings when she saw them all together, especially after her disapproval of *Lady Chatterley's Lover* (vii. 419). At some point during the party, orders were taken for *Boccaccio Story* and *Leda*, but events of the following day led to their being cancelled rapidly.

By the time of the party there had been a 'second phase' of hostile press comment which included more insistent calls for action from the authorities.[74] The general election at the end of May had resulted in defeat for the Conservatives, and on 7 June the new Labour cabinet under Ramsay MacDonald had taken control. The Trotters had no longer anything to fear from the zeal of Joynson-Hicks; but under the Obscene Publications Act of 1857 complaints from members of the public to the Commissioner of Police, as well as articles in the newspapers, would have been sufficient to explain the appearance of two detective inspectors at the Gallery on 5 July, at about 4 p.m.[75] They asked the Trotters to close the exhibition. When this request was refused they went away, but came back an hour later with more policemen in order to confiscate thirteen of the twenty-five paintings on show. The chief criterion for selection, Phillip Trotter concluded, was pubic hair, although *Spring* and *Leda* were no doubt taken for other reasons: naked men embracing and the rape of a woman by a swan. While the thirteen pictures had been turned to the wall in preparation for their removal, the Aga Khan arrived (49th Imam or leader of the Ishmaili sect of Muslims and better known by the general public at this time for his interest in race-horses than in art). He insisted that *Contadini* should be reversed once again so that he, and a far less socially distinguished visitor from Nottingham, who had also expressed an interest, might study its finer points.[76]

In addition to the paintings, the police took away four copies of the Mandrake Press edition of the reproductions, which were on display in the Gallery, and a portfolio of water-colours and drawings by Georg Grosz that had been brought down from the Trotters' living quarters above and left on a shelf by mistake.[77] When the policemen were on the point of impounding the Nonesuch edition of William Blake's *Pencil Drawings*, which happened to be in the Gallery also, they were saved from this absurdity by a visitor who may have been well-intentioned but was certainly not shrewd. (Had they taken this book, their total incompetence in matters of art would have been more easily exposed.) The Trotters were summoned to show on 12 July due cause why the seized objects should not be destroyed – 'or further dealt with according to law';[78] but adjournment was quickly secured until the 18th whereupon the hearing was further postponed until 8 August to allow for the summer holidays of the policeman most involved, Detective Inspector Hester.[79] Throughout the whole affair the police manifested that same deference to class evident in their willingness to allow the Aga Khan a leisurely view of *Contadini*. They allowed the Trotters, for example, to bring to Marlborough Street Police Station an art-expert friend of theirs who had been out of the country when the exhibition was opened; and they arranged for his and the Trotters' special benefit a private view in the cell where Lawrence's pictures were stacked against a wall. As a policeman obligingly held up *Boccaccio Story*, and Phillip Trotter made some observations, the friend pondered for a while and then said that the painting's distinction lay in the way all the different elements in the scene had subtly converging lines. What gave the composition its harmony, he went on, was the meeting of these lines in the painting's central patch of dark, and he lent forward to place his forefinger on the sleeping gardener's pubic hair.[80]

The seizure of half of Lawrence's pictures ought to have led to the closure of the exhibition but enough additional interest had now been created by the police action to make keeping it open a viable commercial proposition. Eventually the majority of the gaps on the walls, eloquent enough in themselves, would be filled by ten of Lawrence's early paintings (mostly and perhaps all of them copies) which Ada brought down from Nottingham.[81] The immediate problem was what to do about those in gaol. Cancelling her arrangements for Baden-Baden, Frieda attended a council of war on 9 July at which tactics were discussed. In addition to the Trotters' own solicitor, St John Hutchinson was present, acting now not for Lawrence but for them; but so also was Percy Robinson, a second solicitor who had been engaged to ensure that, although the police action was not explicitly directed against Lawrence, his obvious interests in the affair were safeguarded.

With a good deal of experience of magistrates' courts, Robinson suggested that the paintings could be recovered simply by giving a firm undertaking that they would never again be exhibited in Britain; but the Trotters were looking for some formula which would be less of an implicit admission to the public that the paintings they had been showing were in fact obscene. To them it seemed there were important civil liberties at stake, as well as their own reputation, and they were reluctant to give in without a fight.

As part of his search for a formula, Phillip Trotter would soon begin collecting photographs of previous treatments of Leda and the swan which were more graphic than Lawrence's and had for years been on public display: a painting by Michelangelo in the National Gallery, for instance, and a late sixteenth-century inkstand in the Wallace Collection where (as he puts it) 'the lady is up and doing, complete master of the situation'.[82] He hoped that at the coming hearing Hutchinson would be able to deploy this kind of material as part of a defence. With the same end in view, he went round all the London galleries, and consulted the Witt Library of reproductions: looking for nudes with pubic hair. To his surprise he could not find any and was obliged to conclude that, 'if the police had visited us as custodians of a rigidly maintained aesthetic convention, their case would have been unassailable'.[83]

Lawrence had chosen to represent pubic hair in his pursuit of naturalness, but there is some evidence that it had a special significance for him. We have no way of knowing whether the phobic dislike of it which he attributes to Parkin in the second version of *Lady Chatterley's Lover* is in any way autobiographical, and whether that might not have some relevance to his supposed objection to Brett's 'pubes'; but Parkin's response does chime in with a story George Neville tells. He describes coming across Lawrence, who was in his early twenties, sketching a female nude, insisting to him that the drawing was incomplete without body hair, and having the additions he then made met with hysterical rage and Lawrence's repeated cry that it was not true, it was not true.[84] Certainly in the final version of the novel, any phobia Lawrence himself may once have had is exorcised and Connie's pubic hair markedly celebrated; and it is no surprise therefore to find the same feature prominent in *Fight with an Amazon*, and other of the seized paintings. Trotter thought that in making it important Lawrence showed himself to be an innovator, which was true in relation to most pictures on display in the galleries but not as far as Picasso and other avant-garde artists of the day were concerned. At the hearing on 8 August, Herbert Muskett, the solicitor acting on behalf of the police and, by ironic chance, the same person who in 1915 had successfully argued that *The Rainbow* should be burned,[85] would predictably claim that the representation of pubic hair was one evident proof of obscenity.[86] It would have done no good to have told him that by 1929 there were plenty of other painters willing to break what Trotter calls a 'rigidly maintained aesthetic convention', because Muskett would have had Picasso's nudes burned just as happily as Lawrence's.

At the meeting on 9 July the Trotters' objections to Robinson's proposal gave the impression that their view of the options available was radically different from his, and this would later lead Lawrence to urge them to subordinate all other considerations to the recovery of the pictures. The incinerated *Rainbow* had risen from the flames but, once a painting was burned, it was gone for ever. Frieda was likewise chiefly concerned to recover the paintings and seems to have participated with energy and enthusiasm in the response to the crisis. She would no doubt have stayed to see it through, had not her involvement been cut short by a telegram from Italy telling her that her husband was dangerously ill and required her presence immediately. Without knowing how the situation in London would be resolved, she left there in time to be in Florence late in the evening of 11 July. Frieda had spent not two but almost three 'coruscating' weeks in England and from all accounts enjoyed every minute.

IV   More Trouble

Lawrence had taken as long to travel from Marseilles to Forte dei Marmi as Frieda had to get to London so that they had both arrived at their different destinations on the same day. He stayed about a mile from the centre of town at the Pensione Giuliani, which he liked because his bedroom reminded him of the Villa Mirenda, he could eat out of doors under a big plane tree, and there was a cat (vii. 348, 346). With the Huxleys' rented villa nearby, he would go there for tea, but also met them on the beach where Maria (if not Aldous) could be found most days after eleven (vii. 351).[87] As the record of his experiences in Australia, America and Mexico show, the author of *Sun* was never enthusiastic about sun-bathing in the company of other people, and he now recorded his impressions of Italian beach life in one of the many poems he was continuing to write.

> The evening sulks along the shore, the reddening sun
> reddens still more on the blatant bodies of these all-but-naked, sea-bathing city people.

> Let me tell you that the sun is alive, and can be angry,
> and the sea is alive, and can sulk,
> and the air is alive, and can deny us as a woman can.

> But the blatant bathers don't know, they know nothing;
> the vibration of the motor-car has bruised their insensitive bottoms
> into rubber-like deadness, Dunlop inflated unconcern.[88]

It was perhaps because Lawrence found the Huxleys preoccupied with this beach-life, and with their several friends in the area, Costanza and Eckhart Petterich among them, that very soon after his arrival on the 22nd (which was a

Sunday) he invited Orioli to join him in Forte for the coming weekend. By the time of his visit, he would have other company in addition to Pino's: that of a young but this time female admirer from America who had been promising to pay Lawrence a visit for some time, and had finally caught up with him.

Maria Cristina Chambers was a Mexican who had gone to the United States at the age of fourteen and was now married to an editor of the American journal, the *Literary Digest*. She wrote short stories in a modest way and had been overwhelmed with admiration when she first read Lawrence's account of Rosolino, his *mozo* in Oaxaca. For a non-Mexican the understanding seemed uncanny. In addition to persuading her husband to print an abridged version of 'The Mozo' in his magazine, she had participated actively in trying to publicise and sell *Lady Chatterley's Lover* in America – so actively and enthusiastically that Lawrence had thought her 'mad' (vi. 518).[89] When Maria Chambers had suggested in the summer of 1928 that she might come and see Lawrence, once he had moved from Florence to the Alps, he warned her that she would probably be disappointed ('You think one day the heavens will open. They will never open. It would be a pity if they did'); pointed out that in a hotel there was not much more to do than talk ('one gets weary of talk'); and concluded, 'And then of course my wife doesn't look on me as a shrine, and objects to that attitude in other people: at which one can't wonder' (vi. 419). These sage remarks did not stop Maria Chambers from arranging to see Lawrence in 1929, by which time, from her home in Long Island, she had been able to meet both Brett and Mabel Luhan when they had been in New York the previous winter.[90]

Her account of her week with Lawrence, still full (thirty-five years later) of the hero-worship of youth, gives little hint of the tension which developed between herself and Maria Huxley (vii. 354, 356), or of how impatient Lawrence himself became with her. The character sketch he wrote for Frieda's benefit on 7 July is unpleasant – 'She's a mixture of the worst side of Arabella – turns up her eyes in that awful indecent fashion – and of Ivy Low – humble, cringing, yet impudent . . . tangled up in her own ego till it's shameful' (vii. 359),[91] although its tone could partly be explained by his letter's recipient, and the fact that by then he was very ill. What she herself had to say includes a description of her last evening with Lawrence, which has some interest. When he came back from tea with the Huxleys she found him 'very silent, lost in some wretched depression'. After dinner they walked to the beach together where Lawrence sang a Mexican song as competently, she thought, as any native speaker.[92] He explained that Nellie Morrison and her Italian companion might turn up in Forte the following day and then surprised her with the news that he himself was leaving. Having made this announcement, he walked quickly back to the Pensione 'without having said even goodnight'. The next day she agonised over whether to go from her room in the Pensione to his in order to help him pack. When she finally did so, she found

494

Lawrence bending over a big trunk, 'breathing painfully from his asthma'. He was grateful for her assistance although, 'sick or not', he was punctilious in insisting that everything should be packed 'just so'. After he had left to be driven by Maria Huxley to Pisa (vii. 359), where he could catch the train to Florence, she never saw him again although Lawrence wrote to her frequently once she was back in America where, at her own request rather than his, she became a sort of unofficial agent, busily keeping an eye on his literary affairs.[93]

If after his major haemorrhage in the summer of 1927, which his doctor had attributed to sea-bathing on a previous visit to the Huxleys, Lawrence already had reasons for thinking that Forte dei Marmi was unlucky, they were strengthened now. The trouble had begun, as it had in Oaxaca, with a violent disturbance of his 'lower man' which yet made his 'chest sore' (vii. 359); but by the time he had fled from Forte dei Marmi, and was occupying one of the beds in Orioli's flat, the more usual feverish symptoms were also well to the fore. Reporting to his brother Julian on 13 July, Aldous Huxley said that of course Lawrence was weaker than when they had both been with him in Les Diablerets – 'coughs more, breathes very quickly and shallowly, has no energy'; but that the impression he gave in Forte was of being 'even worse than he was in Paris in March'.[94] Soon after he arrived in Florence on the 6th, Lawrence heard about the seizure of his paintings and he attributed, and would continue to attribute, to this blow a causal power in making him ill (vii. 364, 446). So bad was he that Orioli, who had after all seen Lawrence ill several times before, panicked and sent the telegram which brought Frieda rushing back from London. In normal circumstances, Lawrence bitterly resented this degree of interference in his private affairs, especially his private medical affairs; but the mildness of his reproofs on this occasion – 'no need for poor Frieda to rush here' (vii. 367) – suggests that he felt Orioli had done the right thing and that he was greatly relieved to have Frieda back.

With her return Lawrence once more rallied; and Frieda was able to bring him up to date on the pictures situation. Whether or not she conveyed to him the combative mood of the Trotters, that quickly became clear in the 'long and interesting letter' from Dorothy Warren to which he replied on 14 July, when he and Frieda were staying at the Hotel Porta Rossa in central Florence. Lawrence was the opposite of what in Secker's volume of *Pansies*, just published, he had called a 'Willy Wet-Leg': someone so resigned that 'when you hit him / he lets you hit him twice'; and in a three-line poem written in Forte dei Marmi he had said, 'How welcome death would be / if first a man could have his full revenge / on our castrated society.'[95] Calmly accepting insult or turning the other cheek, he considered as actions not only wrong in themselves but unhealthy because the resentment which passivity inevitably bred was certain at some point to have a distorting emotional effect. Yet in this case he did all he could to calm Dorothy

Warren down and discourage her from thinking of the High Court, worried that on the way there his pictures could easily be destroyed:

The law, of course, must be altered – it is blatantly obvious. Why burn my pictures to prove it? There is something sacred to me about my pictures, and I will not have them burned, for all the liberty of England. I am an Englishman, and I do my bit for the liberty of England. But I am most of all a man, and my first creed is that my manhood and my sincere utterance shall be inviolate and beyond nationality or any other limitation. To admit that my pictures should be burned, in order to change an English law, would be to admit that sacrifice of life to circumstance which I most strongly disbelieve in.   (vii. 369)

The argument is similar to Birkin's when in *Women in Love* he is discussing with Gerald what can be done if someone steals one's hat,[96] and by extension it is also similar to some of those Lawrence himself had deployed to justify his refusal to respond to patriotic appeals during the war. 'I am an Englishman – but good God, I am a *man* first', he had written to a German acquaintance in 1921 (iv. 133); and this was the point of view he had tried to impress on his Mexican colleagues at the PEN dinner.

Describing to his brother how Lawrence's health seemed to have deteriorated, Aldous Huxley had said: 'He hasn't written a line or painted a stroke for the last 3 months. Just lack of vital strength.'[97] This was far from true and the tonic effect of Frieda's return soon allowed him to begin writing again. In the main it was only his short poems for which he had the energy, but to his last stay in Florence belongs Aldington's anecdote of how Lawrence went into Orioli's bookshop, read through the proofs of an introduction to his translation of Lasca's *Story of Doctor Manente*, which someone else had provided and, dissatisfied with the result, wrote out then and there his own introduction on the back of the galleys, 'quite indifferent to the people coming in and out of the shop and all the resonant Italian voices'.[98]

To an Italian friend who met him on the Lungarno at this time and found him both emaciated and very pale, Lawrence said that he had continued to work even during his illness.[99] If that is so, then the likelihood is that while in bed he had continued to write his poems. A prominent and recurrent theme of these was the state of modern industrial society and the prospects of ever being able to resist its advance. One provocation to think more about such matters had come when he had received in Majorca the latest number of the *London Aphrodite* which included an article by Stephensen entitled, 'The Whirled Around'. The sub-title to this short piece – 'Reflections upon Methuselah, Ichthyphallos, Wheels and Dionysos' – suggests eccentricity (or worse); but in fact it begins with the relatively straightforward suggestion that, caught between utopians like Shaw and Wells on one side and on the other a 'modern Luddite rioter' such as Lawrence, 'singing swan songs aloofly, prophesying the smash-up of the wheels', the only sensible alternative was Communism. 'One soldier in the Red Army', Stephensen wrote, 'can introduce more reality to social discussion than ten drawing-rooms of daring modern novelists and playwrights.' Although he was more flattering to Lawrence than to Shaw – 'both monists, one of intellect, one of emotion' – the problem with the former's work, in Stephensen's drastically simplified view, was that, 'You can never become, by will, a peasant or an animal once you have been fully human.'[100]

Lawrence had brushed aside this further attempt to define him as regressive, telling Stephensen on May Day, that: no, he did *not* think the article he had sent him was 'brilliant'. In his view it was 'not even very estimable', although it 'might have been worse' (vii. 269). Yet reading 'The Whirled Around', and knowing Stephensen, must have helped to prompt various attempts to redefine his own political position in the weeks ahead. In Forte dei Marmi, for example, Lawrence wrote a moving account of how implicated he felt in the fate of the English proletariat, so that although:

> the pomegranate has red flowers outside the window
> and oleander is hot with perfume under the afternoon sun
> and I am 'Il Signore' and they love me here,
> yet I am a mill-hand in Leeds
> and the death of the Black Country is upon me
> and I am wrapped in the lead of a coffin-lining, the living death of my fellow-men.[101]

This sense of being necessarily implicated in the fate of his compatriots, and of having an always undeniable collective as well as individual self, would become more manifest in the months to come. And yet Lawrence's feelings of solidarity with mill-hands in Leeds did not prevent him from writing very shortly afterwards of the need to separate himself off from others: 'The mass are not my fellow-men / I repudiate them as such'; or denying that the usual way of defining social class was relevant: 'Behold the gulf, impassable / between machine-spawn, myriads / mechanical and intellectual, / and the sons of men, with the wind and the fire of life / in their faces, and motion never mechanical in their limbs.'[102] Moreover, if most people were indeed 'machine-spawn' then the only way forward for the remainder was to disengage: in a situation too far gone to admit of effective social action, removing oneself from the group along with a few others, or even one other, was the only solution. Lawrence can talk in his poems of the need for such disengagement and thereby imply that questions of social organisation no longer interest him but then, again only a short time later, can go right back to his old leadership ideas and insist that democracy is not 'the service of demos' but *demos* serving life 'as it gleams on the face of the few, / and the few look into the eyes of the gods, and serve the sheer gods'.[103] One way of explaining

497

these disconcerting shifts would be to say that Lawrence was now making no attempt to reconcile conflicting political attitudes but simply expressing each one as the mood took him. But this would be to ignore what in this instance becomes an important issue of literary genre. The prose texts Lawrence wrote in the last months of his life would show that the impulse to synthesise was never far away; but it was the essence of the short poems to resist overall coherence. 'Live and let live', Lawrence had written in the introduction to Lahr's edition of *Pansies*, 'and each pansy will tip you its separate wink.'[104]

CHAPTER TWENTY-ONE

◆

July 1929–January 1930

BATTLING ON

I Lichtenthal and Plättig

During the three weeks of their separation, Lawrence and Frieda had discussed by post several, different schemes for meeting up again. One was that he should go to England, and another that they should both make their way to either Garda or Como, and look for a house in those areas (vii. 351, 355). By the time Frieda made her decision that they should meet in Baden-Baden for her mother's birthday, her husband's thoughts had taken a different turn. Since first getting to know each other in Irschenhausen two years ago, Lawrence and Max Mohr had continued to correspond, but there had been a recent, more rapid exchange of letters over the possibility of Mohr undertaking a German translation of *Lady Chatterley's Lover*. One attraction of this was that he had agreed anything he wrote would be supervised by the Lawrences; but there were endless complications over publishers' rights. By July it seemed as if it might be useful to discuss those complications in person and that, for this and other reasons, Mohr's frequent invitations to his home near Munich should be taken up. That was what Lawrence had been somewhat unrealistically preparing to do when Frieda suddenly appeared in Florence and insisted on Baden-Baden. They left for Germany on 16 July and stayed, along with the Baroness, in the same Hotel Löwen in Lichtenthal where they had been with the Brewsters the previous September. 'I have Achsah's room', Lawrence wrote to his American friends on the day of the old lady's birthday, 'Frieda has Earl's, and the Schwiegermutter has one of ours' (vii. 378). He once again enjoyed the garden of the old inn – enough to write a poem about it;[1] and he could pass his time going alone to the Kurhaus, sitting under the trees listening to the orchestra and 'looking at the amazing grotesques of people' (vii. 384). But still unwell, he was not at all happy and in what may have been a manifestation of his irritation with Frieda for having made him fall in with *her* plans, he analysed her enthusiasm for Baden-Baden as the obverse of secret hate, and a typical example of German sentimentality. The Germans, he told Orioli,

love things just because they think they have a sentimental reason for loving them – das Heimatland, der Tannenbaum, das Brünnele, das Bächlein – the very words send a

German into a swoon of love, which is as often as not entirely false. They make up their feelings in their heads, while their *real* feelings all go wrong. That's why Germans come out with such startling and really, silly bursts of hatred.   (vii. 384)

It was not only Frieda's plans to which Lawrence was now obliged to accommodate himself but also those of his mother-in-law. She had been looking forward to spending some time in a spa hotel in the mountains about an hour from Baden-Baden and because she could hardly go on her own, and Lawrence was still probably too ill either to stay at the Hotel Löwen by himself or to visit other friends, all 3 of them travelled up to Plättig in the Badischer Schwarzwald on 23 July. The large hotel in Plättig stands on the side of a mountain with the steeple of the small village church in front and the Black Forest all around. It is an idyllic spot but, with 150 fellow guests, and weather which had turned both cold and rainy, Lawrence was miserable. As he sent back corrected proofs of the Lasca story to Orioli a week later, he told him: 'I have to lie under the great feather bolster on my bed, to be warm. I have got a cold, and I simply hate it here' (vii. 396). Left to himself he would have returned to Baden-Baden quickly, but his mother-in-law was keen to stay because she felt it did her so much good. After her initial opposition to Frieda's plans for leaving Ernest Weekley, Lawrence and the Baroness had built up over the years an unusually warm relationship; but there now developed an intense and unpleasant conflict of wills. Stuck on the side of a mountain from where he could do little more than look across the Rhine to the Vosges, and with a wind which he describes as cutting his chest, Lawrence found Frieda's mother 'really rather awful now'. At 78, he complained, she fought viciously for everything that would keep her alive a little longer; and he evoked a grotesquely vivid picture of the Baroness standing in the roadway greedily gulping in air and proclaiming, 'es gibt mir Kraft, es gibt mir Kraft' ('it gives me strength'). Feeling that she would experience an 'ugly triumph' if he died before she did, he explained her state to his sister Ada by saying that she thought 'her time to die might be coming on': 'So she fights in the ugliest fashion, greedy and horrible, to get everything that will keep her alive – food, air, pine-trees, Frieda and me, *nothing* exists but just for the purpose of giving her a horrible strength to hang on a few more years' (vii. 397–8). On several occasions over the previous few months, Lawrence had mentioned the possibility of revising *The Virgin and the Gipsy* for publication.[2] The terrifying figure of the Mater in that novella had not been based on the Baroness; but he must now have felt that it might just as well have been.

While he was in Plättig Lawrence began to translate a second story of Lasca's (vii. 394).[3] Further evidence that he was not completely and continually prostrate are the seven letters and two postcards he wrote from the spa the day before he left; and it was on 2 August also that he posted 'The Risen Lord' to Nancy Pearn.

This longish essay had been requested by an editor of the magazine *Everyman* for a series on 'A Religion for the Young' (vii. 401), and describes what for Lawrence were the three chief features or phases of Christian teaching. Before the war, he wrote, most Italian and many English men identified with the Christ child in the lap of the all-sheltering mother. During the hostilities, that became impossible and the emphasis therefore fell on the image of Christ crucified. What was now required was for the churches to lay stress on the most important aspect of the Christian message: the Resurrection. Here, however, was the one part of the Christian mystery which was misleading for, if Christ rose, it was to live on earth in the flesh not the spirit, 'with hands and feet, then with lips and stomach and genitals of a man.' He returned to 'take a woman to Himself', to have the delight, as well as the nuisance, of children, to make friends and to 'have a man-friend whom He would hold sometimes to His breast, in strong affection, and who would be dearer to Him than a brother, just out of the sheer mystery of sympathy'.[4] Apart from this last touch, which harks back to Lawrence's concern with male companionship, these remarks on 'The Risen Lord' could be read as a commentary on *The Escaped Cock* which the Crosbys were about to publish (the proofs arrived on 8 August – vii. 411). They confirm how tenaciously, even now he was increasingly ill, he continued to associate the concept of a new life with this world rather than the next.

Back in Lichtenthal by 3 August, Lawrence sent Nancy Pearn another newspaper article on the 5th (vii. 405). 'Men and Women', the topic on which he had been asked to reflect by the *Star Review*, accused science of having failed to keep up with modern aspirations towards a labour-free world so that there were still many tasks – washing the dishes, for example – which required physical effort. He felt that although the modern revulsion away from that effort hit women harder than men, it had a general effect which was disastrous. The film, the radio and the gramophone had all been invented because not only physical effort but also physical contact had become repulsive to both sexes: 'The aim is to abstract as far as possible.' It was this move towards abstraction which made human beings necessarily repulsive to one another so that the only solution was for a few individuals 'to try to get back their bodies and preserve the other flow of warmth, affection and physical unison'.[5]

The completion of this piece, as of 'The Risen Lord', was a sign of Lawrence feeling somewhat better; but although he was much happier back at the Hotel Löwen he was still far from recovered and continued to cough 'to the general annoyance or cold commiseration of a nervous universe' (vii. 427). Now that he had prevailed over his mother-in-law, who had not wanted to leave Plättig, his feelings towards her softened; but they would never again recover their former warmth and he found living within her circle of necessarily old friends oppressive. On 11 August 1929 Frieda celebrated her fiftieth birthday with large blue trout, duck, 'fat meringues', a white wine called Gauwinkelheimer and a peach punch which was made with champagne (vii. 427) and which no doubt also contained some soda water (when she had helped prepare the champagne punch for her party at the Warren Gallery on 4 July, her insistence on this addition had shocked Phillip Trotter who had 'come of age in the Black Forest' and thought it an 'unwarrantable adulteration'[6]). Besides dreading the future effect on his wife of four large boxes of chocolates, Lawrence was a little dismayed that five of the nine guests at Frieda's party were over seventy (vii. 420). They must also have struck him as over-weight. Increasingly emaciated, he felt in Baden-Baden that he was surrounded by 'huge German women' who, if they happened to sit not with but actually on him, would be incapable of noticing because 'their bottoms would be too tough for my poor pinching' (vii. 449).

During the first days of his return from the mountains Lawrence waited anxiously for news of the hearing on 8 August that would decide the fate of his paintings. The outcome fully justified the recessive attitude Percy Robinson had advocated and Lawrence had urged the Trotters to adopt. Through St John Hutchinson, they had made it clear that they were as willing as Lawrence to recover the paintings by promising never to show them again; but they simultaneously tried to argue they were not obscene and offered to call a number of famous art experts to vouch for that fact.[7] Frederick Mead, the eighty-two-year-old magistrate, allowed Hutchinson to have his say but implied he felt his offer irrelevant by insisting that it was immaterial whether Lawrence's paintings were works of art because 'the most beautiful pictures in the world might be obscene'.[8] He ordered the paintings to be returned on the condition of their not ever being shown again in Britain, and showed plainly enough what he thought by also ordering that the four copies of the Mandrake Press edition which had been seized should be destroyed. Given that one of these was on vellum and could therefore have been sold for fifty guineas, the financial loss (for Stephensen and Goldston, if not for Lawrence himself) was hardly trivial.

When the news of the judgement came through to Lawrence, first via a telegram and then in letters, he was more angry than relieved; and his anger was intensified by the arrival of copies of some of the hostile press coverage. From the first moment he heard his paintings had been seized, he had tried to relieve his feelings by writing poems which he referred to not as pansies but 'nettles' (vii. 373, 389). Very shortly after his death twenty-five of the more polemical of these were published by Faber and Faber under that title. Given that Lawrence's gift for satire in verse was no more than moderate, this was no great favour. Before he left Baden-Baden he sent to Lahr several drafts of poems which would eventually appear in *Nettles* (vii. 441–3),[9] and at the same time suggested they might found together a fortnightly satirical magazine entitled the *Squib*. Lawrence became quite keen on the idea and three weeks later proposed to Lahr some possible subjects for satirical treatment. Although he explained that he could not himself 'go for Murry', because he had known him too intimately, one of these was a 'Life of JMM by J.C.' a review of which would begin: 'This is a work which cannot be lightly dismissed. The author has gazed into the flowing stream of introspection, and seen, as in a glass, darkly, the great image of – himself' (vii. 484). Some of Lawrence's ideas in his letter to Lahr are funnier than this stumbling allusion to Murry's *Life of Jesus*, and several of his satirical poems are genuinely lively; but in general it would be hard to regret the *Squib* never materialised. He badly wanted to avenge himself on his detractors but two days later told Lahr, 'K.[ot] thinks the "Squib" is a bad idea – perhaps it is. Perhaps one would only collect a little bunch of not very nice people' (vii. 489). He pursued the project for several weeks and sent £10 for the hard-up Davies to act as editor; but when it began to seem that he would be by far the largest contributor, and when Lahr showed no enthusiasm for his insistence on anonymity, it petered out.[10]

The abuse Lawrence was obliged to endure over his paintings sickened him, and made him feel even more violently alienated than usual from his compatriots; but it was not without its compensations. Frieda showed that she understood the connection between notoriety and selling books when, in her report on her English trip for their Majorcan friends, she said, 'But the fun is that all this fuss means lots more money for Lawr's work' (vii. 373). He was amazed when Titus sent him the equivalent of $150 as his share of the profits from the sale of *My Skirmish with Jolly Roger* which had been published as a separate pamphlet in New York (vii. 428–9). It seemed ridiculous as well as embarrassing that such a short text could be on the market there for $3.50 (vii. 446). Secker's edition of 3,000 *Pansies* quickly sold out and for the 500 unexpurgated ones, which were snapped up in 3 days, Lahr would shortly pay him £500 (vii. 502, 428, 445). In this last case, as also in his dealings with Titus, Lawrence was benefiting not only from the publicity which the seizure of the pictures had brought but also very favourable agreements with men who were not full-time, established publishers. In a letter of advice to Davies which he wrote before leaving Baden-Baden, he made a distinction between the 'proper' public of publishers such as Heinemann and Gollancz and an 'improper' one which he felt was almost as big, 'if not bigger' (vii. 448). Writing to Pollinger 10 days later, he redefined this difference as 'the sort of esoteric public within the great stupid exoteric public' and told his agent, 'The thing to do is make the most of this boom of limited editions – it's the only way to make money, and without so much fuss . . . no taxes and all that' (vii. 462). Norman Douglas would not have noticed there had been a boom in limited editions; but the controversy surrounding Lawrence had given him a name which made almost anything he now wrote easy to sell. As the author of a pamphlet that reviewed the difficulties with British law faced by Lawrence and Radclyffe Hall in the late 1920s would put it: 'Thanks to the prosecution and the publicity it entailed, [Lawrence's] work are legion among those who otherwise would probably have thought he was an aircraftsman or a soldier in Arabia.'[11]

There were of course drawbacks in this situation. When in *Point Counter Point* someone suggests that Rampion might want to try private publication, he replies, 'Do you think I am ambitious of having my books sold in the rubber shops?'[12] The kind of publicity Lawrence's work had received must certainly have brought him some members of a rubber-shop public; but a more important disadvantage (in his view) was that the world of limited editions into which he was moving more and more was exclusive to the relatively rich. He was periodically embarrassed by the price of some of his books and persuaded Charles Lahr to charge less for the unexpurgated *Pansies* than he had originally intended (vii. 336). Even so, at 2 guineas Lahr's edition was 4 times the price of the ordinary, unsigned copies of Secker's, and it was not for some time that Secker would bring out a cheap edition at 3s 6d. The fleeting notions of publishing some of his more political pansies as election broadsheets which Lawrence had entertained earlier in the year, and the price he fixed *Lady Chatterley's Lover*, were signs of his wish to reach a large public. Yet he wanted this at the same time as he was anxious to make as much money as he could from the private publishing trade. A Marxist like Stephensen might have been able to analyse this contradiction more competently than Lawrence but, a publisher of expensive books himself, he may not have been any better at living through it. At the end of August, Stephensen visited Eastwood, almost certainly at the invitation of Willie Hopkin.[13] Full of enthusiasm for the miners there, he wrote to Lawrence urging him to declare himself an active Socialist (vii. 460). But Lawrence claimed that the Socialists were even more hostile to him than the Conservatives and remembered that it was under a Labour not a Conservative Home Secretary that his pictures had been seized. It would have been around this time that he wrote 'Choice of Evils':

> If I have to choose between the bourgeois and the bolshevist
> I choose the bourgeois
> he will interfere with me less.

> But in choosing the bourgeois, one brings to pass
> only more inevitably, the bolshevist
> Since the bourgeois is the direct cause of the bolshevist,
> as a half-lie causes the immediate contradiction of the half-lie.[14]

It may well have been in response to Stephensen's challenge that Lawrence wrote 'Nottingham and the Mining Countryside', for whose date of composition the only evidence is the opening phrase, 'I was born nearly forty-four years ago'.

This is a much-quoted essay because of the details about Lawrence's grandfather, a company tailor who made thick flannel vests and moleskin trousers for the miners; its descriptions of some of the houses Lawrence had lived in as a boy; and its lyrical evocation of an Eastwood which was still 'a curious cross between industrialism and the old agricultural England of Shakespeare and Milton and Fielding and George Eliot.' Lawrence's father and his fellow miners are portrayed as uneducated men with a strong sense of community derived from working close to each other and 'practically naked' in the dark intimacy of the pit. They had no idea of pitying themselves until 'agitators and sentimentalists' taught them how to do it. Their love of nature was disinterested whereas their wives were driven by a 'nagging materialism' which made them value the flowers in their garden less for their intrinsic beauty than as possessions. The real tragedy of England, Lawrence goes on, 'is the tragedy of ugliness'. He contrasts with Eastwood what the Italians were able to make of the hilltop which is now Siena, and suggests that more important than anything else is the provision of a beautiful environment. Lawrence can be taken as responding directly to Stephensen when he complains that the English 'nag, nag, nag all the time about politics and wages and all that, like mean narrow housewives'. In a tone which could also have been that in which Mellors would have responded to the Parkin of *The First Lady Chatterley*, he says that they should no longer mind about 'wages and industrial squabbling' but concentrate instead on clearing away the ugliness to which English workers have previously been condemned. This is because, as he had put it earlier in the essay, 'the human soul needs actual beauty even more than bread'.[15]

II Rottach

On her way back from London, Frieda had twisted her ankle again on Milan station (vii. 366) and had arrived in Florence limping. If the Lawrences stayed longer than they expected in Baden-Baden it was partly that the Baroness wanted them to, but partly also because her daughter was following a course of massage to improve her walking. Lawrence also consulted the doctor, the same one he had seen two years before. This time he was told his lungs were so much better he ought not to bother about them, and that what he had to take care of were his bronchials and his asthma (vii. 420–1).[16] The asthma might be 'very bad', he wrote to Maria Chambers on 23 August, but it was 'basically nerves, chagrin' (vii. 440). The doctor's recommendation was now no longer for altitude but for somewhere near the Mediterranean. It may not be a coincidence that, after his recent unhappy experience in Plättig and his memory of how he had felt in Bandol, this was the advice Lawrence would have given himself. For the moment however, he had agreed with Frieda that they would look for a house in the

Florence area and he would shortly send Orioli to inspect some lodgings Giulia Pini had recommended (vii. 455). More immediately, he felt committed to the visit he had said he would make to Max Mohr, even though that meant a return to the mountains. Lawrence left Baden-Baden with Frieda for Munich on 25 August, thankful to escape heavy old German women. The Baroness was wonderful for her age, he had admitted to his sister Emily four days before, but 'still I find her seventy-eight years weigh on me and become oppressive. I get depressed here – which is not usual for me, I am very rarely depressed' (vii. 436).

Mohr lived in a village in the Bavarian Alps at the southern end of a narrow mountain lake called the Tegernsee, some 40 miles southeast of Munich. Only 30 miles from Edgar Jaffe's little house at Irschenhausen, Rottach was high up but at least, Lawrence reminded himself (vii. 459), below the magic 3,000 feet, an altitude he had previously been told it was important to be *above*. Partly because of the contrast with Plättig, he liked the situation very much. He and Frieda had the house Mohr found for them virtually to themselves, and meals could be provided by their landlords who ran the adjoining inn (vii. 463, 470). At $3\frac{1}{2}$ marks a day, this was the opposite of a fashionable spa: the daily tariff at the Plättig hotel had been 11 (vii. 389). Lawrence appreciated the simplicity but Else Jaffe's memory of visiting him there, along with Alfred Weber, is that she found him 'lying in a bare room in the mean village inn. Beside him stood a great bush of pale blue autumn gentians as the only furnishing.'[17] The bareness he clearly did not mind and the flowers gave rise to one of his most famous poems. Drafts of what eventually became 'Bavarian Gentians' occur towards the end of the second notebook in which Lawrence had been jotting down his pansies. It is clear from these that at first his only concern was with the beauty of the flowers. 'Blue and dark', he writes,

> Bavarian gentians, tall ones
> make a dark-blue gloom
> in the sunny room
>
> They have added blueness to blueness, until
> it is dark: beauty
> blue joy of my soul[18]

As he continues to contemplate them, however, and ponders the oxymoron of their blazing darkness, the drafts show that the gentians begin to seem like torches which will lead him down to the underworld where the dead are gathered and where Persephone is once again in the arms of Pluto. The appearance in the notebook, shortly after these first versions of 'Bavarian Gentians', of a first draft of 'The Ship of Death' indicates that, if Lawrence was more contented in Rottach than he had been in Plättig, he was hardly any better. Both poems mark one more stage in a series of efforts to habituate an exceptionally active imagination to the prospect of death. He had made these all his life but they had become markedly more frequent with the composition of *Sketches of Etruscan Places*. The first version of 'Bavarian Gentians' is called 'Glory of Darkness'. What is characteristic in the poem which developed out of it is the invocation of one of Western culture's more familiar paradigms of renewal. Persephone, or Proserpine as the Romans called her, is dragged down into the dark during the winter but bursts forth in splendour at spring-time. Yet in all the extant versions of 'Bavarian Gentians' it is the descent into gloom which is described and made grimly alluring, while the prospective return to light is no more than implied. In Rottach, Frieda remembered listening for her husband's breath through the open door of his bedroom all night with 'an owl hooting ominously from the walnut tree outside'. As the dawn came, the only living thing in the room seemed 'the enormous bunch of gentians . . . on the floor by his bed'.[19] Given Lawrence's condition, it was comforting as well as convenient that in Mohr there was a qualified doctor only five minutes away. He records how Frieda once sent a peasant boy to fetch him because she thought her husband was either dying or already dead; but that after he had rushed over the blue eyes opened and the putative corpse smiled, knowing what Frieda must have been thinking. When, with his usual gift for communicating with children, Lawrence would play with the Mohrs' three-year-old daughter, Frieda asked the father whether he was not worried about infection. 'Nobody can believe', Mohr claims to have replied, 'that any harm can come from Lorenzo.'[20]

In spite of all her massage sessions in Baden-Baden, Frieda was still limping. In what was probably desperation she decided to consult a local farmer who doubled as a bone-setter. He concluded that the ankle bone was resting on the edge of its socket, gave a firm tap and from then on Frieda's ankle steadily improved. Lawrence was enraged: at being told that if the bone had not been reset the socket would have filled up so that his wife would have limped for ever, but also at having paid twelve guineas to a London specialist and then been left owing several more to the doctors in Baden-Baden (vii. 461). The episode intensified his usual suspicion of the medical profession, yet in Rottach he allowed two of its members to make the trip from Munich in order to examine him (vii. 466). At least one of these, however, was unorthodox in his approach, closer in spirit to the bone-setter who had achieved such remarkable results with Frieda. This doctor intimated that he thought he could cure Lawrence within a few weeks, if he followed a special regime chiefly based on diet and breathing exercises. Lawrence had always believed in what, depending on the remedy in question, could be characterised as either folk or alternative medicine; but there were special reasons why in this particular case he should feel encouraged.

Since he first properly formulated it in 1927, Lawrence had stuck to the notion that his illness was associated with the male equivalent of the menopause. In a letter written to Maria Huxley from Lichtenthal on 12 August he had said, 'I'm sorry Aldous isn't well – hope he's not in for one of those long psychological–organic changes that men get, like the change of life in women'; and on 5 September he told Brewster, 'my ill-health is the same as your loss of energy – it's a sort of masculine change of life' (vii. 420, 464). Writing to Aldous Huxley from Rottach on that same day, he indicated that his new doctor, who had been a priest and was no 'ordinary *Artz* at all', had offered confirmation of this view: 'He says that we are all undergoing a great change in our animal man – that includes woman, of course. But especially men between 42 and 49 are in a state of change.' The key to successful management of the transition was diet: 'The great thing is, if you can, to live mainly on the good, rather solid porridges – millet, oatmeal, barley – then raw fruits and vegetables – then yaourt and sour milk and light cheese – and nuts' (vii. 466). According to this new doctor, Lawrence went on, his asthma came from a vagus nerve in a constant state of reaction to food the system did not really want. A persistent protest during Lawrence's latest stay in Germany was that the food was too heavy, and in one of his poems from this period entitled 'Food of the North' he had complained it tasted too much of 'the fat of the pig', and asked to be taken south again where he could be oiled with 'the lymph of silvery trees'.[21] The new doctor's idea that he was suffering from a poisoned system, as well as the change of life, was therefore all the more likely to strike him as reasonable, and he was ready to give his remedies an extended trial.

In some ways Aldous Huxley was the right person to whom Lawrence could explain this new diagnosis: he had a wife who was interested in alternative medicine and he himself (as the future was to prove) was not entirely hostile to it.[22] But he was also the wrong person in that he knew precisely where the vagus nerve was and how it was supposed to operate. Moreover, he had spoken to the specialist who had seen Lawrence in Paris and felt he knew exactly why his friend suffered from 'asthma': if he had increasing difficulty in breathing it was because there were now so few areas of his lungs left undiseased. Huxley's general view in his letters was rigorously scientific and he felt Lawrence was foolish in not admitting what was really wrong with him, and in not seeking orthodox professional advice. 'How horrible this gradually approaching dissolution is', he had told Robert Nichols on 2 August, '– and in this case specially horrible, because so unnecessary, the result simply of the man's strange obstinacy against professional medicine.' Lawrence's new doctor was a professional, with a clinic in Munich; but he was sufficiently unlike the 'scientific doctor' with whom he had broken the appointment in Paris to inspire faith. Following his instructions, and in addition to adopting the new diet, Lawrence began taking small doses of arsenic and phosphorus; but these made him so ill that he quickly gave them up. Although he persisted with the new foods, he was disappointed that they made him feel no better, 'in fact . . . rather worse' (vii. 477). Now convinced it was the altitude which was bad for him, he did not immediately abandon hope; but the note of optimism which had accompanied his report of his first contacts with the new doctor is frail, and it would not be long before he fell back into the depression to which he had recently confessed.

Ill as he was in Rottach, Lawrence expanded the 'Pornography and Obscenity' article he had written for Titus until it was more than twice its original length. This was so that it could appear in a shilling pamphlet series published by Faber and Faber which was called the 'Criterion Miscellany'. Having ended his original article by comparing modern attitudes to sex with the openness of writers like Boccaccio, he now expatiated, with his usual vigour and cogency, on the connections between sex as the 'dirty little secret' of his culture, and that culture's widespread masturbatory tendencies. These extended to writing where, he claimed, 'the sentimentalism and niggling analysis, often self-analysis, of most of our modern literature, is a sign of self-abuse'. Neither the new, scientifically hygienic approach to sex of reformers such as Marie Stopes, nor the emancipation of the bohemians, offered effective ways of escaping secrecy and self-enclosure which would simultaneously preserve the dynamic character of sex, especially as English society was still dominated by Victorians, the 'grey elderly ones' of the last century, 'the eunuch century, the century of the mealy-mouthed lie'. This last emphasis gave Lawrence the opportunity of taking issue with an article on censorship which Joynson-Hicks had recently published in the *Nineteenth Century*, and of pointing out that when the police had raided his picture show they had been so confused about what they were doing that they merely took anything where there was 'the actual sight of a fragment of the human *pudenda*'.[23] Lawrence's pamphlet was published on 14 November as number 5 in the 'Criterion Miscellany' series, Faber and Faber having previously arranged that a rival pamphlet by Joynson-Hicks (*Do We Need a Censor?*) should appear in the same month as number 6. The resulting 'stir' gratified him and he was especially pleased when his own contribution not only sold very well but better than his rival's attempt to explain and justify his recent conduct as Home Secretary (vii. 588, 589).

Wednesday 11 September 1929 was Lawrence's forty-fourth birthday. He was disappointed and surprised that the only people from whom he received greetings were the Brewsters ('Even my sisters forgot me this time'). Their letters and presents made him keener than before that he should have them as neighbours sometime during the coming winter (vii. 478, 481, 482). His intention was still to spend the next few months somewhere in Tuscany, and he planned to travel down to Florence via Venice where he could meet the Trotters who were about to embark on a European holiday. He felt that the exhibition had left both parties with a lot to discuss and settle, face to face. At the last minute, however, the Trotters cancelled this arrangement (tentative in their minds but firm in his) because it did not fit with their plans to visit the castle of Phillip Trotter's business partner in Hungary.[24] Lawrence had felt many times before that Dorothy in particular was unreliable and he exploded with anger, sending them a letter which is now lost but whose first paragraph Phillip Trotter describes as almost reminiscent of 'the relation-severing letter to Bertrand Russell, and the "spit in the face" to Katherine Mansfield'.[25] By the time he wrote to them again on the 16th, after having now received both a letter and a cheque for the few of his paintings which had been sold, Lawrence had calmed down, although he did complain again, in partial explanation of his recent fury, that they never minded leaving him to dangle 'in the thin space of uncertainty, for indecent lengths of time' (vii. 489).

With the Trotters no longer available there was no need to pass through Venice but by the 16th Lawrence had in any case changed his plans. 'The doctors and everybody', he had written to Orioli on 14 September, 'urge that I should *not* go to Florence but to the sea, and insist that if Bandol suited me so well all winter, I should go back there. So I give in, and will go to Bandol straight from here' (vii. 480). This may well be an accurate record of the form the discussion took but, given the predilection Lawrence had already made clear, it is more likely that it was Frieda who gave in, having taken into account what was now her husband's highly critical state. The Lawrences left Rottach on 18 September intending to look for a house in Bandol or, if not there, then in Cassis, a few miles along the coast towards Marseilles.

III Bandol Again

Lawrence had kept in regular contact with Brett since her return to New Mexico in May 1926, but during recent months the relationship had become unusually strained because of confusion and difficulty over his manuscripts and typescripts. Reminded of the potential value of these by Harry Crosby, he had no plans for selling more immediately; but he was nevertheless anxious that as many as possible should be preserved. Careless in the past about what happened to them, he had now come to realise that they could well provide protection against possible hard times ahead, or insurance for Frieda in the increasingly likely event of his death occurring before hers. His problem was to find out where they all now were, and then take the necessary measures to ensure they would not be damaged, lost or stolen in the future.

Lawrence knew that he had left many of them in a small cupboard on the ranch. The experiment of Brett living at Kiowa with Rachel Hawk and her children had lasted only a short time, and she was now there often on her own. At the best of times he had very little confidence in her powers of stewardship, feeling that her irresponsibility (in financial matters especially) sometimes came close to dishonesty. Although he had no very clear memory of the transaction, he accepted that he must at some point have given to Brett the manuscript which he heard she had sold in New York the previous winter; but he became alarmed when Mabel Luhan suggested to him that it might be only the first of several.[26] From Forte dei Marmi he had written a business-like letter to Brett in which he asked her to make a list of the manuscripts at the ranch, have it checked and verified by both Mabel and the local bank manager, send him a copy of the list and then put the manuscripts in one of the bank's safety-deposit boxes under his name (vii. 342–3). Her delay in responding made him nervous and drove Frieda to send Brett three wildly abusive letters in which she accused her of dishonesty and swore that her wish to buy the ranch would never be granted, even if she could somehow raise the necessary money.[27] When the list did arrive Lawrence was dismayed by what seemed to him large gaps. In a letter he wrote to Brett from Rottach on 12 September, he assumed that he had been robbed and, although he stopped short of accusing Brett of being herself the thief, it was only just. Looking down the list, he said, he was amazed to see that 'nearly all the hand-written manuscripts must have disappeared'. If she felt all those she had typed for him at the ranch should be hers, that was surely going 'a bit far'; but in any case he suspected she was hiding something from him, and he hated the idea that 'things aren't straight'. 'You have written so much about loyalty', he went on, 'And if an MS has been stolen, I am not one to break my heart. – But there is more than that' (vii. 475). A few days later however, Lawrence learned that most of the manuscripts not on Brett's list were in the Curtis Brown office in New York.[28] Not having time to write from Rottach, he sent Brett a postcard with the good news as he passed through Munich on the 19th ('so glad'), and wrote to her fully from the south of France ten days later. Unlike Frieda, he had left himself just enough room to be able to say: 'Of course I knew quite well you would not sell my MSS, in spite of what anybody said. But your visitors are another matter: same as anyone's visitors. – And the MSS I gave you, of course you do as you like with. Only I wish you'd tell me' (vii. 505).

The postcard to Brett shows that the Lawrences were in Munich on the 19th but they did not arrive in Bandol until 23 September. This suggests that from Marseilles they had looked around in Cassis but not found anything which suited them. Lawrence was enormously relieved to be back again by the Mediterranean, away from 'the tensions of the north'; and he was particularly pleased by the warm reception he received at the Hotel Beau Rivage: 'so nice, such welcomings' (vii. 491, 492). During his last stay there he had developed good relations with the proprietress, Mme Douillet, and in a letter to Catherine Carswell back in August had cited her, along with the Mirenda peasants and the man who had delivered his mail at Kesselmatte, as examples of ordinary people who showed a genuine liking for his paintings: 'It never occurred to any of them to be shocked.

Yet people who called themselves my dear friends were not only shocked but *mortally offended* by them. But they were just bourgeois' (vii. 418–19).

He would have been perfectly happy to settle in again at Beau Rivage (vii. 493) but, frustrated in her efforts on so many other occasions, Frieda immediately found them a house. The Villa Beau Soleil was very different from the houses the Lawrences had usually lived in. A six-roomed bungalow in a faintly art-deco style, it was part of that rash of modern development along the French Riviera he had previously deplored. When in the middle of October, and at Lawrence's express invitation (vii. 494), the Brewsters came from Capri to spend the winter close to him and Frieda, Achsah was distressed by its ugliness, both outside and in – like Frieda (vii. 537), she attributed its 'heliotrope-tinted walls and gold-framed mirrors' to the house having once been the home of a kept woman.[29] Visiting the Lawrences briefly with Orioli at the beginning of the new year, Norman Douglas would be no more impressed and would later refer to Beau Soleil as 'one of those dreadful little bungalows built of gaudy cardboard – there may have been one or two bricks in it as well – which grow up overnight, like a disfiguring eruption, along that coast'.[30] Contradicting this idea of flimsiness, but not of functional ugliness, Lawrence himself called his new home a 'rather hard square box' (vii. 537).

Without architectural distinction, the Lawrences' house was nonetheless in a fine position, at the inside tip of a spit of land in the irregular western curve of the bay. A pine grove behind protected it from wind off the sea and alongside was a whole field of late-blooming yellow narcissi. From the room in which Lawrence chose to sleep he could lie in bed and watch the movement of the waves. Now more than ever concerned to adapt his own rhythm of life to nature's, he never closed the shutters or drew the curtains.[31] It was a house on the town water supply and came with a *femme de ménage* whose cooking he found not only excellent but also, after Germany, agreeably light (vii. 532). Above all, it boasted central heating. This broke down on one occasion (vii. 580) and, with his commitment to naturalness in all things, Lawrence would come to regret the absence of fire in an open hearth.[32] For a man in his condition, continuous and reliable warmth at all periods of the day was nevertheless a godsend. For the first time the Lawrences were in a house (rather than a hotel) which had 'all the conveniences'. They moved in on 1 October and engaged to stay until March 1930 (vii. 538, 500).

Lawrence was happier in Bandol than he had been in Germany (even in Rottach) but, as far as his health was concerned, he was still no better. 'It is very lovely', he told Else Jaffe, 'the wind, the clouds, the running sea that bursts up like blossom on the island opposite. If only I was well, and had my strength back! But I am so weak. And something inside me weeps black tears. I wish it would go away'

(vii. 510). Mohr, who had either travelled with the Lawrences from Rottach or followed them down shortly after they left, was in Bandol until 21 October, so Frieda had no immediate need for local medical advice (vii. 534, 532). Her husband had in any case recovered much of his old scepticism about doctors, telling Emily on 4 October that they could do nothing for him and were 'merely a fraud' (vii. 511). It was a measure of how desperate he soon became over his state, however, that by mid-October, when he was 'in bed again' and 'feeling pretty rotten', he could write to Caresse Crosby: 'I expect I shall have to go into a sanatorium for a time, unless I pick up very soon. No use dying just yet' (vii. 530). If Lawrence was at last willing to consider the sanatorium, not for its doctors but as a means of building up his strength again, this did not mean he had accepted the associated idea of pulmonary tuberculosis. When Kot suggested that he should come to England in order to be close to the Mundesley and specialist advice, Lawrence replied that if his health got 'very tiresome', and he did decide to live near a sanatorium, it would be one in the south of France. 'But you see', he added, 'it's quite different supervising lungs, which are straightforward, from supervising what is my real trouble, chronic inflammation of the bronchials and all the breathing passages' (vii. 538).

It was rare now for him to get up before noon so that when he speaks of being 'in bed' he means that he was confined to it all day (vii. 536). And yet he still managed to work. On 3 November he told Martin Secker, 'I neither write nor paint – which I suppose is best for my health' (vii. 553). This is the kind of statement that had deceived Aldous Huxley in the past (and risked doing so a couple of months later when Lawrence told Huxley he was doing 'practically nothing' – vii. 608). The only way to explain it is by positing a distinction in Lawrence's mind between large projects like a novel, that required sustained effort over a relatively long period of time, and the shorter ones which his fluency and undiminished powers of concentration allowed him to deal with quickly. It was with these latter, which, when he wrote to Secker or Huxley, he must have felt did not count, that he was fairly consistently occupied in the last three months of 1929; but that was also the period of some of his greatest poetry as well as of a self-assignment that would eventually result in a short book.

Lawrence had written a sufficient number of short newspaper or magazine pieces in the recent past to begin collecting them together in November for the volume that would appear soon after his death as *Assorted Articles*, a dull alternative title to the 'Orts and Slarts' or 'Chips and Faggots' he had first suggested (vii. 584, 607). In this period there were three more pieces, published too late to qualify for inclusion in the volume. The first, written in bed on the morning of 5 October, was probably 'We Need One Another' (vii. 513). With a title which is in itself a gloss on 'The Man Who Loved Islands', this article begins with what had now become a major emphasis in Lawrence's thinking: the folly of ignoring our inevitable reliance on each other. There is no life without relationship. For him of course the supreme relationship is that between a man and a woman which, to be authentic, requires the true contact of sex. Yet there is a rhythm of change in sex which needs to be embraced: it is 'a changing thing, now alive, now quiescent, now fiery, now apparently quite gone, quite gone'; so that although sex means to Lawrence 'the whole of the relationship between man and woman' he has to recognise that 'at periods, the sex-desire itself departs completely. Yet the great flow of the relationship goes on all the same, undying, and this is the flow of living sex'.[33]

The changing rhythm of sex was very much on Lawrence's mind during October 1929 when one of his additional, small-scale projects was expanding *My Skirmish with Jolly Roger* into *A Propos of 'Lady Chatterley's Lover'*. He did this for Stephensen whose anxiety to secure for the Mandrake Press what became a much longer defence of the novel may well have been connected with the commercial success of *My Skirmish* in America. Dispatched to Pollinger on 1 November (vii. 549), it is in a section Lawrence decided to omit from his final text that *A Propos* is closest to the concluding passages in 'We Need One Another'. 'What a downfall', Lawrence writes in this cancelled section, 'when woman longed for a perpetual lover, instead of a husband! . . . What terrible impoverishment of life, sameness, perpetual loverdom!'

Oh! let us get back into the bigger connections. Man is a river of blood, woman is a river of blood, and the phallus makes the connection. But the rivers go their way, the phallus ceases to be, and for a time again the connection is a subtle harmony in apartness, a ripple through space. Until, in the sway of the rhythm of we know not what, the rivers draw near again, and there is a new connection, the phallic touch, and still one more renewal of two beings. But unless there is a sway apart there is no sway together, unless there is the subtle flow of revulsion, away, away, there is no delicate compulsion into a fresh togetherness, and a fresh newness of being. That is the life of man and woman.[34]

In the parts of *A Propos* that were published, Lawrence continues his argument from *My Skirmish* by insisting that there is an absence of genuine feeling and therefore of genuine sexual contact in the modern world; and he mocks George Bernard Shaw for a recent appearance as a spokesman for modern, 'enlightened' attitudes to sex. In a speech on 13 September of which Lawrence must have read a report, Shaw had seemed to scoff at the Pope's objections to the way women were dressing in the 1920s and suggested that, in all matters sexual, it would make more sense to consult Europe's chief prostitute rather than her chief priest.[35] But in Lawrence's view Catholicism, in the Mediterranean countries at least, had retained a proper understanding of sex, having always understood it as the foundation of marriage which was in its turn the real basis of the Church. His lyrical praise of indissoluble marriage – 'perhaps the greatest contribution to the social life of man made by Christianity' – would seem incongruous in reflections on *Lady Chatterley's Lover* did he not then go on to insist that marriage needed to be based on blood rather than mind ('nearly all modern sex is a pure matter of nerves, cold and bloodless'), and to possess a rhythm 'that matches the rhythm of the year'. To rediscover those rhythms there was a need for rituals which would take us back beyond Plato, the Buddha and Jesus, three great leaders who had introduced tragedy into the world by stressing the separation of mankind from his material environment. 'Today', Lawrence wrote, 'is already the day after the end of the tragic and idealist epoch.'[36] When on 15 October Lawrence told Stephensen that he was expanding *My Skirmish with Jolly Roger*, he said that what he was writing gave 'a sort of key to the whole novel – the basic idea' (vii. 531). Yet as so often in his discursive writing, although what he now wrote was closely related to certain aspects of *Lady Chatterley's Lover*, it also looked forward to what would surely have been important new emphases in his work, had there still been far to look.

A Propos is substantial, four times the length of *My Skirmish with Jolly Roger*. It must have meant a busy October; but by 4 November Lawrence had completed two more magazine articles;[37] and three days later he had also sent to Nancy Pearn a lively review of V. V. Rozanov's *Fallen Leaves*, in a translation by Koteliansky (vii. 556).[38] For a desperately sick man, all this writing – lucid, interesting, distinctive – was already an impressive achievement. Yet it was accompanied by two other kinds of composition, less obviously occasional and more consonant with his state of health. One of these derived from a renewed contact with Frederick Carter, the writer/illustrator whose work on the Book of Revelation Lawrence had received when he was in Chapala, and at whose house in Shropshire he had stayed at the beginning of January 1924.[39] He had lost touch with Carter after his return to Europe from Taos but heard of him again through Titus (separated from his wife, Carter now spent a lot of time in Paris). They began to correspond again while Lawrence was last in Baden-Baden (vii. 444), and the idea of a collaboration which would help to get more of Carter's work on Revelation into print was revived. In Bandol Lawrence began preparing himself to write on the subject with a degree of intellectual energy in moving contrast to his physical condition.

He read four manuscripts Carter sent him and the book he had published in 1926 entitled *The Dragon of the Alchemists* (vii. 519, 555). Disappointed that none of these seemed to have quite the magic of the text he had seen in Chapala, he expressed severe criticism of Carter's drawing, which he felt to be too Greek and Jewish in inspiration: 'What fascinates you essentially' he wrote, in phrases perhaps more applicable to himself than his correspondent, 'is the great pagan vision of the eastern Mediterranean, pre-Athenian. I wonder you don't take your inspiration from that world – the Mycenean, Cretan, Etruscan things' (vii. 508).

Yet even in Carter's latest treatment the Book of Revelation continued to fascinate him. He read through the Bible in a modern translation (as far as the New Testament was concerned in the version by James Moffatt published in 1913),[40] and also consulted the two dense volumes of R. H. Charles's *Critical and Exegetical Commentary on the Revelation of St John*. Reminding himself of what Hesiod and Plutarch had to say on cosmogony, he tackled Dean Inge on Plotinus, *Five Stages of Greek Religion* by Gilbert Murray, the *Book of Enoch*, and at least one French book – Alfred Loisy's *L'Apocalypse de Jean*.[41] In addition, Lawrence asked Kot to send him the copy of John Burnet's *Early Greek Philosophers* which he had bought when he was last in London (vii. 518). This book had altered his whole intellectual landscape in 1915, providing him with a vital insight into a pre-Socratic world; and he used it now both as an aid to a reading of Revelation and as the chief source or inspiration for nine epigraphs he had been asked to provide for each section of a new edition of *Birds, Beasts and Flowers* which was to have illustrations by a young artist who had been a contemporary of Barby's at art school, Blair Hughes-Stanton.[42]

What distressed Lawrence particularly about his growing weakness was that it prevented him from walking. 'My health is better', he would optimistically assure Orioli on 9 December, 'but I can't *walk*. I just can't' (vii. 588); and Frieda reported later how it was 'pure agony' for him 'walking to the corner of the little road by the sea, only a few yards!' But in Lawrence there was no necessary correlation between physical and mental frailty, which may be just a small part of what Frieda meant when she said that he was always able to maintain his dignity.[43] He approached matters apocalyptic with a characteristic enthusiasm and vigour, inviting Carter to spend the second half of November at the Beau Rivage as his guest, so that they could discuss the finer points (vii. 562). This visit must have helped to show him just how divergent their interpretations were so that when, by the end of the year, Lawrence had completed what amounted to his own book on Revelation, he had to put it entirely on one side in order to write a 5,000-word introduction to Carter's interpretations in fulfilment of his original promise to help these into print. Describing the imaginative release into the 'grand fields of the sky' which Carter's original manuscript had given him when he first received it in Chapala, Lawrence regretted that now his work had become 'more – more argumentative, shall we say', and admitted that he could not 'see eye-to-eye with Mr. Carter about the Apocalypse itself'. Yet he praised the book as at least a step towards a new vision and a new knowledge, one less dependent on linear logic and scientific modes of thinking.[44]

The need for new ways of thinking had become an important emphasis in his own book. By insisting on it, he was continuing to develop what was already implicit in the well-known poem he must have written a few weeks before, while he was still in Germany:

Thought, I love thought.
But not the niggling and twisting of already existent ideas
I despise that self-important game.
Thought is the welling up of unknown life into consciousness,
Thought is the testing of statements on the touchstone of the conscience,
Thought is gazing on to the face of life, and reading what can be read,
Thought is pondering over experience, and coming to a conclusion.
Thought is not a trick, or an exercise, or a set of dodges,
Thought is a man in his wholeness wholly attending.[45]

'Thought' occurs towards the end of the second notebook Lawrence had been using for his verse. The beginning of a third is roughly coincident with his move to Bandol. This third and last notebook opens with four poems which describe how those parts of the Mediterranean Lawrence could see from his bedroom window conjure up before his mind the old, Homeric world of Greek seafarers, despite the occasional glimpse of a modern ocean liner 'leaving a long thread of dark smoke / like a bad smell'.[46] Next come a number of poems in which he attempts to define the world's creative principle and which include a characteristic insistence that, 'There is no god / apart from poppies and the flying fish, / men singing songs, and women brushing their hair in the sun.'[47] All those poems could still be regarded as pansies or nettles, but they tend to be longer now and more consistently sombre in tone, so that Aldington was perhaps justified in believing that with this third notebook there is a new and different category of composition.[48] An 'Invocation to the Moon', in which Lawrence begs the goddess to give him back his 'lost limbs', and set him again on his 'moon-remembering feet', is related to the reading of ancient cosmologies in which Lawrence was now engaged: in the 'great pagan religions of the Aegean, and Egypt and Babylon', he told Carter at the end of October, it is 'Mother Moon who gives us our body' (vii. 545); but his interest in whatever would throw light on Revelation is more directly reflected in the poem entitled 'Anaxagoras' (one of Burnet's pre-Socratic philosophers).[49] There is now a preoccupation with religious matters, but also the pervasive concern with death already evident in Rottach. Achsah Brewster records an occasion when Lawrence told her and Earl that he had been writing 'some verses about death' and offered to read them out, 'then, shaking his head wistfully, he closed the book, saying, "I can't read them now." '[50]

In the third notebook Lawrence wrote his revised versions of 'Bavarian Gentians' and 'The Ship of Death'. He is likely to have done this in October because both poems precede a cluster of reflections on All Saints' and All Souls' days (1 and 2 November). The haunting beauty of much of Lawrence's poetry at this time is hard to illustrate briefly, but 'After All Saints' Day' (which reworks effectively lines from the first version of 'The Ship of Death') at least suggests the prevailing tone.

Wrapped in the dark-red mantle of warm memories
the little, slender soul sits swiftly down, and takes the oars
and draws away, away, towards dark depths
wafting with warm love from still-living hearts
breathing on his small frail sail, and helping him on
to the fathomless deeps ahead, far, far, from the grey shores
of marginal existence.[51]

Lawrence had always said that the dead lived on in the memory of their loved ones; but the way he had sometimes referred to being haunted by his mother, and translated his guilt at her death into a notion of her soul wandering unexpiated in some undefined region, could sometimes suggest that, for all his constant denials of 'spirit', he believed that there was an after-life. Whether or not he did is a topic on which any biographer is likely to pronounce with trepidation. At least twice in the past Lawrence had appeared to commit himself quite explicitly to belief in the existence of a location where the dead foregather, which was not strictly synonymous with the mind of a surviving friend or relative.[52] More often he had recognised, consciously or unconsciously, that to do this lent support to that dichotomy between body and soul which he felt had bedevilled his own culture, and which he fought against so strenuously. The issue is complicated by the highly personal view he took of dying. For Lawrence, any worthwhile life was punctuated by a series of deaths from which one rose again renewed, and these episodes of renewal were conflated in his own experience with occasions when he had been close to actual physical extinction and lived to tell the tale. Both varieties of experience implied a continuity of death and recovery, the terms of which could never be known beforehand. In which case, Lawrence appears sometimes to hint, the possibility that there was a form of recovery or resurrection which completely transcended our normal experience and understanding could not positively be excluded, even when all the traditionally Christian notions of an after-life could. As he explores these matters in his last poems one of his difficulties is an inevitable reliance on words and images from which traditional concepts are impossible to expel entirely. In one of the re-written versions of 'The Ship of Death', the 'oblivion' to which so many of the final poems yearningly refer is followed by the appearance of a 'horizontal thread / that fumes a little with pallor upon the dark', and the body 'like a worn sea-shell / emerges strange and lovely' before the 'frail soul steps out, into her house again / filling the heart with peace'.[53] Someone who read these lines out of context might well wonder whether they do not represent the return of the black sheep to the fold, and be tempted to imagine that, with death approaching, Lawrence sought consolation in the religious culture which had meant so much to him in his childhood and youth. That this is highly unlikely to have been the case is evident from 'Shadows' which comes only two poems before the end of the third notebook, and is in all probability therefore almost the last, substantial poem Lawrence wrote. To quote from it briefly would not throw sufficient light on one of the more complicated aspects of his thinking, and nor would it do enough to support the contention that, if these so-called last poems had been Lawrence's only publication, they would have been sufficient to ensure that he was not easily forgotten. When 'Bavarian Gentians' or 'The Ship of Death' are inevitable candidates for inclusion in any anthology of poems that deal with death, then so also is, or should be, 'Shadows':

> And if tonight my soul may find her peace
> in sleep, and sink in good oblivion,
> and in the morning wake like a new-opened flower
> then I have been dipped again in God, and new-created.
>
> And if, as weeks go round, in the dark of the moon
> my spirit darkens and goes out, and soft strange gloom
> pervades my movements and my thoughts and words
> then I shall know that I am walking still
> with God, we are close together now the moon's in shadow.
>
> And if, as autumn deepens and darkens
> I feel the pain of falling leaves, and stems that break in storms
> and trouble and dissolution and distress
> and then the softness of deep shadows folding, folding
> around my soul and spirit, around my lips
> so sweet, like a swoon, or more like the drowse of a low, sad song
> singing darker than the nightingale, on, on to the solstice
> and the silence of short days, the silence of the year, the shadow,
> then I shall know that my life is moving still
> with the dark earth, and drenched
> with the deep oblivion of earth's lapse and renewal.
>
> And if, in the changing phases of man's life
> I fall in sickness and in misery
> my wrists seem broken and my heart seems dead
> and strength is gone, and my life
> is only the leavings of a life:
>
> and still, among it all, snatches of lovely
> oblivion, and snatches of renewal
> odd, wintry flowers upon the withered stem, yet new, strange flowers
> such as my life has not brought forth before, new blossoms of me –
>
> then I must know that still
> I am in the hands of the unknown God
> he is breaking me down to his own oblivion
> to send me forth on a new morning, a new man.[54]

519

Earl Brewster noted that whereas in Kesselmatte Lawrence had told the Brewsters' Brahmin friend Mukerji that 'God was an exhausted concept', he now said his attitude had changed and it was with God he wanted to establish a conscious relationship.[55] Yet the God to which Lawrence pledges allegiance in all his prose and poetry of this period is never an anthropomorphic deity, some presence behind or beyond what we experience here, but more akin to a pagan or animist creative force not simply 'manifest' in the universe but identical with it. Here 'God' is the word for that cycle of 'lapse and renewal' with which Lawrence movingly hopes to remain associated. Trusting himself entirely to this power, he cannot know what kind of 'new man' he will become, and it may be, therefore, that the possibility remains open of a newness beyond ordinary human experience. To attempt to conceive what this would be other than in ordinary human terms, however, would have been an affront to his religious materialism. If there is a next world, then there is nothing useful that can be said about it in this. The overwhelming tendency in all Lawrence's last writings is to remain courageously agnostic on the issue (what after all can we know?), and to resist any consolation which was not physically grounded. 'Never', says Earl Brewster in a remark highly significant for an understanding of Lawrence's psychology if not his beliefs, 'did he give me the impression that he thought his recovery doubtful.'[56]

IV Christmas at Beau Soleil

Mme Douillet had good reason to like the Lawrences. Although they might, on this their second stay in Bandol, have withdrawn their own custom earlier than she would have preferred, Lawrence's presence attracted a stream of visitors to her hotel. For reasons which are not clear, Mohr stayed in a rival establishment called Les Goëlands (vii. 501); but Lawrence put Carter up at Beau Rivage and the Brewsters stayed there many weeks as they explored the area for a house in which they could spend the winter. He took a keen interest in their search, joining them when he could in car excursions that impressed upon him the beauty of the surrounding countryside (vii. 558). Eventually, in the middle of November, they settled on a property known as the Château Brun, which stands on a hill four miles from Bandol a few hundred yards off the road to Saint Cyr (vii. 566). Although it is much smaller and less imposing than its name implies, Lawrence took revenge for Achsah's disparaging remarks about his own bungalow by making mild fun of her ambitions to be a *châtelaine* (vii. 566). He nevertheless admired the solid, three-story house they had found and was struck by its cheapness, only 2,500 francs for the whole year, whereas Beau Soleil was 1,000 francs a month (vii. 500). But apart from the usual disadvantages of 'no light nor bath nor water-closet – and water from wells' (vii. 560), the Château Brun came without furniture and the Brewsters' financial affairs were such that they had to wait for money to arrive from America before they could buy any. As a result they did not move out of Beau Rivage until after Christmas by which time Lawrence had given them a refectory table in teakwood, specially made by a local village carpenter.[57]

He was not sympathetic to the Brewsters in their financial difficulties, telling Emily they had been 'very silly' and Brett that, 'People who don't work, and live in comfortable hotels, shouldn't have money problems' (vii. 593, 594). He was amazed that the first and, for a while, only piece of furniture they acquired was a grand piano (vii. 579). The disapproval represented the careful side of Lawrence that would have pleased his mother; yet at the same time he was scornful of anybody who took money too seriously, and uneasy that he himself now had rather a lot. After the crash on Wall Street in late October, he angrily forbade Frieda from bringing him any news of a number of investments which appeared to have been made in the United States on his behalf.[58] According to Brewster this was in protest at the power of money in modern life; but his refusal to be informed was also an admission of its potential power over him. At some point during this period Frieda remembered Lawrence saying to her, 'I shan't die a rich man now', as if his mother's ambitions for him had never been abandoned entirely; but then he added, 'perhaps it's just as well, it might have done something to me.'[59]

Carter became Mme Douillet's customer and the Brewsters' presence brought the Di Chiaras from Capri to Beau Rivage. They arrived at the beginning of December around the same time as Ida Rauh, now finally separated from Andrew Dasburg and wintering in Europe (vii. 588). Talking with Ida increased Lawrence's feeling that he would never get better where he was ('Europe gets me into an inward rage, and keeps my bronchials hellish inflamed', he told Bynner – vii. 574), and that his only hope lay in a return to New Mexico. He worried about the difficulties there might be with immigration and, feeling that a six-month visa would not do, seriously pondered the problem of having himself put on the immigration quota (vii. 628) when those around him were becoming increasingly convinced that he was not only unfit to travel now, but never would be. He wrote several times of going to see the American consul in Marseilles and wondered whether he and Frieda might not sail from there to San Francisco on one of the ships of the Dollar line, so called after its founder Captain Robert Dollar and not because it was especially cheap (vii. 617). In his imagination, the trip to America seems to have become associated with the voyage to a new life in 'The Ship of Death'.

It was as a result of talking with Ida Rauh shortly after Christmas that Lawrence explained to Mabel Luhan what became his last ideas for an ideal community, for Rananim. They had been making plans to come back to the ranch and live near one another, he wrote, and perhaps having a sort of old school, like the Greek philosophers, talks in a garden, that is, under the pine trees. I feel I might perhaps get going with a few young people, building up a new unit of life out there, making a new concept of life. Who knows! we have always talked of it. My being ill so long has made me realise perhaps I had better talk to the young and try to make a bit of a new thing with them, and not bother much more about my own personal life. Perhaps now I should submit, and be a teacher. I have fought so against it. (vii. 616)

An additional difficulty in going back to New Mexico was his wife's hostility to Brett, especially after what had been said in Frieda's three recent letters about the manuscripts. But Lawrence decided that much of her anger was illusion and, as for himself, he was too weak to quarrel (vii. 617). In any case, 'though I am perhaps *more* irascible, being more easily irritable, not being well, still, I think I am more inwardly tolerant and companiable' (vii. 616).

The letters tend to confirm this diagnosis. Hardly anyone now escapes a malicious reference but the malice is very much passing and superficial. Carter remembered that Frieda called it 'spite' and he describes how her request to her husband not to be spiteful merely egged him on so that,

only the more sinister was the curious high whinny of a laugh that he gave when he had achieved the droll revelatory traits of character in his tale. A feminine-sounding laugh it was too, near to a cackle and old-maidish. Uncontrolled, something of sharp disappointment burst out in it, and of malice; ungenial it was, as it something baffled and sterile cried out in him.[60]

At the same time Carter admitted that Lawrence had a 'remarkable feeling for the natural grotesque' in people, and that his observation of others was penetrating and accurate. Nor was malice or spite all he remembered. Visiting Beau Soleil every day for tea during his November stay, he recalled Lawrence happily singing folk songs with the Brewsters – by 10 October Frieda had already made sure she had a piano (vii. 524). Although Lawrence had enough breath for that, in conversation his remarks would sometimes die away with 'a kind of sighing aspiration'. What distressed Carter more however, and what he found most difficult to 'pass over without alarm and even horror', was Lawrence's 'incessant spitting'. Once he was used to someone's presence, he would cough slightly with an 'apologetic throat sound' and then spit carefully into the used envelopes he carried: 'In his jacket pocket he kept them, and they were folded up when used and neatly returned into his pocket again.' Lawrence would discuss his illness, Carter went on, 'as if it were due to throat trouble from a bronchial cold – a weakness of the bronchial tubes that was difficult to overcome – and to get rid of; and it was tiresomely liable to recur. Only that, nothing more.'[61]

It was as Christmas approached that Lawrence heard of Harry Crosby's death in

New York (vii. 600). On a trip back home with Caresse, one ostensible reason for which was the annual Harvard–Yale football game, he had been reunited with one of his many mistresses, a recently married socialite. Shortly afterwards he had shot her before shooting himself in what seemed like a suicide pact.[62] Lawrence's response to the news filtered into his writing on Revelation where he says that 'lovers who shoot themselves in the night, in the horrible suicide of love' have been driven mad by the 'poisoned arrows of Artemis: the moon is against them';[63] but he was shocked as well as distressed. To throw away the precious gift of life seemed to him perverse and, in his current state of thinking especially, irreligious. There had been one brief moment during the war when he had toyed with the idea of killing himself; but in general his attitude to suicide was sternly disapproving and consistent with his having once described it as a 'final act of egotism and vanity' (ii. 335, 247). Although in 'The Ship of Death' he had reflected on suicide – rejecting it on the grounds that Hamlet's 'bare bodkin' could never in fact lead to anything which resembled 'quietus' – and although Barby records how he told her in Bandol (with perhaps Harry Crosby in mind) that his nights had now become so awful, 'At two in the morning, if I had a pistol I would shoot myself', there is no evidence to suggest that killing himself had ever been a *serious* option during the recent months of depression and misery consequent on his illness.[64] Crosby had been in excellent physical health and, explaining to Orioli on 18 December that Caresse was now on her way back to Europe 'with the ashes (his only) in a silver jar', Lawrence concluded that her husband had 'always been *too* rich and spoilt: nothing to do but commit suicide. It depressed me very much' (vii. 601).

On 19 December Harwood Brewster was expected, after her first term at Dartington Hall, the progressive English public school in Devon where she had gone with the eventual hope of becoming a doctor – 'qualify quickly and cure my asthma', had been Lawrence's response when she had initially declared her intentions (vii. 427). By then he had received two Christmas hampers from his sisters who were both making plans to visit him early in the new year. This would give Frieda, Lawrence later explained to them, the opportunity of going to Baden-Baden to see her mother (vii. 621–2). Whether or not Frieda's intention was only to see her mother, there was certainly considerable strain in looking after a man as sick as Lawrence, and it was reasonable to expect that she would at some point need a break. She records how, when she characteristically upbraided him for not getting better while all the natural things around him were flourishing, he replied, 'I want to, I want to, I wish I could.' In the past her no-nonsense approach, and her refusal to treat him as an invalid, had usually had a bracing effect; but now, after she had slept alongside him at his request ('all night I was aware of his aching inflexible chest, and all night he must have been so sadly aware of my healthy body beside him'), she came to the conclusion that there was nothing more that she could do.[65] Sensing this, and long familiar with that instinctive repugnance in Frieda for the weak and unhealthy which he had dramatised in the character of Ursula, Lawrence began to feel that his wife now viewed him with physical distaste. As he would put it to Barby, 'Your mother is repelled by the death in me.'[66]

The day of Harwood's arrival from England coincided with what Lawrence later described as nothing less than the 'tragedy' of the goldfish (vii. 608). At the beginning of their stay in Beau Soleil, the Lawrences had acquired a young cat which, having abandoned its own home, 'howled like a lion on the terrace' to be let into theirs (vii. 537). A yellow or 'marmalade' colour with a white breast, this animal was variously known as 'Monsieur Beau-Soleil', 'Micky' or 'Mickie Mussolini'.[67] Lawrence became very fond of it and Micky spent much of the day on his bed – although he insisted it must always be put out at night in case it became too comfortable and bourgeois.[68] In the second week of December, a grateful Mme Douillet sent the Lawrences two goldfish in a bowl by the intermediary of her mother, and these became the 'bane of the cat's life' (vii. 590). When on the 19th it finally managed to secure one, despite all the precautions that had been taken, Lawrence was furious. Ignoring Frieda's protest that the cat was only obeying its nature, he spanked it in a manner mildly reminiscent of the Bibbles episode. When Micky not unnaturally twisted round on him 'like a Chinese dragon' (vii. 604), he spanked it again and, complaining that it knew the goldfish were not to be touched, refused to be reconciled to the animal for several days.

Confined to his bed again on 23 December with one of the 'linseed poultices' the *femme de ménage* was expert at preparing – 'My bronchials are really awful', he told Gertler, 'It's not the lungs' – Lawrence hated the idea of Christmas and regretted that Frieda thought any celebration necessary: 'Why make merry when one doesn't feel merry' (vii. 602, 606, 605). Yet Achsah Brewster describes what a good host he was at the party the Lawrences gave on Christmas Eve when he served up the contents of his sisters' Christmas hampers, as well as some lemon tarts he had helped to make, and handed out his carefully selected presents. 'He had painted a clock', she says, 'putting a sun-burst design around the face that – "the sun might never set for us".'[69] On New Year's Day he made the effort to go to lunch with the Di Chiaras – it was to having walked into town and sat down in the 'cutting wind' after this occasion that Achsah Brewster attributed his final decline; and more company for him, as well as more custom for Mme Douillet, arrived at Beau Rivage in January. Orioli and Douglas were briefly in Bandol on 4 January, Pollinger was there for the five days until the 20th, and Titus paid a short visit. Of these, Orioli and Pollinger, and perhaps one or both of the others, would have stayed at the hotel at Lawrence's expense.[70] He felt some embarrassment that the house he was living in was too small to accommodate those who were not members of the family; and with his days in Eastwood now so distant, complained that it was a place where you could hear everybody else brushing their teeth (vii. 591).

On 20 January there arrived also in Bandol Andrew Morland, a young doctor from the Mundesley whom Mark Gertler had got to know. Recently married to a woman who suffered from tuberculosis, he may well have been in the south of France to settle her in for the winter.[71] Kot and Gertler had asked him to make the trip from the Cannes area to see Lawrence who had initially been reluctant, especially when a first suggestion was that he might visit Morland rather than Morland visit him – 'I simply don't want to make a three to four hours' journey to talk with a doctor who will want to talk about lungs when the trouble is bronchials' (vii. 575). Later however, with his condition so obviously worsening, he had agreed to be seen. The examination Morland undertook on the morning of the 20th (vii. 625) convinced him that Lawrence had been suffering from pulmonary tuberculosis for a long time;[72] but he was less concerned by that than a general weakened condition. The X-rays he later saw confirmed his initial impression that here was a man with a strong natural resistance to the disease: 'There was a very extensive scarring but only one tiny cavity';[73] but Lawrence was now so drastically enfeebled that his body was very close to a state where it would not be able to resist any more. Morland thought that he ought really to go into a sanatorium but that otherwise he should impose upon himself complete and absolute rest with no more visitors, and no more writing (vii. 626–7).

Up until Morland's visit Lawrence had indeed been writing, most recently a response to a request from Kot for an introduction to his translation of the chapter in Dostoyevsky's *Brothers Karamazov* entitled 'The Grand Inquisitor', that was being published separately, in a limited edition.[74] Before Harwood Brewster went back to England on 14 January (vii. 621), however, she had finished typing Lawrence's short work on Revelation and, since her departure, he had been busy correcting that (vii. 621).[75] Its 25,000 words (20,000 more of what was probably an early draft were discarded before Harwood began typing[76]) have an intellectual drive and coherence hard to associate with a dying man. Especially striking is their opening characterisation of the unpleasant tone of that part of Revelation most easily attributable to its designated author, John of Patmos. He appears to write, Lawrence suggests, from the position of those who know they will be 'saved', and to manifest not only a rancorous hatred of the wealthy and successful, but a lust for vengeance against them in the hereafter. It was this aspect of the Bible's last book, Lawrence explained, which made it so successful in the non-conformist chapels, appealing to people who could not anticipate enjoying the delights of heaven unless they knew that the wicked, the non-elect, would be simultaneously enduring the torments of hell (preferably in that burning lake which the Book of Revelation was first responsible for introducing into Christianity). The tone he defines so well was for Lawrence quintessentially 'democratic', a consequence of losing the capacity to participate by proxy in splendour – in the old Russia, he claims, 'every peasant was consummated in the old dash and gorgeousness of the nobles'[77] – and of therefore deciding that, since one was not oneself going to enjoy privileges, no-one else would either. A supreme manifestation of this democratic, envious attitude, and a pointer towards a possible apocalyptic future for the whole Western world, he now took to be the Russian revolution.

Yet if Lawrence found the tone which the Jewish author of Revelation often adopts repugnant, and such that it was impossible to associate him with the same John who wrote the Gospel, why did the work as a whole so fascinate him? It was because in his view John of Patmos had been adapting previously existing vision narratives with a long history. The text was obviously a palimpsest and what was both thrilling and valuable was the old pagan substratum. That was full of symbols which, in contrast to the one-to-one correspondences of the less satisfactory allegories characteristic of its more recent levels of composition, could stir the feelings without ever being fully interpreted. Although Lawrence himself was now offering an extensive reading of these symbols, he knew that what he said could never be definitive. It was through clusters of images that must often have included symbols of this kind that people in the remote past developed a mode of non-logical, non-linear thinking that there was now a desperate need to recover. For them,

a thought was a completed state of feeling-awareness, a cumulative thing, a deepening thing, in which feeling deepened into feeling in consciousness till there was a sense of fulness. A completed thought was the plumbing of a depth, like a whirlpool, of emotional awareness, and at the depth of this whirlpool of emotion the resolve formed. But it was no stage in a journey. There was no logical chain to be dragged further.[78]

Lawrence had written about the nature of thinking before, in the introduction to his translation of Verga's *Cavalleria rusticana* as well as in the poem on 'Thought', but his treatment in *Apocalypse* (as his book came to be called) is more developed and detailed than it had been before. It represents the last attempt by a man highly gifted in logical argument to describe an alternative to a reductive, bloodless rationality, a final Romantic protest against the more damaging emotional implications of the Enlightenment.

The great virtue of the ancient symbols one could uncover in Revelation was that they put one back in touch with a pre-Christian, pre-Socratic world where man was still at one with the cosmos: a world which predated the sense of apartness from nature that had led to the creation of gods as necessary intermediaries, and introduced the notion of tragedy. Now that the phase of culture dominated by Plato, Jesus or the Buddha was so clearly over (*'All* our present life-forms are evil'[79]), it was time to go back to the old ways. This would not be regression because 'there are two modes of reversion: by degeneration and decadence; and by deliberate return in order to get back to the roots again, for a new start.'[80] The great religions of the more recent past, and Christianity in particular, were all based on the notion of deferral. There was therefore a need to recover the wonder of living in the present and Lawrence ends his book with phrases which, given when they must have been written, have an especially poignant ring. 'For man', he says, 'the vast marvel is to be alive. For man, as for flower and beast and bird, the supreme triumph is to be most vividly, most perfectly alive'; or again, 'We ought to dance with rapture that we should be alive and in the flesh, and part of the living, incarnate cosmos.'[81]

CHAPTER TWENTY-TWO

◆

January–March 1930

VENCE

In the latter half of January, Else Jaffe spent ten days at Beau Soleil and, responding to appeals for assistance from both the Lawrences, Barby came at the end of the month (vii. 622, 630).[1] Despite the regime of rest that Morland had recommended, and Lawrence had agreed to follow, there was no improvement in his condition. His decline was dramatically evident in his weight which had decreased steadily over the previous months. In February he told Emily that, whereas in the spring he had been 'over seven, nearly eight' stones, he was now 'something over' six (vii. 646). More precisely he told Kot that he weighed 'under 45 kgr. – 90 lb' (vii. 643). For a man who was 5 ft 9 in. tall this was dangerously little and Frieda records how grieved she was to see his 'strong, straight, quick legs gone so thin, so thin'.[2] In late November Brewster had been massaging him every day with medicinal oils and reported to Carter his distress on having to recognise the 'emaciated and martyrized' state of Lawrence's body. In what was perhaps the last example of a comparison that had followed Lawrence for much of his adult life, Brewster described it as 'terrifying in its meagreness, just like . . . one of the haggard, medieval, carved figures of the crucified Jesus'.[3]

One of Lawrence's favourite images of resurrection was the almond tree. In two poems in *Birds, Beasts and Flowers* he had described how, in winter, its branches could appear like 'old, twisted implements', and how miraculous it was therefore to see 'iron break and bud, / . . . rusty iron puff with clouds of blossom.'[4] On 30 January 1930 he reported to Mohr, 'The weather is sunny, the almond trees are all in blossom, beautiful, but I am not allowed any more to go out and see them'; and he told Pollinger, 'Weather sunny – they say all the almond blossom is out, lovely up at the Brewsters. I watch the sea and the white foam' (vii. 633, 634). Deciding for himself that he was clearly not getting any better, Lawrence accepted that he would have to try a sanatorium. With the knowledge of his patient's temperament he would have gleaned from Kot and Gertler, as well as his own observation, Morland had recommended one where the regime was not at all strict but more like living in a hotel with medical supervision (vii. 643).[5] Until quite recently, there were still reference books which claimed that Lawrence died in Venice, but the Ad Astra sanatorium was in Vence, a small, strikingly picturesque town on a hill behind Nice. Telling Frieda to bring his papers to his bed, Lawrence tore many of them up with 'a set face' and made everything 'tidy and neat' before helping to pack his own trunk.[6] On 6 February the Lawrences left the cat with Achsah, entrusted their house to Barby and travelled by train to Antibes with Earl Brewster. There they were met by Barby's young artist friend, Blair Hughes-Stanton, who was living in the area and drove them all to Vence. By the time he arrived, Lawrence was exhausted from having had to walk up and down stairs at Toulon station, as well as from the jolts of the journey, and had to be carried into the Ad Astra in Hughes-Stanton's arms.[7]

In spite of an unpleasant blue on the walls of his room and two steep flights of stairs down to the dining room, which also meant two flights back-up, Lawrence found the sanatorium bearable at first (vii. 645). It pleased him that his room had a balcony from which he could see the coastline near Cannes (vii. 641). Breaking Morland's rule about rest, he began writing a review of *Art Nonsense and Other Essays* by the English artist Eric Gill. Before Frieda persuaded him to abandon it, he had denounced Gill as a 'crude and crass amateur' as far as either writing or systematic thinking were concerned, but praised his belief that 'happy, intense absorption in any work, which is to be brought as near to perfection as possible . . . is a state of being with God, and the men who have not known it have missed life itself.'[8] Mention of God brought him back to the subjects which had been preoccupying him most recently, and to the complaint that even in Catholicism a moral God had been substituted for the old notions of one who was vital and magnificent: 'Only in the country, among peasants, where the old ritual of the seasons lives on in its beauty, is there still some living, instinctive "faith" in the God of Life.'[9] These were phrases particularly characteristic of his concerns in this final period of his life as was the fact that the last of several books he read, or began to read, in Vence was a life of Columbus. He still hoped that in March he would be able to go to America, and when Barby came to join Frieda in Vence some time later, she went into Nice in order to make enquiries about visas for them all.[10]

The general weakness which for Lawrence's doctors at the Ad Astra was the most disturbing aspect of his state, would prove fatal when he now developed pleurisy. The condition brought with it great pain and Frieda, who was staying in a local hotel, left disturbing accounts of the occasional nights she spent on a cane chair in his room. On one of these she was glad that Lawrence was slightly deaf and could not hear, amid all the coughing from young and old throughout the building, the girl next door who called out insistently to her mother, 'Mama, mama, je souffre tant!'[11]

On 24 February H. G. Wells, comfortably installed nearby in the appropriately named town of Grasse, came to see Lawrence and concluded that his illness was chiefly a question of hysteria.[12] Once such an admirer of Wells, Lawrence now thought him a 'common temporary soul' and was far more heartened by the visit of the Aga Khan and his wife, especially as that involved some talk of a future exhibition of his paintings in Paris (vii. 653). This was on the 27th. The day before, the American sculptor Jo Davidson had been to make a clay bust of Lawrence. He had been encouraged to visit by Wells but already had a faint connection with the Lawrence circle through his brother-in-law's marriage to Ida Rauh's sister. In Lawrence's opinion the result of Davidson's efforts was mediocre, and having to pose tired him (vii. 653). When Davidson was back in Paris shortly afterwards and reported on Lawrence's condition to Mrs Harry Payne Whitney (a Vanderbilt before her marriage), she asked him to ring Frieda with an offer to cover any medical expenses that might be required.[13] But by then it was too late, and at the end of February 1930 money was in any case no longer one of Lawrence's problems.

When he first arrived at the sanatorium Lawrence had told Kot that his case was not 'desperate' and Emily that he was in 'no sudden danger' (vii. 643, 646). Now painfully made aware that his condition was not improving, he became impatient, telling Orioli and Earl Brewster on 21 February that the Ad Astra did not suit him and he wanted to move (vii. 650). Responding to his protests, Frieda rented a villa in Vence and on 1 March went to bring Lawrence 'home'. It was the first time she could remember him allowing her to put on his shoes.[14] Waiting at the villa as Lawrence staggered up the few steps of the verandah, supported by the driver of the taxi, were Barby and Ida Rauh. Also present was an English nurse whom Frieda had engaged and whose ministrations, in the short time she had to offer them, made Lawrence impatient even though, in Barby's view, 'she was unobtrusive enough, poor thing'.[15] It was this nurse who in 1937 appears to have sent to the *Evening Standard* a page of doodling which she claimed to have found on his breakfast tray the following morning. In addition to a few odd words and an address, both in hand-writing which suggest the page is authentic, it contains the drawing of a cheerful sun in the top right-hand corner and, diagonally opposite (next to a game of noughts and crosses) a peacock. Top left is a railway engine of the short, stubby variety Lawrence would have remembered from his Eastwood days but, diagonally opposite that, a wryly humorous sketch of a fully clothed, 'laid out' corpse, the feet at one end and the beard at the other, both pointing vertically upwards.[16]

Now the crisis had come, the Huxleys were also on hand. They had been in London for a dramatisation of *Point Counter Point* which had not been especially well received – 'Only Mr. D. A. Clarke-Smith's Rampion', *The Times* commented, 'begins to become a human being';[17] but they now arrived in the south of France to see Lawrence and also find a house for the winter. On his visits to the sanatorium in the previous week, Aldous had been upset to find his friend 'such a miserable wreck of himself and suffering so much pain'.[18] He and Maria spent the night of 1 March at Villefranche, just outside Nice, with Robert Nichols and his wife; but on the afternoon of the 2nd, a Sunday, they came to see

Lawrence at the Villa Robermond, as the house Frieda had rented was then called.[19]

Although he was very weak, Lawrence had been sufficiently calm on the day before to raise the question of re-writing a lost will in which he had left everything to Frieda, but she thought it would tire him too much.[20] By Sunday however, his first full day out of the sanatorium, he was semi-delirious. No longer able to contemplate his own dead body with humorous resignation, he complained, with 'startled brilliant eyes', that he could see it lying on the table opposite his bed, and he asked first Barby and then Frieda to put their arms around him.[21] As Maria Huxley, particularly distressed by the sufferings of someone towards whom she had always felt a special affinity, later cradled his head, he said that her hands were like his mother's. According to her, when Frieda went out of the room for a few minutes, he grasped her wrists and called out, 'Maria, Maria, don't let me die.'[22] As far as she was concerned, these would be Lawrence's last words. Hughes-Stanton told his wife that his last words to Frieda were, 'Wind my watch.'[23]

In acute pain, Lawrence had called for morphine and Barby went with Aldous to fetch a local Corsican doctor, Dr Maestracci, who had seen Lawrence the day before and pronounced his case hopeless. Finding that he was not at home, they went on to the hotel where Frieda had stayed in Vence and asked the proprietor to ring the sanatorium. The doctor there was reluctant to be involved further, because it was Sunday evening or because Lawrence had discharged himself against medical advice; but he was eventually persuaded to come and give a morphine injection. This calmed Lawrence ('if I could only sweat I would be better'[24]) and he seemed to sleep, or at least breathe more peacefully. Barby and Aldous felt that he might nevertheless need more morphine later and set off to see if the Corsican doctor was home yet. Again they were disappointed but when they got back to the villa at eleven o'clock they found it did not matter because Lawrence had been dead for about an hour. From time to time, Frieda had been holding his left ankle, which felt so full of life, but suddenly there had been gaps in his breathing and then, as she put it, 'his face changed, his cheeks and jaw sank, and death had taken hold of him'. When she went into his room shortly afterwards and noticed her husband's slippers still impressed with the shape of his feet, she pulled back the sheet covering his face and felt that all suffering had been wiped from it. In one of Lawrence's earliest short stories ('Odour of Chrysanthemums'), the revision of which is generally taken to signal his entry into that most brilliant phase of his career especially marked by *The Rainbow* and *Women in Love*, the heroine Elizabeth Bates feels that the husband lying dead before her is a man she has never properly known. As Frieda now looked at Lawrence's dead body she similarly felt that he was someone whom she had never before seen or known 'in all the completeness of his being'.[25] If that was true for her how much more true must it have been, and still be, for anyone else.

In 'Odour of Chrysanthemums' Elizabeth Bates and her mother-in-law reverently wash the body of the dead miner in preparation for the arrival of a coffin and the undertakers. Because there is no mention in the records of Frieda participating in these rituals, it is likely that Lawrence was 'laid out' by the nurse who was on hand. He was left in one of the bedrooms of the Villa Robermond, his feet covered by a sheet and his 'Greek satyr's beard sticking up'. With a rapidity characteristic of a time when corpses were kept at home, the funeral was fixed for 4 p.m. on 4 March. Achsah Brewster's memory was of ten people in attendance. Apart from Frieda and Barby, this number would have included the Di Chiaras (who had taken a house in the Nice area), Ida Rauh and of course the Huxleys. Achsah was on her own because her husband had only recently left Europe for a short trip to India, but Robert Nichols came over from Villefranche and we know from a long and informative letter which he wrote to a friend on 8 March that Titus was present.[26] Grief and respect may well have brought him down from Paris but there were also a number of on-going business matters which he would have needed to settle with Frieda.

This was the inner group which gathered at the cemetery as the coffin was lowered into the earth, but it has recently become clear that they were not quite alone. Frank Budgen, a painter who was a friend as well as an early critic of Joyce, was also in Vence at this time, helping to keep up the spirits of a fellow artist, Louis Sargent, who had lung trouble and was being treated by the same Dr Maestracci whom Barby and Aldous Huxley had failed to find at home. It was Maestracci who on 3 March told Sargent of Lawrence's death with the result that he and Budgen immediately sent flowers to the Villa Robermond and on the 4th attended Lawrence's funeral with their wives. Excluding the undertakers, Mrs Budgen counted twenty-two people round the grave. Some of these appear to have been there out of mere curiosity although there may well have been one or two from the local expatriate community who, like Sargent and Budgen themselves, had come because they admired Lawrence's work. Frieda had rejected the local English chaplain's offer to say a few prayers at the graveside so that there was no provision for any kind of ceremony.[27] Once the coffin was in the ground but not yet covered over, Budgen felt the lack: 'one of his near friends might have extolled his virtues and celebrated his achievements and the tempo of the proceedings might have been slowed down to advantage'.[28] According to Nichols, Frieda and one or two others dropped a few flowers on the coffin lid but after the earth had been replaced and the undertakers were arranging the various floral tributes round the grave, Frieda urged Lawrence's friends to take them for themselves and wear small bunches or single blooms in their clothes. Only Maria

Huxley refused to do this. Of those present she was the one whose grief was most manifest, with her face greyish so that 'one could see the blue veins of her temples' and tears continually gathering in her light blue, red-lidded eyes.[29]

Nichols describes the grave as being on the lowest terrace of the cemetery, just before the ground fell away into an orange grove. Standing by it, there was a beautiful view into the valley below and, although the day was overcast, one could glimpse the sea glittering through the haze in the distance.[30] Before the year was out, this impressive spot would be visited by two women who had been very important to Lawrence in his early life. His former fiancée Louie Burrows told Ada that she had made the pilgrimage to Vence to see 'the poor lad's grave', and by at least July 1930 Jessie Chambers had placed anemones on it. The news that he had died reaffirmed Jessie in her conviction that Lawrence had been a 'living manifestation of God', and she recorded that on the morning of the death itself she had heard his voice saying, 'as distinctly as if he had been in the room with me: "Can you remember only the pain and none of the joy?"'[31]

Frieda commissioned two Italian workmen to make a headstone in mosaic of a phoenix, but only a week after the funeral she told Bynner that what she really wanted to do was transport Lawrence's body back to the ranch in New Mexico. The difficulty was, she pointed out, enquiring as she did so about the possibility of selling manuscripts, that she might well be short of the necessary money.[32] Under a British statute of 1925 relating to the property of those who, like Lawrence, had died intestate, she was entitled to £1,000, all her husband's personal belongings, and the interest on the rest of the estate until her death; but after that, and given that her children were not Lawrence's, whatever remained would go to her husband's brothers and sisters or their descendants. In her letter to Bynner she describes Lawrence as having left £4,000 but, when in June she had to apply for a 'letter of administration' which meant that the management of the estate was to be shared between her and Lawrence's least favourite sibling, George, she may have been less concerned about more direct access to the remaining £3,000 than the difficulties she might encounter should she want in the future to sell manuscripts or pictures. Her problems were not resolved until November 1932 when she went to the probate section of the High Court and persuaded the judge that there had once been a will in which everything was left to her. Influential in the judge's decision was that she had already arranged to pay £500 each to Emily and George. Disgusted by what she took to be Frieda's mercenary behaviour, and even more antagonistic to her now than she had been during her brother's life-time, Ada angrily refused to involve herself in these dealings.[33]

Exasperated though Aldous Huxley frequently was by Frieda's volatility and lack of either measure or order in practical affairs ('She had relied *totally* on

Lawrence', he concluded, 'and felt completely lost until she found another man to support her'[34]), he proved a loyal friend during all these legal difficulties. More specifically useful to her was Middleton Murry. In the month after Lawrence's death he had hurried to Vence to pay his last respects, a trip which had eventually involved him in sharing Frieda's bed: 'With her, and with her for the first time in my life,' he later recorded, in reference to this episode, 'I knew what fulfilment in love really meant.'[35] At the hearing in November 1932 he was able to testify that when he and Katherine Mansfield were with the Lawrences in 1914 both the men had agreed they should make wills in favour of their wives. That he could produce his own gave added credence to Frieda's claim that it was this 1914 will which had been lost in one of the Lawrences' several trans-continental moves. For her, the sexual episode with Murry was in the nature of unfinished business (which no ghost rose from the dead to prohibit), and her main involvement was not with him but Ravagli. Once she was in complete possession of her dead husband's estate she felt ready to settle in New Mexico with Ravagli and, because this would of course mean his having to resign his commission, able to pay and keep on paying from her own pocket the proportion of his officer's pay which he was in the habit of allocating to his wife.[36] At Kiowa Frieda and Ravagli lived comfortably enough on her income, selling the occasional manuscript to help with their improvement of the ranch buildings or to provide them with alternative accommodation in warmer climes during the bitterly cold winter months. Arranging to have Lawrence's body cremated and his ashes brought to New Mexico, they had built, on a rise just above the ranch at Kiowa, a memorial chapel in which his remains could lie (like the design of this chapel, the grotesquely comic and often rehearsed circumstances surrounding the transport of the ashes are matters from which admirers of Lawrence are happiest turning their eye[37]). 'Losing' Lawrence, both when he abandoned them and when he died, had been deeply traumatic events for Jessie Chambers and Louie Burrows. Frieda by contrast, cheerfully committed to 'life' and deeply suspicious (as Lawrence had always encouraged her to be) of any feelings which threatened to become morbid, appears to have had little difficulty in reconciling a continuing reverence for her second husband with the entirely different life she enjoyed with the man who would eventually become her third, and she was not inclined to compare the relative affluence Lawrence's works now brought her with the miserable poverty in which several of them had been composed. Only after she had agreed to sell an early version of *Sons and Lovers* with annotations in the hand of Jessie Chambers did she write: 'I hope [the sale] is to a nice person because of the Miriam bits in it. I wish I were rich, then I would have a huge fire of all his Mss, that's what [Lawrence] would have liked, you know he hated the personal touch. But I daresay he wanted me to have the money.'[38] Because Frieda's ability to solve complex moral dilemmas in this way was one of her attractions for Lawrence, one dare say also that he would not have begrudged her the money.

The market for Lawrence manuscripts was to fluctuate a good deal but, if there was one at all, it was because by the time of his death he was so well known. An indication of this is the number of obituaries which rapidly appeared, not only in British and American journals, as well as those in France and Germany, but in publications as geographically distant from each other as the *Illustrated Tasmanian Mail* and the *Canadian Forum*.[39] In many of these there is a recognisable pattern. Attention is drawn first to Lawrence's modest social origins (even in 1930 the number of well-known writers from a genuinely working-class background was very small indeed). Tribute is next paid to his exceptional talents and reservations are then expressed about his preoccupation or, in some accounts, obsession with sex. As far as the last two elements are concerned, this is the pattern epitomised in the title of the biography Aldington was to publish in 1950: *Portrait of a Genius, But* . . . 'Genius' allowed one to avoid the responsibility of thinking too closely about what kind of writer Lawrence was, and the 'but' then permitted a very wide range and degree of qualification.

In a discussion of Lawrence's fellow Midlander Lord Byron, Matthew Arnold followed Goethe in noting how difficult it was to separate Byron's writing from a sense of his personality, and Lawrence's case was similarly to become one in which life and art appeared locked together.[40] By 1930 his fame or notoriety had aroused a curiosity about the author of such controversial books which many of his friends and relatives quickly moved to satisfy. Well before Aldington's biography, and within the five years which followed Lawrence's death, Murry, Ada, Mabel Luhan, Catherine Carswell, Frederick Carter, Brett, Helen Corke, the Brewsters, Frieda and Jessie Chambers had all published memoirs or, in Murry's case, a full biographical account; and interest in Lawrence the man had been both satisfied and increased by Huxley's 1932 edition of his letters. The biographers and memorialists of the 1930s had the inestimable advantage of having known their subject (no-one, says Dr Johnson, who has not eaten and drunk with a man should attempt to write his life[41]), but they still found him a difficult person to define adequately. Six days after Lawrence's death Huxley called him 'the most extraordinary and impressive human being [he] had ever known', but by July he was describing Rampion as 'just some of Lawrence's notions on legs. The actual character of the man was incomparably queerer and more complex than that.'[42]

Part of the difficulty for Huxley was that he had only known Lawrence in the last part of his life and it is clear that the young man about whom Jessie Chambers (for example) wrote so well was not the same as the harried and besieged author of *Women in Love* during the war, or the figure who emerges from those war-time experiences. The difficulty was compounded by Lawrence's commitment to spontaneity: his refusal to live according to some idea he had formed of himself. In two paragraphs from an essay in praise of the novel's ability to avoid 'the ugly imperialism of the absolute' which belong in spirit to the last days at the ranch but were probably written a little later, and which represent very well the qualities of Lawrence's late, discursive style, he writes:

Me, man alive, I am a very curious assembly of incongruous parts. My yea! of today is oddly different from my yea! of yesterday. My tears of tomorrow will have nothing to do with my tears of a year ago. If the one I love remains unchanged and unchanging, I shall cease to love her. It is only because she changes and startles me into change and defies my inertia, and is herself staggered in her inertia by my changing, that I continue to love her. If she stayed put, I might as well love the pepper pot.

In this change, I maintain a certain integrity. But woe betide me if I try to put my finger on it. If I say of myself, I am this, I am that! – then, if I stick to it, I turn into a stupid fixed thing like a lamp-post. I shall never know wherein lies my integrity, my individuality, my me. I *can* never know it. It is useless to talk about my ego. That only means I have made up an *idea* of myself, and that I am trying to cut myself out to pattern. Which is no good. You can cut your cloth to fit your coat, but you can't clip bits off your living body, to trim it down to your idea. True, you can put yourself into ideal corsets. But even in ideal corsets, fashions change.[43]

There are cogent psychological reasons for people not wanting to enquire too closely into their integrity, their individuality, their 'me', especially when, in social life as it is presently organised, they can always rely on their friends, acquaintances or biographers to do that for them. But what biographer would be foolish enough to attempt a definition of D. H. Lawrence's 'me', his essential self? All one can do is try to tell a reasonably complete story and leave the reader to draw his or her own conclusions. As anyone who has ever given a moment's thought to the issue will immediately recognise, this is a potentially disingenuous way of stating an aim or intention. Any story requires the selection of material, a choice of emphases and, to become coherent – to qualify as indeed a story – it is also likely to need a good deal of interpretation. The question as so often in literary matters is one of degree. The particular danger in dealing with Lawrence's last years is that many of the episodes in which he was involved will seem to some so unusual or bizarre that there is a danger of pushing interpretation farther than is necessary for common understanding, and of tipping over into apologia. Aware that many of his readers would have found aspects of the life of his friend Richard Savage strange, Dr Johnson warned that no-one could be its proper judge who had 'slumber'd away their Time on the Down of Plenty'.[44] Of the last decade of Lawrence's life, the years in which he had struggled to define the terms of an entirely new way of life after the cataclysm of the war, it might equally be said that no-one is in a position to judge who had not had some personal experience of that cataclysm, or did not also know what it was to battle against an incurable disease. Yet Lawrence himself would have been impatient with these restrictions and contemptuous of anything which might suggest special pleading. With the same gift for a memorable phrase as Johnson, he had asked in *his* biographical account of a friend, written shortly before he left Europe for Ceylon, 'Who dares humiliate the dead with excuses for their living?'[45] What the dead demanded, he wrote, was not 'praise or exoneration' but 'deep, true justice'. He was sufficiently of the nineteenth century to appeal without embarrassment to such a concept; enough of a modern to know the unlikelihood of a justice that was deep and true ever being secured.

CUE-TITLES AND ABBREVIATIONS

A Letters of Lawrence

(i.) James T. Boulton, ed. *The Letters of D. H. Lawrence*, Volume I. Cambridge: Cambridge University Press, 1979.

(ii.) George J. Zytaruk and James T. Boulton, eds. *The Letters of D. H. Lawrence*, Volume II. Cambridge: Cambridge University Press, 1982.

(iii.) James T. Boulton and Andrew Robertson, eds. *The Letters of D. H. Lawrence*, Volume III. Cambridge: Cambridge University Press, 1984.

(iv.) Warren Roberts, James T. Boulton and Elizabeth Mansfield, eds. *The Letters of D. H. Lawrence*, Volume IV. Cambridge: Cambridge University Press, 1987.

(v.) James T. Boulton and Lindeth Vasey, eds. *The Letters of D. H. Lawrence*, Volume V. Cambridge: Cambridge University Press, 1989.

(vi.) James T. Boulton and Margaret H. Boulton, with Gerald M. Lacy, eds. *The Letters of D. H. Lawrence*, Volume VI. Cambridge: Cambridge University Press, 1991.

(vii.) Keith Sagar and James T. Boulton, eds. *The Letters of D. H. Lawrence*, Volume VII. Cambridge: Cambridge University Press, 1993.

B Works of Lawrence

AA *Assorted Articles*. London: Martin Secker, 1930.

BB *The Boy in the Bush*. With M. L. Skinner. Ed. Paul Eggert. Cambridge: Cambridge University Press, 1990.

E[+ no.] Manuscript [+ no.] listed in Warren Roberts, *A Bibliography of D. H. Lawrence*. 2nd edn. Cambridge: Cambridge University Press, 1982.

FLC *The First Lady Chatterley*. Harmondsworth: Penguin Books, 1973.

Hardy *Study of Thomas Hardy and Other Essays*. Ed. Bruce Steele. Cambridge: Cambridge University Press, 1985.

JTLJ *John Thomas and Lady Jane*. Harmondsworth: Penguin Books, 1973.

K *Kangaroo*. Ed. Bruce Steele. Cambridge: Cambridge University Press, 1994.

LCL   *'Lady Chatterley's Lover' and 'A Propos of Lady Chatterley's Lover'*. Ed. Michael Squires. Cambridge: Cambridge University Press, 1993.

MM   *Mornings in Mexico*. London: Martin Secker, 1927.

P   *Phoenix: The Posthumous Papers of D. H. Lawrence*. Ed. Edward D. McDonald. New York: Viking Press, 1936.

P II   *Phoenix II: Uncollected, Unpublished and Other Prose Works by D. H. Lawrence*. Ed. Warren Roberts and Harry T. Moore. London: Heinemann, 1968.

Poems   *The Complete Poems of D. H. Lawrence*. Ed. Vivian de Sola Pinto and Warren Roberts. Revised edn. Harmondsworth: Penguin Books, 1977.

PS   *The Plumed Serpent*. Ed. L. D. Clark. Cambridge: Cambridge University Press, 1987.

Q   *Quetzalcoatl: The Early Version of 'The Plumed Serpent'*. Ed. Louis I. Martz. Redding Ridge, California: Black Swan Books, 1995.

RDP   *Reflections on the Death of a Porcupine and Other Essays*. Ed. Michael Herbert. Cambridge: Cambridge University Press, 1988.

SCAL   *Studies in Classic American Literature*. London: Martin Secker, 1924.

SEP   *Sketches of Etruscan Places and Other Italian Essays*. Ed. Simonetta de Filippis. Cambridge: Cambridge University Press, 1992.

SMOS   *St. Mawr and Other Stories*. Ed. Brian Finney. Cambridge: Cambridge University Press, 1983.

WWRA   *'The Woman Who Rode Away' and Other Stories*. Ed. Dieter Mehl and Chirsta Jansohn. Cambridge: Cambridge University Press, 1995.

C   Other Printed Works

Brett   Dorothy Brett, *Lawrence and Brett: A Friendship*. London: Secker, 1933.

Brewster   Earl and Achsah Brewster, *D. H. Lawrence: Reminiscences and Correspondence*. London: Secker, 1934.

Britton   Derek Britton, *Lady Chatterley: The Making of the Novel*. London: Unwin Hyman, 1988.

Bynner   Witter Bynner, *Journey with Genius*. London: Peter Nevill, 1953.

DHLR   *D. H. Lawrence Review* (1968–).

EY   John Worthen, *D. H. Lawrence: The Early Years 1885–1912*. The Cambridge Biography, Volume I. Cambridge: Cambridge University Press, 1991.

Frieda   Frieda Lawrence, *"Not I, But the Wind . . ."* Santa Fe: Rydal Press, 1934.

JMM John Middleton Murry, *Reminiscences of D. H. Lawrence*. London: Jonathan Cape, 1933.

LT Mabel Luhan, *Lorenzo in Taos*. New York: Knopf, 1932.

Memoirs *Frieda Lawrence: The Memoirs and Correspondence*. Ed. E. W. Tedlock. London: Heinemann, 1961.

Merrild Knud Merrild, *With D. H. Lawrence in New Mexico*. London: Routledge and Kegan Paul, 1964. (Reissue of the book first published in 1938 under the title, *A Poet and Two Painters*.)

Nehls Edward Nehls, ed., *D. H. Lawrence: A Composite Biography*. 3 volumes. Madison: University of Wisconsin Press, 1957–9.

Parmenter Ross Parmenter, *Lawrence in Oaxaca: A Quest for the Novelist in Mexico*. Salt Lake City: Peregrine Smith Books, 1984.

Rudnick Lois Palken Rudnick, *Mabel Dodge Luhan: New Woman, New Worlds*. Albuquerque: University of New Mexico Press, 1984.

SP Catherine Carswell, *The Savage Pilgrimage: A Narrative of D. H. Lawrence*. Cambridge: Cambridge University Press, 1981. (Reprint of the first 1932 edition.)

TE Mark Kinkead-Weekes, *D. H. Lawrence: Triumph to Exile 1912–1922*. Cambridge: Cambridge University Press, 1996.

Tedlock E. W. Tedlock, Jr, *The Frieda Lawrence Collection of D. H. Lawrence Manuscripts: A Descriptive Bibliography*. Albuquerque: University of New Mexico Press, 1948.

D Manuscript Sources

BL British Library
NCL Nottingham County Library
NWU Northwestern University Library, Evanston, Illinois
OCU (Library of) University of Cincinnati
OkTU (Library of) University of Tulsa
UCB Bancroft Library, University of California at Berkeley
UN University of Nottingham Library
UT Harry Ransom Humanities Research Center, University of Texas at Austin
YU Beinecke Library, Yale University, New Haven, Connecticut.

Appendices

THE WRITING LIFE, 1922–1930: PROSE

Note In the following table, the E-numbers in the third column refer to entries in the manuscript section of the second edition of the Roberts bibliography (Warren Roberts, *A Bibliography of D. H. Lawrence* (Cambridge: Cambridge University Press, 1982)). In Roberts, differing versions of a piece are described by adding letters of the alphabet (a, b, c, etc) after the number. In the interests of clarity a full listing of these variant versions has been omitted here. Full accounts of the textual histories of the texts are given in the introductions to the Cambridge editions of Lawrence's works. Where the manuscript has not yet been allocated an E-number the location of the manuscript is given. The entries in the fourth column are of the significant early publications of these pieces in Britain and America. The final column lists, in the order of publication, important subsequent collections or editions in which these prose works appeared. Volumes in the ongoing Cambridge edition are differentiated by being placed in round brackets.

Additional Cue-Titles for the Letters and Works of D. H. Lawrence

AmWWRA	*The Woman Who Rode Away and Other Stories.* New York: Knopf, 1928.
Apocalypse	*Apocalypse and the Writings on Revelation.* Ed. Mara Kalnins. Cambridge: Cambridge University Press, 1980.
BrWWRA	*The Woman Who Rode Away and Other Stories.* London: Martin Secker, 1928.
CentaurRDP	*Reflections on the Death of a Porcupine.* Philadelphia: The Centaur Press, 1925.
Letters (Huxley)	*The Letters of D. H. Lawrence.* Ed. Aldous Huxley. London: Heinemann, 1932.
LL	*The Lovely Lady.* London: Martin Secker, 1933.
Movements	*Movements in European History.* Ed. Philip Crumpton. Cambridge: Cambridge University Press, 1989.
Plays	*The Complete Plays of D. H. Lawrence.* London: Heinemann, 1965.
POS	*The Princess and Other Stories.* Ed. Keith Sagar. Harmondsworth: Penguin, 1971.

This appendix was prepared by Howard J. Booth.

DATE	TITLE	ROBERTS NUMBER OR LOCATION	EARLY PUBLICATION	COLLECTIONS AND LATER PUBLICATION
Jan.–2 April 1922	Translation of *Mastro-don Gesualdo* by Giovanni Verga	E230.9	New York: Thomas Seltzer, 1923	–
probably by 2 April 1922	First version of the introduction to *Mastro-don Gesualdo* by Giovanni Verga, entitled 'Introductory Note'	E231	–	–
probably by 2 April 1922	'Biographical Note' to *Mastro-don Gesualdo* by Giovanni Verga	E231	In 1923 Seltzer edition	–
3 April– 18 May 1922	Translation of short stories by Giovanni Verga published as *Little Novels of Sicily*	E204	(New York: Thomas Seltzer, 1925)	–
c. 1 June– 15 July 1922; revised between 8 Oct. and 16 Oct. 1922, including new last chapter	*Kangaroo*	E182	(London: Martin Secker, 1923)	(*K*)
Aug.–Sept. 1922	Translation of four stories by Giovanni Verga later included in *Cavalleria rusticana and Other Stories*	E62	In *Cavalleria rusticana and Other Stories* (London: Jonathan Cape, 1928)	–
20 Sept.– 31 Oct. 1922	'Pueblos and an Englishman'; split up and revised as 'Certain Americans and an Englishman', 'Indians and an Englishman' and 'Taos'	–	–	–
20 Sept.–Dec. 1922	'Certain Americans and an Englishman'	E63.3	*New York Times Magazine*, 24 Dec. 1922	*P II*

20 Sept.– ?31 Oct. 1922	'Indians and an Englishman'	E170.8	*Dial*, Feb. 1923; *Adelphi*, Nov. 1923	*P*
20 Sept.– ?31 Oct. 1922	'Taos'	E388	*Dial*, March 1923; as 'At Taos, An Englishman Looks at Mexico', *Cassell's Weekly*, July 1923	*P*
c. 19–20 Sept.–Oct. 1922	'November of the year 1916. A woman travelling from New York to the South west . . .'. Titled 'The Wilful Woman' (by Sagar); 'The Luhan Story' (Tedlock)	E432.6	*The Princess and Other Stories*, ed. Keith Sagar (Harmondsworth, 1971)	(*SMOS*)
by 12 Oct. 1922	Review of *Fantazius Mallare* by Ben Hecht	–	In the form of a letter beginning 'Chère Jeunesse' in *Laughing Horse*, Dec. 1922	*P II*
Nov. 1922– Jan. 1923	*Studies in Classic American Literature*, final versions	E382	(New York: Thomas Seltzer, 1923)	*SCAL*
by 1 Feb. 1923	MS entitled 'The Future of the Novel'	E385.5	As 'Surgery for the Novel – Or a Bomb', *Literary Digest International Book Review*, April 1923 (edited version)	As 'Surgery for the Novel – Or a Bomb' in *P*, (*Hardy*)
after 8 Dec. 1922 – proofs by 25 Feb. 1923	'Model Americans' (Review of *Americans* by Stuart Sherman)	E14.3	*Dial*, May 1923	*P*
April 1923	'Au Revoir USA'	–	*Laughing Horse*, Dec. 1923	*P*
10 May– late June 1923	'Quetzalcoatl'	E313	–	*Q*
13–17 Aug. 1923	Revision of Koteliansky and Mansfield's trans- lation of *Reminiscences of Leonid Andreyev*	–	Published over three issues of the *Dial*, June, July and Aug. 1924	–

28 Aug. 1923	'A Spiritual Record' (Review of *A Second Contemporary Verse Anthology*)	–	*New York; Evening Post Literary Review*, 29 Sept. 1923	P
by 17 Sept. 1923	'The Proper Study'	E326	*Adelphi*, Dec. 1923; as 'The Proper Study of Mankind', *Vanity Fair*, Jan. 1924	P
2 Sept.–14 Nov. 1923; new last chapter, with other revisions, *c.* 9 Jan. 1924	*The Boy in the Bush* (by D. H. Lawrence and M. L. Skinner)	E55	(London: Martin Secker, 1924)	(*BB*)
Nov. 1923	'A Britisher Has a Word With an Editor' (MS entitled 'A Britisher Has a Word With Harriet Monroe')	E57.5	[unsigned] *Palms*, V (Christmas 1923)	Edward Nehls, ed., *D. H. Lawrence: A Composite Biography*, vol. II (Madison: University of Wisconsin Press, 1958), *P II*
Oct.–Nov. 1923	'There is no real battle . . .' (fragment related to 'On Being Religious')	E289	*New Mexico Quarterly*, vol. X (Summer 1951)	(*RDP*)
Dec.–early Jan. 1924	'. . . polite to one another . . .' (fragment perhaps related to 'On Coming Home')	E320.8	–	(*RDP*)
by 24 Dec. 1923	'On Coming Home'	E290	–	*P II*, (*RDP*)
by 24 Dec. 1923	'On Being Religious'	E289	*Adelphi*, Feb. 1924	P, (*RDP*)
24 Dec. 1923–by March 1924	'On Being in Love' (notes for 'On Human Destiny')	E288.5	–	(*RDP*)
24 Dec. 1923–by March 1924	'On Human Destiny'	University of California Los Angeles	*Adelphi*, March 1924; *Vanity Fair*, May 1924	*AA, P II,* (*RDP*)
24 Dec. 1923–spring 1924	'On Being a Man'	University of California Los Angeles	*Vanity Fair*, June 1924; *Adelphi*, Sept. 1924	*AA, P II,* (*RDP*)

After 24 Dec. 1923 (possibly the result of the intention to write two pieces 'On Writing a Book' and 'On Reading a Book')	'Books'	E52	–	P, (RDP)
24 Dec. 1923– early 1924	'On Taking the Next Step'	–	–	(RDP)
by 9 Jan. 1924	'Dear Old Horse: A London Letter'	–	Laughing Horse, May 1924	Letters (Huxley)
by 1 Feb. 1924	'Paris Letter'	–	Laughing Horse, April 1926	P
early version by 19 Feb. 1924; final version by 4 April 1924	'The Last Laugh'	E190	Ainslee's, Jan. 1926; The New Decamoran IV (Oxford: Basil Blackwell, 1925)	BrWWRA, AmWWRA, (WWRA)
by 19 Feb. 1924	Review of The Book of Revelation by Dr John Oman (written under the pseudonym L. H. Davidson)	–	Adelphi, April 1924	P II, (Apocalypse)
by 19 Feb. 1924	'A Letter from Germany'	E197	New Statesman and Nation (Autumn Books Supplement), 13 Oct. 1934	P
Early version post 6 Feb. – final version by 4 April 1924	'The Border-Line'	E53	Hutchinson's Magazine, Sept. 1924; Smart Set, Sept. 1924	BrWWRA, AmWWRA and (WWRA). The latter also includes the alternative ending written in Feb. 1928
after 19 Feb.– April 1924	'Jimmy and the Desperate Woman'	E181	Criterion, Oct. 1924; The Best British Short Stories of 1925 (Boston: Small, Maynard and Co. Inc., 1925)	BrWWRA, AmWWRA, (WWRA)

?late Feb. 1924	'A Pure Witch' (fragment)	–	–	(*WWRA*)
by 20 April 1924	'Indians and Entertainment'	E171	*New York Times Magazine,* 26 Oct. 1924; *Adelphi,* Nov. 1924	*MM*
by 23 April 1924	'Dance of the Sprouting Corn'	E83.5	*Theatre Arts Monthly,* July 1924; *Adelphi,* Aug. 1924	*MM*
May–June 1924	'Pan in America'	E300.5	*Southwest Review,* Jan. 1926	*P*
After 18 May– 7 July 1924	'The Woman Who Rode Away'	E439.5	*Dial,* July and Aug. 1925 (2 parts); *Criterion,* July 1925 and Jan. 1926 (2 parts); also *Best British Short Stories of 1926,* ed. Edward J. O'Brien (New York: Dodd Mead and Co., 1926)	*BrWWRA, AmWWRA,* (*WWRA*)
19–23 June 1924	*Altitude*	E13	*Laughing Horse,* Summer 1938	*Plays*
c. early June 1924 first version; mid/ late June– 13 Sept. 1924	*St Mawr*	E352.6 (MS destroyed in Huxley fire)	*St Mawr together with 'The Princess'* (London: Martin Secker, 1925)	(*SMOS*)
22 Aug. 1924	'Just Back from the Snake Dance – Tired Out'	E181.9	*Laughing Horse,* Sept. 1924	*Letters* (Huxley)
26 Aug.–by 30 Aug. 1924	'The Hopi Snake Dance'	E164	*Theatre Arts Monthly,* Dec. 1924	*MM*
1 Sept. 1924	'The Bad Side of Books' (Introduction to E. D. McDonald's *A Bibliography of the Writings of D. H. Lawrence*)	E36	(Philadelphia: Centaur Bookshop, 1925)	*P*

by 28 Sept. 1924	'Epilogue' to *Movements in European History*	E256	*Movements in European History*, introduction by James T. Boulton (Oxford: OUP, 1971)	*(Movements)*
by 12 Sept. 1924	'Climbing Down Pisgah'	E68.5	–	*P*
late Sept.–8 Oct. 1924	'The Princess'	E322.8	*Calendar of Modern Letters*, March, April and May 1925 (3 parts); *St Mawr* together with 'The Princess' (London: Martin Secker, 1925)	*(SMOS)*
19 Nov. 1924– 2 Feb. 1925	*The Plumed Serpent* (MS entitled 'Quetzalcoatl')	E313	(London: Martin Secker, 1926)	*(PS)*
by 10 Jan. 1925	'Corasmin and the Parrots' (MS entitled 'Mornings in Mexico. Friday Morning')	E76	*Adelphi*, Dec. 1925	*MM*
by 10 Jan. 1925	'Market Day' (MS entitled 'Mornings in Mexico. Saturday Morning')	E227.7	As 'The Gentle Art of Marketing in Mexico' in *Travel*, April 1926; as 'Mornings in Mexico. Saturday Morning', *New Criterion*, June 1926	*MM*
by 10 Jan. 1925	'Walk to Huayapa' (MS entitled 'Mornings in Mexico: Sunday Morning')	E421.7	As 'Sunday Stroll in Sleepy Mexico' in *Travel*, Nov. 1926; same title in *Adelphi*, March 1927	*MM*
by 10 Jan. 1925	'The Mozo' (MS entitled: 'Mornings in Mexico: Monday Morning')	E258	*Adelphi*, Feb. 1927; as 'Sons of Montezuma', *Living Age*, 1 April 1927	*MM*
24 Dec. 1924	Preface to *Black Swans* by Mollie Skinner	E49.5	–	*P II*

by 10 Jan. 1925	Re-write of Luis Quintanilla's 'Mexico, Why Not?' as 'See Mexico After by Luis Q'	E357	–	P
Christmas 1924– before 10 Jan. 1925	'Resurrection'	E346.1	–	P, (RDP)
10 Jan.– early March 1925	Fragment beginning 'Man is essentially a Soul . . .'	E226.5	–	(RDP)
mid-March 1925	Noah's Flood (fragment)	E273	–	Plays
?11 March– 25 March 1925	'The Flying-Fish'	E136	–	P, (SMOS)
late March– 7 May 1925	David	E87	David (London: Martin Secker, 1925)	Plays
by 18 April 1925 (with additional material on 9 May)	'Accumulated Mail'	E3	The Borzoi (New York: Knopf, 1925)	(RDP)
June 1925	'Art and Morality'	E24	Calendar of Modern Letters, Nov. 1925; Living Age, 26 Dec. 1925	P, (Hardy)
by 29 June 1925	'The Novel' (MS entitled 'The Modern Novel')	E280	–	CentaurRDP, (Hardy)
June–July 1925	'Morality and the Novel'	E244	Calendar of Modern Letters, Dec. 1925	P, (Hardy)
mid-July–by 25 Aug. 1925	'Him with His Tail in His Mouth'	E161	–	CentaurRDP, (RDP)
mid-July–by 25 Aug. 1925	'Blessed are the Powerful'	–	–	CentaurRDP, (RDP)
mid-July–by 25 Aug. 1925	'. . . . . Love was Once a Little Boy'	E215	–	CentaurRDP, (RDP)
mid-July–by 25 Aug. 1925	'Reflections on the Death of a Porcupine'	E340.4	–	CentaurRDP, (RDP)
mid-July–by 25 Aug. 1925	'Aristocracy'	E23	–	CentaurRDP, (RDP)

mid July–by 25 Aug. 1925	Revision of 'The Crown'	E80	–	*CentaurRDP*, (*RDP*)
by 12 Aug. 1925	Note on 'The Crown'	E81	–	*CentaurRDP*, (*RDP*)
?8 Sept.– 13 Oct. 1925	Review of *Hadrian the Seventh* by Baron Corvo [Frederick Rolfe]	–	*Adelphi*, Dec. 1925	*P*
8 Sept.– 20 Oct. 1925	Review of *Saïd the Fisherman* by Marmaduke Pickthall	–	*New York Herald Tribune: Books*, 27 Dec. 1925; *Adelphi*, Jan. 1927	*P*
by 21 Nov. 1925	Review of *Origins of Prohibition* by J. A. Krout	E297	*New York Herald Tribune: Books*, 31 Jan. 1926	*P*
25 Nov. 1925	'A Little Moonshine with Lemon'	E203.5	*Laughing Horse*, April 1926	*MM*
Nov. 1925	'Europe versus America'	–	*Laughing Horse*, April 1926	*P*
Nov. 1925	'Why the Novel Matters'	E432	–	*P*, (*Hardy*)
Nov. 1925	'The Novel and the Feelings'	E281	–	*P*, (*Hardy*)
2 Nov.– 19 Dec. 1925	'Smile'	–	*Nation and Athenaeum*, 19 June 1926; *New Masses*, June 1926	*BrWWRA*, *AmWWRA*, (*WWRA*)
by 12 Dec. 1925	*Sun* (first version)	E385	*Sun* (London: E. Archer, 1926); *New Coterie*, Autumn 1926	*BrWWRA*, *AmWWRA*, (*WWRA*)
19 Nov.– 29 Dec. 1925	*Glad Ghosts*	E148	*Glad Ghosts* (London: Ernest Benn Ltd., 1926); *Dial*, July and Aug. 1926 (2 parts)	*BrWWRA*, *AmWWRA*, (*WWRA*)
Nov. 1925– before 20 Feb. 1926	'The Late Mr Maurice Magnus'	–	Letter to *New Statesman*, 20 Feb. 1926	*P*, (v.)
by 26 Jan. 1926	*The Virgin and the Gipsy*	E420	(Florence: G. Orioli, 1930)	*Tales* (London: Martin Secker, 1934)

1 Feb.– 25 Feb. 1925	'The Rocking-Horse Winner'	E351	*Harper's Bazaar*, July 1926; *The* *Ghost Book*, ed. Cynthia Asquith (London: Hutchinson, 1926)	*LL*, (*WWRA*)
?April 1926	Review of *Heat* by Isa Glenn	E158	–	*P*
Nov. 1925– April 1926	'American Heroes: A Review of *In the* *American Grain* by William Carlos Williams'	–	*Nation* (New York), 14 April 1926	*P*
27 Feb.–by 13 May 1926	'Two Blue Birds'	E412	*Dial*, April 1927; *Pall Mall*, June 1928	*BrWWRA*, *AmWWRA*, (*WWRA*)
May 1926	'Introduction to *Max Havelaar* by Multatuli (pseudonym of E. D. Dekker)'	–	*Max Havelaar*, trans. W. Siebenhaar (New York: Knopf, 1927)	*P*
late June 1926	'The Nightingale'	E272	*Forum*, Sept. 1927; *Spectator*, 10 Sept. 1927	Frieda, *P*
initial version *c.* 25 June 1926, revised version by early spring 1927 at the latest	'Fireworks'	E134	*Nation and* *Athenaeum*, 16 April 1927; *Forum*, May 1927	First version as 'Fireworks in Florence' in *P*, both versions in (*SEP*)
June–by 10 July 1926	'The Man who Loved Islands'	E227.3	*Dial*, July 1927; *London Mercury*, Aug. 1927	*AmWWRA*, *LL*, (*WWRA*)
20–29 July 1926	'Mercury'	E236	*Atlantic Monthly*, Feb. 1927; *Nation* *and Athenaeum*, 5 Feb. 1927	*P*
by 20 Aug. 1926	Review of *The World* *of William Clissold* by H. G. Wells	–	*Calendar*, Oct. 1926	*P*
?Sept.– Oct. 1926	'Return to Bestwood'	–	–	*P*
?Oct. 1926	'Which Class I Belong To'	E428	–	–

? Oct. 1926	'Getting On'	E144	–	–
6–?11 Oct. 1926	'The Duc de Lauzun'	E106	–	P (as 'The Good Man')
c. 22 Oct. 1926	'In Love' (originally 'More Modern Love')	E170.3	*Dial*, Nov. 1927	*BrWWRA*, *AmWWRA*, (*WWRA*)
mid-Oct.– 1 Dec. 1926	'Man is a Hunter'	E226	–	P
c. 22 Oct. 1926– c. 1 Dec. 1926	*Lady Chatterley's Lover* 1st version	E186	–	*The First Lady Chatterley* with foreword by Frieda Lawrence (New York: Dial Press, 1944); Heinemann edn, London, 1972; Penguin edn, Harmondsworth, 1973
c. 1 Dec. 1926– 25 Feb. 1927	*Lady Chatterley's Lover* 2nd version	E186	–	(Milan: Mondadori, 1954); Heinemann edn, as *John Thomas and Lady Jane*, London 1972; Penguin edn, *JTLJ*
by 9 Nov. 1926	'Coast of Illusion: A Review of *Gifts of Fortune* by H. M Tomlinson'	E145	*T.P.'s and Cassell's Weekly*, 1 Jan. 1927	P
Nov.–early Dec. 1926	Review of *Pedro de Valdivia* by R. B. Cunninghame Graham	E306	*Calendar*, Jan. 1927	P
by 9 Jan. 1927	?'Becoming a Success'	–	Probably an adapted version published as 'Myself Revealed', *Sunday Dispatch*, 17 Feb. 1929	Adapted version as 'Autobiographical Sketch' in *AA*, *P II*

by 25 Feb. 1927	Review of *Nigger Heaven* by Carl Van Vechten, *Flight* by Walter White, *Manhattan Transfer* by John Dos Passos and *In Our Time* by Ernest Hemingway	E271	*Calendar,* April 1927	*P*
by 28 Feb. 1927	'John Galsworthy' (MS entitled 'A Scrutiny of the Work of John Galsworthy')	E171.3	*Scrutinies by Various Writers,* ed. Edgell Rickword (London: Wishart and Co., 1928)	*(Hardy)*
Feb.–11 Mar 1927	'The Lovely Lady'	E216	*The Black Cap.* ed. Cynthia Asquith (London: Hutchinson and Co., 1927)	*LL, (WWRA)* – latter contains both shorter version and, for the first time, the longer version
Feb.–April 1927	'Flowery Tuscany' I–III	E135	*New Criterion,* Oct., Nov. and Dec. 1927, Nov. 1927, Dec. 1927 (three parts); as 'A Year in Flowery Tuscany' in *Travel,* April 1929	*P, (SEP)*
? by 5 May 1927	*The Escaped Cock* (*The Man who Died*) – first half	E116	*Forum,* Feb. 1928	–
probably 26 April 1927	'Making Love to Music'	E221	–	*P*
12 April–27 April 1927	Review of *Solitaria* by V. V. Rozanov	E368	*Calendar,* July 1927	*P*
by 6 June 1927 (first three essays); by 14 June 1927 (next two); by 25 June 'Volterra' written; 'The Florence Museum'	*Sketches of Etruscan Places* – I. Cerveteri II. Tarquinia III. The Painted Tombs of Tarquinia 1 IV. The Painted Tombs of Tarquinia 2 V. Vulci VI. Volterra	E117	'Cerveteri' as 'The City of the Dead at Cerveteri', in *Travel,* Nov. 1927; 'Tarquinia' as 'The Ancient Metropolis of the Etruscans', in *Travel,* Dec. 1927; 'Painted Tombs of	First published as *Etruscan Places* (London: Martin Secker, 1932) – without 'The Florence Museum', *(SEP)*

possibly written July–Oct. 1927	VII. The Florence Museum		Tarquinia', in *Travel*, Jan. 1928; 'Volterra' as 'The Wind-Swept Stronghold of Volterra', in *Travel*, Feb. 1928. The same four Etruscan essays in *World Today* Feb.–May 1928	
probably 30 April 1927	'Flowery Tuscany' IV	E143.7	–	As 'Germans and Latins' in *P*
probably early May 1927	'Germans and English'	E143.7	Published by Insel-Verlag as 'Ein Brief von D. H. Lawrence an das Inselschiff', *Das Inselschiff* (Leipzig, 1927)	In English as 'Germans and English' in *P II*
by 9 May 1927	Introduction to *Mastro-don Gesualdo* by Giovanni Verga	E231	First published in the Jonathan Cape edition of Lawrence's translation of *Mastro-don Gesualdo* (London, 1928)	*P II*
by 9 May 1927	Further version of the *Mastro-don Gesualdo* introduction	E231	–	*P*
by 12 May 1927	Review of *Peep Show* by Walter Wilkinson	E307	*Calendar*, July 1927	*P*
?May 1927	'Things'	E397	*Bookman* (New York), Aug. 1928; *Fortnightly Review*, Oct. 1928	*LL*
probably 12 May– 27 May 1927	'None of That'	E275a	–	*BrWWRA*, *AmWWRA*, (*WWRA*)

?May 1927	'The Man who was Through with the World'	E227.4	ed. John R. Elliot in *Essays in Criticism*, July 1959	*POS*
July 1927–by 25 Sept. 1927	Translation of the remaining 5 stories by Giovanni Verga for what became *Cavalleria rusticana and Other Stories*	–	*Cavalleria rusticana and Other Stories* (London: Jonathan Cape, 1928)	–
3–7 Aug. 1927	'A New Theory of Neuroses: A Review of *The Social Basis of Consciousness* by Trigant Burrow'	E366	*Bookman* (New York), Nov. 1927	*P*
by 28 Sept. 1927	'Translator's Preface' to *Cavalleria rusticana and Other Stories* by Giovanni Verga	E63	Giovanni Verga, *Cavalleria rusticana and Other Stories*, trans D. H. Lawrence (London: Jonathan Cape, 1928)	*P*
Perhaps *c.* 28 Oct. 1927	MS begins 'Nothing depresses me more . . .'	E30	–	As 'Autobiographical Fragment' in *P*; as 'A Dream of Life' in *POS*
?Oct. 1927	'The Undying Man' (unfinished)	E415	–	*P*
by 17 Nov. 1927, lengthened Nov. 1928	*Rawdon's Roof*	E334	*Rawdon's Roof* (London: Elkin Matthews, 1928)	*LL*
c 26 Nov. 1927– 8 Jan. 1928	*Lady Chatterley's Lover* – third version	E186	(Florence: G. Orioli, 1928)	*(LCL)*
by 5 Jan. 1928	Introduction to *The Mother (La Madre)* by Grazia Deledda, trans. Mary G. Steegmann	E248	(London: Jonathan Cape, 1928)	*P*
13–29 April 1928	*Sun* – altered version	E385	*Sun* (Paris: Black Sun Press, 1928)	*(WWRA)*

17–29 April 1928	'Chaos in Poetry' (written as the introduction to Harry Crosby's *Chariot of the Sun*)	E65	*Echanges*, Dec. 1929; Harry Crosby, *Chariot of the Sun* (Paris: Black Sun Press, 1931)	slightly different, probably earlier, version in *P*, with less positive conclusion
probably April 1928	'The "Jeune Fille" Wants to Know' (Lawrence's first title 'The Bogey Between the Generations')	E179	As 'When She Asks Why', *Evening News*, 8 May 1928; as 'Bogey between the Generations' in *Virginia Quarterly Review*, Jan. 1929	*AA*, *P II*
on or by 12 May 1928	'Foreword to *Collected Poems*'	E73	–	As '*Collected Poems*' in *P*; as 'Foreword' in *Poems*
on or by 12 May 1928	'Note to *Collected Poems*'	E73.1	*Collected Poems* (London: Secker, 1928)	–
by 13 May 1928	'Laura Philippine'	E194	*T.P.'s and Cassell's Weekly*, 7 July 1928	*AA*
by 21 May 1928	'Women Always Know Best' (MS entitled 'That Women Know Best')	E390	*Daily Chronicle*, 29 Nov. 1928	ed. Roy Spencer (Santa Rosa, California: Black Sparrow Press, 1994)
by 7 June 1928	'Mother and Daughter'	E279	*Criterion*, April 1929	*LL*
?May 1928	'All There'	E10a	–	*P*
? June 1928	'Thinking About Oneself'	E398	–	*P*
by 27 June 1928	'Insouciance'	E174	As 'Over-Earnest Ladies', *Evening News*, 12 July 1928	*AA*, *P II*
27–28 June 1928	'Master in his Own House' (MS entitled 'Men Must Rule')	E230	*Evening News*, 2 Aug. 1928	*AA*, *P II*

by 2 Sept. 1928	Second half of *The Escaped Cock*	E116	Both parts in *The Escaped Cock* (Paris: Black Sun Press, 1929); as *The Man Who Died* (London: Martin Secker, 1931)	–
by 9 July 1928	'Matriarchy'	E232	As 'If Women Were Supreme', *Evening News*, 5 Oct. 1928	*AA, P II*
by 12 July 1928	'Ownership'	E299	–	*AA, P II*
9–26 July 1928	'The Blue Moccasins'	E50	*Eve: The Lady's Pictorial*, 22 Nov. 1928; *Plain Talk*, Feb. 1929	*LL*
11 July 1928– 17 July 1928	Review of *The Station* by Robert Byron, *England and the Octopus* by Clough Williams-Ellis, *Comfortless Memory* by Maurice Baring, and *Ashenden or the British Agent* by W. Somerset Maugham	E377.5	*Vogue* (London), 20 July 1928	*P*
June–by 18 July 1928	'Autobiography' (autobiographical details for the French publisher Kra)	E31.3	–	Edward Nehls, ed., *D. H. Lawrence: A Composite Biography*, vol. III (Madison: University of Wisconsin Press, 1959)
27 June– 20 Aug. 1928	'Dull London' (MS entitled 'Why I Don't Like Living in London')	E107	*Evening News*, 3 Sept. 1928	*AA, P II*
by 24 Aug. 1928	'Women Are So Cocksure', probably a preliminary draft for 'Cocksure Women and Hensure Men'	E440	–	*P*

by 24 Aug. 1928	'Cocksure Women and Hensure Men'	E70	–	*AA, P II*
by 2 Sept. 1928	'Hymns in a Man's Life'	E165	Trans. Frieda Lawrence in *Buch Des Dankes Für Hans Carossa* (Leipzig: Insel Verlag, 1928); *Evening News*, 13 Oct. 1928	*AA, P II*
by 13 Sept. 1928	'Red Trousers'	E340	As 'Oh! For a New Crusade', *Evening News*, 27 Sept. 1928	*AA, P II*
30 Oct.–3 Nov. 1928	'Is England Still a Man's Country?'	E177	*Daily Express*, 29 Nov. 1928	*AA, P II*
Oct.–early Nov. 1928	Translation of *The Story of Doctor Manente: Being the Tenth and Last Story From the Suppers of A. F. Grazzini called Il Lasca*	E379.9	(Florence: G. Orioli, 1928)	–
30 Oct. 1928– by 5 Nov. 1928	'Sex Locked Out' (MS entitled 'Sex Appeal')	E359.1	*Sunday Dispatch*, 25 Nov. 1928; *Vanity Fair*, July 1929; as 'Men and Peacocks', *Golden Book*, Dec. 1929. (Also published as a booklet, privately and it seems without authorisation, in Dec. 1928: reprinted from the *Sunday Dispatch* version.)	As 'Sex versus Loveliness' in *AA, P II*
by 8 Nov. 1928; lengthened by 23 Feb. 1929	'Do Women Change?'	E96	As 'Women Don't Change', *Sunday Dispatch*, 28 April 1929 and, with the same title, *Vanity Fair*, April 1929	*AA, P II*

Nov.–Dec. 1928	'Introduction to Pictures'	E300	–	*P*
by 24 Nov. 1928	'Enslaved by Civilisation'	E115	As 'The Manufacture of Good Little Boys', *Vanity Fair*, Sept. 1929	*AA, P II*
6–9 Dec. 1928	'Give Her a Pattern' (MS entitled 'Oh These Women')	E147	As 'Woman in Man's Image', *Vanity Fair*, May 1929; as 'The Real Trouble About Women', *Daily Express*, 19 June 1929	*AA, P II*
19 Dec.– 25 Dec. 1928	'New Mexico'	E269	*Survey Graphic*, 1 May 1931	*P*
Dec. 1928	'Introduction to *Pansies*' – first version	E302.5	*Review of English Studies*, vol. 21 (May 1970)	–
by 7 Jan. 1929	'Introduction to *Pansies*' – second version	E303	*Pansies* (London: Martin Secker, 1929)	*Poems*
by 28 Feb. 1929	'Introduction to *Pansies*' – third version	E303	*D. H. Lawrence: Foreword to 'Pansies'*, intro. Keith Sagar (Marlborough: Libanus Press, 1988)	–
by 27 April 1929	'Introduction to *Pansies*' – fourth version	E303	*Pansies* (London: Martin Secker, 1929)	–
late Dec. 1928– by 12 Jan. 1929	'Introduction to These Paintings'	E300	*The Paintings of D. H. Lawrence* (London:Mandrake Press, 1929)	*P*
by 1 Mar 1929	'The State of Funk'	E377	–	*AA, P II*
by 1 Mar 1929	'Introduction to *Bottom Dogs* by Edward Dahlberg'	E54	(London: G. Putnam's Sons, 1929)	*P*
26 Mar–April 1929	'My Skirmish with Jolly Roger' (expanded into *A Propos of Lady Chatterley's Lover*)	E1.5	In popular edition of *Lady Chatterley's Lover* (Paris: privately printed,	*(LCL)*

			1929); and separately in New York by Random House, 1929	
10–15 April 1929	'Making Pictures'	E222	*Creative Art*, July 1929; *Vanity Fair*, Aug. 1929; *Studio*, July 1929	*AA, P II*
19 Apr 1929– 29 Apr 1929	*Pornography and Obscenity* – first, short, version	E322	*This Quarter*, July–Sept. 1929	–
by 1 May 1929	'Pictures on the Walls'	E311	As 'Dead Pictures on the Wall', *Vanity Fair*, Dec. 1929; as 'Pictures on the Walls', *Architectural Review*, Feb. 1930	*AA, P II*
6–16 July 1929	Introduction to the translation of *The Story of Doctor Manente: Being the Tenth and Last Story From the Suppers of A. F. Grazzini called Il Lasca*	E380	(Florence: G. Orioli, 1929)	*P*
July–?Aug. 1929	Translation of *The Story of Doctor Manente: Being the First Story of the Second Supper of A. F. Grazzini called Il Lasca* (unfinished)	–	*Sunday Telegraph*, 25 Oct. 1981	–
by 2 Aug. 1929	'The Risen Lord'	E350	*Everyman*, 3 Oct. 1929	*AA, P II*
by 5 Aug. 1929	'Men Must Work and Women As Well' (MS entitled 'Men and Women')	E235	As 'Men and Women', *Star Review*, Nov. 1929	*AA, P II*

possibly after 5 Sept. 1929	'Nottingham and the Mining Countryside'	E279	*New Adelphi*, June–Aug. 1930; as 'Disaster Looms Ahead, Mining Camp Civilisation, The English Contribution to Progress', *Architectural Review*, Aug. 1930	*P*
by 8 Sept. 1929	*Pornography and Obscenity*, extended version	E322	(London: Faber and Faber, 1929)	*P*
possibly 7 Oct. 1929; written by 4 Nov. 1929	'We Need One Another'	E422.7	*Scribner's Magazine*, May 1930; *Review of Reviews*, June 1930. Separate edition New York: Equinox, 1933 (also includes 'The Real Thing')	*P*
?*c.* 17 Oct. 1929	*A Propos of Lady Chatterley's Lover*	E1.5	(London: Mandrake Press, 1930)	*P II*
by 4 Nov. 1929	'Nobody loves me'	E274	*Life and Letters*, July 1930; *Virginia Quarterly Review*, July 1930	*P*
by 4 Nov. 1929	'The Real Thing'	E337	*Scribner's Magazine*, June 1930; shorter version in *Daily Herald*, 27 and 28 Aug. 1930 (2 parts) as 'Both Sides Lose in Sex War' and 'Love Among the Moderns'	In *We Need One Another* (New York: Equinox, 1933), *P*
by 7 Nov. 1929	'A Remarkable Russian: A Review of *Fallen Leaves* by V. V. Rozanov'	E124	*Everyman*, 23 Jan. 1930	*P*

1 Nov.–by 12 Nov. 1929	'Notes for the Illustrated Cresset Press Edition of *Birds, Beasts and* *Flowers*'	E47.2	(London: Cresset Press, 1930)	P
1 Oct. 1929–by 9 Jan. 1930	*Apocalypse*	E17	(Florence: G. Orioli, 1931)	(*Apocalypse*)
?Dec. 1929	'The Elephants of Dionysos'	E113	–	P
by 6 Jan. 1930	'Introduction to *The* *Dragon of the* *Apocalypse* by Frederick Carter'	E101	*London Mercury*, July 1930	P, (*Apocalypse*)
possibly by 25 Jan. 1930	'Introduction to *The* *Grand Inquisitor* by F. M. Dostoyevsky'	E151	F. M. Dostoyevsky, *The Grand* *Inquisitor*, trans. S. S. Koteliansky (London: Elkin Matthews and Marrot, 1930)	P
end of Feb. 1930 –	Review of *Art* *Nonsense and Other* *Essays* by Eric Gill (unfinished)	E24.5	*Book Collector's* *Quarterly*, Oct.– Dec. 1933	P

THE WRITING LIFE, 1922–1930: POETRY

Because of the point at which it broke off, the corresponding chronological table in *Triumph to Exile* ceased dating DHL's poems mid-way through the composition of *Birds, Beasts and Flowers*. For the sake of a chronological synopsis of that volume, the poems which DHL assembled, in February 1928, for the *Birds, Beasts and Flowers* and *Look! We Have Come Through!* sections of *Collected Poems* are listed at the appropriate rows in this table. The earlier dates of composition of these poems, and of all poems in the volume sections of *Collected Poems*, are shown in square brackets. For the important phase of revision of *Look! We Have Come Through!*, in January–February 1917, readers should consult Mark Kinkead-Weekes's Appendix in the second volume of the biography, and *Triumph to Exile* more generally. In the *Collected Poems* sections, titles which differ substantively from those adopted in *Collected Poems* are shown in the column indicating where the earlier title was adopted: earliest MS/TS; early publication; first collection.

In the table more generally, later titles are shown in round brackets after the earliest title. Titles cancelled in manuscript are not shown. In the *Pansies* section, where a poem has a title restricted to a specific MS/TS, that title is again shown in the MS/TS column. Some variant versions of poems which can be related in a stemma of composition have been included, where the versions are very different or have an intrinsic interest (as in the versions of 'Bavarian Gentians'). Where DHL added location notes to a poem, these are shown in brackets after the title. As distinct from the poems in *Look! We Have Come Through!*, there is only one conspicuously suspect, indeed factitious location note in *Birds, Beasts and Flowers* – that to 'Humming-Bird', located 'Española', New Mexico, when a version of the poem had been published sixteen months before DHL's arrival in New Mexico. Scholars interested in notes verifying the composition dates must await the full manuscript listing of DHL's poetry, to be included in the apparatus volumes of the Cambridge *Poems*.

In the case of *Pansies* and *Nettles*, re-listing titles in volume sequence has been thought to require too much repetition to be useful in this table; titles are shown in their notebook order and form. Capitalisation of poem titles is regularised for *Collected Poems*, but not thereafter. In authorial typescripts DHL tended to follow the convention of most of his publishers, of rendering poem titles in upper case. Reproducing authorial capitalisation from his last verse notebooks not only preserves the possible significance of such capitalisation, but marks a distinction between poems DHL saw through the press and those he left to be published posthumously. Punctuation of titles from the *Nettles* and *Last Poems* notebooks is also preserved in manuscript form, even though the terminal period DHL added to many titles appears to be non-significant. Angle brackets around titles indicate poems which have been cancelled or overwritten.

This appendix was prepared by Christopher Pollnitz.

Additional Cue-Titles

Amores	*Amores.* Duckworth, 1916.
Bay	*Bay.* Beaumont, 1919.
BBF	*Birds, Beasts and Flowers.* Martin Secker, 1923.
BBF (Cresset)	*Birds, Beasts and Flowers.* Illust. Blair Hughes-Stanton. Cresset Press, 1930.
BBF (NY)	*Birds, Beasts and Flowers.* New York: Thomas Seltzer, 1923.
Ench Y	*The Enchanted Years.* Ed. John Calvin Metcalf and James Southall Wilson. New York: University of Virginia, 1921.
ER	*English Review.*
Fire	*Fire and Other Poems.* San Francisco: Grabhorn Press, 1940.
IA	*Imagist Anthology.* New York: Covici Friede, 1930.
LaP	*Last Poems.* Ed. Richard Aldington and Giuseppe Orioli. Florence: G. Orioli, 1932.
Look!	*Look! We Have Come Through!* Chatto and Windus, 1917.
LP	*Love Poems and Others.* Duckworth, 1913.
MC	*Monthly Chapbook.*
Nettles	*Nettles.* Faber, 1930.
NMQ	*New Mexico Quarterly.*
NP	*New Poems.* Martin Secker, 1918.
NR	*New Republic.*
Pansies	*Pansies.* Martin Secker, 1929.
Pansies (PP)	*Pansies.* Privately printed, 1929.
PD	*Poetry and Drama.*
SelP	*Selected Poems.* Ed. Keith Sagar. Harmondsworth: Penguin Books, 1972.
SIP	*Some Imagist Poets.* Boston: Houghton Mifflin, 1915, 1916 and 1917.
Smailes	T. A. Smailes. 'D. H. Lawrence: Seven Hitherto Unpublished Poems', *D. H. Lawrence Review,* iii (Spring 1970), 42–6.
WG	*Saturday Westminster Gazette.*

DATE	TITLE	EARLIEST MS/TS	EARLY PUBLICATION	FIRST COLLECTION
April 1922	Apostrophe to a Buddhist Monk	E19	Brewster 50	*Poems* 760
6–11 Oct. 1922	The Ass (2nd version)	–	–	*BBF*
11 Oct. 1922	Eagle in New Mexico ('Taos')	E47a	–	*BBF*
Oct. 1922	Eagle in New Mexico (2nd version) ('Taos')	E109d?	*NMQ* Nov. 1938	*Fire*
	Eagle in New Mexico (3rd version) ('Taos')	E109e?	–	*BBF*
	Men in New Mexico ('Taos')	E234.5a and E234.5b	–	*BBF*

25 Oct.–8 Nov. 1922	Autumn at Taos ('Taos') The Red Wolf ('Taos') Spirits Summoned West ('Taos')	E31.5 E340.3 E376.4	– – –	*BBF* *BBF* *BBF*
c. 23 March 1922; or Jan. 1923	Elephant ('Kandy')	E47c	*ER* April 1923	*BBF*
late June–July 1922; or Jan. 1923	Kangaroo ('Sydney')	E47c	–	*BBF*
by 1 Feb. 1923	Bibbles ('Lobo')	E47c	–	*BBF*
by 7 Feb. 1923	Mountain Lion ('Lobo')	E47c	–	*BBF*
	The Blue Jay ('Lobo')	E47c	–	*BBF*
by 14 March 1923	The American Eagle ('Taos')	E47a	–	*BBF*
June–July 1923	Autumn in New Mexico (2nd version, 'Autumn at Taos')	–	*Palms* Autumn 1923	–
c. 1 Aug. 1923	The American Eagle (2nd version)	E14b	–	*BBF* (NY)
20 April 1924	O! Americans!	E282a	*NMQ* May 1938	*Fire*
c. 20 Nov. 1923	Change of Life	[E64]; E315a	–	*Fire*
Jan. 1926	Mediterranean in January	E233a	*Laughing Horse* April 1926	*Poems* 814
	Beyond the Rockies	E45a	*Laughing Horse* April 1926	*Poems* 816
Dec. 1926	The Old Orchard Rainbow 'There's no immortal heaven'	E302d E332a E396.3	*Calendar* April 1927 *Calendar* April 1927 –	*Poems* 816 *Poems* 818 –
?June 1927	'There was a gay bird named Christine'	E394.5	–	*Poems* 846
Aug. 1927	August Holidays Bathing Resort Hymn to Nothingness	E29 E40 E164.9	– – –	*Poems* 824 *Poems* 826 *Poems* 823
Nov. 1927–Feb. 1928	**COLLECTED POEMS**			
	PART ONE: **RHYMING POEMS**			
Nov. 1927 [?1908]	The Wild Common	E317 ('Into a deep pond, an old sheep dip')	–	*Amores*
Nov. 1927 [1908]	Dog-Tired	E317	–	*LP*
Jan. 1928 [1908]	From a College Window	E317	–	*NP*

Nov. 1927 [Nov. 1909]	Discord in Childhood	E320.1 ('[A Life History/ Third] Discord')	–	*Amores*
Nov. 1927 [by 20 Jan. 1909]	Cherry Robbers	E317	–	*LP*
Nov. 1927 [late 1909]	Dream-Confused	E317 ('Dream')	*ER* April 1910 ('Wakened')	*LP*
Nov. 1927 [by 20 Jan. 1909]	Renascence	E317 ('Renaissance')	–	*LP*
Nov. 1927 [?May 1909]	Virgin Youth	E317 ('[Movements] 3. The Body Awake')	–	*Amores*
Nov. 1927 [?1907]	Study	E317	–	*Amores*
Jan. 1928 [1906–8]	Twilight	E317 ('Evening of a Week-day')	–	*NP* ('Palimpsest of Twilight')
Nov. 1927 [?Oct. 1909]	Love on the Farm	E320.1 ('A Beloved')	–	*LP* ('Cruelty and Love')
Jan. 1928 [Dec. 1910]	Gipsy	E145.5a ('Self-Contempt')	–	*NP*
Nov. 1927 [Autumn 1911]	The Collier's Wife	–	–	*LP*
Jan. 1928 [1906–8]	Flapper	E317 ('Song')	*Egoist* 1 April 1914 ('Song')	*NP*
Jan. 1928 [?Dec. 1910; or ?April 1918]	Thief in the Night	E269.5	–	*NP*
Nov. 1927 [Dec. 1909–Jan. 1910]	Monologue of a Mother	E320.1	*Poetry* Jan. 1914 ('The Mother of Sons')	*Amores*
Jan. 1928 [1908]	The Little Town at Evening	E317 ('Eastwood – Evening')	*MC* July 1919	*Bay*
Nov. 1927 [1908]	In a Boat	E317	*ER* Oct. 1910 ('Tired of the Boat')	*Amores*
Jan. 1928 [1906–8]	Last Hours	E317 ('The last hours of a holiday')	–	*Bay*
Jan. 1928 [?April 1911]	Flat Suburbs, S.W., in the Morning	E320.1 ('[Transformations] 2. Morning')	–	*NP*

Nov. 1927 [later 1911]	The Best of School	–	*WG* 1 June 1912 ('[The Schoolmaster] VI. The Best of School')	*LP* ('[The School-master] II. The Best of School')
Nov. 1927 [by June 1909]	Dreams Old and Nascent: Old	E317 ('A Still Afternoon in School')	*ER* Nov. 1909	*Amores*
Jan. 1928 [?April 1911]	Suburbs on a Hazy Day	E320.1 ('Transfor-mations/ 4. The Inanimate, that Changes Not in Shape')	–	*NP*
Nov. 1927 [late 1909–early 1910]	Weeknight Service	E317	–	*Amores*
Jan. 1928 [late 1910–early 1911]	A Man Who Died	E320.1 ('Nils Lykke Dead')	*Poetry* Jan. 1914 ('A Woman and Her Dead Husband')	*NP* ('Bitterness of Death')
Jan. 1928 [March 1909]	Letter from Town: On a Grey Morning in March	E317 ('Letter from Town/ The City')	–	*NP* ('Letter from Town: On a Grey Evening in March')
Jan. 1928 [March 1909]	Letter from Town: The Almond-Tree	E317	–	*NP*
Nov. 1927 [later 1911]	Wedding Morn	E213b	–	*LP*
Nov. 1927 [by Jan. 1909]	Violets	E317 ('Violets for the Dead')	*Nation* 4 Nov. 1911	*LP*
Nov. 1927 [1906–8]	Lightning	E317	*Nation* 4 Nov. 1911	*LP*
Nov. 1927 [?Aug. 1909]	End of Another Home Holiday	E317	–	*LP*
Nov. 1927 [Summer 1909]	Baby Running Barefoot	E317 ('Movements/ 1. A Baby Running Barefoot')	*ER* Nov. 1909 ('Baby Movements/ I. Running Barefoot')	*Amores* ('A Baby Running Barefoot')
Jan. 1928 [Summer 1909]	Sigh No More	E320.1	*ER* Oct. 1910	*NP*

	Guards/ A Review in Hyde Park, 1910: The Crowd Watches	E317 '[Movements] 5. The Review of the Scots Guards'	–	*Bay* ('Guards!/ A Review in Hyde Park 1913./ The Crowd Watches')
	[Guards . . .] Evolutions of Soldiers	E317 ('[Movements] 5. The Review of the Scots Guards')	–	*Bay*
Nov. 1927 [?later 1911]	Aware	E213b	–	*LP*
	A Pang of Reminiscence	E213a	–	*LP*
	A White Blossom	E213a	–	*LP*
Nov. 1927 [?April 1911]	Corot	E320.1 ('[Transfor-mations] 6. Corot')	–	*LP*
	Michael Angelo	E320.1 ('[Transfor-mations] 7. Raphael')	–	*LP*
Jan. 1928 [Autumn 1909]	Hyde Park at Night, Before the War: Clerks	E317 ('The Songless/ 1. Tonight')	*ER* April 1910 ('Workaday Evenings/ I. Yesternight')	*NP*
	Piccadilly Circus at Night: Street-Walkers	E317 ('The Songless/ 2. Tomorrow')	*ER* April 1910 ('Workaday Evenings/ II. To-morrow Night')	*NP*
Jan. 1928 [Nov.–Dec. 1917]	After the Opera	E319	*ER* June 1918	*Bay*
Nov. 1927 [?April 1911]	Morning Work	E320.1 ('Transfor-mations/ 3. Men in the Morning')	–	*LP*
	Transformations: I. The Town	E320.1 ('Transfor-mations/ 4. The Inanimate, that Changes Not in Shape')	–	*LP*

	[Transformations:] II. The Earth	E320.1 ('Transformations/ 4. The Inanimate, that Changes Not in Shape')	–	*LP*
	[Transformations:] III. Men	E320.1 ('[Transformations] 5. The Changeful Animate/ Men, whose Shape is Multiform')	–	*LP*
Nov. 1927 [Summer 1909]	A Baby Asleep After Pain	E320.1 ('[Movements] 2. A Baby Asleep after Pain')	*ER* Nov. 1909 ('Baby Movements/ II. Trailing Clouds')	*Amores*
Nov. 1927 [late 1909–early 1910]	Last Lesson of the Afternoon	E320.1 ('[School –] Afternoon')	*WG* 18 May 1912 ('The Schoolmaster/ II. Afternoon in School')	*LP* ('[The Schoolmaster] III. Afternoon in School')
Jan. 1928 [?Feb. 1909]	School on the Outskirts	E317 ('A Snowy Day at School: "Snow, and the silence of snow"')	–	*NP*
Nov. 1927 [Jan.–Feb. 1909]	A Snowy Day in School	E317 ('School')	*WG* 1 June 1912 ('The Schoolmaster/ V. A Snowy Day in School')	*LP* ('[The Schoolmaster] I. A Snowy Day in School')
Nov. 1927 [Autumn 1911]	Whether or Not	–	–	*LP*
Nov. 1927 [by 20 Jan. 1909]	A Winter's Tale	E317	*Egoist* 1 April 1914	*Amores*
Nov. 1927 [?April 1911]	Return	E320.1	–	*LP*
Nov. 1927 [Autumn 1910]	The Appeal	E320.1	–	*LP*
Nov. 1927 [?later 1911]	Lilies in the Fire	E213a	–	*LP*
Nov. 1927 [Feb. 1912]	Red Moon-Rise	E213a	–	*LP*

Nov. 1927 [?May 1910]	Scent of Irises	E320.1	*SIP* (1915)	*Amores*
Nov. 1927 [Oct.–Nov. 1909]	Forecast	E320.1 ('Epilogue from Thelma')	–	*Amores* ('Epilogue')
Nov. 1927 [Sept. 1909]	Prophet	E320.1 ('Discipline')	–	*Amores* ('The Prophet')
Nov. 1927 [by June 1909]	Discipline	E317	*ER* Nov. 1909	*Amores*
Nov. 1927 [?Oct. 1909]	The Punisher	E320.1	*WG* 25 May 1912 ('The School-master/ IV. The Punisher')	*Amores*
Nov. 1927 [March 1911]	Tease	E320.1 ('A Wise Man')	*PD* Dec. 1914 ('Teasing')	*Amores*
Nov. 1927 [later 1911–early 1912]	Mystery	E320.6	–	*Amores*
Nov. 1927 [Autumn 1910]	Repulsed	E320.1 ('Nocturne')	–	*LP*
Nov. 1927 [Oct. 1910]	Coldness in Love	E320.1 ('A Plaintive Confession')	–	*LP*
Nov. 1927 [?Nov. 1910]	Suspense	E320.1 ('Patience')	–	*Amores* ('Patience')
	Endless Anxiety	E320.1 ('Anxiety')	–	*Amores* ('Anxiety')
Nov. 1927 [Dec. 1910]	The End	E320.1 ('To My Mother – Dead')	*Poetry* Dec. 1914 ('Memories')	*Amores*
	The Bride	E320.1 ('The Dead Mother')	–	*Amores*
	The Virgin Mother	E320.1 ('My Love, My Mother')	–	*Amores*
Nov. 1927 [later 1909–early 1910]	At the Window	E317	*ER* April 1910	*Amores*
Nov. 1927 [?Dec. 1910]	Reminder	E320.1	–	*LP*
Nov. 1927–Jan. 1928 [?May–June 1911]	Drunk	E320.1	–	*Amores*
Nov. 1927–Jan. 1928 [Dec. 1910]	Sorrow	E317	*Poetry* Dec. 1914 ('Weariness')	*Amores*
Nov. 1927–Jan. 1928 [Autumn 1910]	Dolour of Autumn	E320.1	–	*Amores*

Nov. 1927–Jan. 1928 [?April 1911]	The Inheritance	E320.1	–	*Amores*
	Silence	E320.1	–	*Amores*
	Listening	E320.1 ('Silence')	–	*Amores*
Nov. 1927–Jan. 1928 [Dec. 1910]	Brooding Grief	E317 ('Brooding')	–	*Amores*
Nov. 1927 [late 1910–early 1911]	Last Words to Miriam	E317 ('Last Words to Muriel')	–	*Amores*
Nov. 1927–Jan. 1928 [?Feb. 1910]	Malade	E320.1	–	*Amores*
Nov. 1927–Jan. 1928 [?later 1911]	Lotus and Frost	E320.2 ('Lotus hurt by the Cold')	–	*Amores* ('Lotus Hurt by the Cold')
Nov. 1927–Jan. 1928 [Autumn 1910]	The Yew-Tree on the Downs	E320.1 ('Liaison')	–	*Amores* ('Liaison')
Nov. 1927–Jan. 1928 [?May 1911]	Troth with the Dead	E320.1	–	*Amores*
	At a Loose End	E320.1 ('Troth with the Dead')	–	*Amores* ('Dissolute')
Nov. 1927–Jan. 1928 [Dec. 1910–early 1911]	Submergence	E320.1	–	*Amores*
Nov. 1927–Jan. 1928 [?May 1911]	The Enkindled Spring	E320.1 ('Troth with the Dead')	–	*Amores*
Nov. 1927–Jan. 1928 [?Dec. 1910]	Excursion Train	E317 ('Honeymoon')	*Egoist* 1 April 1914 ('Honeymoon')	*Amores* ('Excursion')
Nov. 1927–Jan. 1928 [?Autumn 1910]	Release	E320.1 ('Reproach')	–	*Amores* ('Reproach')
Nov. 1927–Jan. 1928 [?later 1911]	These Clever Women	E14.5b ('A Spiritual Woman')	–	*Amores* ('A Spiritual Woman')
Nov. 1927 [later 1910]	Ballad of Another Ophelia	E320.1 ('Ophelia')	*SIP* 1915	*Amores*
Nov. 1927 [later 1911]	Kisses in the Train	E213a	–	*LP*
Nov. 1927–Jan. 1928 [Summer 1909]	Turned Down	E317 ('Lost')	*Egoist* 1 April 1914 ('Fooled')	*Amores* ('Perfidy')
Nov. 1927–Jan. 1928 [early 1911]	After Many Days	E320.1 ('Meeting')	–	*Amores*

Nov. 1927–Jan. 1928 [later 1911]	Snap-Dragon	E320.4	*ER* June 1912	*Amores*
Nov. 1927–Jan. 1928 [?May 1911]	Come Spring, Come Sorrow	E320.1 ('Mating')	–	*Amores* ('Mating')
Nov. 1927–Jan. 1928 [Summer 1911]	The Hands of the Betrothed	E320.1 ('Hands')	–	*Amores*
Nov. 1927–Jan. 1928 [?Spring 1911]	A Love Song	E320.1	–	*Amores*
Jan. 1928 [?later 1911]	Twofold	E320.2 ('Indoors and Out')	–	*NP*
Jan. 1928 [1906–8]	Tarantella	E317	–	*NP*
Jan. 1928 [Autumn 1910]	Under the Oak	E320.1 ('The Appeal')	–	*NP*
Nov. 1927–Jan. 1928 [early 1911]	Brother and Sister	E320.1 ('To Lettice, my Sister')	–	*Amores*
Nov. 1927–Jan. 1928 [?April 1911]	The Shadow of Death	E320.1 ('Blue')	–	*Amores* ('Blue')
Jan. 1928 [early 1909]	Birdcage Walk	E317 ('Triolet')	–	*NP*
Nov. 1927–Jan. 1928 [?later 1911]	In Trouble and Shame	E320.2	–	*Amores*
	Call into Death	E14.5b	–	*Amores* ('Elegy')
Nov. 1927–Jan. 1928 [?later 1911; or Oct. 1913]	Grey Evening	E320.6 ('Afterwards')	*Poetry* Dec. 1914 ('Grief')	*Amores*
	Firelight and Nightfall	E320.6 ('Afterwards')	*ER* Feb. 1914 ('Twilight')	*Amores*
Nov. 1927–Jan. 1928 [?April 1911]	Blueness	E320.1 ('Blue')	–	*Amores* ('The Mystic Blue')
Nov. 1927–Jan. 1928 [Summer 1909]	A Passing-Bell	E317	–	*Amores*
Nov. 1927 [Autumn 1911]	The Drained Cup	–	–	*LP*
Jan. 1928 [?Autumn 1909]	Late at Night	E320.1 ('New Wine')	–	*NP* ('Phantasmagoria')
Jan. 1928 [Nov. 1909]	Next Morning	E320.1 ('A Day in November')	–	*NP*

Jan. 1928 [early 1911]	Winter in the Boulevard	E320.1 ('Winter')	–	*NP*
Jan. 1928 [?April 1911]	Parliament Hill in the Evening	E320.1 ('Transfor-mations/ 1. Evening')	–	*NP*
Jan. 1928 [?Summer 1909]	Embankment at Night, Before the War: Charity	E317 ('Brotherhood')	–	*NP*
	Embankment at Night, Before the War: Outcasts	E317 ('After the Theatre')	–	*NP*
Jan. 1928 [?Oct. 1909]	Sickness	E320.1	–	*NP*
Jan. 1928 [?Dec. 1910]	In Church	E317 ('The Crow')	–	*NP*
Jan. 1928 [1906–8]	Piano	E317 ('The Piano')	–	*NP*
Jan. 1928 [?Dec. 1910]	The North Country	E317 ('The Crow')	–	*NP*
Jan. 1928 [?later 1911]	Love Storm	E320.6 ('Storm in Rose-Time')	–	*NP*
Jan. 1928 [later 1911–1912]	Passing Visit to Helen	E320.4 ('And Jude the Obscure and His Beloved')	–	*NP* ('Intime')
Jan. 1928 [Nov. 1909]	Twenty Years Ago	E320.1 ('[A Life History] Third Harmony')	–	*NP*
Jan. 1928 [?May 1909]	Reading a Letter	E317 ('Reading in the Evening')	–	*NP*
Jan. 1928 [?April 1918]	Seven Seals	–	–	*NP*
Jan. 1928 [later 1911–1912]	Two Wives	E320.4 ('White')	–	*NP*
Jan. 1928 [?April 1918]	Noise of Battle	E320.1 ('The Inheritance')	–	*NP* ('App-rehension')
Jan. 1928 [?Dec. 1910]	At the Front	E317 ('The Crow')	–	*NP* ('Heimweh')
Jan. 1928 [Autumn 1910]	Reality of Peace, 1916	E320.1 ('Unwitting')	–	*NP* ('Débâcle')
Jan. 1928 [1906–8]	Narcissus	E317 ('Dim Recollections')	–	*NP*

Jan. 1928 [late 1917; or April 1918]	Tommies in the Train	E400b	*Poetry* Feb. 1919	*Bay*
Jan. 1928 [1906–8]	On the March	E317 ('On the Road')	–	*Bay*
Jan. 1928 [late 1909–early 1910]	Ruination	E320.1 ('School – I. Morning/ The Waste Lands')	–	*Bay*
Jan. 1928 [late 1917; or April 1918]	The Attack	–	–	*Bay*
	Winter-Lull	E320	–	*Bay*
Jan. 1928 [Spring 1910]	Bombardment	E320.1 ('The town has opened to the sun')	–	*Bay*
Jan. 1928 [early 1909]	Rondeau of a Conscientious Objector	E317 ('Coming Home from School/ Rondeau Redoublé')	*Voices* July 1919	*Bay*
Jan. 1928 [April 1918]	Obsequial Ode	E283c	*Poetry* Feb. 1919 ('Obsequial Chant')	*Bay*
Jan. 1928 [late 1917; or April 1918]	Going Back	E320	–	*Bay*
	Shades	E359.3b	*Poetry* Feb. 1919 ('Pentecostal')	*Bay*
Jan. 1928 [late 1917]	Town in 1917	E320 ('Town')	*ER* June 1918 ('Town')	*Bay* ('Town')
Jan. 1928 [late 1917; or April 1918]	Bread upon the Waters	E319	*Poetry* Feb. 1919	*Bay*
Jan. 1928 [April 1918]	War-Baby	E319	*ER* June 1918	*Bay*
Jan. 1928 [late 1917; or April 1918]	Nostalgia	E276b	*Poetry* Feb. 1919	*Bay*
Nov. 1927 [by June 1909]	Dreams Old and Nascent: Nascent	E317 ('A Still Afternoon in School')	*ER* Nov. 1909	*Amores*
Jan. 1928 [July 1911]	On that Day	E320.1 ('Her Birthday')	*Poetry* Jan. 1914 ('Birthday')	*NP*

Jan. 1928 [early 1910]	Autumn Sunshine	E317 ('Amour')	*Egoist* 1 April 1914 ('Early Spring')	*NP*
	PART TWO: UNRHYMING POEMS LOOK! WE HAVE COME THROUGH!			
Feb. 1928 [Jan. 1912]	Moonrise	E320.4 ('An Address to the Sea')	–	*Look!*
Feb. 1928 [?early 1912]	Elegy ('Eastwood')	–	–	*Look!*
	Nonentity	–	–	*Look!*
Feb. 1928 [?Dec. 1910]	Martyr à la Mode ('Croydon')	E229.5 ('Ah Life, God, Law, whatever name you have')	–	*Look!*
Feb. 1928 [?April–May 1912]	Don Juan	E320.6	*Poetry* Dec. 1914	*Look!*
Feb. 1928 [Jan. 1912]	The Sea ('Bournemouth')	E320.4 ('An Address to the Sea')	*ER* Sept. 1917	*Look!*
Feb. 1928 [?Feb. 1912]	Hymn to Priapus	–	*ER* Sept. 1917 ('Constancy of a Sort')	*Look!*
Feb. 1928 [9–11 May 1912]	Ballad of a Wilful Woman ('Trier')	E320.6 ('Ballad of a Wayward Woman')	–	*Look!*
Nov. 1927 [11 May 1912]	Bei Hennef ('Hennef am Rhein')	E213a	–	*LP*
Feb. 1928 [May 1912]	First Morning ('Beuerberg')	–	–	*Look!*
Feb. 1928 [?late May 1912]	'And oh – That the Man I am might cease to be –' ('Wolfratshausen')	–	–	*Look!*
	She Looks Back ('Beuerberg')	–	–	*Look!*
Feb. 1928 [June–Aug. 1912]	On the Balcony ('Icking')	E318 ('Illicit')	*Poetry* Jan. 1914 ('Illicit')	*Look!*
Feb. 1928 [?6 June 1912]	Frohnleichnam	–	–	*Look!*

Feb. 1928 [June–Aug. 1912]	In the Dark	–	–	*Look!*
	Mutilation ('Wolfratshausen')	–	–	*Look!*
	Humiliation	–	–	*Look!*
	A Young Wife	–	–	*Look!*
	Green ('Icking')	E318	*Poetry* Jan. 1914	*Look!*
	River Roses ('Kloster Schaeftlarn')	E318	*Poetry* Jan. 1914 ('All of Roses/ I')	*Look!*
	Gloire de Dijon ('Icking')	E318	*Poetry* Jan. 1914 ('All of Roses/ II')	*Look!*
	Roses on the Breakfast Table	E318	*Poetry* Jan. 1914 ('All of Roses/ III')	*Look!*
[?1917; later than 1912]	I Am like a Rose	–	–	*Look!*
	Rose of All the World	–	–	*Look!*
Feb. 1928 [June–Aug. 1912]	A Youth Mowing	E318 ('The Mowers')	*Smart Set* Nov. 1913 ('The Mowers')	*Look!*
	Quite Forsaken			*Look!*
	Forsaken and Forlorn	–	–	*Look!*
	Fireflies in the Corn	E318	*Poetry* Jan. 1914	*Look!*
Feb. 1928 [?April–May 1913]	A Doe at Evening ('Irschenhausen')	E97	–	*Look!*
Feb. 1928 [?7 Aug. 1912]	Song of a Man Who Is Not Loved ('Glashütte')	–	–	*Look!*
Feb. 1928 [11–15 Aug. 1912]	Sinners ('Mayrhofen')	–	–	*Look!*
Feb. 1928 [?31 Aug. 1912]	Misery ('Sterzing')	–	–	*Look!*
Jan. 1928 [?Nov. 1912]	Everlasting Flowers ('Lago di Garda')	E320.2 ('From the Italian Lakes')	–	*NP*
Feb. 1928 [?Oct.–Dec. 1912]	Sunday Afternoon in Italy ('Gargnano')	–	–	*Look!*
Feb. 1928 [?Winter 1912–13]	Winter Dawn	–	–	*Look!*
Feb. 1928 [?Oct.–Dec. 1912]	A Bad Beginning	–	–	*Look!*
Feb. 1928 [?Oct.–Dec. 1912]	Why Does She Weep?	–	–	*Look!*

579

Feb. 1928 [?2 Nov. 1912]	Giorno dei Morti	–	*New Statesman* 15 Nov. 1913 ('Service of All the Dead')	*Look!*
Feb. 1928 [?1917; later than 1912]	All Souls	–	–	*Look!*
Feb. 1928 [?Winter 1912–13]	Lady Wife	–	–	*Look!*
	Both Sides of the Medal	–	–	*Look!*
	Loggerheads	E205.8b ('Deadlock')	–	*Look!*
	December Night	–	–	*Look!*
	New Year's Eve	–	–	*Look!*
	New Year's Night	–	–	*Look!*
	Valentine's Night	In E205.8a title was 'Candlemass' (iii. 145, n. 1).	–	*Look!*
	Birth Night	In E205.8a title was 'Eve's Mass' (iii. 145, n. 1).	–	*Look!*
Feb. 1928 [?1917; later than early 1913]	Rabbit Snared in the Night	E330. In MS205.8a title was 'Rabbit Snared in the Dark' (iii. 115).	–	*Look!*
Feb. 1928 [?early 1913]	Paradise Re-entered	E320.6 ('Purity')	–	*Look!*
Jan. 1927 [?April 1918]	Coming Awake	–	–	*NP*
Feb. 1928 [?April 1913]	Spring Morning ('San Gaudenzio')	–	–	*Look!*
Feb. 1928 [?Spring 1913]	Wedlock	–	–	*Look!*
Feb. 1928 [?June–July 1913]	History ('The Cearne')	–	–	*Look!*
Feb. 1928 [Summer 1912]	Song of a Man Who Is Loved	E320.6	–	–
	Song of a Man Who Has Come Through	–	–	*Look!*
	One Woman to All Women ('Kensington')	–	–	*Look!*

Feb. 1928 [Winter 1909–10]	People	E320.1 ('The Street-Lamps')	–	*Look!*
	Street Lamps	E320.1 ('The Street-Lamps')	*Egoist* Jan. 1917	*Look!*
Feb. 1928 [?1915–17]	'She said as well to me'	–	–	*Look!*
Feb. 1928 [?early 1915]	New Heaven and Earth ('Greatham')	–	*SIP* (1917) ('Terra Nuova')	*Look!*
Feb. 1928 [by 28 June 1916]	Elysium	E113.3 ('The Blind')	–	*Look!*
Feb. 1928 [?Summer 1916]	Manifesto ('Zennor')	–	–	*Look!*
Feb. 1928 [?Autumn 1916]	Autumn Rain	–	*Egoist* Feb. 1917	*Look!*
Feb. 1928 [?Winter 1916–17]	Frost Flowers	E142	*ER* Sept. 1917	*Look!*
Feb. 1928 [late Feb. 1917]	Craving for Spring ('Zennor')	–	–	*Look!*
	BIRDS, BEASTS AND FLOWERS			
Feb. 1928 [10–15 Sept. 1920]	Pomegranate ('San Gervasio in Tuscany')	E320.9b	*Dial* (March 1921)	*BBF*
	Peach ('San Gervasio')	E47c	–	*BBF*
	Medlars and Sorb-Apples ('San Gervasio')	E47c	*NR* 5 Jan. 1921	*BBF*
	Figs ('San Gervasio')	E47c ('Fig')	–	*BBF*
	Grapes ('San Gervasio')	E47c	–	*BBF*
Feb. 1928 [?15–16 Sept. 1920]	The Revolutionary ('Florence')	E47c	*NR* 19 Jan. 1921	*BBF*
Feb. 1928 [?Oct. 1920]	The Evening Land ('Baden-Baden')	E47c	*Poetry* Nov. 1922	*BBF*
Feb. 1928 [?July 1920]	Peace ('Taormina')	E47a	*Ench Y* June 1921 ('Slopes of Etna')	*BBF*
Feb. 1928 [15–28 Sept. 1920]	Cypresses ('Fiesole')	E47c	–	*BBF*
Feb. 1928 [by 28 Jan. 1921]	Bare Fig-Trees ('Taormina')	E39	–	*BBF*
	Bare Almond-Trees ('Taormina')	E47c	–	*BBF*

Feb. 1928 [July 1920]	Tropic ('Taormina')	E47a	*Ench Y* June 1921	*BBF*
Feb. 1928 [June–July 1920]	Southern Night ('Taormina')	E47a	–	*BBF*
Feb. 1928 [by 28 Jan. 1921]	Almond Blossom ('Fontana Vecchia')	E12a	*ER* Feb. 1922	*BBF*
Feb. 1928 [4 Feb. 1921]	Purple Anemones ('Taormina')	E47a	–	*BBF*
Feb. 1928 [18–25 Oct. 1920]	Sicilian Cyclamens ('Taormina')	E47a	–	*BBF*
Feb. 1928 [31 Jan. 1921]	Hibiscus and Salvia Flowers ('Taormina')	E47a	–	*BBF*
Feb. 1928 [15 Sept.– ?14 Oct. 1920]	St Matthew	E47c	*Poetry* April 1923	*BBF*
	St Mark	E352.55	*Dial* April 1921	*BBF*
	St Luke	E352.53	*Dial* April 1921	*BBF*
	St John ('San Gervasio')	E352.5	*Dial* April 1921	*BBF*
Feb. 1928 [Oct.–Nov. 1920]	Mosquito ('Siracusa')	E47c	*Bookman* July 1921	*BBF*
Feb. 1928 [by 9 Sept. 1921]	Fish ('Zell-am-See')	E47c	*ER* June 1922	*BBF*
Feb. 1928 [by 17 Sept. 1921]	Bat	E47c	*ER* Nov. 1922	*BBF*
	Man and Bat ('Florence')	E47c	–	*BBF*
Feb. 1928 [by 28 Jan. 1921]	Snake ('Taormina')	E362.7b	*Dial* July 1921	*BBF*
Feb. 1928 [15–30 Sept. 1920]	Baby Tortoise	–	*ER* Nov. 1922	*BBF*
	Tortoise Shell	–	–	*BBF*
	Tortoise Family Connections	–	–	*BBF*
	Lui et Elle	–	–	*BBF*
	Tortoise Gallantry	–	–	*BBF*
	Tortoise Shout	–	–	*BBF*
Feb. 1928 [15–28 Sept. 1920]	Turkey-Cock ('Fiesole')	E47c	*Poetry* Nov. 1922	*BBF*
Feb. 1928 [18 Oct.–4 Nov. 1920]	Humming-Bird ('Española')	E47c	*NR* 11 May 1921	*BBF*

Feb. 1928 [11 Oct. 1922]	Eagle in New Mexico ('Taos')	E47a	–	*BBF*
Feb. 1928 [Jan. 1923]	The Blue Jay ('Lobo')	E47c	–	*BBF*
Feb. 1928 [2 March 1921]	The Ass ('Taormina')	E47a	–	*BBF*
Feb. 1928 [?early 1922]	He-Goat ('Taormina')	E47c	–	*BBF*
Feb. 1928 [? early 1922]	She-Goat ('Taormina')	E47c	–	*BBF*
Feb. 1928 [*c.* late March 1922; or Jan. 1923]	Elephant ('Kandy')	E47c	*ER* April 1923	*BBF*
Feb. 1928 [late June–July 1922; or Jan. 1923]	Kangaroo ('Sydney')	E47c	–	*BBF*
Feb. 1928 [by 1 Feb. 1923]	Bibbles ('Lobo')	E47c	–	*BBF*
Feb. 1928 [by 7 Feb. 1923]	Mountain Lion ('Lobo')	E47c	–	*BBF*
Feb. 1928 [25 Oct.–8 Nov. 1922]	The Red Wolf ('Taos')	E340.3	–	*BBF*
Feb. 1928 [Oct. 1922]	Men in New Mexico ('Taos')	E234.5a	–	*BBF*
Feb. 1928 [25 Oct.–8 Nov. 1922]	Autumn at Taos ('Taos')	E31.5	–	*BBF*
	Spirits Summoned West ('Taos')	E47c	–	*BBF*
Feb. 1928 [by 14 March 1923]	The American Eagle ('Lobo')	E47a	–	*BBF*
later April 1928	[Guards] Potency of Men	E155a	–	–
	Gipsy (2nd 'MS' version)	E155a	–	–
Nov.–Dec. 1928	**The *Pansies* notebook**			
early Nov. or *c.* 17–24 Nov. 1928	'I know a noble Englishman' ('The noble Englishman')	E302d	–	*Pansies* (PP)
	'How beastly the bourgeois is!'	E302d	–	*Pansies*

c. 17–24 Nov. 1928	'If you live among the middle classes' ('Worm either way')	E302d	–	*Pansies*
	Natural Complexion	E302d	–	*Pansies*
	The English Voice ('The Oxford Voice')	E302d	–	*Pansies*
	The Gentleman	E302d	–	*Poems* 830
	What Matters	E302d	–	*Pansies* (PP)
	The Young Are not Mean in Material Things ('A played-out game –'; 'The combative spirit')	E302d	–	*Pansies*
	The Young Want to be Just ('A played-out game –'; 'The combative spirit')	E302d	–	*Pansies*
	Roses	E302d; E302f	–	*Poems* 831
	The Young Are Not Greedy ('A played-out game –'; 'The combative spirit')	E302d	–	*Pansies*
	Middle-Class Children	E302d	–	*Poems* 832
	Know Thyself ('Know thyself, and that thou art mortal')	E302d	–	*Pansies*
Nov.–Dec. 1916; and Nov. 1928	The Gazelle calf	E49a; and E302d	–	*Pansies*
c. 17–24 Nov. 1928	Little Fish	E302d	–	*Pansies*
	The Mosquito ('The Mosquito knows –')	E302d	–	*Pansies*
	Self-Pity	E302d	–	*Pansies*
	Spray	E302d	–	*Pansies*
	Seaweed	E302d	*Dial* July 1929	*Pansies*
	The New Moon ('New Moon')	E302d	–	*Pansies*
	Night	E302d	–	*Poems* 834
	Touch	E302d	–	*Pansies*
	Sex ('Leave sex alone –')	E302d	–	*Pansies*
	Love ('The mess of love –')	E302d	–	*Pansies*

	Fidelity	E302d	–	*Pansies*
	All I ask	E302d	–	*Pansies*
	Female Coercion	E302d	–	*Pansies*
	Energetic Women	E302d	–	*Pansies*
	Volcanic Venus	E302d	–	*Pansies*
	What does she want?	E302d	–	*Pansies* (PP)
	Don't look at Me	E302d	–	*Pansies* (PP)
	Poor Bit of a Wench	E302d	–	*Pansies*
	What ails Thee?	E302d	–	*Pansies*
	Tarts	E302d	–	*Pansies*
	So There!	E302d	–	*Poems* 835
	The worst of the Younger Generation ('Latter-day sinners')	E302d	–	*Pansies*
	The Fate of the Younger Generation ('Fate and the younger generation')	E302d	–	*Pansies*
	Cowardly Man ('Cowards')	E302d	–	*Pansies*
	'Think, the sapphire is only alumina, a sort of aluminium' ('Think – !'; 'Peacock')	E302d	–	*Pansies*
	Think how – ('Paltry-looking people')	E302d	–	*Pansies*
by 24 Nov. 1928	Morality ('Man's image')	E302d	–	*Pansies*
c. 24–29 Nov. 1928	Immorality	E302d	–	*Pansies*
	Censors	E302d	*Dial* July 1929	*Pansies*
	Conscience	E302d	–	*Pansies*
	The Middle Classes	E302d	–	*Pansies*
	Aristocracy ('Aristocracy of the Sun')	E302d	–	*Pansies*
	Democracy	E302d	–	*Pansies*
	A Man	E302d	–	*Pansies*
	Sacred Order of Men ('Sun-men')	E302d	–	*Pansies*
	Sacred Order of Women ('Sun-women')	E302d	–	*Pansies*

	A Lizard ('Lizard')	E302d	*Dial* July 1929	*Pansies*
	Self-Protection	E302d	–	*Pansies*
	Life and the Human Consciousness ('A tale told by an idiot')	E302d	–	*Pansies*
	Being Alive	E302d	–	*Pansies*
	A finished Game ('A played-out game –')	E302d	–	*Pansies*
	The Latent Desire	E302d	–	*Poems* 838
	For all that	E302d	–	*Poems* 838
	Wages	E302d	–	*Pansies*
	Young Fathers	E302d	–	*Pansies*
	Young Men of Today	E302d	–	–
	Love as an Escape	E302d	–	*Poems* 838
	Make a Revolution ('A sane revolution')	E302d	–	*Pansies*
	The Third Thing	E302d	–	*Pansies*
	The Sun in me ('Sun in me')	E302d	–	*Pansies*
	Nemesis	E302d	–	*Pansies*
	What's to be done ('Be still!')	E302d	–	*Pansies*
	Rallying-Point	E302d	–	*Poems* 839
	Today ('Fear of society is the root of all evil')	E302d	–	*Pansies*
	Moon-Memory (Moon memory)	E302d	–	*Pansies*
	Rain in Me ('There is rain in me –')	E302d	–	*Pansies*
	Desire Gone Down into the Sea ('Desire goes down into the Sea –')	E302d	–	*Pansies*
by 29 Nov. 1928	On the Shore ('November by the Sea –')	E302d	*Dial* July 1929	*Pansies*
by 2 Dec. 1928	The Elements ('Elemental')	E302d	–	*Pansies*
	Fire: 'Ah, the fire' ('I wish I knew a woman –'; 'Talk')	E302d	–	*Pansies*

Two Wishes ('I wish I knew a woman –'; 'Talk')	E302d	–	*Pansies*
Elderly Discontented Women	E302d	–	*Pansies*
Old People	E302d	–	*Pansies*
The Grudge of the Old	E302d	–	*Pansies*
To be Old ('Beautiful old age –')	E302d	–	*Pansies*
Desire is Dead	E196.6 'Let the flood rise'; and E302d	–	*Pansies*
Numbness ('Man reaches a point')	E302d	–	*Pansies*
The Grasshopper has become a Burden ('Grasshopper is a burden')	E196.6 'Let the flood rise'; and E302d	–	*Pansies*
It is Finished ('Basta!')	E302d	–	*Pansies*
Tragedy	E302d	–	*Pansies*
The End of Sorrow ('After all the tragedies are over –')	E302d	–	*Pansies*
Nonentity ('Nullus')	E302d	–	*Pansies*
The Salt of the Earth ('Salt of the earth –')	E192a[1]; E302d	–	*Pansies*
Fresh Water	E192a[1]; and E302d	–	*Pansies*
Peace ('Peace and War –')	E192a[1] 'Widdershins', 'War'; and E302d	–	*Pansies*
Gain	E302d	–	–
Glory	E192a[1]; E302d	–	*Pansies*
Fight for Life ('What would you fight for?')	E192a[1]; E302d	*Dial* July 1929	*Pansies*
Woe	E192a[1] 'Woe is over the World'; and E302d	–	*Pansies*

Attila	E192a[1]; E302d	*Dial* July 1929	*Pansies*
Choice	E192a[1]; E302d	–	*Pansies*
Riches	E192a[1] 'To be Rich'; and E302d	–	*Pansies*
Poverty	E192a[1] 'To be poor'; and E302d	–	*Pansies*
Noble	E192a[1] 'To be Noble'; and E302d	–	*Pansies*
Wealth	E192a[1] 'I am Well-off'; and E302d	–	*Pansies*
Intolerance ('Tolerance')	E192a[1] 'Intolerance'; and E302d	–	*Pansies*
Compari	E192a[1]; E302d	–	*Pansies*
Sick	E192a[1]; E302d	–	*Pansies*
One thing I don't want to do ('Cerebral emotions')	E302d	–	*Pansies*
Wellsian Futures	E302d	–	*Pansies*
To a Woman ('To women, as far as I'm concerned')	E302d	–	*Pansies*
I am a Blank ('Blank')	E302d	–	*Pansies*
When I went to the film	E302d	–	*Pansies*
When I went to the Circus	E302d	*Dial* May 1929	*Pansies*
c. 29 Nov.– 2 Dec. 1928 Our day is Over	E302d	–	*Pansies*
Hark in the Dusk!	E302d	–	*Pansies*
Elephants in the Circus	E302d	–	*Pansies*
Elephants Plodding	E302d	–	*Pansies*
On the Drum	E302d	–	*Pansies*
The two performing Elephants ('Two performing Elephants')	E302d	–	*Pansies*

	Twilight	E302d	–	*Pansies*
	Cups	E302d	–	*Pansies*
	Bowls	E302d	–	*Pansies*
	You	E302d	–	*Pansies*
	In the Dark ('After dark')	E302d	–	*Pansies*
2–15 Dec. 1928	To be or thus to be ('To let go or to hold on – ?')	E302d	*Dial* July 1929	*Pansies*
	Swan	E302d	–	*Pansies*
	Religion ('Give us gods')	E302d	–	*Pansies*
	Gods ('Spiral flame')	E302d	–	*Pansies*
	Little-boy brilliants	E302d	–	*Poems* 841
	I heard her say –	E302d	–	*Poems* 842
	What's wrong –	E302d	–	*Poems* 843
	The Ignoble Procession	E302d	–	*Pansies*
	Never, my young men – ('No joy in life –')	E302d	–	*Pansies*
	Money ('Money-madness –')	E302d	–	*Pansies*
	Kill money	E302d	–	*Pansies*
	Sex won't work – ('Wild things in captivity –')	E302d	–	*Pansies*
	Mournful young man ('Mournful young men –')	E302d	–	*Pansies*
	There is no way out	E302d	–	*Pansies* (PP)
	In Nottingham ('Nottingham's New University –')	E302d	–	*Pansies*
	O Start a Revolution	–E302d	–	*Pansies*
	For God's Sake – ('Let us be Men –')	E302d	–	*Pansies*
	Work	E302d	*Dial* July 1929	*Pansies*
	There is nothing but life – ('All that we have is Life –')	E302d	–	*Pansies*
	Things men have made – ('Things Men have made –'; 'Things made by Iron –'; 'New Houses, new Clothes –')	E302d	*Dial* July 1929	*Pansies*

Whatever lives – ('Whatever Man makes –')	E302d	*Dial* July 1929	*Pansies*
Fight O my young men	E302d	–	*Pansies*
Women want fighters for their lovers	E302d	–	*Pansies* (PP)
'It's either you fight or you die'	E302d	–	*Pansies*
'Beware, oh my young men, of rottenness' ('Beware! O my dear young men –')	E302d	–	*Pansies*
Deeper than love ('Underneath –')	E302d	–	*Pansies*; see also *Poems* 844, 954
My father was – ('Red-herring')	E302d	–	*Pansies*
I read a novel – ('I am in a novel –')	E302d	–	*Pansies*
My naughty book	E302d	–	*Pansies* (PP)
Morality of sin ('Our moral age –')	E302d	–	*Pansies*
No Mr Lawrence – !	E302d	–	*Pansies*
'There is a little gentleman' ('The little wowser –')	E302d	–	*Pansies* (PP)
'When you read Shakespeare' ('When I read Shakespeare –')	E302d	–	*Pansies*
Mr Squire Says I'm not lovable	E302d	–	–
'I'm sick of loving women' ('The effort of love –')	E302d	–	*Pansies*
'Any woman who says to me' ('Can't be borne –')	E302d	–	*Pansies*
'Bawdy can be sane and wholesome'	E302d; E302f 'What's sane and what isn't'	–	*Poems* 845, 956
'Oh Juliette' ('Henriette')	E302d	–	*Pansies*
by 15 Dec. 1928	'Thank you, dear Maria' ('To Clarinda')	E302d	–	*Pansies* (PP)

c. 9 Dec. 1928	As for me, I'm a patriot	E24.7; and E302d	–	*Pansies*
	After it's happened ('Now it's happened')	E281.7; and E302d	–	*Pansies*
by 20 Dec. 1928	'When all's said and done'	E302d	–	–
	Demon justice	E302d	–	*Pansies* (PP)
	'Oh be a demon' ('Be a demon!')	E302d	–	*Pansies* (PP)

Uncollected 'Pansies' not in *Pansies* notebook

late Nov. 1928	Amphibian	E192a[1]	Smailes	–
	Salt-licks	E192a[1]	Smailes	–
	The Maleficent Triangle	E192a[1]	Smailes	–
Nov. 1928– 11 Feb. 1929	'Softly, then, softly'	[E367a]; E367b	–	*Fire; Poems* 765
	'Reach over, then, reach over'	E335	–	*Fire; Poems* 763
	'Traitors, oh liars, you Judas lot!'	E405a	–	*Fire; Poems* 762
	'Are you pining to be superior? –'	E22	–	*Fire; Poems* 773
	Fire: 'Wave then'	[E131a]; E315a	–	*Fire; Poems* 783

Collected 'Pansies' not in *Pansies* notebook, E302d

c. 20 Dec. 1928– 7 Jan. 1929	What is man without an income?	E426.5a; E302f	–	*Pansies*
	Altercation	E12.7a; E302f	–	*Pansies*
	The saddest day	E322.5; E302f	–	*Pansies*
	Prestige	E322.5; E302f	–	*Pansies*
	Finding your Level	[E302a]; E302f 'Let me put you in your place –'	–	*Pansies*
	Climbing Up	[E302a]; E302f 'When you climb up to the upper classes –'	–	*Pansies*
	Canvassing for the Election	[E302a]; E302f	–	*Pansies*

A Rise in the World	[E302a]; E302f	–	*Pansies*
	'I rose up in		
	the world –'		
True democracy	E302f	–	*Pansies*
To be superior	E302f	–	*Pansies*
Leda	E302f	–	*Pansies*
Let the dead bury	E302f	–	*Pansies*
their dead –			
A living	E302f	–	*Pansies*
We are transmitters –	E302f	–	*Pansies*
The sea, the sea –	E302f	–	*Pansies*
Good husbands make	E302f	–	*Pansies*
unhappy wives –			
Don'ts –	E302f	–	*Pansies*
The risen lord	E302f	–	*Pansies*
What was lost –	E302f	–	*Pansies*
('The secret waters –')			
Obscenity	E302f	–	*Pansies*
Sex isn't sin –	E302f	–	*Pansies*
The elephant is slow	E302f	–	*Pansies*
to mate –			
Sex and trust –	E302f	–	*Pansies*
My enemy –	E302f	–	*Pansies*
Noli me tangere –	E302f	–	*Pansies*
Chastity	E302f	–	*Pansies*
Let us talk, let us	E302f	–	*Pansies*
laugh –			
Touch comes –	E302f	–	*Pansies*
The root of all our	E302f	–	*Pansies*
evil – ('The root of			
our evil –')			
Many mansions –	E302f	–	*Pansies*
Dead people –	E302f	–	*Pansies*
Courage	E302f	–	*Pansies*
After all the tragedies	E302f	–	*Pansies*
are over –			
Dies Irae	E302f	–	*Pansies*
Dies Illa –	E302f	–	*Pansies*
The death of our	E302f	–	*Pansies*
era –			
When things get	E302f	–	*Pansies*
bad – ('At last')			
You have to pay –	E302f	–	*Pansies*
('Always this paying –')			

	Pathos of youth – ('Poor young things –')	E302f	–	*Pansies*
	Triumph	E302f	–	*Pansies*
	Relativity –	E302f	–	*Pansies*
	Man is immoral – ('Immoral Man')	E302f	–	*Pansies*
	Film passion –	E302f	–	*Pansies*
	It's no good –	E302f	–	*Pansies*
	Up he goes –	E302f	–	*Pansies*
	Have done with it –	E302f	–	*Pansies*
	Maybe!	E302f	–	*Pansies*
	Stand up!	E302f	–	*Pansies*
	Trust	E302f	–	*Pansies*
	Won't it be strange – ?	E302f	–	*Pansies*
	When wilt thou teach the people – ?	E302f	–	*Pansies*
	When the ripe fruit falls –	E302f	–	*Pansies*
	Fire: 'Fire is nice' ('Fire': 'Fire is dearer to us than love or food')	E302f	–	*Pansies*
	Space	E302f	–	*Pansies*
	Wonderful women – ('Wonderful spiritual women')			
	Willy Wet-leg – ('Willy wet-legs')	E302f	–	*Pansies*
18 Jan. 1929	Ships in bottles	E302f	–	*Pansies*
7 Jan.–11 Feb. 1929	Old song	E302g	–	*Pansies*
	Climb down, O lordly mind –	E302g	–	*Pansies*
	Ego bound	E302g	–	*Pansies*
	Jealousy	E302g	–	*Pansies*
	Ego-bound women –	E302g	–	*Pansies* (PP)
	Know deeply, know thyself more deeply –	E302g	–	*Pansies*
	The universe flows –	E302g	–	*Pansies*
	The primal passions –	E302g	–	*Pansies*
	Escape	E302g	–	*Pansies*
	Men are not bad –	E302g	–	*Pansies*
	Stop it –	E302g	–	*Pansies*

	The new word	E302g	–	*Pansies*
	The optimist	E302g	–	*Pansies*
	The sane universe	E302g	–	*Pansies*
	God	E302g	–	*Pansies*
	Sane and insane	E302g	–	*Pansies*
	The rose of England	E302g	–	*Pansies*
	England in 1929	E302g	–	*Pansies*
	Liberty's old story	E302g	–	*Pansies*
	New brooms	E302g	–	*Pansies*
	Police spies	E302g	–	*Pansies*
	Conundrums	E302g	–	*Pansies*
	Vitality	E302g	–	*Pansies*
	The jeune fille	E302g	–	*Pansies* (PP)
	Why – ?	E302g	–	*Pansies*
	What is he?	E302g	–	*Pansies*
	Destiny	E302g	–	*Pansies*
c. 24 Jan.–11 Feb. 1929	'Oh the teeth of the old dogs are dirty & yellow' ('The young and their moral guardians')	E320f; E302g	–	*Pansies* (PP)
	The *Nettles* notebook (*More Pansies*)			
11 Feb.–*c.* 7 March 1929	Image-making love.	E192a[1]	*IA*	*LaP*
	People.	E192a[1]	–	*LaP*
	Desire	E192a[1]	–	*LaP*
	<Love.>	E192a[1]	–	–
c. 20 May 1929	To a certain friend	E192a[1]	–	*LaP*
	The Emotional Friend.	E192a[1]	–	*LaP*
	Correspondence in after years	E192a[1]	–	*LaP*
11 Feb.–*c.* 7 March 1929	The Egoists	E192a[1]	–	*LaP*
	Chimaera	E192a[1]	–	*LaP*
	Ultimate Reality	E192a[1]	*IA*	*LaP*
	Sphinx	E192a[1]	*IA*	*LaP*
	Intimates	E192a[1]	*IA*	*LaP*
	True love at last.	E192a[1]	*IA*	*LaP*
c. 1 June–22 June 1929	Andraitx. – Pomegranate flowers.	E192a[1]	–	*LaP*
	I dare do all.	E192a[1]	–	*LaP*
	Battle of Life.	E192a[1]	–	*LaP*

594

There are too many people.	E192a[1]	–	*LaP*
The Heart of Man.	E192a[1]	–	*LaP*
Moral Clothing	E192a[1]	–	*LaP*
Behaviour	E192a[1]	–	*LaP*
The Hostile Sun	E192a[1]	–	*LaP*
The Church	E192a[1]	–	*LaP*
The Protestant Churches.	E192a[1]	–	*LaP*
Loneliness	E192a[1]	–	*LaP*
The Uprooted.	E192a[1]	–	*LaP*
Delight of being alone.	E192a[1]	–	*LaP*
Refused friendship.	E192a[1]	–	*LaP*
Future Relationships	E192a[1]	–	*LaP*
Future Religion	E192a[1]	–	*LaP*
Future States.	E192a[1]	–	*LaP*
Future War	E192a[1]	–	*LaP*
Signs of the Times	E192a[1]	–	*LaP*
Initiation Degrees	E192a[1]	–	*LaP*
Unhappy Souls	E192a[1]	–	*LaP*
Full life	E192a[1]	–	*LaP*
People who care	E192a[1]	–	*LaP*
Non-existence	E192a[1]	–	*LaP*
All-knowing	E192a[1]	–	*LaP*
Salvation.	E192a[1]	–	*LaP*
Old Archangels	E192a[1]	–	*LaP*
Lucifer	E192a[1]	*IA* April 1930	*LaP*
The Mills of God.	E192a[1]	–	*LaP*
Multitudes.	E192a[1]	–	*LaP*
Fallen Leaves.	E192a[1]	–	*LaP*
The difference.	E192a[1]	–	*LaP*
The breath of life	E192a[1]	–	*LaP*
Vengeance is mine –	E192a[1]	–	*LaP*
Astronomical Changes	E192a[1]	–	*LaP*
Fatality	E192a[1]	–	*LaP*
Free Will.	E192a[1]	–	*LaP*
In a Spanish tram-car.	E192a[1]	–	*LaP*
Spanish privilege	E192a[1]	–	*LaP*
At the bank in Spain.	E192a[1]	–	*LaP*
The Spanish wife.	E192a[1]	–	*LaP*
The painter's wife.	E192a[1]	–	*LaP*
Modern problems.	E192a[1]	–	*LaP*
Dominant woman.	E192a[1]	–	*LaP*

	Men and Women	E192a[1]	–	*LaP*
	The Scientific doctor.	E192a[1]	–	*LaP*
	Healing.	E192a[1]	–	*LaP*
	En masse.	E192a[1]	–	*LaP*
	God and the Holy Ghost.	E192a[1]	–	*LaP*
	Humility	E192a[1]	–	*LaP*
	Proper Pride.	E192a[1]	–	*LaP*
	Humility-mongers.	E192a[1]	–	*LaP*
	Tender Reverence.	E192a[1]	–	*LaP*
	Absolute Reverence.	E192a[1]	–	*LaP*
	Belief.	E192a[1]	–	*LaP*
	Modern Prayer.	E192a[1]	–	*Nettles*
	Bells.	E192a[1]	*London Mercury* March 1930	*LaP*
	The triumph of the machine.	E192a[1]	*London Mercury* June 1930	*LaP*
c. 22 June 1929	Forte dei Marmi	E192a[1]	–	*LaP*
c. 22 June–6 July 1929	Sea-bathers.	E192a[1]	–	*LaP*
	Talk of loyalty	E192a[1]	–	*LaP*
	Talk of faith.	E192a[1]	–	*LaP*
	Leaves of grass, flowers of grass. ('Leaves of Grass, Flowers of Grass'; 'Magnificent Democracy')	E192a[1]	–	*Nettles*
	Amo sacrum vulgus	E192a[1]	–	*LaP*
	Boredom, ennui, depression	E192a[1]	–	*LaP*
	The deadly Victorians	E192a[1]	–	*LaP*
	What are the wild waves saying – ?	E192a[1]	–	*LaP*
	Welcome Death.	E192a[1]	–	*LaP*
	Dark Satanic Mills	E192a[1]	–	*LaP*
	We die together.	E192a[1]	–	*LaP*
	What have they done to you – ?	E192a[1]	–	*Nettles*
	What is a man to do?	E192a[1]	–	*LaP*
c. 7–18 July 1929	City-life ('The People')	E192a[1]	–	*Nettles*
	The factory cities –	E192a[1]	–	*Nettles*
	Cry of the masses –	E192a[1]	–	*Nettles*

	13 Pictures	E192a[1]	–	*LaP*
	Auto da Fe.	E192a[1]	–	*LaP*
	Give me a sponge.	E192a[1]	–	*Nettles*
	Shows.	E192a[1]	–	*LaP*
	Rose and Cabbage. ('A Rose is not a Cabbage')	E192a[1]	–	*Nettles*
	The Gulf	E192a[1]	–	*LaP*
	The Cross.	E192a[1]	–	*LaP*
	Fellow-men	E192a[1]	–	*LaP*
	The Sight of God	E192a[1]	–	*LaP*
	Souls to save	E192a[1]	–	*LaP*
	When most men die.	E192a[1]	–	*LaP*
	Hold Back!	E192a[1]	–	*LaP*
	Impulse.	E192a[1]	–	*LaP*
	Men like Gods	E192a[1]	–	*LaP*
	Man and Machine	E192a[1]	–	*LaP*
	Masses and Classes	E192a[1]	–	*LaP*
	Give us the Thebaïd.	E192a[1]	–	*LaP*
	Side-step, O sons of men!	E192a[1]	–	*LaP*
	On and on and on –	E192a[1]	–	*LaP*
	Oh wonderful machine!	E192a[1]	–	*LaP*
	But I say unto you: Love one another.	E192a[1]	–	*LaP*
	Love thy neighbour –	E192a[1]	–	*LaP*
	As thyself – !	E192a[1]	–	*LaP*
	Lonely, lonesome, loney-o!	E192a[1]	–	*LaP*
?mid-July 1929	À la Manière de D. H. Lawrence [Poem is of doubtful authority]	E1	–	*Poems* 846
c. 19 July 1929	Trees in the Garden ('Lichtent[h]al')	E192a[1]	–	*LaP*
c. 20 July 1929	Storm in the Black Forest.	E192a[1]	–	*LaP*
19 July–24 Aug. 1929	Revolutions as such!	E192a[1]	–	*LaP*
	Robot feelings	E192a[1]	–	*LaP*
	Robot-democracy.	E192a[1]	–	*LaP*
	Real democracy.	E192a[1]	–	*LaP*

Worship.	E192a[1]	–	*LaP*
Classes	E192a[1]	–	*LaP*
Democracy is Service	E192a[1]	–	*LaP*
False democracy and real.	E192a[1]	–	*LaP*
Service.	E192a[1]	–	*LaP*
What are the gods?	E192a[1]	–	*LaP*
The gods! the gods!	E192a[1]	–	*LaP*
Name the gods!	E192a[1]	–	*LaP*
There are no gods –	E192a[1]	–	*LaP*
Food of the North	E192a[1]	–	*LaP*
Retort to Whitman	E192a[1]	–	*LaP*
Retort to Jesus	E192a[1]	–	*LaP*
The deepest sensuality	E192a[1]	–	*LaP*
Sense of truth.	E192a[1]	–	*LaP*
<Beauty and truth.>	E192a[1]	Smailes	–
Satisfaction	E192a[1]	–	*LaP*
Vibration of Justice	E192a[1]	–	*LaP*
Lies	E192a[1]	–	*LaP*
Poison.	E192a[1]	–	*LaP*
Commandments	E192a[1]	–	*LaP*
Emotional lies.	E192a[1]	–	*LaP*
Laughter.	E192a[1]	–	*LaP*
Drawing-room.	E192a[1]	–	*LaP*
Cabbage-roses.	E192a[1]	–	*LaP*
Cold blood.	E192a[1]	–	*LaP*
Sunset	E192a[1]	–	*LaP*
Listen to the band!	E192a[1]	–	*LaP*
The human face.	E192a[1]	–	*LaP*
Portraits	E192a[1]	–	*LaP*
Furniture	E192a[1]	–	*LaP*
Children singing in school.	E192a[1]	–	*LaP*
Keep it up.	E192a[1]	–	*LaP*
Race and battle.	E192a[1]	–	*LaP*
Nothing to save.	E192a[1]	–	*LaP*
Puss-Puss!	E192a[1]; E266b	–	*Nettles*
London Mercury	E192a[1]; E266b	–	*Nettles*
My little critics	E192a[1]; E266b	–	*Nettles*

Emasculation. ('Never had a Daddy')	E192a[1]; E266b	–	*Poems* 658
Editorial Office.	E192a[1]; E266b	–	*Nettles*
British Sincerity	E192a[1]	–	*LaP*
The English are so nice!	E192a[1]	–	*LaP*
The Hills	E192a[1]	–	*LaP*
Tourists	E192a[1]	–	*LaP*
Seekers.	E192a[1]	–	*LaP*
Search for love.	E192a[1]	–	*LaP*
Search for truth.	E192a[1]	–	*LaP*
Lies about love.	E192a[1]	–	*LaP*
Travel is over.	E192a[1]	–	*LaP*
Old Men.	E192a[1]	–	*LaP*
Death.	E192a[1]	–	*LaP*
Bourgeois and Bolshevist	E192a[1]	–	*LaP*
Property and No-property	E192a[1]	–	*LaP*
Cowardice and Impudence.	E192a[1]	–	*LaP*
Lord Tennyson and Lord Melchett.	E192a[1]	–	*LaP*
Choice of evils.	E192a[1]	–	*LaP*
Hard-boiled Conservatives	E192a[1]	–	*LaP*
Solomon's baby	E192a[1]	–	*LaP*
The Property Question	E192a[1]	–	*LaP*
The way out.	E192a[1]	–	*LaP*
St George and the Dragon.	E192a[1]	–	*LaP*
The half-blind.	E192a[1]	–	*LaP*
Minorities in danger.	E192a[1]	–	*LaP*
If you are a man –	E192a[1]	–	*LaP*
Terra incognita.	E192a[1]	–	*LaP*
Climbing down.	E192a[1]	–	*LaP*
Only the best matters	E192a[1]	–	*LaP*
by 19 Aug. 1929 To Pino	E192a[1]	–	*LaP*
19 July–24 Aug. 1929 Broadcasting to the G.B.P.	E192a[1]	–	*LaP*
We can't be too careful	E192a[1]	–	*LaP*

The Member of the British Public ('The Man in the Street')	E192a[1]	–	*Nettles*
Lucky little Britisher ('Britannia's Baby')	E192a[1]	–	*Nettles*
Innocent England	E192a[1]	–	*Nettles*
13000 people.	E192a[1]	–	*Nettles*
Change of Government	E192a[1]	–	*Nettles*
The British Public and the Government. ('The British Workman and the Government')	E192a[1]	–	*Nettles*
The Working Man ('Clydesider')	E192a[1]	–	*Nettles*
The Great Newspaper Editor to his Subordinate.	E192a[1]; E266b	–	*Nettles*
Flapper Vote.	E192a[1]	–	*Nettles*
Glimpses	E192a[1]	–	*LaP*
All sorts of gods.	E192a[1]	–	*LaP*
For a moment.	E192a[1]	–	*LaP*
Goethe and Pose.	E192a[1]	–	*LaP*
Men like Gods.	E192a[1]	–	*LaP*
\<Meditation\>	E192a[1]	–	–
\<The gods are us.\>	E192a[1]	–	–
Thought	E192a[1]	–	*LaP*
Be it so.	E192a[1]	–	*LaP*
Conceit.	E192a[1]	–	*LaP*
Man is more than *homo sapiens*.	E192a[1]	–	*LaP*
Self-conscious people.	E192a[1]	–	*LaP*
Two ways of living and dying.	E192a[1]	–	*LaP*
So let me live	E192a[1]	–	*LaP*
Gladness of Death.	E192a[1]	–	*LaP*
Humanity needs pruning	E192a[1]	–	*LaP*
Self-Sacrifice.	E192a[1]	–	*LaP*
Shedding of blood.	E192a[1]	–	*LaP*

	The old idea of sacrifice	E192a[1]	–	*LaP*
	Self-sacrifice	E192a[1]	–	*LaP*
	Songs I was taught at School ('Songs I Learnt at School/ I. Neptune's Little Affair with Freedom')	E192a[1]	–	*Nettles*
	another song/ The British Boy ('[Songs I Learnt at School] III The British Boy')	E192a[1]	–	*Nettles*
	Another Song I learned at School ('[Songs I Learnt at School] II. My Native Land')	E192a[1]	–	*Nettles*
24 Aug. 1929	'I heard a little chicken chirp'	E192a[1]	–	*LaP*
	"Gross, coarse, hideous –"	E192a[1], E154.7	–	*LaP*
	'Dearly-beloved Mr Squire'	E192a[1]	–	*LaP*
26 Aug.–18 Sept. 1929	Let there be Light!	E192a[1]	–	*LaP*
	God is Born	E192a[1]	–	*LaP*
	\<Butterfly\> (early versions)	E192a[1]	–	–
	The White Horse	E192a[1]	–	*LaP*
	Glory of darkness (early versions, 'Bavarian Gentians')	E192a[1]	–	*LaP*
	Flowers and Men.	E192a[1]	–	*LaP*
	Ship of Death (1st version, 'The Ship of Death')	E192a[1]	–	*LaP*
	Song of Death (1st version)	E192a[1]	–	*LaP*
	Prayer ('Invocation to the Moon')	E192a[1]	–	*LaP*
	The *Last Poems* notebook			
1 Oct.–late Oct. 1929	The Greeks are Coming!	E192a[2]	–	*LaP*

The Argonauts	E192a[2]	–	*LaP*
Middle of the World.	E192a[2]	–	*LaP*
For the heroes are dipped in Scarlet.	E192a[2]	–	*LaP*
Demiurge.	E192a[2]	–	*LaP*
The work of Creation	E192a[2]	–	*LaP*
Red Geranium and Godly Mignonette	E192a[2]	–	*LaP*
Bodiless God.	E192a[2]	–	*LaP*
The Body of God	E192a[2]	–	*LaP*
The Rainbow	E192a[2]	–	*LaP*
Maximus	E192a[2]	–	*LaP*
The Man of Tyre.	E192a[2]	–	*LaP*
They say the sea is loveless.	E192a[2]		*LaP*
Whales weep not!	E192a[2]	–	*LaP*
Invocation to the Moon. (2nd version)	E192a[2]	–	*LaP*
Butterfly (3rd version)	E192a[2]	–	*LaP*
Bavarian Gentians (1st revised version)	E192a[2]	–	*LaP*
Bavarian Gentians (2nd revised version)	E192a[2]	–	*LaP*
Lucifer.	E192a[2]	–	*LaP*
The breath of life.	E192a[2]	–	*LaP*
Silence.	E192a[2]	–	*LaP*
The Hands of God	E192a[2]	–	*LaP*
Pax.	E192a[2]	–	*LaP*
Abysmal Immortality	E192a[2]	–	*LaP*
Only Man	E192a[2]	–	*LaP*
Return of Returns	E192a[2]	–	*LaP*
Stoic.	E192a[2]	–	*LaP*
In the cities	E192a[2]	–	*LaP*
Lord's Prayer	E192a[2]	–	*LaP*
Mana of the Sea	E192a[2]	–	*LaP*
Salt	E192a[2]	–	*LaP*
The Four	E192a[2]	–	*LaP*
The Boundary Stone.	E192a[2]	–	*LaP*
Spilling the Salt.	E192a[2]	–	*LaP*
Walk Warily	E192a[2]	–	*LaP*
Mystic	E192a[2]	–	*LaP*
Anaxagoras	E192a[2]	–	*LaP*

26–29 Oct. 1929 — Mana of the Sea
late Oct.–mid-Nov. 1929 — Salt

	Kissing and horrid strife.	E192a[2]	–	*LaP*
	When Satan fell	E192a[2]	–	*LaP*
	Doors.	E192a[2]	–	*LaP*
	Evil is homeless.	E192a[2]	–	*LaP*
	What then is Evil?	E192a[2]	–	*LaP*
	The Evil World-Soul	E192a[2]	–	*LaP*
	The Wandering Cosmos.	E192a[2]	–	*LaP*
	Death is not Evil, Evil is Mechanical	E192a[2]	–	*LaP*
	Strife	E192a[2]	–	*LaP*
	The late War	E192a[2]	–	*LaP*
	Murder.	E192a[2]	–	*LaP*
	Murderous Weapons	E192a[2]	–	*LaP*
	Departure	E192a[2]	–	*LaP*
	The Ship of Death. (2nd version)	E192a[2]	–	*LaP*
	Difficult death.	E192a[2]	–	*LaP*
	All Souls Day.	E192a[2]	–	*LaP*
	The Houseless Dead.	E192a[2]	–	*LaP*
	Beware the unhappy dead!	E192a[2]	–	*LaP*
	After All Saints Day	E192a[2]	–	*LaP*
	Song of Death. (2nd version)	E192a[2]	–	*LaP*
	The End, the Beginning	E192a[2]	–	*LaP*
	Sleep	E192a[2]	–	*LaP*
	Sleep and Waking	E192a[2]	–	*LaP*
	Fatigue	E192a[2]	–	*LaP*
	Forget	E192a[2]	–	*LaP*
	Know-all.	E192a[2]	–	*LaP*
	Tabernacle	E192a[2]	–	*LaP*
	Temples.	E192a[2]	–	*LaP*
	Shadows.	E192a[2]	–	*LaP*
	Change	E192a[2]	–	*LaP*
	Phoenix.	E192a[2]	–	*LaP*
Oct.–Nov. 1929	Ship of Death (3rd version)	[E360.5] E192b	–	*LaP*
	Prose poems			
12 Nov. 1928	[Section prefaces for *Birds, Beasts and Flowers*]	E47.2	*BBF* (Cresset) June 1930	*Poems* 277–406

mid–Nov. 1929	The Elephants of Dionysos	E113a	–	*P* 59
mid–Nov. 1929	'Fire: did you ever warm your hands' **Uncollected 'Nettles' not in *Nettles* notebook**	E132	Smailes	*SelP* 230
by 13 Dec. 1929	Daddy-Do–Nothing.	E266c	–	*Poems* 582
	Question.	E266c	–	*Poems* 582

Notes and Sources

NOTES

Here and elsewhere, place of publication is London unless otherwise specified.

Preface

1 Originally published in the *Sewanee Review* Leavis's review was collected in *'Anna Karenina' and Other Essays* (1967), pp. 168, 170.
2 *Memoirs* 367.
3 John Worthen, 'Orts and Slarts: Two Biographical Pieces on D. H. Lawrence', *Review of English Studies*, xlvi (February 1995), 28–9.
4 *Letters and Prose Writings of William Cowper*, ed. James King and Charles Ryskamp (Oxford, 1979), i. 20.
5 Brewster 254.
6 George D. Painter, *Marcel Proust* (1959), i. xii. The same phrases reappear in the popular edition of the biography published in 1977 by Peregrine Books.
7 By, among others, Seàn Burke in *The Death and Return of the Author: Criticism and Subjectivity in Barthes, Foucault and Derrida* (Edinburgh, 1992).
8 'The Function of Criticism at the Present Time', in *Complete Prose Works of Matthew Arnold*, ed. R. H. Super (Ann Arbor, 1962), iii. 258.

Chapter One: Ceylon

1 This conflict in DHL, evident enough in his poem 'Piano', is perhaps most impressively dramatised in his description of visiting Maurice Magnus in August 1920 at Montecassino and feeling in the monastery 'all the wonder of the medieval past'. See *Poems* 148 and *D. H. Lawrence: Memoir of Maurice Magnus*, ed. Keith Cushman (Santa Rosa, 1987), pp. 56–7.
2 There is an account of Von Gloeden (1856–1931), who spent most of his adult life in Taormina, in Robert Aldrich, *The Seduction of the Mediterranean: Writing, Art and Homosexual Fantasy* (1993), pp. 143–52. A selection of his photographs, with an introduction by Roland Barthes, was published in Naples in 1978.
3 For details of DHL's contacts with Marie Hubrecht, Jan Juta and Alan Insole see *TE* 578, 597.
4 For a detailed account of the genesis of these three novellas, see the Cambridge edition of *The Fox, The Captain's Doll, The Ladybird* (1992), ed. Dieter Mehl, and my introduction to the Penguin edition of this text (1994).
5 *SP* 117.
6 Ruth Wheelock's friendship with the Lawrences is described in *TE*.

7 Frieda 134. DHL himself described the 'piece of a Sicilian cart' as 'very colourfully painted with two scenes from the life of Marco Visconte' (iv. 206).

8 In 1920 DHL actively pursued with Compton Mackenzie the possibility of buying a boat in which they could both sail away with their wives and a few friends to the South Seas (*TE* 551–2, 594).

9 'The Spirit of Place', first published in the *English Review* (November 1918), 331.

10 *Poems* 289–93. Christopher Pollnitz has established that, although DHL sought to associate 'The Evening Land' with Baden-Baden, it was first composed before his 1921 visit there.

11 The best source for details of the Brewsters is Keith Cushman's interview with Harwood Brewster Picard in *DHLR*, xviii (Fall 1984), 119–217; but see also Keith Cushman, 'Lawrence and the Brewsters', *Journal of the D. H. Lawrence Society*, iv (1987–8), 56–62, and *TE* 640–2.

12 The Brewsters were married on 1 December 1910 in New Haven and left for Europe two days later. Fontana Vecchia was their first home, 'in a way . . . my parent's honeymoon house' as Harwood Brewster puts it (*DHLR*, xviii, 201, 211).

13 Extracts from *Sea and Sardinia* appeared in the *Dial* in October and November 1921. Given that DHL replied to Mabel Sterne's first letter on 5 November, she had probably read only one instalment before sending her invitation (iv. 110).

14 *LT* 4.

15 *SP* 160.

16 Numbers, XXII, 25.

17 *Portrait of a Genius, But* . . . (1950), p. 244.

18 *SEP* 62:14–16.

19 The link between Plato and Jesus is not as idiosyncratic as it might at first appear. In a book DHL was to read in 1929, Dean Inge claims that Platonism was part of the 'vital structure of Christian theology' and suggests the 'utter impossibility' of excising it without 'tearing Christianity to pieces' (W. R. Inge, *The Philosophy of Plotinus*, 2nd edn (1923), i. 12, 14).

20 Frieda 134.

21 *K* 151:36–9.

22 DHL's first impression of Verga had not been favourable. In December 1916 he called *Cavalleria rusticana* 'a veritable blood-pudding of *passion*! . . . not at all good, only, in some odd way, comical, as the portentous tragic Italian is always comical' (iii. 53). He began to change his mind in October 1921 and would have paid a visit to the 81-year-old Verga in Catania had he not died on 27 January 1922, shortly before DHL was about to set out (iv. 105, 186).

23 Nehls, ii. 116.

24 Brewster 249.

25 Ibid. 252.

26 *Portrait of a Genius, But* . . . , p. 248.

27 *Life for Life's Sake: A Book of Reminiscences* (1968), p. 278 (English edition of a book first published in New York in 1940).

28 Brewster 49.

29 Ibid. 260–1.

30 *The Prince of Wales' Eastern Book* (1922), on the third page of the section 'Ceylon to Hong-Kong' (there are no page numbers). The founder of Theosophy, Mme Blavatsky, had been similarly tactless when she was shown the tooth in 1880, describing it as the size of an alligator's. See Peter Washington, *Madame Blavatsky's Baboon: Theosophy and the Emergence of the Western Guru* (1993), p. 67.

31 Although the elephant from the Temple of the Tooth had the place of honour in the procession, it was on this occasion (Sir Percival Phillips noted) bearing a relic 'slightly less precious than the Tooth itself' (*Prince of Wales' Eastern Book*, fourth page). It seems to have been common practice not to risk the actual tooth in the procession. See Lucien Rajakarunayaka, 'The Kandy Perahera', *Serendib* (July–September 1983) 17–20.

32 DHL remembers the devil-dancers in his article 'New Mexico' first published in the *Survey Graphic* on 1 May 1931 but reprinted in *P* 140–7. For these phrases, see pp. 143–4.

33 Fig. 1 suggests where the 'white people in evening dress' referred to in the poem as 'buzzing and crowding the stand upon the grass below and opposite' would have been placed.

34 *Poems* 389.

35 The Prince began his eastern tour on 21 October 1921 and did not get back to England until 20 June 1922.

36 One of the Prince's biographers writes in describing the eastern tour that, 'Melancholy by nature and easily bored, when he was forced to appear at public functions which did not interest him, by his unresponsiveness and air of discontent, he gave colour to the kind of rumour that he was "still suffering from a hangover from the night before" or "was drunk at the time"' (Frances Donaldson, *Edward VIII* (1974), p. 98).

37 Brewster 253.

38 The reference could be to Victor Cunard, correspondent for *The Times* in Italy during the 1920s and 1930s (vii. 367–8, 395, 477).

39 In *Kangaroo* the central character thinks, 'and though he had no antecedents whatsoever yet he felt himself to be one of the responsible members of society, as contrasted with the innumerable irresponsible members' (p. 21:24–7).

As he was sailing away from Ceylon in late April, DHL would write to Lady Cynthia Asquith:

I break my heart over England when I am out here. Those natives are back of us – in the living sense lower than we are. But they're going to swarm over us and suffocate us. We are, have been for five centuries, the growing tip. Now we're going to fall. But you don't catch me going back on my whiteness and Englishness and myself. English in the teeth of all the world, even in the teeth of England. – How England deliberately undermines England. You should see India. Between Lloyd George and Rufus Isaacs etc we are done. (iv. 234)

Isaacs, the former Edward VIII was to note with veiled disapproval, was the first Viceroy of India not to come from the aristocracy. See *A King's Story. The Memoirs of HRM the Duke of Windsor* (1951), p. 177.

DHL would only entertain serious doubts about the legitimacy of Great Britain's imperialist role much later. His feeling that 'natives' were 'lower' than Europeans was (he felt) confirmed in the South Seas, but it was then challenged by his contacts with the Indian population of the American Southwest and Mexico.

40 Brewster 255–6.

41 Ibid. 258.

42 Ibid. 253.

43 Earl Henry Brewster, *The Life of Gotama the Buddha (Compiled Exclusively from the Pali Canon)* (1926).

44 Brewster 260. Morning frost is common in Nuwara Eliya, even in the hottest season. For a description of the journey there from Kandy in DHL's time, see Ali Foad Toulba, *Ceylon: The Land of Eternal Charm* (1926).

45 *SP* 165.

46 Jeffrey Meyers thinks it is 'almost certain' that DHL was already a consumptive as early as 1911; Paul Delany says that DHL's request to his friend Dr Eder in 1915 for something for his influenza was futile because tuberculosis already 'lay at the root of the problem'; and Claire Tomalin has suggested that when DHL was with Katherine Mansfield and Middleton Murry in Cornwall in 1916 he probably gave her his TB: 'This may have been the real *Bludbrüdershaft*, more sinister than Lawrence ever intended' (Meyers, *D. H. Lawrence: A Biography* (1990), p. 73; Delany, *D. H. Lawrence's Nightmare: The Writer and his Circle in the Years of the Great War* (1979), p. 81; and Tomalin, *Katherine Mansfield: A Secret Life* (1987), p. 163). These claims are dealt with in *TE*. Reliance on tuberculosis to explain abnormal behaviour is exemplified in Delany's reference to DHL's 'tubercular rage' (p. 249).

47 In *Below the Magic Mountain: A Social History of Tuberculosis in 20th Century Britain* (1988), Linda Bryder explains that around 90 per cent of the English urban population in DHL's time 'had' TB in the sense that they had been infected early in their lives and still harboured the dormant bacillus in what is known as a focus or site of primary infection (most commonly in the lungs). But as few as 1 per cent developed the disease later in life (pp. 3–4).

48 Practically the only documentary evidence for DHL having been tubercular before the 1920s is a passage in David Garnett's *Golden Echo*, published in 1954, in which he excuses the DHL of 1913 for lacking 'the instincts of a gentleman' in his treatment of Frieda on the grounds that he was ill: 'Once I caught sight of one of Frieda's handkerchiefs, marked with a coronet in the corner, crumpled in Lawrence's hand, after a fit of coughing and spotted with bright arterial blood – and I felt a new tenderness for him and readiness to forgive his bad moods' (p. 254). Many of us spit blood from time to time and it takes a sharp eye to recognise immediately where it comes from and what has caused it to appear. No-one in 1913 confirms David Garnett's diagnosis. A year and a half before, when DHL was suffering from the illness that led him to give up schoolteaching and which was diagnosed as double pneumonia, he had a sputum test which proved negative. 'The report concerning the expectoration', wrote his sister, 'was very satis- factory. No germs were discovered and since then both lungs have almost completely cleared up' (*EY* 323).

49 Brewster 261, 253.

50 Keith Sagar has pointed out that although the much-anthologised 'Humming Bird' is followed in *Birds, Beasts and Flowers* by the word 'Española' (the name of a village near Taos), an identical version of the poem first appeared in May 1921, before DHL went to America. See *D. H. Lawrence: A Calendar of his Works* (Manchester, 1979), p. 102.

The appearance of the word 'Kandy' at the end of 'Elephant' does not therefore guarantee that the poem was composed in Ceylon but – in this case – it makes it likely. Just as likely is that 'Kangaroo' (see p. 50 above), which is followed by the word 'Sydney', was composed in New South Wales.

51 Brewster 250.

52 *EY* 202.

53 Brewster 256; Frieda 135.

54 Brewster 260.

55 The Lawrences were given a beautiful blue rug when they moved to Byron Villas in Hampstead in 1915 (see *TE* 256).

56 Brewster 259.

57 Frieda 117.

58 Brewster 50.

59 In a letter to the author, Harwood Brewster Picard wrote that Mrs Ennis and two other ladies came with them to the perahera and suggested that the Ennises may have had a house in Kandy since her mother refers in letters to their living near. For Mrs Ennis see *Who Was Who. 1929–1940*, ed. Adam and Charles Black (1941), p. 417; the entry under 'Joseph Kirkland' in vol. v of the *Dictionary of American Biography*, ed. Dumas Malone (New York, 1957); and Clyde E. Henson, *Joseph Kirkland* (New York, 1962), p. 129. According to Robert Darroch, the local newspapers indicate that the Ennises were in Nuwara Eliya on the same day as the Lawrences and Brewsters. See 'Letters of Introduction', *Rananim: The Journal of the D. H. Lawrence Society*, i (October 1963), 5.

60 Brewster 51. In the same category of 'reasonable' responses which Earl Brewster seemed able to elicit was DHL's remark that he did not want to write a successor to *Fantasia of the Unconscious* because, 'I would contradict myself on every page' (p. 48).

61 Ibid. 47.

Chapter Two: Australia

1 'The St. Joseph's Ass' appeared in the fourth number of *Adelphi* (September 1925), 284–97. See p. 135 above.

2 It was three years later, when he was in Mexico, that DHL associated his illness in Ceylon with malaria. Kandy itself is too high for the relevant mosquito (although Colombo isn't), but the incubation period is in any case six weeks so that if he did first begin to suffer from the disease in Ceylon, he must have been infected shortly before leaving Sicily (where it was rife).

3 Andrew Wilkin, *Little Novels of Sicily* by Giovanni Verga, translated by D. H. Lawrence (Harmondsworth, 1973), p. 12.

4 Ibid., pp. 155–6.

5 Bruce Steele, 'D. H. Lawrence and J. Elder Walker: An Indian Connection', *Journal of the D. H. Lawrence Society*, iv (1987–8), 63–6.

6 Washington, *Madame Blavatsky's Baboon*, p. 223.

7 There is a full account of Annie Besant in Anne Taylor, *Annie Besant: A Biography* (Oxford, 1992).

8 Siebenhaar's memoir of his contacts with DHL can be found in Nehls, iii. 104–12.

9 Nehls, iii. 105.
10 M. L. Skinner, *The Fifth Sparrow: An Autobiography* (1973), p. 111 (first published by Sydney University Press in 1972).
11 Nehls, ii. 136. This recollection, which is in the form of a letter to R. G. Howarth, first appeared in the Australian journal *Southerly* in 1952 (xiii, 233–5).
12 Nehls, ii. 133. May Gawler's memoir was dictated to her daughter in 1953.
13 After she had come to know him well, Mollie Skinner was able to offer an explanation of why different witnesses report the colour of DHL's eyes so differently. When she was in London in 1924, trying to find a publisher for *Black Swans*, Edward Garnett mentioned to her DHL's 'keen blue eyes': ' "Not always blue Mr Garnett", I interrupted. "Hazel, green, beryl, as the mood takes him" ' (*The Fifth Sparrow*, p. 149). Earlier she describes DHL's eyes as 'flecked with colours, changing like a chameleon with his changing moods' (pp. 111–12).
14 In *Aaron's Rod* the case is complicated by the fact that there are two characters with claims to be regarded as authorial figures, Aaron Sisson and Rawdon Lilly. In the space of less than twenty pages Lilly is described as a 'dark, irascible little man', a 'quiet little individual' and a 'little man'. See the Cambridge edition (1988), ed. Mara Kalnins, pp. 79:17; 88:9; 96:13.
15 This height is taken from the passport which DHL received in 1921 and which is now in UT.
16 *K* 219:22–3; 255:20.
17 *K* 27:7, 11–12.
18 *K* 38:27, 28, 37.
19 Nehls, iii. 134; *The Fifth Sparrow*, p. 114.
20 Only an accident of nature prevented DHL from associating at this time with a quartet of women with the Australian equivalent of blue blood. Katharine Susannah Pritchard was married to the son of a West Australian Premier. In the third week of May her husband learned from his evening paper that DHL was a few miles away in Darlington but his wife was prevented from rushing to pay her respects by the birth of their son the very next day. Since the Lawrences left Perth on 18 May she was able to correspond with DHL but never met him. Already a published writer in 1922, Katharine Pritchard eventually became a highly respected novelist (Nehls, ii. 152–3, 480–1).
21 *The Fifth Sparrow*, p. 27.
22 Ibid., p. 26.
23 The phrase occurs in DHL's preface to *Black Swans* (*BB* 377).
24 *The Fifth Sparrow*, p. 110.
25 Nehls, ii. 134–5; iv. 251.
26 *The Fifth Sparrow*, p. 110.
27 In *The Fifth Sparrow* Mollie Skinner explains that she joined Lady Minto's Nursing Service in Calcutta, Lady Minto being the wife of India's Viceroy at the time (p. 94).
28 *The Fifth Sparrow*, p. 111.
29 Nehls, iii. 105; (iv. 240, 273).
30 *The Fifth Sparrow*, p. 110.
31 Ibid., p. 111.
32 Preface to *Black Swans* (*BB* 377).

33 In his introduction to the Cambridge edition of *The Boy in the Bush*, Paul Eggert describes the way in which Mollie Skinner must have made use of this history in her 'House of Ellis' (*BB* xlvi).

34 *The Fifth Sparrow*, p. 114.

35 Ibid., pp. 114–15.

36 Ibid., p. 114.

37 For details see my introduction to the Everyman's Library edition of *Sons and Lovers* (1991), pp. v–xii.

38 G. H. Neville, *A Memoir of D. H. Lawrence: ('The Betrayal')*, ed. Carl Baron (Cambridge, 1981), p. 35.

39 *The Fifth Sparrow*, pp. 115–16.

40 Ibid., p. 128.

41 Ibid., pp. 115–16.

42 Detailed accounts of the composition of these two novels can be found in the introductions to the Cambridge editions of *Aaron's Rod*, and *Mr Noon* (1984), ed. Lindeth Vasey.

43 R. E. Leake, *Letters of a VAD* (1919), pp. 98–9.

44 Cf. 'he had carried the chunk of lead in his gizzard for ten months, till suddenly it had rolled into his throat and he had coughed it out' (*K* 24:20–2), and *The Fifth Sparrow*, p. 155.

45 For accounts of DHL's collaborations with Louie Burrows and Helen Corke, see *E Y* 242, 255–9.

46 In *Kangaroo* Somers complains to Harriett, 'I want to do something with living people, somewhere, somehow, while I live on the earth. I write, but I write alone. And I live alone. Without any connection whatever with the rest of men.' Harriett accuses him of 'swank' and says, 'I know how much alone you are, with me always there keeping you together' (69:31–7).

47 *BB* xxvii.

48 Nehls, iii. 109.

49 *The Fifth Sparrow*, p. 129. For the changes that were made and DHL's attitude to any alteration of his ending, see *BB* xxxix–xlii above.

50 *K* 15:6–9 and 362 (note on 15:6–9).

51 *K* 14:31, 24, 35–9, 15–16, 4–5. Jessie Chambers refers to how DHL could be transformed by the moon in chapter v of *D. H. Lawrence: A Personal Record* (Cambridge, 1980), pp. 126–8. For Mollie Skinner's nervousness, see *The Fifth Sparrow*, p. 112.

52 *The Fifth Sparrow*, p. 113.

53 Siebenhaar had published *Dorothea: A Lyrical Romance in Verse* in 1909. *Sentinel Sonnets* (1919) was a collaboration with Alfred Chandler.

54 His chief crime was to have collected money at work for the legal costs of the IWW member. See N. Segal, *Who and What was Siebenhaar: A Note on the Life and Persecution of a West Australian Anarchist*, Studies in West Australian History Occasional Papers No. 1 (University of Western Australia, 1988). Siebenhaar's interest and involvement in politics may well have stimulated some of the political discussions in *Kangaroo*. That his views were very different from DHL's does not seem to have affected their relationship.

55 *The Fifth Sparrow*, p. 116.

56 *L'hiver* is the only painting DHL mentions in his letters, but Bruce Steele points out that in May 1922 there were two newly acquired drawings by Claud Lovat Fraser prominently displayed in Melbourne's National Gallery, and that Fraser had married Grace Crawford, a woman DHL had once known well. See *K* 361–2 (note on 10:8) and *EY* 231–3. Fraser's middle name may have influenced DHL's choice of a middle name for Somers, although its appropriateness comes from the critical examination in *Kangaroo* of notions of love to which he himself had once adhered.

57 When DHL wrote this letter to Brewster he was settled by the Pacific shore in Thirroul and struck by not only the '*extraordinary* delicacy of the air' but also, 'the weird bits of creek and marsh, dead trees, sand, and very blue hills'. *L'hiver* had revived his memory of Puvis in general and almost certainly therefore of his most well-known and widely reproduced painting, *Le pauvre pêcheur*. In a sentimentally populist rather than classical manner, *Le pauvre pêcheur* is one of the few paintings by Puvis de Chavannes in which the landscape is as prominent as the figures: a wife picking flowers on the estuary shore, an over-large baby and the poor fisherman himself standing in his diminutive boat in a posture of abject misery. DHL told Brewster that as he looked at *L'hiver* in Melbourne he still hated the 'self-conscious sentiment and rather snivelling outlook' of Puvis (iv. 265). For a critic who had got out of bed on the wrong side, 'snivelling' would not be a bad word for the poor fisherman himself; but DHL must have admired the representation of the landscape behind him and recalled it, or similar representations, as he looked out to where a creek flowed into the sea behind his house.

58 See Nehls, ii. 141.

59 *K* 156:1–8; 382 (note on 156:8); 482.

60 *K* 7:29, 19; 9:35–6; 10:27–32.

61 DHL was later to feel that the egalitarianism could also impart to certain personalities an entirely unaffected willingness to help others which it would be hard to find in Europe. Cf. his warmly appreciative description of the bus-driver who brings the Somerses back from 'Wolloona' (*K* 275–6).

62 In the novel the Somerses have two Gladstone bags and a hat box (*K* 9:14–15). As Robert Darroch has pointed out, this would represent the Lawrences' cabin luggage, which they took with them from the boat on the 27th, and they may have had to collect their trunks later ('Following the Footsteps of Lawrence', *Rananim: The Journal of the D. H. Lawrence Society of Australia*, ii (June 1994), 9).

63 In *D. H. Lawrence in Australia* (Melbourne, 1981), Robert Darroch argues that the Lawrences stayed in Sydney on both Saturday and Sunday night (27 and 28 May 1922), travelling to Thirroul on Monday 29th (p. 34). In the more recent *D. H. Lawrence at Thirroul* (Sydney, 1989), Joseph Davis gives good reasons for thinking they might just as plausibly have moved out of Sydney on the Sunday (pp. 28–30).

64 *D. H. Lawrence in Australia*, p. 36. (On p. 220 of his book, Davis challenges this identification.) Darroch has more recently suggested the daily rate was 15 shillings ('Following the Footsteps of Lawrence', p. 10).

65 Frieda 119.

66 Ibid. 118, 120.

67 *Lawrence at Thirroul*, pp. 31–5.

68 *K* 76–9.

69 Frieda 119.

70 *K* 70:21–2.

71 The manner in which this name is made prominent at the beginning of *Kangaroo* encourages readers to detect in it an allusion to another R. L. S. who was also a writer. DHL had read Stevenson's novels in his youth, and when he went to Bournemouth to recover from the after-effects of pneumonia in the early part of 1912, he was aware that Stevenson had also convalesced there (i. 361). He had read some of his work in 1920 and discussed it with Compton Mackenzie when he visited Capri where he might have met Stevenson's stepson, who was also the co-author with Stevenson of *The Wrecker*, a novel in which one episode begins in Sydney (*K* 316 – note on 10:8). The Scottish writer may have been brought into DHL's mind at this time by the hope he expresses on 30 May of trying to write a 'romance' while he was in New South Wales and of then visiting the South Sea islands (iv. 247). Stevenson had been able to fulfil one of DHL's most cherished ambitions and buy a boat in which he toured the South Seas, and in the early 1890s he had also spent a month in Sydney. Yet what many people would be likely to remember most about him in the 1920s was that he was consumptive (although Stevenson's death was not directly attributable to tuberculosis, he was someone who, almost as much as Keats, had helped to strengthen in the popular mind the illusion that there was some natural association between that disease and the literary life). DHL's implicit identification with Stevenson in 'R. L. Somers' suggests that either he felt no fears whatsoever on his own behalf and regarded the medical reasons for Stevenson's presence in the southern hemisphere as immaterial, or that, at some level of his consciousness, he was anxious to acknowledge a special affinity.

72 *K* xxxvi.

73 In his edition of *Kangaroo*, Bruce Steele gives a full account of DHL's difficulties and how he resolved them (*K* xxxviii).

74 *K* 188:18.

75 *K* 280:17–18; 282:9–11; 284:11, 27–8.

76 Later he would be more vehement about the 'dirt', especially after Frieda had expressed admiration for the novel. Dorothy Brett records that after Frieda had told her and DHL that *Ulysses* was 'a wonderful book', he retorted, 'The last part of it is the dirtiest, most indecent, obscene thing ever written. Yes it is Frieda . . . It is filthy' (Brett 79).

77 For details of DHL's revisions, see *K* xl–xliii.

78 DHL had already begun to think of the after-effects of the war in this way in *Aaron's Rod* where he writes of the 'lightness and an appearance of bright diffidence and humour' in Captain Herbertson: 'But underneath it all was the same as in the common men of all the combatant nations: the hot, seared burn of unbearable experience, which did not heal nor cool, and whose irritation was not to be relieved. The experience gradually cooled on top: but only with a surface crust' (114: 18–23).

79 *K* 280:29.

80 *Poems* 185.

81 For details of DHL's indecision as to how the novel ought to end, see *K* xliii–xlvii.

82 Nehls, ii. 4–5.

83 *K* 110:20, 23–4.

84 The first three of DHL's four short essays on 'Democracy' were published in the *Word* on 18 and 25 October and 6 December 1919 (the fourth never appeared) (*RDP* xliii, 63–83).

85 *K* 175:8–24.

86 DHL's inclination to blame his emotional dependency on his mother is often apparent in *Fantasia of the Unconscious*. An indication of his awareness of his own solipsism is the hostility he developed to Whitman's celebrations of 'merging', or his implicit insistence on 'otherness' in *Birds, Beasts and Flowers*. For discussion of these matters, see David Ellis, 'Lawrence, Wordsworth and "anthropomorphic lust"', *Cambridge Quarterly*, xxiii (1994), 230–42.

There is a clear if indirect connection between the imaginative appropriation of one's surroundings which solipsism involves and a potentially megalomanic claim to more importance in the social world than the circumstances warrant (both rely on what Freud termed the 'omnipotence of thoughts'). In the manuscript version of *Kangaroo*, Somers is told by Jaz that he would be a more appropriate leader of Australia than Cooley. Although he is not himself inclined to disagree, his wife (who has overheard) is, and she pours cold water on the idea in a manner similar to her criticisms of her husband in chapter ix. For the details see *K* xxxvii.

87 See Aldington's introduction to the novel in the Heinemann edition (1955), p. 1.

88 Russel Ward, *The History of Australia, 1901–1975* (London, 1975), p. 142.

89 Several of the very many articles on this issue are referred to in my own 'D. H. Lawrence in Australia: The Darroch Controversy', *DHLR*, xxi (Summer 1989), 167–74. One problem was always how DHL could have described in such fine detail the organisation of Cooley's 'Digger' clubs without inside information from a real member of such a movement (if not from one of its leaders); but the cancelled passage from *Fantasia of the Unconscious* which Bruce Steele prints in the explanatory notes to his edition of *Kangaroo* (*K* 372, note on 92:9) proves that an important part of the description was already in DHL's head before he set foot in Australia.

90 *K* 136:21–2. This account was heavily revised. As Bruce Steel explains, it was in its first version more tenderly homoerotic and includes Cooley's statement, 'I have never loved a man as I have loved you' (*K* xlii, 430).

91 *K* 138:9, 18–25.

92 *K* 143:22–8; 146:39–40; 147:4–9.

93 *K* 474. Although there is no way of knowing how far the second encounter is based on a real event, it nevertheless has interesting implications for the Lawrences' marriage, allowing one to contemplate the irony of a situation where each partner accords the other sexual freedom (pondering what to do about Victoria, Somers dismisses conventional notions of loyalty: 'For [Harriett], too, honour did not consist in a pledged word kept according to pledge, but in a genuine feeling faithfully followed' – *K* 143:11–13), but where only one can then profit from this freedom without self-recrimination.

94 *K* 44:23; 47:9; 92:14.

95 It clearly mattered a great deal to DHL that he should be the initiator in a relationship, whatever its sexual orientation. In *Kangaroo*, Somers is not only a 'small' or 'little' man

but also one frequently cast in the conventionally female and therefore passive role. Ben Cooley is partly responsible for this but it is his lieutenant Jack who most often designates Somers as a woman. He feels that if Somers can be persuaded to join the movement he could be a 'sort of queen bee' around whom the other bees would cluster (95:6); Somers's hesitations he attributes to his being 'slow and backward like a woman' (106:17); and after Jack has been disappointed by him, he is described as feeling a 'he-man contempt' for the 'shifty she-man' (291:5). For other references in the novel to Somers as 'female' see 316:26 and 326:18.

96 The parenthetical phrase is a brutal reminder of the limits of biographical enquiry. It is precise ('twice') and at the same time gratuitous: if DHL had not been moved here to refer to his own recent experience, in however distorted or exaggerated a fashion, what alternative motive could he have had for the phrase's inclusion? Yet with the dubious exception of Earl Brewster, there is no trace of any potential 'blood-brother' for DHL 'since he had left Europe'. Like the sections in the novel concerning Victoria Callcott (which several commentators have suggested might be associated with Laura Forrester) DHL's 'twice' may be an example of the novelist's imagination working with the barest hint. In 'The Art of Fiction', Henry James defines the novelist as someone on whom nothing is lost (*Selected Literary Criticism*, ed. Morris Shapira (1963), p. 57). This might be just as true of fleeting internal observations as of those which are external.

97 *K* 107:11–20.

98 *K* 205:23.

99 *K* 208:8–19.

100 *K* 208:21–2, 37–8; 210:40 – 211:1; 211:16–17.

101 *K* 202:32.

102 Cf. from the fourth (unpublished) section of 'The Crown', 'Everyone knows that the natural activity in the life of a real soldier is drinking, prostitution and homosexuality' (*RDP* 473); but the relation between army life and homosexuality is of course also dealt with in DHL's introduction to the Magnus memoirs, and his short story, 'The Prussian Officer' (first published in 1914).

103 For a detailed account of the essay in which this happens see *TE* 453–7.

104 DHL seems to be recalling here the passage in Dostoyevsky's *The Brothers Karamazov* in which the body of the saintly Zossima begins to stink (a suggestion for him, one suspects, of the corruption underlying Christian ideals).

105 *K* 324:39–40; 325:2–4.

106 It is in *Kangaroo* that Somers elaborates a philosophy of the dark gods in opposition to Christianity and its derivatives. This involves listening attentively to messages which come from below rather than above. The artist justifies his special status by being both unusually sensitive to these messages and also capable of conveying them to a majority of people who dangerously persist in the old, worn-out beliefs because they have not yet been shown anything which might replace them. Cf. *K* 296–7.

107 Nehls, ii. 132.

108 The evidence for this daily routine comes from *K* (162:39; 163:1–5), but there is no reason to doubt it.

109 The doctor Frieda saw is likely to have been Francis Crosslé who had been born in Ireland and had literary interests (in 1931 he published a novel). For details see Davis, *Lawrence in Thirroul*, pp. 56–64.

110 See Tedlock 96.

111 Frieda 120.

112 *D. H. Lawrence in Australia*, p. 59. More recently Darroch has appeared to suggest that what they all indicate is not DHL's satisfaction in having been temporarily free of any developed social contacts in New South Wales, but in having managed to conceal his real identity from those people he did get to know. The phrases I quote will not bear that construction. See Robert Darroch, 'The Evidence of the Letters', *Rananim* (October 1994), 16–18.

113 *K* 183:1.

114 *K* 96:25–40 – 97:1–16.

115 The most disturbing of all occurs in chapter VII, after Somers has decided he will not make love with Victoria. He dreams he is back in Mullumbimby 'bending forward doing some little thing by the couch' when his arms are pinned from behind and he hears

> a man's voice speaking mockingly behind him, with a laugh. It was if he saw a man's face too—a stranger, a rough sort of Australian. And he realized with horror: "Now they have put a sack over my head, and fastened my arms, and I am in the dark, and they are going to steal my little brown handbag from the bedroom, which contains all the money we have"   (144:7–12)

The relevance of this to the final medical inspection during the war might seem evident enough but not so evident (*pace* Freud) is the nature of the connection between homosexuality and money.

116 *K* 262:8, 10–11, 15, 20–33.

117 Nehls, ii. 41. DHL seems to have been particularly friendly with Laura Forrester, sending her three postcards which have survived: from San Francisco, Taos and Mexico City. See Robert Darroch, 'More on Lawrence in Australia', *DHLR*, xx (Spring 1988), 41–2.

118 *K* 353:34–5. As I indicate, there are direct references to the storm in DHL's letters but not to this final excursion. Frieda does however mention it in *"Not I, But the Wind . . ."* (p. 121).

Chapter Three: New Mexico

1 In a revision of chapter XVIII of *Kangaroo* the reasons for DHL's irritation are made very clear (*K* 477). In Bruce Steele's view, DHL decided against inclusion of these New Zealand references before the novel was published (p. xliii).

2 *Katherine Mansfield's Letters to John Middleton Murry*, ed. J. M. Murry (1951), p. 663. The break with Mansfield and Middleton Murry is fully documented in *TE* (see especially pp. 557–64).

3 *SCAL* 134.

4 This 1920 version is reprinted in *The Symbolic Meaning: The Uncollected Versions of 'Studies in Classic American Literature'*, ed. Armin Arnold (Arundel, 1962). For this

quotation see p. 222. Its putative 1918 predecessor was never published in the *English Review* and no manuscript of it from that period has survived.

5 *SCAL* 134, 137, 138.

6 Frieda 150. The film's original title was 'Lost and Found on a South Sea Island'. For details see Ross Parmenter, 'Lawrence's Brush with Hollywood: "Lost and Found"', *Journal of the D. H. Lawrence Society* (1990), 49–59.

7 *LT* 47; Merrild 11.

8 DHL makes no reference in the surviving letters to translating Verga on the *Tahiti* but convincing reasons for thinking he tackled four of the stories later to appear in *Cavalleria Rusticana* (the title story, 'The She-Wolf', 'Fantasticalities' and 'Jelli the Shepherd') are summarised by Keith Sagar in *D. H. Lawrence: A Calendar of his Works*, p. 124.

9 DHL wrote to Mary Cannan about the sale while he was on the *Tahiti* (iv. 287) but although we know he received at least one letter and one telegram during his voyage (iv. 287) the good news may have reached him just before he left Australia. *Hearst's* paid him the money but never in fact published 'The Captain's Doll'. For details see John Worthen, *D. H. Lawrence: A Literary Life* (1989), pp. 116–17. The letter to Mary Cannan shows that DHL believed Mountsier must have been responsible for the transaction, whereas it was Seltzer's doing.

10 The two other books concerned were translations of Arthur Schnitzler's *Casanova's Homecoming* and of the anonymous *A Young Girl's Diary*, which had a foreword by Freud.

11 Bynner 145.

12 Frieda 133.

13 *LT* 4; Rudnick 193. Mabel had seen extracts from *Sea and Sardinia* in the *Dial* (see p. 9 above). When she showed *Sons and Lovers* to her analyst Ely Jelliffe in 1921 he diagnosed in the author 'a severe homosexual fixation' (Rudnick 195). It is possible that John Reed spoke to Mabel about DHL – having read *The Rainbow* for the publisher Benjamin Huebsch, Reed declared that nothing had ever moved him more deeply; and we now know that Mountsier's one-time companion, Esther Andrews, wrote to Mabel enthusiastically about her contacts with DHL (*TE* 375–6, 682).

14 *P* 90 (the date and place appear in the original magazine version only). At one point DHL had thought that 'America, Listen to Your Own' could provide an introduction to *Studies in Classic American Literature* (iii. 591, 627). His piece was immediately followed in the same number of the *New Republic* by a riposte from another, now prominent former member of Mabel Sterne's New York *salon*, Walter Lippmann. He complained that although DHL's 'futurist rage against a museum world' was understandable in Florence, what America needed to combat a pervasive philistinism was more European culture rather than less. Besides, 'Mr Lawrence should study his map. He will see that the Aztecs flourished in Mexico; the Incas in Peru. He will note that it is still a longer and harder journey from America to those excavated ruins than it is to the Milan Cathedral' (15 December 1920, 70–1).

15 Rudnick 23.

16 Daniel Aaron, *Writers on the Left: Episodes in American Literary Communism* (New York, 1974), p. 32.

17 Rudnick is the major source for Mabel's previous life but additional information can be found in Emily Hahn, *Mabel: A Biography of Mabel Dodge Luhan* (Boston, 1977). These secondary sources are in addition to Mabel's own, not always reliable, *Intimate Memories*, published in four volumes between 1932 and 1937.

18 When she published her memoirs the woman being described here chose to be known as Mabel Dodge Luhan. On the principle implied by that choice she ought to have been Mabel Evans Dodge Sterne Luhan, which is one reason for settling for Mabel in much of what follows. The number of people who knew her by her first name was a sign of her power and prominence rather than a gender-dependent inferiority. If she had felt as some feminists from a later generation have about these matters, she would have called herself Mabel Ganson Luhan or simply, Mabel Ganson.

19 Mabel is the undoubted model for Edith Dale in Carl Van Vechten's *Peter Whiffle* (1922), for Gisell Links in Jacques Emile Blanche's *Ameryis* (1922), for Mary Kitteredge in Max Eastman's *Venture* (1927) and also for the unnamed female protagonist of Witter Bynner's satirical play *Cake* (1926).

20 *LT* 70.

21 Rudnick 17.

22 *SMOS* 199:32–3.

23 Mabel writes of having enclosed the necklace in her first letter to DHL, along with some Indian herbs (*LT* 5), but it must have been later that she sent it. After following them to Kandy, it is likely that the necklace only caught up with the Lawrences once they were in Australia (iv. 266–7, 276).

24 *LT* 16.

25 *LT* 36.

26 *SCAL* 138. Soon after his arrival in Taos, in a letter to Catherine Carswell on 29 September, DHL wrote, 'Mabel Sterne has an Indian lover lives with her. She has had two white husbands and one Jew: now this' (iv. 313).

27 *LT* 39.

28 Bynner 2, and F.-J. Temple, 'Au Nouveau Mexique sur les pas de D. H. Lawrence', *Nouvelle Revue Française*, n.s. x (1962), 562–7. Bynner described the panel as 5 feet long and 2 feet high.

29 There are details of Bynner's career in James Kraft's 'Biographical Introduction' to Bynner's *Selected Poems*, ed., and with a critical introduction, by Richard Wilbur (New York, 1977), pp. xviii–lxxx.

30 *LT* 39.

31 Before this wedding took place in December Mabel asked Lawrence to have a man-to-man talk to her only child (himself only twenty) about the responsibilities of marriage. When it was over she asked John Evans what had been said. 'He said for me to be always alone', her son told her, 'Never to let Alice know my thoughts. To be gentle with her when she was gentle, but if she opposed my will, to beat her.' 'Well!' was all his startled mother could find in reply (*LT* 78).

The Hendersons had partly gone to Santa Fe because they believed their daughter was threatened with consumption. High and dry, New Mexico was widely regarded in the 1920s as an excellent environment for those suffering from tuberculosis. There are interesting details about its popularity in this regard in Brenda Maddox, *The Married Man: A Life of D. H. Lawrence* (1994), pp. 319–20.

32 In October DHL would meet at Mabel Sterne's house a young writer named Maurice Lesemann who also testified to his powers of mimicry and described his imitation of Bertrand Russell as 'outrageously irreverent, biting and funny' (Nehls, ii. 487: n. 39).

33 Bynner 7.

34 In October DHL told Mountsier that if he was coming to Taos he could take from Santa Fe, 'the stage motor car which leaves at midday, and gets here at 6.0 or 6.30: a very bumpy bad road over the desert' (iv. 321).

35 *Edge of Taos Desert: An Escape to Reality* (1937). The account of driving to Taos from Santa Fe with Maurice Sterne in 1917 is in chapter IV.

36 *P* 142. The article is entitled 'New Mexico' and was written in December 1928 (see p. 453 above).

37 *LT* 43.

38 There is a detailed description of Mabel's house, and its relation to the design of the Villa Curonia, in Agnesa Lufkin, 'A Rare Place: Mabel Dodge Luhan's Taos Estate', *El Palacio*, lxxxvi (Spring 1980), 29–35.

39 DHL described the house he lived in as being 'just on the Indian reservation' and said it was 'supposed to belong to Tony' (iv. 295, 324).

40 *P* 92–9. The textual history of 'Indians and an Englishman', and its relations to both 'Taos' and 'Certain Americans and an Englishman', are complicated. All three articles appear to have grown out of an essay entitled 'Pueblos and an Englishman' which DHL mailed to Mountsier on 31 October (iv. 324) but then divided and revised over the following weeks. His initial reason for the division was the realisation that the material he had sent to Mountsier would only appear in the *Dial* after Christmas whereas the Bursum Bill would come before Congress in December. (I am grateful to Ian S. MacNiven for this information.)

41 *P* 95.

42 The accusation everyone remembers was made by Norman Douglas and reported by Rebecca West (Nehls, ii. 62).

43 Bynner 7. As 'America, Listen to Your Own' made clear, 'Indian' always meant for DHL the original inhabitants of Central and South as well as North America.

44 See 'Taos', *P* 100–3. It is clear from remarks in his letters that DHL originally thought of 'Taos' as the second part of 'Indians and an Englishman' (iv. 369).

45 DHL had sent his agent what he describes as a 'complete copy' of *Studies* on 2 August 1920 (iii. 582) so that Mountsier could have a clean typescript prepared. Although in September 1922 he asks Mountsier for 'a Manuscript copy' he is almost certainly referring to a typescript. DHL often uses the word 'manuscript' when he means typescript and if he had wanted his original copy he would hardly have used the indefinite article.

46 Rudnick 175. Brian W. Dippie, *The Vanishing American: White Attitudes and US Indian Policy* (Lawrence: Kansas, 1982), pp. 274–9.

47 *P* 90.

48 *P II* 240.

49 *English Review*, xxviii (March 1919), 211, 215. (The *English Review* versions of *Studies in Classic American Literature* are reprinted in Armin Arnold, *The Symbolic Meaning*.

50 These are phrases from references to the Leatherstocking novels in the essay on Cooper published in the *English Review* the month previously. In context, they suggest the application of a private habit of thought to a public domain. As DHL's dreams reveal, the spirit which he often felt was unappeased and inwardly destructive of himself was his mother's. Preceding his reference to the Indians in this first of the two essays on Cooper to appear in the *English Review* is his description of how 'souls that find in death a passionate consummation return to us appeased, and add the beauty and richness of their presence to us' whereas those who are 'caught out of life unliberated' come back as 'girning, terrible ghosts'. 'What is the use of a mother's sacrificing herself for her children', DHL goes on, 'if after death her unappeased soul shall perforce return upon the child and exact from it all the fulfilment that should have been attained in the living flesh, and was not?' (*English Review* (February 1919), 92).

51 *English Review* (March 1919), 212.

52 It is possible that the division of the Cooper material into two was the work of the *English Review*'s editor, Austin Harrison, rather than DHL himself (it was Harrison who had first divided DHL's Hawthorne material into two parts).

53 *SCAL* 42. There are similar complaints in the revision of the original essay on Hector Crèvecoeur's *Letters of An American Farmer* which now includes:

> Hazlitt, Godwin, Shelley, Coleridge, the English romanticists, were, of course, thrilled by the Letters of an American Farmer. A new world, a world of the Noble Savage and Pristine Nature and Paradisal Simplicity and all that gorgeousness that flows out of the unsullied fount of the ink-bottle. Lucky Coleridge, who got no farther than Bristol. Some of us have gone all the way. (*SCAL* 29)

54 *English Review* (March 1919), 206 ('This tiny speech shows us Mrs. Cooper's attitude. She was impatient of her husband's Indian passion. To her the coarse and revolting traits of the savage were most in evidence – as they were to Franklin').

55 *SCAL* 52–3.

56 *SCAL* 63.

57 *English Review* (March 1919), 208, 215.

58 *SCAL* 54, 58–9. *The Pioneers* is set in New York State, where the scenery is quite different from that of New Mexico. It was not written in Europe and appeared well before Taos had been incorporated into the United States. One might have thought, in any case, that when in the first version DHL compared the world of Glimmerglass to the 'lands in ancient poetry' he was already acknowledging that Cooper was no realist. But it is hard to forgive the source of our illusions in the painful period when they have to be shed.

The Indians DHL was now meeting were very different from the tribal groups described in the Leatherstocking novels but in this context America was made all one for him by what he assumed must everywhere be the after-effects of the dispossession of its original inhabitants.

59 *SCAL* 40, 54–5, 57.

60 *English Review* (March 1919), 212–13.

61 *SCAL* 41.

62 'I find all dark people here have a fixed desire to jeer at us: these people here. They jeer behind your back', DHL wrote from Ceylon in April 1922. In August of the following year he wrote to Amy Lowell from an address in New Jersey, 'But I don't care for New York. I feel the people one sees want to jeer at us. They come with a sort of predetermination to jeer' (iv. 225, 487). Similar responses follow Lawrence's arrival in Sydney, Mexico City and Chapala.

63 The notebook which Keith Sagar concludes DHL was using for more translation of Verga on the Tahiti, and which has the same watermark as the third notebook he used for *Kangaroo*, contains two pages of Spanish exercises (Tedlock 272–3). On 24 July he wrote to Achsah Brewster, 'I am now going to start learning Spanish, ready for the Mexicans' (iv. 280).

64 Seltzer's first edition of the novel had been for subscribers only. His difficulties with the law did not end with Judge Simpson's decision on 12 September that each of the three books the New York Society for the Suppression of Vice had found objectionable was 'a distinct contribution to the literature of the present day'. For details see G. Thomas Tanselle, 'The Thomas Seltzer Imprint', *Papers of the Bibliographical Society of America*, lviii (1964), 380–448.

65 DHL's relations with Marsh, who was well connected in both literary and artistic circles, and had managed to combine being editor of several volumes of *Georgian Poetry* with a post as Winston Churchill's private secretary, are well documented in *TE* (see especially pp. 85–6, 814).

66 Rudnick 155.

67 *Women in Love*, ed. David Farmer, Lindeth Vasey and John Worthen (Cambridge, 1987), pp. 137–8.

68 See p. 176 above.

69 *LT* 37.

70 *LT* 90. Cf. also, from the third volume of Mabel's *Intimate Memories* (*Movers and Shakers*, 1936):

> Motoring in Provincetown with Maurice, we had to spend a night somewhere on the way. After riding for miles in the long, summer twilight, I remember standing, dazzled by the light at the hotel desk, in a large, mahogany lobby, hearing Maurice ask for a double room and bath, and feeling perfectly limp and miserable. I had accepted what I called to myself the minor inconvenience of a physical relationship with him to further my scheme, thinking that by so doing I would remove our two bodies from the foreground, since they had become obstacles to the work I planned, and stood in the way of a complete influence over him. (p. 376)

The 'scheme' Mabel refers to was Maurice Sterne's 'artistic metamorphosis' (p. 374). The former lover with whom she does seem to have had a strong physical relationship is John Reed.

71 *LT* 60, 61, 64.

72 Frieda 152.

73 *LT* 59–60.

74 Frieda 136. Frieda gave a further brief account of Mabel's attempt to take DHL from her in the last chapter of her unfinished autobiographical novel, 'And the Fullness Thereof' (*Memoirs* 120).

75 Tony Luhan's Indian wife was called Candelaria. Mabel had compensated her for the loss of her husband by signing a contract which guaranteed Candelaria a life-long income of $35 a month (Rudnick 152–6).

76 Because of its association with French, 'Mond' may have already suggested money, power and influence to DHL; but through Mary Cannan, he had some contact with Henry Ludwig Mond, a leading British industrialist and one of the founders of ICI (Imperial Chemicals Ltd). See *TE* 481. Before leaving Mary, Gilbert Cannan formed a relationship with Gwen Wilson who in January 1920 became Mond's wife. For a short time in 1921 he toured South Africa with both her and Mond in a curious *ménage à trois*: a combination, as DHL wickedly described it, of 'the Mond, the Demi-Monde, and the Immonde' (iii. 502–3).

77 *SMOS* 199:21–2, 25–36; 202:6–9. For the textual history of this fragment (first entitled 'The Wilful Woman' by Keith Sagar), and the deleted sentence, see pp. xix–xxi, 268.

78 The 'woman' in the first work is young and from California; no-one ever accused Mabel of having the sardonic wit of Lou's mother in *St. Mawr*; and Kate Leslie has many of the characteristics of Frieda (as well as DHL himself). Insofar as they could be said to be 'based' on women he had met, the protagonists in these three works are clearly amalgams. When DHL deliberately set out to depict people he knew, his preferred term was 'portrait' or 'sketch'. He did not publish a portrait of Mabel until 'None of That!' (see pp. 360–1 above).

79 The four poems were 'Eagle in New Mexico', 'The Red Wolf', 'Men in New Mexico' and 'Autumn at Taos' (*Poems* 372, 403, 407, 408).

80 See the chapter in *Mr Noon* called 'Aphrodite and the Cow' (pp. 34–43).

81 See *EY* 272–3.

82 *Poems* 412.

83 *Adelphi*, i (October 1923), 374–7.

84 The influence of Freud's disciple Otto Gross on Frieda is described in both *EY* and *TE*.

85 Hecht's first great success in the theatre was *The Front Page* (1928), written in collaboration with Charles MacArthur. His screenplays – also with MacArthur – included *Wuthering Heights* (1939), *Spellbound* (1945) and *Notorious* (1946).

86 Details concerning the launching of *Laughing Horse* can be found in Nehls, ii. 501.

87 'The Sex-Obsessed Mr. D. H. Lawrence' is the heading of the review of *Psychoanalysis and the Unconscious* in the *Brooklyn Eagle* by John V. A. Weaver (28 May 1921).

88 *Fantazius Mallare: A Mysterious Oath* (Chicago, 1922), p. 55.

89 *Laughing Horse*, no. 4 (no date and no page numbers).

90 Ibid.

91 Hecht offers a very brief account of his difficulties in *A Child of the Century* (New York, 1954), p. 180, where he also reprints the list of 'The World's 22 Worst Books' (p. 328) which he published in the *Chicago Literary Times* in 1923. This includes *Women in Love* (but also *Pilgrim's Progress*, *Adam Bede* and *As You Like It*).

92 Bynner 11.

93 *SCAL* 9. This formulation does not appear in the earlier versions but the attitude it summarises is very much implicit in them.

94 *English Review*, xxviii (May 1919), 412.

95 Ibid., 411, 413.

96 *SCAL* 91, 92, 94.

97 *English Review* (May 1919), 414.

98 *SCAL* 98.

99 In an indirect reference to Jessie Chambers, DHL includes in his attack on the understanding woman: ' "I can read him like a book", said my first lover of me. The book is in several volumes, dear' (*SCAL* 98). Another example of the new autobiographical element in the final version is his treatment of the gipsy woman. In the first essay he had said that Hawthorne knew what it was to meet in a crowd 'eyes that answer in instant, mystic, deadly understanding, as the eyes of a gipsy will sometimes answer, out of a crowd' (*English Review* (May 1919), 416). In revision this becomes,

> I always remember meeting the eyes of a gipsy woman, for one moment, in a crowd, in England. She knew and I knew. What did we know! I was not able to make out. But we knew.
>
> Probably the same fathomless hate of this spiritual conscious society in which the outcast woman and I both roamed like meek-looking wolves'   (*SCAL* 98)

For what is obviously another reminiscence of this episode from DHL's youth see *BB* 193:31–7.

100 *SCAL* 165.

101 *SCAL* 169. The change in manner, apparent enough in the quotation from the Whitman essay, can also be illustrated by DHL's treatment of Hestor's daughter Pearl in the *Scarlet Letter* essay. In the first version he writes that Pearl embodies 'the truly deadly principle of betrayal for betrayal's sake' and describes how she 'mocks and tortures Dimmesdale with a subtlety rarer even than her mother's, and more exquisitely poisonous' (*English Review*, 416–17). In the revision he makes very much the same points but in a tone whose difference is evident in his claim that Pearl 'has the pietistic Dimmesdale on toast, spits right in his eye: both his eyes' (*SCAL* 100).

102 *LT* 73–5.

103 DHL had been urging Mountsier to come to Taos for some time. On 19 September he had said, 'If you come, I will ask Mabel Dodge to lend you the Studio, about 100 yards away, and you will eat with us', but ten days later he had referred to hiring the Studio for Mountsier (iv. 316). On 11 October, he had to explain that Mabel 'did not rent her places, because then everybody would say, "you rented it to him, so why not to me" ' (iv. 321). It clearly was not easy to establish straightforward financial arrangements with Mabel. When DHL left the Taos house he wrote a thank-you letter to Mabel but also one to Luhan. In the latter he must have enclosed some money: 'Let me give you some dollars for [the house's] christening' (iv. 346); but a note to Luhan on 15 December suggests the money was returned: 'Why did you send back the cheque?' (iv. 361). All this makes it very doubtful whether he was ever able to pay rent for the Taos house.

104 *LT* 79.

105 See Robert R. White, *The Taos Society of Artists* (Albuquerque 1983).

106 Mabel describes in some detail her early relations with Nina Wilcox (as she then was) in the first volume of her *Intimate Memories* (*Background*), pp. 68–81. Having married someone from their common *milieu* named Bull, Nina Bull became for a while a Christian therapist – a 'Divine Science practitioner' – and treated Mabel herself (Rudnick 134). On 15 December 1922 DHL told Bessie Freeman that Nina – who by that time had been married to Lee Witt for over a year – was going to England in January 'to study some sort of co-ordination healing stunt under some doctor in London' (iv. 361). By 1925 she had become intensely interested in Behaviourism, the very latest therapeutic fashion (vi. 210).

107 Ida Rauh and Max Eastman had been married in 1911. Shortly before the war, when the defence of Indian culture was – like the defence of psychoanalysis or birth-control – still just one of many fashionable causes Mabel supported, she staged a ceremony at her apartment during which a number of people including the Eastmans chewed peyote 'in the Indian manner'. The unhappy consequences, and Eastman's suspicion that Mabel had only pretended to take the hallucinogenic drug herself, helped to confirm his already low opinion of her. See William L. O'Neill, *The Last Romantic: A Life of Max Eastman* (New York, 1978), p. 28.

108 Andrew Dasburg reported that no-one enjoyed playing charades more than DHL and that in the 1950s he could still see him 'on top of a London bus with raincoat and open umbrella commenting on the vileness of the weather' (Nehls, ii. 197).

109 Merrild 291.

110 Ibid. 29.

111 In a letter to Mountsier at the end of November DHL says that the rent for his own cabin would be $100 and that the Danes would pay $50 for theirs – 'till April' (iv. 344), but Merrild's memory was that he and Gótszche were invited to Del Monte as the Lawrence's guests (Merrild, p. 56).

112 *LT* 101

Chapter Four: Christmas at Del Monte

1 Merrild 66–8.

2 Ibid. 73.

3 Ibid. 74.

4 Ibid. 204.

5 In his essay on Dana's *Two Years Before the Mast*, which DHL had finished revising before he went up to Del Monte (iv. 348), there is,

> The more we intervene machinery between us and the naked forces the more we numb and atrophy our own senses. Every time we turn on a tap to have water, every time we turn a handle to have fire or light, we deny ourselves and annul our being. The great elements, the earth, air, fire, water, are there like some great mistress whom we woo and struggle with, whom we heave and wrestle with. And all our appliances do but deny us these fine embraces, take the miracle of life away from us.
>
> (*SCAL* 127)

This passage was already in the essay DHL revised and expresses well one of his more persistent attitudes.

6 For more on this topic see David Ellis, 'Lawrence, Wordsworth and "Anthropomorphic Lust"', *Cambridge Quarterly*, xxiii (Autumn 1994), 230–42. Lawrence's urgent need to feel he was in contact with 'reality' helps to explain his rejection of Brewster's Buddhism.

7 DHL's relations with the male members of the Chambers and Hocking families are described in both *EY* and *TE*.

8 *LT* 109.

9 Merrild 239–40. In Taos DHL had already told Andrew Dasburg that Mabel ought to be tarred and feathered and run out of town on a rail (Nehls, ii. 197). In his parodic recasting of Benjamin Franklin's list of virtues, the fourth – 'Resolution: Resolve to perform what you ought to perform; perform without fail what you resolve' – becomes: 'Resolve to abide by your own deepest promptings, and to sacrifice the smaller things to the greater. Kill when you must, and be killed the same: the must coming from the gods inside you, or from the men in whom you recognize the Holy Ghost' (*SCAL* 23).

10 *LT* 112–13.

11 Around 21 January 1922, DHL wrote to a Mrs Bergman asking her to open the Witts' house for Mountsier, who would be spending the night in Taos, and saying that Frieda would be down some time that week 'for the dentist'. Having gone to Boston after Christmas, the Witts had clearly left their house at the Lawrences' disposal and Mrs Bergman must have had the key. They came back on 13 March, in time to entertain the Lawrences before they left for Mexico (iv. 370, 410).

12 *LT* 114.

13 Mabel Dodge Luhan, *Intimate Memories: Background*, p. 73.

14 See *D. H. Lawrence: Letters to Thomas and Adele Seltzer*, ed. Gerald M. Lacy (Santa Barbara, 1976), pp. 253–4. As well as an interesting selection of the Seltzers' own letters, this edition contains a very useful 'Biographical Narrative' of Lawrence and the Seltzers by Alexandra Lee Levin and Lawrence L. Levin.

15 Ibid., p. 276; Merrild 125. There is a 'Good King Arthur' and of course 'Good King Wenceslas' in the massive BBC Music Library catalogue but no 'Good King Quentin'.

16 After Los Angeles, Seltzer went to San Francisco to meet more cinema contacts and stayed in the same Palace Hotel the Lawrences had patronised. He and his wife must have spent some time with Mountsier at Del Monte because on 7 January they wrote separate letters in which they both thanked him for lending them $100 (*Letters to Thomas and Adele Seltzer*, ed. Lacy, pp. 249–50).

17 Mountsier had been to see the Lawrences while they were in Germany and then Austria in 1921. He had first met DHL when, in the company of Esther Andrews, he went to Cornwall at the end of 1915, but it was not until August 1920 that he became his literary agent (*TE* 344–5, 587).

18 Merrild 129.

19 The information about Mountsier's fall comes from a letter Frieda wrote to her mother on 23 February 1923 (iv. 396). It may be that Lawrence was remembering it when he described the riding accident in *St. Mawr*.

20 Although he had connections with the New York *Sun* newspaper, Mountsier seems in 1922–3 to have had no very settled employment, beyond what was involved in

being DHL's agent. Correspondence between him and DHL before the visit to Del Monte suggests that he had always intended to come to the Taos area for a considerable time (iv. 342), and he certainly stayed there many months after the Lawrences had left.

21 Letters to Mountsier in his papers (NWU) are addressed c/o Higgins, now perhaps the best-known of the Taos painters.

22 In a letter to Koteliansky dated 10 November 1921, Lawrence had complained of Mountsier that he was 'one of those irritating people who have generalised detestations: his particular ones being Jews, Germans, and Bolshevists. So unoriginal. He got on my nerves badly in Germany' (iv. 113).

23 *Our Eleven Million Dollars: Europe's Debt to the United States* was published by Seltzer in 1922. Mountsier's obituary in the New York *Times* on 25 November 1972 also mentions *Soldiers, Sailors and Marines* but there is no mention of this book in the National Union Catalog.

24 Copies Mountsier kept of his letters to Seltzer can be found in the Mountsier papers.

25 On several occasions in his letter Mountsier uses 'we' and at one point he also writes: 'In the matter of your advertising Lawrence wishes, as I do, that the "genius" and "greatest" stuff and any fulsome praise be eliminated.' A copy of the letter is in the Mountsier papers.

26 Seltzer's wife was born Adele Szold in Baltimore in 1876, the daughter of a German-speaking Rabbi. Seltzer himself was born in Russia in 1875 and came to the United States with his family in 1887 (*Letters to Thomas and Adele Seltzer*, ed. Lacy, pp. 171–2).

27 Ibid., p. 186.

28 Ibid., pp. 251, 254.

29 According to his obituarist in the New York *Times*, Mountsier had graduated from the University of Michigan in 1909 before going on to the Ph.D., which he appears not to have completed. For further information about his background, see *TE* 825 and Meyers, *D. H. Lawrence*, pp. 199–200.

30 Discovering that he would have to pay American income tax on his American income, DHL drew up in February 1923 a table of his earnings during the previous year. He calculated that he had received $3,824.67 in royalties from his books (mostly from Seltzer) and a total of $1,615 in payments from the *Dial*, *Hearst's* and Harriet Monroe's *Poetry*. That made a gross income of just under $5,440 from which he subtracted $543.96 as Mountsier's commission, $300 for his train journey from New York and $345.31 for other expenses his agent had incurred, including typing (iv. 400). The problem was what to allow Mountsier in the future, from the contracts with Seltzer he had negotiated, now that he was no longer in DHL's employ. On 3 March 1923 DHL asked him, 'Will you write that you are satisfied if I pay you ten per-cent of all my receipts from Seltzer for this current year? – There will probably be very little from any other source' (iv. 403). Mountsier agreed to this arrangement but there were acrimonious exchanges later over its implementation. (Information from the letters has been supplemented here by reference to DHL's brief diary in UCB.)

31 *Letters to Thomas and Adele Seltzer*, ed. Lacy, p. 191. The large number of letters of rejection in the Mountsier papers suggests that he tried hard to promote Lawrence,

who was both an acquired and minority taste. They also show that, whether through much effort on his own part or not, he was able to secure during Lawrence's first months in America a number of lucrative invitations to lecture. But on 4 December 1922 Lawrence wrote to Koteliansky, 'I am repeatedly asked to go East and lecture. I might be a rich man. But shoulder to shoulder with Gilly and Hughie Walpole, no' (iv. 349). 'Gilly' was Gilbert Cannan.

32 In DHL's final, hand-written version of his chapter on *The Scarlet Letter* one short paragraph reads, 'The fiery heart. A. Mary of the Bleeding Heart. Mater Adolorata! A. Capital A. Adulteress. Glittering with gold thread. Abel. America. Adultery.' This is identical to the printed version except that there the word 'Admirable!' has been tagged on the end (*SCAL* 90). In his chapter on Hawthorne in *Americans*, Sherman quotes from *Endicott and the Red Cross* Hawthorne's own description of a woman wearing an 'A' and his suggestion that it might lead people to believe it meant 'Admirable or anything rather than Adulteress' (pp. 141–2).

33 *P* 316, 315.

34 DHL's original title for this collection of short stories had been 'Black Bread' but it later became *Little Novels of Sicily.*

35 Lawrence had known Meredith Starr in Cornwall (*TE* 386–7). His book consisted of interviews with sixty English novelists (Lawrence not included). Adrian Lawlor's sardonic review in the *Bulletin* suggested that most of them exhibited a 'naive tendency' to 'recommend for the consumption of posterity [their] own particular line of goods' (20 July 1922, p. 25).

36 For details see *Hardy* xlv–xlvi. The new title was the responsibility of the editors of the *Literary Digest International Book Review* where the essay was published, much edited, in April 1923.

37 *Hardy* 151:31–5.

38 Ibid. 154:15–19, 30–1, 8–10.

39 *Poems* 402.

40 Merrild 84.

41 See (iv. 385); Bynner 16; and Merrild 147.

42 Merrild 148–59, 143.

43 There is a reproduction of Merrild's book cover for *The Captain's Doll* volume in *Letters to Thomas and Adele Seltzer*, ed. Lacy, p. 122. On 17 February Seltzer sent Merrild a cheque for $120. This was for three covers at $40 each (p. 259), but he decided against using those for *Studies in Classic American Literature* and *Kangaroo*.

   DHL gave Götzsche's portrait of him to Adele Seltzer later in the year and it is now in UT (iv. 503, and *Letters to Thomas and Adele Seltzer*, ed. Lacy, p. 266).

44 Merrild 82–3.

45 Ibid. 135, 252, 197.

46 Ibid. 126. ('Lawrence wouldn't think of using all that money himself. He didn't feel he had a right to, or even that it belonged to him').

47 Ibid. 136.

48 Ibid. 45–50. The conversation is taken from chapter IV of *Kangaroo* and edited to disguise its origin.

49 A photograph facing p. 138 in Merrild's book shows the fireplace in the Lawrences'

cabin at Del Monte, with one of DHL's watercolours hanging above the mantelpiece. Unfortunately the quality of the photograph is too poor to reveal whether this was the *Death of Procris*. When DHL copied this picture in March 1917 it gave him 'great delight' (iii. 103).

50 Merrild 209–12. 'Making Pictures' was included in *AA* 164–74.

51 Merrild 133–5, 232.

52 Ibid. 85.

53 *LT* 36, 72. For a vivid impression of what Frieda must have looked like when she was smoking, see the last photograph in this book.

54 Bynner 31–2.

55 Merrild 136–8.

56 *Poems*, 395, 399.

57 Merrild 172.

58 Ibid. 172–3.

59 Ibid. 174.

60 Ibid. 175. The blanks in the second of these long quotations are puzzling. Since they cannot stand for 'bitch', a word printed in the quotation before, a possible and potentially significant candidate is 'cunt'.

61 *Letters to Thomas and Adele Seltzer*, ed. Lacy, p. 255. In one of five sketches of DHL reproduced in Merrild's book, Bibbles is sitting on DHL's lap.

62 The crucial document here is a letter to Henry Savage in September 1913 in which DHL admits his lungs are 'crocky' but insists he is not consumptive – 'the type, as they say':

> I am not really afraid of consumption, I don't know why – I don't think I shall ever die of *that*. For one thing, I am certain that when I have been ill, it has been sheer distress and nerve strain which have let go on my lungs. I am one of those fools who take my living damnably hard. And I have a good old English habit of shutting up my rages of trouble well inside my belly, so that they play havoc with my innards. If we had any sense we should lift out hands to heaven and shriek, and tear our hair and our garments, when things hurt like mad. Instead of which, we behave with decent restraint, and smile, and crock our lungs. (ii. 73)

63 Cf. 'Of Lawrence's faults I think the chief one was quick changes of mood and temper. He could be so furious so easily. Up and down his barometer went at a fierce rate. He did not keep anything to himself, but it burst forth and that was not easy to live with' (*FLC* 14).

64 Merrild 203–4, 208. On the subject of DHL's sexual make-up Merrild adds, 'He was not, either, a hermaphrodite, that at least, my eye recorded for a fact!' He does not explain how he had been able to form an impression of the Archbishop of Canterbury's physique.

65 There is more on the tendency to use tuberculosis as an explanation for DHL's rages in David Ellis, 'Explaining the Abnormal: D. H. Lawrence and Tuberculosis', in *Writing the Lives of Writers*, ed. Warwick Gould and Tom Stacey (1997).

66 Merrild 138, 175.

67 JMM 231 (the review had been published in the *Nation and Athenaeum* on 12 August 1922).

Chapter Five: Old Mexico

1 'Au Revoir, U.S.A.', *P* 104.

2 In the 1923 edition of Philip Terry's *Guide to Mexico* (Boston and New York) the Hotel Regis advertised itself as having '500 rooms and 450 baths' with 'all the *comforts and conveniences* of the most modern American hotel'. The rooms without baths cost 'from 4 pesos a day', those with them from 4 to 20. At the Monte Carlo there was a tariff of 4 pesos a day, 'food and all' (iv. 415). On 11 May DHL told Bessie Freeman that 'a peso is about 49 cents American' (iv. 443).

3 The phrase quoted is from *Q* 11. For other descriptions of the Monte Carlo by DHL see (iv. 414–15), and *The Plumed Serpent* where Kate Leslie explains that she has tried some of the big hotels but 'there is such a feeling of lowness about them, awful! I can't stand the feeling of prostitution. And then the cheap insolence of the servants' (p. 23).

4 Bynner 21–2.

5 See *TE* 208–11.

6 *Letters to Thomas and Adele Seltzer*, ed. Lacy, p. 88.

7 The details about Bynner come from James Kraft's 'Biographical Introduction' to his and Richard Wilbur's edition of Bynner's *Selected Poems*. A China enthusiast, Bynner had travelled in the East and some of his work is reminiscent of the earlier poems of Ezra Pound (whom he had met and encouraged in New York). It is a sad comment on the decline in his reputation that he was best known in later life as the perpetrator of one of the period's most successful literary hoaxes. In 1914, with a friend named Arthur Ficke, Bynner quickly composed what he considered parodic equivalents of the new 'modernist' verse (having particularly in mind the 'Imagism' of Amy Lowell and Pound), and very successfully passed them off as the products of a new 'Spectric' School of Poetry, named in honour of the Russian ballet's *Le spectre de la rose*. But it was precisely the new modernist verse which by the 1930s had succeeded in making most of his own work seem hopelessly antiquated. For Bynner's own account of the 'Spectre Hoax', see his *Prose Pieces*, ed. James Kraft (New York, 1979), pp. 314–17.

8 Nehls (ii. 493) has a likely chronology, calculating that Bynner and Johnson arrived in Mexico City on Tuesday 27 March 1923. In a letter Bynner wrote to Alice Corbin Henderson from Puebla on 13 April he remembered their arrival as being on 'Monday night'. See the *Selected Letters of Witter Bynner*, ed. James Kraft (New York, 1981), p. 99.

9 The report of DHL's rage comes from the letter Frieda wrote to Adele Seltzer on the 8th (*Letters to Thomas and Adele Seltzer*, ed. Lacy, p. 88). In 'Quetzalcoatl' DHL gives to the episode which forces the heroine to flee from the stadium the character of a horrific homosexual rape. An old limping horse, making its way out of the ring, is charged by a bull from behind:

> the horse was heaved up absurdly from the rear, with one of the bull's horns between his legs and deep in his body, then he went collapsing down in front, with his rear still heaved up and the bull's horn working vigorously, pushing up and down inside him, while he lay on his neck, all twisted. And a heap of bowels coming out. And the nauseous stench! (p. 8).

Bynner wrote an alternative account of the visit to the bullfight which he published in the American periodical *Pearson's* in June 1924. It is reprinted in his *Prose Pieces*, pp. 53–61.

10 There are details of Gamio's discovery in Parmenter 277–8. As L. D. Clark explains in his 'Sketch of Aztec Mythology', the second possible translation of 'Quetzalcoatl' is 'precious twin' (*PS* 555). DHL writes of 'one great dark, green blot of an obsidian eye' and enamelled fangs in 'Au Revoir, U.S.A.' (*P* 105).

11 DHL especially appreciates Crèvecoeur's tenth letter in which there is an account of two snakes fighting because in it the artist overcomes the ideologue and Crèvecoeur forgets the 'benevolence of nature'. His description is 'as handsome a piece of ophiolatry, perhaps, as that coiled Aztec rattlesnake carved in stone' (*English Review*, January 1919, 15).

12 *P* 104–6.

13 It was DHL who claimed at the time that the photograph was taken during the visit to Cuernavaca (iv. 429, 431, 435). In his memoir Bynner associated it with San Agustin Acolman, an old monastery near Teotihuacán (p. 23).

14 Nehls, ii. 227–8. Details of Beals's career are in ii. 497–8, n.111.

15 These letters to Johnson are in UT. Most of the second is reprinted in *Selected Letters of Witter Bynner*, pp. 100–1.

16 Bynner 37–9. The source of DHL's information would have been L. Gutierrez de Lara and Edgcumb Pinchon, *The Mexican People: Their Struggle for Freedom* (New York, 1914), which he had read by 22 February 1923 (iv. 394). According to Bynner, DHL had this book with him in Orizaba.

17 Like all the postcards these two letters are dated by DHL 21 April (a Saturday). The postmarks of the postcards are dated the 21st, but of the letters, the 23rd.

18 The reforms centred chiefly on a drive against illiteracy. Over 1,000 rural schools were built between 1920 and 1924, more than the total number in the previous fifty years. See Michael C. Meyer and William L. Sherman, *The Course of Mexican History* (New York, 1979), p. 573.

19 *Q* 22. Frieda told Adele Seltzer on 8 April, 'We went to see a learned Mrs Nuttall – she liked us but was frightened of us – belongs to the old sort. When I mentioned Steffens an old American judge (dont know his name) nearly jumped out of his skin' (*Letters to Thomas and Adele Seltzer*, ed. Lacy, p. 88).

20 Bynner 31.

21 Ibid. 61.

22 E. M. Forster, *A Passage to India*, ed. Oliver Stallybrass (1978), p. 70. Compare, in *Kangaroo*: 'It came on to rain—streaming down the carriage windows. Jack lit a cigarette, and offered it to Harriet. She, though she knew Somers disliked it intensely when she smoked, particularly in a public place like this long, open railway carriage, accepted, and sat by the closed window smoking' (76:10–14).

23 See Nehls, ii. 243–4.

24 Ibid. ii. 230 (and 227–9, where Carleton Beals writes about the same occasion).

25 These two letters are in UT.

26 Bynner 80.

27 Díaz was president for all but four years of this long period. He was eventually

overthrown in May 1911 (Meyer and Sherman, *The Course of Mexican History*, pp. 431–510).

28 See L. D. Clark, *Dark Night of the Body. D. H. Lawrence's 'The Plumed Serpent'* (Austin, 1964), for excellent photographs by Laverne Clark of El Manglar, the house in Calle Zaragoza and, above all, Isabel Dolores de Medina in old age.

29 Dr Purnell seems to have been separated from his wife. When he was staying with Johnson in Guadalajara at the beginning of May, Bynner described the Purnells' house as quaint but untidy and added, 'While the mother has been away for some years with all the children, Dr Purnell has lived here as a bachelor; and Idella, returned from college, is more an editor than a housekeeper' (*Selected Letters of Witter Bynner*, p. 103). It was at this time that Idella Purnell launched her poetry magazine *Palms*.

30 Bynner 91–2.

31 This picture of life in Chapala is derived from the letters, published and unpublished, of the Lawrences, Bynner, Johnson and Idella Purnell; 'Quetzalcoatl' and *The Plumed Serpent*; the reminiscences of Frieda, Bynner, Johnson and Idella Purnell; and the latter's unpublished novel 'Friction'.

32 This journey is described in detail in both 'Quetzalcoatl' and *The Plumed Serpent* and there is no other time DHL would have had occasion to make it. According to Capt. Percy Holmes, who was British Vice-Consul in Guadalajara at this time, DHL called on him to ask if he knew of a suitable house to rent on Lake Chapala (Nehls, ii. 232). This would suggest that he stopped in Guadalajara *before* continuing by rail to Ocotlán but I am assured by L. D. Clark that this was not possible.

33 It is in *The Plumed Serpent* (pp. 98–101) that the horror stories are attributed to the German manager of the hotel where Kate stays on her arrival at Lake Chapala. Bynner suggests in his memoir that their source was in fact Scott, the manager of the Arzopalo (pp. 123–8).

34 *PS* 136–7. Bynner's view of how DHL in fact reacted to the supposed break-in is unflattering and malicious. He describes how on the morning of 9 May he and Johnson were summoned urgently round to the Lawrences' house after breakfast and told they must all leave Chapala immediately. Awakened in the night, DHL had seen a hand with a knife break the glass of the pane nearest the lock on his bedroom door. His response had been to rush to Frieda's room, jump in bed with her and, with his head against her shoulder, say, 'They've come!' But when Frieda got up to investigate 'there was no one in his room, in any room, no one in the house, no one in the garden, only the moonlight' (Bynner 160).

There is further confirmation here for the well-known fact that, like many middle-class couples of the period, the Lawrences preferred separate bedrooms when space was available; support also for the idea that DHL was prone to hysteria. It would be comparatively easy to illustrate that tendency but difficult to find much evidence in his life of physical cowardice, although whether that implied charge has been insinuated by Bynner or comes directly from Frieda is not clear from the way his account is written. Bynner later describes himself as being at one with Frieda in the conviction that DHL was simply imagining things, and his tone implies that whereas DHL nervously exaggerated the dangers of Chapala, he himself was perfectly at ease there. In 'Quetzalcoatl', on the other hand, it is Owen Rhys, the character unmistakably based on him, who is the nervous one. He is already at the hotel when Kate arrives at Lake Chapala and tells her that it is a dangerous area: ' "Of course they say it's safe enough now, but a man sleeps on the stairs with a loaded gun." Owen was rolling his eyes in one of his nervous fits. Kate knew he would not stay' (*Q* 62).

35 Bynner 16. In his memoir Bynner claimed that on their first arrival in Mexico City, he and Johnson stayed in the very hotel room at whose window Graham's friend, William Ewart, had been shot (p. 20).

36 Huitzilopochtli was a tribal deity the Aztecs had brought with them to the Valley of Mexico. The myths and legends surrounding Quetzalcoatl are conflicting but he was usually felt to be unenthusiastic about human sacrifice and, as one authority puts it, the 'God of learning and civilisation'. Two other features also made him an appropriate choice for Ramón: that he was sometimes identified with a supposedly historical figure, a priest-king of the Toltecs; and that when Cortés first arrived in Mexico, it was thought by Montezuma – a high-priest before he became the Emperor – that the invader might be a reincarnation of Quetzalcoatl. See George C. Vaillant, *Aztecs of Mexico: Origin, Rise and Fall of the Aztec Nation*, revised by Suzannah B. Vaillant (Harmondsworth, 1965), p. 191; *PS* 556; and Hugh Thomas, *The Conquest of Mexico* (1993), pp. 183–7.

37 Jean-Paul Pichardie, *D. H. Lawrence: la tentation utopique: de Rananim au 'Serpent à Plumes'*, Publications de l'Université de Rouen, no. 137 (1988). This book provides a very thorough study of all the possible literary influences on DHL's novel. What he had read specifically about Mexico when he began 'Quetzalcoatl' – Prescott's *History of the Conquest* and information in Terry's *Guide* mainly – is summarised in *PS* xxv, note 49. He was asking Idella Purnell for Díaz in order to re-read him.

38 *Q* 17.

39 Bynner 71–8; Frieda 138; and, for Johnson's account, Nehls, ii. 235.

40 *P* 105.

41 *Q* 141–4.

42 *Q* 198.

43 *PS* 380:27–8.

44 *Q* 126, 124.

45 The homoerotic overtones of this scene I am discussing are slight. They become striking only in DHL's re-writing for *The Plumed Serpent* of a later encounter in which Ramón persuades Cipriano that he ought to become the living Huitzilopochtli (*Q* 253–4; *PS* 367–9).

46 *Q* 312, 318.

47 *PS* 148, 188, 271.

48 Cf.: 'Fascism won't hold against the lust for anarchy which is at the bottom of the Fascisti themselves. The Fascisti only live because they think they can bully society. It is a great bully movement, just as communism is a bully movement. But communism is a more vital feeling, because of the big grudge that burns in a communist's belly' (*Q* 248). Already in this version of his novel, DHL tries to deal with the charge that his own ideas for the future are reactionary. 'Do you know what Padre Ignacio once said to me, about you', Cipriano tells his friend, 'Ramón Carrasco's future is the past of humanity.' But Ramón responds, 'It is only the spiral of evolution, if you care to see it

that way. We must make a great swerve, and gather up the past, before we can have any future' (*Q* 125).

49 Unpublished letter in UT. Eighteen months later, little boys would point at DHL in the Oaxaca streets and murmur 'Cristo' (Brett 164).

50 Bynner 111.

51 Ibid. 130–3. When *Journey with Genius* appeared Frieda challenged this detail and suggested the boys' arrest might have been a 'subterfuge of Mr Scott's' (the Arzopalo's manager). See *Selected Letters of Witter Bynner*, p. 213.

52 *Q* 132–3.

53 As James Kraft explains, Bynner visited Chapala regularly after 1923 and bought a house there in 1940.

54 *Selected Letters of Witter Bynner*, p. 181.

55 Ibid., pp. 200–1.

56 Cf. Bynner 136.

57 *Q* 43. Johnson was sufficiently struck by this passage to copy it down in a diary he was keeping (now in UT). On the inside front cover of the notebook which contains this diary, his hand-written index includes: 'Pages 4 & 5 – Excerpts from "Quetzalcoatl" (Later "Plumed Serpent") by D. H. Lawrence copied from his MS while I was typing it for him at Chapala (same summer).' Johnson appears to have typed just over four chapters of 'Quetzalcoatl' before Seltzer's typists took over. As L. D. Clark has pointed out to me, there is a change of typewriters at the end of p. 81 of the TS, three pages into chapter V, and also a change of style in the page numbering, from 'p. 81' to '-82-'. The half-page of typescript Johnson used for his note is numbered p. 82. This suggests that although there may have been some plan for Johnson to continue typing 'Quetzalcoatl' after the Lawrences left Guadalajara, he did not do so. In another letter to Idella from this period, Johnson writes, 'What *shall* I charge Lorenzo for the typing? And *how*? By the line, the number of words, number of pages? Or what? Please answer immediately. He's leaving at the end of the week.' Both Johnson's letters are in UT.

58 Nehls, ii. 236. Evidence in Idella Purnell's *Friction* suggests that she was in fact attracted to Johnson.

59 *Q* 70.

60 For DHL's attempts to convince Forster that what he needed was a woman see *TE* 190–2.

61 I am very grateful to Idella Purnell's daughter, Dr Marijane Osborn, for allowing me to see and quote from this novel.

62 In 1926 Idella Purnell must have written to Bynner mentioning certain rumours that disturbed her. In his reply he admitted 'an element of tenderness towards my male friends which verges on the sort of physical attachment the detractors talk about' but implicitly denied being a practising homosexual. In a letter a few months later to Robert Hunt, with whom he was to live from 1930 until Hunt's death in 1964, Bynner warns him about being too frank, 'On the whole . . . I disbelieve in admitting the unsympathetic to knowledge.' For James Kraft, the remarks in the letter to Hunt probably explain those in Bynner's reply to Idella. See *Selected Letters of Witter Bynner*, pp. 118–19.

63 Bynner had also written from Mexico City to warn Idella about DHL. In a letter to her

dated 20 April 1923 he calls him an 'arroyo seco' ('dried-up stream'): 'Already he has turned on an acquaintance of mine in Mexico City: "Go away I don't want to see you any more" ' (UT). The acquaintance was Frederic Leighton – see Bynner 32–3.

64 Both these letters are in UT.

65 JMM 240 (the review of *Fantasia of the Unconscious* was first published in the *Algemeed Handelsblad*).

66 Ibid. 242 (pp. 105–6 of Murry's *Reminiscences* describe how powerfully he was affected by *Fantasia*).

67 *Adelphi*, i (June 1923), 9.

68 *SP* 185.

69 There is an account of how unexpectedly well the *Adelphi* began in F. A. Lea, *The Life of John Middleton Murry* (1959), pp. 110–11.

70 *Adelphi*, i (June 1923), 5–6.

71 Bynner 151.

72 Merrild 139; *LT* 105.

73 *Q* 69, 286. In the penultimate chapter of 'Quetzalcoatl' Kate nevertheless tells Cipriano that she must go home to see her mother and children: 'I said I would go at the end of the month and I must stick to it' (p. 317).

74 Frieda 157.

75 The detail is from 'Friction', but there is no reason to think it unreliable.

76 'Friction', ch. XVI, 'Sailing to Eden'.

77 L. D. Clark, *Dark Night of the Body*, p. 7.

78 Bynner 173–7.

79 The phrase is from 'Friction' but compare also Nehls, ii. 252.

80 Unpublished letter in UT.

81 In an undated letter in UT, Bynner expresses his surprise at learning that he and the other members of his party would need 'a certificate of recent vaccination' to re-enter the United States. From Laredo, DHL wrote to Johnson, 'They will vaccinate at the frontier free of charge. Why pay 3 pesos?' (iv. 468). If he had known this beforehand he would not have needed to send the information to Johnson. Idella Purnell's job at the American Consulate in Guadalajara must have made securing the necessary papers for re-entry comparatively easy.

Chapter Six: New York, Los Angeles, Guadalajara

1 *Letters to Thomas and Adele Seltzer*, ed. Lacy, p. 165.

2 *TE* 344, 564.

3 For letters of apology to the Brewsters and Amy Løwell see (iv. 484–5, 487). That the Lawrences saw Bessie Freeman once can be deduced from (iv. 472–3, 476, 484).

4 Joseph Collins, author of a ferocious attack on Lawrence as a sexual pervert in his *The Doctor Looks at Literature* (New York, 1923), complains, 'But there is a Lawrence cult here and it is growing, particularly amongst those who like to be called Greenwich villagers, the breath of whose nostrils is antinomianism, especially sex antinomianism!' (p. 257).

5 Joseph Wood Krutch, *More Lives Than One* (New York, 1962), p. 172.

6 *The Revealing Eye. Personalities of the 1920s in Photographs by Nickolas Muray and Words by Paul Gallico* (New York, 1967), p. 170. Muray remembered Lawrence being brought to his studio by Mabel Luhan, but that is not possible.

7 Several other occasions on which Frieda and DHL parted in a way which might have been a prelude to a more permanent separation are described in *TE* (cf. pp. 230–6).

8 *SP* 190.

9 *Letters to Thomas and Adele Seltzer*, ed. Lacy, p. 106.

10 F. A. Lea, *The Life of John Middleton Murry* (1959), pp. 117–8.

11 *Memoirs* 229.

12 *LT* 88.

13 How Weekley came to have custody of the children, the legal measures he took to prevent Frieda from seeing them, and the efforts she made to see them nevertheless are matters fully documented in *TE* 80–2, 102, 146–7, 169.

14 *New York Evening Post*, 20 August 1923.

15 Lawrence arrived in Buffalo on the evening of the 22nd and stayed with Bessie Freeman at 10 Saybrook Street. He was still there on Saturday 25th but by Monday 27th had moved to the house of a Mary Wilkeson at 42 Lancaster Avenue (he left Buffalo that evening). *Wilkinson* was Bessie Freeman's maiden name (*LT* 117) so that Mary Wilkeson is likely to have been a friend, rather than a relative of Bessie's.

16 Merrild 312–19; (iv. 495–7); and, for memories of the Lompoc expedition from a poet in the artist community in Carmel, Nehls, ii. 257–9.

17 The information concerning the visit to the opera comes from a letter to Frieda which will be published in vol. viii of the Cambridge edition of DHL's letters; the description of the actor is part of a satirical account DHL provided five years later (Nehls, iii. 289).

18 Merrild 313.

19 *P* 324.

20 *P* 722–3.

21 Skinner, *The Fifth Sparrow*, p. 117.

22 See *BB* 112–14 and the excellent note on 113:2 (pp. 407–8).

23 Merrild 320.

24 *BB* 149:11–20, 25–33. The end of the third notebook coincides with p. 113 of the Cambridge edition so that this passage would have been composed either on DHL's journey south or in Guadalajara. There are many other moments in the novel where DHL's voice and preoccupations are clearly apparent. Late in 1924 Mollie Skinner marked in Edward Garnett's copy of *BB* all the parts which she felt were wholly or partly by DHL. They came to only 37 per cent of the whole novel. For a convincing, closely argued account of why this is likely to have been a gross underestimation, and good reasons for believing that *BB* should be regarded as 'a Lawrence novel', see *BB* xlv–lii.

25 In *Tortoises* sex is implicitly regretted as the cross we all have to bear and an inevitable destroyer of independence.

26 On 7 August DHL had written to Merrild from New York, 'we might find some boat, some sailing ship that would take us to the islands: you as sailors, myself as cook: nominal. Frieda, I suppose, will want to join me at the end of October' (iv. 481). Reporting the 'absolute failure' of DHL's enquiries in Los Angeles Harbour, San

Pedro and Wilmington, Merrild commented, 'It might have been possible for us, individually, to get on ships, but three dilettantes on one ship was too much to expect' (Merrild 319).

27 Merrild 322–9.

28 Information from a letter to be published in vol. viii of the Cambridge edition of DHL's correspondence.

29 The Forsythes had expressed disappointment that he had never used the letters passed on to him via Bessie Freeman before his previous Mexican trip (iv. 498).

30 Merrild 338.

31 Ibid. 338–9.

32 'When Mabel learned that Lawrence was *alone* in Mexico, without his wife and guardian angel Frieda, she knew he was vulnerable and she wrote him at once' (Merrild 354).

33 *LT* 118. With DHL's encouragement secured, Mabel Luhan now wrote a series of letters to him. In what is likely to have been the first of these, she must have accepted his diagnosis of her failings. 'One day', he replied on 8 November, 'I will come to you and take your submission.' In a postscript he explains that 'Frieda and everybody insist on my going to England' and then adds, 'Before very long I hope to come and see you again' (iv. 528).

There may be a gloss on DHL's use of 'submission' here in chapter XI of *BB* where Jack Grant thinks that when he can get into communication 'with his own Lord, he always felt well and right again . . . [Monica] must give up to him. She must give herself up. He demanded this submission as if it were a submission to his mysterious Lord' (167:28–30; 168:3–5).

34 Johnson was the likely source of the rumours Lawrence mentions (see iv. 515).

35 In a review of *The Lost Girl* published in the *Athenaeum* in December 1920 Murry had written, 'Mr Lawrence would have us back to the slime from which we rose'; and referring to the concern with the 'awful African process' in his review of *Women in Love* in the *Nation and Athenaeum* nine months later, he concluded 'by the knowledge that we have we can only pronounce it sub-human and bestial, a thing our forefathers had rejected when they began to rise from the slime' (JMM 217, 227).

36 See ch. II, p. 56 above.

37 *SCAL* 138–9.

38 *BB* xlix.

39 In chapter XII, when Jack is pondering why he is hostile to the Christian notion of 'spirit', the reader is surprised to learn that 'He had a natural dislike of Shelley and vegetarians and socialists and all advocates of "Spirit"' when he has been convincingly presented in the opening of the novel as someone to whom Shelley would mean nothing (*BB* 175:25–6).

40 *SCAL* 96–7.

41 Merrild 340–1.

42 Nehls, ii. 267–8.

43 See an unpublished letter to Bynner, in response to his request for information for *Journey with Genius*, in UT; and Nehls, ii. 267.

44 For the two versions see Nehls, ii. 269–70. In the letter mentioned in the note above,

Idella Purnell describes how DHL one day took her to tea in Guadalajara:

It was as English a tea as could be managed, and in the middle of it some gipsy woman came in, and he very grandly told her to tell our fortunes . . .for which I think he paid a peso. She told me I would have three children, and I don't recall what she told Lawrence; but he was tickled and amused by the whole proceeding.

This incident may have had some influence on the fortune-telling episode in *The Virgin and the Gipsy*. Idella Purnell recalls in this same letter how in 1925 she would find herself cornered in the Los Angeles Public Library and asked ' "Is Lawrence a homo?" At which I, being young, unmarried and a virgin would blush violently and say I didn't think so.' DHL's reputation for homosexuality may well have owed something to the way Joseph Collins interpreted *Women in Love* in his *The Doctor Looks at Literature* (see note 4 above). When Merrild and Gótzsche first arrived in Los Angeles, a contact whose name DHL had given them, the writer Will Comfort, said, 'So you are the two homosexual lovers that stayed with [Lawrence] in the mountains all winter, do tell me about it' and assured them that he had always thought of DHL as a homosexual (Merrild 299).

45 Lea, *The Life of John Middleton Murry*, p. 112.

46 *Adelphi*, i (August 1923), p. 183. Lea points out that a photograph of Mansfield went out with the first number of *Adelphi*.

47 Ibid. i (July 1923), 96.

48 Information from a letter to be published in vol. viii of the Cambridge edition of DHL's correspondence.

49 'Friction', ch. XVI.

50 Merrild 343.

51 Ibid. 345 – 'Lawrence is more human again. At present, he excuses himself on the ground that the air is so changeable that it makes him "crazy" once in a while. A poor excuse!'

52 Ibid. 348.

53 Ibid. 350.

54 Ibid. 329.

55 *BB* 334:12–14, 18–29.

56 Ibid. 335:26–30, 38–40; 336:1–3; 337:9–10; 338:6–8.

57 When Jack returns to Perth after his period in the outback and is expecting to see Monica, he 'was wondering if she would want him to plead and play the humble and say he wasn't good enough for her. Because he wouldn't do it. Not if he never saw her again. All that flummery of love he would not subscribe to' (*BB* 259). It was almost certainly to DHL's 'tanti saluti' letter that Frieda was referring when, back in London, she wrote to Koteliansky on 4 December, 'Another letter from L. *Why* can't he say he will be glad to see me? Always a misery and a pain! It makes me *sick*!' This is the postscript to a note in which she has been pondering on her love for him: 'When you say Lawrence has loved me I have loved him a thousand times more! And to really love includes everything, intelligence and faith and sacrifice – and passion' (*Memoirs* 231).

58 *K* 288:34–5.

59 Merrild 350.

60 The account of the meeting in the restaurant comes from Bynner who also describes

how DHL would complain to Covarrubias about the ugliness of the murals the young Mexican had taken them all to see (Bynner 28–31). In 'Au Revoir, U.S.A.'' DHL writes: ' "Only the ugly is aesthetic now", said the young Mexican artist. Personally he seems as gentle and self-effacing as the nicest of lambs. Yet his caricatures are hideous' (*P* 105).

61 Meyer and Sherman, *The Course of Mexican History*, pp. 549, 579–80.

62 'Don't think of the *world* any more', Lawrence tells Mabel. 'Leave that to me, I am more cunning, and being alone, one must be a serpent as far as the world is concerned' (iv. 540). Jack Grant, for whom 'the world is a snake pit into which one is thrown', thinks to himself, 'But I must be wary. I must not put out my hand to ask them for anything, or they will strike my hand like vipers out of a hole' (*BB* 336:31–2, 8–10).

63 Veracruz was the site in 1914 of the first of the United States' two, significant military interventions in Mexican affairs after the fall of Díaz (US Navy 'bluejackets' occupied the port in the spring of 1914). After an incursion into New Mexico by Pancho Villa in 1916, the American government sent a punitive expedition into northern Mexico which remained there until January 1917 (Meyer and Sherman, *The Course of Mexican History*, pp. 533, 541).

Chapter Seven: European Interlude

1 *SMOS* 218:7; 219:14; 221:34–7; 224:13, 20–1. There is a further account of landing in Havana in *St. Mawr* (*SMOS* 128–9).

2 *RDP* 178:30, 34–6.

3 King appears to have complained that the British Foreign Office had instructed him to do nothing which might offend the US government: 'I have an Englishman wants to get into the United States. Washington has given him a visa, and said: Yes, you can enter whenever you like. Comes a cable from London: Prevent this man from crossing into the United States, Washington may not like it. What can one do?' (*RDP* 182:31–5). As a potential undesirable himself, and someone who felt that in the past he had suffered British government persecution, DHL would have found this anecdote especially striking.

4 *RDP* 183:30–3.

5 *RDP* 183:6–7.

6 JMM 110.

7 *The Savage Pilgrimage* was first published by Chatto and Windus in June 1932 and then, after the withdrawal of this edition, by Secker early in 1933. My quotation is on p. 202 of the second edition. For details see John Carswell's introduction to the reissue of the original version of his mother's book by Cambridge University Press in 1981 (pp. xxv–xxvi).

8 On 27 November 1955 Murry wrote,

Tell me, Frieda, for my own private satisfaction – it shall be buried afterwards – did you love me as much as I loved you in those queer days? It drove me crazy – really crazy, I think – wanting you so badly: the comfort and delight of you, and then feeling Oh God, but Lorenzo will never get over it. I mustn't, I must not. And I sometimes wonder what would have happened if I had not had that awful feeling of loyalty in friendship to L.

From Port Isabel in Texas Frieda replied on 10 December,

> Now I answer your question. I think how it was with me. After our famous journey together, something ultimate and deeply satisfactory and new had happened to me; there it was, just an inner lovely fact, that I accepted without question for ever. I trusted you and what you would do. Of course I wanted to hear from you, but not so much. No, you did the right thing, Lawrence was already very ill. I think you averted an ugly tragedy. (*Memoirs* 367–8)

In *The Married Man: A Life of D. H. Lawrence*, relying perhaps on Frieda's enigmatic, 'Of course I wanted to hear from you', Brenda Maddox has conjectured that what Murry refused Frieda was future cohabitation rather than sexual intercourse (p. 350); but that hardly seems to be the sense of Murry's words, which Frieda's do nothing to contradict. In his diary entry for 18 December 1955, Murry described how Frieda 'wanted us to stay together in Freiburg for a few days' and categorised his refusal of Frieda's request as 'the one and only great renunciation I have made' (Lea, *Life of John Middleton Murry*, p. 118).

9 *SP* 193–4.

10 *LT* 129.

11 Frieda 160. In this same passage, after regretting having made DHL come to Europe, Frieda writes: 'these are the mistakes we make, sometimes irreparable'.

12 *TE* 132 and *passim*.

13 *SP* 202.

14 Brett's unpublished diary, now at NWU, takes the form of a series of letters to the departed Katherine ('Dearest Tig') whose spirit is described as paying periodic visits to Brett's rooms in Pond Street.

15 *SP* 196–7.

16 Brett 23.

17 Ibid. 25–6.

18 *SP* 206.

19 Sean Hignett, *Brett: From Bloomsbury to New Mexico* (1984), p. 143.

20 *SP* 206.

21 *Memoirs* 231. The letter was written from Heath Street on 4 December 1923 and has other impressive moments. '*Sons and Lovers*', Frieda tells Kot, 'is *not* so great a book! I had more to do with that, than any of his others; but you don't want to accept the struggle and chaos of *Women in Love*, it's so upsetting!!' (230–1).

22 An 'N' (for Napoleon) surrounded with an imperial laurel wreath and capped with an imperial crown was what would now be termed the Café Royal's logo. There is an account of these matters in Guy Deghy and Keith Waterhouse, *Café Royal: Ninety Years of Bohemia* (1955), pp. 36–7.

23 *SP* 208–9.

24 *SP* 210–11.

25 Full accounts of Mary Cannan and Mark Gertler can be found in *TE*.

26 Hignett, *Brett*, p. 143.

27 Cf. 'If I went with him, I went with him on personal grounds, I paid no allegiance to the impersonal principle he represented' (JMM 174).

28 *SP* 212.

29 *Son of Woman. The Story of D. H. Lawrence* (1931), p. 388; JMM 175, 192.

30 JMM 175–8.

31 *SP* 212.

32 Ibid.

33 Ibid.

34 Harry T. Moore, *The Priest of Love* (1974), p. 381.

35 Reviewing in the second series of his *Essays in Criticism* Dowden's biography of Shelley, which he found a 'sore trial' for his love of the poet, Arnold complained, 'What a set! what a world! is the exclamation that breaks from us as we come to an end of this history of "the occurrences of Shelley's private life".' Great a man as Arnold was, it is sometimes difficult to distinguish between what is justifiably fastidious and what is merely snobbish in him.

36 *SP* 213.

37 *RDP* 200:14–16.

38 *RDP* 207:11–18.

39 *RDP* 199:35–6.

40 After a somewhat wild youth, George Lawrence had become religious and sternly disapproved of his younger brother's involvement with Frieda while she was still married to Ernest Weekley. He and DHL seem to have had little or no contact after a violent argument in 1915. See *EY* 54; *TE* 295.

41 There is an account of Pryse's influence on DHL in *'Apocalypse' and the Writings on Revelation*, ed. Mara Kalnins (Cambridge, 1980), pp. 5–7.

42 Carter describes this visit in Frederick Carter, *D. H. Lawrence and the Body Mystical* (1932), pp. 33–42.

43 Ibid., p. 32. Expanded by Carter into 'The Ancient Science of Astrology', this joint work was published, after insertions and revisions by Lawrence, in *Adelphi* for April 1924. The article was published under the name of Carter who, in *D. H. Lawrence and the Body Mystical*, later commented that the 'perspicuous reader' might discover in it 'some hints of the Lawrencian purple' (p. 32). What any kind of reader is more conscious of nowadays is how 'Lawrencian' several of the article's ideas seem. In the first section, for example, there is a discussion of the way people in ancient times thought in images whereas we are now reduced to the abstractions of words: 'Our words are dead shells, empty of sensual contact, and only Art, by the stress of powerful rhythm and the energy of association can occasionally put the blood of life into them' (*Adelphi*, i (April 1924), 99).

44 Carter, *D. H. Lawrence and the Body Mystical*, p. 33.

45 Ibid., p. 38.

46 *Laughing Horse*, no. 9, published in December 1923, was described as a 'Southwest Number'. In addition to the song it contained a description by Mabel Luhan of an Indian council meeting in the pueblo, which Tony Luhan had attended, poems by Idella Purnell and Witter Bynner, and a review of the new edition of Natalie Curtis Burlin's *The Indian's Book* (first published in 1907) which praised her for being one of the earliest to defend pueblo culture and regretted her death in Paris two years earlier, shortly before she was due to return to her home in Santa Fe.

47 *Laughing Horse*, no. 10. The 'London Letter' was not collected in either volume of

Phoenix, perhaps because Aldous Huxley had included it in his 1932 edition of DHL's letters (pp. 590–3).

48 *BB* 339:27–9.

49 *BB* 343:27–9.

50 *BB* 346:13–18.

51 *BB* xxxii–xxxiii. In this section of his introduction, Eggert also describes the parallels between Dorothy Brett and Hilda Blessington.

52 In the notebook DHL was using at this time, he heavily revised 'The Last Laugh'. It is in the second, revised version that the Murry figure becomes 'Marchbanks' (earlier he had been 'Joey Pantling'). For DHL's revisions, see appendix III of *WWRA* (pp. 297–301).

53 *WWRA* 122:10, 27; 123:5; 124:40.

54 *WWRA* 123:19.

55 *WWRA* 129:32; 131:11; 132:40.

56 *WWRA* 133:11, 39; 134:1–2, 20–1.

57 *P* 22. Seeing Pan in daylight is fatal but, as DHL goes on to explain, 'you might dimly see him in the night, a dark body within the darkness' (as James does – she and Marchbanks say goodnight to Lorenzo at midnight).

58 *WWRA* 136:28; 137:6–8.

59 *WWRA* 129:32–4.

60 The episode in which the friend forced Brett to touch his penis and then began kissing her until she tore herself away is described in Hignett, *Brett*, pp. 30–1.

61 In view of the common assumption that DHL was in no way *physically* attracted to Brett, it is significant that in the first version of 'The Last Laugh' he describes the policeman as seeing James's 'slim body shining softly within her clothes' like the 'tube of light' in her listening machine (*WWRA* 297).

62 Both letters are quoted in Hignett, *Brett*, pp. 147–9.

63 Barbara Weekley has described how she and Elsa met DHL in the winter of 1923 at 110 Heath Street. Although she was impressed by his 'rather mocking, but brilliant and spirited manner', and thought his eyes 'alive and tender', she found him a 'queer fish, secretly preferring the more ordinary Murry' (who was also present). See 'Step daughter to Lawrence – 1', *London Magazine*, xxxiii (August/September 1993), 32.

64 *LT* 151–2.

65 It is not until July 1926 that one learns from DHL's letters that Milly Beveridge had a flat in Rossetti Garden Mansions, Flood Street, Chelsea (v. 501); but since she was no longer in Paris with Mabel Harrison, she might well have been there by 1924.

66 Frieda 160.

67 For the 'Paris Letter' see *P* 119–22 (and note 70 below).

68 DHL refers to the Gurdjieff Institute as 'that Ouspensky place' because the doctrines of its founder had been popularised in England by one of his former disciples, Peter Ouspensky (although, as far as Katherine Mansfield is concerned, another important intermediary had been her former editor at the *New Age*, A. R. Orage). In the mid-1920s, ignoring DHL's disapproval and always in search of the definitive guru, Mabel Luhan offered Gurdjieff both $1,500 and a site for a new institute in Taos. According

to Peter Washington in *Madame Blavatsky's Baboon*, Gurdjieff took the money but declined the site (p. 257).

69 When DHL sent his very brief remarks on Oman to Murry he said, 'Dont put my name on the review if you use it' (iv. 585), perhaps feeling that he needed a different public persona if what he had to say about an academic work was to be taken seriously. He gave qualified approval to Oman's interpretation but protested that it was only one of the many others possible: 'But why should he appear so unwilling to accept any astrological reference? Why should not the symbols have an astrological meaning, and the drama be also the drama of cosmic man, in terms of the stars?' (*Apocalypse*, ed. Kalnins, p. 41). This was accepting Carter's approach but also (in 'cosmic man') reconciling it with his own.

70 *P* 107, 108, 109. DHL's 'Paris Letter' was not published in *Laughing Horse* until April 1926 and 'Letter from Germany' never appeared there at all: it was not after all a magazine much concerned with European politics and when DHL had sent his first, London letter to Johnson, promising to try to send a similar one every month, he had said, 'Do as you like with it, exactly' (iv. 555). But the German letter did appear in the *New Statesman* on 13 October 1934 where it must have seemed prophetic (as the editors no doubt intended it should).

71 *P* 107; *WWRA* 285:11–12. There are verbal similarities between 'A Letter from Germany' and all three versions of 'The Border-Line', with descriptive phrases being carried forward from the first to the other two. For the first, published version of the story DHL filled out his draft with fresh detail and made the identification of Frieda with the heroine much more apparent. That this detail was probably added when he was no longer in England does not lessen its biographical significance, although it may suggest a *growing* resentment against Murry.

72 *WWRA* 78:17–26, 33–5; 79:18; 81:21, 34–7; 80:29–30; 82:4–5.

73 *WWRA* 85:38–9; 86:13–15, 32–3.

74 *WWRA* 90:5, 25.

75 *WWRA* 94:11–12; 95:24; 93:8; 95:29–30.

76 *WWRA* 96:15–17, 24–8, 33–9; 98:7–13.

77 Lea, *Life of John Middleton Murry*, p. 165.

78 The existence and character of the Murry stories seem to me to indicate that DHL and Frieda must have discussed together her feelings for Murry. Even if the stories were not partly prompted by such discussions (as I think likely), the subject would be hard to avoid once DHL read or showed them to his wife. Whatever was said seems to have made DHL feel that Frieda was once again his and that Murry's company in New Mexico would not represent a sexual threat. Murry himself had different ideas. On 21 July 1932 he wrote in his journal, 'But one thing is absolutely clear to me. If I had gone with Lawrence and Frieda, Frieda would have become my woman' (Lea, *Life of John Middleton Murry*, p. 119).

79 The first version, which is in UT, is a typescript with autograph corrections, twenty-one pages long, dating from 1930. In an entry made in his diary in July 1953 Murry indicated that Brett's and DHL's versions of this episode were true in substance although he describes the miner's wife as living in Mansfield (rather than the Yorkshire of Brett's version and DHL's story). See Lea, *Life of John Middleton Murry*, p. 129.

The aspects for which we have only Brett's word concern the audience for Murry's confession, the exact date of the episode and the degree of DHL's involvement.

80 *WWRA* 100:33, 7–11. Brett is likely to have described to DHL how, when Katherine Mansfield was dying, she asked her to look after the 'little lad' (an episode recalled in her private diary).

81 *WWRA* 101:27–8, 14–16; 105:40–1; 113:23–6.

82 *WWRA* 107:28–31; 118:23–7.

83 *WWRA* 116:23–4; 120:8; 121:2, 5–7.

84 *WWRA* 117: 15–25. The photographs in Lea's biography of Murry, particularly those between pages 48 and 49, seem to support the point DHL makes here.

85 E313a.

86 DHL had taken this scheme seriously enough to first consider launching it with *The Boy in the Bush* (iv. 557). Murry was to provide £500, Koteliansky £200 and DHL himself £300, once he had heard from Seltzer and knew how much he had in the bank (iv. 574).

87 *Adelphi*, i (February 1924), 772–3.

88 Seltzer's letter will appear in vol. viii of the Cambridge edition of DHL's letters.

89 What made Seltzer's news especially disappointing was that he had previously sent a telegram asking if he could dispose of the film rights of *Women in Love* for $5,000. DHL had cabled his agreement in the second week of January (iv. 558). Seltzer described the $600 in the account as including a cheque for $100 from Gótzsche – a contribution perhaps to the boat ticket which DHL would remember in 'The Flying-Fish' as having cost £45 (*SMOS* 217).

90 According to Hignett, 'Murry baited his advances with the possibility of marriage but quickly had second thoughts' (p. 134). On 25 February, in the letter to Kot already referred to (see p. 158 above), she had written, 'I have been Murry's mistress. I shall never be his wife' (*Brett: From Bloomsbury to New Mexico*, p. 147). In the last entry in the private diary which deals with these matters, dated 2 March 1924 and beginning 'Dearest Tig', Brett writes of leaving Murry so that he will have more freedom. Her tone does not suggest she was confident of seeing him in America.

91 *JMM* 194.

92 The month after the Lawrences left England Katherine Mansfield's royalties brought Murry a cheque for £1,000 (Lea, *Life of John Middleton Murry*, p. 124).

93 *SP* 198.

94 *Carrington: Letters and Extracts from the Diaries*, ed. David Garnett (1970), pp. 283–4. DHL particularly annoyed Carrington by accusing her of being 'very rich'. She describes herself as taking the 'shine off his Northampton noise [*sic*]' by pointing out that the annual income of herself and her husband, Ralph Partridge, was only £210; and she characterises DHL as always saying 'yer' rather than 'you'.

Chapter Eight: Back to New Mexico

1 There are details of DHL's financial dealings with Seltzer in Worthen, *D. H. Lawrence: A Literary Life*. See especially pp. 124–7, 135.

2 Ibid., pp. 120–1.

3 During his week in New York, DHL referred to Adele's 'bad influence' and her 'poison-streak' (v. 16, 17). As the letters from Adele to friends published in *Letters to Thomas and Adele Seltzer*, ed. Lacy, make clear, her feelings for DHL remained friendly until he abandoned the Seltzers for Knopf.

4 Information from Keith Cushman.

5 James Woodress, *Willa Cather: A Literary Life* (Lawrence: Nebraska Press, 1987), p. 354.

6 Harriet Monroe published a short account of this meeting in *Poetry*, shortly after DHL's death in 1930. It is reprinted in Nehls, ii. 330. Clearly she had not taken offence to DHL's short riposte to her suggestion (after a trip to Europe) that British poets would not have anything very important to say while their country was still a monarchy and there was an 'oligarchic social system' still in place. 'A Britisher Has a Word with an Editor', as DHL's riposte is called, was written during his time with Idella Purnell in Guadalajara and published in her poetry journal *Palms* (Christmas 1923). For the text see *P II* 299.

7 Brett 41.

8 Ibid. 43.

9 In *Movers and Shakers*, Mabel describes how, as a little girl, she used to watch Alice Sprague walk down Buffalo's Delaware Avenue in the dusk 'more like a creature from one of my favorite books than a flesh-and-blood go-to-the-market-and-dance-at-the-Charity-ball woman, like all the others there' (p. 349). It was Alice Sprague who introduced Mabel to Maurice Sterne.

10 *LT* 141.

11 Details of De Angulo's background come from the introduction to Gui de Angulo, *Jaime in Taos: The Taos Papers of Jaime de Angulo* (San Francisco, 1985), pp. 1–13. The team he worked with in Oaxaca was under the direction of Manuel Gamio, the distinguished Mexican anthropologist with whom DHL was to begin a correspondence in May 1924 (v. 45). It may throw some light on DHL's own stay in Oaxaca that De Angulo is described by his son as working there on 'a quite astonishing large number of languages that winter, in spite of the fact that he had a bad case of malaria' (p. 7).

12 *LT* 142–3.

13 DHL's hostility to Jung (or at least to Jung as mediated through Mabel) is surprising as well as a little ungrateful. Apart from papers and a book by Trigant Burrow (see pp. 368–71 above), *Psychology of the Unconscious* (an early version of Jung's *Symbols of Transformation*) was the only work of psychoanalysis we know DHL to have read (iii. 301). Although he tended to disparage it, he did in fact adopt several of its positions against Freud in his own psychology books. He had far more in common with Jung than with Freud. At the beginning of 1925, when neither DHL nor Mabel were in Taos, Jung paid a short visit to the pueblo in the company of two American admirers and with De Angulo as their guide. After his previous three-week stay, De Angulo was able to introduce Jung to Antonio Mirabal. In his *Memories, Dreams, Reflections* (New York, 1963 – tr. Richard and Claire Winston), Jung describes how impressed he was with Mirabal, whom he refers to by his Indian name of Ochwiay Biano ('Mountain

Lake'), and records two exchanges which illustrate the closeness of his own views to those of DHL. In the first, after Mirabal had explained that the sun was the Indians' father, Jung asked him whether he did not think that it might be 'a fiery ball shaped by an invisible god'. What impressed him was the way Mirabal regarded this suggestion as self-evidently absurd. In the second exchange, Jung responded sympathetically to Mirabal's belief that in helping the sun to fulfil its tasks the Indians were not only working for their own benefit but for that of all the world. He was no more inclined (that is) to treat with contempt either the anti-rationalism of this belief or Mirabal's dismissal of Judeo-Christian monotheism than DHL himself. Like DHL (and like De Angulo) Jung was led to feel strongly that the Indians could help whites to find a better way of life. As De Angulo put it in a letter he wrote to Mabel on 16 January 1925, describing Jung's visit: 'the white American must preserve the Indian, not as a matter of justice or brotherly charity, but in order to save his own neck' (*Jaime in Taos*, p. 87). See also Gerhard Wehr, *Jung: A Biography*, tr. David M. Weeks (1987), pp. 227–32.

14 *LT* 134.

15 *LT* 166.

16 *LT* 173.

17 DHL insisted that the toilet should have a cream background on which he painted 'a great, green snake wrapped around the stem of a sunflower that burned and shone like the Taos sun. On either side of it he painted a black butterfly as large as a plate, a white dove, a dark-brown bullfrog, and a rooster' (*LT* 173–4).

18 *SP* 197.

19 *LT* 174.

20 *LT* 175.

21 *LT* 175–9.

22 *LT* 184 (Jaime's dress is described on pp. 183, 186).

23 *Jaime in Taos*, p. 55; *LT* 186–7. The fact that De Angulo (*pace* DHL) did seriously intend to hitch-hike back to California is not invalidated by his son's gloss on the 18 April letter: 'I don't know anything about Jaime's return trip to Berkeley except that he evidently didn't get enough rides after all and had to catch the train' (*Jaime in Taos*, p. 62).

24 *MM* 99, 113–14.

25 There is a detailed and intelligent account of Commissioner Burke's visit to the pueblo in *Jaime in Taos*, pp. 57–60. See also Rudnick 186.

26 *MM* 101.

27 *Poems* 777.

28 *LT* 280.

29 *LT* 179.

30 The play in question was the one-act, *Where the Cross is Made*. There is information about Rauh's career in her obituary in the New York *Times*, 12 March 1970; and in Van Dere Coke, *Andrew Dasburg* (Albuquerque, 1979), pp. 55–6.

31 Brett 121.

32 At the beginning of *Cake* a 'Lady' is sitting on a throne in the form of a golden eagle and complaining of being bored:

I have had seven husbands – and that's enough, I think
I have come through mysticism, free love, drink.
I am offered everything money can buy,
And yet there's nothing I want – not even to die.

There then follows a short episode with 'The Psychoanalyst'. See Witter Bynner, *Light Verse and Satire*, ed. William Jay Smith (New York, 1978), pp. 102–4.

33 The exact date of the play ('Altitude') cannot be determined but, since Alice Sprague figures in it, composition must have followed her arrival in Taos. Around 12 June, DHL asked Mabel, 'Has your Mrs Sprague come?' (v. 56), and all those who describe the events at Mabel's on the weekend of 21–22 June agree that by that date Alice Sprague was there.

34 For Mary Austin see T. M. Pearce, *Mary Hunter Austin* (New York, 1965).

35 It was in 1914, after John Reed had transferred his affections to another woman, that Mabel attempted to compensate for his loss by driving round several New York orphanages in search of a child to adopt. The eight-year-old Elizabeth was suitably cherubic but proved mentally backward. Rudnick describes Mabel as quickly losing interest, although she did continue to take care of Elizabeth and pay for her education (Rudnick 103).

36 *Complete Plays of D. H. Lawrence* (1963), pp. 535, 542, 540, 544. The *Oxford English Dictionary* (1932) cites an American source for the first use of 'queer' as a derogatory term for a homosexual in 1922 (2nd edn, prepared by J. A. Simpson and E. S. C. Weiner).

37 The absurdity of Hale's estimation nevertheless alerted DHL to the potential value of his manuscripts. 'All this expostulation about the *Sons and Lovers* manuscript makes me feel I ought to be more careful of the rest of my MSS', he wrote, and in a letter to his niece he himself estimated its value at 'three or four thousand' dollars (v. 105, 111). A note in his diary for 30 September records that he had sent seven manuscripts of recent essays to Barmby in New York for safe-keeping (UT). In the 1920s the trade in manuscripts of modern works was just beginning but prices remained low by today's standards. In 1937 T. E. Hanley paid $3,500 for the manuscript of *The Rainbow* and $1,500 for that of *Kangaroo*. See *D. H. Lawrence's Manuscripts: The Correspondence of Frieda Lawrence, Jake Zeitlin and Others*, ed. Michael Squires (1991), pp. 271, 276.

38 *LT* 191.

39 Brett 68

40 According to Mabel Luhan, the name of the Mexican carpenter who was often drunk was Pablo Quintana (*LT* 195). The seven Indians who helped DHL at various times are listed in (v. 38, note 1).

41 UT.

42 Brett 71–2.

43 *P* 27.

44 *P* 22. Cf. in 'The Story of a Panic':
'Pan!', cried Mr Sandbach, his mellow voice filling the valley as if it had been a great green church, 'Pan is dead. That is why the woods do not shelter him.' And he began to tell the striking story of the mariners who were sailing near the coast at the

time of the birth of Christ, and three times heard a loud voice saying: 'The great God Pan is dead.'

(E. M. Forster, *'The Celestial Omnibus' and Other Stories* (1911), p. 8)

45 Brett claimed she had not ridden since she was eight (Brett 46), but she very quickly adapted. There are numerous accounts in her memoir of hunting and fishing. Around 12 June, DHL told Mabel, 'Brett has walked off . . . to try for fish', and on 13 September he explained to Murry, 'Brett shoots rabbits – cottontails they call them here' (v. 57, 121). The typescript of *St. Mawr*, now at UN, shows how inexpert her typing could be.

46 Brett 31, 94; *LT* 202–3.

47 *LT* 185.

48 *Jaime in Taos*, pp. 49–52.

49 *LT* 203–4.

50 *LT* 206–7.

51 *LT* 210.

52 Brett 79. DHL had first read *The Golden Bough* in 1915 (ii. 470). Brett gives no indication of quite when Mabel provided him with an opportunity of looking at it again but there is a phrase in 'Pan in America' (written in April) very like the one she reports: 'What can men who sit at home in their studies, and drink hot milk and have lamb's-wool slippers on their feet, and write anthropology, what can they possibly know about men, the men of Pan' (*P* 29). In the 1920s the complaint that Frazer was a stay-at-home anthropologist who worked too exclusively from documentary evidence was beginning to be common. DHL may have heard it from De Angulo, who had certainly seen plenty of Indians, or inferred it from *The Delight Makers*, a novel by the great excavator of Indian sites, Adolph Bandelier, which Mabel lent him at this time (v. 42). He refers to Bandelier in 'Indians and Entertainment' (*MM* 100). *The Delight Makers* was first published in 1890 but DHL would have seen the second, 1916 edition that included impressive photographs by Frederick Hicks, one of which – of the ceremonial cave in the Rito de los Frijoles (facing p. 384) – may well have had an influence on 'The Woman Who Rode Away'.

53 DHL's descriptions of the hallucinatory effects of the drugs the Indians administer are vivid enough to make one wonder whether he had ever taken any himself. Peyote was used in religious ceremonies by the Indians in the Taos area and on 18 April De Angulo told his wife, 'Some of the many guests [Mabel] has are dabbling in peyote' adding, 'I must say Mabel herself is against peyote and has made Tony abandon it' (De Angulo, *Jaime in Taos*, pp. 56–7).

54 Brett 65–6.

55 Ibid. 105.

56 *LT* 227, 229, 230.

57 *LT* 133–4.

58 *LT* 238.

59 *WWRA* 60:21–4.

60 *LT* 239.

61 See *Adelphi* (July 1924), 150–3 ('Bou-oum or Ou-boum?'). Murry is concerned in his commentary to define the lack of faith which he feels the scenes in the Marabar caves

illustrate, and to associate it with the fact that *A Passage to India* was Forster's first novel for fourteen years. He predicts – accurately as it turned out – that there would not be another: 'It will take him, I imagine, a good deal more than fourteen years to find a word which will evoke a different echo from the primeval cave of Marabar: and I fancy (such is my faith in his intellectual honesty) that he will not speak again without the assurance of a different reply' (151).

62 Already in a letter to Murry from Guadalajara, responding to the idea that England should once again assume world leadership, DHL had said that Englishmen by themselves were not sufficient: 'One hand in space is not enough. It needs the other hand from the opposite end of space, to clasp and form the Bridge. The dark hand and the white' (iv. 520).

63 *SMOS* 26:20; 43:26; 44:12–13.

64 Brett 132. When DHL wrote an introduction to a bibliography of his work in September, he began, 'There doesn't seem much excuse for me, sitting under a little cedar tree at the foot of the Rockies' (*P* 232).

65 *SMOS* xxiv.

66 Brett 132–3.

67 *SMOS* 81:2; 118:1–3.

68 How different can be judged from this passage:

> In the woods and the remote places ran the children of Pan, all the nymphs and the fauns of the forest and the spring and the river and the rocks . . . the nymphs, running among the trees and curling to sleep under the bushes, made the myrtles blossom more gaily, and the spring bubble up with greater urge, and the birds splash with a strength of life. And the little flanks of the fauns gave life to the oak-groves, the vast trees hummed with energy. And the wheat sprouted like green rain returning out of the ground, in the little fields, and the vine hung its black drops in abundance, urging the secret. (*P* 22)

This is 'pastoral', which always attracted DHL, but which he simultaneously despised for its lack of 'reality'.

69 *SMOS* 147:30–1; 155:9–10, 15–34.

70 *SMOS* 144:22, 25–7. For DHL's celebration of the pinetree as 'still within the allness of Pan' and a communicator of 'fierce and bristling' (but not necessarily sexual) energy, see 'Pan in America' (*P* 24–5). The notion of a non-sexual primeval world is already anticipated in 'Au revoir, U.S.A.' (*P* 105–6).

71 *SMOS* 111:36–7; 112:8–11.

72 This detail, along with several others which are in addition to the material in Brett's memoir, can be found in the extract from her unpublished autobiography which appeared in the *South Dakota Review* under the title 'My Long and Beautiful Journey' (v (1967), 19–20).

73 Joseph Foster, *D. H. Lawrence in Taos* (Albuquerque, 1972), pp. 131–144. On the way down from the ranch, Swinburne Hale's new Cadillac 'went through a bridge' and had to be abandoned. Compare (v. 90) for DHL's likely reference to this incident. One remark of DHL's which Foster records does ring true. There were occasional summer storms in the Lobo area during one of which three of the horses at Del Monte were killed by lightning (v. 59). Of the storm which he says broke out while he and his party

were visiting the ranch, Foster reports DHL as saying, 'It's good to have a storm . . . It's real, Brett. It's real' (p. 143).

74 Brett 100–1.

75 Ibid. 134–6.

76 Foster, *D. H. Lawrence in Taos*, p. 166. On pp. xvi–xvii Foster has a long note on the sixty-year-old Martin.

77 'Just Back From the Snake-Dance – Tired Out' was published in *Laughing Horse*, no. ix (September 1924). For Mabel's response to it, and her account of the trip, see *LT* 256–68.

78 The second account of 'The Hopi Snake Dance' can be found in *MM* 135–69. DHL saw the dance at Hotevila which had come into existence only eighteen years before after a split in the nearby village of Oraibi between those Hopi willing to seek an accommodation with Washington and those who remained unco-operative (it was these latter who founded Hotevila). The Bureau of Indian Affairs was often hostile towards the more conservative Hopi. In 1921 one of its agents, Robert Daniel, sent soldiers to forcibly immerse the inhabitants of Hotevila in sheep-dip after a majority of them had refused to submit to a programme of delousing; and in the same year Daniel was overheard to say, 'Snake Dance! I'd snake dance 'em if I had my way about it. I'd bring a troop of soldiers and make them stop it or kill 'em all off.' See Henry C. James, *Pages from Hopi History* (Tucson, 1974), pp. 178, 184; and, for details of the split, Frank Waters, *Book of the Hopi* (New York, 1963), and Harold Courlander, *The Fourth World of the Hopis* (Greenwich: Conn., 1971). I am entirely indebted to Neil Roberts for these references.

79 Forster reprinted his letters home in *The Hills of Devi* (1953).

80 *LT* 267.

81 *LT* 191.

82 Brett 93.

83 Ibid. 146.

84 See p. 147 above. DHL used his characterisation of the Scottish father for his account of the husband in 'The Woman Who Rode Away'; but the situation between him and his daughter is the germ of 'The Princess'.

85 *Hardy* 122:13–17.

86 *SMOS* 196:19.

87 *SMOS* 78–80.

88 *P* 233.

89 Kennerley had sent DHL £25 for the first American edition of *Sons and Lovers* and promised him a further £25; but the second cheque was for £10 only and proved in any case uncashable. In response to the efforts of first Mountsier and then Seltzer, and to a legal action which in 1923 DHL was told would cost him $300–$500 (iv. 376), Kennerley yielded the rights to Seltzer later that year. But despite having reissued the novel several times over the previous ten years, he never sent DHL any more money. For details see the Cambridge edition of *Sons and Lovers* (1992), ed. Helen Baron and Carl Baron, pp. lx–lxiii. The lawyer whom DHL used in his legal action against Kennerley (Benjamin Stern) was also the one he appealed to in his difficulties with Seltzer (v. 298).

90 *P* 232. Ernest Hooley was a stock-exchange speculator from the Nottingham area imprisoned for fraud in 1922. See *EY* 533–4.

91 Arthur Lawrence had died on 10 September 1924. There may be an echo of DHL's last meeting with his father in the fragment, 'A Pure Witch', which was probably written in Europe and certainly finished by June 1924 (*WWRA* xxiv). This begins in an autobiographical mode with the narrator describing a mother who

> adored us children, but the boys more than the girls. She gave *everything* for us: and denied my father her tenderness, almost on principle. He was a tall, bearded, taciturn man with a slight stammer, who grumbled when we made a noise in the house and always wore old, frayed clothes. As children we didn't like him: we adored our mother . . . Then Tom, mother's favourite, died of a slow, fatal illness. And soon she developed cancer. When she was dead, father became <very> old and rather rambling, stuttering worse than ever.

> (*WWRA* 377:11–12 – the arrows surrounding 'very' indicate that it was deleted) This sounds so like the Lawrence family that it is a surprise to discover the narrator is female and the setting for the proposed story upper-middle-class and cosmopolitan.

92 'Climbing Down Pisgah' can be found in *P* 740–4. For the 'Epilogue' and interesting details of reactions to it by Oxford University Press's readers see *Movements in European History*, ed. Philip Crumpton (Cambridge, 1989), pp. xxviii–xxix, 255–66.

93 Brett 124–5.

94 *LT* 270.

95 *LT* 189.

96 *LT* 279.

Chapter Nine: Oaxaca and *The Plumed Serpent*

1 Bynner 251.

2 Brett 153.

3 Ibid. 156.

4 The book may have been *Forjanda patria* ('Forging a Nation'), published in 1916, or the pamphlet guide to Teotihuacán which Gamio brought out in 1921.

5 *Memoirs* 324.

6 Frieda 163. Maugham never used a telephone because of his stammer so that having Haxton make calls for him was not the act of condescension DHL took it for. See Ted Morgan, *Maugham* (New York, 1980), p. 276.

7 Maugham's book with the reference to DHL was published in New York in 1943. DHL had read his *The Moon and Sixpence* in 1922 ('not bad, but forcé' – iii. 566). On 22 May 1922, while he was still in Sydney, he wrote to Mountsier, 'Did you read Somerset Maugham's *Trembling of a Leaf* – ? – Pacific Isles tales? I'll send them to you. Make it not attractive *at all*. Bisogna vederi coi sui occhi' (iv. 246).

8 *Memoirs* 324.

9 The PEN club was founded by Amy Dawson Scott in 1921. In letters to her daughter from that year Scott wrote, 'I've started my international dinner Club. I've called it PEN because it consists of *P*oets, *P*laywrights, *E*ditors and *N*ovelists'; and also,

'Apparently it is the word International that makes the PEN Club attractive.' See
PEN: The Early Years (1971) by the daughter in question (Marjorie Watts), p. 12.

Genaro Estrada was a civil servant who, when Lawrence met him, had published
Poetas nuevas de México (1916).

10 Brett 157; Frieda 162.

11 Roderic Ai Camp, *Mexican Political Biographies: 1935–1975* (Tucson, 1975), p. 261;
Miguel Angel Peral, *Diccionario biográfico mexicano* (Mexico City, 1960-), pp. 660–1.

12 I am very grateful to Ross Parmenter for providing me with a copy of this pamphlet
(dated '24 enero de 1925') and to Derek Utley for translating it.

13 Frieda 162–3; Parmenter 7–9.

14 *The Daybooks of Edward Weston*, ed. Nancy Newhall (Rochester: New York, 1973),
(Mexico), i, 101–2. See also the biographical introduction by Ben Maddow to *Edward
Weston: His Life and Photographs* (New York, 1973).

15 It is clear from DHL's letter that he only received two photographs: 'I think I like the
one with the chin up better than the other looking down: but I like both of them'
(v. 185). Yet there are at least two different poses of DHL looking down – see the
frontispieces to *Letters to Thomas and Adele Seltzer*, ed. Lacy, and to Harry T. Moore's
and Warren Roberts's volume on DHL in Thames and Hudson's 'Literary Lives'
series (1966).

16 Weston's response to DHL's death appeared in a supplement to the *Carmelite*, iii (19
March 1930), but is reprinted in Nehls, ii. 370–2.

17 Nehls, ii. 370–1.

18 Because George Conway was something of a scholar as well as a businessman (see
p. 239 above) the Lawrences might just as plausibly have met the Conways at Zelia
Nuttall's house.

19 There are intriguing details of the Rickards family in Parmenter 26–8.

20 Brett 161.

21 When he went to the Hopi snake dance with Mabel and Tony Luhan, DHL had left the
machine in Santa Fe for repairs but there were difficulties and delays, comparable to
those he and Brett had to endure when it was sent to Veracruz (v. 127, 132, 202, 206).

22 For a full account of García, as well as many other valuable details about the history of
Oaxaca, see Parmenter 1–24.

23 Ibid. xxix–xxx; Howard T. Young, *José Vasconcelos: An Appreciation* (1980),
pp. 189–91.

24 *MM* 41–2. The four opening sketches were originally entitled 'Friday Morning' (now
'Corasmin and the Parrots'), 'Saturday Morning' (now 'Market Day'), 'Sunday
Morning' (now 'Walk to Huayapa') and 'Monday Morning' (now 'The Mozo') but
they have never been printed in that order. 'Market Day' begins, 'This is the last
Saturday before Christmas' i.e., 20 December 1924 (*MM* 79).

For literacy rates see Eyler N. Simpson, *The Ejido: Mexico's Way Out* (Chapel Hill,
1937), p. 659.

25 *PS* 209.

26 Cf. '"Perhaps", you say, "The Virgin of Guadalupe will cure your deafness." She
doesn't, but the Fiesta is lovely round the old Church; and the many paintings of
miracles absorb us' (Brett 159).

27 *MM* 85.

28 Parmenter 55–8; Brett 166. For the Díaz passage, see J. M. Cohen's translation: *The Conquest of New Spain* (Harmondsworth, 1963), p. 233.

29 The detail comes from an interview with the Kulls which Ross Parmenter was able to secure (p. 66).

30 Several of the photographs which record this visit to the ruins of a Zatopec palace have been widely reproduced (see for example Keith Sagar's *Illustrated Biography*, p. 187), and there is an account in Brett 175–7.

31 Parmenter 1.

32 Ibid. 7. Already in Mexico City DHL had described Zelia Nuttall as 'full of news about the murdered Mrs Evans etc' (v. 155).

33 Brett 167.

34 Parmenter has the details on the borrowed furniture (pp. 30–1).

35 'Mexican tradition makes it very plain that obsidian, because of its blood-procuring properties, came to be regarded as the source of all life, as the very principle of existence. Tonacaciuatl, the creative goddess, as we shall see, gave birth to an obsidian knife from which sprang sixteen hundred demigods who peopled the earth' (Lewis Spence, *The Gods of Mexico* (1923), p. 31). Along with whatever book Gamio sent and Zelia Nuttall's *Fundamental Principles of Old and New World Civilizations*, *The Gods of Mexico* must have been very important to DHL in re-writing 'Quetzalcoatl', especially as it contained English translations of some of the 'sacred songs or hymns included in the Mexican MS of Sahagun's *Historia General*, which that most unwearied of workers received at first hand from approved native scribes' (p. 7).

36 *MM* 55.

37 *MM* 74.

38 The evidence that DHL helped Rosalino with his Spanish lessons for an hour every morning comes from Brett 172.

39 *PS* 151:14.

40 *PS* xxxvi.

41 Brett 158.

42 *PS* 37:12–16.

43 *Q* 33.

44 For Archbishop Gillow see Parmenter 35–6 and *passim*. Cipriano reveals his Oaxaca background when Kate's white hands remind him of the Virgin of Soledad (*PS* 71:21–7).

45 *PS* 61:7–8, 174:39.

46 *PS* 420:8–9.

47 There are details of Calles's anti-Catholic legislation in Robert E. Quirk, *The Mexican Revolution and the Catholic Church. 1910–1929* (Bloomington, 1973). In the summer of 1926, Edward Weston and Tina Modotti were in Oaxaca staying at the Francia. They noted Lawrence's signature in the hotel register and decided to call on his former landlord. But when they arrived at Father Rickards's house they found he had been 'arrested and deported to Mexico [City] the night before by the military' – this under laws specifically directed against priests of foreign extraction. As Weston says, 'This was a hint . . . of that which followed in the religious war' (*The Daybooks of Edward Weston*, i, p. 168).

48 Jean Charlot, *The Mexican Mural Renaissance. 1920–25* (New Haven, 1963), pp. 160–1.

49 Bynner 29–31.

50 *PS* 51:24–6, 34–6.

51 *PS* 52:23, 19–20.

52 As Desmond Rochfort has pointed out in *The Murals of Diego Rivera* (1987), Rivera had spent a long time abroad and absorbed many European influences. Yet for Charlot, the shape of his Indians was the one example of the influence which the young disciples of the habitually over-powering Rivera managed to have on him: 'It was Revueltas in his "Devotion to the Virgin of Guadelupe" who first used the hieratic, white-clad Indian and the women wrapped in stylized rebozos that soon became the accepted cyphers of a Mexican mural alphabet' (*The Mexican Mural Renaissance*, p. 154).

53 *PS* 52:17–20. Bynner reports that on the first visit to the murals in 1923 DHL had said:

> You remember, Bynner, the factory town we were taken to, all modern and model? Those rows of new houses, each one neat and up-to-date, but each one like every other. Every new comfort but no old dignity. You should be proud, Covarrubias, of the Indians who wouldn't live in them, left them empty, set up their own shacks on the edge of town. Their benefactors might iron out of the houses all character, all individualism but not out of the Indians. And so those silly socialistic houses stood empty. That would have been a thing to paint. That would have been Mexican!
>
> (Bynner 29)

54 *PS* 453, note on 53:1.

55 *PS* 53:33–5.

56 The sketch is reproduced in *¡Orozco! 1883–1949* (Oxford, 1980), pp. 26–7. See also p. 16.

57 *PS* 53:10–11, 17–20.

58 *PS* 53:36–7, 39–41; 54:1–2, 9–10, 13–14.

59 Cf:

> He would never woo: she saw this. When the power of his blood rose in him, the dark aura steamed from him like a cloud pregnant with power, like thunder, and rose like a whirlwind that rises suddenly in the twilight and raises a great pliant column, swaying and leaning with power, clear between heaven and earth.
>
> Ah! and what a mystery of prone submission, on her part, this huge erection would imply! (*PS* 311:24–5)

60 *PS* 352:4–6, 422:15–16. DHL had often gestured towards a distinction of this kind before but it is in *The Plumed Serpent* that he first attempts to make it anatomically specific.

61 *PS* xl.

62 For descriptions of dancing in *The Plumed Serpent* DHL continued to rely on his memories of New Mexico. As he explained on 10 January 1925 to Edith Issacs, the editor of the *Theatre Arts Monthly* in which his essay on the Hopi snake dance had just appeared, 'There's never a dance down here. They're terribly un-dancy, these Zapotec and Mixtex Indians' (v. 195).

63 There is an account of the craft-based domestic economy of Ramón's hacienda in chapter XI of *PS* ('Lords of the Day and Night'). Cipriano's address to the 'Knights of

Columbus' in chapter xv of *Q*, where he defines what is wrong with Fascism, is only one example among several of more specifically political material which DHL omitted.

64 *PS* 191:13–16.

65 The notebook jottings are described in Tedlock (p. 134) and reprinted in *RDP* 385:2–3.

66 This is the thesis of Jean-Paul Pichardie in *D. H. Lawrence: la tentation utopique* (Rouen, 1988).

67 George L. Mosse, *The Crisis of German Ideology: Intellectual Origins of the Third Reich* (1964). One element of Volkish ideology was the rejection of Christianity in favour of Nordic mythology and the devising of public ceremonies for celebrating the old German gods. In chapter xvii of *The Plumed Serpent* Ramón explains,

> So if I want Mexicans to learn the name of Quetzalcoatl it is because I want them to speak with tongues of their own blood. I wish the Teutonic world would once more think in terms of Thor and Wotan, and the tree Igdrasil. And I wish the Druidic world would see, honestly, that in the mistletoe is their mystery, and that they themselves are the Tuatha De Danaan, alive, but submerged.   (p. 248:31–6)

In 1927 Diego Rivera was on his way to Moscow when he stopped over in Berlin and witnessed an extraordinary sight:

> From behind a clump of trees in the middle of the forest, there appeared a strange cortege. The marching men and women wore white tunics and crowns of *ghui*, the Druidic ceremonial plant. In their hands, they held green branches. Their pace was slow and ritualistic. Behind them four men bore an archaic throne on which was seated a man representing the war god, Wotan. This man was none other than the President of the Republic, Paul von Hindenburg! Garbed in ancient raiment, von Hindenburg held aloft a lance on which supposedly magic runes were engraved. The audience . . . took von Hindenburg for a reincarnation of Wotan. Behind Hindenburg's appeared another throne occupied by Marshall Ludendorff, who represented the thunder god, Thor. Behind the 'god', trooped an honorable train of worshippers composed of eminent chemists, mathematicians, biologists, physicists, and philosophers. Every field of German 'Kultur' was represented in the Grunewald that night.

> (Diego Rivera, with Gladys March, *My Art, My Life: An Autobiography* (New York, 1960), pp. 142–3)

Although Rivera was notorious for his exaggeration there is no reason to doubt that he saw something like what is described here. In a bilingual *Economic and Social Program of Mexico (A Controversy)*, published by the City of Mexico in 1935, one of the participants, a priest, complains,

> Throughout the official educational program there runs a strong strain of Indian nationalism and of opposition to the institutions that came from Europe. In much the same manner as old German gods and pagan habits of pre-Christian Germany are glorified under Hitler, the aztecs are glorified in the official educational program. An almanac is issued by the Government in which day after day Aztec gods and heroes are given the place of honor. On Christmas day, for example, Quetzalcoatl is substituted for Christ.   (p. 134 with the Spanish version on the facing page)

68 *PS* 103:1.

69 *SP* 183; *Listener,* iii (30 April 1930), 753–4.

NOTES TO PAGES 220-5

70 The reference to this interview occurs in the obituary published in the *New York Evening Post* on 3 March 1930.

71 DHL's abandon of his high opinion of *The Plumed Serpent*, or at least his fondness for it, was certainly not immediate. Cf., from a letter to George Conway in June 1925, 'I am about my normal self again – but I shall never forgive Mexico, especially Oaxaca, for having done me in . . . Nevermore need I look on Mexico – but especially Oaxaca. – Yet my "Quetzalcoatl" novel lies nearer my heart than any other work of mine' (v. 263).

72 *RDP* 233:37; 234:38–40. In a philosophical fragment in the same vein as *Resurrection*, which DHL also wrote about this time, and which begins 'Man is essentially a soul', integration is not achieved by the collapse of one principle into another (the Son into the Father) but by the more familiar means of a reconciling agent. Some of the undoubted lyricism of *The Plumed Serpent* is associated with DHL's presentation throughout of the morning star as just such an agent (mediating between day and night), but here what reconciles the opposites of body and spirit is the soul. Continuity with the novel is nevertheless established when he insists that there is an aristocracy of souls – 'the purest, strongest soul-flame is the highest authority in the world' – and re-interprets the notion of freedom:

> There is no such thing as absolute freedom. True, soul is the only authority, and each man primarily obeys his own soul. But obeying his own soul means, to every man, realising that he cannot know his own soul or come at its intimations without help from a purer, stronger being, to whose authority he must submit himself.
>
> (*RDP* 389:35–6; 390:5–9)

73 *P II* 295. The last sentence of the preface begins, 'Tonight is Christmas Eve' (p. 296).

74 *P II* 296.

75 *P II* 294.

76 I am very grateful to Ross Parmenter for supplying me with a copy of the TS of Quintanilla's article, from which I quote. (The strain in Anglo-Mexican relations which Quintanilla mentions was a consequence of the death of Mrs Evans – see p. 211 above.)

77 Parmenter 148. 'See Mexico After, by Luis Q.' appears in *P* 111–16.

78 *Q* 155; *PS* 229:22–4.

79 *Q* 156; *PS* 231:2–3.

80 Pichardie, *D. H. Lawrence: la tentation utopique*, p. 248. The particular critic Pichardie has in mind is Graham Hough whose book on DHL, *The Dark Sun*, appeared in 1956.

81 The phrase comes from the fourth paragraph of Arnold's 'Count Leo Tolstoi' in the second series of his *Essays in Criticism* (1888).

82 *Movements in European History*, ed. Crumpton, 257:18; 258:30–2.

83 *Blake: Complete Writings*, ed. Geoffrey Keynes (Oxford, 1966), p. 629, l. 20.

84 *MM* 1.

Chapter Ten: Brett is Banished

1 Brett 192–3.

2 Ibid. 174.

3 Ibid. 182.

4 This is one of the paintings which was in the possession of Saki Karavas. It is reproduced in Sagar's *Illustrated Biography* (on p. 5 of the inserts between pp. 128 and 129). See Brett 186-7 for an account of DHL's additions.

5 Brett 187.

6 Ibid. 191-2. For Sean Hignett, Brett only began to 'see' Katherine in March 1923, two months after her death (*Brett*, p. 134). That seems reasonable yet it is hard to see what the 'wonderful, mystical experience' she had about this time would be if it was not some kind of spiritual communion with Katherine.

7 *Memoirs* 120-1.

8 It is possible that DHL's note *preceded* the letter to William Hawk on the 6th and was therefore written on the evening of 2 January. When DHL writes to Quintanilla and Ida Rauh after the 9th about Brett's future movements he does not reveal there has been a quarrel; but on the other hand neither is he as circumstantial as in his 6 January letter to William Hawk where he explains that Brett's reasons for not wanting to return to Europe were financial. If his note was written on Friday 2 January, that would have been a lie whereas dating it a week later makes his explanations after the 9th no more than evasions of the whole truth (v. 196, 199).

9 Brett 196.

10 Ibid. 195-6.

11 Ibid. 198, 199-200.

12 Ibid. 201.

13 Ibid. 187-8, 195.

14 Parmenter 213.

15 *Sons and Lovers*, p. 83:2. The person about whom Paul feels guilty is of course his sister but the doll provides a convenient intermediary. The crucial phrase is, 'He seemed to hate the doll so intensely, because he had broken it' (p. 83:10).

16 The text of the cable will be published in vol. viii of the Cambridge edition of Lawrence's letters.

17 Koteliansky had objected that the *Adelphi* was being taken over by Murry and was not open enough to other views. Murry therefore offered the journal to Kot on reasonable terms but the other key members of the *Adelphi* group – J. W. N. Sullivan and H. M. Tomlinson – objected and the deal fell through. Kot then resigned as business manager and 'From that time forward, the *Adelphi* became a one-man concern' (Lea, *Life of John Middleton Murry*, pp. 133-4). DHL had already been exasperated by Murry's account of these disputes, telling him on 17 November, after several previous, perfectly friendly letters, that it had been inevitable he and Kot should come to hate each other and warning him against 'stirring [his] own finger in [his] own vitals' (v. 170).

18 Nehls, i. 284; *TE* 264.

19 Hignett, *Brett*, p. 168.

20 NWU.

21 See Tedlock 58 (whose text has been corrected from the MS). These suggestions for stories occur in the notebook after the four 'Mornings', 'Resurrection' and DHL's re-writing of Quintanilla's essay. On 26 July 1923 Murry had written to Brett from the country, 'It would be nice if you could come down on your motor-bike then we could

go for a few rides together. But I don't suppose you'll be expert enough by then' (OCU).

22 See *EY* 154.

23 One would hardly have expected DHL to be sympathetic to physical determinism. In what is obviously an allusion to Berman's book he writes in *Kangaroo*, 'It may be that there is an insufficient activity of the thyroid glands, or the adrenalin cortex isn't making its secretions, or the pituitary or the pineal body is not working adequately. But this is result, not cause of our neurasthenia and complexes' (*K* 296, 403–4 note on 297:1).

24 *PS* xxxii–xxxiii.

25 Parmenter 318.

26 Frieda 165.

27 *SMOS* 207:3, 8; 208:21; 210:1, 18. When the Lawrences first arrived at the Francia, the landlady had explained to them how thieves could poke long poles with hooks on the end through the bars on the windows. Later Brett was able to examine just such a pole, dropped by a thief she had surprised at his work (Brett 163).

28 *SMOS* 210:31–2, 33, 34; 211:24–7.

29 Frieda 166.

30 Ibid. 166.

31 In a letter to Mabel from Vence early in 1930, Frieda reports that DHL could not eat and was very weak: 'I can't understand it because his lungs are not worse, the doctors say, than the X photograph that was taken in Mexico' (YU).

32 Nehls, ii. 396.

33 Frieda 166–7.

34 Ibid. 167.

35 'Getting On' was never published. The MS is in UT.

36 *SMOS* xxxiv.

37 *Complete Plays of D. H. Lawrence*, pp. 553, 556.

38 Ibid., p. 558.

39 The 'Conway papers', in the Library of Congress, are listed under 'Spanish material. 1: Manuscripts' in the section on 'Sources' at the conclusion of Hugh Thomas's *History of Mexico*. But this must refer to only part of Conway's collection because, as Parmenter points out (p. 348), it was distributed at his death among four different libraries. DHL would remember Conway's hobby when he wrote 'The Lovely Lady' (*WWRA* 247:4).

40 My information is from a letter to Lindeth Vasey from Eileen G. Foote in January 1987. The photocopy of her parents' 'Record of Guests' for 18 March which she provided shows Frieda adding to her name 'Née von Richthofen'.

41 Rosendo Salazar, *Historia de las luchas proletarias de Mexico* (Mexico City, 1938), pp. 178–81.

42 There is an account of *Irradiador* in Amy Conger, *Edward Weston in Mexico* (Albuquerque, 1983), pp. 16–18.

43 Nehls, ii. 369–70.

44 The Australian historian Andrew Moore has discovered in the US archives a letter from W. W. Husband, a second Assistant Secretary at the State Department, acknowl-

edging receipt of the copy of a letter of complaint about his treatment which DHL must have written to the American Vice Consul in Mexico City. Husband comments that DHL's letter 'will be transmitted at once to the District Director at El Paso with directions that a thorough investigation and full reports be made', and he adds, 'It is about the most extravagant complaint that has ever come to my attention.' (I am grateful to Warren Roberts for having passed on Moore's discovery to the editors of vol. v of the Cambridge *Letters*.)

45 *Memoirs* 336. Jeffrey Meyers has suggested that the pressure was applied by Stuart Grummon and refers his readers to the obituary of this career diplomat in the *New York Times* (3 June 1960). But although this obituary confirms that Grummon's first appointment was as a Secretary at the US embassy in Mexico City in 1923, it makes no mention of DHL. It could have been of course that the pressure to which Frieda refers was applied from the capital by telephone. See Meyers, *D. H. Lawrence*, pp. 330, 425 n.11.

46 For my information here, and my quotations, I am indebted to Elizabeth A. Berrio, head of the Historical Reference Library and Reading Room Section at the US State Department (Immigration and Naturalization Service), who has consulted the relevant documents. TB sufferers had first been added to the list of those to be refused entry to the United States by a consolidating statute of 1907. See Maldwyn Allen Jones, *American Immigration* (Chicago, 1960), p. 262.

47 Brett 207.

Chapter Eleven: The Return to the Ranch

1 Widely reproduced, the photograph can be found in Brett's memoir (facing p. 96).
2 There are further details of the Hawk family in Parmenter 269.
3 'D. H. Lawrence and Frieda Lawrence: Letters to Dorothy Brett', ed. Peter L. Irvine and Anne Killey, *DHLR*, ix (Spring 1976), 48.
4 Ibid.
5 Ibid., 49.
6 Brett 220, 224; and Hignett, *Brett*, pp. 171, 175.
7 *DHLR*, ix (Spring 1976), 48.
8 Ibid., 50.
9 Bynner 253.
10 This is how Frieda remembered it in a letter to Kathryn Herbig on 26 April 1938. See *D. H. Lawrence's Manuscripts: The Correspondence of Frieda Lawrence, Jake Zeitlin and Others*, ed. Michael Squires (1991), p. 174.
11 *Complete Plays of D. H. Lawrence*, p. 102.
12 There were originally seventeen scenes and the beginning of an eighteenth but DHL discarded scenes xvi and xvii, rewrote scene xv, and then completed the play with what had once been the beginning of scene xviii but then became scene xvi. In one of the discarded scenes Saul conveniently elaborates on his – and DHL's own – reasons for disliking David: 'This fox, that peepeth round corners! This sly one, that slingeth stones unexpectedly at his enemy.' These details will be available in the forthcoming Cambridge edition of DHL's plays, edited by Hans-Wilhelm Schwarze and John Worthen.

13 The Southwest had intrigued Cather since her first trip in 1912 but it was not until *Death Comes For the Archbishop* (1927) that her fascination found expression in a major work. Writing to a friend in 1932, she described DHL as undoubtedly the most gifted author of his generation but a man whose prejudices got the better of him. For a discussion of Cather, DHL and their representations of the Southwest, see Guy Reynolds, *Willa Cather in Context: Progress, Race, Empire* (1996), pp. 161–4.

14 Foster, *D. H. Lawrence in Taos*, p. 255.

15 Brett 211.

16 *Complete Plays of D. H. Lawrence*, p. 68.

17 Ibid., pp. 92–3.

18 *K* 151–3.

19 *RDP* 239:23, 27; 240:36, 1–3.

20 *D. H. Lawrence and Maurice Magnus: A Plea for Better Manners* was privately printed in Florence in 1924. On p. 9 Douglas quotes the memorandum in which Magnus made him his literary executor. He goes on to imply that DHL was chiefly motivated in his account of Magnus by resentment at having lent money which was never returned, and to claim that he 'has now recouped himself many times over by the sale of the Memoirs' (p. 26). For a full account of DHL's involvement with Magnus see *TE* 537–9, 565–7, 581–5, 703–9.

21 Tomlinson's review was published in the *Weekly Westminster*, iii(n.s.), on 14 February 1925. As venomous remarks in his unpublished correspondence in UT indicate, he did not like DHL; but he was a great admirer of Norman Douglas. The flattering monograph on Douglas which he published in 1931 includes a passage in which he complains that, because of unhelpful genre distinctions, a contemporary novelist like DHL is 'gravely contemplated as a momentous advent, the most poignant expression of soul since nobody knows when' whereas 'Norman Douglas, who has given us some of the best narrative prose we have had this century, has had scant consideration.' 'No critic', he goes on, 'has declared the body of serious work of the author of *Old Calabria* to be worth more than a severely brief if favourable expert opinion, though beside it Lawrence's *Sea and Sardinia* is mainly the captiousness of an avid adolescent with a queasy mind' (pp. 2–3).

22 Muir's essay was published in the *Nation* for 11 February 1925. It also appeared in England in the *Nation and Athenaeum* on 4 July 1925.

23 *RDP* 243:36; 241:11–12.

24 Hignett, *Brett*, p. 175.

25 'Quella sua cupidigia di libertà, di svergognata sincerità interiore lo condusse ad abracciare le teorie di Freud.' Linati's article was entitled, 'Un esploratore di uomini' and appeared in the *Corriere della Sera* on 18 December 1924.

26 Linati had said that DHL was a writer full of Freudian subtleties ('intriso di sottigliezze freudiane') whose sincerity led him to the limits of coherence and decency ('sincero fino all'incoerenza e all'impudicizia'), that he had an almost hallucinatory vision of reality ('una visione quasi allucinata della realtá'), and that his frenetic love of life showed him to be a descendant of the bloodthirsty Elizabethans ('discendente dai sanguigni elisabettiani').

27 DHL had reviewed Sherman's *Americans* in the *Dial* in May 1923 and Sherman

responded with a review of *Studies* in the New York *Evening Post Literary Review* on 20 October of that same year. See p. 90 above.

28 Seligmann's *D. H. Lawrence: An American Interpretation* was enthusiastic but, as Sherman rather cruelly points out, not very well written:

> Mr Seligman's [*sic*] expression of this thought is memorable: 'D. H. Lawrence, like a well tempered chisel or some sharp boring instrument, goes to America's vitals, not to destroy but to strip off the lies and duality and subterfuges that prevent its voice singing out.' One doesn't ordinarily use a 'boring instrument' as a stripping instrument, but when by such an operation one can get 'singing' out of a nation's 'vitals' one shouldn't be too particular.

Sherman's essay was reprinted in *Critical Woodcuts* (New York, 1926). For this quotation see p. 22.

29 Collins, who must have followed DHL's literary career closely, had lived in Europe and obviously knew the European literary scene very well. His chapter includes the photograph which Catherine Carswell took of DHL in Italy in 1921 and liked so much that she used it as the frontispiece to *The Savage Pilgrimage* in 1932. John Carswell, Catherine Carswell's son, has no idea how Collins acquired it.

30 *Critical Woodcuts*, p. 26.

31 The original title for this essay was 'The Modern Novel' (*Hardy* xlix).

32 *Hardy* 164. Early versions of both 'Art and Morality' and 'Morality and the Novel' can be found in the appendices to this edition.

33 Ibid. 171:1–6.

34 *Hardy* 171:21, 24. The notion of a fourth dimension dates back to at least 1875. DHL became familiar with it around 1907 (after it had received a considerable boost from Einstein's *Special Theory of Relativity* in 1905). The possibility that his renewed interest in the mid–1920s stems from his having read and extensively annotated Peter D. Ouspensky's *Tertium Organum: A Key to the Enigmas of the World* in September 1923 is explored in Robert O. Young, '"Where the Trees Come and Go": D. H. Lawrence and the Fourth Dimension', *DHLR*, xiii (Spring 1980) 30–44.

35 *Hardy* 172:20–36.

36 Ibid. 179:21, 29–30.

37 See *TE* 20, 163.

38 *Hardy* 185:10, 15–16 The positions in DHL's three published essays are eloquently elaborated or restated in two further, unpublished ones: 'Why the Novel Matters' and 'The Novel and the Feelings'. From the manuscript evidence Bruce Steele has concluded that these are likely to belong, not to the period at the ranch, but rather to November 1925, when DHL was back in Europe (*Hardy* 1, 193–205).

39 There is an account of the *Signature* in *TE* 261, 264, 269–71, 275–6.

40 Brett 100.

41 Ibid. 209, 215.

42 Brett herself describes how DHL contributed to her painting (Brett 235, 242, 244).

43 *RDP* 352:15.

44 *RDP* 333:2–3, 5–10.

45 *RDP* 333:15–18.

46 *Critical Woodcuts*, p. 24.

47 'So a man can go forth in desire, even to the primrose. But let him refrain from falling all over the poor blossom, as William did. Or trying to incorporate it in his own ego, which is a sort of lust. Nasty anthropomorphic lust' (*RDP* 343). I explain why I think this is a misunderstanding in 'Lawrence, Wordsworth and "anthropomorphic lust"', *Cambridge Quarterly*, xxiii (1994), 230–42.

48 *RDP* 10:14–20.

49 *RDP* 332:9–13.

50 *RDP* 374:35–6; 375:1–2; 376:22–6.

51 *RDP* 325:25–6.

52 *SMOS* 155:30, 32.

53 *RDP* 315:13–20.

54 In his 1974 edition of Brett's memoir, John Manchester, the companion of her last years, writes, 'The whole book was written in bits and pieces as Brett remembered the different episodes. These were then sorted out and put together in small sections separated by a row of three asterisks as though they were undated entries in a diary' (p. ii). This method helps to explain why Brett's chronology is often faulty.

55 'One of the hens persisted in being broody, so we let her sit just seven eggs. They're due to hatch tomorrow or Wednesday' (v. 279).

56 Brett 147.

57 I am aware that this incident could be attributed to nothing more than bad temper. Brett's own refusal to take this interpretative route is evident in the way she links it to DHL's irritation with two puppies on the ranch. In her account, DHL catches sight of these just after he has let the hen out of the box and is walking with her back to the cabin:

> 'I must get rid of those pups', you say, 'I can't stand them. They suck each other all day long, and that is more than I can stomach. I shall give them back to Mabel.' As we go into the kitchen porch, the two pups are lying comfortably in the sun sucking each other happily. 'Look at them', you cry angrily, 'the little beasts!' and you push them apart with your foot and smack them both hard. 'I can't bear it.'   (Brett 147)

The two puppies on the ranch in July 1924 came from Mabel (v. 73), those of a year later had been brought to Kiowa by Trinidad (v. 233–4). The precise pair Brett is remembering here is less important than her decision to associate them with the hens.

58 T. S. Eliot, *Collected Poems: 1909–1965* (1943), p. 210.

59 *RDP* 310:18–22; 313:20–1.

60 *RDP* 275:35–8.

61 *RDP* 356:8–18.

62 *RDP* 309:1, 2, 8–9. (A dummy is what is known in the United States as a pacifier.)

63 *Women in Love*, p. 172:27–8. The chief credit for identifying this as a key concept in DHL's thinking, at a time when he was being seen largely in terms of a simplified liberationist ideology, belongs to Colin Clarke in his *River of Dissolution: D. H. Lawrence and English Romanticism* (1969).

64 *RDP* 292:18–20; 293:23–4.

65 In the original version of 'The Crown' DHL had said of 'the sensitive man':

> He is given up to the flux of reduction, his mouth is upon the mouth of corruption. This is the reason of homosexuality, and of connection with animals. This is the significance of the myths, of Leda, of Europa. This is David turning to Jonathan,

Achilles to Patroclus. This is always the higher, more developed type seeking to revert to the lower. (*RDP* 472)

66 *RDP* 268:24–8.

67 *RDP* 270:12–14.

68 *RDP* 370:9–11.

69 *RDP* 323:32.

70 *RDP* 337:25–7.

71 *RDP* 336:40 and note on 429.

72 *RDP* 359:15–16.

73 *RDP* 325:29–30; 326:4, 10; 327:26–9.

74 *RDP* 331:1–3.

75 For details of Crichton's background see Nehls, ii. 526 n.138.

76 A sentence in the letter of 31 August looks forward to DHL's view of the mining life as it appears in his late autobiographical writings: 'What was there in the mines that held the boy's feelings?', he asks, referring to Crichton's story. 'The darkness, the mystery, the otherworldliness, the peculiar camaraderie, the sort of naked intimacy: men as gods in the underworld, or as elementals' (v. 294).

77 Nehls, ii. 413. This account Crichton gives of the interview dates from c. 1950. The original publication in the New York *World*: 'D. H. Lawrence lives at the Top of the World – A kindly Lion in a New Mexican Lair' (11 October 1925) has many of the same anecdotes but is shorter and less detailed.

Frieda's quarrel with Ford, or Hueffer as he was afterwards known, is descibed in *TE* 225.

78 *Hardy* 182:11.

79 Nehls, ii. 414.

80 Ibid.

81 Brett 243.

82 See Ron Goulart, *An Informal History of Pulp Magazines* (New York, 1972), pp. 31–9.

83 Nehls, ii. 416.

84 In August Mollie Skinner wrote to say that her brother Jack, on whom she had based the hero of 'The House of Ellis', had died. In his letter of condolence, DHL said that if Jack could be described as having had no luck, it was probably because he never really 'wanted to make good.'

> At the bottom of his soul, he preferred to drift penniless through the world. I think if I had to choose, myself, between being a Duke of Portland, or having a million sterling and forced to live up to it, I'd rather, far, far rather be a penniless tramp. There is deep inside one a revolt against the fixed thing, fixed society, fixed money, fixed homes, even fixed love. I believe that was what ailed your brother: he couldn't bear the social fixture of everything. It's what ails me too. (v. 292)

If fixture could not always be avoided physically, nor the need for change and the love of adventure properly satisfied in real life, then for Mollie and himself there was at least the possibility of escape into the imagination: 'And that again is what I think about writing a novel: one can live so intensely with one's characters and the experience, one creates or records, it is a life in itself, far better than the vulgar thing people *call* life, jazzing and motoring and so on.' All literature is an escape but it has been customary to call certain kinds of it 'escapist' because its authors make no attempt to equip their readers more adequately for the lives to which they are eventually obliged to return. As his reply to Crichton on the question of why he wrote shows, DHL had a strong sense of the moral responsibility of the writer and of his duty to try and change people; but he also had a strong need to retreat into the world of his writing, especially at times when his relations with others were particularly bad or, as in 1925, when he was weakened by illness. Yet even in periods when he was most tempted to use writing as a refuge, Lawrence never abandoned his engagement with life's problems although it may well be that, at those times, the solutions he proposes are more strongly marked by wish-fulfilment than at others.

85 Nehls, ii. 416–17.

86 Brett 237–8 (the photograph is in UT).

87 Nehls, ii. 417.

88 Brett 226–7.

89 Advising Brett on her coming trip to Italy, DHL explained to her from New York that a first-class ticket for a small boat would cost $209 but that if she went in a larger one, where the second-class accommodation stood more chance of being comfortable, a first-class ticket would cost $250 and one for the second class, $135 (v. 299). For the Lawrences of course these figures would have to be doubled.

90 Lee Witt was a saw-mill owner who had been a local sheriff. In strictly conventional terms, Nina's marriage to him in 1921 had been almost as much of a *mésalliance* as Mabel's to Tony Luhan: 'People say Nina has eight million', DHL reports at one point (v. 239). On 4 April 1924 DHL noted that she was divorcing her husband, 'rightly', and a year later said that she had suddenly appeared at the ranch with Tony Luhan 'thrilled at getting a divorce from Lee' (v. 22, 237). It seems clear that she was no longer based in Taos in the period between these two remarks.

91 Marguerite Bartelle McDonald, 'An Evening With the Lawrences', *DHLR*, v (Spring 1972), 62–6.

92 *P* 343.

Chapter Twelve: Spotorno

1 For DHL's relations with the Eders see *TE* 133. Another former contact whom DHL is likely to have seen on his return to London is Barbara Low, also an analyst and Edith Eder's sister. In December he mentions having written to her, and her name continues to appear on the lists of people to whom he asks publishers to send his new books (v. 329, 347). But because his post–1916 correspondence with her is lost, she more or less disappears from the story of his life.

2 There is an account of this visit in *SP* 227–9. At one moment during it, in a manner that was 'half shy, half careless', DHL threw a five-pound note across the table for the Carswells' young son, John Patrick. Catherine Carswell took this to be a repayment of money she had given Frieda when the Lawrences were about to leave England in 1919. It was another settling of accounts for a man who hated to be under an obligation.

3 By this time DHL's contact, and the associate editor of the *New York Herald Tribune Books*, was not Stuart Sherman but Irita van Doren (v. 301).

4 The reviews are reprinted in *P*, pp. 327–30, 351–4. DHL sent them off to the Curtis Brown office on 13 and 20 October, respectively (v. 317, 319). What he had to say about *Saïd the Fisherman* appeared in the *New York Herald Tribune Books* on 27 December 1925 but his remarks on Rolfe never seem to have been published there (although they were printed in the December 1925 issue of *Adelphi*).

5 Nehls, iii. 8.

6 Ibid. 9. In a later account of this visit, published in two successive numbers of the *London Magazine*, Barbara Weekley Barr explains that her Nottingham friends were called Hewitt and that the husband was in awe of Weekley who had helped to get him his professorship (xxxiii (August/September 1993), 33).

7 This was not John Grant MacFarlane, whom the Lawrences had met when they were staying in Heath Street in 1923 and who was chiefly a farmer, but George Gordon MacFarlane, author of *The Natural Man*, a war novel DHL admired (v. 315–16). The rent for the flat was two guineas (v. 326).

8 William Gerhardie (formerly spelt Gerhardi) had recently published *The Polyglots: A Novel* (1925). For Gerhardie's malicious but nonetheless interesting and informative impressions of DHL, see Nehls, iii. 10–14. He was one of many to compare DHL with Christ: 'In the sunlight his red-bearded face looked harrowed and full of suffering, almost Christ-like.' He noted that DHL was the principal cook in the house; that Frieda had a tendency to produce parodic versions of her husband's ideas; and he was given a practical illustration of DHL's willingness to help emerging young writers like himself. Yet his most interesting remarks probably concern the conversations he had with DHL about immortality: 'Lawrence's idea of immortal life was not something which would start after death, but a living reality within us going on even now, all the time, though intermittently clouded over by the illusion of time. He grew enthusiastic. Anything true to its own nature, he declared, was immortal' (p. 11).

9 At Kiowa, one of the Lawrences' alternative names for their cat Timsy was 'Miss Wemyss' (v. 306).

10 Nicola Beauman, *Cynthia Asquith* (1987), p. 97. Other details concerning Cynthia Asquith's life are chiefly drawn from this source.

11 Ibid. 171.

12 JMM 118.

13 JMM 119–20.

14 Seelig published a short article about his relations with DHL in *Neue Zürcher Zeitung*, 23 May 1957. For his account of how he and the Lawrences spent their time after he had met them in Lucerne, see Armin Arnold, 'In the Footsteps of D. H. Lawrence', *Texas Studies in Language and Literature*, no. 3 (Summer 1961), 188.

15 There are useful details of DHL's stay in Spotorno in *Omaggio a D. H. Lawrence*, a pamphlet published by the Commune di Spotorno in 1986.

16 Although there is no mention of it in the letters, it is likely to have been during his stay in Spotorno that DHL wrote the short but highly favourable review of *In the American Grain* by William Carlos Williams – it appeared in the *Nation* (New York) on 14 April 1926. Praising Williams for his contribution to the 'sensuous record of Americanization of the white men in America', DHL concluded: 'But if an author rouses my deeper sympathy he can have as many faults as he likes, I don't care. And if I disagree with

him a bit, heaven save me from feeling superior just because I have a chance to snarl. I am only too thankful that Mr Williams wrote his book' (*P* 334, 336).

17 *P* 331–3. This review appeared in the *New York Herald Tribune Books* on 31 January 1926.

18 *WWRA* 174:2–5.

19 *WWRA* 174:12–14.

20 *TE* 422.

21 Beauman, *Cynthia Asquith*.

22 *WWRA* 181:9; 410, note on 176:9.

23 *WWRA* 187:17; 203:29–31; 207:25.

24 *WWRA* 208:13–14; 209:29–31.

25 *WWRA* xxxiii.

26 *WWRA* xxxiii–xxxiv.

27 *WWRA* 183:1; 193:19–20.

28 *MM* 177. After its appearance in *Laughing Horse* (no. 13), 'A Little Moonshine with Lemon' provided a postscript for *Mornings in Mexico*. On 23 June 1924 DHL wrote to Seltzer, 'We are just off back to the ranch, with 12 bottles of smuggled whiskey' (v. 60). 'Schillings' is the name of an American spice company.

29 The piece was reprinted in *P* 117–18.

30 *Poems* 814–15. The second poem which appeared in the April 1926 number of *Laughing Horse* – 'Beyond the Rockies' – has no immediate relevance to DHL's feelings about going back to America.

31 Frieda 200.

32 The letter is in the Koteliansky Papers (BL).

33 This was the Loeb edition of Hesiod's *Homeric Hymns and Homerica*. DHL drew a design based on the frontispiece for Ottoline Morrell to embroider (*TE* 315, 821). He is remembering it in *K* 171:12–17.

34 Brett 273.

35 *WWRA* 243:30–31.

36 Cynthia Asquith, *Haply I May Remember* (1950), p. 189. Lady Cynthia also remembered that her ghost book had 'a very large sale'. Her other contributors included Algernon Blackwood, Enid Bagnold, De la Mare, L. P. Hartley, Desmond McCarthy, Arthur Machen and Oliver Onions.

37 'That little story about the boy who betted on the horse races', DHL wrote to Ada on 3 May 1926, 'was sold in America for £50: and in England from Cynthia I only got £15' (v. 449).

38 Beauman, *Cynthia Asquith*, p. 286.

39 *Memoir of Maurice Magnus*, ed. Cushman, p. 35. In the original Secker edition of 1924, the text reads, ' "Precisely," said D——— . . . ' (p. 18).

40 Douglas was following his usual practice by first of all publishing *Experiments* privately in Florence. It was only in the more commercial editions, published in London and New York, that he decided to fill a thin volume out by including a revised version of *A Plea*. See Roberts, *Bibliography*, pp. 77–83.

41 Douglas's original letter is in UT. In his letter to the *New Statesman* DHL says that he kept what Douglas had written to him 'remembering the care with which he files all his

letters' (v. 396). This is not an intelligible explanation. What is likely is that DHL broke with his usual practice and kept Douglas's letter because he realised the legal situation was complicated and that he needed some insurance.

42 Frieda's remark is reported by Ravagli – see Nehls, iii. 18.

43 Ravagli had been to Taos with Frieda before April 1933, but that is when he went there to live with her on a permanent basis. After Mrs Ravagli had given her consent, Frieda and he were married in Taos on 31 October 1950. But this American marriage was never legally recognised in Italy. When Frieda died in 1956, Ravagli went back to Spotorno and lived with his first, and, in Italian terms, only wife in the Villa Bernarda. See Robert Lucas, *Frieda Lawrence* (1973), pp. 262, 279.

44 The first would then be 'Smile' which describes how a man goes to visit his wife lying dead in the nunnery where she had chosen to retreat and cannot prevent himself from grinning nervously when he views her corpse. This very short sketch, almost certainly provoked by Lawrence's recent meeting with Murry, exploits the way moments of great tension are sometimes likely to be accompanied by inappropriate physiological reactions (in *Sons and Lovers* Paul and his sister giggle hysterically as they prepare a final, fatal dose of pain-killer for their dying mother); but it also implies that people like Murry are so habituated to simulating feeling that they are incapable of genuine grief.

In 'Smile', there is none of that particularity which makes it certain that in 'The Last Laugh', 'The Border-Line' and 'Jimmy and the Desperate Woman' DHL is using Murry as a model; but in July 1926 DHL wrote to Brett: ' "Smile" – that little sketch of the dead wife – came in the English *Nation*. – In the *Adelphi*, the Life of Christ is relegated to the back pages, and our little friend is discovering he is a pantheist: without a Pan, however: fryingpantheist!' (v. 504). The way a mention of the story provokes a reference to Murry here suggests strongly it had been based on him. Nancy Pearn found it hard to place: 'several editors liked it personally but seemed to be afraid of it' (*WWRA* xxix). There is nothing remotely improper in the story so that a likely cause of their fear would be that they recognised it as referring to Murry and thought it dealt too cruelly with his response to Katherine Mansfield's death. What is cruel in 'Smile' is that the wife's corpse seems itself to smile and mock the husband's attempt at grief.

45 *RDP* 375:2.

46 *WWRA* 33:27–9.

47 *'The Woman Who Rode Away' and Other Stories* (1928), pp. 51, 54. This is the version of the story which first appeared in the *New Coterie* in Autumn 1926. For a later version see *WWRA* and p. 407 above.

48 The story of Barby's expulsion is told by A. Alvarez in *Life After Marriage* (1982) and has been confirmed by Barbara Weekley Barr herself.

49 Nehls, ii. 294 and iii. 22.

50 Because of what Barby calls the 'curious streak of conventionality in him which cropped up from time to time', it is possible DHL was as much concerned with the propriety of his sister not travelling alone as with its convenience. Although his friendship with Brett ought to have taught him that, if the Slade did not (in his view) teach you to paint properly, at least it made you indifferent to a number of the more

conventional standards, he was shocked to learn from Barby that she had travelled third-class in Italy: 'An English girl doing that here gives the impression that she is looking for an "adventure"' (Nehls, iii. 20–1).

51 JMM 120–2.

52 Cf. 'To me the venture meant nothing real: a little escapade. I can't believe in "doing things" like that. In a great issue like the war, there was nothing to be "done", in Murry's sense' (*RDP* 249:24–6).

53 J. Middleton Murry, *The Life of Jesus* (1926), p. 147.

54 There is a detailed analysis of the preliminaries of the final break with Murry in Britton 22–7.

55 *The Virgin and the Gipsy* (1930), p. 11 (Secker edition). We learn from *Mr. Noon*, ed. Lindeth Vasey, pp. 125, 314, and from one of Frieda's own memoirs, that in the first months of their courtship and marriage Weekley referred to her as his white snow-flower. Writing to Ada on 15 December 1925 DHL says of Weekley, 'But he's made provision for Frieda in his will!!!! See what it is to leave your husband' (v. 353). In *The Virgin and the Gipsy* DHL writes of the Reverend Mr Saywell, 'Yes, the white snowflower was forgiven. He had even made provision in his will for her' (p. 11).

56 Ibid., p. 175

57 Ibid., p. 132.

58 Barbara Weekley Barr, 'Step-daughter to Lawrence – II', *London Magazine*, xxxiii (Oct./Nov. 1993), 14.

59 *The Virgin and the Gipsy*, p. 36.

60 Ibid., p. 174.

61 'Step-daughter to Lawrence – II', p. 14.

62 For the difficulties with Heseltine see *TE* 672, 866.

63 When Secker was shown the manuscript of *The Virgin and the Gipsy* in Spotorno he did not like it (*WWRA* xxxiv), perhaps because he recognised that publication might bring trouble. All the first editions published in Florence, England and the United States in 1930, after DHL's death, carry the note, 'This work lacks the author's final revision, and has been printed from the manuscript exactly as it stands.' This seems to derive more from anxiety about possible legal difficulties than any sense that the text would strike readers as unfinished.

64 The warmth is partly explained by Brett having sent Frieda some clothes she had acquired during a recent stay with her wealthy family in England (v. 358).

65 Nehls, iii. 21.

66 Frieda 194.

67 DHL had first written to Knopf about *Max Havelaar* on 20 October 1925 (v. 320), in support of an initial approach by Siebenhaar himself. The agreement to publish was dependent on Siebenhaar agreeing to surrender copyright (v. 393). Thus it was only after he had seen the Siebenhaars in Monte Carlo that DHL heard from them that everything had been satisfactorily 'fixed up' (v. 420).

68 Brett 257.

69 *TE* 551, 556, 850; Morgan, *Maugham*, p. 24, 38.

70 Brett 264.

71 Faith Compton Mackenzie, *More Than I Should* (1950), p. 34.

669

72 Brett 265.

73 Brewster 267; but see also Brett 270–2.

74 When Brett did take DHL to her hotel to see the picture, he was not impressed. Partly as a consequence she destroyed it (Brett 275), tackling the same subject again only much later. A reproduction of the second version serves as the frontispiece to Keith Sagar's illustrated *Life of D. H. Lawrence* (1980).

75 Brett 260.

76 Nehls, iii. 26.

77 Brett 274.

78 Brewster 94.

79 *Eve*, 31 March 1926, p. 625, and *Tatler*, 24 March 1926, p. 513. Herm is one of the Channel Islands.

80 *TE* 557.

81 Brett 277–8, 280.

82 The Brewsters knew Lord Grimthorpe but they were particularly close friends of his daughter (information from Keith Cushman)

83 Brett 280.

84 All but the last of my quotations come from the epilogue in John Manchester's edition of Brett's memoir published in Santa Fe in 1974 (while she was still alive). In that edition however DHL is reported as saying, 'Your boobs are all wrong' (p. iii). The phrase I have preferred comes from Sean Hignett's otherwise very similar version of events which he based on 'Brett's own typescript version' of the account she had provided for Manchester (Brett, p. 192). Hignett has suggested to me in a letter that 'boobs' must have been an error of transcription by Manchester.

85 Cf Hignett: 'in the summer of 1970, I met Brett for the first time when she was refusing to travel up from Taos to the ranch to take part in the Festival that was being held there to mark the fortieth anniversary of Lawrence's death. "All those Lawrence scholars want to know is whether I slept with Lawrence and I'm afraid that's my business"' (*Brett*, p. 190).

86 There is a full account of this episode, and DHL's possible allusions to it in *Aaron's Rod*, in *TE* 601–6, 647–50.

87 Koteliansky Papers (BL).

88 *Lawrence and Brett: A Friendship*, with an introduction, prologue and epilogue by John Manchester (Santa Fe, 1974), p. v.

89 As in the crisis with Brett in Mexico, DHL's thoughts seem inevitably to turn to Murry, here perhaps because he was once again – technically speaking – the successful rival.

90 Frieda 195.

91 *Memoirs* 232.

Chapter Thirteen: Florence and England

1 There are details of the organisation of the infamous *squadristi* in Denis Mack Smith, *Mussolini* (1981), p. 47, the chief source of much of my other information on Mussolini.

2 Nehls, iii. 24.

3 Ibid. 662–3 n.8. Mirenda told Nehls:

Lawrence's personality made a favourable impression upon me. Rather tall, slim, with a lively, penetrating eye, a good-humoured smile, hair and moustache blond, tending to red, his parting on the left, at ease in conversation – he expressed himself clearly in Italian. On his temples were a few threads of white hair, which engraved on his frank, intelligent features a peculiar aspect of interior torment. His beard was like that of the Nazarene. (ibid. 59)

4 Ibid. 63. When DHL first met the Wilkinson brothers Walter would have been on a visit to his brother's villa. It is clear that he did not normally live there.

5 Almost everyone who has written about the Lawrences at the Villa Mirenda has assumed that the 'Pietro' who is often referred to in the letters as driving the dog-cart down to Ponte Vingone, accompanying Frieda on shopping exhibitions or stealing Christmas trees, and who is thought by many to have posed for DHL, was Guilia's brother. She did have a brother called Pietro but in April 1926 he was only twelve and too young for all the various functions assigned to the 'Pietro' of the letters. This must therefore have been Pietro Degli Innocenti, often known as 'Piero', who is referred to by Raul Mirenda as Guilia Pini's 'half brother' (Nehls, iii. 61) but who, strictly speaking, was not related to her at all. The credit for clearing up this confusion belongs entirely to Stefania Michelucci who has consulted the local archives and was able to interview Guilia Pini.

6 When she was in a spot as isolated as Fiascherino before the war Frieda had insisted on a piano. For the difficulties of transporting it, see *TE* 99.

7 *SEP* 211:1–2, 16–17; 212:37–8.

8 *SEP* 214:19–20; 215:28–39.

9 *SEP* lxi.

10 *WWRA* 5:1–2.

11 Faith Mackenzie expressed her resentment in her memoir *More Than I Should* (1940), p. 34; and her husband describes how he assured her there was nothing to get upset about in Octave 6 of *My Life and Times* (1967), pp. 84–5.

12 *WWRA* 7:12, 32; 15:32, 34; 16:39–40; 17:1–4.

13 *WWRA* 17:31–40; 18:1–2.

14 This is the view which Mackenzie expresses in a taped interview with David Gerard (NCL).

15 Nehls, i. 71.

16 L. D. Clark points out that unsympathetic reviews of *The Plumed Serpent* were not as numerous as DHL had feared (*PS* xli); but they were numerous enough and must have affected him more than hostile criticism usually did because they were of a novel which he had felt was particularly important to him. A frequent refrain in them which would have depressed DHL was that he was past his best.

17 For 'Fireworks', of which there are two versions, see *SEP* lix–lxi, 203–8, 287–91. Simonetta di Filippis points out its probable connection with a letter DHL wrote to Nancy Pearn on 27 June: '*Vogue* told Richard Aldington to ask me to do them little articles: paying £10 for 1,500 words' (v. 482), although the sketch did in fact appear in the *Nation and Athenaeum* on 16 April 1927 (and in the American *Forum* in the following month).

18 Andro Linklater, *Compton Mackenzie: A Life* (1987), p. 205; Sybille Bedford, *Aldous Huxley: A Biography*, (1973), i. 130, 178.

19 The Wilkinsons left diaries which covered their time in Florence. These were described and quoted from in K. M. Sagar, 'Lawrence and the Wilkinsons', *Review of English Literature*, iii (October 1963), 62–75, but have unfortunately now been destroyed.

20 Stanley Weintraub, *Reggie: A Portrait of Reggie Turner* (New York, 1965), p. 139. DHL had depicted Turner as Algy Constable in *Aaron's Rod* (p. 325, note on 215.1). There are details of 'Botticelli Horne' in G. Orioli, *Adventures of a Bookseller* (1938), p. 117. A tribute to Turner as 'Comus' appears in Max Beerbohm, *And Even Now* (1920).

21 *TE* 598–9, 858.

22 G. Orioli, *Adventures of a Bookseller*, p. 125. Both the context and the language here suggests that the relationship between Orioli and Davis had initially been homosexual, although the Mrs Crocker previously mentioned eventually left her husband in order to marry Davis (see ibid., p. 136).

Taking most of the details of Orioli's life from *Adventures of a Bookseller* is problematic because that work, like his previous travel book *Moving Along* (1934), was composed in collaboration with Norman Douglas. This explains why the memoir is not only lively but also extremely well written. In *Pinorman* (1954), Richard Aldington quotes letters from Orioli in which the English is far from perfect (p. 158), and, in his excellent biography of Douglas (1976), Mark Holloway makes it clear that Douglas did re-write Orioli's books for him (pp. 401–4, 408, 424). Yet there seems little doubt that the main lines of the narrative are his own and the details of his previous life, several of which can be checked from other sources, broadly accurate.

23 In the via Oriuolo (*Adventures of a Bookseller*, p. 254).

24 Private conversation with Barbara Barr and Ianthe Carswell.

25 *Pinorman*, pp. 27–8.

26 For an extended description of this visit to the Sitwells, as well as convincing evidence that DHL borrowed certain characteristics of Lady Ida for Lady Eva Rolleston in *FLC*, see Britton 74–6. The artistic children were of course, in order of seniority, Edith, Osbert and Sacheverell.

27 Linklater, *Compton Mackenzie*, pp. 219–20.

28 Nehls, iii. 74, 71.

29 Ibid. 75, 666 n.60.

30 Gardiner explains that, according to Halliwell's *Dictionary of Archaic and Proverbial Words*, 'Kibbo Kift' meant in Old English 'strength or any proof of great strength' (Nehls, iii. 78). The account of Hargrave with which he provided Nehls is very detailed (pp. 77–80).

31 In both the *Atlantic Monthly* (xxxix) and the *Nation and Athenaeum* (5 February 1927).

32 *P* 35–6.

33 *P* 38.

34 Brewster 296–7.

35 *Badener Tagblatt*, 20 juli 1926.

36 *P* 37.

37 *WWRA* xxxviii–ix.

38 Britton has argued that DHL's treatment of this episode reflects many of the feelings he had had about Brett in Ravello (Britton 42).

39 *WWRA* 168:20–9. In the manuscript, transcribed in the Cambridge edition (pp. 319–39), the wording of this passage is different. DHL typed the version he sent to Nancy Pearn himself and made the alterations as he did so.

40 Robert E. Gajdusek, 'A Reading of *The White Peacock*', in *A D. H. Lawrence Miscellany*, ed. Gajdusek, p. 194.

41 *WWRA* 170:15.

42 Milly Beveridge lived at 20 Rossetti Garden Mansions (vi. 334); the flat the Lawrences rented was number 25 (v. 504). According to Rolf Gardiner, it was owned by a Mrs Stanley Fay (Nehls, iii. 82).

43 For Montague Weekley's account see Nehls, iii. 70, and his taped interview with David Gerard in NCL.

44 Nehls, iii. 83.

45 Aldous Huxley, Introduction to *The Letters of D. H. Lawrence* (1932), p. xxix. The letters Huxley wrote at this time are on the Athenaeum's notepaper. See *Letters of Aldous Huxley*, ed. Grover Smith (1969), pp. 270–1.

46 Richard Aldington, *Life for Life's Sake* (1968), pp. 274–6.

47 A picture of Milly Beveridge's house as it now is accompanies the note on 'D. H. Lawrence in Scotland' by Margaret Needham in the *D. H. Lawrence Newsletter*, n. 49 (Autumn 1991), 15.

48 Linklater, *Compton Mackenzie*, p. 221.

49 *P* 349, 348.

50 *P* 346, 350.

51 The information is from Mrs Margaret ('Peggy') Needham herself.

52 *EY* 6; *TE* 491.

53 Olive Hopkin was interviewed by David Gerard; Britton 128.

54 Britton 145–7.

55 The suggestion that DHL may have begun one or more of his short autobiographical accounts of his last stay in England before it was over comes from Britton (pp. 134, 283 n.45).

56 *P* 257, 264.

57 Britton has discovered that the trial was in Heanor and gives details of the incidents which gave rise to it. He has worked out that DHL must have seen the women in the market-place at Ripley, not Eastwood (pp. 102–3).

58 *P II* 260.

59 *P II* 265. For another occasion on which DHL suggests that economic problems could be solved by nationalisation, see his letter to Bertrand Russell in February 1915 (ii. 282).

60 As H. G. Wells had shown, an enthusiasm for eugenics was not a specifically right-wing phenomenon.

61 *My Friends When Young: The Memoirs of Brigit Patmore* (1968), ed. with an introduction by Derek Patmore, p. 97.

62 In this introduction, reprinted in *P* 236–9, DHL argues that if *Max Havelaar* were no more than a tract (like *Uncle Tom's Cabin*), it would not have kept its interest. In his

view it survives because it has its origins in hate not pity and because its author is
essentially a satirist.

63 *TE* 566, 851.

64 Nehls, iii. 104.

65 *SP* 245.

Chapter Fourteen: Two Lady Chatterleys

1 'Flowery Tuscany: I', *SEP* 226:22–3.

2 In a letter to Montague Weekley DHL wrote:

> I have painted window frames by the mile, doors by the acre, painted a chest of
> drawers till it turned into a bureau, and am not through, by a long chalk. This is
> living heroically, à la Frieda. Mussolini says vivi pericolosamente! and then makes
> millions of laws against anybody who takes a pot shot at him. (v. 570)

According to Denis Mack Smith, the fourth attempt to assassinate Mussolini, which
took place in Bologna in October 1926, was 'used as the final justification for setting up
a totalitarian dictatorship' (*Mussolini*, p. 144).

3 *SEP* 220:40–2; 221:15–16.

4 *Portrait of a Genius, But* . . . , p. 320.

5 The three families on the estate were the Bandelli, Orsini and Pini (v. 607; Frieda 200).
A year or so later the Bandelli appear to have been sent away and replaced by the
Salvestrini (vi. 164, 235, 306, 361).

6 Frieda 203; *FLC* 247; *JTLJ* 17.

7 Frieda 203.

8 Sagar, 'Lawrence and the Wilkinsons', 66. An additional reason for not hearing the
knocking may have been DHL's growing deafness. When she saw him in London the
month before, Catherine Carswell felt that this had got worse. According to her, there
were times when he welcomed some degree of deafness as 'a protection against the
wearisome chatter of the world. When Dorothy Brett would re-charge her listening
machine, I have heard him laugh and ask whether any human conversation was worth
the three shillings needed for a fresh battery' (*SP* 240).

9 *Letters of Aldous Huxley*, ed. Grover Smith, p. 284. As David Bradshaw has pointed out
to me, the articles in question are likely to have been bought by either *Vanity Fair* or
Harper's Magazine.

10 Elsa Weekley was at St Paul's School with her fiancé's sisters and from 1918 the two
families had lived within 500 yards of each other in Chiswick. Although she and
Seaman were engaged in 1926 they did not marry until April 1929. In a letter to James
T. Boulton in 1986, from which this information is derived, Commander Seaman (as
he then was) makes clear that he never met DHL.

11 DHL has Duncan Forbes refer to the difference in *FLC*: 'He gazed at her shrewdly
and ironically. "My dear little Constance," he said, "do you mean that you really *love*
Op? I don't mean *in love* with him . . . It can't be! Nobody ever *loves* anybody
nowadays. They're all too busy being *in love*" ' (p. 212).

12 *WWRA* 140:26–31. DHL's first title for this story was 'More Modern Love'. Both the
quoted phrases were introduced as he typed the manuscript. During that process the

fiancé's awareness of his mistake, as well as his real desire for Hester, are brought out clearly in order to provide a satisfactory ending.

13 *FLC* 9 (the introduction to this edition). In *JTLJ* there is a moment when, 'Constance sat down with her back to a young pine tree, that swayed against her like an animate creature, so subtly rubbing itself against her, the great, alive thing with its top in the wind!' (p. 91)

14 *LCL* xx.

15 *JTLJ* 16.

16 *FLC* 41. DHL's reference to Parkin as a 'black man of the woods' recalls the symbolism he had detected in Hawthorne's *The Scarlet Letter*. There is a deliberately ironic reversal of the usual relationship between wood and town in his description of Connie's reaction to Clifford reading Racine:

> And meanwhile the voice of the other man, Sir Clifford, went on and on, clapping and gurgling with strange sound. Not for one second did she really hear what he said. But it sounded to her like the uncouth cries and howls of barbarous, disconnected savages dancing round a fire somewhere outside of the wood. Clifford was a smeared and painted savage howling in an utterly unintelligible gibberish somewhere on the outskirts of her consciousness. (*FLC* 53–4)

17 In the first two versions, Robin Hood's Well (which can still be visited) is referred to by its real name. In *LCL* it becomes 'John's Well'.

18 *FLC* 109; *The Fox, The Captain's Doll, The Ladybird*, p. 219.

19 *FLC* 125.

20 *FLC* 71 but see also pp. 80–2.

21 They can also be in appalling taste. Cf.:

> There came the banging of guns from the woods.
> 'Hark! They are killing his pheasants!' she said.
> 'Has Clifford gone in his chair?'
> 'Yes! He's gone too – with his gun!'
> 'My God! After the war and all! – and he lets off gunpowder at his own elegant and tame birds! My God! Sits there in a motor-chair and bangs away and bags a few birds, I'll bet!'
> 'Five yesterday!'
> Duncan opened his mouth, and doubled up in mirthless joy. 'I wonder if he cripples any of them in the legs! By Jove, I'll ask him.' (*FLC* 207–8)

22 *FLC* 88, 102, 248.

23 *LCL* 333:35–6.

24 In 1955 Frieda wrote to Harry T. Moore: 'The terrible thing about Lady C. is that L. identified himself with both Clifford and Mellors; that took courage, that made me shiver, when I read it as he wrote it' (*Memoirs* 352).

25 *FLC* 243.

26 'Making Pictures' was first published in the magazine *Creative Art*, v (July 1929). For these quotations see *P II* 602–3.

27 *FLC* 120.

28 As Lawrence put it in a letter to Spud Johnson on 12 December, in blowing back his shirt the wind shows those parts 'other people are pleased to call his *pudenda*, and

which the nuns named his *glorietta*' (v. 600). In the original story, which is the first of the Third Day, the Abbess is alone when she comes across the gardener who is inadvertently exposing himself.

29 Frieda 205.

30 The picture of the negro wedding has been lost. The photograph encaptioned 'African Women take to European Sport: Exotic Push Ball' had appeared in the *Illustrated London News* on 25 December 1926.

31 For an illustration of this famous sculpture see Francis Haskell and Nicholas Penny, *Taste and the Antique* (New Haven, 1981), p. 322. Its influence is perhaps more evident on DHL's later painting *Throwing Back the Apple* than on *Flight Back into Paradise*.

32 Most of DHL's paintings from this period were reproduced in the Mandrake Press edition of 1929 (see pp. 457–9 above). They are easier to consult in *Paintings of D. H. Lawrence*, ed. Mervyn Levy (1964). Most of the originals are either at UT or in Saki Karavas's collection in Taos. For a location list, see Sagar, *Calendar*, p. 267.

33 Both merit entries in the *Dictionary of British Painters: 1880–1940*, compiled by J. Johnson and A. Greutzer (Woodbridge: Sussex, 1976). This is specifically for 'exhibiting artists' (although DHL does not appear!). In a letter written to the Wilkinsons from Bandol in 1928, DHL says he has heard that in London they have been 'Showing A[rthur]'s pictures and selling them – beato lui!' (vii. 81).

34 Sagar, 'Lawrence and the Wilkinsons', 67.

35 *FLC* 156. Cf. also in this passage: 'And with the mystery of the phallus goes all the beauty of the world . . . But for the penis we should never know the loveliness of Sirius or the categorical difference between a pomegranate and an india-rubber ball.' This shows that DHL was not much concerned to make a distinction between the phallus as a *symbol* of life in the body – of what he calls, in 'A Propos of *Lady Chatterley's Lover*', 'godly vitality in a man . . . immediate contact' (*LCL* 382:7–8) – and the specific organ of individual males. The lack of concern was even more in evidence when in *JTLJ* he came to develop further the thoughts in this passage (see *JTLT* 236–9). It is not only for readers without penises that this can cause problems. One of these is: does a satisfactory relationship with the human and natural environment not merely manifest itself in, but *depend on*, having a penis, and a penis in good working order?

36 Frieda 204–5.

37 Sagar, 'Lawrence and the Wilkinsons', 68.

38 Jacques Lassaigne in *A Dictionary of Modern Painting* (1956), p. 212. Magnelli's style in the 1920s is usually described as 'imaginary realism'. In *Alberto Magnelli: L'oeuvre peint* (Paris, 1975), Anne Maisonnier writes of Magnelli's 'retour à la figuration' after World War I and describes it as 'un cheminement progressif vers une nouvelle forme d'abstraction' (p. 19).

39 For details of this visit see *TE* 185–6, 213–14.

40 *LCL* 286:34.

41 This was on 19 December when they all went with Orioli to see a Florentine version of a pantomime based around the clown figure of 'Stenterello'. See Sagar, 'Lawrence and the Wilkinsons', 68.

42 *Calendar of Modern Letters*, iii (April 1926), 77–9.

43 DHL quickly became reconciled to *Mornings in Mexico* deciding that all the essays were 'really good – except, it might be, "Indians and Entertainment"' (v. 580).

44 *P* 355, 358–9. It is possible that during this period DHL also wrote a review of Isa Glenn's *Heat*, a novel which was first published in March 1926 and describes the relations of a US lieutenant in the Philippines with both an American schoolteacher and the daughter of a prominent Spanish family in Manila. The review never appeared in his life-time and is not mentioned in the *Letters*. See *P* 337–41 and Tedlock 256.

45 *P* 362, 363, 366.

46 *Hardy* 209:6, 13–15, 22–3; 210:6–7.

47 In *Psychoanalysis and the Unconscious* Lawrence paraphrases two assertions of Burrow and calls them 'brilliantly true' (p. 206). Burrow had sent two off-prints to DHL in January 1925 and DHL acknowledged receipt of two more in December 1926 (v. 261, 611).

48 *Hardy* 210:15–16; 214:36–7, 19. The meaning and origin of the distinction between individual and social beings become much clearer when the essay is read in conjunction with the 'fragement of an early draft' printed as appendix IV in this edition (pp. 249–52).

49 Nehls, iii. 122.

50 DHL's four sheets of musical notation are reproduced in *A D. H. Lawrence Miscellany*, ed. Moore, between pages 150 and 151. The music consists of a single competently notated vocal line with the text written under the notes. DHL specified that the voice(s) should be accompanied by 'a pipe', tambourine, and a 'tom-tom drum' (v. 557), but he did not provide a musical score for these instruments; he presumably expected one to be produced either in a written arrangement, or extemporaneously in performance. For what was probably the first performance of the music, at the D. H. Lawrence Centre at the University of Nottingham on 20 April 1996, Bethan Jones produced a full score for the appropriate instruments, a copy of which has been deposited (together with a recording of the 1996 performance) in UN.

51 There is an entry on Percy in the *Oxford Companion to the Theatre*, ed. Phyllis Hartnoll (1967), pp. 726–7.

52 Nehls, iii. 121. There is a full resumé of the reception of *The Widowing of Mrs Holroyd* in *A D. H. Lawrence Handbook*, ed. Keith Sagar (Manchester, 1982), pp. 289–94. This gives Percy's 1947 account of Shaw's response ('Compared with that, my prose is machine-made lace. You can hear the typewriter in it'); and Shaw's own version in an article he published in *Time and Tide* in August 1932: 'In my ignorance, I attached no importance to Lawrence until one afternoon at the Stage Society, when I saw a play by him which rushed through in such a torrent of profuse yet vividly effective dialogue, making my own seem archaic in comparison, that I was interested technically' (p. 288).

53 Dicky Pogmore, Alan Chambers and Frances Cooper can all be traced through the index to *EY*.

54 *Sons and Lovers*, ed. Carl and Helen Baron, pp. 85, 525 note on 85:22.

55 E144 (OCU). The first, crossed-out title of this piece was 'My Career'. Another unpublished essay of an autobiographical character, clearly belonging with 'Return to Bestwood' and 'Getting On', is 'Which Class I Belong To' (E428 at OCU). Having

described in this piece his own climb up the social ladder, DHL goes on to say that, if he had to choose between the 'two evils' of working- and middle-class culture, he would plump for the former. Life with people like his father may often be full of obtuseness, prejudice and mass-emotion but 'To enter the middle class, a man has to sacrifice something that is very deep and necessary to him, his natural physical affinity with other men and women.'

56 Cf. *FLC* 33–4 with *JTLJ* 78–9.

57 The Christmas guests at Wragby now not only include Lady Eva but a couple called the Strangeways, the young Harry Winterslow and his much older friend Tommy Dukes. The latter is just beginning to emerge as a spokesman for DHL's own gradually evolving philosophy of 'touch'; yet the role of Dukes, as of all these new characters, is nevertheless at this stage still minor.

58 In all three versions of the novel, Sir Malcolm is a painter and a member of the Royal Academy. This suggests that in creating Connie DHL was thinking of Rosalind Thornycroft (see *TE* 528–9), and several of the early physical descriptions are reminiscent of her. Yet Connie's life-style is aristocratic, like that of Cynthia Asquith (who had also been 'finished' at Dresden), and her behaviour often recalls Frieda. The character is clearly an amalgam, with characteristics borrowed from different women DHL knew.

59 *JTLJ* 85, 109–10. In *FLC* Mrs Bolton had been fifty (p. 91). In the second version DHL makes her forty-five or forty-six (p. 81). Although the shock she expresses at the change in the women of her home town is in the idiom of her character, and very different therefore from DHL's own, the sentiments are similar to those in 'Return to Bestwood': 'The women, though, had changed most. They had got so much cheekier, and commoner. The things they did, and the things they said, you'd never believe. Swear! They'd as leave swear at you as look at you, many of them. Oh, it wasn't like that before the war' (*JTLJ* 110).

60 *JTLJ* 13.

61 For details of Wells's family background, see David C. Smith, *H. G. Wells: Desperately Mortal* (1986), p. 4.

62 *JTLJ* 198, 230–1. See p. 714, n. 84 below.

63 *JTLJ* 365–6, 294–5.

64 *JTLJ* 332, 367.

65 *JTLJ* 369.

66 *Poems* 818. Along with a poem called 'Rainbow', 'The Old Orchard' appeared in *Calendar of Modern Letters*, iv (July 1927), 17–21.

67 *JTLJ* 236, 242.

68 Lady Cynthia's collection was entitled *The Black Cap: New Stories of Murder and Mystery* and published in 1927.

69 *WWRA* 267:12.

70 *WWRA* 254:27–8; 258:5–6; 273:38–274:6.

71 *Sons and Lovers*, p. 448, and *Poems* 101. For 'Spirits Summoned West' see pp. 73–4] above.

72 See *WWRA* xli–xlii.

73 Aldington was the general editor of a series of translations of French memoirs from the eighteenth century. He later described how he asked DHL to write the introduction to Flint's translation of Lauzun but then wrote it himself after 'breakfast-table homilies' convinced him that whatever DHL produced would not be suitable (Tedlock 246). DHL's completed version is more general in tenor than the unfinished one, and it reflects the same disillusionment with politics which Connie and Parkin express in *JTLJ*. Complaining that we can 'only feel things in conventional feeling-patterns', he goes on, 'But at the same time, we know quite well that if all our heads were chopped off, and the working-classes were left to themselves, with a clear field, nothing would have happened, really. Bolshevist Russia, one feels, and feels with bitter regret, is nothing new on the face of the earth . . . So what's the point in a revolution?' (*P* 747, 753).
For the dating of 'Flowery Tuscany' see *SEP* lxv–lxvii.

74 According to Barbara Weekley Barr, DHL had been amused by Anita Loos's 1925 bestseller *Gentlemen Prefer Blondes* (Nehls, iii. 23). Edith Maude Hill had already written the 'Sheik II' to which he refers. Her *The Sheik* (1919) had proved so popular, especially after the film which featured Rudolf Valentino, that in 1925 she published a sequel entitled *Sons of the Sheik*.

75 *Hardy* 211:4–7.

76 There are signs of the re-emergence of DHL's Etruscan interest in 'The Lovely Lady' where Pauline Attenborough has a skull 'like that of some Etruscan woman', and Robert refers to the Etruscan god Tinia (*WWRA* 244:6; 266:14).

77 A letter to Mabel Harrison and the Beveridge sisters, probably written on 22 March and to be published in vol. viii of the letters, allows us to be certain of his date of arrival. It also shows that the visit to Ostia referred to in 'Laura Philippine' (*AA* 18), but also in (vi. 246), took place on his way to, rather than from, Ravello.

Chapter Fifteen: Change of Life

1 Nehls, iii. 143–4.

2 There are several letters from Ravagli in *D. H. Lawrence's Manuscripts*, ed. Squires (1991).

3 *Observer* Colour Supplement, 13 December 1970, p. 20. For Frieda's advice to Barby see Rosie Jackson, *Frieda Lawrence* (1994), p. 77. Barby's reservations about Ravagli are quoted on p. 48 where we learn that Ida Rauh used to call him Frieda's 'ice-cream man'. For evidence that Frieda herself sometimes came to regret his limitations, see *Memoirs* 20–3.

4 See pp. 642–3 above (note 8).

5 *P* 747.

6 The invitation came in a cablegram sent to the Palazzo Cimbrone after DHL and the Brewsters had left. On 3 May, explaining to Brewster why he would not be accepting it, DHL wrote, 'our difficulty is that Frieda wont go near Brett again, and is doubtful of Mabel' (vi. 49).

7 *Fauns and Nymphs* is reproduced in *Paintings*, ed. Levy, facing p. 56. From two

references to it after the Etruscan trip as 'orange-coloured' and 'very orange', it is clear it went through considerable transformation (vi. 133, 196). On 13 August 1928 DHL told Harry Crosby: 'I've got a nice canvas of sun fawn and sun nymphs laughing at the Crucifixion – but I had to paint out the Crucifixion' (vi. 504).

8 There are details of DHL's Uncle George in *EY* 43–4.

9 Brewster 271–8.

10 Earl Brewster's memory was a little different. He recalled driving out to the end of the Sorrento peninsula and 'returning to Sorrento on foot' (p. 120).

11 *AA* 15.

12 DHL's translation was reissued in Jonathan Cape's 'Travellers' Library' (1928). For this reference to the brilliant young Italian, see pp. vi–vii. In an alternative version of the introduction, published in *P*, DHL refers to what had been said to him about Verga in Rome 'the other day' by 'one of the leading literary young Italians' (p. 224). The person referred to seems to have been Lanro de Bosis, a playwright and translator (vi. 40 n.3).

13 From the station at Palo, DHL and Brewster walked the five or so miles to Cerveteri because there was no bus due. The bus got them back to Palo around five o'clock, but they then walked to the sea-shore and back, more than two miles away, while waiting for the train to Cività Vecchia (*SEP* 10:26–7; 25:10).

14 DHL's six sketches were first published in 1932 under the title *Etruscan Places*. His MS, and several references in his letters, indicate that his own preference had been for *Sketches of Etruscan Places*. The MS also shows that he usually preferred to write Etruscan with a small 'e' (*SEP* xlviii).

15 *SEP* 44:20; 45:9–10.

16 *SEP* 17:22–3. Brewster would have been made aware of the different types of phallic stones during his recent trip to India.

17 *SEP* 53:36–40; 54:1–6, 11–14.

18 *SEP* 35:40; 36:1–3; 126–7. For a discussion of this picture which broadly supports DHL's tentative suggestion that its figures are symbolic, see Jacques Heurgon, *La vie quotidienne des Etrusques* (Paris, 1961), pp. 264–9.

19 *SEP* 32:40–1; 36:4–6, 12–13.

20 *The Letters of Virginia Woolf: 'A Change of Perspective'*, ed. Nigel Nicolson (1977), iii, p. 361. Because Brewster also had a shock of white hair, Woolf thought the person sitting next to DHL on the platform bench was Norman Douglas.

21 *SEP* 30:13–18.

22 *SEP* 31:31–40; 32:8, 9–10.

23 *SEP* 158:38–40; 159:1–7.

24 *SEP* 166:22–8.

25 *SEP* 171:39 – 172:7. A description of a visit to this prison in *Adventures of a Bookseller* suggests that DHL picked up his information about the governor's misfortunes from Orioli.

26 For 'The Florence Museum' and convincing speculations about its date of composition, see *SEP* xxxviii and 175–9.

27 *SEP* 33:4–10.

28 Mabel's poem was entitled 'Change' and published in Idella Purnell's *Palms*, ii (1923).

DHL's 'Change of Life', first published in *'Fire' and Other Poems* (San Francisco, 1940), is divided into seven sections. The first three of them take over almost verbatim many of Mabel's lines, but in the fifth he describes how 'Tall virgins of the afterwards / Who have been through the fire' come together with 'men of the afterwards' wearing 'The knowing smile of the final virgin in man.' See *Poems* 770 and Rudnick 195–6. The degree of indebtedness to Mabel makes 'Change of Life' a small item to add to DHL's long list of collaborations.

29 Brewster 123.

30 These quotations are from the version of the story published in the *Forum* in February 1928 and reprinted in *The Escaped Cock*, edited and with a commentary by Gerald M. Lacy (Los Angeles, 1973), pp. 106–7.

31 *Escaped Cock*, ed. Lacy, p. 16.

32 When DHL finally plucked up courage to write to Gertie Cooper on 19 May, he said that for her to be on the road to recovery after 'all those operations' was 'a miracle: *almost* a resurrection' (vi. 63 – my italics).

33 Mabel Harrison and the Beveridge sisters had taken La Massa from the end of February but by 20 April Mary Beveridge had already 'gone back to Scotland' (vi. 39).

34 *SP* 100, 254–5.

35 As the reference to Mary Ellen indicates, not 'There was I, Waiting at the Church' but the less familiar song whose exact words Barbara Weekley Barr can still recall:

> Mary Ellen at the church turned up
> Her Ma turned up and her Pa turned up
> Her sister Gert and her rich uncle Bert
> And the parson in his long white shirt turned up.
> But no bridegroom with the ring turned up
> But a telegraph boy with his nose turned up
> Brought a telegram which said
> That he didn't want to wed
> And they'd find him in the river with his toes turned up.

On the way home from the Villa Poggi, DHL apparently said that he thought Barby's rendition 'quite good'.

36 Nehls, iii. 139.

37 'Making Love to Music' was published for the first time in *P* 160–6. Cf. with the comments on the Etruscan dancers, *SEP* 50:1–20.

38 *Forum* (May 1928), 794. DHL was sent a selection of the complaining letters and on 17 April 1928 told a member of the *Forum*'s editorial staff that he was glad to have seen them: 'Now I know I've committed the unpardonable sin, I feel all right. I was always so afraid I might be saved: like ten dollars in the bank. No more fear of that!' But a week later he complained to a friend that he had never seen 'such a batch of vituperative condemnation' (vi. 370, 378).

39 Because 'None of That!' deals with Mexican matters, Ross Parmenter has conjectured that it was written in Oaxaca. But the initial setting is Venice, where the author meets the Mexican who narrates the story and, in the 1920s at least, DHL seems to have sent stories off to his agent as soon as they were written (Parmenter 223).

40 *WWRA* 215:5, 8, 14; 217:38. It may be because Ethel Cane is described as blond that some commentators have followed Brett's casual suggestion in her memoir that she was modelled on Dora Carrington (Brett 28). DHL had met Carrington again in March 1924 (see pp. 171–2 above), but he hardly knew her well and nearly everything else except hair colour recalls Mabel. That seems to have been changed by DHL in a typically half-hearted attempt to cover his tracks – much as he has the Mexican narrator of 'None of That!' say that Ethel Cane did not come from Boston or New York 'but somewhere else, Omaha or something' (*WWRA* 215:3–4).

In 'The Wilful Woman' DHL had described the clash between the 'child-like' appearance of Mabel ('like an obstinate girl of fourteen') and her 'thick, dark brows like curved horns over the naïve-looking face' (*SMOS* 199:22–9). In 'None of That!' there is a similar clash between Ethel's 'childish' look, her 'warm and naïve and false-innocent' eyes, and the way 'her blond eyebrows gathered together above her nose, in a diabolic manner'. Mabel's memoirs suggest that 'none of that' was one of her characteristic expressions, but the most obvious links between her and Ethel Cane are psychological. Ethel, for example, is described as always needing to meet any man she heard of who had a 'dramatic sense of power'; and also as an extraordinary person who could nevertheless 'only work through individuals, through others' (*WWRA* 215:7, 9, 11–12; 216:14–15).

41 *WWRA* 227:33, 36.

42 *WWRA* 215:19, 21–2, 24–5.

43 In *D. H. Lawrence: A Calendar of his Works*, Sagar says that Nancy Pearn returned the original MS of this story to DHL on 10 June (p. 163). When DHL was thinking which MSS to sell to Harry Crosby almost a year later and sent several to be bound (see pp. 406–7 above), 'Things' and 'None of That!' were closely enough associated in his mind for him to put them both on the same line in the list he drew up in the 'Memorandum Book' now at NWU. All the other items occupy a line of their own (vi. 348 n.5).

44 *The Lovely Lady* (1932), pp. 176–7.

45 It is Keith Cushman in 'The Serious Comedy of "Things"', *Etudes Lawrenciennes* vi (1991), who points out that 'even the detail of the Melvilles' hospital work in Italy during World War I conforms to the Brewsters' experience' (pp. 89–90).

46 The review of *Solitaria* is in *P* 367–71. It was first published in the last number of the *Calendar of Modern Letters* (July 1927). DHL would have liked to have found it a more commercially useful home but all attempts to place it elsewhere failed. The periodical whose refusal excited DHL's sympathy in his letter to Kot on 13 June was probably the *Nation* (vi. 30, 41, 52, 81, 84).

47 *P* 372–6.

48 From a letter to be published in vol. viii of the Cambridge edition of DHL's *Letters*.

49 Both reviews are reprinted in Sagar's *A D. H. Lawrence Handbook*, pp. 296–7.

50 'Flowery Tuscany III', *SEP* 233:37–40.

51 The Sitwells were equally pleased. Osbert remembered that DHL was 'extremely courteous' and that he and Edith spent 'two extremely delightful hours'. He was surprised at what 'a fragile and goatish saint [DHL] was: a Pan and a Messiah', but he

thought the paintings on the walls 'crudely hideous and without any merit save that he painted them' (Nehls, iii. 142–3).

52 *TE* 640, 668, 670.

53 *Letters of Aldous Huxley*, ed. Grover Smith, p. 275.

54 For the equivalent but more hostile references to Maugham, see p. 205 above. In *LCL*, DHL writes of Clifford, 'When he was alone, he tap-tap-tapped on a typewriter, to infinity. But when he was not "working", and she was there, he talked' (p. 83:23–5). Perhaps it was because his father was a miner that DHL had difficulty in regarding writing as proper work. Yet he could on occasions refer to all the hard (writing) work he himself had done in the past.

55 Frieda 208.

56 *Letters of Aldous Huxley*, ed. Grover Smith, p. 288.

57 Frieda 209.

58 *The Escaped Cock*, ed. Lacy, pp. 112–13.

59 The burden of DHL's criticism of *Jane Eyre* is that Mr Rochester, and in particular his 'sex passion', can only be accepted by the heroine after he has been 'burned, blinded, disfigured, and reduced to helpless dependence' (*P* 176–7). In 1919 DHL had been made bitterly angry by what seemed to him the brutality of Frieda's nursing (*TE* 498), and he was later to complain of it to Mabel Luhan (*LT* 61); but during the 1920s his response to her refusal to play the ministering angel was in general positive.

60 It was probably in the spring or summer of 1927 that DHL wrote an interesting opening to a story about a man who was 'through with the world'. This begins by mocking the hermit impulse, but after the protagonist has walked the 'four long miles . . . down the steep side of the mountain' to the local village and later been obliged to make a visit to the city, it begins to endorse the hermit's sense of the 'pollution of people'. This radical ambivalence may be one reason why the story was never finished. What there is of it was published by John R. Elliott Jr in *Essays in Criticism*, xiv (July 1959), 213–21. Tedlock describes the pages on which the MS is written as taken from a notebook 'like those used for the third version of [*Lady Chatterley's Lover*]' and says that it 'probably once contained text for the Etruscan studies' (p. 62). On at least two occasions after his return from his Etruscan trip, DHL talked of wanting to become a hermit (vi. 26, 28).

61 *P* 378. The passage from which this sentence comes might be compared with *somewhat* similar thoughts in Jacques Lacan, 'Le stade du miroir comme formation de la fonction du Je', *Ecrits I* (Paris, 1957), 89–97. Burrow derives the formation of a radically false self from the moment when the child loses its sense of 'unitary consciousness' with the mother; but he has very little to say on how the move to self-consciousness could be managed better, nor on why the recovery of a unitary consciousness would not be regressive. Yet in spite of the exceptional turgidity of his style (commented on by DHL in his review), he is effective in denouncing the falsity of most social contacts. DHL was attracted partly because he recognised the similarity between Burrow's 'images' and his own 'ideals'. In his review, he stresses even more than *The Social Basis of Consciousness* might seem to warrant, the shortcomings of Freudian analysis with its insistence on always applying the 'fixed motive of the incest-complex'; but he is

excellent in making the reader see the force of Burrow's critique of social life. He is right to call the conclusions which lie behind the critique 'almost naïve in their startled emotion'; wrong, perhaps, not to have insisted more on how vague and evasive Burrow is at the points where he needed to be most constructive. There are details of Burrow's career in *A Search for Man's Sanity: The Selected Letters of Trigant Burrow* (New York, 1958).

Chapter Sixteen: *Lady Chatterley's Lover*

1 Nehls, iii. 162.

2 *TE* 70–9, 90–4.

3 Secker had first broached the idea of a *Collected Poems* as long ago as 1919 (iii. 379).

4 Elizabeth Mayer, 'An Afternoon with D. H. Lawrence', *A D. H. Lawrence Miscellany*, ed. Moore, pp. 140–1. Elizabeth Mayer's close friendship with Auden, after she had emigrated to the United States, is described by Humphrey Carpenter, *W. H. Auden* (1981), pp. 275ff.

5 Barby was staying in Cologne with the professor who had first introduced her mother to Ernest Weekley (Nehls, iii. 162).

6 Carossa was seven years older than DHL and had served as a medical officer during the war. He was best known at this time as the author of *Rumänisches Tagebuch* (1924), a volume of war reminiscences from the Romanian campaign (*Oxford Companion to German Literature*, p. 127).

7 *Confessions of a European Intellectual* (New York, 1946), p. 288.

8 'An Afternoon with D. H. Lawrence', p. 141.

9 *P* 244–5.

10 *P* 247. When *'Cavalleria rusticana' and Other Stories* appeared in 1928, DHL's introduction was called a 'Translator's Preface'. It is reprinted in *P* 240–54.

11 *P II* 281–2. There is evidence that the version of this introduction printed in *P* (223–31) must have come first – and can therefore be regarded as a first draft – in its claim on p. 223 that Verga 'was born about 1850, and died, I believe, at the beginning of 1921'. The first sentence of the published introduction informs the reader – accurately – that Verga 'was born in the year 1840, and he died at the beginning of 1922'. In a letter to Christine Hughes on 25 April, DHL complains about the difficulty of finding material on Verga: 'I scour Florence, but Verga had better have been a Hottentot, the Italians would know more about him' (vi. 40). Between this remark and DHL's reporting to Jonathan Cape on 9 May that he had sent the introduction off to Curtis Brown (vi. 53), it is likely that he found the material he was looking for and re-wrote it.

12 For the review of Mann's *Death in Venice*, see *P* 308–13.

13 *P* 248.

14 *P* 249–50.

15 *P* 250.

16 Linda Bryder, *Below the Magic Mountain: A Social History of Tuberculosis in 20th Century Britain* (Oxford, 1988), pp. 69, 178.

17 Courage is not necessarily an attribute which manifests itself uniformly (what attributes

do?). It would certainly be possible to argue that, in refusing the doctor's advice and persistently misdescribing his own real situation, Lawrence lacked courage: was being cowardly. On 27 August, Gertler had told Koteliansky: 'I will write again to Lawrence as soon as I get a new address from him . . . When I write I will tell him what to do, but it is not much use unless he realises that he has lung trouble and not call it, or try to pretend, that it is something else' (Koteliansky Papers. BL). By October, DHL had conceded momentarily that there was something amiss with his lungs, but he refused to acknowledge openly that he was tubercular, which is what Gertler, who has also taken refuge in a euphemism ('lung trouble'), is insisting that he should do. Different readers will judge his behaviour differently; but there may be some need here of the obvious reminder that DHL was an intensely imaginative man who spent most of his life wholly absorbed in imaginary scenarios. When he tells one of his sisters that allowing himself to think too much about Gertie's plight would make him ill (vi. 60), he needs to be taken literally. One sign of his imaginative nature was that he was constantly afflicted with vivid dreams. To Gertie herself he had confessed on 19 May that he had not written because 'I was afraid of all those operations'; but he had also told her that recently he had often dreamed of her sister Frances whose death from tuberculosis he had witnessed in 1918 (vi. 63). It is likely enough that those dreams were as disturbing as those DHL describes in *Kangaroo*.

18 There is an an excellent account of Stevens in F. B. Smith, *The Retreat of Tuberculosis: 1850–1950* (1988), pp. 155–62.

19 In an unpublished letter to Edward McDonald, dated 8 May, Douglas says that he had 'met D. H. Lawrence the other day' (UT).

20 *Life for Life's Sake*, pp. 341–2. Aldington was not an eye-witness but is likely to have had the scene described to him by Orioli, or Frieda (who was also present). See Aldington, *Pinorman*, p. 181.

21 *Memoirs of Maurice Magnus*, ed. Cushman, p. 120.

22 There was a succession of such boys. This one was called Luciano and had been the cause of Douglas having to leave Florence hurriedly in March. For details see Holloway, *Norman Douglas*, pp. 346–59. At this point Douglas had recently bought a flat on the top floor of a building on the Lungarno delle Grazie. Orioli was shortly to move his shop from the Lungarno Corsini to the bottom floor of this same building.

23 The details are from Holloway who quotes Douglas's comic remark to Lytton Strachey that when he did slip into Florence for business, it was 'thickly veiled and wearing blue glasses and a carroty beard' (*Norman Douglas*, p. 335). In this situation, Orioli must have been invaluable (as he later proved invaluable to DHL) in helping to oversee the printing process.

24 The anti-semitic remarks that litter DHL's correspondence are usually more obviously offensive than this. I call them 'casual' in contradistinction to those in the works of writers such as Pound whose anti-semitism is both pondered and political. What DHL says about Jews is often similar to the rapid generalisations which he was inclined to use in his characterisation of other groups: the French, Celts, Indians, etc. One important difference is that, in the case of the Jews, his own impressions are mingled with a number of ugly, rooted prejudices which seem to have been characteristic of Frieda's background. For an excellent treatment of anti-semitism in DHL see Judith

Ruderman, 'D. H. Lawrence and the "Jewish Problem": Reflections on a Self-Confessed "Hebrophobe" ', *DHLR*, xxiii (Summer/Fall 1991), 99–109.

25 *P* 817. 'A Dream of Life' was published in *P* as '[Autobiographical Fragment]'. Keith Sagar was the first to give this unfinished piece the more defining title which I have used.

26 In *The White Peacock*, ed. Andrew Robertson (Cambridge, 1983), the narrator discovers the dead body of the gamekeeper Annable in a local quarry (pp. 152–4).

27 *P* 834. In the transformed Eastwood the Congregational Chapel has clearly been replaced by a building which reflects DHL's contemporary interest in phallus worship.

28 There is no proof that the manuscript DHL is referring to in his letter to Kot is 'A Dream of Life' but it seems highly probable. The date of October 1927 in the text is confirmed by the fact that it appears to have been written on notebook leaves which are 'identical with those of insertion in first volume of third version of *Lady Chatterley's Lover*' (Tedlock 64). See note 68 below.

29 *Throwing Back the Apple* and *Jaguar Leaping at a Man* are reproduced in *Paintings*, ed. Levy, pp. 99, 73. DHL took the jaguar painting with him to Les Diablerets in January 1928 and accidentally left it in his chalet. Telling Juliette Huxley on 8 March that she could either post it to him from London or keep it until he got there, he said that it was '*not* good, *not* finished', that he did not like it, and that it was a 'Miserable thing!' (vi. 313).

30 My quotations are from the version of the story which appeared in the posthumous collection *The Lovely Lady* (1932), pp. 55–6. A different version had already appeared in 1929 as number 7 of 'Woburn Books', a series of limited editions published by Elkin Mathews and Marrot. This was after DHL had spent 'a good hour' lengthening some of the exchanges (vii. 23), allowing the 'book' – 530 signed and numbered copies of which were printed – to stretch to 32 pages. None of his alterations affect the points being made here.

31 Britton 240. Britton's notion of 'Rawdon's Roof' as an act of revenge against the Campbells is part of a general thesis that, after his return from Germany, DHL was suffering from an 'irrational instability', 'diminished judgement' and 'paranoia' (p. 232). This explains why the third version of *Lady Chatterley's Lover* should be, in his view, so much worse than its predecessors. He cites as evidence for this opinion the letters which DHL wrote to the Dobrées and Campbells about proposed visits to Egypt and Ireland (vi. 170, 171, 194–5, 205, 219–20, 282–4, 299–300, 300, 334–5, 337–8), and a letter to Kot complaining that Dobrée had lacked courtesy in not following up his warm invitation to Cairo with a letter explaining why it had needed to be withdrawn (vi. 233–4). The most I can find in any of these is an occasional touch of irritation. On the whole they seem to me charming letters which blankly contradict the terms Britton uses about the DHL of this period. But this is a case where every reader can easily judge for her or himself.

32 *Poems* 28.

33 T. S. Eliot, 'Tradition and the Individual Talent', *Selected Essays* (1951), p. 18. DHL nowhere comments on this precise formulation but, writing to Murry in September 1923, he says, 'This classiosity is bunkum, but still more, *cowardice*' (iv. 500). The context for this remark is Murry's response in the *Adelphi* to attacks on him for his

'Romanticism' in Eliot's *Criterion*. In denouncing the *Criterion*'s championing of 'classical' values DHL can also be taken as attacking the closely associated notions of impersonality.

In *Women in Love* Ursula attacks Loerke's contention that his statuette of a naked, pubescent girl on a massive stallion has no relation to the everyday world with: 'The horse is a picture of your own stock stupid brutality, and the girl was the girl you loved and tortured and then ignored' (p. 432:15–17). DHL deliberately conceived Ursula as naïve and his own intellectual sophistication was immeasurably greater, but his sympathies on this issue were always essentially the same as hers.

34 *Poems* 28.

35 See *P* 252 where the longer of the two introductions can be found (pp. 251–4). Secker's original idea had been to ask Robert Bridges to write an introduction but he must have declined (vi. 395).

36 *W. H. Auden* (1981), p. 118. The letter is quoted in full in Peter Stansky and William Abrahams, *Journey to the Frontier: Julien Bell and John Cornford: Their Lives and the 1930s* (1966), pp. 173–4.

37 *Love Poems and Others* (1913), pp. iii, xxx, and *Poems* 120, 97.

38 *Love Poems and Others*, p. xxxi, and *Poems* 98.

39 *Poems* 84.

40 Many of the changes in *Amores*, DHL's second collection, are equally startling. As Keith Sagar writes in the introduction to the revised edition of a selection of DHL's poetry (Harmondsworth, 1986), 'How ridiculous . . . to suppose that the young man of twenty-two, out of his actual virginity, could have written the version of "Virgin Youth" which appears in *Collected Poems*. It is a poem by the author of *Lady Chatterley's Lover*.' Justifying his decision to print his selection of the early poems as they first appeared in *Love Poems, Amores, New Poems* and *Bay* (the changes to the later collections are minor), Sagar goes on: 'It seems to me much more important that we should have what the young man actually wrote at twenty-two than what Lawrence at forty-two (a much better poet, but a different man with a different demon), thought he should have written' (p. 12).

41 Acton, who had been brought up in the Florence area where his parents had a villa, was still at Oxford. Four years younger than DHL, Scott-Moncrieff is usually associated with Rome (where he died in 1930); but, in *Florence: A Literary Companion* (1991), Francis King describes him as 'one of the many *stranieri inverti* – as the Florentines called them – who could be found in Florence during the wars' (p. 74). When DHL saw Turner on 17 November (vi. 217) he might also have seen Scott-Moncrieff and Acton again. In this context, the paradoxical common feature of all these friends, as well as of Norman Douglas and Orioli of course, was that they were homosexual. This means that one could describe whatever encouragement they gave to DHL in his new plans for publishing *Lady Chatterley's Lover* privately as either equivocal or disinterested. Shortly after DHL's death, Collingwood Gee, another member of the expatriate community in Florence who had been depicted by DHL in *Aaron's Rod* as 'little Mee', and who was once described by Compton Mackenzie as the most completely homosexual man he had ever met, painted DHL offering a reading of *Lady Chatterley's Lover* to Orioli, Turner and Douglas. It is difficult to know whether to attribute the

expression of polite but bored attention on the faces of the listeners in this picture to technical ineptitude or a penetrating realism. In their book on DHL in Thames and Hudson's 'Literary Lives' series (1966), Harry T. Moore and Warren Roberts describe Gee's picture as having been 'painted from memory' in 1933. For Mackenzie's remark see Octave 2 of *My Life and Times* (1963), p. 253.

42 *Letters of Aldous Huxley*, ed. Grover Smith, pp. xxxi–xxxii.

43 See Holloway, *Norman Douglas*, p. 356.

44 DHL's previous relations with Kouyoumdjian are described in *TE* 289–99.

45 DHL's reflections on Arlen are in a memorandum book, now at NWU, which was chiefly used by him to record orders for *Lady Chatterley's Lover* as they came in, calculate how much money he had received, and work out both his net profit (the bill from the printer is included) and Orioli's 10 per cent share. At the beginning, he lists photographs he has posted to London to accompany his Etruscan essays and later there is a list of the paintings that have been sent off to Dorothy Warren. Otherwise there is an occasional note of receiving proofs or sending MSS to Orioli to be bound, but nothing else like his record of Arlen's visit and reflections on it.

46 DHL refers to *The Green Hat* in 'Accumulated Mail' (*P* 803) and at more length in 'The Novel': 'And there is the heroine who is always "pure", usually, nowadays, on the muck-heap! Like the Green Hatted Woman. She is all the time at the feet of Jesus, though her behaviour there may be misleading' (*Hardy* 182:9–12).

47 Kouyoumdjian was not Jewish. For Lady Ottoline's remark see (ii. 473 n.2); and for Rebecca West's, Morgan, *Somerset Maugham*, p. 317. In his book on Arlen in Twayne's 'English Authors Series' (Boston, 1975), Harry Keyishian says that American sales of *The Green Hat* reached 250,000 and that Arlen, 'quotable in himself and the cause of good quotations in others', liked West's remark so much that he would often use it himself (pp. 68, 69).

48 In an unpublished letter to H. M. Tomlinson dated 27 November, Douglas writes, 'D. H. Lawrence is here. Likewise Michael Arlen. We are *lunching* together on Tuesday. What ho! Both of them are pretty damned ill' (UT).

49 Michael Squires has given a detailed account of the chronology of composition in his introduction to the Cambridge edition of *Lady Chatterley's Lover* (pp. xx–xxiv). I have supplemented this with information from the introduction to the forthcoming Cambridge edition of the novel's first two versions, ed. Dieter Mehl and Christa Jansohn.

50 *LCL* 23:26–8.

51 *LCL* 291:7–19.

52 In September 1929 Edward Titus, the American bookshop owner who published a cheap edition of *Lady Chatterley's Lover* in Paris, wrote a letter to DHL which includes: 'Mike [i.e. Arlen] is a tremendous admirer of you and feels greatly elated at having served as one of the characters in Lady Chatterley. He keeps you on a pedestal and he seemed very happy when I told him I would mention him to you when next writing' (vii. 475–6 n.6).

53 *LCL* 71:15.

54 *LCL* 54:9–10.

55 *LCL* 7:33–2.

56 *LCL* 202:8–11, 14–15, 16–21.

57 *JTLJ* 320–5. Parkin averts his face from Connie when he first sees her because he has lost a tooth in the fight. DHL himself had five false teeth as we learn from a letter to Brett, wondering whether she has taken the right decision in having all hers out (vi. 292–3).

58 *LCL* 283:38–9.

59 *LCL* 300:37–40; 301:17, 19–20; 302:8–9.

60 For Hammond, a 'tall thin' writer 'much more closely connected with a typewriter' than with his wife and children, and Charlie May, 'an Irishman, who wrote scientifically about stars', see *LCL* 31:25–6; 32:4–5.

61 *LCL* 223:7–13.

62 An example of a book of this period in which the descriptions of sexual encounters are repetitive would be *My Life and Loves* (1925) by Frank Harris. DHL had glanced at this in Florence, almost certainly in Orioli's bookshop. He thought the way Harris told some things 'unpleasant and humiliating – but probably no more so than a dose of castor oil: and perhaps effective in the same way. It's only furtive things that should be suppressed' (v. 533). He and Harris shared a commitment to openness and he was very much on the side of the author when attempts were made in Paris to suppress *My Life and Loves*. It is possible that Harris's free use of words like 'cunt' in his autobiography had some influence on the evolution of *LCL*.

63 *FLC* 10.

64 *Sons and Lovers*, p. 64:40. Compare also Frieda's reference to this incident in the letters (i. 531).

65 DHL described genuine tragedy as a 'great kick at misery' in a letter about Arnold Bennett's *Anna of the Five Towns* (i. 459).

66 Maria Huxley was a particularly intimate friend of Costanza Petterich. DHL would meet her and her husband Eckart Petterich again in Forte dei Marrni in 1929 (vii. 346).

67 In his 20 December letter, DHL tells Nellie Morrison that he would be willing to have another look at her 'story' (the inverted commas are his), with the alterations he had suggested, and asks if it was the same one that came out in 'that Scotch paper' (vi. 245). Neither the story nor the paper have been identified.

To say that Nellie Morrison had a young Italian lover may be doing her less (or more) justice than she deserves; but when she is mentioned in the letters it is usually together with a certain 'Gino' with whom she certainly travelled to London in the summer of 1926 (v. 525). In May 1927 DHL complains that she served up Gino rather as the Prince of Wales is supposed to have served up naked, on a 'huge silver platter', Cora Pearl, a famous courtesan (vi. 61).

68 The MS of the third version of *Lady Chatterley's Lover* consists of two bound volumes but the first of these begins with an insertion of the pages which had been given to Nellie Morrison and which were taken from another notebook – the same one in which 'A Dream of Life' had probably been written (Tedlock 24–7).

69 *Mango Tree* can be found in *Paintings*, ed. Levy, p. 98. In his *Calendar* of DHL's works, Keith Sagar includes this water-colour in his entries for December 1927 (p. 167), on the evidence of a letter to the Huxleys on 2 April 1928 in which DHL says they already know it (vi. 353). He concludes from this that they must have seen it when they were

with the Lawrences at Christmas. Yet because we know DHL took *Jaguar Leaping at a Man* to Les Diablerets, he may have taken this picture with him also, or even painted it while he was there. See note 29 above.

70 *P* 265.

71 *P* 263–6. This translation of *La madre* was by Mary Steegmann and published under the title *The Woman and the Priest*.

Chapter Seventeen: Last Days at the Villa Mirenda

1 Julian Huxley, *Memories* (1970), p. 156.

2 Juliette Huxley, *Leaves of the Tulip Tree: Autobiography* (1986), pp. 115, 118.

3 *The Science of Life* came out in 1929. It was a follow-up to Wells's *Outline of History* fulfilling the need (he claims in the introduction) for 'the same clearing up and simplifying of the science of life' which that book had given to 'the story of the past'.

For Julian Huxley's response to DHL, see *Memories* (1970), p. 160. His discussions with DHL about 'genetic improvement' make their impact on *Point Counter Point* where the DHL character (Rampion) has made drawings of two outlines of history: his own and that of H. G. Wells. The latter begins with very small monkeys and ends with very large depictions of Wells and the industrialist Sir Alfred Mond. In Rampion's version, the moderns are abortions and in the future little more than heads. DHL's views on these matters would have been partly formed, before he discussed 'genetic improvement' with the Huxley brothers, by having to review the first volume of Wells's *World of William Clissold*.

4 In DHL's re-written version, Philip falls ill once he and Katherine are in Baden-Baden and takes to his bed. This allows his wife to walk alone in the forest where one day Alan appears to her in a kilt and a khaki tunic. Katherine yields to him in 'a complete yielding she had never known before. And among the rocks he made love to her, and took her in the silent passion of a husband, took a complete possession of her.' When the next day she wants to go to meet Alan again, Philip protests he is too ill to be left alone and pleads with her to stay with him. Towards midnight, he begs Katherine to hold him but, as she pushes her arms under his shoulders, Alan enters the room and loosens Philip's hands from around Katherine's neck. Whereupon Philip dies, on his face 'a sickly grin of a thief caught in the very act', and Alan draws his wife to the other bed 'in the silent passion of a husband come back from a very long journey'. For significant differences between this ending and the original magazine version, see pp. 161–3 above.

5 Yvonne Franchetti's husband was both a baron and a concert pianist. Maria Huxley had brought the Franchettis to the Villa Mirenda in June but DHL did not find them sympathetic: 'Maria Huxley came yesterday, with the Franchettis. He is a Jew, Barone Luigi – and rich as Croesus. He plays the piano very well, and is quite nice – but I agree entirely – I have absolutely no basic sympathy with people of "assured incomes". All words become a lie, in their mouth, and in their ears also. I *loathe* rich people' (vi. 81).

In the first version of his poem thanking Maria Huxley for helping to type *LCL*, published in a radically different form as 'To Clarinda' (*Poems* 550–1), DHL refers to her as a 'clever / rascal with a wicked tongue' (E302d).

6 *Leaves of the Tulip Tree*, p. 122.

7 Under pressure from his friends DHL first of all demoted 'John Thomas and Lady Jane' to a subtitle and only then, under further pressure, eliminated it altogether. See Squires, *The Creation of 'Lady Chatterley's Lover'*, p. 14.

8 For DHL's contacts with Juliette Baillot, see *TE* 290.

9 The *Colour Dictionary of Herbs and Herbalism*, ed. Malcolm Stuart (1979), describes coltsfoot as 'still one of the most important herbal remedies for the treatment of coughs' (p. 147).

10 A very likely phrase but in a letter to Juliette on 27 March, DHL refers to Martin Secker as an 'expurgated edition of a man: like so many others' (vi. 344).

11 *Leaves of the Tulip Tree*, p. 125.

12 For Gardiner's account of his visit, see Nehls, iii. 178–83.

13 Bynner 331–5.

14 *Adventures of a Bookseller*, p. 233. Stefania Michelucci, who has been able to interview surviving members of the Salvestrini family, reports them as saying, 'All the peasants of the Villa Mirenda were fascinated by Lawrence and Frieda, who were very generous and would pay for any little service.'

15 Aldington has an effective attack on Orioli's remarks in his book about Orioli, Douglas and Charles Prentice, *Pinorman* pp. 194–8. In the course of it, he suggests that if Douglas's hostility to DHL grew rather than diminished with the passage of time, it was because 'he found that Lawrence's writings, far from disappearing as he expected, stood much higher in general esteem than his own' (p. 182). For evidence that Orioli's English would have needed correction see chapter 13, n.22 above.

16 The Tipographia Giuntina was in the via del Sole which runs off the Piazza Santa Maria Novella and is only five minutes walk from the Lungarno Corsini where Orioli had his shop. It was thus convenient for Orioli to keep an eye on things.

17 Holloway, *Norman Douglas*, p. 356; Squires, *The Creation of 'Lady Chatterley's Lover'*, pp. 13, 11.

18 The Knopfs responded much more favourably than Secker, or Jonathan Cape (vi. 343, 352) – one of the other English publishers Curtis Brown approached – and Blanche Knopf told DHL that they hoped to 'get [the novel] into shape to offer to the public'; but by this time he doubted whether they would be able to do that (vi. 374).

19 DHL had initially estimated the production costs at around £250. Apart from the cost of postage, the final bill for printing and binding came to only £162 (Worthen, *A Literary Life*, pp. 147–8).

20 The $20 piece had been designed in 1907 by Augustus Saint-Gaudens. For this and other information I am grateful to Richard Doty, Curator of Numismatics at the Smithsonian Institute, Washington.

21 Caresse Crosby, *The Passionate Years* (1955), pp. 227–30. It emerges from Harry Crosby's diary, first published by his Black Sun Press in 1929, that he sent the first present of gold to DHL on 29 March and that 'Bill' Sykes did not appear in the rue de Lille with his consignment before 20 June (*Shadows of the Sun: The Diaries of Harry Crosby*, ed. Edward Germain (Santa Barbara, 1977), pp. 184–5, 193).

For further information concerning DHL's relations with the Crosbys, see Geoffrey Wolff, *Black Sun: The Brief Transit and Violent Eclipse of Harry Crosby* (New York, 1976), pp. 194–205, and Edward Weekes, *My Green Age* (Boston, 1973), pp. 243–4. These books assume that Crosby's initial request was for one manuscript ('Sun') which could be published by the private press he and Caresse had recently established. But his first exchanges with DHL suggest that he simply wanted to buy manuscripts (an impression confirmed by their subsequent correspondence).

22 *WWRA* xxxi. DHL had forgotten that, during his last visit to England, he had sent the MS of 'Sun' to Milly Beveridge 'to see if you recognise the garden at Fontana Vecchia, and where you used to sit and sketch, above the Lemon Grove. – Put the MS. in the fire when you've done with it', he added, '– it's no good' (v. 533).

23 Bound together with 'Sun' were the poems 'Eagle in New Mexico', 'Guards', 'Morning Work' and 'Gipsy'. See Carole Ferrier, 'D. H. Lawrence's Poetry, 1920–1928: A Descriptive Bibliography of Manuscripts, Typescripts and Proofs', *DHLR*, xii (Fall 1979), 299. The third part of 'Guards' ('Potency of Man') and the last two stanzas of 'Gipsy' had never been published (vi. 388–9 n.3).

24 In April 1929 DHL reminded Lawrence Pollinger that Crosby's Black Sun Press had produced an edition of 'Sun' 'in its unexpurgated form' (vii. 243).

25 *WWRA* 32:25–6; 38:23. Variants between the two versions of 'Sun' are given on 277–81.

26 The introduction to *Chariot of the Sun* is reprinted in *P* 255–62. The text as it appeared in Crosby's collection has very minor changes throughout but also a re-written ending which is marginally more positive and may well have been altered in proof.

27 There are photographs of the snuff box in UN. In addition to the original inscription (which explains my spelling of Napoleon's family name) there is also: 'for D. H. Lawrence from Harry and Caresse, "the young trees greet the sun". Paris 1928.'

28 Nehls, iii. 62.

29 Five of these six paintings are reproduced in *Paintings*, ed. Levy (pp. 89, 93, 94, 101). The exception is *Dandelions*, now owned by Melissa Partridge.

In his letter to Nehls, Raul Mirenda says that DHL not only painted Piero nude but also 'in the act of leading his oxen to work. To have a model true to life, he made Pini pose beside his oxen, for which he had obtained two fine red muzzles, against the background of a farm threshing floor' (p. 61). Pietro degli Innocenti's son remembered his father saying that DHL painted him in the fields, and Giulia Pini reports that she used to send Pietro to pose for DHL in the evenings; but no-one can confirm Raul Mirenda's memory of Pietro posing nude. (Information from Stefania Michelucci.)

30 Margaret Gardiner does not refer to DHL's visitors by name (she says he called them 'the Virgins'), and she assumed that they were *resident* in Florence. The letters show that on the same day Millicent and Mary Beveridge were due to arrive in Florence, DHL was expecting Nellie Morrison and another unmarried friend, Muriel Moller, to tea (vi. 364). They were Florence residents but Nellie Morrison's relationship with her 'Gino' hardly suggests she would qualify as a virgin, and Margaret Gardiner specifically describes the visitors as sisters.

31 Margaret Gardiner's account first appeared in Nehls, iii. 203–8, and then in her own *A*

Scatter of Memories (1988). Milly Beveridge's feelings about the paintings can be found in an unpublished letter, probably addressed to Catherine Carswell, now in OkTU. She says that she and her sister made it clear to DHL that they loathed them and also that they detested *LCL*. What she admits to not having told him is that they burnt one copy of his novel and gave the other away. Visitors to their house in Inverness-shire in the 1980s were still being shown the fireplace where the burning took place. See Margaret Needham, 'D. H. Lawrence in Scotland', p. 15.

32 *SEP* 123:39–124:3.

33 *The Rape of the Sabine Women, Close-Up* and *Family on a Verandah* can be consulted in *Paintings*, ed. Levy (pp. 64, 48 and 92). In addition to all the pictures mentioned in this section, DHL also continued to work on *The Finding of Moses* and might have painted 'Cigarette', all traces of which have disappeared (vi. 384, 381).

34 For these details, see Enid Hopkin Hilton, *More Than One Life: A Nottinghamshire Childhood with D. H. Lawrence* (Stroud, 1993), pp. 47, 53, 57–8. Enid Hilton was well into her nineties when these memoirs were published and they are full of misremembering. She suggests, for example, that DHL asked her to smuggle into England a few copies of *Lady Chatterley's Lover* and gives an entertaining account of how she did so in her knickers. But no copies of the novel were available before she left the Villa Mirenda. If she did indulge in some smuggling it would have been later in the year when she was on the Continent once again. On 21 October DHL wrote to regret that he had missed seeing her when she had been in Toulon the week before (vi. 594). It is clear from this letter, and another from the same period, that she had been in Milan where a bookseller had refused to sell her a copy of *Lady Chatterley's Lover* after he had asked to see her passport, and realised from her *permesso di soggiorno* that she would be on her way back to England in three days (vi. 595). Because she had been in Italy, she may have picked up copies of the novel from Orioli and felt, after her experience in Milan, that she had better not declare them at the Customs.

Enid Hilton also says that when she saw DHL in the Villa Mirenda she bought *Fire Dance*. In fact, it was in July 1929 that he asked her which of his paintings she would like to keep for him (vii. 372) and September of the same year that he reported to the Warrens that she had insisted on *buying Fire Dance* for £10 (vii. 490). In this picture the male genitalia are more prominent and central than in any other so that her choice reinforces the impression gained from her dealings with *LCL* that she was certainly no prude.

35 Nehls, iii. 189.

36 Ibid.

37 Alfred Weber was the brother of Max and a distinguished intellectual in his own right. His long relationship with Else Jaffe is described in Martin Green, *The von Richthofen Sisters* (1974).

38 On 20 February Aldous Huxley had written to a friend from Les Diablerets, 'We are thinking perhaps next year of going for 6 months to live on D. H. Lawrence's ranch in New Mexico. It sounds very agreeable there and would be a good place for writing, if in the meantime I collect good store of matter. But all this is dim' (*Letters of Aldous Huxley*, ed. Grover Smith, p. 295).

39 The MS of 'Laura Phillipine' (E194a) has unfortunately been lost.

40 The original version of 'That Women Know Best' has been published by Black Sparrow Press, with a short introduction by Roy Spencer (Santa Rosa, 1994). For a different version of the episode involving DHL's parents, see *Sons and Lovers*, p. 49:10–15.

41 *The Lovely Lady*, pp. 96, 104, 98.

42 Ibid., pp. 94, 100, 108, 113. A modern reader who agrees in general with my characterisation of this story as urbane is likely to find a departure from an otherwise successfully maintained tone where DHL is discussing the strain which her work imposes on Virginia:

> She had to do it it all off her nerves. She hadn't the same sort of fighting power as a man. Where a man can summon his old Adam in him to fight through his work, a woman has to draw on her nerves, and on her nerves alone. For the old Eve in her will have nothing to do with such work. So that mental responsibility, mental concentration, mental slogging wear a woman out terribly, especially if she is head of a department, and not working for somebody. (pp. 105–6)

43 Brewster 281–2.

Chapter Eighteen: The Search for Health

1 Brewster 282.

2 *The Parlour Song Book: A Casquet of Vocal Gems*, ed. Michael Turner (1972), p. 260. (I am grateful to Peter Preston for this reference.)

In what is likely to have been a preliminary attempt at one of his articles for the *Evening News* ('Women are so Cocksure'), DHL describes how his mother used to insist on her children attending the Temperance or 'Band of Hope' meetings. There they heard the story of the 'heroic youth' who had taken the pledge but whose 'cruel comrades' tried to force him to drink some beer. Although he clenched his teeth, one of them was missing so that 'through the narrow gap beer trickled down his gullet' and he died of a broken heart. 'My mother', DHL comments, 'though a woman with a real sense of humour, kept her face straight and stern while we recounted this fearsome episode' (*P* 167).

3 Brewster 282.

4 From 1929, when it was granted independent commune status, it has been called Saint-Nizier-du-Moucherotte. Previously it was dependent on Pariset. Relatively fashionable and bustling in the 1920s and 1930s, much of the village was destroyed during World War II. In DHL's time it was linked to Grenoble by a tramway.

5 Brewster 284–5.

6 *AA* 34, 36.

7 In 'Master in His Own House' DHL claimed that if women were now busy colonising many traditional masculine fields, including politics, it was because men had become indifferent to them; and he contrasted indifference with the insouciance which the over-earnest ladies of his previous piece lacked. That meant not being anxious whereas indifference was the result of 'a certain deadness or numbness' and was nearly always accompanied by 'a pinch of anxiety' (*AA* 61). In 'Dull London' he did little more than explain that a town, which as a young man he had found so exciting, was now depressing for him, chiefly because of its climate.

8 *AA* 156, 160.

9 *The Escaped Cock*, ed. Lacy, p. 35.

10 DHL would have read about the Osiris myth in Frazer's *Golden Bough*, but he had been reminded of it recently in his correspondence with Harry Crosby (vi. 301).

11 *The Escaped Cock*, ed. Lacy, p. 43.

12 Ibid., p. 57.

13 Ibid., pp. 50, 51. 'Spirits Summoned West' (see pp. 73–4 above) is a different case because it is deeply enigmatic and there had been no previous history of hostility.

14 *Letters of Aldous Huxley*, ed. Grover Smith, p. 299.

15 Byron's 'Prisoner of Chillon' was first published in 1816.

16 Brett and Mabel Luhan had been attempting to arrange an exhibition of DHL's paintings in New York for some time. They negotiated first with Elizabeth Hare, a wealthy patroness of the arts whom the Lawrences had visited at her house on Long Island when they were staying with Nina Witt in September 1925, and who had Santa Fe connections (v. 304). She eventually wrote to DHL and seemed willing to make the necessary arrangements (vi. 437). The advantage of Stieglitz's offer was that it came from a well-known artist with an established reputation for mounting important exhibitions.

17 The address was no. 44, which Enid Hilton says she and her husband shared with the historian R. H. Tawney (*More Than One Life*, p. 64). For DHL's time there, see *TE* 419–25.

18 Brewster 286.

19 *AA* 63, 65–6, 52, 56. The second article was entitled 'Ownership'. Neither it nor 'Matriarchy' found a home in the newspapers or journals before their publication in *AA*.

20 The publishing house was called Kra. Its literary director, Philippe Soupault, was a young author associated with the *transition* circle and other avant-garde groups. See Nehls, iii. 702, n.408.

21 *P II* 300–2.

22 DHL's mini-career as journalist could be said to have begun when in June 1926 he received through Richard Aldington a request from *Vogue* for 'little articles' (v. 482). Since he was writing his review of Robert Byron and others two years later, the editors of *Vogue* cannot have much liked the pieces they were offered first. On 20 August 1928, DHL asked Nancy Pearn, 'Did *Vogue* print that review? I'll bet not!' (vi. 516).

23 *P* 383–7.

24 *AA* 75–6. This article was published in *Forum* in January 1929. The likely preliminary draft, mentioned in n. 2 above, comes to a somewhat abrupt stop as DHL attempts to describe 'three sisters' whose family name is clearly Von Richthofen: 'One started out to be learned and to give herself to social reform . . . The second obstinately decided to live her own life . . . The aim of the third was to gather roses, whilst she might.' Now,

> The age of fifty draws near. All three are in a state of vital bankruptcy of the modern woman of that age. The one is quite cynical about reform, the other begins to realize that the 'self' she was so cocksure about doesn't exist, and she wonders what does exist. To the third the world is a dangerous and dirty place, and she doesn't know where to put herself. (*P* 168–9)

It must have been clear to DHL that he could not go on quite like this in a newspaper article.

25 *AA* 88, 91, 93.

26 Mukerji might well have been in Switzerland in connection with the publication there of a French translation of his autobiography: *Brahmane et paria* (Geneva, 1928).

27 Brewster 289. *North Sea* is reproduced in *Paintings*, ed. Levy, p. 103; *The Milk White Lady* is in UT. Two other small oils DHL appears to have completed in Gsteig are *Fire in the Sands* and *Pietà*. Both are at present unlocated although when *Pietà* was auctioned at Sotheby's in 1984 it was reproduced in the catalogue (vii. 199 n. 1).

28 Brewster 288.

29 For an account of DHL's alterations to 'The Blue Moccasins' as well as of an earlier, abandoned version of the story, see Tedlock 68–71. The story was first collected in *The Lovely Lady* (pp. 131–60).

30 Brewster 287.

31 Nellie Morrison had of course been shocked by *Lady Chatterley's Lover* but, more importantly, so had Millie Beveridge. It may be no coincidence that DHL saw neither of the Beveridge sisters after their hostile response to *Dandelions* in spring 1928. He felt that Kot, Secker and Nancy Pearn disapproved; and would later defend the novel in letters to Rolf Gardiner, Lady Ottoline Morrell and his sister Ada (vii. 88, 105, 127). But very few of his long-standing relationships seem to have been destroyed by its publication.

32 Brewster 171.

33 Brewster 292. Margaret Needham's recollections are recorded on an audio tape, co-produced by D. Seymour and J. P. Aitin and distributed by the University of Nottingham (1988).

34 *AA* 158. It is strange that one of the most characteristically English of DHL's writings should have been written in response to a request from Anton Kippenberg, head of the firm (the Insel-Verlag, Leipzig) which published German translations of DHL's work. What he asked for was a contribution to a Festschrift for Hans Carossa – *Buch des Dankes für Hans Carossa* (1928). It was Frieda who performed the difficult task of translating DHL's article into German.

35 *D. H. Lawrence: A Personal Record*, by E. T. (Jessie Chambers) (1935), p. 198.

36 The degree of his hostility can be judged by the fact that on 10 September, shortly after Emily and her daughter had left, he was prepared to write to Ada:

> Peg has improved in appearance, at least. But she's hardly a man's woman. My god, these mincing young females all mincing together in a female bunch, they little know what a terrible blank they're preparing for themselves later, when this mincing young female business wears itself out. Are *all* young Englishwomen instinctively homosexual? looks like it, to me. Of course, I'm only speaking of the instinct, not of any practice. But the instinct sends a man's feelings recoiling to the ultimate pole. My God! – what a ghastly mess 'purity' is leading to! – But don't say anything – this is absolutely between you and me. (vi. 554)

37 In Jan Gordon, *Modern French Painters* (1923), p. 143, the Braque painting is one of several in which scraps of newsprint and a stringed instrument appear. It is usually referred to as *Nature Morte (1914)*.

38 Number 13 of *transition* was described as an 'American Number', even though its frontispiece was a photograph of Joyce. At its inception, the journal had been jointly edited by Eugene Jolas and Elliot Paul but by this stage Jolas was the sole editor. 'Work in Progress' had been temporarily suspended for numbers 9 and 10.

39 Brewster 293.

40 Ibid. 298.

41 Giulia Pini's version is that her family left the Villa Mirenda because it was too hard to make a living there (information from Stefania Michelucci).

42 Brewster 298.

43 Ibid. 299.

44 *Letters of Aldous Huxley*, ed. Grover Smith, p. 302.

45 There is no reference in the letters to the Huxleys being with DHL on the boat trip to Port Cros but confirmation of their presence comes from one of the poems (or 'pansies') he would write when he had moved to Bandol. Unpublished before its appearance in the 'Uncollected Poems' section of *Poems* (p. 842), 'I heard her say' reveals that the sea was rough, they were all 'nearly sea-sick', and that the Huxleys had their young son with them. Like the poem just above in DHL's notebook, 'Little-Boy Brilliant' (*Poems* 841), the hostile tone of 'I heard her say' indicates how upset DHL had been by *Point Counter Point*.

46 Brewster 286.

47 *Life for Life's Sake*, p. 299.

48 There is a minor indication of how Aldington's touchiness distorted his numerous accounts of fellow writers when he complains in *Portrait of a Genius, But* . . . : 'I now regret very much the money I spent in sending telegrams from Port Cros with prepaid answers to Lawrence (whose reply always was "Waiting for Frieda"), only to find his letters to other people reporting blandly that there was "no sign" of me!' (p. 336). In postcards DHL sent on 5 and 6 October he does say that there has been as yet 'no sign' of the Aldingtons; but on the 8th he reports that they have telegraphed and that he has told them he is going to wait for Frieda (vi. 585–6). Aldington would not have seen all these letters, but he is quick to jump to the conclusion that DHL told lies.

49 *No Tomorrow* (1929) was published in the United States only. As Brigit Patmore makes clear in *My Friends When Young* (1968), Aldington had been interested in her for some time (pp. 101–2).

50 Brigit Patmore first published her reminiscences of DHL in the *London Magazine* (June 1957) but they were reprinted in Nehls and again in her *My Friends When Young*. For the remarks here, and Aldington's references, see Nehls, iii. 253, 255.

51 Orioli went ahead with Douglas's book of limericks and Acton's translation, both of which ran into trouble. DHL reports that the police visited a man in Sussex who had received a subscription copy of the *Limericks* (vii. 142); and the British Home Office prompted the Italian authorities into an unsuccessful prosecution of *The Last of the Medici*. For details of this prosecution, see Ornella De Zordo, *Una proposta anglofiorentina degli anni trenta: The Lungarno Series* (Florence, 1981), pp. 47–8.

52 Lasca's career is described in Robert J. Rodini, *Antonfrancesco Grazzini* (Madison: Wis., 1970).

53 See Ornella De Zordo, 'Lawrence's Translations of Lasca: A Forgotten Project', in *Critical Assessments: D. H. Lawrence*, ed. David Ellis and Ornella De Zordo (1992), iv, pp. 169–78.

In Lasca's story, the somewhat 'insolent and forward' Manente is kidnapped by Lorenzo de'Medici after a drinking bout, and very elaborate arrangements are then made to convince his family and friends that he has died of the plague. Affairs of state next preoccupy Lorenzo for a while and by the time he remembers the joke he has played and releases Manente, the doctor's wife has remarried. So convinced has everyone been that he is dead that when he returns home he is either not recognised or taken for an evil spirit. Lorenzo finally resolves the resulting complications by arranging for someone to impersonate a magician and convince people that what has happened was the result of necromancy. After suitable arrangements have been made for the child with which the wife is newly pregnant, Manente recovers his home and family, and life returns to normal.

In the introduction to the story which DHL would write in the following year, he describes it as 'perhaps the best Florentine beffa, or burla (practical Joke) on record', and is right to point to the skill with which the various narrative strands are intertwined. As he says, the doctor's mental toughness when he is being kept in prison and subjected (like Malvolio) to mild forms of sensory deprivation is interesting, and it seems to go along with a certain period toughness in the narrator's underlying assumptions: though Manente is dismayed to have lost his property there is no indication that he suffers from sexual jealousy. See *The Story of Doctor Manente being the Tenth and last story from the 'Suppers' of A. F. Grazzini called il Lasca*, translation and introduction by D. H. Lawrence (Florence, 1929).

54 Nehls, iii. 259.

55 For *John Bull*'s attack on DHL over *The Rainbow*, see *TE* 672–5.

56 The articles from *John Bull* (20 October) and the *Sunday Chronicle* (14 October) are reprinted in Nehls, iii. 262–5.

57 Nehls, iii. 260.

58 DHL had first heard of this book from Harold Mason, the publisher of *Reflections on the Death of a Porcupine*, who may have been responsible for sending it to him (vi. 548 n.1).

59 *AA* 78, 26, 46. In *AA*, 'Sex Locked Out' became 'Sex versus Loveliness' and 'Women Don't Change', 'Do Women Change?' Although, like the other two, this last piece was sent off at the beginning of November, it did not appear in the *Sunday Dispatch* until April of the following year after Lawrence had responded to a request to lengthen it (vii. 117–8).

60 *K* 262:15.

61 Charles Doyle, *Richard Aldington: A Biography* (1989), p. 124.

62 *Death of a Hero* (1984), p. 222. This edition by Hogarth Press restores numerous cuts made by Chatto and Windus in 1929.

63 Nehls, iii. 254. The post-war misogyny so stridently exhibited by Aldington had already been announced by DHL when, in revising *Studies in Classic American Literature*, he wrote: 'The colossal evil of the united spirit of Woman. WOMAN, German woman or American woman, or every other sort of woman in the last war, was something frightening. As every *man knows*' (*SCAL* 94).

64 *Death of a Hero*, p. 7.

65 See the letter to Gertler on 9 October 1916 which begins, 'Your terrible and dreadful picture has just come. This is the first picture you have ever painted: it is the best modern picture I have seen. I think it is great, and true. But it is horrible and terrifying' (ii. 660).

66 Mosley became a junior member of the Labour government which came to power in 1929 but he resigned in the following year.

67 The chief victim of the charms of the novel's vamp (Lucy Tantamount) is described as a 'murderee' by Spandrell who explains, 'It takes two to make a murder. There are born victims, born to have their throats cut, as the cut-throats are born to be hanged' (*Point Counter Point* (1928), p. 209). In *Women in Love* Birkin says, 'No man . . . cuts another man's throat unless he wants to cut it, and unless the other man wants it cutting. This is a complete truth. It takes two people to make a murder: a murderer and a murderee. And a murderee is a man who is murderable' (p. 33:15–18).

68 *Point Counter Point*, p. 130.

69 Ibid., p. 157.

70 See, for example, chapter xxvi ('Philip Quarles's Notebook') where Quarles says that Rampion lives in a more satisfactory way than anyone he knows:

He lives more satisfactorily, because he lives more realistically than other people. Rampion, it seems to me, takes into account all the facts (whereas other people hide from them, or try to pretend that the ones they find unpleasant don't or shouldn't exist), and then proceeds to make his way of living fit the facts.   (p. 440)

DHL's short story 'Smile' is described on p. 670 above (note 44).

71 Ibid., p. 231.

72 Like Brett, Beatrice has never got over the shock of being pawed by a man her father's age when she was a very young girl. 'Have you seen Aldous' book *Point Counter Point*', DHL would write to her in November 1928. 'Mark Rampion is supposed to be me! Poor me! And poor you!! Do you recognise yourself? Aldous knows about as much as a pump, about us or anybody' (vii. 27). The last sentence may have been partly prompted by DHL's guilty sense that some of the details of Burlap's sexual dealings with Beatrice could only have come from what he had told Huxley about Brett and Murry.

73 In a letter to a friend, Murry claimed that the portrait had not affected him in the way one of DHL's short stories once had because he had never admired Huxley in the same way: 'D. H. L. can stick the barb deep, and A. H. can't.' He said that the chief result had been to convince him he was right in wanting to call his next book *God* – 'I'm grateful to Burlap for making me realise this clearly.' Yet in quoting this further example of Murry's extraordinary power of rationalisation, F. A. Lea points out that he had at first been so outraged by Burlap that he wanted to challenge Huxley to a duel, a prospect to which (Lea adds) 'only Max Beerbohm could have done justice' (Lea, *John Middleton Murry*, p. 159).

74 Nehls, iii. 253, 266.

75 *Richard Aldington: An Autobiography in Letters*, ed. Norman T. Gates (University Park: Pa., 1992), pp. 88, 93.

76 For Brigit Patmore's version, see Nehls, iii. 260. In a letter written to H. D. on 20 March 1929, quoted in Doyle, *Richard Aldington*, p. 122, Aldington says that DHL

openly sided with Arabella 'in a series of demented scenes from some southern Wuthering Heights'.

77 *Richard Aldington*, ed. Gates, p. 93.

Chapter Nineteen: Bandol

1 See Huxley's letter to his brother Julian from Paris on 22 February 1929 (*Letters of Aldous Huxley*, ed. Grover Smith, p. 307).

2 Christopher Pollnitz does the calculations in his 'Cough Prints and Other Intimacies: Considerations in Editing Lawrence's Later Verse', in *Editing D. H. Lawrence: New Versions of a Modern Author* ed. Charles L. Ross and Dennis Jackson (Ann Arbor, 1995), pp. 153, 168.

3 DHL's first, draft introduction to *Pansies* was published by David Farmer in the *Review of English Studies*, xxi (1970), 180–4.

4 Aldington assumed that DHL must have begun writing his pansies on Port Cros because one ('I am in a Novel') deals with the discomfort of having been portrayed as Rampion in *Point Counter Point*, while another is entitled 'Attila', and during their time on the island Aldington had lent Lawrence a book about Attila which he read with great interest (*Life for Life's Sake*, p. 301). But Lawrence wrote down the first batch of his pansies in a notebook which still exists and both 'I am in a Novel' and 'Attila' appear too late in the sequence to suggest that they were written anywhere else but in Bandol. Because MSS exist which show that DHL sometimes composed poems on loose sheets, the order in which he entered them in this, and later notebooks, cannot be an infallible guide to the sequence of composition. There is, however, enough intermittent concordance between a number of pansies and remarks in the letters to suggest that, broadly speaking, the two do coincide.

The notebook in which DHL wrote his first pansies (E302d) is in UT. (There is a detailed description of it in Tedlock 104–12.) The order in which the poems were originally entered is difficult to work out because several leaves have become detached. In my own remarks I rely on Christopher Pollnitz who has convincingly demonstrated that three loose leaves relegated by Tedlock to the end of his descriptive listing really belong at the beginning ('Cough Prints and Other Intimacies', p. 156). This means that the earliest poems do appear to be concerned with Port Cros matters. The very first, 'I Know a Noble Englishman', seems to be a record of Arabella Yorke's no doubt jaundiced view that Aldington's philandering came from the fact that, like Don Juan, he really hated women and was covertly homosexual; and, following that, there are a number of poems, such as the one that eventually became 'The Oxford Voice', which appear to satirise Aldington's public school manner. The seventh in the sequence is called 'What Matters'. In its original form especially, this develops into such a close verse equivalent of the letter which DHL wrote to Huxley from Port Cros, after having just read *Point Counter Point*, that in addition to indicating how much his complaints about murder, suicide and rape owe to conversations with Aldington, it also suggests that DHL might well have begun his pansies on the island after all. That is to say that Aldington's hypothesis is not disproved simply because he happened to have chosen the wrong illustrations.

5 *Poems* 466, 467.

6 *Review of English Studies*, vxxi (1970), 181–4.

7 *Poems* 507. In the notebook version of this poem 'other flesh' is a substitution for 'Another's flesh'.

8 In a letter to Maria Huxley on 24 February 1929 DHL mentions a 'circus on the beach' that he had been too depressed to go to (vii. 190). Yet several poems about performing elephants, included in the batch of pansies he sent off on 7 January, suggest that a circus had been to Bandol earlier. In her memoir, Frieda says '*We* went to the beautiful circus' (p. 211 – my italics). Information about the African bowls and cups which so impressed DHL, and which he writes about both in his pansies and in his letters, comes from Brewster Ghiselin (Nehls, iii. 293), one of the young men who later visited him in Bandol. It is Ghiselin who explains that they were sold in 'a bookshop kept by a Frenchman who had lived in Africa'.

9 *Poems* 490.

10 *SEP* 39:11–12.

11 Nehls iii. 291; Frieda 211.

12 'New Mexico' (*P* 141–7) was first published in the *Survey Graphic*, 1 May 1931. It is described on p. 62, above.

13 The title referred to what DHL felt was the emasculation of little boys of his time by the schoolmistresses of the relatively new national education system. He compared their fate with the freedom of his father's generation, but also recalled how enraged one of his schoolmasters had been at his disinclination to admit to his own first name: '"David, David", he raved, "David is the name of a great and good man. You don't like the name David? You don't like the name David!" He was purple with indignation. But I had an unreasonable dislike of the name David, and still have, and he couldn't force me into liking it' (*AA* 123–4). As John Worthen has pointed out to me, DHL's Nottingham High School algebra book is signed 'H. Lawrence'.

14 Frieda 211.

15 The *New Coterie* ran from Summer 1925 to Autumn 1927. Associated with it were writers such as H. E. Bates, Louis Golding, Hugh MacDiarmed and James Hanley. Lahr's shop was described by Rhys Davies as a place where there was 'a coming and going of post-Marx exiles from Central Europe'. He said that 'studious Jews' argued there, 'including an impressive melancholic named Koteliansky', and 'free-lance journalists and translators dropped in for obscure Socialist and Communist periodicals' (*Print of a Hare's Foot: An Autobiographical Beginning* (New York, 1969), pp. 114–15).

16 In an unpublished dissertation entitled, 'The Lost Ladies: The Marketing and Sale of the Florentine Editions of *Lady Chatterley's Lover*' (UN), Helen Stone has calculated that Lahr and his wife took 28 copies of the first edition of *Lady Chatterley's Lover*. DHL reports in his letter that they managed to sell 112 of the second (vii. 140). Some of these were posted directly to individuals from Florence after Lahr had sent Orioli a subscribers' list (vii. 88). Lahr bought the copies of the second edition at a guinea and sold them for 30 shillings.

17 In one of his pansies from this time, DHL writes, 'There is no way out, we are all caged monkeys / blue-arsed with the money bruise' (*Poems* 485).

18 Nehls, iii. 280.

19 Nehls, iii. 277, 303–4.

20 *Print of a Hare's Foot*, p. 137. For details of Katherine Mansfield's two visits to the Hotel Beau Rivage, see Antony Alpers, *The Life of Katherine Mansfield* (1980), pp. 186, 265.

21 *Print of a Hare's Foot*, pp. 142–3.

22 Lindsay describes his meetings with Frieda and Orioli in Nehls, iii. 300–3. Details of the Fanfrolico Press can be found in Craig Munro, *Wild Man of Letters: The Story of P. R. Stephensen* (Melbourne, 1984).

23 DHL had received copies of *The Times Literary Supplement* and the *London Illustrated News* throughout his recent stay in Italy, and on occasions from as early as the summer of 1924 (vii. 336 n.1). From a letter to Secker on 28 February 1929 which ends with 'Thanks for the papers' (vii. 196), it would seem Secker kept on sending them when the Lawrences were in Bandol.

24 Stephensen had come to Oxford in 1924 as a Rhodes scholar. See Munro, *Wild Man of Letters*, p. 24.

25 Ibid., pp. 67, 75. Flaherty was staying in La Colle sur Loup which is close to Vence.

26 Ibid., p. 88. The original terms were an advance of £250 and a 10% royalty but, chiefly to avoid the 20% tax on royalties, Lawrence had these changed to a flat permissions fee of £250 and a royalty of only 5% (vii. 130–1).

27 DHL's interest in reaching a working-class public was stimulated by his correspondence with Charles Wilson, a journalist and poet from the North East, who had first written to him towards the end of 1927 (vi. 229), and who was later to invite both Joyce and Huxley to lecture to the Durham miners. In response to what seems to have been a request from Wilson for some kind of 'message' for the miners, DHL sent him five of his recent pansies on 28 December. The first two are 'political' in the sense indicated by these phrases from the opening paragraphs of the letter which included the pansies:

> You've got to smash money and this beastly *possessive* spirit. I get more revolutionary every minute, but for *life's* sake. The dead materialism of Marx socialism and soviets seems to me no better than what we've got. What we want is life, and *trust*: men trusting men, and making living a free thing, not a thing to be *earned*. (vii. 99)

On 11 January 1929, DHL told Davies that Stephensen 'liked the *Pansies*, was pining to take a pamphlet or broadside from them, for the working-classes' (vii. 128). DHL was attracted by the idea and on 18 March, to the dismay of his agent Pollinger ('He's crazy'), suggested that he might have some of his pansies done as 'a broadside at 2d., for the election' – due to take place on 30 May (vii. 218). On 18 April he told Charles Lahr, 'I have no MS here now from which to choose an election broadside. But *you* choose one, and let me know, and we can go ahead with that' (vii. 256). A month later, however, he admitted to Kot that he felt 'hesitant about a broadside for electioneering purposes – it's not quite my line' (vii. 282).

28 While he was in Bandol DHL also painted a curiously ugly frontispiece ('Venus in the Kitchen', reproduced in *Paintings*, ed. Levy, p. 104) for a book of aphrodisiac recipes which Norman Douglas was collecting and Orioli planning to publish (vii. 124, 134); and he drew the picture of a naked man and woman facing each other

which appeared on the last page of the Mandrake Press edition of his paintings (vii. 135).

29 *Renascence of Men*, *Spring* and *Summer Dawn* are all reproduced in *Paintings*, ed. Levy, pp. 92, 96. It is in the first piece in *MM* ('Corasmin and the Parrots') that DHL says the Aztec belief in 'suns' pleases his fancy better than 'the long and weary twisting of the rope of Time and Evolution, hitched on to the revolving hook of a First Cause. I like to think of the whole show going bust, *bang*!' (p. 15).

30 For *Dance Sketch* see *Paintings*, ed. Levy p. 61.

31 *Leda* and *Singing of Swans* can be found on pp. 77 and 97 of *Paintings*, ed. Levy.

32 Nehls, iii. 297.

33 *Poems* 436.

34 Ibid. 438–9. This poem is not in E302d but does appear in the typescript sent to Curtis Brown on 7 January (DHL posted two copies but retained one for himself). Its title appears in the draft contents list at the back of E302d. According to Christopher Pollnitz, this notebook had been filled by 20 December at the latest. The composition of 'Won't It Be Strange–?' is likely, therefore, to have been between that date and the posting of the typescript on 7 January. Davies's presence in Bandol between 18–22 December narrows down the likely period still further.

35 Nehls, iii. 283.

36 *AA* 40. In *AA* this article became 'Give her a Pattern'.

37 Nehls, iii. 285. Brewster Ghiselin's memoirs of DHL were first published in the *Western Humanities Review*, xxi (Autumn 1958).

38 *TE* 386, 400. Discussing the Hebridean songs in 'Indians and Entertainment' DHL writes:

> Sometimes the song has merely sounds, and a marvellous melody. It is the seal drifting in to shore on the wave, or the seal woman, singing low and secret, departing back from the shores of men, through the surf, back to the realm of the outer beasts that rock on the waters and stare through glistening, vivid, mindless eyes.
>
> (*MM* 103–4)

39 Nehls, iii. 292.

40 Ibid. 294.

41 Robert Gathorne-Hardy was with Ottoline Morrell when she received DHL's letter containing this suggestion. She handed it to him and, as he read it, 'watched me solemnly, with eyes that seemed to be looking, remote from the material world, only at inward things. / "I don't think it would," she said seriously; and then, shaking her head and with a great burst of laughter, "in fact, I'm quite sure it wouldn't"' (*Ottoline: The Early Memoirs of Lady Ottoline Morrell*, ed. and with an introduction by Robert Gathorne-Hardy (1963), p. 55).

42 Neither of the poems in question was published during DHL's life-time but he must have heard about them from Huxley who had by this time probably already written the essay on Swift which appeared in his collection *Do What You Will* (1929). A passage in this essay reads:

> Nor can I refrain from mentioning that line, which Swift thought so much of that he made it the culmination of several poems:
>
>> Oh, Celia, Celia, Celia . . . !

The monosyllabic verb, which the modesties of 1929 will not allow me to reprint, rhymes with 'wits' and 'fits'. (p. 94)

43 The second *Pansies* introduction is reprinted in *Poems* 417–21. For Ghiselin's memory of DHL's remarks to Barby, see Nehls, iii. 289.

44 Nehls, iii. 295, 296.

45 *P* 552.

46 Jack Lindsay, whom DHL asked (through Stephensen – vii. 168) to check the facts in his introduction about syphilis among the Tudor and Stuart families, assumed that their source was a book DHL could have come across in Sydney: *Post Mortem: Essays, Historical and Medical* (1923) by an Australian doctor, Charles MacLaurin (Nehls, iii. 302). In the first chapter of *Post Mortem* ('The Case of Ann Boleyn') MacLaurin does say that Henry VIII was a victim of the syphilis which 'supposed to have been introduced by Columbus' men, ran like a whirlwind through Europe', and he also claims that Mary Tudor 'grew up, as one can see from her well-known portrait, probably a hereditary syphilitic' (pp. 14, 16); but low-grade speculation of this kind must have been very common, and there are no very strict parallels between MacLaurin's work and DHL's.

47 *P* 559, 564.

48 The claim comes in the chapter 'Greatness and Decline' (on p. 142 of the Phoenix Library edition of 1928 which DHL probably used). *Art* was first published in 1914.

49 *P* 565–6.

50 Fry thought it would be hard to exaggerate the importance of the still-lifes in 'the expression of Cézanne's genius', and he claimed that one had to recognise in Cézanne's early paintings 'his heroic, his almost contemptuous candour, and the desperate sincerity of his work' (pp. 52, 27).

51 Too technical for his taste perhaps, but not for his knowledge as DHL shows at the end of his essay when he reels off for comic effect all the fashionable technical terms of painters and their critics (*P* 582–3). If he needed any help for this pyrotechnic display, Barby could have provided it.

52 On p. 64 of his book Fry speaks of the 'necessity which Cézanne felt so strongly of discovering always in the appearance of nature an underlying principle of geometric harmony'.

53 *P* 577.

54 *P* 567–8.

55 *P* 579.

56 *Cézanne: A Study of his Development* (1927), p. 69.

57 *P* 569–70.

58 *P* 569.

59 *P* 571.

60 *P* 575.

61 *P* 553.

62 Because there is no surviving MS of the introduction, we cannot know whether DHL had given it a title of his own. An MS entitled 'Introduction to Pictures', which seems to date from this period and is probably a first attempt at what we know as 'Introduction to These Paintings', is extant. An essay on the curse of self-consciousness

and of working the body from the mind, the only references to art in this fragment occur in its title and first paragraph. See *P* 765–71 and Tedlock 172–3.

63 *Letters of Aldous Huxley*, ed. Grover Smith, p. 307.

64 Cf. 'I hear that the police stopped a copy of Douglas' *Limericks* in the post, and the Chief of Police went to interview the man it was addressed to, somewhere in Sussex. But then I think the limericks are just indecent. Why didn't Douglas keep them out of the post? – so bad for everybody else' (vii. 142).

65 The relevant extract from *The Parliamentary Debates*, House of Commons, 5th series, ccxxx (28 February 1929) is reprinted in Nehls, iii. 308–11. Joynson-Hicks was questioned on the issue of DHL's typescripts by F. W. Pethick-Lawrence (no relation), the Labour MP for East Leicester who was deputising for Ellen Wilkinson, the better-known Labour MP for Middlesbrough East. But the moving spirit could well have been Oswald Mosley, a close friend of the Hutchinsons (vii. 161, 162).

66 In a letter to Pollinger on 27 March, Secker referred to a group of pansies 'which Lawrence himself removed and of which typescript has reached me separately' (vii. 237 n.2).

67 This was the position DHL took in a letter to Ottoline Morrell on 5 February 1929 (vii. 164); and Brewster Ghiselin remembered that, although he was not best pleased by *Point Counter Point* and entirely rejected the portrait of himself as Rampion, he 'again and again gave evidence of strong affection for Huxley himself' (Nehls, iii. 291).

68 A chronologically confused account of how *Bottom Dogs* came to be sent to DHL can be found in chapter xxvii of *The Confessions of Edward Dahlberg* (New York, 1971). His claim there that Arabella Yorke herself sent the manuscript to DHL is not supported by DHL's surviving letters to him. According to Dahlberg, it was Constant Huntington, the managing director of the American publishers Putnam's in London, who pressed him to ask Lawrence for a foreword (pp. 212, 215). The only book by DHL which Dahlberg describes himself as admiring in his *Confessions* is *Studies in Classical American Literature*; but his views may have been coloured by his dislike of the *Bottom Dogs* foreword. On 7 May 1929 DHL wrote to Dahlberg from Majorca,

Sorry you feel a bit irritated by my preface to your book. But it's quite simple to suppress it altogether in U.S.A. – make no mention of it, and it doesn't exist. – It won't hurt *English* sales, as Putnam knows, even if it is a bad Sales-letter in America. – I can't help it, anyhow – I had to write what I felt. (vii. 272)

Dahlberg was born in 1900. For information about his background, see Fred Moramarco, *Edward Dahlberg* (New York, 1972), pp. 19–25.

69 *P* 267, 269, 270, 272.

70 *AA* 152. 'Myself Revealed' was republished in *AA* as 'Autobiographical Sketch'. It may well have been an adaptation of the article which DHL sent Nancy Pearn on 9 January 1927 and which she referred to as 'Becoming a Success' (v. 620 n.4).

71 *AA* 101, 102, 103.

Chapter Twenty: Old Haunts and New

1 *Print of a Hare's Foot*, pp. 154–5. In later life Davies would explain that he once shared a bed with DHL and this is the most likely occasion to which he was referring. Sharing

hotel beds was common among men from his and DHL's background, but, a homosexual himself, Davies would impart this information as part of his insistence that he had never detected any signs of homosexuality in DHL. He was someone exceptionally discreet about his sexual orientation so that DHL would be by no means the only friend not to have recognised it. For these details I am grateful to D. A. Callard who is preparing a biography of Davies.

2 *Confessions of Edward Dahlberg*, p. 227.

3 There are many documents which relate to DHL's 1929 Paris stay but in none of them is Mabel Harrison mentioned. This might seem at first a consequence of her and Millicent Beveridge's disapproval of *Lady Chatterley's Lover*, but if Mabel Harrison had been at home refusing to meet DHL some hint of that situation ought to be apparent in the letters. On 24 June 1929 DHL told Secker to send her and Millicent Beveridge a copy of *Pansies*. He had only six author's copies at his disposal and the only other non-family-member included in his list was Juliette Huxley (vii. 347).

4 On 19 January DHL had told an American friend that the Customs in New York had wanted to confiscate *Sun* 'because it contained the word "womb"' (vii. 145). His information would have come from Crosby who describes in his diary for 6 December 1928 how 'Sun had been held up at the Customs because of the use of the word "womb" but had been released by our bribing with two gold coins – the low-down bastards' (*Shadows of the Sun*, ed. Germain, p. 215). For details of the pirated edition, see Roberts, *A Bibliography of D. H. Lawrence*, p. 566.

5 Throughout most of 1928, *The Escaped Cock* was being considered for publication by Crosby Gaige, an American publisher of limited editions. But early in 1929 DHL learned that he was only prepared to publish the first part (vii. 62, 111, 121).

6 Cf. DHL's commentary on Shelley and the 'Ode to a Skylark' in *Hardy* 71:5–33.

7 *Shadows of the Sun*, ed. Germain, p. 241. As the editor explains on p. 226, the more uncomplimentary phrases in this entry were crossed out by Caresse Crosby after her husband's death.

8 *LCL* 306:38–9. Davies has an account of DHL going to see Groves, finding his office closed and taking this as a sign that he should not deal with him: 'I think he had consulted his midriff on the pavement. He refused to meet or correspond with the pirate after that' (Nehls, iii. 314).

9 Nehls, iii. 315.

10 Ibid.

11 *Letters of Aldous Huxley*, ed. Grover Smith, p. 313. The Huxleys blamed Frieda for her apparently casual approach to DHL's illness, as well as her unwillingness or inability to make him seek orthodox medical advice. In August, Maria wrote to her what seems to have been an admonitory letter (vii. 417), but Aldous thought that telling Frieda she was a 'a fool and a criminal' had no more effect than 'telling an elephant. So it's hopeless. Short of handcuffing him and taking him to a sanatorium by force, there's nothing to be done' (*Letters of Aldous Huxley*, ed. Grover Smith, p. 314).

12 *Print of a Hare's Foot*, p. 157.

13 Sylvia Beach, *Shakespeare and Company* (New York, 1959), pp. 92–3. It was during DHL's negotiating trip to Beach's shop that Dahlberg first met him (*Confessions of Edward Dahlberg*, p. 225). Of this occasion Davies wrote, 'I went for a walk while Miss

Beach turned *Lady Chatterley*, and a small fortune, down. Publication of *Ulysses* had fulfilled her' (*Print of a Hare's Foot*, p. 156).

14 There are more details concerning Titus in Billy Klüver and Julie Morton, *Kiki et Montparnasse. 1900–1930* (Paris, 1989). See especially p. 242, n.7 (third column) and the fine photograph by André Kertész on p. 187 of Titus looking into his own bookshop window. He called his press 'At the Sign of the Black Manikin'.

15 Nehls, iii. 313.

16 *LCL* lvii. In a statement DHL drew up in his memorandum book on 26 March he estimated his profit as £1,239 16s 3d (vii. 230 n.1).

17 DHL had replied to Holliday's letter around 15 February (vii. 176–7). The amount he had been sent is recorded in his memorandum book.

18 *LCL* 306:30–2. The first six pages of 'A Propos of *Lady Chatterley's Lover*' in the Cambridge edition are based on DHL's autograph MS of 'My Skirmish With Jolly Roger'.

19 *LCL* 307:27–30.

20 *LCL* 308:20–6. This is the second of two extracts from DHL which Michel Foucault quotes in *La volonté de savoir* (Paris, 1976), p. 208, vol. i of his *Histoire de la sexualité* (the first extract is from *The Plumed Serpent*). For someone concerned to show that, far from being secret or 'repressed' during the late nineteenth and early twentieth centuries, sex was talked and written about more than it ever had been before, the choice is apt.

21 *LCL* 309:4–7.

22 *LCL* 309:22–4.

23 *LCL* 310:2, 23, 27–30.

24 After repeating the accusation which he attributes to smart young people, DHL goes on,

> But perhaps the mentality of a boy of fourteen, who still has a little natural awe and proper fear in face of sex, is more wholesome than the mentality of the young cocktaily person who has no respect for anything, and whose mind has nothing to do but play with the toys of life, sex being one of the chief toys, and who loses his mind in the process. Heliogabalus indeed! (*LCL* 310:14–19)

Writing to the Crosbys on 7 June, DHL says, 'With life as it is today, the battle is everything. But of course if you don't really believe in anything, there's nothing to fight for. Anyhow Heliogabalus is all bunk – he was so bored he went cracked, out of boredom' (vii. 323).

One of the reasons for Harry Crosby's interest in Varius Avitus Bassianus, who as Heliogabalus (or more accurately Elagabalus) was Roman Emperor in 218–22 AD, was that he chose to call himself by the name of the Syro-Phoenician sun god whose high priest he had been from an early age. For a highly coloured account of his career from *The Augustan History*, see *Lives of the Later Caesars*, tr. Anthony Birley (1976). The entry in Crosby's diary for 25 August 1928 begins, 'Read a chapter on the extravagances of Heliogabalus (they are magnificent what of it if he did have megalomania it is better to exalt oneself into Sun than to whimper in the dust)' (*Shadows of the Sun*, ed. Germain, p. 202).

25 Crosby had begun to rent an old mill on his friend Armand de la Rochefoucauld's estate in summer 1928. He christened it 'Le Moulin du Soleil' and equipped it with ten bedrooms, a swimming pool and a large banqueting hall. In addition to his race-

horses, he kept there 'cockatoos, a ferret, a cheetah, a macaw, a couple of whippets, two carrier pigeons, four donkeys, nine ducks . . . and a python' (Wolff, *Black Sun*, p. 227).

26 Davies says that the 'curly-brimmed grey felt hat and a long, thick overcoat' which DHL had 'obtained in Toulon for [his] visit to the capital' made him look at first glance 'like a dimly goatish upholder of bourgeois principles' (*Print of a Hare's Foot*, p. 155).

27 Caresse Crosby, *The Passionate Years*, pp. 231–2.

28 For accounts of DHL's attack, see *The Passionate Years*, p. 232, and Wolff, *Black Sun*, p. 234. On 20 May, DHL wrote to Crosby, 'Frieda would love a little gramophone, but *no* Joyce – and please, not till we get a house' (vii. 291). A gramophone was sent on to the Lawrences via the Huxleys in Forte dei Marmi but by the time it reached Florence they had left for Germany. When they decided to go to Bandol again rather than return to Italy, the gramophone was forwarded to them by Orioli, along with many other of their belongings, including DHL's typewriter (vii. 493). On 9 November 1929 DHL was able to write to Caresse Crosby, 'The gramophone is at the station – imagine!' (vii. 557). Five days later he told the Mohrs that he was only allowing Frieda to play it in the kitchen 'with the doors shut. I do mortally hate it' (vii. 566).

29 In *Bibliography of James Joyce: 1882–1941* (New Haven, 1953), p. 173, John J. Slocum and Herbert Cahoon explain that this recording was made in November 1926 and that there were only thirty copies.

30 Geoffrey Wolff, *Black Sun*, p. 206.

31 *Shadows of the Sun*, ed. Germain, p. 245.

32 Richard Ellmann, *James Joyce* (1982), p. 615.

33 *The Finding of Moses* was the painting which Stephensen and Goldston had chosen to reproduce in their prospectus for their edition of DHL's paintings (vii. 199).

34 See p. 94 above.

35 *AA* 169, 172.

36 *Women in Love*, p. 89:10–11.

37 'A Jixless Errand', *Time and Tide*, x (15 March 1929), 284. DHL's encouragement of Rebecca West shows great forbearance. She certainly calls him a 'great man' but if Joynson-Hicks is not worthy to 'tie his shoestring' it is because DHL has reached 'lofty spiritual heights' in works other than those in which improper words appear. The use of those words she attributes to a 'neurotic compulsion' (p. 285). Her article is also homophobically concerned with Radclyffe Hall's *The Well of Loneliness* which had been successfully prosecuted by the government in 1928. The furore over that book helped fuel some of the indignation against DHL and make censorship a prominent public issue.

38 Nehls, iii. 304.

39 Richard Aldington described this notebook in his introduction to *Last Poems* (1932), pp. 5–6.

40 *Poems* 604.

41 *Poems* 610, 617.

42 *Poems* 613.

43 'In a Spanish Tram-Car', 'Spanish Privilege', 'At the Bank in Spain' and 'The Spanish Wife'. The following poem – 'The Painter's Wife' – would seem to be concerned with someone DHL had met in Majorca (*Poems* 617–19).

44 *Poems* 620.

45 Ibid.

46 Graves has a not altogether complimentary account of Nichols in *Goodbye to All That* (1929). DHL had known Nichols briefly during the war, declaring on 17 November 1915, 'I liked seeing you and knowing you very much' (ii. 443).

47 The details are from Paul Hogarth's as yet unpublished *Escape to the Sun: Travels in the Footsteps of D. H. Lawrence*. Hogarth's impressive series of paintings of all the places in which DHL lived was exhibited in London in 1994. From his Majorcan connections he has discovered that DHL was introduced in Palma to Joan Junyer, a local painter who took the Lawrences to see his well-known painter uncle, Sebastia Junyer, an intimate friend of Picasso in his Barcelona period. Joan Junyer, who was twenty-five in 1929, recalled DHL as 'good-looking, Christ-like, with reddish hair and sensitive hands'.

48 One resident to whom DHL later wrote was Edward Huelin. He lived in San Agustan, the same suburb of Palma where the Lawrences' hotel was to be found, and was trying to become a writer. It was Huelin's brother-in-law who was British Vice-Consul on the island (vii. 373 n.1).

49 There is an account of *This Quarter* in William Wiser, *The Crazy Years: Paris in the Twenties* (1983), pp. 62-5.

50 *This Quarter*, (July–September 1929), 21, 24, 27.

51 The prospective buyer was Jack Young-Hunter, whose land bordered Mabel Luhan's (vii. 287-8).

52 *AA* 182-3, 186. When this article was reprinted in *AA* it became 'Pictures on the Walls'.

53 The issue had already come up with *Collected Poems*. In writing to both Secker and Pollinger about the proposed signed copies for this edition, DHL claimed they cost nothing extra to produce, and pointed out that a down-payment for his signature would have the advantage of being exempt from the government's 20% tax on royalties. Secker had in fact offered 20% for DHL's signature but he insisted on $33\frac{1}{3}$% (vi. 471-2). It clearly annoyed him that, having established the principle for *Collected Poems*, he had to re-establish it for *Pansies*.

54 Before his discussions with Lahr, DHL had sent, via an intermediary who was probably Ada, a copy of the poems to Guy Aldred, a publisher committed to radical causes. The foreword which accompanied this copy has an emphasis like the one in 'Pornography and Obscenity' on the importance of resisting mob reactions: 'If the mass wave is enervating emotionalism, oppose it. If the mass wave is arrogant fascism, oppose it. If it is destructive communism, oppose it. The mass is always wrong. Mankind only lives on the strength of its vigorous minority of opposition' (*D. H. Lawrence: Foreword to Pansies*, ed. Keith Sagar (Libanus Press, 1988), p. 8). In Sagar's introduction to this edition, there are interesting details about Aldred which may explain why he was not interested in DHL's proposition (pp. 2-3). It is argued by Sagar, and confirmed by Pollnitz, that this foreword is the same as the one DHL had sent to Secker on 28 February (vii. 195-6). It was his third attempt to introduce the poems, after the first draft introduction (published in the *Review of English Studies*) and the one confiscated by the police. In Majorca, in response to Secker's anxieties, he wrote a fourth, which he describes as 'perfectly proper' (vii. 267) but which explains to readers of the Secker

edition that about a 'dozen poems' have been 'perforce omitted' and complains about the 'nanny-goat-in-a-white-petticoat silliness of it all' (*Poems* 423).

55 Although Lahr was the actual publisher, the inside cover of the unexpurgated edition gives not only Stephensen's name but also the address of the Mandrake Press in Museum Street.

56 *Poems* 446. Provocative lines from the first, notebook version (e.g. 'Every single erection of his is an erection of mean spite') disappear from the published version of this poem. But they had already disappeared by the time of the typescript confiscated by the police. The process which led to their elimination seems to have been more one of normal revision than self-censorship.

57 *Poems* 475, 485, 491, 493, 539, 541, 562.

58 The Guardia portraits suggest some physical deterioration even in comparison with photographs taken of DHL by the American journalist and photographer Robert H. Davis a year before. Like others, Davis had expected DHL to be 'a strapping fellow with a fierce beard' and was surprised to find him so slight and frail. For comments on this and other portraits of DHL, see David Ellis, 'Images of D. H. Lawrence: On the Use of Photographs in Biography', in *The Portrait in Photography*, ed. Graham Clarke (1992), pp. 155–72.

59 Catherine Carswell talks of a rumour reaching England that DHL had 'only a few days, possibly only a few hours to live. Several of his friends, including ourselves, were rung up on the telephone by unknown editors, while the sound of the sharpening of obituarists' quills made itself heard' (*SP* 282). On 2 June DHL told Ada, 'Your letter yesterday – sorry you were worried – those fool newspapers! I always say they are pining to announce one's death. But they're too "previous" ' (vii. 318).

60 JMM 123.

61 One of the poems DHL wrote at this time is 'Correspondence in After Years':

> A man wrote to me: We missed it, you and I.
> We were meant to mean a great deal to one another;
> but we missed it.
> And I could only reply:
> A miss is as good as a mile
> mister! (*Poems* 603)

This appears in the notebook five poems before 'Intimates' and would therefore seem to prove that the latter must have been written in Majorca. But Christopher Pollnitz has pointed out to me that, along with 'To a certain friend' and 'The Emotional Friend', 'Correspondence in After Years' was interlined in pencil over a seemingly unrelated poem, 'Love', which had been entered in ink and then deleted in pencil.

62 Chopin and George Sand were in Majorca 8 November 1838 – 13 February 1839. Her account of the stay was published as *Un hiver à Majorque* in 1842.

63 Frieda 212.

64 The *TLS* review is republished in R. P. Draper, *The Critical Heritage* (1970), pp. 309–11.

65 Munro, *Wild Man of Letters*, p. 85.

66 Frieda 212.

67 The niece of a president of Magdalene College, Oxford, and goddaughter of Henry

James, Dorothy Warren was born more into the intellectual than social aristocracy of English society although, as Trotter writes, 'The family is Norman.' He describes himself as coming from a 'Scottish Border family' and explains that he was educated at Charterhouse before serving in the Welsh Guards during World War I (Nehls, iii. 695 n.337).

68 Phillip Trotter describes how, shortly before DHL's exhibition opened, his wife received a favourable offer for her two floors in Maddox Street: 'Dorothy left the decision to me, pointing out that Lawrence had been throughout *menfichiste* about the exhibition' (Nehls, iii. 300). It certainly was not any sense of loyalty to DHL that prevented her from selling.

Stephensen's dislike of Dorothy Warren is made clear in a letter to DHL reproduced in Craig Munro, 'The D. H. Lawrence – P. R. Stephensen Letters', *Australian Literary Studies*, xi (May 1984), 300–1. An original autograph, there is some doubt whether this letter was ever sent. Writing to her and Trotter on 16 September 1929, DHL insisted that Stephensen had never written a word against them (vii. 489); but that his views had nevertheless been made clear, if not directly then through third parties, is evident in DHL's letter to Ada a fortnight before (vii. 458).

69 Hutchinson's words come from *The Times*' report of the hearing held on 8 August (9 August 1929).

70 Nehls, iii. 340. The shilling was for the catalogue which was meant to secure entry.

71 See DHL's poem '13,000 People' (*Poems* 577).

72 Nehls, iii. 326.

73 *SP* 284.

74 On 16 June the critic in the *Observer* had said, 'Pornography is probably the worst form of lewd expression, and when undeniable skill is present to increase its effect, a firm stand should be taken against any display of it.' More directly, one of the *Daily Telegraph*'s critics wrote on 27 June, under the title 'A Disgraceful Exhibition', 'So long as the exhibition remains open it must be a standing source of amazement that the authorities permit the public display of paintings of so gross and obscene a character' (Nehls, iii. 336, 339).

75 The day after the Labour cabinet had taken control, DHL wrote to Emily optimistically hoping that things would be easier for him now Labour were in charge, and saying that he would have voted Labour 'without hesitation' (vii. 327). A few months later, in defence of his own record in office, Joynson-Hicks, or Viscount Brentford as he had by then become, pointed out that, whereas all plays had to have a licence from the Lord Chamberlain before they could be performed, a British Home Secretary had no power to censor books before they were published and could only decide whether or not to prosecute in response to a complaint. The situation was similar with paintings. He noted with satisfaction that 'a prosecution resulting in the withdrawal of certain paintings by a well-known writer from exhibition' had been directed by his 'successor in office' (Viscount Brentford, *Do We Need A Censor?*, Criterion Miscellany, no. 6 (1929), p. 17). The justification for the seizure of DHL's typescripts of *Pansies* was a law governing the transport of obscene matter by the post.

76 Nehls, iii. 343–7.

77 Grosz's book, deliberately shocking in its representation of fat, often naked, members

of the German middle classes and its detailed depiction of female pudenda, had already been successfully prosecuted for obscenity in Germany. See Martin Kane, *Weimar Germany and the Limits of Political Art: A Study of the Work of George Grosz and Ernst Toller* (1987), pp. 51–3. It was returned to the Trotters on the grounds that it had not been offered for sale.

78 This is the phrase used in *The Times* report of the hearing.

79 Nehls, iii. 360.

80 Ibid. 350–1.

81 For Trotter's list of the replacements, which included the copy of Fra Angelico's *Flight into Egypt*, see Nehls, iii. 371.

82 Nehls, iii. 363. Trotter apparently raised with Stephensen and Goldston the possibility of a book in which images like these would appear alongside some of DHL's paintings. See Munro, 'D. H. Lawrence – P. R. Stephensen Letters', 300.

83 Nehls, iii. 363.

84 G. H. Neville, *A Memoir of D. H. Lawrence (The Betrayal)*, ed. Carl Baron (1981), pp. 81–3. There is an attempt to interpret this episode, and the references to pubic hair in *JTLJ* (see p. 341 above), in David Ellis, 'D. H. Lawrence and the Female Body', *Essays in Criticism*, xlvi (April 1996), 136–52.

85 *TE* 278.

86 Nehls, iii. 382. Cf. also Frederick Hollis, *The Law and Obscenity* (1932), pp. 16–17.

87 In her account of visiting DHL in Forte dei Marmi ('Afternoons in Italy with D. H. Lawrence'), published in the *Texas Quarterly*, vii (Winter 1964), 114–20, Maria Cristina Chambers implies that the Pensione Giuliani was next door to the Huxleys' house. She describes going to the beach with DHL on a number of occasions.

88 *Poems* 625.

89 The strange letter to which he was responding is published in Michael Squires, 'Two Newly Discovered Letters of D. H. Lawrence', *DHLR*, xxiii (Spring 1991), 31. It was Maria Chambers who had first informed DHL that copies of *Lady Chatterley's Lover* were selling in New York for $50.

90 That Maria Chambers got to know Brett and Mabel Luhan emerges from DHL's letters to them (vii. 204, 343). In the earliest of his letters to her, which dates from November 1927, he asks, 'Is it possible you really are the godmother of Rosalino – the actual Rosalino of Oaxaca? Or do you mean, in the spirit merely? (Pardon the merely)' (vi. 210). Ross Parmenter, who researched Maria Chambers's background, could not find an answer to this question. See Parmenter 107–8.

91 DHL would be likely to remember Ivy Low in this context because in 1914 her passionate enthusiasm for his work had led her to visit him in Italy also. For an account of her trip to Fiascherino, and other details of Ivy Low's life, see *TE*, 117–18, 427, 785.

92 A notebook which DHL was using at the time of *The Boy in the Bush* contains in his hand the words and music of five songs in Spanish: 'Cielito Lindo', 'Pajarerea', 'Mi Vieja Amor', 'La Borrachita' and 'Nortena' (Tedlock 134).

93 Chambers, 'Afternoons in Italy with D. H. Lawrence', 117–18. They were afternoons because DHL had told her that he 'liked to work in the mornings' (p. 114).

94 *Letters of Aldous Huxley*, ed. Grover Smith, p. 313.

95 *Poems* 559, 628.

96 *Women in Love*, p. 29:11–32.

97 *Letters of Aldous Huxley*, ed. Grover Smith, p. 313.

98 *Portrait of a Genius, But* . . ., p. 102.

99 Aldo Sorani, 'Incontri con D. H. Lawrence', in *Pegaaso: Rassegna di lettere e arte* (Florence, 1932), p. 709.

100 *London Aphrodite*, v (April 1929), 338–41.

101 *Poems* 629. The poem is called 'We Die Together' and comes ten poems after 'Forte dei Marmi'. Evidence for believing that it was indeed written there can be found in the article by Maria Chambers cited in note 87 above. Of the maid at the Pensione Giuliani she writes, 'Fifteen years old and with a madonna face, Mariuccia was the maid-of-all-work in the pensione; but in her busy world there existed only one *signore*. Simply and superbly, "Il Signore" was D. H. Lawrence'; and she refers also to the 'pomegranate hedge that separated the pensione from the next villa' (pp. 114, 116).

102 See 'Fellow-Men' and 'The Gulf' (*Poems* 638, 635). That the last in sequence of these two poems comes eighteen entries before 'Trees in the Garden', which describes the garden of the Hotel Löwen and has the word 'Lichtental' (*sic*) written under it, strongly suggests that they both belong to DHL's stay in Florence.

103 'Democracy is Service' (*Poems* 650).

104 *Poems* 417. There is an almost identical phrase in the first draft introduction.

Chapter Twenty-One: Battling On

1 See chapter 20, n.102 above

2 On 3 April 1929 DHL had told Pollinger about the 'little novel' which he had written two years before but which wanted 'doing over'; on 2 August he spoke to Nancy Pearn of re-writing it if he ever got 'into the mood'; and on 14 September he mentioned it to Pollinger again as something he might 're-cast' (vii. 236, 402, 481). Hardly any of DHL's works are finished in the sense that, given the opportunity, he would not have revised them; but *The Virgin* is as finished as most others. The re-casting he had in mind, therefore, is likely to have been related to the ethics of his portrayal of the Weekley family.

3 The story of a poor man (Gabbriello) who looks sufficiently like his rich neighbour Lazzero to be able to impersonate him once he has drowned is the first in the series from Lasca's 'Second Supper'. DHL translated three quarters of it, probably while he was still in Germany. The part he completed was published in the *Telegraph* Sunday magazine on 25 October 1981. For further details, see Ornella De Zordo, 'Lawrence's Translations of Lasca: A Forgotten Project', pp. 172, 177.

4 *AA* 111, 113–14.

5 *AA* 131, 145. 'Men and Women' was republished in *AA* as 'Men Must Work and Women as Well'.

6 Nehls, iii. 343.

7 The five experts who had promised to come forward if required were Augustus John, Colin Agnew, Glyn Philpot, Tancred Borenius and Sir William Orpen. After 'Introduction to These Paintings' Roger Fry was understandably reluctant, but he and Lytton Strachey did sign a general protest against the *principle* of censorship in art

which was largely drafted by Geoffrey Scott – editor of Boswell and author of *The Architecture of Humanism* (1914) – who was very active in the dispute (Nehls, iii. 364–70).

8 *The Times* report (9 August 1929). In his pamphlet in the 'Criterion Miscellany' series, Joynson-Hicks would write: 'To discriminate in favour of a book which in the opinion of many will debauch the young, because in the minds of some it is a work of art, seems to me quite impossible' (*Do We Need a Censor?*, pp. 18–19).

9 The poems were 'Puss-Puss', 'London Mercury', 'My Little Critics', 'Editorial Office', 'The Great Newspaper Editor and his Subordinates' (*Poems* 581–4) – all of which appeared in *Nettles* (1930) – and 'Never had a Daddy'.

10 During October 1929, in a gesture of witless malice, Lahr printed for private distribution thirty or so copies of DHL's spoof announcement of the life of Murry, together with the opening sentences DHL had suggested in his letter, i.e., 'John Middleton was born in the year of the Lord 1891. It happened also to be the most lying century since time began, but what is that to an innocent babe!' For details see Roberts, *Bibliography of D. H. Lawrence*, p. 142.

11 Hollis, *The Law and Obscenity*, p. 30.

12 *Point Counter Point*, p. 129.

13 Stephensen had met Hopkin at Frieda's party at the Warren Gallery on 4 July and got on with him 'marvellously well. Some reality in such people' (Munro, 'D. H. Lawrence – P. R. Stephensen Letters', p. 300).

14 *Poems* 664.

15 *P* 133, 135, 136, 137, 140, 138. 'Nottingham and the Mining Countryside' was first published in the special commemorative number of Murry's *New Adelphi* shortly after DHL's death (iii, June–August 1930). In August it also appeared in the *Architectural Review* as 'Disaster Looms Ahead, Mining Camp Civilisation, the English Contribution to Progress'.

16 This was comforting news yet in describing his lungs as 'healed' (vii. 420, 421) DHL was implicitly admitting that it was not catarrh which had been affecting them previously.

17 Nehls, iii. 426.

18 The various drafts of 'Bavarian Gentians' can be consulted in Appendix 1 of D. H. Lawrence, *Selected Poems*, ed. Mara Kalnins (1992), pp. 263–5. For a circumstantial account of the evolution of the poem see Keith Sagar, 'The Genesis of Bavarian Gentians', *DHLR*, viii (Spring 1975), 47–53.

19 Frieda 213.

20 Nehls, iii. 397.

21 *Poems* 652.

22 In the late 1930s both the Huxleys became disciples of F. M. Alexander who taught that posture was the key to health. They were sent by him to Dr J. E. R. McDonagh who believed that many or most disorders were caused by intoxication of the intestines and who consequently imposed upon them a regime of 'colonic lavages, vaccine injections and diet' (Bedford, *Aldous Huxley*, i, pp. 311–13).

23 *Pornography and Obscenity* (1929), pp. 16, 20, 25–6, 31. Joynson-Hicks's article, which is entitled ' "Censorship" of Books' and signed 'Brentford', appeared in the August

number of the *Nineteenth Century* (pp. 207–11) and is a short preliminary version of his pamphlet *Do We Need a Censor?*

24 In addition to helping his wife with her gallery, Phillip Trotter was involved in the mining of a 'green translucent stone' which could be found in the area of this castle and which he and his partner called 'Styrian jade' (Nehls, iii. 696 n.337).

25 Nehls, iii. 400.

26 Hignett, *Brett*, 203.

27 Ibid. 206–8.

28 DHL may have forgotten that he had sent many of his MSS to New York in September 1924 (vii. 474–5 n.3); but a more likely explanation of the confusion is that the Curtis Brown agent there – no longer Barmby but Edwin Rich – had sent him an incomplete list (vii. 472).

29 Brewster 303.

30 Nehls, iii. 422.

31 Nehls, iii. 412; Frieda 304.

32 Squatting miner-like in front of an open fire in the house the Brewsters eventually rented, DHL told Achsah that 'man lived by the elements and should not deny fire' (Carter, *D. H. Lawrence and the Body Mystical*, p. 52; Brewster 306). The 'poem to fire' she describes him writing at the time is a moving and evocative poem in prose. The MS is described in Tedlock (213–14) and the text reprinted in Keith Sagar's Penguin selection of DHL's poetry (1972), pp. 230–1.

33 *P* 194–5.

34 The cancelled passage is printed in the 'Explanatory Notes' of *LCL* (pp. 370–1).

35 Shaw's speech was delivered at the Wigmore Hall in London to the Third International Conference of the World League for Sexual Reform. Teasing the Establishment with the idea that the fewer clothes women wore the less alluring they would be, he demonstrated that Michel Foucault was not the first to understand the importance of paradox in debates about sex. 'Modern women', *The Times* (14 August 1929) reported Shaw as suggesting, 'would probably be shocked by pictures of those Victorian ladies, with every contour emphasized and upholstered. The Victorian age was an exceedingly immoral age, affected with the disease of exhibitionism.'

36 *LCL* 321:17; 323:15–16; 326:31–2; 330:28–9.

37 In 'The Real Thing' DHL claims that the fight for women's liberation was already won and in danger of going too far. It had begun in a protest by women at the way their husbands and lovers had lost their 'instinctive hold on the life-flow and the life-reality'. Now that it was the 'great woman-spirit that sways mankind', young men had responded by becoming cynical and emptying themselves of feeling so that both sexes were beginning to wonder whether they had lost the 'real thing'. The real thing as far as he was concerned, DHL went on, what made life good to him, was the sense that he was somewhere in touch with the 'vivid life of the cosmos', even when he was ill. The question therefore became: 'How to be renewed, reborn, revivified?' In what seems like a private allusion to his recent experiment with alternative medicine, he concluded that 'getting into contact again with the *living* centre of the cosmos' was the only solution rather than 'some trick with glands or secretions, or raw food, or drugs' (*P* 196–203).

There are already traces in this piece of DHL's renewed contact with the Brewsters but, in the third article from October or early November ('Nobody Loves Me'), he begins with an analysis of something Achsah Brewster had said to him as she and her husband breathlessly arrived at Kesselmatte one afternoon during the summer of 1928. Looking round at the surrounding mountains, Achsah had declared that they made her feel she had lost all her 'cosmic consciousness' and all her 'love of humanity'. (Much struck by the phrases at the time, DHL had reported them in a letter he wrote to Maria Huxley in mid-July 1928 – vi. 462.) DHL makes gentle fun of the New England transcendentalism he feels these remarks imply and, given that it was after all the 'loving forebears' of the present generation of young people who had 'brought on the Great War', he is not surprised that it is now so totally rejected. Yet for the young to repudiate *any* form of connection with the cosmos or humanity was to throw the baby out with the bathwater. Refusing to force their feelings in a sympathetic direction had left many of them with no feelings at all and, the young women especially, forlorn at being unloved (*P* 204, 207).

38 The review was in response to an implicit appeal from Stephensen who on 31 October claimed to have published the book solely as a favour to Kot and was convinced it would not sell (Munro, 'D. H. Lawrence – P. R. Stephensen Letters', p. 315). Trying to attract some attention to Kot's work gave DHL the opportunity to repeat his belief that the remarkable coruscations of Russian literary culture in the nineteenth century, and of Dostoyevsky in particular, were the consequence of a feudal culture being too suddenly confronted with Western ideas. On members of the intelligentsia the effect was the deprivation of any natural centre and condemnation to a bewildering succession of simulated rather than real feeling which was the archetypal modern condition. Nancy Pearn was able to place DHL's review in *Everyman* (23 January 1930). It is reprinted in *P* 388–92.

39 See p. 154 above.

40 In a previously unpublished passage from the MS of DHL's book on Revelation, *Apocalypse*, printed as an appendix in the Cambridge edition, DHL begins, 'After reading the Old Testament', and goes on to say how grateful he is 'to the new translations of the Bible. A translation like Moffatt's frees the book from the pompous snoring of the old Elizabethan language and the parson's voice combined.' After a few more sentences he writes, 'The beauty of Isaiah is even greater, now it is more intelligible, the loss of the Elizabethan gilding gives it its own poetry' (p. 153). The hostility to the Authorised Version is strange in view of its influence on DHL's own prose style; but he is writing here of the pleasure which comes from seeing very familiar material in a new light.

41 Achsah Brewster talks of DHL reading Inge and Murray (Brewster 305); the other authors are referred to in his letters (vii. 519, 539, 578, 589, 599).

42 For the effect of Burnet's book on DHL, see *TE* 245–6. The epigraphs are reprinted in *P* 65–8. They include some direct quotation from Burnet's pre-Socratics but also contributions in a similar style. He sent them off to Hughes-Stanton around 12 November (vii. 563), explaining to Pollinger on the 25th,

the "bits" to go in front of the *Birds Beasts* sections are part original and sometimes quotations from the fragments of Xenophanes and Empedokles and others, but I should like it all put in inverted commas, and let them crack their wits (the public) to find out what is ancient quotation and what isn't. (It is nearly all of it me.)

(vii. 573)

It was after his return to Europe in 1925 that DHL must have been introduced to Hughes-Stanton by Barbara Weekley. At that time, the young artist and his wife were living in a basement flat in Hammersmith Terrace, close to the river. When the Thames overflowed its banks in February 1926 the flat was flooded and its occupants nearly drowned. This explains the reference in DHL's letter of 30 August 1929, expressing pleasure that Hughes-Stanton would be providing the illustrations for the new Cresset Press edition of *Birds, Beasts and Flowers*: 'Regards to you both – and for god's sake, don't go into a *cellar*. If it must be among the corpses, let it at least be a modest above-ground mausoleum!' (vii. 457).

43 Frieda 305, 306.

44 *Apocalypse*, ed. Kalnins, pp. 45:36; 47:7; 54:28. Carter chose *not* to include the introduction in his *Dragon of Revelation* (1930).

45 The version of this poem printed here is the one established by Christopher Pollnitz with (above all) 'niggling' in the second line replacing the 'juggling' of the version in *Poems* 673. This is the one occasion I have departed from the text of *Poems* even though, as the forthcoming Cambridge edition of DHL's poetry will show, it is often unsatisfactory.

46 'The Greeks Are Coming!' (*Poems* 687).

47 'The Body of God' (*Poems* 691).

48 See Aldington's introduction to *Last Poems* in *Poems* (p. 592). Another of his views – that for some time DHL used the final two notebooks simultaneously, with the second serving as a repository for rough drafts and the third for final versions, has been convincingly challenged by Keith Sagar in 'The Genesis of "Bavarian Gentians"', *DHLR*, viii (Spring 1975).

49 *Poems* 696, 708.

50 Brewster 309.

51 *Poems* 723.

52 In his introduction to *Fantasia of the Unconscious* (1923), DHL writes: 'I am sorry to say I believe in the souls of the dead. I am almost ashamed to say that I believe the souls of the dead in some way re-enter life and pervade the souls of the living; so that life is always the life of living creatures, and death is always our affair. This bit, I admit, is bordering on mysticism. I'm sorry, because I don't like mysticism' (p. 18); and in his essay on Poe in *Studies in Classic American Literature* he says of Ligeia's return from the dead, 'For it is true, as William James and Conan Doyle and the rest allow, that a spirit can persist in the afterdeath. Persist by its own volition. But usually, the evil persistence of thwarted will, returning for vengeance on life' (*SCAL* 77).

53 *Poems* 719–20. A third, much shorter typescript version of 'The Ship of Death' exists in which there is no return from oblivion. See Keith Sagar, 'Which "Ship of Death"?', *DHLR* xix (1987), 181–4. Much of the time in his last poems DHL seems to be equating 'oblivion' with finally being granted a full and restorative night's sleep.

54 *Poems* 726. A preliminary title for this poem was 'Pauses'.

55 Brewster 224.

56 Ibid.
57 Brewster 306.
58 Ibid. 225. A note in the Curtis Brown archive in UT gives the value of DHL's American share holdings in October 1929 as $3134.25.
59 Frieda 314.
60 Nehls, iii. 413–14.
61 Ibid. 414–16.
62 The event was sufficiently sensational, and the protagonists sufficiently prominent, to make the front pages of the newspapers in America. For a detailed account, see Wolff, *Black Sun*, pp. 273–305.
63 *Apocalypse*, ed. Kalnins, p. 77:19–21.
64 *Poems* 717, 957; Nehls, iii. 427.
65 Frieda 303.
66 Nehls, iii. 428.
67 The first name is found in the letters (vii. 603); the second in Frieda 303; and the third in Brewster 305.
68 Frieda 301.
69 Brewster 307.
70 DHL referred on 6 January to the visit of Orioli and Douglas (vii. 614); and Douglas himself said that the last time he saw him was on the 4th (Nehls, iii. 422). On 15 January DHL told Kot that Pollinger had arrived that day (vii. 620). On 23 January he wrote to Titus, 'Thank you for the cheque for 7,692 francs which you gave me when you were here last week' (vii. 625–6).

 DHL had promised Orioli that he would put him up at Beau Rivage if his own house was too full (vii. 588). When he writes to Pollinger the assumption is always that his agent will go to Beau Rivage as his guest and on 15 January DHL talks of having 'got' him there (vii. 622).
71 In a letter to Gertler on 25 February 1930, after DHL's move to the sanatorium in Vence, Morland writes that his wife would be going to see DHL 'in about a week's time'. See George J. Zytaruk, 'The Last Days of D. H. Lawrence: Hitherto Unpublished Letters of Dr Andrew Morland', *DHLR*, i (Spring 1968), 44–50. Writing to Morland on 30 January, DHL suggests that the signed copy of *Lady Chatterley's Lover* he wants to give him should be sent to Mrs Morland and asks, 'What is her address in Mentone?' (vii. 631).
72 In the memoir Morland wrote for Harry T. Moore in 1952, he said that DHL had probably been suffering from TB 'for ten or fifteen years'; but when pressed by Moore, he admitted that the first stages of the disease were very difficult to determine: 'I do not think the childhood illnesses or the pneumonia at sixteen had any bearing on the tuberculosis. The onset of this probably predated his first attack of haemorrhage by at least a few months or possibly considerably longer' (Nehls, iii. 424, 729 n.398).
73 Nehls, iii. 425.
74 The publishers were Elkin Matthews and Marrot, the same London firm which in 1928 had been responsible for a limited edition of 'Rawdon's Roof'. Providing an introduction was no hardship for DHL given that the issues raised by Ivan Karamazov's story of Jesus returning to earth, only then to receive a dressing-down

from the head of the Spanish Inquisition in Seville, were the same as those he had been discussing in his work on Revelation. Jesus, DHL felt obliged to conclude, had been wrong in basing Christianity on too idealistic a view of human nature. He agreed with Ivan's Grand Inquisitor that, if a recognition of the need of the great mass of the people to be commanded implied a love of them more contemptuous than that of Jesus, it was also more true: grounded on what they actually were, rather than on what they ought to be. Moreover for Jesus to have turned his back on material questions and the power which inevitably went with them, to have rendered unto Caesar the things which were Caesar's, was a grave error: 'ignoring money and leaving it to the devil means handing over the great mass of men to the devil'. Because most men are not able to see the difference between life-values and money-values, those who like Jesus possessed that ability had the responsibility to be power lords as well as religious leaders. Only through them could ordinary people be put in touch with the greater life: 'The sight of a true lord, a noble, a nature-hero puts the sun into the heart of the ordinary man, who is no hero, and therefore cannot know the sun direct.' Ramón Carrasco could not have put it better (*P* 286, 290). For a description of Koteliansky's translation, published in July 1930 at 3 guineas in an edition of 300 copies, see Roberts, *Bibliography of D. H. Lawrence*, p. 277. DHL's introduction made up 16 of the book's 56 pages.

75 Brewster 307.
76 *Apocalypse*, ed. Kalnins, p. 37.
77 Ibid., 71:13−14.
78 Ibid., 93:16−22.
79 Ibid., 126:34.
80 Ibid., 137:11−13.
81 Ibid., 149:13−15, 19−20.

Chapter Twenty-Two: Vence

1 Nehls, iii. 413.
2 Frieda 303.
3 Nehls, iii. 413.
4 *Poems* 301, 304.
5 Nehls, iii. 425.
6 Frieda 306.
7 See Nehls, iii. 430; and Frieda 306. The detail about Hughes-Stanton carrying DHL comes from a letter Ida Hughes-Stanton wrote to James T. Boulton in 1989. She says that this took place when Hughes-Stanton brought DHL *out* of the Ad Astra but other records suggest that Frieda ordered a taxi on that occasion.
8 *P* 396. In a note which accompanied the review when it appeared in the *Book Collector's Quarterly* (Oct.–Dec. 1932), Frieda described it as 'unfinished' (*P* 393).
9 *P* 393, 396.
10 Nehls, iii. 435.
11 Frieda 308.
12 Nehls, iii. 435.

13 Ibid. 433–4; 728 n. 384.

14 Frieda 308.

15 Nehls, iii. 435.

16 The doodle, on what appears to be a compliments slip of the *New English Weekly*, is reproduced in Nehls, iii. 440.

17 *The Times*, 31 January 1930.

18 *Letters of Aldous Huxley*, ed. Grover Smith, pp. 330–1.

19 Harry T. Moore records that the name of the house was later changed to the Villa Aurella (*The Priest of Love*, p. 503). It has now been pulled down and replaced with an apartment block.

20 Nehls, iii. 435.

21 Ibid. 435–6.

22 Bedford, *Aldous Huxley*, i, 224.

23 Ida Hughes-Stanton, in the letter to James T. Boulton (1989).

24 Frieda 309.

25 Ibid. 310.

26 In his letter to Dr and Mrs Henry Head, Nichols referred to Titus as 'Thys, the Paris publisher of *Lady Chatterley's Lover*'. It is from his letter that I have taken the detail about DHL's 'Greek satyr's beard'. See Bedford, *Aldous Huxley*, vol. i, p. 225.

27 Nehls, iii. 448.

28 Budgen knew Stephensen and the quotation is from a letter to him. I take both it, and the information about Budgen and Sargent, from an as yet unpublished article by Christopher Pollnitz: '"No Form or Appropriate Ceremony". An Account of DHL's Funeral'.

29 Bedford, *Aldous Huxley*, vol. i, p. 225.

30 Ibid., p. 227.

31 Nehls, iii. 449, 471–2, 481. It is Barbara Barr who reports the wording of Louie Burrows's letter to Ada. Confirmation that she did indeed visit the grave comes from a letter from Herbert Read to James T. Boulton in which Read claimed that, when he saw her in Vence, she 'obbviosly had never renounced her love and devotion for Lawrence'. See *Lawrence in Love: Letters to Louie Burrows*, ed. James T. Boulton (Nottingham, 1968), p. xxviii.

32 *Memoirs* 241.

33 *The Times*' report of the hearing is reprinted in Nehls, iii. 477–8. Frieda's agreement with Emily and George made it something of a formality although she was still required to convince the judge that a will had once existed.

34 Lucas, *Frieda Lawrence*, p. 254.

35 Lea, *Life of Middleton Murry*, p. 165.

36 Lucas, *Frieda Lawrence*, p. 262.

37 Lucas (pp. 268–70) gives one version of the story but there are several others. In his, Ravagli left the ashes on a station plaform but other accounts describe their being thrown into the Mediterranean. Once they (or their substitute) were at the ranch Frieda supposedly set them in concrete to prevent them being stolen by Mabel Luhan.

38 *D. H. Lawrence's Manuscripts*, ed. Squires (1991), p. 167.

39 The piece in the Australian journal was published in March 1930 and signed 'Nettie

Palmer', that in the *Canadian Forum* appeared in May under the pseudonym 'Inconstant Reader'. For a careful study of obituaries of DHL see Dennis Jackson, '"The Stormy Petrel of Literature is Dead": The World Press Reports D. H. Lawrence's Death', *DHLR*, xiv (Spring 1981), 33–72.

40 See Arnold's essay on Byron in the second series of his *Essays in Criticism* (1888).

41 James Boswell, *The Life of Johnson* (London, 1927), p. 449.

42 *Letters of Aldous Huxley*, ed. Grover Smith, pp. 332, 340.

43 'Why the Novel Matters', *Hardy* 196:35 – 197:12.

44 Johnson, *Life of Richard Savage*, ed. Clarence Tracy (Oxford, 1971), p. 140.

45 *Memoir of Maurice Magnus*, ed. Cushman, p. 101.

ACKNOWLEDGEMENTS

My collaborators on this project, John Worthen and Mark Kinkead-Weekes, have been unfailingly helpful and generous: I could not have managed without them. With their own work largely over, their friendly encouragement never slackened and they were there at the last, to help me across the finishing line. If the rules for biography were the same as those for the marathon, I would have been disqualified. Other readers of my preliminary drafts from whom I have benefited a great deal include Michael Black, Howard Booth, David Bradshaw, Jon Kear, Howard Mills and Christopher Pollnitz; and I am especially grateful to Howard Booth and Christopher Pollnitz for the two appendices. I owe a special debt to Lindeth Vasey who read my text with an acuteness of attention which I am only half relieved it is never likely to receive from anyone else. More generally, I would like to thank Frank Cioffi for attempting to clarify my thoughts on biography and Dennis Enright for continuing to speak to me even after he had discovered I was involved in writing one.

In the increasingly hectic life of British academics, research has become impossible without grants. I am very grateful to the Director of the Humanities Research Center in North Carolina, as well as to his assistants and whole staff, for making my year there so enjoyable. Since returning from the USA I have been lucky enough to secure a grant from the Leverhulme foundation; and before going I benefited from two travel bursaries from the British Academy. Members of my own university have been continuously supportive and I am grateful to colleagues, mostly but not only in English, who have patiently endured my enquiries. Although the Library staff at the University of Kent at Canterbury will no doubt be glad to see the back of me, I remain warmly appreciative of their helpfulness and co-operation.

When responsibilities for this biography were being divided, John Worthen complained that, whereas I would be able to request travel grants for exotic places, all he could apply for was the bus fare to Eastwood. Volume iii has in fact required a good deal of travelling, and left me in the debt of many people. To list their names here is a poor return for their kindness. In the USA I was fortunate to meet Harwood Brewster Picard shortly before she died and learned a great deal from her account of her parents. Ross Parmenter took my wife and me on a 'Walk to Huayapa' we will never forget, and has been throughout remarkably generous. If there were a book for every phase of Lawrence's life as detailed as *Lawrence in Oaxaca* this biography would hardly be necessary. Several leading Lawrence scholars in America made me feel very much at home there: I think particularly of Keith Cushman, James Cowan, Dennis Jackson, Judith Ruderman and Michael Squires; and although I have never met Idella Purnell's daughter, Marijane Osborn, I have been grateful for both her assistance and her permission to quote from her mother's as yet unpublished autobiographical novel.

In Italy, my path was initially smoothed by Ornella De Zordo who has written an excellent book on the publishing venture into which Orioli was tempted by the success of *Lady Chatterley's Lover*. Simonetta de Filippis has always been a friend in need and, more recently, I have received important information from the indefatigable Stefania Michelucci. When I was obliged to be in Florence (hard fate), Frank and Melba Woodhouse were unfailingly hospitable and also provided useful facts about the 1920s when the British Institute which is now in their charge was so important to expatriates. The present occupants of the Villa Mirenda could not have been more co-operative, and I am especially grateful to Roberto Nanni. Barbara Weekley Barr now lives in a village to the south of Florence, and the sense she is so generously willing to impart of what it was like to know Lawrence excites and chastens in equal measure.

Someone who also knew Lawrence, and who has been as generous with her time as Barbara Weekley Barr, is Margaret ('Peggy') Needham. Her name brings me back to England where my debts are legion. Keith Sagar is a pioneer in Lawrence studies who has never had his proper due. No-one could have handed over valuable material with less fuss or egotism, and I retain a warm memory of an evening at his house when Mark Kinkead-Weekes and I were both invited to try on the summer jacket which had once belonged to Lawrence, only to discover it was a no better fit for either of us than the glass slipper for Cinderella's ugly sisters. For matters American I have relied a good deal on my colleague at Kent, Arnold Goldman; James T. Boulton and Mara Kalnins have regularly supplied me with useful information and advice, and I have learned a lot from two research students from Nottingham University, Bethan Jones and Helen Stone. When I had to deal with documents in Spanish I could not have done without my old friend Derek Utley. Many more names come to mind, of individuals who have been helpful but to mention them all in any detail might seem like an attempt to give more importance than it deserves to the end result of all their helpfulness. To show that I have not forgotten however, I would like to thank the following for their help: Al Alvarez, Michael Arlen, Linda Bree, Janet Byrne, D. A. Callard, John and Ianthe Carswell, Henry Claridge, L. D. Clark, John Court, Francesco and Paola Donfrancesco, Denis Donoghue, Paul Eggert, Jay Gertzman, William Graves, Edward Greenwood, Sean Hignett, Paul Hogarth, Rosemary Howard, Stella and Michael Irwin, Martin Kane, Francis King, Jonathan Lamb, Nigel

Lewis, Ian McNiven, Dieter Mehl, Neloufer de Mell, David Mendel, Alan Millen, Leigh Mueller, Jeff Nosbaum, Erik Petersen, Eldon Pethybridge, Peter Preston, Guy Reynolds, Neil Roberts, Cornelia Rumpf-Worthen, Andrews Reith, Doreen Rosman, Martin Scofield, Naomi Segal, R. K. de Silva, Bruce Steele, Brian Vickers and John Wiltshire.

According to my daughters, dedicating an academic book always runs the risk of sounding what they call naff. If it were not for that, the dedicatee would certainly have been their mother, Geneviève, who has lived with D. H. Lawrence longer than she cares to remember, provided an incalculable degree of support and, when a particular line of enquiry proved fruitless or the behaviour of my subject more baffling than usual, habitually pardoned my French.

As far as publication rights are concerned, I am especially grateful for the permission of the Literary Executor of the Estate of Frieda Lawrence Ravagli, Gerald Pollinger, and Laurence Pollinger Limited – as well as of Lawrence's publishers, Messrs William Heinemann Ltd and Cambridge University Press in Great Britain, and Viking Press and Cambridge University Press in the USA – to quote from D. H. Lawrence's and Frieda Lawrence's published and unpublished works and letters. For access to, and permission to quote from, published and unpublished documents, as well as for the use of photographs, I must thank: Barbara Weekley Barr, Sybille Bedford, the Beinecke Rare Book and Manuscript Library at Yale University, the British Library, the Caresse Crosby Photograph Collection (Special Collection/Morris Library, Southern Illinois University at Carbondale), the Center for Creative Photography at the University of Arizona in Tucson, the Harry Ransom Humanities Research Center of the University of Texas at Austin, William Heinemann Ltd, Mara Kalnins, Mrs Alexandra Lee Levin, the Museum of Modern Art in Oxford, Stefania Michelucci, Margaret Needham, the Library of Northwestern University, the Library of Nottingham University, Nottingham County Libraries, Melissa Partridge, Keith Sagar and the Shiller-Nationalmuseum Deutsches Literaturarchiv in Marbach am Neckar.

INDEX

Acton, Harold, visits DHL at Villa Mirenda with Reggie Turner, 385; homosexuality of, 385n; Orioli publishes his translation of *The Last of the Medici*, 443, 443n

Ad Astra, DHL enters, 529; dislikes it and wishes to leave, 530; Huxleys visit DHL at, 530; F removes DHL from, 530; *see also* Vence

Adelaide (Australia), Ls visit art gallery in, 35

Adelphi, 135; DHL's translation of Verga's 'History of the St Joseph's Ass' in, 24, 24n, 135; 'Spirits Summoned West' in, 74, 135; DHL receives copy of first number and dislikes it, 118–19; J. M. Murry's first editorial for, 118, 119; 'The Proper Study' in, 128; Murry's October editorial for, 135; Murry's support for DHL in, 135; extract from *Fantasia of the Unconscious* in, 135; poems from *Birds, Beasts and Flowers* in, 135; DHL dislikes Murry's editorials for, 135; Katherine Mansfield's work in, 135; 'On Being Religious', 'On Human Destiny', 'On Being a Man' in, 144, 152; a tool for recovering England's intellectual leadership, 144–5; Murry's reminiscences of reunion with DHL in, 145; Murry and DHL disagree over its viability, 150; attribution of 'The Ancient Science of Astrology' to Frederick Carter in, 154n; DHL reviews Oman's Revelation book in, 160, 160n; Locke-Ellis its chief financial backer, 168; Murry's 'Heads or Tails?' in, 169–70; possibility of Murry giving it up, 172; review of *A Passage to India* in, 190, 190n; Koteliansky and Murry struggle for control of, 231, 231n; DHL wishes no more of his work in, 285; *see also* Murry, John Middleton

Adventure, DHL's enjoyment of, 262–3

Aga Khan, the, demands to *see Contadini*, 490–1; visits DHL in Ad Astra, 529–30

Aldington, Richard, on DHL's east–west waverings, 11; impressed by DHL's demonstration of jungle noises, 14–15; on DHL in *Portrait of a Genius, But...*, 15, 535;

on DHL in *Life for Life's Sake*, 15; mistaken on source for para-military information in *Kangaroo*, 45, 45n; on Orioli's 'sense of life', 306; renews contact with DHL in England, 312; living with Arabella Yorke, 312; H. D. refuses to divorce, 312; on DHL's visit to Reading, 313; Ls invite him and Arabella to Villa Mirenda, 313; discusses Etruscan matters with DHL, 313; period when the Ls lived with him, H.D. and Arabella, 318; arrives at Villa Mirenda, 321; on DHL at Villa Mirenda, 321–2; editing translations of French memoirs, 345n; he and Arabella offer money to DHL, 385; on Norman Douglas's envy of DHL, 404, 404n; likes *Lady Chatterley's Lover*, 437; arrives at 'la Vigie' with Arabella and Brigit Patmore, 441; worried about DHL's condition, 442; gives DHL advice on Grazzini translation, 443; on DHL's hurt at attacks on *Lady Chatterley's Lover*, 443; working on *Death of a Hero*, 445–6; misogyny in *Death of a Hero*, 446; DHL's reaction to *Death of a Hero*, 446; tensions over Arabella–Patmore situation, 449, 449n; comments on DHL's 'pansies', 451n; 'Ronald' in 'The Noble Englishman' probably based on him, 485; on DHL's introduction to the *Story of Doctor Manente*, 496; on the last stage of DHL's poetry, 517, 517n; *see also* H. D.; Yorke, Dorothy; and Patmore, Bridgit

Aldred, Guy, DHL sends him unexpurgated *Pansies* for consideration, 485n

America, DHL's fascination with and possibility of going to, 7; DHL avoiding confrontation with, 8; DHL's continued wavering on decision to go to, 9, 10; DHL's money in, 21; animism in, 34; DHL still planning voyage to, 34; DHL gets visas for, 50; DHL books tickets to, 53; DHL's apprehension about going to, 54; DHL on, in 'Au Revoir, U.S.A.', 102; DHL on, 65–6, 67, 67n, 265; DHL on romantic views of, 66–7, 67n, 68; DHL on wilfulness of Americans, 70; effect

Dahlberg, Edward, DHL writes foreword to
Bottom Dogs by, 468, 468n, 469; DHL
compares *Bottom Dogs* to *Point Counter
Point*, 469; comments on Grand Hotel
de Versailles, 472
Daily Telegraph (London), encourages
authorities to close DHL exhibition, 490n
Daily Telegraph (Sydney), DHL's use of in
Kangaroo, 39
Danes, the, *see* Götzsche, Kai; Merrild, Knud
Darlington (Australia), Mollie Skinner's guest
house in, 26; *see also* Leithdale
Darroch, Robert, on *Kangaroo* and DHL's stay
in Australia, 37, 37n, 45, 45n, 50, 51, 51n
Darrow, Clarence, represents Ben Hecht on
obscenity charges, 75
Dasburg, Andrew, part of Mabel Sterne's New
Mexico coterie, 82; on DHL's love of
charades, 82n; DHL describes to him an
appropriate fate for Mabel, 86n; moves to
Santa Fe with Ida Rauh, 181; visited by Ls
and Brett in Santa Fe, 204; he and Rauh
drive Ls to Del Monte, 241; DHL writes to
him on pace of recovery, 244; Mabel
interfering in relationship with Rauh, 413;
Rauh separated from, 521; *see also* Rauh,
Ida
Davidson, Jo, sculpts bust of DHL, 530
Davies, Rhys, visits DHL in Bandol, 455–6;
DHL likes *The Withered Root* by, 455;
witness to Ls' rows, 456; on DHL in
Horizon and *Print of a Hare's Foot*, 456–7;
contributor to *London Aphrodite*, 458; visits
DHL with P. R. Stephensen, 458; gives
DHL silk dressing gown for Christmas
present, 461; posts 'improper' pansies to
Secker for DHL, 468; travels to Paris with
DHL, 471; stays at Grand Hotel de
Versailles with DHL, 472; homosexuality
of, 472n; account of DHL's illness, 473–4;
on DHL and Sylvia Beach's negotiations,
474n; on DHL's desire to 'reach the
masses', 475; returns to England, 478; on
DHL's reaction to poems being seized, 479;
DHL writes to him about Majorca, 482;
inclined to make a fuss over F, 488–9;
financial difficulties of, 503; DHL writes on
'proper' and 'improper' publishing publics
to, 503
Davis, Irving, Orioli's London business partner,
306; DHL blames higher *Lady Chatterley's
Lover* prices on him and Orioli, 435
Davis, Joseph, on DHL's stay in and around
Sydney, 37n, 38
De Angulo, Jaime, meets Mabel Sterne in San
Francisco, 175; background, 175–6, 176n;

discusses linguistic matters with Tony
Luhan, 176; practises amateur
psychoanalysis on Clarence Thompson,
176; interests Mabel in Jung, 176; returns
to Taos with Tony Luhan, 176; DHL's
opinion of, 178–9; sets out to walk to
California, 179, 179n; on Ls, 186;
contracted malaria in Oaxaca, 235
Dekker, E. D., *Max Havelaar* by, 43; *see also*
Siebenhaar, William
Delany, Paul, on DHL's tuberculosis, 19n
Deledda, Grazia, DHL writes introduction to
her translation of *La madre*, 396–7; wins
1926 Nobel Prize for Literature, 397; *La
madre* entitled *The Woman and the Priest* in
translation, 397n
Del Monte ranch, DHL plans to rent cabin on,
83; Ls move to, 84; conditions at, 84, 85;
visitors to, 87, 93; Ls leave, 99; Brett to
return to, 228; Rauh and Dasburg drive Ls
to, 241; Brett to remain there rather than
going to Kiowa, 241; Brett assumes she will
stay on after Ls have left, 263–4; *see also*
Hawks, the
Dennis, George, DHL reads *Cities and
Cemeteries of Etruria* by, 304; DHL requests
copy of Dennis's book from Secker, 365
Diablerets, Les (Switzerland), DHL leaves
Jaguar Leaping at a Man in, 381n; Ls leave
for, 397; Ls with Huxleys in, 398; F leaves,
401; DHL leaves, 401
Diaz, Bernal, DHL's use of *True History of the
Conquest of Mexico* by, 110, 110n, 211
Díaz, Porfirio, 107, 107n, 108, 109, 210; house of
brother used in 'Quetzalcoatl'/*The Plumed
Serpent*, 108; Oaxacan population under,
209
Di Chiara, Anna and Ferdinando, DHL sees
them in Capri, 290; Brewsters stay in villa
of, 332, 460; at Hotel Beau Rivage, 521;
they lunch with DHL on New Year's Day,
524; at DHL's funeral, 532
Dobrée, Bonamy, DHL meets him through
Gertler, 318; invites Ls to Egypt, 377; DHL
invites his wife to Villa Mirenda, 377–88;
letter from DHL on reactions to *Lady
Chatterley's Lover* to, 434
Doctor Looks at Literature, The, *see* Collins,
Joseph
Dodge, Mabel, *see* Sterne, Mabel
Doolittle, Hilda, *see* H. D.
Dos Passos, John, DHL reviews *Manhattan
Transfer* by, 337
Dostoyevsky, Fyodor, possible allusion to *The
Brothers Karamozov* in *Kangaroo*, 49n;
DHL compares him to John Fenimore

LIFE

thinking of writing a book on the Etruscans, 296;
returns to warm welcome at the Villa Bernarda,
296; uncertain plans, settles on Florence, 297; to
Pensione Lucchesi in Florence, 298; wants to
prepare for Etruscan book, 298; he and F move
into Villa Mirenda, 299; likes the Villa Mirenda
very much, 298–9; writes 'The Nightingale' and
'Two Blue Birds', 300; encourages Rachel Hawk
and son to move to Kiowa, 302; worried about
his sisters because of miners' strike, 303; worried
about writing future and money, 303–4; writes to
Mabel regularly about her memoirs, 304;
continues plans for Etruscan book, 304; types F's
translation of *David*, 304–5; enjoys the
Wilkinsons' company, 305; gets to know Orioli
through Reggie Turner, 306; Turner introduces
him to the Sitwells, 306–7; visits the Sitwells
outside Florence, 307; working on 'The Man
Who Loved Islands', 307; wishes to go to
London to oversee *David* production, 307; leaves
for Baden-Baden, 307; with F's mother in
Baden-Baden, 307–8; he and F probably visit
altar to Mercury, 309–10; to London, 311; he
and F rent flat in Chelsea, 311; Huxley,
Koteliansky and Rolf Gardiner visit, 312; with F
spends weekend with Aldingtons, 313; visits
Beveridge sisters in Scotland, 313; visits Fort
William and the Isle of Skye, 313; reviews Wells's
The World of William Clissold, 314; to
Nottingham, 314; travels with Eddie Clarke and
Peggy King to Mablethorpe, 314; concerned
about Gertie Cooper's health, 314–15; joined by
F and moves to Sutton-on-Sea, 315; to Emily's
house in Nottingham, 315–16; sees Ada in Ripley,
316; visits Eastwood for the last time, 316; may
have now begun 'Return to Bestwood', 316;
returns to F in London, 318; sees many people
during last days in London, 318; researches
Etruscans at the British Museum, 318; Dorothy
Richardson takes him to the Untermeyers' party,
318; sees the Carswells and Koteliansky before
leaving, 319; leaves England for last time, 319;
sees Mabel Harrison in Paris, 319; back at the
Villa Mirenda, 319; Aldingtons visit, 321; he and
F work on the Villa Mirenda, 322; they visit
Huxleys in Florence, 323; Maria gives him
canvasses, 323; begins *The First Lady Chatterley*,
324; has trouble resolving class struggle in *The
First Lady Chatterley*, 327–8; change in attitude
to politics, 328; finishes *The First Lady Chatterley*
and immediately begins rewrite (*John Thomas
and Lady Jane*), 326; knows *Lady Chatterley* book
will be controversial, 327; growing enthusiasm
for painting, 328, 329, 330; considers a London
exhibition, 330; resents negative responses to his
paintings, 332; visits the Stentorello Theatre in

Florence with Orioli and the Wilkinsons, 335,
335n; has Christmas party for the peasants on
the estate, 331–2;

1927:

Earl Brewster visits, 332; he and Brewster visit
Magnelli's studio, 332–3; Huxleys visit with
Mary Hutchinson, 333–4; falls ill after finishing
John Thomas and Lady Jane, 334; thinking of
selling Kiowa, 339; writes 'The Lovely Lady' for
Cynthia Asquith, 343, 345; writes first two parts
of 'Flowery Tuscany', 345, 345n; Seltzers ask
him to return to them, 345; leaves for Rome and
stays with Christine Hughes, 346–7; with the
Brewsters in Ravello, 347, 349; working on *Fauns
and Nymphs* at Brewsters', 349; walking with
Earl on the Sorrento peninsula, 350; takes
Etruscan tour with Earl, 350–4; back at the Villa
Mirenda, 355; not getting along with Barby on
current visit, 357; Edith and Osbert Sitwell visit,
366; writes new introduction to *Mastro-don
Gesualdo*, 350; takes Christine Hughes and
daughter to the Uffizi, 366; completes the six
Sketches of Etruscan Places, 351; renews lease on
the Villa Mirenda, 358; dismayed by new taxes
on royalties, 359; writes 'None of That!', 360;
writes 'Things', 361, 361n; tells Brewsters that
'Things' is not about them, 362; reviews Walter
Wilkinson's *The Peep Show*, 363–4; health makes
him unable to return to London to help with
David, 364; worried about money, 366; driven by
Maria Huxley to Forte dei Marmi, 366; planning
Etruscan trip with F, 367; serious haemorrhages
confine him to bed, 367; finishes review of
Trigant Burrow's *The Social Basis of
Consciousness*, 369, 369n; takes train to Villach,
Austria, 371; translating more Verga, 371; wishes
to help Gertie Cooper out financially, 371–2; to
Else Jaffe's house in Irschenhausen, 372;
responds favourably to Secker's idea for a
Collected Poems, 372; enjoys Irschenhausen, 372;
Schoenberner and Carossa visit and Carossa
gives him a false diagnosis, 373–4; Max Mohr
visits, 377; finishes translating Verga stories for
Cavalleria rusticana, 374; to Baden-Baden, 376;
has medical exam, 376; unwilling to enter a
sanatorium, 376–7; takes cold air cure but is
unimpressed, 377; unsure of where to go for
winter, 377–8; he and F return to Villa Mirenda,
378; attempts to help Koteliansky, 379;
reconciled with Norman Douglas, 379–80; writes
'Dream of Life' for Kotelinsky, 380; completes
Throwing Back the Apple and *Jaguar Leaping at a
Man*, 381; sends 'Rawdon's Roof' to Pearn, 382;
working on *Collected Poems*, 382, 383, 384; car
trip to San Gimignano with the Wilkinsons, 385;

INDEX

Lawrence, David Herbert (*cont.*)
trip into Florence makes him ill, 385; determines
to publish *Lady Chatterley's Lover* privately, 386;
Michael Arlen visits for tea, 386, 387; begins
final revision of *Lady Chatterley's Lover*, 388;
irritated by Christmas plans, 394–5; enjoys
Christmas dinner with Huxleys at the
Petterichs', 395; has trouble getting *Lady
Chatterley's Lover* typed, 396, 397; finishes
Mango Tree, 396;

1928:

departure for Switzerland delayed by illness,
397; at the Chateau Beau Site in Les Diablerets,
398; begins to enjoy Les Diablerets, 399; picnic
on the Pillon Pass, 399, 428; writes new ending
for 'The Border-Line' because of lost proofs,
399; sends off *Collected Poems*, 399; preparing
expurgated *Lady Chatterley's Lover* for Knopf
and Secker, 399, 400; has difficulty deciding on
title for *Lady Chatterley's Lover*, 400, 400n;
develops good relationship with Juliette Huxley,
400; Rolf Gardiner visits, 401; Max Mohr visits,
402; Juliette accompanies him to Aigle on leaving
Les Diablerets, 401; meets F in Milan, 403;
return to Villa Mirenda, 403; working on private
publication of *Lady Chatterley's Lover*, 404–5;
angry at Curtis Brown for not finding a UK
publisher for *Lady Chatterley's Lover*, 405;
receives five gold $20 coins from Harry Crosby,
405; re-handwrites 'Sun' for Crosby with new
ending, 405; has Orioli bind up MSS for Crosby,
407; asks that Crosby not be so generous, 408;
paints *Dandelions* and several other paintings,
409; Margaret Gardiner visits, 410, 412;
Beveridge sisters visit and 'loathe' *Dandelions*,
410, 410n; Dorothy Warren invites him to
exhibit paintings at her gallery, 411; his
suspicions about F and Ravagli, 412–13; renews
Villa Mirenda lease for six months, 413; Enid
Hilton and husband visit, 411, 412; has Hiltons
transport paintings to Warren in London, 412;
still unsure of whether to exhibit, 412; making
plans to return to America, 414; writes 'When
She Asks Why', 414; sends 'Laura Phillipine' to
Pearn, 414; becoming more secure financially,
415; sends 'Mother and Daughter' to Pearn, 415;
reconciled with Ottoline Morrell, 416–17; to
Turin, Chambéry, Aix-les-Bains, and Grenoble
with the Brewsters, 421; to Saint-Nizier, 421;
required to leave Hotel des Touristes, Saint-
Nizier, because of cough, 421–2; to Chexbres-
sur-Vevey, 422; writes 'Over-Earnest Ladies' in
Chexbres, 422; writes 'Master in His Own
House' and 'Dull London' in Chexbres, 423;
working on the second part of *The Escaped Cock*,

423–4; Huxleys visit and take him to Château de
Chillon, 424; asks Orioli to oversee the packing
of his paintings, 424–5; reconsiders where to
exhibit paintings, 425; receives first copy of *Lady
Chatterley's Lover* from Orioli, 425–6; worried
about Customs interference with *Lady
Chatterley's Lover*, 426; directing *Lady
Chatterley's Lover* sales, 427; leaves Chexbres for
Gstaad, 427; he and F move to Chalet
Kesselmatte, 427–8; feels isolated at Chalet
Kesselmatte, 428; writes 'Matriarchy', 428; has
Enid Hilton and Koteliansky hold returned
copies of *Lady Chatterley's Lover*, 426; writes
autobiographical sketch for a French publisher,
429, 429n; sends Pearn reviews for *Vogue*, 429;
sends 'Red Trousers' to Pearn, 430; meets
Mukerji and Boshi Sen, 431; paints *Sun-Men
Catching Horses* for Crosby, as well as *Contadini*,
North Sea, *Accident in a Mine* and *The Milk
White Lady*, 432; writes 'The Blue Mocassins'
and asks the Brewsters how to end it, 433; illness
not improving, 434; excited over *Lady
Chatterley's Lover* activities, 434–5; asks Orioli to
make false dust-jackets for *Lady Chatterley's
Lover*, 434–5; *Lady Chatterley's Lover* becomes a
crusade for him, 435; has had Tipographia
Guitina produce 200 cheap *Lady Chatterley's
Lover* copies, 435; doubles the price for the last
200 higher-quality copies of *Lady Chatterley's
Lover*, 435; at farewell party for Brewsters, 436;
writes 'Hymns in a Man's Life', 436; considers
Port Cros in travel plans, 437; pleased by the
Aldingtons' liking of *Lady Chatterley's Lover*,
437–8; dislikes Joyce's 'Work in Progress' in
transition, 438; has to give up US exhibition
plans because of US Customs, 438–9; America
eliminated from travel plans, 439; leaves for
Baden-Baden, 439; staying outside Baden-Baden
with Brewsters, F, and F's mother, 439–40;
decides to go to Port Cros, 440; travels with
Brewsters to Le Lavandou, 440; sees *Ben Hur* in
Strasbourg and hates it, 440; meets Else Jaffe
and Alfred Weber in Le Lavandou, 440, 441;
visits Port Cros with Huxleys, Else and Weber,
441; to Port Cros to stay with Aldingtons, 441;
catches cold from F, 442; translating Grazzini's
Story of Doctor Manente, 443; hurt by attacks on
Lady Chatterley's Lover, 443, 444; writes 'Is
England Still a Man's Country?', 'Sex Locked
Out' and 'Women Don't Change' on Port Cros,
445; his reaction to Aldington's *Death of a Hero*
and Mohr's *Venus in den Fischen*, 446; receives
and reacts to Huxley's *Point Counter Point*,
446–7; reaction to 'Rampion' portrait in *Point
Counter Point*, 447; decides to leave Port Cros,
449; responds warmly to letter from David

748

Chambers, 450; at Hotel Beau Rivage, Bandol, 451; begins writing pansies, 451–3; unsure where to go next, 453, 454; concerned about *Lady Chatterley* non-payers, 454; worries over piracy of *Lady Chatterley's Lover*, 454; sends 'Enslaved by Civilisation' to Pearn, 454; receives many visitors in Bandol, 455; reacts to Murry's version of his presence at Mansfield's death, 457; no desire to renew friendship with Murry, 457; completes six paintings in Bandol, 457, 458; very interested in idea for book of his paintings, 458; he and F spend Christmas alone, 460; likes Rhys Davies, 461;

1929:

invites Ghiselin to spend his vacation with them, 461; writes second introduction to *Pansies*, 462–3; sends *Pansies* TS to Curtis Brown's office (is seized by UK Customs), 462; to Ottoline Morrell on *Lady Chatterley's Lover* and 'basic physical realities', 462, 462n; writes essay on painting for P. R. Stephensen, 463–6; hears of Scotland Yard seizures of *Lady Chatterley's Lover*, 466–7; tries to get *Pansies* TS returned, 467; revising and working on new pansies, 467–8; arranges for 'improper' pansies to reach Secker, 468; anger at Joynson-Hicks over seizures, 468; less angry about *Point Counter Point* and still quite fond of Huxley, 468, 468n; writes foreword to Dahlberg's *Bottom Dogs*, 468, 468n, 469; sends Brewsters and his sisters copies of *Lady Chatterley's Lover*, 469; tells Ada to read 'Myself Revealed' in *Sunday Dispatch*, 469; Ada's visit depresses him, 469–70; sends £50 to Ada, 470; to Paris with Davies, 471, 472; lunch with Crosbys, 472; seriously ill, 473; stays with Huxleys in Suresnes for a week, 473; abandons plan to get X-rayed, 474; Sylvia Beach may have suggested Edward Titus as publisher of French edition of *Lady Chatterley's Lover*, 475; makes deal with Titus for 3,000 *Lady Chatterley's Lover* copies (later authorises second and third printing), 475; writes 'My Skirmish with Jolly Roger' for Titus's edition, 475–6; spends weekend with Crosbys, 477; breaks records over F's head, 477; dislike of Joyce confirmed by recording of him reading from *Ulysses*, 477; second visit to Crosbys', 477; confirms deal with Titus, 478; receives £1,200 from Titus, 475; he and F leave for Spain, 478; writes 'Making Pictures' in Barcelona, 478; decides to go to Majorca, 479; corresponds with Secker over the pansies, 479; congratulates Rebecca West on her article attacking Joynson-Hicks, 479, 479n; continues to write short poems, 479–80, 480n; sees Robert Nichols in Majorca, 481; he and F move from

the Hotel Royal to the Principe Alfonso, 481; his opinion of Majorca, 481, 482; house-hunting cut short by shivering fit, 481–2; meets the Majorcan expatriate community, 482; writes 'Pornography and Obscenity' for Titus, 482–3; receiving proofs for edition of paintings, 483; Italy plans, 483–4; sends 'Pictures on the Wall' to Pearn, 484; impatient with publishers, 484; negotiates signed edition of *Pansies* through Pollinger, 484, 484n; irritated by Secker's suggested cuts to *Pansies*, 484, 485; makes unexpurgated *Pansies* deal with Lahr, 485, 485n; writes fourth *Pansies* introduction for Secker, 485n; irritated by reports of impending death, 486, 486n; discourages Murry from visiting, 487; writes to Mohr on his health in Majorca, 487; trip to Valldemosa and Soller, 487; Pollinger warns of threat of arrest if he returns to England, 487; exhibition of paintings opens at the Warren Gallery, 487; he and F leave Majorca, and part in Marseilles, 487–8; arrives in Forte dei Marmi, 493; 3,500 visit exhibition of his paintings in first week, 489; pleased that Ada likes paintings, 490; hopes new Labour government will be better for him, 490n; continuing to write poems, 493; invites Orioli to Forte, 493–4; Maria Cristina Chambers joins him in Forte, 494; police seize thirteen of his paintings, 490; Maria Huxley takes him to Pisa, 495; travels to Florence, 495; stays in Orioli's flat while ill, 495; relieved at F's return, 495; F takes him to Hotel Porta Rossa in Florence, 495; corresponds with Warren over court case, 495–6; still writing poems, 496; to Baden-Baden, 499; to Plättig with F and F's mother, 500; battle of wills with F's mother, 500; on Baroness von Richthofen's greed for life, 500; considers rewriting *The Virgin and the Gipsy*, 500, 500n; sends 'The Risen Lord' to Pearn, 500; returns from Plättig, 501; sends 'Men and Women' to Pearn, 501; better but still ill, 501; paintings to be returned to him, 502; angry over court case outcome and press coverage, 502; writing 'nettles', 502; suggests 'Squib' idea but soon abandons it, 502–3; Titus sends £150 for 'My Skirmish' pamphlet in NY, 503; burgeoning sales from increased notoriety, 503–4; embarrassed by price of limited editions, 504; writes 'Choice of Evils', 504; writes 'Nottingham and the Mining Countryside', 504–5; looking for house in Florence, 505–6; he and F leave for Munich, 506; to Rottach to see Max Mohr, 506; likes Rottach situation, 506; begins writing 'Bavarian Gentians' 506, 506n; examined by two doctors, 507; associates illness with male menopause, 507–8; interested in new doctor's approach but depressed when no results are seen,

Lawrence, David Herbert (*cont.*)
Spring: changes to, 458–459; seized by police, 490;
Summer Dawn: and physical intimacy between males, 459;
Sun-Men Catching Horses: paints for Crosby, 432; Emily King posts to Crosby, 437;
Throwing Back the Apple: completed within a month of returning to Villa Mirenda, 381;
Under the Haystack: melancholy and static, 409;
Yawning: similar pose to *Fire Dance*, 409

Plays

'Altitude': DHL begins in June but abandons, 181, 181n; portraits of Mabel Sterne's circle in, 182;
The Daughter-in-Law: similar situation to that in 'Whether or Not', 384;
David: DHL writes for Ida Rauh, 238; working on, 244; relation to the Bible, 245; sympathises with Saul, 245; similar themes to 'Noah's Flood', 245; length of, 245, 245n; DHL finishes, 245; reads to Rauh, 246; Rauh's reaction to, 246–7; DHL on, 247; conflation of power and sexual potency in, 261; New York Guild Theatre considers producing, 264; F translates into German, 296; DHL types F's translation, 304–5; DHL wishes to oversee first staging in London, 307; waiting for rehearsals to begin, 315; Phyllis Whitworth organising London production, 318; DHL writes music for, 339, 339n; Whitworth asks for help in preparing subscription performance, 364; Koteliansky to DHL on the performance, 364–5; negative reviews, 365;
'Noah's Flood': for Ida Rauh, 238; the Great White Bird image, 238; unfinished, 238; similar themes to *David*, 245;
The Widowing of Mrs Holroyd: Whitworth arranges a production of, 339;

Poetry

'All-Knowing': very short, 480;
'All Saints' Day': and DHL's prevailing tone of the time, 517–18;
'The American Eagle': political poem written at Del Monte, 92;
Amores: changes to, in *Collected Poems*, 385n;
'Anaxagoras': and DHL's interest in Revelation, 517;
'Andraitx—Pomegranate Flowers': written in Majorca, 479;
'Autumn at Taos': written in Taos, 73, 73n;
'Bavarian Gentians': drafts begun in Rottach, 506, 506n; on death, 506–7, 519; first version called 'Glory of Darkness', 507; revised, 517;

'Beyond the Rockies': in special DHL issue of *Laughing Horse*, 278n;
'Bibbles': on DHL's dog, 92; finished, 96;
Birds, Beasts and Flowers: most of the poems written in Fontana Vecchia, 6; Keith Sagar on, 20n; DHL's awareness of own solipsism in, 45n; 'Kangaroo', 50; 'Spirits Summoned West', 73; finished at Del Monte, 92; 'The American Eagle', 'Bibbles', 'The Blue Jay', 'Mountain Lion', 92; correcting proofs for, 122; poems from in *Adelphi*, 135; felicity of description in best of these poems, 143; DHL writing little poetry between their publication and beginning to write pansies, 343, 451; chooses epigraphs for new edition of, 516, 516n; image of almond tree in, 528;
'The Blue Jay': written at the Del Monte, 92;
'The Body of God': one of several poems attempting to define the world's creative principle, 517;
'Change of Life': borrows from Mabel's poem on menopause, 355, 355n;
'Choice of Evils': on choice between the bourgeois and the bolshevist, 504;
Collected Poems: Secker suggests, 372, 372n; DHL preparing, 382; regrets absence of biographical framework for, 382–3; provides Secker with two introductions, 383; mentions Chambers, Corke and (obliquely) Burrows in introduction, 383; alters some poems in, 383, 384, 385; finishes work on, 399; interest in poetry revived by, 451; DHL negotiates deal with Secker for signed copies, 484n;
'Corot': removal of references to 'God' in *Collected Poems*, 384;
'Correspondence in After Years': and Murry's letter of concern, 487n;
'Democracy is Service': return to leadership ideas in, 497;
'Eagle in New Mexico': written in Taos, 73, 73n;
'Elephant': celebrates the Kandy perahera, 16; discrepancy between the Prince of Wales and the festival, 17; where the 'white people' were in relation to the festival, 17n; perhaps only writing done in Ceylon, 20; question of its place of composition, 20n;
'The Evening Land': and complex feelings on America, 7;
'Fatality': on becoming 'finally self-centred', 480;
'Fellow-Men': on separation from others, 497, 497n;
'Food of the North': complaint of heavy German food in, 508;
'Forte dei Marmi': and arrival in Italy, 480;
'The Greeks Are Coming!': written on return to Bandol, 517;

Lawrence, David Herbert (*cont.*)

'Letter from Germany': on post-war state of Germany, 160; in *New Statesman* in 1934, 160n; similar descriptions to 'The Border-Line', 160, 160n;

'A Little Moonshine with Lemon': in *Laughing Horse*, 277; contrasts Kiowa and Villa Bernarda, 277–8; provides postscript to *Mornings in Mexico*, 278n;

Little Novels of Sicily: translation of Verga stories, 24n, 91, 91n, 371;

'London Letter': in *Laughing Horse*, 155; uncollected, 155n; effect on final chapter of *The Boy in the Bush*, 156;

The Lost Girl: DHL completes, 6; wins James Tate Black Memorial prize, 10;

'Love': and '...... Love Was Once a Little Boy', 255;

'The Lovely Lady': written for Asquith, 343; takes from Poe's 'Ligeia' and *The Picture of Dorian Gray*, 344; connection to DHL's mother, 344–5; shortens for Asquith, 345;

'...... Love Was Once a Little Boy': Susan the cow features in, 254–5; and relationship with external world, 255; disillusioned commentary on 'Love', 255–6; equality and difference in, 260; and DHL's illness, 261;

'Making Love to Music': on sex and dancing, 359; Pearn cannot place, 359–60; elaborated on in 'A Dream of Life', 380–1;

'Making Pictures': Merrild quotes from, 94; on painting at the Villa Mirenda, 328; in *Creative Art*, 328n; written in Barcelona, 478; in the *Studio* with *The Finding of Moses*, 478; on importance of 'visionary awareness', 478; DHL refers to his copying in, 478–9;

'Man is a Hunter': discrepancy between hunter and hunted in, 321;

'The Man Who Loved Islands': Mackenzie's reaction to, 301, 302; 'nearly done', 303; ponders the mix between privacy and social contact, 307; posted to Pearn, 310; Mackenzie pressures Secker not to include in the *Woman Who Rode Away* collection, 310; most philosophical of DHL's fiction, 310; relationship between language and society in, 311; on the impossibility of separating ourselves from others, 311; Cathcart based on both Mackenzie and DHL, 311; on use of Mackenzie in, 362; MS included in Crosby package, 407;

'Master in His Own House': for the *Evening News*, 423, 423n;

Mastro-don Gesualdo: Verga translation, 13, 20, 24, 350, 350n, 371, 374–5, 375n;

'Matriarchy': for the *Evening News*, 428; on women

in post-war Britain overwhelming men, 428–9; *Evening News* will not publish, 429n;

'Men and Women': *Star Review* requests, 501; name changed in *Assorted Articles*, 501n;

'Mercury': based on visit to altar to Mercury in Baden-Baden, 309; Achsah Brewster on, 309; fictionalisation in, 309–10; appears in *Atlantic Monthly* and *Nation and Athenaeum*, 309n;

'Morality and the Novel': art to reveal relationship between man and universe, 250–1; in *Calendar of Modern Letters*, 251;

Mornings in Mexico: DHL writes opening chapters around Christmas, 210, 210n, 223, 226; on Oaxacan illiteracy in 'The Walk to Huayapa', 210; visit to market subject of fourth 'Morning', 211, 223; Father Rickards's garden described in first sketch, 212, 224; portrait of Rosalino in third sketch, 212; compared to *The Plumed Serpent*, 223–4; first sketch intended for *Vanity Fair*, 226; 'A Little Moonshine and Lemon' provides postscript for, 278n; misgivings about, 336, 336n;

'Mother and Daughter': 415–16, 416n; may have been prompted by Mary Foote, 415;

Movements in European History: effect of working on, 153; DHL uses pseudonym L. H. Davidson for, 160; writes new 'Epilogue' which Oxford University Press refuses to print, 202, 224;

Mr Noon: left unfinished, 6, 32, 32n; on writer's block with, 39; on Sallie Hopkin, 73, 73n;

'Myself Revealed': DHL tells Ada to read, 469; in *Sunday Dispatch*, 469; Pearn probably adapts from longer piece, 469, 469n;

'My Skirmish with Jolly Roger': foreword to Titus edition of *Lady Chatterley's Lover*, 475; basis of 'A Propos of *Lady Chatterley's Lover*', 475n, 514, 515; offers defence of language in *Lady Chatterley's Lover*, 475–6; Foucault uses passage from, 476n; Swift's 'Celia' cited in, 476n; criticism of Home Secretary in, 476; criticises 'modern young jazzy' people in, 476; contains Harry Crosby's criticism of *Lady Chatterley's Lover*, 477; published as pamphlet in NY, 503;

'New Mexico': DHL remembers Buddhist dancers in, 16n; records first impressions of New Mexico, 62; commissioned to write it via Mabel, 453;

New Poems: preface to, 42;

'The Nightingale': comments on Keats and Murry's *Keats and Shakespeare* in, 300; protests against self-pity, 300;

'Nobody Loves Me': completed, 515; sparked by Achsah Brewster's comment, 515n;

'None of That!': portrait of Mabel Sterne in,

Europe to see mother and children, 119; her children a source of conflict with DHL,119; admits DHL is correct on some matters concerning children, 119; holds DHL firmly to intention of leaving Chapala, 120; on lake trip, 120–1; she and DHL leave Chapala, 121; vaccinated to re-enter the US, 121, 121n; she and DHL move into Birkindele, 122; spends most of time with DHL in the countryside, 122–3; determined to go to England on her own, 124; previous separations from DHL, 124, 124n; to Adele Seltzer on anger with DHL, 124; J. M. Murry on her anger with DHL, 125; possibility of leaving DHL, 124, 125, 126; writes to Bynner on happiness at Chapala, 125; possibility of physical abuse between DHL and her, 125; her financial dependence on DHL, 125; uses Mary Cannan's flat in England, 126; moves in with Carswells, 126; might not have sent letter breaking with DHL, 130; she and DHL correspond on length of her stay in Europe, 130, 132, 135; her complaints about DHL's attachment to monogamous 'loyalty', 133; DHL's distrust of new closeness between Murry and her, 135; his warnings to her, 135; DHL receives two letters from, 138; DHL informs her that he is returning to England, 138–9; she writes to Koteliansky on her love for DHL, 139n; explains the point/aim of *Adelphi*, 144; her relationship with Murry, 145, 145n, 146, 163, 164; meets DHL in London, 145; settles into 110 Heath Street with DHL, 146; worries about DHL's health in England, 146; writes that making DHL return was a mistake, 147, 147n; Brett unaware of Murry's attraction to, 148; she and DHL at Christmas meal with Brett, 148; visits Emily King in Nottingham, 269–70; disagrees with Koteliansky over DHL's greatness, 149, 149n; issue of Murry and her, at Café Royal dinner, 151; behaviour at dinner, 151–2; stays in London while DHL visits family, 153; on Koteliansky's condemnation of Brett, 158; decides to return to America with DHL, and make second visit to mother, 158; visits daughters in England, 159; clothes-shopping in Paris, 159; visits Gurdjieff Institute with DHL, 159; indentification of her with heroine in 'The Border-Line', 160, 160n; 'queen bee' or 'q-b' DHL's nickname for, 161; relations with Murry after DHL's death, 163; sexual relations with DHL,

163–4; possibly discusses Murry with DHL, 165n; more Paris sightseeing, 165; DHL on why she was attracted to Murry, 167; she and DHL make arrangements to leave England, 170; stays in Seltzers' NY flat with Brett, 174; she and DHL spend time with Willa Cather, 174; Harriet Monroe shows them around Chicago, 175; writes to Mabel on the value of *Sons and Lovers* MS, 183, 190; dances with Thompson at Mabel's dance, 188; talks with Mabel, 189; disbelieves DHL's claims to psychic powers, 189; on *St. Mawr*, 191; sexual relations with DHL implied in *St. Mawr*, 193–4; possibly attracted to Swinburne Hale, 194; does housework at Kiowa, 195; enjoys horseback riding, 195; preparing to leave for Mexico, 202; she and Brett a possible element in Mabel's breakdown, 203; she and DHL catch the 'flu in Mexico City, 205–6; leaves for Oaxaca, 208; getting to know Oaxaca with DHL and Brett, 210–11; her growing irritation with Brett, 212; she and DHL move to Father Rickards's, 212; , 225, 226–7, 228, 229; DHL's use of her in developing female response in *The Plumed Serpent*, 216; her unfinished autobiographical novel, 226–7; ultimatum regarding Brett, 227; wishes to see mother and children, 227; calls on Brett, 229; sees Brett off with DHL, 229; writes friendly note to Brett in Mexico City, 231; on kindness of Oaxacan expatriate community during DHL's illness, 235; upset and sick at DHL's state on trip to Mexico City, 236; plans to return to England, 236; to Mabel on X-ray of DHL's lungs, 237, 237n; told of DHL's tuberculosis, 237; to Brett about return to Kiowa, 237; on delay at the US border, 239–40; renewed tension with Brett, 2–243; reading the Books of Samuel, 244; nephew Friedel visits, 245; her liking for Willa Cather, 246; working on the ranch, 252–3; DHL's relations with, 256, 257; her resentment of Ford Maddox Ford, 261–2; teamwork with DHL on Crichton interview, 262; she and DHL leave Kiowa, 263; happy to see children again, 270; at Ada Clarke's, 270–2; returns to London, 271; she and DHL have lunch with the Asquiths, 271–2; to Baden-Baden to see mother, 273; likes their landlord at Villa Bernarda, 274; eventually brings Ravagli to Taos and later marries him, 282, 282n; hostility to Brett revives, 288–9; relations with DHL poor,

Luhan, Tony (*cont.*)
drives Ls to Taos, 62; Ls' house supposedly
owned by, 63, 63n; takes DHL to Apache
reservation, 63; takes part in Jicarillo
celebrations, 64; Mabel on relationship
with, 68; in planned DHL–Mabel
collaboration, 71, 72, 72n; DHL tries to pay
him for use of house, 80n; DHL compares
to Mabel's dog, 80, 81; marries Mabel, 113;
DHL to Mabel on her marriage to, 132;
discusses Indian linguistics with De Angulo,
176; returns to Taos with De Angulo, 176;
his portrait in 'Altitude', 182; visits the
Lobo with Mabel and Thompson, 186;
leaves angrily for the pueblo, 188; pact with
Thompson against DHL, 189; takes Ls to
Hopi ceremony, 196; drives Mabel to Santa
Fe, 203; drives Ls and Brett to Santa Fe,
204; *see also* Sterne, Mabel Dodge

Macdonald, Edward, preparing bibliography of
DHL's work, 201; DHL writes to him on
need to return to Europe, 243; his
bibliography prompts idea for collection of
essays, 251; DHL writes to him to on taking
it easy and the way the old hang on to life,
308
MacDonald, Ramsey, 166–7, 490
MacGregor, Genaro Fernández, review of
Aaron's Rod by, 206
Mackenzie, Edward Montague Compton, DHL
and he pursue possibility of sailing around
the world, 7n; DHL writes about South
Seas to, 56; dictating at 2:00 am, 262; DHL
sees in London, 269; claims to be
unbothered by 'Two Blue Birds', 301, 310;
and 'The Man Who Loved Islands', 301,
310; on DHL's fictional portraits of others,
302, 302n; his financial situation, 303–4;
invites DHL to see his new islands, 307; no
time for DHL to visit islands in Scotland,
313; a contributor to 'What Women Have
Taught Me' series, 415
Mackenzie, Faith Compton, DHL sees in
London, 269; DHL asks to look after Brett
in Capri, 269; DHL sees her in Capri, 290;
bitterly resents 'Two Blue Birds', 301, 301n,
302; *see also* Mackenzie, Edward Montague
Compton
Macy, John, DHL meets, 123; rejects 'The
Proper Study', 128; *see also* Nation
Maddox, Brenda, on F's and Murry's
relationship, 145n
Magnelli, Alberto, Brewster takes DHL to meet,
332–3; painting style of, 332–3, 333n; DHL
compares his own work to, 334

Magnus, Maurice, DHL had visited in 1920, 5n;
DHL's introduction to *Memoirs of the
Foreign Legion* by, 6, 48n, 230, 281;
homosexuality of, 6; tries to borrow money
from DHL, 6; suicide of, 6; Norman
Douglas on DHL's handling of *Memoirs of
the Foreign Legion*, 248, 248n, 282; DHL's
response to Douglas over *Memoirs of the
Foreign Legion*, 282
Majorca (Spain), Ls plan to go to, 479; Ls' hotels
in, 481; DHL's and F's opinions of, 481;
DHL feeling 'pretty well' in, 487; Ls travel
around, 487; George Sand and Chopin in,
487, 487n
Manby hot springs, 84, 98
Mandrake Press, *see* Goldston, Edward;
Stephensen, Percy Reginald
Manglar, El, model for Ramón's hacienda, 108
Mansfield, Katherine, possibility of her having
contracted tuberculosis from DHL, 19n;
DHL sends her peace-offering from
Wellington, 55, 55n; death of, 55, 99; piece
by her in first *Adelphi*, 118; Gorky
translation by her and Koteliansky, 122;
works by her in *Adelphi*, 135; her picture in
first *Adelphi*, 135n; Murry–Brett affair
begins after death of, 148; Brett's diary as
letters to, 148n; devotion of Koteliansky and
Brett to, 158; dies at Gurdjieff Institute,
160; requests that Brett look after Murry,
166n; royalties go to Murry after her death,
171, 171n; her tuberculosis compared with
DHL's, 196; Brett's visions of, 226, 226n;
Murry's posthumous collections by, 252;
Murry's posthumous promotion of, 262;
and 'Smile', 283n; DHL on Murry's
presence at death of, 457
Marchbanks, Bill, 36, 53
Marsh, Edward Howard ('Eddie'), DHL's
relations with, 69, 69n; DHL tells him of
indecisiveness of his travel plans, 104
Mason, Harold Trump, suggests a collection of
DHL's essays, 251; Ls dine with him and
his wife, 265; DHL tells him of Russia
plans, 279; tells DHL about *To the Pure*,
444n
Masters, Edgar Lee, 65
Maugham, William Somerset, DHL meets, 205;
on DHL in *Introduction to English and
American Literature*, 205, 205n; DHL on
The Moon and Sixpence and *Trembling of a
Leaf* by, 205n; DHL critical of, 366, 366n;
DHL reviews *Ashenden or the British Agent*
by, 430
Maupassant, Guy de, DHL compares to James
Fenimore Cooper and Hardy, 66

COLLEGE OF MARIN

3 2555 00127704 0